Big Data Analytics

S Chandramouli
Associate Director
Cognizant Technology Solutions

Asha A George
PPM and Strategy Consultant
Verbat Technologies

C R Rene Robin
Professor (CSE) and Dean (Innovation)
Sri Sairam Engineering College
Chennai

D Doreen Hephzibah Miriam
Founder and Director
Computational Intelligence Research Foundation
Chennai

J Jasmine Christina Magdalene
Assistant Professor
PG Department of Computer Applications
Bishop Heber College
Tiruchirappalli

All rights reserved. No part of this book may be modified, reproduced or utilised in any form, or by any means, electronic or mechanical, including photocopying, recording or by any information storage and retrieval system, in any form of binding or cover other than in which it is published, without permission in writing from the publisher.

BIG DATA ANALYTICS

UNIVERSITIES PRESS (INDIA) PRIVATE LIMITED

Registered Office
3-6-747/1/A & 3-6-754/1, Himayatnagar, Hyderabad 500 029, Telangana, India
info@universitiespress.com; www.universitiespress.com

Distributed by
Orient Blackswan Private Limited

Registered Office
3-6-752 Himayatnagar, Hyderabad 500 029, Telangana, India

Other Offices
Bengaluru, Chennai, Guwahati, Hyderabad, Kolkata,
Mumbai, New Delhi, Noida, Patna, Visakhapatnam

© Universities Press (India) Private Limited 2024
First published 2024

ISBN: 978-93-93330-46-8

Cover and book design
© Universities Press (India) Private Limited 2024

Typeset in Bembo MT Pro 12 by
SRS Publishing Services, Puducherry

Printed in India by
B.B. Press, Noida 201 301

Published by
Universities Press (India) Private Limited
3-6-747/1/A & 3-6-754/1, Himayatnagar, Hyderabad 500 029, Telangana, India

Disclaimer
Care has been taken to confirm the accuracy of information printed in this book. The author and the publisher, however, cannot accept any responsibility for errors or omissions or for consequences from application of the information in this book and make no warranty, express or implied, with respect to its contents. This textbook does not constitute a standard, specification or regulation. The trademarks or manufacturer's names appear/are used in this book only because they are considered essential to the object of subject discussion and do not necessarily constitute endorsement of product/standard by the author or publisher. All products and company names are trademarks™ or registered® trademarks of their respective holders. Use of them do not imply any affiliation with or endorsement by them.

Contents

Preface	xxii
Acknowledgements	xxv
About the Authors	xxviii

Chapter 1 Introduction to Data Analytics   1

	1.1	Introduction	1
	1.2	What Is Data?	2
		1.1.1 Data Relationships	2
		1.1.2 Data Models	3
	1.3	Types of Data	11
	1.4	Nature of Data	12
	1.5	Data Visualization	14
	1.6	Data Analysis Methods	19
		1.6.1 Correlation	19
		1.6.2 Regression	21
		1.6.3 Forecasting	22
		1.6.4 Clustering	22
		1.6.5 Classification	25
	1.7	Web Data	25
		1.7.1 Evolution of Analytic Scalability	26
		1.7.2 Reporting vs. Analysis	30

Summary | Multiple Choice Questions | Short-answer Questions | Essay-type Questions

Chapter 2 Data Analytics Life-cycle   61

	2.1	Introduction	61
	2.2	Business Drivers for Analytics	62
		2.2.1 Increasing Profitability and Growth	62
		2.2.2 Strengthening Customer Experience and Intimacy	62
		2.2.3 Driving Digital Transformation and Innovation	63
		2.2.4 Managing Regulatory and Compliance Risks	63
		2.2.5 Increasing Operational Efficiency	63
	2.3	Typical Analytical Architecture	64
		2.3.1 Data Analytical Architecture	64
		2.3.2 Challenges of Conventional Systems	66

	2.4	Analytic Processes and Tools	67
		2.4.1 Types of Analytics	67
		2.4.2 Modern Data Analytic Tools	69
	2.5	Data Analytic Life-cycle	71
		2.5.1 Need of Data Analytic Life-cycle	71
		2.5.2 Phases of Data Analytic Life-cycle	71
	2.6	Key Roles for Successful Analytic Projects	75
	2.7	Modern-day Intelligence	76
		2.7.1 Business Intelligence vs. Data Science	76
		2.7.2 Intelligent Data Analysis	78

Summary | Multiple Choice Questions | Short-answer Questions | Essay-type Questions

Chapter 3 Fundamentals of Big Data — 97

3.1	Introduction to Big Data	97
3.2	Big Data Concepts and Terminology	97
	3.2.1 Big Data Processing Activities	98
	3.2.2 Common Terminologies	98
3.3	Fundamentals of Big Data Types	101
3.4	Big Data Analytics	103
	3.4.1 Text Analytics	104
	3.4.2 Audio Analytics	105
	3.4.3 Video Content Analytics	106
	3.4.4 Social Media Analytics	106
	3.4.5 Predictive Analytics	107
3.5	Distributed File System in Big Data	108
3.6	Big Data Characteristics	110
	3.6.1 The 5 *V*'s of Big Data	110
	3.6.2 Challenges of Processing Big Data	111
3.7	Drivers for Big Data	114

Summary | Multiple Choice Questions | Short-answer Questions | Essay-type Questions

Chapter 4 Big Data Analytics Technology — 124

4.1	Introduction to Big Data Analytics	124
4.2	Big Data Analysis Framework	125
4.3	Approaches for Big Data Analysis	128
4.4	Understanding Text Analytics and Big Data	130
	4.4.1 Text Mining Process	130
	4.4.2 Applications of Text Analytics	138

	4.5	Predictive Analysis of Big Data	138
		4.5.1 Predictive Analytics Models	139
		4.5.2 Predictive Analytics Algorithms	142
	4.6	Procedural vs. Functional Programming Models for Big Data	146
	4.7	Big Data Integration Process	147
	4.8	Big Data Technology Landscape	149
		4.8.1 Big Data Architecture	150
		4.8.2 Big Data Storage	151
	4.9	Big Data Key Roles	155

Summary | Multiple Choice Questions | Short-answer Questions | Essay-type Questions

Chapter 5 Fundamentals of Hadoop — 179

	5.1	Introduction	179
	5.2	Problems with Traditional Large-scale Systems	179
	5.3	Five *V*'s of Big Data	181
	5.4	What Is Hadoop?	183
	5.5	History of Hadoop	184
	5.6	Why Hadoop?	185
	5.7	Different Flavors of Hadoop	188
	5.8	Different Modes of Hadoop	188
		5.8.1 Standalone Mode	188
		5.8.2 Pseudo-distributed Mode (Single-node Cluster)	189
		5.8.3 Fully Distributed Mode	189
	5.9	Core Components of Hadoop	190
	5.10	Hadoop Ecosystem	191
	5.11	Data Ingestion Layer	191
	5.12	ETL and ELT	193
	5.13	Ingestion Tools in Hadoop Ecosystem	193
	5.14	Data Storage Layer	195
		5.14.1 Data Storage Tools	196
	5.15	Processing Layer	197
	5.16	Analysis Layer	199
	5.17	Management and Coordination	203
	5.18	Anatomy of a Hadoop Cluster: HDFS Architecture	204
	5.19	Data Locality in Hadoop	211
	5.20	Configuration Files in Hadoop	213
	5.21	Limitations of Hadoop	215
	5.22	Distributed Cache in Apache Hadoop	215

5.23		Apache Hadoop and RDBMS	216
5.24		Problems with Small Files in Hadoop	217
5.25		Security in Hadoop	217
5.26		File System Check in Hadoop	218
5.27		Starting and Stopping Hadoop	218
5.28		Edit Log and FSImage in Hadoop	218
5.29		Communication Protocols	219
	5.29.1	Three Common Types of Failures	219
5.30		Hadoop Safe Mode	220
5.31		Hadoop 1 and Hadoop 2	220
5.32		Hadoop 2 and Hadoop 3	221
5.33		Start Hadoop Daemons Command	221
5.34		Yarn Architecture	222
5.35		Apache Spark Architecture	224
5.36		Zeppelin Architecture	226
5.37		Hadoop Streaming	227
5.38		Other Hadoop Commands	227
5.39		NoSQL Concepts	228
	5.39.1	CAP Theorem	229
	5.39.2	ACID and BASE Models	229
	5.39.3	Advantages and Disadvantages of NoSQL	230

Summary | Multiple Choice Questions | Short-answer Questions | Essay-type Questions

Chapter 6 Hadoop Distributed File System 264

6.1		Introduction	264
6.2		Virtualization	264
6.3		Downloading VMware	266
6.4		Installing VMware	268
6.5		VirtualBox	275
	6.5.1	VirtualBox Installation Steps	275
6.6		HDP Sandbox Download and Installation	281
6.7		Ambari Administration	289
6.8		HDFS Command Line Interface	300
	6.8.1	JPS Command	301
	6.8.2	List of Files	301
	6.8.3	File Management	302
	6.8.4	Upload and Download Files	303
	6.8.5	Ownership and Validation	304

	6.9	VMware vs. VirtualBox	304
	6.10	HDFS Features	306
	6.11	HDFS Architecture	310
	6.12	HDFS Read Request	313
	6.13	HDFS Write Request	314
	6.14	HDFS Blocks	316
	6.15	Data Racks	317
	6.16	HDFS Block Replication	317
	6.17	Rack Awareness Algorithm	318
	6.18	Data Integrity in HDFS	319
	6.19	Data Locality in HDFS	320
	6.20	Distributed Cache in HDFS	322
	6.21	HDFS Serialization	322
	6.22	HDFS Web UI	323
	6.23	Directory Creation in HDFS: Java Program	327
	6.24	Append Data to HDFS File: Java Program	328
	6.25	File Read from HDFS: Java Program	328
	6.26	File Write to HDFS: Java Program	330
	6.27	Connecting HDFS from Python	331
	6.28	Snakebite Command Reference for CLI	332
	6.29	When to Avoid Using HDFS	333

Summary | Multiple Choice Questions | Short-answer Questions | Essay-type Questions

Chapter 7 MapReduce 357

	7.1	Introduction	357
	7.2	MapReduce Features	358
	7.3	Advantages of MapReduce	360
	7.4	A Real-world Problem	362
	7.5	Real-time Use Cases of MapReduce	365
	7.6	MapReduce Phases	366
		7.6.1 Splitting	366
		7.6.2 Mapping Phase	367
		7.6.3 Shuffling	368
		7.6.4 Reducing Phase	369
	7.7	Programming for Word Count Example	372
	7.8	How to Run the Word Count Example	375
	7.9	MapReduce Job	377
	7.10	Hadoop Mapper	378

7.11	Hadoop Reducer	379
7.12	Hadoop Key-Value Pair	381
7.13	Input Format in MapReduce	383
7.14	InputSplit in MapReduce	385
7.15	Hadoop Record Reader	386
7.16	MapReduce Partitioner	388
	7.16.1 MapReduce Combiner	389
7.17	Shuffling and Sorting in MapReduce	391
	7.17.1 Hadoop Output Format	392
7.18	Input Split vs. HDFS Block in MapReduce	394
7.19	MapOnly Job in MapReduce	394
7.20	Hadoop Speculative Execution	396
7.21	Hadoop Counters	397
7.22	Hadoop Optimization	399
7.23	MapReduce Performance Tuning: Best Practices	400
	7.23.1 System Level Best Practices	400
	7.23.2 Application Level Best Practices	401
7.24	YARN	402

Summary | Multiple Choice Questions | Short-answer Questions | Essay-type Questions

Chapter 8 Hadoop Ingestion   426

8.1	Introduction	426
8.2	Data Ingestion Types	426
	8.2.1 Real-time Data Ingestion (RTDI)	427
	8.2.2 Batch-based Data Ingestion (BBDI)	427
	8.2.3 Lambda Architecture Data Ingestion (LADI)	428
8.3	Benefits of Data Ingestion	428
	8.3.1 Data Ingestion Tools Selection	428
8.4	Introduction to Sqoop	430
8.5	Features of Sqoop	431
8.6	Basic SQL Commands and Connecting from Cloudera	432
8.7	Basic Sqoop Commands from Cloudera Command Prompt	434
8.8	Sqoop Importing	436
8.9	Sqoop Incremental Import	439
8.10	Sqoop Export	439
8.11	Advantages of Sqoop	441
8.12	Disadvantages of Sqoop	442

8.13	Need for Apache Flume		442
8.14	Apache Flume Architecture		443
8.15	Features of Apache Flume		446
8.16	Data Flow in Flume		447
8.17	Failure Handling in Flume		448
8.18	Flume Disadvantages		448
8.19	Apache Flume Applications		449
8.20	Apache Flume Installation in Windows 10		449
8.21	Messaging System		454
8.22	Apache Kafka		455
	8.22.1	Features of Kafka	456
	8.22.2	Need for Kafka	456
	8.22.3	Kafka Use Cases	456
8.23	Kafka Architecture and Terminologies		456
8.24	Kafka Replication		460
8.25	Kafka Producers		461
8.26	Kafka: Consumer and Consumer Groups		464
8.27	Quick Introduction to Impala		466
8.28	Quick introduction to Apache NiFi		467

Summary | Multiple Choice Questions | Short-answer Questions | Essay-type Questions

Chapter 9 Hive   477

9.1	Introduction to Hive		477
9.2	Need for Hive		477
9.3	Features of Hive		478
9.4	Limitations of Hive		479
9.5	Hive Architecture		480
	9.5.1	Hive Clients	480
	9.5.2	Hive Services	480
9.6	Workflow in Hive		483
9.7	Hive vs. Traditional Database		485
9.8	Installing and Configuring Hadoop on Ubuntu		486
9.9	Installing and Configuring Hive		492
9.10	Creating and Using a Database in Hive		496
	9.10.1	Introduction to Hive Data Types	496
	9.10.2	Categorization of Data in Hive	497
	9.10.3	Creating and Using a Database: An Example	498

9.11	Creating an Internal/Managed Table in Hive	498
9.12	Loading Data into a Table	499
	9.12.1 Creating a Table Using LIKE	499
	9.12.2 Adding Data Using INSERT INTO Table	500
	9.12.3 Adding Data Using INSERT OVERWRITE	500
9.13	Altering, Truncating and Dropping a Table	500
9.14	Creating an External Table	501
9.15	MapReduce Programs Through Hive	501
9.16	Hive Commands – Loading, Filtering, Grouping	502
9.17	Data Types, Operators	503
9.18	Relational Operators in Hive QL	503
9.19	Arithmetic Operators in Hive QL	505
9.20	Hive Logical Operators	506
9.21	Hive Complex Operators	506
9.22	Joins, Groups	506
9.23	Map Join	509
	9.23.1 Parameters of Hive Map Side Join	509
9.24	Bucket Join	510
	9.24.1 Real-estate Example	510

Summary | Multiple Choice Questions | Short-answer Questions | Essay-type Questions

Chapter 10 HBase — 523

10.1	Introduction	523
10.2	Features of HBase	524
10.3	Architecture of HBase	525
	10.3.1 HMaster	526
	10.3.2 Region Server	526
10.4	Managing Large Datasets with HBase	532
10.5	HBase Compaction	534
	10.5.1 Minor Compaction	535
	10.5.2 Major Compaction	536
10.6	Schema Design	537
	10.6.1 Table Schema	537
	10.6.2 HBase Row-key Design	538
	10.6.3 Schema of Column Families	541
10.7	Other Factors in HBase Schema Design	541
	10.7.1 Region Split	541
	10.7.2 Load Balancing	543

	10.7.3	Data Replication	543
	10.7.4	HBase Crash Recovery	544
	10.7.5	Data Recovery	544
10.8	HBase Coprocessor	546
10.9	Setting HBase Environment	548
10.10	Creating HBase Tables	550
10.11	Listing all Tables	550
10.12	Adding Data to a Table	551
10.13	Getting a Row of Data	551
10.14	Scanning a Table	552
10.15	Counting the Number of Rows in a Table	552
10.16	Altering a Table	552
10.17	Deleting a Table Row, Column	553
10.18	Disabling and Enabling a Table	553
10.19	Truncating and Dropping a Table	554
10.20	Determining if Table Exists	555
10.21	Creating a Hive External Table Stored by HBase	555
	10.21.1	Defining an External Table over HBase Tables	556
	10.21.2	Mapping Specific HBase Columns and Column Families	556
	10.21.3	Working Hive with HBase (Integration)	557
10.22	Advanced Indexing in HBase	558
10.23	HIndex	559
	10.23.1	Writing Data with Index	559
	10.23.2	Reading Data with Index	559
	10.23.3	HIndex Features	560
10.24	HBase Admin API	560
10.25	HBAse Client API	561
	10.25.1	`Put` Method	561
	10.25.2	`Get` Method	561
10.26	Using HBase in Hadoop Applications	561
10.27	HBase Advanced Usage	563
	10.27.1	Filters	563
	10.27.2	The Filter Hierarchy	563
	10.27.3	Comparison Operators	564
	10.27.4	Comparators	564
	10.27.5	Comparison Filters	564
10.28	Dedicated Filters	565
10.29	Decorating Filters	566

	10.30	Counters	566
		10.30.1 Single Counters	567
		10.30.2 Multiple Counters	567
	10.31	Coprocessors	568
		10.31.1 The Coprocessor Class	568
		10.31.2 Coprocessor Loading	568
		10.31.3 Loading from the Configuration	569
	10.32	HTablepool	570
	10.33	HBase Security and Grant	570
		10.33.1 `grant`	570
		10.33.2 `revoke`	570
		10.33.3 `user_permission`	570
	10.34	HBase vs. HDFS	571
	10.35	Applications of HBase	571

Summary | Multiple Choice Questions | Short-answer Questions | Essay-type Questions

Chapter 11 Hadoop Streaming   588

11.1	Introduction	588
11.2	Real-time Analytics	588
	11.2.1 Choosing the Proper Tool for Real-time Analytics	589
	11.2.2 Apache Spark Streaming	589
	11.2.3 Apache Samza	590
	11.2.4 What Would a Perfect Solution Entail?	591
	11.2.5 Challenges to Be Solved	591
11.3	Thread Pooling	593
11.4	Stream Computing	594
11.5	The Future of Data Streaming	595
11.6	Stream Computing's Advantages in the Big Data world	596
11.7	How Streaming Works	598
11.8	Real-time Streams vs. Batch Processing	598
11.9	Hadoop Streaming	599
	11.9.1 Hadoop Streaming Characteristics	600
	11.9.2 Specifying Other Plugins for Jobs	601

Summary | Multiple Choice Questions | Short-answer Questions | Essay-type Questions

Chapter 12 Pig Latin   607

12.1	Introduction	607
12.2	Basic Features of Apache Pig	608

12.3	Apache Pig Architecture	608
	12.3.1 Using the Interactive Pig Shell	609
	12.3.2 Using Batch Processing	609
12.4	Interpreting Pig Scripts	611
12.5	Apache Pig Installation on Ubuntu	612
12.6	Grunt Shell Commands	613
12.7	Pig Data Model	615
	12.7.1 Pig Data Types	616
	12.7.2 Pig Latin Statements	618
	12.7.3 Pig Arithmetic Operators	619
	12.7.4 Pig Comparison Operators	621
	12.7.5 Pig Type Construction Operators	621
	12.7.6 Pig Relational Operators	621
12.8	Advanced Pig Latin	624
	12.8.1 Built-in Functions in Pig	624
	12.8.2 Apache Pig User-Defined Functions (UDF)	626
12.9	Making Pigs Fly by Optimizing Pig Scripts	628
	12.9.1 Advanced Joins	629
	12.9.2 Handling Key Skew	630
	12.9.3 "On the Fly" Replanning by the Pig Community	631
12.10	Algebraic Function in Pig	633
12.11	Accumulator	634
12.12	Writing a Function	634
	12.12.1 Writing a Filter Function	634
	12.12.2 Writing a Load and Store Function	634
12.13	Comparison of Pig with Hive and MapReduce	636
	12.13.1 Apache Pig vs. MapReduce	637
	12.13.2 Apache Pig vs. Hive	637

Summary | Multiple Choice Questions | Short-answer Questions | Essay-type Questions

Chapter 13 Fundamentals of Spark — 648

13.1	Introduction	648
13.2	Apache Spark in Hadoop Ecosystem	649
13.3	History of Spark	650
13.4	Versions of Spark	651
	13.4.1 Spark 3.0	652
13.5	Spark Ecosystem	653
	13.5.1 Spark Ecosystem: Supporting Languages	654
	13.5.2 Spark Ecosystem: Spark Core	655

		13.5.3 Spark Ecosystem: Spark SQL	655

- 13.5.3 Spark Ecosystem: Spark SQL — 655
- 13.5.4 Spark Streaming — 657
- 13.5.5 Spark MLlib — 658
- 13.5.6 Spark GraphX — 658
- 13.5.7 SparkR — 659
- 13.5.8 Cluster Management — 659
- 13.6 Design Principles of Apache Spark — 662
- 13.7 Advantages of Spark — 663
- 13.8 Disadvantages of Apache Spark — 667
- 13.9 Installation of Apache Spark on Windows — 670
- 13.10 Apache Spark Physical Architecture — 677
- 13.11 Apache Spark Layered Architecture — 681
  - 13.11.1 Resilient Distributed Dataset (RDD) — 681
  - 13.11.2 Directed Acyclic Graph (DAG) — 683
- 13.12 Ways to Create RDD in Spark — 684
- 13.13 Paired RDD — 685
- 13.14 Features of Spark RDD — 685
- 13.15 Persistence and Caching Mechanisms in Apache Spark — 687
- 13.16 Operations of Apache Spark RDD — 689
  - 13.16.1 Transformations — 690
  - 13.16.2 Actions — 692
- 13.17 Limitations of Apache Spark RDD and Ways to Overcome It — 693
- 13.18 Directed Acyclic Graph (DAG) — 695
- 13.19 DAG in Apache Spark — 695
  - 13.19.1 Need for DAG in Apache Spark — 695
  - 13.19.2 Working Principle of DAG in Spark — 696
- 13.20 Applications of Apache Spark — 697
  - 13.20.1 Streaming Data — 697
- 13.21 Spark in Real-world — 699
- 13.22 Use Cases of Spark — 700
- 13.23 Spark vs. Hadoop — 702
- 13.24 Sample Program — 705

Summary | Multiple Choice Questions | Short-answer Questions | Essay-type Questions

Chapter 14 Introduction to NoSQL Database Concepts — 735

- 14.1 Introduction — 735
- 14.2 Relational Databases — 735

14.3	NoSQL Definition	737
14.4	Types of NoSQL Databases	737
	14.4.1 Column Family Databases	737
	14.4.2 Key-Value Pair Database	739
	14.4.3 Document Store	740
	14.4.4 Graph Database	741
14.5	Examples of NoSQL Databases	743
14.6	Advantages of NoSQL Databases	743
14.7	NoSQL Usage	745
14.8	SQL vs. NoSQL	747
14.9	NewSQL	747
14.10	ACID	748
	14.10.1 Atomicity	749
	14.10.2 Consistency	749
	14.10.3 Isolation	750
	14.10.4 Durability	751
14.11	BASE	752
14.12	Two-phase Commit	753
	14.12.1 Commit–request Phase	754
14.13	Schema	756
	14.13.1 Sharding and Share Nothing Architecture	757
	14.13.2 Partitioning Horizontal and Vertical Data	757
	14.13.3 Four Basic Strategies for Shard Structure	760
14.14	Brewer's CAP Theorem	764
14.15	Cassandra – Definition and Features	766
	14.15.1 Definition	766
	14.15.2 Features	766
	14.15.3 Key Structures in Cassandra	772
	14.15.4 Cassandra Advantages and Use Cases	776
14.16	MongoDB	776
	14.16.1 Architecture of MongoDB	777
	14.16.2 MongoDB Advantages and Use Cases	778
14.17	HBase	778
	14.17.1 HBase Architecture	779
14.18	Comparing Cassandra, MongoDB, and HBase	780

Summary | Multiple Choice Questions | Short-answer Questions | Essay-type Questions

Chapter 15 Cassandra Data Model 791

- 15.1 Introduction 791
- 15.2 Use Cases of Cassandra 792
- 15.3 Cassandra Installation in Windows Environment 792
  - 15.3.1 Installing Python 2.7.x Edition 792
  - 15.3.2 Installing Apache Cassandra 796
- 15.4 Cassandra Basic CQL 798
- 15.5 How to Create, Alter, Drop and Use Keyspace in Cassandra 801
  - 15.5.1 Create Keyspace 801
  - 15.5.2 Simple Strategy 802
  - 15.5.3 Network Topology Strategy 803
- 15.6 Column Families 805
  - 15.6.1 Types of Columns 805
- 15.7 Cassandra Table 806
  - 15.7.1 Inserting and Displaying Data from the Table 807
  - 15.7.2 Updating the Table Data 807
- 15.8 Data Types in Cassandra 808
  - 15.8.1 Collection Data Type in Cassandra 809
- 15.9 Cassandra BATCH 812
- 15.10 Difference Between Cassandra and RDBMS 812
- 15.11 Denormalization 814
- 15.12 Design Patterns 814
  - 15.12.1 Coexistence Patterns 815
- 15.13 RDBMS Migration Patterns 815
- 15.14 CAP Patterns 816
- 15.15 Temporal Patterns 817

Summary | Multiple Choice Questions | Short-answer Questions | Essay-type Questions

Chapter 16 Cassandra Architecture 824

- 16.1 Introduction 824
  - 16.1.1 Cassandra Architecture 824
  - 16.1.2 Features of Cassandra 827
- 16.2 Cassandra's Peer-to-Peer Approach 828
- 16.3 Gossip and Failure Detection 829
- 16.4 SS Tables and Commit Log 832
  - 16.4.1 Partition and Token 833
  - 16.4.2 Compression Offset Map 834
  - 16.4.3 Cassandra Commit Log 834

16.5	Cassandra Memtable		835
	16.5.1	Memtable Allocation Types	836
	16.5.2	Slab Allocator	837
	16.5.3	Memtable Flush	837
	16.5.4	Row Cache	838
	16.5.5	Cassandra Memtable Metrics	839
16.6	Hashing to the Rescue		839
16.7	Compaction in Cassandra		840
16.8	Tombstones in Cassandra		841
16.9	Hinted Handoff		842
16.10	Anti-entropy and Read Repair		844
	16.10.1	Anti-entropy	844
	16.10.2	Read repair	845
16.11	Bloom Filters in Cassandra		846
	16.11.1	Bloom Filter	846
	16.11.2	Changing Bloom Filter	847
16.12	Load Balancing in Cassandra		847
16.13	Cassandra Read Process		851
	16.13.1	Example of Cassandra Read Process	852
16.14	Cassandra Write Process		853
16.15	Staged Event-Driven Architecture (SEDA)		854
16.16	Cassandra Migration		855
	16.16.1	Migration Approaches	855
	16.16.2	Partition Key Cache	856
	16.16.3	Partition Summary	856
	16.16.4	Partition Index	857
	16.16.5	Cache Migration Pattern	857
	16.16.6	Estimating a Migration	858
16.17	Streaming		858
	16.17.1	Streaming Based on Netty	858
	16.17.2	Zero-copy Streaming	859
	16.17.3	Parallelizing of Streaming of Keyspaces	860

Summary | Multiple Choice Questions | Short-answer Questions | Essay-type Questions

Chapter 17 MongoDB 874

17.1	Introduction	874
17.2	History of MongoDB	875

17.3	MongoDB Environment Setup	875
	17.3.1 Install MongoDB on Windows	875
	17.3.2 Starting the MongoDB Server	882
17.4	MongoDB Schema Design	884
17.5	Key Features of MongoDB	887
17.6	RDBMS vs. MongoDB	889
17.7	MongoDB Query Language (MQL)	890
17.8	MongoDB Database, Collection and Documents	890
17.9	MongoDB Server	891
17.10	MongoDB Client Through the JavaScript's Shell	891
17.11	CRUD Operation in MongoDB	891
	17.11.1 Creating Database in MongoDB (C of CRUD)	892
	17.11.2 Creating Collection in MongoDB	892
	17.11.3 Listing Down the Databases Available in MongoDB	892
	17.11.4 Inserting Records into Collection (Table)	893
	17.11.5 Showcasing the Current Database Used	896
	17.11.6 Showcasing the Tables (Collections) in the Current Database	897
	17.11.7 Reading Collections in MongoDB (R of CRUD)	897
	17.11.8 Updating documents in MongoDB (U of CRUD)	898
	17.11.9 Delete Operation in MongoDB (D of CRUD)	899
	17.11.10 Dropping (Deleting) a Particular Database	899
17.12	`Pretty()` Method	900
17.13	AND in MongoDB	900
17.14	OR in MongoDB	901
17.15	Using AND and OR Together	902
17.16	NOR in MongoDB	902
17.17	NOT in MongoDB	904
17.18	Creating and Querying Through Indexes	904
	17.18.1 The `createIndex()` method	905
	17.18.2 MongoDB's `dropIndex()` Method	906
	17.18.3 The `dropIndexes()` Method	906
	17.18.4 The `getIndexes()` Method	906
17.19	Mongo Compass	906
	17.19.1 MongoDB Connection	906
	17.19.2 Creating Database in Compass	908
	17.19.3 Adding Documents in Compass	910

	17.19.4 MongoDB View	911
	17.19.5 Filters in Compass	913
	17.19.6 Sorting in Compass	914
	17.19.7 Limit Option in Compass	914
	17.19.8 Skip Option in Compass	915
	17.19.9 Project Option in Compass	916
	17.19.10 Dropping a Database in Compass	917
	17.19.11 Dropping a Collection in Compass	918
	17.19.12 Importing Documents in Compass	918
	17.19.13 Aggregations Option in Compass	919
	17.19.14 Schema Option in Compass	920
	17.19.15 Update MongoDB Compass with the Latest Version	921

Summary | Multiple Choice Questions | Short-answer Questions | Essay-type Questions

Chapter 18 Big Data Visualizations — 940

18.1	Introduction	940
18.2	History of Data Visualization	941
18.3	Big Data Visualization	942
18.4	Importance of Big Data Visualization	943
18.5	How Does Data Visualization Work?	943
18.6	Types of Data Visualization	944
18.7	Challenges of Big Data Visualization	951
18.8	Introduction to Tableau	951
	18.8.1 Features of Tableau	951
	18.8.2 Tableau Product Suite	952
	18.8.3 Installation of Tableau	952
	18.8.4 Tableau for Big Data Visualization	955
18.9	Python for Data Visualization	960
	18.9.1 Installation of Python	960
	18.9.2 Visualization of Data Using Python	964
	18.9.3 Matplotlib	964

Summary | Multiple Choice Questions | Short-answer Questions | Essay-type Questions

Chapter 19 Business Implementation of Big Data — 973

19.1	Introduction	973
19.2	Big Data in Business	974
	19.2.1 Big Data in Marketing	974
	19.2.2 Big Data in Banking Sector	977

19.2.3 Big Data in Healthcare Sector 979
19.2.4 Big Data in Education Sector 981
19.3 Security in Big Data 983
19.3.1 User Access Control 983
19.4 Big Data on Cloud 986
19.5 Best Practices in Big Data Implementation 988
19.6 Latest Trends in Big Data 991
19.6.1 Big Data Analytics Will Incorporate Artificial Intelligence 991
19.6.2 The Use of Blockchain for Data Security Will Increase 991
19.6.3 The Internet of Things (IoT) Will Drive Streaming Analytics Adoption 991
19.6.4 The Rise of DataOps 992
19.6.5 Data-as-a-Service (DaaS) 992
19.6.6 Data Mesh 993
19.6.7 Synthetic Data 993
19.6.8 Empowerment of Self-service Analytics 993
19.6.9 Data Democratization 994
Summary | Multiple Choice Questions | Short-answer Questions | Essay-type Questions

Chapter 20 Limitations of Hadoop and Solutions to Overcome Them 1002

20.1 Introduction 1002
20.2 Problem with Small Files 1002
20.3 Vulnerability 1003
20.4 Long Processing Time 1003
20.5 Not Easy to Use 1004
20.6 Supports Only Batch Processing 1005
20.7 No Delta Iteration 1005
20.8 Security Issues 1006
Summary | Multiple Choice Questions | Short-answer Questions | Essay-type Questions

Chapter 21 Big Data Case Studies 1009

21.1 Applications of Big Data in the Retail Industry 1009
21.1.1 Customer Segmentation 1009
21.1.2 Inventory Management 1010
21.1.3 Price Optimization 1011
21.1.4 Fraud Detection 1011
21.1.5 Supply Chain Optimization 1012
21.1.6 Predictive Analytics 1013

		21.1.7 Customer Experience	1014
		21.1.8 Social Media Analysis	1015
		21.1.9 Store Layout Optimization	1016
	21.2	Applications of Big Data in the Logistics Industry	1017
		21.2.1 Route Optimization	1017
		21.2.2 Supply Chain Visibility	1018
		21.2.3 Risk Management	1018
		21.2.4 Fleet Management	1019
		21.2.5 Warehouse Optimization	1020
		21.2.6 Pricing Optimization	1020
		21.2.7 Quality Control	1021
		21.2.8 Environmental Sustainability	1022
	21.3	Applications of Big Data in the Manufacturing Industry	1022
		21.3.1 Predictive Maintenance	1022
		21.3.2 Quality Control	1023
		21.3.3 Supply Chain Optimization	1024
		21.3.4 Production Optimization	1024
		21.3.5 Energy Efficiency	1025
		21.3.6 Product Development	1026
		21.3.7 Risk Management	1027
		21.3.8 Warranty Analytics	1027
		21.3.9 Customer Analytics	1028
	21.4	Applications of Big Data in the Travel Industry	1028
		21.4.1 Customer Service	1028
		21.4.2 Predictive Maintenance	1029
		21.4.3 Weather Forecasting	1030
		21.4.4 Customer Sentiment Analysis	1030
		21.4.5 Destination Management	1031
		21.4.6 Operational Efficiency	1032
		21.4.7 Revenue Management	1032

Summary

Appendix A: Model Questions   1034
Appendix B: Capstone Projects   1040
Appendix C: Model Syllabi   1045
Index   1052

Preface

The phrase "Big Data" refers to the enormous volumes of data produced and gathered by organizations in various fields, including business, science, and social media. These data are often complex and heterogeneous, requiring new methods and tools for their storage, processing, and analysis. Some emerging technologies to handle Big Data include distributed file systems like Hadoop, parallel computing frameworks like Spark, and non-relational databases like NoSQL. Big Data can be characterized by Volume, Velocity, Variety, Veracity and Value, collectively referred to as the $5V$'s. "Volume" describes the data's overall size, ranging from terabytes to petabytes and beyond. "Velocity" refers to the rate at which data are generated and processed, which may occur in real-time or segments. "Variety" refers to the diversity of the data sources and formats, including structured, semi-structured, or unstructured data. "Veracity" is the term used to describe the accuracy and dependability of the data, which noise, consistency issues, or incompleteness might impact. "Value" characterizes the potential benefits and insights derived from the data, which can help organizations make better decisions and improve their performance.

Big Data Analytics extracts valuable insights from large and complex datasets using various methods, tools, and techniques. It is a rapidly evolving field with applications in multiple domains such as business, science, engineering, health, education, social media, and more. Big Data Analytics can help organizations improve decision-making, optimize operations, enhance customer experience, and create new products and services. It can help organizations gain valuable insights from their data, enhance performance, and create new opportunities for innovation. This book aims to provide a comprehensive and easy-to-understand overview of Big Data Analytics for beginners who want to learn the basics of Big Data Analytics as well as for advanced readers who want to enhance their knowledge and skill in this exciting field. It covers the basic concepts and principles of Big Data Analytics, the leading technologies, and tools used to handle Big Data, the key challenges and issues faced by Big Data analysts, and the various applications and benefits of Big Data Analytics across different domains and sectors.

This book aims to provide a thorough and approachable introduction to the fascinating field of Big Data Analytics by studying it in logical parts, namely, Introduction, Ingestion and Storage, Processing, Analysis, Management and Coordination, and Business Implementation and Case Studies.

The book first introduces the concept of Data and Data Models, and discusses the various Data Analysis methods, Data Analytics lifecycle, typical analytical architecture, and the different phases of the Data Analytics lifecycle. It covers the fundamentals of Big Data which include: Big Data Concepts and Terminology, Big Data Analytics, Framework for Big Data Analysis, Approaches for Analysis of Big Data, Introduction to

Big Data Frameworks such as Hadoop, HDFS, MapReduce, Hive, HBase, Pig, Spark and NoSQL.

Next, the chapters deal at length with the data ingestion layer, which is the first layer where the data is gathered from different sources like RDBMS, web, or local file systems, into a single place for further analysis. Some Big Data ingestion tools such as Apache Kafka, Apache NiFi, Talend, and Snitch are also discussed. We explore how the Data Storage layer works as the destination layer in the data ingestion framework and the source layer in the Processing and Analysis framework. Here, we also analyze how data governance policies and compliance requirements are built into this layer for security and privacy, and delineate the basis for optimal storage format, i.e., SQL or NoSQL, and data warehouse or data lake, depending on use cases.

After examining the essentials of data ingestion layer, the discussion shifts to how the data collected from the previous layer is processed, i.e., translated, optimized, and made ready for easy and smooth analytics. The chapters emphasize on the need for efficient design of the processing layer to enable the smooth flow of data through the rest of the data pipeline. This part introduces the frameworks and techniques for processing large-scale data in parallel and distributed manner, such as MapReduce, Spark, Flink, and Beam. It also covers the concepts and applications of batch, stream, and interactive processing, as well as the challenges and solutions of data integration, cleansing, and transformation.

We then move on to Data Analysis. The Data Analysis layer helps to analyze the data that are coming out of the processing layer. We describe processing frameworks like Pig, Apache Hive, Apache Mahout, and others, which can be used to mine the data for business insights by pulling data either from the data storage layer or directly from the source. Here, we also elaborate on the creation of data models through presentation and visualization tools for evaluation of Big Data projects by end-users or business users. The use of Tableau, Microsoft Power BI, Qlik Sense, and Klipfolio for custom-built or real-time visualization is discussed. After Data Analysis comes Management and Coordination. The Management and Coordination layer helps in overall management of the Hadoop ecosystem. The chapters that deal with this concept provide a bird's-eye view of coordination across Hadoop ecosystem layers.

The concluding chapters of the book expounds on the business implementation of Big Data. Here, we cover Big Data Implementation and Workflow, Operational Databases, Graph Databases in a Big Data environment, Real-time Data Streams and Complex Event Processing, the application of Big Data in a business scenario, Security and Governance for Big Data, Big Data on Cloud, best practices in Big Data implementation, latest trends in Big Data, Big Data computation and limitations, the limitations of Hadoop and ways to overcome them. Chapter 21, the last chapter, illustrates the implementation of Big Data through illuminating case studies in retail, logistics, manufacturing and travel industry.

The book provides a comprehensive and in-depth coverage of Big Data concepts and is replete with diagrams to drive home the ideas discussed in the text. The book also contains objective, short-answer, and essay-type questions to evaluate the reader's knowledge and comprehension of the subject. The questions also help the reader to prepare for exams or interviews, as they are designed to test the reader's understanding of the topics at varied levels and depth. Therefore, the book is an invaluable resource to understand the subject clearly and systematically, and is a must-read for those interested in Big Data Analytics, whether they are students, researchers, practitioners, or managers. Through this book, we hope to inspire readers to explore the potential of Big Data Analytics for solving real-world problems and creating value for society.

S Chandramouli
Asha A George
C R Rene Robin
D Doreen Hephzibah Miriam
J Jasmine Christina Magdalene

Acknowledgements

The journey through traditional Project Management, Agile Project Management, Program and Portfolio Management along with use of artificial intelligence, machine learning, blockchain technologies and Big Data Analytics in the field, has been very rewarding, as it has given me the opportunity to work for some of the best organizations in the world and learn from some of the best minds. Along the way, several individuals have been instrumental in providing me with the guidance, opportunities and insights needed to excel in project and portfolio management. I wish to personally thank Mr Ramesh Dhanakoti, Mr Sriram Vaithamanithi and Mr Alexis Samuel, Senior Vice Presidents, Cognizant Technology Solutions; Mr Hariharan Mathrubutham, Ex Vice President, Cognizant Technology Solutions; Mr Krishna Prasad Yerramilli, Vice President, Cognizant Technology Solutions; Mr Dharmendraraj Govindarajan Nagarajan, Associate Vice President, Cognizant Technology Solutions; and Mr Balasubramanian Narayanan, Senior Director, Cognizant Technology Solutions, for their inspiration and help in creating this book. They have immensely contributed to improve my skills.

This book is a result of my association with many highly reputed professionals in the industry. I was fortunate to work with them and in the process, acquire knowledge that helped me in molding my professional career. I am obliged to Mr V Chandrasekar, Ex CIO, Standard Chartered Bank, for demonstrating how the lives, thoughts and feelings of others in professional life are to be valued. He is a wonderful and cheerful man who inspired me and gave me a lot of encouragement when he launched my first book, *Virtual Project Management Office*.

My parents (Mr Subramanian and Ms Lalitha) have always been enthusiastic about this project. Their unconditional love and affection provided the much-needed moral support. My son, Shri Krishna, and daughter, Shri Siva Ranjani, constantly added impetus to my motivation to work hard. This book would not have been possible without the constant inspiration and support of my wife, Ramya. She was unfailingly supportive and encouraging during the long months that I had spent glued to my laptop while writing this book. Last and not the least, I beg forgiveness from all those who have been with me over the course of the years and whose names I have failed to mention here.

S Chandramouli

My sincere thanks to the Chairman of Verbat Technologies, Dr Saju Varghese, and my colleagues for their invaluable insights and support throughout the exacting research that has gone into this book and the laborious writing process.

It is teamwork that makes the dream work. This cannot be truer than for my wonderful team of co-authors, to whom I am very grateful. Our multiple knowledge-sharing sessions and discussions on various topics related to Big Data Analytics have culminated in the creation of this book with the hope that it will help to shorten the learning curve for anyone interested in the subject, whether he/she is a college student or an IT professional.

I am indebted to my family and friends, who were my punching board and soothing balm during the stressful days; my parents for their tough love, which I appreciate only now; and my brother and sister for their inspiration. Last but not least, I am thankful to my husband, George, for his patient love and support that gives my life an extra dimension, and to my wonderful son, Steven, whose encouragement never fails to motivate me.

And above all, I want to thank God, without whose grace, love, and blessings none of this would have been possible.

Asha A George

Writing technical books is the pre-eminent desire of any teacher. It makes the academician migrate from teaching learning to learning teaching. However, it is not possible to be a good author without the support of family members. My gratitude goes to my lovely wife Dr Doreen Hephzibah Miriam, my daughter Geona and son Joanez. I also thank the Chairman and CEO of Sairam Group of Institutions Dr Sai Prakash LeoMuthu and my colleagues. My Ph.D. research scholars provided great support and were a driving force to update my knowledge. My special thanks to the publisher for giving me this wonderful opportunity to be a part of this book.

C R Rene Robin

Authoring a book is a great piece of evidence for outcome-based education. I would like to thank my husband Dr C R Rene Robin, parents Dr N Durairaj and Dr Mrs Florance Durairaj, and my children Geona and Joanez for their immense support and motivation to write this book. I am obliged to my mentor who has contributed a lot in bringing out the best in me. The hard work and dedication shown by the CIRF team at the time of preparation of this book are praiseworthy. I thank everyone in the publishing team for bringing this work to fruition.

D Doreen Hephzibah Miriam

I express my deepest gratitude to the Almighty for providing me with the strength and inspiration to contribute towards this comprehensive and well-crafted book. It is only through His grace and guidance that I have been able to achieve this milestone. I am truly humbled and grateful for the opportunities that have come my way, including the chance to write chapters in this book. I would like to thank Dr Chandramouli, for being a constant source of encouragement and for being the person to bring to me this wonderful opportunity, thereby enabling me to pursue my passion for writing. I owe a great deal of thanks to my son Pranav Jayden Samuel, my family and friends for their unwavering support throughout this journey. Their love, encouragement and patience have been a source of inspiration for me. They have been my sounding board, my cheerleaders and my pillars of strength. Without them, I would not have been able to complete this book. Finally, I am indebted to all those who have believed in me and supported me on this journey.

J Jasmine Christina Magdalene

We are grateful to Universities Press (India) Private Limited, who came forward to publish this book. Messrs Thomas Mathew Rajesh, Kallol Das and Ramesh of Universities Press were always kind and understanding. Mr Ramesh reviewed this book with abundant patience and helped us say what we had wanted to, improvising each page of this book with care.

S Chandramouli
Asha A George
C R Rene Robin
D Doreen Hephzibah Miriam
J Jasmine Christina Magdalene

About the Authors

Dr S Chandramouli, PhD, PfMP, PMP, PMI-ACP, is an alumnus of Indian Institute of Management Kozhikode (IIM-K). He is a Certified Global Business Leader from Harvard Business School. He is a prolific writer of business management articles dealing with technology management, delivery management, competitiveness, IT, organizational culture, and leadership. He is a certified "Green Belt" in six-sigma methodology and a certified master practitioner in Neuro Linguistic Programming (NLP). He has presented papers on Project Management in various international forums. His paper on "Best Practices of
Agile Program Management – SCRUM TEA Model" won an award at "Program and Portfolio Management Conference". Another paper titled "Strategy Based Service Model – DISCO PMO" won an award at International IT Service Management Conference. He has 30 publications to his credit in National and International Journals and Conferences.

Chandramouli has a good record of delivering large-scale, mission-critical projects including those that use blockchain technology, AI, Big Data Analytics and machine learning, on time and within budget to the customer's satisfaction. A formerly active member of PMI's Organization Project Management Maturity Model (OPM3) and Project Management Competency Development Framework (PMCDF) assignments, he has been an invited speaker at various technology and management conferences. In addition, he has addressed more than 15,000 software professionals worldwide on a variety of themes associated with Blockchain, AI, machine learning, Big Data Analytics, delivery management, competitiveness, and leadership.

Asha A George, CGEIT, PfMP, PMP is a Certified Blockchain Expert and Certified Cryptocurrency Expert from Blockchain Council. She is a consultant with over 20 years of project program portfolio management experience, including 10 years as a portfolio manager running the Program Management Office (PMO). A technology enthusiast, learner, educator and mentor, she is passionate about developing the next generation of talents in areas of innovative technology, P3M, leadership and communication. She also holds recognized certifications in Six-Sigma, COBIT,
ITIL, Scrum and other project management and governance fields.

Asha is a specialist in enterprise project management office and methodologies, having established the PMO in major organizations, formalizing and aligning the methodologies, frameworks, matrices and KPIs with organizational maturity to ensure measurable business results and continuous improvement. She has successfully led complex cross-country transformation, data migration, systems integration, software development and process improvement projects throughout her professional career.

Dr C R Rene Robin is currently Professor in the Department of Computer Science and Engineering, and Dean (Innovation) at Sri Sairam Engineering College, Chennai. He received his M.E. (CSE) and Ph.D. (CSE) degrees from CEG, Anna University, India, in 2006 and 2011, respectively. His areas of interest include Data Science, Ontological Engineering, Knowledge Management, E-Learning, and Semantic Web. He has successfully guided 11 students in their Ph.D. Programmes, and currently 07 research scholars are doing their research under him. He is a doctoral committee member of Anna University, and other universities. He  is a senior member of IEEE, lifetime member of ISTE and member of several professional bodies. He has 80 publications to his credit in national and international journals and conferences. He has designed and developed an innovation ecosystem integrated with UN's SDG and in line with NEP 2020 for the higher education institutions.

Dr D Doreen Hephzibah Miriam is the Founder and Director of Computational Intelligence Research Foundation (CIRF). She is a Data Scientist and a Machine Learning and Deep Learning trainer and a keynote speaker. She received her B.Tech. in Information Technology from Madras University, Chennai, M.E. in Computer Science and Engineering and Ph.D. degree in Computer Science and Engineering from Anna University, Chennai. Her research interests include Parallel and Distributed Computing, Peer-to-peer Computing, Grid Computing, Cloud Computing and Big Data Analytics. She has delivered more than  500 keynote addresses, conference talks and handled hands-on session for corporates, faculty, and students on topics such as Data Engineering, Blockchain, Software Testing, Cybersecurity, Cloud Computing and Digital Educational Tools for teaching and learning. She has published about 30 papers in International and National Journals and Conferences. She is a life member of ISTE.

J Jasmine Christina Magdalene is Assistant Professor and aspirant Research Scholar in the Department of Computer Applications at Bishop Heber College, affiliated to Bharathidasan University, Tiruchirappalli, India. With over 14 years of teaching experience, Jasmine is an expert in her field, with a passion for data analytics, Internet of Things, cloud computing, and machine learning. She uses practical examples and real-world case studies, to guide her students through the fundamentals of these technologies, explaining complex concepts in a clear and concise manner.

CHAPTER 1

Introduction to Data Analytics

> **LEARNING OBJECTIVES**
>
> In this opening chapter, we discuss the basics of data, its type and nature. The chapter also examines the standard methods to visualize data and the various data analysis models. It also enumerates the differences between reporting and analytics and provides a brief about the different analytic processes and tools.

1.1 INTRODUCTION

Big Data, data analytics, and data sciences are all current trending topics on which much research is being done. And rightfully so. Organizations are continually looking to evaluate and obtain the right tools and techniques to solve complex problems and gain business advantage through data. Of these techniques, forecasting and predictive modeling play a prominent role, and are widely used in AI, decision support systems, data mining, and management, to name a few. As a result, these fields are the biggest consumer of large-scale data or Big Data. As per the research based on Zion Market Research study, predictive analytics industry gathered revenue about US$ 8.12 billion in 2020 and is set to garner revenue of approximately US$ 39.1 billion by 2028.

The basic principle of analytics is to collect raw data from multiple sources, crunch and clean them to extract useful information, and exploit the emerging patterns that can be further processed and analyzed to identify new insights, opportunities, problems, and causes.

Data is continuously growing. Data analytics is a crucial driver for business strategy and success in today's data-rich world. So is the technology used to store and process the said data. However, just like the 'Garbage-In–Garbage-Out' concept, the insights drawn from these tremendous volumes of data are hugely dependent on the tools and methods used and the perception and analytical skills of the data scientists and analysts who work on the data.

1.2 What Is Data?

"Data! Data! Data! I can't make bricks without clay!"—Sir Arthur Conan Doyle.

Data (*singular: datum*) is collected and analyzed to enable relevant decision-making. Some of the most critical decisions of governments, organizations, and people worldwide are based on organized data.

Man has been collecting data since time immemorial. The emergence of libraries is man's first attempt at collecting and storing data for study, and has been recorded as far back as in the 2nd century in Babylon. The Great Library of Alexandria (300 BC – 48 AD) is considered the most extensive data collection in the ancient world. However, by the 1640s, the word 'data' was often referred to as a term used in calculations.

The **Hollerith Tabulating Machine**, created by Herman Hollerith, an American inventor and statistician, is considered the precursor of the electronic computer. The machine was built to record statistics by electrically reading and sorting punched cards. Hollerith's machine was used by the United States Census Office to successfully tabulate census data like age, race, gender, employment status, profession, occupation, age, relationship to head of the family, and marital status, to list a few. This allowed the 1890 Federal Census count to be tallied in six months against the estimated ten years.

Do You Know?

The Tabulating Machine Company was founded in 1896 by Herman Hollerith, the father of modern automated computation. In 1911, Tabulating Machine company merged with two other companies to form the Computing Tabulating Recording Company or CTR. In 1924, the Computing Tabulating Recording Company was renamed International Business Machines Corporation, better known as IBM.

Today data is synonymous with computer storage, memory, and processing. Social websites like Facebook, Twitter, Instagram, and e-Commerce websites like Amazon, Flipkart, Alibaba, and other industry-specific websites in Education, Healthcare, and Banking, all contain a humungous amount of corresponding data that impact everyone across the world.

1.1.1 Data Relationships

Hollerith's machine and further advancements in punched card automation made it possible to process and analyze large amounts of data. This shifted the focus to data storage and collection. The invention of computers and the subsequent need for greater data storage resulted in the development of semiconductor memory chips and floppy disks in the mid-to-late 1900s. Finally, the World Wide Web transformed the world as we know it in the 1990s. The web popularized the Internet and paved the way for the information superhighway. With more data and data types being assessed daily via the Internet, new ways for collecting, consuming, and analyzing it became imperative.

Unless it is organized and ordered in a comprehensible language, any set of data cannot yield helpful information and oft-times, if not assessed correctly, can produce chaotic results. Therefore, to extract the best possible value from the data, specific models (refer Section 1.1.2 Data Models) are used for storing and retrieving data from systems. The key to building these models is understanding the relationship within the data, i.e., between the data fields or entities/units.

There are three types of data relationships:

- **One-to-one:** One record or field in a table is connected to one and only one record/field of another table. E.g., a passport number can belong to only one person or a unique employee ID is associated to only a single person.
- **One-to-many:** One record or field is connected to one or more records of another table. E.g., one employee (Employee ID) can have multiple addresses or one employee can have multiple contact numbers.
- **Many-to-many:** Both tables have duplicate values. E.g., for books and authors, multiple authors could write a book, and an author may have written multiple books.

Suppose a data unit does not have a relationship or link with another entity. In that case, it is of no value in the grand scheme of the data organization structure.

1.1.2 Data Models

Data models are a structural representation of how data is stored in a database. It describes the design of a database representing the entities, attributes, and the relationship among data, its constraints, and others.

There are typically three stages to developing a data model (Fig 1.1):

- **Conceptual data model:** This high-level design displays only the entities and their relationships. The goal is to define and structure the business's scope, rules, and procedures. Therefore, the physical characteristics of the data are not considered at this stage.
- **Logical data model:** In this stage, more detail is built into the data design with data attributes like data types, length, and other characteristics. This logical design helps form a database blueprint, bridging the application and developer specifications.
- **Physical data model:** While the conceptual and logical data models are produced independently of any software or data storage structure, the physical data model is the schema or framework of how the data is physically stored within a database. Hence, in-depth knowledge of the database system and its performance constraints is required. This stage defines referential integrity, performance tuning, indexing, and triggers.

Two types of data modeling typically used in database management systems are Object-based data models and Record-based data models.

4 ● Big Data Analytics

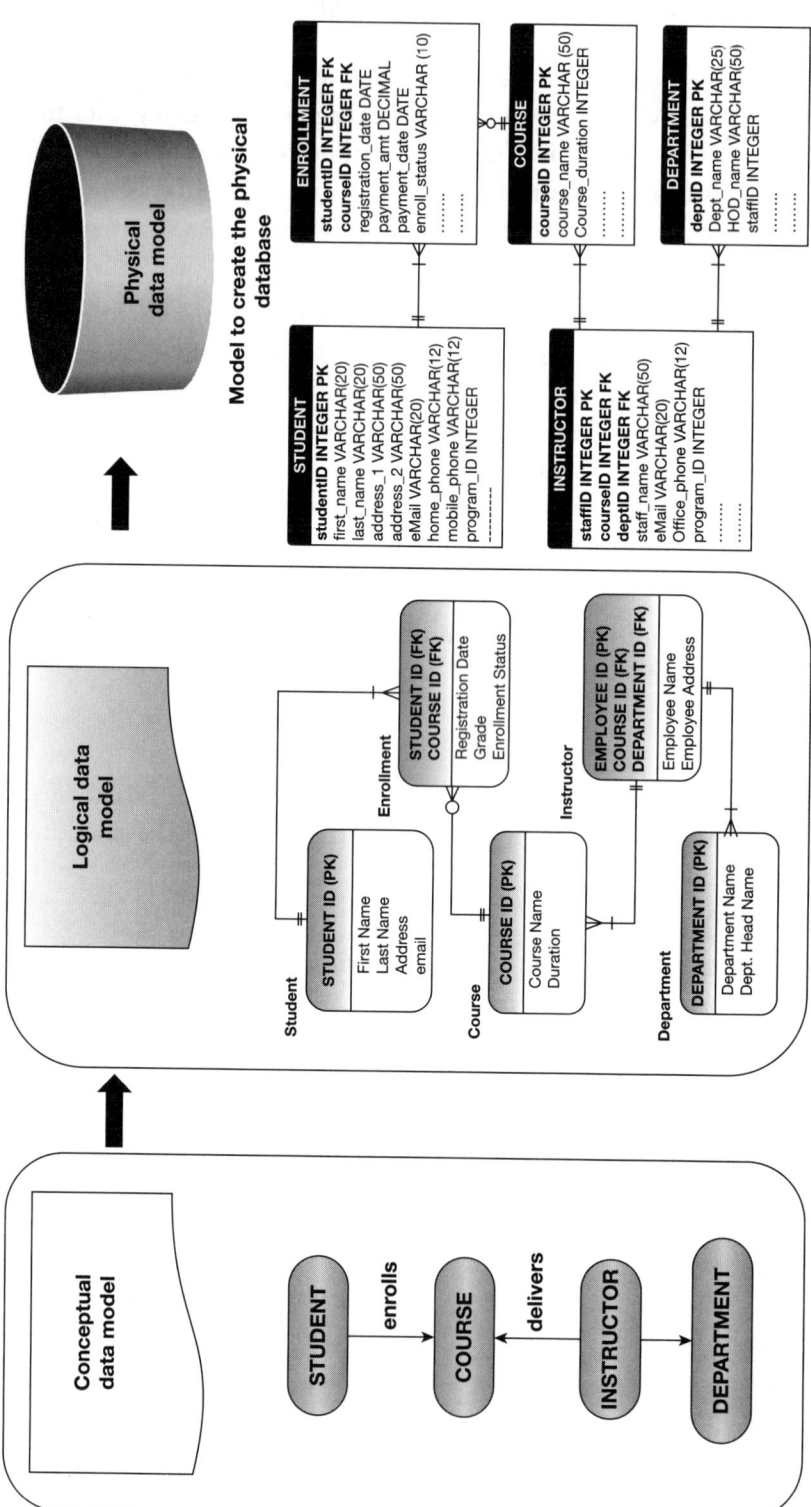

Figure 1.1 Stages of a data model

Object-based Data Models

Object-based data models are built at the conceptual stage while designing a database. The entities are abstract. However, once designed, they can be used to create a relational database. There are two object-based data models commonly used.

1. Entity-Relationship Data Model: Dr Peter Chen introduced the Entity-Relationship or ER data model in 1976. It is a diagrammatic representation of the relationship between entities (Fig 1.2). The ER diagram consists of three main components:

- **Entity:** The object or component of the data is typically represented as a rectangle.
- **Attribute:** The entity's property is an oval in the ER diagram. e.g., Employee id, Name, DOB, and Address can be the attributes of entity Employee.
- **Relationship:** The associated relationship between entities, e.g., one-to-one, one-to-many/many-to-one, and many-to-many, are represented by connecting lines. M, N and 1 represent the relationship between entities. This indicates that there are possibly M Students who can choose N number of Courses and all the students have only one Instructor (1).

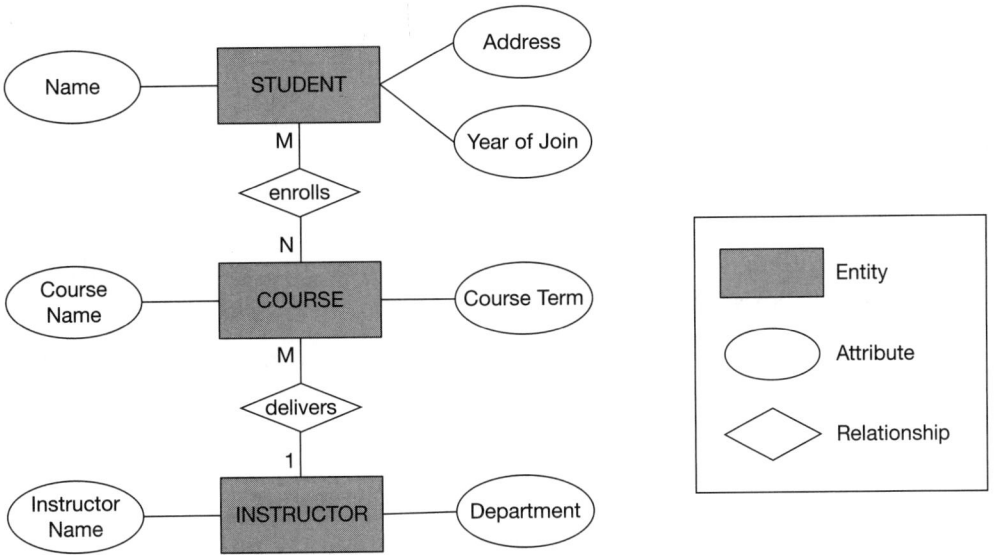

Figure 1.2 Representation of a basic ER model

Diamond shapes in the diagram represent the actions between the entities. ER diagrams are used to represent the logical structure of a database. However, it is difficult to represent complex relationships in an ER model.

2. Object-Oriented Data Model: The Object-Oriented Data Model (OODM) is built around objects where an object is a grouping of data and its behavior. It took on with the advent of object-oriented programming (OOP). It is a combination of OOP and a relational database model. OODM can cater to data complexity and has high flexibility and efficiency in retrieving and expanding objects. It consists of five components:

- **Object:** The real-world entity that consists of data and code encapsulated into a single unit. Example EMPLOYEE or STUDENT. The object is akin to a relational data model (refer Record-Based Data Models).
- **Attribute:** The characteristic or properties of the object like Employee ID, Department, Grade of the object EMPLOYEE or Roll no, Class, Grade of the object STUDENT. An attribute is similar to the column of a relational data model.
- **Method:** Represents the object's behavior like obtaining the Student's marks or leave taken by the Employee.
- **Class:** A collection of objects that share similar attributes and methods. An object is an instance of a class. For example, a Student and an Employee are of the same class.
- **Inheritance:** A new class can inherit the attributes and methods of the original or base class. For example, both Class Student and Employee are inherited from the base class Person.

The OODM is quite popular as it is easily understandable, and the code can be reused due to inheritance. In addition, the same inheritance concept also allows for a low cost of maintenance.

Record-Based Data Models

In the Record-Based Data Model, the database is organized in a specific fixed format of records. The records have a fixed number of fields or attributes, and each field is generally of a fixed length. There are typically three kinds of record-based data models most prevalent in database management.

1. Hierarchical Model: The hierarchical model stores the data in an upside-down tree structure. The structure consists of a root record or table called a **parent** having the other branches or **child** tables linked to it, forming a one-to-one or one-to-many relationship (Fig. 1.3). A parent node can have several child nodes; however, a child can have only one

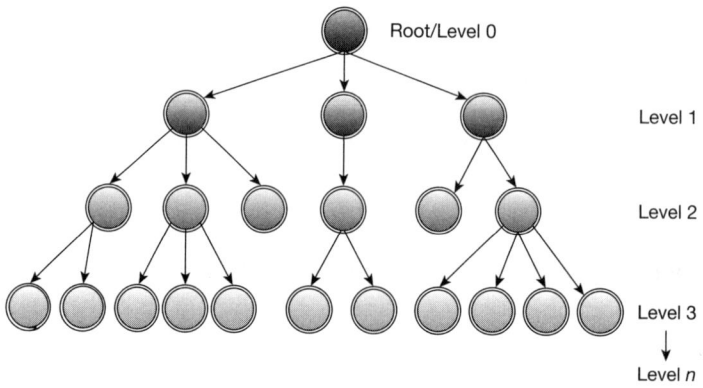

Figure 1.3 Hierarchical model

parent node. The root record at level 0 is the first entity to be traversed in the data model. Any information search in this type of database follows a linear top-down approach that starts at level 0 and traverses down the entire model till the desired information is found. Hence accessing information at the top levels of the tree is quick but gets extremely slow for information stored further down the lower levels.

This type of database was mainly used in Mainframe computers: the Windows Registry and the mobile edition of RDM (Raima Database Manager) use hierarchical databases.

Characteristics
- A hierarchical tree structure is used to store data.
- One-to-one and one-to-many relationships.
- Predefined relationships between root, parent, and child records.
- Parent and child records are linked together via pointers.
- All child nodes are deleted if the parent is deleted.
- Provides fast navigation and direct access to data.
- Disk input and output are minimized as parent and child records are stored close to each other in hierarchical order.

Advantages
- An ideal model for inherently hierarchical data, like organization staff and departments, geographical locations.
- Simple and easy to understand as the relationship between records is predefined.
- Minimized disk input/output as parent and child records are stored close to each other.
- Referential integrity is maintained as any change to the parent automatically reflects in all the child nodes under it.
- Easy to update, delete and create new data information.

Disadvantages
- A many-to-many relationship is not supported.
- Redundancy and duplication of data, since inter-linkages between nodes are not supported.
- Sophisticated relationships are not supported; hence the model does not accurately describe the full relationship between all the records.
- Complexity in design, since adding a new data field or record calls for reworking the whole database structure.
- Reorganization or movement of records from one level to another is restrictive/challenging.
- Programmers and developers need a detailed understanding of the data structure and its storage to access or implement it.
- Retrieving information can get very slow as database size increases and information is required from the lowermost levels.

2. Network Model: C W Bachman developed the network model in 1965 as an enhanced version of the hierarchical data model. It is similar to the hierarchical data model, i.e., the data is organized in an upside-down tree structure. However, the key difference is that the network data model allows the child node to have multiple parents (Fig. 1.4). The parents are called the **occupiers** in network databases, and the child nodes are called the **members**.

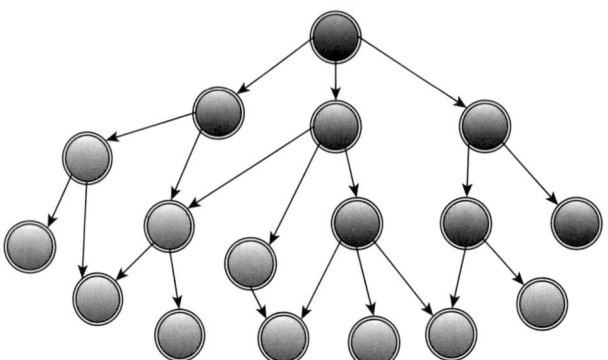

Figure 1.4   Network model

The model also performs better than the hierarchical model by establishing a standard language called CODASYL (Conference on Data System Languages). The network database arranges its data with pointers and has a standard navigational language. With many-to-many relation support, the network model is helpful in geographic information systems with road intersections to multiple branches.

Characteristics
- Data is stored in an upside-down tree structure.
- Supports one-to-one, one-to-many, and many-to-many relationship.
- The parent record is called an occupier, and the child is called a member.
- Parent and child records are linked together via pointers.

Advantages
- It has all the advantages of the hierarchical data model and a more straightforward navigation and data search due to its flexibility.
- Simple structure including multi-parent support.
- It supports complex data models as multiple relations can be created between the data.
- The many-to-many relationship enables a database of larger quantities of information.
- Better access to data.

Disadvantages
- More complex than the hierarchical model, as records are maintained using pointers.
- Data relationships must be predefined.
- Database alteration or addition of a new data field or record requires many pointer adjustments making implementation quite complex.
- Programmers and developers need a detailed understanding of the data structure and its storage to access or implement it.

3. Relational Model: Edgar F Codd introduced the relational data model in 1970. This model stores the data as **tuples** in two-dimensional tables represented by rows and columns forming relations. Data can be easily expanded by increasing the number of rows or columns to create records or attributes/fields respectively.

A unique identifier or key identifies each record in a table, and these keys are used to represent the relationship between records from different tables. This allows basic tables to be created, and their data may be cross-referenced by utilizing one table's primary key and another table's foreign key (Fig. 1.5). Both tables must share at least one column to perform or establish a relational join.

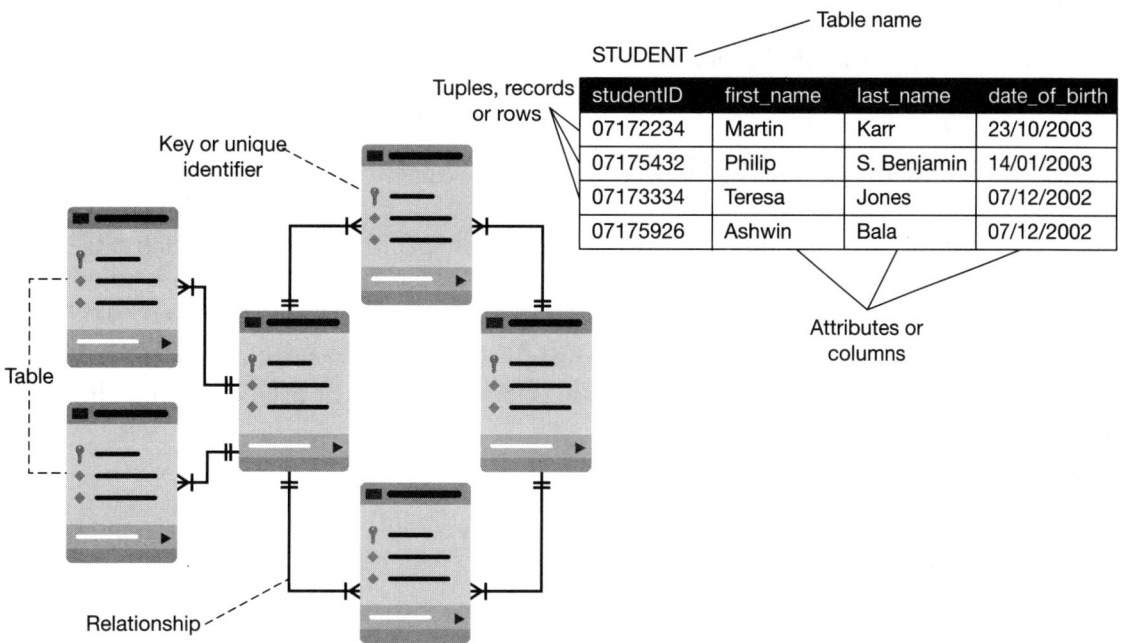

Figure 1.5 Relational model

Since the data is structured, a standard language called Structured Query Language (SQL) was also created to access the relational database and is the de-facto standard for accessing data today.

Database management systems based on the relational data model are called Relational Database Management Systems (RDBMS). Oracle, MySQL, IBM DB2, Hive, and Microsoft Azure SQL Database are some of the top RDBMS today.

Characteristics
- It is a record-based model that comprises a **set of relations** or tables of values.
- Each relation can be represented as a table with columns representing **attributes** and rows representing **records** or entities.
- Every relation or table in the database must be unique and identified by an entity name, say, Student, Faculty.

- The relation records are also **tuples** and are of a fixed format.
- No relation can have duplicate records.
- Attributes represent the type of entity information, e.g., student id, name. No two attributes in a table can have the same attribute name.
- Each data value in a record is called a **field**.
- Attributes and records need not be ordered in any specific format.

Advantages
- It has a simple database design with a tabular view supporting large amounts of data.
- It is scalable as records and attributes can be added to the table.
- Programmers and developers need not know the tables' physical representation or detailed storage to access or update data. Only the entity/attribute names are required.
- Many-to-many relationships between datasets are possible with primary and foreign keys.
- Data redundancy and duplication are avoided as specific data within each table has relations via primary and foreign key concepts.
- Easy extraction of data with the use of SQL language.
- High data security as only the database administrator can access the data.
- Normalization ensures that the database is sturdy, devoid of data anomalies, and has optimized storage space.

Disadvantages
- Performance in accessing and retrieving data is affected if the SQL query to the database involves many tables between which relationships need to be established.
- Higher cost in hardware and related software for setting up and implementing the RDBMS solutions.
- Well-trained professionals are required for the maintenance and administration of RDBMS for the effective and efficient running of the system.

While the record-based and relational data models are helpful for efficient storage, the **dimensional model** focuses on faster retrieval. Ralph Kimball developed it in 1996 to optimize data retrieval speeds for analytic purposes in a data warehouse.

The dimensional models are denormalized data structures and appear like a star with a central or primary table called the **fact table** with surrounding tables connected to it called **dimension tables** or **star schema**. The fact table contains the measurements, metrics, or factual data about a business process and the foreign key to the dimension tables. In contrast, the dimension tables contain detailed or descriptive data.

Another variant of the dimensional model is the **snowflake schema**. It is similar to the star schema, except for the normalized dimension tables. Thus, the dimension table can split into multiple tables giving a snowflake appearance to the schema.

1.3 Types of Data

It makes little difference if we can store and access vast amounts of data, if we cannot analyze or comprehend it. That is where data analysis comes into the picture, where understanding the different data types is critical. To get the most accurate insights in market research and data sciences, a proper understanding of essential data is needed by applying suitable statistical measurements that fit our needs and goals.

At a high level, data can be categorized into two types as shown in Fig. 1.6.

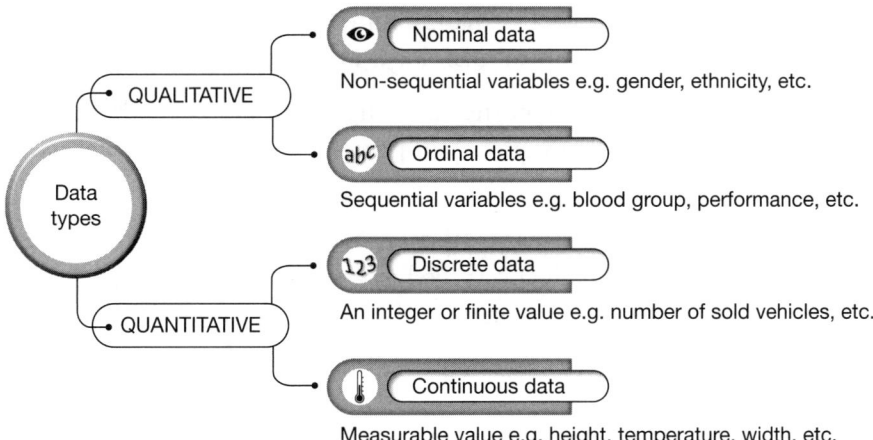

Figure 1.6 Types of data

Quantitative Data

Quantitative data refers to **numerical data**, i.e., any data dealing with numbers or anything that can be measured, e.g., age, height, weight, temperature, and prices.

Discrete data and **continuous data** are the two types of quantitative data.

Discrete: The quantitative data is considered discrete if it can be counted. They are typically represented as integers like the number of students in a class, the number of visits to the doctor, and the number of vehicles owned. The discrete data variables can take only specific values and cannot be subdivided into smaller parts—for instance, a soccer game score of 5 goals. A score of 5½ goals is not practical. Discrete data is typically represented in bar and pie charts.

Continuous: Quantitative data is referred to as continuous data if it can be measured. It can take a range of values from lowest to highest. It can be divided and measured to decimal places, e.g., temperature, weight, and car speed. Continuous data is typically represented as histograms.

Qualitative Data

Qualitative data is also referred to as **categorical data**. It deals with characters and attributes that cannot be numerically measured, e.g., educational background, people, or focus groups' opinions on a specific brand or product, etc. Words, pictures, or symbols are typically used to represent them.

Nominal data and **ordinal** data are the two types of qualitative data.

Nominal: Nominal data is a type of data used to label variables without providing any quantitative value. It comes from the Latin term 'nomen', which means name. They do not have any inherent order or sequence. Some of the examples of nominal data are:

- Eye color (blue, brown, grey, black, hazel.)
- Nationality (Indian, American, German, Chinese, Italian.)
- Subjects (Maths, Physics, Chemistry, Biology, History.)

Nominal data can be analyzed by hypothesis testing or grouping method, i.e., grouping into categories and calculating the frequency or percentage. They are typically represented as a pie chart.

Ordinal: Ordinal data refers to a categorical data variable with a set order or scale, e.g., a preference set of "Most likely, Likely, Least likely, Not likely." Researchers use this type of data to scale responses. Some of the examples of ordinal data are:

- Service satisfaction (Very satisfied, Satisfied, Indifferent, Dissatisfied, Very dissatisfied)
- Winning order (First, Second, Third)
- Student grades (A-Excellent, B-Good, C-Satisfactory, D-Unsatisfactory, F-Fail)

Binary: Another type of data is binary data. It can be categorized as either nominal or ordinal. Only two values represent binary data: Yes/No, True/False, On/Off, or Male/Female. It can also hold the value of 0/1, in which case it can be termed as a quantitative data type based on the nature of its application.

1.4 NATURE OF DATA

The nature of data plays a vital role in understanding how the data must be collected, stored, and analyzed. There is a wide variety of data available, and the ability to categorize or classify such data ensures that the data collected is less redundant and more of value.

Data generated for analytics comes from three primary sources:

Transaction Data

Transaction data is the traditional business data stored by practically all organizations. Examples of transaction data are personnel or customer files, commercial transactions, financial/medical/government/education records, etc. They can be classified as administrative data collected as part of management and operational needs. They are typically stored in structured or relational database systems.

However, in some instances, the data may be unstructured and produced in formats that cannot be directly stored in relational databases but require fast processing, e.g., huge volumes of electronic invoices (e-invoicing) coming in at a great pace from a multinational business.

Data in the form of images, pictures, pdf, etc., would need alternative storage and processing methods. Again, understanding the source and nature of data can help identify the required technology.

Social Data

Social data is also referred to as human-sourced data. It is the data of human interactions produced in social networks.

This data can be quantitative; for example, the number of product clicks, or qualitative; like why a group or community would prefer or reject a specific product. Social data is rarely structured and is often ungoverned by standard rules. Social or human-sourced data are found in mobile data texts, user-generated maps, social networks like Facebook and Twitter, blogs, comments and discussion forums, videos from YouTube and Vimeo, pictures from Instagram and Pinterest, and many more internet sources. Data from these sources are used for sentiment analysis, trend topics analysis, etc.

Machine Data

Machine-generated data is gaining ground with the advent of the Internet of Things. It is all-encompassing as it contains a real-time record of all user behavior and activity and transactions and information from applications, servers, networks, and mobile devices. There will be a prolific rise in machine data with smartwatches, fitness trackers, smart mobiles, medical sensors, and the growth of smart cities and smart homes.

Machine-generated data is well structured in nature. However, its high speed and size creation in real-time poses a challenge for traditional data storing and processing approaches.

Machine-generated data is sourced from:

- Fixed sensors like security or surveillance videos, traffic webcams, RFID, weather sensors, etc.
- Mobile or tracking sensors like mobile phones, GPS receivers, satellite images, etc.
- Data from computer systems, e.g., data logs.

Once the source and nature of the data are understood, the data team can figure out the technical aspects related to how the data should be collected, how it should be stored, the best-suited architecture required, the corresponding hardware and software, the apt algorithms or techniques to use for data processing and many more.

The nature of data can be classified based on its mode of representation:

Numerical (quantitative): Data is numerical when the values are represented either as a numerical measurement, say 1.95, or a numerical value like 1 or 0 to represent 'Yes' or 'No.'

Descriptive (qualitative): Data is said to be descriptive if it consists of textual comments or statements about a subject. All qualitative data are descriptive.

Graphical or symbolic: Charts, maps, graphs, and flowcharts fall under this category, where the nature of data is a visual representation.

Based on time factor
- **Time-dependent:** There can be multiple event occurrences during a time period. Data value measurement examples are blood pressure, stock prices during the day, precipitation, etc.
- **Time-independent:** The data value occurs once or is not time-dependent, e.g., heart attack, stock market crash, cyclone occurrence, etc.

Based on variables
- **Univariate data**: Refers to data that has one characteristic for measurement. For example, the number of members in a family.
- **Bivariate data**: Refers to data when two characteristics are measured simultaneously. For example, the sex and age of the members of a family.
- **Multivariate data**: When multiple characteristics are measured. For example, the family size, income, and savings of families in a city.

Temporal: Data that is temporary or valid only for a given or prescribed time.

Categorical: Data that can be classified or stored into groups, for example, race, film genres, animal species, etc.

Dimensionality of Data

Dimensionality refers to the level of attributes that a data can have. Data can be of high dimension or low dimension. High-dimensional data are when the number of dimensions or attributes is relatively high and vice-versa for low-dimensional data. E.g., a high-resolution image of a vast color landscape would be of high dimension compared to a black-and-white cartoon image of a cat.

Understanding the nature of data allows data analysts and scientists to determine the kind of machine learning model to build, to identify the inputs and outputs for the process that are easy to measure and valuable to predict, for better insights and visual representation.

1.5 DATA VISUALIZATION

The primary form of information display is tables and graphs. While tables display information quantitatively in the form of rows and columns, graphs or charts visually display how the data relate to each other and make it more easily perceivable. This enables data analysts to study and understand the patterns and outliers in large datasets.

Introduction to Data Analytics • 15

The approaches listed below are most often utilized for information visualization.

- **Line chart:** The line chart is the most straightforward technique providing a two-dimensional view of a relationship by joining the data points (Fig. 1.7 (a)). It shows the variation of one variable plotted on the vertical axis with the regular progression of the second variable plotted on the horizontal axis. It is typically used to show the trend in data over time. Several line plots on the chart can represent trends among multiple variables.
- **Bar chart:** They are used to compare variables in the form of a horizontal or vertical bar where the length and height of the bar represents the respective values. The data plotted is categorical, where one axis represents the categories being compared while the other axis represents the respective numerical value (Fig. 1.7 (b)).

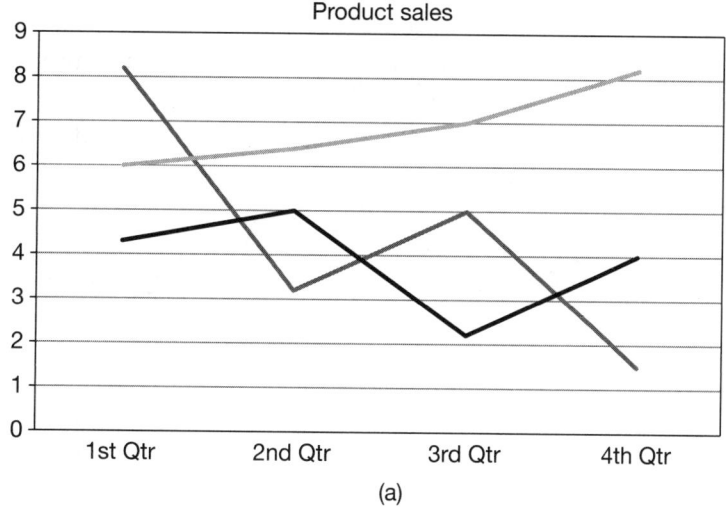

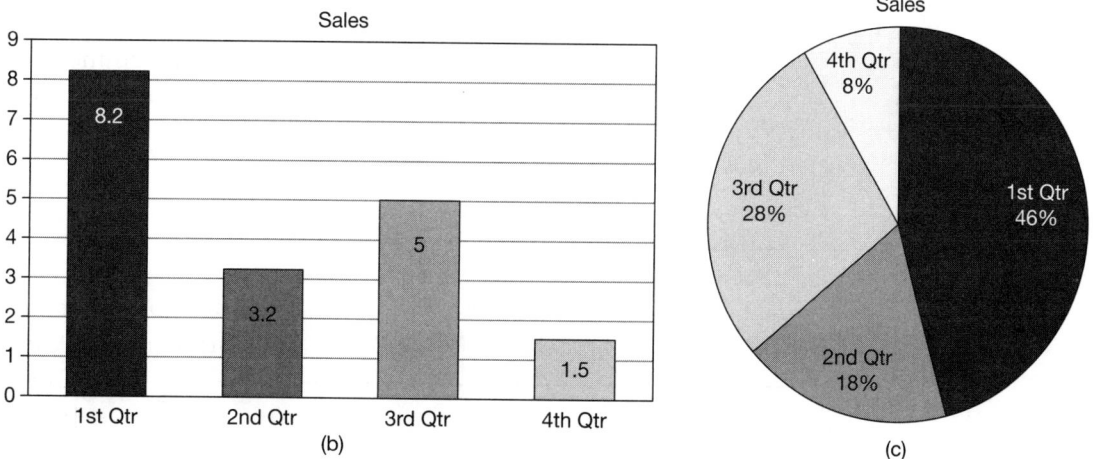

Figure 1.7 (a) Line chart, (b) Bar chart and (c) Pie chart

- **Pie chart:** Pie charts provide a visual representation of how a group is broken down into minor elements or categories. It is represented as a circular graph called a pie that is 100% of the group, wherein each pie slice represents a category proportional to the quantity. A pie chart is ideal in scenarios where the categories are limited to 5 or 6 (Fig. 1.7 (c)).
- **Histogram:** Histograms represent the frequency distribution of variables measured on discrete intervals or bins. The bar area is proportional to the frequency of a variable, and the width is equal to the interval. The intervals are continuous and set by the x-axis, while the y-axis shows the value occurrences (Fig. 1.8 (a)). It is typically used when dealing with large Datasets and helps detect any gaps or outliers in the data.

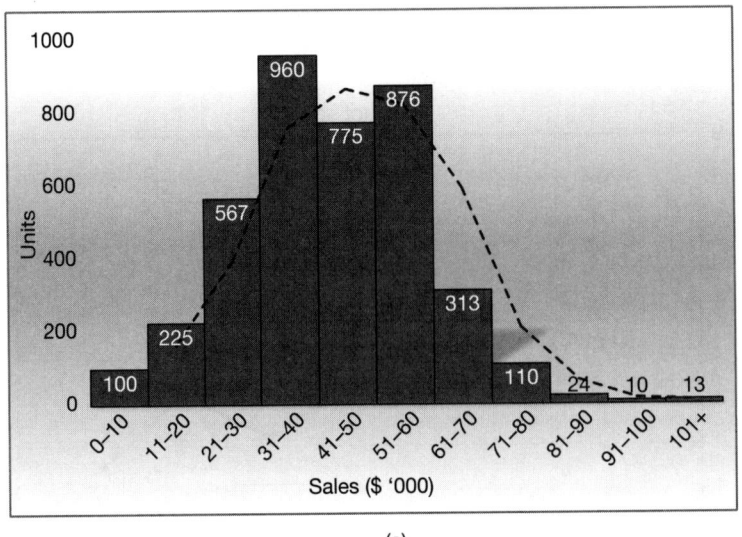

(a)

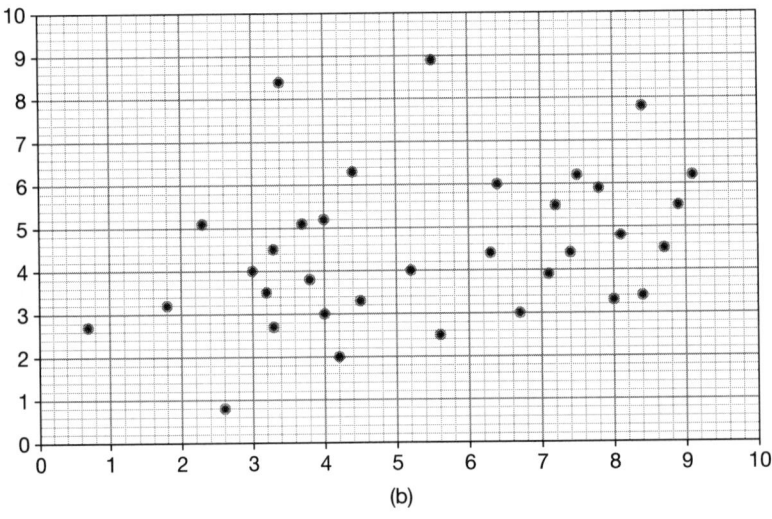

(b)

Figure 1.8 (a) Histogram and (b) Scatter plot

- **Scatter plot:** A scatter plot or graph is used to observe the relationship between variables. The values of two variables plotted along the x and y-axis can reveal a pattern or existence of any correlation in a dataset. Scatter plots are used to identify correlations, unexpected gaps, or outliers in data analysis (Fig. 1.8 (b)).
- **Time-series:** Time-series graphs are used to visualize trends or seasonality in data over time (Fig. 1.9). The data is plotted across the x-y axis, where the x-axis shows the time increments like hourly, daily, monthly, and yearly, and the y-axis is the value of the variable being measured. The plotted points are joined by a continuous line, thus depicting how the value of the variable changes over time.

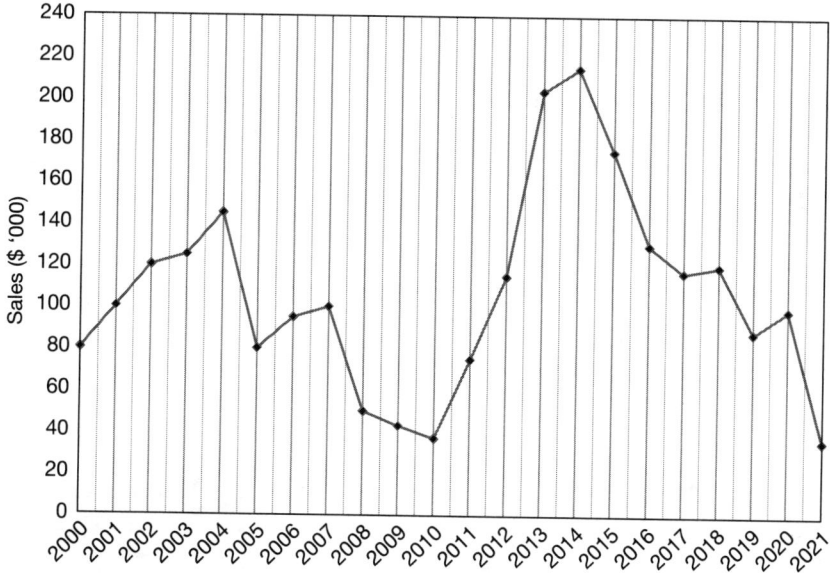

Figure 1.9 Time-series graph

- **Box plot:** A box plot, also known as box-and-whisker plot, is a graphical method of displaying variations in datasets.

    It is a standardized way of comparing Distribution between many groups using a five-number summary (Fig 1.10), namely, Minimum – the lowest data point, First Quartile Q1 – the median of the lower half of the dataset, Median – middle value of the dataset, Third Quartile Q3 – the median of the top half of the dataset and Maximum – the largest data point. The box plots help understand multiple datasets from independent related sources, skewed distributions, and detect the presence of outliers.
- **Word cloud:** A word cloud is employed when the source data is text-based. It is also known as text clouds or tag clouds and displays keyword information on web pages (tags). It is rendered in various sizes, depending on how frequently they are used in the study context. The frequency or importance of a word is directly proportionate to its size (Fig. 1.11 (a)).

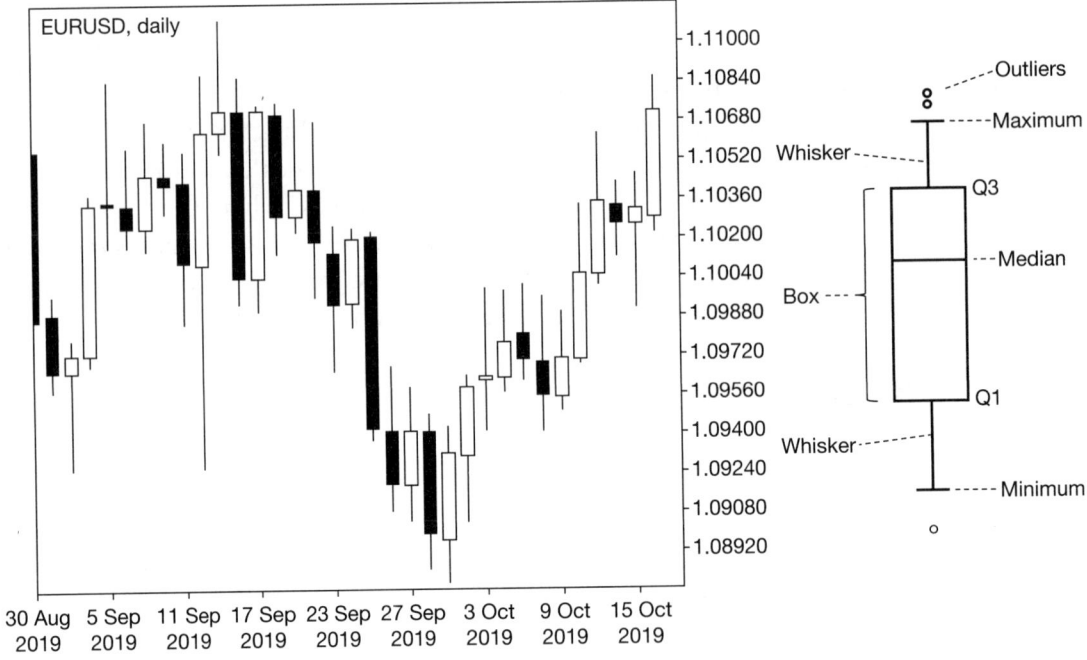

Figure 1.10 Box plot showing fluctuation in EUR/USD currency pair in a 5-trading platform

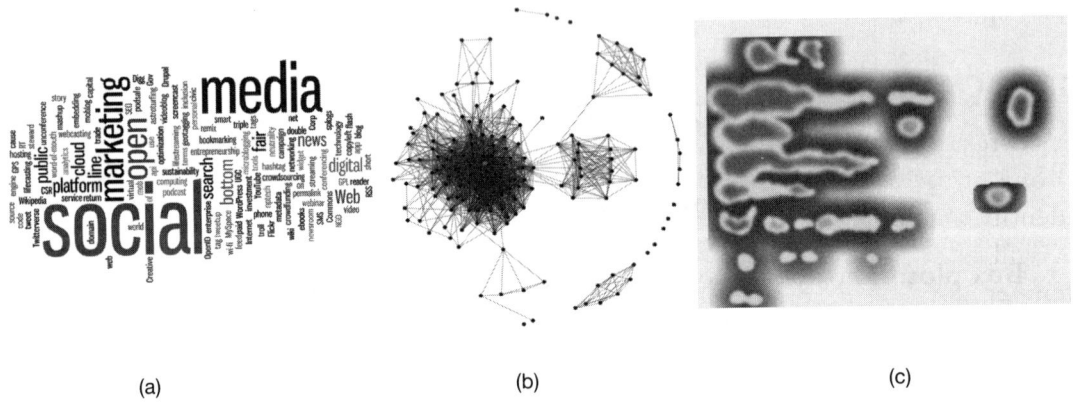

Figure 1.11 (a) Word cloud, (b) Network graph and (c) Heat map

- **Network diagrams:** Network diagrams or graphs show interconnections between entities or nodes. Connections or links between the nodes represent the relationship. It is generally used to analyze social networks to understand how people are connected. Various aspects of the relationship can be communicated by varying the color, width/size, and arrowheads of the nodes or relationship lines (Fig. 1.11 (b)).
- **Heat map:** It is a method of graphically representing numerical data using a hot-to-cold or cold-to-hot color scheme. Businesses typically use it to understand

their web page user behavior in real-time. For example, they provide an efficient way to identify, at a glance, the most popular and least popular elements or sections on a page by the number of mouse clicks or hovers represented by a predetermined color spectrum.

There are numerous other visualization techniques. Data scientists and data analysts sometimes use a combination of various visualization plots and methods to produce the right chart that fits the purpose. These depend on the variables under study and the question that needs answering. We will delve deeper into data visualization techniques and models in *Chapter 18: Big Data Visualizations*.

1.6 DATA ANALYSIS METHODS

Today when we say 'data,' we mean 'Big Data.' We have gone beyond just storing data as strings or numbers. Instead, data is transactional and comes in machine data form derived from IoT sensors like satellites, cameras, and smart meters. There is also streaming data from the web and social media platforms like video uploads, likes, and tweets that can provide valuable insights into consumer behavior and marketing trends.

Data analysis is collecting, cleaning, organizing, transforming, and modeling the data to extract useful information to support business decision-making. Depending on the industry and the purpose of the analysis, data analysts and scientists use various analysis methods and techniques to uncover and visualize the data trends and patterns. Some of the commonly used analysis methods are described below.

1.6.1 Correlation

A correlation model is applied to identify the relationship between two variables. It is one of the essential data analytics tools that can help define trends and predict and identify the root cause for specific scenarios. For example, it shows how much variable X will change if there is a change in variable Y. Examples are correlation between temperature and ice-cream sales, age and blood pressure, and education and income earned.

Typically, scatter plot graphs are used to visually analyze the relationship between two variables by plotting one variable (X-axis) against the other (Y-axis). The correlated data can match any of the four types below:

Positive Correlation

A dataset is considered to have a positive correlation if any increase in variable 'A' results in an increase in variable 'B' or a decrease in variable 'A' results in a decrease in variable 'B'. In other words, both variables move in the same direction, e.g., the correlation between age and blood pressure. A positive correlation will form an upward slope (Fig. 1.12).

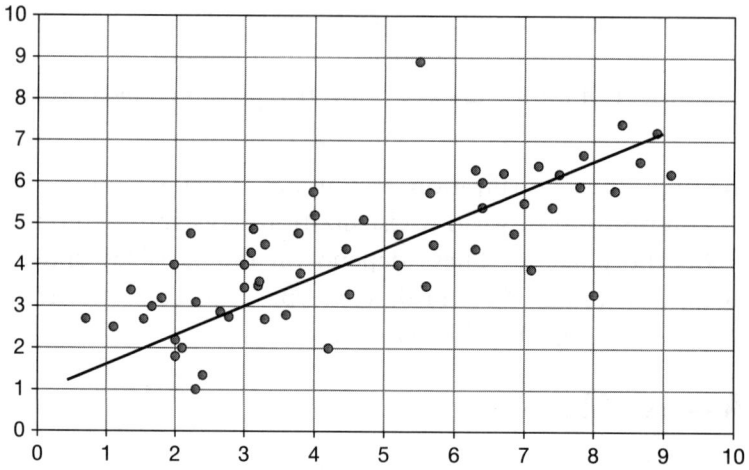

Figure 1.12 Positive correlation

Negative Correlation

If the growth of one causes the decline of the other, the dataset is said to have a negative correlation. For example, age and agility. As one increases in age, the less agile they become. A negative correlation forms a downward slope line (Fig. 1.13).

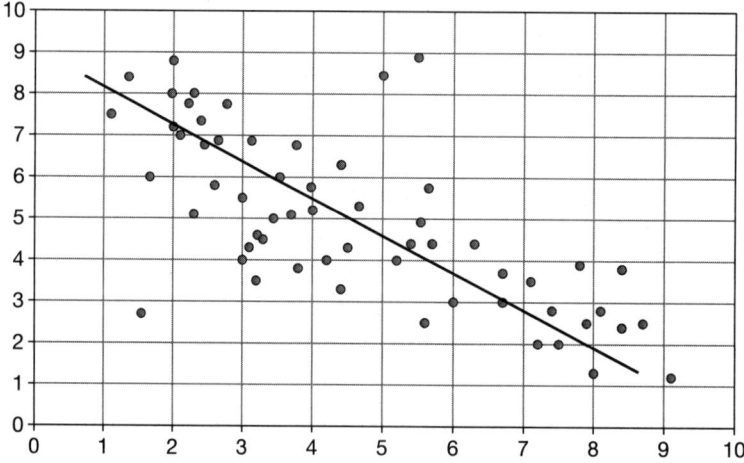

Figure 1.13 Negative correlation

Zero Correlation

When there is no detectable trend between the two variables, the dataset is said to have no correlation or zero correlation. Here the data will be scattered, and there is no discernable pattern. For example, a person's complexion and height or a person's intellect and happiness. The graph does not represent an upward or downward linear line, when plotted (Fig. 1.14).

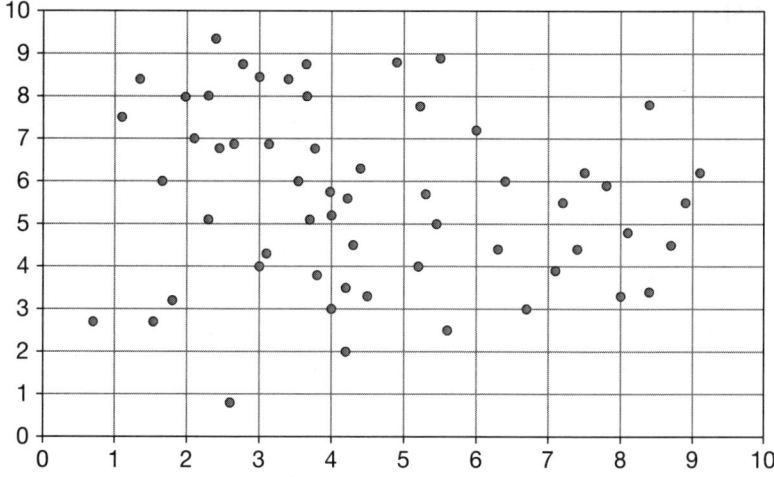

Figure 1.14 Zero correlation

Spurious Correlation

A spurious correlation is when a significant correlation is observed between two variables that have no causal connection but are influenced by a third or unknown factor. Common well-cited spurious correlations are the death rate by drowning with higher ice cream sales and more iPhone sales to death from falling downstairs. However, it is essential to note that correlation does not mean causality. Though some spurious correlations are apparent, it is essential to note that there could be instances where the data pairing looks plausible but is, in reality, unauthentic.

1.6.2 Regression

Regression is widely used for forecasting and prediction. The premise is to predict an outcome variable called a **dependent variable** based on input variables called **independent variable** or **predictor variable**. It is typically used to predict an actual value (output), whether past, current, or future, based on previously collected data or information. For example, predicting the precipitation in a particular year based on rainfall data from the available years. While the dependent variable is the total rainfall, the predictor variable could be the monthly rainfall volume. However, there are multiple predictor variables used in regression analysis. In this example, the other predictors could be the temperature, soil moisture, wind velocity, and others to predict the total precipitation (rainfall) in a future or gap year.

It is also used to deduce causal relationships between the independent and dependent variables. In regression, the output is always quantitative, and the model can work only if we know the previous input and output data figures. Scatter plot graphs are widely used to represent regression models.

1.6.3 Forecasting

Forecasting is predicting or estimating the future value of data by analyzing trends based on past and present data. It is best used where numerical historical information is available and past trends are assumed to continue into the near future. For example, hourly electricity demand at home or annual company profits. It should be noted that forecasting techniques do not predict the future. Instead, it gives a calculated estimation of what could happen based on what has already happened.

The most commonly used quantitative forecasting technique is the **time-series forecasting** method. A time-series is a set of numerical measurements of the same entity taken at equally spaced intervals over time. The analysis output enables us to make informed predictions of future values.

Time-series data has five components:

1. **Level**: The base value of the series if it were a straight line.
2. **Trend**: The overall increasing or decreasing direction of the series.
3. **Seasonality**: When repeated behavior in the data occurs at regular intervals, e.g., vacations in December.
4. **Cycles**: When a series follows an up-and-down pattern that is not seasonal.
5. **Noise**: An unexplained variation in the pattern.

While all time-series graphs generally have the level and noise, the components of trend, seasonality, and cycles are optional factors that enable a better understanding of the dataset and making of informed decisions.

1.6.4 Clustering

Clustering is the technique of grouping data or objects with similar characteristics in a dataset. It is assumed that the entities of a particular group are comparatively more similar to the entities of another group. Clustering follows a single-phase approach, where we provide the input data to the system without knowing the output or groupings. Instead, the technique identifies patterns in data by using distance measures to group or separate data points.

This technique allows us to set the clustering parameters that align with our business strategy and goals. For example, cluster analysis is typically used in market research for customer segmentation. People are grouped based on their responses to several variables, for example, identifying customer segments based on their purchasing power to offer discounts for specific products. Google and Amazon use clustering algorithms in their search results to present users with links or products that are relevant to them.

There are four types of clustering, as follows:

Connectivity-based Clustering

Connectivity-based clustering is also known as hierarchical clustering. It goes by the premise that the data point closest to it is more related than the point away from it. Two methods are used for connectivity-based clustering:

(i) **Method 1**: All data points are taken as one big cluster and then partitioned into smaller groups or sets as their distance increases Fig. 1.15 (a).

(ii) **Method 2**: Each data point is taken as an individual cluster and joined with another data point or group of data points similar to it till a big cluster is reached Fig. 1.15 (b).

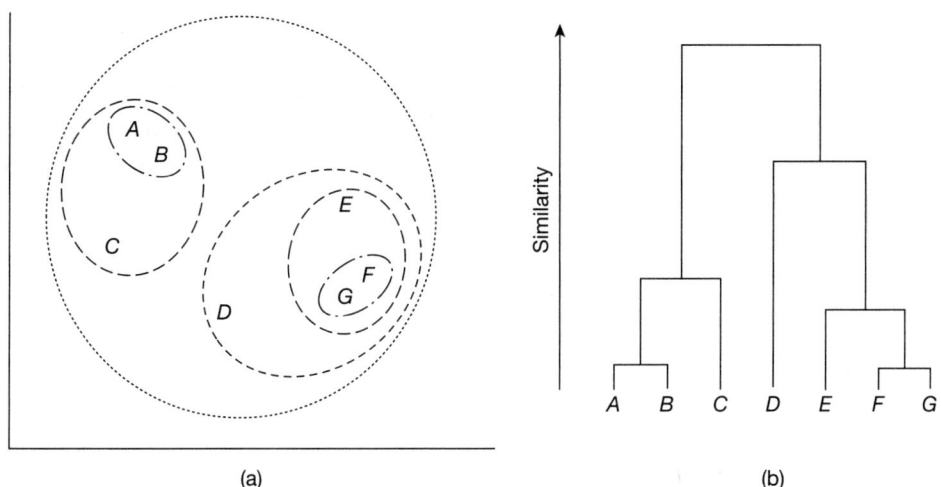

Figure 1.15 Connectivity-based clustering

Though simple to interpret, the connectivity-based technique gets complex and time-consuming when working with too many outliers. Hence the model is typically used when working with small datasets.

Centroid-based Clustering

In this technique, the data is first randomly grouped into clusters. Each cluster consists of data points that are closest to it (Fig. 1.16).

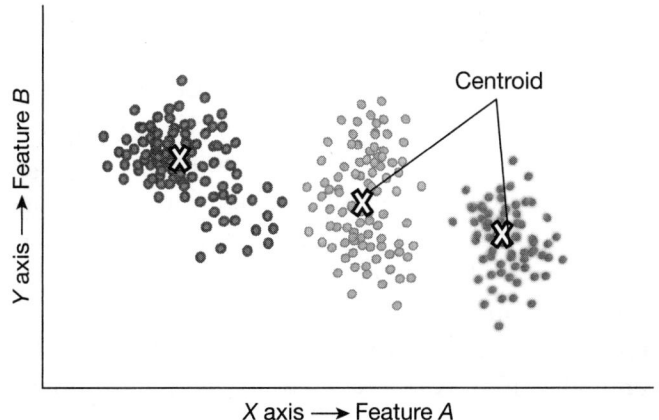

Figure 1.16 Centroid clustering representing three clusters

The centroid is calculated as the average of all the data points in the cluster and plotted. The data points are then revisited to determine whether any data point is closer to the cluster of another centroid than its assigned centroid. If they are closer to another centroid, it is redistributed to the cluster of that centroid. The process is repeated iteratively till all data points are in the clusters containing the centroid closest to them, thus reaching the optimal grouping.

Density-based Clustering

Density-based clustering connects areas of high density (Fig. 1.17). It is assumed that the more densely populated the data points are together, the more the chances that the data belongs to the same group. In this methodology, a random data point is selected, and the distance between each data point and the data points around it is measured. If the data points are within a certain predetermined distance, they are considered related and grouped. The process will iterate by selecting random data points until the best clusters can be identified within the distance threshold. Unlike distribution-based clustering, the outliers are not assigned to any cluster.

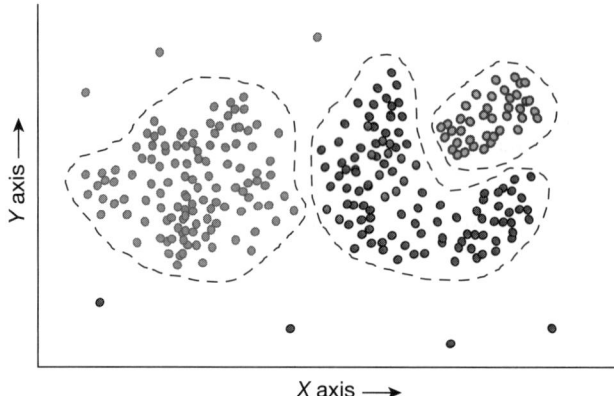

Figure 1.17 Density-based clustering

Distribution-based Clustering

The distribution clustering model is based on the probability that a particular data point belongs to a cluster. Around each possible centroid, the algorithm defines the density distributions for each cluster, quantifying the probability of belonging based on these distributions. The graph represents the density distributions of the data points (Fig. 1.18). If a data point is close within the density circle or centroid, it is a 100% probability that it is part of the specific group. The farther away it gets, the lesser the probability that the data point belongs to the group.

Thus the premise is based more on probability than definitive fact, as is the case in other clustering techniques. However, distribution-based clustering is also significant in assigning outliers to clusters.

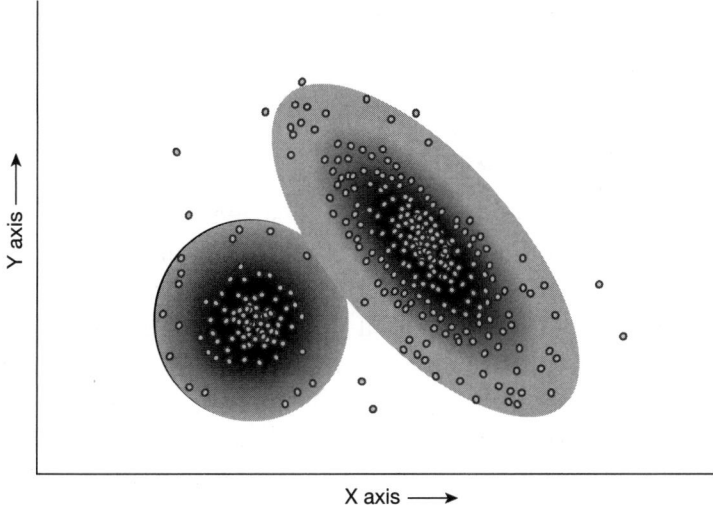

Figure 1.18   Distribution-based clustering

1.6.5 Classification

Classification is a technique used to analyze and group data into categories or classes using algorithms. In this model, the output dataset is labeled, i.e., the resultant data is qualitative and known. The classification model is a two-stage process:

1. **The training stage**: In this stage, a set of training data is built that constitutes a set of attributes and the expected outcome. The algorithm is trained on a massive set of correctly classified data to ensure that the points in the dataset are classified correctly to reach the right outcome. For example, a set of symptoms based on clinical data is constructed to classify a particular disease.
2. **The classification stage**: Once the model is built, the algorithm is run on test data to estimate the accuracy and precision of the classification rules. Finally, the model predicts the target class for each case in new datasets.

The classification method uses mathematical techniques such as decision trees, linear programming, neural network, statistics, and others. When data is classified into two classes like Yes/No, Good/Bad, and Male/Female, it is called **binary classification**. E.g., spam detection and customer churn prediction. When data is classified into three or more classes, it is called **multinomial classification**. E.g., classifying fruits into apples, bananas, oranges, or classifying buildings, lakes, and forests from hyperspectral imaging.

1.7   Web Data

Web data is the most widely used source of Big Data today, and it is extensive. This data can be from enterprise portals, online business applications, social media, and social networks. According to a Cisco study, 74.4 billion networked devices will be linked by 2025. This is a massive volume of data that businesses can exploit through web data integration.

1.7.1 Evolution of Analytic Scalability

Organizations have used technology and data analytics since the 1960s to gain a competitive edge on each other. However, the advent of the Global Internet, Data Warehouse, and ELTs in the 90s revolutionized analytics. With web applications, globalization, mobile computing, and social networks like Amazon, Google, Facebook, and LinkedIn, organizations are now dealing with voluminous data that are unstructured and heterogeneous.

The traditional data processing and analytics using RDBMS and Enterprise Data Warehousing are unfeasible for processing such a fast-rising amount of data. However, technology has evolved in the past decade or two, ushering in the foundation for modern analytics architecture. Some technologies capable of handling big unstructured data are MPP, Cloud Computing, and MapReduce.

We need a structure in unstructured voluminous data before it can be analyzed. This would require consolidation of data from various heterogeneous sources, preprocessing for data cleansing, and consolidation of the data quality to make it workable for accessing and analyzing. This requires high processing power and scalability when working with massive data.

Symmetric Multiprocessing (SMP) Architecture

In symmetric multiprocessing or SMP databases, data is stored in servers called nodes. In this system, multiple identical processors (Fig. 1.19) work in parallel to execute independent programs and tasks concurrently. However, they share the same **main memory** and input/output devices via a data bus or switch. Though the SMP architecture can work well with small to medium data volumes, it becomes a bottleneck when huge volumes are involved due to the shared memory constraint.

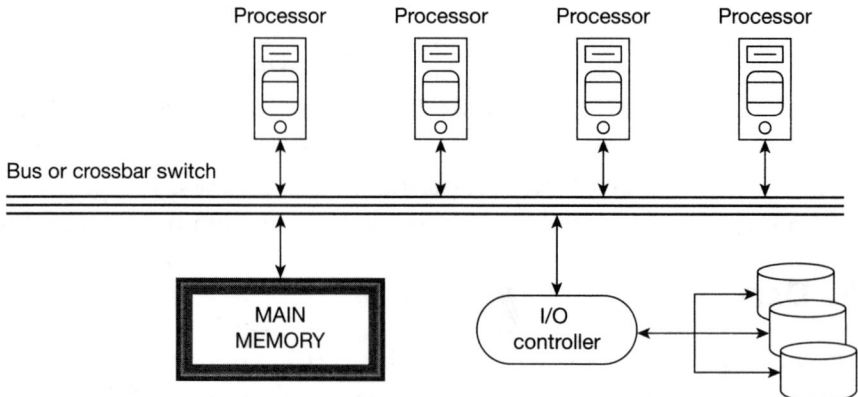

Figure 1.19 Symmetric multi-processing architecture

Hence, a system upgrade is required to scale up, leading to high costs and downtime. In addition, its reliance on shared resources makes SMP databases less fault-tolerant and less efficient. Oracle and Sybase work on the SMP database.

Massively Parallel Processing (MPP)

The MPP or massively parallel processing architecture addresses the drawbacks of scalability inherent in the SMP architecture. Each processor or **compute node** or **node** works independently with its operating system, dedicated memory, and disk storage (Fig. 1.20). Thus, the compute nodes are independent of each other and communicate only via a high-speed communication system or interconnect. This environment is called the 'shared-nothing' environment.

When requested, MPP systems use a **control node** to identify the right query plan. The control node plans and distributes the work to the compute nodes, which will work in parallel to retrieve data from their respective disks and execute the task in a shorter period.

MPP systems can be linearly scaled up by adding more nodes. The system can take advantage of the computing time by breaking the workload into smaller tasks. However, if there are dependencies between the tasks, then the efficiency of information communication between the different processing units becomes key. Thus, the system needs to be optimized to deal with caching, data distribution and sorting, and storage. The setting up and database management of MPP systems is complex. Teradata and Azure SQL Data Warehouse are built on MPP architecture.

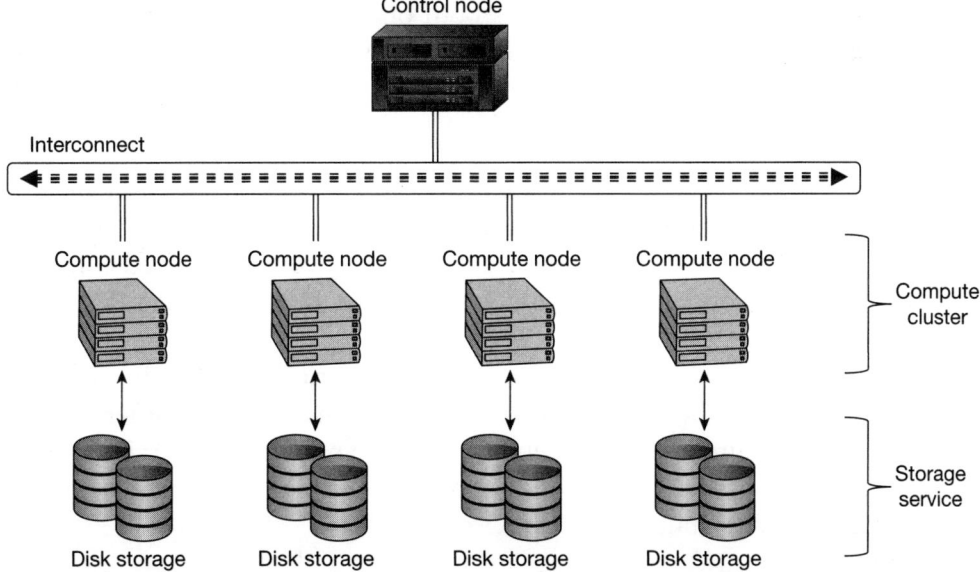

Figure 1.20 Massively parallel processing architecture

Cloud Computing

Cloud computing is more cost-effective and less complex than MPP data operation. In addition, cloud computing brings elasticity to MPP architecture, paving the way for on-demand MPP architecture. The critical aspects of cloud computing are:

- **On-demand self-service:** The user can monitor, prioritize and manage the computing resource for query/analytics and leave the infrastructure maintenance and resource pooling to the service provider.
- **Broad network accessibility:** Data storage and computing is performed over the internet, giving anyone access to it irrespective of their location or device used (such as a laptop or mobile device).
- **Elasticity and scalability:** Cyclical changes in demand can be efficiently managed by scaling in and scaling out as required without a massive impact on time and resources.
- **Economical:** It is a pay-as-you-go model where the user is charged according to the usage of services, i.e., storage processing power. Hence based on the required nodes, a user can increase or decrease their subscription over time. This model provides flexibility, agility, and a low cost of ownership.
- **Continuity and security:** Automatic snapshots and backups ensure that data is stored across different nodes. This supports business continuity by enabling users to work without interruption in the event of a disaster or incident. In addition, the cloud data is kept more secure through encryption services and VPNs.

Organizations that handle growing data volumes are steadily opting for cloud data warehouses or a hybrid model that includes both on-premises and cloud. For example, Amazon Redshift and Microsoft Azure SQL Data Warehouse are cloud storage and computing platforms.

Grid Computing

Grid computing is a large-scale distributed computing method where a network of computers, irrespective of their geographical location, share resources like processing power, memory, and storage to accomplish a task. Thus, every authorized computer has access to the entire network's collective processing power and storage capacity, making it a supercomputer.

A primary computer or server(s) called the **control node** acts as the administrator for the whole network. The rest of the computers in the network either provide the resources or use the resources from the network resource pool (Fig. 1.21). As a result, grid computing is more economical as the work is split and distributed over the network, thus efficiently utilizing the computer's idle time.

Organizations use grid computing to optimize and share data resources and computational power across networks, pool them for large workloads, and enable collaboration. However, there could be constraints when nodes work with large data volumes where network bandwidth may be a bottleneck.

Introduction to Data Analytics • 29

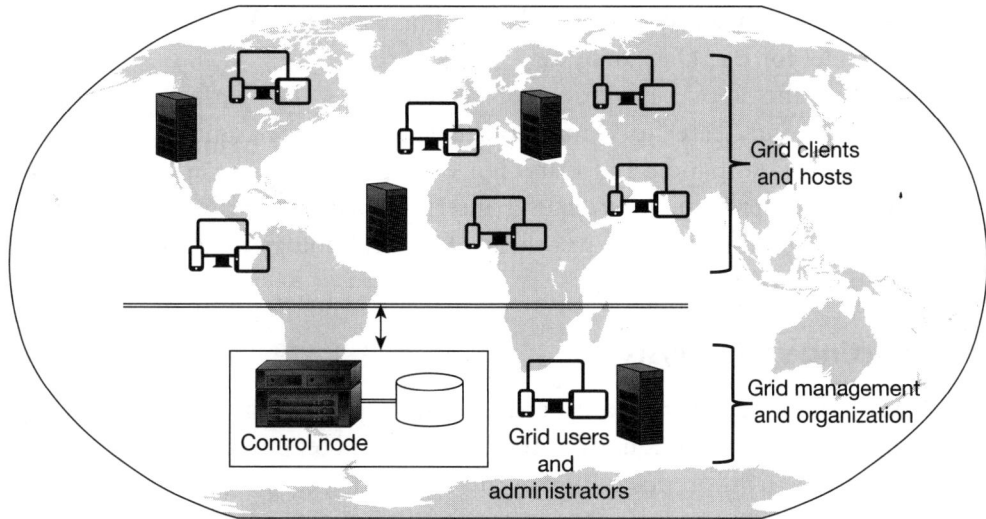

Figure 1.21 Grid computing architecture

MapReduce

It is important to note that MapReduce is not a database. Instead, it is a programming model or framework that can organize how vast volumes of data are processed and computed. MapReduce works in three stages: Map, Shuffle and Reduce (Fig. 1.22).

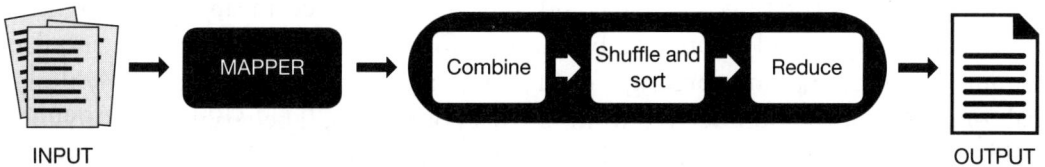

Figure 1.22 Basic MapReduce flow

Map: The map phase or mapper function is to process the input data, typically in the form of files or directories, and generate key-value pairs that will be useful for identifying the presence of a data or a block of data in a storage environment.

Shuffle and Sort: In this stage, the framework shuffles and sorts the unstructured data output from the mapper function and transfers them as an input to the reducer function. While the shuffling process collects similar work units and groups them by key, the sorting process sorts the data by key into the required order. Shuffling can start before the Map phase is completed, saving time.

Reduce: In the final Reduce stage, the reducer function takes the sorted results from the map function and does an aggregation or summation to produce the final result.

MapReduce works well with data-intensive operations but not if it is CPU-intensive. Furthermore, as MapReduce is not a database, there is no indexing mechanism or built-in security. It is, however, an effective programming model for performing large-scale data analysis using multiple machines in the cluster. For example, Apache Hadoop uses the MapReduce model for Big Data analysis.

As seen from the above evolution of technologies, no perfect technology can effectively and efficiently cater to voluminous data. Hence the right set of technologies needs to be integrated to handle Big Data. For example, Hive is an application that runs on top of Hadoop to provide a better user interface, while Pig is a scripting language. Spark, BigQuery, and Snowflake are just some of the technology platforms that have their foundation in Big Data Analytics.

1.7.2 Reporting vs. Analysis

Both analysis and reporting are crucial areas of web analytics. However, unfortunately, both terms are used interchangeably. Hence, it is essential that we clearly understand the difference between the two and their purpose in organizational decision-making.

Reporting is collating existing information and presenting it in a comprehensive and user-friendly way based on the audience's needs. The data is presented in a specific manner that is defined, objective and accurate. The purpose of reporting is for organizations to track and analyze their business's performance and overall health, thus guiding improvement and growth opportunities. E.g., financial reports, inventory stock reports, and market analysis report.

Analysis is interpreting the data and reports to extract meaningful insights for better understanding and improving business performance. Analysis is about enquiring, examining, comparing, interpreting, confirming, or predicting. This is done by using or 'analyzing' the information derived from raw data or reports. The analysis aims to answer specific business questions of why/when/how by providing key findings and actionable recommendations.

Both reporting and analysis are done with graphs, charts, tables, and other data visualization tools. However, the three key differentiators between the two are:

1. While reporting shows **what** is happening, analysis attempts to explain **why**.
2. Reporting provides **information** while analysis reveals **insights**.
3. In reporting, data from statistic reports, dashboards, and alerts are **pushed** to the users. While in analysis, users **pull** the required data for examination and interpretation.

In today's data-driven world of data analytics, the best organizational decisions are made when the right reports are generated to draw meaningful insights aligned to the organization's business strategy.

By implementing the appropriate data analytics tool, businesses can increase revenue and decrease costs. Data is out there, and the challenge is not in acquiring the data but extracting, cleansing, and storing the required data. Businesses can address analytics and reporting needs by leveraging specialized analytical tools like Power BI, Hadoop, Tableau, Azure Analytics, and Knime that fit their organizational data needs towards decision-making insights.

SUMMARY

Data is information that is collected and analyzed to enable relevant decision-making. Organizations are continually looking to evaluate and obtain the right tools and techniques to solve complex problems and gain business advantage through data. The basic principle of analytics is collecting raw data from multiple sources, crunching and cleansing them to extract useful information, and exploiting patterns that can be further processed and analyzed to gain new insights, opportunities, problems, and causes.

Data Models are used to extract the best possible value from data systems. Data modeling is creating a conceptual model of how data is stored in a database. It describes the design of a database representing the entities, attributes, and the relationship among data, its constraints, and others. It occurs in three stages:

1. **Conceptual data model:** High-level design representing the business view of the data entities and their relationship.
2. **Logical data model:** A more detailed and logical representation of the data with attributes like data types, length, and other characteristics.
3. **Physical data model:** Represents the schema or framework of physically stored data in a database.

Data modeling builds data integrity and normalization. Models typically used in database management systems are object-based and record-based data models.

Data analytics is the science of storing, accessing and examining large volumes of data to analyze, interpret and draw conclusions. Understanding the type and nature of the data is required to analyze the data correctly and know which tools and techniques are best applied. At the highest level, data is of two kinds:

1. **Quantitative data:** Quantifiable data can be measured by numerical variables, e.g., age, height, weight, temperature, and prices. It is further divided into discrete data and continuous data.
2. **Qualitative data:** Also referred to as categorical data, it deals with characters and attributes that cannot be numerically measured, e.g., educational background, ethnicity, and hair color. Qualitative data is further divided into nominal and ordinal data.

A basic understanding of quantitative and qualitative data is required to comprehend how the data is to be collected and processed. Data generated from social media applications will be quite different from conventional or corporate applications.

The nature of data plays an important role in understanding how the data must be collected, stored, and analyzed. Categorizing or classifying such data ensures that the data collected is less redundant and more of value.

Data generated for analytics comes from three primary sources: transaction, social, and machine data.

The nature of data can be classified based on its mode of representation:

- **Numerical (quantitative):** Data is numerical when the values are represented as numbers, e.g., 1.95, 1, 0, 1125, etc.

- **Descriptive (qualitative):** Data consists of textual comments or statements about a subject.
- **Graphical or symbolic**: Visually represented data, e.g., charts, maps, graphs, and flowcharts.
- **Based on time factor**: Data can be time-dependent, i.e., multiple occurrences of the event during a time period, or time-independent where the occurrence is not time-dependent, e.g., occurrence of a heart-attack.
- **Based on variables**: Data can be univariate, bivariate, or multivariate based on the number of attributes or characteristics attributed to the data.
- **Temporal**: Data that is temporary or valid only for a given or prescribed time.
- **Categorical**: Data that can be classified or stored into groups, for example, race, film genres, animal species, etc.
- **Dimensionality**: Data can be of high dimension or low dimension. In high-dimensional data, the number of dimensions or attributes is relatively high, vice-versa for low-dimensional data.

Various data analytics technologies and techniques are used to comprehend the data. Some of the research methods used in analyzing the relationship between data variables to support business strategic and operational decision-making are:

- **Correlation**: The model applied to identify the relationship between two variables in a dataset.
- **Regression**: The model applied to predict a dependent variable when the value of the independent variable is given.
- **Forecasting**: Model used for predicting or estimating the future value of data by analyzing trends based on past and present data.
- **Clustering**: Model to identify discrete groups by organizing items into groups or clusters based on their similar characteristics.
- **Classification**: Model used to analyze and group data into labeled categories or classes.

Both analysis and reporting are crucial areas of data analytics. Both reporting and analysis are done with graphs, charts, tables, and other data visualization tools. While reporting shows what is happening, analysis attempts to explain why.

    Data scientists, analysts, and researchers need to use the right chart type to make sense of the data. Commonly used graphical charts in data sciences and statistics are bar charts, pie charts, line charts, histograms, scatter plots, box plots, time-series graphs, network charts, and heat maps.

    The data analytics strategy to be adopted by an organization depends on the quality and quantity of data at hand, the current state of data analytics, and the primary area that needs focus. There are currently many data mining, data analytics, and business intelligence (BI) tools in the market such as Hadoop, Power BI, Tableau, Qlik, Azure Analytics, Knime, and others that can meet the current need with the capability to scale up as required.

EXERCISES

Multiple Choice Questions

1. **Which of the following is not a type of data relationship?**
   A. One-to-One
   B. One-to-Many
   C. Many-to-Many
   D. Many-to-One
   Answer: D
   Explanation: There are three types of data relationships:
   One-to-one: One record or field in a table is connected to one and only one record/field of another table.
   One-to-many: One record or field is connected to one or more records of another table.
   Many-to-many: Both tables have duplicate values. E.g., Books and Authors - multiple authors could write a book, and an author may have written multiple books.

2. **Which of the following represents a structural representation of how data is stored in a database?**
   A. Data model
   B. Types of data
   C. Clustering
   D. Data analysis method
   Answer: A
   Explanation: Data models are a structural representation of how data is stored in a database. It describes the design of a database representing the entities, attributes, and the relationship among data, its constraints, and others.

3. **Which of the following is not a stage of developing a data model?**
   A. Conceptual data model
   B. Logical data model
   C. Physical data model
   D. Hierarchical data model
   Answer: D
   Explanation: There are typically three stages to developing a data model: They are Conceptual data mode, Logical data model and Physical data model.

4. **This high-level design displays only the entities and their relationships:**
   A. Conceptual data model
   B. Logical data model
   C. Physical data model
   D. Hierarchical data model
   Answer: A
   Explanation: Conceptual data model: This high-level design displays only the entities and their relationships. The goal is to define and structure the business's scope, rules, and procedures. The physical characteristics of the data are not considered at this stage.

5. **In this stage, more detail is built into the data design with data attributes like data types, length, and other characteristics:**
   A. Conceptual data model
   B. Logical data model
   C. Physical data model
   D. Hierarchical data model
   Answer: B

Explanation: Logical data model: In this stage, more detail is built into the data design with data attributes like data types, length, and other characteristics. This logical design helps form a database blueprint, bridging the application and developer specifications.

6. **In this stage, in-depth knowledge of the database system being used and its performance constraints are required:**
   A. Conceptual data model
   B. Logical data model
   C. Physical data model
   D. Hierarchical data model
   Answer: C
   Explanation: Physical data model: While the conceptual and logical data models are produced independently of any software or data storage structure, the physical data model is the schema or framework of how the data is physically stored within a database. Hence, an in-depth knowledge of the database system being used and its performance constraints are required. In this stage, referential integrity, performance tuning, indexing, and triggers are defined.

7. **In this stage, referential integrity, performance tuning, indexing, and triggers are defined.**
   A. Conceptual data model
   B. Logical data model
   C. Physical data model
   D. Hierarchical data model
   Answer: C
   Explanation: Same as for Question 6.

8. **In ER diagram, this represents the object or component of the data and is typically represented as a rectangle.**
   A. Entity
   B. Attribute
   C. Relationship
   D. Connectivity
   Answer: A
   Explanation: The ER diagram consists of three main components:
   Entity: The object or component of the data is typically represented as a rectangle.
   Attribute: The entity's property is represented as an oval in the ER diagram. E.g., Employee id, Name, DOB, address can be the attributes of entity Employee.
   Relationship: The associated relationship between entities, E.g., one-to-one, one-to-many/many-to-one and many-to-many are represented by connecting lines.

9. **This is represented as an oval in the ER diagram:**
   A. Entity
   B. Attribute
   C. Relationship
   D. Connectivity
   Answer: B
   Explanation: Same as for Question 8.

10. **In Object-Oriented Data Model (OODM), this represents a real-world entity:**
    A. Object
    B. Attribute
    C. Method
    D. Inheritance
    Answer: A

Explanation: Object: A real-world entity that consists of data and code encapsulated into a single unit. Example: EMPLOYEE or STUDENT. The object is akin to a relational data model.

11. **In an Object-Oriented Data Model (OODM), this represents characteristics of the object:**
    A. Object behavior
    B. Attribute
    C. Method
    D. Inheritance
    Answer: B
    Explanation: Attribute: The characteristic or properties of the object like Employee ID, Department, Grade of the object EMPLOYEE or Roll no, Class, Grade of the object STUDENT. An attribute is similar to the column of a relational data model.

12. **In an Object-Oriented Data Model (OODM), this represents the object's behavior:**
    A. Object exception
    B. Attribute
    C. Method
    D. Inheritance
    Answer: C
    Explanation: Method represents the object's behavior like obtaining the student's marks or the employee leave taken.

13. **In an Object-Oriented Data Model (OODM), this represents the Collection of Objects:**
    A. Class
    B. Attribute
    C. Object group
    D. Inheritance
    Answer: A
    Explanation: Class is a collection of objects that share similar attributes and methods. An object is an instance of a class. For example, a Student and an Employee are of the same class.

14. **In an Object-Oriented Data Model (OODM), this represents the property of a new class inheriting the attributes and methods of the original or base class:**
    A. Class
    B. Attribute
    C. Object group
    D. Inheritance
    Answer: D
    Explanation: Inheritance: A new class can inherit the attributes and methods of the original or base class. E.g., both Class Student and Employee are inherited from the base class Person.

15. **This record-based data model stores the data in an upside-down tree structure.**
    A. Hierarchical model
    B. Network model
    C. Relational model
    D. Object model
    Answer: A

Explanation: The hierarchical model stores the data in an upside-down tree structure. The structure consists of a root record or table called a parent having the other branches or child tables linked to it, forming a one-to-one or one-to-many relationship

16. **In a hierarchical data mode, a parent node can have several child nodes; however, a child can only have one parent node.**
    A. True   B. False
    Answer: A
    Explanation: In a hierarchical data mode, a parent node can have several child nodes; however, a child can only have one parent node. The root record at level 0 is the first entity to be traversed in the data model. This type of database was mainly used in Mainframe computers: the Windows Registry and the mobile edition of RDM (Raima Database Manager) use hierarchical databases.

17. **This type of database was mainly used in Mainframe computers:**
    A. Hierarchical model   B. Network model
    C. Relational model   D. Object model
    Answer: A
    Explanation: Same as for Question 16.

18. **Hierarchical data model does not support one-to-many relationship.**
    A. True   B. False
    Answer: B
    Explanation: Following are the characteristics of the hierarchical model:
    - A hierarchical tree structure is used to store data.
    - One-to-one and one-to-many relationship.
    - Predefined relationships between root, parent, and child records.

19. **Hierarchical data model does not support many-to-many relationship.**
    A. True   B. False
    Answer: A
    Explanation: A many-to-many relationship is not supported. Redundancy and duplication of data as inter-linkages between nodes are not supported.

20. **In this type of model, retrieving information can get very slow as database size increases and information is required from the lowermost levels:**
    A. Hierarchical model   B. Network model
    C. Relational model   D. Object model
    Answer: A
    Explanation: The characteristics of hierarchical model are: Programmers and developers need a detailed understanding of the data structure and its storage to access or implement it. Retrieving information can get very slow as database size increases and information is required from the lowermost levels.

21. **CODASYL in network model stands for:**
    A. Conference on Digital Support Languages
    B. Conference on Data Support Languages
    C. Classic On-premise Data System Languages
    D. Conference on Data System Languages
    Answer: D
    Explanation: Network data model is a network-enhanced version of the hierarchical data model. The model also performs better than the hierarchical model by establishing a standard language called CODASYL (Conference on Data System Languages). The network database arranges its data with pointers and has a standard navigational language.

22. **Network model does not support many-to-many relationship.**
    A. True   B. False
    Answer: B
    Explanation: The network database arranges its data with pointers and has a standard navigational language. With many-to-many relation support, the network model is helpful in geographic information systems with road intersections to multiple branches.

23. **Hive is an example of:**
    A. Hierarchical model   B. Network model
    C. Relational model   D. Unstructured model
    Answer: C
    Explanation: Database management systems based on the relational data model are called Relational Database Management Systems (RDBMS). Oracle, MySQL, IBM DB2, Hive, and Microsoft Azure SQL Database are some of the top RDBMS in use today.

24. **In a relational model, Attributes and Records need to be ordered in a specific format:**
    A. True   B. False
    Answer: B
    Explanation: Relational model characteristics are: No relation can have duplicate records. Attributes represent the type of entity information, e.g., student id, name. No two attributes in a table can have the same attribute name. Each data value in a record is called a field. Attributes and records need not be ordered in any specific format.

25. **In a relational model, data redundancy and duplication are avoided as specific data within each table has relations via _____.**
    A. Primary Key   B. Primary and Foreign Key
    C. Foreign Key   D. Relationship Key
    Answer: B
    Explanation: Data redundancy and duplication are avoided as specific data within each table has relations via primary and foreign key concepts.

26. **Higher cost is involved in setting up and implementing hardware and related software in which type of data model?**
    A. Hierarchical model
    B. Network model
    C. Relational model
    D. Unstructured model
    Answer: C
    Explanation: Following are the disadvantages of Relational model: The efficiency of accessing and retrieving data is affected if the SQL query to the database involves many tables among which relationships need to be established. The cost of hardware and related software for setting up and implementing the RDBMS solutions is higher. Well-trained professionals are required for the maintenance and administration of RDBMS for the effective and efficient running of the system.

27. **This model is a denormalized data structure and appears like a star with a central or primary table called the fact table.**
    A. Hierarchical model
    B. Network model
    C. Relational model
    D. Dimensional model
    Answer: D
    Explanation: The dimensional models are denormalized data structures and appear like a star with a central or primary table called the fact table with surrounding tables connected to it called dimension tables or star schema.

28. **This table contains the measurements, metrics, or factual data about a business process and the foreign key to the dimension tables.**
    A. Data table
    B. XML table
    C. Dimension table
    D. Fact table
    Answer: D
    Explanation: The fact table contains the measurements, metrics, or factual data about a business process and the foreign key to the dimension tables. In contrast, the dimension tables contain detailed or descriptive data.

29. **Another variant of the dimensional model is _____.**
    A. Fact schema
    B. Snowflake schema
    C. Star schema
    D. Moon schema
    Answer: B
    Explanation: Another variant of the dimensional model is the snowflake schema. It is similar to the star schema, except the dimension tables are normalized. Thus, the dimension table can split into multiple tables giving a snowflake appearance to the schema.

30. **At a high level, data in analytics can be categorized into two types:**
    A. Structured and Unstructured data
    B. Quantitative data and Qualitative data
    C. Real and False data
    D. Primary and Secondary data
    Answer: B

Explanation: To get the most accurate insights in market research and data sciences, a proper understanding of essential data is a must. For this, we apply suitable statistical measurements that fit our needs and goals. At a high level, data can be categorized into two types: (1) Quantitative data and (2) Qualitative data.

31. **Two types of quantitative data are:**
    A. Discrete and Continuous
    B. Nominal and Ordinal
    C. Structured and Semi-structured
    D. Easy and Difficult
    Answer: A
    Explanation: Discrete data and continuous data are the two types of quantitative data. Quantitative data is considered discrete if it can be counted. Quantitative data is referred to as continuous data if it can be measured. It can take a range of values from lowest to highest.

32. **This type of data is typically presented in a bar and pie charts:**
    A. Discrete
    B. Continuous
    C. Nominal
    D. Ordinal
    Answer: A
    Explanation: The discrete data variables can take only specific values and cannot be sub-divided into smaller parts. For instance, a soccer game score of 5 goals. A score of 5½ goals is not practical. Discrete data is typically represented in bar and pie charts.

33. **This can take only specific values and cannot be subdivided into smaller parts:**
    A. Discrete
    B. Continuous
    C. Nominal
    D. Ordinal
    Answer: A
    Explanation: Same as for Question 32.

34. **This type of data is typically presented in a histogram:**
    A. Discrete
    B. Continuous
    C. Nominal
    D. Ordinal
    Answer: B
    Explanation: Quantitative data is referred to as continuous data if it can be measured. It can take a range of values from lowest to highest. It can be divided and measured to decimal places, e.g., temperature, weight, car speed, etc. Continuous data is typically represented as histograms.

35. **Quantitative data is also referred to as categorical data.**
    A. True
    B. False
    Answer: B
    Explanation: Qualitative data is also referred to as categorical data. It deals with characters and attributes that cannot be numerically measured, e.g., educational background, people or focus groups' opinions on a specific brand or product, etc.

36. **Nominal data is a type of data used to label variables without providing any quantitative value. It comes from the Latin term 'nomen,' which means?**
    A. No Man B. Name
    C. No Mean D. Normal
    Answer: B
    Explanation: Nominal data is a type of data used to label variables without providing any quantitative value. It comes from the Latin term 'nomen,' which means name. They do not have any inherent order or sequence.

37. **This type of data can be analyzed by hypothesis testing.**
    A. Ordinal data B. Discrete data
    C. Continuous data D. Nominal data
    Answer: D
    Explanation: Nominal data can be analyzed by hypothesis testing or grouping method, i.e., grouping into categories and calculating the frequency or percentage. They are typically represented as a pie chart.

38. **Service Satisfaction is an example for:**
    A. Ordinal data B. Discrete data
    C. Continuous data D. Nominal data
    Answer: A
    Explanation: Ordinal data refers to a categorical data variable that has a set order or scale to it, e.g., a preference set of "Most likely, Likely, Least likely, Not likely." Researchers use this type of data to scale responses. Service satisfaction can have a preference set as (Very satisfied, Satisfied, Indifferent, Dissatisfied, Very dissatisfied). So, it is ordinal data.

39. **This type of data represents only two values:**
    A. Discrete B. Continuous
    C. Nominal D. Binary data
    Answer: D
    Explanation: Binary data can be categorized as either nominal or ordinal. Only two values represent binary data: Yes/No, True/False, On/Off, or Male/Female. It can also hold the value of 0/1, in which case it can be termed as a quantitative data type based on the nature of its application.

40. **This has a pre-defined data model and is typically stored in a tabular format with rows and columns:**
    A. Structured data B. Semi-structured data
    C. Quasi-structured data D. Unstructured data
    Answer: A
    Explanation: Structured data has a pre-defined data model and is typically stored in a tabular format with rows and columns. It is specific and consistent in format, having discrete fields that can be accessed separately or with vital relational fields that can be mapped with data from other fields.

41. **SQL or relational databases, comma-separated value (.csv) files, and Excel files are examples of:**
    A. Structured data   B. Semi-structured data
    C. Quasi-structured data   D. Unstructured data
    Answer: A
    Explanation: SQL or relational databases, comma-separated value (.csv) files, and Excel files are examples of structured data.

42. **It is a structured data that does not have a pre-defined data model. It is not stored in a relational database.**
    A. Structured data   B. Semi-structured data
    C. Quasi-structured data   D. Unstructured data
    Answer: B
    Explanation: Semi-structured data is structured data that does not have a pre-defined data model. It is not stored in a relational database. However, it does have some organization that makes it easy to analyze.

43. **This type of data contains tags or other elements like metadata with defined properties, which introduce a hierarchy and define how the data is stored:**
    A. Structured data   B. Semi-structured data
    C. Quasi-structured data   D. Unstructured data
    Answer: B
    Explanation: Semi-structured data is structured data that does not have a pre-defined data model. It is not stored in a relational database. However, it does have some organization that makes it easy to analyze. The data contains tags or other elements like metadata with defined properties, which introduce a hierarchy and define how the data is stored. Hence it is called a self-describing structure.

44. **This type of data has self-describing structure:**
    A. Structured data   B. Semi-structured data
    C. Quasi-structured data   D. Unstructured data
    Answer: B
    Explanation: Same as for Question 43.

45. **It consists of textual content with erratic data formats that can be formatted with effort:**
    A. Structured data   B. Semi-structured data
    C. Quasi-structured data   D. Unstructured data
    Answer: C
    Explanation: Quasi-structured data consists of textual content with erratic data formats that can be formatted with effort, software system tools, and time. An example of quasi-structured data is the data about web pages a user visited and the order in which the web pages were visited. A hyperlink is another example of quasi-structured data.

46. **Hyperlink in a page is an example of:**
    A. Structured data
    B. Semi-structured data
    C. Quasi-structured data
    D. Unstructured data
    Answer: C
    Explanation: Same as for Question 45.

47. **This data does not have a pre-defined or specific format like stream data from social network feeds IoT devices:**
    A. Structured data
    B. Semi-structured data
    C. Quasi-structured data
    D. Unstructured data
    Answer: D
    Explanation: Unstructured data does not have a pre-defined or specific format like stream data from social network feeds IoT devices. It can be images (.jpeg, .png), text files, pdf files, sound files (.wav, .mp3), video files (.mp4, .avi), etc.

48. **It is the most prevalent data used in organizations today for business intelligence and analytics due to its ease of readability by humans.**
    A. Structured data
    B. Semi-structured data
    C. Quasi-structured data
    D. Unstructured data
    Answer: D
    Explanation: Unstructured data is the most flexible type of data due to the absence of a schema. It is the most prevalent data used in organizations today for business intelligence and analytics due to its ease of readability by humans. However, it requires major preprocessing before it is analyzed by a computer.

49. **It shows the variation of one variable plotted on the vertical axis with the regular progression of the second variable plotted on the horizontal axis:**
    A. Line chart
    B. Bar chart
    C. Pie chart
    D. Histogram
    Answer: A
    Explanation: The line chart is the most straightforward technique providing a two-dimensional view of a relationship by joining the data points. It shows the variation of one variable plotted on the vertical axis with the regular progression of the second variable plotted on the horizontal axis. It is typically used to show the trend in data over time. Several line plots on the chart can represent trends among multiple variables.

50. **It is typically used to show the trend in data over time.**
    A. Line chart
    B. Bar chart
    C. Pie chart
    D. Histogram
    Answer: A
    Explanation: Same as for Question 49.

51. **The data plotted is categorical, where one axis represents the categories being compared while the other axis represents the respective numerical value.**
    A. Line chart
    B. Bar chart
    C. Pie chart
    D. Histogram
    Answer: B
    Explanation: Bar charts are used to compare variables in the form of a horizontal or vertical bar where the length or height respectively of the bar represents the value. The data plotted is categorical, where one axis represents the categories being compared while the other axis represents the respective numerical value.

52. **This provide a visual representation of how a group is broken down into smaller elements or categories:**
    A. Line chart
    B. Bar chart
    C. Pie chart
    D. Histogram
    Answer: C
    Explanation: Pie charts provide a visual representation of how a group is broken down into smaller elements or categories. It is represented as a circular graph called a pie that is 100% of the group, wherein each pie slice represents a category proportional to the quantity. A pie chart is ideal in scenarios where the categories are limited to 5 or 6.

53. **This is ideal in scenarios where the categories are limited to 5 or 6.**
    A. Line chart
    B. Bar chart
    C. Pie chart
    D. Histogram
    Answer: C
    Explanation: Same as for Question 52.

54. **This represents the frequency distribution of variables measured on discrete intervals:**
    A. Line chart
    B. Bar chart
    C. Pie chart
    D. Histogram
    Answer: D
    Explanation: Histograms represent the frequency distribution of variables measured on discrete intervals or bins. The bar area is proportional to the frequency of a variable, and the width is equal to the interval. The intervals are continuous and set by the x-axis, while the y-axis shows the value occurrences within that interval. It is typically used when dealing with large datasets and is helpful to detect any gaps or outliers in the data.

55. **It is typically used when dealing with large datasets and is helpful to detect any gaps or outliers in the data.**
    A. Line chart
    B. Bar chart
    C. Pie chart
    D. Histogram
    Answer: D
    Explanation: Same as for Question 54.

56. **This is used to observe the relationship between variables. The values of two variables plotted along the x- and y-axis can reveal a pattern or existence of any correlation in a dataset.**
   A. Scatter plot
   B. Time-series graph
   C. Box plot
   D. Word cloud
   Answer: A
   Explanation: A scatter plot or graph is used to observe the relationship between variables. The values of two variables plotted along the x- and y-axis can reveal a pattern or existence of any correlation in a dataset. Scatter plots are used to identify correlations, unexpected gaps, or outliers in data analysis.

57. **This is used to visualize trends or seasonality in data over time.**
   A. Scatter plot
   B. Time-series graph
   C. Box plot
   D. Word cloud
   Answer: B
   Explanation: Time-series graphs are used to visualize trends or seasonality in data over time. The data is plotted across the x-y axis where the x-axis shows time increments in hourly, daily, monthly or yearly intervals, and the y-axis is the value of the variable that is being measured. The plotted points are joined by a continuous line, thus depicting how the value of the variable changes over time.

58. **This is also called as whisker plot:**
   A. Scatter plot
   B. Time-series graph
   C. Box plot
   D. Word cloud
   Answer: C
   Explanation: A Box plot, also known as Box-and-Whisker plot, is a graphical method of displaying variations in datasets. It is a standardized way of comparing distribution among many groups using a five-number summary, namely Minimum – the lowest data point, First Quartile Q1 – median of the lower half of the dataset, Median – the middle value of dataset, Third Quartile Q3 – median of the top half of the dataset and Maximum – the largest data point. The box plots help understand multiple datasets from independent related sources, skewed distributions, and the presence of outliers.

59. **This is employed when the source data is text-based:**
   A. Scatter plot
   B. Time-series graph
   C. Box plot
   D. Word cloud
   Answer: D
   Explanation: A word cloud is employed when the source data is text-based. It is also known as text cloud or tag cloud and displays keyword information on web pages (tags). It is rendered in various sizes, depending on how frequently they are used in the study context. The frequency or importance of a word is directly proportional to its size.

Introduction to Data Analytics • 45

60. **Businesses typically use it to understand their web page user behavior in real time.**
    A. Scatter plot
    B. Time series graph
    C. Box plot
    D. Heatmap
    Answer: D
    Explanation: Heat Map is a method of graphically representing numerical data using a hot-to-cold or cold-to-hot color scheme. Businesses typically use it to understand how their web pages are accessed by users in real time. For example, they provide an efficient way to identify, at a glance, the most popular and least popular elements or sections on a page by the number of mouse clicks or hover represented by a predetermined color spectrum.

61. **If any increase in variable 'A' results in an increase in variable 'B' or a decrease in variable 'A' results in a decrease in variable 'B', it is called as _____.**
    A. Positive correlation
    B. Negative correlation
    C. Zero correlation
    D. Spurious correlation
    Answer: A
    Explanation: A dataset is considered to have a positive correlation if any increase in variable 'A' results in an increase in variable 'B' or a decrease in variable 'A' results in a decrease in variable 'B'. In other words, both variables move in the same direction, e.g., the correlation between age and blood pressure. A positive correlation will form an upward slope.

62. **If the growth of one causes the decline of the other, it is called as _____.**
    A. Positive correlation
    B. Negative correlation
    C. Zero correlation
    D. Spurious correlation
    Answer: B
    Explanation: If the growth of one causes a decline of the other, the dataset is said to have a negative correlation. For example, age and agility. As one increases in age, the less agile they become. A negative correlation forms a line with a downward slope.

63. **When there is no detectable trend between the two variables, the dataset is said to have _____.**
    A. Positive correlation
    B. Negative correlation
    C. Zero correlation
    D. Spurious correlation
    Answer: C
    Explanation: When there is no detectable trend between the two variables, the dataset is said to have no correlation or zero correlation. Here the data will be scattered, and there is no discernable pattern. For example, a person's complexion and height or the intellect of a person and happiness. The graph does not represent an upward or downward linear line, when plotted.

64. **When a significant correlation is observed between two variables that have no causal connection but are influenced by a third or unknown factor, it is known as:**
    A. Positive correlation
    B. Negative correlation
    C. Zero correlation
    D. Spurious correlation
    Answer: D
    Explanation: A spurious correlation is when a significant correlation is observed between two variables that have no causal connection but are influenced by a third or unknown factor. Common well-cited spurious correlations are the death rate by drowning with higher ice cream sales and more iPhone sales to death from falling down the stairs.

65. **In time series, the base value of the series, if it were a straight line, is called as:**
    A. Level
    B. Trend
    C. Cycles
    D. Noise
    Answer: A
    Explanation: A time series is a set of numerical measurements of the same entity taken at equally spaced intervals over time. Time-series data has five components:
    1. Level – The base value of the series if it were a straight line.
    2. Trend – The overall increasing or decreasing direction of the series.
    3. Seasonality – When repeated behavior in the data occurs at regular intervals.
    4. Cycles – When a series follows an up-and-down pattern that is not seasonal.
    5. Noise – An unexplained variation in the pattern.

    While all time-series graphs generally have the same level and noise, the components of trend, seasonality, and cycles are optional factors that enable a better understanding of the dataset and making of informed decisions.

66. **This is the technique of grouping data or objects with similar characteristics in a dataset:**
    A. Clustering
    B. Regression
    C. Correlation
    D. Sampling
    Answer: A
    Explanation: Clustering is the technique of grouping data or objects with similar characteristics in a dataset. It is assumed that the entities of a particular group are comparatively more similar than the entities of another group.

67. **This clustering is also known as hierarchical clustering:**
    A. Connectivity-based clustering
    B. Centroid-based clustering
    C. Density-based clustering
    D. Distribution-based clustering
    Answer: A

Explanation: Connectivity-based clustering is also known as hierarchical clustering. It goes by the premise that the data point closest to it is more related than the point away from it.

68. **This model is typically used when working with small datasets:**
    A. Connectivity-based clustering
    B. Centroid-based clustering
    C. Density-based clustering
    D. Distribution-based clustering
    Answer: A
    Explanation: Though simple to interpret, the connectivity-based technique gets complex and time-consuming when working with too many outliers. Hence the model is typically used when working with small datasets.

69. **In this technique, the data is first randomly grouped into clusters. Each cluster consists of data points that are closest to it.**
    A. Connectivity-based clustering
    B. Centroid-based clustering
    C. Density-based clustering
    D. Distribution-based clustering
    Answer: B
    Explanation: In this technique, the data is first randomly grouped into clusters. Each cluster consists of data points that are closest to it. The centroid is calculated as the average of all the data points in the cluster and plotted.

70. **In this methodology, a random data point is selected, and the distance between each data point around it is measured. If the data points are within a certain predetermined distance, they are considered related and grouped.**
    A. Connectivity-based clustering
    B. Centroid-based clustering
    C. Density-based clustering
    D. Distribution-based clustering
    Answer: C
    Explanation: Connecting areas of high density define density-based clustering. It is assumed that the more densely populated we are together, the more the chances that we belong to the same group. In this methodology, a random data point is selected, and the distance between each data point around it is measured. If the data points are within a certain predetermined distance, they are considered related and grouped.

Short-answer Questions

1. **Write notes on the three types of data relationships.**
   There are three types of data relationships:
   One-to-one: One record or field in a table is connected to one and only one record/field of another table. E.g., a passport number or a unique employee id can belong to only one person.
   One-to-many: One record or field is connected to one or more records of another table. E.g., One employee (Employee ID) can have multiple addresses or one employee can have multiple contact numbers.

Many-to-many: Both tables have duplicate values. E.g., Books and authors – multiple authors can write a single book, and an author may have written multiple books.

Suppose a data unit does not have a relationship or link with another entity. In that case, it is of no value in the grand scheme of the data organization structure.

2. **What is data model?**
   Data models are a structural representation of how data is stored in a database. It describes the design of a database representing the entities, attributes, and the relationship among data, its constraints, and others.

3. **What is conceptual data model stage?**
   This high-level design displays only the entities and their relationships. The goal is to define and structure the business's scope, rules, and procedures. The physical characteristics of the data are not considered at this stage.

4. **What is logical data model stage?**
   In this stage, more detail is built into the data design with data attributes like data types, length, and other characteristics. This logical design helps form a database blueprint, bridging the application and developer specifications.

5. **What is physical data model stage?**
   Physical data model: While the conceptual and logical data models are produced independently of any software or data storage structure, the physical data model is the schema or framework of how the data is physically stored within a database. Hence an in-depth knowledge of the database system being used and its performance constraints is required. In this stage, referential integrity, performance tuning, indexing, and triggers are defined.

6. **What are the two types of data modeling?**
   Two types of data modeling typically used in database management systems are Object-based data models and Record-based data models.

7. **What is object-based data model?**
   Object-based data models are built at the conceptual stage while designing a database. The entities are abstract. However, once designed, they can be used to create a relational database.

8. **What are the types of object-based data models?**
   There are two object-based data models commonly used.
   1. Entity Relationship data model
   2. Object-oriented data model

9. **Write short notes on Entity Relationship Data Model.**
   It is a diagrammatic representation of the relationship among entities. The ER diagram consists of three main components:

Entity: The object or component of the data is typically represented as a rectangle.
Attribute: The entity's property is represented as an oval in the ER diagram. E.g., Employee id, Name, DOB, and address can be the attributes of entity Employee.
Relationship: The associated relationship between entities, E.g., one-to-one, one-to-many/many-to-one and many-to-many are represented by connecting lines.

10. **Write short notes on Object-Oriented Data Model.**

    The Object-Oriented Data Model (OODM) is built around objects where an object is a grouping of data and its behavior. It took on after the advent of Object-Oriented Programming (OOP). It is a combination of OOP and relational database model. OODM can cater to data complexity and has high flexibility and efficiency in retrieving and expanding objects.

11. **What are the components of Object-Oriented Data Model?**

    It consists of five components:
    Object: The real-world entity that consists of data and code encapsulated into a single unit. Example EMPLOYEE or STUDENT. The object is akin to a relational data model.
    Attribute: The characteristic or properties of the object, like Employee ID, Department, Grade of the object EMPLOYEE or Roll no., Class, Grade of object STUDENT. An attribute is similar to the column of a relational data model.
    Method: Represents the object's behavior like obtaining the student's marks or leave taken by the Employee.
    Class: A collection of objects that share similar attributes and methods. An object is an instance of a class. For example, a Student and an Employee are of the same class.
    Inheritance: A new class can inherit the attributes and methods of the original or base class. E.g., both classes Student and Employee are inherited from the base class Person.

12. **What is Record-based data model?**

    In the Record-based data model, the database is organized in a specific fixed format of records. The records have a fixed number of fields or attributes, and each field is generally of a fixed length. There are typically three kinds of record-based data models most prevalent in database management, 1. Hierarchical model 2. Network model and 3. Relational model.

13. **What is Hierarchical model?**

    The hierarchical model stores the data in an upside-down tree structure. The structure consists of a root record or table called a parent having the other branches or child tables linked to it, forming a one-to-one or one-to-many relationship. A parent node can have several child nodes; however, a child can only have one parent node. The root record at level 0 is the first entity to be traversed in the data model.

14. **Write any 4 characteristics of Hierarchical data model?**
    - A hierarchical tree structure is used to store data.
    - One-to-one and one-to-many relationship.
    - Predefined relationships between root, parent, and child records.
    - Parent and child records are linked together via pointers.

15. **Write any 4 advantages of Hierarchical data model?**
    Advantages
    - An ideal model for inherently hierarchical data, like organization staff, departments, and geographical locations.
    - Simple and easy to understand, as the relationship between records is predefined.
    - Minimized disk input/output as parent and child records are stored close to each other.
    - Easy to update, delete and create new data information.

16. **Write any three disadvantages of Hierarchical data model?**
    Disadvantages
    - A many-to-many relationship is not supported.
    - Redundancy and duplication of data as inter-linkages between nodes are not supported.
    - Sophisticated relationships are not supported; hence the model does not accurately describe the full relationship between all the records.

17. **Write short notes on Network data model.**
    C W Bachman developed the network model in 1965 as an enhanced version of the hierarchical data model. It is similar to the hierarchical data model, i.e., the data is organized in an upside-down tree structure. However, the key difference is that the network data model allows the child node to have multiple parents. The parents are called the occupiers in network databases, and the child nodes are called the members.

18. **What are the top characteristics of Network data model?**
    - Data is stored in an upside-down tree structure.
    - Supports one-to-one, one-to-many, and many-to-many relationship.
    - Parent record is called an occupier, and child is called a member.
    - Parent and child records are linked together via pointers.

19. **List down any three advantages of Network data model.**
    - It has all the advantages of the hierarchical data model and more straightforward navigation and data search due to its flexibility.
    - It is a simple structure including multi-parent support.
    - It supports complex data models as multiple relations can be created between the data.

20. **List down any three disadvantages of the network model.**
    - More complex than the hierarchical model, as records are maintained using pointers.
    - Data relationships must be predefined.

- Database alteration or addition of a new data field or record requires many pointer adjustments making implementation quite complex.

21. What is Relational model?
Edgar F Codd introduced the relational data model in 1970. This model stores the data as tuples in two-dimensional tables represented by rows and columns forming relations. Data can be easily expanded by increasing the number of rows or columns to create records or attributes/fields respectively.

22. List down any three characteristics of the Relational model.
- It is a record-based model that comprises a set of relations or tables of values.
- Each relation can be represented as a table with columns representing attributes and rows representing records or entities.
- Every relation or table in the database must be unique and identified by an entity name, say, Student, Faculty.

23. Write any three advantages of the Relational model.
- It has a simple database design with a tabular view supporting large amounts of data.
- It is scalable as records and attributes can be added to the table.
- Programmers and developers need not know the tables' physical representation or detailed storage to access or update data. Only the entity/attribute names are required.

24. Write any three disadvantages of the Relational model.
Disadvantages
- Performance in accessing and retrieving data is affected if the SQL query to the database involves many tables between which relationships need to be established.
- Higher cost in hardware and related software for setting up and implementing the RDBMS solutions.
- Well-trained professionals are required for the maintenance and administration of RDBMS for the effective and efficient running of the system.

25. Describe Quantitative data.
Quantitative data refers to numerical data, i.e., any data dealing with numbers or anything that can be measured, e.g., age, height, weight, temperature, prices. Discrete data and continuous data are the two types of quantitative data.

26. What is Discrete data?
The quantitative data is considered discrete if it can be counted. They are typically represented as integers like the number of students in the class, the number of visits to the doctor, the number of vehicles owned, etc. The discrete data variables can take only specific values and cannot be subdivided into smaller parts—for instance, a soccer game score of 5 goals. A score of 5½ goals is not practical. Discrete data is typically represented in bar and pie charts.

27. **What is Continuous data?**
    Quantitative data is referred to as continuous data if it can be measured. It can take a range of values from lowest to highest. It can be divided and measured to decimal places, e.g., temperature, weight, and car speed. Continuous data is typically represented as histograms.

28. **What is Qualitative data?**
    Qualitative data is also referred to as categorical data. It deals with characters and attributes that cannot be numerically measured, e.g., educational background, people's, or a focus group's opinions on a specific brand or product. They are typically represented by words, pictures, or symbols.
    Nominal data and ordinal data are the two types of qualitative data.

29. **What is Nominal data?**
    Nominal data is a type of data used to label variables without providing any quantitative value. It comes from the Latin term 'nomen', which means name. They do not have any inherent order or sequence. Some of the examples of nominal data are:
    - Eye color (blue, brown, grey, black, hazel.)
    - Nationality (Indian, American, German, Chinese, Italian.)

30. **What is Ordinal data?**
    Ordinal data refers to a categorical data variable that has a set order or scale to it, e.g., a preference set of "Most likely, Likely, Least likely, Not likely." Researchers use this type of data to scale responses. Some of the examples of ordinal data are:
    - Service satisfaction (Very satisfied, Satisfied, Indifferent, Dissatisfied, Very dissatisfied)
    - Winning order (First, Second, Third)

31. **What is Binary data?**
    Another type of data is binary data. It can be categorized as either nominal or ordinal. Only two values represent binary data: Yes/No, True/False, On/Off, or Male/Female. It can also hold the value of 0/1, in which case it can be termed as a quantitative data type based on the nature of its application.

32. **What is the nature of data?**
    Data is multi-dimensional. It can be Structured, Semi-structured, Quasi-structured, or Unstructured.

33. **What is Structured data?**
    Structured data has a pre-defined data model and is typically stored in a tabular format with rows and columns. It is specific and consistent in format, having discrete fields that can be accessed separately or with vital relational fields that can be mapped with data from other fields. Thus, data can be accessed and aggregated from any location in the database, making it the ideal kind of data to analyze and process.

34. What is Semi-structured data?

Semi-structured data is structured data that does not have a pre-defined data model. It is not stored in a relational database. However, it does have some organization that makes it easy to analyze. The data contains tags or other elements like metadata with defined properties which introduce a hierarchy and define how the data is stored. Hence, it is called a self-describing structure. Extensible Markup Language (XML) files, JavaScript Object Notation (JSON) files, TCP/IP packets are examples of semi-structured data.

35. What is Quasi-structured data?

Quasi-structured data consists of textual content with erratic data formats that can be formatted with effort, software system tools, and time. An example of quasi-structured data is the data about web pages a user visited and the order in which the web pages were visited. A hyperlink is another example of quasi-structured data.

36. What is Unstructured data?

Unstructured data does not have a pre-defined or specific format. Streamed data from social network feeds and IoT devices are examples. It can be images (.jpeg, .png), text files, pdf files, sound files (.wav, .mp3), video files (.mp4, .avi), etc. It is the most flexible form of data due to the absence of a schema. Hence it is the most prevalent data used in organizations today for business intelligence and analytics due to its ease of readability by humans. However, major preprocessing is required before the data is analyzed by a computer. AI and sophisticated machine learning methods are currently making huge progress towards making unstructured data machine-readable.

37. What is Line Chart?

Line chart is the most straightforward technique providing a two-dimensional view of a relationship by joining the data points. It shows the variation of one variable plotted on the vertical axis with the regular progression of the second variable plotted on the horizontal axis. It is typically used to show the trend in data over time. Several line plots on the chart can represent trends among multiple variables.

38. What is Bar Chart?

Bar charts are used to compare variables in the form of a horizontal or vertical bar where the length or height respectively of the bar represents the value. The data plotted is categorical, where one axis represents the categories being compared while the other axis represents the respective numerical value.

39. What is Pie Chart?

Pie charts provide a visual representation of how a group is broken down into smaller elements or categories. It is represented as a circular graph called a pie that is 100% of the group, wherein each pie slice represents a category proportional to the quantity. A pie chart is ideal in scenarios where the categories are limited to 5 or 6.

40. What is Histogram?

Histograms represent the frequency distribution of variables measured on discrete intervals or bins. The bar area is proportional to the frequency of a variable, and the width is equal to the interval. The intervals are continuous and set by the x-axis, while the y-axis shows the value occurrences within that interval. It is typically used when dealing with large datasets and is helpful to detect any gaps or outliers in the data.

41. What is Scatter plot?

A scatter plot or graph is used to observe the relationship between variables. The values of two variables plotted along the x- and y-axis can reveal a pattern or existence of any correlation in a dataset. Scatter plots are used to identify correlations, unexpected gaps, or outliers in data analysis.

42. What is Time-series graph?

Time-series graphs are used to visualize trends or seasonality in data over time. The data is plotted across the x-y axis where the x-axis shows the time increments like hourly, daily, monthly or yearly intervals, and the y-axis is the value of the variable that is being measured. The plotted points are joined by a continuous line, thus depicting how the value of the variable changes over time.

43. What is Box Plot?

A Box plot, also known as Box-and-Whisker plot, is a graphical method of displaying variations in datasets.

It is a standardized way of comparing distribution between many groups using a five-number summary, namely Minimum – the lowest data point, First Quartile Q1 – median of the lower half of the dataset, Median – middle value of dataset, Third Quartile Q3 – median of the top half of the dataset and Maximum – the largest data point. The box plots help understand multiple datasets from independent related sources, skewed distributions, and detect the presence of outliers.

44. Write short notes on Word Cloud.

A word cloud is employed when the source data is text-based. It is also known as text cloud or tag cloud and displays keyword information on web pages (tags). It is rendered in various sizes, depending on how frequently they are used in the study context. The frequency or importance of a word is directly proportional to its size.

45. What is Network Diagram?

Network diagrams or graphs show interconnections between entities or nodes. Connections or links between the nodes represent the relationship. It is generally used to analyze social networks to understand how people are connected. Various aspects of the relationship can be communicated by varying the color, width/size, and arrowheads of the nodes or relationship lines.

46. What is Heatmap?

Heatmap is a method of graphically representing numerical data using a hot-to-cold or cold-to-hot color scheme. Businesses typically use it to understand their web page user behavior in real-time. For example, they provide an efficient way to identify, at a glance, the most popular to least popular elements or sections on a page by the number of mouse clicks or hover represented by a predetermined color spectrum.

47. Write short notes on Correlation model.

A Correlation model is applied to identify the relationship between two variables. It is one of the essential data analytics tools that can help define trends, predict and identify the root cause for specific scenarios. For example, it shows how much variable X will change if there is a change in Y; for example,, between temperature and ice-cream sales, age and blood pressure, education and income earned.

48. What is Positive Correlation?

A dataset is considered to have a positive correlation if any increase in variable 'A' results in an increase in variable 'B' or a decrease in variable 'A' results in a decrease in variable 'B'. In other words, both variables move in the same direction, e.g., the correlation between age and blood pressure. A positive correlation will form an upward slope.

49. What is Negative Correlation?

If the growth of one causes the decline of the other, the dataset is said to have a negative correlation. For example, age and agility. As one increases in age, the less agile they become. A negative correlation forms a line with downward slope.

50. What is Zero Correlation?

When there is no detectable trend between the two variables, the dataset is said to have no correlation or zero correlation. Here the data will be scattered, and there is no discernable pattern. For example, a person's complexion and height or the intellect of a person and happiness. The graph does not represent an upward or downward linear line when plotted.

51. What is Spurious Correlation?

A spurious correlation is when a significant correlation is observed between two variables that have no causal connection but are influenced by a third or unknown factor. Common well-cited spurious correlations are the death rate by drowning with higher ice cream sales, and more iPhone sales with death from falling down the stairs. However, it is essential to note that correlation does not mean casualty. Though some spurious correlations are apparent, it is essential to note that there could be instances where the data pairing looks plausible but is, in reality, unauthentic.

52. What is Regression?

Regression is widely used for forecasting and prediction. The premise is to predict an outcome variable called a dependent variable based on input variables called independent variable or predictor variable. It is typically used to predict an actual value (output), whether past, current, or future, based on previously collected data or information.

53. What is Forecasting?
Forecasting is predicting or estimating the future value of data by analyzing trends based on past and present data. It is best used where numerical historical information is available, and past trends are assumed to continue into the near future. For example, hourly electricity demand at home or annual company profits. It should be noted that forecasting techniques do not predict the future. Instead, it gives a calculated estimation of what could happen based on what has already happened.

54. What is time-series forecasting method?
The most commonly used quantitative forecasting technique is the time-series forecasting method. A time series is a set of numerical measurements of the same entity taken at equally spaced intervals over time. Analysis of the output enables us to make informed predictions of future values.

55. What are the components of time-series data?
Time-series data has five components:
1. **Level**: The base value of the series if it were a straight line.
2. **Trend**: The overall increasing or decreasing direction of the series.
3. **Seasonality**: When repeated behavior in the data occurs at regular intervals, e.g., vacations in December.
4. **Cycles**: When a series follows an up-and-down pattern that is not seasonal.
5. **Noise**: An unexplained variation in the pattern.

56. What is Clustering?
Clustering is the technique of grouping data or objects with similar characteristics in a dataset. It is assumed that the entities of a particular group are comparatively more similar to each other than the entities of another group. Clustering follows a single-phase approach, where we provide the input data to the system without knowing the output or groupings. The technique identifies patterns in data by using distance measures to group or separate data points.

57. What are the types of Clustering?
There are four types of clustering:
1. Connectivity-based clustering
2. Centroid based clustering
3. Density-based clustering
4. Distribution-based clustering

58. What is connectivity-based clustering?
Connectivity-based clustering is also known as hierarchical clustering. It goes by the premise that the closest data points are more related to each other are than to the points that are farther away.

59. What are the methods used in connectivity-based clustering?

Two methods are used for connectivity-based clustering:
1. **Method 1**: Each data point is taken as an individual cluster and joined with another data point or group of data points similar to it till a big cluster is reached.
2. **Method 2**: All data points are taken as one big cluster and then partitioned into smaller groups or sets as their distance increases.

Though simple to interpret, the connectivity-based technique gets complex and time-consuming when working with too many outliers. Hence the model is typically used when working with small datasets.

60. What is centroid-based clustering?

In this technique, the data is first randomly grouped into clusters. Each cluster consists of data points that are closest to it. The centroid is calculated as the average of all the data points in the cluster and plotted. The data points are then revisited to determine whether any data point is closer to a cluster of another centroid than its assigned centroid. If they are closer to another centroid, it is redistributed to the cluster of that centroid. The process is repeated iteratively till all data points are in the clusters containing the centroid closest to them, thus reaching the optimal grouping.

61. What is density-based clustering?

Connecting areas of high density define density-based clustering. It is assumed that the more densely populated we are together, the more the chances that we belong to the same group. In this methodology, a random data point is selected, and the distance between each data point around it is measured. If the data points are within a certain predetermined distance, they are considered related and grouped. The process is iterated by selecting random data points until the best clusters can be identified within the distance threshold. Unlike distribution-based clustering, the outliers are not assigned to any cluster.

62. What is distribution-based clustering?

The distribution clustering model is based on the probability that a particular data point belongs to a cluster. Around each possible centroid, the algorithm defines the density distributions for each cluster, quantifying the probability of belonging based on these distributions. The graph represents the density distributions of the data points. If a data point is close within the density circle or centroid, it is a 100% probability that it is part of the specific group. The farther away it gets, the less the probability that the data point belongs to the group.

63. What is Classification?

Classification is a technique used to analyze and group data into categories or classes using algorithms. In this model, the output dataset is labeled, i.e., the resultant data is qualitative and known.

64. What are the two stages of the classification model?
1. The Training Stage
2. The Classification Stage

65. What is the Training Stage in the classification model?
In this stage, a set of training data is built, that constitutes a set of attributes and the expected outcome. The algorithm is trained on a massive set of correctly classified data to ensure that the points in the dataset are classified correctly to reach the right outcome. For example, a set of symptoms based on clinical data is constructed to classify a particular disease.

66. What is the Classification Stage in the classification model?
Once the model is built, the algorithm is run on test data to estimate the accuracy and precision of the classification rules. Finally, the model is set to predict the target class for each case in new datasets.

The classification method uses mathematical techniques such as decision trees, linear programming, neural network, statistics, and others. When data is classified into two classes like Yes/No, Good/Bad, Male/Female, it is called binary classification. E.g., spam detection and customer churn prediction. When data is classified into three or more classes, it is called multinomial classification. E.g., classifying fruits into apples, bananas, oranges, or classifying buildings, lakes, and forests from hyperspectral imaging.

67. Write notes on Web data.
Web data is the most widely used source of Big Data today, and it is extensive. This data can be from enterprise portals, online business applications, social media or social networks. According to a Cisco study, about 74.4 billion networked devices will be linked by 2025. That is a massive volume of data that businesses can exploit through web data integration.

68. Write short notes on Symmetric Multiprocessing (SMP) Architecture.
In symmetric multiprocessing or SMP databases, data is stored in servers called nodes. In this system, multiple identical processors work in parallel to execute independent programs and tasks concurrently. However, they all share the same main memory and input/output devices via a data bus or switch. Though the SMP architecture can work well with small to medium data volumes, it becomes a bottleneck when huge volumes are involved due to the shared memory constraint.

69. Write short notes on Massively Parallel Processing architecture.
The MPP or massively parallel processing architecture addresses the drawbacks of scalability inherent in the SMP architecture. Each processor or compute node works independently with its operating system, dedicated memory, and disk storage. Thus, the compute nodes are independent of each other and communicate only via a high-speed communication system or interconnect. This environment is called the 'shared-nothing' environment.

70. What is Cloud Computing?

Cloud computing has taken the load off the MPP data operation personnel regarding the cost and complexity of managing the system. In addition, cloud computing brings elasticity to MPP architecture, paving the way for on-demand MPP architecture.

71. List down any three aspects of the Cloud Computing.

The critical aspects of cloud computing are:

On-demand self-service: The user can monitor, prioritize and manage the computing resource for query/analytics and leave the infrastructure maintenance and resource pooling to the service provider.

Broad network accessibility: Data storage and computing is performed over the internet, giving anyone access to it irrespective of their location or device.

Elasticity and scalability: Cyclical changes in demand can be efficiently managed by scaling in and scaling out as required without a massive impact on time and resources.

72. What is Grid Computing?

Grid computing is a large-scale distributed computing method where a network of computers, irrespective of their geographical location, share resources like processing power, memory and storage, to accomplish a task. Thus, every authorized computer has access to the entire network's collective processing power and storage capacity, making it a supercomputer.

73. Write short notes on MapReduce.

MapReduce is a programming model or framework that can organize how vast volumes of data are processed and computed. It is not a database. MapReduce works in three stages: Map, Shuffle and Reduce.

74. What is Reporting?

Reporting is the process of collating existing information and presenting it in a comprehensive and user-friendly way based on the audience's needs. The data is presented in a specific manner that is defined, objective and accurate. The purpose of reporting is for organizations to track and analyze their business's performance and overall health, thus guiding improvement and growth opportunities. E.g., financial reports, inventory stock reports and market analysis reports.

75. What is Analysis?

Analysis is the process of interpreting the data and reports to extract meaningful insights for better understanding and improving business performance. Analysis is about enquiring, examining, comparing, interpreting, confirming, or predicting. This is done by using or 'analyzing' the information derived from raw data or reports. Analysis aims to answer specific business questions of why/when/how by providing key findings and actionable recommendations.

76. What are the key differences between Reporting and Analysis?

Both reporting and analysis are done with graphs, charts, tables, and other data visualization tools. However, the three key differentiators between the two are:
1. While reporting shows what is happening, analysis attempts to explain why.
2. Reporting provides information while analysis reveals insights.
3. In reporting, data from statistic reports, dashboards, alerts, etc., are pushed to the users. In analysis, on the other hand, users pull the required data for examination and interpretation.

Essay-type Questions

1. Write an essay on Data Relationships.
2. Write an essay on data model. What are the stages to develop a data model?
3. Write an essay on Entity Relationship data model.
4. Write an essay on Object-Oriented Data model.
5. What is Record-based data model? Explain Hierarchical model in detail.
6. What is Record-based data model? Explain Network model in detail.
7. What is Record-based data model? Explain Relational model in detail.
8. What are the types of data at high level? Explain Quantitative data in detail.
9. What are the types of data at high level? Explain Qualitative data in detail.
10. Explain Structured, Semi-structured, Quasi-structured and Unstructured data in detail.
11. Explain Line Chart, Bar Chart, Pie Chart and Histogram.
12. Explain Box plot, Word Cloud, Network Diagram and Heatmap.
13. Explain Correlation in detail, with its types.
14. Explain Regression in detail.
15. Explain Forecasting in detail.
16. What is Clustering? Explain connectivity-based Clustering in detail.
17. What is Clustering? Explain centroid-based Clustering in detail.
18. What is Clustering? Explain density-based Clustering in detail.
19. What is Clustering? Explain distribution-based Clustering in detail.
20. What is Classification? Explain its stages.
21. What are SMP and MPP in the data model world?
22. What is Cloud Computing? Explain the critical aspects of Cloud Computing.
23. What is Grid Computing? Explain its critical aspects.
24. Compare and Contrast Reporting and Analysis.

CHAPTER 2

Data Analytics Life-cycle

> **LEARNING OBJECTIVES**
>
> This chapter explores the various business drivers for analytics and discusses the typical data analytical architecture. It explains the types of analytics used and provides an overview of the standard tools used for data analytics. It then explains the data analytic life-cycle and compares the characteristics of business intelligence with data science.

2.1 Introduction

According to a Gartner 2017 report, 85% of analytics and Big Data projects fail. Not having a clear business case is one of the main reasons for the failure. There has to be a business objective that aligns with the organization's strategy. However, that, in itself, is not enough. The organization must also have the necessary resources in terms of technology as well as analytics and Big Data skillset. An understanding of data analytics, data availability, and how it can benefit the business needs, can potentially address project management and organizational issue-driven failures.

As organizations evolve with Big Data, they discover the limitations of the traditional data architecture and business intelligence systems. Changing an existing analytics architecture is quite complex, especially as businesses move from the conventional Business Intelligence (BI) to the Data Science projects to maintain their competitive edge.

Corporations like Amazon, Netflix, and Starbucks have successfully implemented analytics programs and are taking advantage of the benefits. An organization that can leverage data from multiple sources, including social media, the Internet of Things, video surveillance, and various other data sources, can emerge as market or brand leaders of their domain.

2.2 BUSINESS DRIVERS FOR ANALYTICS

We are in a generation where vast volumes of data from an ever-widening stream of sources flood a business daily. Data analytics can turn this data into insight, and insight into action with intelligent data. However, for a business to make the right decisions on data strategy, it is essential to understand what drives the business.

Business drivers are conditions, processes, or activities that are vital in maximizing a company's growth and business value. Drivers vary significantly with each industry. Some of the key business drivers for an organization to implement a data and analytics program are:

2.2.1 Increasing Profitability and Growth

Finance is the fuel that runs the business. A key measure determining an organization's success is how efficiently it can turn revenue into profit. As a result, organizations continuously look for new revenue streams to spur growth.

An analytics system can enable the business to study the existing data and identify avenues for growth. Using data analytics to gain deeper insights allows us to find pockets of growth that may be overlooked. It can help the company understand customer interactions with the product or services, linkages to seasons and demographics, future market conditions, and other varying factors. Data-driven analytics can predict niche markets, identify new products or services, or a combination that can help realize the customers' full profit potential. This can enable customer conversion with targeted marketing, campaigns, incentives, and promotions.

Amazon, Netflix, e-Bay, Starbucks are a few data-driven companies that leverage Big Data Analytics to increase revenue.

2.2.2 Strengthening Customer Experience and Intimacy

The customer is a crucial asset to any business. Social media platforms like Facebook, Twitter, and Instagram produce sheer volumes of customer data, their behaviors, and preferences. Technology can now be leveraged to collect customer data in near real-time, enabling an organization to find the customer's pulse, needs, and wants. Building an emotional connection and trust with our customers can trigger customer loyalty and reduce churn.

Predictive analysis on customer transactions and various other socio-economic and geographical data can enable organizations to better understand their customer base, the peer influences among customers, and predict future behaviors. This understanding can lead to initiatives that can proactively cater to customer needs, problems, and expectations, thus fostering positive customer experience and intimacy, leading to customer retention and increasing the customer base.

For example, gaming corporations use data analytics mechanisms to make in-game adjustments and balance customer skill and gameplay, thus maximizing customer retention and in-app purchases or ad views.

2.2.3 Driving Digital Transformation and Innovation

Companies are transforming their products and customer relationships by leveraging Digital Transformation. Digital transformation is the organizational change of integrating existing technologies, processes, and capabilities that enable the organization to innovate and rapidly adapt to changing circumstances. It impacts people, processes, and technology.

In today's digitally advanced environment, data analytics is the technology that can deliver transformational value. Data-driven insights that were previously too costly to process are a thing of the past. Instead, data analytics can picture the organization's past successes and failures, spot trends for strategic decisions and future growth channels. In addition, new insights can lead to business innovation.

Data analytics initiatives can transform the business with better customer relationships, data-driven decision-making, enhanced business intelligence, competitive services, products, innovative branding strategies, and more.

For example, a self-service real-time analytics platform that facilitates access to various data linked to user types can promote innovation and data accessibility at multiple levels across the business.

2.2.4 Managing Regulatory and Compliance Risks

Data analytics can help organizations enable strategic initiatives and decision-making. It can also help simplify and improve the efficiency of the organization's compliance and regulatory processes, irrespective of the industry. All companies are expected to comply with the government and other regulatory laws like SOX, anti-money laundering, CPSC and other regulatory laws. Companies can build analytics programs to continuously monitor and receive insights into the effectiveness of its compliance and control framework model. "Data-driven" compliance programs can help identify existing risks and their status as well as identify new and emerging risks for which controls need to be established.

2.2.5 Increasing Operational Efficiency

Operational efficiency involves process improvement, customer/employee feedback, technology transformations, and organizational matrices. Organizations use multiple systems, processes, and procedures for their business operations. Over the years, systems get outdated, processes redundant and overall, they drive up costs that are not always obvious. Analytics solutions can help capture and sieve through the disparate data from varying formats of logs, text, images, videos and predict leakages or disruptions in processes, hardware/software inefficiencies, and other bottlenecks that otherwise are hard to interpret.

By leveraging data analytics, organizations can identify the areas or infrastructure elements that need to be replaced. It can predict the need for maintenance well in advance, before the occurrence of productivity breakdowns or other critical cost impacts that affect output and efficiency.

A holistic view and analysis of the operations with data analytics can enable organizations to identify areas where the processes can be strengthened, performance measures fine-tuned, errors eliminated and wastages reduced to improve the bottom-line. In addition, the appropriate analytical solutions with automation can bring down production costs and ensure that people are employed on the right work.

Demonstrating growth potential is critical to establishing value. Connecting one or more of these drivers to the organization's strategic goals can set the right path towards promoting data analytical programs.

2.3 Typical Analytical Architecture

2.3.1 Data Analytical Architecture

Data Architecture is a set of systems, policies, and technology that determines what kind of data gets collected and how it is extracted, processed, and stored within a database system.

The analytics architecture is a crucial facet of business intelligence. Data, in itself, is useless unless we can extract value out of it. With the advent of relational databases or the RDBMS in the 1970s, business users could query the data and make fact-based decisions instead of intuitive ones. However, organizational data existed in disjointed systems, and analysts mainly worked in isolation using spreadsheets.

The advancements in hardware, scalability and storage capabilities from the 1980s onward made it possible to transform all the data into a central repository – the data warehouse (DW) or the enterprise data warehouse (EDW). This paved the way for storing historical data over time and making it system-ready for data analysis.

A typical analytical architecture can be divided into three sections (Fig. 2.1).

Data Management

The captured data from multiple sources is combined into the staging area(s) in the data management layer. Then, processes like normalization, transformations, validations, cleansing, and other optimization techniques are executed to organize the data into a single consistent schema for loading into the data warehouse or SQL storage.

The data warehouse can be at the departmental or enterprise level based on the organization's preferred data storage and access mechanism. The data in the warehouse is in a structured format and hence ready for users to build reports or dashboards geared towards analysis or decisions.

Data Analytics

The data analytics layer is where the data users/analysts/scientists build the analytical data models that help the organization make data-driven business decisions. Data from the DW is organized and quickly sorted into database systems and data marts for later access.

Data marts are a subset of data created from the data warehouse. It enables the end-user to easily access readily available and relevant data with a faster processing time. Data marts are department- or domain- or subject-specific. A hybrid data mart can have a combination

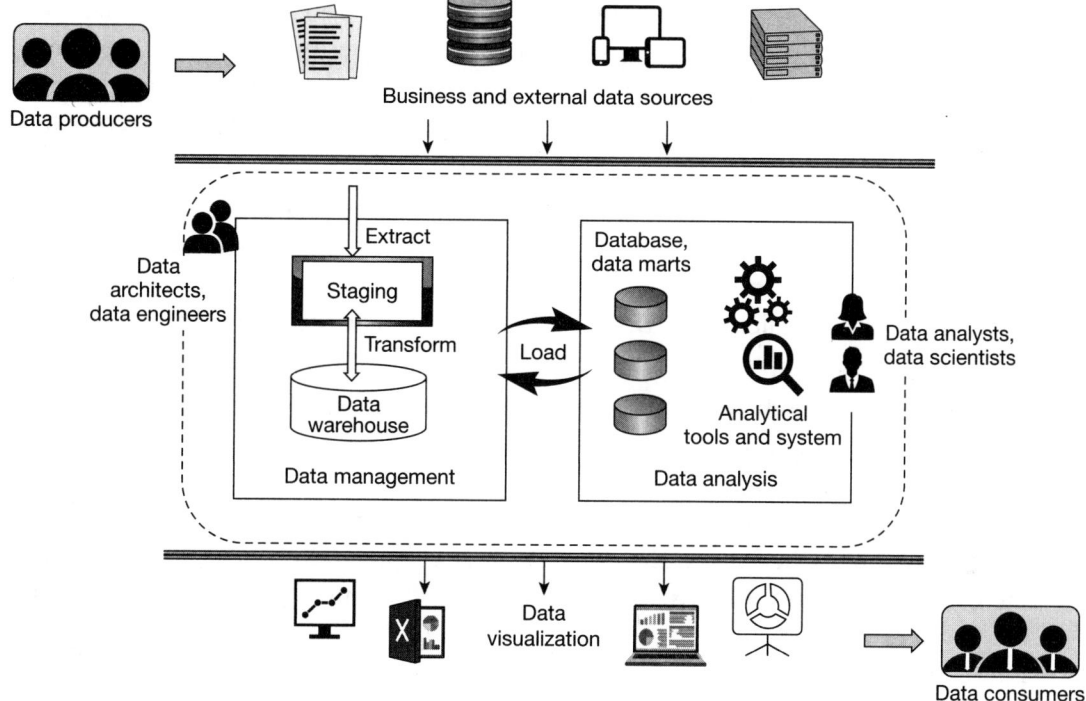

Figure 2.1 Typical data analytics architecture

of data from the data warehouse and other sources. Here, data analysts and scientists also use ETL (extract, transform, load) integration methods to build the data model.

The analytical models are built using tools like R and Python programming, Excel, Tableau, Power BI, and other analytics tools for business intelligence. The BI and analytics (refer to Section 2.4.1: Types of Analytics) done in the typical analytical architecture is primarily **descriptive** (what happened) and **diagnostic** (why did it happen).

Data Visualization

This layer is the data output layer. The summary of the analytical findings and insights is translated into a visual context for consumers or decision-makers to benefit. Data visualization is a quick and easy technique to convey information comprehensibly using visual information like charts, graphs, maps, infographics, dashboards.

Visual information is easier to absorb and process than numbers and texts. Therefore, the visualization layers leverage tools like Microsoft BI, Tableau, Sisence, QlikView to manipulate, format, and deliver data in an efficient, visually appealing, and comprehensible way.

Today, data architecture is not just about storing data. It is about how well the model supports the collection, collation, enrichment, and analysis of the data. The right data architecture can ensure the best data quality for new insights, automation, better reporting, and experience.

2.3.2 Challenges of Conventional Systems

One of the biggest challenges of the typical data architecture that data analysts and data scientists face is the limitation of implementing advanced analytics with predictive modeling, machine learning, and various automation techniques.

While traditional data architecture with the data warehouse is still prevalent, it is not without challenges. Big Data has brought in increased demands for more predictive analytics, so as to forecast the future and prescribe how the business should change now to stay competitive in the future.

Some of the main challenges with the conventional architecture model are:

1. **High costs**: The cost of storage for large volumes of data is high. Database resources are expensive when handling increasing data volumes and processing capabilities. It is nearly impossible to scale up on-premise storage capabilities to ensure system performance without incurring exceedingly high costs.
2. **Source data limitations**: A typical data warehouse is not built for Big Data analysis. Because of the restrictions to the amount of data that can be stored, businesses limit the data they store to what is required for their reporting needs rather than storing the entire raw data that may potentially be required for the future.
3. **Lack of flexibility**: As businesses are becoming more agile, the need of the hour is an efficient architecture that can support quick on-demand changes. The typical data architecture, once built, is relatively rigid. Any change to a data model with its processing and testing could take months for implementation and is not cost-effective.
4. **Degrading performance**: The rigid structure of the architecture forces organizations to implement add-ons and tools that can use parallel processing and other performance optimization techniques to meet the business requirements of accelerated data retrieval and real-time reporting. This leads to multiple isolated data sources, redundant architecture, and inefficient methods of ETL (Extract, Transfer and Laod) processing. This negatively impacts the performance of the data architecture.
5. **Limitations of analytics landscape**: Another critical requirement in today's Big Data world is the need for complex datasets, both structured and unstructured. Social media data containing texts, videos, audios, images are not stored in data warehouses. To add to the complexity, competitive organizations aim to augment their facilities with machine learning and AI to address future-looking questions.

A well-designed data architecture takes on an enterprise-level view instead of a domain-specific data model or database-level architecture model. As a result, it can help develop effective data analytics platforms from which organizations can draw meaningful and valuable insights for value-added strategic planning and effective decision-making. This leads to better business performance and competitive advantages.

Today, we are in an era of real-time, automated, and predictive analytics. The evolution of business analytics would need an enhanced and extended architecture where vast chunks of data – the Big Data that is drawn from a combination of storage repositories like data lakes and real-time cloud data.

2.4 ANALYTIC PROCESSES AND TOOLS

We shall now examine the types of analytics and tools available for processing Big Data and storing large datasets.

2.4.1 Types of Analytics

There are four main types of analytics – descriptive, diagnostic, predictive, and prescriptive – used by business users and analysts to gain insights (Fig. 2.2).

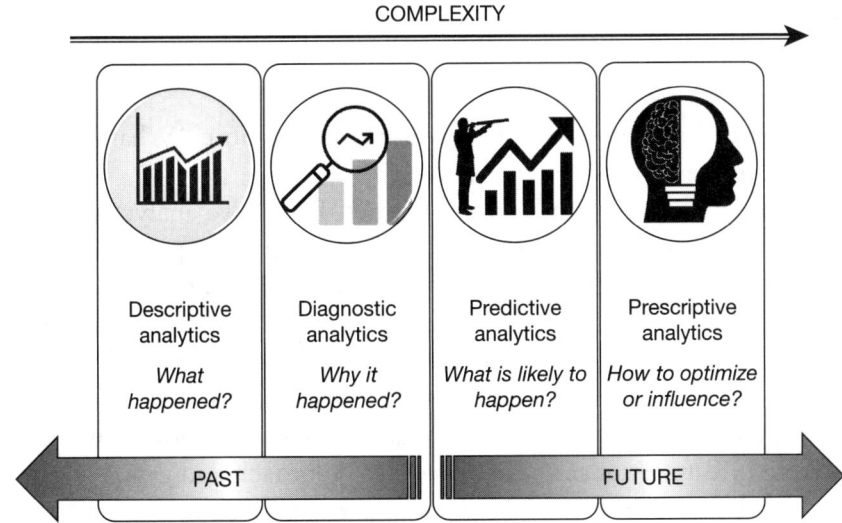

Figure 2.2 Types of data analytics

Descriptive Analytics

This type of analytics answers the question, "What happened in the past, and what we can learn from it?"

Organizations use it to identify trends, past occurrences, and areas for improvement by extracting, cleaning, and analyzing already-captured raw data. It is the most commonly used analytics that works with traditional statistical functions of mean, median, percentages, and other arithmetic operations on existing historical data.

The essential techniques used in descriptive analytics are data aggregation and data mining, which will be explained later in Chapter 3. By summarizing the data into meaningful and applicable measurements in the form of reports, departments across the organization will draw insights from their past performances and work towards the success of their business, like service improvements, targeted marketing, and others.

Diagnostic Analytics

This analytics answers the question, "Why did the past results occur?"

While descriptive analytics was about what happened, diagnostic analytics is about **why it happened**. Diagnostic analytics provides in-depth insights into what caused a particular event or outcome by looking at both internal historical data and external data, typically using ratios, probabilities, likelihoods, and distribution of outcomes for the analysis. Organizations use it to identify the 'root cause' or causal relationship in a particular situation or scenario.

Some techniques used in diagnostic analytics are correlation, drill-down, regression, classification, and others. However, while diagnostic analysis helps us determine the factors that contributed to an outcome, it provides limited, if any, actionable insights. For example, it can find the factors or root cause of why sales increased or decreased in a particular period or what caused network congestion, but it does not indicate how to resolve it.

Predictive Analytics

As the name suggests, Predictive Analytics answers the question, "What is likely to happen in the future so that we can respond proactively?"

It is used to predict future trends and outcomes. Predictive analytics uses the findings of descriptive and diagnostic analytics to detect clusters and exceptions and finally lead to providing accurate predictions. Businesses use advanced machine learning algorithms like Random Forest, Support Vector Machines, Time Series, and many traditional forecasting techniques to arrive at the outcome. However, it should be noted that predictive analytics can only forecast what *might* happen and not what *will* happen.

It is a valuable forecasting tool used by organizations to support complex forecasts in sales and marketing. Businesses can take a proactive approach and gain a competitive edge by understanding the probabilities of an event occurring based on a given set of variables. For example, Netflix uses data (watch history, preferences, demographics, etc.) on each user to create or promote their shows/movies, leading to customer retention of over 91%.

Prescriptive Analytics

Prescriptive Analytics answers the question, "What decisions and actions should be taken now to eliminate a problem or potential problem or to cultivate a promising opportunity/trend?"

It is the most advanced form of analytics as it can suggest all favorable outcomes according to a specified course of action. It can also suggest various courses of action to get to a particular outcome by simulating various scenarios. For example, while predictive analytics would give the school board a good idea of which set of students was most likely to enroll, prescriptive analytics will provide insights on who is most likely to enroll in their school and the most likely approach that could convince them that the school is the best match for them.

Prescriptive analytics uses tools and technologies like artificial intelligence, machine learning and neural network algorithms that constantly learn and update the relationship between the action and the outcome to provide recommendations of the subsequent steps that should be taken. The data source includes internal data of the organization and external data that may influence the algorithm. Prescriptive analytics is used across industries like retail, healthcare and education. Utility businesses, gas producers and pipeline companies, for example, employ prescriptive analytics to discover variables impacting oil price and gas in order to secure the best terms and hedge risks in the energy industry.

The common link in all the above analytics is data. The data analytics strategy to adopt depends on the quality and quantity of data at hand, the current state of data analytics in the organization, and the critical area that needs to be focused on. Based on the information obtained/assessed, companies can design, implement and launch their data analytics solution.

2.4.2 Modern Data Analytic Tools

Hadoop

Hadoop or Apache Hadoop is a Big Data tool developed by the Apache Software Foundation for distributed data processing and storage of large datasets across clusters of computers. The framework consists of three core components that form the main services of the Hadoop ecosystem, namely.

- **HDFS** – HDFS or Hadoop Distributed File System is the primary data storage system used by Hadoop applications. It provides robust storage, scalability, high availability, and fault tolerance. In addition, it is cost-effective and supports the deployment of Big Data applications and frameworks over it.
- **MapReduce** – It is the data processing component of Hadoop.
- **YARN** – YARN or Yet Another Resource Negotiator is the operating system of Hadoop that monitors and manages the resources.

Applications like Hive (data warehouse application), Pig (high-level programming language for querying and analyzing data), HBase (open-source non-relational distributed database), Mahout (platform for Machine Learning applications), and Spark (distributed processing system for large-scale data processing) are some of the other components in the Hadoop ecosystem.

Hadoop and its applications are elaborated on in later chapters.

R Programming

R is an open-source tool that facilitates wide-scale statistical analysis, data visualization, and data science. R is the go-to programming language for data scientists and analysts due to its vast array of packages and libraries. **CRAN** (R Archive Network), the main repository for R packages, contains over 17000 packages of algorithms and modules that can cater to practically any analytical model and computational needs. R also has a massive collection of graphical libraries like ggplot2, plotly, RGL, and others, capable of creating almost any type of high-quality graph.

The language is versatile and can work seamlessly with other programming languages like Python, Java, C, and C++. Furthermore, R is platform-independent and can run efficiently on multiple operating systems like Windows, MacOS, UNIX, and Linux. In addition, it is highly portable and can be integrated with other technologies like Hadoop, Spark, and various other database management systems.

Though R is free-to-use software, its downside is the weak security and a steep learning curve. It is also memory-intensive and slower when compared to other programming languages like Python and MATLAB. However, it is an evolving language with constant upgrades and packages to bridge the gaps.

Tableau

Tableau is an end-to-end data analytics platform that can connect data (structured, semi-structured, unstructured) from any source or platform in real-time, be it SQL or NoSQL databases, Hadoop, Hive, Spark, and others, without the user having to be tech-savvy. According to Gartner Magic Quadrant, its ease of use, self-service data visualization, smart dashboards, and high performance makes it the leader in Business Intelligence tools.

Its best feature is its high computational capability and interactive visualization. Some of the products in the Tableau ecosystem are:

- **Tableau Desktop** – Core component where all the development takes place.
- **Tableau Server** – Core administrative component for security, integration, automation/scheduling at the server level.
- **Tableau Online** – Tableau analytics platform hosted in the cloud.
- **Tableau Reader** – Free tableau software where analysts can share their visualizations built on Tableau Desktop for collaboration. However, users would need Tableau Reader to open the file.
- **Tableau Viewer** – Role-based licensed product for business organizations to empower people with dashboards/visualizations and trusted content to make data-driven decisions without putting data security at risk.
- **Tableau Public** – Free Tableau software to produce data visualizations.

The platform provides flexible settings and agility to meet changing business demands. However, to exploit the full capability of Tableau, users need to have in-depth training and knowledge.

Qlik

Qlik is another data analytics tool that is quickly gaining a solid community base with its end-to-end data integration (ETL) solution-cum-analytics engine, and BI and data visualization tool. The front-end UI is browser-based, where users can view/share documents and collaborate on the insights in real-time or offline. The documents and reports are hosted on the internet by the **QlikView Server**. The server is responsible for the client-server communication between the user and the QlikView Back-End system.

The back-end system consists of **QlikView Developer** or **QlikView Desktop** for designers and developers to produce their work. The **QlikView Publisher** distributes the documents to the various QlikView servers and users. The QlikView Publisher is also responsible for data loading, security, and user roles and privileges. It is cost-effective with efficient in-memory storage and speed of delivery, irrespective of the number of users and data requests. Its downside is the need for high technical expertise to develop the applications and scripts.

In today's hypercompetitive world, enterprises must be quick in their decision-making. With the internet and mobile technologies, sophisticated data analytics tools like Microsoft Azure Analytics, Power BI, RapidMiner, Knime, Splunk, Talend, and many others, businesses can make strategic and operational decisions from anywhere, anytime.

2.5 DATA ANALYTIC LIFE-CYCLE

2.5.1 Need of Data Analytic Life-cycle

A data project inherently comes with questions, especially when dealing with a humungous volume of data. What are the goals of the project? What and where is the data? Where and how to begin?

A data analytics project necessitates understanding the business problem, understanding and preparing the data that could potentially address the problem, exploratory analysis of the data to build an analytics model, executing the model and validating the results, and finally communicating the findings to the business. Due to the complexities and ambiguity in data, the process is unfathomable unless a systematic structure or methodology is followed.

Hence, the need arises for a process with an organized set of tasks and activities that the team can follow. A well-defined process can provide the direction and method to extract information from the data as it gets processed, tested, used, and analyzed. It enables the data experts to ascertain that they are proceeding in the right direction to accomplish business goals. At any stage, based on lessons learned and insights during analysis, the team can make strategic decisions on whether to move forward with the existing research or retrace with different variable sets/methods or redo the analysis completely.

Thus, it offers a systematic way to manage data for converting it into information that can fulfill organizational and project goals.

2.5.2 Phases of Data Analytic Life-cycle

The key to managing a successful data analytics project that can bring value to an organization is to understand the data analytics life-cycle. Today, there is no single standard methodology followed universally by all data analysts/scientists. However, a typical data analysis project life-cycle fundamentally follows six phases (Fig. 2.3). The maximum duration is spent on the first three phases, i.e., Discovery, Data Preparation, and Model Planning, where the project team needs to understand and prepare the data and design the models. The subsequent phases, though complex, are somewhat shorter in duration.

The analytic data life-cycle is iterative, and the teams can move forward and backward through the phases.

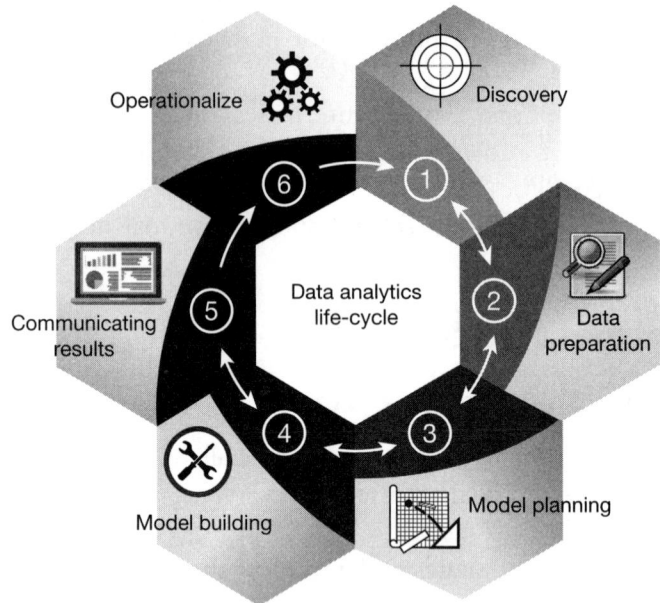

Figure 2.3 Typical phases of a data analytics project

A brief description of the different phases in the life-cycle is provided below:

Phase 1: Data Discovery

The key output of the Discovery phase of a data project is to define the business objective. This involves defining the business problem in terms of an analytical challenge that is to be addressed with the analytics project, identifying the existing resources in terms of data, people, and technology to achieve the set goal(s), and drafting a timeline for the end-to-end execution of the solution.

The activities of this phase are:

- Gathering of business requirements, challenges and source of information.
- Assessment of existing models related to past projects, if any, to determine the appropriate analysis method required for developing the model.
- Requirement analysis of existing skills, in-house resources and infrastructure, and the domain knowledge required to fulfill the data model.
- Define the purpose of the data in terms of problem statement explaining the current situation and future impact, project objectives, success and failure criteria, key performance indicators, high-level timeline, and resource requirement.
- Develop the initial hypothesis set (IHs) to test with data at later phases.

Phase 2: Data Preparation

The Data Preparation phase involves the cleansing and transforming the raw accumulated data prior to processing and analysis. The data from various identified sources is collected, mixed, and merged. The key objective of this phase is to prepare a scalable analytics sandbox platform with available data that can be used in subsequent phases for modeling and analysis.

The activities of this phase are:

- Identify the data sources and the quantity, quality, and structure of the data that can be acquired.
- Collection of data. Typically, three data collection methods are used.
    1. Data Entry using manual entry or from systems within the organization via APIs, SQL database and plug-ins
    2. Data Acquisition from external sources
    3. Signal Reception where data is acquired from digital devices like IoT and other control devices.
- Prepare the sandbox or staging area with ample space to Extract, Load, and Transform (ELT) the data and load the datasets.
- Understand the gaps in data and evaluate the work to be done on the dataset for it to be useful. This can be done using various visualization tools, from Excel for small data to Alteryx, Python, or R for larger datasets.
- Cleansing the data by filling in missing variables, removing erroneous data and duplicates, masking sensitive information, standardizing the structure, and other cleansing activities.
- Data validation procedures are conducted after each round of cleansing activity.
- Transforming and enriching the data. Data transformation is the process of updating the format or values of source data to the required one for better user understanding. Enriching is the process of appending data with information from other related sources to provide deeper insights.

Data preparation activities are performed multiple times before the data is ready for the Model Planning process.

 Phase 3: Model Planning

The Model Planning phase analyzes the enriched data and identifies a suitable data model that achieves the project goal. It involves various techniques and methods like clustering, regression, classification using decision trees, neural networks and others to identify the features and relationship between variables for applying to the model. A data model is nothing but a conceptual model that organizes data elements and standardizes how they relate to one another. It emulates a possible real-world scenario.

The various activities in this phase are:

- Study the dataset structures with reference to the initial hypothesis identified in the Data Discovery phase and ascertain the right set of variables that the project needs to focus on.
- Create the initial data models using analytic software packages like Matlab, SAS, RStudio, or by designing a customized set of algorithms.
- Establish the approach, tools, techniques, and analytical workflow.
- Document the assumptions made at each stage of devising the preliminary model(s).

Phase 4: Model Building

As the name suggests, the data analytics team builds and operates the data model designed during the Model Building phase. In addition, datasets are developed for **training** (labeled data for algorithms to learn how to process information and produce sophisticated results), **testing** (unlabeled data executed on the model to validate if the algorithm was trained effectively), and **production** purposes.

This phase determines whether the model being built meets the business objective as defined in the Data Discovery phase. It is a cyclic process that repeats itself between model planning and building, multiple times, before the model is deemed robust and accurate enough to meet business needs.

If the results are invalid, the project team must revisit the previous phases 1–3. If valid, the project can move on to the next phase.

Phase 5: Communicating Results

The Result Communication phase is crucial as it can set the project for success or failure. The phase consists of presenting the data analysis findings to the stakeholder in a simple comprehensible manner.

The project team must identify the essential findings and insights of the analysis, connect the findings with the hypothesis, and share the relevant top results that have business value for the stakeholder. These results must be linked to the success criteria defined in the Discovery phase.

The optimal way to summarize and convey the findings is through appealing visual charts with data points and animation. Tableau, Power BI, and Cognos are some powerful visualization tools.

It should be noted here that when the findings are presented to the stakeholders, there may be queries or new understanding that may necessitate revisiting the Model Building phase.

Phase 6: Operationalize

In the Operationalize phase, the data is moved from the sandbox to the production environment to monitor and validate the results to check if they match the expected business goal. It is recommended to be deployed in iterations rather than a full-scale rollout. If any discrepancy is found, it is easy to move back to the previous life-cycle phases and update the input variables for the correct output.

If the findings fit the objectives, then a detailed report that includes but is not limited to the key findings, coding, technical papers, test results, and all other details documented during the course of the life-cycle is finalized.

As data quality degrades over time, it is essential to re-evaluate the data model at intervals to enrich and add new features to ensure that it is kept relevant for business use.

2.6 KEY ROLES FOR SUCCESSFUL ANALYTIC PROJECTS

In the simplest form, we have seen that data analytics collects information or data on specific topics or focus areas, analyzes and interprets the said data, and finally presents the findings via comprehensive reports or dashboards.

However, like any project, a data analytics project has several key players essential for the project's success. Any data project ideally should be linked to the organization's strategic goal and will have the backup of the Executive Sponsor. The sponsor can be an individual or a group of senior-level executives like the CEO, CFO or CIO. The sponsor's responsibility is to ensure that the project's goals are aligned with the overall organization strategy.

The Data Analytics project execution team typically has the following roles.

Project Manager / Project Lead

The role of the project manager (PM) in a data analytics project is to ensure the successful delivery of the project in terms of the scope, budget, and timelines without compromising on quality. The PM is responsible for engaging the right resources and managing them, communicating regularly and effectively with the stakeholders, and ensuring that business benefits are delivered in the best way possible.

Business Analyst

They do the liaison between the business and the IT team. The business analyst is expected to be aware of the IT domain and be able to speak the business language. The individual is the functional expert with a clear understanding of the project goals, in-depth business knowledge, including the organizations' business processes, and knowledge of the depth and breadth of the data.

The business analyst works closely with data architects, analysts, and engineers to identify if the correct data exists and check the completeness and condition of the data. The Business Analyst collects the raw usage data and transfers it to the Data Analyst/Architect to execute this data.

Data Architect

Data architects visualize, design, create and manage an organization's data architecture. They prepare data in a framework that can be used by data scientists, data engineers, or data analysts. They analyze the existing organization data platforms and the platforms in the marketplace and define which data components to use, like Hive, MapReduce, Pig, etc. for designing the enterprise data management framework model. The model helps outline and communicate the project's scope, including master data, reference data, metadata, and others.

Their role entails evaluating the various technical designs by conducting proofs-of-concept to recommend and design a holistic and optimized analytics platform.

Data Analyst

Data Analysts work on the existing raw data creating a simplified data model in a language that is familiar to the end-users. They gather, clean, understand, organize and analyze the data using various analytics and visualization tools like R, Python, SQL, and others, to present their findings/results in formats that can be automatically updated and accessed.

They spot essential patterns within the data, which help them create meaningful reports that provide insights for strategic business decisions.

Data Scientists

While Data Analysts typically work with structured data, Data Scientists work with highly complex digital data. They design and construct data modeling processes to create algorithms, prototypes and predictive models, and perform custom analysis. Their skills include advanced statistical analysis, a comprehensive understanding of machine learning, artificial intelligence and data conditioning.

The data scientist essentially identifies patterns and trends from past and present data to formulate questions that could be key to the organization's success and derive reliable predictions for the future.

Data Engineer

Data engineers build and optimize systems that the data analysts and data scientists work on. They are responsible for creating and managing the data pipeline, monitoring and testing the system for optimized performance, and ensuring availability, accessibility, and consistency of the datasets.

Many of the responsibilities of the roles overlap based on the size of the analytics project. For example, large-scale data science projects have many more roles like the product developer, reporting developer, platform architect or system administrator and data liaison.

2.7 Modern-day Intelligence

"Today people are information-rich and time-poor."—Marty Neumeier.

2.7.1 Business Intelligence vs. Data Science

Organizations depend on **Business Intelligence** (BI) systems to guide executives, managers, and other business users for decisions and strategic planning. BI combines data analysis, data mining, data visualization, and reporting capabilities to help organizations make better data-driven decisions.

The business Intelligence process consists of five steps:

Step 1 – Integrate data from source systems and load it into a data warehouse or other data repository.

Step 2 – Prepare the data for analysis by organizing the datasets into data models or OLAP cubes.

Step 3 – Run analytical queries or processes on the data. This is typically done by the analysts/business users/data scientists.

Step 4 – Build the resultant findings using data visualization tools/systems into dashboards, charts, portals.

Step 5 – Use the information to make actionable decisions to fulfill a strategic goal.

BI systems are used by organizations to track KPIs and measure the performance of a department or organization as a whole. This can enable the business to address problems more proactively. For example, BI tools can track marketing campaign metrics to measure unit performance and plan for future campaigns. BI information can be shared with business users via dashboards with drill-down features. In addition, the visualization can be shared on the company portal, promoting data transparency and a single source of truth.

Business Intelligence is usually based on descriptive and diagnostic analytics by analyzing historical or real-time data of events that have already occurred or are currently occurring. However, some what-if queries can be run on the BI system to bring a predictive analytics element to the BI process. Nevertheless, the analytics scenarios are pretty limited.

This is where **Data Science** comes in. Data Science is a discipline that uses computer science and statistical methodology to make valuable predictions and gain insights. It involves

- Data analysis techniques like Data wrangling EDA (exploratory data analysis)
- Programming languages like Python, R, Java
- Machine Learning techniques, e.g., Deep Learning, Dimensionality Reduction, and other algorithms
- Linear Algorithms, Statistics, and other mathematical modeling processes.
- Data visualization.

Data scientists are the actual actors in the data science field and typically work only on Big Data. Once BI has translated the data to insights, data scientists run predictive and prescriptive analysis on a combination of historical data real-time, and unstructured data. They theorize solutions to problems and present data visualizations in a way that reveals trends and forecasts.

A unique aspect of data science is the application of machine learning and AI to create a self-sustaining data mechanism that can adapt over time to new data.

Some of the characteristics of BI and Data Science given in Table 2.1:

Table 2.1 Characteristics of BI and Data Science

	Business Intelligence	Data Science
Ownership	IT owned	Analytics owned
Key player	Data analyst	Data scientist
Data storage	Mostly in data warehouses	A data lake, data platforms like Hadoop
Process	Transforms raw data into meaningful datasets, and extracts and analyzes the information to derive insights.	Gathers and analyzes the raw data using statistical techniques and algorithms to uncover hidden patterns and derive insights
Nature of data	Structured data, some unstructured	Structured, semi-structured, unstructured
Analytical models	Descriptive, diagnostic	Predictive, prescriptive
Methods	OLAP, ETL	Machine learning, Data wrangling
Outcome	Operational, lower value	High-value generation

Data Science can be said to be an evolution of BI. In other words, BI provides the foundational insights from structured historical data, which Data Science combines with less structured data types to forecast how present trends might change or develop in the future.

2.7.2 Intelligent Data Analysis

Intelligent Data Analysis (IDA) refers to the use of analysis, classification, conversion, extraction, organization, and reasoning methods to extract valuable knowledge from Big Data using techniques in various disciplines, such as artificial intelligence, high-performance computing, pattern recognition, and statistics.

The IDA process generally consists of three stages:

1. **Data preparation** – Selecting the required data from the relevant data source and integrating this into a dataset for the data mining stage.
2. **Data mining** – Involves the extraction and working out of rules and patterns in large complex datasets using specific methods or algorithms under the discipline of statistics, machine learning, and artificial intelligence.
3. **Result Validation and Explanation** – This stage deals with the validation/verification of the rules and patterns produced by the mining algorithms and provides intuitive communication of results.

IDA is used in different Web information analysis, economic data analysis, Big Data analysis, medical informatics and image analysis. For example, Big Data intelligence involves using Artificial Intelligence and Machine Learning to provide actionable data analytics models and transform Big Data into insights for data scientists, BI analysts and strategists, and other relevant users to take the next actionable steps.

SUMMARY

According to a Gartner 2017 report, 85% of analytics and Big Data projects fail. Not having a clear business case is one of the main reasons for the failure. Thus, there has to be a business objective that aligns with the organization's strategy. For a business to make the right decisions on data strategy, it is essential to understand what drives the business.

Business drivers are conditions, processes, or activities vital in maximizing a company's growth and business value. Some of the key business drivers to implement a data and analytics program are:

- Increasing profitability and growth
- Strengthening customer experience and intimacy
- Driving digital transformation and innovation
- Managing regulatory and compliance risks
- Increasing operational efficiency.

The foundation of an exemplary data analytics system is a stable and robust data analytics architecture. Data Architecture is a set of systems, policies and technology that determines what kind of data gets collected and how it is extracted, processed, and stored within a database system. The right data architecture can ensure the best data quality for new insights, automation, better reporting, and experience.

However, the traditional data architecture with the data warehouse model cannot cope with the increased business demands that Big Data has brought in. The need of the hour is more predictive analytics to forecast the future and prescribe how the business should change to stay competitive for the future. The challenges in the typical architecture model with the evolution of Big Data are high costs, source data limitations, rigid architecture, poor and degrading performance, and fundamental limitations of the analytics landscape to handle unstructured data and advanced analytics.

In today's data-driven world of data analytics, the best organizational decisions are made when proper reports that can draw meaningful insights aligned to the organization's business strategy are generated. There are four types of analytics:

1. **Descriptive analytics** is all about "What happened in our past and what can we learn from it?"
2. **Diagnostic analytics** is about why it happened, i.e., "Why did the past results occur?"
3. **Predictive analytics** addresses the question, "What is likely to happen in the future and how can we respond proactively?"
4. **Prescriptive analytics** answers the question, "What decisions and actions should be taken now to eliminate a problem or potential problem or to cultivate a promising opportunity/trend?"

With the internet and mobile technologies, sophisticated data analytics tools like Microsoft Azure Analytics, Power BI, RapidMiner, Knime, Splunk, Talend, and many others, businesses can make strategic and operational decisions from anywhere, anytime.

A structured data analytics life-cycle offers a systematic way to manage data for converting it into information that can fulfill organizational and project goals. A data analytics life-cycle is circular or iterative. The main six phases are:

1. **Data Discovery** – Defining the business goal and identifying the needed resources for data, people, and technology to achieve the set goal. The initial hypothesis (IH) is set at this time.
2. **Data Preparation** – Capturing the source data from disparate sources, cleansing, validating, transforming, enriching, and storing the data.
3. **Model Planning** – Analyzing the enriched data using various analytical techniques and methods like clustering classification. Identifying a suitable data model achieves the project goal.
4. **Model Building** – Building the planned analytical model and testing/validating it.
5. **Communicating Results** – Presenting the findings/results in an appealing and comprehensible way using reports, dashboards, or other data visualization methods.
6. **Operationalize** – Deploying in a production environment.

The success of a data analytics project is dependent on the project team behind it. Some of the critical roles in a typical data analytics project are the project manager, business analyst, data analyst, data architect, data scientist, data engineer, product developer, reporting developer, platform architect, and a few others. The three roles distinct to a data analytics project are the data analyst, the data scientist, and the data architect/engineer. Many of the responsibilities of the roles overlap based on the size of the analytics project.

EXERCISES

Multiple Choice Questions

1. **Which of the following is not a business driver for analytics?**
   A. Increasing profitability and growth
   B. Strengthening customer experience and intimacy
   C. Increasing data engineers motivation
   D. Driving digital transformation and innovation
   Answer: C
   Explanation: Data analytics has nothing to do with increasing the motivation of employees, as it is more subjective in nature.
   However, the business drivers for analytics include: increasing profitability and growth, strengthening customer experience and intimacy, driving digital transformation and innovation and managing regulatory compliance risks.

2. This is a set of systems, policies, and technology that determines what kind of data gets collected and how it is extracted, processed, and stored within a database system.
   A. Data mining
   B. Data visualization
   C. Data analytics
   D. Data architecture
   Answer: D
   Explanation: Data Architecture is a set of systems, policies, and technology that determines what kind of data gets collected and how it is extracted, processed, and stored within a database system. The data analytics layer is where the data users/analysts/scientists build the analytical data models that help the organization make data-driven business decisions.

   Data visualization layer is the data output layer. The summary of the analytical findings and insights is translated into a visual context for consumers or decision-makers to benefit. Data mining involves the extraction and working out of rules and patterns in large complex datasets using specific methods or algorithms under the discipline of statistics, machine learning, and artificial intelligence.

3. This layer is where the data users/analysts/scientists build the analytical data models that help the organization make data-driven business decisions.
   A. Data mining
   B. Data visualization
   C. Data analytics
   D. Data architecture
   Answer: C
   Explanation: Same as for Question 2.

4. This layer is the data output layer. The summary of the analytical findings and insights is translated into a format for consumers or decision-makers to benefit.
   A. Data mining
   B. Data visualization
   C. Data analytics
   D. Data architecture
   Answer: B
   Explanation: Same as for Question 2.

5. This involves the extraction and working out of rules and patterns in large complex datasets using specific methods or algorithms under the discipline of statistics, machine learning, and artificial intelligence.
   A. Data mining
   B. Data visualization
   C. Data analytics
   D. Data architecture
   Answer: A
   Explanation: Same as for Question 2.

6. Which of the following is not the section of a typical analytical architecture?
   A. Data management
   B. Data analytics
   C. Data visualization
   D. Data reporting

Answer: D

Explanation: A typical analytical architecture can be divided into three sections: data management, data analytics and data visualization.

The captured data from multiple sources is combined into the staging area(s) in the data management layer. The data analytics layer is where the data users/analysts/scientists build the analytical data models that help the organization make data-driven business decisions. Data Visualization layer is the data output layer. The summary of the analytical findings and insights is translated into a visual context for consumers or decision-makers to benefit.

7. **What is Data Mart?**
    A. Data marts are a subset of data created from the data warehouse.
    B. Data mart is a place where the raw data is stored from the user.
    C. It answers the question, "Why did the past results occur?"
    D. It answers the question, "What happened in our past, and what can we learn from it?"
    Answer: A
    Explanation: Data from the Data Warehouse is organized and quickly sorted into database systems and data marts for later access. Data marts are a subset of data created from the data warehouse. It enables the end-user to easily access readily available and relevant data with a faster processing time. Data marts are department- or domain- or subject-specific. A hybrid data mart can have a combination of data from the data warehouse and other sources.

8. **ETL Stands for:**
    A. Explain, Transform, Load
    B. Extract, Transform, Load
    C. Extract, Translate, Lock
    D. Extract, Transform, Lock
    Answer: B
    Explanation: A hybrid data mart can have a combination of data from the data warehouse and other sources. Here, data analysts and scientists also use ETL (extract, transform, load) integration methods to build the data model.

9. **Microsoft BI, Tableau, Sisence and QlikView are the tools used in:**
    A. Data Management   B. Data Analytics
    C. Data Visualization   D. Data Reporting
    Answer: C
    Explanation: Visual information is easier to absorb and process than numbers and texts. Therefore, the visualization layers leverage tools like Microsoft BI, Tableau, Sisence, QlikView to manipulate, format, and deliver data in an efficient, visually appealing, and comprehensible way.

10. **Which of the following is not a challenge with the conventional Architecture model?**
    A. High cost
    B. Source data limitations
    C. Too much of flexibility
    D. Degrading performance
    Answer: C
    Explanation: One of the biggest challenges of the typical data architecture that data analysts and data scientists face is the limitation of implementing advanced analytics with predictive modeling, machine learning, and various automation techniques. Some of the main challenges with the conventional architecture model are: higher cost, source data limitations, lack of flexibility and degrading performance.

11. **How many types of data analytics are there?**
    A. 2
    B. 3
    C. 4
    D. 8
    Answer: C
    Explanation: There are four main types of analytics – descriptive, diagnostic, predictive, and prescriptive – used by business users and analysts to gain insights.

12. **This type of analytics answers the question, "What happened in our past, and what can we learn from it?"**
    A. Descriptive
    B. Diagnostic
    C. Predictive
    D. Prescriptive
    Answer: A
    Explanation
    Descriptive Analytics: This type of analytics answers the question, "What happened in our past, and what can we learn from it?" Organizations use it to identify trends, past occurrences, and areas for improvement by extracting, cleaning, and analyzing already-captured raw data.

13. **It is the most commonly used analytics using statistical functions of mean, median, percentages, and other arithmetic operations on existing historical data.**
    A. Descriptive
    B. Diagnostic
    C. Predictive
    D. Prescriptive
    Answer: A
    Explanation: Descriptive analytics is the most commonly used analytics using statistical functions of mean, median, percentages, and other arithmetic operations on existing historical data. The essential techniques used in descriptive analytics are data aggregation and data mining.

14. **This type of analytics answers the question, "Why did the past results occur?"**
    A. Descriptive
    B. Diagnostic
    C. Predictive
    D. Prescriptive
    Answer: B

Explanation: Diagnostic Analytics answers the question, "Why did the past results occur?" While descriptive analytics was about what happened, diagnostic analytics is about why it happened. Diagnostic analytics provides in-depth insights into what caused a particular event or outcome by looking at both internal historical data and external data, typically using ratios, probabilities, likelihoods, and distribution of outcomes for the analysis.

15. **Organizations use it to identify the 'root cause' or causal relationship in a particular situation or scenario:**
    A. Descriptive
    B. Diagnostic
    C. Predictive
    D. Prescriptive
    Answer: B
    Explanation: Organizations use diagnostic analysis to identify the 'root cause' or causal relationship in a particular situation or scenario. Some techniques used in diagnostic analytics are correlation, drill-down, regression, classification, and others.

16. **This answers the question, "What is likely to happen in the future so that we can respond proactively?"**
    A. Descriptive
    B. Diagnostic
    C. Predictive
    D. Prescriptive
    Answer: C
    Explanation: As the name suggests, Predictive Analytics answers the question, "What is likely to happen in the future so that we can respond proactively?" It is used to predict future trends and outcomes. Predictive analytics uses descriptive and diagnostic analytics findings to detect clusters and exceptions and finally lead to providing accurate predictions.

17. **This answers the question, "What decisions and actions should be taken now to eliminate a problem or potential problem or to cultivate a promising opportunity/trend?"**
    A. Descriptive
    B. Diagnostic
    C. Predictive
    D. Prescriptive
    Answer: D
    Explanation: Prescriptive Analytics answers the question, "What decisions and actions should be taken now to eliminate a problem or potential problem or to cultivate a promising opportunity/trend?" It is the most advanced form of analytics as it can suggest all favorable outcomes according to a specified course of action. It can also suggest various courses of action to get to a particular outcome by simulating various scenarios.

18. **This uses tools and technologies like artificial intelligence, machine learning, neural network algorithms:**
    A. Descriptive
    B. Diagnostic
    C. Predictive
    D. Prescriptive

Answer: D

Explanation: Prescriptive analytics uses tools and technologies like artificial intelligence, machine learning and neural network algorithms that constantly learn and update the relationship between the action and the outcome to provide recommendations of the subsequent steps that should be taken.

19. **The key output of this phase of a data project is to define the business objective:**
    A. Data Discovery
    B. Data Preparation
    C. Model Planning
    D. Model Building

    Answer: A

    Explanation: The key output of the Discovery phase of a data project is to define the business objective. This involves defining the business problem in terms of an analytical challenge that is to be addressed with the analytics project, identifying the existing resources in terms of data, people, and technology to achieve the set goal(s), and drafting a timeline for the end-to-end execution of the solution.

20. **The analytic data life-cycle is:**
    A. Step-by-step Approac
    B. Iterative Approach
    C. Incremental Approach
    D. Hybrid Approach

    Answer: B

    Explanation: The maximum duration is spent on the first three phases, i.e., Discovery, Data preparation, and Model planning, where the project team needs to understand and prepare the data and design the models. The subsequent phases, though complex, are somewhat shorter in duration. The analytic data life-cycle is iterative, and the teams can move forward and backward through the phases.

21. **In the data analytic life-cycle, the maximum duration is spent on the first three phases.**
    A. True
    B. False

    Answer: A

    Explanation: Same as for Question 19.

22. **This phase involves the cleansing and transforming of raw accumulated data prior to processing and analysis.**
    A. Data Discovery
    B. Data Preparation
    C. Model Planning
    D. Model Building

    Answer: B

    Explanation: The Data Preparation phase involves the cleansing and transforming of raw accumulated data prior to processing and analysis. The data from various identified sources is collected, mixed, and merged. The key objective of this phase is to prepare a scalable analytics sandbox platform with available data that can be used in subsequent phases for modeling and analysis.

23. **This phase analyzes the enriched data:**
    A. Data Discovery
    B. Data Preparation
    C. Model Planning
    D. Model Building
    Answer: C
    Explanation: The Model Planning phase analyzes the enriched data and identifies a suitable data model that achieves the project goal. It involves various techniques and methods like clustering, regression, classification using decision trees, neural networks and others to identify the features and relationship between variables that could be applied to the model.

24. **This organizes data elements and standardizes how they relate to one another. It emulates a possible real-world scenario.**
    A. Data Discovery
    B. Data Preparation
    C. Data Presentation
    D. Data Model
    Answer: D
    Explanation: The Model Planning phase analyzes the enriched data and identifies a suitable data model that achieves the project goal. It involves various techniques and methods like clustering, regression, classification using decision trees, neural networks and others to identify the features and relationship between variables for applying to the model. A data model is nothing but a conceptual model that organizes data elements and standardizes how they relate to one another. It emulates a possible real-world scenario.

25. **The data analytics team builds and operates the data model designed in this phase:**
    A. Data Discovery
    B. Data Preparation
    C. Model Planning
    D. Model Building
    Answer: D
    Explanation: As the name suggests, the data analytics team builds and operates the data model designed during the Model Building phase. In addition, datasets are developed for training (labeled data for algorithms to learn how to process information and produce sophisticated results), testing (unlabeled data executed on the model to validate if the algorithm was trained effectively), and production purposes.

26. **This phase determines whether the model being built meets the business objective:**
    A. Data Discovery
    B. Data Preparation
    C. Model Planning
    D. Model Building
    Answer: D
    Explanation: Model Building phase determines whether the model being built meets the business objective as defined in the Data Discovery phase. It is a cyclic process that repeats itself between model planning and building multiple times before the model is deemed robust and accurate enough to meet business needs.

27. **In this phase, the data is moved from the sandbox to the production environment to monitor and validate if the results match the expected business goal:**
    A. Data Discovery
    B. Data Preparation
    C. Model Planning
    D. Operationalize
    Answer: D
    Explanation: In the Operationalize phase, the data is moved from the sandbox to the production environment to monitor and validate if the results match the expected business goal. It is recommended to be deployed in iterations rather than a full-scale rollout. If any discrepancy is found, it is easy to move back to the previous life-cycle phases and update the input variables for the correct output.

28. **The role of this person in a data analytics project is to ensure the successful delivery of the project in terms of the scope, budget, and timelines without compromising on quality:**
    A. Business Analyst
    B. Project Manager
    C. Data Architect
    D. Data Analyst
    Answer: B
    Explanation: The role of the project manager (PM) in a data analytics project is to ensure the successful delivery of the project in terms of the scope, budget, and timelines without compromising on quality. The PM is responsible for engaging the right resources and managing them, communicating regularly and effectively with the stakeholders, and ensuring that business benefits are delivered in the best way possible.

29. **The _____ is expected to be aware of the IT domain and be able to speak the business language.**
    A. Business Analyst
    B. Project Manager
    C. Data Architect
    D. Data Analyst
    Answer: A
    Explanation: The business analyst is expected to be aware of the IT domain and be able to speak the business language. The individual is the functional expert with a clear understanding of the project goals, in-depth business knowledge, including the organizations' business processes, and knowledge of the depth and breadth of the data.

30. **This role analyzes the existing organization data platforms and the platforms in the marketplace and defines which data components to use:**
    A. Business Analyst
    B. Project Manager
    C. Data Architect
    D. Data Analyst
    Answer: C
    Explanation: Data architects visualize, design, create and manage an organization's data architecture. They prepare data in a framework that can be used by data scientists, data engineers, or data analysts. They analyze the existing organization data platforms and the platforms in the marketplace and define which data components to use, like Hive, Map Reduce, Pig, for designing the enterprise data management framework model.

31. **They spot essential patterns within the data, which that help them create meaningful reports that provide insights for strategic business decisions.**
    A. Business Analyst
    B. Project Manager
    C. Data Architect
    D. Data Analyst
    Answer: D
    Explanation: Data analysts work on the existing raw data creating a simplified data model in a language that is familiar to the end-users. They gather, clean, understand, organize and analyze the data, using various analytics and visualization tools like R, Python, SQL, and others, to present their findings/results in formats that can be automatically updated and accessed.
    They spot essential patterns within the data, which help them create meaningful reports that provide insights for strategic business decisions.

32. **They work with highly complex digital data. They design and construct data modeling processes to create algorithms, prototypes, predictive models and perform custom analysis:**
    A. Business Analyst
    B. Project Manager
    C. Data Architect
    D. Data Scientist
    Answer: D
    Explanation: While Data Analysts typically work with structured data, Data Scientists work with highly complex digital data. They design and construct data modeling processes to create algorithms, prototypes, predictive models and perform custom analysis. Their skills include advanced statistical analysis, a comprehensive understanding of machine learning, artificial intelligence, data conditioning.

33. **They are responsible for creating and managing the data pipeline, monitoring and testing the system for optimized performance, and ensuring availability, accessibility, and consistency of the datasets:**
    A. Business Analyst
    B. Project Manager
    C. Data Engineer
    D. Data Scientist
    Answer: C
    Explanation: Data engineers build and optimize the systems that the data analysts and data scientists work on. They are responsible for creating and managing the data pipeline, monitoring and testing the system for optimized performance, and ensuring availability, accessibility, and consistency of the datasets.

Short-answer Questions

1. **Write short notes on Business Drivers.**
   We are in a generation where vast volumes of data from an ever-widening stream of sources flood a business daily. Data analytics can turn this data into insight and insight into action with intelligent data. However, for a business to make the right decisions on data strategy, it is essential to understand what drives the business.

Business drivers are conditions, processes, or activities that are vital in maximizing a company's growth and business value. Drivers vary significantly with each industry.

2. **List down any four key business drivers for an organization to implement a data and analytics program.**
   1. Increasing profitability and growth
   2. Strengthening customer experience and intimacy
   3. Driving digital transformation and innovation
   4. Managing regulatory and compliance risks

3. **Increasing profitability and growth is one of the key business drivers for an organization to implement the data analytics program. Please justify.**
   Using data analytics to gain deeper insights allows us to find pockets of growth that may be overlooked. It can help the company understand customer interactions with the product or services, linkages to seasons and demographics, future market conditions, and other varying factors. This can enable customer conversion with targeted marketing, campaigns, incentives, and promotions. Amazon, Netflix, e-Bay and Starbucks are a few data-driven companies that leverage Big Data Analytics for increased revenue.

4. **Strengthening customer experience and intimacy is one of the key business drivers for an organization to implement data analytics program. Please justify.**
   The customer is a crucial asset to any business. Building an emotional connection and trust with our customers can trigger customer loyalty and reduce churn. Predictive analysis on customer transactions and various other socio-economic and geographical data can enable organizations to better understand their customer base, the peer influences among customers, and predict future behaviors. This understanding can lead to initiatives that can proactively cater to customer needs, problems and expectations, thus fostering positive customer experience and intimacy, leading to customer retention and increasing the customer base.

5. **Driving digital transformation and innovation is one of the key business drivers for an organization to implement data analytics program. Please justify.**
   Companies are transforming their products and customer relationships by leveraging Digital Transformation. Digital transformation is the organizational change of integrating existing technologies, processes and capabilities that enable the organization to innovate and rapidly adapt to changing circumstances. Data analytics initiatives can transform the business with better customer relationships, enhanced business intelligence, competitive services, products, innovative branding strategies, and more.

6. **Managing regulatory and compliance risks is one of the key business drivers for an organization to implement data analytics program. Please justify.**
   Data analytics can help organizations enable strategic initiatives and decision-making. However, it can also help simplify and improve the efficiency of the organization's compliance and regulatory processes. Companies can build analytics programs to continuously monitor and receive insights into the effectiveness of its compliance and control framework model. "Data-driven" compliance programs can help to identify existing risks and their status as well as identify new and emerging risks.

7. **Increasing operational efficiency is one of the key business drivers for an organization to implement data analytics program. Please justify.**
   Operational efficiency involves process improvement, customer/employee feedback, technology transformations, and organizational matrices. By leveraging data analytics, organizations can identify which areas or infrastructure elements need to be replaced. It can predict the need for maintenance well in advance before the occurrence of productivity breakdowns.

8. **What is analytical architecture?**
   The analytics architecture is a crucial facet of business intelligence. Data, in itself, is useless unless we can extract value out of it. With the advent of relational databases or the RDBMS in the 1970s, business users could query the data and make fact-based decisions instead of intuitive ones. The advancements in hardware, scalability and storage capabilities from the 1980s onward made it possible to transform all the data into a central repository – the data warehouse.

9. **Define data management.**
   The data warehouse can be at the departmental or enterprise level, based on the organization's preferred data storage and access mechanism. Processes like normalization, transformations, validations, cleansing, and other optimization techniques are executed to organize the data into a single consistent schema for loading into the data warehouse or database. The data in the warehouse is in a structured format and hence ready for users to build reports or dashboards geared towards analysis or decisions.

10. **Define Data Analytics.**
    Data from the DW is organized and quickly sorted into database systems and data marts for later access. It enables the end-user to easily access readily available and relevant data with a faster processing time. The data analytics layer is where the data users/analysts/scientists build the analytical data models that help the organization make data-driven business decisions.

11. **Write short notes on Data Visualization.**
    Data architecture is not just about storing data. It is about how well the model supports the collection, collation, enrichment, and analysis of the data. The right data architecture can ensure the best data quality for new insights, automation, better

reporting, and experience. Data visualization layers leverage tools like Microsoft BI, Tableau, Sisence and QlikView to manipulate, format, and deliver data in an efficient, visually appealing, and comprehensible way.

12. **Write short notes on the challenges of conventional systems.**
    One of the biggest challenges of the typical data architecture that data analysts and data scientists face is the limitation of implementing advanced analytics with predictive modeling, machine learning, and various automation techniques.
    While traditional data architecture with the data warehouse is still prevalent, it is not without challenges. Big Data has brought in increased demands for more predictive analytics to forecast the future and prescribe how the business should change now to stay competitive for the future.

13. **Write any three challenges with the conventional architecture model.**
    1. **High costs** – The cost of storage for large volumes of data is high. Database resources are expensive when handling increasing data volumes and processing capabilities. It is nearly impossible to scale up on-premise storage capabilities to ensure system performance without incurring exceedingly high costs.
    2. **Source data limitations** – A typical data warehouse is not built for Big Data analysis. Because of the restrictions to the amount of data that can be stored, businesses limit the data they store to what is required for their reporting needs rather than storing the entire raw data that may potentially be required for the future.
    3. **Lack of flexibility** – As businesses are becoming more agile, the need of the hour is an efficient architecture that can support quick on-demand changes. The typical data architecture, once built, is relatively rigid. Any change to a data model, with its processing and testing, could take months for implementation and is not cost-effective.

14. **What are the types of analytics?**
    There are four main types of analytics – descriptive, diagnostic, predictive, and prescriptive – used by business users and analysts to gain insights.

15. **Write short notes on descriptive analytics.**
    Descriptive analytics are the most commonly used analytics using statistical functions of mean, median, percentages, and other arithmetic operations on existing historical data. The essential techniques used in descriptive analytics are data aggregation and data mining. By summarizing the data into meaningful and applicable measurements in the form of reports, departments across the organization will draw insights from their past performances and work towards the success of their business.

16. **Write short notes on diagnostic analytics.**
    Diagnostic analytics provides in-depth insights into what caused a particular event or outcome by looking at both internal historical data and external data. Organizations

use it to identify the 'root cause' or causal relationship in a particular situation or scenario. Some techniques used in diagnostic analytics are correlation, drill-down, regression, classification, and others.

17. **Write short notes on predictive analytics.**

    Predictive analytics is used to predict what is likely to happen in the future so that we can respond proactively. Businesses use advanced machine learning algorithms like Random Forest, Support Vector Machines, Time Series, and many traditional forecasting techniques to arrive at the outcome. For example, Netflix uses data (watch history, preferences and demographics on each user to create or promote their shows/movies, leading to customer retention of over 91%.

18. **Write short notes on prescriptive analytics.**

    The most advanced form of predictive analytics can suggest all favorable outcomes according to a specified course of action. It can also suggest various courses of action to get to a particular outcome by simulating various scenarios. The data source includes the internal data of the organization and external data that may influence the algorithm. Prescriptive analytics is used across industries like retail, healthcare, education and the energy industry.

19. **Write short notes on R Programming environment.**

    R is an open-source tool that facilitates wide-scale statistical analysis, data visualization, and data science. The CRAN (R Archive Network) contains over 17000 packages of algorithms and modules that can cater to practically any analytical model and computational needs. R is platform-independent and can run efficiently on multiple operating systems like Windows, MacOS, UNIX, and Linux.

20. **Write short notes on Tableau.**

    Tableau is an end-to-end data analytics platform that can connect data (structured, semi-structured, unstructured) from any source or platform in real-time, be it SQL or NoSQL databases, Hadoop, Hive, Spark, and others without the user having to be tech-savvy. According to Gartner Magic Quadrant, its ease of use, self-service data visualization, smart dashboards, and high performance make it the leader in Business Intelligence tools.

21. **What are the products in Tableau ecosystem?**

    Some of the products in the Tableau ecosystem are:
    - **Tableau Desktop** – Core component where all the development takes place.
    - **Tableau Server** – Core administrative component for security, integration, automation/scheduling at the server level.
    - **Tableau Online** – Tableau analytics platform hosted in the cloud.
    - **Tableau Reader** – Free tableau software where analysts can share their visualizations built on Tableau Desktop for collaboration. However, users would need Tableau Reader to open the file.

- **Tableau Viewer** – Role-based licensed product for business organizations to empower people with dashboards/visualizations and trusted content to make data-driven decisions without putting data security at risk.
- **Tableau Public** – Free Tableau software to produce data visualizations. The platform provides flexible settings and agility to meet changing business demands. However, to exploit the full capability of Tableau, users need to have in-depth training and knowledge.

22. Write short notes on Qlik.

Qlik is another data analytics tool that is quickly gaining a solid community base with its end-to-end data integration (ETL) solution. The front-end UI is browser-based, where users can view/share documents and collaborate on the insights in real-time or offline. It is cost-effective with efficient in-memory storage and speed of delivery, irrespective of the number of users and data requests. Its downside is the need for high technical expertise to develop the applications and scripts.

23. What is the need for Data Analytic Life Cycle?

A data project inherently comes with questions, especially when dealing with a humungous volume of data. Due to the complexities and ambiguity in data, the process is unfathomable unless a systematic structure or methodology is followed. A well-defined process can provide the direction and method to extract information from the data as it gets processed, tested, used, and analyzed. It enables the data experts to ascertain that they are proceeding in the right direction to accomplish business goals.

24. Describe data discovery phase of Data Analytic Life Cycle.

Discovery is the first phase of a data project, which involves defining the business objective and identifying the existing resources in terms of data, people, and technology to achieve the set goal(s). The activities of this phase include gathering of business requirements, challenges, source of information, and high-level timeline.

25. Describe the data preparation phase of the Data Analytic Life Cycle.

The data preparation phase involves the cleansing and transforming raw accumulated data prior to processing and analysis. The data from various identified sources is collected, mixed, and merged. The key objective of this phase is to prepare a scalable analytics sandbox platform with available data that can be used for modeling and analysis in subsequent phases.

26. Describe the data model planning phase of the Data Analytic Life Cycle.

A data model is nothing but a conceptual model that organizes data elements and standardizes how they relate to one another. It involves various techniques and methods like clustering, regression, classification using decision trees, neural networks and others to identify the features and relationship between variables for applying to the model. It documents the assumptions made at each stage of devising the preliminary model(s).

27. **Describe the model building phase of the Data Analytic Life Cycle.**
    The model building phase determines whether the data model being built meets the business objective as defined in the Data Discovery phase. It is a cyclic process that repeats itself between model planning and building, multiple times before the model is deemed robust and accurate enough to meet business needs. If the results are invalid, the project team must revisit the previous phases 1–3.

28. **Describe the "communicating the results" phase of the Data Analytic Life Cycle.**
    The result communication phase is crucial as it can set the project for success or failure. The optimal way to convey the findings is through appealing visual charts with data points and animation. Tableau, Power BI, and Cognos are some powerful visualization tools. When the findings are presented to the stakeholders, there may be queries or new understandings that require revisiting the Model Building phase.

29. **Describe the "operationalize phase" of the Data Analytic Life Cycle.**
    It is recommended to be deployed in iterations rather than a full-scale rollout. In the operationalize phase, the data is moved from the sandbox to the production environment to monitor and validate if the results match the expected business goal. If any discrepancy is found, it is easy to move back to the previous life-cycle phases and update the input variables for the correct output.

30. **What are the roles of a Project Manager in an analytic project?**
    The role of the project manager in a data analytics project is to ensure the successful delivery of the project in terms of the scope, budget, and timelines without compromising on quality. The PM is responsible for engaging the right resources and managing them, communicating regularly and effectively with the stakeholders, and ensuring that business benefits are delivered in the best way possible.

31. **What are the roles of a Business Analyst in an analytic project?**
    Business Analysts are the liaison between the business and the IT team. They are expected to be aware of the IT domain and be able to speak the business language. The Business Analyst collects the raw usage data and transfers it to the Data Analyst/Architect to for execution. The individual is the functional expert with a clear understanding of the project goals and is expected to have in-depth business knowledge, including the organizations' business processes.

32. **What are the roles of a Data Architect in an analytic project?**
    Data architects prepare data in a framework that can be used by data scientists, data engineers, or data analysts. Their role entails evaluating the various technical designs by conducting proofs-of-concept to recommend and design a holistic and optimized analytics platform.

33. **What are the roles of a Data Analyst in an analytic project?**
    Data Analysts work on the existing raw data creating a simplified data model in a language that is familiar to the end-users. They gather, clean, understand, organize

and analyze the data, using various analytics and visualization tools like R, Python, SQL, and others, to present their findings/results in formats that can be automatically updated and accessed.

They spot essential patterns within the data, which help them create meaningful reports that provide insights for strategic business decisions.

34. What are the roles of Data Scientists in an analytic project?
While Data Analysts typically work with structured data, Data Scientists work with highly complex digital data. Their skills include advanced statistical analysis, a comprehensive understanding of machine learning, artificial intelligence and data conditioning. The data scientist essentially identifies patterns and trends from past and present data to formulate questions that could play a key role in the organization's success.

35. What are the roles of a Data Engineer in an analytic project?
Data engineers are the people who build and optimize the systems that the data analysts and data scientists work on. They are responsible for creating and managing the data pipeline, monitoring and testing the system for optimized performance, and ensuring availability, accessibility, and consistency of the datasets. Many of the responsibilities of the roles overlap, based on the size of the analytics project.

36. Write notes on Business Intelligence (BI) systems.
Organizations depend on Business Intelligence (BI) systems to guide executives, managers, and other business users for decisions and strategic planning. BI combines data analysis, data mining, data visualization, and reporting capabilities to help organizations make better data-driven decisions.

37. Write short notes on Intelligent Data Analysis.
Intelligent Data Analysis (IDA) refers to the use of analysis, classification, conversion, extraction, organization, and reasoning methods to extract valuable knowledge from Big Data, using techniques from various disciplines such as artificial intelligence, high-performance computing, pattern recognition, and statistics.

38. What are the three stages of Intelligence Data Analysis (IDA)?
The IDA process generally consists of three stages:
1. **Data preparation** – Selecting the required data from the relevant data source and integrating this into a dataset for the data mining stage.
2. **Data mining** – Involves the extraction and working out of rules and patterns in large complex datasets using specific methods or algorithms under the discipline of statistics, machine learning, and artificial intelligence.
3. **Result validation and explanation** – This stage deals with the validation/verification of the rules and patterns produced by the mining algorithms and provides intuitive communication of results.

39. What are the applications of Intelligence Data Analysis (IDA)?
IDA is used in different Web information analysis, such as economic data analysis, Big Data analysis, medical informatics and image analysis. For example, Big Data

intelligence involves using Artificial Intelligence and Machine Learning to provide actionable data analytics models and transforms Big Data into insights for data scientists, BI analysts and strategists, and other relevant users to take the next actionable steps.

40. **What is Data Mart?**
    Data from the data warehouse is organized and quickly sorted into database systems and data marts for later access. Data marts are a subset of data created from the data warehouse. It enables the end-user to easily access readily available and relevant data with a faster processing time. Data marts are department- or domain- or subject-specific. A hybrid data mart can have a combination of data from the data warehouse and other sources.

Essay-type Questions

1. Write short notes on Business Drivers for Analytics. How do organizations use it for increasing the profitability and strengthening customer experience?
2. Write short notes on Business Drivers for analytics. How do organizations use it to drive digital transformation and innovation and manage regulatory and compliance risks?
3. Write short notes on Business Drivers for analytics. How do organizations use it for increasing operational efficiency?
4. Explain a typical Analytical Architecture in detail.
5. What are the challenges of Conventional Systems? Explain with examples.
6. What are the types of Analytics? Explain in detail.
7. What is Tableau? What are the components of its eco-system?
8. Write an essay on Qlik.
9. What is the need of Data Analytic Life-cycle?
10. Explain the data discovery phase of the Data Analytic Life-cycle.
11. Explain the data preparation phase of the Data Analytic Life-cycle.
12. Explain the model planning phase of the Data Analytic Life-cycle.
13. Explain the model building phase of the Data Analytic Life-cycle.
14. Explain the communicate results phase of the Data Analytic Life-cycle.
15. Explain the various roles for successful Analytic projects.
16. Explain Business Intelligence in detail.
17. Explain Intelligent Data Analysis in detail.

CHAPTER 3

Fundamentals of Big Data

LEARNING OBJECTIVES

This chapter introduces the concept of Big Data and the terminologies used for discussing Big Data. It elaborates on the types of Big Data and explains the importance of Distributed File System for storing Big Data. The chapter also provides an overview of the characteristics and challenges of Big Data before dealing at length with the business drivers of Big Data.

3.1 INTRODUCTION TO BIG DATA

Big Data is an umbrella term for datasets that traditional technologies or tools cannot practically handle due to their high volume, velocity, and variety. The term Big Data is also used when referring to computing systems or technologies used to handle this type of data.

There is no specific size definition for Big Data, and it varies from organization to organization. On the other hand, Big Data is defined as a collection of Big Datasets that are too large and complicated for typical database management systems to handle.

The rise of digitization, eCommerce, social media usage, IoT, video, and music streaming websites, etc., and the plummeting cost of technology enabled the popularity of Big Data. Businesses constantly produce and collect Big Data to process, analyze, and extract valuable information that can benefit the organization or business.

3.2 BIG DATA CONCEPTS AND TERMINOLOGY

The aspects of Big Data are:

- First, the data grows exponentially with time.
- The collected data is retained as raw as feasible for better flexibility later in the pipeline.

- Third, the term is all-encompassing to include the dataset and the tools and techniques used to process and analyze the data.

3.2.1 Big Data Processing Activities

Big Data processing has the same approach as processing traditional structured transaction data. However, because of Big Data's inherent complexities, and computational and storage needs, the activities within the processes and the tools used would vary.

Data Mining: Data is gathered from multiple sources such as relational databases, web, media, cloud, etc. Tools and techniques like ETL explore and analyze the data to find patterns and correlations. Techniques like clustering, neural networks, classification trees, and logistic regression are used. While the data is cleaned, categorized, labeled, and validated to specific requirements, the collected data is retained as raw as feasible for better flexibility later in the pipeline.

Data Storing: The analyzed data is stored in distributed databases like NoSQL databases, as they are designed for fault tolerance and scalability needs, critical for Big Data storage. Document-oriented databases, graph databases, and columnar databases are examples of NoSQL databases.

Data Computing and Analysis: Once stored, the data is processed to extract real value. The processing of large datasets is an iterative process to gather the various types of insights as per need. Batch and real-time processing are the two types of computational methods used. Work is broken into smaller units in batch processing, scheduled, calculated, and assembled for the final result or answers. Real-time like stream processing is used if processed information is needed immediately, and the system needs to react to information as soon as it becomes available.

Data Consumption and Visualization: The processed data is displayed visually, making it easy for the end-user to identify trends and pull insights. The data is also stored in data marts or business areas that may need it for their processing and studies.

3.2.2 Common Terminologies

Algorithm: Algorithms, in the context of Big Data, are mathematical and analytical formulas or rules or statistical processes implemented in the software to perform data analysis to solve a complex mathematical or computational problem. For example, algorithms are used in machine learning, data processing, search engine optimization, etc.

Artificial intelligence: Artificial Intelligence or AI is a combination of algorithms fed into machine systems to perform tasks typically requiring human intelligence, such as speech recognition, visual perception, decision-making, language translation, self-learning, predictions, etc. Big Data Analytics can employ AI for improved data analysis, whereas AI requires enormous data and can leverage Big Data to learn and enhance decision-making processes.

Batch processing: Batch processing is a computing method that involves processing enormous datasets that are not time-sensitive. Batch processing jobs are executed when the most available computing resources are utilized for a specific schedule. Human intervention is not required once the batch starts running.

Behavioral analytics: It is an area of data analytics that collects and analyzes data of the users' digital experience with a particular digital product or app to predict future actions. Behavioral analytics can provide insights into user behavior on eCommerce platforms, gaming sites, web/mobile applications, etc., and help companies design or improve their digital products to maximize their business outcomes.

Cloud computing refers to computing infrastructure and resources, including software and data, stored on remote servers that users can access via the internet. Cloud computing provides on-demand services, flexible scaling, resource pooling, and many other cost benefits. Infrastructure (IaaS), Platform (PaaS), or Software-as-a-Service (SaaS) models on the cloud can help companies process and analyze large datasets without worrying about the infrastructure, storage, or maintenance costs. For example, MongoDB and MapR are cloud computing platforms used in Big Data.

Clustered computing: Clustered computing is the process of pooling the resources of multiple servers (clusters) to complete tasks. It involves a cluster management layer that handles communication between the nodes for loading balancing, parallel processing, etc.

Data aggregation: The act of gathering raw data from numerous sources and presenting it in a summary style for data analysis or reporting is known as data aggregation.

Data analytics: The process of discovering and evaluating data is known as data analytics. Large datasets are needed to uncover hidden patterns, trends and correlations, and derive valuable insights and predictions for the business. Big Data Analytics is done with the aid of specialized tools and software. A **Big Data analyst** specializes in analyzing Big Data and interprets and reports on the analytical findings.

Data cleansing: Data cleansing is a stage of data processing where corrupt, invalid, inaccurate, or erroneous data are identified and resolved/corrected/removed from the record or dataset. This ensures more accuracy and reliability of the data for processing.

Data lake: Data lake is an extensive repository of unprocessed raw data, including unstructured, semi-structured, and structured data. Data scientists use it to harness the power of Big Data for analysis.

Data mart: Data mart is a subset of Data Warehouse in a department or domain. It is subject-specific to enable the end-user to easily access readily available and relevant data with a faster processing time.

Data mining: Data mining identifies patterns in large datasets using statistics, machine learning techniques, or artificial intelligence.

Data model/modeling: A data model is a system for organizing and storing data that includes but is not limited to object definition, attributes, integrity rules, etc. Data modeling is the process of creating a data model that supports business processes.

Data processing: Data processing is a part of data analytics. It is the process of collecting and transforming raw data into a meaningful or usable format by machines or businesses to gain insights for decision-making.

Dataset: A dataset or dataset is a collection of data. A dataset, in its simplest form, is a tabular file organized as rows and columns. A dataset can also be a zip file or a folder containing many files. The term "Big Data" refers to enormous, complicated databases.

Data replication: For high availability and fault tolerance, data replication is the act of writing or duplicating (storing) the same data at several places or sites (nodes).

Data science: Data science is a multidisciplinary field that incorporates statistics, mathematics, computer science, data mining, data visualization, machine learning, and other disciplines to solve complex problems by transforming the data into valuable insights. A **data scientist** is a person with business domain expertise, who is well-skilled in the data sciences to analyze and extract/uncover value for the business.

Data size: It is related to data measurement or how much storage the data consumes. There is no specific size defined for Big Data. Instead, Big Data is determined by volume, velocity, and various other factors. But in general, data is assumed to be more than one terabyte (TB) and estimated to contain petabytes, exabytes, and zettabytes of information.

    1 Gigabyte (GB) = 1,024 Megabytes
    1 Terabyte (TB) = 1,024 GB
    1 Petabyte (PB) = 1,024 TB
    1 Exabyte (EB) = 1,024 PB
    1 Zettabyte (ZB) = 1,024 EB

Data warehouse: Data warehouse is a repository of processed/structured enterprise-wide data, both current and historical, from diverse sources used by the organization for analytics and reporting. Collecting, storing, and managing the warehouse data to provide meaningful business insights is called **data warehousing**.

ETL: ETL (extract, transform, and load) refers to the process of 'extracting' raw data from multiple sources, 'transforming' by cleaning and enriching the data to make it analysis-ready, and 'loading' it into a data warehouse or appropriate repository for usage.

Internet of things: It is a group of (network of) interconnected computing devices that can perceive, produce, gather, and share data via sensors over the internet.

Machine-generated data: Machine-generated data (MGD) is information that is generated by software or digital devices without human intervention, e.g., APIs, change events, sensor data, etc.

Machine learning: Machine learning is an area of computer science that deals with creating systems that learn and improve as more data is fed into them without needing to be explicitly programmed.

Metadata: Metadata is data that contains granular information and descriptive details about other data. E.g., Meta tag on the web page.

NoSQL: NoSQL stands for "not SQL" and refers to non-relational database management systems. It is well-suited for Big Data systems as it is schema-free, flexible, and supports distributed architecture.

Structured data: Refers to data with a well-defined structure and conforms to a data model. They can easily be stored and accessed by traditional data management systems.

Unstructured data: Unstructured data refers to data that does not have a pre-defined data model or schema and cannot be stored in a traditional database system (DBMS).

Visualization: It is a visual representation of processed data in graphs, scatter charts, images, etc., to communicate information more effectively and accelerate the rate of insight retrieval for organizations.

V's of Big Data: Big Data is typically characterized by five words starting with the letter V: Volume – a large amount of data, Velocity – the speed of data generation and movement, Variety – data diversity, Veracity – accuracy of data, Value – a benefit that Big Data can bring to the user. Visualization, Viscosity, and Virality have been added to the mix recently.

Some of the technology and tools used by Big Data are R and Python, Hadoop, Spark, Hive, MapReduce, Mongo dB, etc.

3.3 FUNDAMENTALS OF BIG DATA TYPES

Big Data is multi-dimensional. It needs to go through the ETL (extract, transform, load) process before it can be analyzed. The ETL process varies based on the data type. Big Data can be classified into four types (Fig. 3.1.) – Structured, Semi-structured, Quasi-structured, or Unstructured.

Structured Data

Structured data has a pre-defined data model and is typically stored in a tabular format with rows and columns. It is a highly organized, specific, and consistent format defined by set parameters. Structured data is the most straightforward type because it requires little or no preparation before processing. It has discrete fields that can be accessed separately or with vital relational fields mapped with data from other fields. For example, the Employee file in an organization's database containing the employee's personal information can easily be mapped to the payroll or department files. Thus data can be seamlessly stored and accessed or aggregated from any location in the database, making it the ideal kind of data to analyze and process. In addition, structured data is quite robust. As a result, the time

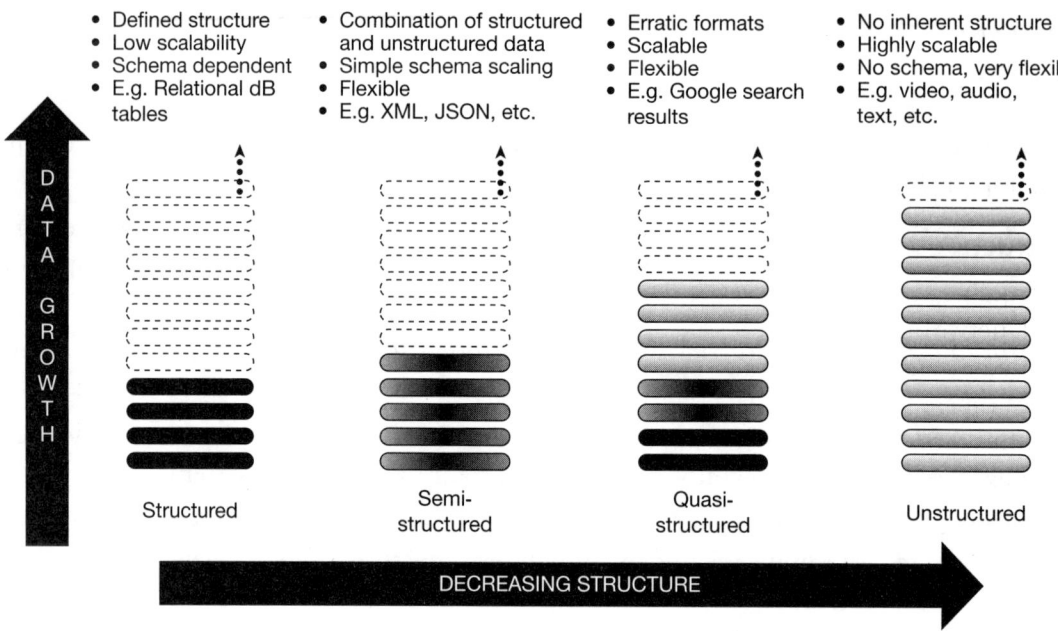

Figure 3.1 Types of Big Data

required to define and enable the communication between the data sources is significantly reduced, thus expediting the delivery of actionable insight.

However, the fixed format makes it less flexible, with comparatively poor scalability. SQL or relational databases, comma-separated value (.csv) files, and Excel files are examples of structured data. Data post the ETL processing is stored in a **data warehouse** system for reporting and analysis.

Semi-structured Data

Semi-structured data is structured data that does not have a pre-defined data model or schema. It is considered to be in between structured and unstructured data. A relational database is not used to store it. However, it has some arrangement that makes it simple to examine. This can be metadata, which is inherent data, like time, location, device ID, semantic tag, or other elements. These tags or metadata contain distinct properties which introduce a hierarchy and define how the data is stored. Hence it is called a self-describing structure.

For example, an email contains information like the timestamp, email address of sender and receiver, IP address, and other information specific to the email. Hence while the email content and other factors are unstructured, some components allow the data to be grouped in a structured format.

Though not as robust as structured data, it allows for better flexibility, scalability, and data portability. Extensible Markup Language (XML) files, JavaScript Object Notation (JSON) files, TCP/IP packets, and sensor data are examples of semi-structured data. The data is best managed in NoSQL, i.e., non-relational databases.

Quasi-structured Data

Quasi-structured data consists of textual content with erratic data formats that can be formatted with effort, software system tools, and time. An example of quasi-structured data is clickstream data, i.e., data about web pages a user visited and in what order it was visited, Google search results, web page data for scrapping, etc.

Unstructured Data

Unstructured data does not have a pre-defined or specific format, e.g., stream data from social network feeds, emails, etc. Any data with an unfamiliar structure or model is classified as unstructured data. The source data is typically huge with an intricate mix of images (.jpeg, .png), text files, pdf files, sound files (.wav, .mp3), video files (.mp4, .avi), etc. Thus processing and preparing unstructured data to determine value out of it is quite complex and time-consuming.

Unstructured data is stored in NoSQL databases or **data lakes**. The data is preserved in its raw format in data lakes, making it more malleable. It is the most flexible form of data due to the absence of a schema. Hence it is the most prevalent data used in organizations today for business intelligence and analytics due to its ease of readability by humans. However, it requires major processing before being analyzed by a computer. AI and sophisticated machine learning methods are making massive progress towards making unstructured data machine-readable.

3.4 BIG DATA ANALYTICS

Big Data is pointless unless we can extract value to drive evidence-based decision-making. There are two main processes for extracting value from Big Data – Data Management and Analytics (Fig. 3.2).

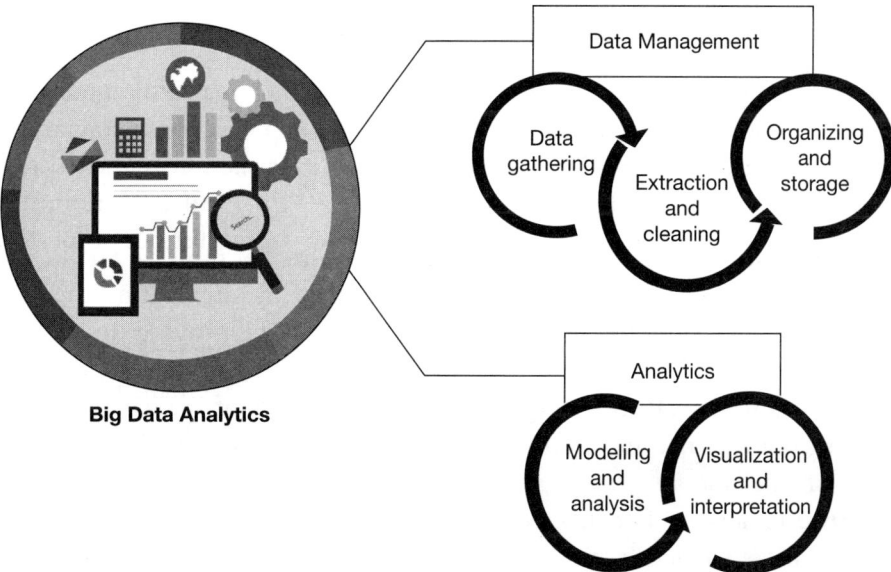

Figure 3.2 Big Data Analytics: High-level processes

Data Management involves the technology and process of gathering, organizing, and storing the data securely to retrieve data for analysis efficiently. The sub-processes within data management are data gathering, extraction, cleaning, organizing, and storing for data retrieval.

Analytics refers to the methods for analyzing and extracting insight from large amounts of data. The sub-processes within analytics are modeling and analysis, visualization, and interpretation.

Big Data consists of massive and diverse volumes of exponentially growing data, and the analytic techniques used to extract information are generally quite complex. Thus, **Big Data Analytics** is the complex process of examining Big Data sets using advanced analytics like predictive modeling, machine learning algorithms, and other statistical methods to uncover information that helps organizations make informed business decisions.

Large volumes of data such as email, video, sensor data, texts, and photos, are analyzed using Big Data Analytics. Following are some of the analyzing techniques that are used. In many instances, a combination of the techniques is applied.

3.4.1 Text Analytics

Text analytics refers to techniques used to extract meaningful information from textual data. For example, people's interactions in current times are primarily digital in tweets, blogs, comments, surveys, reviews, and forum discussions. This huge unstructured data database can be capitalized by research, government, security, and business agencies to extract valuable information. Typically, organizations use text analytics software that leverages machine learning and NLP algorithms to find common themes and trends within enormous amounts of text.

A typical text analytics workflow consists of

1. **Data gathering** where data is collected from within the organization (emails, surveys, structured database, etc.) and external agencies (social media posts, reviews, etc.).
2. **Data preparation** where the unstructured data is broken down and prepared for deeper analysis. Some of these methods are:
   - **Tokenization**, where the text is separated into smaller units called tokens. Tokens can be a word, character, or subword. This helps in interpreting the meaning of the text by analyzing the sequence of the words and removing unwanted content or spaces.
   - **Part of Speech (PoS) Tagging** is where the part of speech of every token is identified, i.e., whether a noun, pronoun, adjective, or some other speech modifier. E.g., in *"the little girl"*, *'the'* is an article; *'little'* is an adjective, and *'girl'* is a noun.
   - **Chunking** assigns PoS-tagged tokens to text phrases. E.g., in *"the little girl is playing in the meadow"*; *'the little girl'* is a noun phrase, *'is playing'* is a verb phrase, and *'in the meadow'* is a prepositional phrase.

- **Syntax Parsing** is where a semantic structure is assigned to the text based on some rules.
- **Lemmatization and Stemming** where different forms of suffixes and prefixes of a word or token are grouped as a common word, e.g., *play, plays, playing, played,* will be reduced to *play*.

3. **Text analytics**, where the relevant information is extracted from the prepared data and analytics like topic extraction, sentiment analysis, and clustering, can be conducted.

   - **Text extraction** is extracting data keywords from textual data, like trending terms, titles, company names, and many more. Marketing teams typically use this to identify frequently discussed topics and current trends. It can also effectively summarize data from multiple documents or sources by extracting only the relevant information or phrases.
   - **Sentiment analysis** analyzes opinionated texts containing people's opinions about entities like products, individuals, and event organizations. For example, businesses may increase customer happiness, discover product flaws, perform market research and manage brand reputation, among other things, by studying their customers' feelings, likes, and dislikes about their goods.
   - **Clustering** is the technique of bringing together large quantities of unstructured data that are similar to each other into a cluster (Section 1.6.4). Clustering text data has several use cases from document retrieval, fake news identification, customer support issue analysis, etc. For example, Google algorithms break down web pages and tag them. Then, when a topic is searched for, the pages containing the highest count of the searched word will appear first in the results.

Once the text analysis is done and verified, the output can be fed into data visualization systems. Finally, the results are viewed to identify patterns, trends, and actionable insights that enable the business to make data-driven decisions.

3.4.2 Audio Analytics

Audio analytics is the process of analyzing and extracting information from unstructured audio data captured by digital devices. The primary application area of audio analytics is in call-centers, healthcare, and smart cities. Advanced algorithms are used to process sound, similar to how the human ear processes it.

Audio analytics is used in:

- Speech-to-text or Speech recognition, where AI and machine learning methods transcribe audio files to text. Speech analytics technology provides automatic transcription. In healthcare, it allows doctors and medical providers to monitor compliance in real-time.

- The sound or audio classification technique is the process of listening to and analyzing audio recordings to classify the sounds into specific categories.
    1. **Acoustic data classification** identifies where the sound was recorded, e.g., restaurants, fields, offices, oceans, etc.
    2. **Music classification** is based on the musical instrument or genre of the music.
    3. **Environment sound classification** takes account of sounds in various surroundings like a car horn, breaking glass, children laughing, gunshot, etc. Its key usage is in event detection systems.
    4. **Natural language utterance classification** is the analysis of speech based on the dialects, semantics, and other features of the spoken language. This classification algorithm is used in chatbots in customer service, education, training, and other related areas.
- **Sound event detection** is the method to recognize an audio signal within large audio data streams at the time when it happens. Audio analytics that run on video surveillance can cut through the noise and identify target sounds like a gunshot, car crash, breaking glass, or other atypical sounds that will enable security forces or personnel to respond faster to violent outbreaks or security-related scenarios.

3.4.3 Video Content Analytics

Video content analytics (VCA) is the process of monitoring, analyzing, and understanding the behavior of objects from video streams. The most common use is in security. However, VCA has applications in many industries.

Security: Facial recognition or license plate recognition are used by law enforcement on real-time or archived video footage to locate miscreants or unauthorized personnel.

Smart Cities: VCA is helpful in crowd and traffic management. It can detect and warn of increased traffic, enabling accident prevention and traffic congestion measures.

Sports: Video analysis of a team's play or an athlete's technique can help improve performance.

Retail: VCA can help retailers better understand their consumer behavior. Smart algorithms using facial recognition, age, gender, gaze, detect movement patterns, and other factors that can provide retailers insights to drive product placement, price, layout optimization, and staffing decisions.

3.4.4 Social Media Analytics

Social media analytics refers to the analysis of structured and unstructured data from social media channels like social networks (Facebook, LinkedIn), media (YouTube, Instagram), social news (Reddit, Newsvine, Digg), blogs and microblogs (Blogger, WordPress, Twitter, Tumblr), Wikis (Wikipedia, WikiHow, Fandom), review sites, mobile apps (find my friend, WhatsApp) and many others and evaluation of that data to make business decisions.

Organizations use Social Media Analytics to:

- identify customer sentiments towards a product or service.
- understand the competition/competitors and their effectiveness.
- track online conversations and use the insights for business leverage.
- track the effectiveness of a social media campaign and make tactical adjustments, if required.
- spot the latest or popular trends and many more.

Text analytics, video analysis, sentiment analysis, social listening, social influence analysis, social monitoring and campaign analysis are some of the components of social media analytics.

3.4.5 Predictive Analytics

Predictive analytics involves a variety of technologies and techniques comprising Big Data, data mining, statistical modeling, machine learning and various mathematical processes that predict future outcomes based on historical and current data (Section 2.4.1). Organizations use predictive analytics to detect trends and forecast events and situations that should occur at a specific time, based on supplied parameters. Some of the techniques used in predictive analytics are data mining, decision trees, regressions like linear and multinomial logit models, and machine learning techniques like neural networks. Some of the algorithms used in predictive analytics are discussed hereunder.

Random Forest Model: It is a classification algorithm that consists of multiple decision trees (Fig. 3.3) used widely in classification and regression problems. The premise for this model is that the results from a collection of decision trees can be aggregated into one final result.

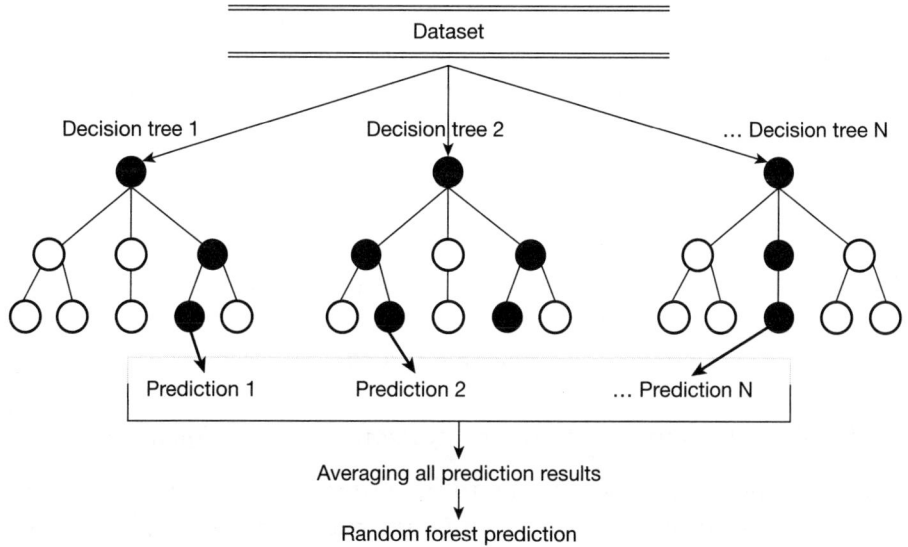

Figure 3.3 Random forest structure

Gradient Boosted Model (GBM): GBM also uses decision trees. However, unlike Random Forest where the decision trees are unrelated, each tree is built by adjusting or correcting the errors from the previous tree. Models are built sequentially, and each subsequent model attempts to correct the errors of the previous model.

K-means: This is a centroid-based clustering algorithm (Section 1.6.4) that looks for a fixed number (k) of clusters in a dataset. The data points in the cluster are averaged, which refers to the 'means' in the K-means; that is, finding the centroid. It starts with a group of randomly selected centroids. It then performs iterative calculations until the centroids' position is optimized or until the defined number of iterations is completed.

Prophet: This algorithm is used in time-series or forecast models with strong seasonal effects and several seasons of historical data. The prophet is quite flexible and can accommodate assumptions related to missing data, outliers, and shifts in trends. This is commonly used for capacity planning, e.g., inventory planning, sales quotas, and resource allocations.

Predictive analytics is used in sales forecasting, assessing risk, customer targeting, fraud detection, business outcomes, clinical decisions, support in healthcare, etc.

3.5 Distributed File System in Big Data

Traditional data is structured and stored in pre-configured and fixed models of files/records/tables assessed by relational database systems like SQL Server, MySQL, Oracle dB, etc. It is typically stored and maintained using a centralized database architecture that is easy to store and process. The database in this architecture is stored and maintained in a single location (Fig. 3.4) like a CPU server or mainframe and accessible from many points via LAN/WAN. This reduces data redundancy and the cost of processing. While this database architecture is robust and cheaper to install, secure, and maintain, the downside is that it can work only with small, simple datasets. In other words, the greater the data in a relational database, the longer each processing takes. The centralized database system is not equipped to process high volumes of complex data, that is, Big Data.

Big Data cannot fit into traditional relational databases as it consists of unstructured and semi-structured data. In addition, the speed and complexity of Big Data alone can cause stress to traditional data storage systems.

Storage for Big Data should cater to
- Voluminous high-velocity data to the extent of petabytes, zettabytes, or exabytes coming in at real-time or near real-time.
- Complex, varied datasets of innumerable unstructured data of images, videos, text, audio, and others.
- Scalability that allows for scaling out or horizontal scaling model.

The file management system that can cater to Big Data is the distributed file system (DFS). The DFS is a collection of autonomous systems distributed across multiple locations/servers that can be accessed from any server/computer via LAN or WAN. The whole premise of the distributed file system is to distribute data across multiple clusters or nodes and utilize

Fundamentals of Big Data • 109

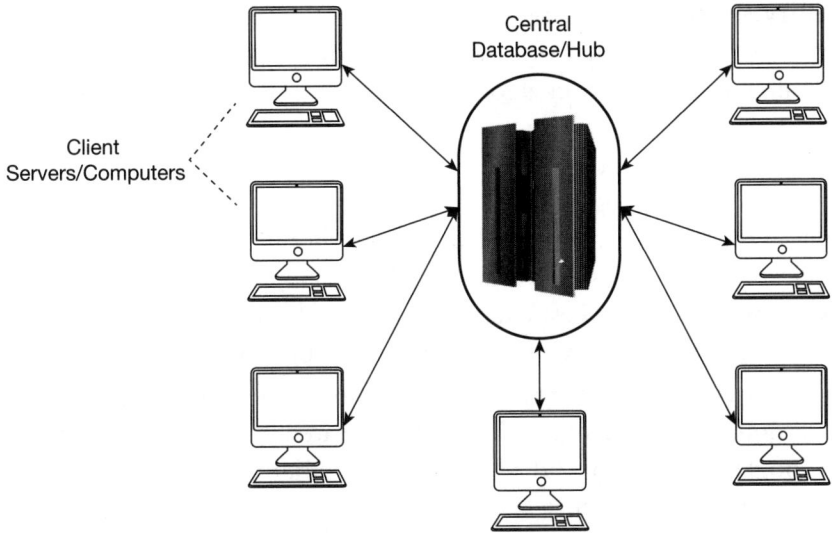

Figure 3.4 Centralized database architecture

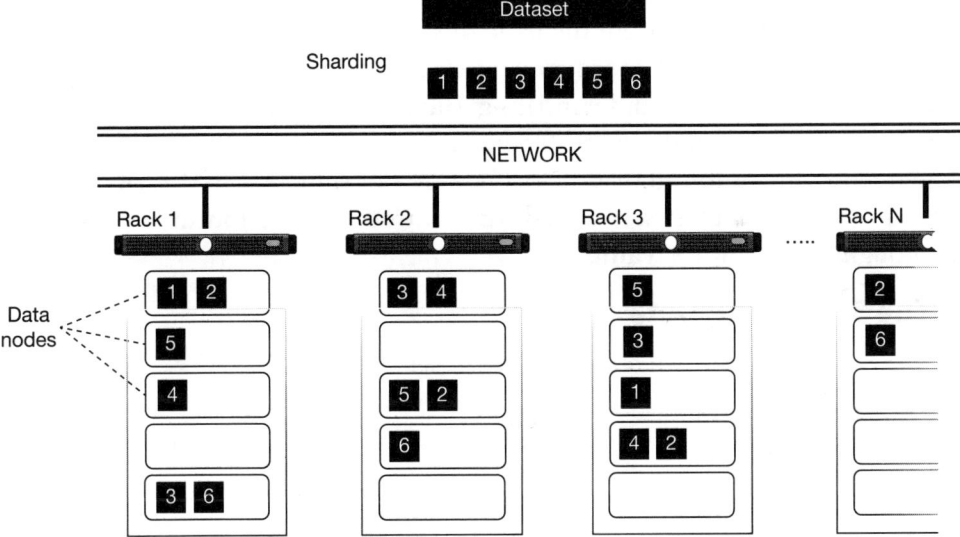

Figure 3.5 Distributed file system

the computing power of each node to process information. As seen in Fig. 3.5, each block of dataset is distributed across multiple nodes. This provides the following advantages:

1. **Fault Tolerance:** It supports fault tolerance by data partitioning and replication. Each node has storage and processing capability, and the concept is to divide and distribute data across multiple nodes. The file system replicates and distributes at least one copy on a different rack. For example, in Fig. 3.5, data block four is replicated in rack 1, rack 2 and rack 3. Hence the data is available even if one computer/server or node fails.

2. **Scalability:** DFS works on multiple parallel reads and writes. As the data grows, the infrastructure can be scaled out by adding more racks or clusters to the file system without affecting application algorithms. A good DFS should be able to scale down and be space- and time-efficient.
3. **Transparency**: Though DFS is a collection of systems that people can access and store files, users and programmers view it as a single entity. It would seem they are working on their local machine to a user, even though that may not be the case. Users and applications can access and share data concurrently without any interference. For example, User A could access data block 2 of rack one, and User B can access block 2 of rack three concurrently without experiencing any disruption.

However, this is a very complex system to maintain. For example, if a user changes a data block on one node, these changes need to be updated across all the data replications of this block. Google File System (GFS), HDFS, and Microsoft DFS are examples of some of the best distributed file systems.

3.6 BIG DATA CHARACTERISTICS

To fully comprehend the complexities of Big Data, it is important to understand the core characteristics that set it apart from the basic or small data. In 2001, Gartner analyst Doug Laney introduced the 3 V's of information assets attributed to Big Data, namely **Volume**, **Velocity**, and **Variety**, thus differentiating Big Data as data that arrives at increasing volumes, higher velocity, and remarkable variety.

Subsequently, it was found that the 3 V's were not sufficient to describe Big Data. So in time, two more attributes were added. IBM introduced the fourth V – **Veracity**, and Oracle brought in the fifth – **Value**.

3.6.1 The 5 V's of Big Data

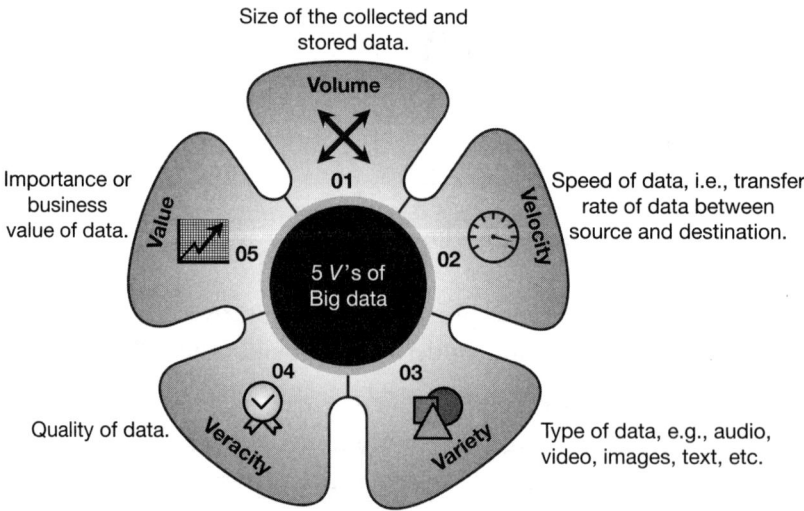

Figure 3.6 Big Data characteristics

Volume

Volume refers to the quantity of data collected and stored from various sources. For example, Big Data solutions would need to process high volumes of data generated from social networks, web pages, sensors/IoT, daily transactions, etc. Big Data volumes are typically over 1TB. International Data Corporation (IDC) predicts the global data to reach 175 ZB by 2025, with 49% of the world's data residing in public clouds.

Velocity

The pace at which data is created, the rate at which it changes, and the multiple speeds at which incoming information must be linked for processing are called velocity. It concerns the rate at which data flows from numerous sources such as social networking sites, sensors, mobile apps, and programs. This can be real-time, near real-time, batch data, or continuous streaming data.

Variety

Variety refers to the different data forms in Big Data, both structured, unstructured, and semi-structured, making it difficult to sort and interpret. The complexities involved in storing, mining, and analyzing raw data like text, photos, videos, music, emails, monitoring equipment, etc., are unfathomable. While organizations store tabular structured data in relational databases, over 90% of the Big Data is unstructured and cannot be maintained by traditional database management systems. Hence variety is a key attribute that needs to be considered in building Big Data applications.

Veracity

The quality and correctness of the data obtained are referred to as veracity. To extract value from Big Data, the data must be devoid of uncertainties. Information extracted from Twitter feeds, customer browsing habits, and customer sentiments is not an exact science. Big Data analytic solutions need to address these uncertainties to produce accurate results.

Value

Value refers to the usefulness and benefits that the business can derive from the data. In the raw state, the value of Big Data is low compared to volume. However, a high business value is obtained as the Big Data gets mined and analyzed.

3.6.2 Challenges of Processing Big Data

A well-executed Big Data strategy can streamline operational costs, reduce time to market and launch new products, and enable a data-driven culture.

Organizations adopting Big Data strategies must cater to the challenges in working with the process of storing and analysis of huge volumes of data. Due to the complexities and characteristics of Big Data, data management teams must plan and be ready to face unprecedented or evolving issues while implementing or deploying Big Data solutions. A few of the common challenges are discussed hereunder.

Accessing and Managing Big Data Volumes

Most organizations already have high volumes of data stored before planning out Big Data initiatives. These data are typically housed in disparate systems or silos. The main challenge is in consolidating the exponentially growing data from the various internal and external sources, social media pages, sensor data, ERP applications, emails, etc. Enterprises must analyze the existing software and hardware architecture to check scalability. Suppose the architecture does not support the storage and processing of growing volumes of data over time. Then organizations need to invest in new hardware or alternative solutions that may not be time- or cost-effective. Regular system and stress tests must be conducted to analyze the resilience and performance of the solution. Corrective and/or preventive actions will ensure the Big Data systems are kept updated and help the data management teams efficiently prepare and deal with system failures.

Managing Data Quality Issues

A typical overlook is the business value the data is expected to deliver. It is essential to focus on the outcome expected while planning and deciding on the technology. Storing high volumes of irrelevant data has no value. Instead, the focus should be on quality data storage. The accuracy of the analytics is a function of the reliability of the data. Organizations obtain data from a variety of sources. The data generated from these sources must have inherent value relevant to the business. Some of the questions that must be asked while investing in integration technology are:

- What data sources must the platform support?
- Is it scalable to the current volumes and future estimated volumes collected?
- Does it offer the data transformations required for data consistency?
- Is the data structured or real-time via social media, sensors, etc., or a combination of these?
- Are master data management and data governance capabilities required?

Poor data collection leads to poor and limited data quality, leading to inaccurate reporting, misalignment, and flawed decision-making. Hence the Big Data teams must ensure that the proper integration tools that fit the purpose are evaluated and used.

Standard data integration tools are IBM Infosphere, QlikView, Informatica, Oracle Data Integration Cloud Service, Talend Data Studio, etc.

Selection of the Right Solution Tools

Generating timely reports and insights is another challenge and key purpose of working with Big Data. With the availability of advanced technology and Big Data, enterprises are investing in ETL and analytics tools with real-time capabilities to compete against their market counterparts.

Availability of Big Data Skills and Knowledge-base

An effective Big Data team includes data scientists, data analysts, data engineers, and other professionals with expertise in running Big Data tools and/or managing the Big Data environment. It is their collective effort and it provides the business with valuable insights from Big Data.

Acquiring Big Data specialists with the right skill-set is a challenge, and acquiring the wrong skill-set can also be detrimental. There are two employee knowledge base challenges faced within companies:

- **Lack of skilled Big Data staff:** Companies address this challenge by recruiting skilled professionals. With the advancement of Big Data tools and technology evolving rapidly, the companies also need to invest in regular training programs for their existing data staff. Some companies look to invest in AI, or Machine Learning powered analytical solutions that can be managed by professionals who do not necessarily need high data science expertise. Many organizations have a Chief Data Officer whose role includes making strategic decisions regarding Big Data initiatives.
- **Lack of Big Data awareness among non-data professionals:** If the awareness of the large data projects is limited to just the data teams, it may result in implementation failure or poor adoption of Big Data systems or processes within the organization. Employees may not appreciate the criticality of data storage, backup, and the importance of following the workflow procedures. Organizational change management, Big Data workshops and training are critical to spreading employee awareness on what data is, the company's sources and technologies, storage, processing, and importance.

All the employees must understand the benefits that the organization hopes to realize from the innovative Big Data solutions and their role and responsibility in supporting the initiative.

Governance and Data Security

Organizations with huge data stores and marts are a treasure trove for malicious hackers and cyber-attacks. When Big Data is involved, it is crucial to invest in additional security and safety measures and protocols. Security breaches, data harvesting, customer privacy, and other data leaks can cost the company millions of dollars if not more in reputation alone, thus critically damaging the business. Unfortunately, most organizations either deprioritize or overlook the importance of data security while dealing with complex Big Data solutions. It later becomes a challenge to implement privacy protection and process data mining without exposing sensitive information. In addition, Big Data solutions use multiple third-party tools and cloud services and infrastructure for hosting or processing Big Data operations. Some potential threats could arise when:

- Data is collected from multiple sources indiscriminately resulting in harmful or invalid data.
- Data sourced from insecure channels are gathered, making the destination systems vulnerable to attacks and malware.
- Data repositories do not have the necessary safeguards in places like encryption, access controls, and firewalls.
- Standardized compliance protocols and procedures with regular/real-time monitoring are not implemented across all channels.

Implementing tools that support data encryption and segregation, identity and access authorization control, endpoint security, real-time monitoring, and other Big Data security tools can address the Big Data challenges.

Most of the above challenges contribute to resistance to Big Data adoption. Companies selecting Big Data analysis tools without due diligence on their capability and features can substantially lose money, time and effort. For example, Spark, Hadoop, MapReduce, Cassandra, etc., are Big Data tools, but many, including data professionals, are not aware of their full functionalities. The ideal way to get the best out of Big Data is to consider all the challenges upfront, recruit the right professionals or seek Big Data consultancy expertise to identify the right tools and technology. Then, based on the company's strategy, core needs, and scenario, Big Data consultants can advise on the best tool for analysis or storage, so that the organization can get the best value for money out of their investments.

Ongoing training programs and seminars can reduce the challenges, improve adoption and enable the organization to capitalize on the insights provided by Big Data.

3.7 Drivers for Big Data

The current digital revolution has seen massive data growth. As a result, companies store voluminous data by transforming their business with data-driven decisions and strategies. With the right tools and infrastructure, analytics-driven decision-making is on the rise, leaning towards real-time and predictive.

Some of the Big Data business drivers are:

Digitization

As per Statista, the market and consumer data statistics provider, the 2022 average daily social media usage of internet users is 147 minutes per day. Data created worldwide has been projected to reach 79 zettabytes and double by 2025. Digital mediums have become the delivery mechanism for most businesses. Some consumers spend daily around 4+ hours on digital devices or applications. Each click or message produces essential data that can be mined and utilized to study customer behavior/sentiment for targeted marketing or development of products, etc.

Identify Business Performance Strategy

Data is connected from all levels/departments within an organization. Big Data analysis of the matrices, performance indicators, and critical success factors collated from all levels, along with external data like similar industry information, global best practices and indicators with key questions, can enable the leadership to understand the current performance of the organization and future potential. This insight can lead businesses to create new strategies or enhance existing strategic initiatives proactively.

Innovate Products and Services

The current market environment is quite dynamic. Harnessing Big Data can enable companies to find new ways to proactively keep ahead of the curve and consequently increase the top-line revenue. Organizations can look beyond the traditional approach of reactive and reflective actions using internal data. Instead, with Big Data, the source of information is limitless. With Big Data Analytics, businesses can identify their service or product positions and predict future customer/global needs to build innovative solutions and products proactively.

Increasing Data Variety and Complexity

Organizations have a plethora of data like pdf files, videos, emails, web information, etc., at their disposal. Unfortunately, many complex data are not leveraged due to a lack of necessary tools, technology, or understanding. Traditional data storage systems constrain companies since they are not equipped to take advantage of the value of Big Data. Millions of dollars are lost on opportunities missed in the time spent on collating essential data and filtering out irrelevant information. Companies can produce highly actionable insights from multiple sources by taking advantage of Big Data tools and techniques, thus saving time and costs.

Affordable Technology and Hardware

As data grows within an organization at an exponential rate, storage and scalability without negatively impacting performance are the key challenges. However, the cost of data storage and processers is reducing. Hence hardware costs are not a deterrent to Big Data initiatives. In addition, Big Data solutions are available on open-source frameworks like Apache Hadoop.

Distributed storage systems on the cloud allow organizations to license the storage and processing capacity and scale up or down as required. This enables organizations to commence Big Data projects without worrying about the high infrastructure and maintenance costs.

Predictive analytics with Big Data Analytics tools enable businesses to make better decisions and optimize operational efficiencies. For example, the insights into customer pain points and behavior patterns can allow companies to streamline their digital marketing strategies to enhance the overall consumer experience leading to more sales and revenue. In addition, the insights gleaned from Big Data can identify targeted promotions and offers, and help in gaining a competitive edge over the competitors.

SUMMARY

According to Gartner, Big Data is high-volume, high-velocity, and/or high-variety information assets requiring new processing forms to enable enhanced decision-making, insight discovery, and process optimization.

The key aspects of Big Data are:

- The data grows exponentially with time.
- The data is too voluminous to be processed and analyzed by conventional techniques.
- The term is all-encompassing to include the dataset and the tools and techniques used to process and analyze the data.

The nature of Big Data warrants it to be analyzed for data categorization and labeling before going through the computation process for extracting insights. Big Data consists of unstructured data, semi-structured data, and quasi-structured data.

Structured data has a pre-defined data model and is typically stored in a tabular format with rows and columns. It is a highly organized, specific, and consistent format defined by set parameters.

Semi-structured data is structured data that does not have a pre-defined data model or schema. It is considered to be in between structured and unstructured data. A relational database is not used to store it.

Quasi-structured data consists of textual content with erratic data formats that can be formatted with effort, software system tools, and time. E.g., Clickstream data.

Unstructured data does not have a pre-defined or specific format, e.g., stream data from social network feeds, emails, etc. Any data with an unfamiliar structure or model is classified as unstructured data. They are stored in NoSQL databases.

Big Data cannot fit into traditional relational databases because of its complex structure and high volume, velocity, and variety. The file management system that can cater to Big Data is the Distributed File System (DFS). It is a collection of autonomous systems distributed across multiple locations/servers that can be accessed from any server/computer via LAN or WAN. The system can distribute data across multiple clusters or nodes and utilize the computing power of each node to process information. In addition, it provides the fault tolerance, scalability, and transparency features required for Big Data storage.

Big Data is not defined by its size but by its inherent characteristics of **Volume** (a large amount of data), **Velocity** (the speed of data generation and movement), **Variety** (data diversity), **Veracity** (accuracy of data), and **Value** (a benefit that Big Data can bring to the user).

Big Data Analytics is the complex process of examining Big Data sets using advanced analytics like predictive modeling, machine learning algorithms, and other statistical methods to uncover information that helps organizations make informed business decisions. Text analytics, video content analytics, social media analytics, and predictive analytics are some of the analyzing techniques used.

The everyday challenges of processing Big Data are:

1. Accessing and managing Big Data volumes
2. Managing data quality issues
3. Selection of the right solution tools
4. Availability of Big Data skills and knowledge-base
5. Governance and data security.

Companies store voluminous data by transforming their business with data-driven decisions and strategies. With the right tools and infrastructure, analytics-driven decision-making is on the rise. Predictive analytics with Big Data Analytics tools enables businesses to make better decisions and optimize operational efficiencies. In addition, the insights into customer pain points and behavior patterns can allow companies to streamline their digital marketing strategies leading to more sales and revenue.

EXERCISES

Multiple Choice Questions

1. **This is a computing method that involves processing enormous datasets that are not time-sensitive:**
   A. Algorithm
   B. Batch processing
   C. Behavioral analytics
   D. Cloud computing
   Answer: B
   Explanation: Batch processing is a computing method that involves processing enormous datasets that are not time-sensitive. Batch processing jobs are executed when the most available computing resources are typically performed to a specific schedule. Human intervention is not required once the batch starts running.

2. **It is an area of data analytics that collects and analyzes data of the users' digital experience with a particular digital product:**
   A. Algorithm
   B. Batch processing
   C. Behavioral analytics
   D. Cloud computing
   Answer: C
   Explanation: Behavioral Analytics is an area of data analytics that collects and analyzes data of the users' digital experience with a particular digital product or app to predict future actions. Behavioral analytics can provide insights into user behavior on eCommerce platforms, gaming sites, web/mobile applications, etc., and help companies design or improve their digital products to maximize their business outcomes.

3. **This refers to computing infrastructure and resources, including software and data stored on remote servers that users can access via the internet:**
   A. Algorithm
   B. Batch processing
   C. Behavioral analytics
   D. Cloud computing
   Answer: D
   Explanation: Cloud computing refers to computing infrastructure and resources, including software and data, stored on remote servers, that users can access via the internet. Cloud computing provides on-demand services, flexible scaling, resource pooling, and many other cost benefits. Infrastructure (IaaS), Platform (PaaS), or Software-as-a-Service (SaaS) models on the cloud can help companies process and analyze large datasets without worrying about the infrastructure, storage, or maintenance costs. For example, MongoDB and MapR are cloud computing platforms used in Big Data.

4. **This is the process of pooling the resources of multiple servers to complete tasks:**
   A. Algorithm
   B. Batch processing
   C. Clustered computing
   D. Cloud computing
   Answer: C
   Explanation: Clustered computing is the process of pooling the resources of multiple servers (clusters) to complete tasks. It involves a cluster management layer that handles the communication between the nodes for loading, balancing, parallel processing, etc.

5. **The act of gathering raw data from numerous sources and presenting it in a summary style for data analysis or reporting is known as:**
   A. Data aggregation
   B. Batch processing
   C. Clustered computing
   D. Cloud computing
   Answer: A
   Explanation: The act of gathering raw data from numerous sources and presenting it in a summary style for data analysis or reporting is known as data aggregation.

6. **The process of discovering and evaluating data is known as:**
   A. Data aggregation
   B. Data analytics
   C. Clustered computing
   D. Cloud computing
   Answer: B
   Explanation: The process of discovering and evaluating data is known as data analytics. Large datasets are used to uncover hidden patterns, trends, and correlations and derive valuable insights and predictions for the business. Big Data Analytics is done with the aid of specialized tools and software. A Big Data analyst specializes in analyzing Big Data and interprets and reports on the analytical findings.

7. **This is a stage of data processing where corrupt, invalid, inaccurate, or erroneous data are identified and resolved:**
   A. Data Lake
   B. Data cleansing
   C. Data mining
   D. Cloud computing
   Answer: B
   Explanation: Data cleansing is a stage of data processing where corrupt, invalid, inaccurate, or erroneous data are identified and resolved/corrected/removed from the record or dataset. This ensures more accuracy and reliability of the data for processing.

8. **This is an extensive repository of unprocessed raw data:**
   A. Data Lake
   B. Data cleansing
   C. Data mining
   D. Data Mart
   Answer: A
   Explanation: Data Lake is an extensive repository of unprocessed raw data, including unstructured, semi-structured, and structured data. Data scientists use it to harness the power of Big Data for analysis.

9. **This is a subset of Data Warehouse that is specific to the department, domain, or subject, to enable the end-user:**
   A. Data Lake
   B. Data cleansing
   C. Data mining
   D. Data Mart
   Answer: D
   Explanation: Data Mart is a subset of Data Warehouse that is department-, domain- or subject-specific to enable the end-user to easily access readily available and relevant data with a faster processing time.

Short-answer Questions

1. **List down a few aspects of Big Data.**
   The aspects of Big Data are:
   - First, the data grows exponentially with time.
   - The collected data is retained as raw as feasible for better flexibility later in the pipeline.
   - Third, the term is all-encompassing to include the dataset and the tools and techniques used to process and analyze the data.

2. **What is Data Mining?**
   Data Mining: Data is gathered from multiple sources like relational databases, web, media, cloud, etc. Tools and techniques like ETL explore and analyze the data to find patterns and correlations. Techniques like clustering, neural networks, classification trees and logistic regression are used. While the data is cleaned, categorized, labeled, and validated to specific requirements, the collected data is retained as raw as feasible for better flexibility later in the pipeline.

3. **Define Algorithm.**
   Algorithms, in the context of Big Data, are mathematical and analytical formulas or rules or statistical processes implemented in the software to perform data analysis to solve a complex mathematical or computational problem. For example, algorithms are used in machine learning, data processing, search engine optimization, etc.

4. **Define Artificial Intelligence.**
   Artificial Intelligence or AI is a combination of algorithms fed into machine systems to perform tasks that typically require human intelligence, such as speech recognition, visual perception, decision making, language translation, self-learning, predictions, etc. Big Data Analytics can employ AI for improved data analysis, whereas AI requires enormous data and can leverage Big Data to learn and enhance the decision-making processes.

5. **What is Batch Processing?**
   Batch processing is a computing method that involves processing enormous datasets that are not time-sensitive. Batch processing jobs are executed when the most

available computing resources are typically performed to a specific schedule. Human intervention is not required once the batch starts running.

6. **What is Behavioral Analytics?**
   Behavioral Analytics is an area of data analytics that collects and analyzes data of the users' digital experience with a particular digital product or app, to predict future actions. Behavioral analytics can provide insights into user behavior on eCommerce platforms, gaming sites, web/mobile applications, etc., and help companies design or improve their digital products to maximize their business outcomes.

7. **What is Cloud Computing?**
   Cloud computing refers to computing infrastructure and resources, including software and data, stored on remote servers that users can access via the internet. Cloud computing provides on-demand services, flexible scaling, resource pooling, and many other cost benefits. Infrastructure (IaaS), Platform (PaaS), or Software-as-a-Service (SaaS) models on the cloud can help companies process and analyze large datasets without worrying about the infrastructure, storage, or maintenance costs. For example, MongoDB and MapR are cloud computing platforms used in Big Data.

8. **What is Clustered Computing?**
   Clustered computing is the process of pooling the resources of multiple servers (clusters) to complete tasks. It involves a cluster management layer that handles the communication between the nodes for loading balancing, parallel processing, etc.

9. **What is Data Aggregation?**
   The act of gathering raw data from numerous sources and presenting it in a summary style for data analysis or reporting is known as data aggregation.

10. **What is Data Analytics?**
    The process of discovering and evaluating data is known as data analytics. Large datasets are needed to uncover hidden patterns, trends, and correlations and derive valuable insights and predictions for the business. Big Data Analytics is done with the aid of specialized tools and software. A Big Data analyst specializes in analyzing Big Data and interprets and reports on the analytical findings.

11. **What is Data Cleansing and Data Lake?**
    Data cleansing is a stage of data processing where corrupt, invalid, inaccurate, or erroneous data are identified and resolved/corrected/removed from the record or dataset. This ensures more accuracy and reliability of the data for processing.

    Data Lake is an extensive repository of unprocessed raw data, including unstructured, semi-structured, and structured data. Data scientists use it to harness the power of Big Data for analysis.

12. **What is Data Mart?**
    Data Mart is a subset of Data Warehouse that is department-, domain-, or subject-specific to enable the end-user to easily access readily available and relevant data with a faster processing time.

13. **What is Data Modeling?**
    A data model is a system for organizing and storing data that includes but is not limited to object definition, attributes, integrity rules, etc. Data modeling is the process of creating a data model that supports business processes.

14. **What is Data Processing?**
    Data processing is a part of data analytics. It is the process of collecting and transforming raw data into a meaningful or usable format by machines or businesses to gain insights for decision-making.

15. **Define Dataset.**
    A dataset or dataset is a collection of data. A dataset, in its simplest form, is a tabular file organized as rows and columns. A dataset can also be a zip file or a folder containing many files. The term "Big Data" refers to enormous, complicated databases.

16. **Define Data Replication?**
    For high availability and fault tolerance, data replication is the act of writing or duplicating (storing) the same data at several places or sites (nodes).

17. **What is Data Science?**
    Data science is a multidisciplinary field that incorporates statistics, mathematics, computer science, data mining, data visualization, machine learning, and other disciplines to solve complex problems by transforming the data into valuable insights. A data scientist is a person with business domain expertise and is well-skilled in the data sciences to analyze and extract/uncover value for the business.

18. **Define Data Size.**
    Data Size is related to data measurement or how much storage the data consumes. There is no specific size defined for Big Data. Instead, Big Data is determined by volume, velocity, variety, veracity and value. But in general, data is assumed to be more than one terabyte (TB) and estimated to contain petabytes, exabytes, and zettabytes of information.

    1 Gigabyte (GB) = 1,024 Megabytes
    1 Terabyte (TB) = 1,024 GB
    1 Petabyte (PB) = 1,024 TB
    1 Exabyte (EB) = 1,024 PB
    1 Zettabyte (ZB) = 1,024 EB

19. **Define Data Warehouse.**
    Data warehouse is a repository of processed/structured enterprise-wide data, both current and historical, from diverse sources used by the organization for analytics and reporting. Collecting, storing and managing the warehouse data to provide meaningful business insights is called data warehousing.

20. **What is ETL? What do you mean by Internet of Things?**
    ETL (extract, transform, and load) refers to the process of 'extracting' raw data from multiple sources, 'transforming' by cleaning and enriching the data making it analysis-ready, and 'loading' it into a data warehouse or appropriate repository for usage.
    <u>Internet of Things:</u> It is a group of (network of) interconnected computing devices that can perceive, produce, gather, and share data via sensors over the internet.

21. **What is MGD in Big Data?**
    Machine-generated data (MGD) is information that is generated by software or digital devices without human intervention, e.g., APIs, change events, sensor data, etc.

22. **What is Metadata? What does NoSQL stand for?**
    Metadata is data that contains granular information and descriptive details about other data. E.g., Meta tag on the web page.
    NoSQL stands for "not SQL" and refers to non-relational database management systems. It is well-suited for Big Data systems as it is schema-free, flexible, and supports distributed architecture.

23. **What is Data Management?**
    Data Management involves the technology and process of gathering, organizing, and storing the data securely to retrieve data for analysis efficiently. The sub-processes within data management are data gathering, extraction, cleaning, organizing and storing for data retrieval.

24. **Define Analytics.**
    Analytics refers to the methods for analyzing and extracting insight from large amounts of data. The sub-processes within analytics are modeling and analysis, visualization, and interpretation.

25. **What is Text Analytics?**
    Text Analytics refers to techniques used to extract meaningful information from textual data. For example, people's interactions in current times are primarily digital, in tweets, blogs, comments, surveys, reviews, and forum discussions. This huge unstructured data database can be capitalized by research, government, security, and business agencies to extract valuable information. Typically organizations use text analytics software that leverages machine learning and NLP algorithms to find common themes and trends within enormous amounts of text.

26. **What is Text Extraction?**
    Text extraction is extracting data keywords from textual data like trending terms, titles, company names, and many more. Marketing teams typically use this to identify frequently discussed topics and current trends. It can also effectively summarize data from multiple documents or sources by extracting only the relevant information or phrases.

27. What is Sentiment Analysis?
Sentiment analysis analyzes opinionated texts containing people's opinions about entities like products, individuals, and events organizations. For example, businesses may increase customer happiness, discover product flaws, perform market research and manage brand reputation, among other things, by studying their customers' feelings, likes, and dislikes about their goods.

28. Define Audio Analytics.
Audio Analytics is the process of analyzing and extracting information from unstructured audio data captured by digital devices. The primary application area of audio analytics is in call-centers, healthcare, and smart cities. Advanced algorithms are used to process sound, similar to how the human ear processes it.

29. Define Social Media Analytics.
Social media analytics refers to the analysis of structured and unstructured data from social media channels like social networks (Facebook, LinkedIn), media (YouTube, Instagram), social news (Reddit, Newsvine, Digg), blogs and microblogs (Blogger, WordPress, Twitter, Tumblr), Wikis (Wikipedia, WikiHow, Fandom), Review sites, mobile apps (find my friend, WhatsApp) and many others and evaluation of that data to make business decisions.

30. What is Predictive Analytics?
Predictive analytics involves a variety of technologies and techniques comprising Big Data, data mining, statistical modeling, machine learning, and various mathematical processes that predict future outcomes based on historical and current data. Organizations use predictive analytics to detect trends and forecast events and situations that could occur at a specific time, based on supplied parameters. Some of the techniques used in predictive analytics are data mining, decision trees, regressions like linear and multinomial logic models, and machine learning techniques like neural networks.

Essay-type Questions
1. Write an essay on Big Data Processing activities.
2. Write an essay on different types of Big Data.
3. What is Text Analytics? Explain in detail.
4. What is Audio Analytics? Explain in detail.
5. What are Video Analytics and Social Media Analytics? Explain in detail.
6. What is Predictive Analytics? What are the algorithms used for Predictive Analysis?
7. Why is Distributed File System used in Big Data?
8. What are the challenges of processing Big Data?
9. What are the drivers for Big Data?

CHAPTER **4**

Big Data Analytics Technology

> **LEARNING OBJECTIVES**
>
> This chapter takes a close look at the framework needed for Big Data Analysis and the difference approaches to leverage Big Data efficiently. It elaborates on text and predictive analysis, procedural and functional programming and the Big Data integration process. The chapter also provides a comprehensive view of the landscape of Big Data technology and provides a brief note on the key roles that could be played by a Big Data specialist.

4.1 INTRODUCTION TO BIG DATA ANALYTICS

It is purported that only around 20% of the worldwide data is structured. That would mean there exists 80–90% of unstructured data that carries a wealth of information that could be a gold mine for organizations worldwide if they tap into its potential. This is where Big Data Analytics comes into the picture.

Data analytics analyzes datasets to evaluate, condense, and extract value and insights for sensible business decisions. R and Python are popular programming languages with rich libraries used by data analysts and data scientists for statistical analytics and scientific computing.

Before the advent of Big Data, Microsoft Excel was the most widely used tool used by companies to address their data analytics needs. However, new technologies like the Hadoop framework with HDFS and MapReduce programming languages have come into play with Big Data. In addition, frameworks like Apache Spark can process and extract patterns and information in real time.

Big Data Analytics benefit organizations in better decision making, increasing productivity, improving customer service, lowering costs, increasing profits, and much more. However, there are potential drawbacks, especially in the hardware and technology needs like storage and network bandwidth that come with handling the complex volumes of Big Data. In addition, integrating legacy systems and architecture with Big Data architecture adds time and cost. Security is also a concern when high volumes of sensitive data make it attractive targets for cyber-attacks.

4.2 BIG DATA ANALYSIS FRAMEWORK

The 21st century has seen the automation of business processes and digitization that has led to an explosion in data volumes, including continuous streaming of data from the internet. In addition, new storage and processing technology trends are emerging that can integrate the data generation and data processing tools comprising IoT, AI, quantum computing, edge computing, augmented analytics, and hybrid clouds, among others. Therefore, organizations must keep up with the evolving technologies to stay relevant in the Big Data world.

With exponentially growing data, it is essential that the Big Data Analytics solutions, when implemented, should achieve long-term success and be flexible enough to cater to organizational changes, technologies, and strategies. A framework can provide the organization with a structure that considers all organizational capabilities starting from the definition of a Big Data strategy to the technical tools and capabilities required.

The overlying layer of a Big Data analysis framework is the Business Issue Understanding. A successful Big Data Analytics practice must commence with a solid, grounded business strategy considering the problems or issues to be solved, expectations of the results or possible solution definition, alignment with the financial objectives and long-term goals, and other essential aspects.

There are six aspects to the Big Data technology agnostic framework (Fig. 4.1).

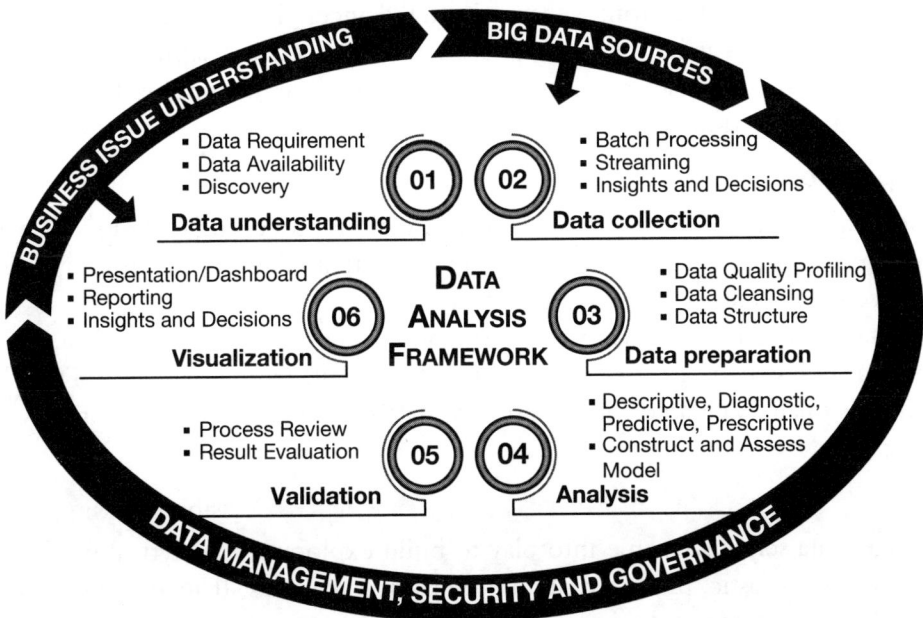

Figure 4.1 Data analysis framework steps

Data Understanding

The first step, after understanding the business needs, is to understand the data requirements and availability. In most instances, a repository of organizational data in the form of historical or transactional data already exists. Typically in data analytics projects, the business analysts or data analysts work backward from the hypothesis or expected outcomes to the available data.

Working backward helps to understand the data requirements and focus only on the structure of the required data, i.e., whether structured, unstructured, or semi-structured, its sources, accessibility, i.e., whether static or streaming, along with additional data requirements to generate the best value from data and analytics. In addition, understanding the data will enable the organization to plan out the Big Data enterprise's storage infrastructure, processing, and architecture needs.

Data Collection

This stage decides how to ingest the data from the various sources and what type of storage is best suited for the data, i.e., whether cloud, on-premise or hybrid, and whether any pre-requisite schema definitions or alterations are required to store the data.

Data can be structured in the form of excel or RDBMS files or unstructured like text files, image files, videos, audio files, emails, social media data, etc., or semi-structured like metadata, JSON, XML data, sensor data, and so on. Big Data would be a combination of all the varieties of data. Typically, companies acquire external data and combine it with internal transactional or stored historical data.

The data is gathered from various sources based on the business need. Other than transactional data from an internal data store, data can be sourced from Data-as-a-Service companies or streaming data from websites or IoT devices. The data is then deposited in a database or storage for further processing. Storage can be a data warehouse, Data Lake, or a combination of on-premise and cloud storage architecture. Many cloud storage services come with data collection tools.

Data Preparation

Once the data is collected from different sources, various processing techniques are applied to make it ready for analysis. This is an essential step that takes the maximum time to get the most accurate results or insights from data.

The data is cleaned by removing any erroneous, irrelevant, or duplicate data, addressing missing data and structural errors like misspellings, data ambiguity, etc. The cleaned, labeled data is finally validated for consistency, data quality, and quantity for downstream processing.

Analysis

At this stage, data scientists come into play to build exploratory analytical models related to descriptive, diagnostic, predictive, and prescriptive analytics. It incorporates many Big Data techniques and technologies that utilize statistics, computer science, and applied mathematics to build data models. Some of the analysis techniques used for Big Data are given below:

A/B testing is where control (A) and alternative (B) versions of a variable are tested to compare the performance using statistical analysis. The technique is best used in webpage optimization.

Data Mining is where data patterns, trends, and other valuable information are extracted from raw/large datasets using statistics and machine learning procedures to draw useful information and predict outcomes. For example, data mining is used to identify product associations, improve market segmentation, build anti-fraud systems, etc.

Machine learning (ML) originated from Artificial Intelligence. It used data and algorithms to build automated analytical models that can self-learn without having to be explicitly programmed for each different task. For example, chatbot, predictive analytics, and medical diagnosis are fields that use ML.

Natural Language Processing (NLP) is a branch of Artificial Intelligence that uses Big Data and algorithms to understand and interpret the human language. NLP is typically used in text analytics, smart assistants, and language translation.

Other techniques include statistics, spatial modeling, network analysis, and many more. The end goal is to find key insights for business planning. The technologies that process, manage, and analyze Big Data are expansive and continue to evolve over time.

Validation

At this stage, the business or user team evaluates the model. Next, tests are conducted to verify the process and ascertain that the business logic at various node points is correct. Finally, the model outputs are tested using testing datasets, and results are validated to ensure that the outcome is as expected.

Visualization

The results and insights of the analysis in the form of graphs or charts are presented to the business for data-driven decision-making. It is ideal for building a storyline linking the insights to actionable recommendations and execution plans. In addition, dashboards and dynamic user interfaces are built that can automate the process in day-to-day decision-making or operational decisions with email notifications or custom alerts.

Data governance and security are primary concerns when working with massive volumes of data and complex technology. Hence, an end-to-end data management setup with a centralized governance structure is essential. In addition, effective access control will provide an insight into executed data processes, data profiles in the connected data stores, metadata, and other touchpoints to ensure that business and regulatory policies are being complied with.

Thus, adopting the proper framework can provide a single solution that gives complete visibility and data management for Big Data to succeed and even trigger actions based on predefined parameters.

4.3 APPROACHES FOR BIG DATA ANALYSIS

With the advancement of technology to process voluminous data faster and efficiently, organizations leverage Big Data to identify opportunities and risks and answer critical business questions related to market insights by tracking customer behavior and market trends, develop product features by analyzing customer needs and preferences and identify efficient ways of doing business to improve their bottom line.

There are common approaches to Big Data analysis that can be broadly divided into descriptive analysis, exploratory data analysis, confirmatory data analysis, predictive analysis, and inferential analysis.

Descriptive Analysis

Descriptive analysis or statistics helps to describe and summarize the basic features of a dataset using numerical calculations and tables. It allows the data analyst or data scientist to understand the data better.

Frequency distribution, variability, and measures of central tendency are some types of descriptive analysis.

Frequency distribution or simply **distribution** summarizes the frequency of every possible value of a variable plotted on a graph or table either as numbers or percentages, or percentiles to depict each possible outcome of an event. Frequency distributions are quite helpful in summarizing large datasets and assigning probabilities; for example, the bell curve.

The Measure of central tendency is used to estimate the center or average of a dataset by calculating its **mean** (average of response values), **mode** (most frequent response value), and **median** (precise center of the dataset).

The measure of variability or dispersion identifies how to spread out or disperse the response values by calculating the **range** (the difference between the two extreme values, i.e., largest and lowest values), **standard deviation** (amount of variation of a set of values from the mean value), and **variance** (square of standard deviation). Variance depicts the degree of spread. The greater the variance relative to the mean, the greater the spread.

Netflix adopts descriptive analysis to identify TV and movie shows or themes trending on their platform and display them on the users' home page. Other usages are polling predictions, monitoring progress to goals, financial statement analysis, and many more.

Exploratory Data Analysis

Exploratory data analysis (EDA) is an approach to analyzing and summarizing the main characteristics of data using visual techniques like statistical graphics and other data visualization methods. EDA typically follows descriptive data analysis, where the calculated numerical data values are plotted graphically to understand trends and patterns. There are three types of exploratory data analysis.

Univariate analysis where the characteristics and effects of a single variable on a set of data are explored, e.g., mean of population distribution. Univariate analysis results can be visualized with bar graphs, histograms, box plots, etc.

Bivariate analysis where the correlation between two variables is explored. For example, ice-cream sales with the temperature or traffic accidents with age group. Scatter plots and histograms can be used to represent bivariate analysis visually.

Multivariate analysis where comparative analysis of multiple variables is done. Multivariate analysis is the most complex. Cluster analysis, multiple regression analysis, PCA, and factor analysis are just a few ways to perform multivariate analysis. In addition, scatter plots, contour plots, and multi-dimensional plots can be used to visualize multivariate analysis results.

EDA establishes the data's underlying structure and the key variables, and helps to estimate parameters, find missing data, fix anomalies, and improve margins of error. In other words, it explains the data with the fewest possible predictor variables. R and S-PLUS are programming packages used for EDA.

Confirmatory Data Analysis

While exploratory data analysis summarizes the data with the fewest possible predictor variables, confirmatory data analysis (CDA) is used to confirm or reject the model. The main aim is to challenge the model and quantify the extent of deviation from the proposed model.

CDA involves testing hypotheses and producing estimates, regression, and variance analyses.

Predictive Analysis

The predictive analysis calculates the approximated or most likely future outcome from historical or past data. Organizations leverage Big Data and Machine Learning to forecast potential scenarios to help drive strategic decisions.

Predictive analysis is explained in detail in Section 4.7.

Inferential Analysis

Inferential analysis is a statistical approach to making inferences, theories, or conclusions by analyzing a sample sector or dataset for a result and making inferences about the entire sector or population based on that result. In other words, it works on probability by taking a small sample instead of working on the whole population. The inferential analysis is mainly used in

- Estimations; e.g., calculating the per capita income of a whole state or country using a random sample dataset of people from across the state or areas.
- Testing hypothesis; in statistical hypothesis testing, the **null hypothesis** predicts no effect or relationship between variables except for sampling error, while the **alternative hypothesis** predicts the existence of an effect or relationship. For

example, the effectiveness of a treatment by calculating the mean difference between the treatment group and the control (placebo) group. If the results are statistically significant, you can conclude your hypothesis to be true.

The best technique to use for data analysis is based on the use case and area of the application. For example, when working with Big Data, a combination of approaches is generally adopted, starting with descriptive and exploratory data analysis and then developing predictive models to forecast future outcomes.

4.4 Understanding Text Analytics and Big Data

We briefly discussed text analytics in Chapter 3 (refer to Section 3.4.1). Text analytics relates to techniques used to extract meaningful information from textual data. In Big Data, the textual data is an unending panorama of unstructured and semi-structured data covering publications, webpages, social media, blogs, discussion forums, technical documentation, emails and news, to list a few.

Text analytics is also referred to as text mining, or KDT (Knowledge Discovery in Text). It is an extension of data mining. It measures unstructured content using linguistic rules, natural language processing, and machine learning to derive insights and patterns.

4.4.1 Text Mining Process

Figure 4.2 provides a generalized representation of the text mining process. Unstructured and semi-structured/quasi-structured data from multiple sources is collected and preprocessed to extract and keep only the pertinent information from the data, thus making it suitable for analysis.

The resulting process provides "structured" or "semi-structured" information that can be further used to create a model. Finally, analytical techniques are executed or repeated until a pattern matching a set rule is found and applied to the text to annotate. This

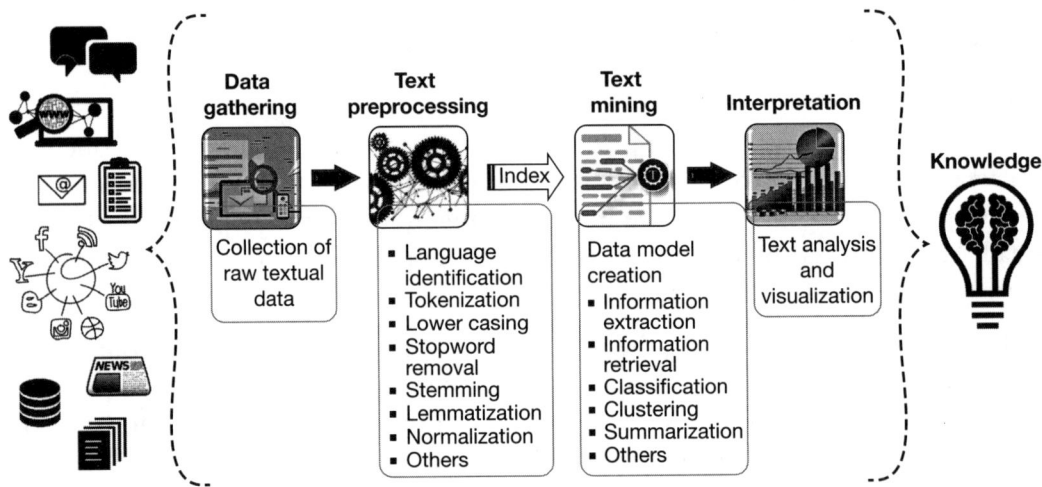

Figure 4.2 General text analytics process

complex set of analytic tools and techniques involves statistics, machine learning, NLP, etc., to gain insights for informed decision-making.

Data Gathering

Data Gathering is the first step in the text analytics process. Unstructured or semi-structured datasets like full-text documents, HTML files, blogs, newspaper articles, academic papers, etc., are collected from multiple sources. Text data sources include Library databases, Social media, Open sources, Web scraping, Language corpora, etc.

Based on the purpose of the application, say for research, the source could be created by the organization in the form of survey responses, questionnaire responses, or transcripts. Other sources could be collated from third parties such as British National Corpus, audio/video data transcription, Google Books Ngram Viewer, JSTOR, Science Direct, Wikisource, etc.

Text Preprocessing

Text preprocessing is perhaps the most crucial stage in text mining as it cleans and removes anomalies and redundancies from the raw data text and prepares it for further processing. When correctly done, text preprocessing results in a dataset that is clean and easier to understand and analyze. This ensures a higher possibility of accurate results.

A set of techniques or methods are applied to the data based on the use case in question. Each step reduces the problem dimensionality. Following are some of the standard text cleaning or pre-processing steps:

Tokenization: Tokenization breaks a stream of textual data into words, terms, sentences, symbols, or some other meaningful elements called tokens. A tokenizer separates information into units that may be considered distinct from unstructured data and natural language text. Tokenization can be broadly classified into four types:

1. **Sentence tokenization** is splitting the text of journals or documents into individual sentences. For example, consider the following text:

   > The platform delivers complete and authentic content. It is a simple language and easy to understand.

   The tokenization function will generate two sentences, as below:
   ["**The platform delivers complete and authentic content.**"]
   ["**It is a simple language and easy to understand.**"]

2. **Word tokenization** will split the sentences into words. A common algorithm used is splitting based on white space.
   ["**The**", "**platform**", "**delivers**", "**complete**", "**and**", "**authentic**", "**content.**", "**It**", "**is**", "**a**", "**simple**", "**language**", "**and**", "**easy**", "**to**", "**understand.**"]

3. **Character tokenization**, as the name suggests splits the sentence to characters. For example:

   > The platform delivers complete and authentic content.

will generate

["T", "h", "e", "p", "l", "a", "t", "f", "o", "r", "m", "d", "e", "l", "i", "v", "e", "r", "s", "c", "o", "m", "p", "l", "e", "t", "e", "a", "n", "d", "a", "u", "t", "h", "e", "n", "t", "i", "c", "c", "o", "n", "t", "e", "n", "t", "."]

4. **Subword tokenization** is where frequently occurring words remain as a whole while rare words are split into frequent subwords. It forms a balance between word and character tokenization.

   Consider the strings "**deliver**", "**delivers**", "**delivered**" and "**delivering**". One valid subword tokenization of above words would be [**deliver, ##s**], [**deliver, ##ed**], and [**deliver, ##ing**] where the double-hashtag represents a prefix subtoken of the initial string "**deliver**".

   Extracting the subtokens such as "**##ing**," "**##s**," "**##ly**," "**##ed**," and similar others over an English corpus would help in fitting fewer words in a model that restricts the number of tokens.

Gensim, NLTK, Keras, and spaCy are some of the tokenization tools. However, as demonstrated in the word tokenization example above, a few functions of the word tokenizers are whitespace tokenizers.

There are many others. For example, in NLTK, consider the sentence "**You're very lucky. So…off you go!**"

The WordPunct tokenizer will split the words as:
[You] ['] [re] [very] [lucky] [.] [So] […] [off] [you] [go] [!]

PunktWordTokenizer will split the words as:
[You] ['re] [very] [lucky.] [So] […] [off] [you] [go] [!]

Pattern tokenizer:
[You're] [very] [lucky.] [So…off] [you] [go!]

Tokenization helps interpret the text's meaning by analyzing the sequence of the words. The resulting tokens help in understanding the context and developing the analytical model.

Lower Casing: The lower casing is a standard text preprocessing technique where the input text is converted to a lower case format. Hence '**Big Data**', '**Big Data**', '**Big Data**', and '**BIG data**' are converted to '**Big Data**' and treated the same way.

The lower casing is quite helpful in reducing duplication and getting the correct counts or term frequency–inverse document frequency (TF-IDF) values. TF-IDF indicates the number of times a particular word (say 'data') appears in a document divided by the total number of words in the document. However, Lower Casing is not a useful function when applying POS tagging. The same work may have different meanings, e.g., '**Major**' is a military ranking and noun, while '**major**' can be an adjective, meaning "very important". Capital letters are significant for extracting information, like names and locations. Similarly, in sentiment analysis, the meaning attached to **a big miss in service**' differs from '**a BIG miss in service**' as the latter may refer to anger, disappointment, or frustration.

Stemming: Finding a word's root and cutting it off at its stem is a procedure known as stemming. For example, applying stemming to the words 'feels' and 'feeling', will stem the suffix into 'feel'. Stemming is a rule-based algorithm; sometimes, the word may lose its meaning with stemming. For example, applying stemmer to the following sentences:

[**The platform delivers completely and authentic content. It is a simple language and easy to understanding.**]

produces

[**The platform deliv complet and authent content. It is a simple language and easy to understand**].

As the above example shows, the stemmer removed the suffix '**ers**', '**ic**' and others, thus giving wrong English words like '**deliv**,' '**authent**'.

The efficiency of information retrieval systems is increased by stemming. It is used in Natural Language Processing (NLP) and Natural Language Understanding (NLU). Porter stemmer and snowball stemmer are common stemming methods used.

Lemmatization: Lemmatization is also used in NLP and NLU. It is similar to stemming in that it reduces the words to their stem words. But unlike stemming where the prefix or suffix is blindly cut out, lemmatization ensures the base word result is proper and reveals its intended meaning. For instance, the stemmer tool would stem '**diversifying**' and '**diversified**' to give an illogical word '**diversifi**.' However, lemmatization would convert the words to the root word or *lemma* '**diversify**'. As a result, lemmatization is slower than the stemming process.

Example: Lemmatization of

[**The platform delivers completely and authentic content. It is a simple language and easy to understanding.**]

produces

[**The platform deliver complete and authentic content It be a simple language and easy to understand**].

Stop word removal: Stop words commonly occur, such as 'a', 'an', 'but', 'the', etc., that do not provide significant information for downstream analysis. These words do not offer much value in terms of analysis of the whole sentence and hence can be removed. There are stop word packages for all major languages, for example, spaCy, NLTK, etc. In the English language, the common stop words include articles, pronouns, prepositions, conjunctions, and others.

Stop word removal is done after tokenization. It helps in bringing more focus to the essential information in the text. In addition, it can potentially help in:

- Improving performance as fewer words are left, thereby increasing accuracy in clustering and classification.

- Preventing stop words from being indexed.
- Decreasing dataset size, thus reducing the time to train the model.
- Enabling faster retrieval of data from the database. For example, Google applies stop word removal in its search engine.

However, it should be used with discretion. The stop words may provide valuable information in POS tagging and sentiment analysis. For example, the stop word removal function on the text '**I was not happy with their service.**' gives the output '**happy service**,' which is an incorrect sentiment.

Some of the other methods, also used in normalizing the text during preprocessing, are

- Removal of punctuations
- Spellchecks
- Removal of frequent words: The word **data** or **Big Data** would be quite common and repeatedly occur when analyzing textual content of books and articles of Big Data. Hence it can be removed to improve computational speed.
- Removal of rare words
- Removal of emojis and emoticons: Quite common in Twitter, Instagram, and social media platform texts as they do not contain any valuable information. However, for sentiment analysis, the emojis and emoticons would convey information on the sentiment and should not be removed.
- Converting emojis and emoticons to words
- Removal of URLs
- Removal of HTML tags, etc.

The first step to any analytics exercise is to understand the problem that needs to be addressed, whether it is document summarization, fraud detection, lead generation, etc. All the above text preprocessing methods need not be conducted on text data. Instead, the required preprocessing steps must be chosen based on the use case.

POS Tagging, Parsing, and Indexing

Part-of-Speech (POS) tagging: POS tagging is an NLP process where each word in a sentence is tagged to its part of speech. It is instrumental in providing a linguistic indicator of how a term is used within the scope of a phrase, sentence, or document. The word is tagged or annotated as a proper noun – NN, verb – VBZ (like works, gives, plays), determiner – DT, adjective – JJ, adverb – RB, preposition – IN, conjunction pronoun – PRPS, etc.

For example:

Tagged	The platform delivers complete and authentic content.						
	The	platform	delivers	complete	and	authentic	content
	↓	↓	↓	↓	↓	↓	↓
	DT	NN	VBZ	JJ	CC	JJ	NN

There are two types of POS taggers: 1. Rule-based, and 2. Stochastic.

As the name suggests, **a rule-based POS tagger** tags the word by the grammatical rules of a particular language. It is done by analyzing the meaning of the preceding and the succeeding word. Brill's tagger is an example of a rule-based tagger.

Stochastic (or statistical) POS Tagger tags a word by using word frequency measurement or tag sequence probabilities. In frequency measurement, the tag is applied to the unclear word if the word frequently occurs in the training set. In the probability method, the best tag for a given word is determined by the probability it occurs with the n previous tags. Finally, the highest occurring tag is applied to the word. This approach is also known as the n-gram approach.

POS tagging is crucial for the subsequent processing of text. POS tagging is used in information retrieval, information extraction, text-to-speech applications, and higher NLP tasks like translation, semantics analysis, etc. It is typically done after tokenization or after some or all preprocessing steps. nltk.tag package in Python, TextBlob, spaCy, and Parts-of-speech.info are some tools used for POS tagging.

Parsing: Finding a text's syntactic structure is a process of parsing. It follows POS tagging as the algorithm uses the grammar of the language the text is written in. In addition, parsing is used in NLP to report any syntax or commonly occurring errors. There are two types of parsing – shallow parsing and deep parsing. An essential representation of the two processes is given in Fig. 4.3.

- **Shallow parsing** is also referred to as **chunking**. It is the process of analyzing a sentence and extracting phrases to group them into noun phrases, verb phrases, etc. It is used in less complex NLP applications, for instance, text mining and information extraction.

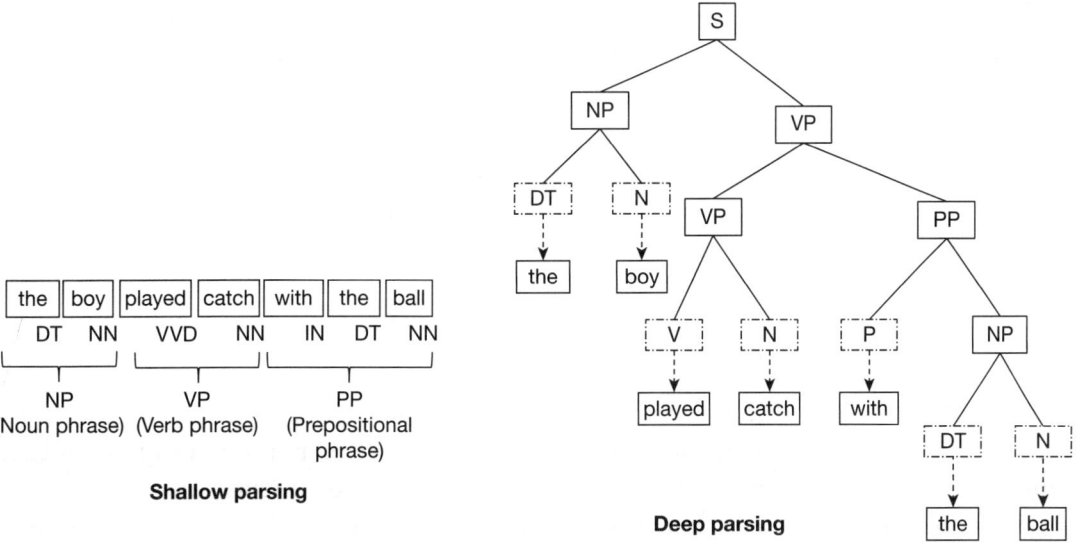

Figure 4.3 Shallow parsing vs. Deep parsing

- **Deep parsing** gives more structure to the POS-tagged text. It is represented as a tree structure and used in complex NLP applications like dialogue systems such as the Watson QA system.

Text Index: Text Indexing is a processing step to extract statistics considered necessary for representing the information available and/or to allow a fast search of its content. The most popular text indexing technique for data retrieval is **inverted indices**. The method consists of two indexed tables – the document table that consists of the document id and a list of pointers or tokens. The token terms are grouped in alphabetical order, and an array-like structure is formed containing the doc ID and the terms grouped, creating an inverted index (Fig. 4.4).

Doc ID	Document
1	Document I
2	Document II
3	Document III
4	Document IV

Term dictionary (Sorted alphabetically)	Frequency of appearance of term in the documents (I-IV)		Document ID list			
Token term a	4	→→	1	2		
Token term b	9	→→	1	2	3	4
Token term c	1	→→	3	4		
Token term d	3	→→	2			
Token term e	2	→→	2	3	4	
Token term f	5	→→	1	2		
.... Token term x	...n	→→	3			

Figure 4.4 Inverted index

Text Mining

The text mining process step deals with constructing the training dataset. There are five commonly used techniques in text mining.

Information Extraction (IE): Information Extraction, commonly referred to as IE, is the process of extracting meaningful information from a massive set of unstructured or semi-structured text formats. The technique includes tokenization and identification of named entities, key phrases, sentence segmentation, and parts of speech to establish the relationship between entities and attributes.

The extracted entities, their attributes and relationships, and other related information are stored in a database for easy access and retrieval.

Information Retrieval (IR): Information Retrieval or IR is extracting relevant information and associated patterns based on a particular set of words or phrases. While IE focuses more on text extraction, IR is all about retrieving a set of documents that are relevant to the users' information needs. For example, web search engines like Google extensively use information retrieval systems. The IR system does not directly provide the same document or information. Instead, the system reports on the existence and location of documents that might contain the required information.

Text Categorization: Text categorization, in text analytics, assigns categories to unstructured text documents based on their content. The categories may have a hierarchical structure and are predefined with descriptors like concepts, patterns, rules, etc. A text document is assigned to a category if it matches the descriptors/rules. For example, news articles are categorized based on topic or theme, categorizing web pages under hierarchical definitions, and others. Some algorithms used in text categorization are decision trees, SVM, K-nearest neighbor, and neural networking.

At times text categorization is identified with **text classification**. Classification uses a combination of NLP and machine learning to categorize text documents based on their contents.

Clustering: Text clustering is the technique of automatically organizing unclassified, unlabeled textual data into groups or clusters of documents for further analysis. It works on the premise that the content of documents in a specific cluster is similar to the content in other clusters.

Unlike categorization, text clustering groups documents together without predefined categories or topics as references. Instead, it classifies based on similarity measures between documents. K-means is a commonly used algorithm in text clustering. Text clustering finds applications in customer segmentation, identifying anomalies, data exploration, etc.

Summarization: Text summarization is the process of condensing textual material while maintaining the essential points and purposes of the original. It provides a synopsis of massive textual data for making a concise and intelligible summary of important points of a document. This is extremely useful in automated content research, patent research, science, and R&D, where an abstract of the paper can be made. In addition, text summarization integrates the various methods that use text categorization, such as decision trees, neural networks, swarm intelligence, or regression models.

Data Interpretation

The text analysis model is created using one or more algorithms. Analysis can be done as a stand-alone or integrated with larger models. Patterns within the data are analyzed via records or information management systems. Once the text analysis is complete, the output information is fed to data visualization systems. The results can be visualized in charts, graphs, networks, correlation maps, dendrograms, infographics, or dashboards. Interactive data visualization enables businesses to spot trends and use the insights gleaned for decision-making.

4.4.2 Applications of Text Analytics

Some of the most used applications of text analytics are given hereunder.

Fraud Detection: Financial institutions and insurance companies can use text mining techniques for fraud detection. The system can analyze extensive collections of customer files and automatically flag customers or files with a high probability of fraud for the officials' focus.

Contextual Ad Placement: Digital advertising is a growing field in text analytics and mining applications. Text mining helps companies understand a webpage's context and place targeted ads to enable higher ROI, personalization, and re-engagement. For example, while reading an article on indoor plants, you may get an ad from plant nurseries due to their relevance.

Social Media Monitoring: Social media is a valuable market and customer intelligence source. Text analytics is used in social media (or the voice of the customer) to extract opinions, emotions, and overall public sentiment towards the enterprise's brand, services, or product. Enterprises use sentiment analysis to analyze the textual content through word choice, including chat acronyms, emojis, and others, to quantify customer sentiment, whether positive, negative, or neutral, and better understand how they connect with the customers.

Content Enrichment: Huge volumes of pre-existing data are available on the web. Text mining technology can pore through massive amounts of documents and textual information to collect, tag, organize and summarize information relevant to your writing topic. This makes it the ideal solution for content enrichment.

Customer Care Service: Companies are adopting text analytics tools to improve their services and enhance customer experience. Analyzing textual data from various sources, including surveys, user feedback, chats, discussion forums and other mediums, can minimize the company's reaction time to proactively and efficiently resolve customer complaints.

There are ample text analytics applications in the real world like business intelligence, crime prediction and prevention, spam filtering, risk management, regulatory compliance, and many more.

Thematic, IBM Watson, Lexalytics, Google Cloud NLP, MonkeyLearn, RapidMiner, and Amazon Comprehend are some standard text analytics tools.

4.5 Predictive Analysis of Big Data

Predictive analytics refers to using historical data, machine learning, and artificial intelligence to predict what will happen in the future. Predictive analytics utilizes statistical modeling, data mining, machine learning, and deep learning algorithms to extract the required information from Big Data and predict behavioral project patterns for the future. This will enable enterprises to change their strategy for revenue growth, operational efficiencies and risk reduction. For example, predictive analytics is used by retail companies like Walmart and Amazon to understand customers' buying behavior and purchase patterns to identify high-value customers, strategize promotions, cross-sell, and work on many other tactical plans.

Python, R, and MatLab are commonly used languages in predictive analytics.

The basic process of predictive analytics is represented in Fig. 4.5. Once historical data is collected and cleaned, it is analyzed to retrieve all the valuable insights or patterns from the Big Data that will help tackle the problem. The data is now fed into a mathematical model or a machine-learning algorithm to build the predictive model. The model aims to identify key trends and patterns in the data to isolate factors that have driven specific outcomes.

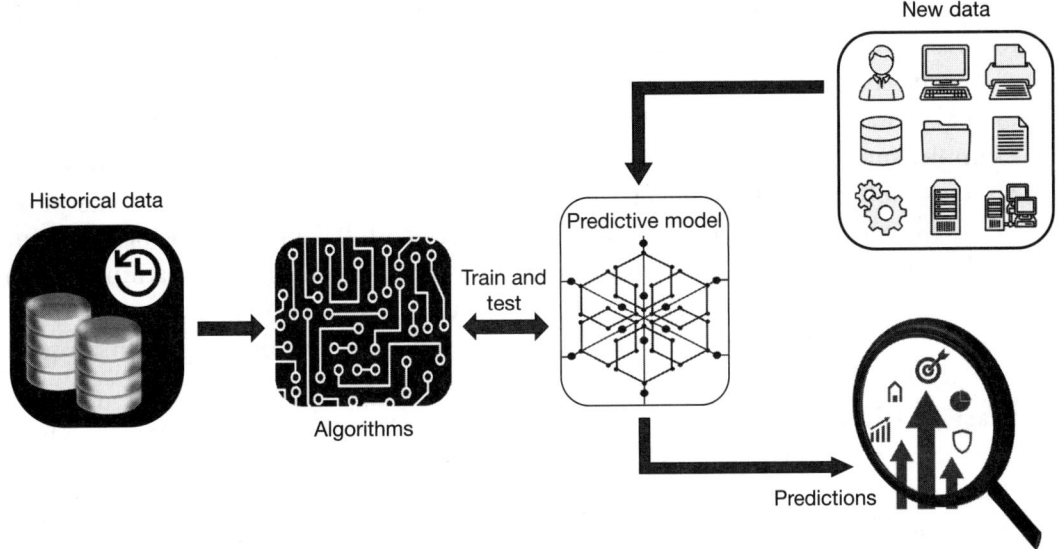

Figure 4.5 Predictive analytics process

Building the model typically involves randomly splitting the input data into training and testing datasets. The predictive model is first built using the training dataset. The accuracy of the model is then validated using the testing dataset. This is an iterative process, and any of the insignificant predictor variables identified during the testing stage must be filtered out to improve the efficiency of the predictive model. The model is then applied to the new or current data to predict the likely future outcome.

Training the model using terabytes of Big Data helps achieve more accurate domain predictions or problem predictions. Once the predictive model is built and validated, it must be retrained and tested periodically to adjust for changing behavior patterns.

4.5.1 Predictive Analytics Models

Predictive analytics works best when multiple modeling methods are combined. Traditional models involve statistics and data mining techniques like regression, classification, and clustering. Supervised models use machine learning techniques like deep learning, neural networks, etc. Some of the predictive analytical models are listed below:

1. **Regression Modelling:** Regression models are used in statistical analysis to understand the relationship between variables and their associated strengths. Regression models are used by organizations to determine which independent or predictor variables (input) hold the most influence on over-dependent (output) variables. It is called simple regression when only one dependent and independent variable exists. While on the other hand, when many independent variables influence one dependent variable, we call it multiple regression. Many regression algorithms depend on the relationship between the variables, like linear regression, muli-linear regression, time-series regression, logistic regression model, etc.

   Businesses leverage regression models are used to analyze the relevant features of their datasets and identify correlations to make essential business decisions. For example, suppose the likelihood of an online purchase is dependent on the ease of online search and cost of delivery. In that case, the regression model can show which of the two variables, i.e., online search or delivery cost, has a stronger association with the likelihood of purchase. Say the cost of delivery has a stronger association, then the business can focus on addressing delivery cost or related aspects. Linear regression, lasso regression, decision trees, random forest, and SVM are some algorithms used in regression modeling.

2. **Classification Model:** The classification model is used in predictive analytics to sort or categorize the data by broadly analyzing historical data. It can be **binary**, i.e., the result is classified into two discrete classes: 'Yes/No', 'High/Low', 'Good/Bad', etc. The model addresses questions corresponding to "Will the company stock increase in the market?" or "What is the likelihood of customer churn?" or "Is the email spam?" and similar other business questions. **Multi-class** classifies the data into more than two classes, e.g., movie classification, document classification, customer classification, etc.

   The classification model is simple and can be easily retrained with new data. Some popular algorithms used in the classification model are KNN, random forest, decision trees, logistic regression and SVM, among others.

3. **Clustering Model:** The clustering model is a time-effective way to quickly sort through the vast arena of Big Data and deliver the answers. It is widely used for targeted marketing campaigns. The model segregates the data into clusters or groups that have similar attributes. For example, algorithms can efficiently sort customers into similar groups based on common characteristics and buying patterns. This can enable companies to devise selective and focused promotion strategies.

   There are two types of clustering – **hard clustering**, which categorizes whether the data point belongs to the data cluster, and **soft clustering**, which assigns the probability of the data point joining a cluster. In soft clustering, the data point can belong to more than one cluster. The most used clustering algorithm is K-means.

4. **Outliers Model:** The outlier model predicts abnormal activities and transactions. The model identifies unusual data that deviates from the norm in isolation or with different categories and numbers. It can detect atypical data entries within a dataset and accurately predict fraudulent transactions. The anomaly detection can also predict the possibility of fraud or other losses that can cost the company millions of rupees, besides loss of reputation.

   For example, a spike in a credit card withdrawal in a single day that is not typical behavior of the customer may be cause for concern. Isolation forest and SVM are algorithms used in the outlier model.

5. **Time-series Model:** The time-series model uses Big Data to observe past data patterns to predict future patterns. The time-series model uses time as an input parameter. The model uses different data points at specific periods from historical data, say past 5+ years or more, to develop a numerical metric that will predict trends for the future period using that metric. Time-series forecasting is one of the often-used predictive analytics models in business since it can take several input variables simultaneously.

   Time-series predictions are not exact. The model can only predict the highest likelihood of a situation occurring in a specific period. For example, climate forecasting, demand forecasting, the pandemic spread forecasting, and so on. The forecast's accuracy depends on the quality and quantity of clean data and on suppressing data fluctuations and irregularities or outliers like seasonality. Regression algorithms like Autoregressive Integrated Moving Average (ARIMA) are used in the time-series mining function.

6. **Machine Learning:** Machine learning deals with complex data relationships by applying predictive and statistical algorithms that enable the model to automatically learn and improve as more data is fed to it without being explicitly programmed. It is an iterative process where the dataset is divided into training and testing sets. The model is trained with the training set, and the performance is tested with the testing set. With each iteration, the model gradually learns and improves performance.

   The two main approaches to machine learning are unsupervised and supervised learning. **Unsupervised learning** is where the machine learning model is fed with unlabeled data to identify interesting patterns or structures within the data. The machine learning model is trained using a labeled dataset in supervised learning. The model produces an output variable that can easily be assessed for accuracy by comparing it to the labeled input.

   Machine Learning-based predictive analytics has many industrial applications like medical diagnoses in healthcare, in cybersecurity by predicting and preventing cyberattacks, preventing fraudulent transactions and activities in financial services, identifying leads and prospects in sales and marketing, and many more.

Some of the challenges of predictive modeling are:

- Possibility of errors in data labeling that can cause skewed or incorrect results.
- Limited or inconsistent data collection and cleaning procedures.

- Shortage of massive data for training sets that have more variables or predictors.
- Predicts or forecasts about the likelihood of an event, but without providing insights on the best course of action to be taken.
- Results that are dependent on many variables, assumptions, and probability factors that can fluctuate or be subject to bias.

4.5.2 Predictive Analytics Algorithms

1. **Decision Trees:** Decision trees are classification-based algorithms represented graphically like a top–down tree structure, starting with the root node from where the decision tree starts, and branching out with alternative choices or decisions till it arrives at a final decision. Three nodes represent the tree.
   - **Decision node** branches to a course of action or alternative choices where a decision must be made. It is represented as a square.
   - **The chance node** is represented as a circle that indicates the probability of a result.
   - **The end node or leaf node** is the final node or decision that cannot be divided further.

   There are two kinds of trees: **classification trees**, where the responses are categorical, and **regression trees**, where the response variable is continuous or numerical. Decision trees can get quite complex and large as the branches and variables increase. The complexity is typically controlled by **pruning** or intentionally removing the levels of questions for the best fit.

2. **Linear Regression Algorithms:** Linear regression is used to find the linear relationship between a dependent or response variable and the independent or predictor variables. The goal is to form a formula or regression coefficient that describes the dependent variable in terms of the independent variable. Once this relationship is quantified, the dependent variable can be predicted for any instance of an independent variable. For example, defining the likelihood of having blood pressure (dependent variable) in relation to age, weight, and sex (predictor variables). A scatter plot can show whether the relationship is linear or not. The regression coefficient is shown by the slope of the line in the scatter plot.

3. **Logistic Regression Algorithms:** Logistic Regression is a supervised classification algorithm. It is used to predict the probability of the occurrence of an event. The output variable is finite (Yes/No, 0/1, true/false) rather than continuous with infinite values, as seen with linear regression. The output of logistic regressions closer to 1 indicates that the variable fits within the category, and those closer to 0 indicate that the input variable is not likely to fit within the category.

    Logistic regression can be used to identify prospective customers or the winning chances of an election candidate.

4. **Random Forest:** Random Forest is a variation of decision and regression trees and uses both to organize and label the data. The random forest algorithm is

well-adapted to classify large volumes of data. Instead of constructing a single complex tree with many branches of logic, a random forest constructs many simple small trees (refer to Fig. 3.3: Random forest structure), each unrelated to the other. Each tree evaluates the instances of data and determines a categorization. Once all the trees complete their data evaluation, the process merges the individual results to create a final category prediction, and this method is known as an **ensemble method**.

5. **Clustering algorithms:** Clustering algorithms organize data into groups whose data points or members are similar (refer Chapter 1, Section 1.6.4). Commonly used clustering algorithms are:
   - *K-means clustering* is an unsupervised clustering algorithm that computes centroids and iterates the process until the optimal centroid is found. The input parameter is the K-th cluster or number of clusters. K centroids are randomly placed, and data points are assigned to the nearest centroid to form a cluster. By placing data points in clusters so that their combined squared distance from the cluster's centroid is minimized, centroids are calculated. The less variation within clusters, the more similar the data points are within the same cluster.

     K-Means is used in customer or market segmentation applications, identifying crime localities, optimizing delivery stores, and other real-world use cases.
   - *Hierarchical-based clustering:* The hierarchical-based clustering algorithm is unsupervised. The number of clusters is not predefined. Instead, the algorithm starts by identifying each data point as a cluster, identifies two clusters closest (most similar) to each other, and merges them. The process of merging (refer Fig. 1.16) continues iteratively until all the clusters are merged.

     The final output is represented as a dendrogram. Branches or **clades** closer to the same height are considered similar, while clades with different heights are dissimilar. Pearson's correlation coefficient, Jaccard similarity coefficient, and Gower's similarity coefficient are commonly used to measure the similarity.
   - *Density-based clustering:* Density-based clustering algorithms are useful to avoid outliers and noise. The algorithm identifies clusters of arbitrary shapes. The algorithm detects areas of concentrated data as well as areas that are sparse. The key premise is that for each cluster point, the neighborhood of a given radius (**Eps**) must contain at least a minimum number of points called **Minpts**. There are three points – the **core point** that has most Minpts within Eps, the **border point** that has fewer Minpts but still sits within Eps of the core point, and **the noise point**, which is neither a core point nor border point and, as such, does not form part of the cluster. Noise point is also referred to as an **outlier**.

     Density-based clustering is used in model building and unsupervised machine learning as it is self-learning and automatically detects patterns.

6. **Deep Learning:** Artificial neural networks are used in deep learning, a type of machine learning, to carry out complex calculations on vast volumes of data. The purpose is to program a computer to emulate the human brain, i.e., process data, identify patterns and make an informed decision. Deep learning algorithms can

work with almost any kind of data. However, solving complicated problems requires substantial computing power and large amounts of labeled data. Convolutional Neural Networks (CNNs), Recurrent Neural Networks (RNNs), Multilayer Perceptions (MLPs), and Self-Organizing Maps (SOMs) are examples of deep learning methods.

Automated driving uses deep learning to automatically detect stop signs, traffic lights, obstacles, and pedestrians. In addition, deep learning-enabled microscope is used in medical research to detect cancer cells.

7. **K-Nearest Neighbour (KNN):** KNN is a supervised classification algorithm. It uses labeled points (trained data) to learn how to label new points. Labeled points closest to the new point are considered their neighbors or '**K**'. The distance between the new data point (test data) and the training data is calculated and sorted. The K-nearest neighbors are determined based on the minimum distance values. The category is then assigned to the test data based on the neighbors' majority voting or consensus.

   The higher the value of K or neighbors to be considered, the more effective the algorithm is. Lower values of K may result in overfitting, and very high values may result in a generic model that is difficult to predict. Euclidean distance, Manhattan, and Minkowski are distance metrics commonly used in KNN algorithms. KNN is often used in search applications, recommendation systems, and preprocessing of data.

8. **Fuzzy Logic Algorithm:** Fuzzy logic is used in prediction problems with uncertain or imprecise data. The approach is based on the principle that a value can be between completely True and completely False, i.e., it can take any real value between 0 and 1. The logic consists of 4 parts – the **rule base** that contains all fuzzy rules and if/then conditions, **fuzzification** that converts the inputs (crisp values like temperature, pressure, etc. from sensors) to fuzzy sets, **and inference** that determines the degree of match between the fuzzy sets and rules to decide which rules are to be implemented. Then, the designated rules are combined to form the control actions, and finally, the **defuzzification** process converts the fuzzy sets to crisp values.

   Fuzzy logic is used in cruise control to adjust the throttle setting to set car speed and acceleration. Other applications include washing machines, vacuum cleaners, traffic control, NLP, antiskid braking systems, and many more.

9. **Neural Network:** Neural Network is a machine learning algorithm that attempts to simulate the human brain. The algorithm is used to train a network with a set of training data and then test it with a group of test data to check the accuracy. The process continues till the network is stable and able to classify data accurately at all times. A neural network consists of three layers – outer, hidden, and output. The **outer layer** takes in the information or data from the outside world and processes and categorizes it for the next layer, the hidden layer. The **hidden layer** consists of many layer(s) that generate results using multiple algorithms and processes like cross-validation, back propagation, feed-forward calculations, and many others depending on the AI or ML application. The **output layer** then generates the finished product.

The output layer may have only one output node if the question is binary or more than one node if the question is a multiclass classification problem.

The algorithm is adaptable, self-learning, and highly fault-tolerant, with high accuracy rates and the ability to work with large volumes of data. Neural network algorithms are used in speech recognition, handwriting recognition, image labeling, face recognition, and financial predictions, to name a few. Convolutional neural networks, recurrent neural networks, and modular neural networks are some examples of neural network types.

10. **Support Vector Machine (SVM):** SVM is a supervised machine learning algorithm best used for classification techniques. For a simple example, let us take two classes. First, the algorithm works by making a separating line between the two classes. Data points on either side of the line represent two categories (refer to Fig. 4.6). The separating line is called the **hyperplane**. Next, the SVM algorithm finds the points closest to the line from both classes. These points are called **support vectors**. The margin is the separation between the line and the support vectors. The most advantageous hyperplane is the one for which the margin is most significant. The linear hyperplane is affected by this procedure.

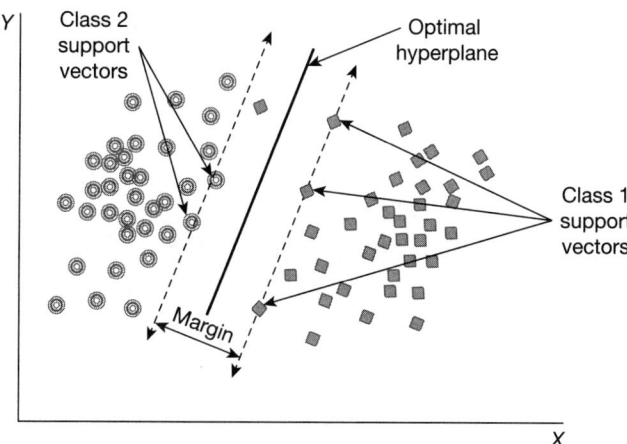

Figure 4.6 Linear SVM representation

The above example is for linear SVM, i.e., two-dimensional or linearly arranged data. However, SVM can also compute non-linear data using kernel function by adding a third dimension, Z.

The algorithms mentioned above are only a few examples of those utilized in predictive analysis. Naive Bayes, YOLO, Gradient Boosted model, Prophet, ensemble models, and many more are a growing number of algorithms used in predictive analytics.

4.6 PROCEDURAL VS. FUNCTIONAL PROGRAMMING MODELS FOR BIG DATA

The various Big Data platforms and tools like MapReduce, Pig, Hive, and others use programming models within their software systems to address the business problems that need to be solved. Programming models or paradigms are concepts or methods used to structure the code. For example, three programming paradigms organize code in data sciences – Object-Oriented Programming (OOP), Procedural Programming, and Functional Programming. In OOP, the code is organized into logical entities: the object or class. The objects contain both the data and the methods that affect that data, thus securing the mutability of data.

OOP, procedural, and functional programming approaches are all supported by Python, the high-level programming language. Scala is a blend of OOP and functional programming. The programming paradigms typically followed in Big Data are procedural and functional programming models.

The code is written in a sequential series of computational steps or tasks in a procedural programming model. It is also structured programming and follows a top-to-bottom execution style. There is no grouping of code into logical entities or organizing data and logic in objects. The procedure is just a series of clearly defined steps that need to be executed. A given procedure can be called at any point during the execution of a program, including by other procedures or by itself. This reusability of the program code is a significant advantage of the procedural programming model.

A common technique used in procedural programming is **iteration**, where a program repeats a series of steps *n* number of times or till the controlling condition becomes false. This technique is useful in task automation.

COBOL, Matlab, and C# are examples of Procedural Programming languages.

The functional programming model is a declarative programming paradigm where the code is organized as functions with clearly defined tasks. The function holds the logic, and the language implementation carries out the computation. The data is passed to the function as parameters, and the computation produces consistent outputs solely dependent on the inputs to the function. The key principle of the paradigm is the execution of a series of mathematical functions, and it has no dependency on the series of steps that precede the function.

Functions can be constructed out of other functions and call themselves recursively. This is best suited for running parallel and concurrent program execution. Hence it is the most prominent programming model in defining Big Data distributed processing workflows.

Languages that support functional programming include Python, Lisp, R, Scala, and F#.

Table 4.1 gives a side-by-side comparison of the procedural and functional programing models.

Table 4.1 Procedural and functional programming models

Procedural	Functional
The code is written in a sequential series of computational steps or tasks.	The code is organized as logical or mathematical functions within its program structure.
Statements are structured into procedures.	Stateless, i.e., it avoids changing state and mutable data. It depends only on the input arguments.
It tells the computer what to do.	It describes the result required.
It supports conditional statements, function calls, loops, and iterations.	It supports function calls, including recursive.
It does not support parallel programming.	It supports parallel programming.

A very simplistic example of procedural code to add two by defining a *procedure_add* procedure to illustrate the concept.
`num = 0`
`  def procedure_add():`
`    global num`
`    num += 2`
`    return num`
`procedure_add()    #output = 2`
`procedure_add()    #output = 4`
`procedure_add()    #output = 6`
The output result is 6. Each step executes the procedure sequentially.
	A very simplistic example of functional code to add two by defining a *function_add* function to illustrate the concept.
	`num = 0`
	`def function_add(num):`
	`    num += 2`
	`    return num`
	`function_add()    #output = 2`
	`function_add()    #output = 2`
	`function_add()    #output = 2`
	The output result is 2. Each function is independent of the steps that precede it.

Languages – COBOL, C#, Python, Matlab	Languages – LISP, Scala, R, F#

Functional, procedural, or a combination of both programming styles are used in Machine Learning, Deep Learning, and Data Manipulation.

4.7 BIG DATA INTEGRATION PROCESS

Big Data integration is a set of processes, tools, and technology used to retrieve information from massive heterogeneous sources and transform it into meaningful information for data analysis. Therefore, the Big Data Integration process needs to address the complex dimensions of Big Data, viz., the 5 *V*'s.

The two data integration processes used in Big Data are ETL and ELT. The letters stand for:

E – Extract or extraction is the process of pulling or extracting the data from various source systems, having different formats like flat files, XML, relational dB, NoSQL, etc. The data is extracted into the staging area or datastore.

T – The process of altering the information's structure to integrate with the target data systems is known as transformation, or transform. This involves the cleansing and converting or scrubbing raw data into a format ready for use in data analysis.

L – Load or loading refers to storing or depositing the transformed data into a data warehouse, data lake, or any data storage system.

ETL (Extract, Transform, Load) is preferred when dealing with smaller datasets, usually structured data requiring complex transformations. It is generally used with batch processing in data warehouse environments. The **ELT** (Extract, Load, Transform) integration method is used when dealing with massive volumes of structured and unstructured data of very high complexity. ELT is preferred over ETL in Big Data when scalability and faster data ingestion needs become a key factor in processing.

Figure 4.7 illustrates the high-level difference between the two integration processes. The main distinction is that ELT lacks a staging area. In ETL, the data is first converted/transformed in the temporary staging area before loading into the central repository or data warehouse. In ELT, the raw data is directly loaded into the repository or data lake where all the transformation occurs. In both the integration processes, the transformed data, i.e., the cleaned and enriched data, is finally transmitted to visualization or analysis systems.

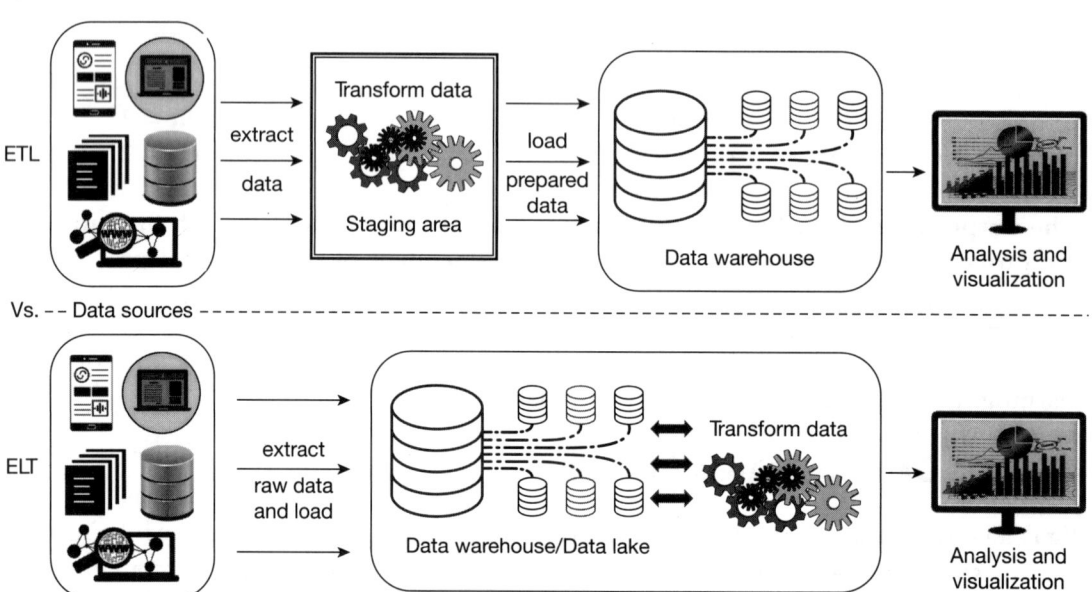

Figure 4.7 ETL and ELT integration process

The ETL and ELT integration procedures are contrasted in Table 4.2

Giving due diligence during the planning phase concerning Big Data integration solutions' performance, governance and security, can avoid the typical post-implementation issues related to infrastructure and performance. Furthermore, Big Data integration technology continues to improve with the cloud and other advancements. Therefore, the Big Data Integration system must ideally be set up to leverage the evolving technologies.

Table 4.2 Integration procedures – ETL and ELT

ETL	ELT
Transforms and integrates data with analytics	Transforms and integrates data with analytics
Represents **E**xtract, **T**ransform, **L**oad.	Represents **E**xtract, **L**oad, **T**ransform.
Implemented in business environments that are geared towards batch processing mode.	Implemented in business environments that require high-volume or real-time, or on-demand data usage.
Best suited for smaller datasets up to terabytes of data requiring complex transformations.	Technology is modeled to cater to the complexities and enormity of Big Data with a focus on speed and efficiency.
Supports relational or structured, or semi-structured data.	Datasets can consist of any data type from structured, unstructured, and/or semi-structured data sources.
Data is transformed in the interim staging area before loading onto the database or data warehouse.	There is no staging area. Instead, data is transformed directly into the central repository or data lake.
Longer waiting period as the data needs to be transformed before it can be loaded to its final destination.	Provides faster loading as raw data is directly loaded into the data repository without transforming.
A new type of analysis is difficult as the data is transformed and stored in specific formats identified during the design stage. Therefore, a change may require a complete modification to the OLAP warehouse.	Offers more flexibility as the full raw data is stored in the data lake. As a result, analysts/data scientists can determine the exact data they require to transform and analyze.
Higher cost of maintenance and hardware with growing scalability and storage requirements.	Lower cost of ownership as it leverages Big Data processing frameworks and cloud-based data warehouse/data lake systems
More secure as data is transformed before it is loaded.	All the sensitive data is directly loaded and would require more privacy safeguards.
Resources with knowledge of ETL technology are available.	Resources with knowledge of ELT technology are not easily available.
Examples of tools are IBM Datastage, Oracle Data Integrator, SAS Data Management, Informatica PowerCenter, etc.	Examples of tools are Hevo, Luigi, Blendo, Kafka, Talend, etc.

4.8 BIG DATA TECHNOLOGY LANDSCAPE

The Big Data technology landscape is fast emerging as one of the most powerful tool for data management, analytics and storage. Big Data is finding tremendous use in improving customer relationships, developing customized marketing campaigns and taking other actions to increase revenue and profits.

4.8.1 Big Data Architecture

Big Data contains different forms of data in many formats such as images, audio, video, and texts that combine structured, unstructured, and semi-structured data. The complexities involved in storing, mining and analyzing such data are immeasurable.

Figure 4.8 represents the data pipeline landscape of a generic two-tier architecture involving a data warehouse and a data lake. The Big Data landscape consists of five main sections – the data ingestion layer, the data storage layer, the data processing layer, the analytics layer, and the data management and security layer.

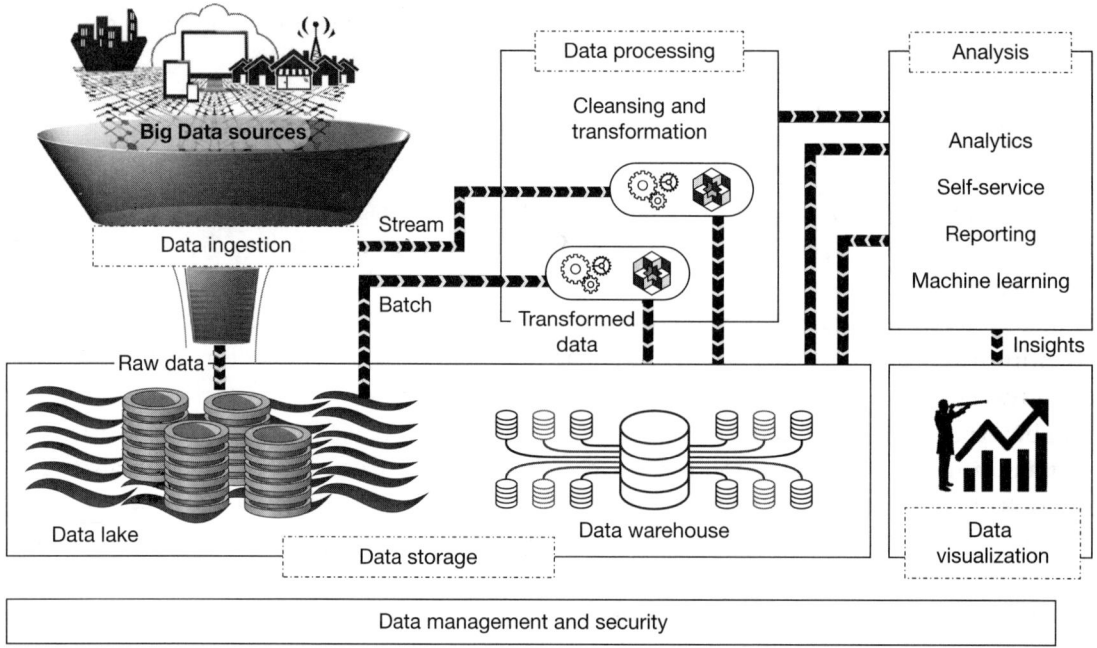

Figure 4.8 Big Data Analytics landscape

The data pipeline begins with the **data ingestion layer**. The layer transports data from the source or multiple sources and delivers it to the data storage site or landing area for further processing. A good architecture system can push or pull all data formats. Data sources are prioritized and categorized for routing to the correct destinations. Slight transformations in data are also made for smooth transmission. The data can be ingested in batches, streamed in real-time, or both.

In **batch processing**, the data is moved in discrete chunks at scheduled intervals, triggered events, or other logical conditions. The data is stored in the raw format in data lakes without any major transformation. This makes the ingestion process fast and more cost-efficient. In addition, storing historical data is advantageous when the purpose of data is yet to be defined.

In **stream processing**, the data is ingested in real-time or near real-time as and when the data becomes available or recognized by the ingestion layer. For example, data is streamed for applications that require live monitoring like stock market trading, multi-player game interactions, and real-time fraud detection. Stream data is collected and sent for processing as soon as it is received.

The data needs to be pre-processed, whether it is batch or stream data. Data processing is done in the **processing layer**, where the data is cleaned and transformed to make it analytics-ready. The process includes, but is not limited to, structuring or enriching by combining multiple datasets, normalization to reduce inconsistencies and redundancies, cleansing datasets by removing corrupted or duplicate data, and addressing missing and unformatted data. The processed or transformed data is then piped to the analytics layer for insight analysis or to the storage layer for analysis at a later time.

The **storage layer** provides the storage infrastructure, whether the massive raw unstructured historical data in data lakes or the structured architecture of the data warehouse. The storage layer focuses on the ideal way to store the various data types and models. The data warehouse contains organized, structured, and protected data. Transaction logs, relational databases, metadata, and transformed or derived data can be securely stored in the data warehouse. The summarized data can be piped and stored in data marts for specific or specialized processing or analytics by the consumers.

The **analysis layer** is the engine where the information and insights are extracted from the data. The transformed data undergoes complex procedures with entity identification, model building, analytical algorithms, and machine learning capabilities for advanced analytics and experiments. The results or insights can be visualized through pre-built reports or dashboards. A key layer component is model management, where the models are continuously trained for improved accuracy. The analysis layer can also provide consumers with a data pipeline for self-service, like building their customized reports or dashboards or analysis experiments if they are not outright clear on the information or insight contained within the data.

The outcome of the analyzed data is presented through business intelligence and advanced visualization tools for data-driven strategic and operational insights for decision-making. A good data pipeline must also have a robust **data management and security layer** to ensure that the Big Data landscape adheres to the best practices, governance, and compliance. Governance procedures must be defined, built, and followed throughout the data pipeline, from ingestion to consumption, including data privacy and security. Centralized monitoring tools can be adapted to monitor performance, database queries, and optimization needs.

4.8.2 Big Data Storage

Data warehouses and data lakes are the most widely used storage repositories for Big Data. Data warehouses were the first storage architecture used for data analytics. With the advent of Big Data and digitization, organizations and enterprises were flooded with high volumes of raw unstructured, heterogeneous data that had potential value. Data lakes were the solution to store these vastly changing multi-format multi-source data for evolving business use cases.

In recent years, various data lakes have emerged that combine the data management capability of data warehouse architecture and the flexibility of data lakes. This merged storage system is referred to as the Data Lakehouse. All three storage systems can store large amounts of information from multiple sources within an organization or in the cloud.

Data Warehouse

The data warehouse acts as a repository to store the organizational data from internal and external sources, including text files, emails, customer feedback, application data and logs, business, transactional data, and many more (Fig. 4.9). The warehouse is optimized for relational data from transaction systems. The data structure is hierarchical with the predefined schema to optimize fast SQL queries.

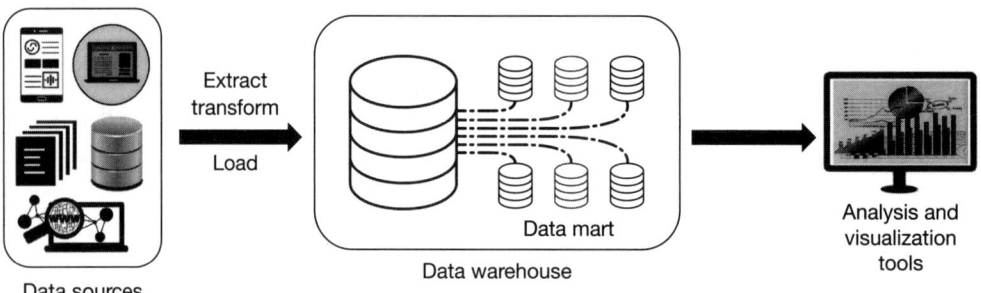

Figure 4.9 Simplified enterprise data warehouse landscape

The enterprise data warehouses (EDW) are designed for BI, reporting, and analysis purposes. Some of the main components of an EDW architecture are:

- ETL tool that extracts, transforms, and loads the enterprise data into the Data Warehouse. It integrates data from both operational systems and external information providers. The ETL process is done in a staging area.
- A main central repository that stores raw data, summary data, and metadata. Data is stored as OLAP (online analytical processing) cubes for rapid data analysis.
- Data warehouses - these may or may not have data marts. Data marts are subunits of the data warehouse and act as a repository for specific departments or lines of business.
  There are two approaches. The top-down or Inmon methodology is most common, where the data is first centralized within the data warehouse and then fed into the data marts. The second approach is the bottom-up or Kimbell methodology, where departmental or mission-critical data marts are first set up for analytic purposes and finally transferred into the data warehouse.
- Analytical, data mining, and reporting tools.
- Analysts or engineers who can securely and safely explore new datasets in a sandbox environment without following the data warehouse's protocols.

Pros
- Stored in files and folders in relational files, thus easy for data discovery and query.
- Data is cleaned and prepped before storage, making it easy for analysts to work on data.
- Strong built-in security protocols that protect the data.

Cons
- An enormous amount of redundancy.
- Prior ETL means some relevant data value may get lost in the process.
- Lack of data flexibility – works well with only structured data. Hence, it is not the ideal solution for the advanced analytics of Machine Learning and AI.
- Not cost-effective for storing and analyzing unstructured or streaming data.
- High maintenance costs.

IBM Db2 Warehouse, Amazon Redshift, and Google BigQuery are popular Data Warehouse solutions on the cloud used by enterprises.

Data Lake

Data Lakes are most appropriate for Big Data. Data lakes can store a massive amount of disparate, unfiltered data that can be used later by the analytics team. The raw data consisting of structured, semi-structured, or unstructured data, e.g., spreadsheets, relational database files, mobile apps, logs, XML, social media, sensors, and other IoT data, is directly loaded into the Data Lake in an open format that can be used for a future purpose. Analysts process the required datasets for insight analysis when a purpose or analytics project is defined.

Data is extracted, loaded, and later transformed (Fig. 4.10) for analysis. The ELT process is simple as there is no schema defined. Hence, it is the ideal architecture for machine learning, predictive analytics, and other AI solutions. Furthermore, Data Lake has a flat architecture where every data element is tagged with metadata, allowing fast access across huge datasets. As a result, data lakes have high scalability regardless of the volume or format of data.

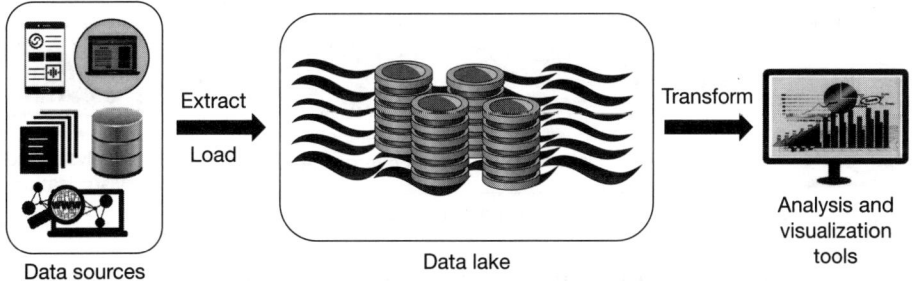

Figure 4.10 Simplified data lake landscape

However, the lack of a standardized structure complicates the analytics process as engineers and scientists need advanced coding knowledge to incorporate changes.

Pros
- Can handle both structured, semi-structured, and unstructured data.
- Data is not pre-modeled. Analysts and scientists have immediate access to raw data offering the flexibility to ask questions.
- Centralization of data from disparate sources and flexible accessibility of data across the globe.
- Metadata, tagging, etc., enables real-time and advanced analytic scope.
- Architecture can effectively handle stream, batch, and complex data processing.
- Scalable, cost-effective solution for any data type.

Cons
- Requires careful planning in designing the data lake and building the complex pipeline.
- It takes more time to get a queryable dataset.
- High risk in security, privacy, and access control.
- Requires careful planning and time to ensure data quality and reliability. Lack of governance procedures could turn the lakes into data swamps where the data is inaccessible or holds no value or consequence.

Hadoop is an example of Data Lake architecture that can be implemented on-premise and in the cloud.

Data Lakehouse

Data Lakehouse is an evolving Big Data storage architecture that aims to combine the benefits of the data warehouse and the data lake, thus eliminating the drawbacks of both. This hybrid model is called the Data Lakehouse. It has a dual-layer architecture (Fig. 4.11) with the warehouse layer sitting over the data lake layer, thus providing the much-needed governance and quality controls that were weak in data lakes, while also having the flexibility and lower TCO (Total Cost of Ownership) storage advantages.

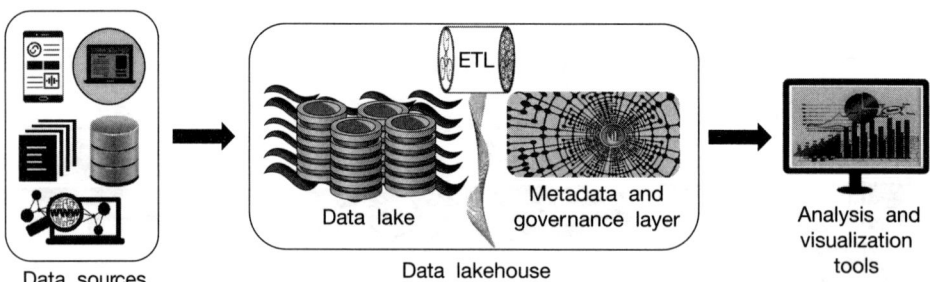

Figure 4.11 Simplified data lakehouse landscape

The Data Lakehouse approach starts with the ingestion of structured and unstructured data directly into the Data Lake. Then a structure and schema are applied by enabling ACID, which is the acronym for Atomic, Consistent, Isolated, Durable transactional processes of the data warehouse model. ACID transaction support enables data consistency and reliability. Finally, schema management is enforced, allowing for governance directly on the data lake, thus improving data quality and integrity across the pipeline.

An API layer of metadata APIs, data frame APIs, and others help faster processing for advanced analytics, machine learning, AI, and research solutions.

Pros
- Can store unlimited structured, unstructured, and semi-structured data.
- ACID capabilities of Atomicity, Consistency, Isolation, and Durability are maintained.
- Comparatively easier to build a pipeline.
- Cost-effective to maintain.
- Reduced data redundancy.
- Enforces schema and data integrity.
- Enables strong data governance and security mechanisms.
- Supports a wide variety of open-source tools and libraries with APIs that support data scientists and architects in analyzing data for advanced analytics and machine learning experiments.

Cons
- A relatively new concept of architecture that is still evolving.

Databricks with Delta Lake is a well-known Data Lakehouse platform.

4.9 BIG DATA KEY ROLES

The core of any Big Data Analytics team is the data analysts, data engineers, and data scientists. The roles may overlap based on the organization's size, business domain, available skill sets, and infrastructure. But each position has distinct responsibilities. To put it simply, the data engineer directs the data to a central place where the data analyst investigates and examines the data before presenting the findings to the company so they may make data-driven choices. The data scientists also analyze data to gain actionable insights. However, they use advanced techniques to design predictive models and machine learning techniques for data mining. They also create programs to automate data collection and processing.

Data Analyst

The primary role of data analysts is to gather, organize, analyze, and interpret data to identify data-led insights that can guide organizations in making informed, critical business decisions.

Though not necessarily an expert in data sciences or software engineering, a data analyst will have good statistical knowledge, critical thinking, problem-solving skills, a strong understanding of the business domain, and data visualization skills. They should also be good at the Big Data tools and technology like Hadoop, MatLab, R, SAS, Scala, etc.

The data analyst typically works with structured data. For example, in the Big Data world, data analysts work with SQL and NoSQL and have skills in programming languages like Python and R. They form the liaison between the data and the business in providing business insights. Hence a good data analyst will have soft skills such as communication, stakeholder management, presentation, technical competence, and business acumen.

Data analysts explore the data from multiple standpoints and perform cleaning and transformation operations to discover trends in the data. In addition, they help identify areas for deeper analysis or new paths the company can potentially explore.

Fundamental aspects of a Big Data analyst:

- Analyzes data to gain actionable insights for the organization.
- Works on answering specific questions for the business, which is mostly based on descriptive or diagnostic.
- Typically works with structured data using SQL
- Presents the insights to the business via dashboards using business intelligence software like Tableau and statistical software like SAS.
- Skilled in mathematics, statistics, advanced Excel, data mining, data warehousing, and business intelligence.

Data Scientist

A data scientist's job is to use machine learning and algorithms to evaluate and understand raw data to provide commercial solutions. The difference between the data analyst and the data scientist is that while the primary role of the former is to present the data facts, the latter focuses on identifying analytics problems that offer the most significant opportunity for the business.

Data Scientists work on large datasets of structured, unstructured, and semi-structured data. Data munging and cleaning take a lot of time for data scientists. Data scientists have advanced knowledge in Machine Learning and Deep Learning. They use these techniques with other statistical methods and simulations to move into predictive and prescriptive analytics, making predictions about future events and actions for possible outcomes.

Data scientists possess strong technical and mathematical abilities such as machine learning, deep learning, statistical modeling, Big Data, and advanced programming skills in R, Python, SAS, SPSS, and coding in other statistical software packages. They are also excellent storytellers who can describe difficult results and convey them from a business viewpoint since they have exceptional communication and presentation abilities.

Fundamental aspects of a data scientist:

- Analyze data to gain actionable insights for the organization.
- Clean, extract and explore data from different sources comprising large datasets of structured, unstructured, and semi-structured data.
- Validate data to ensure accurate, comprehensive, and uniform information.
- Research, design, and implement statistical models and algorithms to mine Big Data.

- Write programs to automate and simplify data collection and processing using tools like TensorFlow and PyTorch to develop and train Machine Learning Models.
- Deep statistical, mathematical, and computer science knowledge.
- Programming in analytics software packages like R, Python, SAS, SPSS, MATLAB, etc.
- Statistical analysis using machine learning and deep learning algorithms such as natural language processing, logistic regression, Random Forest, etc.
- Analyze and interpret data by identifying patterns and trends to discover solutions and opportunities.
- Strong storytelling capability to break down complex findings and present them from a business perspective using visualization and other means.

Data Engineer

The primary responsibility of data engineers or data architects is to design and develop the infrastructure and architecture that enables the data access, utilization, and value capture. They design, build, integrate, and maintain data from various sources to ensure that the data is accessible to the data analysts and data scientists for their operations. They have a solid technical background with the ability to create and manage scalable ETL (extract, transform, load) systems, with a good understanding of batch and real-time data integration, data replication, data streaming, virtualization, and various other technological processes.

Data engineers are the first to onboard to prepare and build data extraction processes and data pipelines that automate data from various internal and external source systems. In addition, they are responsible for the maintenance and performance optimization of the pipelines and the creation of custom transformations or data gathering routines that ETL and ELT tools cannot handle.

They have a strong technical background in software development and/or data management and programming languages. A data engineer is skilled in various Big Data technologies like Hadoop, Python, Hive, Cloud Computing, etc.

Data engineers work with the business and IT teams to manage the broader infrastructure and data models. They need to understand how the data applications are structured, test data pipelines, and monitor how data is used. This makes sure the appropriate data is saved and provided to the business units, data scientists, and analysts on time so that they can extract valuable information.

Fundamental Aspects of a Big Data Engineer

- Design, build and manage data extraction processes and data pipelines from various sources.
- Develop, test, improve and maintain Big Data architectures, data pipelines, data warehouses, data lake solutions, and other processing systems.
- Ensure that the correct data is stored and distributed to the data scientists/analysts and business units promptly to extract useful information.

- Optimize and improve existing data quality and data governance processes to improve performance and stability.
- Work closely with IT, business, and data teams to manage the broader infrastructure and data models.
- Good technical background in software development and/or data management, programming languages, Big Data technologies like Hadoop, Python, Hive, Cloud Computing, etc.

SUMMARY

Data analytics analyzes datasets to evaluate, condense, and extract value and insights for sensible business decisions. R and Python are popular programming languages with rich libraries used by data analysts and data scientists for statistical analytics and scientific computing. New technologies like the Hadoop framework with HDFS and MapReduce programming languages have come into play with Big Data. In addition, frameworks like Apache Spark can process and extract patterns and information in real time.

Big Data Analytics benefit organizations in better decision making, increasing productivity, improving customer service, lowering costs, increasing profits, and much more. A successful Big Data Analytics practice must commence with a solid, grounded business strategy considering the problems or issues to be solved, expectations of the results or possible solution definition, alignment with the financial objectives and long-term goals, and other essential aspects.

The six aspects of a Big Data technology agnostic framework are:

1. **Data Understanding:** Understand the data requirements and their availability within the organization. Understanding the data will enable the organization to plan out the Big Data enterprise's storage infrastructure, processing, and architecture needs.
2. **Data Collection:** This stage decides how to ingest the data from the various sources and determine the type of storage that is best suited for the data, i.e., whether cloud, on-premise, or hybrid, and any pre-requisite schema definitions or alterations would be appropriate for such storage.
3. **Data Preparation:** Application of various processing techniques to make it ready for analysis. This is essential to get the most accurate results or insights from data.
4. **Analysis:** Build exploratory analytical models for descriptive, diagnostic, predictive, and prescriptive analytics. Some of the analysis techniques are data mining, machine learning, and NLP.
5. **Validation:** Tests are conducted to verify the process and ascertain that the model output is as expected.
6. **Visualization:** The results and insights of the analysis in the form of graphs or charts are presented to the business for data-driven decision-making.

The five common approaches to Big Data analysis are descriptive analysis, exploratory data analysis, confirmatory data analysis, predictive analysis, and inferential analysis.

Text analytics and Predictive analytics are common analytics procedures conducted on Big Data.

Text analytics is also referred to as text mining, or KDT (Knowledge Discovery in Text). It measures unstructured content using linguistic rules, natural language processing, and machine learning to derive insights and patterns. There are ample applications of text analytics in the real world like crime prediction and prevention, spam filtering, risk management, regulatory compliance, fraud detection, social media monitoring, and many more.

Predictive analytics refers to using historical data, machine learning, and artificial intelligence to predict what will happen in the future. This will enable enterprises to change their strategy for revenue growth, operational efficiencies, and risk reduction. Traditional predictive models involve statistics and data mining techniques like regression, classification, and clustering. Supervised models use machine learning techniques like deep learning and neural networks.

Some of the algorithms used in predictive analytics are linear regression, logistic regression, Random Forest, K-means clustering, K-Nearest Neighbour (KNN), Support Vector Machine (SVM), Naïve Bayes, and Prophet.

Big Data contains different forms of data such as images, audio, video, and texts that combine structured, unstructured, and semi-structured formats. Storing, mining, and analyzing such data are quite complex. The Big Data landscape consists of five main layers:

1. **Data ingestion layer:** The layer transports data from the source or multiple sources and delivers it to the data storage site or landing area for further processing. The data can be ingested in batches, streamed in real-time, or both.
2. **Data storage layer:** The storage layer focuses on the ideal way to store the various data types and models. Data can be stored in traditional Data Warehouses or Data Lakes.
3. **Data processing layer:** The data is cleaned and transformed to make it analytics-ready.
4. **The analytics layer** is where advanced analysis is done on the transformed data to extract information and insights. Finally, the results and insights are visualized through pre-built reports or dashboards.
5. **Data management and security layer:** The layer ensures that the Big Data landscape is secure and adheres to the best practices, governance, and compliance procedures.

Data warehouses and data lakes are the most widely used storage repositories for Big Data. Data warehouses were the first storage architecture used for data analytics. With the advent of Big Data and digitization, organizations and enterprises are flooded with high volumes of raw unstructured, heterogeneous data that has potential value. Data lakes are the solution to store these vastly changing multi-format multi-source data for evolving business use cases.

Big Data integration is a set of processes, tools, and technology used to retrieve information from massive heterogeneous sources and transform it into meaningful information for data analysis. The two data integration processes used in Big Data are ETL and ELT. The letters stand for E – Extract (the process of pulling or extracting the data from various source systems), T – Transform (the process of cleansing, scrubbing, or transforming the structure of the information so that it can integrate with the target systems for analysis), and L – Load (the process of storing or depositing the transformed data into a data warehouse or data lake or any data storage system).

ETL (Extract, Transform, Load) model is adopted when dealing with smaller datasets, usually structured data requiring complex transformations. It is generally used with batch processing in data warehouse environments. In ETL, the data is first transformed in the temporary staging area before loading into the central repository or data warehouse.

The ELT (Extract, Load, Transform) integration method is used when dealing with massive volumes of structured and unstructured data of very high complexity. First, the raw data is directly loaded into the repository or data lake without any transformation. Then, the relevant dataset is cleaned and scrubbed within the data lake when required. The ELT model is used in Data Lake architecture.

In recent years, various data lakes have emerged that combine the data management capability of data warehouse architecture and the flexibility of data lakes. This merged storage system is referred to as the Data Lakehouse. All three storage systems can store large amounts of information from multiple sources within an organization or in the cloud.

EXERCISES

Multiple Choice Questions

1. **Frequency distribution, variability, and measures of central tendency are some types of:**
   A. Confirmatory analysis
   B. Descriptive analysis
   C. Exploratory analysis
   D. Predictive analysis.
   Answer: B

   Explanation: Descriptive analysis or statistics helps to describe and summarize the basic features of a dataset using numerical calculations and tables. It allows the data analyst or data scientist to understand the data better. Frequency distribution, variability, and measures of central tendency are some types of descriptive analysis.

2. **Which of the following is not a type of exploratory analysis?**
   A. Univariate analysis
   B. Bivariate analysis
   C. Multivariate analysis
   D. Triple variate analysis
   Answer: D

Explanation
The three types of exploratory data analysis are:
- Univariate analysis where the characteristics and effects of a single variable on a set of data are explored, e.g., the mean of a population distribution. Univariate analysis results can be visualized with bar graphs, histograms, box plots, etc.
- Bivariate analysis where the correlation between two variables is explored. For example, ice-cream sales with the temperature or traffic accidents with age group. Scatter plots and histograms can be used to represent bivariate analysis visually.
- Multivariate analysis where comparative analysis of multiple variables is done. Multivariate analysis is the most complex. Cluster analysis, multiple regression analysis, principal component analysis (PCA), and factor analysis are just a few ways to perform multivariate analysis. In addition, scatter plots, contour plots, and multi-dimensional plots can be used to visualize multivariate analysis results.

3. **This is used to challenge the model:**
   A. Confirmatory analysis
   B. Descriptive analysis
   C. Exploratory analysis
   D. Predictive analysis
   Answer: A
   Explanation: While exploratory data analysis summarizes the data with the fewest possible predictor variables, confirmatory data analysis (CDA) is used to confirm or reject the model. The main aim is to challenge the model and quantify the extent of deviation from the proposed model.
   CDA involves testing hypotheses and producing estimates, regression, and variance analyses.

4. **This calculates the approximated or most likely future outcome from historical or past data:**
   A. Confirmatory analysis
   B. Descriptive analysis
   C. Exploratory analysis
   D. Predictive analysis
   Answer: D
   Explanation: Predictive analysis calculates the approximated or most likely future outcome from historical or past data. Organizations leverage Big Data and Machine Learning to forecast potential scenarios to help drive strategic decisions.

5. **This works on probability by taking a small sample instead of working on the whole population:**
   A. Confirmatory analysis
   B. Inferential analysis
   C. Exploratory analysis
   D. Predictive analysis
   Answer: B
   Explanation: Inferential analysis is a statistical approach to making inferences, theories, or conclusions by analyzing a sample sector or dataset for a result and making inferences about the entire sector or population based on that result. In other words, it works on probability by taking a small sample instead of working on the whole population. Inferential analysis is mainly used in Estimations and Hypothesis.

6. **This breaks stream of textual data into words, terms, sentences, symbols:**
   A. Tokenization	B. Lower casing
   C. Stemming	D. Lemmatization
   Answer: A
   Explanation: Tokenization breaks a stream of textual data into words, terms, sentences, symbols, or some other meaningful elements called tokens. A tokenizer separates information into units that may be considered distinct from unstructured data and natural language text.

7. **"Big Data" is converted to "Big Data" in:**
   A. Tokenization	B. Lower casing
   C. Stemming	D. Lemmatization
   Answer: B
   Explanation: Lower casing is a standard text preprocessing technique where the input text is converted to a lower-case format. Hence "Big Data", "Big Data", "Big Data", and "BIG data" are converted to "Big Data" and treated the same way. The lower casing is quite helpful in reducing duplication and getting the correct counts or TF-IDF values.

8. **"feels" and "feeling" are converted to "feel" in:**
   A. Tokenization	B. Lower casing
   C. Stemming	D. Lemmatization
   Answer: C
   Explanation: Finding a word's root and cutting it off at its stem is a procedure known as stemming. For example, applying stemming to the words "feels" and "feeling" will stem the suffix into "feel". Stemming is a rule-based algorithm.

9. **This ensures the base word result is proper and reveals its intended meaning:**
   A. Tokenization	B. Lower casing
   C. Stemming	D. Lemmatization
   Answer: D
   Explanation: Lemmatization is used in NLP and NLU. It is similar to stemming in reducing the words to their stem words. But unlike stemming, where the prefix or suffix is blindly cut out, lemmatization ensures the base word result is proper and reveals its intended meaning. For instance, the stemmer tool would stem "diversifying" and "diversified" to give an illogical word, "diversifi". However, lemmatization would convert the words to the root word or lemma, "diversify". As a result, lemmatization is slower than the stemming process.
   Example: Lemmatization of
   [The platform delivers completely and authentic content. It is a simple language and easy to understanding.]

   produces

   [The platform deliver complete and authentic content It be a simple language and easy to understand].

10. **This assigns categories to unstructured text documents based on their content. The categories may have a hierarchical structure and are predefined with descriptors:**
    A. Text categorization
    B. Text clustering
    C. Summarization
    D. Text split
    Answer: A
    Explanation: Text categorization in text analytics assigns categories to unstructured text documents based on their content. The categories may have a hierarchical structure and are predefined with descriptors like concepts, patterns, rules, etc. A text document is assigned to a category if it matches the descriptors/rules. For example, news articles categorized based on topic or theme, web pages categorized under hierarchical definitions, and others. Some algorithms used in text categorization are decision trees, SVM, K-nearest neighbor, and neural networking.

11. **This is the technique of automatically organizing unclassified, unlabeled textual data into groups of documents for further analysis:**
    A. Text categorization
    B. Text clustering
    C. Summarization
    D. Text split
    Answer: B
    Explanation: Text clustering is the technique of automatically organizing unclassified, unlabeled textual data into groups or clusters of documents for further analysis. It works on the premise that the content of documents in a specific cluster is similar to the content in other clusters. Unlike categorization, text clustering groups documents together without predefined categories or topics as references. Instead, it classifies based on similarity measures between documents. K-means is a commonly used algorithm in text clustering. Text clustering finds applications in customer segmentation, identifying anomalies, data exploration, etc.

12. **This is the process of condensing textual material while maintaining the essential points and purposes of the original:**
    A. Text categorization
    B. Text clustering
    C. Summarization
    D. Text split
    Answer: C
    Explanation: Text summarization is the process of condensing textual material while maintaining the essential points and purposes of the original. It provides a synopsis of massive textual data for making a concise and intelligible summary of important points of a document. This is extremely useful in automated content research, patent research, Science and R&D, where an abstract of the paper can be made. In addition, text summarization integrates the various methods that use text categorization, such as decision trees, neural networks, swarm intelligence and regression models.

13. **This is used by organizations to determine which independent or predictor variables (input) holds the most influence on over-dependent (output) variable:**
    A. Regression modelling
    B. Classification modelling
    C. Clustering model
    D. Outliers model
    Answer: A
    Explanation: Regression models are used in statistical analysis to understand the relationship between variables and their associated strengths. Regression models are used by organizations to determine which independent or predictor variables (input) hold the most influence on over-dependent (output) variables.

14. **This model addresses questions corresponding to "Will the company stock increase in the market?" or "What is the likelihood of customer churn?"**
    A. Regression modelling
    B. Classification modelling
    C. Clustering model
    D. Outliers model
    Answer: B
    Explanation: The classification model is used in predictive analytics to sort or categorize the data by broadly analyzing historical data. It can be binary, i.e., the result is classified into two discrete classes: 'Yes/No', 'High/Low', 'Good/Bad', etc. The model addresses questions corresponding to "Will the company stock increase in the market?" or "What is the likelihood of customer churn?" or "Is the email spam?" and similar other business questions. Multi-class classifies the data into more than two classes, e.g., movie classification, document classification, customer classification, etc.

15. **This model segregates the data into groups that have similar attributes:**
    A. Regression modelling
    B. Classification modelling
    C. Clustering model
    D. Outliers model
    Answer: C
    Explanation: The clustering model is a time-effective way to quickly sort through the vast arena of Big Data and deliver the answers. It is widely used for targeted marketing campaigns. The model segregates the data into clusters or groups that have similar attributes. For example, algorithms can efficiently sort customers into similar groups based on common characteristics and buying patterns. This can enable companies to devise selective and focused promotion strategies.

16. **This model identifies unusual data that deviates from the norm in isolation or with different categories and numbers:**
    A. Regression modelling
    B. Classification modelling
    C. Clustering model
    D. Outliers model
    Answer: D
    Explanation: The outlier model predicts abnormal activities and transactions. The model identifies unusual data that deviates from the norm in isolation or with different categories and numbers. It can detect atypical data entries within a dataset

and accurately predict fraudulent transactions. The anomaly detection can also predict the possibility of fraud or other losses that can cost the company millions of rupees, besides loss of reputation.

17. **This model uses different data points at specific periods from historical data, say the past 5+ years or more, to develop a numerical metric that will predict trends for the future:**
    A. Regression modelling
    B. Classification modelling
    C. Clustering model
    D. Time-series model
    Answer: D
    Explanation: The time-series model uses Big Data to observe past data patterns to predict future patterns. The time-series model uses time as an input parameter. The model uses different data points at specific periods from historical data, say the past 5+ years or more, to develop a numerical metric that will predict trends for the future period using that metric. Time-series forecasting is one of the most often-used predictive analytics models in business since it can take several input variables simultaneously.

18. **The goal of this model is to form a formula or regression coefficient that describes the dependent variable in terms of the independent variable:**
    A. Linear regression algorithm
    B. Logistic regression algorithm
    C. Random forest algorithm
    D. Deep learning algorithm
    Answer: A
    Explanation: Linear regression is used to find the linear relationship between a dependent or response variable and the independent or predictor variables. The goal is to form a formula or regression coefficient that describes the dependent variable in terms of the independent variable. Once this relationship is quantified, the dependent variable can be predicted for any instance of an independent variable.

19. **This model can be used to identify prospective customers or the winning chances of an election candidate:**
    A. Linear regression algorithm
    B. Logistic regression algorithm
    C. Random forest algorithm
    D. Deep learning algorithm
    Answer: B
    Explanation: Logistic regression is a supervised classification algorithm. It is used to predict the probability of the occurrence of an event. The output variable is finite (Yes/No, 0/1, true/false) rather than continuous with infinite values, as seen with linear regression. The output of logistic regression closer to 1 indicates that the variable fits within the category, and that closer to 0 indicates that the input variable is not likely to fit within the category. Logistic regression can be used to identify prospective customers or the winning chances of an election candidate.

20. **Instead of constructing a single complex tree with many branches of logic, this constructs many simple small trees:**
    A. Linear regression algorithm
    B. Logistic regression algorithm
    C. Random forest algorithm
    D. Deep learning algorithm
    Answer: C
    Explanation: Random Forest is a variation of decision and regression trees and uses both to organize and label the data. The Random Forest algorithm is well-adopted to classify large volumes of data. Instead of constructing a single complex tree with many branches of logic, a random forest constructs many simple small trees, each unrelated to the other. Each tree evaluates the instances of data and determines a categorization. Once all the trees complete their data evaluation, the process merges the individual results to create a final category prediction, and this method is known as an ensemble method.

20. **This begins with the data ingestion layer:**
    A. Data pipeline
    B. Data warehouse
    C. Data lake
    D. Data Lake Home
    Answer: A
    Explanation: The data pipeline begins with the data ingestion layer. The layer transports data from the source or multiple sources and delivers it to the data storage site or landing area for further processing. A good architecture system can push or pull all data formats.

21. **This acts as a repository to store the organizational data from internal and external sources, including text files, emails, customer feedback, application data and logs, business, transactional data, and many more:**
    A. Data pipeline
    B. Data warehouse
    C. Data lake
    D. Data Lake Home
    Answer: B
    Explanation: The data warehouse acts as a repository to store the organizational data from internal and external sources, including text files, emails, customer feedback, application data and logs, business, transactional data, and many more. The warehouse is optimized for relational data from transaction systems. The data structure is hierarchical with the predefined schema to optimize fast SQL queries.

22. **This can store a massive amount of disparate, unfiltered data that can be used later by the analytics team:**
    A. Data pipeline
    B. Data warehouse
    C. Data lake
    D. Data Lake Home
    Answer: C
    Explanation: Data Lakes are most appropriate for Big Data. Data lakes can store a massive amount of disparate, unfiltered data that can be used later by the analytics

team. The raw data consisting of structured, semi-structured, or unstructured data, e.g., spreadsheets, relational database files, mobile apps, logs, XML, social media, sensors, and other IoT data, is directly loaded into the Data Lake in an open format that can be used for a future purpose. Analysts process the required datasets for insight analysis when a purpose or analytics project is defined.

23. **This is an evolving Big Data storage architecture that aims to combine the benefits of the data warehouse and the data lake, thus eliminating the drawbacks of both.**
    A. Data pipeline
    B. Data warehouse
    C. Data lake
    D. Data Lake Home
    Answer: D
    Explanation: Data Lakehouse is an evolving Big Data storage architecture that aims to combine the benefits of the data warehouse and the data lake, thus eliminating the drawbacks of both. This hybrid model is called the Data Lakehouse. It has a dual-layer architecture with the warehouse layer sitting over the data lake layer, thus providing the much-needed governance and quality controls that were weak in data lakes, while also having the flexibility and lower TCO (Total Cost of Ownership) storage advantages.

Short-answer Questions

1. **What is Descriptive Analysis?**
   Descriptive analysis or statistics helps to describe and summarize the basic features of a dataset using numerical calculations and tables. It allows the data analyst or data scientist to understand the data better.
   Frequency distribution, variability, and measures of central tendency are some types of descriptive analysis.

2. **What is Exploratory Data Analysis?**
   Exploratory data analysis (EDA) is an approach to analyzing and summarizing the main characteristics of data using visual techniques like statistical graphics and other data visualization methods. EDA typically follows descriptive data analysis, where the calculated numerical data values are plotted graphically to understand trends and patterns.

3. **What are the types of Exploratory Data Analysis?**
   There are three types of exploratory data analysis.
   - Univariate analysis where the characteristics and effects of a single variable on a set of data are explored, e.g., the mean of a population distribution. Univariate analysis results can be visualized with bar graphs, histograms, box plots, etc.
   - Bivariate analysis where the correlation between two variables is explored. For example, ice-cream sales with the temperature or traffic accidents with age group. Scatter plots and histograms can be used to represent bivariate analysis visually.

- Multivariate analysis where comparative analysis of multiple variables is done. Multivariate analysis is the most complex form of analysis. Cluster analysis, multiple regression analysis, PCA, and factor analysis are just a few ways to perform multivariate analysis. In addition, scatter plots, contour plots, and multi-dimensional plots can be used to visualize multivariate analysis results.

EDA establishes the data's underlying structure, the key variables, estimating parameters, missing data, anomalies, and margins of error. In other words, it explains the data with the fewest possible predictor variables. R and S-PLUS are programming packages used for EDA.

4. What is Confirmatory Data Analysis?

While exploratory data analysis summarizes the data with the fewest possible predictor variables, confirmatory data analysis (CDA) is used to confirm or reject the model. The main aim is to challenge the model and quantify the extent of deviation from the proposed model.

CDA involves testing hypotheses and producing estimates, regression, and variance analyses.

5. What is Predictive Analysis?

Predictive analysis calculates the approximated or most likely future outcome from historical or past data. Organizations leverage Big Data and Machine Learning to forecast potential scenarios to help drive strategic decisions.

6. What is Inferential Analysis?

Inferential analysis is a statistical approach to making inferences, theories, or conclusions by analyzing a sample sector or dataset for a result and making inferences about the entire sector or population based on that result. In other words, it works on probability by taking a small sample instead of working on the whole population. Inferential analysis is mainly used in estimation and testing hypothesis.

7. What is Tokenization?

Tokenization breaks a stream of textual data into words, terms, sentences, symbols, or some other meaningful elements called tokens. A tokenizer separates information into units that may be considered distinct from unstructured data and natural language text.

8. What is Lower Casing?

Lower casing is a standard text preprocessing technique where the input text is converted to a lower-case format. Hence, "Big Data", "Big Data", "Big Data", and "BIG data" are converted to "Big Data" and treated the same way.

Lower casing is quite helpful in reducing duplication and getting the correct counts or TF-IDF values. However, it is not a useful function when applying POS tagging. The same work may have different meanings, e.g., "Major" is a military ranking and noun, while "major" can be an adjective meaning something very important. Capital letters are significant for extracting information, like names and locations. Similarly, in sentiment analysis, the meaning attached to "a big miss in service" differs from "a BIG miss in service" as the latter may refer to anger, disappointment, or frustration.

9. **What is Stemming?**

   Finding a word's root and cutting it off at its stem is a procedure known as stemming. For example, applying stemming to the words 'feels' and 'feeling' will stem the suffix into 'feel'. Stemming is a rule-based algorithm; sometimes, the word may lose its meaning with stemming. For example, applying stemmer to the following sentences:

   [The platform delivers complete and authentic content. It is a simple language and easy to understand.]

   produces

   [The platform deliv complet and authent content. It is a simple language and easy to understand].

   As the above example shows, the stemmer removed the suffix 'ers,' 'e,' 'ic' and others, thus giving wrong English words like 'deliv,' 'authent.'

   The efficiency of information retrieval systems is increased by stemming. It is used in Natural Language Processing (NLP) and Natural Language Understanding (NLU). Porter Stemmer and Snowball Stemmer are the common stemming methods used.

10. **What is Lemmatization?**

    Lemmatization is also used in NLP and NLU. It is similar to stemming in that it reduces the words to their stem words. But unlike stemming, where the prefix or suffix is blindly cut out, lemmatization ensures the base word result is proper and reveals its intended meaning. For instance, the stemmer tool would stem 'diversifying' and 'diversified' to give an illogical word 'diversifi'. However, lemmatization would convert the words to the root word or lemma 'diversify'. As a result, lemmatization is slower than the stemming process.

    Example: Lemmatization of

    [The platform delivers complete and authentic content. It is a simple language and easy to understand.]

    produces

    [The platform deliver complete and authentic content. It be a simple language and easy to understand].

11. **What is Stop-word removal?**

    Stop words commonly occur, such as 'a', 'an', 'but', 'the', etc., that do not provide significant information for downstream analysis. These words do not offer much value in terms of analysis of the whole sentence and hence can be removed. There are stop-word packages for all major languages, for example, spaCy, NLTK, etc. In the English language, the common stop words include articles, pronouns, prepositions, conjunctions, and others.

12. **What are the advantages of the Stop-word removal?**

    Stop-word removal is done after tokenization. It helps in bringing more focus to the essential information in the text. In addition, it can potentially help in:
    - Improving performance as fewer words are left, thereby increasing accuracy in clustering and classification.
    - Preventing stop words from being indexed.
    - Decreasing dataset size, thus reducing the time to train the model.
    - Enabling faster retrieval of data from the database. For example, Google applies stop-word removal in their search engine.

    However, it should be used with discretion. The stop-words may provide valuable information in POS tagging and sentiment analysis. For example, the stop word removal function on the text 'I was not happy with their service.' gives the output 'happy service', which is an incorrect sentiment.

13. **What is POS Tagging?**

    Part-of-Speech (POS) tagging is an NLP process where each word in a sentence is tagged to its part of speech. It is instrumental in providing a linguistic indicator of how a term is used within the scope of a phrase, sentence, or document. The word is tagged or annotated as a proper noun - NN, verb - VBZ (like works, gives, plays), determiner - DT, adjective - JJ, adverb - RB, preposition - IN, conjunction pronoun - PRPS, etc.

14. **What are the types of POS Taggers?**

    There are two types of POS taggers: 1. Rule-based, and 2. Stochastic.

    As the name suggests, a rule-based POS tagger tags the word by the grammatical rules of a particular language. It is done by analyzing the meaning of the preceding and the succeeding word. Brill's tagger is an example of a rule-based tagger.

    Stochastic (or Statistical) POS Tagger tags a word by using word frequency measurement or tag sequence probabilities. In frequency measurement, the tag is applied to the unclear word if the word frequently occurs in the training set. In the probability method, the best tag for a given word is determined by the probability it occurs with the *n* previous tags. Finally, the highest occurring tag is applied to the word. This approach is also known as the *n*-gram approach.

15. **What is Parsing?**

    Finding a text's syntactic structure is the process of parsing. It follows POS tagging as the algorithm uses the grammar of the language the text is written in. In addition, parsing is used in NLP to report any syntax or commonly occurring errors. There are two types of parsing – shallow parsing and deep parsing. Shallow parsing is also referred to as chunking. It is the process of analyzing a sentence and extracting phrases to group them into noun phrases, verb phrases, etc. It is used in less complex NLP applications, for instance, text mining and information extraction.

Deep parsing gives more structure to the POS-tagged text. It is represented as a tree structure and used in complex NLP applications such as dialogue systems like the Watson QA system.

16. What is Text Index?

Text Indexing is a processing step to extract statistics considered necessary for representing the information available and/or to allow a fast search of its content. The most popular text indexing technique for data retrieval is inverted indices. The method consists of two indexed tables – the document table that consists of the document id and a list of pointers or tokens. The token terms are grouped in alphabetical order, and an array-like structure is formed containing the doc ID and the terms grouped, creating an inverted index.

17. What is Information Extraction (IE) in text mining?

Information Extraction, commonly referred to as IE, is the process of extracting meaningful information from a massive set of unstructured or semi-structured text formats. The technique includes tokenization and identification of named entities, key phrases, sentence segmentation, and parts of speech to establish the relationship between entities and attributes.

The extracted entities, their attributes and relationships, and other related information are stored in a database for easy access and retrieval.

18. What is Information Retrieval (IR) in text mining?

Information Retrieval or IR is extracting relevant information and associated patterns based on a particular set of words or phrases. While IE focuses more on text extraction, IR is all about retrieving a set of documents that are relevant to the users' information needs. For example, web search engines like Google extensively use information retrieval systems. The IR system does not directly provide the same document or information. Instead, the system reports on the existence and location of documents that might contain the required information.

19. What is Text Categorization in the text mining process?

Text categorization in text analytics assigns categories to unstructured text documents based on their content. The categories may have a hierarchical structure and are predefined with descriptors like concepts, patterns, rules, etc. A text document is assigned to a category if it matches the descriptors/rules. For example, news articles are categorized based on topic or theme, web pages are categorized under hierarchical definitions, and others. Some algorithms used in text categorization are decision trees, SVM, K-nearest neighbor, and neural networking.

At times, text categorization is identified with text classification. Text Classification uses a combination of NLP and machine learning to categorize text documents based on their contents.

20. **What is Text Clustering in the text mining process?**
Text clustering is the technique of automatically organizing unclassified, unlabeled textual data into groups or clusters of documents for further analysis. It works on the premise that the content of documents in a specific cluster is similar to the content in other clusters.

Unlike categorization, text clustering groups documents together without predefined categories or topics as references. Instead, it classifies based on similarity measures between documents. K-means is a commonly used algorithm in text clustering. Text clustering finds applications in customer segmentation, identifying anomalies, data exploration, etc.

21. **What is Summarization in the text mining process?**
Text summarization is the process of condensing textual material while maintaining the essential points and purposes of the original. It provides a synopsis of massive textual data for making a concise and intelligible summary of important points of a document. This is extremely useful in automated content research, patent research, Science and R&D, where an abstract of the paper can be made. In addition, text summarization integrates the various methods that use text categorization, such as decision trees, neural networks, swarm intelligence, and regression models.

22. **Write any three applications of Text Analytics.**
    - **Fraud Detection**: Financial institutions and insurance companies can use text mining techniques for fraud detection. The system can analyze extensive collections of customer files and automatically flag customers or files with a high probability of fraud for the officials' focus.
    - **Contextual Ad Placement**: Digital advertising is a growing field in text analytics and mining applications. Text mining helps companies understand a webpage's context and place targeted ads to enable higher ROI, personalization, and re-engagement. For example, while reading an article on indoor plants, you may get an ad from plant nurseries due to their relevance.
    - **Social Media Monitoring**: Social media is a valuable market and customer intelligence source. Text analytics is used in social media (or the voice of the customer) to extract opinions, emotions, and overall public sentiment towards the enterprise's brand, services, or product. Enterprises use sentiment analysis to analyze the textual content through word choice, including chat acronyms, emojis, and others, to quantify customer sentiment, whether positive, negative or neutral, and better understand how they connect with the customers.

23. **What is Predictive Analytics?**
Predictive analytics refers to using historical data, machine learning, and artificial intelligence to predict what will happen in the future. Predictive analytics utilizes statistical modeling, data mining, machine learning, and deep learning algorithms to

extract the required information from Big Data and behavioral project patterns for the future. This will enable enterprises to change their strategy for revenue growth, operational efficiencies, and risk reduction. For example, predictive analytics is used by retail companies like Walmart and Amazon to understand customers' buying behavior and purchase patterns to identify high-value customers, strategize promotions, cross-sell, and many other tactical plans.

24. **What is Regression Modelling?**
Regression models are used in statistical analysis to understand the relationship between variables and their associated strengths. Regression models are used by organizations to determine which independent or predictor variables (input) hold the most influence on over-dependent (output) variables. It is called simple regression when only one dependent and independent variable exists. While on the other hand, when many independent variables influence one dependent variable, we call it multiple regression. Many regression algorithms depend on the relationship between the variables, like linear regression, multi-linear regression, time-series regression, logistic regression model, etc.

25. **What is Classification Model?**
Classification model is used in predictive analytics to sort or categorize the data by broadly analyzing historical data. It can be binary, i.e., the result is classified into two discrete classes: 'Yes/No', 'High/Low', 'Good/Bad', etc. The model addresses questions corresponding to "Will the company stock increase in the market?" or "What is the likelihood of customer churn?" or "Is the email spam?" and other similar business questions. Multi-class classifies the data into more than two classes, e.g., movie classification, document classification, customer classification, etc.

The classification model is simple and can be easily retrained with new data. Some popular algorithms used in the classification model are KNN, Random Forest, Decision Trees, Logistic Regression, and SVM, among others.

26. **What is Clustering Model?**
The clustering model is a time-effective way to quickly sort through the vast arena of Big Data and deliver the answers. It is widely used for targeted marketing campaigns. The model segregates the data into clusters or groups that have similar attributes. For example, algorithms can efficiently sort customers into similar groups based on common characteristics and buying patterns. This can enable companies to devise selective and focused promotion strategies.

27. **What are the types of Clustering?**
There are two types of clustering – hard clustering, which categorizes whether the data point belongs to the data cluster, and soft clustering, which assigns the data probability of the data point of joining a cluster. In soft clustering, the data point can belong to more than one cluster. The most used clustering algorithm is K-means.

28. What is Outlier model?

The outlier model predicts abnormal activities and transactions. The model identifies unusual data that deviates from the norm in isolation or with different categories and numbers. It can detect atypical data entries within a dataset and accurately predict fraudulent transactions. The anomaly detection can also predict the possibility of fraud or other losses that can cost the company millions in loss of reputation.

For example, a spike in a credit card withdrawal in a single day that is not typical behavior of the customer may be cause for concern. Isolation forest and SVM are algorithms used in the outlier model.

29. What is Time-series model?

The time-series model uses Big Data to observe past data patterns to predict future patterns. The time-series model uses time as an input parameter. The model uses different data points at specific periods from historical data, say the past 5+ years or more, to develop a numerical metric that will predict trends for the future period using that metric. Time-series forecasting is one of the most often-used predictive analytics models in business since it can take several input variables simultaneously.

30. What is Decision Tree?

Decision trees are classification-based algorithms represented graphically like a top-down tree structure, starting with the root node from where the decision tree starts, then branching out with alternative choices or decisions till it arrives at a final decision. Three nodes represent the tree.
- Decision node branches to a course of action or alternate choices where a decision must be made. It is represented as a square.
- The chance node is represented as a circle that indicates the probability of a result.
- The end node or leaf node is the final node or decision that cannot be divided further.

31. What are the types of decision trees?

There are two kinds of trees: classification trees, where the responses are categorical; and regression trees, where the response variable is continuous or numerical. Decision trees can get quite complex and large, as the branches and variables increase. The complexity is typically controlled by pruning or intentionally removing the levels of questions for the best fit.

32. Explain Linear Regression algorithm.

Linear regression is used to find the linear relationship between a dependent or response variable and the independent or predictor variables. The goal is to form a formula or regression coefficient that describes the dependent variable in terms of the independent variable. Once this relationship is quantified, the dependent variable can be predicted for any instance of an independent variable. For example, defining the likelihood of having blood pressure (dependent variable) in relation to age, weight, and sex (predictor variables). A scatter plot can show whether the relationship is linear or not. The regression coefficient is shown by the slope of the line in the scatter plot.

33. **Explain Logistic Regression algorithm.**

    Logistic Regression is a supervised classification algorithm. It is used to predict the probability of the occurrence of an event. The output variable is finite (Yes/No, 0/1, True/False) rather than continuous with infinite values, as seen with linear regression. The output of logistic regression closer to 1 indicates that the variable fits within the category, and those closer to 0 indicate that the input variable is not likely to fit within the category. Logistic regression can be used to identify prospective customers or the winning chances of an election candidate.

34. **What is Random Forest algorithm?**

    Random Forest is a variation of decision and regression trees and uses both to organize and label the data. The Random Forest algorithm is well-adapted to classify large volumes of data. Instead of constructing a single complex tree with many branches of logic, a random forest constructs many simple small trees, each unrelated to the other. Each tree evaluates the instances of data and determines a categorization. Once all the trees complete their data evaluation, the process merges the individual results to create a final category prediction, and this method is known as an ensemble method.

35. **What is Deep Learning?**

    Artificial neural networks are used in deep learning, a type of machine learning, to carry out complex calculations on vast volumes of data. The purpose is to program a computer to emulate the human brain, i.e., process data, identify patterns and make an informed decision. Deep learning algorithms can work with almost any kind of data. However, solving complicated problems requires substantial computing power and large amounts of labeled data. Convolutional Neural Networks (CNNs), Recurrent Neural Networks (RNNs), Multilayer Perceptions (MLPs), and Self-Organizing Maps (SOMs) are examples of deep learning methods. Automated driving uses deep learning to automatically detect stop signs, traffic lights, obstacles, and pedestrians. In addition, deep learning enabled microscope is used in medical research to detect cancer cells.

36. **What is KNN?**

    K-Nearest Neighbour (KNN): KNN is a supervised classification algorithm. It uses labeled points (trained data) to learn how to label new points. Labeled points closest to the new point are considered their neighbors or 'K'. The distance between the new data point (test data) and the training data is calculated and sorted. The K-nearest neighbors are determined based on the minimum distance values. The category is then assigned to the test data based on the neighbors' majority voting or consensus. The higher the value of K or neighbors to be considered, the more effective the algorithm is. Lower values of K may result in overfitting, and very high values may result in a generic model that is difficult to predict. Euclidean distance, Manhattan, and Minkowski are distance metrics commonly used in KNN algorithms. KNN is often used in search applications, recommendation systems, and preprocessing of data.

37. **What is Fuzzy Logic Algorithm?**
Fuzzy logic is used in prediction problems with uncertain or imprecise data. The approach is based on the principle that a value can be between completely True and completely False, i.e., it can take any real value between 0 and 1. The logic consists of 4 parts – the rule base that contains all fuzzy rules and if/then conditions, fuzzification that converts the inputs (crisp values like temperature, pressure, etc., from sensors) to fuzzy sets, and inference that determines the degree of match between the fuzzy sets and rules to decide which rules are to be implemented. Then, the designated rules are combined to form the control actions, and finally, the defuzzification process converts the fuzzy sets to crisp values. Fuzzy logic is used in cruise control to adjust the throttle setting to set car speed and acceleration. Other applications include washing machines, vacuum cleaners, traffic control, NLP, antiskid braking systems, and many more.

38. **What is Neural Network?**
Neural Network is a machine learning algorithm that attempts to simulate the human brain. The algorithm is used to train a network with a set of training data and then test it with a group of test data to test the accuracy. The process continues till the network is stable and able to classify data accurately at all times. A neural network consists of three layers – outer, hidden, and output. The outer layer takes in the information or data from the outside world and processes and categorizes it for the next layer, the hidden layer. The hidden layer consists of many layer(s) that generate results using multiple algorithms and processes like cross-validation, back propagation, feed-forward calculations, and many others depending on the AI or ML application. The output layer then generates the finished product. The output layer may have only one output node if the question is binary or more than one node if the question is a multiclass classification problem.

39. **What is SVM?**
SVM is a supervised machine learning algorithm best used for classification techniques. For a simple example, let us take two classes. First, the algorithm works by making a separating line between two classes. Data points on either side of the line represent two categories, as shown in the figure below:

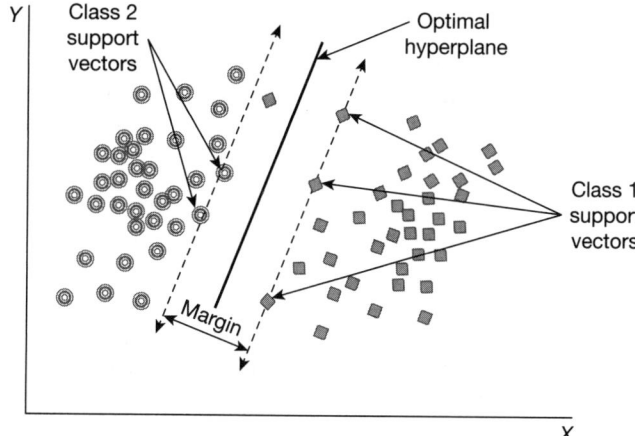

The separating line is called the hyperplane. Next, the SVM algorithm finds the points closest to the line from both classes. These points are called support vectors. The margin is the separation between the line and the support vectors. The most advantageous hyperplane is the one for which the margin is most significant. The linear hyperplane is affected by this procedure. The above example is for linear SVM, i.e., two-dimensional or linearly arranged data. However, SVM can also compute non-linear data using kernel function by adding a third dimension, Z.

40. What is functional programming model?

The functional programming model is a declarative programming paradigm where the code is organized as functions with clearly defined tasks. The function holds the logic, and the language implementation carries out the computation. The data is passed to the function as parameters, and the computation produces consistent outputs solely dependent on the inputs to the function. The key principle of the paradigm is the execution of a series of mathematical functions, and it has no dependency on the series of steps that precede the function.

41. What is Data Pipeline?

The data pipeline begins with the data ingestion layer. The layer transports data from the source or multiple sources and delivers it to the data storage site or landing area for further processing. A good architecture system can push or pull all data formats. Data sources are prioritized and categorized for routing to the correct destinations. Slight transformations in data are also made for smooth transmission. The data can be ingested in batches, streamed in real-time, or both.

42. What is Data Warehouse?

The data warehouse acts as a repository to store the organizational data from internal and external sources, including text files, emails, customer feedback, application data and logs, business, transactional data, and many more. The warehouse is optimized for relational data from transaction systems. The data structure is hierarchical with the predefined schema to optimize fast SQL queries.

43. What is Data Lake?

Data Lakes are most appropriate for Big Data. Data lakes can store a massive amount of disparate, unfiltered data that can be used later by the analytics team. The raw data consisting of structured, semi-structured, or unstructured data, e.g., spreadsheets, relational database files, mobile apps, logs, XML, social media, sensors, and other IoT data, is directly loaded into the Data Lake in an open format that can be used for a future purpose. Analysts process the required datasets for insight analysis when a purpose or analytics project is defined.

44. What is Data Lakehouse?

Data Lakehouse is an evolving Big Data storage architecture that aims to combine the benefits of the data warehouse and the data lake, thus eliminating the drawbacks of both. This hybrid model is called the Data Lakehouse. It has a dual-layer architecture with the warehouse layer sitting over the data lake layer, thus providing the much-needed governance and quality controls that were weak in data lakes while also having the flexibility and lower TCO (Total Cost of Ownership) storage advantages.

Essay-type Questions

1. What are the six steps or aspects to the Big Data technology agnostic framework?
2. Explain the different approaches of Big Data analysis in detail.
3. Explain Text Pre-processing stage in detail.
4. Explain POS Tagging, Parsing and Indexing in detail.
5. Explain Text Mining process in detail.
6. Explain Data Interpretation process in detail.
7. What is Predictive Analysis? Explain in detail along with the various predictive analysis models.
8. Explain the various Predictive Analytics algorithms in detail.
9. Explain Procedural vs. Functional Programming Models for Big Data with simple examples.
10. Explain the difference between ETL and ELT in detail.
11. Explain Big Data Architecture in detail.
12. Explain Big Data warehouse concept in detail.
13. Explain Data Lake concept in detail.
14. Explain Data Lakehouse concept in detail.

CHAPTER **5**

Fundamentals of Hadoop

> **LEARNING OBJECTIVES**
>
> In the previous chapters, we had discussed about the fundamentals of Big Data, the steps in doing analytics in Big Data and the details of Big Data Frameworks. In this chapter, we will learn about the problems with traditional large-scale systems and how Hadoop can help to resolve them. We will also examine Hadoop Architecture and Hadoop Ecosystem in detail.

5.1 Introduction

In this chapter, we will discuss about the problems with traditional large-scale systems and how Hadoop can act as a solution for the same. We will also discuss about Hadoop Architecture and Hadoop Ecosystem in detail.

5.2 Problems with Traditional Large-scale Systems

In a traditional approach, the data generated out of the organizations such as banks or stock markets and hospitals is given as input to the data system. A data system would then extract this data, and it would convert the data into a proper format and load this data onto the database. Now the end users can generate reports and perform analytics by acquiring this data. But as this data grows, it becomes a very challenging task to manage and process this data, and this is one of the fundamental drawbacks of using the traditional approach. Traditional Large Systems worked on a single machine with high-capacity CPUs, high storage databases, and higher memories. However, **expanding this beyond a limit** is not possible. Moreover, it takes a **higher processing time** on traditional systems due to the mega-size of the data. It also succumbs to the **single point of failure** (Refer Fig. 5.1), which means that if a single server machine crashes, then the entire system crashes, and it is a significant risk of traditional large-scale systems. These conventional methods store

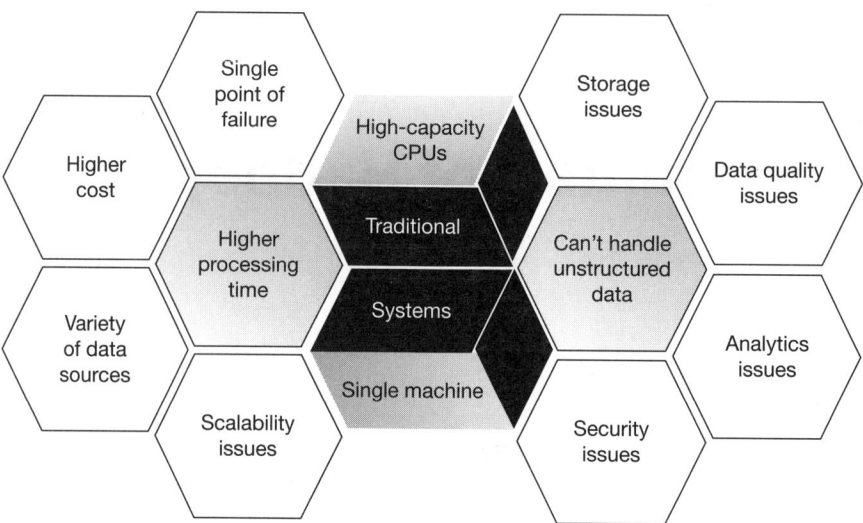

Figure 5.1 Limitations of traditional systems

the data and information in databases in rows and columns in a very structured format and **cannot handle unstructured data formats**. There are three categories of data.

1. **Structured data:** Data is in proper format; for example, the data present within the databases, the CSV files, and the Excel spreadsheets.
2. **Unstructured data:** This is the opposite of structured data, and it does not have any associated format; for example, image files, audio files and video files.
3. **Semi-structured data:** Here, the data has some form; for example, the data present within emails, log files, and Word document.

The growth of structured data is saturated. However, the data from modern-day businesses are too big and include sources like information from sensors, information weblogs, and trading information from the stock market. People tried increasing the database size and CPU capacity. However, it came to a limit where **database can't scale any further**, leading to a single point of failure.

Traditional methods of data storage have the following constraints:

- **Storage:** Data is vast; storing a massive amount of information is a challenge.
- **Security:** Due to the giant size, keeping the data secure is another challenge.
- **Analytics:** Analyzing data is difficult due to the enormous variety of data.
- **Data Quality:** Data is messy, inconsistent, and incomplete.
- **Discovery**: Algorithm to find patterns and insights are complicated.

Big Data systems emerged due to limitations in traditional systems as enterprises endeavour to gain valuable insights using the power of the internet, along with their internal and third-party data sources. Due to the growing volumes and intricacies of Big Data, the processing systems need the capability for heavy computations and complex algorithms are required for advanced data analytics. Advanced data analytics is used today for machine learning, predictive analytics, pattern identification, fraud detection and abundant exploratory analytics that need semi-structured and unstructured data processing. Big Data processing involves heavy computations and long processing hours that the traditional database systems are not equipped to handle. The traditional systems are built essentially for OLTP (Online Transaction Processing) and have limited scalability without incurring high cost and effort. Big Data systems, on the other hand, can process large heterogeneous volumes of data more efficiently and faster. Big Data systems support distributed architecture, have easy scalability, can ingest data from diverse sources, and perform real-time analytics and visualizations that are impossible using traditional systems.

The *V*'s of Big Data help to overcome the above problems of large-scale systems and indicate the requirements for a new approach. Currently, we are living in the mobile and social media revolution phase. The advent of social media sites such as Facebook, Twitter, LinkedIn, and several other social media applications has led to exponential growth of data. Automatic sensors (weather sensors and video surveillance cameras) are also sources of data. Such data proliferation has resulted in the Internet of Things. For example, Google's driverless car needs loads of data like GPS information and varieties of images from several cameras.

5.3 FIVE *V*'S OF BIG DATA

Volume: The structured data's growth is saturated. The popularity of unstructured data is growing fast (Fig. 5.2). It is growing at an exponential rate; handling volume of data is the need of the hour. The only technology that can address this is Big Data; this is another reason why Big Data has become so popular in the recent past.

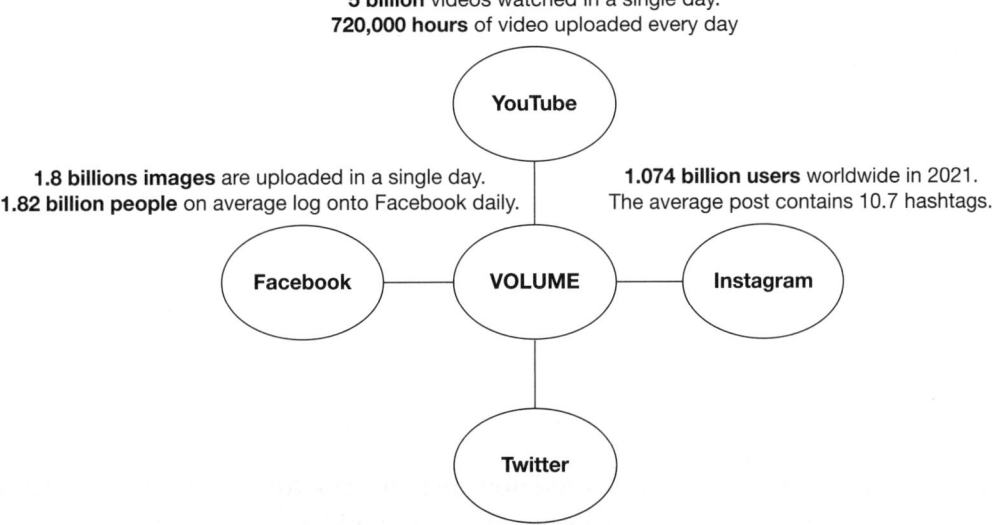

Figure 5.2 Volume of Data

Variety: Initially, we stored the data and information in databases in rows and columns in a structured format. Big Data is in several forms (states) such as email documents, sensor data, mobile devices data, etc. Data are Structured, Semi-Structured, and Unstructured. We need to have different, higher-end computing capabilities to process this data. Since Big Data is in several forms and variety of sources, handling variety (Fig. 5.3) is one of the characteristics of Big Data.

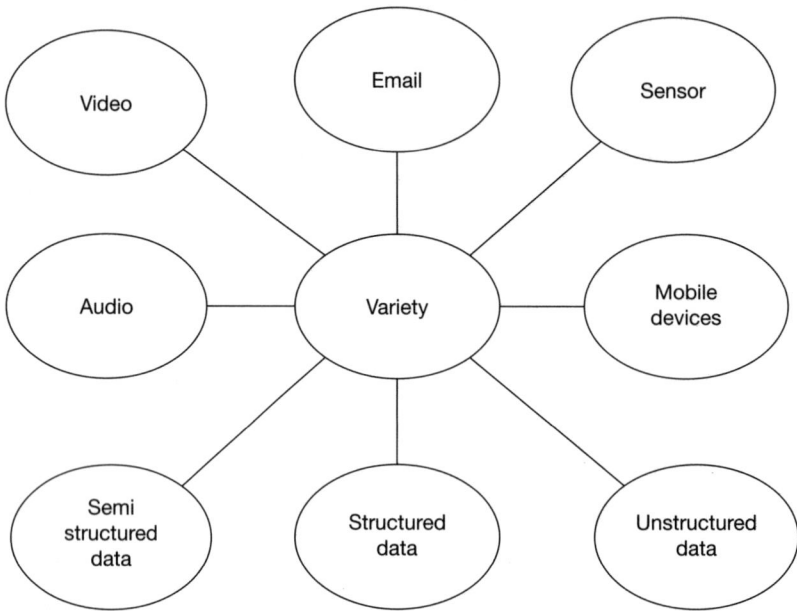

Figure 5.3 Variety of data

Velocity: Velocity is the speed of the collected data. It also refers to the speed in which the collected data is analyzed, and used (Fig. 5.4). For example, Google Map provides "the time to reach" the destination, using "real-time traffic data" based on the distance between the two places, the traffic in that place, current location using GPS, and all other relevant live (real-time) information. Since the traffic data is live (real-time), the speed of refreshing the data is very important here.

Veracity: Veracity means the quality of the data, the cleanliness of the data, meaningful data and trust in the data (Fig. 5.5). It is essential to have volumes of data at high speed, but it needs to be accurate with high quality, be relevant/meaningful and received at the right time to build confidence on the outcome of the analysis.

Value: Value is an integral part of data and plays an important role. If there is no meaningful value in the data, there is no need to analyze it. Data should add value to the end customer for impactful business insights.

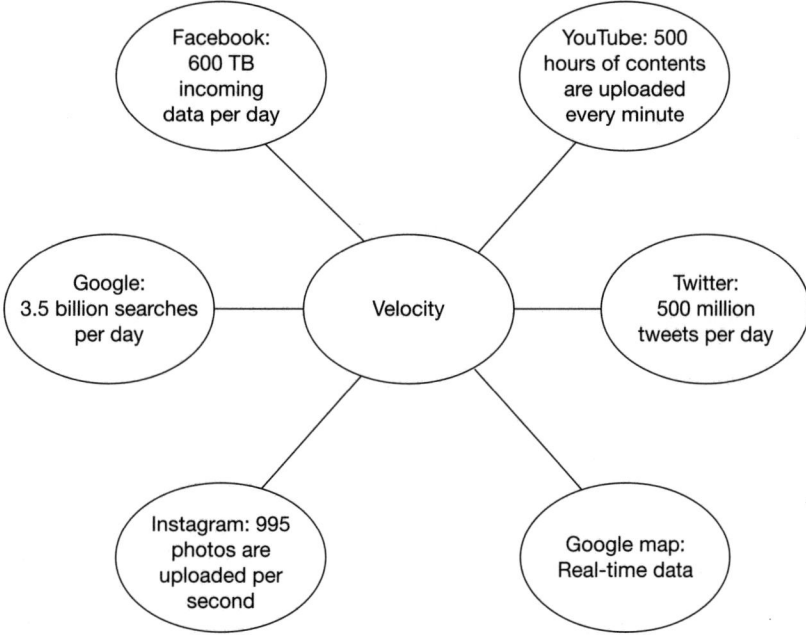

Figure 5.4 Velocity of data

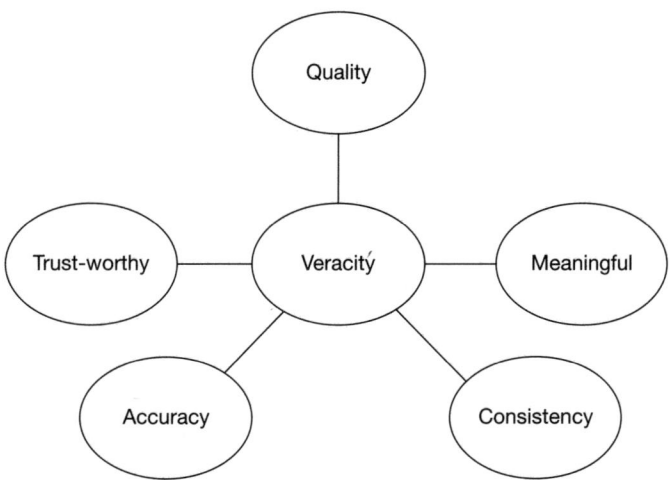

Figure 5.5 Veracity of data

5.4 What Is Hadoop?

Hadoop is the solution to the "Big Data" problems. This modern-day Big Data software overcomes the difficulties of the traditional large-scale systems. Apache Hadoop is a free open-source platform for distributed storage and distributed processing of extensive datasets on a computer cluster. It enables expanding memories in a distributed environment, thus overcoming the single point of failure problem. It can handle structured and unstructured data. Open source means it is freely available, and we can change its source code as per our requirements.

Distributed Software platform means it is a bunch of software that runs on a cluster of computers instead of just running on a single computer. It is a platform for ample data storage as well as Big Data processing. Hadoop runs on a cluster of computers inside a rack. It leverages the power of multiple computers for handling Big Data that uses distributed storage. Distributed storage is one of the main concepts of Hadoop. Big Data deals with terabytes of data/information. While adding more and more computers to the cluster, their hard drives will become part of the data storage. Hadoop offers parallel processing that can take advantage of all the individual CPUs. The horizontal scaling of the Hadoop cluster is linear.

5.5 History of Hadoop

During the 2000s when the number of data found on websites/internet began to rise to millions and billions, it was a bit difficult and time-consuming to quickly retrieve the data and information we were looking for. Doug Cutting and Mike Cafarella (2002) teamed up to create a web crawler called Nutch to address these issues. It is powerful to download web pages and store data. Apache Lucene was the first search engine to systematically sort, store, and retrieve such large amounts of data. But the performance of Nutch and Lucene was limited. These could not handle a large amount of data and information. The Big Data revolution started with Google, when the technology company shared its solution with the world through a white paper published in 2003 (Fig. 5.6). It was called GFS (Google File System), and MapReduce white paper (2004), which was the seed of the modern-day Hadoop. It opened the world's eyes to see how massive data can be stored and processed. In 2005, Doug Cutting and Mike Cafarella worked on implementing GFS and MapReduce into Nutch. In 2006, Doug Cutting joined Yahoo and worked extensively to transform this technology. Since 2006, the technology has continued to evolve. The ecosystem surrounding the technology has also continued to grow. In 2007, Doug Cutting gave the name "Hadoop" and also the mascot of Hadoop, the yellow elephant. Hadoop was the name of Doug Cutting's son's elephant toy; it was a yellow stuffed elephant. GFS is the concept behind HDFS (Hadoop Distributed File System). MapReduce is Hadoop's solution for distributed storage of information (distributed processing). In 2008, Yahoo successfully tested Hadoop with 1000 nodes. However, till 2008, Big Data was used only by dot-com companies like Google and Yahoo, and Facebook. Other organizations did not try this (Big Data).

In 2008, Yahoo released Hadoop as open-source project to ASF (Apache Software Foundation). An organization named "Cloudera" saw this as an opportunity, and came forward for a solution, to provide "support as a service". Several other companies joined this Big Data revolution after that. Cloudera foundation is a very critical item on the whole roadmap of the Big Data Hadoop revolution. Doug Cutting is the chief architect of Big

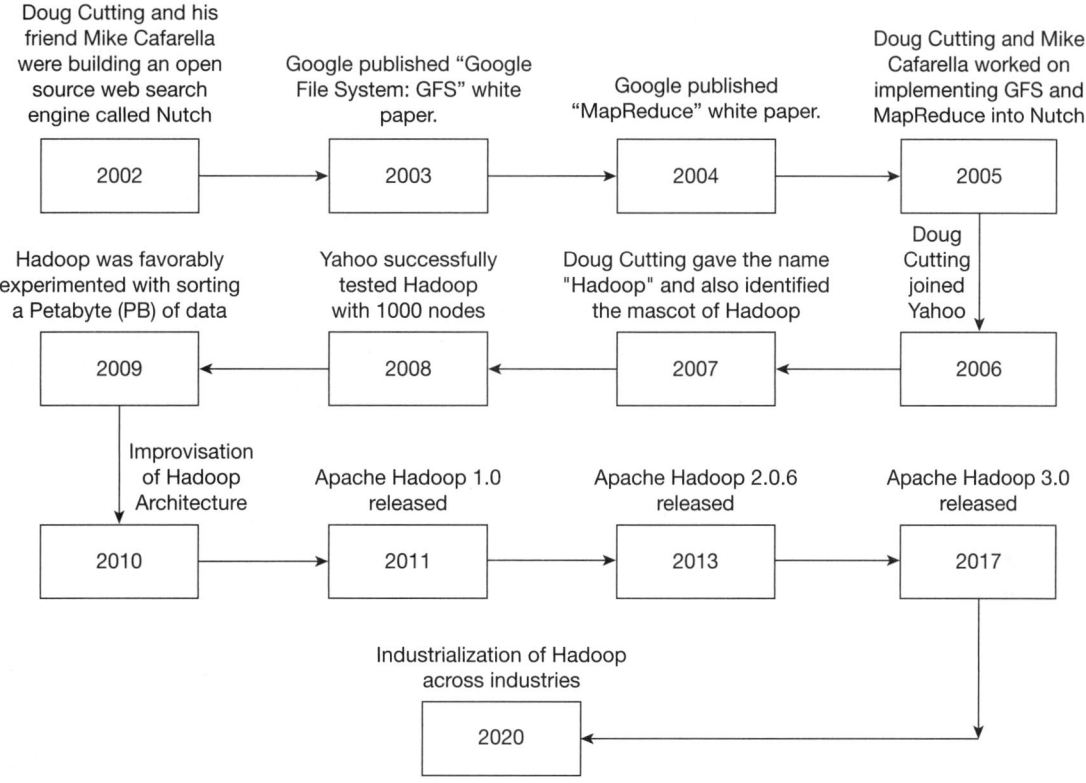

Figure 5.6 History of Hadoop

Data at Cloudera. Big Data gives a competitive advantage to modern-world organizations since it is a disruptive growing technology. Domains like Banking, Finance, Pharma, and Security use Big Data.

In 2009, Hadoop was favorably experimented with for sorting a Petabyte (PB) of data, handling billions of searches, and also indexing millions of web pages in less than 17 hours' time. Doug Cutting left Yahoo and joined Cloudera for spearheading Hadoop to other industries. In December of 2011, Apache Software Foundation released Apache Hadoop version 1.0. And later, in Aug 2013, Version 2.0.6 was available. In December 2017, Apache Software Foundation released the Hadoop version 3.0.

5.6 Why Hadoop?

In this section we shall examine some of the essential features offered by the Hadoop framework.

Hadoop is the solution to the "Big Data" problems (Table 5.1). In this framework, the code travels to the nodes where the data is present. Hadoop is different from a single-machine system. In the traditional approach, while executing a software program, the data is transferred from the data center onto the program execution machine. For example, let us say the data required by our program does exist at some data centers in India, and the program that requires this data does exist in Australia. Let us assume the data needed by a program is around 500 terabytes in size; transferring such a massive volume of data from India to Australia would consume a lot of bandwidth and time. Hadoop eliminates this problem by moving the code of few megabytes in size in Australia to the data center located in India. Then it compiles and executes the code locally on that data. Since this code is a few megabytes in size compared to the input data, which is 500 terabytes in size, this saves a lot of time and bandwidth.

Highly Economical: The first important feature offered by Hadoop is, it is a cost-effective system. Hadoop does not require any expensive or specialized hardware. In other words, it can be implemented on simple hardware referred to as commodity hardware (low cost per GB, singular cluster stores Petabytes of data). Its distributed file system has the provision of rapid data transfer rates among nodes. Hadoop also supports a heterogeneous cluster, and this is one of the most important features offered by the Hadoop framework. A heterogeneous cluster refers to a cluster within which each node can be from a different vendor, and each node could be running a different version and a different flavor of the operating system.

High Reliability: The next important feature on the list is, Hadoop supports a large cluster of nodes. Therefore a Hadoop cluster can be made up of hundreds and thousands of nodes. One of the main advantages of having a large cluster is that it offers more computing power and a huge storage system. Hadoop views all the data distributed across all hard drives in clusters as one single file system. It also keeps backup copies of all data in the cluster. In case of failures, it automatically recovers and makes that data resilient and reliable.

High Availability: Hadoop offers distributed data. The Hadoop framework takes care of splitting and distributing data across all the nodes within a cluster. It also replicates the data over the entire cluster. It is fault-tolerant. Distributed processing distributes the data's processing. Data continues to be available in Hadoop even if there is hardware failure. If any of the nodes within the cluster fails, the Hadoop framework will replace that particular machine (node) with another machine. It also replicates all the configuration settings and the data from this failed machine onto another newly replicated machine. Admins need not worry about all this once the automatic failover management is configured on the cluster. By default, each block creates three replicas across the cluster data. Moreover, we can change it as per need. So if any node goes down, we can recover data on that node from the other node.

High Scalability: Scalability refers to adding or removing the nodes, and adding or removing the hardware components to or from the cluster. We can easily add or remove a node to or from a cluster without bringing down or affecting the cluster operation. Even the individual hardware components such as RAM and hard drives can be added or removed from a cluster. Hadoop can utilize Amazon Web Services or Google, or any other vendors that sell cloud services. It adds as many computers as possible to handle the data. It is possible to add any number of nodes, enhancing the performance dramatically. Here, the data nodes (worker nodes)/Node manager can be scaled horizontally. The Name node works in a master service mode. Only data node/node manager runs on the worker nodes. Master nodes run the management services. There are only a few master nodes (often virtualized). Companies like Amazon, Facebook, Microsoft, Google, Yahoo, IBM, and General Electric run massive Hadoop clusters to store and process massive amounts of data.

High Throughput: Hadoop supports parallel processing of data. Therefore, the data can be processed simultaneously across all the nodes within the cluster, thus saving a lot of time. The amount of work done in unit time is Throughput. HDFS works on the model of the "Write Once and Read Many" principle. It simplifies the data coherency issues as data that is once written, cannot be modified. Thus, it provides high throughput data access. Hadoop works on the Data Locality principle. This principle states, "move the computation to data instead of moving the data to computation". In other words, computation is moved to the node where the data resides. This principle reduces network congestion and, therefore, enhances the overall system throughput.

No Schema: Apache Hadoop stores huge files as they are (raw). without specifying any schema.

Easy to use: There is no need for clients to deal with distributed computing; the framework takes care of all things. So it is easy to use.

Table 5.1 Why Hadoop

S. No	Characteristic	Remarks
1	Highly Economical	It runs on commodity hardware (Low cost per GB; Singular cluster stores petabytes of data).
2	High Reliability	In case of failures, it automatically recovers and makes that data resilient and reliable.
3	High Availability	It is Fault-tolerant. Distributed processing distributes the data's processing. Data is highly available in Hadoop despite the hardware failure.
4	High Scalability	It is possible to add any number of nodes enhancing the performance dramatically.
5	High Throughput	Hadoop works on the Data Locality principle, according to which it is better to move the computation.
6	No Schema	Apache Hadoop stores huge files as they are (raw) without specifying any schema.
7	Easy to use	No need for clients to deal with distributed computing; the framework takes care of all things. So it is easy to use.

5.7 Different Flavors of Hadoop

Various Flavors of Hadoop are classified as Open Source/Not an Open Source and also based on its front-end system (Table 5.2).

- Apache Hadoop (open source): Front end is Apache Ambari
- Horton work (open source): Front end Apache Ambari
- Cloudera (partially open source): Front end Cloudera manager
- Map R (not an open source): Front end Map R control system

Table 5.2 Different flavors of Hadoop

S.No	Name	Open Source	Front End
1	Apache Hadoop	Open Source	Apache Ambari
2	Horton work	Open Source	Apache Ambari
3	Cloudera	Partially Open Source	Cloudera Manager
4	Map R	Not an Open Source	Map R control system

Hartonworks was founded in 2011 by Rob Bearden. He co-founded the company with Yahoo, the same software team that helped develop Hadoop. The company provides us with a framework for integrating critical tools in Apache's Hadoop tools for Big Data management. This way, users do not have to bother to install the software/hardware they need individually. All they have to do is to select the tools (software) that will go into the desired configuration. These tools can all be easily installed on our computer without any problems. This is called HDP (Hartonworks Data Platform). Ambari is the management and administration software tool of HDP, which is acting on the 8080 port.

5.8 Different Modes of Hadoop

There are three modes of Hadoop System, namely standalone, pseudo-distributed mode and fully distributed mode (Table 5.3).

- Standalone Mode
- Pseudo-distributed Mode (single-node cluster)
- Fully distributed mode (or multiple node cluster)

5.8.1 Standalone Mode

Standalone Mode/Single Mode is the default mode of Hadoop, a non-distributed mode that runs as a single Java process. This mode uses the local file system for input and output operation and is useful for debugging. This mode does not offer a truly distributed environment. It does not support fully distributed HDFS. The usage of this model is minimal and used for experimentation and testing.

Table 5.3 Different modes of Hadoop system

S.No	Mode	Remarks
1	Standalone	Standalone Mode/Single Mode is the default mode of Hadoop, a non-distributed mode that runs a single Java process. This mode uses the local file system for input and output operation and is useful for debugging.
2	Pseudo Distributed (Single-node Cluster)	Hadoop runs on a single node in a pseudo (false) distributed mode, just like the Standalone mode. The difference is that each Hadoop daemon runs in a separate Java process in Pseudo-Distributed Mode. Whereas in Local mode, each Hadoop daemon runs as a single Java process.
3	Fully Distributed (Multi-node Cluster)	Fully distributed mode allows different nodes for Master and Slave. In this mode, all daemons execute in separate nodes forming a multi-node cluster. Thus, we enable specific nodes for Master and Slave. We use this model in the production environment, where 'n' number of machines form a cluster in which Hadoop daemons run.

5.8.2 Pseudo-distributed Mode (Single-node Cluster)

Hadoop runs on a single node in a pseudo (false) distributed mode, just like the standalone mode. The difference is that while each Hadoop daemon runs in a separate Java process in pseudo-distributed mode, in the local mode, each Hadoop daemon runs as a single Java process. Again the usage of this model is minimal, and it can only be used for experimentation. In pseudo-distributed mode, we need configuration for all the files. In this case, all daemons run on one node, and thus, both Master and Slave nodes are the same. The pseudo mode is suitable for both development and in the testing environment. In the pseudo mode, all the daemons run on the same machine.

- The configuration is required in the given four files for this model, namely, core-site.xml, hdfs-site.xml, mapred-site.xml.
- Used for real code to test in HDFS.
- Pseudo-distributed cluster is a cluster where all daemons are running on one node itself.
- Here, one node will be used as Master Node / Data Node / Job Tracker / Task Tracker.
- Replication factor is one for HDFS, which means that it is a single-node cluster.

5.8.3 Fully Distributed Mode

Fully distributed mode allows different nodes for Master and Slave. In this mode, all daemons execute in separate nodes forming a multi-node cluster. Thus, we enable specific nodes for Master and Slave. We use this model in the production environment, where n number of machines forms a cluster in which Hadoop daemons run. Name Node runs on one cluster and Data Nodes are run on the other hosts. Therefore, Node Manager installs on every Data Node. And it is also responsible for the execution of the task on every single Data Node. The Resource Manager manages all these Node Managers and receives the processing requests. After that, it passes the parts of the request to the corresponding Node Manager.

5.9 Core Components of Hadoop

In Hadoop, HDFS and MapReduce are considered as the core components. HDFS is the storage layer of Hadoop.

HDFS: It stands for the Hadoop distributed file system. HDFS is the Hadoop version of GFS (Google File System). This system allows the distribution and storage of Big Data across the cluster of computers. It makes all the hard drives on the cluster look like a single giant file system. HDFS works on storing lesser number of large files rather than a vast number of small files. It maintains redundant copies of the data block, so that if one of the computers fails, data can be recovered from the backup. HDFS helps data to create a backup of itself (Replication) to a specified/configured number of copies. It provides high throughput access to an application by accessing it in parallel.

The main features of HDFS are:

- HDFS can store data types of any format – structured, semi-structured and unstructured.
- HDFS is designed to support applications that deal with enormous datasets of megabytes to petabytes. HDFS supports write-once-read-many semantics on files.
- Data is processed in parallel on a cluster of nodes. In addition, computation happens in the DataNodes where the data resides. This reduces network congestion, cuts processing time and enables high throughput.
- Data (data blocks) is replicated across the nodes in a large cluster. Hence data processing is not impacted if any node or hardware fails, thus ensuring high reliability, availability and fault tolerance.
- It is highly scalable and designed to support thousands of nodes within a single cluster.

MapReduce: MapReduce is a programming model that allows the processing of data across the entire cluster at a very high level. It is the data processing layer of Hadoop. MapReduce works by breaking the processing into two phases: mappers and reducers. Mappers write an application that processes the extensive structured and unstructured data stored in HDFS. Mappers can transform the data in parallel across the entire computing cluster in an efficient manner by dividing the submitted job into a set of independent tasks (sub-jobs). Reduce is the second phase of processing. Reducers aggregate the data together. There are creative ways we can put mappers and reducers together to solve complex problems.

5.10 Hadoop Ecosystem

The success of the Hadoop framework has led to the development of an array of software (systems). Hadoop, along with this set of related software, makes up the Hadoop ecosystem. The primary purpose of this ecosystem is to enhance the functionality and increase the efficiency of the Hadoop framework (Refer Fig. 5.7).

There are different ways of organizing these systems, which have lots of complex interdependencies. We will look into these ancillary systems/components one by one.

Hadoop ecosystem				
Ingestion	Storage	Processing	Analysis	Management and coordination
Apache Sqoop (RDBMS connector)	HDFS (Structured data)	MapReduce (Data processing)	Pig (Scripting)	ZooKeeper Apache Ambari Cloudera Manager Map R control system Hortonworks Oozie (Workflow monitoring)
Apache Flume (Data collection)	HBASE (Unstructured, columnar store)	Yarn (Cluster resource management)	Hive (SQL query)	
Apache Kafka (Streaming)	MongoDB	Spark	Spark SQL	
Apache Impala	Apache Cassandra		Spark GraphX	
Apache Nifi			Apache Mahout (Machine learning)	
Storm (Streaming)			Tableau (Visualization)	
Change Data Capture (CDC)			Drill (Interactive analytics)	

Figure 5.7 Hadoop ecosystem

We know that Big Data is a combination of structured, semi-structured and unstructured data. Big Data Framework is an ecosystem of tools and methods that can store, process and handle the data with the organizational aim to benefit from the potential of Big Data. The component of the framework can generally be divided into five components: 1. Data Ingestion Layer (Sqoop, Flume, etc.) 2. Data Storage Layer (HDFS/HBASE, etc.) 3. Processing engine (Map Reduce, etc.) 4. Analysis Layer (Pig, Hive, etc.) 5. Management and Coordination Layer (ZooKeeper, Apache Ambari, etc.)

5.11 Data Ingestion Layer

The data ingestion layer is the first layer where the data is gathered from different sources like RDBMS, web, or local file systems into a single place for further analysis (Fig. 5.8).

The sourced information is integrated and ingested into a Big Data framework like Hadoop, Spark, or Storm. This is a critical stage of the framework as the data quality and quantity are crucial for determining the most accurate end result of the Big Data solution. This layer not only extracts the data from assorted sources but also validates, cleans (noise reduction), normalizes (compress), prioritizes, and processes (integrate) the data in a format that can be ingested into the Storage layer (data destination) of Hadoop for further analysis. Some Big Data ingestion tools are Apache Kafka, Apache Nifi, Talend, and Stitch.

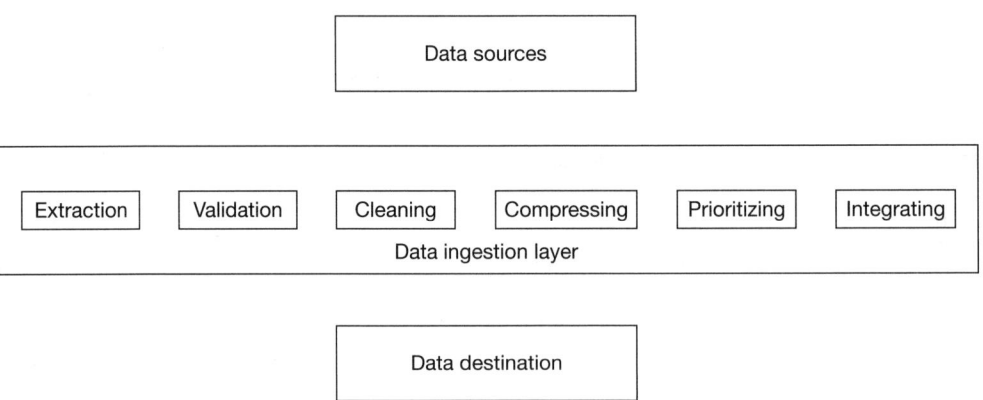

Figure 5.8 Data ingestion layer

Batching ingestion and streaming ingestion are the two different types of data ingestion methodology (Fig. 5.9). Batching methodology ensures that the data gets ingested from the source to the destination in a periodic interval (say every 30 minutes). The streaming methodology helps the real-time data to get ingested into the destination system continuously in real time. Data ingestion software provides various data ingestion APIs through which the data can be extracted easily in various formats.

Figure 5.9 Batching and streaming of data ingestion

5.12 ETL AND ELT

ETL (Extract Transform and Lead) and ELT (Extract Load and Transform) are the two ways in which data can be ingested into the target system (Fig. 5.10). ETL stands for Extract, Transform and Load. ELT stands for Extract, Load and Transform. In ETL, a temporary staging database is used, where the data is first extracted and then transformed before loading into the source system. ETL is used when the source and target databases are different, data volume is low, and data transformation are complex and when the data is structured. In ELT, staging database is not used as the data is straightaway extracted and loaded into the source system and the transformation happens in the source system itself. ELT is used when the source and target databases are same, data volume is large, and data transformation is less complex and the data is unstructured.

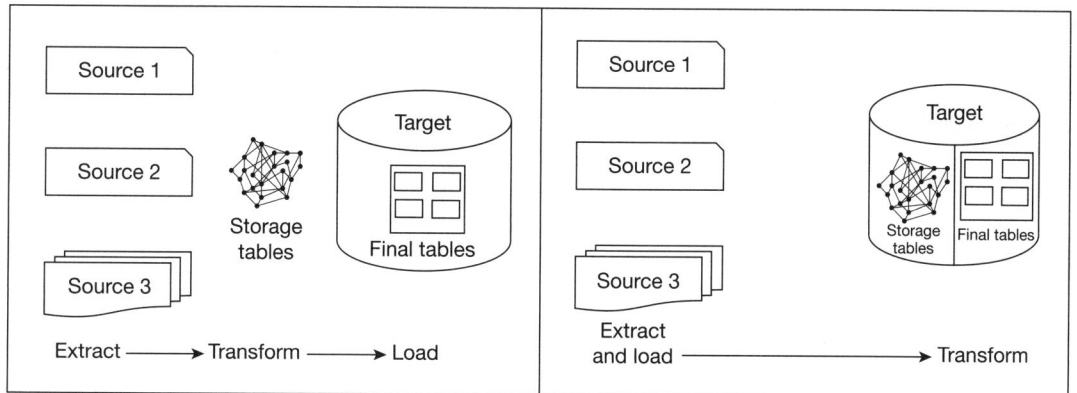

Figure 5.10 ETL and ELT

5.13 INGESTION TOOLS IN HADOOP ECOSYSTEM

Data Ingestion Layer (Fig. 5.11) uses tools like Sqoop and Flume for the data ingestion purpose.

Sqoop: Sqoop (SQL + Hadoop) transfers (bulk-data) processing data from a database/datastore to Hadoop. It is a way of binding the Hadoop database into a relational database. Sqoop is a connector between Hadoop and the legacy databases. We can import data from Sqoop into a cluster; export it to my SQL, and also retrieve the results from the SQL database. It is compatible with all types of databases such as Teradata, MySQL, Oracle, and Postgre.

Flume and Chukwa: Usually, Hadoop starts its work by taking static information loaded into HDFS. But tools like Chukwa and Flume are used to load all the continuous logs from different computers into HDFS and analyze them. There are two systems called agent and collector. An agent works on every computer to pick up and send data. The collector receives the data sent by the agent and sends it to HDFS. The Chukwa device has a tube-like structure with different collection and processing stages. Each of these

Hadoop ecosystem				
Ingestion	Storage	Processing	Analysis	Management and coordination
Apache Sqoop (RDBMS connector)	HDFS (Structured data)	MapReduce (Data processing)	Pig (Scripting)	ZooKeeper Apache Ambari Cloudera Manager Map R Control System Hortonworks Oozie (Workflow monitoring)
Apache Flume (Data collection)	HBASE (Unstructured, columnar store)	Yarn (Cluster resource management)	Hive (SQL query)	
Apache Kafka (Streaming)	MongoDB	Spark	Spark SQL	
Apache Impala	Apache Cassandra		Spark GraphX	
Apache NiFi			Apache Mahout (Machine learning)	
Storm (Streaming)			Tableau (Visualization)	
Change Data Capture (CDC)			Drill (Interactive analytics)	

Figure 5.11 Ingestion layer of Hadoop ecosystem

levels is connected by different interfaces. So even if the update changes later, there will be no reduction in its current status. HICC (Hadoop Infrastructure Care Center) is also an interface for web pages that facilitates the disclosure of information. This allows information to be effectively disclosed, monitored, and selective decisions made accordingly.

Flume: It is a way of transporting weblogs at a vast scale and reliably to a given cluster. So let us say we have a fleet of web servers; flume can listen to the weblogs coming in from these web servers in real-time and publish them into the cluster in real-time for processing by Storm or Spark streaming. This tool is similar to Chukwa that helps with batch processing but in a much shorter time, sending out logs. Chukwa sends logs in batch format every 5 minutes, while Flume picks up and sends logs coming in at the same time. It picks up logs as they fall and sends them in a continuous streaming manner.

Kafka: It solves a similar problem like Sqoop, although it is more general-purpose. It can collect data of any sort from a cluster of computers, from a group of web servers, and broadcast the data into the Hadoop cluster as well.

Apache Impala: Impala is an MPP (Massive Parallel Processing) SQL written in C++ and Java and is an open-source software. It is the highest performing SQL engine that gives an RDBMS-like experience. Impala can be used for data ingestion and data analysis since it connects directly to HBase and HDFS.

Apache NiFi: It is another easy-to-utilize data ingestion tool that provides a strong and secure system to process and distribute information, as it uses SSL, SSH, HTTPS, and encrypted contents. It supports robust and scalable directed graphs of data routing, transformation, and system reconciliation logic. It traces the data flow from the start to the end. It presents a seamless experience between design, control, feedback, and monitoring.

Apache Storm: Storm is a way of processing, streaming real-time data from the sensors or the web. Spark streaming solves the same problem, however apache storm does it quickly and differently; it does not have to be a batch anymore.

Change Data Capture (CDC): This ensures the changes made in the source databases are captured and replicated in the destination databases. The replication can be made in batching mode and real-time mode, depending on the need.

5.14 DATA STORAGE LAYER

Data storage layer (Refer Fig. 5.12) is the destination layer in the data ingestion framework. It is the source layer in the processing and analysis framework. The processed or unprocessed data is stored in this layer in a format easily understood by the data analysis tools. Data governance policies and compliance requirements are built in this layer for security and privacy. The type of data determines the optimal storage format or database, i.e., SQL or NoSQL. Depending on the use case, data storage can be a data warehouse or data lake.

Hadoop ecosystem				
Ingestion	Storage	Processing	Analysis	Management and coordination
Apache Sqoop (RDBMS connector)	HDFS (Structured data)	MapReduce (Data processing)	Pig (Scripting)	ZooKeeper Apache Ambari Cloudera Manager Map R Control System Hortonworks Oozie (Workflow monitoring)
Apache Flume (Data collection)	HBASE (Unstructured, columnar store)	Yarn (Cluster resource management)	Hive (SQL query)	
Apache Kafka (Streaming)	MongoDB	Spark	Spark SQL	
Apache Impala	Apache Cassandra		Spark GraphX	
Apache NiFi			Apache Mahout (Machine learning)	
Storm (Streaming)			Tableau (Visualization)	
Change Data Capture (CDC)			Drill (Interactive analytics)	

Figure 5.12 Storage layer of Hadoop ecosystem

5.14.1 Data Storage Tools

HDFS, HBase, MongoDB and Cassandra are the tools of the storage layer.

HDFS: This system allows the distribution of storage of Big Data across a cluster of computers. It makes all the hard drives on the cluster look like a single giant file system.

HBase: HBase is a "No SQL" database with columnar data store, written in Java, meant for large transaction rates. It was previously called as Google Big Table (GBT) and later renamed as HBase. HBase is a way of exposing the data on the cluster to transactional platforms for low latency operations. It can store massive amount of data (Terabytes and Petabytes). It has easy-to-use Java APIs for client access. It stores the data in Key/Value pair. It is well-suited for OLAP system. HBase is a fault-tolerant column-oriented non-relational (NoSQL) DBMS that runs on top of HDFS. It is part of the Hadoop ecosystem and provides random real-time read-write access to data in the Hadoop file system. HBase is very effective for handling large, sparse datasets typical of Big Data. HBase applications are written in Java. It also supports writing applications in Apache Avro, REST and Thrift. HBase comprises of a set of standard tables with rows and columns having mandatory primary keys to access the tables. In HBase, all the attributes are grouped together into column families in a table and stored. The table schema and the column families must be predefined. However, new columns can be added to families at any time, making the schema flexible and adaptable to changes.

The main characteristics of HBase are:

- HBase stores non-relational data that is accessed via the HBase API. The data is stored in a tabular format for rapid reads and writes.
- HBase is schema-less. It defines only column families.
- It supports distributed storage.
- It supports real-time query processing.
- HBase internally uses Hash tables and it stores the data in indexed HDFS files for faster lookups.
- It supports Java APIs and Thrift and REST APIs for non-Java applications.
- HBase offers atomic read and write (i.e., only one read or write operation can be performed at a time), on a row level.
- It is a column family-oriented database. Any number of columns can be added at any time.
- There are no data types in HBase. Data is stored as byte arrays in the HBase table column.
- It supports data replication over clusters.
- HBase is horizontally scalable through sharding. The database allows for automatic and manual splitting of regions into smaller sub-regions, once it reaches threshold size.

Cassandra and MongoDB: They are both columnar data stores and are good choices for exposing data for real-time usage in a web application. Cassandra DB sits between real-time applications and the cluster. Cassandra and MongoDB are external databases that might integrate with the Hadoop cluster. Cassandra is also distributed.

5.15 PROCESSING LAYER

We talked about the data storage part of Hadoop (mainly, HDFS and Hbase), and this processing layer consists of various tools for its data processing (Fig. 5.13). The data collected from the previous layer is processed, i.e., translated, optimized, and made ready for easy and smooth analytics. The efficient design of the processing layer enables the smooth flow of data through the rest of the data pipeline.

Hadoop ecosystem				
Ingestion	Storage	Processing	Analysis	Management and coordination
Apache Sqoop (RDBMS connector)	HDFS (Structured data)	MapReduce (Data processing)	Pig (Scripting)	ZooKeeper Apache Ambari Cloudera Manager Map R Control Aystem Hortonworks Oozie (Workflow monitoring)
Apache Flume (Data collection)	HBASE (Unstructured, columnar store)	Yarn (Cluster resource management)	Hive (SQL query)	
Apache Kafka (Streaming)	MongoDB	Spark	Spark SQL	
Apache Impala	Apache Cassandra		Spark GraphX	
Apache NiFi			Apache Mahout (Machine learning)	
Storm (Streaming)			Tableau (Visualization)	
Change Data Capture (CDC)			Drill (Interactive analytics)	

Figure 5.13 Processing layer of Hadoop ecosystem

MapReduce: MapReduce is a programming model that allows the processing of data across the entire cluster at a very high level. It is the data processing layer of Hadoop. MapReduce works by breaking the processing into two phases: mappers and reducers. Mappers write an application that processes extensive structured and unstructured data stored in HDFS. Mappers can transform the data in parallel across the entire computing cluster in an efficient manner by dividing the submitted job into a set of independent tasks (sub-jobs). Reduce is the second phase of processing. Reducers aggregate that data together. There are creative ways in which we can put mappers and reducers together to solve complex problems. There are several ways to execute MapReduce operations:

- Hadoop's original method using the Java MapReduce program to process structured, semi-structured and unstructured data.
- Using Pig scripting to execute MapReduce jobs to process structured, semi-structured and unstructured data.
- Using Hive Query Language (HQL) for MapReduce program to process structured data.

Yarn: This stands for Yet Another Resource Negotiator. We talked about the data storage part of Hadoop (HDFS). The data processing part of Hadoop is called Yarn. It is the system resource manager that manages the resources on the computing cluster. It allows various types of data processing engines, such as real-time streaming engine, data science engine, and batch processing engine. It decides what gets to run tasks, what time, what nodes are available for extra work, which nodes are available, and which ones are not available. It is a kind of heartbeat that keeps the cluster going. Yarn allows parallel processing of the distributed data across Hadoop clusters in HDFS.

Spark: It is one of the most exciting open-source cluster computing frameworks in the Hadoop ecosystem that sits at the same MapReduce level used for real-time processing. It runs queries on the data. Like MapReduce, it requires some programming. Spark scripts are written using either Python or Java or the Scallop programming language. Spark is currently a fascinating technology. It is an excellent choice to quickly, efficiently and reliably process data on a Hadoop cluster. It is also very versatile; it can do things like handling SQL queries, executing machine learning across an entire cluster of information, and handle streaming data in real-time. Data parallelism is a form of parallelization across multiple processes in parallel computing environments. It means distributing data across nodes, which operate on the data-parallel. It works on fault-tolerant systems like HDFS, and it is built on top of Yarn. This is because with Yarn, combining different tools like Apache Spark for better processing of the data is easily possible. The topology of Hadoop and Spark are the same, which is a master/slave topology. In Hadoop, in HDFS, the master node is known as the name node. The slave nodes are known as data nodes and also called workers. They are better when they are paired with each other. Spark processes data a hundred times faster than MapReduce; it gives us the results faster, and it performs quick analytics also. Spark applications can run on Yarn, leveraging the Hadoop cluster. The Hadoop cluster is usually set up on commodity hardware, so we get better processing. Low-cost hardware is used, which helps to cut the implementation cost. Apache Spark can use HDFS as storage, so there is no need for different storage space; it can operate on HDFS itself. These are the benefits of combining Spark and Hadoop to analyze Big Data.

The main features of Spark are:

- Spark runs on memory (RAM) that makes the processing much faster, giving quick access and, in turn, accelerating the speed of analytics. It contains RDD (Resilient

Distributed Dataset), which saves time in reading and writing operations, making it faster than Hadoop.
- Spark can work with interactive SQL, batch processing, real-time processing, stream analytics and machine learning. With the diverse set of analytics and algorithms, Spark can perform better analytics.
- It supports multiple languages like Java, Python, Scala, R, and SQL.
- Spark can process real-time streaming data.
- Spark can run in a standalone mode with resource managers like Mesos or in the cloud.

5.16 ANALYSIS LAYER

Data analysis (Fig. 5.14) layer helps to analyze the data that comes out of the processing layer. This layer uses processing frameworks like Pig, Apache Hive, Apache Mahout, and others for advanced analytics. The data is mined for business insights by pulling data either from the data storage layer or directly from the source. Intense interactive querying and complex algorithms are executed in this layer. Data models are created. The end-user or business user can evaluate the value of the Big Data project through presentation and visualization tools. The data can be presented via custom-built or real-time visualization dashboards, BI tools, system alerts, and recommendation systems. Tableau, Microsoft Power BI, Qlik Sense, and Klipfolio are a few examples of visualization tools used for Big Data.

Hadoop ecosystem				
Ingestion	Storage	Processing	Analysis	Management and coordination
Apache Sqoop (RDBMS connector)	HDFS (Structured data)	MapReduce (Data processing)	Pig (Scripting)	ZooKeeper Apache Ambari Cloudera Manager Map R Control System Hortonworks Oozie (Workflow monitoring)
Apache Flume (Data collection)	HBASE (Unstructured, columnar store)	Yarn (Cluster resource management)	Hive (SQL query)	
Apache Kafka (Streaming)	MongoDB	Spark	Spark SQL	
Apache Impala	Apache Cassandra		Spark GraphX	
Apache NiFi			Apache Mahout (Machine learning)	
Storm (Streaming)			Tableau (Visualization)	
Change Data Capture (CDC)			Drill (Interactive analytics)	

Figure 5.14 Analysis layer of Hadoop ecosystem

Pig: Pig is a high-level scripting language that works on top of MapReduce, and uses Java, Python, and SQL style syntax. It is a high-level programming API that allows writing simple scripts called Pig Latin that looks like SQL. The programs created with it are called Pig Programs. In some cases, it allows to chain together queries and get complex answers. Such programs are written using MapReduce algorithms and run on the Hadoop cluster. Pig can be easily integrated into a handful of applications designed to analyze contemporary problems.

The Pig developers coined certain principle strategy statements linking it with the name.

- *Pigs eat anything*, i.e., they can operate on any data irrespective of relational, unstructured, metadata, databases, key values, and other aspects.
- *Pigs live anywhere*, i.e., it is a parallel data processing language that can work on any parallel processing framework.
- *Pigs are domestic animals*, i.e., it is designed to be easily controlled and modified by its users
- *Pigs fly*, i.e., data needs to be processed quickly and consistently at all times.

Pig programs are converted to Hadoop jobs to enable Hadoop to process Big Data in a distributed and parallel manner. The Apache Pig has two main aspects to its architecture – **Pig Latin** which is a high-level data-flow procedural language used for scripting in Pig, and the **Pig Engine** that converts the Pig-Latin scripts into MapReduce jobs via the compiler. Like Hive, Pig also has two execution modes – **local mode** that is used for analyzing small datasets and the **MapReduce mode** which is the default mode where queries are written in Pig Latin and later converted to MapReduce jobs and run on Hadoop clusters. In the local mode the input and output data are stored in the local file system. In MapReduce mode, the input and output data are present on HDFS.

The main characteristics of Pig are:

- It is a parallel data flow language that can have simple linear dataflows or complex workflows where data is joined or split.
- It handles all kinds of data, i.e., structured, unstructured or semi-structured.
- It works well with huge volumes associated with Big Data.
- It uses HDFS for retrieving and storing data.
- It provides its own scripting language, Pig Latin, that is simple and very similar to SQL.
- Pig data model is fully nestable with atomic values, tuples, bags (lists), and maps.
- Pig can process multiple queries in parallel, reducing the amount of coding required compared to Java.
- It contains a set of build-in functions, like eval, load/store, date and time, string, math, bag, and tuple functions and many more.
- It has a vast set of operators like Diagnostic Operators (Dump, Describe, LOAD, Explain, etc.), Grouping and Joining (GROUP, COGROUP, CROSS, etc.)

Combining and Splitting (UNION, SPLIT, etc.) and Filtering (FILTER, DISTINCT, etc.) and others.
- Pig provides support for user-defined functions or UDFs written in Java, JavaScript, Jython, Python, Ruby and Groovy.

The Pig compiler receives the raw data from Hadoop file system – HDFS. After MapReduce jobs are completed, the processed files are stored back in HDFS. The Pig tool is specifically helpful in ETL processes where large volumes data transformation and loading takes place.

The advantages of Pig over other parallel processing platforms are:
- It is highly effective for vast heterogeneous data like Big Data.
- It provides a high level of abstraction for processing, over MapReduce.
- Pig Latin scripting language is easy to learn and write as compared to Java and other complex programming languages. A user without advanced programming skills or basic skills in SQL can pick up and quickly write MapReduce jobs.
- Less effort is required to program in Apache Pig due to the availability of built-in operators and functions. Less lines of code are needed compared to Java, thereby reducing the development time.
- Users can write their own UDFs.
- It is procedural in nature. Hence the user can control the execution at every stage. For example, UDFs can be introduced at specific points in the data pipeline as required.
- Apache Pig optimizes the execution tasks automatically, which is transparent to the users.

Pig can also execute its job in Apache Tez or Apache Spark. Apache Pig is designed for ETL processes and hence not best suited for real-time analysis. It works well for iterative processing and research on raw data, for example to build behavior prediction models.

Hive: This also sits on top of the MapReduce and solves similar problems as Pig, but it directly looks like SQL database; it can be connected through a shell client and ODBC.

This is also a language that can function like SQL. But if Pig is a scripting language, Hive is a query language. Those familiar with the programming language will choose Pig to write Transformation Logic. Those who work in ETL and Data Warehousing and are well-versed in SQL will choose Hive. The two languages are used for doing almost the same job but differ only in the methods of accessing the data. Hive was initially developed by Facebook but is now owned by Apache. It is closely integrated with Hadoop for batch processing jobs. It is highly scalable and works best with structured data. Hive was designed to work across huge distributed database using an SQL-like interface called HQL or Hive-QL. This reduces the learning curve of users who are not familiar with Java coding, but have a basic understanding of SQL. Instead of building MapReduce programs in Java, users can easily access the data using the SQL-like queries. Hive can work on two modes – the local mode for processing smaller datasets on a single node existing in the local machine and the MapReduce mode when working on the Hadoop environment where data is divided across multiple data nodes.

The main features of Hive are:

- It is a distributed, fault-tolerant data storage tool that sits on Hadoop. It is built for Online Analytical Processing (OLAP).
- It is an open-source framework used to store and process petabytes of data using SQL. It can leverage both MapReduce and Apache Tez.
- Hive is designed for managing and querying structured data that is stored in tables. Tables and databases are first created and then data is loaded into the tables.
- Hive can process unstructured data into a structured form.
- Hive is best used for ETL, reporting and data analysis tasks.
- Hive provides plenty of built-in functions. Programmers can use both pre-defined functions and tailored UDFs (User Defined Functions).
- Hive framework supports several optimization techniques for optimizing the query for better performance.
- Hive stores schema information in a component called Metastore.
- Hive supports multi-table inserts.
- Hive supports multiple data formats like comma-separated value (.csv) TextFile, RCFile, ORC, and Parquet.
- Hive uses Derby database for single-user metadata storage that is typically used for testing purposes. MySQL or Oracle is used for multiple-user metadata or shared metadata.

Spark SQL: It is a Spark module for structured data processing, and you can run modified Hive queries on existing Hadoop deployments. Spark SQL is the new module in Spark, and it integrates relational processing with Spark's functional programming API. It supports querying of data either by SQL or via Hive query language. It provides support for various data sources, and makes it possible to read SQL queries with code transformation. Hence, Spark SQL has become a very powerful tool.

Spark streaming: It is the component of the Spark, which is used to process real-time streaming data, and is a useful addition to the core Spark API. It enables high throughput fault tolerant stream processing of live data streams.

Spark GraphX: This is the graph computation engine. It is the Spark API for graphs and graph parallel computation. It has got a set of fundamental operators, like sub-graph, joint purchases etc.

Apache Mahout: This is part of Apache open-source project that helps customers to create scalable machine learning algorithms, which work well in a distributed environment. It supports various machine learning algorithms including Naïve Bayes Classification, Clustering and Recommendation. It is possible to analyze large sets of data quickly. This is the basis for the development of artificial intelligence. Mahout algorithms enable machines to detect a pattern independently from excess data in HDFS and transform machines to be capable of moving to the next level. We can use Apache Mahout to manipulate the data in HDFS on MapReduce.

Tableau: This data visualization software helps to take quick business decisions and also helps to solve business problems easily and quickly by providing limitless data exploration possibilities. It supports Big Data. Its smart dashboards are able to refresh automatically based on the data refresh.

Apache Drill: This is part of Apache open-source project that helps customers to create interactive analytics. It integrates with Hive easily and also helps to visualize the data. It also has its own SQL Query Engine.

5.17 MANAGEMENT AND COORDINATION

Management and coordination layer (Fig. 5.15) helps in the overall management of Hadoop ecosystem to give a birds-eye view and overall coordination across Hadoop ecosystem layers.

Hadoop ecosystem				
Ingestion	Storage	Processing	Analysis	Management and coordination
Apache Sqoop (RDBMS connector)	HDFS (Structured data)	MapReduce (Data processing)	Pig (Scripting)	ZooKeeper Apache Ambari Cloudera Manager Map R Control System Hortonworks Oozie (Workflow monitoring)
Apache Flume (Data collection)	HBASE (Unstructured, columnar store)	Yarn (Cluster resource management)	Hive (SQL query)	
Apache Kafka (Streaming)	MongoDB	Spark	Spark SQL	
Apache Impala	Apache Cassandra		Spark GraphX	
Apache NiFi			Apache Mahout (Machine learning)	
Storm (Streaming)			Tableau (Visualization)	
Change Data Capture (CDC)			Drill (Interactive analytics)	

Figure 5.15 Management and coordination layer of Hadoop ecosystem

ZooKeeper: It is a technology for coordinating everything on the cluster to keep track of which nodes are up and which nodes are down. It is a reliable way of keeping track of shared states. This tool is used to integrate various utilities that run separately. It starts work on alternative functions, maintains all of them, thinking from all angles such as which node, where it comes from, and what to do alternatively, even if one of the more than 50 computers running on the cluster crashes.

Apache Ambari: Apache Ambari sits on top of everything, gives a birds-eye view of the cluster, visualizes what is running on the cluster, and what systems are using how many resources. It executes Hive queries or imports databases into the Hive.

Cloudera Manager: This runs in a central server which hosts UI Web server and application logics to manage end-to-end applications of CDH (Cloudera distributed Hadoop).

It helps to run/switch off various services of CDH. It also helps to deploy various services of CDG quickly by automating the deployment process.

MAP R Control System: MAP R Hadoop replaces HDFS with its file system called as MAP R FS (MAP R File System). MAP R Control System provides complete end-to-end management services for MAP R Hadoop.

Hortonworks: It provides management and administrative support works for Cloudera Horton. The Hortonworks Data Platform of Apache Hadoop is a massively scalable and 100% open-source platform for storing, processing and analyzing large volumes of data. It is designed to deal with data from many sources and formats in a very quick, easy and cost-effective manner. The Hortonworks Data Platform consists of the essential set of Apache Hadoop projects including MapReduce, Hadoop Distributed File System (HDFS), HCatalog, Pig, Hive, HBase, ZooKeeper and Ambari. Hortonworks is the major contributor of code and patches to many of these projects. These projects have been integrated and tested as part of the Hortonworks Data Platform release process, and installation and configuration tools have also been included.

Oozie (Workflow monitoring): It is a way of scheduling jobs on your cluster. Suppose you have a task that needs to happen on the Hadoop cluster that involves many different steps and maybe many other systems. In that case, Oozie is a way of scheduling all these things together into jobs that can run on the specified schedule (time). It is used to run a series of interdependent jobs. That means it is easier to handle jobs that can run independently. Oozie is used for keeping the output of one job as input for another to start its operation. It creates a map called DAG (Directed Acyclical Graphs) to clearly describe the interactions of different jobs and the sequence in which they should be executed. One node is used for action and the other for determining actions. The action node is for action. These include adding files to HDFS, running MapReduce, starting Pig/Hive, and downloading data from various sources. Finally, the control node determines the actions. It determines the outcome of a job, where to go next, and where to start next for any kind of ending. The Start, End, and Error nodes all fall under the category of nodes that determine these actions.

5.18 ANATOMY OF A HADOOP CLUSTER: HDFS ARCHITECTURE

In HDFS, appending the content to the end of the file is supported but it cannot be updated at an arbitrary point. It is suitable for large datasets of gigabytes to terabytes in size.

It can store all types of data (structured, unstructured) that run on commodity hardware. It is a distributed file system with an inbuilt fault-tolerant mechanism. It provides high throughput access detecting the faults and enables quick automatic recovery from failure, as part of its core architectural goal. It can scale to hundreds of nodes in a single cluster. It is portable from one platform to another. Any machine that supports Java can run the Name Node or the Data Node software.

It follows master/slave architecture (Fig. 5.16), so the master node is the name node, and slave nodes are known as data nodes. Another node is known as the secondary name node. The name node is the master daemon, and you can think of it as the king. There is a helper daemon, a secondary name node; you can think of it as a minister. The pawns represent the slave nodes or slave Damon's data node which contains the actual data. Whenever a file is stored in HDFS, it gets distributed and stored in the data nodes. HDFS creates an abstraction layer so that the entire HDFS can be seen as a single unit.

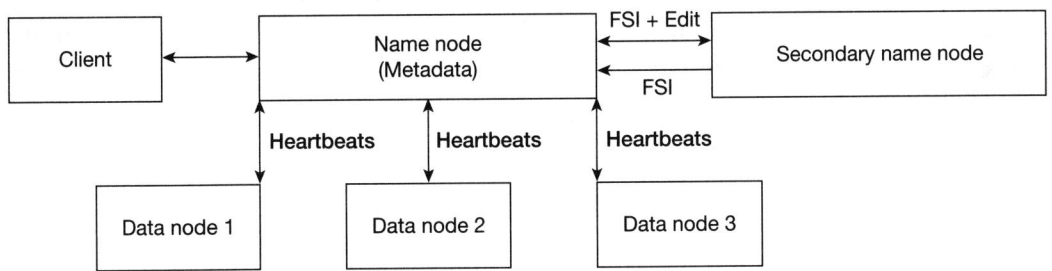

Figure 5.16 Core HDFS architecture

Name Node

It is the master daemon, and it manages the data node. The Name Node is the arbitrator and repository for all HDFS metadata. User data never flows through the Name Node, which preserves only the metadata. Metadata means data about the data. It supports user quotas and access permissions. It is like a sheet or a file having information on what data block is stored in which data node. Other metadata includes the filename, size, replication factor, etc. Name Node takes care of the replication factor of all the blocks. It manages the file system namespace, which includes the opening, renaming, and closing of files and directories. It serves the request from the clients and regulates clients' access to files. Name Node receives heartbeat and block reports from all Data Nodes that ensure Data Node is alive. If the Data Node fails, the Name Node chooses new Data Nodes for new replicas.

The Secondary Name Node

It does an essential task known as Checkpointing, which combines edit logs with FSImage. Let us say that I have set up my Hadoop cluster 5 days back, and whatever transactions that happen with every new data block are stored in HDFS. Every transaction is combined in a file known as an FSImage. This FSImage resides in the disk. There's one more similar file which is known as an edit log. Edit logs store only the latest transaction data. Checkpointing is the task of combining the edit log with the FSImage. Checkpointing happens after every hour (configurable). The secondary name node first copies the FSImage and the edit log and adds them together in order to get the updated FSImage. This FSImage is copied back to the name node, and now the name node has an updated FSImage. In the meantime, a new edit log is created when the Checkpointing is happening. This process continues and it helps the name node to always keep an updated copy.

Data Nodes

These are the slave Daemons, where the actual data is stored. Whenever a client gives a read or write request, the data node serves it. The data node stores the data as data blocks. Racks arrange the data nodes. We can set up different data nodes in racks.

If the client requests to read a particular file (Fig. 5.17), it will first go to the name node. Since the name node contains the metadata, it knows precisely where the file is. So it will give the IP addresses of the data nodes with different data blocks of that particular file. It tells the client that you can go to this IP address, and you can go to this data node to read the file. The client, in turn, goes to the different data nodes, where the data block is present to serve the read request.

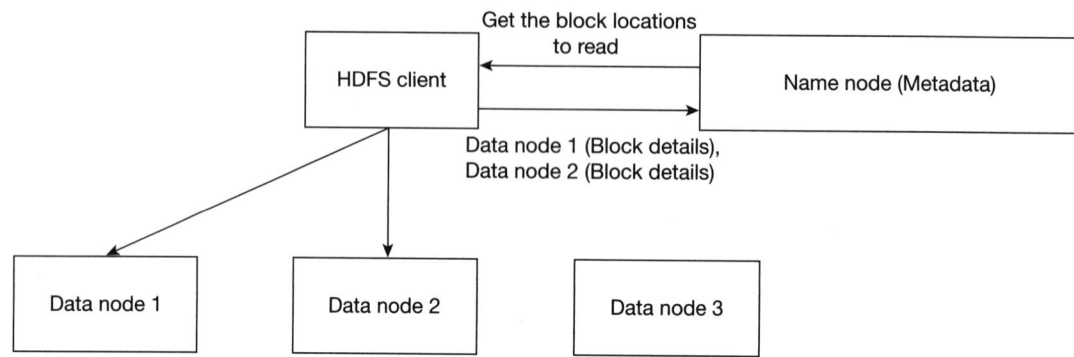

Figure 5.17 Core HDFS architecture: Read request

Now, let's say the client wants to write (Fig. 5.18). Again it will contact the name node to get the metadata. It will check whether space is available or not. And then, it will give the IP addresses of the data nodes, where a client could write the file.

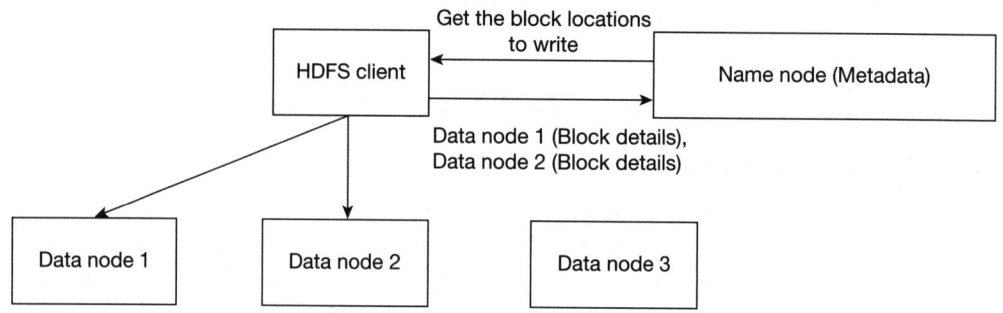

Figure 5.18 Core HDFS architecture: Write request

The data node serves the entire read–write request as per the above procedure.

HDFS Block Replication

HDFS is a fault-tolerant system. Whenever you write a file into HDFS, the HDFS system breaks down the file into different blocks of size 128 megabytes, except the last block (which will have the remainder of the file). These blocks are distributed across the Hadoop cluster.

By doing this, the time taken to store this data onto the disk is significantly reduced. The total time taken to store this entire data onto the disk equals storing one part of the data. It will store all the parts of the data simultaneously on different machines to provide high availability. By default, their replication factor is set to three. If we consider the default replication factor set, there will be three copies for each part of the data on three different machines. To reduce the bandwidth and latency time, it would store two copies of the same part of the data on the nodes present within the same rack, and the last copy would be stored on a node present on a different rack. Another advantage of distributing this data across the cluster is that while processing this data, it reduces time, as this data can be processed simultaneously. The decision to replicate the blocks is taken by the name node. The number of replicas of a file (called replication factor) can be given as a parameter in HDFS and stored in the name node.

The block size and its replication factor are also configurable on a per-file basis. The list of all blocks on a Data Node is available in data reports. If the HDFS cluster crosses multiple data centers, then a replica in the local data center is favored over that in any remote replication. It receives heartbeat and block reports from each of the data nodes.

HDFS Blocks

In HDFS, each file is divided and stored as a block. The default measurement of each block is 128 megabytes. A file of 380 megabytes (Fig. 5.19), divides into three blocks; the first block will be 128 megabytes; the second will be 128 megabytes, and the third will occupy whatever the remaining size of the file (124 megabytes).

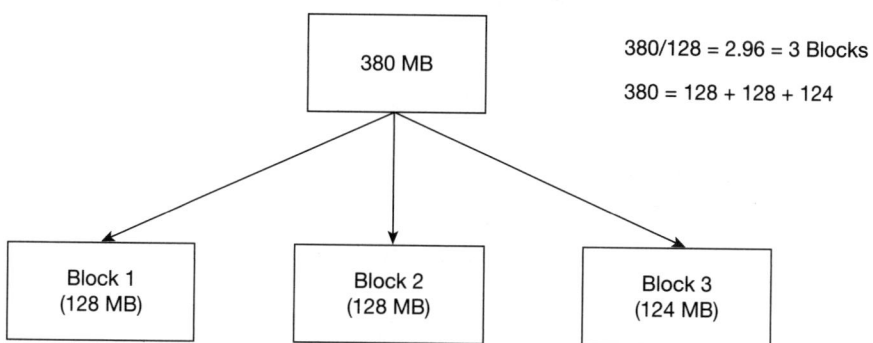

Figure 5.19 HDFS blocks formation: Example 1

Now let us say that we have a file size of 500 megabytes (Fig. 5.20); how many blocks will it create? It is four blocks. The first three blocks will be 128 megabytes, and the last block will occupy the remaining file size (116 megabytes).

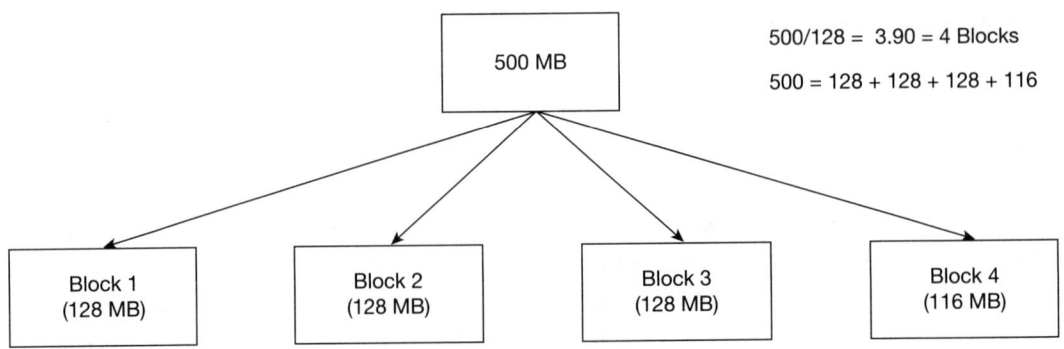

Figure 5.20 HDFS blocks formation: Example 2

Whenever we dump the file into HDFS, it is first divided into blocks, and then each of the blocks is copied as per the replication factor. So, if replication factor equals three, it means that there are three similar blocks in the Hadoop cluster.

Data Racks

A rack consists of multiple nodes (Fig. 5.21), usually 30 to 40 nodes. Each of these nodes, in turn, stores multiple data blocks. Within a rack, Hadoop stores its data in two different data nodes. Communication between nodes present in the same rack is usually faster than the nodes across multiple racks. The concept of choosing the closest data node is called as rack awareness.

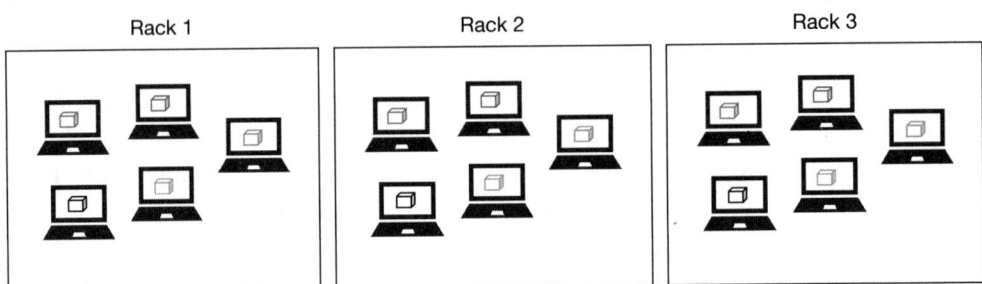

Figure 5.21 Data racks

Rack Awareness Algorithm

The rack awareness algorithm says the local rack stores the first replica of a block, and the next two replicas will be there in a different rack. So, we store a data block in the local rack (rack one) to decrease the latency.

1. Each node will have only one replica of the block.
2. Each rack will have maximum of two replica of the block.
3. The number of racks to be used will be lesser than the replication factor.

If we have the replication factor as 3 then (as per rule 3) only 2 racks are to be used to store the replicated blocks.

Fundamentals of Hadoop • 209

If we have a file with 248 megabytes (Fig. 5.22), Block 1 is 128 megabytes, and Block 2 is 120 megabytes. Block one is there three times, and block two is also multiplied three times.

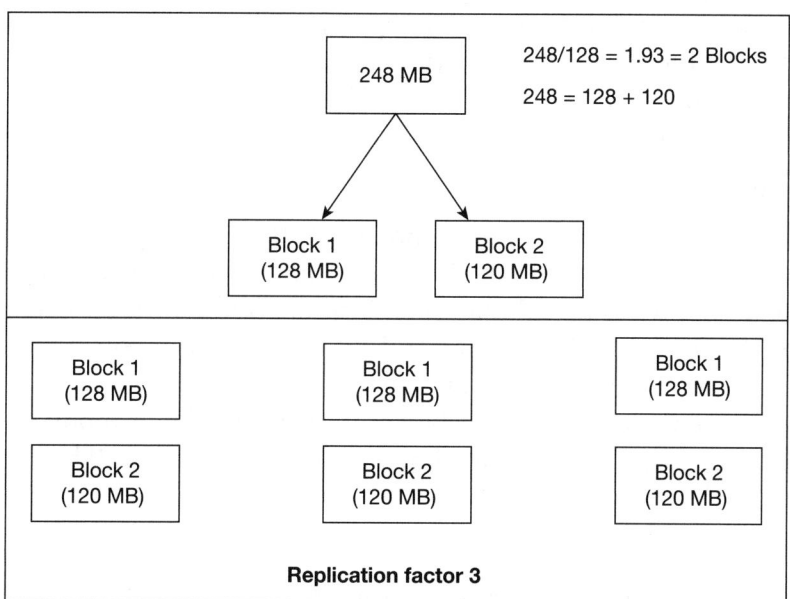

Figure 5.22 Replication factor

Now, let us try to store these blocks (six blocks in total) in racks by applying rack awareness algorithm. Replication factor is three and hence we can use maximum of two racks to store the duplicated data (as per Rule 3). A rack cannot have more than 2 replica blocks. Block 1 is stored in Rack 1. Other two copies of Block 1 are storied in Rack 2. Block 2 is stored in Rack 3 and other two copies are stored in Rack 1 (Fig. 5.23).

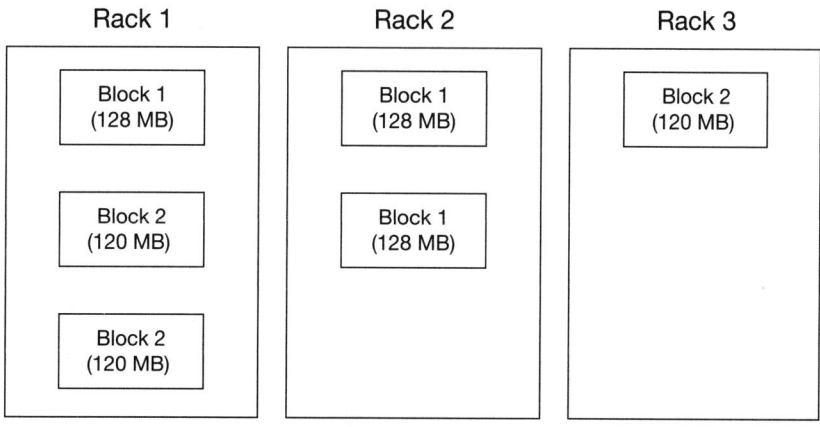

Figure 5.23 Replication across racks

When any data nodes go down, the system can recover the data block from the two other data nodes. This rack awareness algorithm provides fault tolerance.

Hadoop Class Path

CLASSPATH includes all directories containing jar files required to start/stop Hadoop daemons. For example, HADOOP_HOME/share/Hadoop/common/lib contains all the utility jar files. We cannot start/stop Hadoop daemons if we don't set CLASSPATH. We can set CLASSPATH inside /etc/hadoop/hadoop-env.sh file. The CLASSPATH gets automatically added on the next run of Hadoop. That is, you don't need to add CLASSPATH in the parameters each time you run it.

Hadoop Metrics

Metrics is the statistical information exposed by the Hadoop daemons. It is used for monitoring, performance tuning, and debugging. By default, there are many metrics available readily for troubleshooting. Hadoop framework uses Hadoop metrics properties for 'Performance Reporting' and also controls the reporting for Hadoop. The API provides an abstraction to implement it on top of a variety of metrics client libraries. Client library is configurable based on need. Different modules of the same application can use the same metrics implementation libraries. This file is present inside /etc/hadoop.

Data Integrity in Hadoop

Data Integrity ensures that no data loss or corruption happens while storing or processing the data. In Hadoop, the amount of data being written or read is large in volume, so the chances of data corruption are more. Hadoop has a checksum mechanism to tackle this data integrity issue. It computes the checksum while writing the data to the disk for the first time (Fig. 5.24).

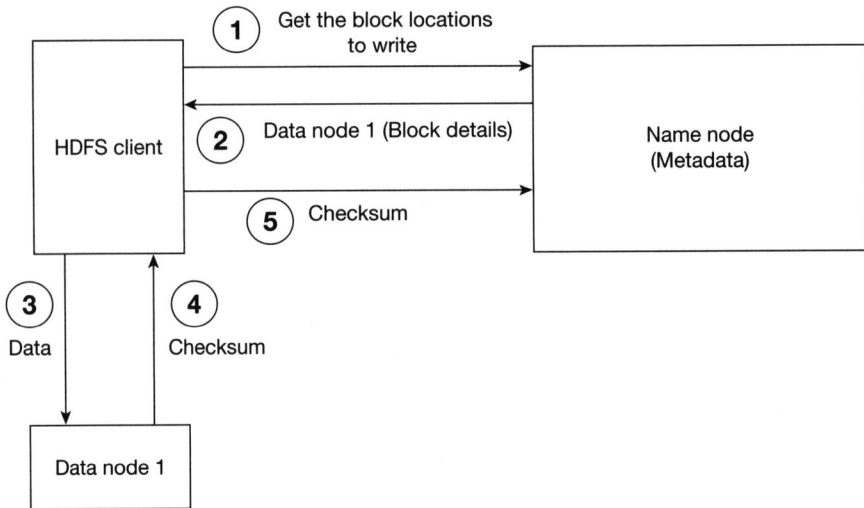

Figure 5.24 Data integrity in Hadoop (Checksum): Write

It checks again while reading the data (Fig. 5.25) from the disk. If the new checksum matches the original checksum, it means the data is uncorrupted.

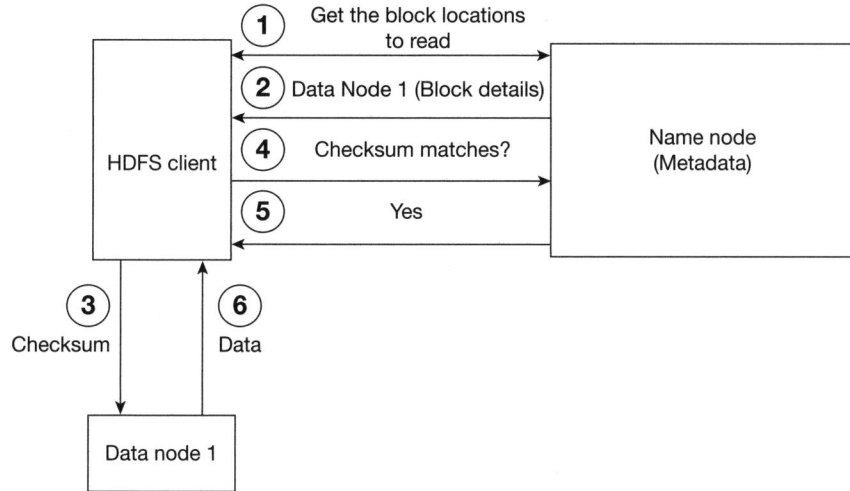

Figure 5.25 Data integrity in Hadoop (Checksum): Read

HDFS uses a more efficient algorithm called CRC-32C to calculate the checksum. DataNodes are responsible for calculating the checksum for the received data before storing the data. Hadoop computes the checksum for the data it receives from clients and other DataNodes during the replication stage. Hadoop can heal the corrupted data by copying one of the good replicas to produce the new replica, an uncorrupt replica. If a client detects an error when reading a block, it reports "the wrong block and the DataNodes it was trying to read" to the NameNode before throwing a Checksum Exception. The NameNode marks the block replica as corrupt, so it doesn't direct any more clients to it or copy this replica to other DataNodes for replication. Instead, it sends a copy of the block from another DataNode to replicate (copy). Thus, its replication factor returns to the expected level. Once this has happened, the corrupt replica gets deleted.

5.19 Data Locality in Hadoop

Inter-rack: Hadoop's major drawback is cross–switch network traffic due to the massive volume of data. It moves extensive amount of data to the computation spot. In this case, usually, data and code reside in different racks (Fig. 5.26) creating heavy traffic across the racks. In this scenario, mapper runs on a different rack due to resource constraints.

Intra-rack: In this scenario the code runs on a different node but the same rack. In such a case, the proximity of the data is closer to the computation of the same rack. Due to constraints, it is not always possible to execute the mapper on the same data node.

This is also called as Rack Locality, which refers to moving the computation (code) close to the rack, where the actual data resides, instead of moving extensive amount of data to the computation spot. However, heavy traffic resides within the rack, as the data gets moved across multiple nodes (Fig. 5.27).

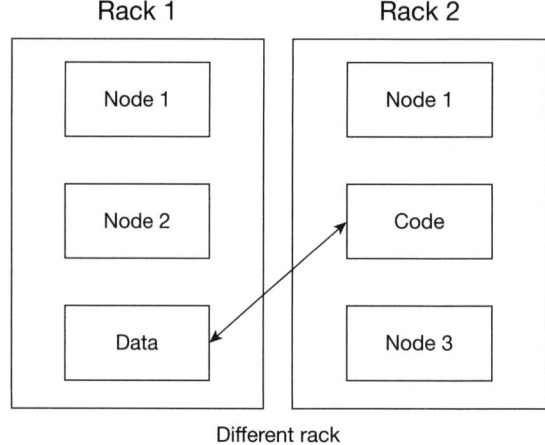

Figure 5.26 Inter-rack sync

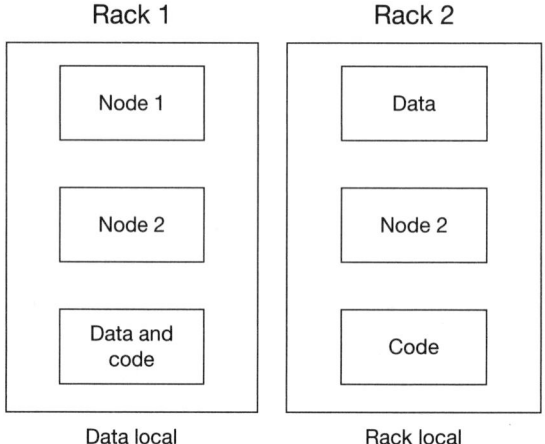

Figure 5.27 Data local and Rack local

Data Locality (Fig. 5.28) refers to moving the computation (code) closer to the node where the actual data resides, instead of moving extensive amount of data to the computation spot.

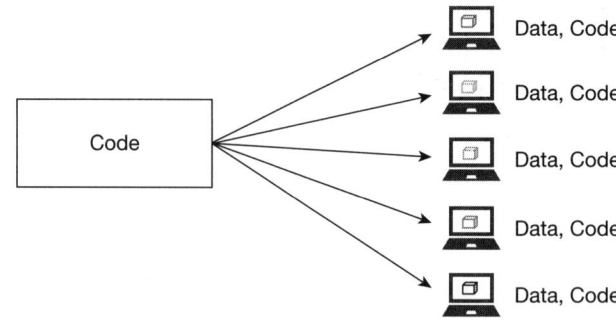

Figure 5.28 Data local

Data local is the most preferred scenario. Data locality increases the overall throughput of the system. In Hadoop, HDFS stores datasets divided into blocks and stored across the data nodes in the Hadoop cluster. When a user runs the code (MapReduce job code), the NameNode sends this code to the data nodes on which data is available related to the MapReduce job.

5.20 CONFIGURATION FILES IN HADOOP

In Hadoop, custom configuration (Fig. 5.29) is required in four Hadoop files. They are:
1. core-site.xml
2. hdfs-site.xml
3. mapred-site.xml
4. yarn-site.xml

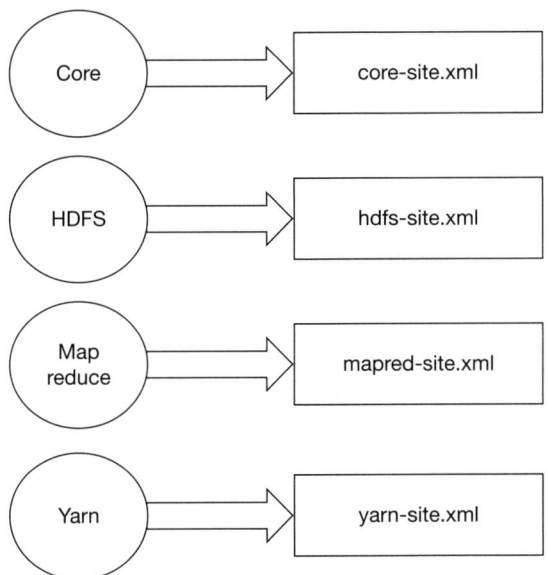

Figure 5.29 Configuration files in Hadoop

Core-site.xml: It contains configuration settings for Hadoop core (Table 5.4), such as inputs and output settings that are common to HDFS and MapReduce. It uses host name and port. The most commonly used port is 9000.

```
<Configuration>
<Property>
<Name>fs.default.name</name>
<Value>hdfs: //localhost:9000</value>
</property>
</configuration>
```

Table 5.4 Hadoop configuration file descriptions

S. No	Configuration File Names	Descriptions
1	core-site.xml	It contains configuration settings for Hadoop core, such as input and output settings that are common to HDFS and MapReduce. It uses Host name and port. The most commonly used port is 9000.
2	hdfs-site.xml	This file contains the configuration setting for HDFS daemons, name node and secondary node, and data nodes. hdfs-site.xml also specifies the default block replication and permission checking on HDFS.
3	mapred-site.xml	In this file, we specify a framework name for MapReduce. We can specify it by setting the mapreduce.framework.name.
4	yarn-site.xml	This file provides configuration setting for Node Manager and Resource Manager.

hdfs-site.xml: This file contains the configuration setting for HDFS daemons. hdfs-site.xml also specify default block replication and permission checking on HDFS.

```
<configuration>
<property>
<name>dfs.replication</name>
<value>1</value>
</property>
</configuration>
```

The three main hdfs-site.xml properties are:

1. **dfs.name.dir** gives you the location where NameNode stores the metadata (FSImage and edit logs). It also specifies where DFS should locate – on the disk or in the remote directory.
2. **dfs.data.dir** gives the location of DataNodes where it stores the data.
3. **fs.checkpoint.dir** is the directory on the file system, on which secondary NameNode stores the temporary images of edit logs. These Edit Logs and FSImage will merge for backup.

mapred-site.xml: In this file, we specify a framework name for MapReduce. We can specify by setting the mapreduce.framework.name. It also can specify job tracker location.

```
<configuration>
<property>
<name>mapreduce.framework.name</name>
<value>yarn</value>
</property>
</configuration>
```

yarn-site.xml: This file provides the configuration setting for Node Manager and Resource Manager.

```
<configuration>
<property>
<name>yarn.nodemanager.aux-services</name>
<value>mapreduce_shuffle</value>
</property>
</configuration>
```

5.21 LIMITATIONS OF HADOOP

The issue with small files: Hadoop is not suited for small files. A small file means it is significantly smaller than the HDFS default block size (default 128MB). HDFS can't handle a large number of such small files. HDFS works well with a small number of large files for storing datasets rather than a large number of small files. If one uses a significant number of small files, this will overload the name node since the name node stores the namespace of HDFS. HBase helps to overcome these small file issues.

Processing speed: With parallel and distributed algorithm, MapReduce processes large datasets. MapReduce performs the tasks of both Mapping process and Reduce process. MapReduce takes a lot of time to perform these tasks. It increases the latency as the data gets distributed and processed over the clusters in MapReduce.

Batch processing: Hadoop, by default, supports the batch processing of data, analyzing the data already stored in the database or files. It does not process the live streaming of data. The system's overall performance is slow as the MapReduce framework does not leverage the cluster's memory to its maximum.

Iterative processing: Hadoop is not the right fit for iterative cyclic processing. Hadoop does not support cyclic data flow with the chain of stages, in which the input to the next upcoming stage is the output of the previous stage.

Vulnerable by nature: Hadoop is wholly composed of the most popular language called Java, which has been heavily exploited by cyber-criminals, and is susceptible to various security breaches.

Security: Hadoop can be challenging in managing complex applications involving security. Hadoop is missing encryption at storage and network levels, which is a vital point of concern. Hadoop supports Kerberos authentication, which is very hard to manage.

5.22 DISTRIBUTED CACHE IN APACHE HADOOP

In Hadoop, the data chunks process happens independently in parallel among DataNodes. The distributed cache contains common files accessible by all the DataNodes, which include read-only text files, Archive files, Jar Files, etc. Hadoop will make these cache files available on each data node where map/reduce tasks are running (Fig. 5.30).

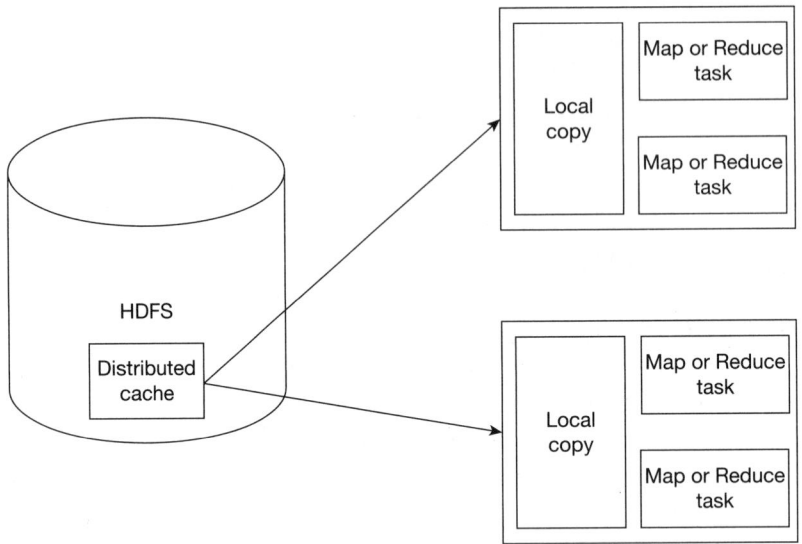

Figure 5.30   Caching mechanism in Hadoop

An application that requires distributed cache should make sure that the files are available on URLs. The URLs can be either hdfs:// or http://. The Hadoop framework will duplicate the cache file on all the data nodes before starting tasks on those nodes. The default size of the distributed cache is 10 GB, which can be modified using local cache size.

5.23 APACHE HADOOP AND RDBMS

Apache Hadoop is the database's future because it stores and processes many varieties of data, which is not easily possible with the traditional database.

Architecture: Traditional RDBMS has ACID properties. Hadoop, on the other hand, is a distributed computing framework having two main components: Distributed file system (HDFS) and MapReduce.

Data acceptance: RDBMS accepts only structured data. In the case of Hadoop, it can receive both structured as well as unstructured data. Data acceptance is an excellent Hadoop feature, as we can store everything in our database, and there will be no data loss.

Scalability: RDBMS is a traditional database that provides vertical scalability. So if the data increases for storing, then we have to increase a particular system configuration. Hadoop provides horizontal scalability. We can add one or more nodes to the cluster if there is any requirement to increase the data storage. In vertical scaling, more disk space is added to get more memory (single computer). In horizontal scaling, computers are added, spreading out data across clusters (more computers, no upper bound); which also distributes storage and processing leading to "no downtime" and "inexpensive" technique of scaling.

OLTP and OLAP: Traditional database (relational database) system supports Online Transaction Processing (OLTP), which is real-time data processing. Apache Hadoop supports large-scale OLAP (Online Analytical Processing).

Cost: Traditional database systems are usually licensed software; therefore, we have to pay for the software. Whereas Hadoop is an open-source framework, so we don't have to pay for the software.

5.24 Problems with Small Files in Hadoop

Hadoop is not suited for small data. Hadoop HDFS cannot support the random reading of small files, which are smaller than the HDFS block size (default 128 MB). If we store these vast numbers of small files, HDFS can't handle these. HDFS works very well with a small number of large files. However, a large number of many small files overload the NameNode as it holds the namespace of the HDFS file system.

Solution: HAR (Hadoop Archive) Files is the solution for handling small file issues in the Hadoop ecosystem. HAR introduces a new layer on top of HDFS, which provides an interface for file accessing. Using the Hadoop archive command, we can create HAR files. This file runs a MapReduce job to pack the archived files into a smaller number of HDFS files. Since each HAR file access requires two index files, this makes it slower. Sequence files also deal with small file problems. In this, we use the filename as a key and the file contents as the value. For example, if we have 10,000 files of 100 KB, we can write a program to put them into a single sequence file. And then, we can process them in a streaming fashion.

5.25 Security in Hadoop

Apache Hadoop uses Kerberos for managing the security. A client needs to take three simple steps to access (Fig. 5.31) service when using Kerberos. Each of these steps involves exchange of message with a server. The steps are Authentication step, Authorization step and the Service Request Step.

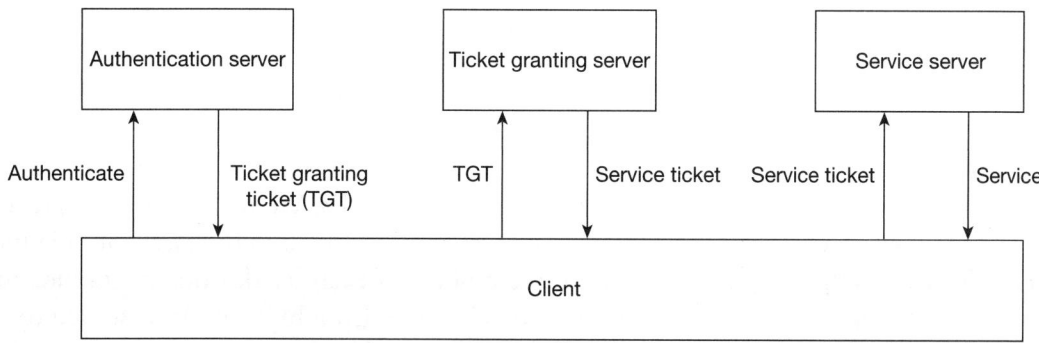

Figure 5.31 Security mechanism in Hadoop

Authentication step: The client first authenticates itself to the authentication server. Then, it receives a timestamped Ticket-Granting Ticket (TGT).

Authorization step: The client uses the TGT to request a service ticket from the Ticket Granting Server.

Service Request step: The client now uses the service ticket to authenticate itself to the server.

5.26 FILE SYSTEM CHECK IN HADOOP

Hadoop HDFS uses the fsck (file system check) command to check for various discrepancies, reporting the problems with the files in HDFS, such as missing blocks for a file or under-replicated blocks. It does not correct the errors. Usually, NameNode automatically corrects most of the recoverable failures. File system check ignores open files but provides an option to select all files during the reporting. The HDFS fsck command runs as bin/hdfs fsck. File system check can run on the whole file system or a subset of files.

5.27 STARTING AND STOPPING HADOOP

The sbin directory inside the Hadoop directory stores the script files. By following methods we can restart the NameNode:

1. You can stop the NameNode individually using /sbin/hadoop-daemon.sh stop namenode
2. You can start the particular NameNode using /sbin/hadoop-daemon.sh start namenode
3. You can stop all the demons using: /sbin/stop-all.sh
4. You can start all the demons using: /sbin/start-all.sh

5.28 EDIT LOG AND FSIMAGE IN HADOOP

The NameNode uses a transaction log called the EditLog to record every change that occurs to file system metadata. The entire file system namespace, including mapping blocks to files and file system properties, is stored in a file called the FSImage. While starting the namenode, the latest FSImage file is loaded into "in-memory."

"In-Memory" (for easy, quick processing) stores the metadata information. For each block metadata, it consumes 150 bytes in "in-memory." Let us say we have a file called "file.txt" that is 1GB (1000MB), and our block size is 128 MB. We will end up with seven 128MB blocks and a 104MB block. The NameNode keeps track of the fact that "file.txt" in HDFS maps to these eight blocks and three replicas of each block (totaling 24 blocks). One block of metadata storage is equivalent to 150 bytes (roughly). In this case, there are eight blocks, with the replication factor 3, totaling 24 blocks. Hence 150 bytes × 24 = 3600 bytes of metadata will be created.

In-memory contains two types/forms of metadata.

1. File metadata (file details)
2. Bitmap metadata (Block to DataNode(s) mapping is available in Bitmap metadata.)

For each file,

> type tag: To indicate whether it is a file or a directory.
> name tag: file name
> replication tag: replication factor for that particular file
> perferredBlockSize tag: default block size
> permission: permission for that client
> blocks: we may have one or more number of blocks for a particular file. All block(s) will be part of blocks tag.
> block: It contains ID (id tag), generated timestamp (genstamp tag), number of bytes (numBytes tag).

5.29 COMMUNICATION PROTOCOLS

All HDFS communication protocols form a cover on top of the TCP/IP protocol, Client protocol, and Data Node protocol (Fig. 5.32).

1. The client talks to the NameNode using Client protocol.
2. The DataNodes talk to the NameNode using the Data Node protocol.
3. A Remote Procedure Call (RPC) abstraction wraps both the Client Protocol and the Data Node Protocol.
4. Name node never initiates Remote Procedural Calls (RPC). It only responds to RPC requests issued by DataNodes or clients.
5. **Cluster rebalancing** moves data from one DataNode to another if the free space on a DataNode falls below a certain threshold.

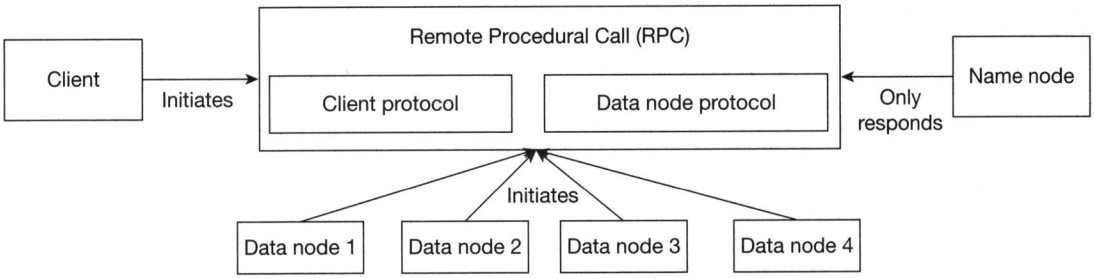

Figure 5.32 Communication mechanism in Hadoop

5.29.1 Three Common Types of Failures

The three common types of failures are – NameNode failures, indicating that the name node is not starting; Data Node failures, indicating that the data node is not starting; and Network Partitions, indicating that the network gets partitioned and only a portion of the overall network will work.

Data integrity – checksum: When a client creates an HDFS file, it computes a checksum of each block of the file and stores these checksums in a separate hidden file in the same

HDFS namespace. The NameNode can be configured to support maintaining multiple copies of the FSImage and EditLog.

Backups: Snapshots support storing a copy of data at a particular instant of time. One usage of the snapshot feature may be to roll back a corrupted HDFS instance to a previously known good point in time.

Staging: When the local file accumulates data over one chunk size, the client contacts the NameNode. The client flushes the chunk of data from the local buffer to the specified DataNode. When a file is closed, the local buffer's remaining un-flushed data is transferred to the DataNode. The client then tells the NameNode that the file is closed. If the name node dies before the file is closed, the file is lost. File close $\rightarrow$ Flush.

5.30 HADOOP SAFE MODE

Safe mode: On start-up, name nodes enter into a special mode: safe mode. Replication of data blocks does not occur when the NameNode is in the safe mode state. During the name node daemon start up, the NameNode enters safe mode for a certain period. The administrator can also enter the safe mode manually with the below command (in the case of maintenance/up-gradation of the cluster).

```
hadoop dfsadmin-safemode enter
```

At the startup of NameNode, it loads the file system namespace from the last saved FSImage into its main memory, and edits the log file. It merges edits log file on FSImage, resulting in a new file system namespace. Then it receives block reports containing information about block location from all the data nodes. NameNode leaves safe mode after the DataNodes have reported that most blocks are available.

```
hadoop dfsadmin –safemode get: To know the status of Safe mode
bin/hadoop dfsadmin –safemode enter: To enter Safe mode
hadoop dfsadmin –safemode leave: To come out of Safe mode
NameNode front page shows whether safe mode is on or off
```

5.31 HADOOP 1 AND HADOOP 2

In Hadoop V1.0, there was only one name and because of that (Table 5.5), there was single point of failure and high availability was not present. In addition to metadata management, the name node was also managing the resource management work (job tracker) which was temporary but consumed lot of time. So the resource management related work was completely given to YARN in the next version (Hadoop 2.0).

Table 5.5 Hadoop 1.0 vs. Hadoop 2.0

S. No	Hadoop 1.0	Hadoop 2.0
1	One Name Node and Name Spaces	Multiple Name Node and Name Spaces
2	One Name Node	Active Name Node, Standby Name Node and Secondary Name Node
3	High Availability not present	High Availability present
4	Job Tracker and Task Tracker	YARN

5.32 HADOOP 2 AND HADOOP 3

In Hadoop V2.0, java version 7 was supported (Table 5.6). In Hadoop 3.0, the next latest version of java (Java 8) is supported. Fault tolerance was achieved through replication in the Hadoop V2.0, However it was achieved through coding in Version 3.0.

Table 5.6 Hadoop 2.0 vs. Hadoop 3.0

S. No	Hadoop 2.0	Hadoop 3.0
1	Java 7 Supported	JAVA 8 Supported
2	Fault Tolerance by Replication	Erasure Coding
3	Data Balancing by HDFS Balancer	Intra Data Load Balancer
4	200% overhead in storage Space	50% overhead in storage Space
5	SPOF: Manual Intervention	SPOF: Auto Recovery

5.33 START HADOOP DAEMONS COMMAND

The following command line commands are used to start and stop various Hadoop daemons (like dfs and Yarn).

- To start all the hadoop daemons use: ./sbin/start-all.sh
- To stop all the Hadoop daemons use: ./sbin/stop-all.sh
- To start all the dfs daemons together using ./sbin/start-dfs.sh
- To stop all the dfs daemons together using ./sbin/stop-dfs.sh
- To start all the Yarn daemons together using ./sbin/start-yarn.sh
- To stop all the Yarn daemons together using ./sbin/stop-yarn.sh

The following command line commands are used to start and stop name node, data node, resource manager and history server.

```
Map Reduce Job history server using /sbin/mr-jobhistory-daemon.sh start history server
./sbin/hadoop-daemon.sh start namenode
./sbin/hadoop-daemon.sh start datanode
./sbin/yarn-daemon.sh start resourcemanager
./sbin/yarn-daemon.sh start nodemanager
./sbin/mr-jobhistory-daemon.sh start historyserver
```

5.34 YARN ARCHITECTURE

When Hadoop came up with its new version (2.0), it introduced Yarn as the new framework. Yarn stands for Yet Another Resource Negotiator. Again, it is a master/slave topology (Fig. 5.33). The master daemon is known as resource manager, and slave Daemons are known as node managers.

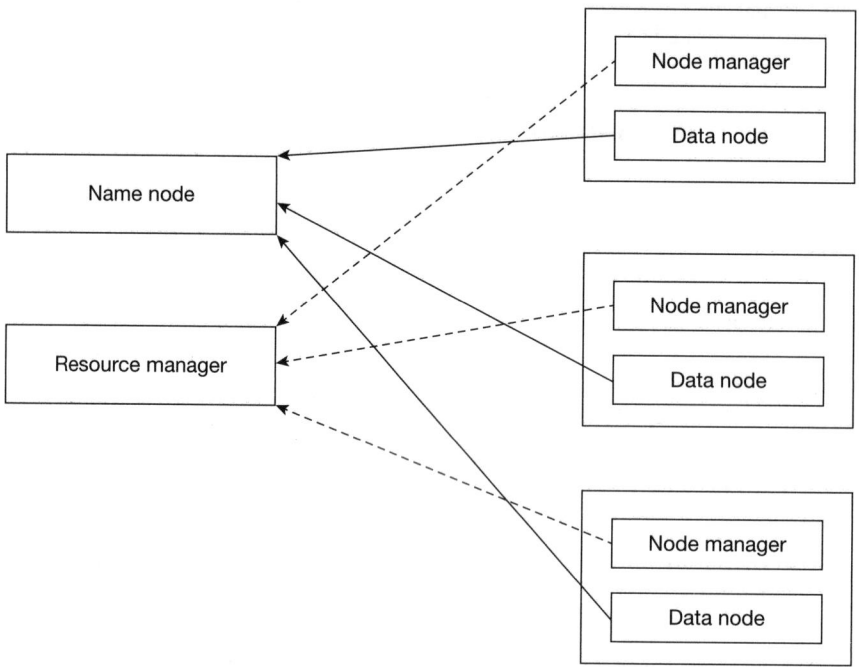

Figure 5.33 YARN resource manager

Yarn Resource Manager: This is the master daemon, and it receives the processing request, and whenever a client comes up with a request, it comes to the resource manager first because the resource manager manages all the slave nodes or node managers. The resource manager takes the request and passes the request to the corresponding node managers.

Yarn Node Manager: Node managers are the slave demons installed on every data node. Data is divided into blocks and stored in the data nodes. A data manager is also present in the data node to process all the data. It is responsible for the execution of the tasks on every single data node.

So, the client comes up with a request to the yarn resource manager to process the data. The resource manager passes on the request to the node manager. The node manager has a container and app master. The app master is launched for every specific application code, every job, or every client's processing task. The application master (the app master) is responsible for handling and taking care of all the required resources to execute the code.

If there is a requirement for any resource, it is the app master which asks for the resources from the resource manager. The resource manager provides the app master with all the resources, and then it asks the node managers to start a container. A container is a place where the actual execution happens (Fig. 5.34).

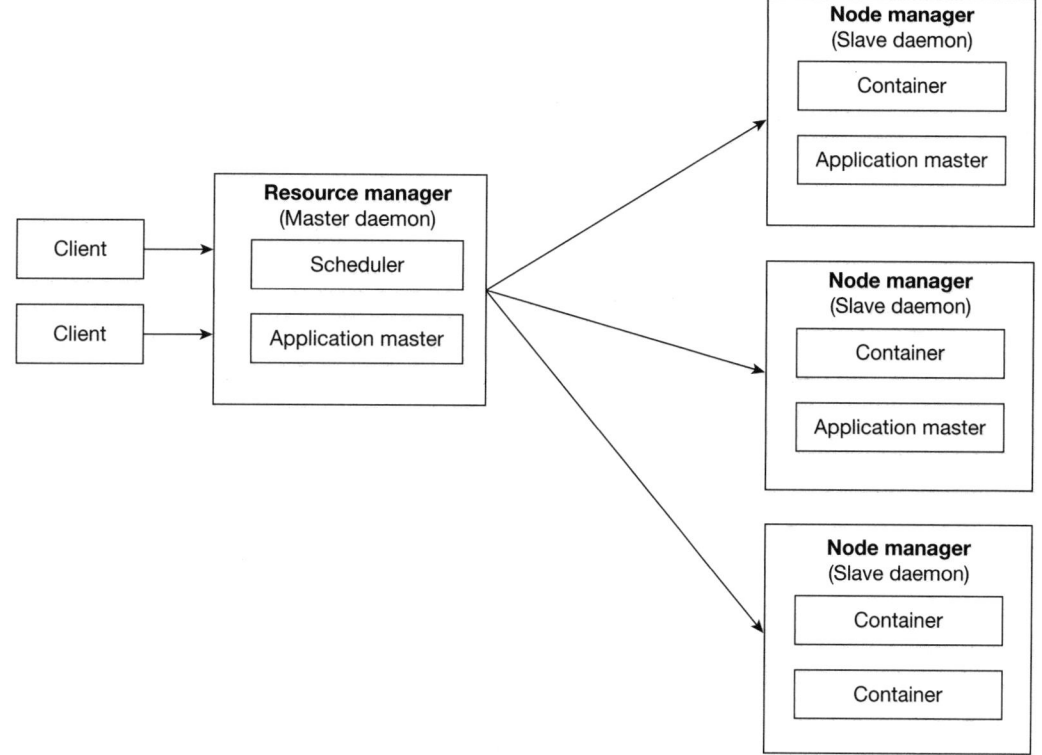

Figure 5.34 YARN architecture

Both HDFS and Yarn follow a master-slave topology. The master in HDFS is the name node, and the master in Yarn is the resource manager. The slave Daemons in HDFS are the data nodes (where all the data is stored), and in Yarn, it is a node manager (This is where the data is processed in a container). The app master takes care of all the resources that are necessary in order to execute the program. The data node and the node manager will lie in the same machine, but it is not necessary that the name node and the resource manager would be in the same machine. Name node can be in a different machine, and a resource manager can be in another machine.

Example 1: Facebook has 21 petabytes of storage in a single HDFS cluster, and they have got two thousand machines per cluster and 32 gigs of ram per machine; they run 15 MapReduce tasks. Each of these machines runs 15 MapReduce tasks, and 1200 machines have eight cores each, and 800 machines have 16 cores each, and there are 12 terabytes of data per machine. So, it is a total of 21 terabytes of configured storage capacity. It is larger than the previously known Yahoo cluster; which was 14 petabytes.

Example 2: Spotify uses Hadoop for generating music recommendations. When you listen to music, some new songs are recommended to you, which belong to the same genre that you have been listening to. It is done by Big Data analysis with Hadoop. Spotify has got sixteen hundred and fifty (1650) nodes, and they have 65 petabytes of storage approximately. Spotify has 70 terabytes of RAM, and they run more than 25,000 daily Hadoop jobs and have 43,000 virtualized cores; so it is an even larger cluster than Facebook.

5.35 APACHE SPARK ARCHITECTURE

It has been a thriving open-source community and is the most active Apache project that supports real-time processing. It has a lot of Spark components for various purposes (Fig. 5.35).

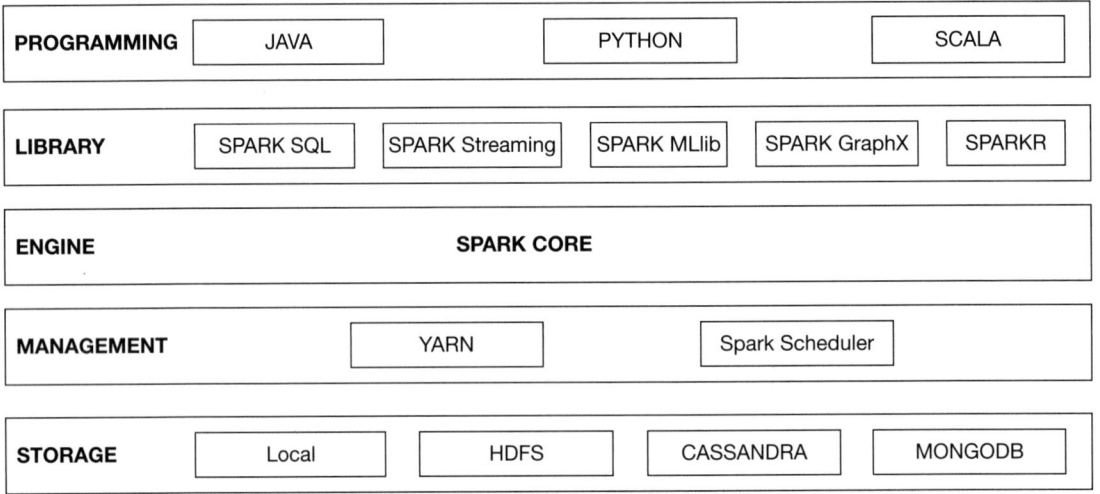

Figure 5.35 SPARK architecture

Spark core engine: The core engine is for the entire Spark framework; every component is part of the core engine. It is the primary engine for large-scale parallel and distributed data processing. The core is the distributed execution engine. Java and Python APIs offer a platform for distributed ETL development, and other additional libraries are on top of the core. It is responsible for scheduling, distributing, and monitoring jobs in a cluster and interacting with the storage systems.

Spark SQL: It is a Spark module for structured data processing, and can be used to run modified Hive queries on existing Hadoop deployments. Spark SQL is the new module in Spark, and it integrates relational processing with Spark's functional programming API. It supports querying of data either by SQL or via a Hive query language. First, we have the "data source universal API" for loading and storing structured data; it supports Hive JSON JDBC, etc. It also supports third-party integration through Spark packages.

Spark streaming: The Spark component is used to process real-time streaming data and is a valuable addition to the core Spark API. It enables high throughput, fault tolerance, and stream processing of live data streams.

Spark MLlib: This is the machine learning library for Spark, used to implement machine learning.

Spark GraphX: This is the graph computation engine. It is the Spark API for graphs and graph parallel computation. It has got a set of fundamental operators, like subgraph, joint purchases, etc.

SparkR: This is the package for Spark language to enable users to leverage Spark power from the shell. You can write all codes in the shell, and Spark will process it for you.

Spark context is the central point (Fig. 5.36) and entry point of the Spark shell. The driver program runs the application's main function, and this is where Spark context is created. Spark context represents the connection to the entire Spark cluster. It helps to create resilient distributed datasets, accumulators and broadcast variables on that cluster. Only one Spark context may be active at a time. You must stop any active Spark context before creating a new one.

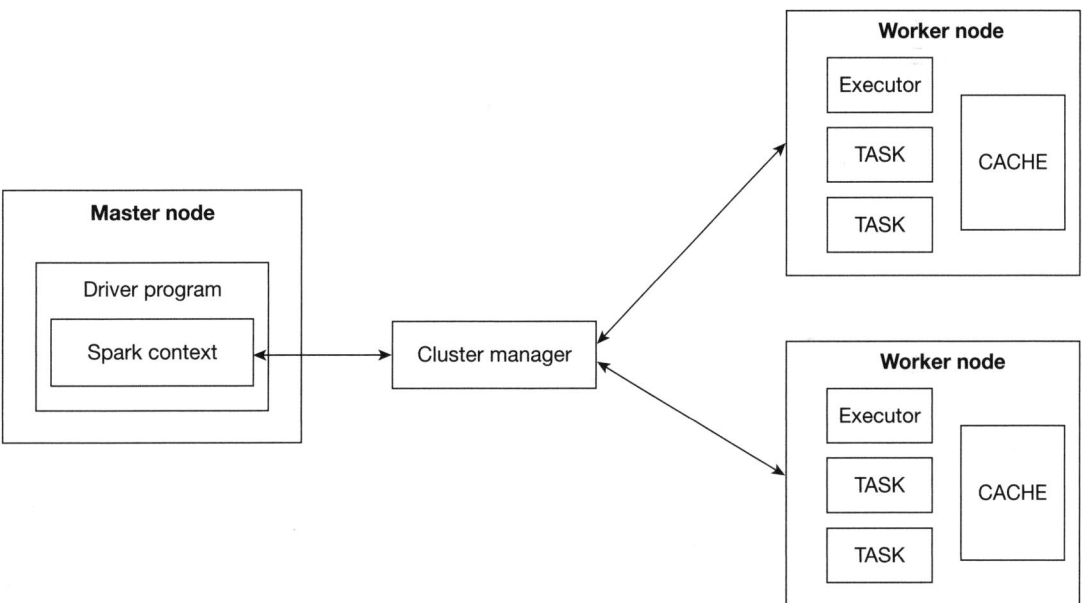

Figure 5.36 SPARK architecture: Cluster manager

The driver program runs on the master node of the Spark cluster. It schedules the job execution and negotiates with the cluster manager. The cluster manager is an external service responsible for acquiring resources on the Spark cluster and allocating them to a Spark job. In the worker node, we have got the executors. The executor is a distributed agent that is responsible for the execution of tasks. Every Spark application has its executor process. Executors usually run for their entire lifetime of the Spark application. This phenomenon is also known as the static allocation of executors. You can also opt for dynamic allocations of executors where you can add or remove Spark executors dynamically to match with the overall workflow. When a client submits a user application code, the driver converts the code containing transformations and actions into logically directed acyclic graph (DAG).

At this stage, the driver program performs certain kinds of optimizations like pipelining transformations. It then converts the logical DAG into physical execution of a plan with a set of stages. After creating a physical execution plan, it creates more physical execution units (referred to as tasks under each state). Then, these tasks are bundled to be sent to the Spark cluster, so the driver program negotiates for the resources with the cluster manager.

On behalf of the driver, the cluster manager launches the executors on the worker nodes. Before the executors begin execution, they first register themselves with the driver program so that the driver gets a holistic view of all the executors. Now, the executors will execute the various tasks assigned to them by the driver program.

5.36 Zeppelin Architecture

Zeppelin (Fig. 5.37) is used to visualize the data. It uses K-means, which is one of the simplest unsupervised learning algorithms that can solve the well-known clustering problem.

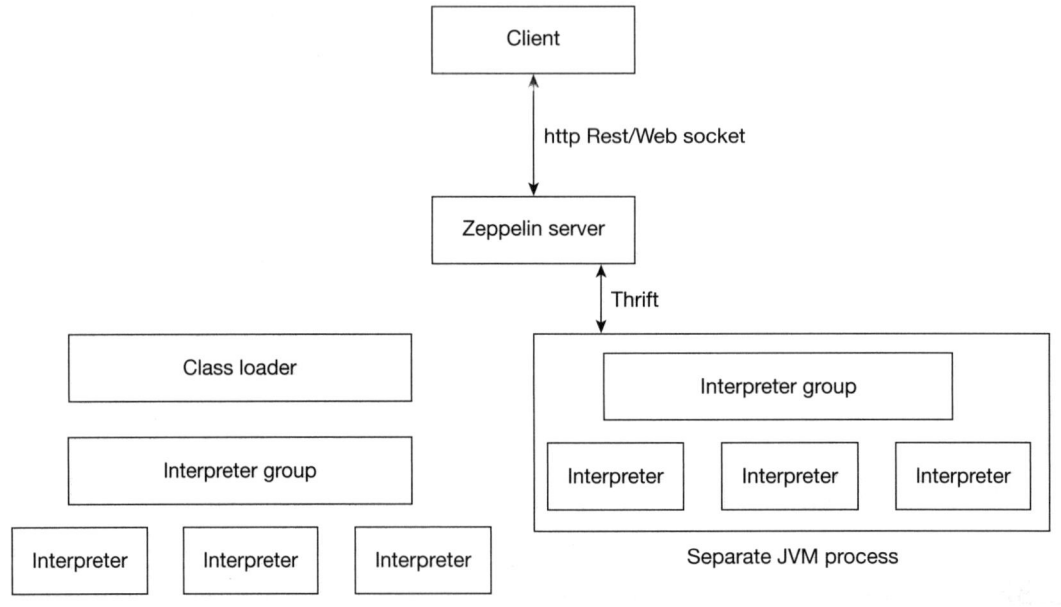

Figure 5.37 Zeppelin architecture

Zeppelin Client connects with Zeppelin Server through Http Rest (or) Web Socket protocol.

Zeppelin Server connects with the data source through the interpreter using Thrift protocol in Java Virtual Machine Process. It can also connect to the interpreter using the class loader.

It uses K-means clustering method. The procedure of K-means follows a simple and easy way to classify a dataset to a certain number of clusters, which is fixed before performing the clustering method. The main idea is to define case centroids for each cluster.

Example: Let us say that we want to cluster a total population of a specific location, and we want to cluster them into four different clusters, namely Groups one, two, three, and four. So the main thing that we should keep in mind is that the objects within the group should be as similar as possible, but there should be as much difference as possible between the objects in different groups. It means that the points lying in the same group should have similar characteristics, and they should be different from the points lying in another cluster. The attributes of the objects are allowed to determine which object should be grouped.

5.37 HADOOP STREAMING

Hadoop distribution provides generic application programming interface (API). This allows writing Map and Reduce jobs in any desired programming language. The utility allows creating/running jobs with any executable as Mapper/Reducer.

For example:

```
hadoop jar hadoop-streaming-3.0.jar \
-input myInputDirs \
-output myOutputDir \
-mapper /bin/cat \
-reducer /usr/bin/wc
```

In the example, both the Mapper and Reducer are executables that read the input from stdin (line by line) and emit the output to stdout. The utility allows creating/submitting Map/Reduce job, to an appropriate cluster. It also monitors the progress of the job until it is completed. Hadoop Streaming uses both streaming command options as well as generic command options. Be sure to place the generic options before the streaming. Otherwise, the command will fail.

The general line syntax is as shown below:

Hadoop command [genericOptions] [streamingOptions]

5.38 OTHER HADOOP COMMANDS

Following command line commands are used in Hadoop for various purposes, as mentioned below:

```
Move to the ~/hadoop-3.1.2 directory

01. hadoop version (To display Hadoop version)
02. hadoop fs –mkdir /path/directory_name
03. hadoop fs -ls
04. hadoop fs -ls -R (display entries in all sub directory path)
05. hadoop fs -put <localsrc> <dest>
06. hadoop fs -copyFromLocal <localsrc> <hdfs destination>
07. hadoop fs -moveFromLocal <localsrc> <dest>
08. hadoop fs -get <src> <localdest>
09. hadoop fs -moveToLocal <src> <localdest>
10. hadoop fs –cat /path_to_file_in_hdfs
11. hadoop fs -mv <src> <dest>
12. hadoop fs -cp <src> <dest>
13. hadoop fs –rm <path>
14. hadoop fs –expunge (makes the trash empty.)
15. hadoop fs -chown [-R] [owner] [:[group]] <path>  (change owner)
16. hadoop fs -setrep <rep> <path> (Set replication factor)
17. hadoop fs -df [-h] <path> (display file details)
```

5.39 NoSQL Concepts

NoSQL databases gained popularity with the advent of web-based applications and Big Data where vast amounts of continuously growing data are stored and retrieved. It is a non-relational data management system with flexible data structures that can store structured, semi-structured and unstructured data. The term NoSQL refers to 'Not Only SQL' or 'Not SQL' which means that NoSQL supports SQL as well as other features.

Some of the main features of NoSQL databases are as below.

- It does not have a rigid pre-defined schema. It supports data changing over time and dissimilar data can be stored together, which is not the case with SQL databases.
- It supports auto-sharding that allows for automatic horizontal scaling and failover capabilities. Data loads and queries are automatically balanced among servers and any failure is switched quickly and transparently without any disruption.
- NoSQL allows for automatic database replication, thus maintaining high availability in case of outages.
- There is no standard based query language like SQL for RDBMS. Selection methods and low-level data manipulation are enabled through simple object-oriented APIs.
- NoSQL databases have integrated caching capability where frequently used data is kept in system memory rather than in a separate caching layer.

NoSQL database systems like MongoDB, Redis, HBase, and Neo4j are becoming popular as emphasis increases on scalable storage that involves terabytes and petabytes of data without compromising on speed and accuracy. That would entail a compromise or variation on distributed system CAP requirements and ACID rules on how transactions are handled.

5.39.1 CAP Theorem

CAP stands for **C** – Consistency, **A** – Availability, and **P** – Partition Tolerance, the three characteristics desired for distributed systems with replicated data.

CAP theorem is also referred to as Brewer's Theorem. CAP theorem postulates that a distributed system cannot guarantee the optimal levels of consistency, availability and partition tolerance, all at the same time. There has to be a trade-off.

In a NoSQL type distributed database system, the data is stored or processed via multiple computers or nodes, while giving the impression of a single working unit to the user. The desired system characteristics are as follows:

- **Consistency:** Consistency means that all nodes will have the same view of the data at any given time. This implies that data written to one node must instantly be replicated to other nodes in the distributed cluster. Consistency is quite relevant for banking apps where the exact value of user account must be displayed.
- **Availability:** Availability means all working nodes in a cluster must get a valid response to a request even if one or more nodes are down. E-Commerce businesses need to have highly available databases where the shopping cart is available 24/7.
- **Partition Tolerance:** Partition Tolerance means that the cluster continues to work despite any number of breaks in communication between the nodes in the system. Partition tolerance is a must for any reliable distributed data store.

With reference to CAP theorem, a NoSQL database management system can deliver consistency and partition tolerance at the expense of availability, e.g. MongoDB, and HBase, or provide availability and partition tolerance at the cost of consistency, e.g. CassandraDB, and CouchDB.

5.39.2 ACID and BASE Models

Relational database management systems are said to be ACID compliant. ACID is an acronym for:

- A – **A**tomic, which means that a transaction or operation either fails or succeeds as a unit. There is no partial completion of a transaction.
- C – **C**onsistent, which means that system-defined constraints or rules will not be violated. The structural integrity of the database will always be maintained.
- I – **I**solated means that multiple transactions running at the same time will run independent of each other. A transaction will not interact or interfere with any transactions that are still in progress.
- D – **D**urable: Once a transaction is completed, the data is saved and will persist even if the system crashes or powers down.

ACID transactions ensure that the database is in a consistent state after running multiple sets of operation. Relational databases like MySQL, PostgreSQL, Oracle, and other RDBMS can guarantee ACID properties of transactions, while NoSQL databases work well on clusters and are more attuned to the complexities of Big Data to cater to speed and scalability. Hence ACID standards are relaxed in NoSQL databases. However, MongoDB and RavenDB are known to be fully ACID compliant, while other NoSQL databases like CouchDB, Redis and many others provide various degrees of ACID compliance.

NoSQL database is typically said to be BASE compliant. BASE is an acronym for:

- BA – **B**asically **A**vailable, which means the availability of data is ensured by spreading data across many storage systems with a high degree of replication. This replication of the data across the database cluster nodes guarantees data availability even if segment failure were to occur.
- S – **S**oft state, means that data consistency is not enforced by the database, but is the responsibility of the developers.
- E – **E**ventually consistent means the system will eventually become consistent once it stops receiving inputs. This is vastly different from the ACID model, which requires a prior transaction to be completed and the database to be consistent before the next transaction executes.

The BASE model prioritizes availability over consistency. The BASE database model is simpler as compared to the robust model of ACID compliant databases. However, BASE model databases are more difficult to implement and the transactions take more time to complete compared to ACID. Cassandra, Redis, DynamoDB and Couchbase conform to BASE principles.

5.39.3 Advantages and Disadvantages of NoSQL

Advantages of NoSQL

- NoSQL is highly flexible and can store and combine any data type including semi-structured and unstructured data.
- NoSQL is built to address the complexities (volume, velocity and variety) of Big Data without impacting performance and latency.
- It has a flexible schema model that can be altered without any downtime.
- It provides fast performance and horizontal scalability.
- High availability with easy replication and no single point of failure.

Disadvantages of NoSQL

- NoSQL is less mature than RDBMS databases with limited query and backup capabilities.
- There is no standardization. Hence the model and query language is dependent on the NoSQL system.
- Data consistency is not a priority and data duplication and other inconsistencies can occur when multiple transactions are performed simultaneously.
- The learning curve is high.

NoSQL is best suited for applications where flexible and fast data storage is a priority with emphasis on having minimal or no code changes or additional IT infrastructure. However, if complex and dynamic querying and security is a significant concern then traditional RDBMS systems may be the best option. NoSQL databases are best suited for web, mobile, IoT, and other digital economy businesses.

SUMMARY

Traditional Large Systems worked on a single machine with high-capacity CPUs, high storage databases, and higher memories. However, expanding this beyond a limit is not possible. Moreover, these systems take a higher processing time due to the mega-size of the data. It also succumbs to the single point of failure.

The five *V*'s of Big Data help to overcome the above problems of large-scale systems and indicate the requirements for a new approach: Volume, Variety, Velocity, Veracity and Value.

The Big Data revolution started with Google. They were gracious enough to share that solution with the world through a white paper published in 2003. It was called GFS (Google File System), and MapReduce white paper (2004), which was the seed of the modern-day Hadoop.

Hadoop is the solution to the "Big Data" problems. In this framework, the code travels to the nodes where the data is present. Hadoop is different from a single-machine system.

Characteristics of Hadoop: Highly economical, high reliability, high availability, high scalability, high throughput, no schema and easy to use.

Various flavors of Hadoop are classified as Open Source/Not an Open Source and are based on Hadoop's front-end system:

- Apache Hadoop (open source): Front end is Apache Ambari
- Horton work (open source): Front end is Apache Ambari
- Cloudera (partially open source): Front end is Cloudera manager
- Map R (not an open source): Front end is Map R control system.

There are three modes of Hadoop System, namely Standalone, Pseudo-distributed mode and Fully distributed mode.

Hadoop ecosystem is software built directly on the Hadoop platform, and it also consists of various ancillary systems. There are different ways of organizing these systems, with several complex interdependencies.

The five major components of the Hadoop ecosystem are 1. Data ingestion layer (Sqoop, Flume etc.) 2. Data storage layer (HDFS/HBASE etc.) 3. Processing engine (MapReduce etc.). 4. Analysis layer (Pig, Hive etc.) 5. Management and coordination layer (ZooKeeper, Apache Ambari etc.).

ETL (Extract, Transform and Load) and ELT (Extract, Load and Transform) are the two ways in which data can be ingested into the target system. ETL stands for Extract, Transform and Load. ELT stands for Extract, Load and Transform.

HDFS: It stands for the Hadoop Distributed File System. HDFS is the Hadoop version of GFS (Google File System). This system allows the distribution of the storage of Big Data across the cluster of computers. It makes all the hard drives on the cluster look like a single giant file system.

HBase: HBase is a "No SQL" database with columnar data store, written in Java and meant for large transaction rates. It was previously called as Google Big Table (GBT) and later renamed as HBase. HBase is a way of exposing the data on the cluster to transactional platforms for low latency operations.

MapReduce: MapReduce, at a very high level, is a programming model that allows processing of data across the entire cluster. It is the data processing layer of Hadoop. MapReduce works by breaking the processing into two phases: mappers and reducers.

In HDFS, appending the content to the end of the file is supported. However, the content cannot be updated at an arbitrary point. HDFS is suitable for large datasets of gigabytes to terabytes in size. It can store all types of data (structured, unstructured) that run on commodity hardware.

Name node: It is the master daemon, and it manages the data node. The Name Node is the arbitrator and repository for all HDFS metadata. User data never flows through the Name Node, which preserves only the metadata.

Secondary name node: It does an essential task known as Check-pointing, which combines edit logs with FS image.

Data nodes: These are the slave daemons, where the actual data is stored. Whenever a client gives a read or write request, the data node serves it. The data node stores the data as data blocks. Racks arrange the data nodes. We can set up different data nodes in racks.

Data racks: A rack consists of multiple nodes, usually 30 to 40 nodes. Each of these nodes, in turn, store multiple data blocks.

Data integrity ensures that no data loss or corruption happens while storing or processing the data. In Hadoop, the amount of data being written or read is large in volume, so the chances of data corruption are more. Hadoop has a checksum mechanism to tackle this data integrity issue.

Data locality refers to moving the computation (code) close to the node, where the actual data resides on, instead of moving extensive amount of data to the computation spot.

The issue with small files: Hadoop is not suited for small files. A small file means it is significantly smaller than the HDFS default block size (128MB). HDFS cannot handle a large number of such small files.

Apache Hadoop is the database's future because it stores and processes many varieties of data, which cannot be easily stored on a traditional database.

Hadoop is not suited for small data. Hadoop HDFS cannot support the random reading of small files, which are smaller than the HDFS block size (default 128 MB). If we store these vast numbers of small files, HDFS cannot handle these. HDFS works very well with a small number of large files. However, a large number of many small files overload the NameNode as it holds the namespace of the HDFS file system.

Safe mode: On start-up, name nodes enter into a special mode: safe mode. Replication of data blocks does not occur when the NameNode is in the safe mode state. During the name node daemon start up, the NameNode enters safe mode for a certain period. The administrator can also enter the safe mode manually for maintenance or up-gradation of the cluster.

Yarn architecture: When Hadoop came up with its new version (2.0), it introduced Yarn as the new framework. Yarn stands for Yet Another Resource Negotiator. It is a master/slave topology. The master daemon is known as resource manager, and slave daemons are known as node managers.

Zeppelin is used to visualizing the data. It uses K-means, which is one of the simplest unsupervised learning algorithms that solve the well-known clustering problem.

EXERCISES

Multiple Choice Questions

1. A data present in CVS file format is an example of _____.
   A. Structured data
   B. Unstructured data
   C. Semi Structured data
   D. Mixed data
   Answer: A
   Explanation
   1. **Structured data:** This type of data is in proper format; for example, the data present within the databases, the CSV files, and the Excel spreadsheets.
   2. **Unstructured data:** This is the opposite of structured data, and it does not have any associated format, for example, the image files, the audio files, and the video files.
   3. **Semi-structured data:** Here, the data has some form; for example, the data present within emails, log files, and Word documents.

2. A data present in Excel sheet file is an example of _____.
   A. Structured data
   B. Unstructured data
   C. Semi-structured data
   D. Mixed data
   Answer: A
   Explanation: Same as for Question 1.

3. **A data present in an Image file is an example of _____.**
   A. Structured data
   B. Unstructured data
   C. Semi Structured data
   D. Mixed data
   Answer: B
   Explanation: Same as for Question 1.

4. **Data present in Word document is an example of _____.**
   A. Structured data
   B. Unstructured data
   C. Semi Structured data
   D. Mixed data
   Answer: C
   Explanation: Same as for Question 1.

5. **A data present in Email is an example of _____.**
   A. Structured data
   B. Unstructured data
   C. Semi Structured data
   D. Mixed data
   Answer: C
   Explanation: Same as for Question 1.

6. **The growth of structured data is saturated.**
   A. True
   B. False
   Answer: A
   Explanation: The growth of structured data is saturated. However, the data from modern-day businesses are too big these days. Sources like information from sensors, information weblogs, and trading information from the stock market are examples.

7. **The structured data growth is saturated. The popularity of unstructured data is growing fast. This represents _____ of the Five *V*'s.**
   A. Volume
   B. Velocity
   C. Variety
   D. Veracity
   Answer: A
   Explanation
   Five *V*s of Big Data – Volume: The structured data's growth is saturated. The popularity of unstructured data is growing fast. It is growing at a very exponential rate; handling volume of data is the need of the hour. The only technology that can address this is Big Data; this is another reason why Big Data has become so popular in the recent past.

8. **Big Data is in several forms (states), such as email documents, sensors data, mobile devices data, etc. This represents _____ of the Five *V*'s.**
   A. Volume
   B. Velocity
   C. Variety
   D. Veracity
   Answer: C
   Explanation
   Five *V*s of Big Data – Variety: Initially, we stored the data and information in databases in rows and columns in a structured format. Big Data is in several forms

(states) such as email documents, sensor data, mobile devices Data, etc. Data are Structured, Semi-Structured, and Unstructured. We need to have different, higher-end computing capabilities to process this data. Since Big Data is in several forms and variety of sources, handling variety is one of the characteristics of the Big Data.

9. **This represents the speed of the collected data:**
   A. Volume   B. Velocity
   C. Variety   D. Veracity
   Answer: B
   Explanation: Velocity is the speed of the collected data. It also refers to the speed in which the collected data is analyzed and used.

10. **Google Map provides alerts on "the time to reach" the destination, using "real-time traffic data" based on the distance between the two places and the traffic in that place (real time data). This is an example of:**
    A. Volume   B. Velocity
    C. Variety   D. Veracity
    Answer: B
    Explanation: Google Map uses real-time traffic data based on the distance between the two places, the traffic in that place, current location using GPS, and all other relevant live (real time) information. Since the data is processed real-time, the speed of refreshing the data is very important here. Velocity is the speed of the collected data. It also refers to the speed in which the collected data is analyzed and used.

11. **This represents the Quality of the data:**
    A. Volume   B. Velocity
    C. Variety   D. Veracity
    Answer: D
    Explanation: Veracity means the quality of the data, the cleanliness of the data, meaningful data and trust in the data. It is essential to have volumes of data at high speed, but it needs to be accurate with high quality, be relevant and meaningful and received at the right time to ensure confidence on the outcome of the analysis.

12. **Data should add this to the end customer in order to have impactful business insights:**
    A. Volume   B. Velocity
    C. Variety   D. Value
    Answer: D
    Explanation: Value is an integral part of data and plays an important role. If there is no meaningful value out of the data, there is no need to analyze. Data should add value to the end customer in order to have business impactful insights.

13. **Which of the following is not a characteristic of the Hadoop software?**
    A. Open Source
    B. Distributed

C. Single Point of Failure
D. It can handle structured and unstructured data.
Answer: C
Explanation: Apache Hadoop is a free open-source platform for distributed storage and distributed processing of extensive datasets on a computer cluster. It enables expanding memories in a distributed environment, thus overcoming the single point of failure problem. It can handle structured and unstructured data. Open source means it is freely available, and we can change its source code as per our requirements.

14. **This represents that Hadoop is freely available, and we can change its source code as per our requirements:**
    A. Open Source
    B. Distributed
    C. Single Point of Failure
    D. It can handle structured and unstructured data.
    Answer: A
    Explanation: Same as that for Question 13.

15. **Hadoop runs on a cluster of computers inside a _____.**
    A. Cluster   B. Rack
    C. Computer   D. Laptop
    Answer: B
    Explanation: Hadoop runs on a cluster of computers inside a rack. It leverages the power of multiple computers for handling Big Data that uses distributed storage. Distributed storage is one of the main concepts of Hadoop.

16. **Horizontal scaling of the Hadoop cluster is _____.**
    A. Linear   B. Non-linear
    C. Exponential   D. Not possible
    Answer: A
    Explanation: Big Data deals with terabytes of data/information. While adding more and more computers to the cluster, their hard drives become part of the data storage. Hadoop offers parallel processing that can take advantage of all the individual CPUs. The horizontal scaling of the Hadoop cluster is linear.

17. **This was the first search engine to systematically sort, store, and retrieve large amounts of data:**
    A. Google   B. Microsoft Edge
    C. Yahoo   D. Apache Lucene
    Answer: D
    Explanation: During the 2000s when the number of data found on websites/internet began to rise to millions and billions, it was difficult and time-consuming to

quickly retrieve the data and information we were looking for. Doug Cutting and Mike Cafarella (2002) teamed up to create a web crawler called Nutch to address these issues. It was a powerful tool to download web pages and store data. Apache Lucene was the first search engine to systematically sort, store, and retrieve such large amounts of data.

18. **Big Data revolution started with _____.**
    A. Google
    B. IBM
    C. Twitter
    D. Facebook
    Answer: A
    Explanation: The performance of Nutch and Lucene was limited. These could not handle a large amount of data and information. The Big Data revolution started with Google, when the technology company shared its solution with the world through a white paper published in 2003. It was called GFS (Google File System), and MapReduce white paper (2004), which was the seed of the modern-day Hadoop. It opened the world's eyes to see how massive data can be stored and processed.

19. **GFS is an expansion of _____.**
    A. Geographic File System
    B. Geographic Factoring System
    C. Google File System
    D. Google Facebook System
    Answer : C
    Explanation: Same as that for Question 18.

20. **GFS is the concept behind _____.**
    A. Hive
    B. HDFS
    C. HBase
    D. NoSQL
    Answer: B
    Explanation: GFS is the concept behind HDFS (Hadoop Distributed File System). MapReduce is Hadoop's solution for distributed storage of information (distributed processing). In 2008, Yahoo successfully tested Hadoop with 1000 nodes.

21. **Which of the following is not the principle of Hadoop?**
    A. The code travels to the nodes where the data is present.
    B. The data is transferred from the data center onto the program execution machine.
    C. It is cost-effective.
    D. It does not require any expensive or specialized hardware.
    Answer: B
    Explanation: In Hadoop framework, the code travels to the nodes where the data is present. Hadoop is different from a single-machine system. In the traditional approach, while executing a software program, the data is transferred from the data center onto the program execution machine. Hadoop eliminates this problem by moving the code, then compiling and executing the code locally on that data.

22. **This refers to a cluster within which each node can be from a different vendor, and each node could be running a different version and a different flavor of the operating system.**
    A. Homogeneous cluster
    B. Heterogeneous cluster
    C. Common cluster
    D. Centralized cluster
    Answer: B
    Explanation: Hadoop supports a heterogeneous cluster, and this is one of the most important features offered by the Hadoop framework. A heterogeneous cluster refers to a cluster within which each node can be from a different vendor, and each node could be running a different version and a different flavor of the operating system.

23. **If any node goes down in the Hadoop cluster, what will happen?**
    A. The data in the cluster is lost.
    B. Hadoop Admins need to run the recovery command.
    C. Hadoop framework will replace that particular machine (node) with another.
    D. Hadoop developer can run the recovery command.
    Answer: C
    Explanation: High availability is an important feature offered by Hadoop. The Hadoop framework takes care of splitting and distributing the data across all the nodes within a cluster. It also replicates the data over the entire cluster. It is fault-tolerant. Distributed processing distributes the data's processing. Admins need not worry about all this once the automatic failover management is configured on the cluster.

24. **This refers to adding or removing the nodes, and adding or removing the hardware components to or from the cluster:**
    A. Availability
    B. Scalability
    C. Throughput
    D. Distributed
    Answer: B
    Explanation: Scalability refers to adding or removing the nodes, and adding or removing the hardware components to or from the cluster. We can easily add or remove a node to or from a cluster without bringing down or affecting the cluster operation.

25. **Hadoop can utilize Amazon Web Services or Google, or any other vendors that sell cloud services.**
    A. False
    B. True
    Answer: B
    Explanation: Scalability refers to adding or removing the nodes, and adding or removing the hardware components to or from the cluster. Hadoop can utilize Amazon Web Services or Google, or any other vendors that sell cloud services. It is possible to add any number of nodes, enhancing the performance dramatically.

26. **The amount of work done in a unit time is called as:**
    A. Availability
    B. Scalability
    C. Throughput
    D. Distributed
    Answer: C
    Explanation: Hadoop supports parallel processing of data. Therefore, the data can be processed simultaneously across all the nodes within the cluster, thus saving a lot of time. The amount of work done in a unit time is Throughput.

27. **HDFS works in the principle of:**
    A. Write Many and Read Once
    B. Write Many and Read Many
    C. Write Once and Read Once
    D. Write Once and Read Many
    Answer: D
    Explanation: The HDFS works in the model of the "Write Once and Read Many" principle. It simplifies the data coherency issues as the data written once; one cannot modify it. Thus, it provides high throughput data access.

28. **This principle states, "move the computation to data instead of moving the data to computation".**
    A. No schema
    B. Data locality
    C. Computation locality
    D. Dynamic computation
    Answer: B
    Explanation: Hadoop works on the Data Locality principle. This principle states that computation has to be moved close to data instead of moving the data to computation. This principle reduces network congestion and therefore, enhances the overall system throughput.

29. **All the following are different flavors of Hadoop, except:**
    A. Apache Hadoop (open source): Front end is Apache Ambari
    B. Horton work (open source): Front end is Apache Ambari
    C. Map R (not an open source): Front end is Map R control system
    D. Apache Hadoop (open source): Front end is Cloudera Manager
    Answer: D
    Explanation: Various Flavors of Hadoop are classified base on Open Source/Not an Open Source and its front end system is as follows: 1. Apache Hadoop (open source): Front end is Apache Ambari. 2. Horton work (open source): Front end is Apache Ambari. 3. Cloudera (partially open source): Front end, Cloudera manager. 4. Map R (not an open source): Front end, Map R control system

30. **All the following are different modes of Hadoop, except:**
    A. Stand-alone mode
    B. Pseudo-distributed mode
    C. Fully distributed mode
    D. Redistributed mode
    Answer: D
    Explanation: There are three modes of Hadoop System, namely Stand-alone, Pseudo-distributed mode (single-node cluster) and fully distributed mode (multiple node cluster)

31. **Which of the following mode is the default mode of Hadoop?**
    A. Stand-alone mode
    B. Pseudo-distributed mode
    C. Fully distributed mode
    D. Redistributed mode
    Answer: A
    Explanation: Standalone Mode/Single Mode is the default mode of Hadoop, a non-distributed mode that runs a single Java process. This mode uses the local file system for input and output operation and is useful for debugging. This mode does not offer a truly distributed environment. It does not support fully distributed HDFS.

32. **Each Hadoop daemon runs as a single Java process in this mode:**
    A. Stand-alone mode
    B. Pseudo-distributed mode
    C. Fully distributed mode
    D. Redistributed mode
    Answer: A
    Explanation: Hadoop runs on a single node in a pseudo (false) distributed mode, just like the stand-alone mode. The difference is that each Hadoop daemon runs in a separate Java process in pseudo-distributed mode, whereas in local mode, each Hadoop daemon runs as a single Java process.

33. **Hadoop daemon runs in a separate Java process in this mode:**
    A. Stand-alone mode
    B. Pseudo-distributed mode
    C. Fully distributed mode
    D. Redistributed mode
    Answer: B
    Explanation: Same as that for Question 32.

34. **This mode can be used for the experimentation purpose:**
    A. Stand-alone mode
    B. Pseudo-distributed mode
    C. Fully distributed mode
    D. Redistributed mode
    Answer: A
    Explanation: Hadoop runs on a single node in a pseudo (false) distributed mode, just like the stand-alone mode. The difference is that each Hadoop daemon runs in a separate Java process in pseudo-distributed mode, whereas in local mode, each Hadoop daemon runs as a single Java process. The usage of this model is minimal, and it can only be used for experimentation.

35. **This mode allows different nodes for Master and Slave:**
    A. Stand-alone mode
    B. Pseudo-distributed mode
    C. Fully distributed mode
    D. Redistributed mode
    Answer: C
    Explanation: Fully distributed mode allows different nodes for Master and Slave. In this mode, all daemons execute in separate nodes forming a multi-node cluster. Thus, we enable specific nodes for Master and Slave.

Fundamentals of Hadoop • 241

36. **This mode is mostly used in the production environment:**
    A. Stand-alone mode
    B. Pseudo-distributed mode
    C. Fully distributed mode
    D. Redistributed mode
    Answer: C
    Explanation: Fully distributed mode allows different nodes for Master and Slave. In this mode, all daemons execute in separate nodes forming a multi-node cluster. Thus, we enable specific nodes for Master and Slave. We use this model in the production environment, where n number of machines form a cluster in which Hadoop daemons run.

37. **Which of the following are considered as core components of Hadoop?**
    A. HDFS and MapReduce
    B. Hive and MapReduce
    C. HBase and MapReduce
    D. Flume and MapReduce
    Answer: A
    Explanation: HDFS and MapReduce are considered as core components of Hadoop. HDFS is the storage layer of Hadoop.

38. **HDFS works on storing larger number of small files rather than the small number of large files.**
    A. True
    B. False
    Answer: B
    Explanation: HDFS works on storing fewer number large files rather than the vast number of small files. It maintains redundant copies of the given data block, so that if one of the computers fails, data can be recovered from the backup. HDFS creates backup (Replication) to a specified/configured number of copies.

39. **Data processing layer of Hadoop is called as _____.**
    A. MapReduce
    B. Hive
    C. HBase
    D. Flume
    Answer: A
    Explanation: MapReduce at a very high level is a programming model that allows processing the data across the entire cluster. It is the data processing layer of Hadoop. MapReduce works by breaking the processing into two phases: mappers and reducers.

40. **Sqoop belongs to which layer of Hadoop ecosystem?**
    A. Data Ingestion layer
    B. Data Storage layer
    C. Processing Engine layer
    D. Analysis layer
    Answer: A
    Explanation: The Five major components of the Hadoop ecosystem are 1. Data ingestion layer (Sqoop, Flume, etc.) 2. Data storage layer (HDFS/HBase, etc.) 3. Processing engine (MapReduce, etc.). 4. Analysis layer (Pig, Hive etc.) 5. Management and coordination layer (ZooKeeper, Apache Ambari, etc.)

41. **Flume belongs to which layer of the Hadoop ecosystem?**
    A. Data Ingestion layer
    B. Data Storage layer
    C. Processing Engine layer
    D. Analysis layer
    Answer: A
    Explanation: Same as that for Question 40.

42. **HDFS belongs to which layer of the Hadoop ecosystem?**
    A. Data Ingestion layer
    B. Data Storage layer
    C. Processing Engine layer
    D. Analysis layer
    Answer: B
    Explanation: Same as that for Question 40.

43. **Pig belongs to which layer of the Hadoop ecosystem?**
    A. Data Ingestion layer
    B. Data Storage layer
    C. Processing Engine layer
    D. Analysis layer
    Answer: D
    Explanation: Same as that for Question 40.

44. **ZooKeeper belongs to which layer of the Hadoop ecosystem?**
    A. Data Ingestion layer
    B. Data Storage layer
    C. Processing Engine layer
    D. Management layer
    Answer: D
    Explanation: Same as that for Question 40.

45. **This layer talks about moving the data from multiple assorted sources into a single place for further analysis:**
    A. Data Ingestion layer
    B. Data Storage layer
    C. Processing Engine layer
    D. Analysis layer
    Answer: A
    Explanation: Data ingestion layer talks about moving the data from multiple assorted sources into a single place for further analysis. This layer not only extracts the data from assorted sources but also validates, cleans (reduces noise), normalizes (compresses), prioritizes and processes (integrates) the data in a format that can be ingested into the Storage layer (data destination) of Hadoop for further analysis.

46. **Batching ingestion and streaming ingestion are the two different types of data ingestion methodology.**
    A. True
    B. False
    Answer: A
    Explanation: Batching ingestion and streaming ingestion are the two different types of data ingestion methodology. Batching methodology ensures the data is ingested from the source to the destination in a periodic interval (say every 30 minutes). The streaming methodology ensures that real-time data is ingested into the destination system continuously at real time.

47. **ETL stands for _____.**
    A. Eliminate, Transform and Load
    B. Extract, Transit and Load
    C. Extract, Transform and Load
    D. Extract, Transform and Lock
    Answer: C
    Explanation: ETL (Extract, Transform and Lead) and ELT (Extract, Load and Transform) are the two ways in which data can be ingested into the target system. ETL stands for Extract, Transform and Load. ELT stands for Extract, Load and Transform. In ETL, a temporary staging database is used, where the data is first extracted and then transformed before loading into the Source System.

48. **In ETL, staging database is not used.**
    A. True
    B. False
    Answer: B
    Explanation: ETL is used when the source and target databases are different, data volume is low, and data transformation is complex, and when the data is structured. In ELT, staging database is not used as the data is straightaway extracted and loaded into the source system and the transformation happens in the source system itself. ELT is used when the source and target databases are same, data volume is large, and data transformation is less complex, and when the data is unstructured.

49. **ELT is used when the source and target databases are same, data volume is large, and data transformation is less complex, and when the data is unstructured.**
    A. True
    B. False
    Answer: A
    Explanation: In ELT, staging database is not used as the data is straightaway extracted and loaded into the source system and the transformation happens in the source system itself. ELT is used when the source and target databases are same, data volume is large, and data transformation is less complex, and when the data is unstructured.

50. **This can be considered as a connector between Hadoop and the legacy databases:**
    A. Flume
    B. HDFS
    C. Hive
    D. Sqoop
    Answer: D
    Explanation: Sqoop (SQL + Hadoop) transfers (bulk-data) processing data from a database/datastore) to Hadoop. It is a way of binding the Hadoop database into a relational database. Sqoop is a connector between Hadoop and the legacy databases. We can import data from Sqoop into the cluster, export it to mySQL, and retrieve the results from the SQL database. It is compatible with all types of databases such as Teradata, MySql, Oracle, Postgre.

51. **It is a way of transporting weblogs, at a vast scale and reliably, to your cluster:**
    A. Flume
    B. HDFS
    C. Hive
    D. Sqoop
    Answer: A
    Explanation: Flume is a way of reliably transporting weblogs at a vast scale to your cluster. Let us say you have a fleet of web servers; flume can listen to the weblogs coming in from these web servers in real-time and publish them into your cluster in real-time for processing by Storm or Spark streaming.

52. **This is an MPP (Massive Parallel Processing) SQL written in C++ and Java:**
    A. Flume
    B. HDFS
    C. Impala
    D. Sqoop
    Answer: C
    Explanation: Impala is an MPP (Massive Parallel Processing) SQL written in C++ and Java and is an open-source software. It is the highest performing SQL engine that gives an RDBMS-like experience. Impala can be used for data ingestion and data analysis since it connects directly to HBase and HDFS.

53. **CDC belongs to which layer of the Hadoop ecosystem?**
    A. Data ingestion layer
    B. Data storage layer
    C. Processing engine layer
    D. Management layer
    Answer: A
    Explanation: Change Data Capture (CDC) ensures that the changes made in the source databases are captured and replicated in the destination databases. The replication can be made in batching mode and real time mode depending on the need.

54. **Destination layer of Data Ingestion Layer is called as _____.**
    A. Data ingestion layer
    B. Data storage layer
    C. Processing engine layer
    D. Management layer
    Answer: B
    Explanation: Data storage layer is the destination layer in the data ingestion framework. It is the source layer in the processing and analysis framework.

55. **HDFS, Hbase, MongoDB and Cassandra are the tools of _____.**
    A. Data Ingestion layer
    B. Data Storage layer
    C. Processing engine layer
    D. Management layer
    Answer: B
    Explanation: Data storage layer is the destination layer in the data ingestion framework. It is the source layer in the processing and analysis framework. HDFS, Hbase, MongoDB and Cassandra are the tools of the storage layer.

56. **This is a "No SQL" database with columnar data store, written in Java, meant for large transaction rates:**
    A. HDFS
    B. Hive
    C. HBase
    D. Cassandra
    Answer: C
    Explanation: HBase is a "No SQL" database with columnar data store, written in Java, meant for large transaction rates. It was previously called as Google Big Table (GBT) and later renamed as HBase.

57. **This was previously called as Google Big Table (GBT):**
    A. HDFS
    B. Hive
    C. HBase
    D. Cassandra
    Answer: C
    Explanation: Same as for Question 56.

58. **YARN stands for _____.**
    A. Yet Another Replica Negotiator
    B. Yet Another Resource Negotiator
    C. Yet Another Resource Navigator
    D. Yet Another Real Node
    Answer: B
    Explanation: YARN stands for Yet Another Resource Negotiator. The data processing part of Hadoop is called Yarn. Yarn is the system resource manager that manages the resources on the computing cluster. It allows various types of data processing engines, such as real-time streaming engine, data science engine, and batch processing engine.

59. **Pig is a scripting language, Hive is a query language.**
    A. True
    B. False
    Answer: A
    Explanation: Pig is a scripting language, Hive is a query language. Those familiar with the programming language will choose Pig to write Transformation Logic. Those who work in ETL and Data Warehousing and are well-versed in SQL will choose Hive. Otherwise, the two are used to do almost the same job. These differ only in the methods of accessing the data.

60. **This is a part of Apache open-source project that helps customers to create scalable "Machine Learning" Algorithms:**
    A. Tableau
    B. Apache Spark
    C. Apache Hive
    D. Apache Mahout
    Answer: D
    Explanation: Apache Mahout is part of Apache open-source project that helps customers to create scalable "Machine Learning" Algorithms, which works well in a distributed environment. It supports various Machine Learning algorithms including Naïve Bayes Classification, Clustering and Recommendation.

61. **This is a data visualization software that helps to take quick business decisions and solve business problems easily and quickly.**
    A. Mahout
    B. Tableau
    C. Spark
    D. Drill
    Answer: B
    Explanation: Tableau is a data visualization software that helps to take quick business decisions and also solve business problems easily and quickly by providing limitless data exploration possibilities. It supports Big Data. Its smart dashboards are able to refresh automatically based on the data refresh.

62. **This is part of Apache open-source project that helps customers to create interactive analytics.**
    A. Mahout
    B. Tableau
    C. Spark
    D. Drill
    Answer: D
    Explanation: Apache Drill is part of Apache open-source project that helps customers to create interactive analytics. It integrates with Hive easily. It also helps to visualize the data. It also has its own SQL Query Engine.

63. **This layer gives a birds-eye view and also provides overall coordination across Hadoop ecosystem layers:**
    A. Data Ingestion layer
    B. Data Storage Layer
    C. Processing engine Layer
    D. Management Layer
    Answer: D
    Explanation: Management and coordination layer helps in the overall management of Hadoop ecosystem to give a birds-eye view and also provide overall coordination across Hadoop ecosystem layers.

64. **This is a system for workflow monitoring and is a way of scheduling jobs on your cluster:**
    A. Oozie
    B. Pig
    C. ZooKeeper
    D. Flume
    Explanation: Oozie (Workflow monitoring) is a way of scheduling jobs on your cluster. So, suppose you have a task that needs to happen on the Hadoop cluster that involves many different steps and maybe many other systems. In that case, Oozie is a way of scheduling all these things together into jobs that can run on the specified schedule (time). It is used to run a series of interdependent jobs.

65. **The secondary name node does an essential task known as _____.**
    A. Checkpointing
    B. Clustering
    C. Rack formation
    D. Data localization
    Answer: A
    Explanation: The secondary name node does an essential task known as Checkpointing, which combines edit logs with FS image. Checkpointing is the

task of combining the edit log with the FS image. Checkpointing happens after every hour (configurable). The secondary name node first copies the FS image and the edit log and adds them together in order to get the updated FS image. This FS image is copied back to the name node, and now the name node has an updated FS image.

66. **Default Block size of HDFS is _____.**
    A. 128 KB
    B. 646 MB
    C. 646 KB
    D. 128 MB
    Answer: D
    Explanation: HDFS is a fault-tolerant system. Whenever you write a file into HDFS, the HDFS system breaks down the file into different blocks of size 128 megabytes, except the last block (which will have the remainder of the file). These blocks are distributed across the Hadoop cluster.

67. **Default replication factor of HDFS is _____.**
    A. 6
    B. 3
    C. 1
    D. 2
    Answer: B
    Explanation: Default replication factor of HDFS is 3. It is configurable. Whenever we dump the file into HDFS, it is first divided into blocks, and then each of the blocks is copied as per the replication factor. So, if replication factor equals three, it means that there are three similar blocks in the Hadoop cluster.

68. **A rack usually consists of _____.**
    A. 3 to 4 nodes
    B. 300 to 400 nodes
    C. 30 to 40 nodes
    D. 3000 to 4000 nodes
    Answer: C
    Explanation: A rack consists of multiple nodes, usually 30 to 40 nodes. Each of these nodes, in turn, store multiple data blocks. Within a rack, Hadoop stores its data in two different data nodes.

69. **Which of the following is not part of the rack awareness algorithm?**
    A. Each node will have only one replica of the block.
    B. Each rack will have maximum of two replica of the block.
    C. Number of racks to be used will be lesser than the replication factor.
    D. Number of racks to be used will be thrice the replication factor.
    Answer: D
    Explanation: The rack awareness algorithm says the local rack stores the first replica of a block, and the next two replicas will be stored in a different rack. So, we store a data block in the local rack (rack one) to decrease the latency.
    1. Each node will have only one replica of the block.
    2. Each rack will have maximum of two replica of the block.
    3. Number of racks to be used will be lesser than the replication factor.

70. **Hadoop uses this mechanism to tackle the data integrity issue:**
    A. Checksum
    B. Replication
    C. Rack Awareness
    D. Distributed Data
    Answer: A
    Explanation: Data Integrity ensures that no data loss or corruption happens while storing or processing the data. In Hadoop, the amount of data being written or read is large in volume, so the chances of data corruption are more. Hadoop has a checksum mechanism to tackle this data integrity issue. It computes the checksum while writing the data to the disk for the first time. It checks again while reading the data from the disk. If the new checksum matches the original checksum, it means the data is uncorrupted.

71. **HDFS uses this efficient algorithm to calculate the checksum:**
    A. CRC-62C
    B. CRC-32C
    C. CRC-12C
    D. CRC-32B
    Answer: B
    Explanation: HDFS uses an algorithm called CRC-32C, which is very efficient to calculate the checksum. DataNodes are responsible for calculating the checksum for the received data before storing the data. Hadoop computes the checksum for the data it receives from clients and other DataNodes during the replication stage.

72. **Hadoop provides:**
    A. Horizontal Scalability
    B. Vertical Scalability
    C. Zigzag Scalability
    D. Does not support Scalability
    Answer: A
    Explanation: RDBMS is a traditional database that provides vertical scalability. So if the data increases for storing, then we have to increase the particular system configuration. Hadoop provides horizontal scalability. We can add one or more nodes to the cluster if there is any requirement to increase the data storage.

73. **In this scaling, more disk space is added to get more memory (single computer):**
    A. Horizontal Scalability
    B. Vertical Scalability
    C. Zigzag Scalability
    D. Does not support Scalability
    Answer: B
    Explanation: In vertical scaling, more disk space is added to get more memory (single computer). In horizontal scaling, computers are added, spreading out data across clusters (more computers. no upper bound). This distributes storage and processing leading to "no downtime" and is also "inexpensive."

74. **Apache Hadoop uses this for managing the security:**
    A. Hive
    B. Kerberos
    C. ZooKeeper
    D. MapReduce
    Answer: B

Explanation: Apache Hadoop uses Kerberos for managing the security. A client needs to take three simple steps to access service when using Kerberos. Each of these steps involves exchange of message with a server. The steps are Authentication step, Authorization step and the Service request Step.

Short-answer Questions

1. **What are the categories of data in the Big Data world?**
   There are three categories of data.
   1. **Structured data:** This type of data is in the proper format; for example, the data present within the databases, the CSV files, and the Excel spreadsheets.
   2. **Unstructured data:** It is the opposite of structured data, and it does not have any associated format, for example, the image files, the audio files, and the video files.
   3. **Semi-structured data:** Here, the data has some form; for example, the data present within the emails, the log files, and the Word document.

2. **What is Hadoop?**
   Hadoop is the solution to the "Big Data" problems. This modern day Big Data software overcomes the difficulties of the traditional large-scale systems. Apache Hadoop is a free open-source platform for distributed storage and distributed processing of extensive datasets on a computer cluster. Expanding memories in a distributed environment is possible on Hadoop. It overcomes the single point of failure problem. It can handle structured and unstructured data. Open source means the software is freely available, and we can change its source code as per our requirements.

3. **What are the different flavors of Hadoop?**
   Various flavors of Hadoop are classified as Open Source/Not an Open Source and its front end system.
   - Apache Hadoop (open source): Front end is Apache Ambari
   - Horton work (open source): Front end is Apache Ambari
   - Cloudera (partially open source): Front end is Cloudera manager
   - Map R (not an open source): Front end is Map R control system

4. **What are the different modes of Hadoop?**
   There are three modes of Hadoop System, namely,
   - Standalone mode
   - Pseudo-distributed mode (single-node cluster)
   - Fully distributed mode (or multiple node cluster)

5. **Write notes on Standalone Mode of Hadoop.**
   Standalone Mode/Single Mode is the default mode of Hadoop, a non-distributed mode that runs a single Java process. This mode uses the local file system for input and output operation and is useful for debugging. It does not offer a truly distributed environment or support a fully distributed HDFS. The usage of this model is minimal and used for experimentation and testing.

6. **Write notes on Pseudo-distributed Mode of Hadoop.**
   Hadoop runs on a single node in a pseudo (false) distributed mode, just like the Standalone mode. The difference is that each Hadoop daemon runs in a separate Java process in Pseudo-distributed Mode, whereas in Local mode, each Hadoop daemon runs as a single Java process. The usage of this model is minimal, and it can only be used for experimentation. In pseudo-distributed mode, we need configuration for all the files. In this case, all daemons run on one node, and thus, both Master and Slave nodes are the same. The pseudo mode is suitable for both development and in the testing environment.

7. **Write notes on fully distributed mode of Hadoop.**
   Fully distributed mode allows different nodes for Master and Slave. In this mode, all daemons execute in separate nodes forming a multi-node cluster. Thus, we enable specific nodes for Master and Slave. We use this model in the production environment, where n number of machines form a cluster in which Hadoop daemons run. The Name Node runs on one host and Data Nodes run on the other hosts. Therefore, Node Manager installs on every Data Node. And it is also responsible for the execution of the task on every single Data Node. The Resource Manager manages all these Node Managers. It receives the processing requests and then passes the parts of the request to the corresponding Node Manager.

8. **What is HDFS?**
   It stands for the Hadoop distributed file system. HDFS is the Hadoop version of GFS (Google File System). This system allows the distribution of the storage of Big Data across the cluster of computers. It makes all the hard drives on the cluster look like a single giant file system. HDFS works on storing fewer number large files rather than a vast number of small files. It maintains redundant copies of the data block, so if one of the computers fails, the system can easily recover. The files are backed up (replication) to a specified/configured number of copies. It provides high throughput access to an application by accessing in parallel.

9. **What is MapReduce?**
   MapReduce, at a very high level, is a programming model that allows processing the data across the entire cluster. It is the data processing layer of Hadoop. MapReduce works by breaking the processing into two phases: mappers and reducers. Mappers write an application that processes extensive structured and unstructured data stored in HDFS. Mappers can transform the data in parallel across the entire computing cluster in an efficient manner by dividing the submitted job into a set of independent tasks (sub-jobs). Reduce is the second phase of processing. Reducers aggregate the data together. There are creative ways we can put mappers and reducers together to solve complex problems.

10. **What is Velocity?**
    Velocity is the speed of the collected data. It may also refer to the speed in which the collected data is analyzed and used. For example, Google Map provides alerts on

"the time to reach" the destination using "real-time traffic data" based on the distance between the two places, the traffic in the place, current location of the user (using GPS), and all other relevant live (real-time) information. Since it shows the live (real-time) traffic data, the speed of refreshing the data is very important here.

11. **What is Veracity?**
    Veracity means the quality of the data, the cleanliness of the data, meaningful data and trust in the data. It is essential to have volumes of data at high speed, but it needs to be accurate, with high quality, be relevant/meaningful and also be available at the right time, so that there will be a confidence on the outcome of the analysis.

12. **What is Hadoop?**
    Hadoop is the solution to the "Big Data" problems. This modern-day Big Data software overcomes the difficulties of the traditional large-scale systems. Apache Hadoop is a free open-source platform for distributed storage and distributed processing of extensive datasets on a computer cluster. Using Hadoop, expanding memories in a distributed environment becomes possible. The distributed characteristics of Hadoop helps to overcome the single point of failure problem. It can handle structured and unstructured data. Open source means it is freely available, and we can change its source code as per our requirements.

13. **How is Hadoop economical in nature?**
    The first important feature offered by Hadoop is, it is a cost-effective system. Hadoop does not require any expensive or specialized hardware. In other words, it can be implemented on simple hardware referred to as commodity hardware (low cost per GB; a singular cluster stores petabytes of data). Its distributed file system has the provision of rapid data transfer rates among nodes. Hadoop also supports a heterogeneous cluster, and this is one of the most important features offered by the Hadoop framework. A heterogeneous cluster refers to a cluster within which each node can be from a different vendor, and each node could be running a different version and a different flavor of the operating system.

14. **Write notes on high reliability of Hadoop.**
    High Reliability: Hadoop supports a large cluster of nodes. Therefore, a Hadoop cluster can be made up of hundreds and thousands of nodes. One of the main advantages of having a large cluster is that it offers more computing power and a huge storage system. Hadoop views the data distributed across all hard drives in clusters as one single file system. It also keeps backup copies of all data in the cluster. In case of failures, it automatically recovers and makes that data resilient and reliable.

15. **Write notes on high availability of Hadoop.**
    High availability: The Hadoop framework takes care of splitting and distributing the data across all the nodes within a cluster. It also replicates the data over the entire cluster. It is fault-tolerant. Distributed processing means the processing of the data is distributed. Data is highly available in Hadoop even if there is hardware failure.

If any of the nodes within the cluster fails, the Hadoop framework will replace that particular machine (node) with another machine. And it also replicates all the configuration settings and the data from this failed machine onto another newly replicated machine. Admins need not worry about such failures once the automatic failover management is configured on a cluster. By default, each block creates three replicas across the cluster data. Moreover, we can change it as per the need. So, if any node goes down, we can recover data on that node from the other node.

16. **Write notes on high scalability of Hadoop.**
    High Scalability: Scalability refers to adding or removing the nodes and adding or removing the hardware components to or from the cluster. We can easily add or remove a node to or from a cluster without bringing down or affecting the cluster operation. Even the individual hardware components such as RAM and hard drives can be added or removed from a cluster. Hadoop can utilize Amazon Web Services or Google, or any other vendors that sell cloud services. We can add as many computers as possible to handle the data. It is also possible to add any number of nodes to enhance the performance dramatically. Here, the data nodes (worker nodes)/node manager can be scaled horizontally. The Name node works in a master service mode. Only data node/node manager runs on the worker nodes. Master nodes run the management services. There are only a few master nodes (often virtualized). Companies like Amazon, Facebook, Microsoft, Google, Yahoo, IBM, and General Electric run massive Hadoop clusters to store and process massive amounts of data.

17. **Write notes on high throughput of Hadoop.**
    High Throughput: Hadoop supports parallel processing of data. Therefore, the data can be processed simultaneously across all the nodes within the cluster, thus saving a lot of time. The amount of work done in a unit time is Throughput. The HDFS also works in the model of "Write Once and Read Many" principle. It simplifies the data coherency issues as one cannot modify the data that has been written once. Thus, it provides high throughput data access. Hadoop works on the Data Locality principle. This principle states that computation has to be moved to the node where data is present instead of moving the data to computation to improve throughput and reduce network congestion.

18. **Write notes on Standalone Mode of Hadoop.**
    Standalone Mode/Single Mode is the default mode of Hadoop. It is a non-distributed mode that runs a single Java process. This mode uses the local file system for input and output operation and is useful for debugging. It does not offer a truly distributed environment. It also does not support fully distributed HDFS. The usage of this model is minimal and used for experimentation, testing.

19. **Write notes on Pseudo-distributed Mode of Hadoop.**
    Hadoop runs on a single node in a pseudo (false) distributed mode, just like the standalone mode. The difference is that each Hadoop daemon runs in a separate Java

process in pseudo-distributed mode, whereas in local mode, each Hadoop daemon runs as a single Java process. The usage of this model is minimal, and it can only be used for experimentation. In pseudo-distributed mode, we need configuration for all the files. In this case, all daemons run on one node, and thus, both Master and Slave nodes are the same. The pseudo mode is suitable for both development and in the testing environment.

20. **Write notes on Fully Distributed Mode of Hadoop.**
    Fully distributed mode allows different nodes for Master and Slave. In this mode, all daemons execute in separate nodes forming a multi-node cluster. Thus, we enable specific nodes for Master and Slave. We use this model in the production environment, where n number of machines form a cluster in which Hadoop daemons run. The Name Node runs on one host and the Data Nodes run on the other hosts. Therefore, Node Manager installs on every Data Node. And it is also responsible for the execution of the task on every single Data Node. The Resource Manager manages all these Node Managers and also receives the processing requests. After that, it passes parts of the request to the corresponding Node Manager.

21. **What is Hadoop ecosystem?**
    The success of the Hadoop framework has led to the development of an array of software (systems). Hadoop, along with this set of related software, makes up the Hadoop ecosystem. The primary purpose of this ecosystem is to enhance the functionality and increase the efficiency of the Hadoop framework. There are several ways of organizing these systems, each of which has lots of complex interdependencies.

22. **What are the components of Hadoop ecosystem?**
    The five major components of the Hadoop ecosystem are 1. Data Ingestion Layer (Sqoop, Flume, etc.) 2. Data Storage Layer (HDFS/HBase, etc.) 3. Processing Engine (MapReduce, etc.). 4. Analysis Layer (Pig, Hive, etc.) 5. Management and Coordination Layer (ZooKeeper, Apache Ambari, etc.)

23. **Write notes on Data Ingestion Layer**
    Data ingestion layer talks about moving the data from multiple assorted sources into a single place for further analysis. This layer not only extracts the data from assorted sources but also validates, cleans (reduces noise), normalizes (compresses), prioritizes and processes (integrates) the data in a format that can be ingested into the Storage Layer (data destination) of Hadoop for further analysis.

24. **Write notes on Batching ingestion and Streaming ingestion.**
    Batching ingestion and Streaming ingestion are the two different types of data ingestion methodology. Batching methodology ensures the data is ingested from the source to the destination in a periodic interval (say every 30 minutes). The streaming methodology ensures that real-time data is ingested into the destination system continuously in real-time. Data ingestion software provides various data ingestion APIs through which the data can be extracted easily in various formats.

25. **Write notes on ETL and ELT.**
    ETL (Extract, Transform and Lead) and ELT (Extract, Load and Transform) are the two ways in which data can be ingested into the target system. ETL stands for Extract, Transform and Load. ELT stands for Extract, Load and Transform. In ETL, a temporary staging database is used, where the data is first extracted and then transformed before loading into the source system. ETL is used when the source and target databases are different, data volume is low, and data transformation are complex, and when the data is structured. In ELT, staging database is not used as the data is straightaway extracted and loaded into the source system and the transformation happens in the source system itself. ELT is used when the source and target databases are same, data volume is large, data transformation is less complex and when the data is unstructured.

26. **Write short notes on Sqoop.**
    Sqoop (SQL + Hadoop) transfers (bulk data) processing data from a database/datastore to Hadoop. It is a way of binding the Hadoop database into a relational database. Sqoop is a connector between Hadoop and the legacy databases. We can import data from Sqoop into a cluster; export it to my SQL, and also retrieve the results from the SQL database. It is compatible with all types of databases such as Teradata, Mysql, Oracle and Postgre.

27. **Write short notes on Chukwa.**
    The Chukwa device has a tube-like structure with different collection and processing stages. Each of these levels is connected by different interfaces. So even if the update changes later, there will be no reduction in its current status. HICC (Hadoop Infrastructure Care Center) is also an interface for web pages that facilitate the disclosure of information. This allows information to be effectively disclosed, monitored, and selective decisions made accordingly.

28. **Write short notes on Flume.**
    Flume: It is a way of transporting weblogs at a vast scale and reliably to your cluster. Let us say you have a fleet of web servers; flume can listen to the weblogs coming in from these web servers in real-time and publish them into your cluster in real-time for processing by Storm or Spark streaming. This tool is similar to Chukwa that helps with batch processing but in a much shorter time, sending out logs. Chukwa sends logs in batch format every 5 minutes, while Flume picks up and sends logs coming in, at the same time. It picks up logs as they fall and sends them in a continuous streaming manner.

29. **Write short notes on Kafka.**
    Kafka: It functions like Sqoop, although it is more general-purpose. It can collect data of any sort from a cluster of computers or from a group of web servers, and broadcast it into the Hadoop cluster.

30. **Write short notes on Impala.**
    Apache Impala: Impala is an MPP (Massive Parallel Processing) SQL written in C++ and Java and is open-source software. It is the highest performing SQL engine that gives an RDBMS-like experience. Impala can be used for data ingestion and data analysis since it connects directly to HBase and HDFS.

31. **Write short notes on NiFi.**
    Apache NiFi: It is an easy-to-utilize data ingestion tool that provides a strong and secure system to process and distribute information, as it uses SSL, SSH, HTTPS, encrypted contents. It supports robust and scalable directed graphs of data routing, transformation, and system reconciliation logic. It traces the data flow from starting to end and presents a seamless experience between design, control, feedback, and monitoring.

32. **Write short notes on Apache Storm.**
    Apache Storm: Storm is a way of processing and streaming real-time data from the sensors or the web. Spark streaming solves the same problem; however, Apache Storm does it quickly and differently. It does not have to be a batch anymore with Storm.

33. **Write short notes on CDC.**
    Change Data Capture (CDC): This ensures that the changes made in the source databases are captured and replicated in the destination databases. The replication can be made in batching mode and real-time mode, depending on the need.

34. **Write short notes on HBase.**
    HBase is a "No SQL" database with columnar data store, written in Java, and meant for large transaction rates. It was previously called as Google Big Table (GBT) and later renamed as HBase. HBase is a way of exposing the data on the cluster to transactional platforms for low latency operations. It can store massive amount of data (Terabytes and Petabytes). It has easy-to-use Java APIs for client access. It stores the data in Key/Value pair. It is well-suited for OLAP system.

35. **Write short notes on Yarn.**
    Yarn: It stands for Yet Another Resource Negotiator. The data processing part of Hadoop is called Yarn. Yarn is the system resource manager that manages the resources on the computing cluster. It allows various types of data processing engines, such as real-time streaming engine, data science engine, and batch processing engine. It decides what gets to run tasks and at what time, what nodes are available for extra work, which nodes are available, and which ones are not available. It is a kind of heartbeat that keeps the cluster going. Yarn allows parallel processing of the distributed data across Hadoop clusters in HDFS.

36. **Write short notes on Spark.**
    Spark: It is one of the most exciting open-source cluster computing frameworks in the Hadoop ecosystem. It sits at the same MapReduce level used for real-time processing. It runs queries on the data. Like MapReduce, it requires some programming. Spark

scripts are written using either Python or Java or the Scallop programming language. Spark is, at present, a fascinating technology. It is an excellent choice to quickly, efficiently and reliably process data on a Hadoop cluster. It is also very versatile; it can do things like handling SQL queries, executing machine learning across an entire cluster of information, and handle streaming data in real-time.

37. **Write short notes on Pig.**
    Pig: Pig is a high-level scripting language that works on top of MapReduce, and uses Java, Python, and SQL style syntax. It is a high-level programming API that allows writing simple scripts that look like SQL, called Pig Latin. The programs created with this script are called Pig Programs. In some cases, it allows queries to be chained together and get complex answers. Such programs are written to MapReduce algorithms and run on the Hadoop cluster. Pig can be easily integrated into a handful of applications designed to analyze contemporary problems.

38. **Write short notes on Hive.**
    Hive sits on top of the MapReduce and solves a similar problem as Pig, but it directly looks like an SQL database; it can be connected through a shell client and ODBC. This is also a language that can function like SQL. But if Pig is a scripting language, Hive is a query language. Those familiar with the programming language will choose Pig to write Transformation Logic. Those who work in ETL and Data Warehousing and are well-versed in SQL will choose Hive. Otherwise, the two are used to do almost the same job. These differ only in the methods of accessing the data.

39. **Write short notes on Spark SQL.**
    Spark SQL is a Spark module for structured data processing. We can run modified Hive queries on existing Hadoop deployments. Spark Sql is the new module in Spark, and it integrates relational processing with Spark's functional programming API. It supports querying of data, either by SQL or via Hive query language. It provides support for various data sources and makes it possible to read SQL queries with code transformation. That is why Spark SQL has become a very powerful tool.

40. **Write short notes on Spark Streaming.**
    Spark Streaming: It is the component of the Spark, which is used to process real-time streaming data, and is a useful addition to the core Spark API. It enables high throughput fault tolerance stream processing of live data streams.

    Spark Graph X: This is the graph computation engine, and is the Spark API for graphs and graph parallel computation. It has got a set of fundamental operators like sub-graph, joint purchases, etc.

41. **Write short notes on Apache Mahout.**
    Apache Mahout: This is part of Apache open-source project that helps customers to create scalable "Machine Learning" algorithms that work well in a distributed environment. It supports various Machine Learning algorithms including Naïve

Bayes Classification, Clustering and Recommendation. Using Mahout, it is possible to analyze large sets of data quickly.

This is the basis for the development of Artificial Intelligence. There is no need to explicitly say through programs what machines should do in this section. Such Mahout algorithms enable machines to detect a pattern independently from excess data in HDFS and transform machines into those capable of moving to the next level.

42. **Write short notes on Tableau.**
Tableau: This data visualization software helps to take quick business decisions and also to solve business problems easily and quickly by providing limitless data exploration possibilities. It supports Big Data. Its smart dashboards are able to refresh automatically based on the data refresh.

43. **Write short notes on Apache Drill.**
Apache Drill: This is part of Apache open-source project that helps customers to create interactive analytics. It integrates with Hive easily. It also helps to visualize the data. It also has its own SQL Query Engine.

44. **Write short notes on ZooKeeper.**
ZooKeeper is a technology for coordinating everything on the cluster to keep track of the nodes that are up and those that are down. It is a reliable way of keeping track of shared states. This tool is used to integrate various utilities that run separately. For example, ZooKeeper starts work on alternative functions, maintains all of them, thinks from all angles, such as which node, where it comes from, and what to do alternatively, even if one of the more than 50 computers running on the cluster crashes.

45. **Write short notes on Apache Ambari.**
Apache Ambari sits on top of everything, giving a birds-eye view of the cluster. It visualizes what is running on the cluster, and what systems are using how many resources. It executes Hive queries or imports databases into the Hive.

46. **Write short notes on Hortonworks.**
Hortonworks: It provides management and administrative support works for Cloudera Horton. The Hortonworks Data Platform of Apache Hadoop is a massively scalable and 100% open-source platform for storing, processing and analyzing large volumes of data. It is designed to deal with data from many sources and formats in a very quick, easy and cost-effective manner.

47. **Write short notes on Oozie.**
Oozie (Workflow Monitoring): It is a way of scheduling jobs on your cluster. Suppose there is a task that needs to happen on the Hadoop cluster, which involves many different steps and maybe many other systems. In that case, Oozie is a way of scheduling all these things together into jobs that can run on the specified schedule

(time). It is used to run a series of interdependent jobs. That means, it is easier to handle jobs that can run independently.

48. **Write short notes on Name Node.**
    Name Node: It is the master daemon, and it manages the data node. The Name Node is the arbitrator and repository for all HDFS metadata. User data never flows through the Name Node, which preserves only the metadata. Metadata means the data about the data. It supports user quotas and access permissions. It is like a sheet or a file having information on what data block is stored in which data node.

49. **Write short notes on Secondary Name Node.**
    Secondary Name Node: It does an essential task known as checkpointing, which combines edit logs with FS image. Let us say a Hadoop cluster was set up 5 days back, and the transactions that happen with every new data block are stored in HDFS. Every transaction is combined in a file known as an FS image. This FS image resides in the disk. There is one more similar file which is known as an edit log. Edit logs store only the latest transaction data. Checkpointing is the task of combining the edit log with the FS image.

50. **Write short notes on Data Node.**
    Data Nodes: These are the slave daemons, where the actual data is stored. Whenever a client gives a read or write request, the data node serves it. The data node stores the data as data blocks. Racks arrange the data nodes. We can set up different data nodes in racks.

51. **Write short notes on HDFS block replication.**
    HDFS Block Replication: HDFS is a fault-tolerant system. Whenever you write a file into HDFS, the HDFS system breaks down the file into different blocks of size 128 megabytes, except the last block (which will have the remainder of the file). These blocks are distributed across the Hadoop cluster. By doing this, the time taken to store this data onto the disk is significantly reduced. The total time taken to store this entire data onto the disk equals storing one part of the data.

52. **Write short notes on Rack.**
    A rack consists of multiple nodes, usually 30 to 40 nodes. Each of these nodes, in turn, store multiple data blocks. Within a rack, Hadoop stores its data in two different data nodes. Communication between nodes present in the same rack is usually faster than the nodes across multiple racks. The concept of choosing the closest data node is called as rack awareness.

53. **Write short notes on rack awareness algorithm.**
    The rack awareness algorithm says that the local rack stores the first replica of a block, while the next two replicas are stored in a different rack. So, we store a data block in the local rack (rack one) to decrease the latency.
    1. Each node will have only one replica of the block.

2. Each rack will have maximum of two replicas of the block.
3. Number of racks to be used will be lesser than the replication factor.
If we have the replication factor as 3 then (as per rule 3) only two racks are to be used to store the replicated blocks.

54. **Write short notes on Hadoop Metrics.**
    Metrics is the statistical information exposed by the Hadoop daemons, used for monitoring, performance tuning, and debugging. By default, there are many metrics available for troubleshooting. Hadoop framework uses Hadoop metrics properties for 'Performance Reporting' and also controls the reporting for Hadoop. The API provides an abstraction to implement it on top of a variety of metrics client libraries. Client library is configurable based on need. Different modules of the same application can use the same metrics implementation libraries. This file is present inside /etc/hadoop.

55. **Write short notes Data Integrity in Hadoop.**
    Data Integrity ensures that no data loss or corruption happens while storing or processing the data. In Hadoop, the amount of data being written or read is large in volume, so the chances of data corruption are more. Hadoop has a checksum mechanism to tackle this data integrity issue. Hadoop computes the checksum while writing the data to the disk for the first time. It checks again while reading the data from the disk. If the new checksum matches the original checksum, it means the data is uncorrupted.

56. **Write short notes Inter Rack.**
    Inter Rack: Hadoop's major drawback is cross-switch network traffic due to the massive volume of data. This moves the extensive amount of data to the computation spot. In this case, usually, data and code reside in different racks creating heavy traffic across the racks. In this scenario, mapper runs on a different rack due to resource constraints.

57. **Write short notes on Intra Rack.**
    Intra Rack: In this scenario the code runs on a different node but the same rack. In such a case, the data is closer to the computation of the same rack. Due to constraints, it is not always possible to execute the mapper on the same data node.
    This is also called as Rack Locality, which refers to moving the computation (code) close to the rack, where the actual data resides, instead of moving extensive amount of data to the computation spot. However, heavy traffic resides within the rack, as the data gets moved across multiple nodes.

58. **Write short notes on data locality.**
    Data Locality refers to moving the computation (code) close to the node where the actual data resides, instead of moving extensive amount of data to the computation spot. Data local is the most preferred scenario. Data locality increases the overall

throughput of the system. In Hadoop, HDFS stores datasets divided into blocks and each dataset is stored across the data nodes in the Hadoop cluster. When a user runs the code (MapReduce job), the NameNode sends this code (MapReduce job code) to the data nodes on which data is available related to the MapReduce job.

59. **Write short notes on issues with small files in Hadoop.**
    Hadoop is not suited for small files. A small file means it is significantly smaller than the HDFS default block size (default 128MB). HDFS can't handle a large number of such small files. It works well with a small number of large files for storing datasets rather than a large number of small files. If one uses a significant number of small files, this will overload the name node since the name node stores the namespace of HDFS. HBase helps to overcome these small file issues.

60. **Write short notes on the processing speed of Hadoop.**
    Processing Speed: With parallel and distributed algorithm, MapReduce processes large datasets. MapReduce performs the tasks of both Mapping process and Reduce process. MapReduce takes a lot of time to perform these tasks. It increases the latency as the data gets distributed and processed over the clusters in MapReduce.

61. **Write short notes on Security of Hadoop.**
    Security: Hadoop can be challenging in managing complex applications involving security. Hadoop is missing encryption at storage and network levels, which is a vital point of concern. Hadoop supports Kerberos authentication, which is very hard to manage.

62. **What is "Distributed Cache" in Apache Hadoop?**
    In Hadoop, the data chunks process happens independently in parallel among DataNodes. The distributed cache contains common files accessible by all the DataNodes, which include read-only text files, archive files, jar files, etc. Hadoop will make these cache files available on each data node where map/reduce tasks are running. An application that requires distributed cache should make sure that the files are available on URLs. URLs can be either hdfs:// or http://. Hadoop framework will duplicate the cache file on all the data nodes before starting tasks on those nodes. The default size of the distributed cache is 10 GB, which can be modified using local cache size.

63. **What is Kerberos?**
    Apache Hadoop uses Kerberos for managing the security. A client needs to take three simple steps to access service when using Kerberos. Each of these steps involves exchange of message with a server. The steps are Authentication step, Authorization step and the Service Request Step. The client first authenticates itself to the authentication server. Then, it receives a timestamped Ticket-Granting Ticket (TGT). The client uses the TGT to request a service ticket from the Ticket Granting Server. The client now uses the service ticket to authenticate itself to the server.

64. What is File System Check in Hadoop?

Hadoop HDFS uses the fsck (file system check) command to check for various discrepancies, reporting the problems with the files in HDFS, such as missing blocks for a file or under-replicated blocks. It does not correct the errors. Usually, NameNode automatically corrects most of the recoverable failures. File system check ignores open files but provides an option to select all files during the reporting. The HDFS fsck command runs as bin/hdfs fsck. File system check can run on the whole file system or a subset of files.

65. How are communication protocols taken care of in Hadoop?

All HDFS communication protocols cover the top of the TCP/IP protocol, client protocol, and data node protocol.
1. The client talks to the NameNode using client protocol.
2. The DataNodes talk to the NameNode using the data node protocol.
3. A Remote Procedure Call (RPC) abstraction wraps both the client protocol and the data node protocol.
4. Name node never initiates RPC. It only responds to RPC requests issued by DataNodes or clients.
5. Cluster rebalancing moves data from one DataNode to another if the free space on a DataNode falls below a certain threshold.

66. What is safe mode in Hadoop?

Safe mode: On start-up, name nodes enter into a special mode: safe mode. Replication of data blocks does not occur when the NameNode is in the safe mode state. During the name node daemon start up, the NameNode enters safe mode for a certain period. The administrator can also enter the safe mode manually with the below command (in the case of maintenance/up-gradation of the cluster):

hadoop dfsadmin –safemode enter

67. Write notes on Hadoop V 1.0.

In Hadoop V1.0, there was only one name and because of that, there was single point of failure and high availability was not present. In addition to metadata management, the name node was also managing the resource management work (job tracker), which was temporary but consumed a lot of time. So, the resource management related work was completely given to YARN in the next version (Hadoop 2.0).

68. Write notes on Hadoop V 2.0 and V 3.0.

In Hadoop V2.0, Java version 7 was supported. In Hadoop 3.0, the next latest version of Java (Java 8) is supported. Fault tolerance was achieved through replication in the Hadoop V2.0, However, it was achieved through coding in Version 3.0.

69. Write short notes on Yarn architecture.

When Hadoop came up with its new version (2.0), it introduced Yarn as the new framework, and it stands for Yet Another Resource Negotiator. It is a master/slave topology. The master daemon is known as resource manager, and slave daemons are known as node manager.

70. Write short notes on Yarn resource manager.
Yarn Resource Manager: This is the master daemon, and it receives the processing request, and whenever a client comes up with a request, it comes to the resource manager first because the resource manager manages all the slave nodes or node managers. The resource manager takes the request and passes the request to the corresponding node managers.

71. Write short notes on Yarn node manager.
Yarn Node Manager: Node managers are the slave daemons installed on every data node. Data is divided into blocks and stored in the data nodes. A data manager is also present in the data node to process all the data. It is responsible for the execution of the tasks on every single data node. If there is any requirement for any resource, it is the app master which asks for the resources from the resource manager. The resource manager provides the app master with all the resources, and then it asks the node managers to start a container. A container is a place where the actual execution happens.

72. Write short notes on Spark core engine.
Spark core engine: The core engine is for the entire Spark framework; every component is part of the core engine. It is the primary engine for large-scale parallel and distributed data processing. The core is the distributed execution engine. Java and Python APIs offer a platform for distributed ETL development, and other additional libraries are on top of the core. It is responsible for scheduling, distributing, and monitoring jobs in a cluster and interacting with the storage systems.

73. Write short notes on Spark SQL.
Spark SQL: It is a Spark module for structured data processing, and you can run modified Hive queries on existing Hadoop deployments. Spark SQL is the new module in Spark, and it integrates relational processing with Spark's functional programming API. It supports querying of data either by SQL or via a Hive query language. First, we have the "data source universal API" for loading and storing structured data; it supports Hive JSON JDBC, etc. It also supports third-party integration through Spark packages.

74. Write short notes on Zeppelin.
Zeppelin is used to visualizing the data. It uses K-means, which is one of the simplest unsupervised learning algorithms that solve the well-known clustering problem. Zeppelin client connects with Zeppelin Server through Http Rest (or) Web Socket protocol.

Zeppelin Server connects with the data source through interpreter using Thrift protocol in Java Virtual Machine Process. It can also connect to the interpreter using the class loader.

Essay-type Questions

1. What are the problems with traditional large-scale systems?
2. Write an essay on the five *V*'s of Big Data.
3. Write an essay on the history of Hadoop.
4. What are the advantages of using Hadoop?
5. Write an essay on the different flavors of Hadoop.
6. Write an essay on the core components of Hadoop.
7. Explain the Hadoop ecosystem and its five major components.
8. Explain HDFS architecture in detail.
9. Explain HDFS block replication mechanism in detail.
10. What is Rack? What is Rack Awareness Algorithm?
11. What are the limitations of Hadoop?
12. Compare and contrast Apache Hadoop with RDBMS.
13. What are the problems with small files in Hadoop? How can these problems be resolved?
14. How security is taken care of in Hadoop?
15. Write an essay on EditLog and FSI image in Hadoop.
16. Write an essay on Hadoop 1 and 2.
17. Write an essay on Yarn Architecture.
18. Write an essay on Apache Spark Architecture.
19. Write an essay on Zeppelin Architecture.

CHAPTER 6

Hadoop Distributed File System

LEARNING OBJECTIVES

In the previous chapters, we had discussed about the problems with traditional large-scale systems and how Hadoop can act as a solution for the same. In this chapter, we will discuss about HDFS (Hadoop Distributed File System), which is an important component of the Hadoop ecosystem. HDFS is the storage layer of Hadoop. It stands for the Hadoop distributed file system. We will discuss about the design of HDFS, its concepts, Command Line Interface, and Hadoop file system interfaces.

6.1 Introduction

HDFS is the storage layer of Hadoop. It stands for the Hadoop distributed file system. HDFS is the Hadoop version of GFS (Google File System), proven at very large scales. There are also other distributed file systems built with Google. Still, GFS was chosen because it had evolved to handle very large datasets, could scale to hundreds of thousands of nodes, and maintain high performances even under conditions of failure. HDFS allows the distribution of Big Data storage across the cluster of computers. It makes all the hard drives on the cluster look like a single giant file system. HDFS works by storing a fewer number of large files rather than a vast number of small files. Before looking into the architecture of HDFS, first, let us understand the details of virtualization, how to install Virtual Box, and how to load HDP Sandbox Cloudera installation into the Virtual Box.

6.2 Virtualization

Virtualization is a relatively old technology, and the concept is still relevant today for building cloud computing strategies. Virtualization is creating a virtual version of storage networking servers or applications. The hypervisor concept enables Virtualization. A hypervisor is software that runs above the physical server (hardware) or host. It pulls the resources from the physical server and allocates them to the virtual environments.

The Type 1 Hypervisor is simply deployed on top of the actual server (Fig. 6.1). Type 1 hypervisors are also called bare-metal hypervisors. Type 1 is the most frequently used hypervisor; it is most secure and lowers the latency. Typical examples are VMware ESX, Microsoft Hyper-V and Xen.

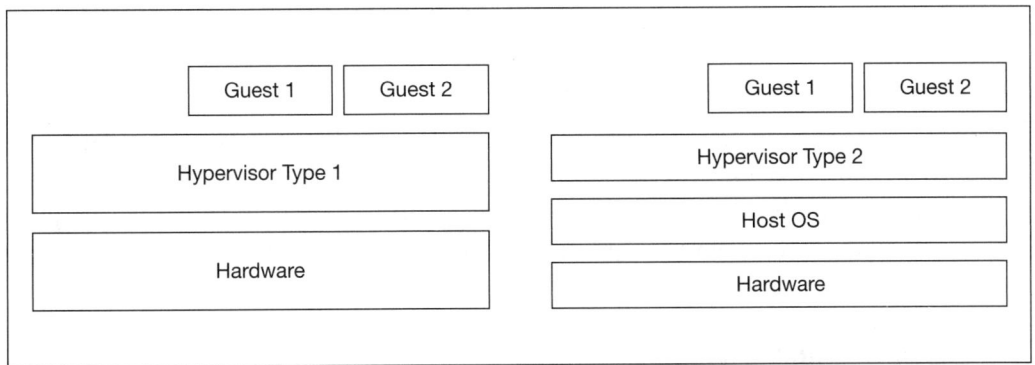

Figure 6.1   Hypervisor Type 1 and Type 2

In Type 2 Hypervisor, there is a layer of host Operating System (Fig. 6.2) between the physical server and the hypervisor, used for end-user Virtualization. Example: Oracle VirtualBox, VMware Workstation. They have a higher latency than a Type 1 hypervisor (Fig. 6.1).

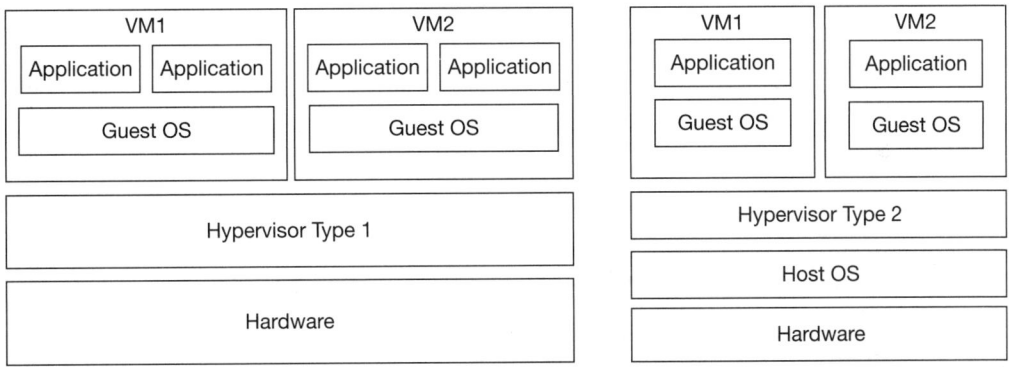

Figure 6.2   Host OS in Hypervisor Type 2

After installing the hypervisor, building virtual environments or virtual machines (VM) is easy. VM is simply a software-based computer that runs like a physical computer; they have an operating system and applications. The hypervisor manages the resources allocated to these virtual environments from the physical server.

It is possible to run different operating systems on different virtual machines as the VMs are independent of one another. They are also highly portable. It is possible to easily move a virtual machine from one hypervisor to another on a completely different device almost instantaneously, giving flexibility and portability within the environment. The first advantage of virtual machines is that it is cost-saving, as it is possible to run multiple virtual environments from one piece of infrastructure. It drastically reduces the physical infrastructure footprint and saves the maintenance cost. The next advantage is agility and speed. Creating a virtual machine environment is relatively quick and straightforward. Further, using a virtual machine lowers the downtime as it is possible to move a virtual machine very easily from one hypervisor to another on a different physical server.

Why do we use Hypervisor?

Hypervisors enable the usage of most of the available resources of a system and give more IT mobility because the guest VMs are independent of the host hardware. This implies that they can be simply transported across servers. It also reduces the space usage, the energy used and the maintenance requirements since a hypervisor allows numerous virtual computers to operate on a single physical server.

6.3 Downloading VMware

VMware Workstation and Oracle VirtualBox are famous virtualization software that allow multiple operating systems to run together on the same physical system. Let us discuss how we can download and install the VMware Workstation player on the Windows 10 operating system. First, open the browser and search for VMware Workstation (Fig. 6.3) for windows, and choose the link from VMware.com; just click on that link.

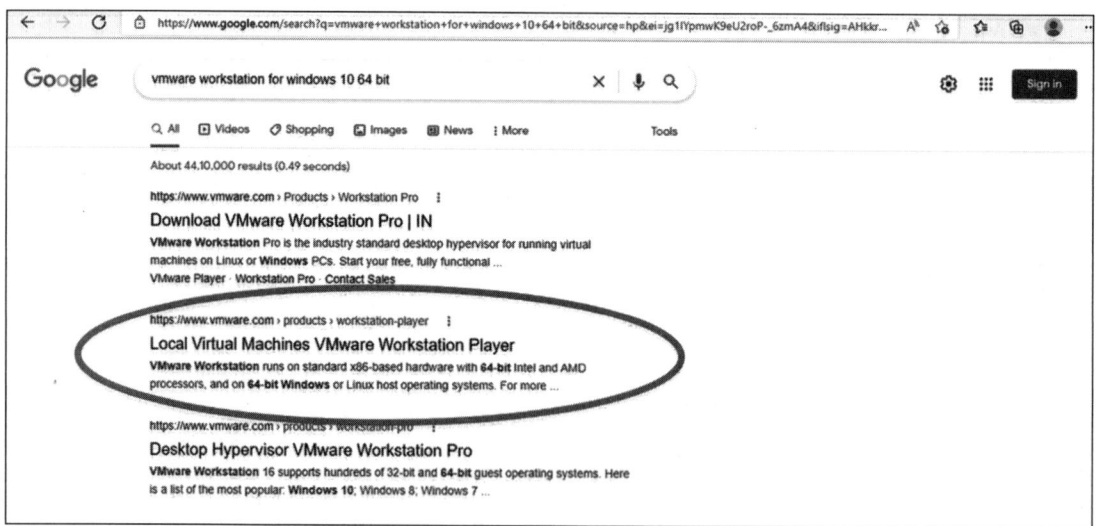

Figure 6.3 Google Browser search for VMware workstation player download

The link will take us to the vmware.com home page; navigate to the menu titled "workspace", scroll down to the link where "workstation Player" is displayed (Fig. 6.4). Click on that link.

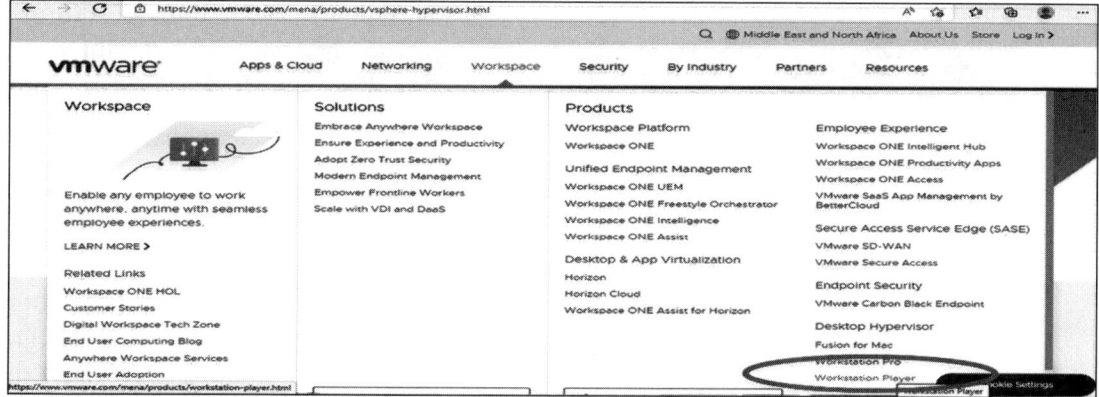

Figure 6.4 VMware home page: Workstation Player link to download

Clicking on the "Workstation Player" link will take us to another page from where we can download VMware Workstation player by clicking "DOWNLOAD FOR FREE" button (Fig. 6.5).

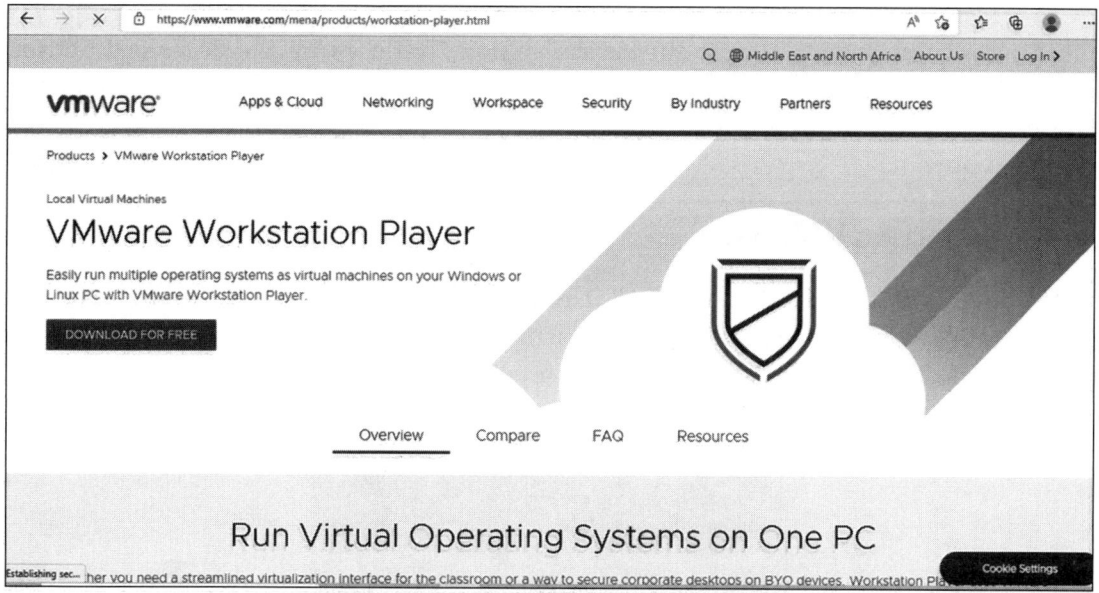

Figure 6.5 Products menu: VMware Workstation Player link to download

Clicking on the "DOWNLOAD FOR FREE" button will take us to another screen where we can select the version to be downloaded. Version 16 is the latest version. Click "Go To Downloads" button (Fig. 6.6).

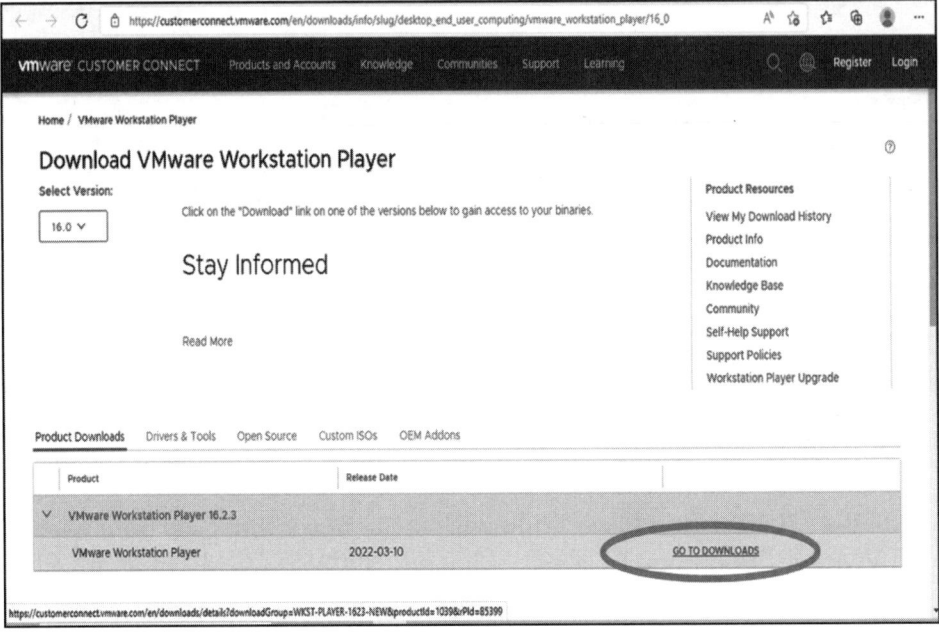

Figure 6.6 VMware Workstation Player Version selection to download

This is the latest version; so just choose this option, and click on the download button. You will see that the download of the executable file will start. Wait for the download of this executable file. Once this executable file is downloaded, click on the executable file, and then open it.

6.4 Installing VMware

After downloading the VMware workstation software, double click on the .exe file. A screen below will appear asking to confirm whether the software from VMware is a genuine one, Do you allow the VMware installation launcher to install in the system? Click "Yes" button to continue with the installation launcher (Fig. 6.7).

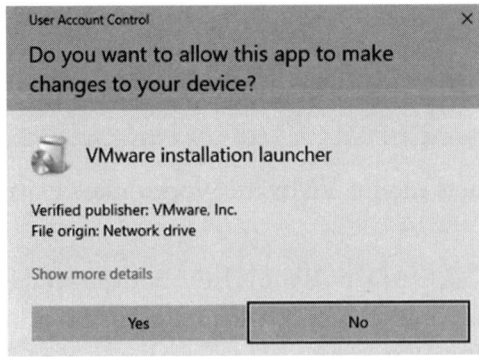

Figure 6.7 VMware installation launcher permission

When we click the "Yes" button, VMware WorkStation 16 player Setup will start installation of the WorkStation player. Click "Next" button (Fig. 6.8).

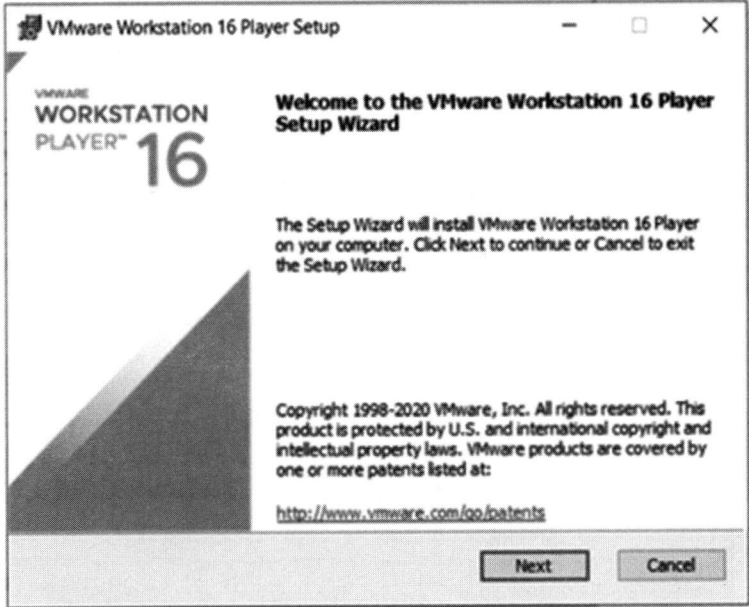

Figure 6.8 VMware installation Welcome Screen

When we click "Next" button, it will ask for the license agreement. Click the accept icon tick mark and click "Next" in the screen (Fig. 6.9).

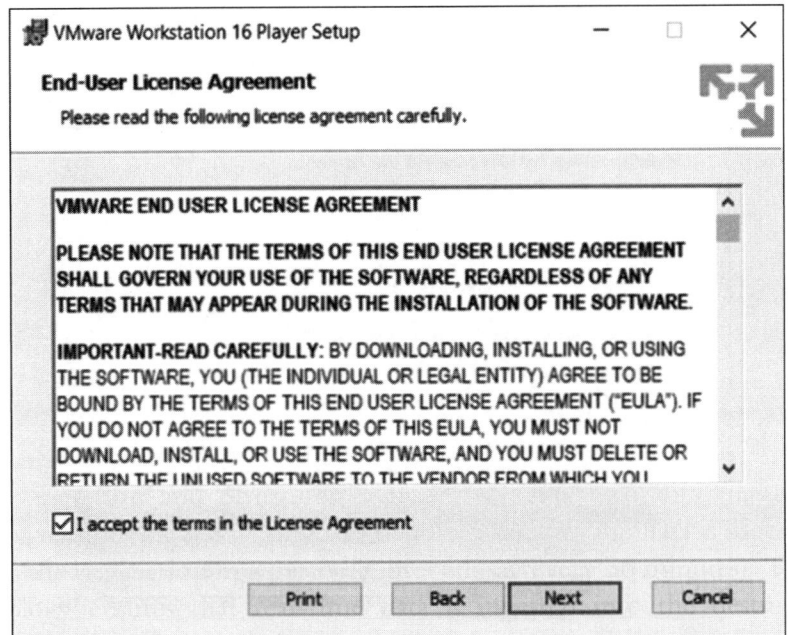

Figure 6.9 VMware installation License Agreement

When we click "Next" button, it will take us to the Custom Setup details, like where the VMware workstation is to be installed; click on the Change button if required. If you don't have a good reason to change it, just leave it as default and also you will see this option for enhanced keyboard driver. A reboot will be required to use this feature (Fig. 6.10).

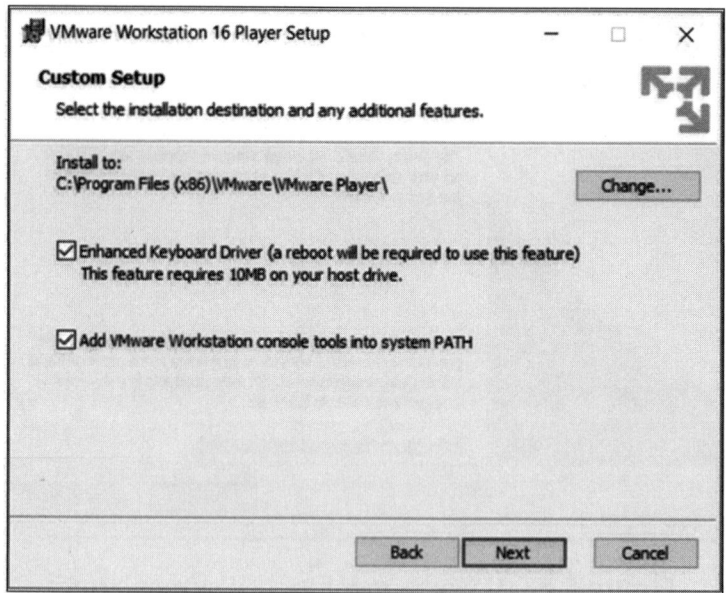

Figure 6.10   VMware installation Custom Setup selection

It will take us through the "User Experience Settings". Ensure tick mark is there in the first option (Check for Product updates on startup). Click "Next" (Fig. 6.11).

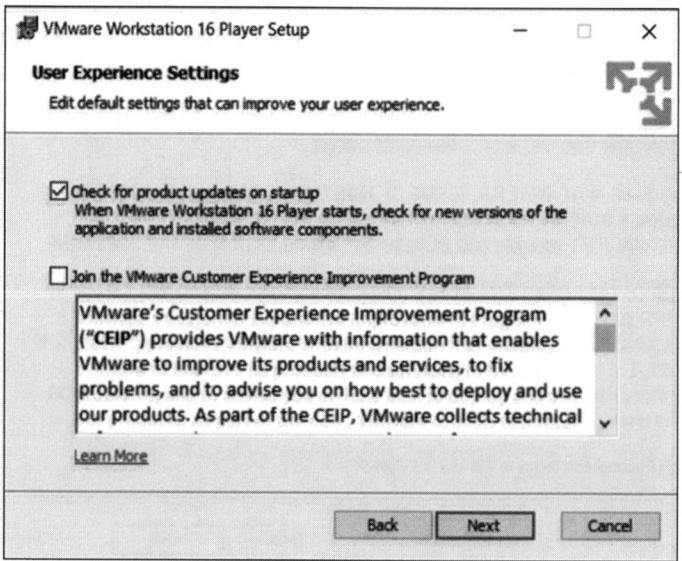

Figure 6.11   VMware installation User Experience settings

It will take us through the "Shortcuts" selection (Fig. 6.12). Select both the options; it will create a short cut on the desktop and in the startup menu Folder. Click "Next".

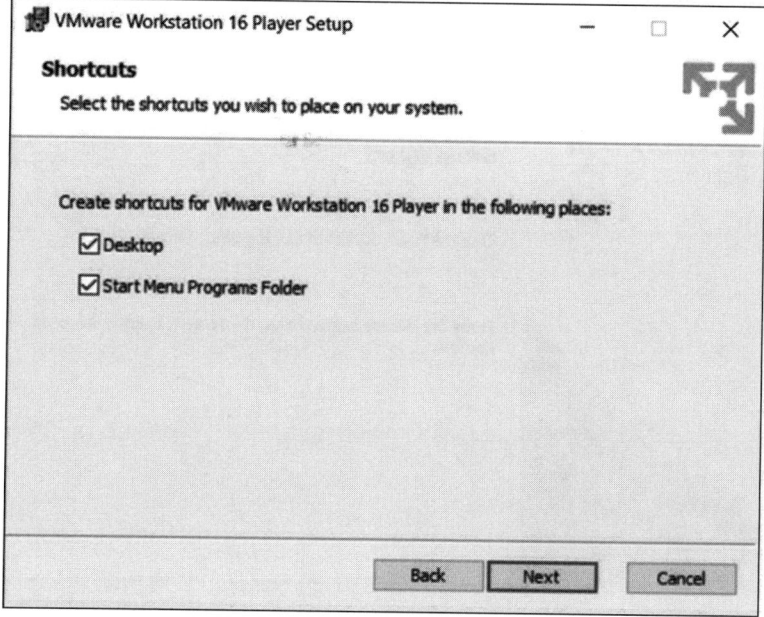

Figure 6.12 VMware installation Shortcut settings

Now all the installation details are captured; it is time to install and it will ask for the confirmation button. Click "Install" button (Fig. 6.13).

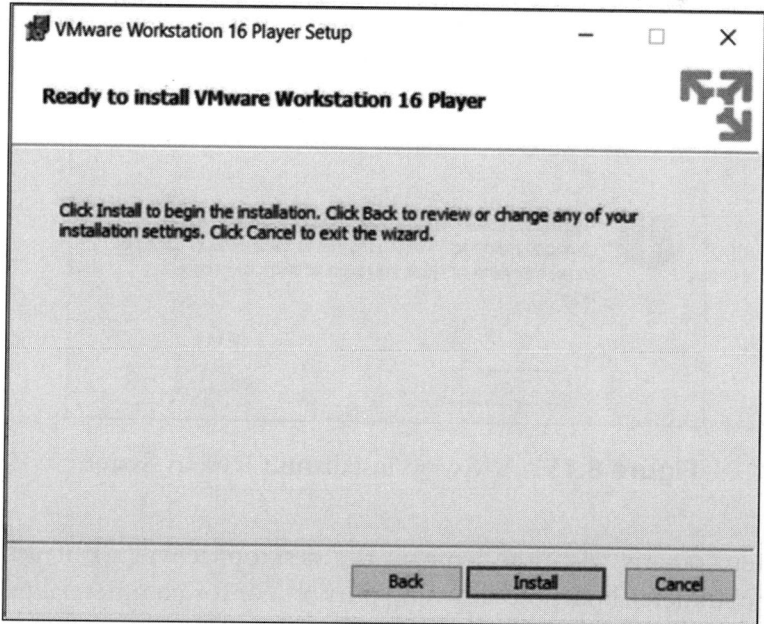

Figure 6.13 VMware installation Ready to Install screen

Once the installation is over, we will get the below screen. Click "Finish" Button (Fig. 6.14).

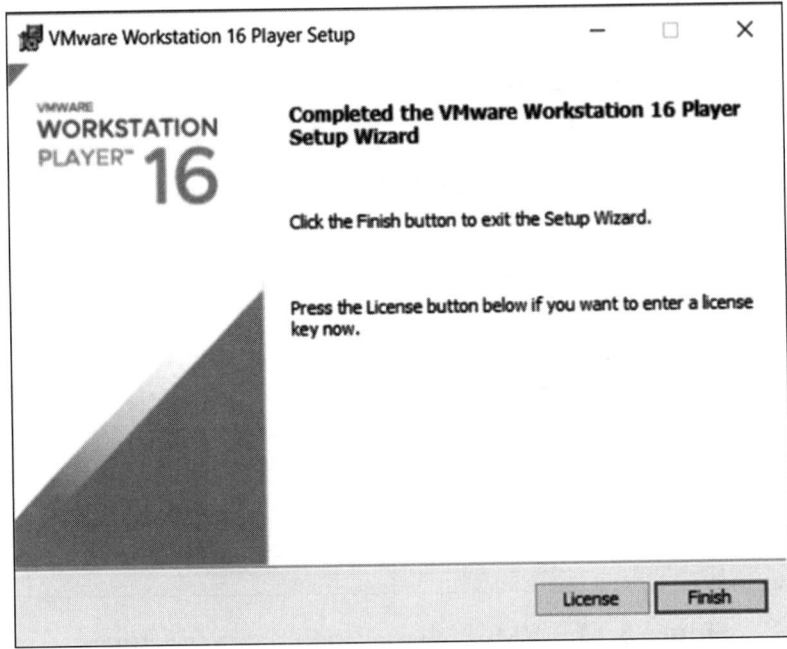

Figure 6.14 VMware installation Finish screen

It will ask us to restart the system once installation is finished (Fig. 6.15). Click Yes and then proceed with the next step after the restart.

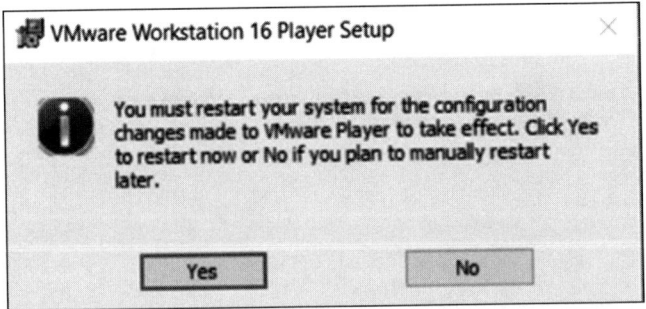

Figure 6.15 VMware installation Restart System

Once the system restarts, click the icon on the desktop; it will ask if we are using the Player for noncommercial purpose (learning purpose) or for commercial purpose (license key is required). We can choose the former option (Fig. 6.16).

Hadoop Distributed File System • 273

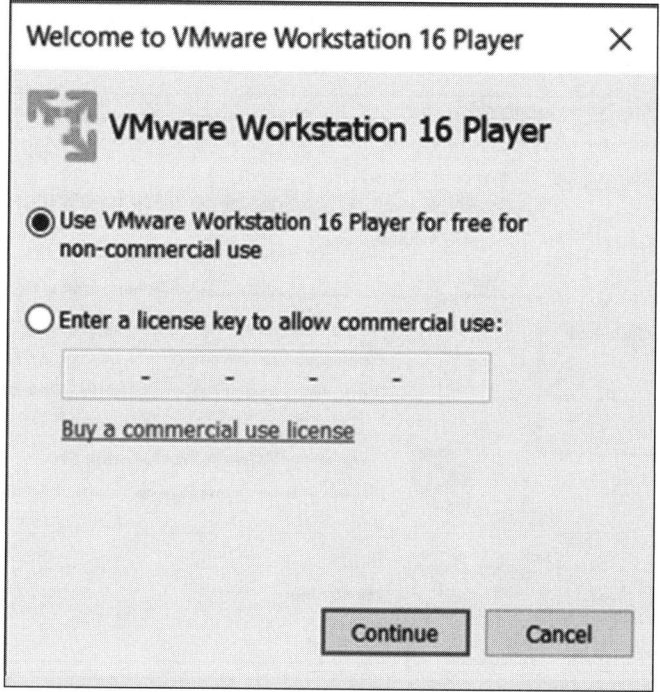

Figure 6.16 VMware Welcome screen

We are going to install Cloudera HDP Sandbox version in VMware. So, login to Cloudera.com and download VMware version of the Sandbox (Fig. 6.17).

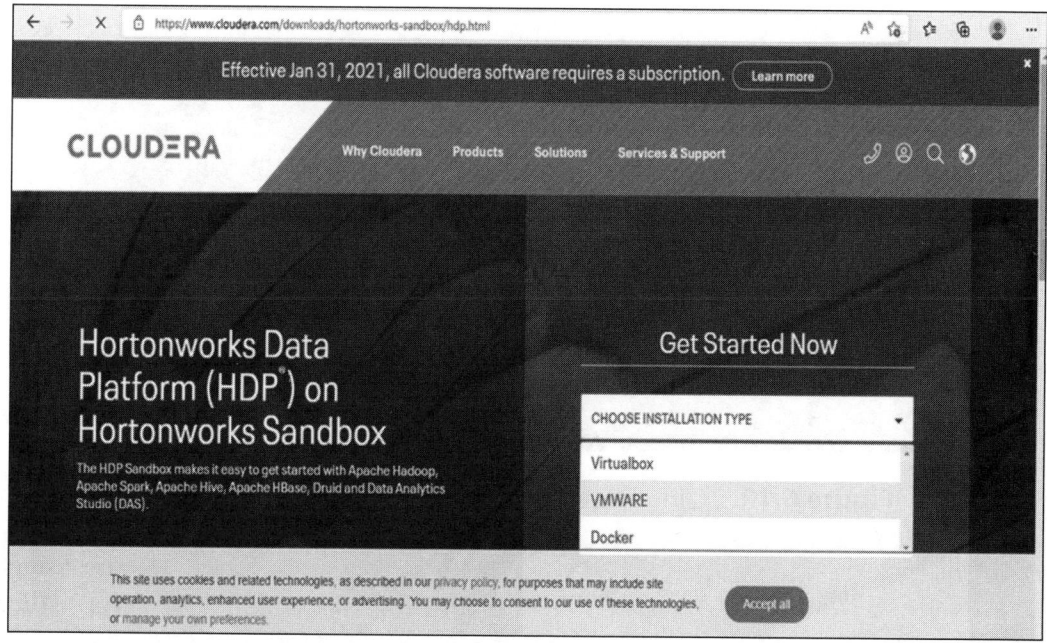

Figure 6.17 Cloudera HDP VMWARE version download

Once the VMware version of the HDP Sandbox is downloaded, import it from VMware workstation by clicking File menu and Open menu (Fig. 6.18).

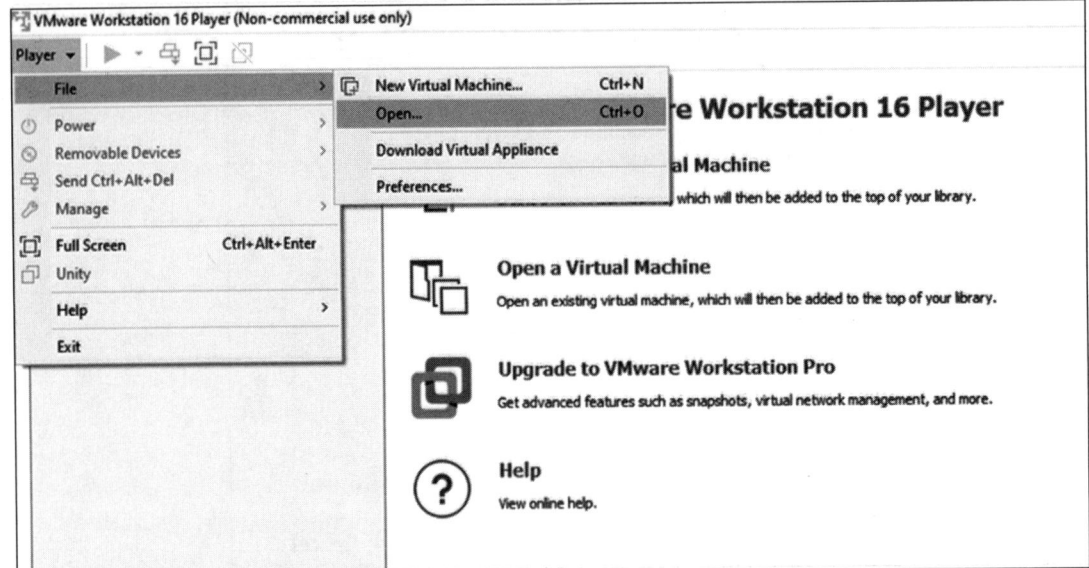

Figure 6.18 Importing Cloudera HDP VMWARE version to VMware Workstation player

The below screen will appear once the Cloudera HDP got installed into VMware Player. This indicates that we are ready to start using Hadoop system of Cloudera using VMware (Fig. 6.19).

Figure 6.19 Cloudera screen when we start the Sandbox

6.5 VIRTUALBOX

VirtualBox is virtualization software that allows multiple operating systems and runs them together on the same physical PC. It is Type 2 hypervisor software. Virtualization technology allows us to run multiple operating systems on the same physical hardware and run them simultaneously.

6.5.1 VirtualBox Installation Steps

Let us discuss downloading and installing Oracle VirtualBox on Windows 10 operating system. Oracle VirtualBox is a hosted hypervisor (Type 2) for free and open-source virtualization. It allows you to install many operating systems virtually on your host operating system, so if we want to install Ubuntu operating system virtually on the Windows operating system, we can do that using VirtualBox. However, we are going to import HDP Sandbox from Cloudera. For installing VirtualBox, let us open our favorite browser and search for VirtualBox (Fig. 6.20). The first link which will appear here will be from virtualbox.org. So, we are going to click on this link.

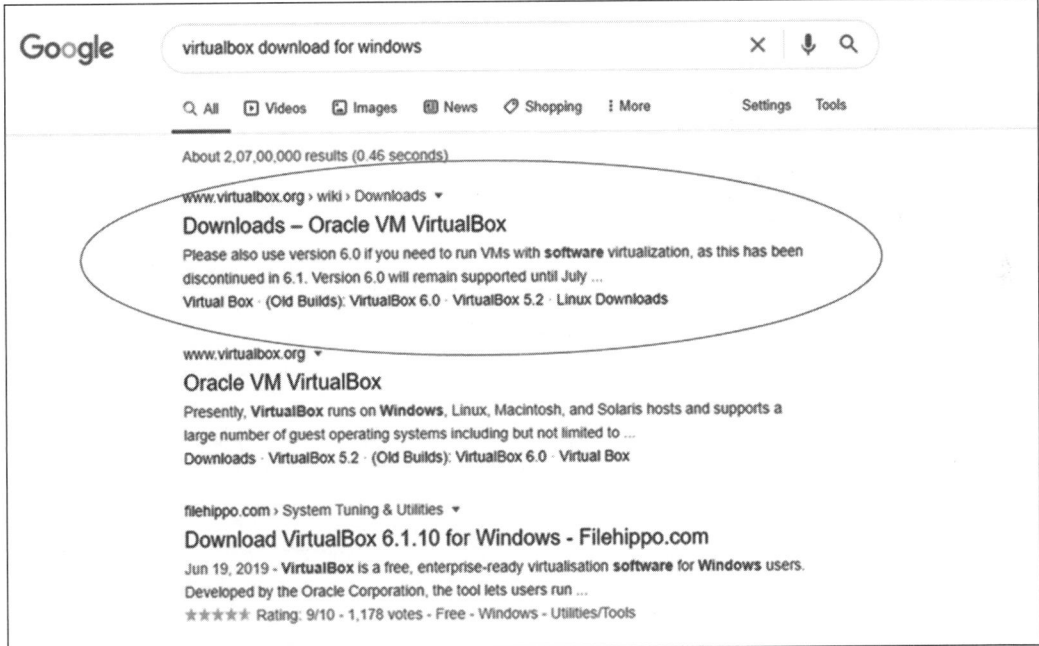

Figure 6.20 Oracle VirtualBox download link from the Google Chrome browser

Once this website opens, if you are not directly redirected to the Downloads page, you can click on Download link and see the Downloads interface (Fig. 6.21).

Figure 6.21 Oracle VirtualBox home screen: Download interface

We want to download the VirtualBox for Windows (Fig. 6.22); so we will select Windows hosts, and once it is clicked, the download of this VirtualBox exe (about 108 MB) starts.

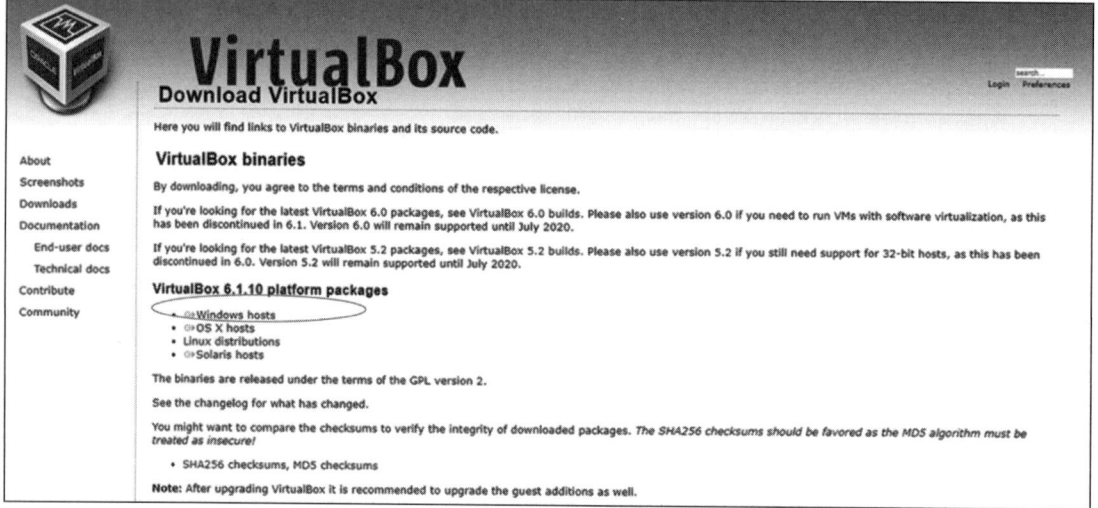

Figure 6.22 Oracle VirtualBox 6.1.10 platform packages: Windows hosts

Once this executable file is downloaded, we can click on the executable file, and then minimize the browser. The first window looks like this (Fig. 6.23), so we are going to click on the next button.

Hadoop Distributed File System • 277

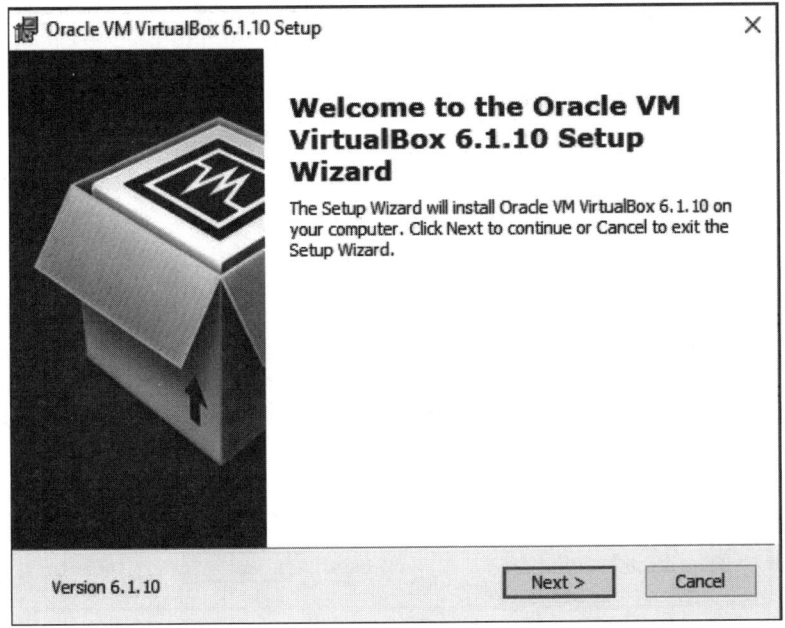

Figure 6.23 Oracle VirtualBox 6.1.10 Setup Wizard screen

And it will ask for the location where our VirtualBox is to be installed; so if you don't have a good reason to change this part, go ahead and click Next (Fig. 6.24) and leave everything as default.

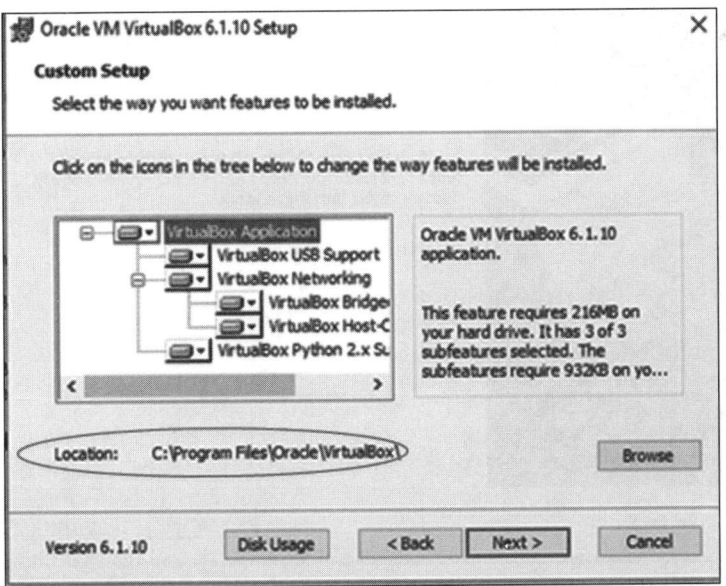

Figure 6.24 Oracle VirtualBox 6.1.10 Custom Setup screen

When we click Next, the below screen appears asking for a few details in Custom Setup (Fig. 6.25). Select all the options given and click on Next button.

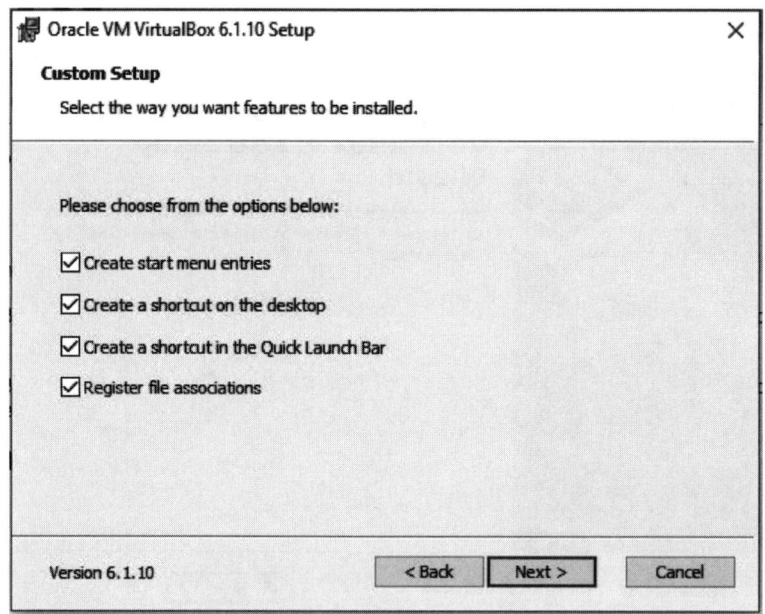

Figure 6.25 Oracle VirtualBox 6.1.10 Custom Setup options

When we click on Next, the below screen appears giving a warning that states "It will reset the network connection" (Fig. 6.26), Click "Yes" button.

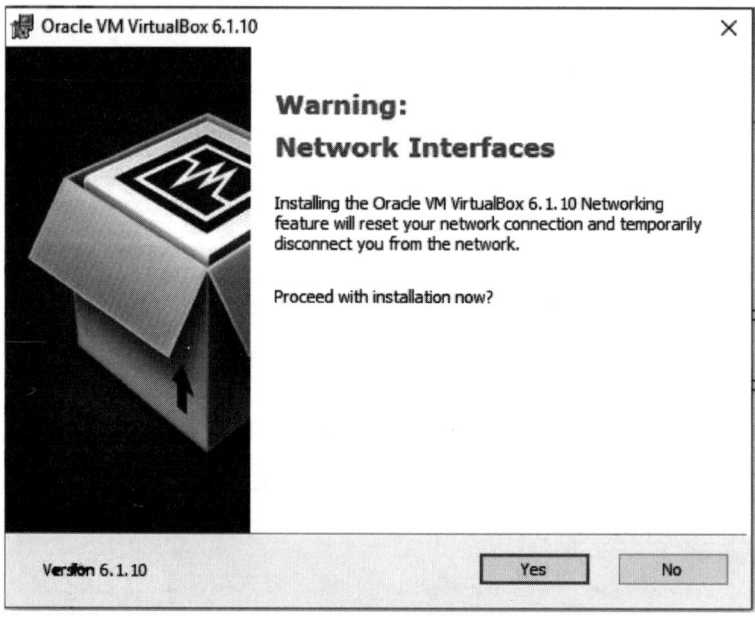

Figure 6.26 Oracle VirtualBox 6.1.10 Network Interfaces warning

When we click Yes Button, the below screen appears (Fig. 6.27) indicating that the Virtual Box is ready to install. Click "Install" button.

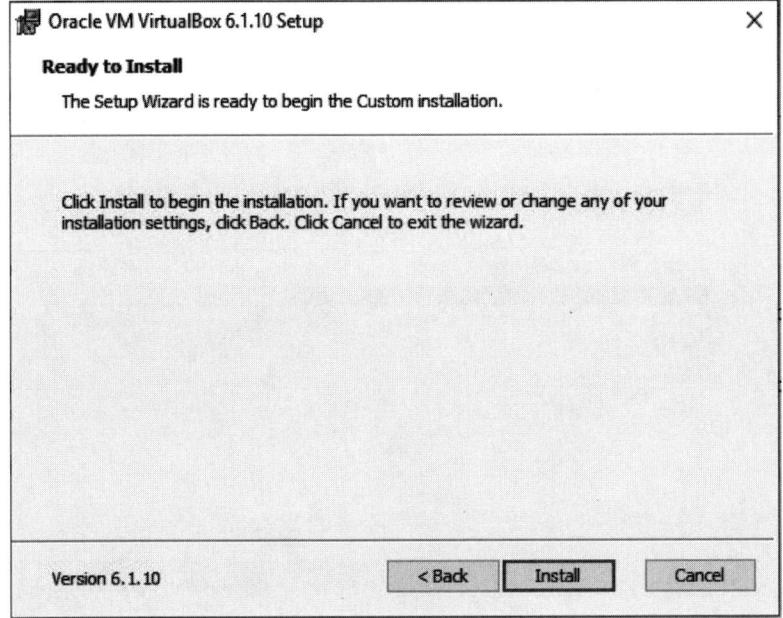

Figure 6.27 Oracle VirtualBox 6.1.10 Ready to Install screen

When we click the "Install" button, the below screen appears indicating the setup wizard is installing the Virtual Box. Wait until the installation is complete (Fig. 6.28).

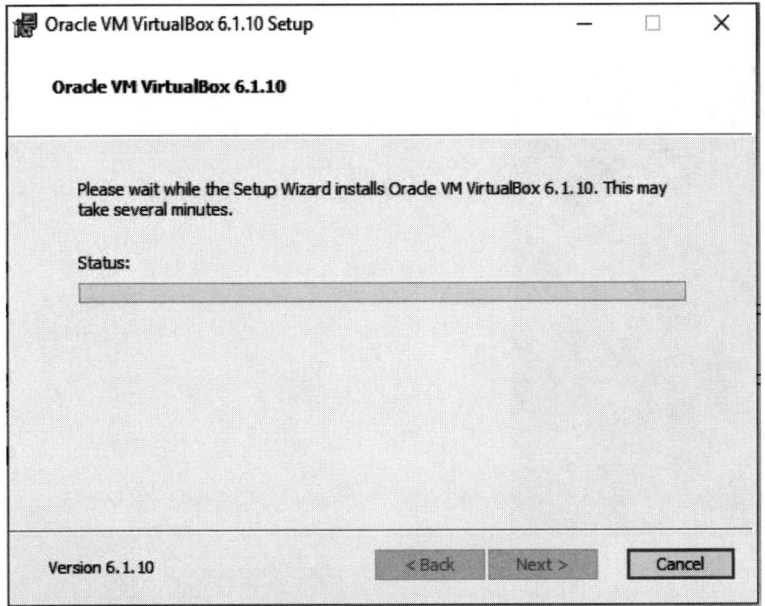

Figure 6.28 Oracle VirtualBox 6.1.10 Installation Status screen

The below screen with a green-mark (Fig. 6.29) status appears indicating the setup wizard is installing the Virtual Box. Wait until the installation completes.

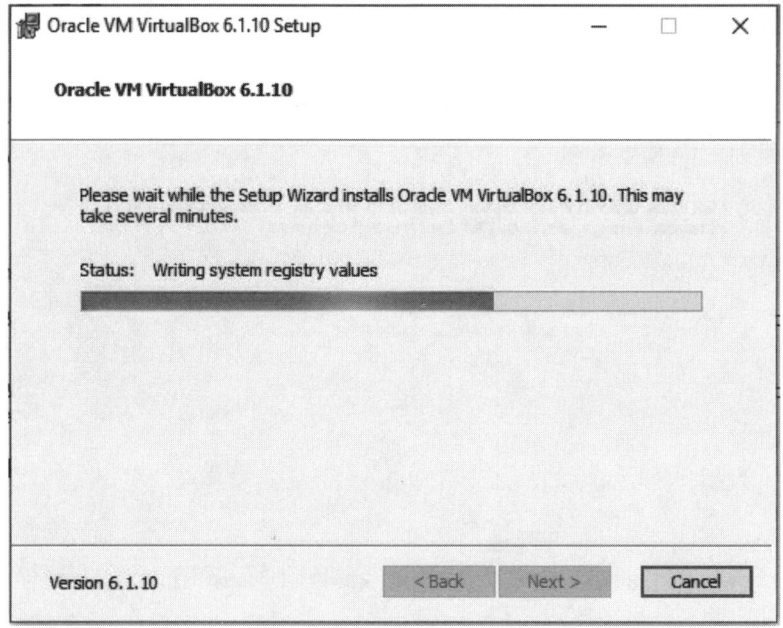

Figure 6.29 Oracle VirtualBox 6.1.10 Installation Status screen: Green Status

When the installation completes, the below screen appears (Fig. 6.30). Click the "Finish" button to finish the installation.

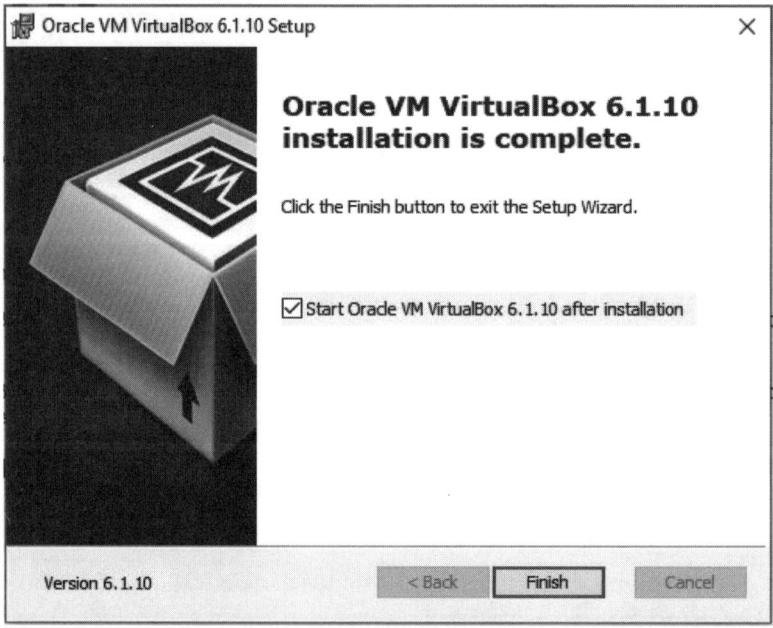

Figure 6.30 Oracle VirtualBox 6.1.10 Installation Completion screen

When we click on "Finish", the below screen appears indicating that the virtual box got installed. This is the screen of the Oracle Virtual Box Manager (Fig. 6.31).

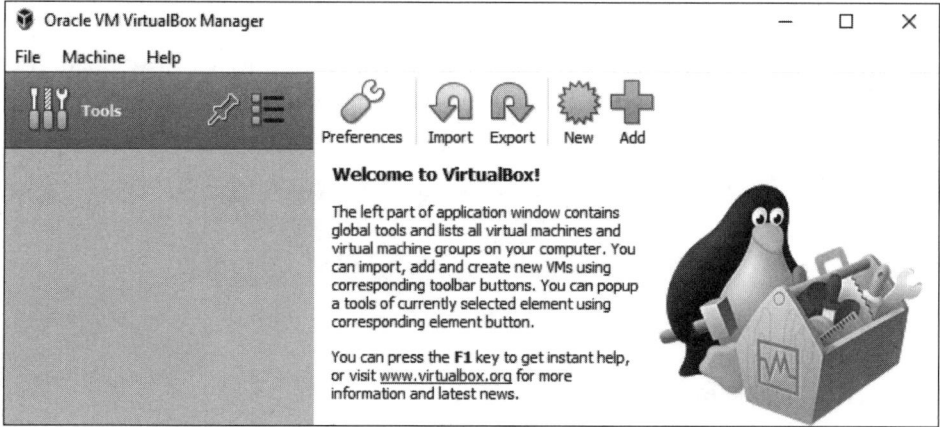

Figure 6.31 Oracle VirtualBox Manager home screen

6.6 HDP Sandbox Download and Installation

In this section, let us look into the details of setting up the sandbox provided by Horton box (Cloudera). Cloudera Hadoop file system interface is an easy-to-use, web-based GUI for accessing HDFS. It offers read and write access to HDFS through a rich, consistent, and intuitive Hadoop interface suitable for both experienced users and new adopters.

Horton box is a perfect software provided by Hortonworks. It is ideal for hands-on use on a machine or laptop and is freely available. It is suitable for day-to-day work and is a single-node Hadoop cluster. The minimum requirement for the machine should be a CPU with 64-bit supported OS. We shall use the 64-bit Windows operating system. The minimum need to install the sandbox is 8 GB RAM. We suggest having 16 GB RAM.

Enabling Virtualization

Go to BIOS in the Windows operating system by pressing the F10 key, and it will go to the machine BIOS. In the BIOS, go to the system configuration, check for the virtualization technology or tab, and enable it (Fig. 6.32) since that is a requirement. Once we allow this, save the configuration, exit and start the machine. This is the first step to install the setup.

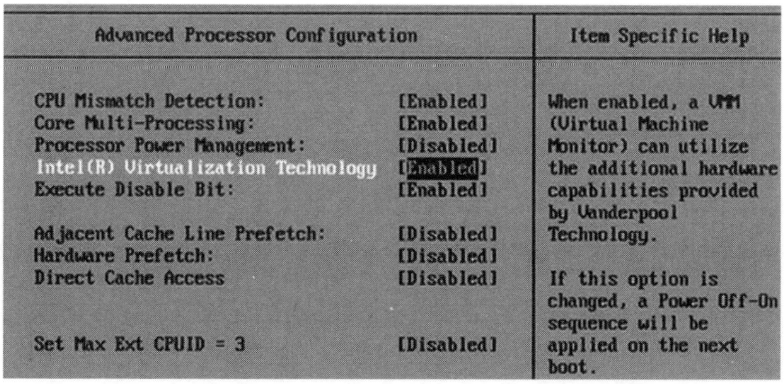

Figure 6.32 Virtualization enabled screen

Downloading HDP Sandbox

Now, let us go to the Cloudera website (www.cloudera.com) to download the HDP sandbox. Click "Products" menu and click "Downloads" menu (Fig. 6.33).

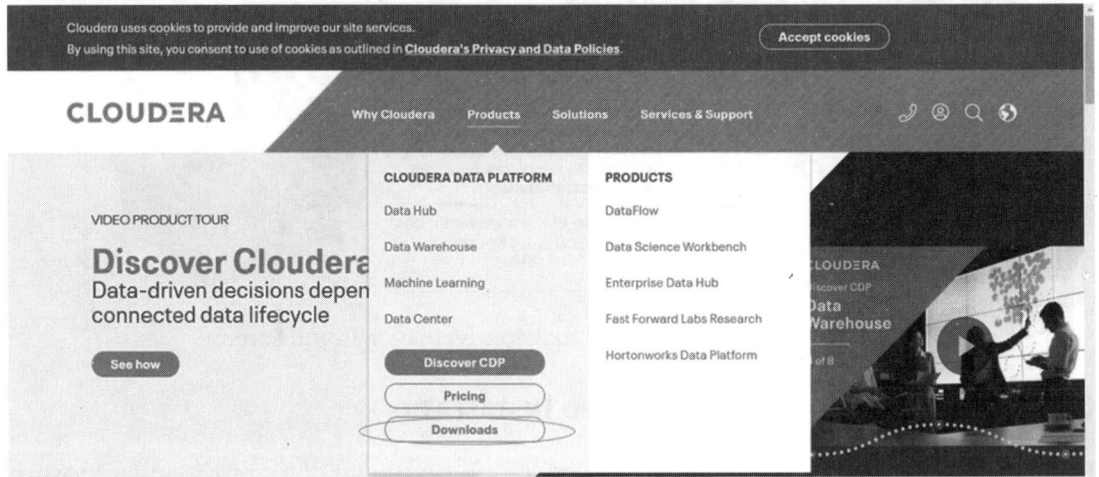

Figure 6.33 HDP Cloudera Download

When we click "Downloads" menu, it will lead to the page below. Click on "Download the Hortonworks (Fig. 6.34) Sandbox."

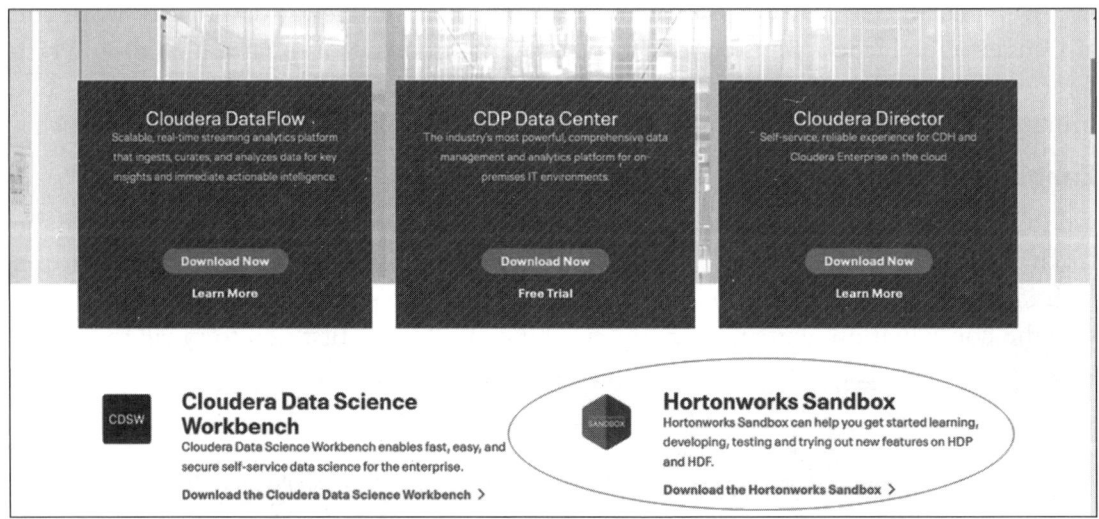

Figure 6.34 HDP Cloudera Download: Hortonworks Sandbox

In the next screen, click "Download Now" button of Hortonworks HDP (Fig. 6.35).

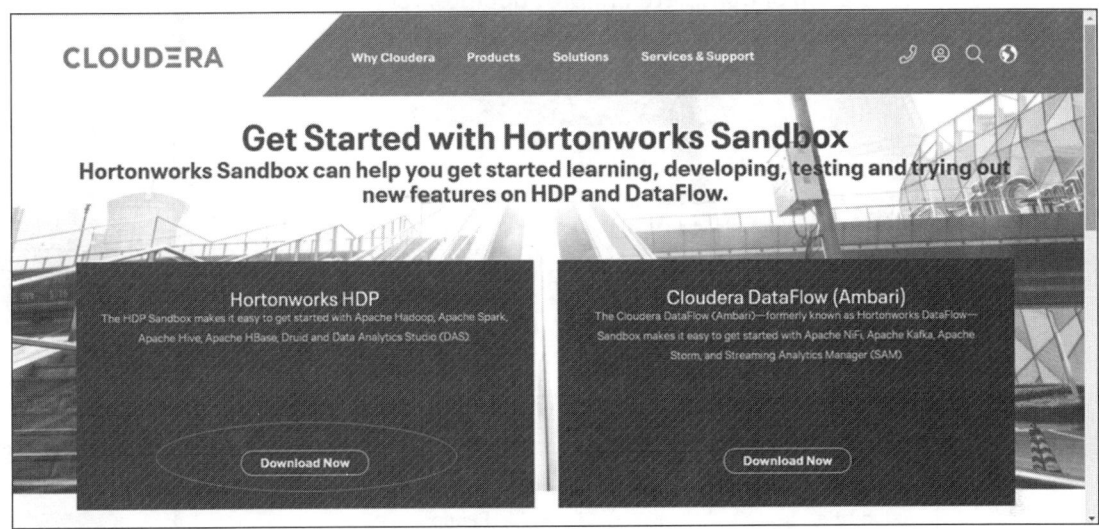

Figure 6.35 HDP Cloudera Download: Hortonworks HDP

In the next screen, choose the installation type as "Virtualbox" (Fig. 6.36).

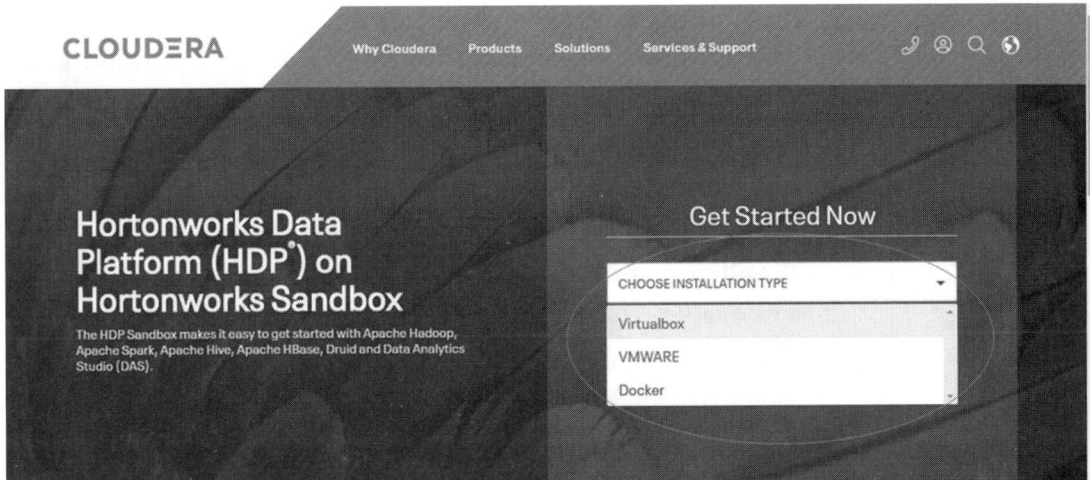

Figure 6.36 HDP Cloudera Download: Installer Type (Virtualbox)

The next screen asks us to fill out the form (Fig. 6.37) you may have to fill in the form, name, and other details, and submit it.

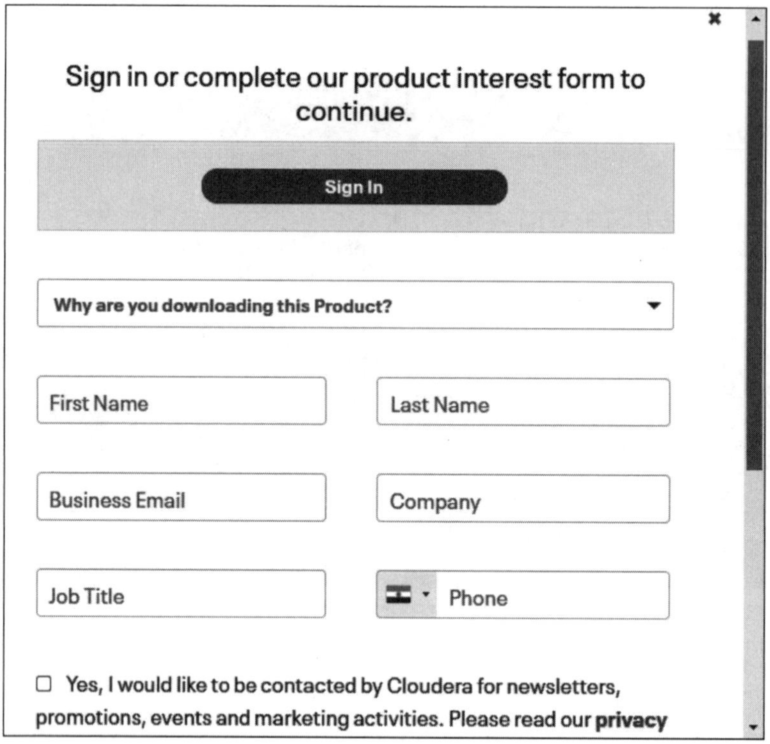

Figure 6.37 HDP Cloudera Download: Sign-in form

Before it starts downloading, it will ask to accept the Terms (Figure 6.38), select it and click "submit". The file size is about 11 GB file, so it may take quite long to download based on our internet bandwidth.

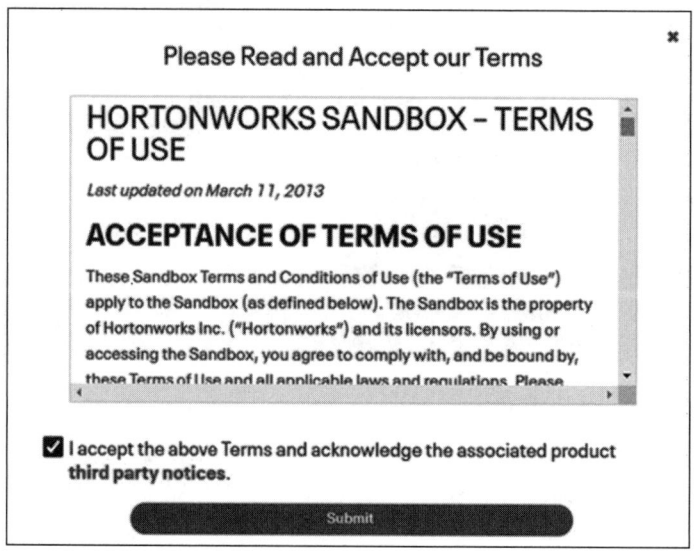

Figure 6.38 HDP Cloudera Download: Acceptance screen

Check for the correct version before downloading it. We are going to work on Windows. Recent available version is the 3.0.1 version (Fig. 6.39). You can download it for VirtualBox.

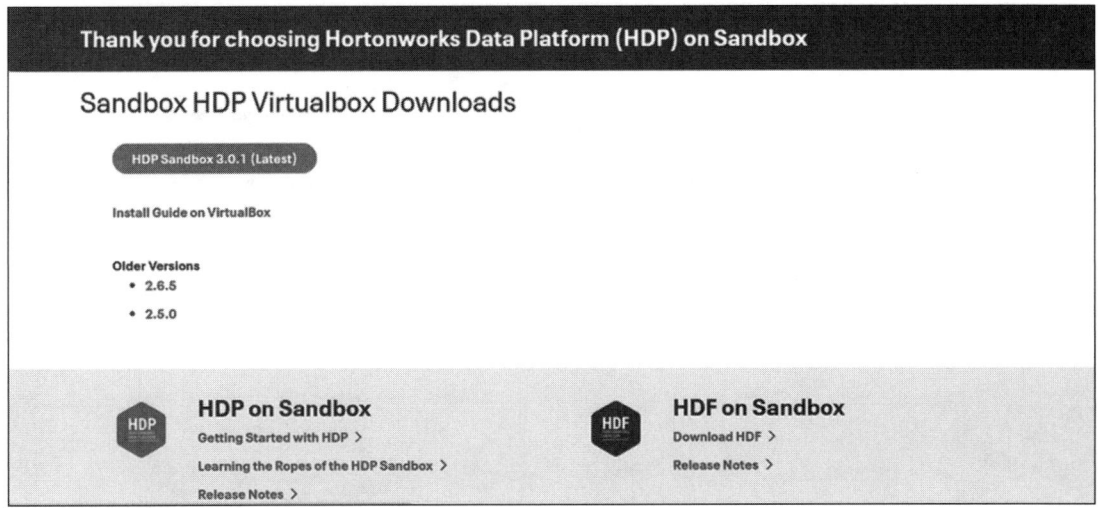

Figure 6.39 HDP Cloudera Download: Sandbox HDP VirtualBox version

Remember we have the download for VirtualBox, not VMware or docker; Oracle provides the VirtualBox. We have already installed the virtual box and have now downloaded the sandbox. Let us start the Oracle Virtual Machine. Click "File" menu (Fig. 6.40) and select "Import Appliance."

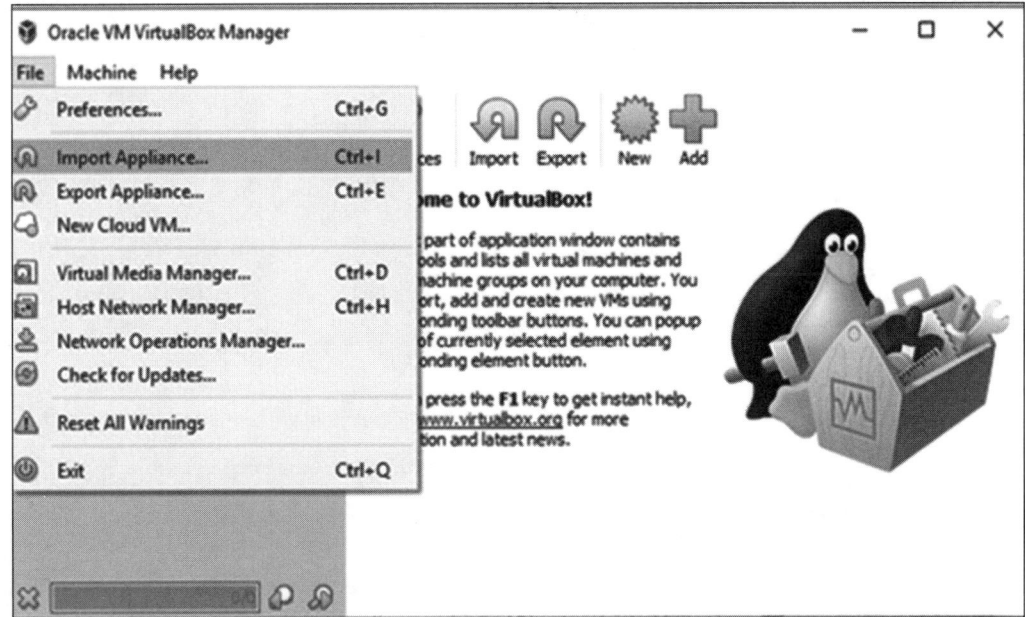

Figure 6.40 Oracle VirtualBox Import Appliance menu

Now let us go to the file where we have downloaded the 11 GB OVA file. Import the appliance. Click Next, and this is the configuration (Fig. 6.41).

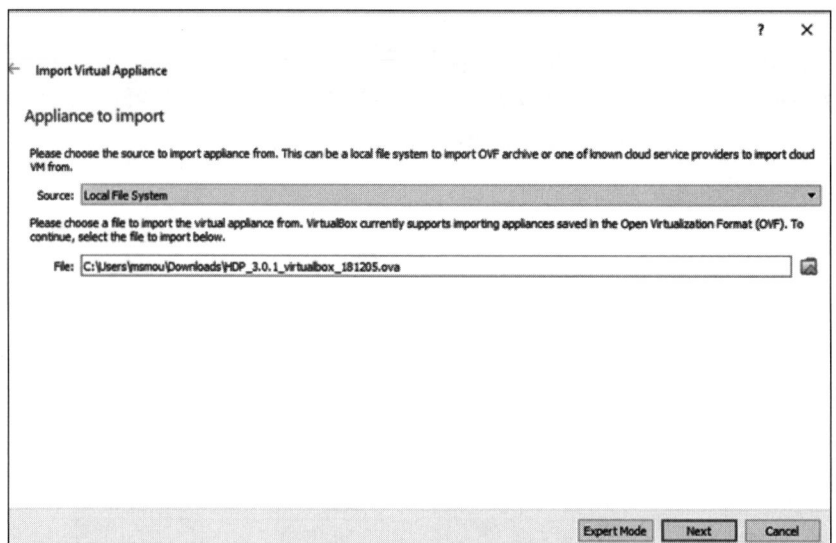

Figure 6.41 Oracle VirtualBox Appliance Import Screen

In the next screen, Click "Import" button (Fig. 6.42).

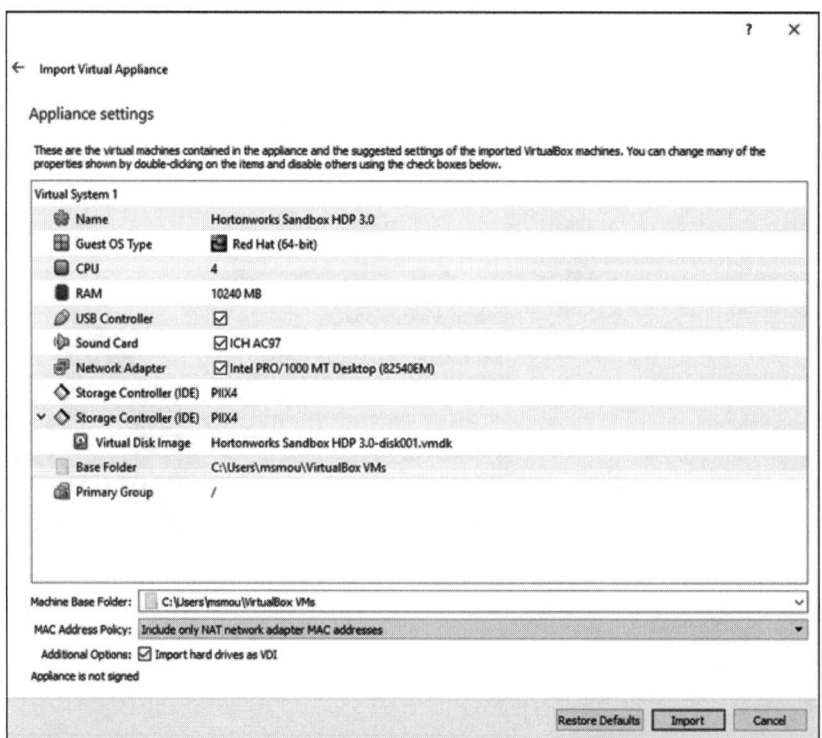

Figure 6.42 Oracle VirtualBox import Appliance settings

When you click "Import", it will show the progress of the import as below (Fig. 6.43).

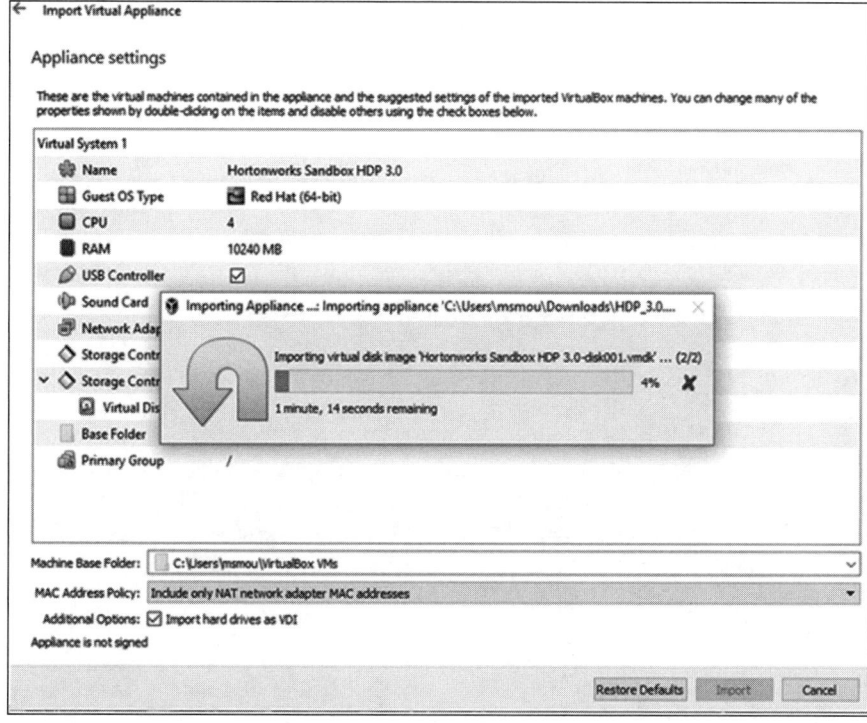

Figure 6.43 Oracle VirtualBox import Appliance status

Once you import the appliance, select the sandbox image. If you have 16 GB RAM and a good laptop, do not change the default settings. Once imported, you will see a screen similar to the one below (Fig. 6.44). Click start to start the Hortonworks Sandbox.

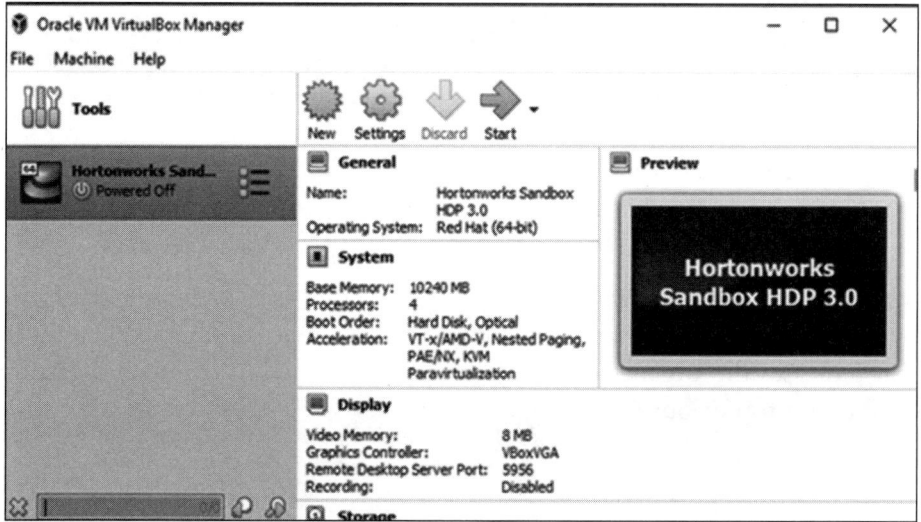

Figure 6.44 Oracle VirtualBox with Hortonworks Sandbox HDP 3.0

Go to the USB setting; you have to unselect if the mouse pointer is selected. When the Sandbox started, it will show the message as below (Fig. 6.45). For Virtualbox, the welcome Screen URL is given below in the message.

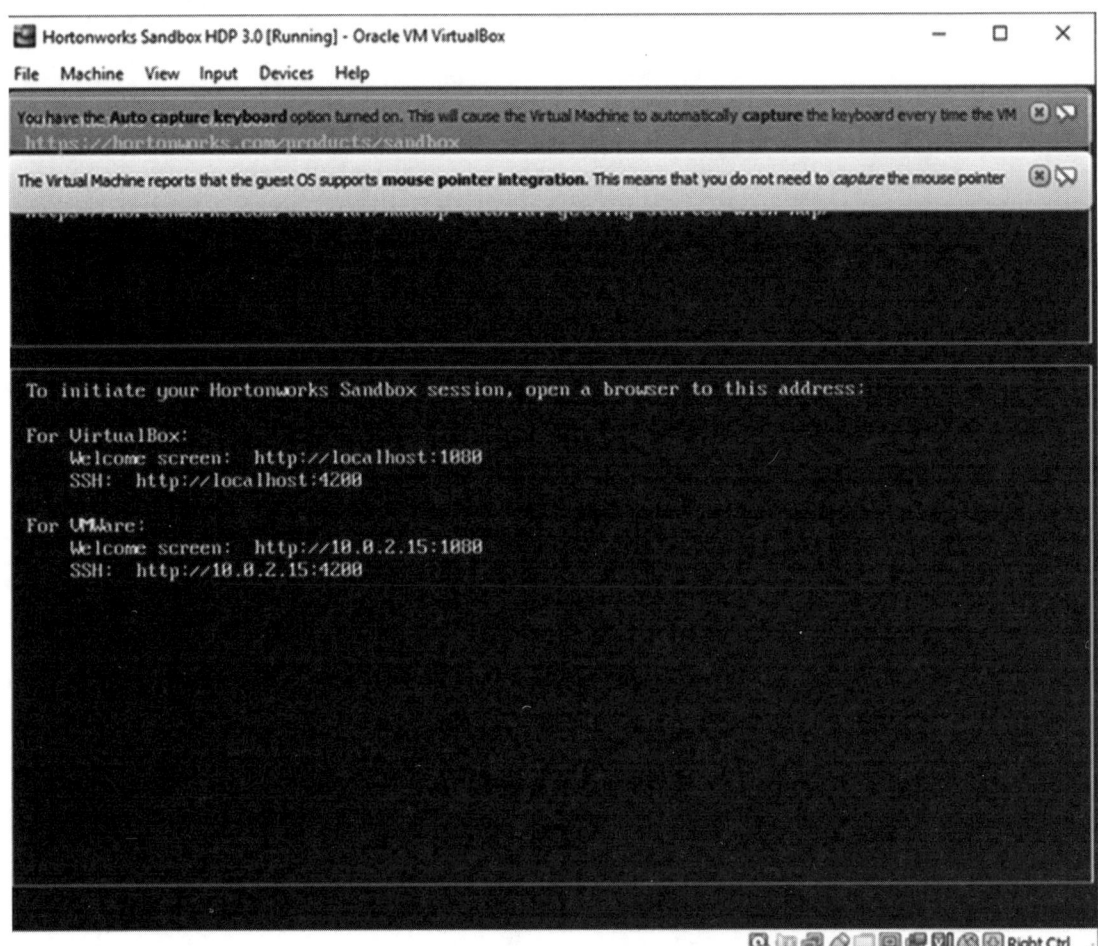

Figure 6.45   Oracle VirtualBox with Hortonworks Sandbox HDP 3.0: Successful Power on

When we open any web browser and ping the virtual box welcome screen URL, if it opens up, it will indicate that the sandbox started successfully. The below diagram (Fig. 6.46) indicates the organization of VirtualBox, Virtual Machine and Hortonworks HDP Sandbox on top of our Operating System.

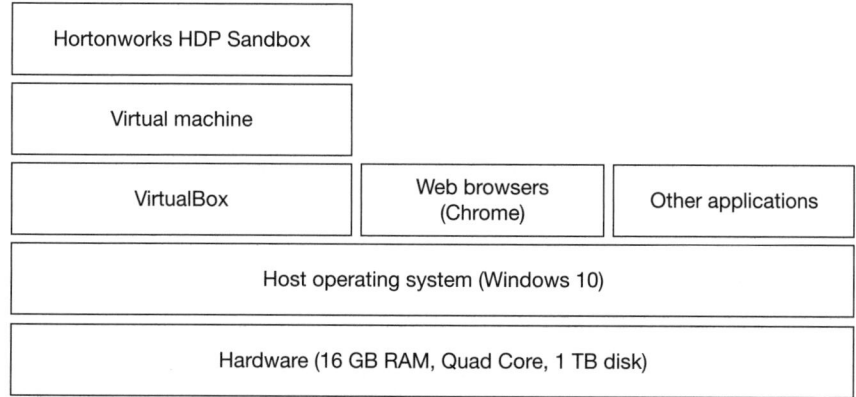

Our personal computer/Machine

Figure 6.46 Architecture diagram of VirtualBox with Virtual Machine

Let us ping the HDP Sandbox welcome screen URL (localhost:1080): Refer Fig. 6.47.

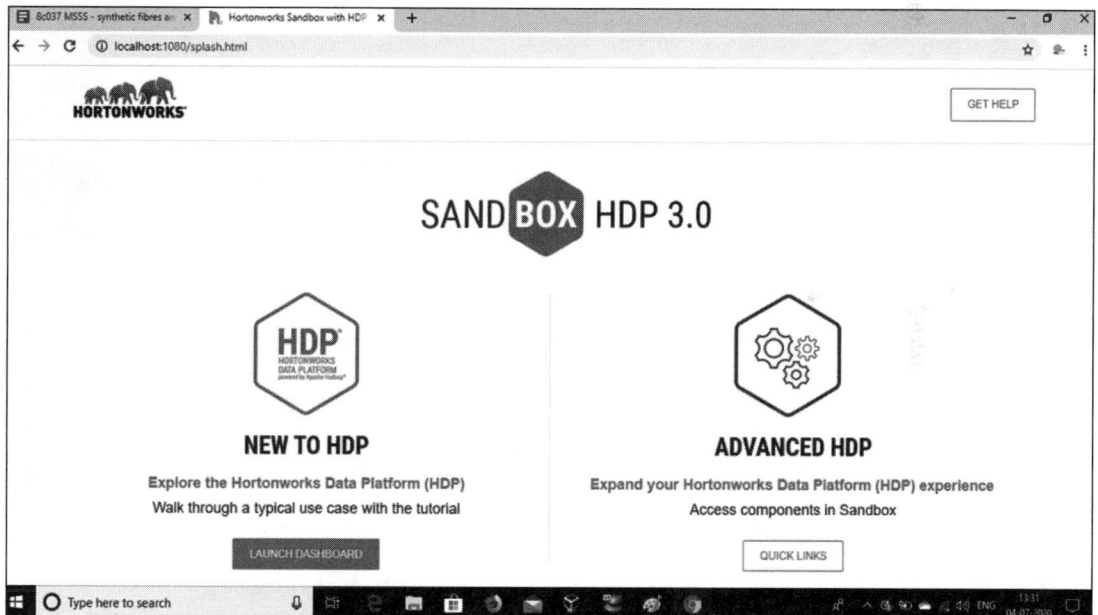

Figure 6.47 Sandbox HDP welcome screen

When we click the "LAUNCH DASHBOARD" Button, a screen of Ambari opens (asking to login).

6.7 Ambari Administration

We are using Hortonworks Sandbox HTP 3.0. So, this is the Sandbox version that we have on Oracle VirtualBox. The Ambari services are installed on 8080 port (the links are available in 1080 port). It will take us to the Ambari login page (Fig. 6.48). We need to type in the administration password. Hadoop console comes up with two players: we can use the Ambari tool or use the console. There are two ways to work with Hadoop. Either we can use the command prompt or use the console.

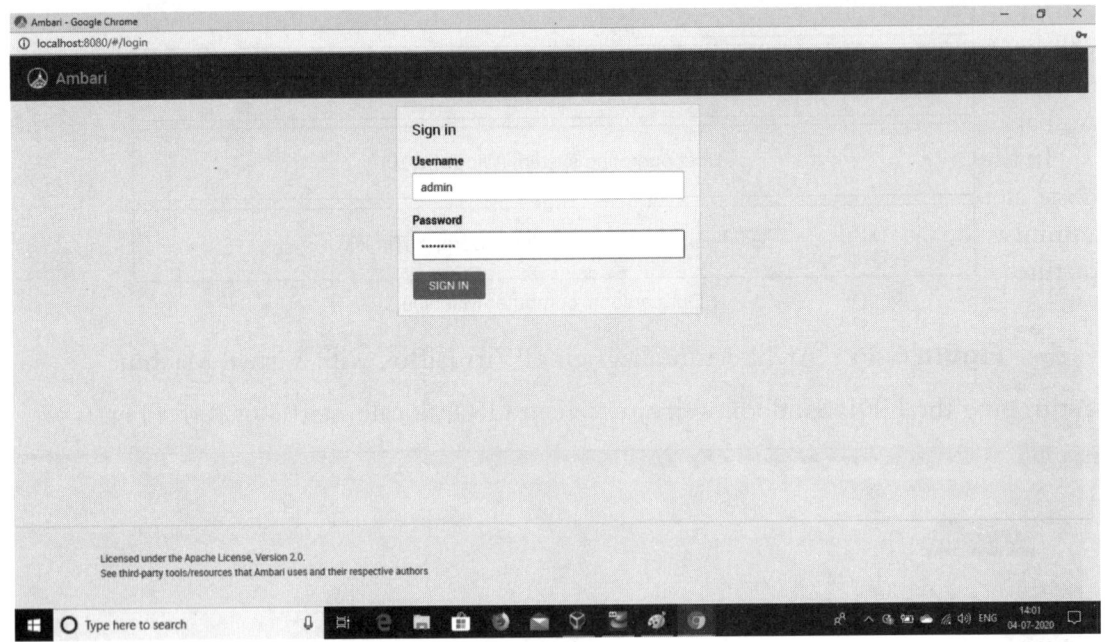

Figure 6.48 Ambari login screen

When we click "sign in", we should be able to see the dashboard. Table 6.1 shows the default user id and password installed by the HDP Sandbox 3.0 Version.

Table 6.1 Default username and password for HDP Sandbox

User	Password	Role	Services
admin	Refer to Admin Password Reset	System Administrator (Ambari Admin)	Ambari
maria dev	maria dev	Spark and SQL Developer	Hive, Zeepelin, Mapreduce/Tez/ Spark, Pig, Solir, Hbase/Phoenix, Sqoop, NiFi, Storm, Kafka, Flume
raj_ops	raj_ops	Hadoop Warehouse Operator	Hive/Tez, Ranger, Falcon, Knox, Sqoop, Oozie, Flume, Zookeeper
holger_gov	holger_gov	Data Steward	Atlas
amy_ds	amy_ds	Data Scientist	Spark, Hive, R, Python, Scala

Ambari administration console is one of the tools we can use for Hadoop administration. If you have worked with the administration of WebLogic, WebSphere, or any other tool, you will be aware that these always come with a console. Similarly, Ambari is one of the console applications using which we can manage the various managerial and administerial activities of Hadoop. To start the console part of Ambari, we must start the Ambari server and Ambari agent. These are the two required components. However, if we have installed the Cloudera HDP Sandbox, it will be installed automatically, and the server and agent will be up and running with the sandbox. Now, let us go to the browser (IE, chrome, or Mozilla). Type HTTP forward slash 8080. It will take us to the login page called an Ambari console.

In the Ambari console (Fig. 6.49), we can see the various tabs like dashboard, services, host, alert, and Cluster admin. On the left is the dashboard section of the Ambari administration console. This contains several metrics that give the Hadoop cluster's overall picture.

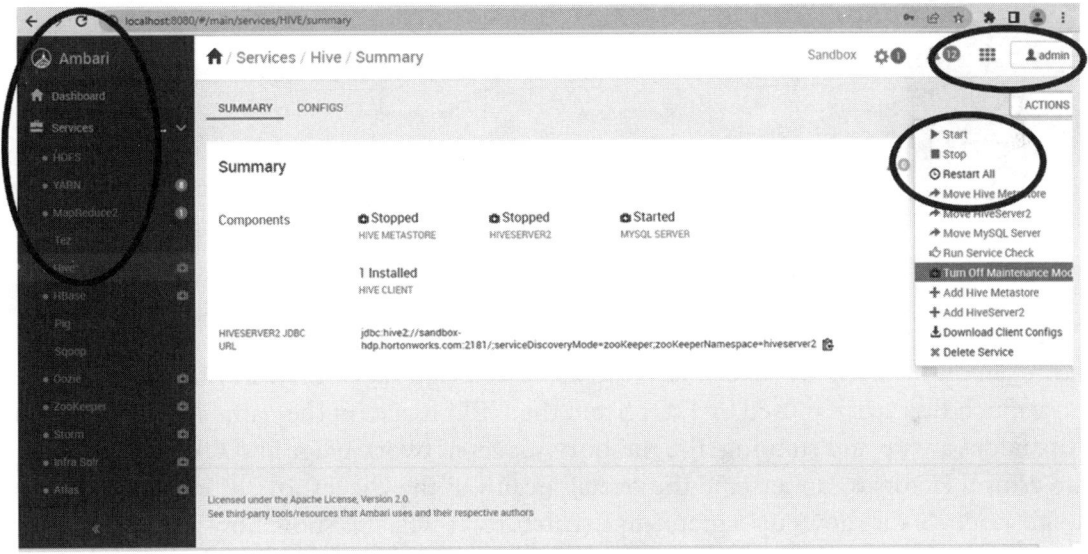

Figure 6.49 Ambari admin console

In the right-hand corner, we can see which user has logged in. Let us move on to the dashboard. This is the service section, and it has got all the services available in this sandbox. It displays all the available services in the sandbox, whether or not they are active and running. The green ones are the active ones, and the ones that are in red are actually in the maintenance mode. We may see a few services highlighted with some numbers, which means that these have some unresolved issues. For example, if there are connection issues, it will be critical because these services will not be able to take any request and serve. You can start the console, stop it, do a restart all, or just put it on the maintenance mode. The currently available services are HDFS, MapReduce, Yarn, Hive, Pig, Zookeeper, and Ambari metrics.

By default, we can see the metrics, Heatmaps, and Config History on the main screen. Metrics (Fig. 6.50) give the details of the metrics at all levels, like HDFS Data usage, HDFS links, Memory usage, Network usage, CPU usage and Cluster load.

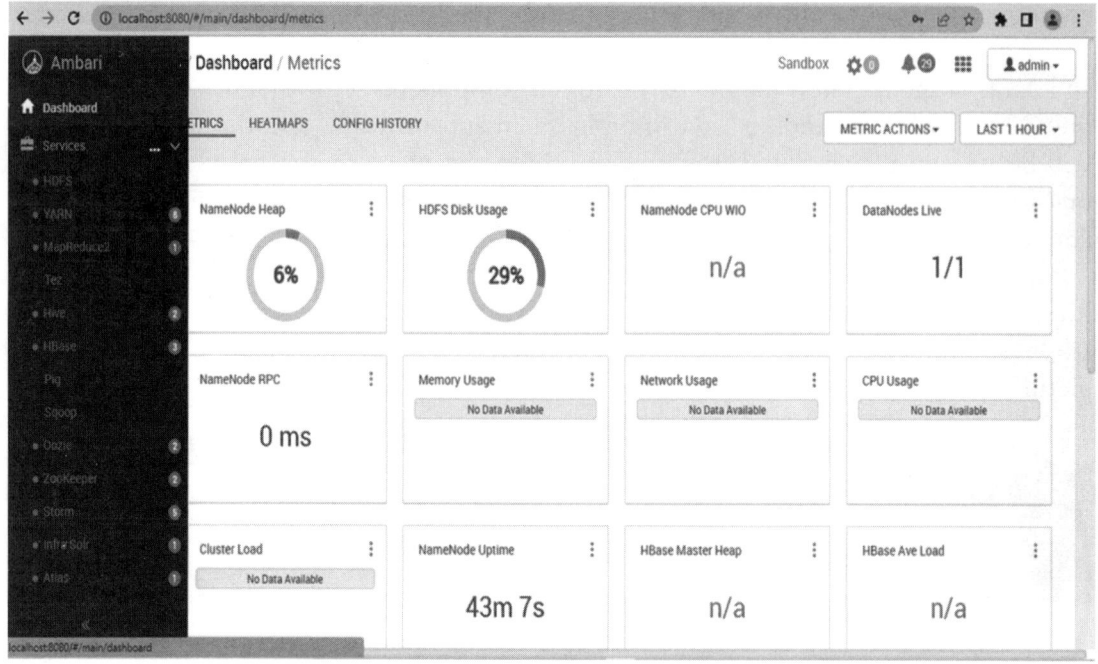

Figure 6.50 Ambari admin console: Metrics tab

For example, we will be able to see the amount of memory used in the name node or how much disk space is used by HDFS and the CPU usage on the name node, how many data nodes are up and running, the memory usage, network usage and CPU usage. These are critical factors to understand the overall health of the cluster. In our case, it is just one single node. So, it shows up a graph-like structure. It will also show how the resources are used in the cluster and how long a name node is up and running. In case of any restarts or failures (crash), we will easily get to know the details of the failure and the time since when the cluster is in a backup mode. Similarly, we have the heap usage on the resource manager, which shows how many node managers are currently live or lost (unhealthy). Such details are available on this dashboard and are filtered for the last hour; but we can go back, to say 24 hours, one week, or one year. We have specific additional metrics that we can add. For example, HDFS, HBase, Yarn, or anything you want to add, can be added using the dropdown.

There is a heatmap tab (Fig. 6.51) that will show a heatmap based on the usage, like the disk used by the HDFS. Config history is an important section. In the entire Ambari page, we will quickly get to know the changes related to any service. We can roll back specific changes related to any services. New properties can be replaced by old properties easily.

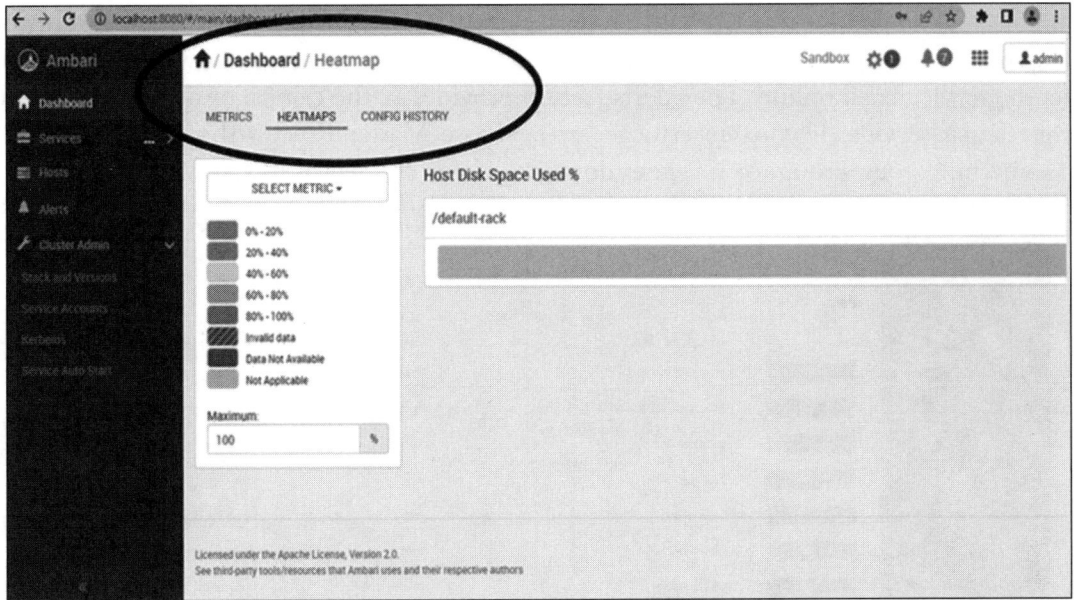

Figure 6.51 Ambari admin console: Heatmap tab

The dashboard area contains all the services. It has a services section, host section, alerts, and custom cluster administration.

The next section is the host (Fig. 6.52). We have only one node cluster, which is the sandbox, but in an enterprise project, you may have more than one node. If we want to add more nodes to the cluster, all we must do is click on Add New Host. Provide all the details and go through confirming the host and assigning the slave configuration. Then we can start and test it. This is one of the easy ways to scale up and scale down.

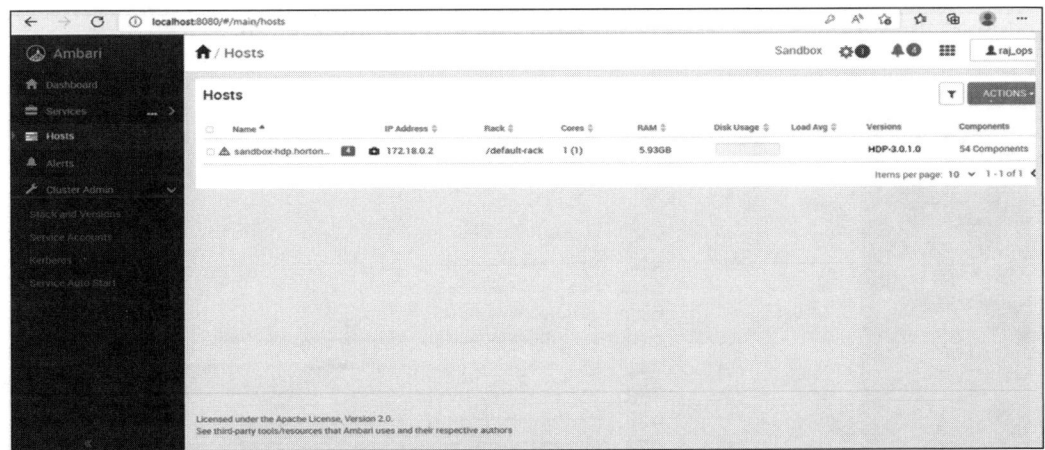

Figure 6.52 Ambari admin console: Host tab

Next, we will talk about the Alert (Fig. 6.53). It shows all the elements which need immediate attention from the Ambari administrators. If some background services are running or stopped, or if you want to restart everything, this small section will help. It will keep track of all the services, irrespective of the time it takes to start or how long it takes to get the service back online. The Alerts section provides all the critical or other alerts about a particular service. If you see critical (crit), HBase Master Process shows critical (crit). If something goes wrong, or if it goes down, or if it is crashed, it lists down all the alerts.

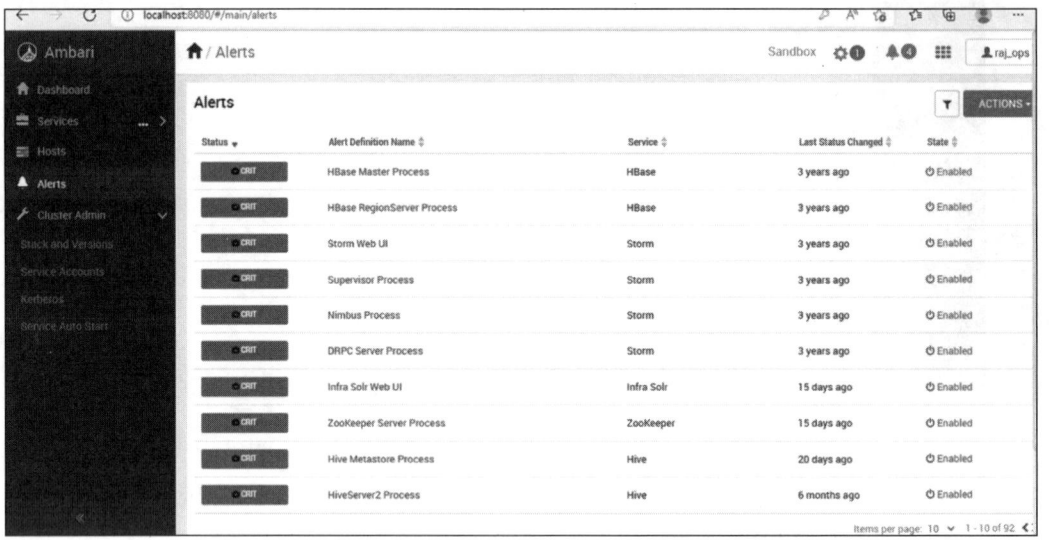

Figure 6.53   Ambari admin console: Alerts tab

The first option in the Cluster Admin section is "Stacks and Version". This is the section where we have all the services (Fig. 6.54) listed along with their version, status, and description of the concerned service. This is very useful when writing our programs to interact with certain applications. For example, certain scripting is limited to certain version of the services. So, we need to pay attention on the version.

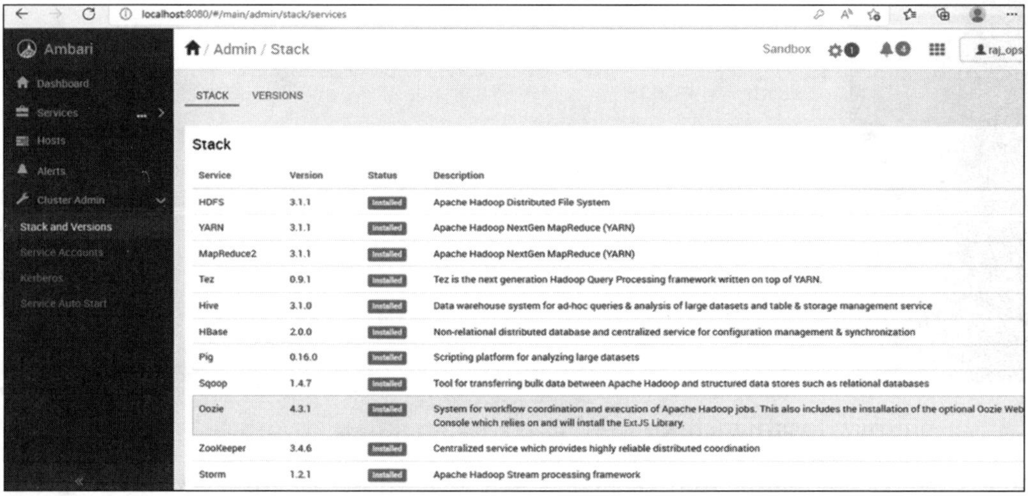

Figure 6.54   Ambari console: Stack and versions

Let us look at the "Service account (Fig. 6.55)". These are the users who are associated with a particular usage service. For example, it shows how to group users on Hadoop. The Hive is the user for accessing all the Hive-related queries. Similarly, we have all the users listed for each of the services.

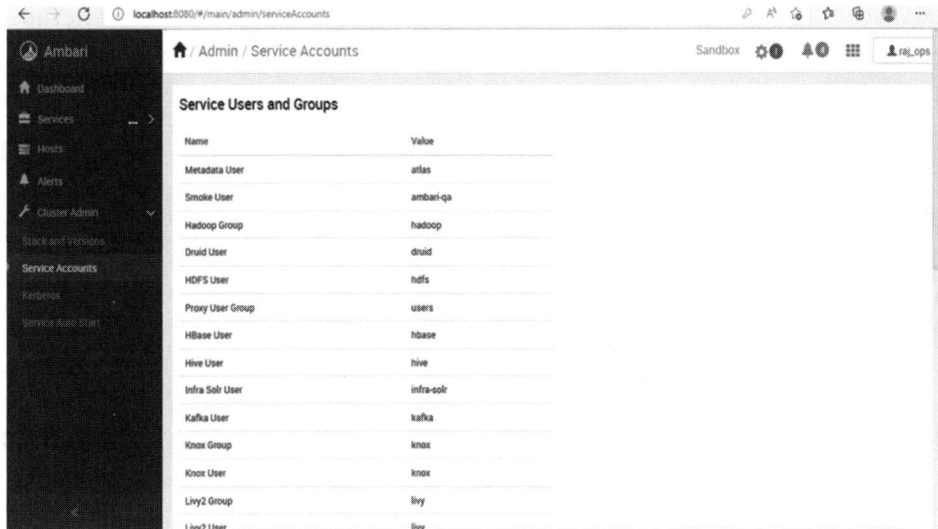

Figure 6.55 Ambari console: Service accounts

Kerberos is another security feature provided by Hortonworks (Fig. 6.56) in a data platform. Most organizations use Kerberos. All the authentications to Hadoop services happen through Kerberos. Kerberos is a service that provides security and access related to Hadoop resources.

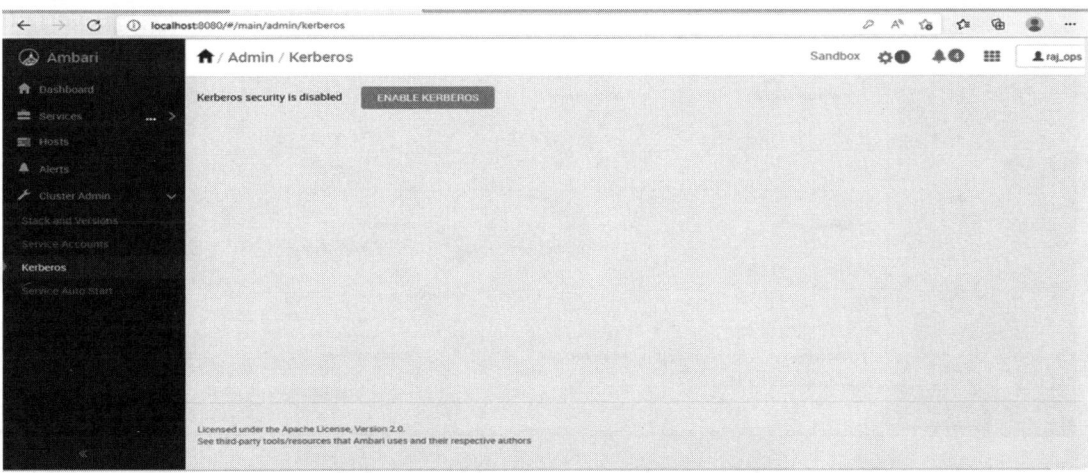

Figure 6.56 Ambari console: Kerberos

The last section under "Cluster Admin" is "Service Auto Start". In this section, we can set only certain services to be active when the cluster is up (Fig. 6.57).

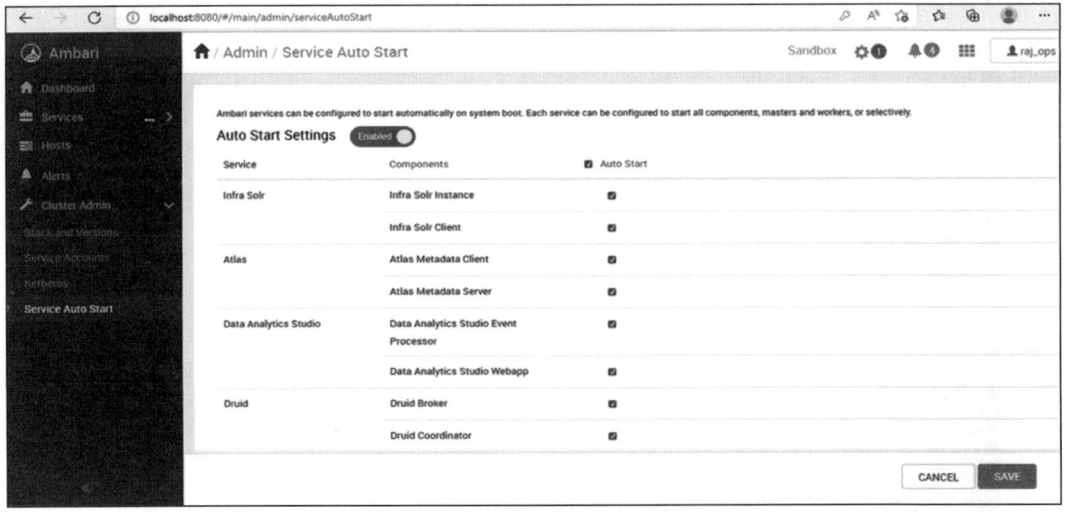

Figure 6.57 Ambari console: Service Auto Start

There is no point in getting all these services up and running at the same time since it takes a lot of resources on our cluster. Based on the need, we enable the required services. For example, if we use Kafka, we can make a checkmark and then hit the save button. When our cluster goes down, we can bring our cluster back online, and these services will be turned on automatically.

The top right section is the user we have logged in to. There are a couple of settings to manage Ambari (Fig. 6.58).

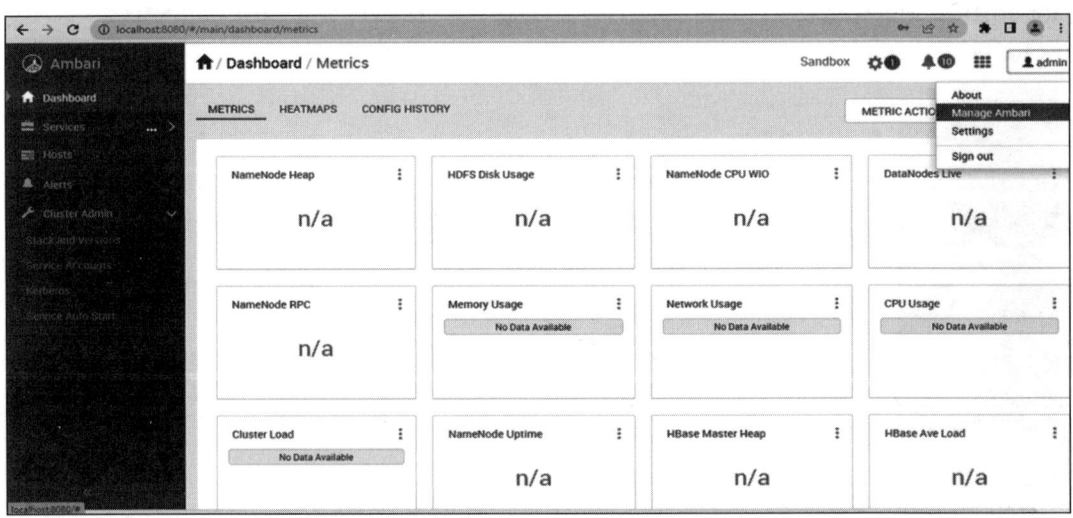

Figure 6.58 Ambari console: Manage Ambari menu

Since we logged in as Admin, we can go to Manage Admin and see the cluster management options. We can see the Apache Ambari version (Fig. 6.59) and check whether it is current or not.

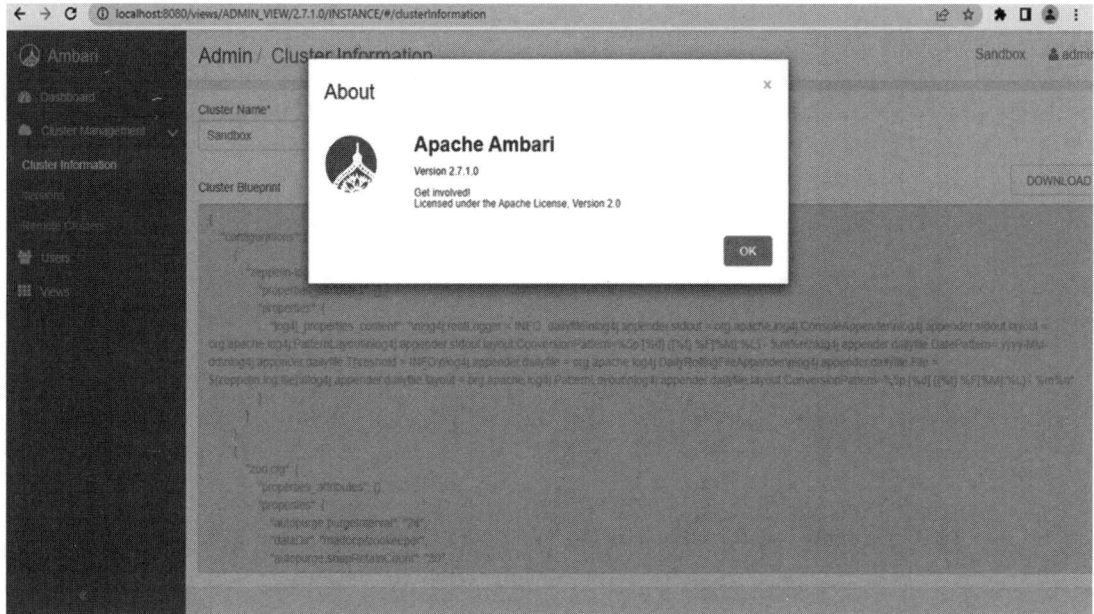

Figure 6.59 Apache Ambari version

We can add remote clusters, which will be displayed here. If we want to add more users, we can do it here in this section (Fig. 6.60).

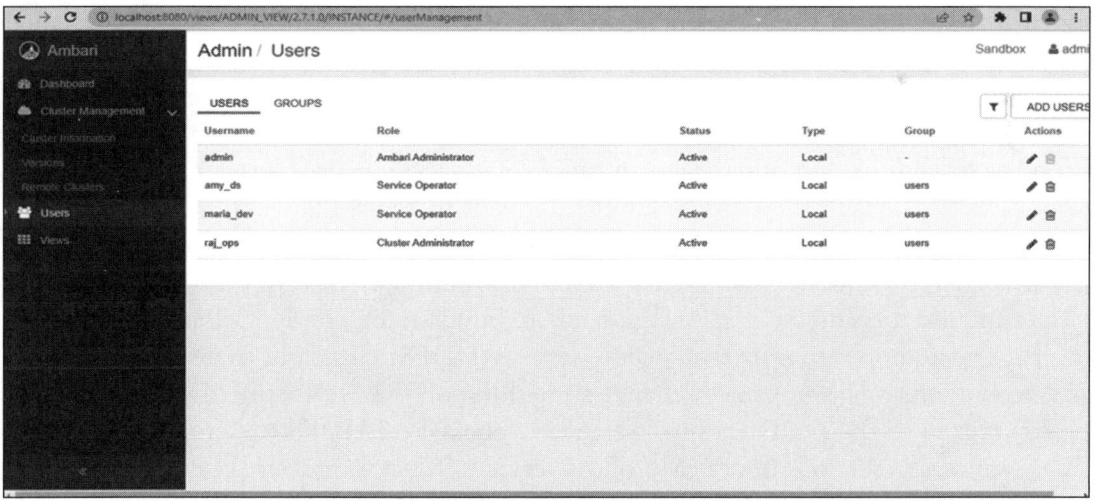

Figure 6.60 Ambari Users menu

The Hortonworks Sandbox comes with a few standard users; Admin and Maria Dev are some of the existing users. We can create a group with these users (Fig. 6.61). First, create a group and then assign users so that we can give privileges to a particular group and not to the users directly. This is one of the best practices.

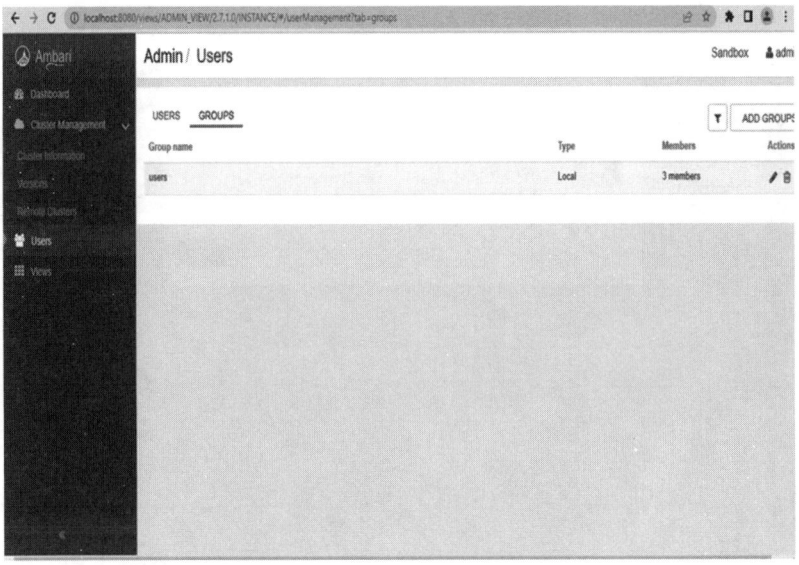

Figure 6.61   Ambari User groups

We have an option to download the client configuration. For example, we need to have some client config details for the Hive. If we download the client config, we will be easily able to configure the Hive client and then start using it. We can also delete the services. We may fix the errors by restarting the services most of the time. Let us say there is something corrupted, then it wouldn't turn in green, and it will even give us a detailed message so that we can go back and check a particular issue.

Let us click on "HDFS" in the services; we can see here, the number of nodes and data nodes. In our case, it is just one-on-one. It will give the details on whether my name node has started. In case of any issue, it will provide the relevant alerts. It will show heat maps on the usage. In the configuration part, we can change any configuration and hit the Save button, and it will go ahead and do the config (file update in the background). For example, if you want to set the data node maximum heap size to be 10 GB, you must scroll to it and then hit Save; it will go back and update the configuration of HDFS. So, this page corresponds to only this specific service (HDFS). Similarly, there are a couple of advanced configs. If you want to change something on the HDFS site, the configuration is only related to the HDFS site (as we already clicked on HDFS to come to this page). There are several sections under each of the services. If we want to make any changes, we have to go to a particular config section, change the values, and hit the Save button. For example, there is a timeout setting; instead of 120, we can make it 180 and then hit Save. It will update the corresponding config table accordingly.

In the same way, the configurations are available for Hive servers (Services). The meta store heap size and the memory limit will be under the settings of Hive. If we want to change the port information, all we have to do is change the port. It will require a restart of the services. If we make any change to configs, it will indicate that a restart is needed. So, in that case, we can go ahead and do the restart.

The Cluster Information tab (Fig. 6.62) will display the current version of the HDP installed. The version installed in our machine is shown as HDP 3.0.1.0 and we need to use this version while referring the help documents.

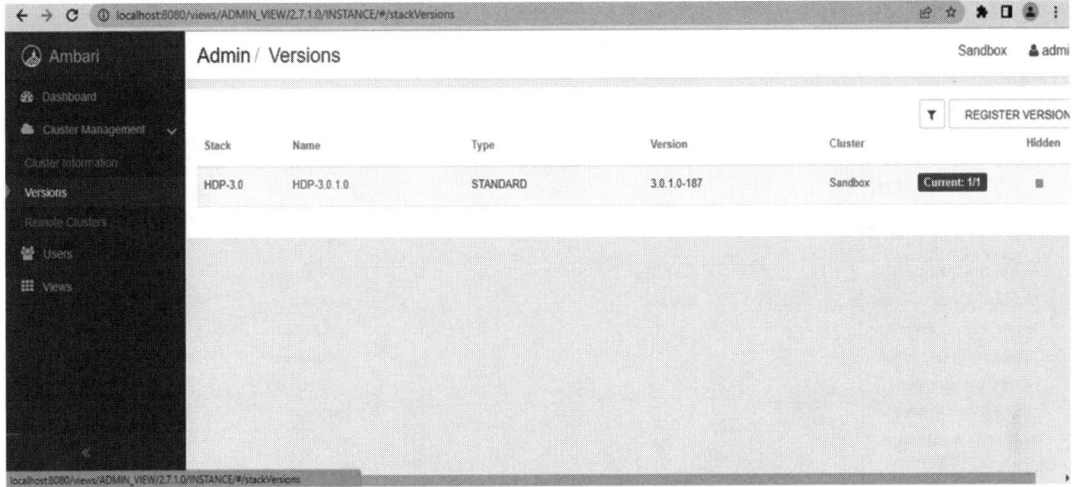

Figure 6.62 Ambari: HDP versions

Cloudera website has the documentation for HDP for all the versions. We need to choose the appropriate version of the installed Cloudera HDP version to go through the Help documents. In our machine, we have installed HDP version 3.0.1 and hence we need to refer to the documents related to this version (Fig. 6.63).

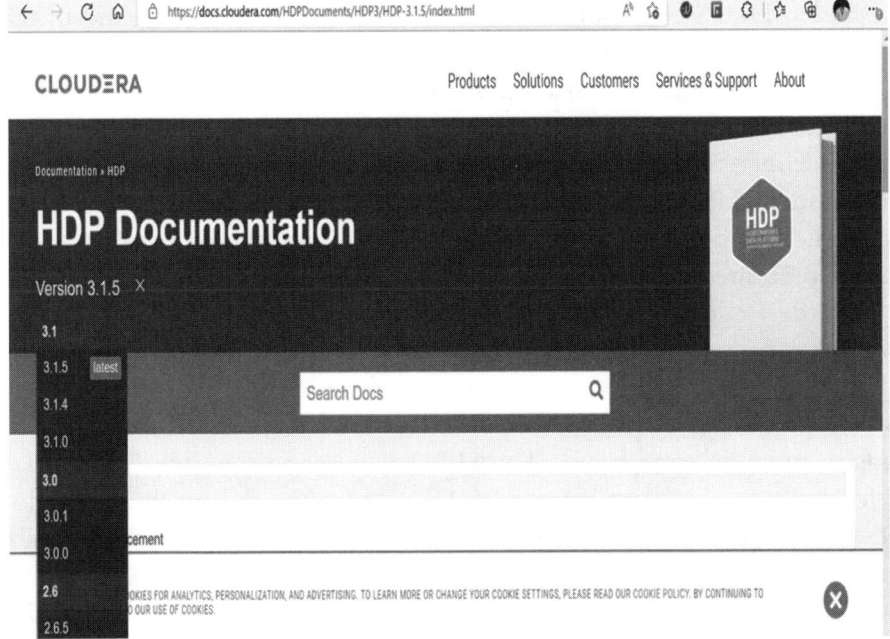

Figure 6.63 HDP Documentation

When we click on the installed version, it takes us to another page where all the helping documents related to Concepts, Installation and Upgrade, and How To documents are available for reference (Fig. 6.64).

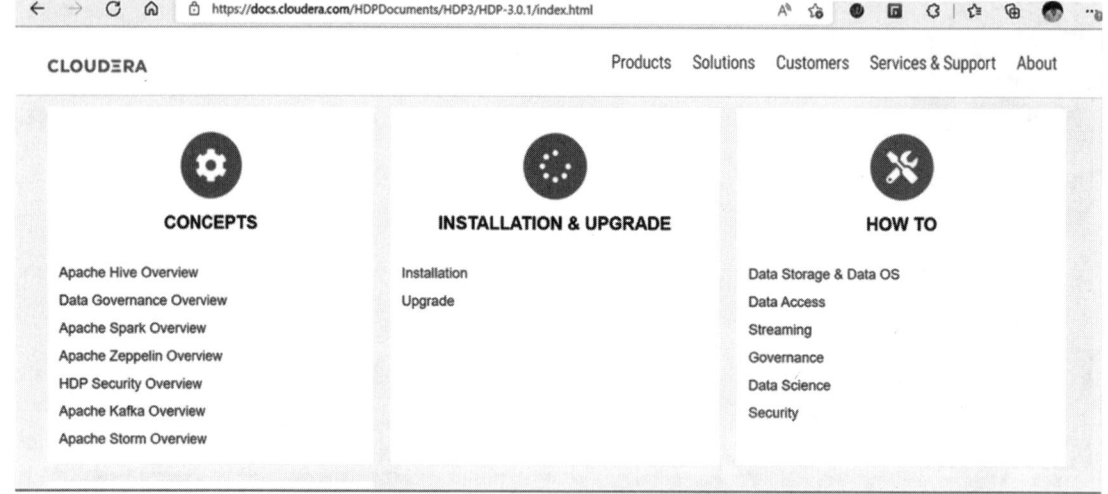

Figure 6.64   HDP Documentation details

6.8   HDFS COMMAND LINE INTERFACE

The HDFS Command Line Interface (Hadoop Distributed File System CLI), also called "fs", is a set of command-line tools that allow users to interact with a Hadoop cluster or a single node in a cluster. HDFS command-line interface (CLI) is a sub-command of namenode. It helps access the Hadoop Distributed File System from the command line. HDFS Shell Commands is the first shell utility that enables us to control our HDFS deployment from the command line; it helps to interact with a running Hadoop cluster without logging in to any of the DataNode servers. Shell Commands provide the ability to create and execute various commands on individual nodes within a distributed Hadoop cluster.

It supports commonly used functionalities such as listing files in a directory, copying a file to a different directory, deleting a file, etc. Before starting to use this tool, you need to install Java, the Hadoop development environment from Apache, and then the binary dump available at http://hadoop.apache.org.

The HDFS Command Line Interface is a Java program that provides a command-line interface to the Hadoop Distributed File System. It has no direct dependency on any other Hadoop modules except Java. The HDFS command-line interface (CLI) is a user interface for bulk-moving data between HDFS and our local machine. It allows us to access the entire Hadoop Distributed File System (HDFS) in Java code without writing any Java code. Only the streaming commands are written in Java code; everything else is in the pure, portable shell script, a console-based utility for managing HDFS. It provides terminal support for Windows, Linux, Solaris and Mac OS X platforms. It allows us to create files, modify file attributes, rename files, move files, delete/truncate/append files, list directories and submit jobs to the cluster. The HDFS command line interface allows users to start, stop, and list the names of Hadoop daemons.

6.8.1 JPS Command

To check the list of Hadoop services that are up and running, we can use the "jps" command (Fig. 6.65). The below screenshot indicates that Name Node, Jps, Journal Node, Unix Authentication Service, Ambari Server, DFS Admin, Data Node, Tag Synchronizer, and OozieCLI are up and running.

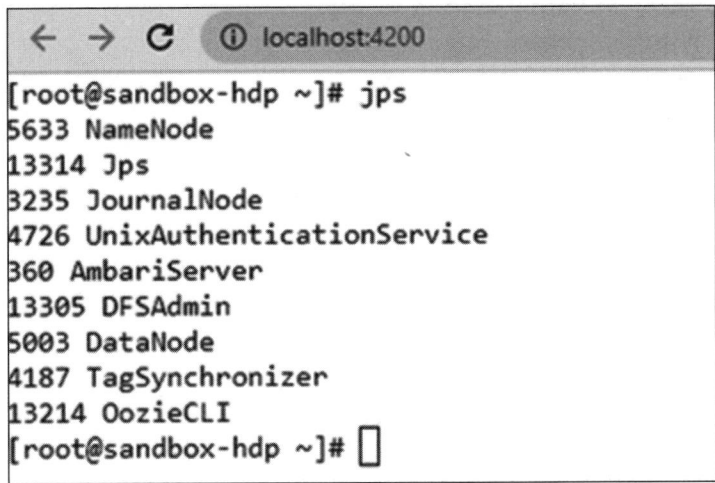

Figure 6.65 HDFS CLI Command: jps command

6.8.2 List of Files

Table 6.2 indicates the details of the list commands in HDFS, which include listing all the files with permissions (ls), listing down the directories (ls -d), listing down the file details in human readable format (ls -h), listing down the files recursively in all the directories and subdirectories (ls -R), and listing down the files inside a directory with the specific structure.

Table 6.2 HDFS CLI commands: List of files

S. No	HDFS Command	Description
		List Files
1	ls	List files with permissions and other details
2	ls-d/hadoop	Directories are listed as plain files
3	ls-h/data	Human readable format
4	ls-R/hadoop	Recursively list all files in hadoop directory and all subdirectories
5	ls/hadoop/dat*	List all the files inside hadoop directory which starts with 'dat'.

The below screenshot shows that while the ls command is used, it lists down only one file in the current directory. After that, the make directory command (mkdir) is executed (Fig. 6.66) to create a new directory called "test". Then, when we use the ls command again and it displays the newly created directory.

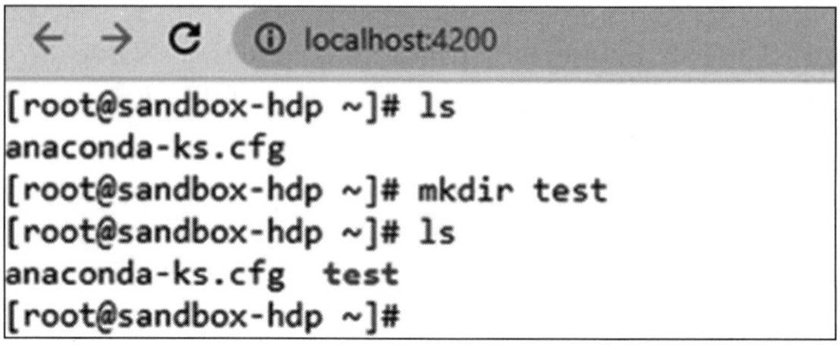

Figure 6.66 HDFS CLI Command: mkdir command

6.8.3 File Management

Table 6.3 lists down the file management commands, which include creating a directory (mkdir), removing the directory (rmdir), displaying the contents of the file (cat), showing the size of the file (du), merging multiple files (getmerge), counting the number of directories (count), changing the replication factor (setrep) and moving files from the source to the destination (mv). The commands for deleting HDFS files and directories work in a similar way to those in the Linux file system – we need to use the command –rm –r (recursive delete) to delete directories and files in them. The command -lsr can be used to recursively list directories and files in a specific folder.

Table 6.3 HDFS CLI commands: File management

S. No	HDFS Command	Description
		File Management
1	mkdir	Creates a directory named path in HDFS
2	rm	To Remove File or a Directory
3	rmr	Removes the file that identified by path
4	rmdir	Delete a directory
5	put	Upload a file/folder from the local disk to HDFS
6	cat	Display the contents for a file
7	du	Shows the size of the file on hdfs.
8	dus	Directory/file of total size
9	get	Store file/folder from HDFS to local file
10	getmerge	Merge multiple files in an HDFS
11	count	Count number of directory, number of files and file size
12	setrep	Changes the replication factor of a file
13	mv	HDFS Command to move files from source to destination

This Hadoop command (mv) is run like the -get commands, but with one difference – it removes the file from the HDFS location on a successful copy operation. This command is similar to the UNIX cp command and is used to copy files from one directory to another in the HDFS file system. The command cat is similar to the Unix cat command and displays the contents of a file.

6.8.4 Upload and Download Files

Table 6.4 lists down the commands related to the upload and download of files, which include moving the file/folder from the local to HDFS (moveFromLocal), moving a file from HDFS to local (moveToLocal), copying files from source to destination (cp), displaying the last kilobyte of the file (tail), creating, changing and modifying time stamps of a file (touch), creating a new file on HDFS with size 0 bytes (touchz), appending the content to the file which is present in HDFS (appendToFile), copying a file from local file system (copyFromLocal), copying files from HDFS to local file system (copyToLocal). The main difference between copying the files and moving the files is that while copying the files, it creates a duplication whereas when moving the files, it will not create duplication and there will be only one copy.

Table 6.4 HDFS CLI commands: Upload and download files

S. No	HDFS Command	Description
		Upload and Download Files
1	moveFromlocal	Move file/folder from local disk to HDFS
2	moveToLocal	Move a File from HDFS to Local
3	cp	Copy files from source to destination
4	tail	Display last kilobyte of the file
5	touch	Create, change and modify timestamps of a file
6	touchz	Create a new file on HDFS with size 0 bytes
7	appendToFile	Append the content to the file which is present on HDF
8	copyFromLocal	Copy file from local file system
9	copyToLocal	Copy files from HDFS to local file system

The below screenshot (Fig. 6.67) indicates that a new file is created when we use the touch command.

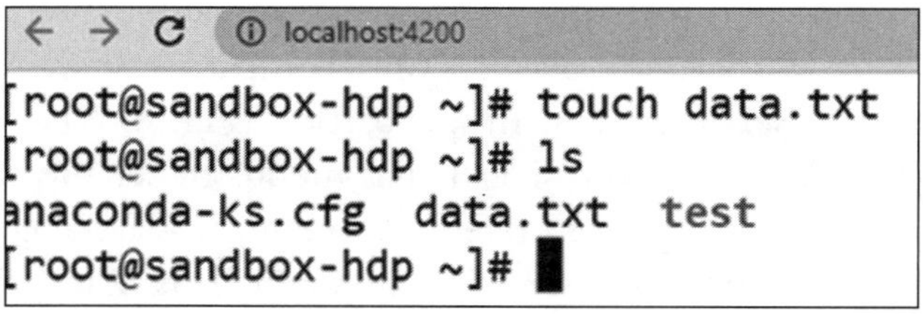

```
[root@sandbox-hdp ~]# touch data.txt
[root@sandbox-hdp ~]# ls
anaconda-ks.cfg  data.txt  test
[root@sandbox-hdp ~]#
```

Figure 6.67 HDFS CLI Command: touch command

6.8.5 Ownership and Validation

Table 6.5 lists the commands related to the ownership of the files and changing the permissions of the file, which include checking the checksum information of a file (checksum), changing the group association of files (chgrp), changing the permission of a file (chmod) and changing the owner and group of a file (chown).

Table 6.5 HDFS CLI commands: Ownership and Validation

S. No	HDFS Command	Description
		Ownership and Validation
1	checksum	Return the checksum information of a file
2	chgrp	Change group association of files/change the group of a file or a path
3	chmod	Change the permissions of a file
4	chown	Change the owner and group of a file

The below screenshot (Fig. 6.68) indicates that while we remove command (rm) with the file name, it removes the file permanently. It is confirmed by using the list command (ls).

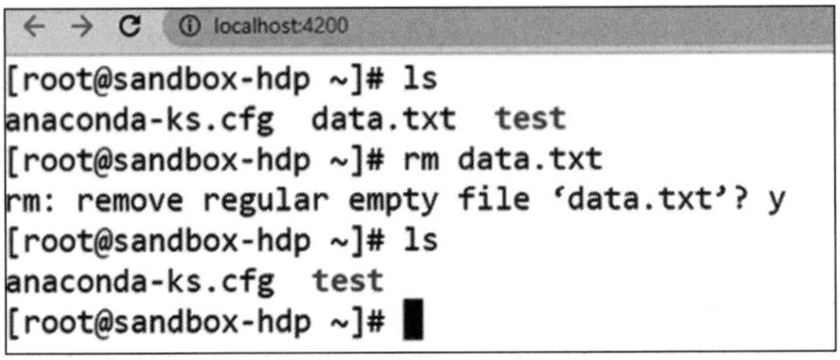

```
[root@sandbox-hdp ~]# ls
anaconda-ks.cfg  data.txt  test
[root@sandbox-hdp ~]# rm data.txt
rm: remove regular empty file 'data.txt'? y
[root@sandbox-hdp ~]# ls
anaconda-ks.cfg  test
[root@sandbox-hdp ~]#
```

Figure 6.68 HDFS CLI command: rm command

6.9 VMWARE VS. VIRTUALBOX

Let us compare two of the most popular free hypervisors (Table 6.6), VMware workstation player and Virtualbox. These two hypervisors are the most popular ones available to download for free today. VirtualBox is compatible with Linux, Windows, Mac OS and Solaris. On VirtualBox's website, you can even access the unsupported versions of VirtualBox for older operating systems like Windows XP or Windows Vista. There are many options to download VirtualBox, and it is compatible with virtually anything. However, the VM ware Workstation player is only compatible with Windows and Linux.

Let us compare the user interfaces: In VirtualBox (Fig. 6.69), we have five buttons at the top and a big gray pane at the side. It has menus to set the Preferences, Import, Export, New, and Add. Through the Preference menu, it is possible to select the input language, and it is user-intuitive and user-friendly. VirtualBox manager is self-explanatory and pretty easy to use.

Hadoop Distributed File System • 305

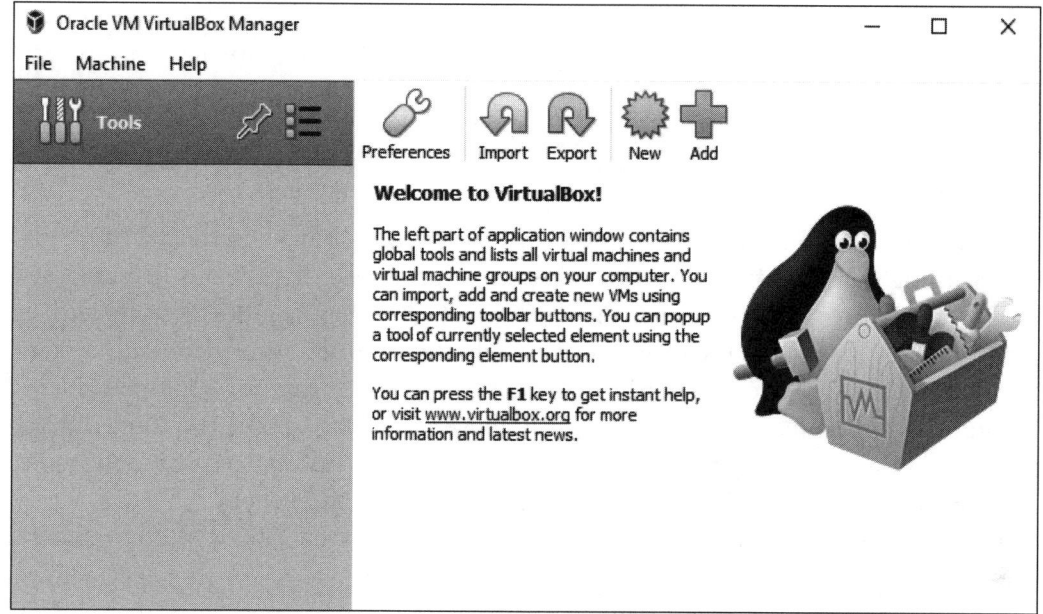

Figure 6.69 Oracle VM VirtualBox Manager home screen

VMware workstation is also user-friendly (Fig. 6.70). Each action is in large bold text with a description under it. It has menus like "Create a new virtual machine", "Open a virtual machine", "Upgrade to VMware Workstation Pro", and "Help".

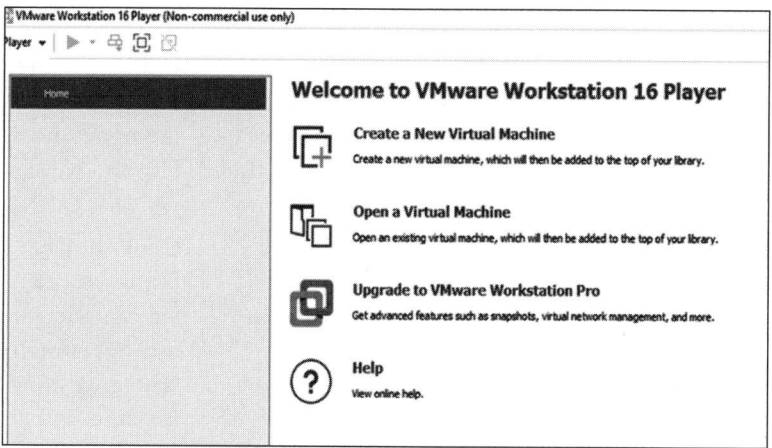

Figure 6.70 VMware Workstation home screen

It is easy to create a new virtual machine; all we have to do in VirtualBox is click on the blue New button at the top. Next, we can select a name for our operating system and where we want the virtual machine to be stored. As for OS compatibility, VirtualBox is compatible with six different operating systems, including Windows, Linux Solaris and

OS/2, and Mac OS. When we click Next after specifying the storage location, it gives us an option to select a memory size; this is self-explanatory. It tells you the recommended amount of ram, and it tells you the meaning of the color codes – green, which is good, and red, which is not recommended. Now we can select how big we want the hard disk to be and where we want it stored. VirtualBox does not ask to choose an iso. So we have to do that in settings after creating the VM.

We have to click the big "create a new virtual machine" button in the VMware player. The first thing that the player asks us to do is to select an iso. If the iso is detected, it will use easy install; beginners will love the easy install, and they can go through with that. Next, it asks us for a Windows product key, what edition we want to install, a name, a password, and confirm the password. Again, this is extremely easy for beginners. Now we can enter the virtual machine's name and the location of the virtual machine. Then, we select how big we want the hard disk to be and choose the option to split it into multiple files, if needed. VMware player supports Windows, Linux and others.

The difference between VMware Work Station and Virtual Box is listed in Table 6.6.

Table 6.6 Difference between VMware Workstation and VirtualBox

S. No	Features	VMware Workstation Player	Virtual Box
1	Operating System Support	Only compatible with Windows and Linux.	Compatible with Linux, Windows, Mac OS, and Solaris.
2	User Interface	It has menus like "Create a new virtual machine," "Open a virtual machine," "Upgrade to VMware Workstation Pro," and then "Help."	Five buttons at the top and a big gray pane at the side. It has menus to set the preferences, Import, Export, New, and Add
3	New Virtual Machine Creation	Click the big "Create a new virtual machine button" in the VMware player.	Click the blue "New" button at the top. Next, we can select a name for our operating system and where we want the virtual machine to be stored.

6.10 HDFS Features

HDFS, HBase, MongoDB, and Cassandra are the tools of the storage layer of Hadoop (Fig. 6.71).

Hadoop ecosystem				
Ingestion	Storage	Processing	Analysis	Management and coordination
Apache Sqoop (RDBMS connector)	HDFS (Structured data)	MapReduce (Data processing)	Pig (Scripting)	ZooKeeper Apache Ambari Cloudera manager Map R control system Hortonworks Oozie (Workflow monitoring)
Apache Flume (Data collection)	HBASE (Unstructured, columnar store)	Yarn (Cluster resource mgmt)	Hive (SQL query)	
Apache Kafka (Streaming)	MongoDB	Spark	Spark SQL	
Apache Impala	Apache Cassandra		Spark GraphX	
Apache NiFi			Apache Mahout (Machine learning)	
Storm (Streaming)			Tableau (Visualization)	
Change data capture (CDC)			Drill (Interactive analytics)	

Figure 6.71 Hadoop ecosystem with HDFS

The basic version of Hadoop 1.0 consists of HDFS and MapReduce components only. Later, all other features are added on top of the Hadoop system. So, HDFS is the primary component of the Hadoop system. It is the backbone upon which the open-source Hadoop ecosystem has been built. It is a file system used mainly for storage. Hive, Spark, and other features support HDFS. It provides random read/write access to application data files. In addition, HDFS permits authentication for access control, quotas for storage limits, and access policies specifying whether clients can read, write, append, truncate, create new files or directories, or execute arbitrary programs in the file system. The implementation of abstracted interfaces allows applications to use HDFS.

HDFS was designed to provide Hadoop with a high-quality, open-source data flow platform. In addition, it includes all the critical components implemented in Java that are required for operational use. The HDFS API is also designed to be evolvable so that the user can confidently deploy it in production environments without the risk of being locked into any specific version of HDFS for the future. This HDFS file system is similar to GFS (Google File System) and presents an open interface for users and application developers. HDFS supports data availability and automatic corruption detection and recovery for large files.

Furthermore, we can tune HDFS for different applications and different environments. HDFS maintains redundant copies of the data block; so if one of the computers fails, it can recover. It will create a backup of itself (replication) to a specified/configured number of copies. It provides high throughput access to an application by accessing data in parallel.

In a nutshell, the following are the Hadoop HDFS Features (Fig. 6.72):

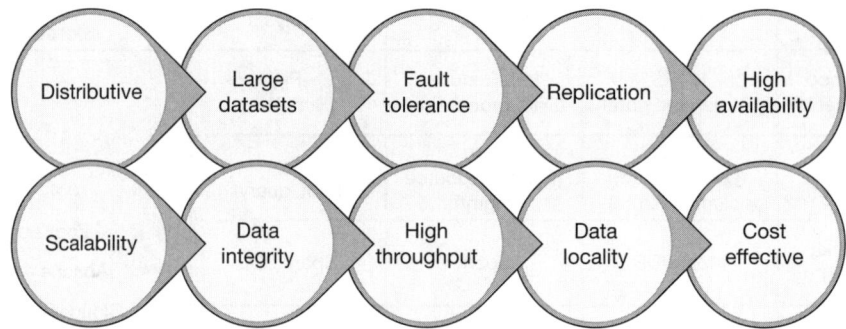

Figure 6.72 HDFS features

Distributive

HDFS is a pure Java implementation program. It attempts to design and implement a file system that will handle large amounts of data. The Hadoop Distributed File System (HDFS) design is based on Google's core distributed file system, which was proven at very large scales. A Distributed File System (DFS) is a file system distributed among numerous file servers or locations. It enables programs to access and store isolated data the same way as they access and save local files, allowing programmers to access files from any network or computer. HDFS breaks up the data into little chunks and distributes it among the cluster's DataNodes. The Hadoop Distributed File System allows MapReduce to process a fraction of enormous datasets divided into blocks in several nodes, in parallel. The Distributed File System (DFS) will enable users of physically distributed computers to exchange data and resources using a common file system.

Large Dataset

Hadoop Distributed File System (HDFS) is an advanced filesystem used in today's world for storing and retrieving large-scale datasets. The HDFS is suitable for large datasets that are gigabytes to terabytes in size. It can store all types of data (structured, unstructured) that run on commodity hardware. HDFS is a highly available, fault-tolerant, distributed file system designed to scale to cluster sizes of 100s of nodes, handling terabytes of data with thousands of clients. Hadoop interfaces allow programs and applications to read and write data stored on Hadoop-compatible file systems like Google File System (GFS) and Amazon Elastic Block Store (EBS). It offers low latency, high bandwidth, and infinite scalability, making it a top choice for distributed storage environments. These interfaces in the Hadoop Distributed File System (HDFS) allow clients to interact with files larger than 1 TB efficiently. HDFS is designed to be extremely fault tolerant and scales up very well (maximum theoretical scalability of HDFS is estimated to be 1 million nodes, each with 200 terabytes of raw capacity).

Fault Tolerance

HDFS is a general-purpose, fault-tolerant, distributed file system. It is a distributed file system with an inbuilt fault-tolerant mechanism. HDFS's ability to replicate blocks of files and store them across nodes in a large cluster provides fault tolerance and reliability because the data blocks are replicated across multiple data nodes. Thus, a server failure will not damage the file. If you keep a 2 GB file on HDFS, it will eventually take up 6 GB. The Name Node updates the metadata regularly and keeps the replication factor consistent. It provides high throughput access detecting the faults and enables quick automatic recovery from failure, which is the core architectural goal of HDFS. HDFS is designed to scale easily across the petabytes (1000 terabytes). At the same time, it offers reliability and fault tolerance.

Cost Effective

HDFS (Hadoop Distributed File System) is an open-source file system that stores and manages data in clusters of commodity servers. It is a cost-efficient, high-performance, fault-tolerant, highly scalable storage architecture with a loosely coupled processing model capable of serving large files to thousands of clients simultaneously. HDFS provides efficient support for process abstraction, low latency operations on large datasets, secure data transfer across heterogeneous computer clusters, efficient scheduling on a variety of hardware configurations and a good quality of life for applications.

Replication and Availability

HDFS is intended to run on commodity hardware developed by Apache Software Foundation. It is designed to allow data to be stored across multiple machines with high availability. Compared to traditional RAID-based systems, HDFS provides higher data availability, specific hardware requirements, and reduced manual tuning. When High Availability daemons are enabled, HDFS will start a sufficient number of DataNodes. The replication factor of data blocks will be determined by the user configuration parameter. The replication factor is dependent on the capacity of DataNode to store blocks, which is also dependent on the available storage capacity of the DataNode's volumes and bandwidth speed to access these volumes.

HDFS is a high-availability distributed file system designed to provide high availability and scalable storage for very large datasets across clusters of networked computers and storage servers and have become the preferred solution for Big Data applications.

Scalability

There are many benefits to using HDFS. The main one is unstructured nature of data in Hadoop, which allows you to store any type of file in it. Another major benefit is scalability. Scalability refers to the ability to extend or contract (shrink) the cluster. Unlike relational databases where our data can grow only vertically (more hard drives), with HDFS we can add more nodes to our cluster to increase storage capacity. This, along with high availability, makes Hadoop a reliable base for virtually any business project. We may scale Hadoop HDFS in two ways.

Vertical scaling: We can increase the number of discs on the cluster nodes. We shall need to change the configuration files and add entries for the newly inserted drives to do so, even if this results in minimal downtime. As a result, most individuals favour the second scaling method, namely, horizontal scaling.

Horizontal Scaling: In this method, new nodes are added to the cluster on the fly without any downtime. Without incurring any downtime, we can add as many nodes to the cluster as we want in real-time. Hadoop offers this as a one-of-a-kind functionality.

HDFS is a multi-computer distributed file-system capable of scalability from gigabytes to petabytes of data across thousands of commodity systems. HDFS is unusual in that it was built from the ground up with excellent data integrity, high availability, and performance in mind. It can scale to hundreds of nodes in a single cluster. It is portable from one platform to another. HDFS gives application developers and architects a rich and powerful programming model and a beautiful, straightforward execution framework to map each programmer's design.

High Throughput

Throughput is the quantity of work accomplished in a given length of time. It describes how quickly data is accessible from the system and is commonly used to assess its performance. When we wish to complete a job or operation in HDFS, the work is divided and shared across many systems. As a result, all the systems will work independently and in parallel to complete the tasks that have been allocated to them. Thus, the task will be accomplished relatively quickly. It provides high throughput access detecting the faults and enables quick, automatic recovery from failure, which is the core architectural goal of HDFS. It provides high throughput access to application data and metadata. This file system is designed for high performance to support large data transfers while retaining low latency. HDFS achieves this by replicating metadata on multiple servers. Duplicate copies of the metadata are arranged in triplicate, so that there is no information loss in case of server failure.

Data Locality

HDFS is a distributed file system with built-in support for high data reliability, high data availability, and data locality. Data local is the most preferred scenario. Data locality increases the overall throughput of the system.

HDFS has many benefits that can solve a wide variety of business needs. There are also several challenges to be overcome with HDFS as the technology seeks to revolutionize data storage, but we can overcome those challenges. The Apache Hadoop ecosystem provides a complete array of tools and utilities to build a reliable cluster for reliable data storage, similar to enterprise-class storage systems. Furthermore, they can be built using enterprise-class hardware.

6.11 HDFS Architecture

In HDFS, appending the content to the end of the file is supported, but it cannot be done at an arbitrary point (Fig. 6.73).

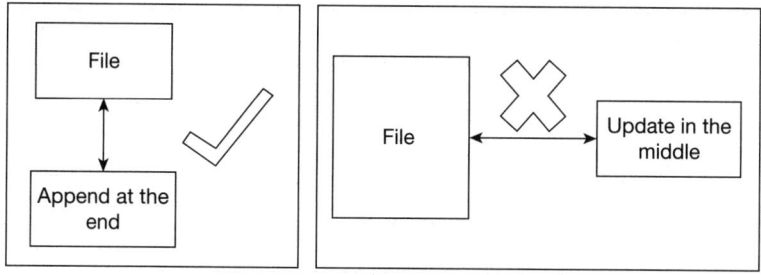

Figure 6.73 HDFS: Appending at the end

HDFS follows a master/slave architecture (Fig. 6.74), so the master node is the name node, and slave nodes are known as data nodes. Another node is known as the secondary name node. The name node is the master daemon, and you can think of it as the king. There is a helper daemon, a secondary name node; we can think of it as a minister. The pawns represent the slave nodes or slave daemon's data node which contains the actual data. Whenever a file is stored in HDFS, it gets distributed and stored in the data nodes. HDFS creates an abstraction layer; we can see the entire HDFS as a single unit.

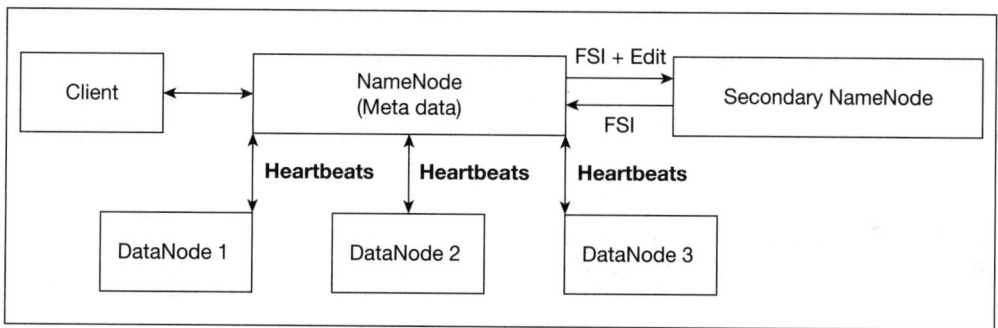

Figure 6.74 Core HDFS architecture

HDFS is a way to organize extensive collections of data efficiently and cost-effectively through an architecture that enables data sharing. The HDFS architecture has four main components: storage nodes (data nodes), the name system (name node), the secondary name system (secondary name node), and clients. HDFS offers clients high availability and scalability for massive file sets and multiple application write access. Currently, it is used mainly for storing and retrieving vast amounts of unstructured data often generated by scientific applications such as image processing or seismic analysis.

HDFS was primarily created to deal with large, unstructured datasets with a massive number of files or blocks that are beyond the capability of a single server. HDFS as such, allows users to write once and read multiple times as is reflected in its architecture design.

NameNode

The main component in HDFS is a NameNode that manages all Hadoop data blocks. It is the master daemon, and it manages the data node. The NameNode is the arbitrator and repository for all HDFS metadata. Any machine that supports Java can run the NameNode or the DataNode software. It does not store the user data and preserves only the metadata. Metadata means data about the data. It supports user quotas and access permissions. It is like a sheet or file with information on what data block is stored in which data node. NameNode takes care of the replication factor of all the blocks. It manages the file system namespace, including the opening, renaming, and closing of files and directories. It serves the request from the clients and regulates clients' access to files. The DataNodes are managed and maintained by the NameNode. It defines how a file's blocks are mapped to DataNodes. NameNode records each modification to the file system namespace. It keeps track of where each block of a file is located. NameNode receives heartbeat and block reports from all DataNodes to ensure that DataNode is alive. If the DataNode fails, the NameNode chooses new DataNodes for new replicas.

Secondary NameNode

The NameNode combines the FS image and edit logs files when it starts up to restore the current file system namespace. Unfortunately, the size of edit logs grows too high because the NameNode operates continuously for an extended period without being restarted. Hence, NameNode will take a long time to restart. This problem is solved by using a secondary NameNode. It does an essential task known as Checkpointing, which combines edit logs with FS images.

Let us say that I had set up my Hadoop cluster 5 days back, and whatever transactions that happen with every new data block are stored in HDFS. Every transaction is combined in a file known as an FS image. This FS image resides in the disk. There's one more similar file which is known as an edit log. Edit logs store only the latest transaction data. Checkpointing (Fig. 6.75) is the task of combining the edit log with the FS image.

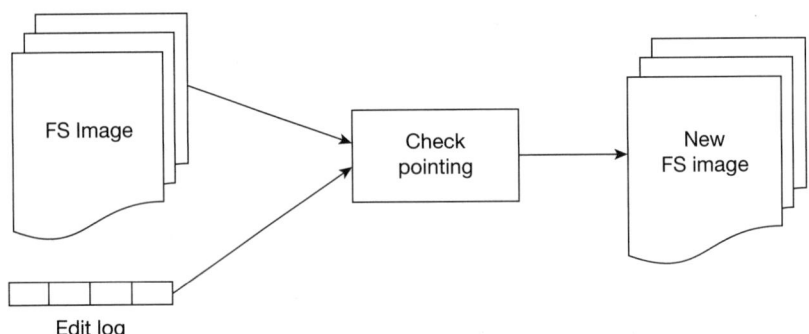

Figure 6.75 HDFS checkpointing

Checkpointing happens after every hour (configurable). The secondary name node first copies the FS image and the edit log (Fig. 6.76) and adds them together to get the updated new FS image. This new FS image is copied back to the name node, and now the name node has an updated FS image. In the meantime, a new edit log is created at the time when the checkpointing happens. This process continues, and it helps the name node always to keep an updated copy.

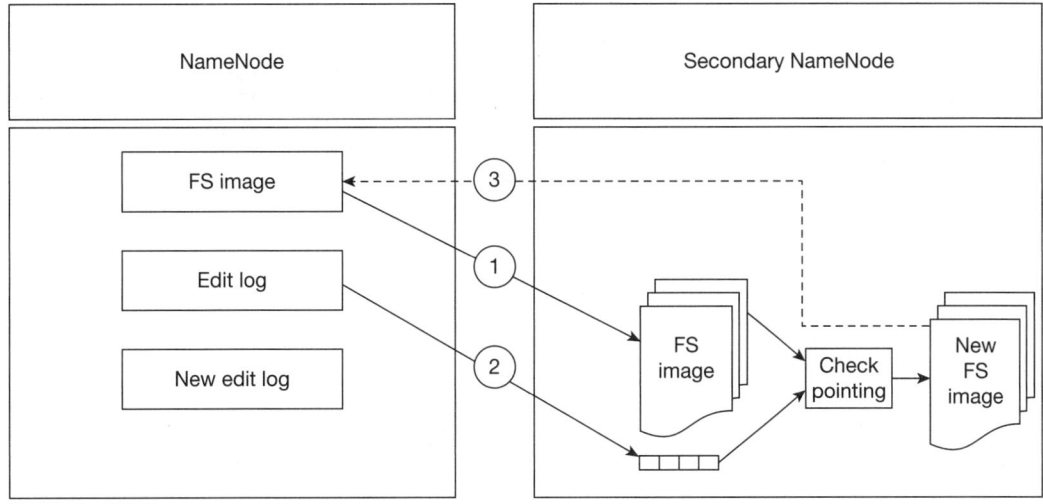

Figure 6.76 HDFS checkpointing: Steps

Backup Node

The Checkpoint node and the Backup node, both provide the checkpointing capability. The backup node maintains an in-memory, up-to-date replica of the file system namespace in Hadoop. It is constantly in sync with the state of the current NameNode. To construct a checkpoint in the HDFS architecture, the backup node does not need to download the FS image and change files from the current NameNode. This is because, in memory, it already has an up-to-date state of the namespace.

Data Nodes

These are the slave daemons, where the actual data is stored. Whenever a client gives a read or writes request, the data node serves it. DataNodes are low-cost commodity servers. The data node stores the data as data blocks (file chunks) and is in charge of operating read/write requests from clients. DataNodes conduct block formation, replication, and deletion based on the NameNode's instructions. To report the health of HDFS, DataNodes transmit a pulse to NameNode. DataNodes also deliver NameNode block reports, which comprise a list of the blocks it contains.

6.12 HDFS Read Request

If the client requests to read a particular file (Fig. 6.77), it will first go to the name node (through the distributed file system API). The client opens the file using the Distributed File System object's `open()` method. Then, to discover the positions of the blocks for the first few blocks in the file, Distributed File System uses RPC to contact the namenode. The namenode delivers the addresses of the data nodes that hold a copy of each block and their proximity.

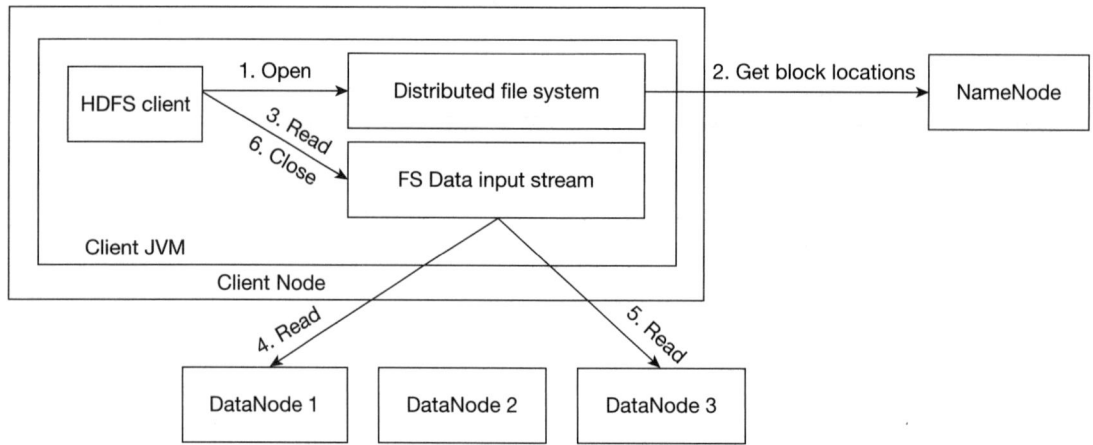

Figure 6.77 HDFS Read Request steps

The client receives an FS Data Input Stream from Distributed File System to read data from. As a result, FS Data Input Stream surrounds the DFS Input Stream, which is responsible for data node and namenode I/O. On the stream, the client calls `read()`. DFS Input Stream connects to the nearest data node for the first block in the file after storing the data node addresses. The data node streams data back to the client, allowing the client to read from the stream many times.

NameNode determines if the client has appropriate credentials to access the data. The name node knows precisely where the file is. If the client has proper credentials, it will give the IP addresses of the data nodes with different data blocks of that particular file. Along with the IP addresses, NameNode sends the client a security token, which it must provide to DataNode before accessing the data for authentication. It tells the client that you can go to this IP address and go to this data node to read the file. The client, in turn, goes to the different data nodes, where the data block is present to serve the read request.

If a data node fails to communicate with the DFS Input Stream, it will attempt the next closest data node for that block. It will also remember unsuccessful data nodes so that it does not have to retry them for subsequent blocks. The DFS Input Stream likewise verifies the checksums for the data sent to it from the data node. Before the DFS Input Stream attempts to read a replica of the block from another data node, it reports any corrupt blocks to the namenode. If the DataNode goes down unexpectedly while reading a file, the client will go back to the NameNode, and the NameNode will share another location where that block is present. The client calls `close()` on the FSDataInputStream once it has done reading the data.

6.13 HDFS Write Request

Now let us say the client wants to write. Again, it will contact the name node (through the distributed file system) to get the metadata (Fig. 6.78). But first, it will check whether space is available or not. The client communicates with the distributed file system API and requests a slave location from NameNode, which will give the IP addresses of the data nodes, where a client could write the file. The client can start writing data to the DFSDataOutputStream returned by the Distributed File System using Create() method. DFSDataOutputStream separates data into packets when the client writes it, which it writes to an internal queue called the data queue.

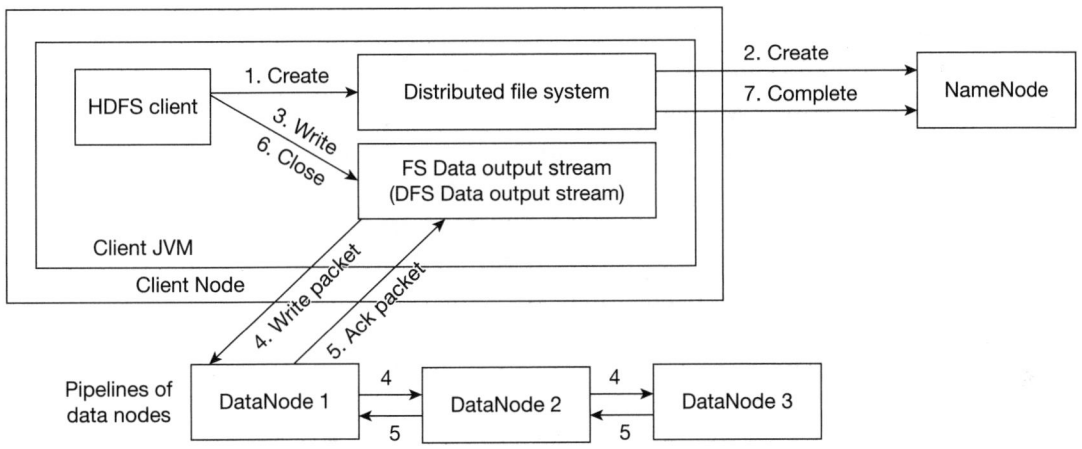

Figure 6.78 HDFS Write request

The RPC call between DistributedFileSystem and NameNode is used to create a new file in the filesystem namespace with no blocks. The NameNode verifies that the client has the appropriate rights and that the file does not already exist. Next, the NameNode creates a record of the new file if the client has adequate rights and no file with the same name already exists. Otherwise, the client will receive an I/O exception, and the file will not be created. Next, the client gets an FSDataOutputStream from the DistributedFileSystem, which the client uses to begin writing data. FSDataOutputstream encapsulates a DFSOutputStream responsible for communication with the DataNodes and NameNode.

The DFSOutputStream separates the client's data into packets and sends it to an internal queue called the data queue as soon as the client starts submitting data. This data queue is used by DataStreamer, which tells the NameNode to allocate additional blocks by selecting a list of suitable DataNodes to store the replicas. A list of DataNode forms a pipeline. The replication factor determines the number of DataNodes in the pipeline. We will assume the replication factor is three in this case, so there are three nodes in the pipeline. The DataStreamer sends packets to the pipeline's first data node, storing them and transmitting them to its second data node. Similarly, the second data node saves the packet and sends it to the pipeline's third (and final) data node.

The ack queue, which DFSDataOutputStream maintains, is a queue of packets waiting to be acknowledged by data nodes. The third DataNode acknowledges the second DataNode, the second DataNode acknowledges the first DataNode, and the first

DataNode acknowledges the last DataNode (in the case of default replication factor). Only after all data nodes in the pipeline have acknowledged a packet is it removed from the ack queue. Once the requisite replicas have been built, DataNode transmits the acknowledgment (3 by default). All of the blocks are similarly stored and duplicated on the various data nodes, with the data blocks being copied in parallel.

When the client has completed writing data to the stream, it uses `close()`. This operation sends all remaining packets to the data node pipeline and waits for acknowledgments before sending a signal to the namenode that the file is finished. The namenode already knows what blocks make up the file, so it has to now wait for the blocks to be copied minimally before returning successfully. Regardless of our replication factor, the client sends just one copy of data, whereas DataNodes duplicate the blocks. As a result, writing a file in Hadoop HDFS is not expensive since several blocks are written parallel on different DataNodes. It provides a final acknowledgment to the client when the requisite copies have been generated.

6.14 HDFS Blocks

HDFS is a fault-tolerant system. Whenever we write a file into HDFS, it breaks down the file into different blocks of 128 megabytes, except the last block (which will have the remainder of the file). For example, a file of 380 megabytes (Fig. 6.79) divides into three blocks; the first block will be 128 megabytes; the second will be 128 megabytes, and the third will occupy the remaining size of the file (124 megabytes).

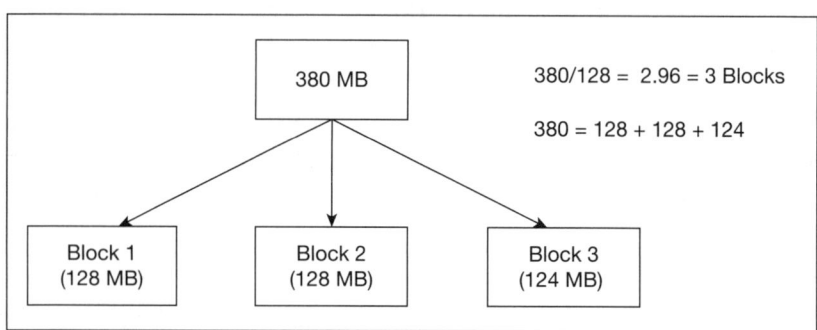

Figure 6.79 HDFS blocks formation: Example 1

The data blocks are distributed across the Hadoop cluster. By doing this, the time taken to store the data onto the disk is significantly reduced. The total time to store this entire data onto the disk equals to the time for storing one part of the data. It will store all the parts of the data simultaneously on different machines to provide high availability.

Now let us say that we have a file size of 500 megabytes (Fig. 6.80); how many blocks will it create? It will create four blocks. The first three blocks will be 128 megabytes, and the last block will occupy the remaining file size (116 megabytes).

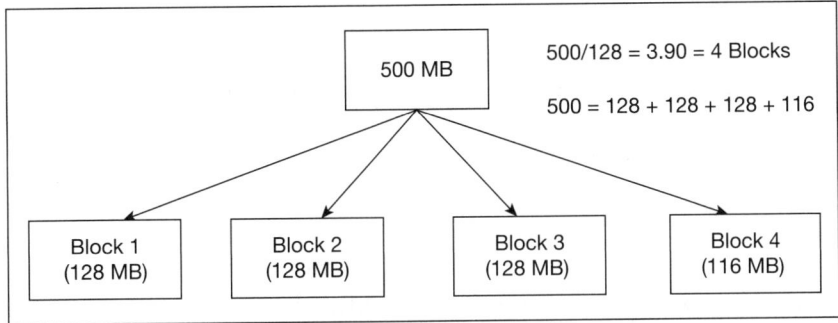

Figure 6.80 HDFS blocks formation: Example 2

Whenever we dump the file into HDFS, it is first divided into blocks, and then each of the blocks is copied as per the replication factor. So, the replication factor equals three means that there are three similar blocks in the Hadoop cluster.

6.15 Data Racks

A rack consists of multiple nodes (Fig. 6.81), usually 30 to 40 nodes. Each of these nodes, in turn, stores multiple data blocks. Within a rack, Hadoop stores its data in two different data nodes. Communication between nodes present in the same rack is usually faster than that with nodes across multiple racks. The concept of choosing the closest data node is called rack awareness.

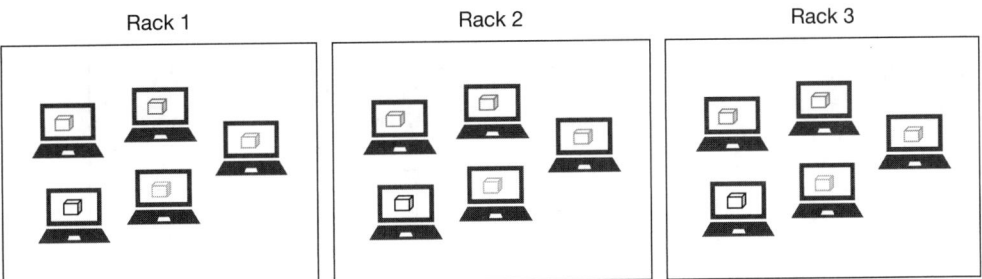

Figure 6.81 Data racks

6.16 HDFS Block Replication

The number of replicas of a file can be given as a parameter in HDFS, and is called the replication factor stored in the name node. By default, the replication factor is set to three. If we consider the default replication factor set, there will be three copies for each data part on three different machines. To reduce the bandwidth and latency time, it would store two copies of the same part of the data on the nodes present within the same rack, and the last copy would be stored on a node present on a different rack. Another advantage of distributing this data across the cluster is that processing this data takes less time, as this data can be processed simultaneously. The block size and its replication factor are also configurable on a per-file basis. The list of all blocks on a DataNode is available in data reports. If the HDFS cluster crosses multiple data centers, then a replica in the local data center is favored over that in any remote replication. This is because it receives heartbeat and block reports from each data node.

6.17 RACK AWARENESS ALGORITHM

The rack awareness algorithm says the local rack stores the first replica of a block, and the subsequent two replicas will be there in a different rack. So, we store a data block in the local rack (rack one) to decrease the latency.

1. Each node will have only one replica of the block.
2. Each rack will have a maximum of two replicas of the block.
3. The number of racks to be used will be lesser than the replication factor.

If we have the replication factor of three, then (as per rule 3) only two racks will be used to store those replicated blocks. Let us say we have a file with 248 megabytes (Fig. 6.82), Block 1 is 128 megabytes, and Block 2 is 120 megabytes. Block one is multiplied three times, and block two is also multiplied three times.

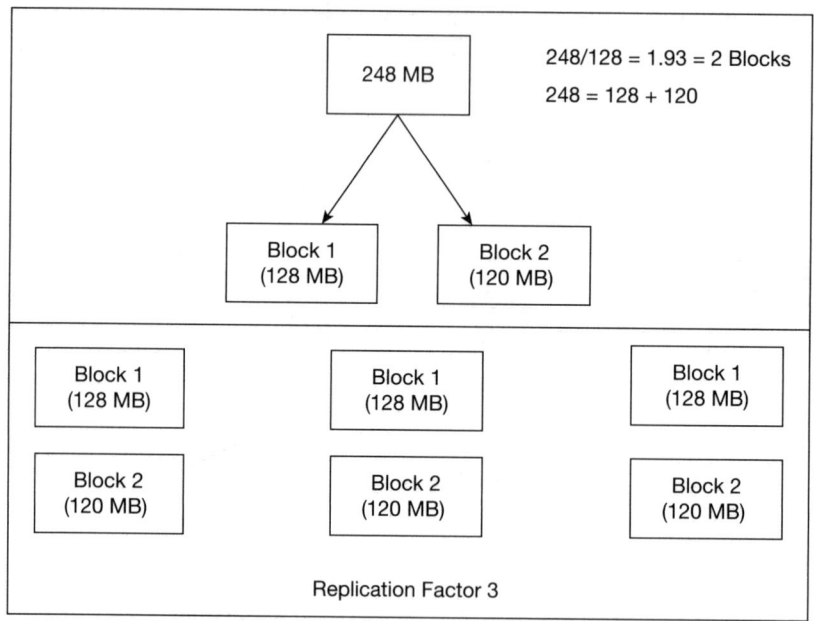

Figure 6.82 Replication factor

Now, let us try to store these blocks (six blocks in total) in racks by applying rack awareness algorithm. Replication factor is three and hence we can use a maximum of two racks to store the duplicated data (as per Rule 3). A rack can't have more than 2 replica blocks. Block 1 is stored in Rack 1 along with its replica (Fig. 6.83). Another copy of Block 1 is storied in Rack 2. Similarly, Block 2 is stored in Rack 1 along with its replica. Another copy of Block 2 is stored in Rack 2.

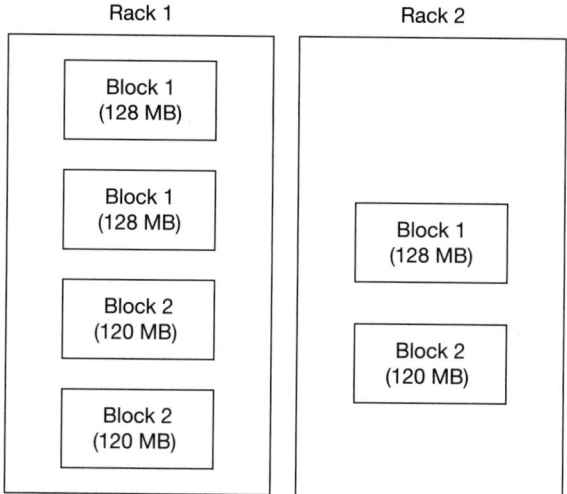

Figure 6.83 HDFS blocks: Racks and replication

When any data nodes go down, the system can recover the data block from the two other data nodes. This rack awareness algorithm provides fault tolerance.

6.18 Data Integrity in HDFS

Data integrity ensures that no data loss or corruption happens while storing or processing the data. In Hadoop, the amount of data being written or read is large in volume, so the chances of data corruption are more. Hadoop has a checksum mechanism to tackle this data integrity issue. Hadoop computes the checksum while writing the data to the disk for the first time (Fig. 6.84).

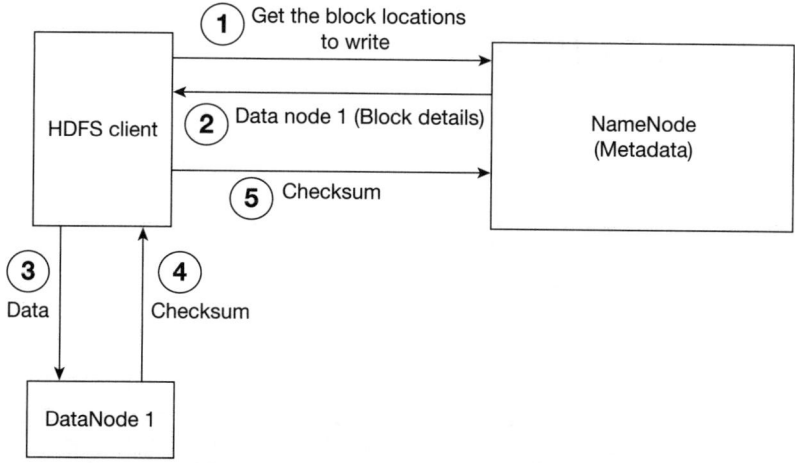

Figure 6.84 Data integrity in Hadoop (Checksum): Write

It checks again while reading the data (Fig. 6.85) from the disk. If the new checksum matches the original checksum, it means the data is uncorrupted.

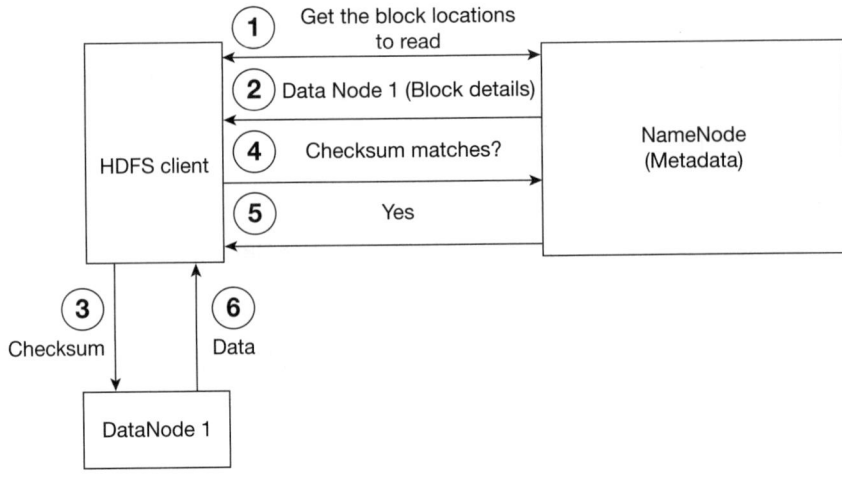

Figure 6.85 Data integrity in Hadoop (checksum): Read

HDFS uses an efficient algorithm called CRC-32C to calculate the checksum. DataNodes are responsible for calculating the checksum for the received data before storing the data. Hadoop computes the checksum for the data they receive from clients and other DataNodes during the replication stage. Hadoop can heal the corrupted data by copying one of the good replicas to produce a new, uncorrupt replica. If a client detects an error when reading a block, it reports "the wrong block and the DataNodes it was trying to read" to the NameNode before throwing a Checksum Exception. The NameNode marks the block replica as corrupt; so it does not direct any more clients to the corrupt block or copy this replica to other DataNodes. Instead, it sends a copy of the block from other DataNodes to replicate (copy), so that its replication factor returns to the expected level. Once this has happened, the corrupt replica gets deleted.

6.19 DATA LOCALITY IN HDFS

Inter Rack Hadoop's major drawback is cross-switch network traffic due to the massive volume of data. This moves the extensive amount of data to the computation spot. In this case, usually, data and code reside in different racks (Fig. 6.86) creating heavy traffic across the racks. In this scenario, the mapper runs on a different rack due to resource constraints.

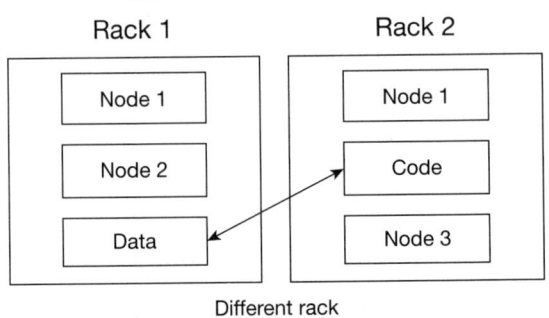

Figure 6.86 Intra rack sync

Intra Rack In this scenario the code runs on a different node but in the same rack. In such a case, the proximity of the data is closer to the computation of the same rack. Due to constraints, it is not always possible to execute the mapper on the same data node.

This is also called as Rack Locality, which refers to moving the computation (code) close to the rack where the actual data resides, instead of moving extensive amount of data to the computation spot. However, heavy traffic resides within the rack, as the data gets moved across multiple nodes (Fig. 6.87).

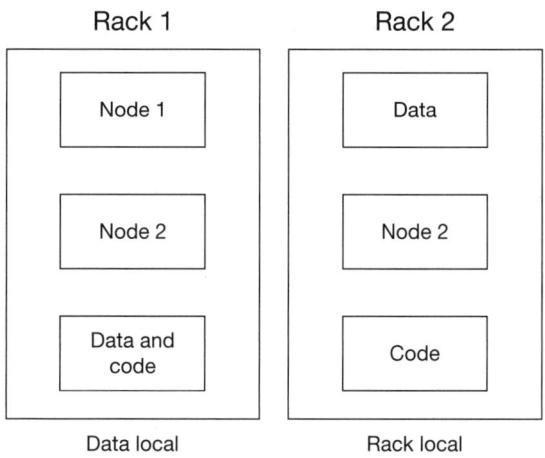

Figure 6.87 Data local and Rack local

Data locality (Fig. 6.88) refers to moving the computation (code) closer to the node, where the actual data resides, instead of moving extensive amount of data to the computation spot.

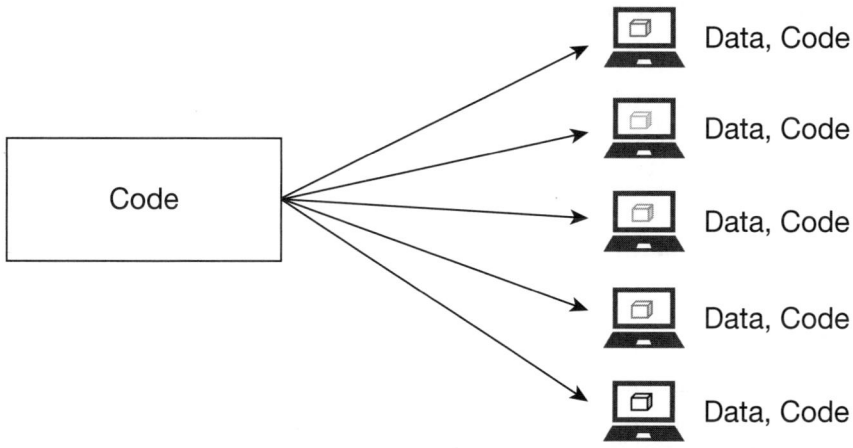

Figure 6.88 Data local

Data local is the most preferred scenario. Data locality increases the overall throughput of the system. In Hadoop, HDFS stores datasets divided into blocks and stored across the data nodes in the Hadoop cluster. When a user runs the code (MapReduce job), the NameNode sends this code (MapReduce job code) to the data nodes on which data related to the MapReduce job is available.

6.20 Distributed Cache in HDFS

In Hadoop, the data chunks process happens independently in parallel among DataNodes. The distributed cache contains common files accessible by all the DataNodes, which includes read-only text files, archive files, jar files, etc. Hadoop will make these cache files available on each data node where map/reduce tasks are running (Fig. 6.89).

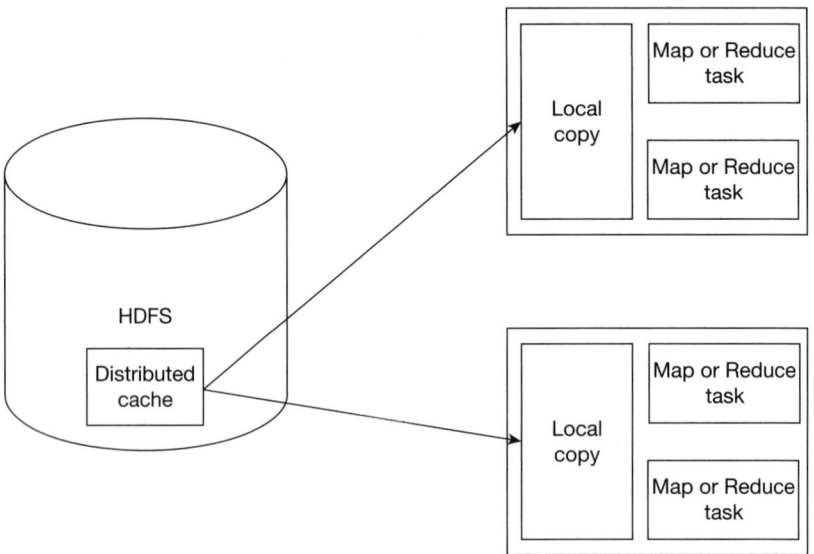

Figure 6.89 Caching mechanism in Hadoop

An application that requires distributed cache should make sure that the files are available on URLs. URLs can be either hdfs:// or http://. Hadoop framework will duplicate the cache file on all the data nodes before starting tasks on those nodes. The default size of the distributed cache is 10 GB, which can be modified using local cache size.

6.21 HDFS Serialization

Serialization is turning an object into a format that can be stored on a disk or transmitted over the network. Data serialization is the conversion of internal or external program states to a format that can be stored in persistent memory, such as disk storage or memory buffers. General serialization includes conversion of simple data types such as integers and strings to more advanced formats such as XML and message-oriented middleware.

Data is inherently hierarchical, so HDFS provides several serialization options. The default DataInputStream/DataOutputStream implementations are based on XML serialization of the Java Data object. HDFS Data Serialization Option is a feature that allows developers to control the way that HDFS stores and reads the data serialization of complex objects. The HDFS data serialization options determine the format in which a FileSystem implementation stores the HDFS data. With HDFS Data Serialization, we can choose from various serialization formats for HDFS data. There are many factors to consider when serializing data, which is why HDFS has provided multiple serialization options. By default, a FileSystem implementation stores its data in a binary format. The default serialization strategy for HDFS coordinates is simple but it can have performance issues under high throughput loads. This new feature of customizing HDFS serialization is located in the DFS. Data node.du.reserved is the configuration property of the hdfs-site.xml file. By default, this property is set to −1, which enables compatibility with previous versions of HDFS and uses the current HDFS default serialization behavior. HDFS offers four data serialization options. By setting this property to 4 or higher, client applications can use custom serialization handlers to better control the serialization behavior for versioned objects stored. The HDFS Data Serialization option supports a controlled approach to inter-process communication and reliability, using a standard data model for data serialization and data transfer. However, this is an advanced feature not intended for most users of Hadoop, and its usage requires strong technical skills and good familiarity with Hadoop. The HDFS data serialization framework provides an extensible mechanism for packaging data into the Hadoop Distributed File System (HDFS) and creating instances of these data types either directly or via other data types.

There are two main methods to serialize data to an HDFS file system. With the first method, you use the DataOutputStream.writeBytes(byte[] buffer) method, which copies the data to an HDFS file in binary format. The second option uses the DataOutputStream.writeObject(Object object) method, serializing the object to an HDFS file in binary form. The data serializer class offers a choice of different serialization formats, from XML to binary. Using the type parameter makes it possible to specify precisely which format is desired for a particular job. The HDFS Data Transfer Service helps users instantaneously move large amounts of data between Hadoop clusters and cloud storage services, such as Amazon S3 and Azure Data Lake Store. The HDFS library provides a rich set of data types, valuable functions, and both static and dynamic storage organization to tailor your data to your application. There are several ways to store critical scientific data in HDFS files.

6.22 HDFS Web UI

Hadoop provides a Web User Interface for HDFS. The HDFS Web User Interface is beneficial in a pseudo-distributed environment and is an essential tool in a fully distributed environment. For example, if we are using Hadoop in the pseudo-distributed mode, we need to type http://localhost:50070/ into our web browser and port 50070 on the localhost host. We need to replace 'localhost' with the real hostname of the cluster computer in a fully dispersed mode. The following is a summary of the HDFS file system, which can be found on the overview page (Fig. 6.90). This overview includes the details of when the sandbox server was started, its version, compiled date, Cluster ID and Block Pool ID.

At the bottom of the Overview, it displays the Summary details, which include whether the Security is On/Off, SafeMode is On/Off, the number of files and directories, the number of blocks created, replicated block number, and heap memory used.

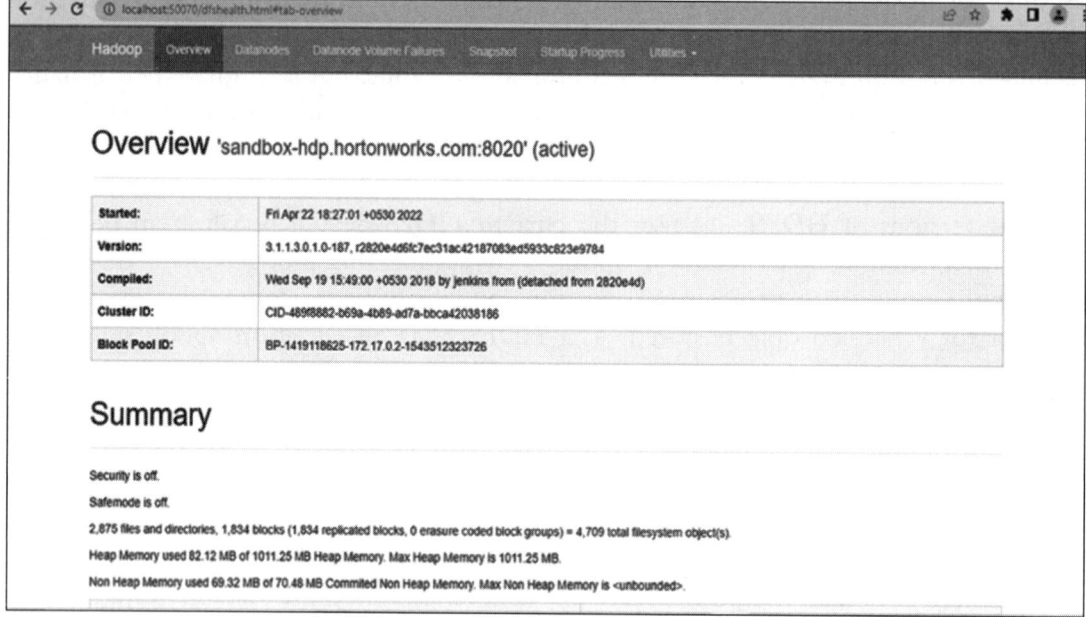

Figure 6.90 HDFS Web UI: Overview

The bottom of the summary page (Fig. 6.91) also includes DFS memory used, non-DFS memory used, live nodes details, block deletion start time and last checkpoint time.

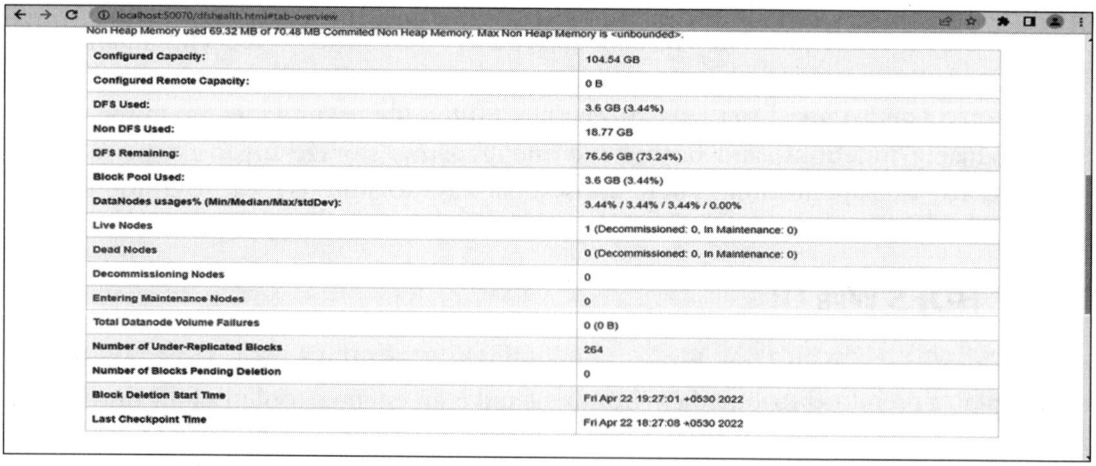

Figure 6.91 HDFS Web UI: Bottom of the Summary page

The DataNodes menu displays (Fig. 6.92) the details of the data node usage histogram.

Figure 6.92 HDFS Web UI: DataNodes

The DataNodes menu (tab) also displays the names of the data node (Fig. 6.93), its HTTP address, when it was last contacted, last block report date, the capacity of the data nodes, the number of blocks within the specific data node, Block Pool used (percentage of the data node used) and its version.

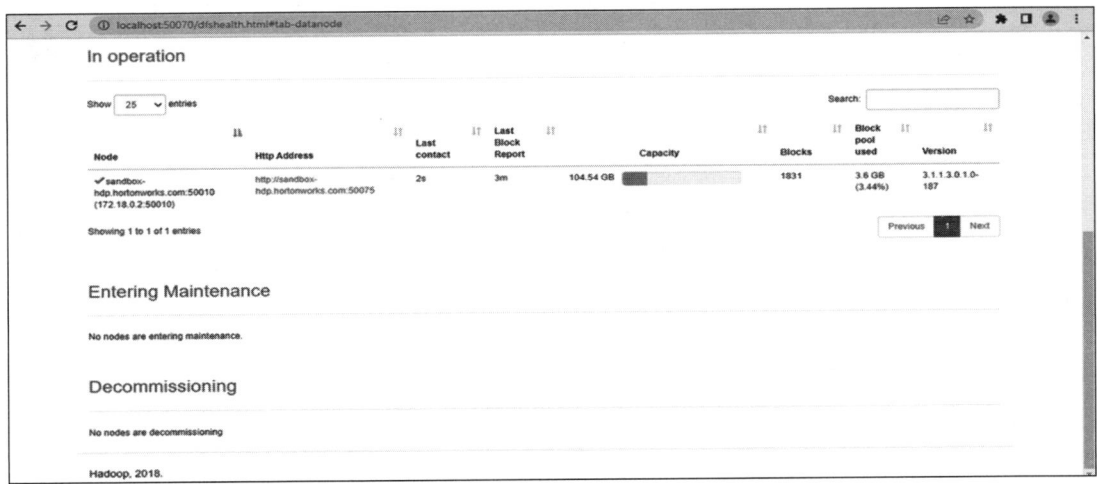

Figure 6.93 HDFS Web UI: DataNodes

The Datanode Volume Failures tab will display the details of the volume failures of the data node (Fig. 6.94). In our case, there was no volume failure and hence it displays "There are no reported volume failures".

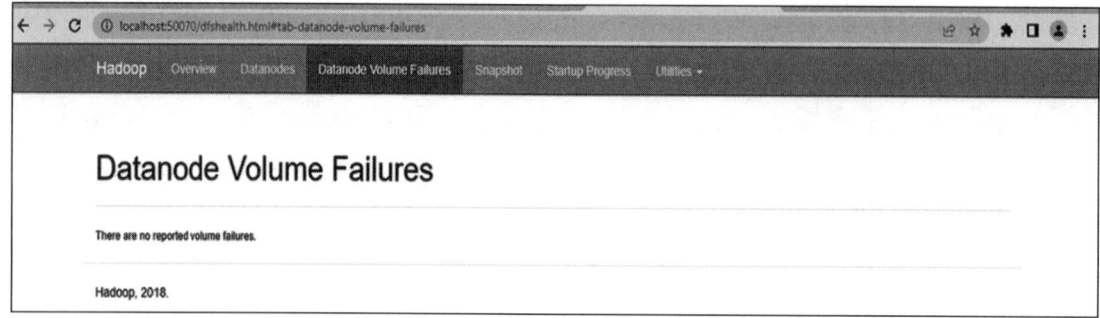

Figure 6.94 HDFS Web UI: Datanode Volume failures

The Snapshot tab will display (Fig. 6.95) the details of the Snapshot summary, which includes Snapshottable directories details like Path, Snapshot number, Snapshot quota, Modification Time, Permission, Owner and Group details. It also displays the details of Snapshotted directories details like Snapshot ID, Snap Shot Directory and modification time.

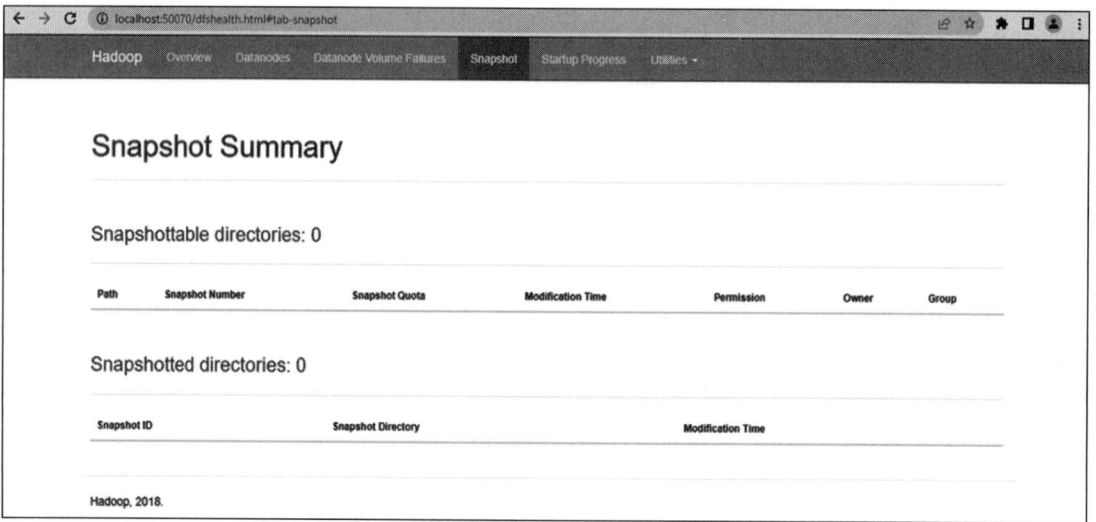

Figure 6.95 HDFS Web UI: Snapshot Summary

We may also explore a list of folders (Fig. 6.96) and file contents by browsing the HDFS file system.

Note: By default, the HDFS Web UI is read-only, with no ability to create or modify files or directories. We may browse the file system from the Utility option on the screen.

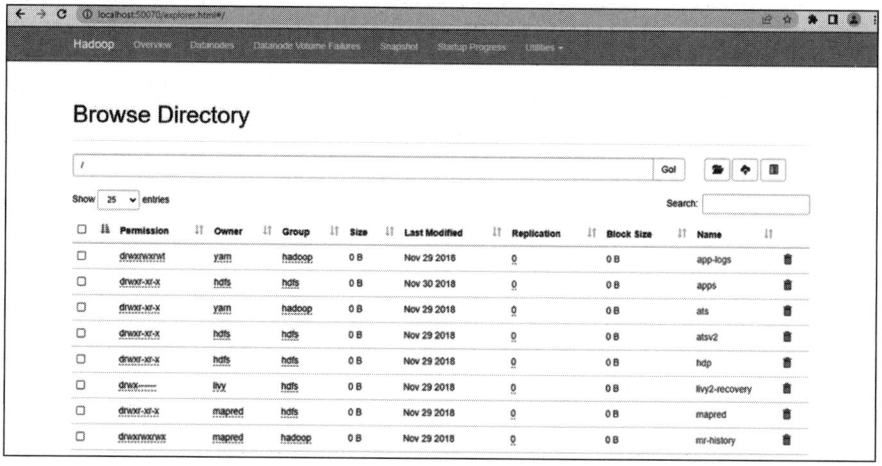

Figure 6.96 HDFS Web UI: List of folders

6.23 Directory Creation in HDFS: Java Program

Creating a directory to HDFS is straightforward; run hadoop fs -mkdir to create a directory in the local filesystem of HDFS. Next, we develop our own Java software to create a directory in the local file system of HDFS. The most straightforward approach to acquire the cluster's configuration is to use the configuration object, which will read the configuration files from the class path and read and load all the data required by the program. We will acquire the File System object (Fig. 6.97) by utilizing the URL. The DistributedFileSystem object will be returned as the file system. All admin-related functionality such as creating a file or directory and deleting a file is provided by the Hadoop FileSystem class. Under HDFS, the mkDirs method is used to create a directory. The Directory Name which we want to create is passed as parameter for the Path. String directoryName = "bigdata/testdirectory"; Path path = new Path(directoryName); Then, File System object uses the path to create the directory using fileSystem.mkdirs(path);

```
import org.apache.hadoop.conf.Configuration;
import org.apache.hadoop.fs.FileSystem;
import java.net.URI;
public class CreateDirectoryInHDFS
{
        public static void main() throws Exception
        {
                Configuration configuration = new Configuration();
                configuration.set("fs.defaultFS", "hdfs://localhost:9000");
                FileSystem fileSystem = FileSystem.get(configuration);
                String directoryName = "bigdata/testdirectory";
                Path path = new Path(directoryName);
                fileSystem.mkdirs(path);
        }
}
```

Figure 6.97 HDFS Java Program: Creating folders

6.24 APPEND DATA TO HDFS FILE: JAVA PROGRAM

The most straightforward approach to acquiring the cluster's configuration is to use the Configuration object, which will read the configuration files from the class path and read and load all the data required by the program. We shall acquire the File System object by utilizing the URL. The DistributedFileSystem object will be returned as the file system. FSDataOutputStream object is created. And then Buffered Writer object is created to append the file (Fig. 6.98).

```
import org.apache.hadoop.conf.Configuration;
import org.apache.hadoop.fs.FileSystem;
import java.net.URI;

public class CreateDirectoryInHDFS
{
    public static void main() throws Exception
    {
        Configuration configuration = new Configuration();
        configuration.set("fs.defaultFS", "hdfs://localhost:9000");
        FileSystem fileSystem = FileSystem.get(configuration);
        //Create a path
        String fileName = "test.txt";
        Path hdfsWritePath = new Path("bigdata/testdirectory/" + fileName);
        FSDataOutputStream fsDataOutputStream = fileSystem.append(hdfsWritePath);
        BufferedWriter bufferedWriter = new BufferedWriter(new OutputStreamWriter(fsDataOutputStream,StandardCharsets.UTF_8));
        bufferedWriter.write("Java API to append data in HDFS file");
        bufferedWriter.newLine();
        bufferedWriter.close();
        fileSystem.close();
    }
}
```

Figure 6.98 HDFS Java Program: Appending a file

6.25 FILE READ FROM HDFS: JAVA PROGRAM

This program can also be modified a little bit, to accept an argument that is nothing more than a fully qualified HDFS path to a file that we will read and show on the screen. Currently the fully qualified HDFS path is hard-coded in this program. The Hadoop fs -cat command will be emulated by this software. We require a few important facts regarding the cluster, such as the name and node details. During cluster setup, the information is already supplied in the configuration files. The simplest approach to acquiring the cluster's configuration is to use the Configuration object (config), which will read the configuration files from the class path and read and load all the data required by the program (Fig. 6.99).

```java
import org.apache.hadoop.conf.Configuration;
import org.apache.hadoop.fs.FileSystem;
import java.net.URI;

public class FileReadFromHDFS
{
        public static void main() throws Exception
        {
                //Setup the configuration object.
                final Configuration config = new Configuration();

                //File to read in HDFS
                String uri = "hdfs://localhost:50070/file.txt"

                //Get the filesystem - HDFS
                final FileSystem fs = FileSystem.get(new URI(uri), config);

                FSDataInputStream in = null;

                try
                {
                        //Open the path mentioned in HDFS
                        in = fs.open(new Path(uri));
                        IOUtils.copyBytes(in, System.out, 4096, false);
                        System.out.println("End Of file: HDFS file read complete");
                }
                finally {
                IOUtils.closeStream(in);
                        }
        }
}
```

Figure 6.99 HDFS Java Program: Reading a file from HDFS

Using the URL we gave as the program input, we shall acquire the File System object. This will return the DistributedFileSystem object(fs), and after we have got the file system object, we shall need the input stream (in) for the file we want to read. Calling the open method on the file system object(fs) with the HDFS URL of the file, we want to read returns of the input stream (in). Then we shall use Hadoop's IOUtils class's copyBytes function to read the entire file's contents from the input stream and print them on the screen.

6.26 FILE WRITE TO HDFS: JAVA PROGRAM

```java
import org.apache.hadoop.conf.Configuration;
import org.apache.hadoop.fs.FileSystem;
import java.net.URI;

public class FileWriteToHDFS
{
        public static void main(String[] args) throws Exception
        {
                //Source file in the local file system
                String localSrc = args[0];
                //Destination file in HDFS
                String dst = args[1];

                //Input stream for the file in local file system to be written to HDFS
                InputStream in = new BufferedInputStream(new FileInputStream(localSrc));

                //Get configuration of Hadoop system
                Configuration conf = new Configuration();
                System.out.println("Connecting to -- "+conf.get("fs.defaultFS"));

                //Destination file in HDFS
                FileSystem fs = FileSystem.get(URI.create(dst), conf);
                OutputStream out = fs.create(new Path(dst));

                //Copy file from local to HDFS
                IOUtils.copyBytes(in, out, 4096, true);

                System.out.println(dst + " copied to HDFS");

        }
}
```

Figure 6.100 HDFS Java Program: Writing a file to HDFS

Writing a file to HDFS is straightforward; run hadoop fs -copyFromLocal to copy a file from the local filesystem to HDFS. Next, we develop our own Java software to write a file from the local file system to HDFS. Two parameters are inputs to the program (Fig. 6.100). The first parameter (args[0]) specifies the file's location on the local file system to be transferred to the HDFS destination, which is specified in the second parameter (args[1]). The first parameter, the file's location in the local file system, will be used to build an InputStream using the BufferedInputStream object. Because we are still addressing a file from the local file system rather than HDFS, the input stream objects are ordinary java. io stream objects rather than Hadoop libraries. Now we must build an output stream to the HDFS file location, where we may write the file's contents from the local file system. We first need to know a few essential characteristics of the cluster, such as its name and node data. During cluster setup, the information is already supplied in the configuration files (conf). The most straightforward approach to acquiring the cluster's configuration is to use the Configuration object, which will read the configuration files from the class path and read and load all of the data required by the program. We shall acquire the File System object by utilizing the URL we gave as the program's input and the settings we generated. Next, the DistributedFileSystem object will be returned as the file system. The output stream to the file to which we want to write the file's contents from the local file system is required after acquiring the file system object. The file's location in HDFS, which we gave to the application as the second parameter, will then be used to invoke the create function on the file system object. OutputStream out = fs.create(new Path(dst)); Finally, we'll utilize Hadoop's `IOUtils` class's `copyBytes` function, passing the input and output stream objects. The input stream will then be read 4096 bytes at a time and written to the output stream, which will copy the entire file from the local file system to HDFS.

6.27 CONNECTING HDFS FROM PYTHON

Snakebite is a Python package produced by Spotify. This package provides a Python client module that allows Python applications to use HDFS programmatically. To connect directly with the NameNode, the client library utilizes protobuf messages. Protocol Buffers (Protobuf) is a cross-platform data format for serializing structured data. This platform is free and open-source. JSON saves data in a human-readable text format, whereas protobuf is a binary data-interchange format. Protobuf may be used to create programs that communicate with one another via a network or to store data. Protobuf messages are used for the following: (1) When we require quick serialization/deserialization, (2) When it is critical to maintaining safety, (3) When adherence to the schema is necessary, (4) When we want to cut down on code. Based on the client library, the Snakebite package also contains a command-line interface for HDFS. The Snakebite package is installed and configured in this part. Snakebite's client library is thoroughly explained with several examples, and Snakebite's built-in CLI is offered as a Python replacement for the HDFS DFS command. Python 2 and python-protobuf 2.4.1 or above are required for Snakebite. Python 3 is not supported right now. Snakebite is a Python package that can be installed using pip:

```
$ pip install snakebite
```

First, we need to create a client Object from snakebite.client (Fig. 6.101) by importing the object into the Python program. This client object can work as HDFS Client and can be used to run multiple commands like creating a directory (mkdir), removing a directory (delete), displaying the content of the directory (ls), and copying the HDFS file to Local (copyToLocal), or simply reading a file from HDFS (text).

```
from snakebite.client import Client

//This creates a client Object
client = Client('localhost', 9000)

//Creating a directory

for p in client.mkdir(['/bigdata/test', '/input'], create_parent=True):
    print p

//{'path': '/bigdata/test', 'result': True}
//{'path': '/input', 'result': True}


for x in client.ls(['/']):
    print x


for p in client.delete(['/bigdata', '/input'], recurse=True):
    print p

//{'path': '/foo', 'result': True}
//{'path': '/input', 'result': True}

//copies the file /input/test.txt from HDFS
// and places it under the /tmp directory on the local filesystem.

for f in client.copyToLocal(['/input/test.txt'], '/tmp'):
    print

//{'path': '/tmp/input.txt', 'source_path': '/input/input.txt', 'result': True, 'error': ''}


//To simply read the contents of a file that resides on HDFS, the text() method can be used.

for l in client.text(['/input/test.txt']):
    print l

//I am calm
//I am cool
//I am intelligent
```

Figure 6.101   HDFS Python program using Snakebite package

6.28 SNAKEBITE COMMAND REFERENCE FOR CLI

The Snakebite CLI client supports a comprehensive set of file manipulation commands, which are shown below. Snakebite, without any parameters, can be used to display this list from the command line. Use snakebite [cmd] —help to get assistance for a specific command, where cmd is a valid Snakebite command.

The below table describes the syntax of CLI with various general options (Fig. 6.102).

```
snakebite [general options] cmd [arguments]
general options:
  -D --debug       Show debug information
  -V --version     Hadoop protocol version (default:9)
  -h --help        show help
  -j --json        JSON output
  -n --namenode    namenode host
  -p --port        namenode RPC port (default: 8020)
  -v --ver         Display snakebite version
```

Figure 6.102 HDFS Python program using Snakebite CLI: General options

Figure 6.103 describes the syntax of CLI with the various possible commands.

```
snakebite [general options] cmd [arguments]

commands:
  cat [paths]                   copy source paths to stdout
  chgrp <grp> [paths]           change group
  chmod <mode> [paths]          change file mode (octal)
  chown <owner:grp> [paths]     change owner
  copyToLocal [paths] dst       copy paths to local file system destination
  count [paths]                 display stats for paths
  df                            display fs stats
  du [paths]                    display disk usage statistics
  get file dst                  copy files to local file system destination
  getmerge dir dst              concatenates files in source dir into destination local file
  ls [paths]                    list a path
  mkdir [paths]                 create directories
  mkdirp [paths]                create directories and their parents
  mv [paths] dst                move paths to destination
  rm [paths]                    remove paths
  rmdir [dirs]                  delete a directory
  serverdefaults                show server information
  setrep <rep> [paths]          set replication factor
  stat [paths]                  stat information
  tail path                     display last kilobyte of the file to stdout
  test path                     test a path
  text path [paths]             output file in text format
  touchz [paths]                creates a file of zero length
  usage <cmd>                   show cmd usage

to see command-specific options use: snakebite [cmd] --help
```

Figure 6.103 HDFS Python Program using Snakebite CLI: Command options

6.29 WHEN TO AVOID USING HDFS

There are several situations where HDFS may not be a suitable fit, as in the following examples.

HDFS is unsuitable for storing data for applications that require fast data access. Because the information for each file must be saved on the NameNode and retained in memory, HDFS is not appropriate for storing a large number of tiny files. Also, HDFS isn't designed for instances when multiple/simultaneous writes to the same file are required.

SUMMARY

HDFS is the storage layer of Hadoop. It stands for the Hadoop Distributed File System. HDFS is the Hadoop version of GFS (Google File System), proven at very large scales.

HDFS allows the distribution of Big Data storage across a cluster of computers. It makes all the hard drives on the cluster look like a single giant file system. HDFS works on storing fewer large files rather than a vast number of small files.

Virtualization creates a virtual version of storage networking servers or applications. The hypervisor concept enables virtualization. A hypervisor is software that runs above the physical server (hardware) or host. It pulls the resources from the physical server and allocates them to virtual environments.

The Type 1 hypervisor is simply deployed on top of the actual server. They are also called bare-metal hypervisors. Type 1 is the most frequently used hypervisor; it is most secure and low in latency. Examples: VMware ESX, Microsoft Hyper-V, Xen.

In Type 2 hypervisor, there is a layer of host Operating System between the physical server and the hypervisor, used for end-user virtualization.

Because the guest VMs are independent of the host hardware, hypervisors enable the usage of most of a system's available resources and give it more IT mobility. This implies that these resources can be simply transported across servers. Because a hypervisor allows numerous virtual computers to operate on a single physical server, it reduces the space usage, the energy used and the maintenance requirements.

VMware workstation and Oracle VirtualBox are two famous virtualization software that allows multiple operating systems and runs them together on the same physical system.

VirtualBox is virtualization software that allows multiple operating systems and runs them together on the same physical PC; it is a Type 2 hypervisor software.

Cloudera Hadoop file system interface is an easy-to-use, web-based GUI for accessing HDFS. It offers read and writes access to HDFS through a rich, consistent, and intuitive Hadoop interface suitable for both experienced users and new adopters.

Ambari administration console is one of the tools we can use for Hadoop administration. To start the console part of the Ambari, we must start the Ambari server and Ambari agent. These are the two required components. However, if we have installed the Cloudera HDP Sandbox, it will be installed automatically, and the server and agent will be up and running with the sandbox.

Kerberos is another security feature provided by Hortonworks in a data platform. Most organizations use Kerberos. All the authentications to Hadoop services happen through Kerberos. Kerberos is a service that provides security and access related to Hadoop resources.

The Hortonworks Sandbox comes with a few standard users; admin and maria_dev are some of the existing users. We can create a group and then assign users so that we can give privileges to a particular group and not to the users directly. This is one of the best practices.

The HDFS command-line interface is a Java program that provides a command-line interface to the Hadoop Distributed File System. It has no direct dependency on any other Hadoop modules except Java. To check the list of Hadoop services that are up and running, we can use the "jps" command.

The following are other useful HDFS commands:

Listing down the directories (ls -d), Listing down the file details in human-readable format (ls -h), Listing down the files recursively in all the directories and subdirectories (ls -R), Listing down the files inside a directory with the specific structure (dat*). If the option -R recursively removes the directory and all its contents, the option -skipTrash ignores the recycle bin, if enabled, and removes the specified files immediately.

Listing down the file management commands include Creating a directory (mkdir); Removing the directory (rmdir); Displaying the contents of a file (cat); Showing the size of a file (du); Merging multiple files (getmerge); Counting the number of directories (count); Changing the replication factor (setrep); and Moving files from the source to the destination (mv). The commands for deleting HDFS files and directories work in a similar way to those in the Linux file system. We need to use the command -rm -r (recursive delete) to delete directories and files in them. The command -lsr can be used to recursively list directories and files in a specific folder.

This Hadoop command (mv) is run like the -get command, but with one difference – it removes the file from the HDFS location on a successful copy operation. This command is similar to the UNIX cp command and is used to copy files from one directory to another in the HDFS file system. The command cat is similar to the Unix cat command and displays the contents of a file.

Listing down the commands related to the upload and download of files include Moving a file/folder from the local to HDFS (moveFromLocal); Moving a file from HDFS to local (moveToLocal); Copying files from source to destination (cp); Displaying the last kilobyte of the file (tail); Creating, changing and modifying time stamps of a file (touch); Creating a new file on HDFS with size 0 bytes (touchz); Appending the content to a file which is present in HDFS (appendToFile); Copying a file from local file system (copyFromLocal); and Copying files from HDFS to local file system (copyToLocal). The difference between copying the files and moving the files is that while copying the files it will create duplication, whereas when moving the files ,it will not create duplication and there will be only one copy.

Listing down the commands related to the ownership of the files and changing the permissions of the file include Checking the checksum information of a file (checksum); Changing the group association of files (chgrp); Changing the permission of a file (chmod); and Changing the owner and group of a file (chown).

VirtualBox is compatible with Linux, Windows, Mac OS, and Solaris. On VirtualBox's website, you can even access older unsupported versions of VirtualBox that supports older operating systems like Windows XP or Windows Vista. There are many options to download VirtualBox, and it is compatible with virtually anything. However, the VMware Workstation player is only compatible with Windows and Linux.

In VirtualBox, we have five buttons at the top and a big gray pane at the side. It has menus to set the preferences, import, export, New, and Add. Through the Preference menu, it is possible to select the input language. It is user-intuitive and user-friendly. VirtualBox manager is self-explanatory and pretty easy to use.

VMware workstation is also user-friendly. Each action is in large bold text with a description under it. It has menus like "Create a new virtual machine," "Open a virtual machine," "Upgrade to VMware Workstation Pro," and then "Help."

HDFS, HBase, MongoDB, and Cassandra are the tools of the storage layer of Hadoop.

The basic version of Hadoop 1.0 consists of HDFS and MapReduce components only. Later, all other features were added on top of the Hadoop system. So, HDFS is the primary component of the Hadoop system.

Distributive: HDFS is a pure Java implementation program. It attempts to design and implement a file system that will handle large amounts of data. The Hadoop Distributed File System (HDFS) design is based on Google's core distributed file system, which was proven at very large scales. A Distributed File System (DFS) is a file system distributed among numerous file servers or locations. It enables programs to access and store isolated data the same way as they access and save local files, allowing programmers to access files from any network or computer.

Besides, HDFS is designed to handle large datasets. It is fault-tolerant, cost-effective, provides high data availability, is scalable, has high throughput, and has built-in support for high data reliability, high data availability, and data locality.

HDFS follows a master/slave architecture, so the master node is the name node, and slave nodes are known as data nodes.

A rack consists of multiple nodes, usually 30 to 40 nodes. Each of these nodes, in turn, store multiple data blocks. Within a rack, Hadoop stores its data in two different data nodes. Communication between nodes present in the same rack is usually faster than the nodes across multiple racks. The concept of choosing the closest data node is called rack awareness.

Rack Awareness Algorithm: The rack awareness algorithm says the local rack stores the first replica of a block, and the subsequent two replicas will be stored in a different rack.

In Hadoop, the data chunks process happens independently in parallel among DataNodes. The distributed cache contains common files accessible by all the DataNodes, which include read-only text files, archive files, jar files, etc. Hadoop will make these cache files available on each data node where MapReduce tasks are running.

Serialization is turning an object into a format that can be stored on a disk or transmitted over the network. Data serialization is the conversion of internal or external program states to a format that can be stored in persistent memory, such as disk storage or memory buffers. General serialization formats include simple data types such as integers and strings to more advanced formats such as XML and message-oriented middleware.

There are two main methods to serialize data to an HDFS file system. With the first method, you use the DataOutputStream.writeBytes(byte[] buffer) method, which copies the data to an HDFS file in binary format. The second option uses the DataOutputStream. writeObject method, serializing your object to an HDFS file in binary form. The data serializer class offers a choice of different serialization formats, from XML to binary.

Hadoop provides a Web User Interface for HDFS. The HDFS Web User Interface is beneficial in a pseudo-distributed environment and is an essential tool in a fully distributed environment. For example, if we are using Hadoop in the pseudo-distributed mode, we need to type http://localhost:50070/ into our web browser and port 50070 on the localhost host. We need to replace 'localhost' with the real hostname of the cluster computer in a fully dispersed mode.

The most straightforward approach to acquiring the cluster's configuration is to use the Configuration object, which will read the configuration files from the class path and read and load all of the data required by the program. We shall acquire the File System object by utilizing the URL. The DistributedFileSystem object will be returned as the file system. All admin-related functionality, like creating a file or directory, or deleting a file, is provided by the Hadoop FileSystem class. Under HDFS, the mkDirs method is used to create a directory. The Directory Name which we want to create is passed as parameter for the Path. String directoryName = "bigdata/testdirectory"; Path path = new Path(directoryName); Then, File System object uses the path to create the directory using fileSystem.mkdirs(path);

Connecting HDFS from Python: Snakebite is a Python package produced by Spotify. This package provides a Python client module that allows Python applications to use HDFS programmatically. To connect directly with the NameNode, the client library utilizes protobuf messages.

Protocol Buffer (Protobuf) is a cross-platform data format for serializing structured data. This platform is free and open-source. JSON saves data in a human-readable text format, whereas protobuf is a binary data-interchange format. Protobuf may be used to create programs that communicate with one another via a network or to store data.

Protobuf messages are used for the following: (1) When we require quick serialization/ deserialization, (2) When it is critical to maintain safety, (3) When adherence to the schema is necessary, (4) When we want to cut down on code.

Snakebite without any parameters can be used to display this list from the command line. Use snakebite [cmd] — help to get assistance for a specific command, where cmd is a valid snakebite command.

When to Avoid Using HDFS: There are several situations where HDFS may not be a suitable fit, as in the following cases. HDFS is unsuitable for storing data for applications that require fast data access. Because the information for each file must be saved on the NameNode and retained in memory, HDFS is not appropriate for storing a large number of tiny files. Also, HDFS isn't designed for instances when multiple/simultaneous writes to the same file are required.

EXERCISES

Multiple Choice Questions

1. **HDFS is the _____ layer of Hadoop system.**
   A. Ingestion
   B. Storage
   C. Processing
   D. Analysis
   Answer: B
   Explanation: HDFS is the storage layer of Hadoop. It stands for the Hadoop Distributed File System. HDFS is the Hadoop version of GFS (Google File System), proven at very large scales.

2. **Creating a virtual version of storage networking servers (or) application is called as _____.**
   A. Hypervisor
   B. Installation
   C. Upgradation
   D. Virtualization
   Answer: D
   Explanation: Virtualization is creating a virtual version of storage networking servers or applications. The hypervisor concept enables virtualization.

3. **This is the common name of a software that runs above the physical server (hardware) or host:**
   A. Hypervisor
   B. Cloud
   C. Virtual software
   D. Supervisor
   Answer: A
   Explanation: A hypervisor is software that runs above the physical server (hardware) or host. It pulls the resources from the physical server and allocates them to the virtual environments.

4. **This type of Hypervisor is simply deployed on top of the actual server:**
   A. Type 1
   B. Type 2
   C. Type 3
   D. Type 4
   Answer: A
   Explanation: The Type 1 Hypervisor is simply deployed on top of the actual server. These hypervisors are also called bare-metal hypervisors. Type 1 is the most frequently used hypervisor; it is most secure and lowers the latency. Examples: VMware ESX, Microsoft Hyper-V, Xen.

5. **This type of Hypervisor has a layer of host Operating System between the physical server and the hypervisor:**
   A. Type 1
   B. Type 2
   C. Type 3
   D. Type 4
   Answer: B

Explanation: In Type 2 hypervisor, there is a layer of host operating system between the physical server and the hypervisor, used for end-user virtualization. Examples: Oracle VirtualBox, VMware Workstation. They have a higher latency than a Type 1 hypervisor.

6. **Oracle VirtualBox and VMware Workstation are examples of this type of Hypervisor:**
   A. Type 1
   B. Type 2
   C. Type 3
   D. Type 4
   Answer: B
   Explanation: In Type 2 hypervisor, there is a layer of host Operating System between the physical server and the hypervisor, used for end-user virtualization. Examples: Oracle VirtualBox, VMware Workstation. They have a higher latency than a Type 1 hypervisor.

7. **This enables the usage of more of a system's available resources and gives more IT mobility:**
   A. Hypervisor
   B. Cloud
   C. Virtual software
   D. Supervisor
   Answer: A
   Explanation: Because the guest VMs are independent of the host hardware, hypervisors enable the usage of more of a system's available resources and gives more IT mobility. This implies that they can be simply transported across servers.

8. **This virtualization software is Type 2 hypervisor from Oracle Software:**
   A. Microsoft Hyper-V
   B. Xen
   C. VMware Work Station
   D. VirtualBox
   Answer: D
   Explanation: Oracle VirtualBox is a Type 2 hypervisor software. Virtualization technology allows us to run multiple operating systems on the same physical hardware and run them simultaneously.

9. **This runs on 8080 port and is mainly used for administration purpose:**
   A. VirtualBox
   B. Ambari
   C. Cloudera
   D. VMware work station
   Answer: B
   Explanation: Cloudera Hadoop file system interface is an easy-to-use, web-based GUI for accessing HDFS. The Ambari services are installed on 8080 port (the links are available in 1080 port). Ambari administration console is one of the tools we can use for Hadoop administration.

10. **Right now, how many node managers are alive? This detail can be obtained from?**
    A. Metrics part of the Ambari console
    B. Config part of the Ambari console

C. Heatmap part of the Ambari console
D. This detail is not available in Ambari console.
Answer: C

Explanation: By default, we can see the metrics, heatmaps, and config history on the main screen of the console. Metrics gives the details of the metrics at all levels, like HDFS data usage, HDFS links, memory usage, network usage, CPU usage, and cluster load. Similarly, the resource manager provides information on heap usage. The dashboard also provides information on the number of node managers that are currently live or lost (unhealthy).

11. **This is another security feature provided by Hortonworks in a data platform:**
    A. Ambari Console
    B. Oracle VirtualBox
    C. VMware workstation
    D. Kerberos
    Answer: D

    Explanation: Kerberos is another security feature provided by Hortonworks in a data platform. Most organizations use Kerberos. All the authentications to Hadoop services happen through Kerberos. Kerberos is a service that provides security and access related to Hadoop resources.

12. **CLI in HDFS is called as:**
    A. Cross Line Interface
    B. Command Line Interface
    C. Class Level Interface
    D. Configuration Level Interface
    Answer: B

    Explanation: The HDFS Command Line Interface (Hadoop Distributed File System CLI), also called "fs," is a set of command-line tools that allow users to interact with a Hadoop cluster or a single node in a cluster.

13. **To check the list of Hadoop services that are up and running, we can use this command:**
    A. Rmdir
    B. Chmod
    C. JPS
    D. LS
    Answer: C

    Explanation: To check the list of Hadoop services that are up and running, we can use the "jps" command.

14. **Which command is used to list down only the directories in a folder?**
    A. ls -d
    B. ls
    C. ls -R
    D. ls -h
    Answer: A

    Explanation: Listing all the files with permissions (ls), Listing down the directories (ls -d), Listing down the file details in human readable format (ls -h), Listing down the files recursively in all the directories and subdirectories (ls -R), Listing down the files inside a directory with the specific structure (dat*).

15. **Which HDFS command is used to list down the size of the file?**
    A. count B. mkdir
    C. rmdir D. du
    Answer: D
    Explanation: Creating a directory (mkdir); Removing the directory (rmdir); Display the content of the file (cat); Showing the size of the file (du); Merging multiple files (getmerge); Counting the number of directories (count); Changing the replication factor (setrep) and Moving files from the source to the destination (mv).

16. **Which HDFS command is used to recursively delete directories and files?**
    A. lsr B. rm -r
    C. rmdir D. du
    Answer: B
    Explanation: The commands for deleting HDFS files and directories work in a similar way to those in the Linux file system - we need to use the command -rm -r (recursive delete) to delete directories and files in them - the command -lsr can be used to recursively list directories and files in a specific folder.

17. **Which HDFS command is used for moving the file/folder from the local to HDFS?**
    A. moveFromLocal B. moveToLocal
    C. cp D. touch
    Answer: A
    Explanation: Moving the file/folder from the local to HDFS (moveFromLocal); Moving a file from HDFS to local (moveToLocal); Copying files from source to destination (cp), Displaying the last kilobyte of the file (tail); Creating, changing and modifying time stamps of a file (touch).

18. **Which HDFS command is used for moving a file from HDFS to local?**
    A. moveFromLocal B. moveToLocal
    C. cp D. touch
    Answer: B
    Explanation: Same as for Question 17.

19. **Which HDFS command is used for copying files from source to destination?**
    A. moveFromLocal B. moveToLocal
    C. cp D. touch
    Answer: C
    Explanation: Same as for Question 17.

20. **Which HDFS command is used to create, change and modify time stamps of a file?**
    A. moveFromLocal B. moveToLocal
    C. cp D. touch

Answer: D
Explanation: Same as for Question 17.

21. **Which of the following command is used for displaying the last kilobyte of the file?**
    A. tail
    B. touch
    C. touchz
    D. appendToFile
    Answer: A
    Explanation: Displaying the last kilobyte of the file (tail); Create, change and modify time stamps of a file (touch); Creating a new file on HDFS with size 0 bytes (touchz); Appending the content to the file which is present in HDFS (appendToFile); Copying file from local file system(copyFromLocal); Copying files from HDFS to local file system (copyToLocal). The main difference between copying the files and moving the files is that while copying the files it will create duplication, when moving the files there will be no duplication but only one copy.

22. **Which of the following command is used for creating a new file on HDFS with size 0 bytes?**
    A. tail
    B. touch
    C. touchz
    D. appendToFile
    Answer: C
    Explanation: Same as for Question 21.

23. **Which of the following HDFS command is used for checking the checksum information of a file?**
    A. checksum
    B. chgrp
    C. chmod
    D. chown
    Answer: A
    Explanation: Checking the checksum information of a file (checksum); Changing the group association of files (chgrp); Changing the permission of a file (chmod); Changing the owner and group of a file (chown).

24. **Which of the following HDFS command is used for changing the group association of files?**
    A. checksum
    B. chgrp
    C. chmod
    D. chown
    Answer: B
    Explanation: Same as for Question 23.

25. **Which of the following HDFS command is used for changing the permission of a file?**
    A. checksum
    B. chgrp
    C. chmod
    D. chown
    Answer: C
    Explanation: Same as for Question 23.

26. **Which of the following HDFS command is used for changing the owner and group of a file?**
    A. checksum
    B. chgrp
    C. chmod
    D. chown
    Answer: D
    Explanation: Same as for Question 23.

27. **VMware Workstation can work with Solaris.**
    A. True
    B. False
    Answer: B
    Explanation: VirtualBox is compatible with Linux, Windows, Mac OS, and Solaris. On VirtualBox's website, you can even access older unsupported versions of VirtualBox that supports older operating system like Windows XP or Windows vista. There are many options to download VirtualBox, and it is compatible with virtually anything. However, the VMware Workstation player is only compatible with Windows and Linux.

28. **VMware Workstation player is only compatible with Windows and Linux.**
    A. True
    B. False
    Answer: A
    Explanation: Same as for Question 27.

29. **Which of the following is not a storage layer of the Hadoop ecosystem?**
    A. HDFS
    B. Flume
    C. MongoDB
    D. Cassandra
    Answer: B
    Explanation: HDFS, HBase, MongoDB, and Cassandra are the tools of the storage layer of Hadoop.

30. **DFS in HDFS stands for:**
    A. Data File System
    B. Distributed File System
    C. Data Flow System
    D. Distributed Flow System
    Answer: B
    Explanation: The Hadoop Distributed File System (HDFS) design is based on Google's core distributed file system, which was proven at very large scales. A Distributed File System (DFS) is a file system distributed among numerous file servers or locations. It enables programs to access and store isolated data the same way as they access and save local files, allowing programmers to access files from any network or computer.

31. **Maximum theoretical scalability of HDFS is estimated to be of ___ million nodes, each with ___ terabytes of raw capacity.**
    A. 200, 2
    B. 2, 200
    C. 200, 1
    D. 1, 200

Answer: D

Explanation: HDFS is designed to be extremely fault tolerant and scales up very well (maximum theoretical scalability of HDFS is estimated to be of 1 million nodes, each with 200 terabytes of raw capacity).

32. **If you keep a 2 GB file on HDFS, it will eventually take up ___ GB.**
    A. 6 GB
    B. 2 GB
    C. 4 GB
    D. 10 GB
    Answer: A

    Explanation: HDFS is a distributed file system with an inbuilt fault-tolerant mechanism. HDFS's ability to replicate blocks of files and store them across nodes in a large cluster provides fault tolerance and reliability because the data blocks are replicated across multiple data nodes. Thus, a server failure will not damage the file. If you keep a 2 GB file on HDFS, it will eventually take up 6 GB.

33. **This refers to the ability to extend or contract (shrink) the cluster:**
    A. Useability
    B. Scalability
    C. Manageability
    D. Controllability
    Answer: B

    Explanation: Scalability refers to the ability to extend or contract (shrink) the cluster. Unlike relational databases where our data can grow only vertically (more hard drives), with HDFS, we can add more nodes to a cluster to increase storage capacity. This, along with high availability, makes Hadoop a reliable base for virtually any business project.

34. **Increasing the number of discs on the cluster's nodes is called as:**
    A. Vertical scaling
    B. Horizontal scaling
    C. Peer Level scaling
    D. Down scaling
    Answer: A

    Explanation: We can increase the number of discs on the cluster's nodes with vertical scaling. We shall have to change the configuration files and add entries for the newly inserted drives to do so, even if this results in minimal downtime. As a result, most individuals favour the second scaling method, horizontal scaling.

    With horizontal scaling, we can add new nodes to the cluster on the fly without any downtime. Without incurring any downtime, we can add as many nodes to the cluster as we want in real-time. Hadoop offers this as a one-of-a-kind functionality.

35. **This will incur mininum down period:**
    A. Vertical scaling
    B. Horizontal scaling
    C. Peer Level scaling
    D. Down scaling
    Answer: A

    Explanation: Same as for Question 34.

36. **This will add new clusters on the fly, without down time:**
    A. Vertical scaling
    B. Horizontal scaling
    C. Peer Level scaling
    D. Down scaling
    Answer: B
    Explanation: Same as for Question 34.

37. **Quantity of work accomplished in a given length of time is called as:**
    A. Work done
    B. Effectiveness
    C. Throughput
    D. Efficiency
    Answer: C
    Explanation: Throughput is the quantity of work accomplished in a given length of time. It describes how quickly data is accessible from the system and is commonly used to assess its performance. When we wish to complete a job or operation in HDFS, the work is divided and shared across many systems. As a result, all the systems will work independently and in parallel to complete the tasks that have been allocated to them. As a result, the task will be accomplished relatively quickly.

38. **The process of moving the computation close to where the actual data resides on the node in HDFS is called as:**
    A. Node locality
    B. Server locality
    C. Computation locality
    D. Data locality
    Answer: D
    Explanation: Data locality is the process of moving the computation close to where the actual data resides on the node. This minimizes network congestion and increases the overall throughput of the system.

39. **It is the master daemon, and is the arbitrator and repository for all HDFS metadata:**
    A. Name node
    B. Secondary node
    C. Data node
    D. Backup node
    Answer: A
    Explanation: The main component in HDFS is a NameNode that manages all Hadoop data blocks. It is the master daemon, and it manages the data node. The NameNode is the arbitrator and repository for all HDFS metadata. Metadata means data about the data. It supports user quotas and access permissions.

40. **It does an essential task known as Checkpointing, which combines edit logs with FS images:**
    A. Name node
    B. Secondary node
    C. Data node
    D. Backup node
    Answer: B
    Explanation: The NameNode combines the FS image and edits log files when it starts up to restore the current file system namespace. Unfortunately, the size of edit

logs grows too high because the NameNode operates continuously for an extended period without being restarted. Hence, NameNode will take a long time to restart. This problem is solved by using a secondary NameNode. It does an essential task known as Checkpointing, which combines edit logs with FS images.

41. **This maintains an in-memory, up-to-date replica of the file system namespace in Hadoop:**
    A. Name node
    B. Secondary node
    C. Data node
    D. Backup node
    Answer: D
    Explanation: The Checkpoint node and the Backup node, both provide the checkpointing capability. The backup node maintains an in-memory, up-to-date replica of the file system namespace in Hadoop. It is constantly in sync with the state of the current NameNode. To construct a checkpoint in the HDFS architecture, the backup node does not need to download the FS image and change files from the current NameNode. This is because, in memory, it already has an up-to-date state of the namespace state.

42. **These are the slave daemons, where the actual data is stored:**
    A. Name node
    B. Secondary node
    C. Data node
    D. Backup node
    Answer: C
    Explanation: Data nodes are the slave daemons where the actual data is stored. Whenever a client gives a read or write request, the data node serves it. Data nodes are low-cost commodity servers. The data node stores the data as data blocks (file chunks). DataNode is in charge of operating read/write requests from clients.

43. **Whenever we write a file into HDFS, it breaks down the file into different blocks of ___ megabytes, except the last block.**
    A. 32
    B. 100
    C. 128
    D. 64
    Answer: C
    Explanation: HDFS is a fault-tolerant system. Whenever we write a file into HDFS, it breaks down the file into different blocks of 128 megabytes, except the last block (which will have the remainder of the file). For example, a file of 380 megabytes divides into three blocks; the first block will be 128 megabytes; the second will be 128 megabytes, and the third will occupy the remaining size of the file (124 megabytes).

44. **Hadoop has this mechanism to tackle this data integrity issue:**
    A. Security
    B. Checksum
    C. Data locality
    D. Rack awareness
    Answer: B
    Explanation: Data Integrity ensures that no data loss or corruption happens while storing or processing the data. In Hadoop, the amount of data being written or read is

large in volume; so the chances of data corruption are more. Hadoop has a checksum mechanism to tackle this data integrity issue. Hadoop computes the checksum while writing the data to the disk for the first time. It checks again while reading the data from the disk. If the new checksum matches the original checksum, it means the data is uncorrupted.

45. **This contains common files accessible by all the Data Nodes:**
    A. Serialization   B. Distributed cache
    C. Custom file   D. Configuration file
    Answer: B
    Explanation: In Hadoop, the data chunk process happens independently in parallel among data nodes. The distributed cache contains common files accessible by all the data nodes, which include read-only text files, archive files, jar files, etc. Hadoop will make these cache files available on each data node where map/reduce tasks are running.

46. **Turning an object into a format that can be stored on a disk or transmitted over the network is called as:**
    A. Serialization   B. Caching
    C. Checksum   D. Check point
    Answer: A
    Explanation: Serialization is turning an object into a format that can be stored on a disk or transmitted over the network. Data serialization is the conversion of internal or external program states to a format that can be stored in persistent memory, such as disk storage or memory buffers. General serialization formats simple data types such as integers and strings to more advanced formats such as XML and message-oriented middleware.

47. **This is the package used in Python to connect to HDFS:**
    A. Snakebite   B. Cobra Bite
    C. Connect HDFS   D. Pyte Connect
    Answer: A
    Explanation: Snakebite is a Python package produced by Spotify. This package provides a Python client module that allows Python applications to use HDFS programmatically. To connect directly with the NameNode, the client library utilizes protobuf messages. Protocol Buffer (Protobuf) is a cross-platform data format for serializing structured data. This platform is free and open-source. JSON saves data in a human-readable text format, whereas protobuf is a binary data-interchange format.

Short-answer Questions

1. **Write short notes on HDFS.**
   HDFS is the storage layer of Hadoop. It stands for the Hadoop Distributed File System. HDFS is the Hadoop version of GFS (Google File System), proven at

very large scales. There are other distributed file systems built at Google. However, GFS was chosen because it had evolved to handle very large datasets, could scale to hundreds of thousands of nodes, and maintain high performances even under failure conditions. HDFS allows the distribution of Big Data storage across the cluster of computers. It makes all the hard drives on the cluster look like a single giant file system.

2. **What is Virtualization?**
   Virtualization is creating a virtual version of storage networking servers or applications. The hypervisor concept enables Virtualization. A hypervisor is a software that runs above the physical server (hardware) or host. It pulls the resources from the physical server and allocates them to virtual environments.

3. **What are Type 1 and Type 2 Hypervisors?**
   The Type 1 Hypervisor is simply deployed on top of the actual server. It is also called bare-metal hypervisor. Type 1 is the most frequently used hypervisor; it is most secure and lowers the latency. Examples: VMware ESX, Microsoft Hyper-V, Xen.
   In a Type 2 Hypervisor, a layer of host Operating System between the physical server and the hypervisor is used for end-user Virtualization. Example: Oracle VirtualBox, VMware Workstation. They have a higher latency than a Type 1 Hypervisor.

4. **Why do we use Hypervisor?**
   The guest VMs are independent of the host hardware. Hence, hypervisors enable the usage of more of a system's available resources and give more IT mobility. This implies that they can be simply transported across servers. In addition, because a hypervisor allows numerous virtual computers to operate on a single physical server, it reduces the space usage, the energy used, and the maintenance requirements.

5. **Give any two examples of Virtualization software.**
   VMware Workstation and Oracle VirtualBox are two famous virtualization software that allow multiple operating systems and run them together on the same physical system.

6. **Write short notes on Oracle VirtualBox.**
   VirtualBox is virtualization software that allows multiple operating systems and runs them together on the same physical PC; it is a Type 2 Hypervisor software. Virtualization technology allows us to run multiple operating systems on the same physical hardware and run them simultaneously.

7. **Write short notes on the Cloudera Hadoop file system.**
   Cloudera Hadoop file system interface is an easy-to-use, web-based GUI for accessing HDFS. It offers read and write access to HDFS through a rich, consistent, and intuitive Hadoop interface suitable for both experienced users and new adopters. Horton box is perfect software provided by Hortonworks. It is suitable for day-to-day work; this is a single-node Hadoop cluster.

8. **Write short notes on Ambari Administration.**
   The Ambari services are installed on 8080 port (the links are available in 1080 port). It will take us to the Ambari login page. We need to type in the administration password. Hadoop console comes up with the two players; we can use the Ambari tool or console. There are two ways to work with Hadoop. Either we can use the command prompt or use the console.
   The Ambari administration console is one of the tools we can use for the Hadoop administration. To start the console part of the Ambari, we must start the Ambari server and Ambari agent. These are the two required components.

9. **Write short notes on Ambari Admin Console.**
   By default, we can see the metrics, heatmaps, and config history on the console's main screen. Metrics give the details of the metrics at all levels, like HDFS Data usage, HDFS links, Memory usage, Network usage, CPU usage and Cluster load. Similarly, we have the heap usage on the resource manager, which shows how many node managers are currently live or lost (unhealthy).

10. **Write short notes on Kerberos.**
    Kerberos is a security feature provided by Hortonworks in a data platform. Most organizations use Kerberos. All the authentications to Hadoop services happen through Kerberos. Kerberos is a service that provides security and access related to Hadoop resources.

11. **Write short notes on HDFS Command Line Interface.**
    The HDFS Command Line Interface (Hadoop Distributed File System CLI), also called "fs", is a set of command-line tools that allow users to interact with a Hadoop cluster or a single node in a cluster. HDFS command-line interface (CLI) is a sub-command of NameNode. It helps to interact with a running Hadoop cluster without logging in to any DataNode server. Shell Commands provide the ability to create and execute various commands on individual nodes within a distributed Hadoop cluster. In addition, it provides terminal support for Windows, Linux, Solaris and Mac OS X platforms.

12. **Write short notes on JPS Command.**
    To check the list of Hadoop services that are up and running, we can use the "jps" command.

13. **How to use the list command in HDFS?**
    Listing all the files with permissions (ls); Listing down the directories (ls -d); Listing down the file details in a human-readable format (ls -h); Listing down the files recursively in all the directories and subdirectories (ls -R); Listing down the files inside a directory with the specific structure (dat★).

14. **What are the different file management commands in HDFS?**
    Creating a directory (mkdir); Removing the directory (rmdir); Displaying the content of the file (cat); Showing the size of the file (du); Merging multiple files (getmerge); Count the number of directories (count); Changing the replication factor (setrep); Moving files from the Source to the destination (mv). The commands for deleting HDFS files and directories work in a similar way to those in the Linux file system – we need to use the command -rm -r (recursive delete) to delete directories and files in them; the command -lsr can be used to recursively list directories and files in a specific folder.

15. **What are the different commands for uploading and downloading files in HDFS?**
    Moving the file/folder from the local to HDFS (moveFromLocal); Moving a file from HDFS to local (moveToLocal); Copying files from source to destination (cp); Displaying the last kilobyte of the file (tail); Creating, changing and modifying time stamps of a file (touch); Creating a new file on HDFS with size 0 bytes (touchz); Appending the content to the file which is present in HDFS (appendToFile); Copying file from the local file system (copyFromLocal); Copying files from HDFS to the local file system (copyToLocal). The main difference between copying the files and moving the files is that while copying the files, it will create the duplication whereas while moving the files, it will not create duplication and there will be only one copy.

16. **What are the different commands for File Ownership and Validation?**
    Checking the checksum information of a file (checksum); Changing the group association of files (chgrp); Changing the permission of a file (chmod) and Changing the owner and group of a file (chown).

17. **Make a quick comparison of VMware and VirtualBox.**
    These two hypervisors are the most popular ones available to download for free today. VirtualBox is compatible with Linux, Windows, Mac OS and Solaris. On VirtualBox's website, you can even access older unsupported versions of VirtualBox that support older operating systems like Windows XP or Windows Vista. There are many options to download VirtualBox, which is compatible with virtually anything. However, the VMware Workstation player is only compatible with Windows and Linux.

18. **List a few of the storage layers of the Hadoop system.**
    HDFS, Hbase, MongoDB, and Cassandra are the tools of the storage layer of Hadoop.

19. **Write short notes on Hadoop 1.0.**
    The basic version of Hadoop 1.0 consists of HDFS and MapReduce components only. Later, all other features are added on top of the Hadoop system. So, HDFS is the primary component of the Hadoop system. HDFS is the backbone upon which

the open-source Hadoop ecosystem has been built. We can simply say that HDFS is a file system used mainly for storage. Hive, Spark, and other features support HDFS.

20. **Explain the distributive nature of HDFS.**
    The Hadoop Distributed File System (HDFS) design is based on Google's core distributed file system, proven at very large scales. A Distributed File System (DFS) is a file system distributed among numerous file servers or locations. It enables programs to access and store isolated data the same way they access and save local files, allowing programmers to access files from any network or computer. HDFS breaks up the data into little chunks and distributes it among the cluster's DataNodes. For example, the Hadoop Distributed File System allows MapReduce to process a fraction of enormous datasets divided into blocks across several nodes in parallel. The Distributed File System (DFS) will enable users of physically distributed computers to exchange data and resources using a common file system.

21. **Explain the large Dataset nature of HDFS.**
    The HDFS is suitable for large size datasets of gigabytes to terabytes. It can store all types of data (structured and unstructured) that runs on commodity hardware. HDFS is a highly available, fault-tolerant, distributed file system designed to scale to cluster sizes of 100s of nodes, handling terabytes of data with thousands of clients. Interfaces in the Hadoop Distributed File System (HDFS) allow clients to efficiently interact with files larger than 1 TB. HDFS is extremely fault-tolerant and scales up very well (maximum theoretical scalability of HDFS is estimated to be 1 million nodes, each with 200 terabytes of raw capacity).

22. **Explain the Fault Tolerance nature of HDFS.**
    HDFS is a distributed file system with an inbuilt fault-tolerant mechanism. HDFS's ability to replicate blocks of files and store them across nodes in a large cluster provides fault tolerance and reliability because the data blocks are replicated across multiple data nodes, and a server failure will not damage the file. For example, keeping a 2 GB file on HDFS will eventually take up 6 GB. The name node updates the metadata regularly and keeps the replication factor consistent. It provides high throughput access to detecting faults and enables quick automatic recovery from failure, which is the core architectural goal of HDFS. HDFS is designed to scale easily across the petabytes (1000 terabytes). At the same time, it offers reliability and fault tolerance.

23. **Explain the cost-effective nature of HDFS.**
    HDFS (Hadoop Distributed File System) is an open-source file system that stores and manages data in a cluster of commodity servers. It is a cost-efficient, fault-tolerant, highly scalable storage architecture with a loosely coupled processing model capable of serving large files to thousands of clients simultaneously. HDFS provides efficient support for process abstraction, low latency operations on large datasets, secure data transfer across heterogeneous computer clusters, efficient scheduling on various hardware configurations, and good quality of life for applications.

24. **Explain the replication and availability nature of HDFS.**
    HDFS is intended to run on commodity hardware developed by Apache Software Foundation. It is designed to allow data to be stored across multiple machines with high availability. HDFS provides higher data availability, specific hardware requirements, and reduced manual tuning compared to traditional RAID-based systems. When high-availability daemons are enabled, HDFS will start sufficient numbers of DataNodes. The user configuration parameter will determine the replication factor of data blocks. The replication factor is dependent on the capacity of DataNode to store blocks, which is also dependent on the available storage capacity of DataNode's volumes and bandwidth speed to access these volumes.
    HDFS is a high-availability distributed file system designed to provide highly available and scalable storage for very large datasets across clusters of networked computers and storage servers. It has become the preferred solution for Big Data applications.

25. **Explain the scalability nature of HDFS.**
    There are many benefits to using HDFS. The main one is the unstructured nature of data in Hadoop, which allows us to store any type of file in it. Another major benefit is scalability. Scalability refers to the ability to extend or contract (shrink) the cluster. Unlike relational databases, where our data can grow only vertically (more hard drives), with HDFS, we can add more nodes to our cluster to increase storage capacity. This, along with high availability, makes Hadoop a reliable base for virtually any business project. We may scale Hadoop HDFS in two ways: vertical scaling and horizontal scaling.

26. **What is the difference between Vertical Scaling and Horizontal Scaling?**
    Vertical scaling: We can increase the number of discs on the cluster's nodes. We shall need to change the configuration files and add entries for the newly inserted drives to do so even if this results in minimal downtime. As a result, most individuals favour the second scaling method, horizontal scaling.
    Horizontal Scaling: In this method, we can add new nodes to the cluster on the fly without any downtime. Without incurring any downtime, we can add as many nodes to the cluster as we want in real-time. Hadoop offers this as a one-of-a-kind functionality.

27. **Explain the High Throughput nature of HDFS.**
    Throughput is the quantity of work accomplished in a given length of time. It describes how quickly data is accessible from the system and is commonly used to assess its performance. When we wish to complete a job or operation in HDFS, the work is divided and shared across many systems. As a result, all the systems will work independently and in parallel to complete the tasks that have been allocated to them. As a result, the task will be accomplished relatively quickly. It provides high throughput access to detecting faults and enables quick, automatic recovery from failure, which is the core architectural goal of HDFS. It provides high-throughput access to application data and metadata. This file system is designed for high performance to support large

data transfers while retaining low latency. HDFS achieves this by replicating metadata on multiple servers. Duplicate copies of the metadata are arranged in triplicate; so any one server can fail without information loss.

28. **Explain the Data Locality nature of HDFS.**

    Data Locality is moving the computation close to where the actual data resides on the node. This minimizes network congestion and increases the overall throughput of the system.

29. **Write short notes on NameNode of HDFS.**

    The main component in HDFS is a NameNode that manages all Hadoop data blocks. It is the master daemon, and it manages the data node. The NameNode is the arbitrator and repository for all HDFS metadata. Any machine that supports Java can run the NameNode or the DataNode software. It does not store the user data and preserves only the metadata. Metadata means data about the data. It supports user quotas and access permissions.

30. **Write a short note on the secondary NameNode.**

    The NameNode combines the FS image and edit logs files when it starts up to restore the current file system namespace. Unfortunately, the size of edit logs grows too high because the NameNode operates continuously for an extended period without being restarted. NameNode will take a long time to restart because of this. This problem is solved by using a secondary NameNode. It does an essential task known as Checkpointing, which combines edit logs with FS images.

31. **Define Checkpoint in HDFS**

    Checkpointing happens after every hour (configurable). The secondary NameNode first copies the FS image and the edit log and adds them together to get the updated new FS image. This new FS image is copied back to the name node, and now the name node has an updated FS image. In the meantime, a new edit log is created when the Checkpointing is happening. This process continues and it helps the name node always to keep an updated copy.

32. **Write short notes on the Backup node.**

    The Checkpoint node and the Backup node, both provide the checkpointing capability. The backup node maintains an in-memory, up-to-date replica of the file system namespace in Hadoop. Therefore, it is constantly in sync with the state of the current NameNode. Therefore, to construct a checkpoint in the HDFS architecture, the backup node does not need to download the FSI image and change files from the current NameNode. This is because, in memory, it already has an up-to-date state of the namespace.

33. **Write short notes on DataNodes of HDFS.**

    Datanodes are the slave daemons where the actual data is stored. Whenever a client gives a read or write request, the data node serves it. DataNodes are low-cost commodity servers. The DataNode stores the data as data blocks (file chunks). DataNode is in charge of operating read/write requests from clients. DataNodes conduct block formation, replication, and deletion based on the NameNode's instructions. To report on the health of HDFS, DataNodes transmit a pulse to NameNode. DataNodes also deliver NameNode block reports, which comprise a list of the blocks it contains.

34. **Write short notes on HDFS blocks.**
    HDFS is a fault-tolerant system. Whenever we write a file into HDFS, it breaks down the file into different blocks of 128 megabytes, except the last block (which will have the remainder of the file). For example, a file of 380 megabytes divides into three blocks; the first block will be 128 megabytes; the second will be 128 megabytes, and the third will occupy the remaining size of the file (124 megabytes). The data blocks are distributed across the Hadoop cluster. By doing this, the time taken to store the data on the disk is significantly reduced. The total time to store this entire data onto the disk equals the time taken for storing one part of the data.

35. **Write short notes on Data Racks in HDFS.**
    A rack consists of multiple nodes, usually 30 to 40 nodes. Each of these nodes, in turn, stores multiple data blocks. For example, Hadoop stores its data in two different data nodes within a rack. Therefore, communication between nodes present in the same rack is usually faster than the nodes across multiple racks. The concept of choosing the closest data node is called Rack Awareness.

36. **Write short notes on the HDFS block replication mechanism.**
    The number of replicas of a file can be given as a parameter in HDFS, called the replication factor, stored in the NameNode. By default, their replication factor is set to three. Considering the default replication factor set, there will be three copies for each data part on three different machines. To reduce the bandwidth and latency time, it would store two copies of the same part of the data on the nodes present within the same rack, and the last copy would be stored on a node present on a different rack.

37. **Write short notes on Rack Awareness Algorithm.**
    The rack awareness algorithm says that the local rack stores the first replica of a block, while the subsequent two replicas are stored in a different rack. So, we store a data block in the local rack (rack one) to decrease the latency.
    1. Each node will have only one replica of the block.
    2. Each rack will have a maximum of two replicas of the block.
    3. The number of racks to be used will be lesser than the replication factor.

38. **Write short notes on Data Integrity in HDFS.**
    Data Integrity ensures that no data loss or corruption happens while storing or processing the Data. In Hadoop, the amount of data being written or read is large in volume, so data corruption is more likely. Hadoop has a checksum mechanism to tackle this data integrity issue. Hadoop computes the checksum while writing the data to the disk for the first time.

It checks again while reading the data from the disk. If the new checksum matches the original checksum, it means the data is uncorrupted.

39. **What is Data Locality in HDFS?**
    Hadoop's major drawback is cross-switch network traffic due to the massive volume of data. Extensive amount of data is moved to the computation spot. In this case, usually, data and code reside in different racks, creating heavy traffic across the racks. The mapper runs on a different rack in this scenario due to resource constraints.
    Data Locality refers to moving the computation (code) close to the node where the actual data resides instead of moving an extensive amount of data to the computation spot.

40. **Write short notes on Distributed Cache in HDFS.**
    In Hadoop, the data chunk process happens independently and in parallel among DataNodes. The distributed cache contains common files accessible by all the DataNodes, including read-only text files, archive files, jar files, etc. Hadoop will make these cache files available on each data node where map/reduce tasks are running. An application that requires distributed cache should make sure that the files are available on URLs. URLs can be either hdfs:// or http://. Hadoop framework will duplicate the cache file on all the data nodes before starting tasks on these nodes. The default size of the distributed cache is 10 GB, which can be modified using the local cache size.

41. **What is HDFS Serialization?**
    Serialization turns an object into a format that can be stored on a disk or transmitted over the network. Data serialization is the conversion of internal or external program states to a format that can be stored in persistent memory, such as disk storage or memory buffers. General serialization formats include simple data types such as integers and strings, and more advanced formats such as XML and message-oriented middleware.

42. **What are the methods to serialize data to an HDFS File System?**
    There are two main methods to serialize data to an HDFS file system. With the first method, we can use the DataOutputStream.writeBytes (byte[] buffer) method, which copies the data to an HDFS file in binary format. The second option uses the DataOutputStream.writeObject (Object object) method, serializing the object to an HDFS file in binary form. The data serializer class offers a choice of different serialization formats, from XML to binary. Using the type parameter makes it possible to specify precisely which format is desired for a particular job.

43. **Write short notes on HDFS Web UI.**
    Hadoop provides a Web User Interface for HDFS. The HDFS Web User Interface is beneficial in a pseudo-distributed environment and is an essential tool in a fully distributed environment. For example, if we are using Hadoop in the pseudo-distributed mode, we need to type http://localhost:50070/ into our web browser

and port 50070 on the localhost host. We need to replace 'localhost' with the real hostname of the cluster computer in a fully dispersed mode.

44. **Write short notes on connecting to HDFS from Python.**
    Snakebite is a Python package produced by Spotify. This package provides a Python client module that allows Python applications to use HDFS programmatically. To connect directly with the NameNode, the client library utilizes protobuf messages. Protocol Buffers (Protobuf) is a cross-platform data format for serializing structured data. This platform is free and open-source. JSON saves data in a human-readable text format, whereas protobuf is a binary data-interchange format.

43. **When should the use of HDFS be avoided?**
    There are several situations where HDFS may not be a suitable fit, such as the following:
    HDFS is unsuitable for storing data for applications that require fast data access. Because the information for each file must be saved on the NameNode and retained in memory, HDFS is not appropriate for storing many tiny files. In addition, HDFS isn't designed for instances when multiple/simultaneous writes to the same file are required.

Essay-type Questions

1. What is Virtualization? Why do we use Hypervisor? Explain its two types.
2. Write notes on HDFS Command Line Interface.
3. Explain JPS Command, List of Files Command, File Management commands, Upload and Download commands, and Changing the ownership of the files of HDFS.
4. Compare and contrast VMware and Virtual Box.
5. Explain Hadoop V1.0 Ecosystem with HDFS.
6. Explain various HDFS Features.
7. Explain HDFS Architecture and its various components in detail.
8. Explain the HDFS Read Request process in detail.
9. Explain HDFS Write Request in detail.
10. Explain HDFS blocks formation, data replication, and rack awareness in detail.
11. Explain the Data Integrity and Data Locality concept of HDFS.
12. Explain Data Distributed Cache and Serialization concept in HDFS.
13. Explain the concept of writing a file to HDFS using a Java program.
14. Explain the concept of connecting to HDFS using Python.

CHAPTER 7

MapReduce

> **LEARNING OBJECTIVES**
>
> In the previous chapters we had discussed about HDFS (Hadoop Distributed File System), which is an important component of the Hadoop ecosystem. In this chapter, we will discuss about the next important core component of the Hadoop ecosystem, MapReduce. We will discuss about the anatomy of a MapReduce job run, failures, job scheduling, shuffle and sort, task execution, MapReduce types and formats, and MapReduce features.

7.1 Introduction

MapReduce is a parallel processing technique for processing data, particularly Big Data, distributed on a commodity cluster. Suppose that we have a large file, say a few Tera Bytes in size, it will take a long time if we process it serially from top to bottom. On the other hand, MapReduce is designed to process our data in parallel. Our file of Tera Bytes size is broken into chunks and processed in parallel. MapReduce is frequently used to speed up computation by breaking the file down into smaller files and simultaneously solving each smaller file in parallel using multiple computers or CPUs.

If somebody asks you to count the number of words in the whole of a newspaper, how will you do it? You will count the words for each paragraph, thereby for each page. And then, you will sum up the numbers on each page. That is a simple process. However, it may take much time considering the number of pages. Assume that the newspaper has ten pages. Now, if we assign ten people to do the same job by, say, giving one page to each person, it may now take lesser time than when the words are counted by a single person. Let us assume that there are five paragraphs on each page. There are fifty paragraphs (because there are ten pages in total). Now, fifty people are allocated to count the words in each paragraph. So, it may now take much lesser time than that taken by ten persons, earlier. This is the concept behind MapReduce.

Suppose a job is assigned to a single computer to process Big Data; it may take time to analyze and display the result. Instead, when we bring in multiple computers, the job could be broken down into smaller chunks. If we give each computer one of these chunks to process individually but in parallel with other computers, the job will be done faster and quicker. This parallel processing is the logic behind MapReduce.

As the business grows, it can be challenging to understand what the customers need and identify patterns in the saved data. This is where MapReduce comes in. This technique can be used to sift through oceans of information and find those important nuggets that will propel the customer's business forward. MapReduce is a programming model and an associated implementation for processing and generating large datasets with a parallel, distributed algorithm on a cluster. First developed at Google, MapReduce is a paradigm for distributed Big Data processing on large clusters. Hadoop's open-source software has become increasingly popular and is being widely implemented based on this programming model. As organizations continue to work with Big Data, MapReduce offers a way to tackle large amounts of data.

The "MapReduce System" (also called "infrastructure" or "framework") orchestrates the processing by marshaling the distributed servers, running the various tasks in parallel, managing all communications and data transfers between the different parts of the system, and providing solutions for redundancy and fault tolerance.

7.2 MAPREDUCE FEATURES

MapReduce, Yarn and Spark are the tools of the processing layer of Hadoop (Fig. 7.1).

Hadoop ecosystem				
Ingestion	Storage	Processing	Analysis	Management and coordination
Apache Sqoop (RDBMS connector)	HDFS (Structured data)	MapReduce (Data processing)	Pig (Scripting)	ZooKeeper Apache Ambari Cloudera manager Map R control system Hortonworks Oozie (Workflow monitoring)
Apache Flume (Data collection)	HBASE (Unstructured, columnar store)	Yarn (Cluster resource mgmt)	Hive (SQL query)	
Apache Kafka (Streaming)	Mongo DB	Spark	Spark SQL	
Apache Impala	Apache Cassandra		Spark GraphX	
Apache NiFi			Apache Mahout (Machine learning)	
Storm (Streaming)			Tableau (Visualization)	
Change data capture (CDC)			Drill (Interactive analytics)	

Figure 7.1 Hadoop ecosystem

Big Data on Hadoop HDFS is not typically stored in a single place. Instead, the information is broken into pieces and stored in DataNodes. As a result, all data is not kept in a single area. Thus, a native client program such as Java or other similar applications will be unable to process the data in its original structure, necessitating the development of a custom framework capable of processing the fragmented data blocks contained in the corresponding DataNodes. Hadoop MapReduce processing is used to complete the task (Fig. 7.2).

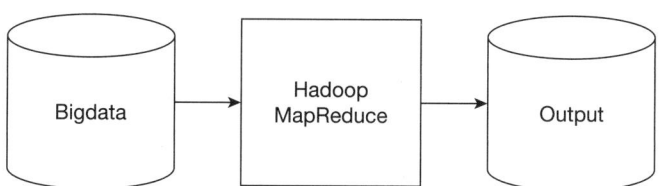

Figure 7.2 Hadoop MapReduce basic architecture

MapReduce is a programming model that processes and analyzes huge datasets logically into separate clusters. While Map sorts the data, Reduce segregates the data into logical clusters. Before 2004, vast amounts of data were stored on single servers; if any program ran a query, logical integration of the search results and analysis of the data was a nightmare as it took a lot of time. Google introduced MapReduce in December of 2004, and the analysis of datasets was done in less than 5 minutes rather than ten to twelve days. Queries could run simultaneously on multiple servers, search results were logically integrated, and data could be analyzed in real-time. The Unique Selling Proposition (USPs) of MapReduce is its fault tolerance and scalability. A parallel computation engine (MapReduce) distributes work across nodes responsible for mapping/reducing tasks. It works in two stages – the 'map' stage and the 'reduction' stage. A MapReduce program is composed of a `Map()` procedure that performs filtering and sorting (such as sorting students by the first name into queues, one queue for each name) and a `Reduce()` procedure that performs a summary operation (such as counting the number of students in each queue, yielding name frequencies).

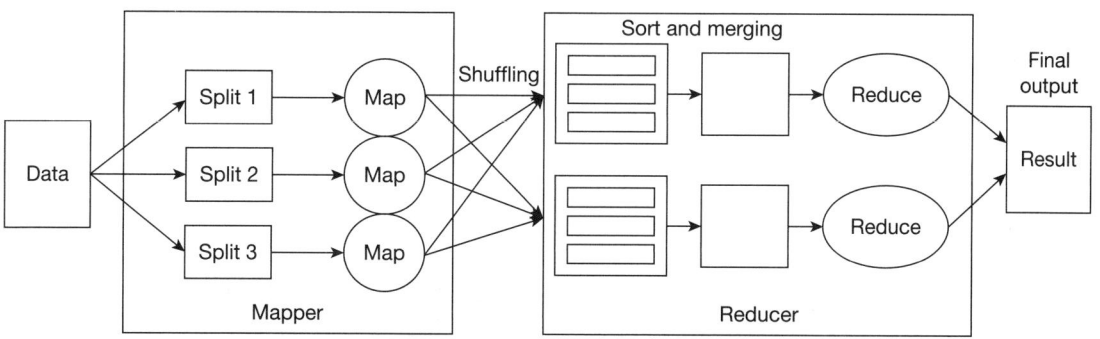

Figure 7.3 Hadoop MapReduce phases

The MapReduce framework has various options and features (Fig. 7.3) that we can use to help meet our business requirements in different ways. We can use it to examine a huge set of data and create subsets, perform advanced functions such as filtering and sorting, merge datasets, or use its automatic sorting capabilities. MapReduce is not just an approach to perform bulk actions on Big Data sets but also a gateway to enter the world of parallel programming and distributed data processing.

A MapReduce task works with a Key-Value pair; thus when we talk about a Map, we're talking about a Map that accepts a Key-Value as input and returns a list of Key-Value as output. This list of Key-Value pairs is shuffled, and the Reducer receives the Key input as well as a list of Values. Finally, the Reducer provides us with a list of Key-Value pairs (Fig. 7.4).

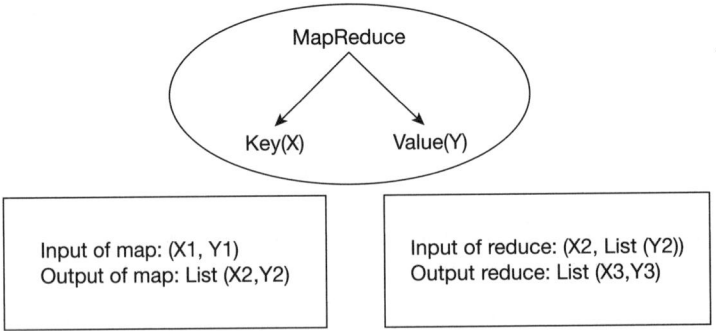

Figure 7.4 Hadoop MapReduce Input and Output

7.3 Advantages of MapReduce

This technique has two distinct benefits, namely, Parallel Processing and Data Locality.

Parallel Processing

Parallel processing is the first benefit. We can always process the data in parallel using MapReduce. As seen in Fig. 7.5, there are four Slave Machines, each of which has some data. The data is processed in parallel using Hadoop MapReduce, which speeds up the process. What occurs here is that Hadoop HDFS divides the entire chunk of data into HDFS Blocks, which are then processed by MapReduce, resulting in faster processing.

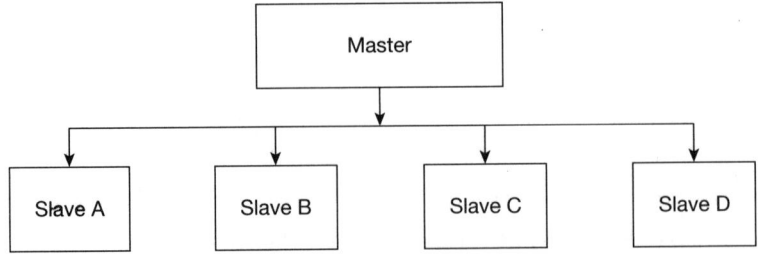

Figure 7.5 Hadoop MapReduce parallel processing

Data Locality

Hadoop MapReduce provides a flexible feature in that it allows us to process data regardless of its location. The data we moved into the Hadoop cluster is separated into HDFS blocks, and then saved in Slave Machines or DataNodes. MapReduce detects and routes processing and logic to the appropriate Slave Nodes or DataNodes, where the data is stored as HDFS blocks (Fig. 7.6).

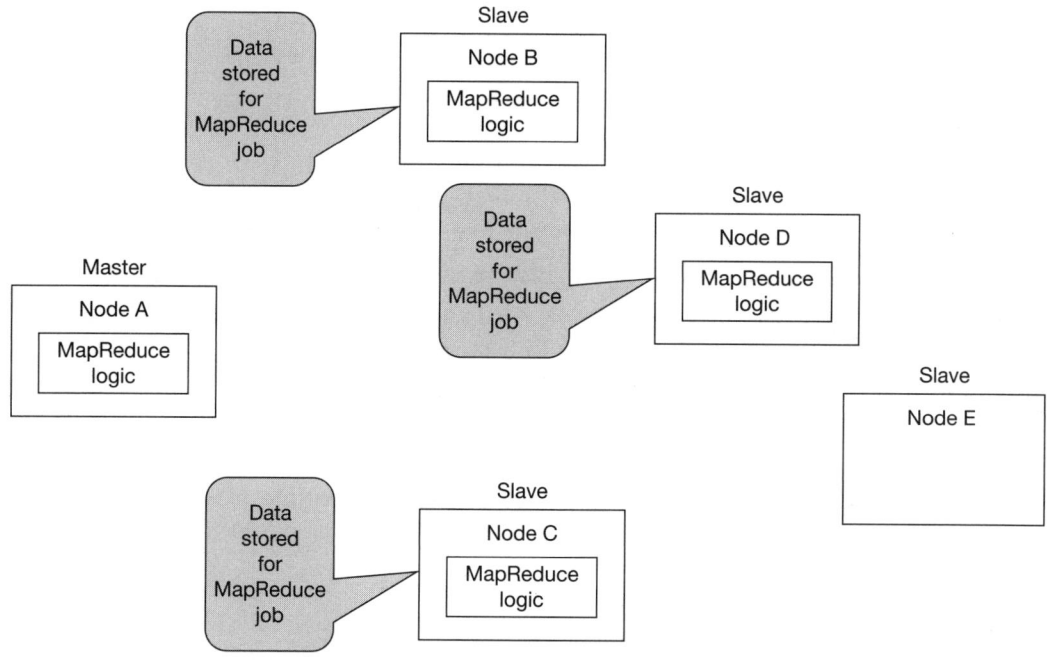

Figure 7.6 Hadoop MapReduce data locality

The processing is carried out in parallel on a smaller amount of data in various places. This saves a significant amount of time and network bandwidth necessary to transport Big Data from one location to another. However, remember that the data we are processing is Big Data broken down into pieces. If we move the Big Data directly over the network channels into a centralized computer and process it, we will lose (block) all of the network bandwidth.

So, when we use Hadoop MapReduce, we are not just "Parallel Processing", we're also processing the data on the appropriate Slave Nodes or DataNodes where the chunks of data are located, thus saving a lot of "Network Bandwidth", which is quite helpful. Then, finally, the Slave Machines finish processing the data stored on the Slave Machines and transfer the results back to the Master Machine because the results are not as large as the blocks saved on the Slave Machines. As a result, it will not consume much bandwidth.

The Slave Machines return the result to the Master Machine, which aggregates the results and sends the final result to the Client Machine that submitted the task.

7.4 A REAL-WORLD PROBLEM

Let us take a real-world problem and see how to solve it. "A Big Online Store" wants to calculate its total sales city-wise for 2021 in India. The details are stored in the below format (Table 7.1):

Table 7.1 MapReduce Real-world Problem: A Big Online Store: Basic data

S. No	Date	City Name	Amount
1	12/01/2021	Chennai	12,20,500
2	15/01/2021	Trichy	50,10,450
3	02/02/2021	Coimbatore	12,325
4	03/03/2021	Madurai	14,500

In a traditional computing environment, how will we solve this problem? We may be using a hash table, where the key is the city name and the amount is the value, but if we run the terabyte of data, which "A Big Online Store" has, it will take a long time to read and process it. It may also run out of memory because of the massive amount of data. So, the better approach may be to split the data into smaller parts or blocks and store them in different machines. Then, we will find the total sales for each city stored in the corresponding machine and in the end, we will combine the results from each machine to get the final output. But first, let us look at the challenges associated with the traditional approach:

Critical path problem: The time it takes to complete the project without postponing the following milestone or the actual completion date is the critical path problem. As a result, if one of the machines causes a delay, the entire process will be delayed.

Problem of reliability: What if one of the machines handling a portion of the data fails? It becomes difficult to take this failover.

Equal-split issue: How can we break down the data into smaller chunks so that each computer has an equal amount of data? In other words, how to distribute the data evenly such that no single system is overburdened or underused.

Single-split failure: We won't be able to compute the outcome if any of the machines fails to produce output. As a result, there should be a method to assure the system's fault tolerance capabilities.

Aggregation of the result: A method needs to be in place to aggregate the results generated by each machine.

We have the MapReduce framework to address reliability, split issue, and split failure. MapReduce enables us to do parallel calculations without worrying about dependability and fault tolerance issues. As a result, MapReduce allows us to build code logic without worrying about the system's architecture difficulties.

Because of this reason, "A Big Online Store" wants to use the MapReduce technique to solve this problem. There are two phases in the MapReduce job: the Map phase and the Reduce phase. It splits the whole data into chunks based on months. Each mapper gets the data for one month, so we have 12 mappers who get the data for each month. And they work on it in parallel at the same time.

The first map will give the first record as the name of the city and the value of sales and write it on the index card (Fig. 7.7). They get the data for the same city on the same pile as they pile up. Now, the mapper job is over. The output of the mapper will be as follows (Table 7.2).

Table 7.2 MapReduce Real-world Problem: A Big Online Store: Mapper

M1	M2	M3	M10	M11	M12
Chennai: 10 K	Chennai:11 K	Chennai: 12 K	Chennai: 9 K	Chennai: 8 K	Chennai: 12 K
Trichy: 12 K	Trichy: 6 K	Trichy: 7 K	Trichy: 7 K	Trichy: 7.1 K	Trichy: 6. 7 K
Coimbatore: 13 K	Coimbatore: 9 K	Coimbatore: 9.7 K	Coimbatore: 9.8 K	Coimbatore: 10 K	Coimbatore: 11 K
Madurai: 1 K	Madurai: 1.1 K	Madurai: 1.5 K	Madurai: 1.51 K	Madurai: 1.6 K	Madurai: 1.87 K

The reducer will get these piles of cards; we can pair each reducer with the city they are responsible for. For example, we can tell Reducer 1 that it will be responsible for Chennai. We can tell Reducer 2 that it will be accountable for Trichy. We can tell Reducer 3 that it will be responsible for Coimbatore. Finally, we can tell Reducer 4 that it will be responsible for Madurai. The reducers retrieve the piles of cards for their cities. Then, they add all values of all the cards to a pile and get the total sales per city.

MapReduce is made up of two tasks: Map and Reduce. Mapper Maps input key-value pairs to a set of intermediate key-value pairs. Maps are the individual tasks that perform input records into intermediate records. So, we say that intermediate output records index cards and mappers work in parallel. These records are key-and-value pairs. In our example, the key is a city, and value is the sales total for each particular piece of input. So, the map generates its intermediate records of key-value pairs.

After the mapper finishes, the next phase in MapReduce is called shuffling and sorting (Fig. 7.8). Shuffling is the movement of intermediate records from mappers to reducers. So, exchanging the intermediate outputs from the map tasks to where the reducers require them is called shuffling. It is the movement of records from mappers to reducers. As the term MapReduce indicates, the reduction step occurs after the mapper phase has been finished. First, the Reducer receives the output of a Mapper or a map job (key-value pairs). Then, the Reducer receives the key-value pair from numerous map tasks. The Reducer then condenses these intermediate data tuples (intermediate key-value pair) into a smaller collection of tuples or key-value pairs, which serve as the final output (Table 7.3).

364 • Big Data Analytics

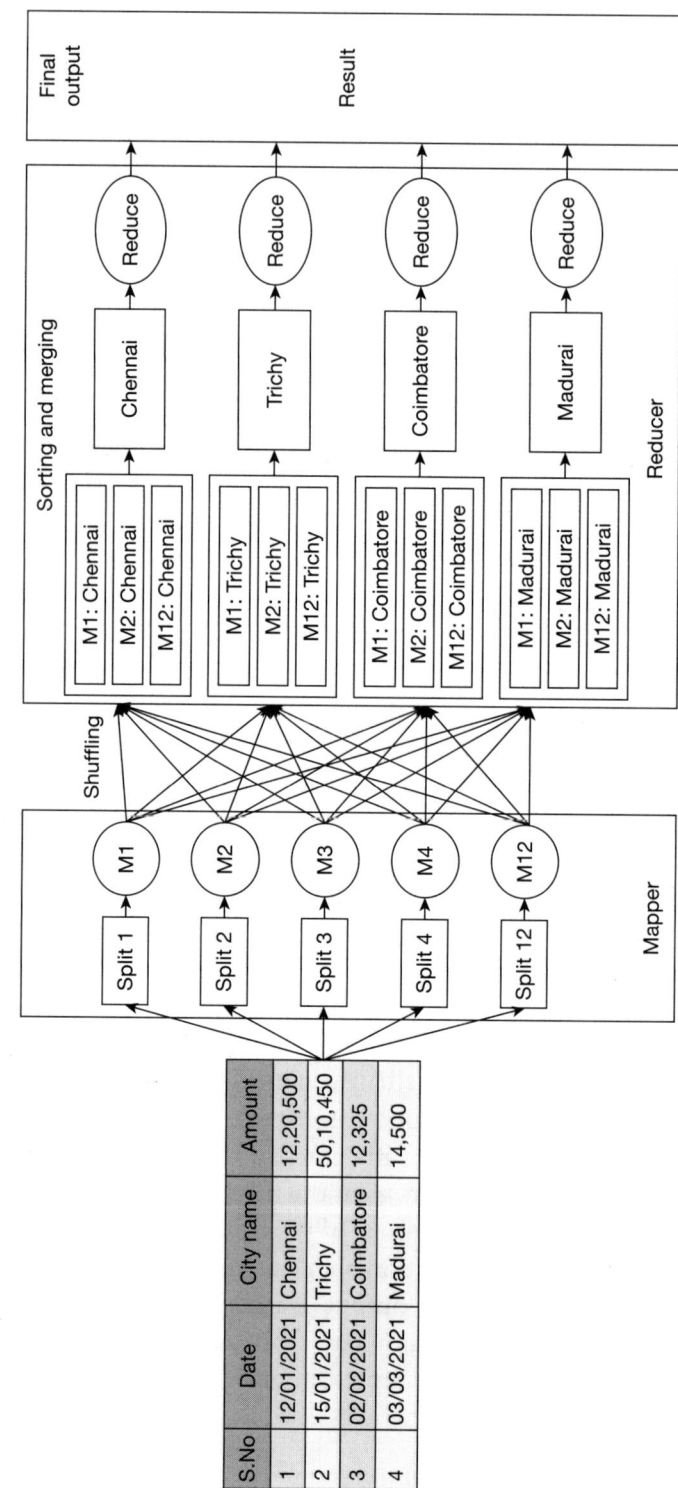

Figure 7.7 Hadoop MapReduce: A Big Online Store

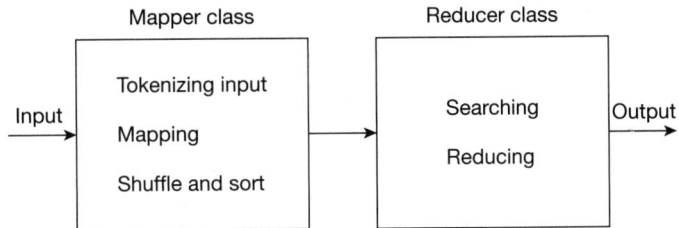

Figure 7.8 Hadoop MapReduce: Mapper and Reducer class flow

Table 7.3 MapReduce Real-world Problem: A Big Online Store: Final output

Months	Chennai (Reducer 1)	Trichy (Reducer 2)	Coimbatore (Reducer 3)	Madurai (Reducer 4)
M1	10 K	12 K	13 K	1 K
M2	11 K	6 K	9 K	1.1 K
M3	12 K	7 K	9.7 K	1.5 K
M10	9 K	7 K	9.8 K	1.51 K
M11	8 K	7.1 K	10 K	1.6 K
M12	12 K	6.7 K	11 K	1.87 K
Months	Chennai (Reducer 1)	Trichy (Reducer 2)	Coimbatore (Reducer 3)	Madurai (Reducer 4)
Total	62 K	45.8 K	62.5 K	8.58 K

The Mapper class is the initial step in utilizing MapReduce to process data. Record Reader processes each input record and creates the key-value pair for that record. This intermediate data is saved to the local disk by Hadoop's Mapper store. The MapReduce Program denotes a block of work that comprises a single map job.

Reducer Class: The reducer receives the intermediate output from the mapper, processes it, and creates the final output, which is then saved in HDFS.

Driver Class: Driver Class is the most important part of a MapReduce task. It is in charge of configuring a MapReduce job to run in Hadoop. We provide Mapper and Reducer Class names that are lengthy and include data types and task names.

7.5 REAL-TIME USE CASES OF MAPREDUCE

MapReduce is designed to handle very-large-scale data in petabytes and terabytes. It works well on write-once and read-many datasets. MapReduce allows parallelism. The Map and Reduce operations are performed by the same processor. These operations are provisioned near the data as data locality is preferred. In other words, we will move the application to the data and not the other way around. Commodity hardware and storage are leveraged in MapReduce to keep things cost-effective, and the runtime takes care of splitting and moving data for operations. Some of the real-time uses of MapReduce are as follows:

Data-intensive computing would include sorting large and small sets of data/stream data and structured data. Data mining operations include probabilistic approaches such as Bayes classification. Search engine operations include the rendering of keywords in the scene and page ranking. Enterprise analytics ensures the business is operating smoothly and with the best decision-making data available. Gaussian analysis for locating extra-terrestrial objects in astronomy uses very large datasets and semantic Web and Web 3.0.

7.6 MAPREDUCE PHASES

Let us look at an example, the MapReduce Word Count Process, in order to understand the MapReduce Phases.

7.6.1 Splitting

As per the diagram (Fig. 7.9), we have an Input from HDFS, and this Input gets divided into various Inputs. This process is called Input Splitting, and the entire Input gets divided into splits of data based on the new line character.

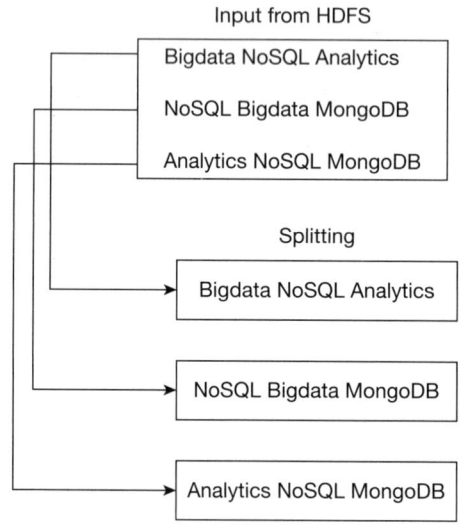

Figure 7.9 Hadoop MapReduce: Word count program: Splitting

Input Files: Input files hold the data for a MapReduce process, and input files are commonly kept in HDFS. The format of these files can be whatever you choose, including line-based log files and binary forms.

Input Format: It specifies how these input files should be divided and read. It chooses the files or other objects that will be utilized as Input. Input Format creates Input Split.

Input Split: Input Format creates Input Split to properly represent the data processed by a single Mapper (we will understand the mapper below). Each split gets its map task; therefore, the total number of map tasks equals the total number of input split. Finally, the split is separated into records, and the mapper will process each record individually.

Record Reader: It talks with Hadoop MapReduce's Input Split and turns data into key-value pairs that the mapper can read. By default, text input format is used to turn Input into a key-value pair. The Record Reader talks with the Input Split until the file reading is finished. Each line in the file is given a byte offset (a unique integer). These key-value pairs are then passed to the mapper to be processed further.

The first line is the first Input, i.e., **Bigdata NoSQL Analytics**. The second line is the second Input, i.e., **NoSQL Bigdata MongoDB**; similarly, the third Input is **Analytics NoSQL MongoDB**.

7.6.2 Mapping Phase

The assigned input split is read from HDFS, where split could be a file block by default. Furthermore input is parsed into records, as key-value pairs. The map function is applied to each record to return 0 or more new records (Fig. 7.10). These intermediate outputs are stored in the local file system as a file. They are sorted first by bucket number, and then by a key. At the end of the map phase, information is sent to the master node after its completion.

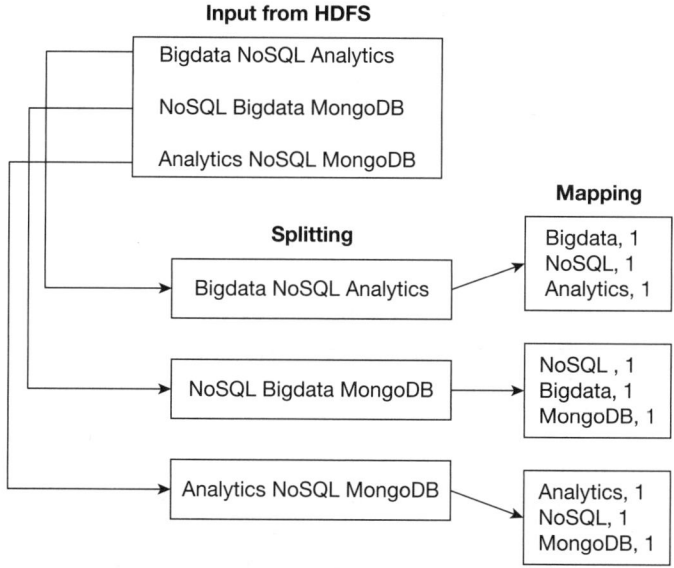

Figure 7.10 Hadoop MapReduce: Word count program: Mapping

Mapper: Each input record (from Record Reader) is processed and a new key-value pair is created by Mapper, which is entirely distinct from the input pair. Mapper's output is referred to as intermediate output because it is written to the local disk. The Mapper's output is not kept on HDFS since it is transitory data, and uploading to HDFS would result in redundant copies (also, HDFS is a high-latency system). The output of the mapper is transferred to the combiner for additional processing.

Combiner: The 'Mini-reducer' is another name for the Combiner. Hadoop MapReduce Combiner conducts local aggregation on mappers' output, reducing data travel between the mapper and reducer (we will see Reducer below). Following the completion of the combiner function, the output is handed to the partitioner for further processing.

Partitioner: If we are working on more than one reducer in Hadoop MapReduce, Partitioner comes into play (partitioner is not used if there is only one reducer). The output of the combiners is sent into the partitioner, which partitions the data. The output is partitioned and then sorted on the basis of the key. The partition is determined using the hash function and the key (or a subset of the key). Each combiner output is partitioned in MapReduce based on the key value, with a record with the same key value going into the same partition, and then each partition is delivered to a reducer. Partitioning allows the map output to be distributed evenly throughout the reduction.

When each line passes through the Mapping Function, the mapping will create the list of key-value pairs. **For Example,** in **Bigdata**, the function will read every word of the line and will mark one (1) after the comma. It will mark one (1) as a Value, like **Bigdata, 1 NoSQL, 1 and Analytics, 1**. Here the question is, why are we putting one (1) after each word? It is because **Bigdata** is one count, so **Bigdata, 1**. Similarly, **NoSQL, 1** and **Analytics, 1** have one count; that is why we mark one (1) as a value. Similarly, for second-line or say, line 2, we have **NoSQL Bigdata MongoDB**. In the same fashion, the Mapping Function again creates the list of key-value pairs for it, and thus as per the count, the key-value pair list will be **NoSQL,1 Bigdata,1** and **MongoDB,1**. We will get the same as the Mapping Function for line 3, i.e., **Analytics, 1 NoSQL, 1** and **MongoDB,1**.

7.6.3 Shuffling

The output is shuffled and sent to the reduction node (a normal slave node, but the reduce phase will run here; hence it is called a reducer node). The shuffle (Fig. 7.11) refers to the physical movement of data through a network. Once the mappers have completed their work, their output would have been shuffled on the reducer nodes; the intermediate result is combined and sorted before being sent into the reduce phase.

In this phase, for every key, there is a list prepared. So the shuffling step will find the appearance of Key **Bigdata**, and it will add the values to the list. Let us see what is happening here. As we can see, there are two incoming arrows, the first arrow comes from List 1, and another arrow is from List 2, so the result will be **Bigdata (1, 1)**.

Similarly, when we see the word **NoSQL**, another list will be prepared for Values again for NoSQL. As we can see, three incoming arrows point to Shuffling, which means the word **NoSQL** will be picked up from List 1, List 2 and List 3, respectively, i.e., the final result after Shuffling will be **NoSQL, (1, 1, 1)**.

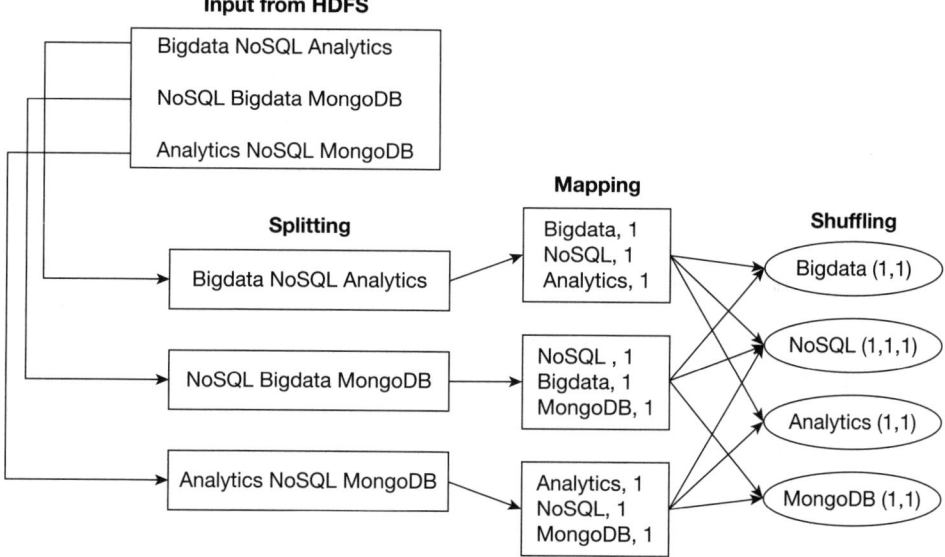

Figure 7.11 Hadoop MapReduce: Word count program: Shuffling

In the same fashion, we will get the rest of the words like **Analytics (1, 1)** and **MongoDB (1, 1)** along with their list of Values or say, the list of Count as per the availability of words in the respective lists.

In the Sort phase, a merge sort of all map outputs occurs in a single run and finally in the reduced phase, a user-defined reduced function is applied to the merged run. The arguments are the keys and the corresponding list of values. The output is written to a file in HDFS. The mappers on each of the nodes are assigned to each input split.

7.6.4 Reducing Phase

The reducing phase takes the collection of intermediate key-value pairs generated by the mappers as input and applies a reducer function to each of them to produce the output. The reducer's output is the final output saved in HDFS (Fig. 7.12).

The intermediate outputs are stored in the local file system; a partitioner then assigns the records to the reducer. In the shuffling phase, the intermediate key-value pairs are exchanged by all nodes. The key-value pairs are then sorted by applying the key and reduced function. Again, the output is stored in HDFS based on the specified output file format. The job input is specified in key-value pairs. Each job consists of two stages. First, a user-defined map function is applied to each input record to produce a list of intermediate key-value pairs. Second, a user-defined reduced function is called once for each key to stay in the map output. Then the list of intermediate values associated with that key is passed. The essentials of each MapReduce phase are as follows; first, the

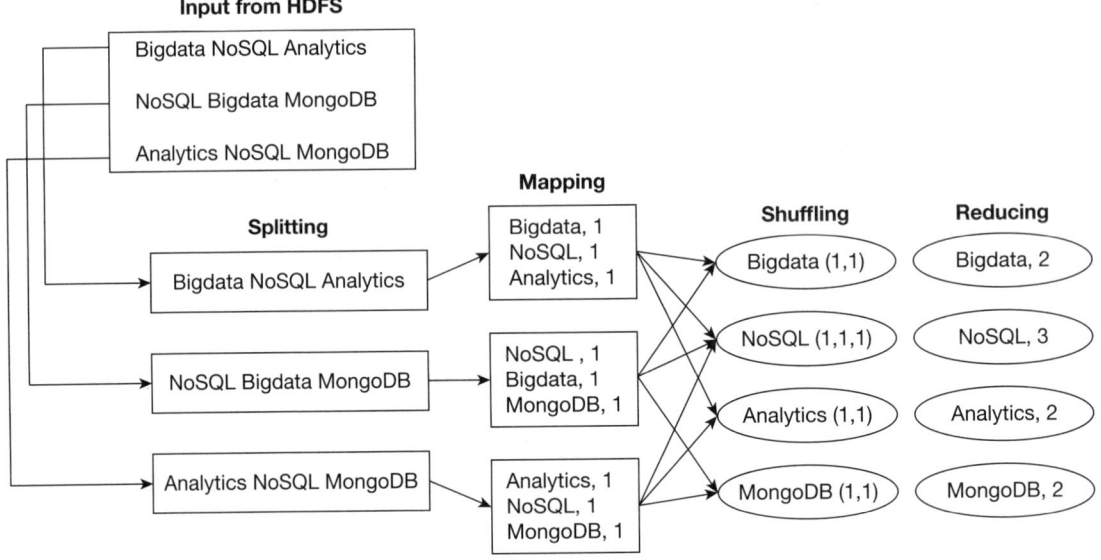

Figure 7.12 Hadoop MapReduce: Word count program: Reducing

number of reduced tasks can be defined by the users; second, each reduced task is assigned a set or record groups that are intermediate records corresponding to a group of keys; third, for each group, a user-defined reduced function is applied to the recorded values and the reduced tasks are read from every map task. Each read returns the record groups for the respective reduce tasks.

Reduce phase cannot start until all mappers have finished processing. So, combining the output is an essential step, once all the tasks are completed.

Now come to the Reducing Phase in our example; in this phase, we start aggregating the Values present in the list against every Key. So for **Bigdata**, there are two values present in the list, i.e., **(1, 1)** and these values will be submitted, so **Bigdata, 2**. Similarly, for **NoSQL**, the Value will be sum, i.e., **(1, 1, 1)** and the submission will be **NoSQL, 3**. Similarly, for **Analytics** and **MongoDB**; the submission for Reducing Function will be **Analytics, 2** and **MongoDB, 2**, respectively.

The OutputFormat determines how these output key-value pairs are written in output files by RecordWriter. Hadoop's OutputFormat instances write files to HDFS or the local disk. As a result, OutputFormat instances write the reducer's final output to HDFS.

The final result will be sent to the customer, as shown in Fig. 7.13.

To summarize, data flow in MapReduce involves the combination of many processing phases such as Input Files, Hadoop InputFormat, InputSplits, RecordReader, Mapper, Combiner, Partitioner, Shuffling and Sorting, Reducer, RecordWriter, and OutputFormat. As a result, all of these components are critical to Hadoop MapReduce operation.

MapReduce • 371

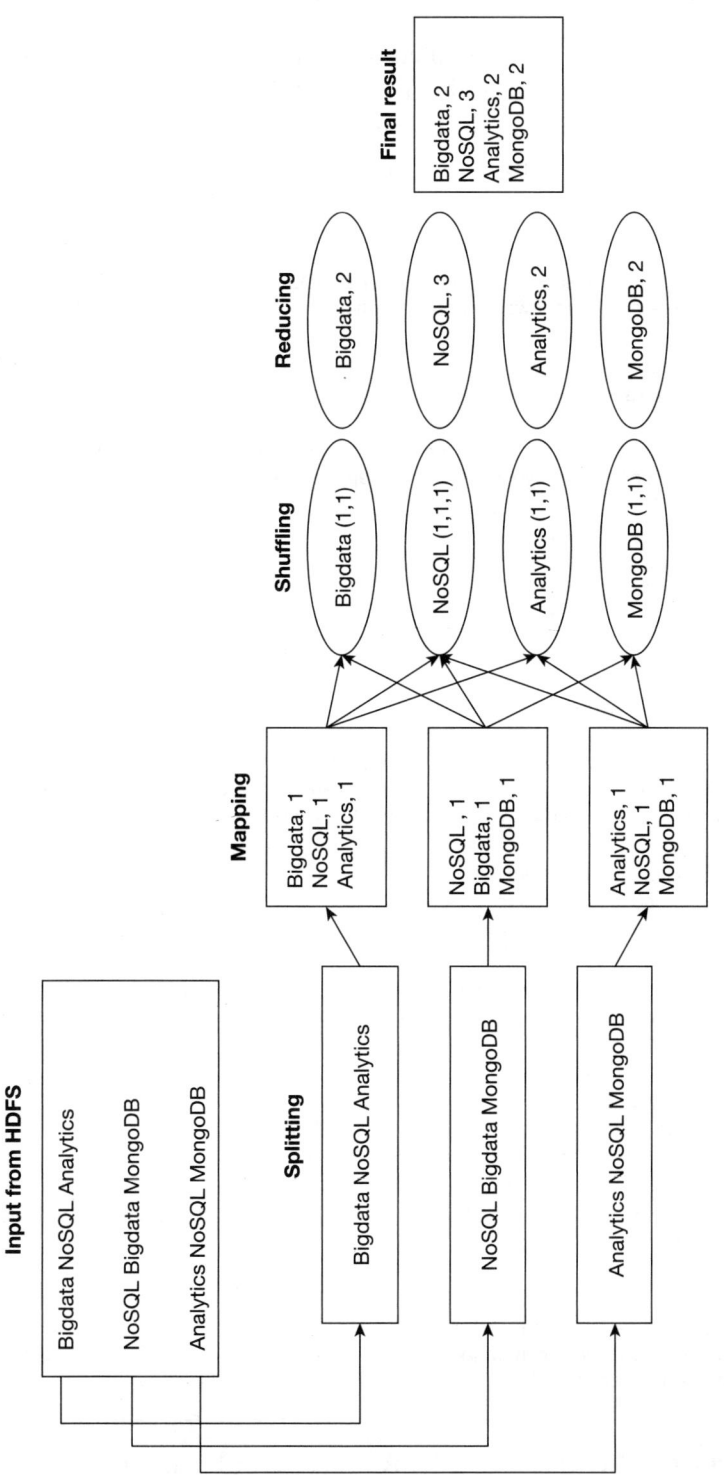

Figure 7.13 Hadoop MapReduce: Word count program: Final result

7.7 PROGRAMMING FOR WORD COUNT EXAMPLE

It is better to use Eclipse, that is installed by default in Cloudera, to run the Java program as it has sophisticated futures to upload external libraries. Let us look into the details of import package in the Word Count Java Program. We are using Java native packages only in two places: IO Exception to handle Input Output Exception and the Regex Pattern, which is helpful to extract words from input files (Fig. 7.14).

```
//The only standard Java classes you need to import are IOException and regex.Pattern.
//You use regex.Pattern to extract words from input files.

import java.io.IOException;
import java.util.regex.Pattern;

//This application extends the class Configured, and implements the Tool utility class.
//Then, we use ToolRunner to run your MapReduce application.

 import org.apache.hadoop.conf.Configured;
 import org.apache.hadoop.util.Tool;
 import org.apache.hadoop.util.ToolRunner;

//The Logger class sends debugging messages from inside the mapper and reducer classes.

import org.apache.log4j.Logger;

//We need the Job class to create, configure, and run an instance of  MapReduce application.
//We extend the Mapper class with your own Mapclass and add your own processing instructions.
//We extend Reduce class to create and customize our own Reduce class.

import org.apache.hadoop.mapreduce.Job;
 import org.apache.hadoop.mapreduce.Mapper;
 import org.apache.hadoop.mapreduce.Reducer;

//Use the Path class to access files in HDFS.
//In your job configuration instructions, you pass required paths using the FileInputFormat and FileOutputFormat classes.

import org.apache.hadoop.fs.Path;
 import org.apache.hadoop.mapreduce.lib.input.FileInputFormat;
 import org.apache.hadoop.mapreduce.lib.output.FileOutputFormat;

//Writable objects have convenience methods for writing, reading, and comparing values during map and reduce processing.
//You can think of the Text class as StringWritable

import org.apache.hadoop.io.IntWritable;
 import org.apache.hadoop.io.LongWritable;
 import org.apache.hadoop.io.Text;
```

Figure 7.14 Hadoop MapReduce: Word count program: Part 1

The main class named "WordCount" extends the Configured Class (for Hadoop configuration) and it also implements Tool Class (from Hadoop util package): Refer Fig. 7.15.

```
//WordCount includes main and run methods, and the inner classes Map andReduce.
//The class begins by initializing the logger.

public class WordCount extends Configured implements Tool {

  private static final Logger LOG = Logger.getLogger(WordCount.class);

//The main method invokes ToolRunner,

  public static void main(String[] args) throws Exception {
    int res = ToolRunner.run(new WordCount(), args);
    System.exit(res);
  }


//The run method configures the job

public int run(String[] args) throws Exception {

//Create a new instance of the Job object.

Job job = Job.getInstance(getConf(), "Wordcount");

//Set the JAR to use, based on the class in use.

job.setJarByClass(this.getClass());

//Set the input and output paths for your application.

    FileInputFormat.addInputPaths(job, args[0]);
    FileOutputFormat.setOutputPath(job, new Path(args[1]));

//Set the map class and reduce class for the job

    job.setMapperClass(Map.class);
    job.setReducerClass(Reduce.class);

//Use a Text object to output the key

    job.setOutputKeyClass(Text.class);
    job.setOutputValueClass(IntWritable.class);

//In Unix, 0 indicates success, and anything other than 0 indicates a failure.

    return job.waitForCompletion(true) ? 0 : 1;
}
```

Figure 7.15 Hadoop MapReduce: Word count program: Part 2

The map class extends Mapper Class. It splits the overall file based on the pattern specified. When each line passes through the Mapping Function, the mapping will create the list of key-value pairs (Fig. 7.16).

```
//The Map class (an extension of Mapper) transforms key/value input into intermediate key/value pairs

  public static class Map extends Mapper<LongWritable, Text, Text, IntWritable> {
    private final static IntWritable one = new IntWritable(1);
    private Text word = new Text();

//Create a regular expression pattern you can use to parse each line of input text on word boundaries

    private static final Pattern WORD_BOUNDARY = Pattern.compile("\\s*\\b\\s*");

//Hadoop invokes the map method once for every key/value pair from your input source.

    public void map(LongWritable offset, Text lineText, Context context)
        throws IOException, InterruptedException{

//Convert the Text object to a string.

      String line = lineText.toString();
      Text currentWord = new Text();

//Use the regular expression pattern to split the line into individual words based on word boundaries.

      for ( String word : WORD_BOUNDARY.split(line)) {
        if (word.isEmpty()) {
          continue;
        }
        currentWord = new Text(word);
        context.write(currentWord,one);
      }
    }
  }
```

Figure 7.16 Hadoop MapReduce: Word count program: Part 3

Now come to the Reducing Phase; in this phase, we start aggregating the values present in the list against every key (Fig. 7.17).

```
//The reducer processes each pair, adding one to the count for the current word in the key/value pair to the overall count of that word from all mappers

  public static class Reduce extends Reducer<Text, IntWritable, Text, IntWritable> {
    @Override public void reduce(Text word, Iterable<IntWritable> counts, Context context)
        throws IOException, InterruptedException{
      int sum = 0;
      for (IntWritablecount : counts) {
        sum += count.get();
      }
      context.write(word, new IntWritable(sum));
    }
  }
}
```

Figure 7.17 Hadoop MapReduce: Word count program: Part 4

7.8 HOW TO RUN THE WORD COUNT EXAMPLE

First, we need to create a structure as shown in Fig. 7.18 in order to run the Word Count Program. We need to create a directory called Wordcount_classess and a sub-directory below that titled "org".

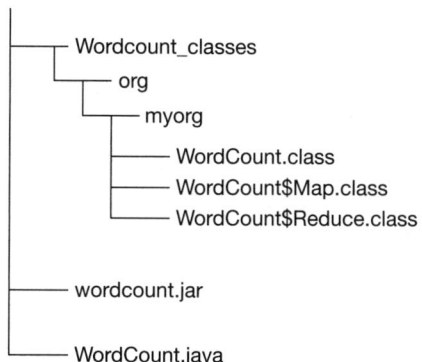

Figure 7.18 Hadoop MapReduce: Word count program: Directory structure

The following command is run in order to create a jar file (wordcount.jar).

```
$ jar -cvf wordcount.jar -C wordcount_classes/ .
added manifest
```

We create the input directory /user/cloudera/wordcount/input: by logging in as HDFS super user and giving permission to the folders created.

```
$ sudo su hdfs
$ hadoop fs -mkdir /user/cloudera
$ hadoop fs -chown hdfs /user/cloudera

$ hadoop fs -mkdir /user/cloudera/wordcount /user/cloudera/wordcount/input
```

We create three files: file0, file1 and file2, with the contents as below. Then, we move these files into the HDFS input directory.

```
$ echo "Bigdata NoSQL Analytics" > file0
$ echo "NoSQL Bigdata MongoDB" > file1
$ echo "Analytics NoSQL MongoDB" > file2

$ sudo su hdfs
$ hadoop fs -put file* /user/cloudera/wordcount/input
```

We will then take this sentence through the corresponding steps of splitting, mapping, shuffling, and reducing. The MapReduce process begins with the input phase, which refers to providing data for which the MapReduce process is performed. The next step is the splitting phase, which refers to converting a job submitted by the client into several tasks. In this example, the job is split into tasks, one for each sentence. Then the mapping phase refers to generating a key-value pair for the input; since this example is about counting words, the sentence is now split into words by using the substring method to generate words from lines. The mapping phase will ensure that the words generated are converted into keys, and a default value of 1 is allotted to each key or word in the sentence in the next step. The shuffling phase refers to sorting the data based on these keys, the words sorted into ascending order. The last phase is the reducing phase; in this phase, the data is reduced based on the repeated keys by incrementing the value of each key, where there is a duplicate word.

The word "Bigdata" is repeated; therefore, the reducer will delete the key and increase the value depending on the number of occurrences of the key.

We can run the wordcount program with the below command:

```
$ sudo su hdfs
$ hadoop jar wordcount.jar org.myorg.WordCount /user/cloudera/wordcount/input /user/cloudera/wordcount/output
```

When we examine the output folder, there is a new file created (part-r-00000). When we display its contents (using cat command), it gives the following output indicating the count of the words.

```
$ hdfs dfs -cat /user/cloudera/wordcount/output/part-r-00000
Analytics 2
Bigdata 2
MongoDB 2
NoSQL 3
```

1. The map method of the Mapper implementation processes one line of input at a time. The StringTokenizer breaks the line into tokens separated by whitespace and produces a key-value pair of <word, one>.
   - The 1st map emits: <Bigdata, 1> <NoSQL, 1> <Analytics, 1>
   - The 2nd map emits: <NoSQL, 1> <Bigdata, 1> <MongoDB, 1>
   - The 3rd map emits: <Analytics, 1> <NoSQL, 1> <MongoDB, 1>
2. Wordcount also specifies a combiner. Hence, the output of each map is passed through the local combiner (which is the same as the Reducer as per the job configuration) for local aggregation, after being sorted on the keys.
3. The Reducer implements the Reduce method to sum up the values and the occurrence counts for each key. So, the output of the job is:
   <Analytics, 2> <Bigdata, 2> <MongoDB, 2> <NoSQL, 2>.
4. The Run method specifies various facets of the job such as the input/output paths (passed via the command line), key-value types, input/output formats, etc., in the JobConf. It then calls the JobClient.runJob to submit the job and monitor its progress.

7.9 MapReduce Job

A job is a MapReduce program (class) that causes multiple Map and Reduce functions to run parallel over the life of the program. Many copies of Map and many copies of Reduce functions are forked for parallel processing, across the input dataset. Table 7.4 lists the various methods and their descriptions of MapReduce job.

Table 7.4 MapReduce class methods

Methods	Description
Counters getCounters()	This method is used to get the counters for the job.
long getFinishTime()	This method is used to get the finish time for the job.
Job getInstancel()	This method is used to generate a new Job without any cluster.
Job getInstance(Configuraton conf)	This method is used to generate a new Job without any cluster and provided configuration.
Job getlnstance(Configuraton conf, String jobName)	This method is used to generate a new Job without any cluster and provided configuration and job name.
String geJobfile()	This method is used to get the path of the submitted job configuration.
String geJobName()	This method is used to get the user-specified job name.
JobPriority getPriority()	This method is used to get the scheduling function of the job.
void setJarByClass(Class< ?>c)	This method is used to set the job by providing the class name with .class extension.
void setJobName(String name)	This method is used to set the user-specified job name.
void setMapOutputKeyClas;(Class<?>class)	This method is used to set the key class for the map output data.
void setMapOutputValueClass(Class<?>class)	This method is used to set the value class for the map output data.
void setMapperClass(Class<? extends Mapper> class)	This method is used to set the Mapper for the job.
void setNumReduceTasks(int tasks)	This method is used to set the number of reduce tasks for the job
void setReducerClass(Class<?extends Reducer> class)	This method is used to set the Reducer Class

A task is a Map or Reduce function executed on a subset of this data. With this understanding of jobs and tasks, the application master and node manager functions become easier to comprehend. First, the application master is responsible for executing a single application or MapReduce job. It divides the job requests into tasks and assigns these tasks to node managers running on one or more slave nodes. The node manager has several dynamically created resource containers. The size of a container depends on the number of resources it contains, such as memory, CPU disk, and network i/o. It executes map and reduce tasks by launching these containers when instructed by the MapReduce application master, MapReduce, and associated tasks. The mapping process is an initial step in processing individual input records. Node managers can keep track of individual map tasks and run them in parallel. A map job runs as a part of a container execution by the node manager on a particular data node. Within a cluster, the application master keeps track of a MapReduce job. A Hadoop MapReduce job is submitted by a client in the form of an input file or several input splits of files containing data. The MapReduce application master will distribute the input split to separate node managers. The MapReduce application master then coordinates with these node managers and will resubmit the task to an alternative node manager if any given data node should fail. The resource manager gathers the final output and informs the client of the success or failure status.

7.10 HADOOP MAPPER

Each input record is processed by the Mapper job, which creates new key-value pairs. The key-value pairings do not have to be identical to the input pair. The result of the mapper job is the whole collection of these key-value pairs. Before publishing the output for each mapper task, the output is partitioned according to the key and sorted. All the values for each key are clustered together in this partitioning. Each input split created by the job's input format creates one map task in the MapReduce frame. Data must first be turned into key-value pairs before being sent to the Mapper because the latter understands only key-value pairs. Table 7.5 lists down various methods and descriptions of the Hadoop mapper class.

Table 7.5 Mapper class methods

Methods	Description
void cleanup(Context context)	This method can be called only once at the end of the task.
void map(KEYIN key, VALUEIN value, Context context)	This method can be called only once for each key-value in the input split.
void run(Context context)	This method can be overridden to control the execution of the Mapper.
void setup(Context context)	This method can be called only once at the beginning of the task.

Let us take a look at how Hadoop generates key-value pairs.

The logical representation of data is called InputSplit. A MapReduce application refers to a unit of work that comprises of a single map job. Record Reader connects with the InputSplit and turns data into key-value pairs that the Mapper can read. TextInputFormat is used by default to turn input into a key-value pair. Until the file reading is finished, the RecordReader talks with the Inputsplit. As indicated earlier, the Mapper only understands key-value pairs of data; hence, data must first be turned into key-value pairs.

Let us see how Hadoop Mapper Works:
For the Hadoop Mapper, InputSplits turns the physical representation of the block into logic. Two InputSplits are required to read a 100MB file. For each block, one InputSplit is formed, with one RecordReader and one Mapper for each InputSplit.

The number of splits for a specific file may be customized by adjusting the mapred.max.split.size parameter during job execution, which does not always rely on the number of blocks.

The RecordReader's job is to read and transform data into key-value pairs until the file is finished. RecordReader assigns a byte offset (unique number) to each line in the file. In addition, the Mapper receives this key-value pair. Intermediate data is the mapper software's output (key-value pairs that are understandable to reduce).

7.11 HADOOP REDUCER

Reducer in Hadoop takes the Mapper's output (intermediate key-value pair) and processes it to create the Reducer's output. The reducer's output is the final output saved in HDFS (Fig. 7.19).

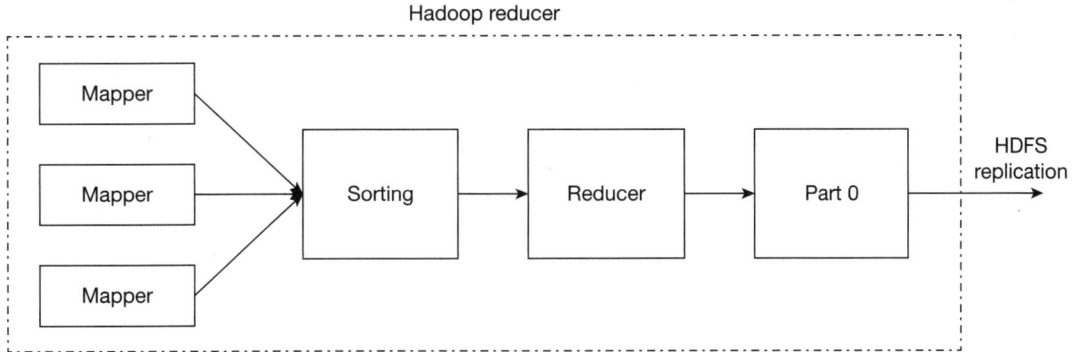

Figure 7.19 Hadoop MapReduce: Reducer

We usually conduct aggregation or summation type computations in the Hadoop Reducer. Let us now see how to modify the number of reducers in Hadoop MapReduce and how many such reducers are necessary for Hadoop. Table 7.6 lists down the methods and descriptions of the Reducer Class.

Table 7.6 Reducer class methods

Methods	Description
void cleanup(Context context)	This method can be called only once at the end of the task.
void map(KEYIN key, Iterable<VALUEIN> values, Context context)	This method can be called only once for each key.
void run(Context context)	This method can be used to control the tasks for the Reducer.
void setup(Context context)	This method can be called only once at the beginning of the task.

The Reducer processes the mapper's output. It generates a new set of outputs after processing the data. Finally, HDFS saves the output data.

Hadoop Reducer takes a collection of intermediate key-value pairs (Fig. 7.20) generated by the mapper as input and applies a Reducer function to each one. This data (key, value) may be aggregated, filtered, and combined in various ways for various processes. Reducer handles the intermediate values provided by the map function for a specific key before generating the output (zero or more key-value pairs).

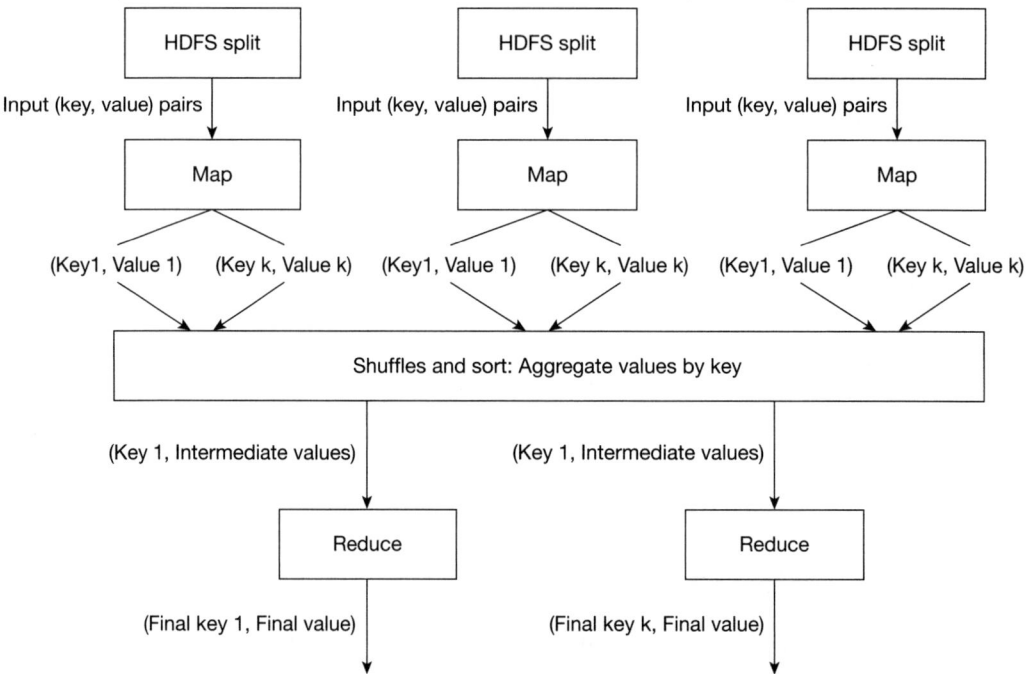

Figure 7.20 Hadoop MapReduce: Reducer – Full flow

One-to-one mapping occurs between keys and reducers. Because reducers are independent of one another, they execute in parallel. The number of reducers is determined by the user and is set to 1 by default.

Reducer Phases of MapReduce

In Hadoop MapReduce, there are three phases of Reducer: 1. Shuffle phase 2. Sort phase 3. Reduce phase

Shuffle Phase: The sorted output from the mapper is the input to the Reducer during the Shuffle Phase of the MapReduce Reducer. During the Shuffle phase, the framework uses HTTP to retrieve the appropriate division of all mappers' output.

Sort Phase: The input from multiple mappers is sorted again in this step based on related keys in distinct Mappers. The shuffle and sort processes happen at the same time.

Reduce Phase: After shuffling and sorting, the reduction job collects the key-value pairs in this step. Finally, the output of the reduction task is sent to the Filesystem using the OutputCollector.collect() function. The output of the Reducer is not sorted.

Number of Reducers

With the help of Job.setNumreduceTasks(int), the user sets the number of reducers for the job. The correct number of reducers is 0.95 or 1.75 multiplied by (<no. of nodes> * <no. of the maximum container per node>). With 0.95, all reducers immediately launch and transfer map outputs as the maps finish. With 1.75, the first round of reducers is finished by the faster nodes, and the second wave of reducers is launched, doing a much better job of load balancing.

Hadoop Reducer is the second phase of MapReduce processing. The Hadoop Reducer performs aggregation or summation computations in three stages (shuffle, sort, and reduce). As a result, HDFS saves Reducer's final output.

7.12 HADOOP KEY-VALUE PAIR

The record object that the MapReduce job gets for execution is the key-value pair. RecordReader converts data into a key-value pair by default using TextInputFormat. What is a key-value pair in MapReduce? How are key-value pairs formed in Hadoop using InputSplit and RecordReader? What is the basis for key-value pair generation in Hadoop MapReduce?

Hadoop is mainly used for data analysis. In data analysis, we look at statistical and logical strategies for describing, illustrating, and evaluating data. Hadoop works with data that is structured, unstructured, or semi-structured. When the schema is static in Hadoop, we may work directly on the column rather than keys and values; but, when the schema is not fixed, we must work on keys and values. The person examining the data chooses the keys and values, which are not fundamental aspects of the data.

Hadoop's MapReduce component is responsible for data processing. Hadoop MapReduce is a software framework that makes it simple to write applications that handle the massive amounts of organized and unstructured data contained in the Hadoop Distributed File System (HDFS). MapReduce divides the processing into two stages: the Map phase and the Reduce phase. As input and output, each step has a key-value.

Key Value Pair Generation in Mapreduce

Let us have a look at how Hadoop MapReduce generates key-value pairs (Fig. 7.21). Before delivering data to the mapper in the MapReduce process, it must first be turned into key-value pairs, as the mapper only understands key-value pairs of data.

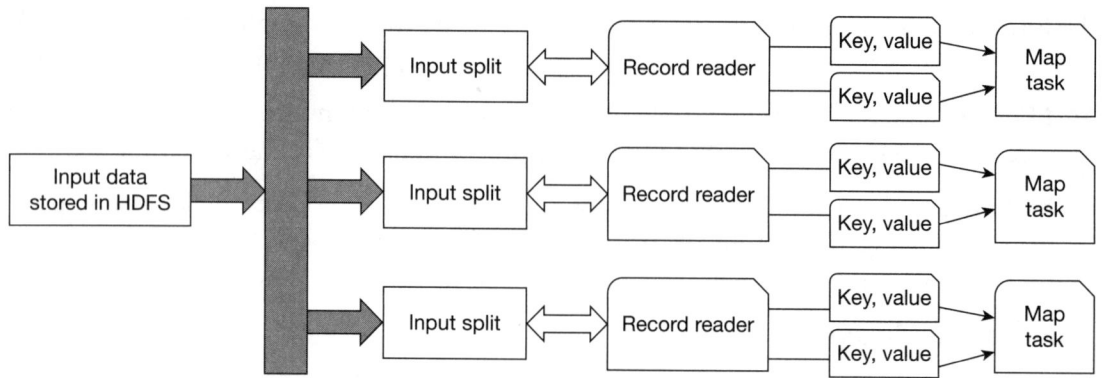

Figure 7.21 Hadoop MapReduce: Key-value pair

Input Split: The logical representation of data is called InputSplit. The InputSplit displays the data that each separate Mapper will process.

RecordReader

This component interfaces with the InputSplit and turns the Split into records in the form of key-value pairs that the Mapper can read. RecordReader converts data into a key-value pair by default using TextInputFormat. Until the file reading is finished, the RecordReader talks with the InputSplit.

In MapReduce, the Map function processes a single key-value pair and outputs a set of key-value pairs, while the Reduce function processes values grouped by the same key and outputs a second set of key-value pairs. The Map's output types should match the Reduce's input types, as seen below:

- **Map:** $(K1, V1) \rightarrow$ list $(K2, V2)$
- **Reduce:** $\{(K2, \text{list } (V2 \,)\} \rightarrow$ list $(K3, V3)$

In Hadoop, the creation of a key-value pair is dependent on the dataset and the desired output. The key-value pair is defined in four places in general: 1. Map input, 2. Map output, 3. Reduce input, and 4. Reduce output.

Map Input: By default, Map-input will use the line offset as the key and the text of the line as the value. We may change them by utilizing a custom Input format.

Map Output: The primary purpose is to filter data and offer an environment for data grouping depending on the key. **Key:** The key will be the field/text/object on which the data must be sorted and aggregated on the reducer side. **Value:** This is the field/text/object that each particular reduction method will handle.

Reduce Input: Reduce's input is Map's output; therefore it is the same as Map-output.

Reduce Output: It is dependent on the output required.

InputSplit and RecordReader use TextInputFormat to construct the key-value pair in Hadoop. As a result, Key is the byte offset of the line's start inside the file, and Value is the line's content, omitting line terminators.

7.13 INPUT FORMAT IN MAPREDUCE

Hadoop Input Format examines the job's Input specification. Input Format divides the input file into Input Splits, each assigned to a different Mapper. Let us look at Input Format in Hadoop MapReduce, how to send data to the mapper, and the many forms of Input Format in Hadoop, such as FileInputFormat, TextInputFormat and KeyValueTextInputFormat.

The data for a MapReduce task is initially saved in input files, which are commonly kept in HDFS. Although the format of these files is variable, binary and line-based log files can be utilized. We specify how these input files are divided and read using InputFormat.

The InputFormat class is a core component of the Hadoop MapReduce system, and it includes the following features:

- The InputFormat determines which files or other objects should be utilized for input.
- The Data divides are defined by InputFormat, which determines the size of each Map jobs as well as the probable execution server.
- The RecordReader is defined by InputFormat and is responsible for reading real records from the input files.

In MapReduce, we have two methods for getting data to the mapper: getsplits() and createRecordReader().

Table 7.7 shows the many forms of Input Format in Hadoop.

Hadoop FileInputFormat: It is the basic class for all InputFormats that work with files. Hadoop FileInputFormat determines the location of data files in the input directory. FileInputFormat is given a path containing files to read when we start a Hadoop job. All files are read by FileInputFormat, which separates the files into one or more InputSplits.

TextInputFormat: It is MapReduce's default InputFormat. Each line of each input file is treated as a distinct record by TextInputFormat, which does not do any processing. This is helpful for unformatted data or records that are based on lines, such as log files. When paired with the file name, the key is the byte offset at the beginning of the line inside the file (not the entire file, only one split); thus it will be unique. The contents of the line, except line terminators, are the required values.

KeyValueTextInputFormat: It works in a similar way to TextInputFormat in that each line of input is treated as a single record. While TextInputFormat treats the full line as the

Table 7.7 Input formats in MapReduce

Input Formats in MapReduce	
Hadoop's FileInputFormat	It is the basic class for all Input formats that work with files.
TextInputFormat	It is MapReduce's default InputFormat. Each line of each input file is treated as a distinct record by TextInputFormat.
KeyValueTextInputFormat	KeyValueTextInputformat uses a tab character ('/t') to divide the line into key and value.
SequenceFileInputFormat	This is a Hadoop Input format that reads sequence files. Series files are binary files that hold binary key-value pairs in a sequence.
SequenceFileAsTextInputFormat	Another kind of SequenceFileInputFormat is SequenceFileAsTextInputFormat, which transforms sequence file key values to Text objects.
SequenceFileAsBinaryInputFormat	Hadoop SequenceFileAsBinaryInputFormat is a SequenceFileInputFormat that extracts the keys and values of a sequence file as an opaque binary object.
NlineInputFormat	Hadoop NlineInputFormat is a variant of TextInputFormat in which the keys are the line's byte offset and the values are the line's contents.
DBInputFormat	Hadoop DBInputFormat is a JDBC-based InputFormat for reading data from a relational database.

value, the KeyValueTextInputFormat uses a tab character ('/t') to divide the line into key and value. The value is the remainder of the line following the tab character, whereas the key is everything up to the tab character.

SequenceFileInputFormat: This is a Hadoop Input Format that reads sequence files. Series files are binary files that hold binary key-value pairs in a sequence. Sequence files compress data in blocks and allow for direct serialization and deserialization of a variety of data types (not just text). Both the Key and the Value are user-defined in this case.

SequenceFileAsTextInputFormat: Another kind of SequenceFileInputFormat is SequenceFileAsTextInputFormat, which transforms sequence file key values to Text objects. The keys and values are converted using the 'tostring()' function. This InputFormat converts sequence files into streamable input.

SequenceFileAsBinaryInputFormat: Hadoop SequenceFileAsBinaryInputFormat is a SequenceFileInputFormat that extracts the keys and values of a sequence file as an opaque binary object.

NLineInputFormat: Hadoop NLineInputFormat is a variant of TextInputFormat in which the keys are the line's byte offset and the values are the line's contents. With TextInputFormat and KeyValueTextInputFormat, each mapper receives a variable number of lines of input, which changes depending on the size of the split and the length of the lines. We use NLineInputFormat if we want our mapper to accept a set number of lines of input. N is the number of lines of input received by each mapper. Each mapper receives precisely one line of input by default (N=1). If N=2, each split will have two lines. The first two key-value pairs will be given to one mapper, while the second two key-value pairs will be given to another mapper.

DBInputFormat: Hadoop DBInputFormat is a JDBC-based InputFormat for reading data from a relational database. We must be careful not to overwhelm the database from which we are reading too many mappers since it lacks portioning capabilities. As a result, it is excellent for importing tiny datasets and also merging them with huge datasets from HDFS using MultipleInputs. LongWritables is the key, and DBWritables is the value.

To summarize, InputFormat specifies how input files should be divided and read. RecordReader is defined by InputFormat. Different sorts of InputFormats can be used for various purposes.

7.14 INPUTSPLIT IN MAPREDUCE

In Hadoop MapReduce, the logical representation of data is called InputSplit. In a MapReduce application, it refers to a unit of work that comprises a single map job. The data handled by each Mapper is represented by Hadoop InputSplit. The split is broken down into tracks. As a result, the mapper goes over each record (which is a key-value pair). The length of an InputSplit is measured in bytes, and each InputSplit has storage locations (hostname strings). MapReduce places map tasks as near to the divided data as feasible using storage locations. To reduce job duration, map tasks are performed in the order of size of the splits, with the greatest split being handled first (greedy approximation approach). The crucial thing to remember is that InputSplit does not really contain the input data; it is only a reference to it.

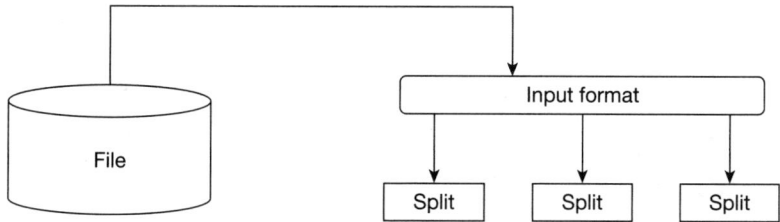

Figure 7.22 Hadoop MapReduce: File → Input Format → Split

Because an InputFormat forms InputSplit (Fig. 7.22), we don't have to deal with it directly as a user (InputFormat creates the InputSplit and divides it into records). By default, FileInputFormat splits a file into 128MB chunks (the same as blocks in HDFS), and we may alter this number by adjusting the mapred.min.split.size parameter in mapred-site.xml or overriding the parameter in the Task object used to submit a specific MapReduce job. By designing a custom InputFormat, we can additionally control how the file is split.

Changing Split Size in Hadoop

In Hadoop, InputSplit is user-defined. In the MapReduce application, the user may control the split size based on the size of the data. As a result, the total number of map jobs equals the total number of InputSplits. By executing 'getSplit(),' the client (who is performing the job) may compute the work's splits, which are then submitted to the application master, who utilizes the storage locations to schedule map tasks that will process the splits on the cluster. The map task then gives the split to the createRecordReader() method on InputFormat, which generates a RecordReader for the split. The map task then passes the RecordReader to the map function.

Finally, InputSplit contains a reference to the data, not the data itself. It is used in the MapReduce program or other processing algorithms to process data. As a result, the split is separated into records, with the map processing each record (a key-value pair).

7.15 Hadoop Record Reader

The data processing model of MapReduce is basic. The Map and Reduce functions use key-value pairs as inputs and outputs. In Hadoop MapReduce, the map and reduce functions use the following general form:

- `map:` $(K1, V1) \rightarrow \text{list}(K2, V2)$
- `reduce:` $(K2, \text{list}(V2)) \rightarrow \text{list}(K3, V3)$

Before processing, it must first determine which data to process, which is accomplished using the InputFormat class. The class InputFormat selects the file from HDFS that should be sent to the map method. An InputFormat is also in charge of producing and splitting InputSplits into records. In HDFS, the data is split into a number of splits (usually 64/128mb). This is known as inputsplit, and it refers to the amount of data processed by a single map.

The getSplits() function is called by the InputFormat class, which computes splits for each file and delivers them to the JobTracker, which schedules map jobs to process them on TaskTrackers at their storage locations. The split is then sent to the task tracker's createRecordReader() function on InputFormat to get a RecordReader for that split. The RecordReader takes data from its source and turns it into key-value pairs that the mapper can understand.

Hadoop RecordReader converts data into key-value format and provides key-value pairs (Fig. 7.23) for the mapper using the data inside the bounds established by the input split. The "start" byte position in the file where the RecordReader should begin creating key-value pairs and the "end" byte position in the file where it should cease reading records are the "start" and "end," respectively. The data is imported from its source and then turned into key-value pairs appropriate for reading by the Mapper in Hadoop RecordReader. It keeps in touch with the input split until the file reading is finished.

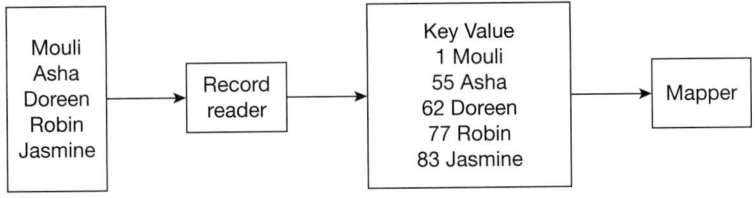

It converts data into key-value format

Figure 7.23 Hadoop MapReduce: Hadoop Record Reader

How RecordReader Works

A RecordReader is more than a record iterator, and the map operation generates a key-value pair from one record that is supplied to the map function. Using mapper's run function, we can observe this:

```
[php]public void run(Context context) throws IOException,
InterruptedException{
<pre>setup(context);
while(context.nextKeyValue())
{
map(context.setCurrentKey(),context.getCurrentValue(),context)
}
cleanup(context);
}[/php]
```

Following setup(), nextKeyValue() will be called on the context to populate the mapper's key and value objects. By means of context, the key and value are retrieved from the record reader and provided to the map() function to conduct its work. A key-value pair (K, V), as an input to the map function, is processed according to the logic specified in the map code. The next KeyValue() function returns False when the RecordReader reaches the end of the record. In order to generate key-value pairs, a RecordReader normally keeps between the borders set by the InputSplit, but this is not required. A custom implementation can read data from outside the InputSplit, although this is not recommended.

Types of Hadoop Record Reader in MapReduce

The InputFormat defines the RecordReader instance. TextInputFormat is used by default to turn input into a key-value pair. There are two types of RecordReaders provided by TextInputFormat: 1. Line Record Reader 2. Sequence File Record Reader.

In Hadoop, the Line RecordReader is the default RecordReader provided by text input format. It considers each input file line as a new value, with the associated key being byte offset. If the split is not the first, LineRecordReader always skips the first line (or a portion of it). Instead, it reads one line after the split's border (if data is available, it is not the last split). SequenceFileRecordReader reads data specified by the header of a sequence file.

Maximum Size for a Single Record

A single record can only be processed up to a certain size. The argument below can be used to set this value.

> [php]conf.setInt("mapred.linerecordreader.maxlength", Integer.MAX_VALUE);[/php]
>
> A line with a size greater than this maximum value (default is 2,147,483,647) will be ignored.

7.16 MAPREDUCE PARTITIONER

The Partitioner in MapReduce is in charge of dividing the intermediate mapper output's key. The partition is determined using the hash function and the key (or a subset of the key). The number of reduction tasks determines the overall number of divisions. In this section, we shall discover why Hadoop partitioners are needed, what the default Hadoop partitioner is, how many Hadoop practitioners are necessary, and what bad partitioning in Hadoop means. We shall also explore the ways to combat poor partitioning of MapReduce.

The Partitioner is in charge of partitioning (Fig. 7.24) the keys of the intermediate map output. The partition is determined using the hash function and the key (or a subset of the key). Each mapper output is partitioned based on the key-value, with records, and the same key value going into the same partition (within each mapper) after which each partition is given to a reducer. The partition class decides where a given (key-value) pair will be stored. The partition phase comes after the map phase but before the reduce phase.

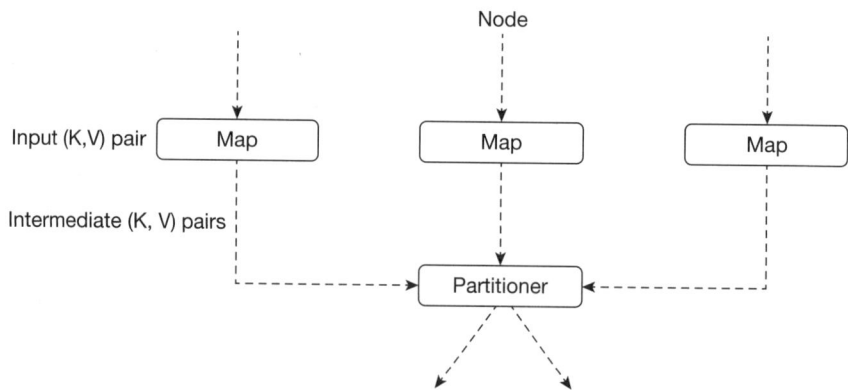

Figure 7.24 Hadoop MapReduce: Partitioner

Need for the Partitioner

The MapReduce job takes an input dataset and outputs a list of key-value pairs, which is the outcome of the map phase, in which the input data is split into tasks, each task processes the split, and each map outputs a list of key-value pairs. The map output is then delivered to the reduce task, which applies the user-defined reduce function on the map outputs. However, the map output is partitioned and sorted based on the key before the reduce step. This partitioning indicates that all the values for each key are grouped. All the values of a single key go to the same reducer, allowing the map output to be distributed evenly throughout the reducer. Hadoop MapReduce's Partitioner guides the mapper output to the reducer by deciding which reducer is accountable for a given key.

Hash Partitioner is the default Hadoop partitioner in Hadoop MapReduce, which computes a hash value for the key and allocates the partition based on this result. In Hadoop, the total number of partitioners is equal to the number of reducers, i.e., The data will be partitioned according to the number of reducers specified by the JobConf. setNumReduceTasks() function. As a result, a single reducer processes the data from a single partitioner. And only when there are numerous reducers is a partitioner generated.

Poor Partitioning

Let us say one key occurs more frequently than the others in data input. In this case, we send data to partitions using two mechanisms. First, the key that appears more frequently will be transferred to a single partition. All other keys will be assigned to partitions based on their hashCode(). However, if the hashCode() function does not evenly divide other key data over the partition range, data will not be transmitted to the reducers equitably. Poor data partitioning means that certain reducers will have more data input than others, implying that they will have more work to accomplish. As a result, the entire task will be delayed while one reducer completes its disproportionately high portion of the load. To address Hadoop MapReduce's bad partitioner, we may develop a Custom partitioner, which allows the workload to be shared equally among multiple reducers.

7.16.1 MapReduce Combiner

When we execute a MapReduce task on a huge dataset, the Mapper generates large blocks of intermediate data and sends them to the Reducer for further processing, causing massive network congestion. The Hadoop Combiner function in the MapReduce architecture is essential for decreasing network congestion. The MapReduce combiner is also known as a 'Mini-reducer'. The Combiner's main task is to process the Mapper's output data before sending it on to Reducer. It is optional to utilize the Combiner and it runs after the Mapper and before the Reducer.

Without Combiner

The input is divided into two mappers (Fig. 7.25), generating six keys. Now that we have six key-value intermediate data, the next Mapper will send it directly to the Reducer, using some network traffic bandwidth. This means that some time is taken to transfer data between the two machines. If the data is large, it will take longer to transmit to the Reducer. Suppose we employ a Hadoop combiner between the Mapper and the Reducer. In that case, the Combiner shuffles intermediate data (six key-value pairs) before passing it to the reduction, creating four key-value pairs as an output.

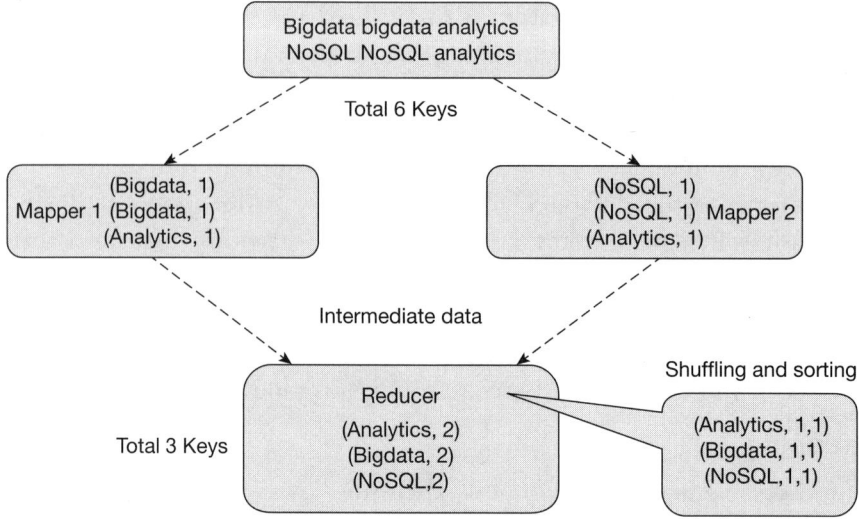

Figure 7.25 Hadoop MapReduce: Without Combiner

With Combiner

The Reducer now only has to handle three key-value pairs created by two combiners. As a result, the reduction is only run three times to create the final output, which improves overall speed (Fig. 7.26).

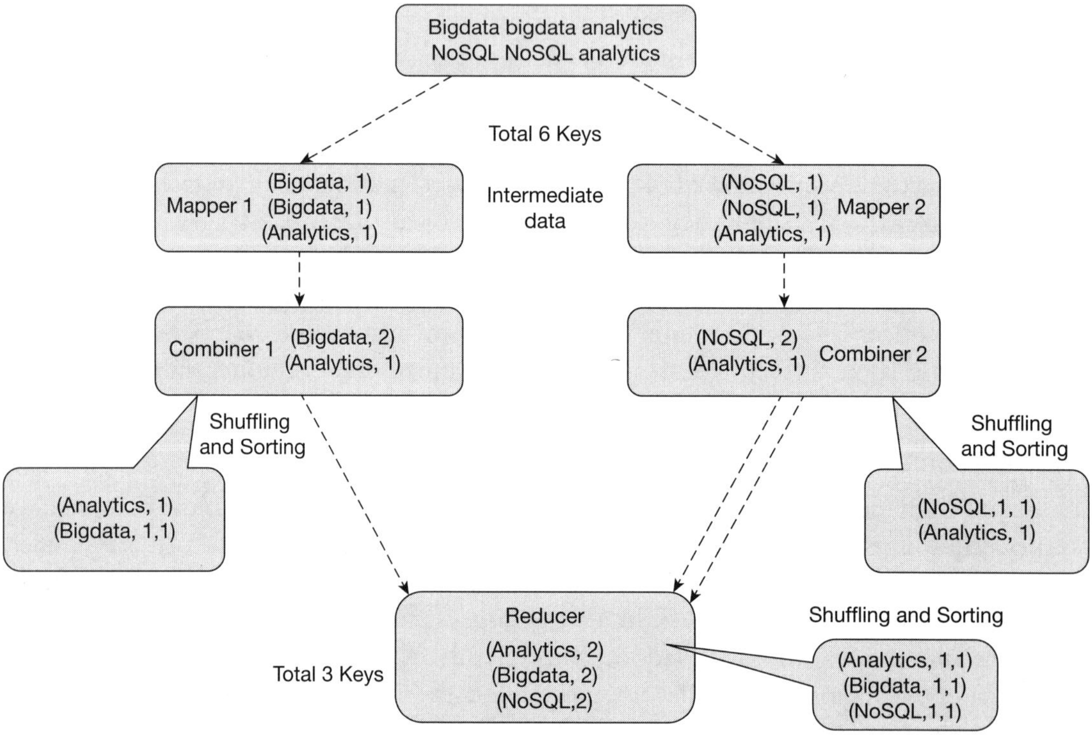

Figure 7.26 Hadoop MapReduce: With Combiner

MapReduce Combiner's Benefits: Hadoop Combiner speeds up data transfers between the Mapper and Reducer. It reduces the quantity of data that the Reducer needs to process. The Reducer's overall performance is improved by the Combiner.

Hadoop Combiner's Drawbacks in MapReduce: There are various drawbacks to using Hadoop Combiner: (1) Because the Hadoop combiner's execution cannot be guaranteed, MapReduce jobs cannot rely on it. (2) The key-value pairs are saved in Hadoop on the local filesystem, and the Combiner is invoked afterward, resulting in costly disk IO.

7.17 SHUFFLING AND SORTING IN MAPREDUCE

Shuffling is the Hadoop word for the process of transferring intermediate output from mappers to reducers. A reducer receives one or more keys and their associated values. The mapper's intermediated key-value is automatically ordered by the key.

In Hadoop, the shuffle phase passes the map output from a Mapper to a Reducer in MapReduce. In MapReduce, the sort phase is responsible for combining and sorting map outputs. The mapper's data is aggregated by key, distributed across reducers, and then sorted by key. Each reducer obtains all values associated with the same key. Hadoop's shuffle and sort phases happen simultaneously and are handled by the MapReduce framework. Let us take a closer look at both of these procedures now:

Shuffling: Shuffling is the process of passing data from mappers to reducers (Fig. 7.27), or the method by which the system sorts the map output and passes it on to the reducer as input. As a result, the reducers require the MapReduce shuffle step; otherwise, they would have no input (or input from every mapper). Because shuffling may begin before the map phase is completed, it saves time and allows the chores to be completed faster.

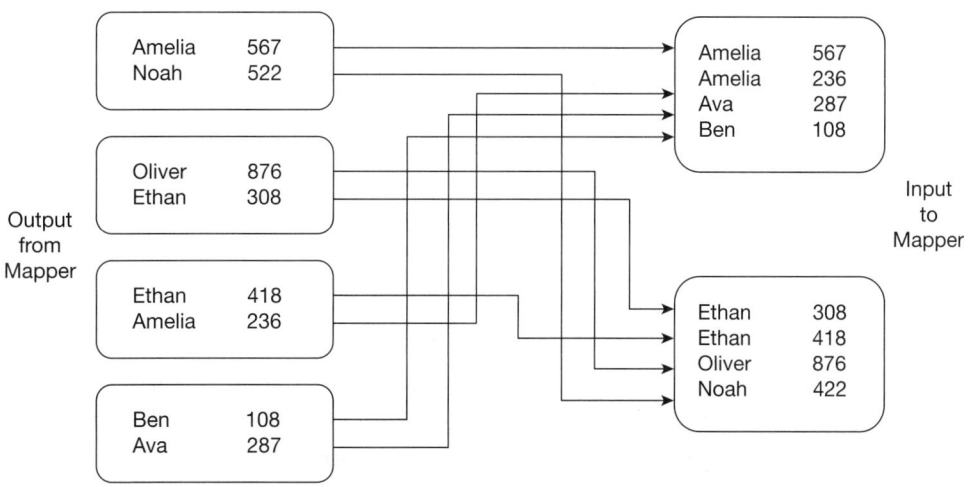

Figure 7.27 Hadoop MapReduce: Shuffling

Sorting: The keys supplied by the mapper are automatically sorted by the MapReduce Framework, i.e., all intermediate key-value pairs in MapReduce generated by the mapper are sorted by key and not by value before commencing the reduction. The reducer's values are not ordered; they can be in any sequence. Sorting in Hadoop makes it easier for reducers to determine when a new reduce process should begin. The reducer will save time as a result of this. The reducer starts a new reduce process when the next key in the sorted input data is different from the preceding one. Each reduction job receives key-value pairs as input and outputs key-value pairs.

If you specify zero reducers (setNumReduceTasks(0)), no shuffling or sorting is done in Hadoop MapReduce. The MapReduce operation then comes to a halt at the map phase, which does not contain any sorting (so even the map phase is faster).

In MapReduce, secondary sorting is also used. If we want to sort the values of reducers, we utilize the secondary sorting strategy, which allows us to sort the values supplied to each reducer (in ascending or descending order).

7.17.1 Hadoop Output Format

Hadoop RecordWriter accepts Reducer's output data and writes it to output files. The Output format determines how these output key-value pairs are recorded in output files by RecordWriter. The functions OutputFormat and InputFormat are quite similar. Hadoop's OutputFormat instances are used to write to files on HDFS or local drive. The output format for a MapReduce task is described by OutputFormat based on the output specification. The MapReduce task checks to see if the output directory already exists. The RecordWriter implementation provided by OutputFormat is used to write the job's output files. A FileSystem is used to store the output files. The output directory is configured using the FileOutputFormat.setOutputPath() function. Each Reducer creates a new file in a shared output directory. Table 7.8 lists various Hadoop output formats in MapReduce.

Types of Hadoop Output Formats

TextOutputFormat: TextOutputFormat is the default Hadoop reduction Output Format in MapReduce. It writes (key-value) pairs on individual lines of text files, and its keys and values can be of any type since TextOutputFormat converts them to strings using toString(). The tab character that separates each key-value combination can be adjusted using the MapReduce.output.textoutputformat.separator parameter. Because KeyValue separates lines into key-value pairs based on a configurable separator, TextOutputFormat is used to read these output text files.

SequenceFileOutputFormat: It is an intermediate format used between MapReduce jobs, which quickly serializes arbitrary data types to the file. The corresponding SequenceFileInputFormat deserializes the file into the same types and presents the data to

Table 7.8 Output formats in MapReduce

Output Formats in MapReduce	
TextOutputFormat	TextOutputFormat is the default Hadoop reduction Output Format in MapReduce. It writes (key,value) pairs on individual lines of text files,
SequenceFileOutputFormat	It is an intermediate format used between MapReduce jobs, which quickly serializes arbitrary data types to the file.
SequenceFileAsBinaryOutputFormat	It is a variant of SequenceFileInputFormat that writes binary keys and values to a sequence file.
MapFileOutputFormat	It is a Hadoop Output Format variant of FileOutputFormat that is used to write output as map files.
MultipleOutputs	It allows data to be written to files with names determined from the output keys and values, or from any string.
LazyOutputFormat	LazyOutputFormat is an OutputFormat wrapper that ensures that the output file is produced only when the record for a certain partition is emitted.
DBOutputFormat	In Hadoop, the DBOutputFormat Output Format is used to write to relational databases and HBase.
Output Formats in MapReduce	Hadoop DBInputFormat is a JDBC-based InputFormat for reading data from a relational database.

the next mapper in the same manner as it was emitted by the previous reducer, because these are compact and easily compressible. The static methods on SequenceFileOutputFormat govern compression.

SequenceFileAsBinaryOutputFormat: It is a variant of SequenceFileInputFormat that writes binary keys and values to a sequence file.

MapFileOutputFormat: It is a Hadoop Output Format variant of FileOutputFormat that is used to write output as map files. Because the keys in a MapFile must be inserted in the correct order, we must guarantee that the reducer emits keys in the correct order.

MultipleOutputs: It allows data to be written to files with names determined from the output keys and values, or from any string.

LazyOutputFormat: Even if the output files are empty, FileOutputFormat will occasionally generate them. LazyOutputFormat is an OutputFormat wrapper that ensures that the output file is produced only when the record for a certain partition is emitted.

DBOutputFormat: In Hadoop, the DBOutputFormat Output Format is used to write to relational databases and HBase. It saves the output of reduction to an SQL table. It takes key-value pairs with a type that extends DBwritable as the key. With a batch SQL query, the returned RecordWriter publishes just the key to the database.

7.18 INPUT SPLIT VS. HDFS BLOCK IN MAPREDUCE

HDFS Block: A block on a hard disk is a continuous storage space for data. FileSystem stores data as a collection of blocks in general. Similarly, HDFS maintains each file as a block. The Hadoop program is in charge of spreading data across numerous nodes.

Hadoop's InputSplit: InputSplit represents the data that will be processed by a single Mapper. The split is separated into records, and the map processes each record (which is a key-value pair). The number of InputSplits equals the number of map tasks. The data for a MapReduce task is initially saved in input files, which are commonly kept in HDFS. The InputFormat variable specifies how these input files will be divided and read. InputFormat is in charge of generating InputSplit.

Block vs. Input Split Size: The default size of an HDFS block is 128 MB, but we may change it to meet our needs. Except for the last block, which might be the same size or less, the file's blocks are all of the same size and stored in Hadoop FileSystem. In **InputSplit**, the split size is set to be nearly equal to the block size, by default. InputSplit is user-defined, and the user may set the split size in the MapReduce program based on the size of the data.

Data Representation: The physical representation of data is called a block. A small amount of data can be read or written on it. The logical representation of data in the block is called InputSplit. It is used in the MapReduce program or other processing algorithms to process data. The data in InputSplit is a reference to the data, not the data itself.

Consider the following scenario: we need to store a file in HDFS. HDFS organizes files into chunks. The smallest unit of data that may be saved or retrieved from the disk is the block, which has a default size of 128MB. HDFS divides files into blocks and stores them on separate cluster nodes. If we have a file that is 130 MB in size, HDFS will split it into two blocks. Now, if we try to run a MapReduce operation on the blocks, it will fail since the second block is missing. However, InputSplit solves this issue by including a position for the next block and constructing a single block by a logical grouping of blocks.

7.19 MAPONLY JOB IN MAPREDUCE

MapReduce is a software framework that makes it simple to create applications that handle the massive amounts of organized and unstructured data contained in Hadoop's Distributed Filesystem (HDFS). Map and Reduce are two fundamental operations performed by the MapReduce algorithm. The Hadoop Map phase turns a collection of data into another set of data, with each piece split down into tuples (key-value pairs). The Hadoop Reduce phase takes the map result as input and combines the data tuples depending on the key, changing the value of the key appropriately.

From the word-count example, we can deduce that there are two sets of parallel processes: Map and Reduce. In the map process, the first input is split to distribute the work among all the Map nodes, and then each word is identified and mapped to the number 1; in the Reduce process, the first input is split to distribute the work among all the Reduce nodes, and then each word is identified and mapped to the number 1. As a result, the pairings are known as tuples (key-value pairs).

Three words are supplied to the first mapper node. As a result, the node's output will be three key-value pairs, each with a distinct key and a value of 1, and the procedure will be repeated for all nodes. Subsequently, these tuples are sent to the reducer nodes, where the partitioner kicks in. Finally, it does shuffling to send all tuples with the same key to the same node. As a result, the reduction procedure entails an aggregate of values or, more precisely, an action on values that share the same key.

Consider a scenario in which we only need to operate and no aggregation is required; in this case, we will use Hadoop's MapOnly job. The map does all tasks with its InputSplit in a Hadoop MapOnly job, while the reducer performs none. The final result is the map output in this case (Fig. 7.28).

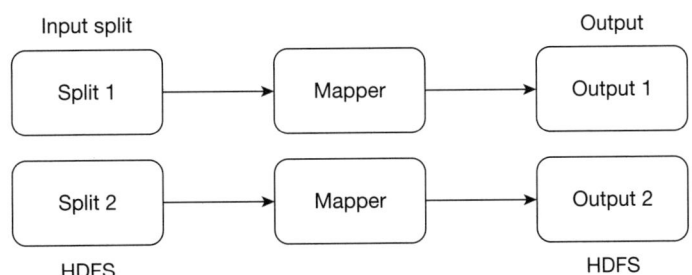

Figure 7.28 Hadoop MapReduce: MapOnly job

We can escape Hadoop's Reduce Phase by setting jobs with setNumreduceTasks(0) in the driver settings. As a result, the number of reducers will be set to 0, and the lone mapper will be responsible for completing the assignment.

Advantages of a Hadoop MapOnly Job

There are key, sort, and shuffle phases in between the map and reductions stages. Sort and shuffle are in charge of ascending the keys and then grouping items based on the same keys. This step is quite costly, and if we don't need it, we should skip it. By skipping it, we will also skip the sort and shuffle phases. This also reduces network congestion because in shuffling, a mapper's output travels to the reducer, and large data must travel to the reducer when the data size is large.

In a map-only task, the output of the mapper is written to the local disk before it is sent to the reducer, whereas in a map-only job, the output is sent straight to HDFS. This saves time and money in the long run.

7.20 HADOOP SPECULATIVE EXECUTION

Slow-running jobs are not fixed or diagnosed by Apache Hadoop. Instead, it tries to identify when a work is taking longer than planned and creates a backup task that is similar to the original (the backup task is called as speculative task). In Hadoop, this is known as speculative execution (Fig. 7.29).

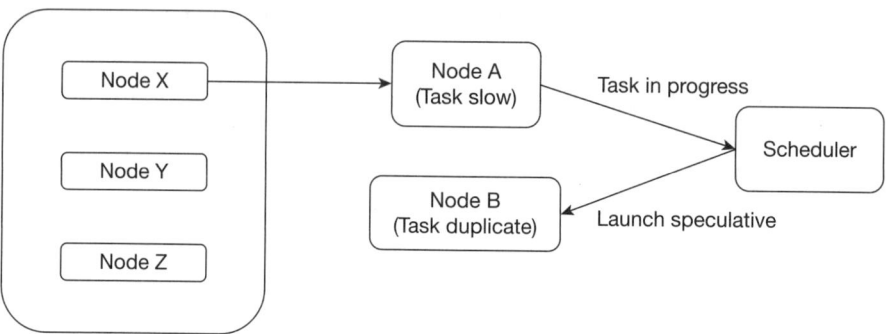

Figure 7.29 Hadoop MapReduce: Speculative execution

MapReduce in Hadoop divides jobs into tasks, which operate in parallel rather than sequentially, reducing the total execution time. However, slow tasks (even if they are small in number) impede the overall execution of a job; hence this model of execution is sensitive to them.

There might be various reasons for task slowdowns, such as hardware failure or software misconfiguration. However, it may be difficult to pinpoint the problem because the tasks still finish properly, even if they take longer than intended. Therefore, Hadoop tries to discover slow-running activities and launch backup tasks instead of diagnosing and fixing them. In Hadoop, this is known as speculative execution. In Hadoop, these backup activities are known as Speculative tasks.

Now, let us take a look at Hadoop's speculative execution mechanism: All of the job's tasks are initiated in Hadoop MapReduce. The speculative tasks are launched for those tasks that have been operating for a long period (at least one minute) and have not made significant progress compared to the other tasks in the job. If the original task completes before the speculative task, the speculative task is destroyed; on the other hand, the original task is killed if the speculative task completes before it.

In certain circumstances, speculative execution is advantageous because in a Hadoop cluster with 100s of nodes, problems such as hardware failure or network congestion are prevalent, and performing parallel or duplicate tasks would be preferable since we wouldn't have to wait for the problem's job to complete. However, if two duplicate jobs are initiated at the same time, cluster resources would be wasted.

In Hadoop, speculative execution is a task optimization strategy that is enabled by default. In mapred-site.xml, you may deactivate speculative execution for mappers and reducers, as seen below:

```
[php]<property>
<name>mapred.map.tasks.speculative.execution</name>
<value>false</value>
</property>
<property>
<name>mapred.reduce.tasks.speculative.execution</name>
<value>false</value>
</property>[/php]
```

Why is it necessary to disable Speculative Execution? The primary goal of speculative execution is to minimize job execution time; however, redundant jobs impair clustering efficiency. Because duplicate tasks are completed during speculative execution, overall throughput may be reduced. As a result, some Hadoop cluster managers prefer to disable speculative execution.

7.21 HADOOP COUNTERS

Hadoop Counters (Fig. 7.30) allow you to track the status of a map/reduce process or the number of operations it does. Counters in Hadoop MapReduce are an excellent way to collect statistics on a MapReduce task, whether for quality control or application-level statistics. They can also be used to diagnose problems. Counters are global Hadoop counters established by the MapReduce framework or by applications. Each Hadoop counter has an "Enum" for its name (Counter) and it can store a long type of value. Counters are grouped into groups containing counters from a specific Enum class. Hadoop Counters substantiate the following: 1. Bytes are read and written in the correct order. 2. The proper number of tasks are initiated and completed effectively. 3. The quantity of CPU and memory used by the task and cluster nodes is adequate.

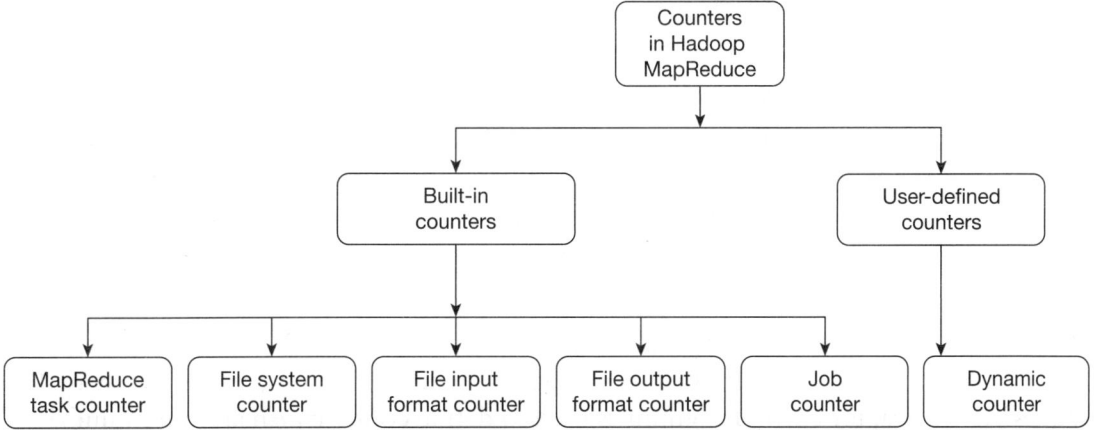

Figure 7.30 Hadoop MapReduce: Type of counters

Hadoop MapReduce Counter Types

MapReduce Counters are divided into two categories: 1. MapReduce that has built-in counters. 2. Counters that are defined by the user/custom counters in MapReduce.

MapReduce built-in counters: For each task, Hadoop keeps a set of built-in Hadoop counters that indicate different metrics, such as the number of bytes and records consumed, allowing us to ensure that the intended amount of input is consumed and the expected amount of output is created. Hadoop Counters are organized into groups, and the built-in counters are divided into many groups. Task counts (which are updated as the task progresses) or job counters are found in each group (which are updated as a job progresses).

MapReduce Task Counters in Hadoop

During the execution of a job, the Hadoop Task Counter captures certain information (such as the number of records read and written). The Map Input Records counter, for example, is the job counter that counts the number of input records read by each map task. Hadoop task counters are kept by each task attempt and communicated to the application master regularly so that they may be aggregated worldwide.

Counters on the FileSystem

In Hadoop MapReduce, Hadoop FileSystem Counters collect data such as the number of bytes read and written by the file system. The names and descriptions of the file system counters are listed below: FileSystem bytes read – The number of bytes read by the map and reduce jobs from the filesystem. FileSystem bytes are written – The amount of data written to the filesystem due to map and reduce processes.

Hadoop FileInputFormat Counters: By using FileInputFormat, you may reduce the number of bytes read by map processes.

Hadoop Map counts for FileOutputFormat: Reduction takes information from several bytes written by map tasks (for map-only jobs) or via FileOutputFormat for reduce tasks.

Job Counters for MapReduce: The job-level statistics are measured by the MapReduce Job counter, not the numbers that change while a task is executing. Total Launched Maps, for example, counts the number of map tasks launched during the course of a job (including tasks that failed). Because the application master maintains MapReduce Job counters, these Hadoop Counters, unlike all other counters, including user-defined ones, do not need to be communicated across the network.

User-defined Counters: In addition to the built-in counters in MapReduce, user code can establish a set of counters in the mapper or reducer, which are then increased as requested. In Java, for example, 'enum' is used to define counters. An arbitrary number of enums, each with an arbitrary number of fields, can be defined by a task. The group name is the enum's name, and the counter names are the enum's fields.

Hadoop MapReduce Dynamic Counters: Because the fields of a Java enum are defined at compile time, we can't use enums to build new counters in Hadoop MapReduce at

7.22 HADOOP OPTIMIZATION

There are several approaches to improving Hadoop optimization. Let us take a look at each one individually:

Proper Configuration of the Cluster: The command -noatime option is used to mount the correct configuration of the cluster DFS and MapReduce storage. This turns off access time and improves I/O performance. RAID should be avoided on TaskTracker and data node computers since it slows them down. To guarantee that all of your disks' I/O capacity is utilized, make sure mapred.local.dir and dfs.data.dir point to one directory on each of them. Ascertain that the health of your disk drives is being monitored intelligently. MapReduce jobs are fault-tolerant; however, tasks must be re-executed if a disk fails. With tools like Ganglia and Hadoop monitoring metrics, you can keep track of swap and network utilization graphs. If you see swap being used, reduce the amount of RAM allocated to each task in mapred.child.java.opts.

LZO Compression Usage: For intermediate data, this is always a smart idea. LZO (Lempel–Ziv–Oberhumer) intermediate data compression will assist almost any Hadoop project that generates a significant quantity of map output. Although LZO adds a little CPU overhead and it saves time during the shuffle by minimizing the amount of disk IO. Set mapred.compress.map.output to true to enable LZO compression. One of the essential Hadoop optimization approaches is clustering.

Tuning the number of MapReduce jobs: Reduce the number of jobs if each one takes 30-40 seconds or more. The following steps are required to begin the mapper or reducer process: first, start JVM (load JVM into memory), initialize JVM, and finally, de-initialize JVM after processing (mapper/reducer). All of these JVM activities are time-consuming. Consider the scenario where the mapper does a job for 20–30 seconds, and we need to launch, initialize, and end the JVM, which might take a long time. It is suggested that the work be run for at least 1 minute. If a project requires more than 1TB of input, you should consider raising the input dataset's block size to 256MB or even 512MB. The command Hadoop distcp –Hdfs.block.size=$[256*1024*1024] can be used to modify the block size of existing files. You should raise the number of mapper jobs to a multiple of the number of mapper slots in the cluster as long as each task runs for at least 30–40 seconds. Do not plan too many reduce tasks—the number of reduce tasks should be equal to or slightly less than the number of reduce slots in the cluster for most workloads.

Combiner between Mapper and Reducer: It is recommended to utilize a Combiner to conduct some aggregation before the input reaches the reducer if your approach includes computing aggregates of any kind. The MapReduce framework cleverly combines data to decrease the amount of data that must be written to disk and moved between the Map and Reduce stages of processing.

Appropriate Writeable type for data: A lot of data users who are new to Hadoop Streaming or moving to Java MapReduce frequently employ the Text writable type inappropriately. Although Text is easy, converting numeric data to and from UTF8 strings is inefficient and can take up a substantial amount of CPU time. Consider utilizing binary Writables like IntWritable, Floatwritable, and others when dealing with non-textual data.

Reusage of Writeable: Many MapReduce users make the frequent error of allocating a new Writable object for each output from a mapper or reducer.

7.23 MAPREDUCE PERFORMANCE TUNING: BEST PRACTICES

Hadoop performance tuning can assist you in improving the performance of your Hadoop cluster and ensuring that you get the best results possible while implementing Hadoop programming in Big Data firms. To do so, repeat the steps below until the desired result is obtained in the most efficient manner.

Run the job → Find the bottleneck → Fix the bottleneck.

The initial step in Hadoop performance tuning is to run a task, identify bottlenecks, and resolve them using the methods listed below to achieve the best results. You must repeat the preceding steps until you reach a satisfactory level of performance.

7.23.1 System Level Best Practices

Following are the MapReduce Performance Tuning best practices at the system level:

- Hadoop run-time parameters tuning
- Memory tuning
- Minimize the Map Disk Spill
- Fine-tune the tasks of the Mapper

Hadoop Run-time Parameters Tuning: Hadoop offers a variety of performance tweaking options for CPU, memory, storage, and network. The majority of Hadoop operations are not CPU constrained; instead, memory and disk spillage are prioritized. Tweaking Hadoop run-time parameters delves further into the mechanics of Hadoop performance tuning.

Memory Tuning: In MapReduce performance optimization, the most general and popular rule is to use as much RAM as possible without triggering swapping. The mapred.child.java.opts parameter for task memory may be found in your configuration file. For improved memory performance, you may use Ganglia, Cloudera Manager, or Nagios to monitor memory utilization on the server.

Minimize the Map Disk Spill: In Hadoop, the performance bottleneck is frequently the Disk IO. There are a number of factors that may be tweaked to reduce spillage, including Mapper output compression and using 70% of heap memory for spill buffer in ion mapper.

However, it is best not to spill more than once because you will have to re-read and re-write all of your data three times in the IO.

Fine-tune Mapper tasks: In contrast to reducer tasks, the number of mapper tasks is implicitly specified. Controlling the number of mappers and the size of each task is the most typical technique to improve Hadoop mapper performance. Hadoop divides huge files into smaller bits so that the mapper may process them in parallel. However, starting a new mapper task takes a few seconds, which is an overhead that should be avoided. The following are some suggestions: JVM job can be reused. Aim for map chores that take 1–3 minutes to complete. If the average mapper running duration is less than one minute, raise mapred.min.split.size to assign fewer mappers per slot and decrease mapper initialization costs. For a group of smaller files, use the Combine file input format.

7.23.2 Application Level Best Practices

Let us now discuss the tips to improve the application-specific performance in Hadoop. Following are the MapReduce Performance Tuning best practices at the Application level:

- Reduce the output of the mapper
- Reducer load balancing
- Speculative execution

Reduce the output of the mapper: Because the mapper output is sensitive to disk IO, network IO, and memory sensitivity during the shuffle phase, minimizing it can significantly increase overall performance. The following are some ideas for attaining this: Filter the records on the mapper side rather than the reducer. Use little data to create your map output key and map output value in MapReduce. Finally, compress the output of the mapper.

Reducer load balancing: Reducer tasks that are not balanced cause another performance problem. Compared to other reducers, certain reducers consume the majority of the output from the mapper and run exceptionally lengthy. The techniques for addressing this are as follows: Build a better hash function in the Partitioner class. Using MultipleOutputs, create a preprocess task to split keys. Then, in a separate map-reduce task, process the specific keys causing the issue.

Speculative Execution: When tasks take a long time to complete, it impacts MapReduce workloads. The method of speculative execution, which backs up slow processes on different computers, solves this problem. To enable speculative execution, set the configuration parameters 'mapreduce.map.tasks.speculative.execution' and 'mapreduce.reduce.tasks.speculative.execution' to true.

If the task progress is delayed owing to memory constraints, this will shorten the job execution time.

7.24 YARN

YARN or Yet Another Resource Negotiator was adopted into the core Hadoop framework with Hadoop 2.0. In Hadoop 1.0, the MapReduce job execution is controlled by two types of processes: a master process called JobTracker that runs on a separate node and sub-processes called TaskTrackers that run on the DataNodes. The JobTracker schedules the MapReduce jobs to the TaskTrackers and monitors them. The TaskTrackers execute the map and reduce tasks and report back to the JobTracker. This is a master–multiple slave concept. If the master, i.e., the JobTracker fails, all the running jobs will stop, making JobTracker the single point of failure. In addition, a JobTracker may also incorrectly blocklist or remove a TaskTracker from the list if the TaskTracker slows down or stops running due to inefficient resource allocation. YARN overcomes these bottlenecks with multiple master-slave concept. If a master fails, another master takes over its function and the job execution resumes.

In Hadoop 2.0 architecture, YARN takes over the resource management and job scheduling function which allows MapReduce to deal only with the data processing aspect.

The main components of YARN are:

- **Container:** Container is the physical resources available like memory, CPU, and network allocation. Containers can be regarded as the resource pool where YARN applications (a MapReduce or DAG jobs) are run. The resources of the data server are divided into containers so that parallel processing is enhanced. One data server can host multiple containers to support multiple compute jobs.
- **ResourceManager:** The ResourceManager is the core component of YARN that manages resource allocation and monitoring in the cluster. The ResourceManager consists of the ApplicationManager which accepts or rejects the application when it is submitted by the client, and the Scheduler which performs the scheduling function based on the resource needs of the application.
- **NodeManager:** The NodeManager runs on the slave nodes. It is responsible for managing resources of individual compute nodes in a Hadoop cluster. It controls the application and workflow on that specific node and sends heartbeats with the health status of the node to the ResourceManager.
- **ApplicationMaster:** The ApplicationMaster negotiates resource Containers from the ResourceManager and works with the NodeManager(s) to execute and monitor the progress of a single application. Here, a Hadoop application refers to a single job or a DAG of jobs. Every application has a unique ApplicationMaster attached to it.

The ResourceManager provides for high scalability as nodes in the cluster expand to work petabytes of data. YARN schedulers manage and allocate cluster resources. It can use multiple resource types like CPU, GPU and memory for scheduling. There are three types of schedulers:

- FIFO (first-in–first-out), where each application is placed in a queue in the order of submission. When the first submitted application is completed, the scheduler serves

the next application. This method is not suited for large clusters as the serving rate is low. Small applications need to wait till the large jobs are complete if they are later in the queue.
- Capacity scheduler allows for sharing resources in large clusters. It supports multi-tenancy and provides each organization a minimum-capacity guarantee. Each application in the queue is executed based on the capacity allocated. In addition, any excess capacity that is not being used will be assigned to applications running below capacity. Capacity scheduler set-up can ensure that no single application or queue has an unfair advantage over the resources in the cluster.
- Fair scheduler dynamically balances resources across all applications in a queue. It does not reserve capacity. All the cluster resources are provided to an application if the application is the only one running. As soon as another application starts, freed up task containers from the first application are allocated to it. After the application completes, the containers are given back to the first application if it is still running or assigned to new applications as required. This allows for high cluster utilization where each application gets the same average amount of resources in time.

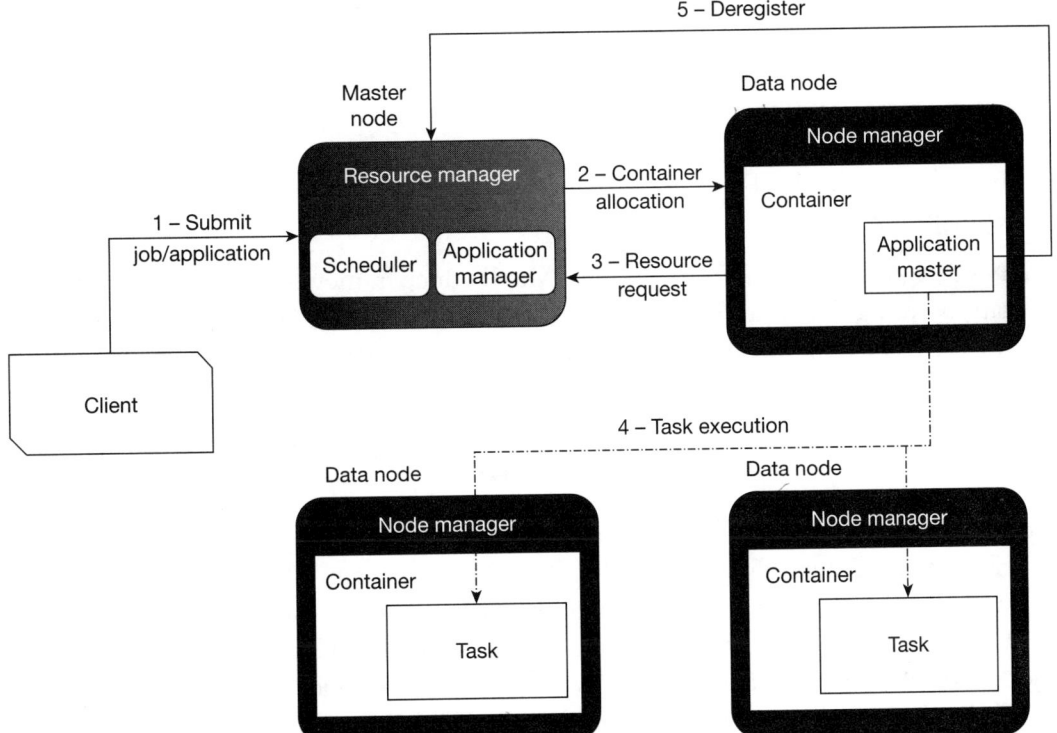

Figure 7.31 YARN workflow sequence

The sequence of steps in the YARN workflow (Fig. 7.31) is as follows:

1. The client submits MapReduce jobs or application to the ResourceManager with the required specifications. The ResourceManager scheduler then requests the

ApplicationManager to identify available NodeManagers to take up the request and schedules the job. As there can be multiple applications submitted, the ResourceManager needs to check the available capacity to see if the application can be launched.

2. The ResourceManager (RM) allocates a Container that can launch the ApplicationMaster. Once confirmed, the RM contacts the NodeManager (of the specific node) for resource allocation. The NodeManager launches the ApplicationMaster process within the Container.

3. The ApplicationMaster registers with the ResourceManager. This allows the Client program to get the node details from the ResourceManager to communicate with the ApplicationMaster directly. The ApplicationMaster will negotiate with the ResourceManager (ApplicationManager) to allocate containers if additional resources are needed. The ApplicationMaster is responsible for the execution and monitoring of all the individual tasks for the application.

4. The application code is executed in the Container(s). The ApplicationMaster launches the Container by providing the Container Launch Specification to the NodeManager(s). The launch specification allows the Container to directly communicate with the ApplicationMaster to get the status, and progress updates. The ApplicationManager monitors the end-to-end lifecycle of the application and can reallocate resources when a NodeManager fails.

5. Once the processing tasks are successfully completed, the ApplicationMaster deregisters with the ResourceManager and shuts down to free up its container for repurposing.

YARN's design not only caters to Hadoop MapReduce framework, but also to distributed applications using other frameworks as well. YARN supports multiple data processing engines such as batch, stream, interactive, and graph processing, all of which can work together efficiently.

SUMMARY

MapReduce is a parallel processing technique for processing data, Big Data in particular, which is distributed on a commodity cluster. The "MapReduce System" (also called "infrastructure" or "framework") orchestrates the processing by marshalling the distributed servers, running the various tasks in parallel, managing all communications and data transfers between the various parts of the system, and providing solutions for redundancy and fault tolerance.

MapReduce is a programming model that processes and analyzes huge datasets logically into separate clusters. While Map sorts the data, Reduce segregates the data into logical clusters. The Unique Selling Proposition (USP) of MapReduce is its fault tolerance and scalability.

A MapReduce Task works with a Key-Value pair; thus when we talk about a Map, we are talking about a Map that accepts a Key-Value as input and returns a list of Key-Value as output. This list of Key-Value pairs is shuffled, and the Reducer receives the Key input as well as a list of Values. Finally, the Reducer provides us with a list of Key-Value pairs. MapReduce technique has two distinct benefits, namely, Parallel Processing and Data Locality.

Parallel processing: Parallel processing is the first benefit. We can always process the data in parallel using Map Reduce.

Data locality: Hadoop MapReduce provides a flexible feature in that it allows us to process data regardless of its location. The data we moved into the Hadoop Cluster is separated into HDFS Blocks, then saved in Slave Machines or DataNodes. MapReduce detects and routes processing and logic to the appropriate Slave Nodes or DataNodes, where the data is stored as HDFS Blocks.

After the mapper finishes, there is one more phase in MapReduce, called shuffling and sorting. Shuffling is the movement of intermediate records from mappers to reducers. Exchanging the intermediate outputs from the map tasks to where the reducers require them is shuffling. As the term MapReduce indicates, the reduction step occurs after the mapper phase has been finished. The Reducer receives the output of a Mapper or a map job (key-value pairs) and the key-value pair from numerous map tasks. It then condenses the intermediate data tuples (intermediate key-value pair) into a smaller collection of tuples or key-value pairs, which serve as the final output.

Reducer Class: The reducer receives the intermediate output from the mapper, processes it, and creates the final output, which is then saved in HDFS.

Driver Class: A Driver Class is the most important part of a MapReduce task. It is in charge of configuring a MapReduce job to run in Hadoop. We provide Mapper and Reducer Classes names that are lengthy and include data types and task names.

Input Files: Input files hold the data for a MapReduce process, and input files are commonly kept in HDFS. The format of these files can be whatever you choose, including line-based log files and binary forms.

Input Format: It specifies how these input files should be divided and read. It chooses the files or other objects that will be utilized as input. Input Format creates Input Split.

Input Split: Input Format creates Input Split to properly represent the data that will be processed by a single Mapper. Each split gets its own map task; therefore the total number of map tasks equals the total number of Input Splits. The split is separated into records, and the mapper will process each record individually. In Hadoop MapReduce, the logical representation of data is called Input Split.

Record Reader: It talks with Hadoop MapReduce's Input Split and turns data into key-value pairs that the mapper can read. Text Input Format is used by default to turn input into a key-value pair. Until the file reading is finished, the Record Reader talks with the Input Split. Each line in the file is given a byte offset (a unique integer). These key-value pairs are then passed to the mapper to be processed further. A Record Reader is more than a record iterator, and the map operation generates a key-value pair from one record that is supplied to the map function. We can observe this using the mapper's run function.

Mapper: Each input record (from Record Reader) is processed and a new key-value pair is created by Mapper, which is entirely distinct from the input pair. Mapper's output is referred to as intermediate output because it is written to the local disk. The Mapper's output is not kept on HDFS since it is transitory data, and uploading to HDFS would result in redundant copies (also HDFS is a high-latency system). The output of the mapper is transferred to the combiner for additional processing.

In MapReduce, the Map function processes a single key-value pair and outputs a set of key-value pairs, while the Reduce function processes values grouped by the same key and outputs a second set of key-value pairs. The Map's output types should match the Reduce's input types, as seen below:

- Map: $(K1, V1) \rightarrow$ list $(K2, V2)$
- Reduce: $\{(K2, \text{list}(V2)\} \rightarrow$ list $(K3, V3)$

In Hadoop, the creation of a key-value pair is dependent on the dataset and the desired output. The key-value pair is defined in four places in general: 1. Map input, 2. Map output, 3. Reduce input, and 4. Reduce output.

MapReduce Combiner: When we execute a MapReduce task on a huge dataset, the Mapper generates large blocks of intermediate data, which is then sent on to the Reducer for further processing, causing massive network congestion. The Hadoop Combiner function in the MapReduce architecture is important for decreasing network congestion. The MapReduce combiner is also known as a 'Mini-reducer'. The Combiner's main task is to process the Mapper's output data before sending it on to the Reducer. It is optional to utilize and runs after the Mapper and before the Reducer.

Partitioner: If we are working on more than one reducer in Hadoop MapReduce, Partitioner comes into play (for one reducer, partitioner is not used). The output of the combiners is sent into the partitioner, which partitions the data. The output is partitioned and then sorted on the basis of the key. The partition is determined using the hash function and the key (or a subset of the key). Each combiner output is partitioned in MapReduce based on the key value, with a record with the same key value going into the same partition, and then each partition is delivered to a reducer. Partitioning allows the map output to be distributed evenly throughout the reduction.

In the sort phase, a merge sort of all map outputs occurs in a single run and finally in the reduced phase a user-defined reduced function is applied to the merged run; the arguments are the keys and the corresponding list of values. The output is written to a file in HDFS. The mappers on each of the nodes are assigned to each input split.

The intermediate outputs are stored in the local file system; thereafter a partitioner assigns the records to the reducer. In the shuffling phase, the intermediate key-value pairs are exchanged by all nodes. The key-value pairs are then sorted by applying the key and reduced function. Reduce phase cannot start until all mappers have finished processing.

MapReduce Job: A job is a MapReduce program (class) that causes multiple Map and Reduce functions to run parallel over the life of the program. Many copies of Map and many copies of Reduce functions are forked for parallel processing, across the input dataset. A task is a Map or Reduce function executed on a subset of this data.

Reducer in Hadoop takes the Mapper's output (intermediate key-value pair) and processes them to create the output. The reducer's output is the final output saved in HDFS.

Shuffling is the Hadoop word for the process of transferring intermediate output from mappers to reducers. A reducer receives one or more keys and their associated values. The mapper's intermediated key-value is automatically ordered by key.

Shuffle Phase: The sorted output from the mapper is the input to the Reducer during the Shuffle Phase of the MapReduce Reducer. During the Shuffle phase, the framework uses HTTP to retrieve the appropriate division of all mappers' output.

Sort Phase: The input from multiple mappers is sorted again in this step based on related keys in distinct Mappers. The shuffle and sort processes happen at the same time.

Reduce Phase: After shuffling and sorting, the reduction job collects the key-value pairs in this step. Finally, the output of the reduction task is sent to the Filesystem using the OutputCollector.collect() function. The output of the Reducer is not sorted.

Map Input: By default, Map input will use the line offset as the key and the text of the line as the value. We may change them by utilizing a custom input format.

Map Output: The primary purpose is to filter data and offer an environment for data grouping depending on the key.

Key: The key will be the field/text/object on which the data must be sorted and aggregated on the reducer side.

Value: This is the field/text/object that each particular reduction method will handle.

Reduce Input: Reduce's input is Map's output; therefore it is the same as Map-Output.

Reduce Output: It is dependent on the output required.

InputSplit and RecordReader use TextInputFormat to construct the Key-value pair in Hadoop. As a result, Key is the byte offset of the line's start inside the file, and Value is the line's content, omitting line terminators.

Hadoop Input Format examines the job's Input Specification. Input Format divides the input file into Input Splits, each assigned to a different Mapper.

The data for a MapReduce task is initially saved in input files, which are commonly kept in HDFS. Although the format of these files is variable, binary and line-based log files can be utilized. We specify how these input files are divided and read using InputFormat.

Sorting: The keys supplied by the mapper are automatically sorted by the MapReduce Framework, i.e., all intermediate key-value pairs in MapReduce generated by the mapper are sorted by key and not by value before commencing the reduction. The reducer's values are not ordered; they can be in any sequence. Sorting in Hadoop makes it easier for reducers to determine when a new reduce process should begin. The reducer will save time as a result of this. When the next key in the sorted input data is different from the preceding key, the reducer starts a new reduce process. Each reduction job receives key-value pairs as input and outputs key-value pairs.

Hadoop OutputFormat: Hadoop RecordWriter accepts Reducer's output data and writes it to output files. The OutputFormat determines how these output key-value pairs are recorded in output files by RecordWriter. The functions OutputFormat and InputFormat are quite similar. Hadoop's OutputFormat instances are used to write to files on HDFS or local drive. The output format for a MapReduce task is described by OutputFormat based on the output specification. The MapReduce task checks to see if the output directory already exists. The RecordWriter implementation provided by OutputFormat is used to write the job's output files. A FileSystem is used to store the output files. The output directory is configured using the FileOutputFormat. setOutputPath() function. Each Reducer creates a new file in a shared output directory.

MapOnly job in MapReduce: MapReduce is a software framework that makes it simple to create applications that handle the massive amounts of organized and unstructured data contained in Hadoop's Distributed File System (HDFS). Map and Reduce are two fundamental operations performed by the MapReduce algorithm. The Hadoop Map phase turns a collection of data into another set of data, with each piece split down into tuples (key-value pairs). The Hadoop Reduce phase takes the map result as input and combines the data tuples depending on the key, changing the value of the key appropriately.

Hadoop Speculative Execution: Slow-running jobs are not fixed or diagnosed by Apache Hadoop. Instead, it tries to identify when a work is taking longer than planned and creates a backup task that is similar to the original (the backup task is called as speculative task). In Hadoop, this is known as speculative execution.

Hadoop Counters allow us to track the status of a map/reduce process or the number of operations it does. Counters in Hadoop MapReduce are a good way to collect statistics on a MapReduce task, whether for quality control or application-level statistics. They can also be used to diagnose problems. Counters are global Hadoop counters that are established by the MapReduce framework or by applications. Each Hadoop counter has an "Enum" for its name and a long data type for its value. Counters are grouped into groups, each of which contains counters from a certain Enum class. Hadoop Counters substantiate the following: 1. Bytes are read and written in the right order. 2. The proper number of tasks are initiated and completed effectively. 3. The quantity of CPU and memory used by the task and cluster nodes is adequate.

Hadoop MapReduce Counter Types: MapReduce Counters are divided into two categories: 1. MapReduce that has built-in counters. 2. Counters that are defined by the user/custom counters in MapReduce.

MapReduce Performance Tuning Best Practices: Hadoop performance tuning can assist you in improving the performance of your Hadoop cluster and ensuring that you get the best results possible while implementing Hadoop programming in Big Data firms.

The initial step in Hadoop performance tuning is to run a task, identify bottlenecks, and resolve them to achieve the best results.

EXERCISES

Multiple Choice Questions

1. **In MapReduce program, map segregates the data into logical clusters, reduce sorts the data.**
   A. True B. False
   Answer: B
   Explanation: MapReduce is a programming model that processes and analyzes huge datasets logically and sorts it into separate clusters. While Map sorts the data, Reduce segregates the data into logical clusters. A MapReduce program is composed of a Map() procedure that performs filtering and sorting (such as sorting students by the first name into queues, one queue for each name) and a Reduce() procedure that performs a summary operation (such as counting the number of students in each queue, yielding name frequencies).

2. **If one of the machines causes a delay, the entire process will be delayed. This is called as:**
   A. Critical path problem B. Problem of reliability
   C. Equal-split issue D. Single-split failure
   Answer: A
   Explanation: The time it takes to complete the project without postponing the following milestone or the actual completion date is the critical path problem. As a result, if one of the machines causes a delay, the entire process will be delayed.

3. **What happens if one of the machines handling a portion of the data fails? It becomes difficult to take this failover. This is called as:**
   A. Critical path problem B. Problem of reliability
   C. Equal-split issue D. Single-split failure
   Answer: B
   Explanation: If one of the machines handling a portion of the data fails, it becomes difficult to take this failover. This is called as Problem of Reliability.

4. **How data is distributed evenly such that no single system is overburdened or underused. This is called as:**
   A. Critical path problem
   B. Problem of reliability
   C. Equal-split issue
   D. Single-split failure
   Answer: C
   Explanation
   Equal-split issue: How can we break down the data into smaller chunks so that each computer has an equal amount of data? In other words, it is the challenge of distributing the data evenly such that no single system is overburdened or underused.

5. **We won't be able to compute the outcome if any of the machines fails to produce output. This is called as:**
   A. Critical path problem
   B. Problem of reliability
   C. Equal-split issue
   D. Single-split failure
   Answer: D
   Explanation: We won't be able to compute the outcome if any of the machines fails to produce output. As a result, there should be a method to assure the system's fault tolerance capabilities. This is called as Single-split Failure.

6. **These hold the data for a MapReduce process, and are commonly kept in HDFS:**
   A. Input files
   B. Input format
   C. Input split
   D. Record reader
   Answer: A
   Explanation: Input files hold the data for a MapReduce process, and input files are commonly kept in HDFS. The format of these files can be whatever you choose, including line-based log files and binary forms.

7. **These specify how the input files should be divided and read:**
   A. Input files
   B. Input format
   C. Input split
   D. Record reader
   Answer: B
   Explanation: Input Format specifies how the input files should be divided and read. It chooses which files or other objects will be utilized as Input. Input Format creates Input Split.

8. **The total number of map tasks equals the total number of:**
   A. Input files
   B. Input format
   C. Input split
   D. Record reader
   Answer: C
   Explanation: Input Format creates Input Split to properly represent the data processed by a single mapper. Each split gets its map task; therefore, the total number of map tasks equals the total number of Input Split. Finally, the split is separated into records, and the mapper will process each record individually.

9. **This talks with the Input Split until the file reading is finished:**
   A. Input files
   B. Input format
   C. Input split
   D. Record reader
   Answer: D
   Explanation: Record Reader talks with Hadoop MapReduce's Input Split and turns data into key-value pairs that the mapper can read. By default, text Input Format is used to turn Input into a key-value pair. The Record Reader talks with the Input Split until the file reading is finished. Each line in the file is given a byte offset (a unique integer). These key-value pairs are then passed to the mapper to be processed further.

10. **This is responsible for executing a single application or MapReduce job:**
    A. Node manager
    B. Application master
    C. Name node
    D. Data node
    Answer: B
    Explanation: The application master is responsible for executing a single application or MapReduce job. It divides the job requests into tasks and assigns those tasks to node managers running on one or more slave nodes. The node manager has several dynamically created resource containers. The size of a container depends on the number of resources it contains, such as memory, CPU disk, and network I/O. It executes Snap and Reduce tasks by launching these containers when instructed by the MapReduce application master, MapReduce, and associated tasks.

11. **This can keep track of individual map tasks and run them in parallel:**
    A. Node manager
    B. Application master
    C. Name node
    D. Data node
    Answer: A
    Explanation: The mapping process is the initial step in processing individual input records. Node managers can keep track of individual map tasks and run them in parallel. A map job runs as part of a container execution by the node manager on a particular data node. Within a cluster, the application master keeps track of a MapReduce job. A Hadoop MapReduce job is submitted by a client in the form of an input file or several input splits of files containing data.

12. **Output from this is the final output saved in HDFS:**
    A. Mapper
    B. Reducer
    C. Combiner
    D. Shuffler
    Answer: B
    Explanation: Reducer in Hadoop takes the Mapper's output (intermediate key-value pair) and processes them to create the output. The reducer's output is the final output saved in HDFS.

13. **This is the basic class for all InputFormats that work with files:**
    A. FileInputFormat
    B. KeyValueTextInputFormat
    C. SequenceFileInputFormat
    D. TextInputFormat

Answer: A

Explanation: Hadoop's FileInputFormat is the basic class for all InputFormats that work with files. Hadoop FileInputFormat determines the location of data files in the input directory. FileInputFormat is given a path containing files to read when we start a Hadoop job. All files are read by FileInputFormat, which separates them into one or more Input Splits.

14. **It is MapReduce's default InputFormat:**
    A. FileInputFormat
    B. KeyValueTextInputFormat
    C. SequenceFileInputFormat
    D. TextInputFormat
    Answer: D
    Explanation: TextInputFormat is MapReduce's default InputFormat. Each line of each input file is treated as a distinct record by TextInputFormat, which does not do any processing. This is helpful for unformatted data or records that are based on lines, such as log files.

15. **This uses a tab character ('/t') to divide the line:**
    A. FileInputFormat
    B. KeyValueTextInputFormat
    C. SequenceFileInputFormat
    D. TextInputFormat
    Answer: B
    Explanation: KeyValueTextInputFormat works in a similar way to TextInputFormat in that each line of input is treated as a single record. While TextInputFormat treats the full line as the value, the KeyValueTextInputFormat uses a tab character ('/t') to divide the line into key and value. The value is the remainder of the line following the tab character, whereas the key is everything up to the tab character.

16. **This is a JDBC-based InputFormat for reading data from a relational database:**
    A. FileInputFormat
    B. DBInputFormat
    C. SequenceFileInputFormat
    D. TextInputFormat
    Answer: B
    Explanation: Hadoop DBInputFormat is a JDBC-based InputFormat for reading data from a relational database. We must be careful not to overwhelm the database from which we are reading too many mappers since it lacks portioning capabilities. As a result, it is excellent for importing tiny datasets and also merging them with huge datasets from HDFS using MultipleInputs. LongWritables is the key, and DBWritables is the value.

17. **This function in the MapReduce architecture is essential for decreasing network congestion:**
    A. Mapper
    B. Reducer
    C. Combiner
    D. Shuffler
    Answer: C
    Explanation
    MapReduce Combiner: When we execute a MapReduce task on a huge dataset, the Mapper generates large blocks of intermediate data, and sends them to the

Reducer for further processing, causing massive network congestion. The Hadoop Combiner function in the MapReduce architecture is essential for decreasing network congestion.

18. **This is the default Hadoop reduction output format in MapReduce:**
    A. MapFileOutputFormat
    B. LazyOutputFormat
    C. SequenceFileOutputFormat
    D. TextOutputFormat
    Answer: D
    Explanation: TextOutputFormat is the default Hadoop reduction Output Format in MapReduce. It writes (key-value) pairs on individual lines of text files, and its keys and values can be of any type since TextOutputFormat converts them to strings using toString().

19. **This format is an OutputFormat wrapper that ensures that the output file is produced only when the record for a certain partition is emitted.**
    A. MapFileOutputFormat
    B. LazyOutputFormat
    C. SequenceFileOutputFormat
    D. TextOutputFormat
    Answer: B
    Explanation
    LazyOutputFormat: Even if the output files are empty, FileOutputFormat will occasionally generate them. LazyOutputFormat is an OutputFormat wrapper that ensures that the output file is produced only when the record for a certain partition is emitted.

20. **Consider a scenario in which we only need to operate and no aggregation is required; in this case, we will use:**
    A. Aggregate only
    B. Map only
    C. Reduce only
    D. Output only
    Answer: B
    Explanation: Consider a scenario in which we only need to operate and no aggregation is required; in this case, we will use Hadoop's 'Map-Only job'. The map does all tasks with its InputSplit in a Hadoop Map-Only job, while the reducer performs none. The final result is the map output.

21. **This, in Hadoop MapReduce, is an excellent way to collect statistics on a MapReduce task, whether for quality control or application-level statistics:**
    A. Mapper
    B. Reducer
    C. Counter
    D. Splitter
    Answer: C
    Explanation: Hadoop Counters allow to track the status of a map/reduce process or the number of operations it does. Counters in Hadoop MapReduce are an excellent way to collect statistics on a MapReduce task, whether for quality control or application-level statistics. They can also be used to diagnose problems.

Short-answer Questions

1. **Write short notes on MapReduce and its importance.**
   MapReduce is a parallel processing technique for processing data, particularly Big Data, distributed on a commodity clus ter. Supposing we have a large file, say a few Tera Bytes in size, it will take a long time if we process it serially from top to bottom. On the other hand, MapReduce is designed to process our data in parallel. Our file of Tera Bytes size is broken into chunks and processed in parallel. MapReduce is frequently used to speed up computation by breaking the file down into smaller files and simultaneously solving each smaller file in parallel using multiple computers or CPUs.

2. **Compare MapReduce with counting the number of words in a newspaper.**
   For counting the number of words in a newspaper, we will count the words in each paragraph, thereby for each page. And then, we will sum up the numbers on each page. This is a simple process. However, it may take much time considering the number of pages. Assuming that the newspaper has ten pages, if we have ten people to do the same job, we can give one page to each person. It may now take lesser time to count the words than the previous method. Let us assume that there are five paragraphs on each page. There are fifty paragraphs (because there are ten pages in total). Now, if fifty people are allocated to count the words in each paragraph, it may now take much lesser time than when one person counts the number of words on a single page. This is the concept behind MapReduce.

3. **Write short notes on Map and Reduce portions of MapReduce.**
   The Unique Selling Proposition (USP) of MapReduce is its fault tolerance and scalability. A parallel computation engine (MapReduce) distributes work across nodes responsible for mapping/reducing tasks. It works in two stages - the 'map' stage and the 'reduction' stage. A MapReduce program is composed of a Map() procedure that performs filtering and sorting (such as sorting students by the first name into queues, one queue for each name) and a Reduce() procedure that performs a summary operation (such as counting the number of students in each queue, yielding name frequencies).

4. **Write short notes on the key-value pair of MapReduce.**
   A MapReduce Task works with a Key-Value pair; thus, when we talk about a Map, we are talking about a Map that accepts a Key-Value as input and returns a list of Key-Value as output. This list of Key-Value pairs is shuffled, and the Reducer receives the Key input and a list of Values. Finally, the Reducer provides us with a list of Key-Value pairs.

5. **How does parallel processing help MapReduce?**
   Parallel Processing is the benefit of using MapReduce. We can always process the data in parallel using MapReduce. The data is processed in parallel using Hadoop

MapReduce, which speeds up the process. What occurs here is that Hadoop HDFS divides the entire chunk of data into HDFS Blocks, which are then processed by MapReduce, resulting in faster processing.

6. **How is data locality taken care of in the MapReduce concept?**
   Hadoop MapReduce provides a flexible feature in that it allows us to process data regardless of its location. The data we move into the Hadoop Cluster is separated into HDFS Blocks, then saved in Slave Machines or DataNodes. MapReduce detects and routes processing and logic to the appropriate Slave Nodes or DataNodes, where the data is stored as HDFS Blocks.
   The Processing is carried out in parallel on a smaller amount of data in various places. This saves a significant amount of time and network bandwidth necessary to transport Big Data from one location to another.

7. **"A Big Online Store" wants to calculate its total sales city-wise for 2021 in India. How can this be solved using the traditional computing environment?**
   In a traditional computing environment, we may solve this problem by using a hash table, where the key is the city name and the amount is the value. However, if we run the terabyte of data which "A Big Online Store" has, it will take a long time to read and process it. It may also run out of memory because of the massive amount of data.

8. **What is the critical path and reliability problem of the traditional approach system of using a hash table?**
   Critical Path Problem: The time it takes to complete a project without postponing the following milestone or the actual completion date is the critical path problem. As a result, if one of the machines causes a delay, the entire process will be delayed.
   Problem of reliability: This occurs when one of the machines handling a portion of the data fails. It becomes difficult to take this failover.

9. **What is the Equal-split issue and Single-split failure of the traditional approach system of using the hash table?**
   Equal-split issue: This is the problem of breaking down the data into smaller chunks so that each computer has an equal amount of data. In other words, the data has to be distributed evenly such that no single system is overburdened or underused.
   Single-split failure: We won't be able to compute the outcome if any of the machines fails to produce output. As a result, there should be a method to assure the system's fault tolerance capabilities.

10. **Write small notes on Mapper class.**
    The Mapper class is the initial step in utilizing MapReduce to process data. Next, the record reader processes each Input record and creates the key-value pair for that record. This intermediate data is saved to the local disk by Hadoop's Mapper store. The MapReduce program denotes a block of work that comprises a single map job.

11. **What are the Reducer class and Driver class of the MapReduce program?**
    Reducer Class: The reducer receives the intermediate output from the mapper, processes it, and creates the final output, saved in HDFS.
    Driver Class: A Driver Class is an essential part of a MapReduce task. It is in charge of configuring a MapReduce job to run in Hadoop. We provide Mapper and Reducer Classes names that are lengthy and include data types and task names.

12. **What is splitting?**
    Input from HDFS gets divided into various sub-inputs. This process is called Input Splitting, and the entire Input gets divided into splits of data based on the new line character.

13. **What are input files and input format in MapReduce?**
    Input Files: Input files hold the data for a MapReduce process. They are commonly kept in HDFS. The format of these files can be whatever you choose, including line-based log files and binary forms.
    Input Format: It specifies how these input files should be divided and read. It chooses the files or other objects that will be utilized as Input. Input Format creates Input Split.

14. **What is Record Reader in MapReduce?**
    Record Reader: It talks with Hadoop MapReduce's Input Split and turns data into key-value pairs that the mapper can read. Text Input Format is used by default to turn input into a key-value pair. Until the file reading is finished, the Record Reader talks with the Input Split. Each line in the file is given a byte offset (a unique integer). These key-value pairs are then passed to the mapper to be processed further.

15. **What is Combiner in MapReduce?**
    Combiner: The 'Mini-reducer' is another name for the combiner. Hadoop MapReduce Combiner conducts local aggregation on mappers' output, reducing data travel between the mapper and the reducer. Following the completion of the combiner function, the output is handed to the partitioner for further processing.

16. **What is Partitioner in MapReduce?**
    If we are working on more than one reducer in Hadoop MapReduce, Partitioner comes into play (for one reducer, partitioner is not used). The output of the combiners is sent into the partitioner, which partitions the data. The output is partitioned and then sorted based on the Key. The partition is determined using the hash function and the Key (or a subset of the Key). Each combiner output is partitioned in MapReduce based on the key-value, with a record with the same key value going into the same partition. Then each partition is delivered to a reducer. Partitioning allows the map output to be distributed evenly throughout the reduction.

17. **Write notes on Shuffling in MapReduce.**
    The shuffle refers to the physical movement of data through a network. Once the mappers have completed their work, their output is shuffled on the reducer nodes;

the intermediate result is combined and sorted before being sent into the Reduce phase. In this phase, for every Key, there is a list prepared. So the Shuffling step will find the appearance of Key Bigdata, and it will add the Values to the list.

18. **Write notes on the Reducer phase of MapReduce.**
    It takes the collection of intermediate key-value pairs generated by the mappers as input and applies a reducer function to each of them to produce the output. The reducer's output is the final output saved in HDFS. First, the intermediate outputs are stored in the local file system; then, a partitioner assigns the records to the reducer. In the shuffling phase, the intermediate key-value pairs are exchanged by all nodes. The key-value pairs are then sorted by applying the Key and reduced function. Again, the output is stored in HDFS based on the specified output file format. Reduce phase cannot start until all mappers have finished processing. So, combining the output is an essential step once all the tasks are completed.

19. **Define a job in MapReduce Program.**
    A job is a MapReduce program (class) that causes multiple maps and reduces functions to run parallel over the program's life. Many copies of the map and many copies of reduced functions are forked for parallel processing across the input dataset.

20. **What are application master and node manager in MapReduce Program?**
    The application master is responsible for executing a single application or MapReduce job. It divides the job requests into tasks and assigns the tasks to node managers running on one or more slave nodes. The node manager has several dynamically created resource containers. The size of a container depends on the number of resources it contains, such as memory, CPU disk, and network i/o. It executes snap and reduced tasks by launching these containers when instructed by the MapReduce application master, MapReduce, and associated tasks.

21. **How does Hadoop generate key-value pairs?**
    The logical representation of data is called InputSplit. A MapReduce application refers to a unit of work that comprises a single map job. Record Reader connects with the InputSplit and turns data into key-value pairs that the Mapper can read. TextInputFormat is used by default to turn input into a key-value pair. Until the file reading is finished, the RecordReader talks with the Inputsplit. Because the Mapper only understands key-value pairs of data, data must first be turned into key-value pairs before being sent to it.

22. **How does Hadoop Mapper work?**
    For the Hadoop mapper, InputSplits turns the physical representation of the block into logic. Two InputSplits are required to read a 100MB file. For each block, one InputSplit is formed, with one RecordReader and one Mapper for each InputSplit. The number of splits for a specific file may be customized by adjusting the mapred. max.split. Size parameter, during job execution, does not always rely on the number of blocks.

23. **What is the job of a record reader?**
    The RecordReader's job is to keep reading and transforming data into key-value pairs until the file is finished. RecordReader assigns a byte offset (unique number) to each line in the file. In addition, the mapper receives this key-value pair. Intermediate data is the output of the mapper software (key-value pairs which are understandable to reduce).

24. **How does Hadoop Reducer work?**
    Reducer in Hadoop takes the Mapper's output (intermediate key-value pair) and processes them to create the Reducer output. The Reducer's output is the final output saved in HDFS. We usually conduct aggregation or summation type computations in the Hadoop Reducer.

25. **How does the shuffle phase work in MapReduce?**
    Shuffle Phase: The sorted output from the Mapper is the input to the Reducer during the Shuffle Phase of the MapReduce Reducer. During the Shuffle phase, the framework uses HTTP to retrieve the appropriate division of all mappers' output.
    Sort Phase: The input from multiple mappers is sorted again in this step based on related keys in distinct Mappers. The shuffle and sort processes happen at the same time.

26. **How does the user set the number of reducers in MapReduce?**
    With the help of Job.setNumreduceTasks(int), the user sets the number of reducers for the Job. The correct number of reducers is 0.95 or 1.75 multiplied by (<no. of nodes> * <no. of the maximum container per node>). With 0.95, all reducers immediately launch and transfer map outputs as the maps finish. With 1.75, the first round of reducers is finished by the faster nodes, and the second wave of reducers is launched, doing a much better job of load balancing.
    Hadoop Reducer is the second phase of MapReduce processing. The Hadoop Reducer performs aggregation or summation computations in three stages (shuffle, sort, and reduce). As a result, HDFS saves Reducer's final output.

27. **Write short notes on Hadoop's FileInputFormat.**
    Hadoop's FileInputFormat is the introductory class for all InputFormats that work with files. Hadoop FileInputFormat determines the location of data files in the input directory. FileInputFormat is given a path containing files to read when starting a Hadoop job. All files are read by FileInputFormat, which separates them into one or more InputSplits.

28. **Write short notes on Hadoop's TextInputFormat.**
    TextInputFormat is MapReduce's default InputFormat. Each input file line is treated as a distinct record by TextInputFormat, which does not do any processing. This is helpful for unformatted data or records based on lines, such as log files. When paired with the file name, the key is the byte offset at the beginning of the line inside the file (not the entire file, only one split). Thus, it will be unique. The contents of the line, except line terminators, are the value.

29. **Write short notes on Hadoop's KeyValueTextInputFormat.**
    KeyValueTextInputFormat works similarly to TextInputFormat in that each line of input is treated as a single record. While TextInputFormat treats the entire line as the value, the KeyValueTextInputFormat uses a tab character ('/t') to divide the line into key and value. The value is the remainder of the line following the tab character, whereas the key is everything up to the tab character.

30. **Write short notes on Hadoop's SequenceFileInputFormat.**
    SequenceFileInputFormat is a Hadoop Input Format that reads sequence files. Series files are binary files that hold binary key-value pairs in a sequence. Sequence files compress data in blocks and allow for direct serialization and deserialization of various data types (not just text). Both the Key and the Value are user-defined in this case.

31. **Write short notes on Hadoop's SequenceFileAsTextInputFormat.**
    SequenceFileAsTextInputFormat is a kind of SequenceFileInputFormat, which transforms sequence file key values to text objects. The keys and values are converted using the 'tostring()' function. This InputFormat converts sequence files into streamable input.

32. **Write short notes on Hadoop's SequenceFileAsBinaryInputFormat.**
    Hadoop SequenceFileAsBinaryInputFormat is a SequenceFileInputFormat that extracts the keys and values of a sequence file as an opaque binary object.

33. **Write short notes on Hadoop's NLineInputFormat.**
    Hadoop NLineInputFormat is a variant of TextInputFormat in which the keys are the line's byte offset, and the values are the line's contents. With TextInputFormat and KeyValueTextInputFormat, each Mapper receives a variable number of input lines, which changes depending on the size of the split and the length of the lines. We use NLineInputFormat if we want our Mapper to accept a set number of input lines. N is the number of lines of input received by each Mapper. Each Mapper receives precisely one line of input by default (N=1). If N=2, each split will have two lines. The first two Key-Value pairs will be given to one Mapper, while the second two Key-Value pairs will be given to another mapper.

34. **Write short notes on Hadoop's DBInputFormat.**
    Hadoop DBInputFormat is a JDBC-based InputFormat for reading data from a relational database. We must be careful not to overwhelm the database from which we are reading too many mappers since it lacks portioning capabilities. As a result, it is excellent for importing tiny datasets and also merging them with huge datasets from HDFS using MultipleInputs. LongWritables is the key, and DBWritables is the value.

35. **Write short notes on InputSplit in MapReduce.**
    In Hadoop MapReduce, the logical representation of data is called InputSplit. A MapReduce application refers to a unit of work that comprises a single map job.

Hadoop InputSplit represents the data handled by each Mapper. The split is broken down into tracks. As a result, the Mapper goes over each record (a key-value pair). The length of an InputSplit is measured in bytes, and each InputSplit has storage locations (hostname strings). MapReduce places map tasks near the divided data as feasible using storage locations. To reduce job duration, map tasks are performed in the order of size of the splits, with the greatest split being handled first (greedy approximation approach). The crucial thing to remember is that InputSplit does not contain the input data; it is only a reference to the data.

36. **Write short notes on MapReduce Partitioner.**

    The Partitioner in MapReduce divides the intermediate mapper output's key. The partition is determined using the hash function and the key (or a subset of the key). The number of reduction tasks determines the overall number of divisions.

37. **Write short notes on MapReduce Combiner.**

    When we execute a MapReduce task on a huge dataset, the Mapper generates large blocks of intermediate data and sends them to the Reducer for further processing, causing massive network congestion. The Hadoop Combiner function in the MapReduce architecture is important for decreasing network congestion. The MapReduce combiner is also known as a 'Mini-reducer'. The Combiner's main task is to process the Mapper's output data before sending it on to Reducer. It is optional to utilize and runs after the Mapper and before the Reducer.

38. **What are the benefits of MapReduce Combiners, and what are the drawbacks?**

    Hadoop Combiner speeds up data transfers between the Mapper and Reducer. It reduces the quantity of data that the Reducer needs to process. The Combiner improves the Reducer's overall performance.

    There are various drawbacks to using Hadoop Combiner in MapReduce: (1) MapReduce jobs cannot rely on Hadoop combiner because the Hadoop combiner's execution cannot be guaranteed. (2) The key-value pairs are saved in Hadoop on the local filesystem, and the Combiner is invoked afterward, resulting in costly disk IO.

39. **Write short notes on TextOutputFormat of Hadoop.**

    TextOutputFormat is the default Hadoop reduction Output Format in MapReduce. It writes (key, value) pairs on individual lines of text files, and its keys and values can be of any type since TextOutputFormat converts them to strings using toString(). The tab character that separates each key-value combination can be adjusted using the MapReduce.output.textoutputformat.Separator parameter. Because KeyValue separates lines into key-value pairs based on a configurable separator, TextOutputFormat is used to read these output text files.

40. **Write short notes on SequenceFileOutputFormat of Hadoop.**

    It is an intermediate format used between MapReduce jobs, which quickly serializes arbitrary data types to the file. The corresponding SequenceFileInputFormat deserializes the file into the same types and presents the data to the next Mapper in the same manner as the previous Reducer emitted it because these are compact and easily compressible. The static methods on SequenceFileOutputFormat govern compression.

41. **Write short notes on SequenceFileAsBinaryOutputFormat of Hadoop.**
    SequenceFileAsBinaryOutputFormat is a variant of SequenceFileInputFormat that writes binary keys and values to a sequence file.

42. **Write short notes on MapFileOutputFormat of Hadoop.**
    It is a Hadoop Output Format variant of FileOutputFormat that is used to write the output as map files. Because the keys in a MapFile must be inserted correctly, we must guarantee that the Reducer emits keys in the correct order.

43. **Write short notes on LazyOutputFormat of Hadoop.**
    Even if the output files are empty, FileOutputFormat will occasionally generate them. LazyOutputFormat is an OutputFormat wrapper that ensures that the output file is produced only when the record for a certain partition is emitted.

44. **Write short notes on DBOutputFormat of Hadoop.**
    In Hadoop, the DBOutputFormat Output Format is used to write to relational databases and HBase. It saves the output of reduction to a SQL table. It takes key-value pairs with a type that extends DBwritable as the key. The returned RecordWriter publishes just the key to the database with a batch SQL query.

45. **Write short notes on the MapOnly job in MapReduce.**
    Consider a scenario in which we only need to operate and no aggregation is required; in this case, we will use Hadoop's 'Map-Only job'. The map does all tasks with its InputSplit in a Hadoop Map-Only job, while the Reducer performs none. The final result is the map output in this case.

46. **What are the advantages of a Hadoop MapOnly job?**
    There is a key, sort, and shuffle phase between the map and reduction stages. Sort and shuffle are in charge of ascending the keys and then grouping items based on the same keys. This step is quite costly, and if we don't need it, we should skip it. By skipping it, we will also skip the sort and shuffle phases. This also reduces network congestion because a mapper's output travels to the Reducer in shuffling, and large data must travel to the Reducer when the data size is large. In a map-only task, the output of the Mapper is written to the local disk before being sent to the Reducer, whereas in a map-only job, the output is sent straight to HDFS. This saves time and money in the long run.

47. **Define Hadoop speculative execution.**
    Slow-running jobs are not fixed or diagnosed by Apache Hadoop. Instead, it tries to identify when work takes longer than planned and creates a backup task similar to

the original (the backup task is called a speculative task). In Hadoop, this is known as speculative execution.

48. **Why is it necessary to disable speculative execution?**
The primary goal of speculative execution is to minimize job execution time. However, redundant jobs impair clustering efficiency. In addition, because duplicate tasks are completed during speculative execution, overall throughput may be reduced. As a result, some Hadoop cluster managers prefer to disable speculative execution.

49. **Define Hadoop Counters.**
Hadoop Counters allow the user to track the status of a map/reduce process or the number of operations it does. Counters in Hadoop MapReduce are a good way to collect statistics on a MapReduce task, whether for quality control or application-level statistics. They can also be used to diagnose problems. Counters are global Hadoop counters established by the MapReduce framework or by applications. Each Hadoop counter has an "Enum" for its name and a long data type for storing its value.

50. **What are the types of Hadoop MapReduce Counters?**
MapReduce Counters are divided into two categories: 1. MapReduce that has built-in counters. 2. Counters defined by the user/custom counters in MapReduce. In MapReduce built-in counters, for each task, Hadoop keeps a set of built-in Hadoop counters that indicate different metrics, such as the number of bytes and records consumed, allowing us to ensure that the intended amount of input is consumed and the expected amount of output is created. Hadoop Counters are organized into groups, and the built-in counters are divided into many groups. Task counts (updated as the task progresses) or job counters are found in each group (updated as the job progresses).

51. **How does proper configuration of the cluster help in Hadoop optimization?**
The command -noatime option is used to mount the correct configuration of the cluster DFS and MapReduce storage. This turns off access time and improves I/O performance. RAID should be avoided on TaskTracker and data node computers since it slows them down. To guarantee that all of the disks' I/O capacity is utilized, make sure mapred.local.dir and dfs. data.dir point to one directory on each of them. Ascertain that the health of the disk drives is monitored intelligently. MapReduce jobs are fault-tolerant; however, tasks must be re-executed if a disk fails. With tools like Ganglia and Hadoop monitoring metrics, we can keep track of swap and network utilization graphs. If we see swap being used, we have to reduce the amount of RAM allocated to each task in mapred.child.java.opts.

52. **How does tuning the number of MapReduce help in Hadoop Optimization?**
Tuning the number of MapReduce jobs: Reduce the number of jobs if each one takes 30–40 seconds or more. The following steps are required to begin the mapper or reducer process: first, start JVM (load JVM into memory), initialize JVM,

and finally, de-initialize JVM after processing (mapper/reducer). All of these JVM activities are time-consuming. Therefore, we should raise the number of mapper jobs to a multiple of the number of mapper slots in the cluster as long as each task runs for at least 30–40 seconds. However, we cannot plan too many reduced tasks—the number of reduced tasks should be equal to or slightly less than the number of reduced slots in the cluster for most workloads.

53. **How does combiner help in Hadoop Optimization?**
    Combiner between Mapper and Reducer: It is recommended to utilize a Combiner to conduct some aggregation before the input reaches the reducer if your approach includes computing aggregates of any kind. The MapReduce framework cleverly combines data to decrease the amount of data that must be written to disk and moved between the Map and Reduce stages of processing.

54. **How does an appropriate writable type of data help in Hadoop Optimization?**
    Appropriate writeable type for data: Many data users who are new to Hadoop Streaming or moving to Java MapReduce frequently employ the Text writable type inappropriately. Although Text is easy, converting numeric data to and from UTF8 strings is inefficient and can take up a substantial CPU time. Instead, consider utilizing binary Writables like IntWritable, FLoatWritable, and others when dealing with non-textual data.

55. **Write short notes on MapReduce Performance Tuning Best Practices.**
    Hadoop performance tuning can assist you in improving the performance of your Hadoop cluster and ensure that you get the best results possible while implementing Hadoop programming in Big Data firms. Repeat the steps below until the desired result is obtained most efficiently. Run the job → Find the bottleneck → Fix the bottleneck.
    The initial step in Hadoop performance tuning is to run a task, identify bottlenecks, and resolve them. After that, you must repeat the preceding steps until you reach a satisfactory level of performance.

56. **What are the different system-level best practices for MapReduce Performance Tuning?**
    Following are the MapReduce Performance Tuning best practices at the system level:
    - Hadoop run-time parameters tuning
    - Memory tuning
    - Minimize the map disk spill
    - Fine tune the tasks of the mapper.

57. **How does Hadoop run-time parameter tuning help in Hadoop performance?**
    Hadoop run-time parameter tuning: Hadoop offers a variety of performance tweaking options for CPU, memory, storage, and network. Most Hadoop operations are not CPU constrained; instead, memory and disk spillage are prioritized.

Tweaking Hadoop run-time parameters delves further into the mechanics of Hadoop performance tuning.

58. **How does memory tuning help Hadoop performance?**
    Memory tuning: The most general and popular rule in MapReduce performance optimization is to use as much RAM as possible without triggering swapping. The mapred.child.java.opts parameter for task memory may be found in the configuration file. For improved memory performance, Ganglia, Cloudera Manager, or Nagios may be used to monitor memory utilization on the server.

59. **How does Minimize the Map Disk Spill help in Hadoop Performance?**
    In Hadoop, the performance bottleneck is frequently the Disk IO. Several factors may be tweaked to reduce spillage, including Mapper output compression and using 70% of heap memory for spill buffer in ion mapper. However, it is best not to spill more than once because you will have to re-read and re-write all of your data, three times the IO.

60. **How do Tasks of the fine-tuning mapper help Hadoop performance?**
    Tasks of the Mapper are fine-tuned. In contrast to reducer tasks, the number of mapper tasks is implicitly specified. Controlling the number of mappers and the size of each task is the most typical technique to improve Hadoop mapper performance. Hadoop divides huge files into smaller bits so that the mapper may process them in parallel. However, starting a new mapper task takes a few seconds, which is an overhead that should be avoided. The following are some suggestions: JVM job can be reused. Aim for map chores that take 1–3 minutes to complete. If the average mapper running duration is less than one minute, raise mapred.min.split.size to assign fewer mappers per slot and decrease mapper initialization costs. For a group of smaller files, use the Combine file input format.

61. **List the various application level best practices of Hadoop.**
    Following are the MapReduce performance tuning best practices at the Application level:
    - Reduce the output of the mapper
    - Reducer load balancing
    - Speculative execution.

62. **How does reducing the mapper's output help Hadoop performance?**
    The mapper output is sensitive to disk IO, network IO, and memory during the shuffle phase. Hence, minimizing it can greatly increase overall performance. The following are some ideas for attaining this: Filter the records on the mapper side rather than the reducer. Use little data to create your map output key and map output value in MapReduce. Finally, compress the output of the mapper.

63. **How does Reducer Load Balancing help Hadoop performance?**
    Reducer Load Balancing: Reducer tasks that aren't balanced cause performance problem. Compared to other reducers, certain reducers consume the majority of the output from the mapper and run exceptionally lengthy. The techniques for load balancing are as follows: Build a better hash function in the Partitioner class. Using MultipleOutputs, create a preprocess task to split keys. Then, in a separate map-reduce task, process the specific keys causing the issue.

64. **How does speculative execution help Hadoop performance?**
    Speculative Execution: When tasks take a long time to complete, it impacts MapReduce workloads. The method of speculative execution, which backs up slow processes on different computers, solves this problem. To enable speculative execution, set the configuration parameters 'mapreduce.map.tasks.speculative.execution' and 'mapreduce.reduce.tasks.speculative.execution' to true. If the task progress is delayed owing to memory constraints, this will shorten the job execution time.

Essay-type Questions

1. Write an essay on the different features of MapReduce.
2. What are the advantages of the MapReduce framework?
3. Write an essay on the job in MapReduce.
4. Write an essay on Hadoop Mapper.
5. Write an essay on Hadoop Reducer.
6. Write an essay on Hadoop Key-Value Pair.
7. Write an essay on InputFormat in MapReduce.
8. Write an essay on InputSplit in MapReduce.
9. Write an essay on Hadoop Record Reader.
10. Write an essay on MapReduce Partitioner.
11. Write an essay on MapReduce combiner.
12. Write an essay on shuffling and sorting in MapReduce.
13. Write an essay on Hadoop Output Format.
14. Explain Input Split vs. HDFS Block in MapReduce.
15. Explain the MapOnly job in MapReduce.
16. Explain Hadoop Speculative Execution.
17. Explain Hadoop Counters.
18. Explain Hadoop Optimization.
19. Explain MapReduce Performance Tuning System-level best practices.
20. Explain the best practices of MapReduce Performance Tuning Application.

CHAPTER 8

Hadoop Ingestion

LEARNING OBJECTIVES

In the previous chapters, we had discussed about HDFS (Hadoop Distributed File System) and MapReduce. Any robust data ecosystem requires effective data input technologies, called the data ingestion layer. We may gain a new perspective on our data with an automated data flow. Analysts may focus on analysis instead of regular data operations with the data ingestion layer. This chapter discusses the details of some of the famous data ingestion tools.

8.1 Introduction

In this era of Big Data, businesses are exposed to an ever-increasing quantity of data streams from a range of sources. These datasets are essential for such corporate houses to improve their marketing approach. Therefore, businesses must harvest data from all available sources and consolidate it in one area for optimal analytics and data management to make better decisions based on these facts. This is when data ingestion tools come in handy. Data ingestion tools are software applications that automatically harvest data from a range of sources and streamline the transmission of different data streams to a single storage location (Fig. 8.1).

In addition to data extraction and transmission, data ingestion solutions may help with data processing, modification, and formatting, helping businesses complete analytics tasks faster.

8.2 Data Ingestion Types

Data ingestion may be done in three ways: real-time, batches, or a hybrid of the two in a system known as lambda architecture. Depending on their business goals, IT infrastructure and financial constraints, companies might choose one of these categories.

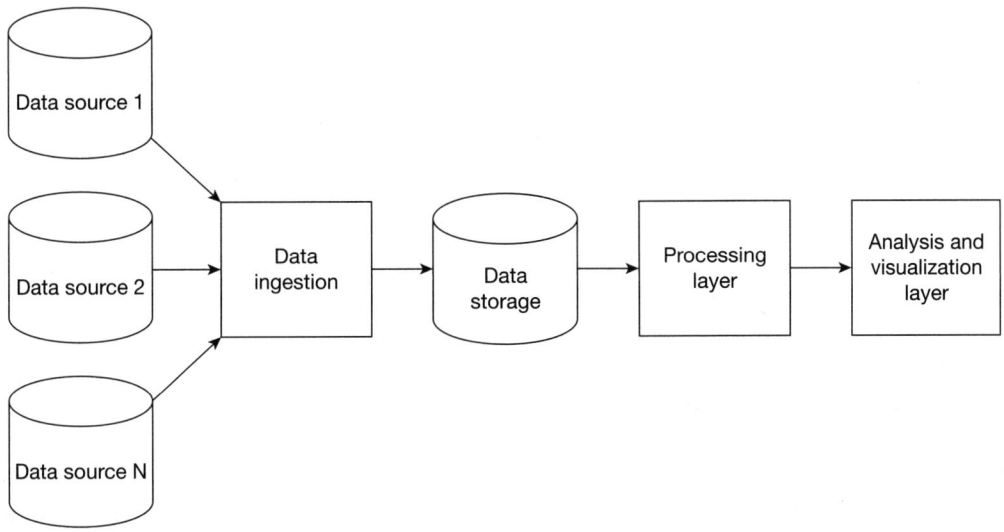

Figure 8.1 Data Ingestion – Basic architecture

8.2.1 Real-time Data Ingestion (RTDI)

The practice of gathering and sending data from source systems in real-time utilizing methods such as change data capture is known as real-time data ingestion. Change Data Capture (CDC) watches transaction or redo logs in real time and transports altered data without interfering with database operations. A company may gain a better knowledge of their business by combining and analyzing data from both on-premises and cloud settings. Real-time data input for analytical or transactional processing allows firms to make important operational choices while the data is still current. For time-sensitive use cases, such as stock market trading or power grid monitoring where companies must respond quickly to new information, real-time ingestion is critical. When it comes to making quick operational choices and recognizing and acting on fresh insights, real-time data pipelines are essential. In order to feed strong analytics solutions, real-time data intake necessitates the transfer of large volumes of data from many sources without affecting source systems and with sub-second latency. Real-time data intake is a vital step in collecting and delivering large amounts of high-velocity data – in a variety of formats – in the period required for businesses to maximize their value.

8.2.2 Batch-based Data Ingestion (BBDI)

The technique of gathering and sending data in batches at regular times is known as batch-based data intake. Simple schedules, trigger events, or any other logical ordering can be used by the ingestion layer to gather data. When firms need to collect certain data points daily or simply don't need data for real-time decision-making, batch-based ingestion is beneficial. Traditional batch approaches impose unpleasant delays when moving data. The data is already out of date by the time it is gathered and provided. Therefore, it cannot be used to make real-time operational decisions.

8.2.3 Lambda Architecture Data Ingestion (LADI)

Lambda architecture is a data intake system that combines real-time and batch processing. Batch, serving, and speed layers make up the setup. The first two levels index data in batches, but the speed layer indexes data that hasn't been picked up by the slower batch and serving layers yet. Data is available for querying with low latency thanks to this continuous hand-off between levels.

8.3 BENEFITS OF DATA INGESTION

Data ingestion technology has various benefits that enable teams to manage data more efficiently and gain a competitive advantage. Businesses may collect data from several places and bring it to a single environment for rapid access and analysis through data ingestion. When combined with ETL systems, advanced data intake pipelines may transform various data types into predefined formats and transport them to a data warehouse. Data intake automates some of the tasks engineers manually did, allowing them to focus on more critical tasks. With real-time data input, firms can see issues and opportunities more quickly and make better decisions. In addition, data engineers may use data ingestion technologies to ensure that their apps and software tools send data quickly and provide a more significant user experience.

8.3.1 Data Ingestion Tools Selection

Data ingestion software has a variety of features and capabilities. We may need to examine several variables (parameters) before deciding on the right tool for the ingestion (Fig. 8.2).

- Is the data organized, semi-structured, or unstructured when it arrives?
- Will data be ingested and processed in real time or in batches?
- What is the frequency of the ingestion?
- What is the maximum amount of data that an ingestion tool can handle?
- Is there any sensitive information that must be hidden or protected?

Data ingestion software may be utilized in a variety of ways. Every day, for example, they can import millions of records into Salesforce. Alternatively, they may guarantee that data is shared between apps on a regular basis. Ingestion software may also transport marketing data to a BI platform for further analysis.

Some of the famous Hadoop ecosystem ingestion layer tools (Fig. 8.3) are Apache Sqoop (RDBMS Connector), Apache Flume (Data Collection), Apache Kafka (Streaming), Apache Impala, Apache NiFi, Storm (Streaming), and Change Data Capture (CDC).

While data input methods appear to work similarly to ETL systems, there are significant differences. Data ingestion entails getting data from the source and transferring

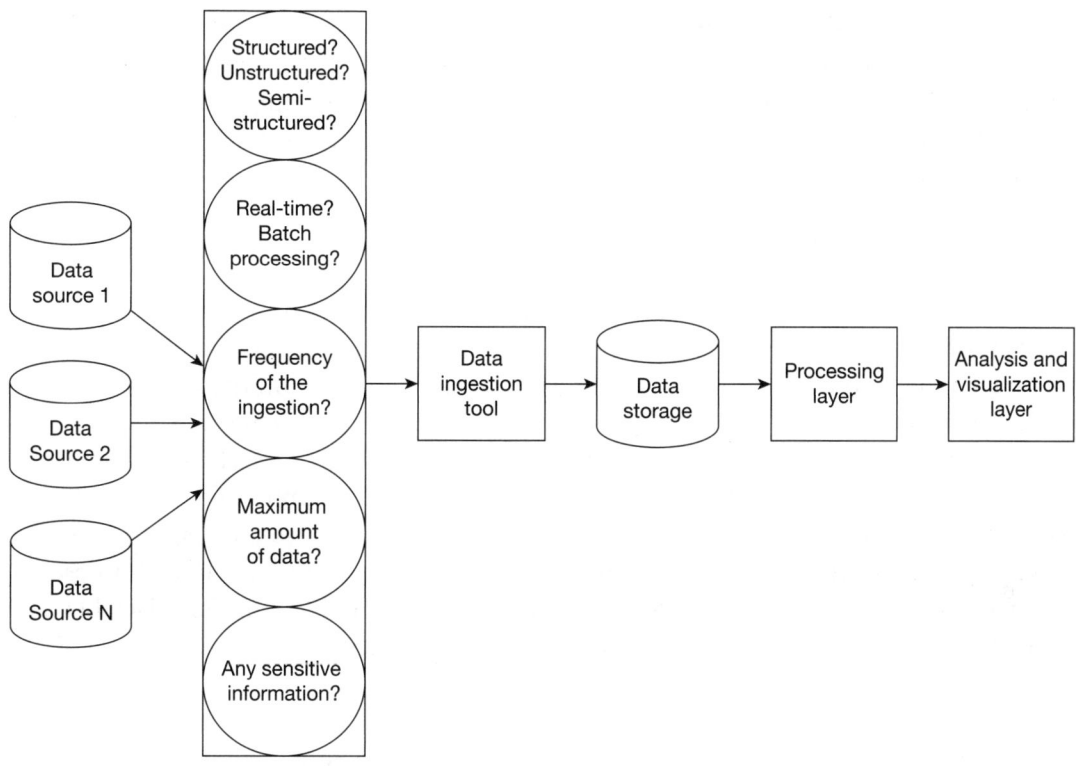

Figure 8.2 Data Ingestion – Basic architecture with ingestion factors

Hadoop ecosystem				
Ingestion	Storage	Processing	Analysis	Management and coordination
Apache Sqoop (RDBMS connector)	HDFS (Structured data)	MapReduce (Data processing)	Pig (Scripting)	ZooKeeper Apache Ambari Cloudera manager Map R control system Hortonworks Oozie (Workflow monitoring)
Apache Flume (Data collection)	HBASE (Unstructured, columnar store)	Yarn (Cluster resource management)	Hive (SQL query)	
Apache Kafka (Streaming)	MongoDB	Spark	Spark SQL	
Apache Impala	Apache Cassandra		Spark GraphX	
Apache NiFi			Apache Mahout (Machine learning)	
Storm (Streaming)			Tableau (Visualization)	
Change data capture (CDC)			Drill (Interactive analytics)	

Figure 8.3 Hadoop ecosystem with data ingestion

it to the target site. ETL, on the other hand, is a data ingestion technique that comprises data extraction, transfer and data transformation before it is delivered to the intended destination. Strim and other ETL platforms may perform aggregating, cleansing, splitting, and joining transformations. The goal is to ensure that the data is delivered in a way that satisfies the needs of the intended receiver.

8.4 Introduction to Sqoop

Loading enormous amounts of data from many sources into Hadoop clusters is required for Hadoop analytics. The actual game begins for Hadoop developers once the data is put into HDFS. They modify and analyze the data to gain insights from the HDFS data. As a result, for this study, data from relational database management systems must be moved to HDFS. Writing MapReduce code to import and export data from a relational database to HDFS is challenging and time-consuming. Loading massive volumes of data into Hadoop from several sources and processing it is challenging. Before choosing the appropriate data load strategy, it is important to maintain and assure data consistency while also ensuring acceptable resource use. Apache Sqoop is a Hadoop tool that transfers data between HDFS (Hadoop storage) and relational database servers, including MySQL, Oracle RDB, SQLite, Teradata, Netezza, and Postgres. Sqoop is a command-line interface that allows data to be moved from relational databases to Hadoop.

Sqoop may be installed with the help of plugins from the Sqoop extension framework. Several real-world Sqoop instances use connectors for different databases such as SQL Server, IBM DB2, MySQL, and PostgreSQL. These connections transport data quickly and efficiently. One of these is the JDBC connection, which is accessible by JDBC. In addition, companies are creating their own Sqoop connections. These APIs are accessible for anything from enterprise data warehouses to NoSQL datastores. Aggregates require the reduction phase. Apache Sqoop, on the other hand, just imports and produces data and does not aggregate it. The map task will launch several mappers based on the number of mappers given by the user. A piece of data will be assigned to each mapper task for Sqoop import. Sqoop uniformly distributes the input data across the mappers to achieve high performance. The mappers then connect to the database using JDBC and get the data allocated by Sqoop, which is subsequently written to HDFS, Hive, or HBase, depending on the CLI settings. Flume and Sqoop vary primarily because Flume exclusively ingests unstructured or semi-structured data into HDFS. At the same time, Sqoop can import and export structured data from RDBMS and Enterprise data warehouses to HDFS and vice-versa (Fig. 8.4).

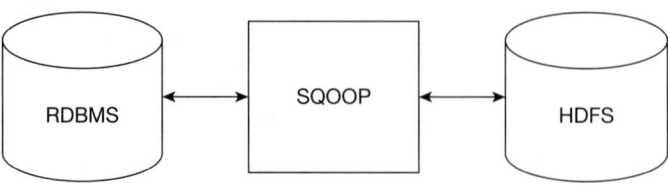

Figure 8.4 Hadoop Sqoop basic structure

8.5 FEATURES OF SQOOP

The diagram below (Fig. 8.5) demonstrates several Sqoop functionalities. Sqoop supports a variety of common relational databases, including MySQL, PostgreSQL, Oracle, SQL Server, and DB2. Each of these connections understands how to communicate with the DBMS with which it is attached. A generic JDBC connector is also available for connecting to any database that supports Java's JDBC interface. Sqoop Big Data also has optimized MySQL and PostgreSQL connectors that employ database-specific APIs to handle bulk transfers effectively. Furthermore, Sqoop in Big Data supports a wide range of third-party data store interfaces, including corporate data warehouses (such as Netezza, Teradata, and Oracle) and NoSQL stores (such as Couchbase). However, these connectors are not included in the Sqoop package and must be downloaded separately and attached to an existing Sqoop installation.

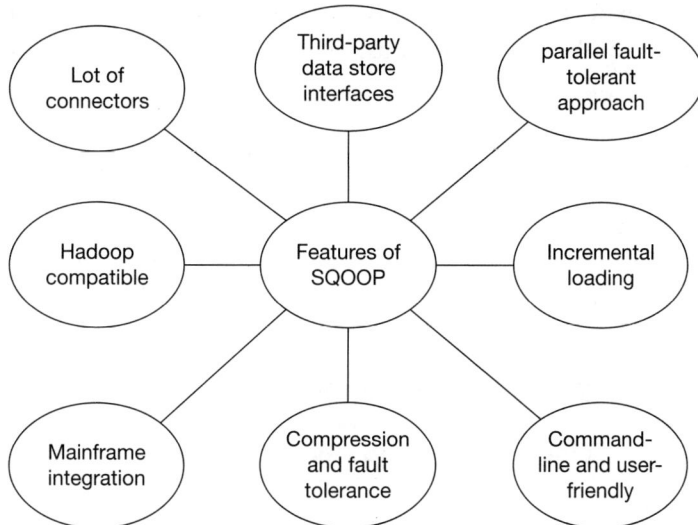

Figure 8.5 Hadoop Sqoop: Basic features

Sqoop imports and exports data using the MapReduce architecture, which provides a parallel fault-tolerant technique. Sqoop got its name from the phrase "SQL to Hadoop & Hadoop to SQL." Because the data is transferred and stored in Hadoop, Sqoop allows us to offload part of the ETL (Extract, Load, and Transform) processing onto low-cost, fast, and efficient Hadoop processes. Cloudera first designed and managed Sqoop. Apache later fostered it on July 23, 2011. In April 2012, the Apache group promoted the Sqoop project to top-level project status. Sqoop is also used to import data from external datastores into Hadoop ecosystem products such as Hive and HBase. Sqoop can export data from MySQL/PostgreSQL/Oracle/SQL Server/DB2 to HDFS/hive/Hbase and vice-versa. As a result, it facilitates the transmission of enormous volumes of data from one location to another. It supports incremental loading of a single table or a free-form SQL query and saved tasks that may be run several times to import database changes made since the previous import. Sqoop is a popular tool for transporting data from RDBMS files to Hadoop for MapReduce processing and other reasons.

Sqoop can do parallel data transfers, making such transfers quicker and less expensive. It also helps with mainframe sequential data integration. This approach reduces mainframe usage while lowering the cost of executing specialized activities on mainframe hardware. Sqoop performs data security activities with the help of Kerberos. After data has been analyzed, Sqoop allows us to compress it. It is incredibly strong and efficient in nature and its operations are generally straightforward. Sqoop uses the command-line interface to handle user commands. Sqoop's CLI for importing and exporting data simplifies the life of developers. They must provide fundamental data such as database authentication, source, destination, and operations, among other things. It handles everything else. Sqoop internally turns the command into MapReduce jobs, which are then executed on HDFS. It may communicate with the user via other means, such as Java APIs. Sqoop can only import and export data in response to user requests and cannot aggregate data. It simplifies the import and export of data using the YARN, thus providing fault tolerance to parallelism.

8.6 Basic SQL Commands and Connecting from Cloudera

Before importing and exporting data using Sqoop, we must first understand the fundamental SQL procedures. Table 8.1 illustrates how to enter SQL prompt using the Cloudera Command Prompt. It also specifies the command (Cloudera) to see if MySQL is already installed on the machine.

Table 8.1 Cloudera command prompt commands for SQL

Cloudera Command Prompt Commands	
sudo service mysqld status	To check the status of mysql
mysql -u root -h local host -p -	To get into mysql prompt((it will ask for password: Give "cloudera")
MySQL Command to Be Used in MySql Prompt	
show databases	To list the databases
use retail db	To use retail db database
show tables	To list down all the tables in the database
select count(l) from orders	Describe orders, list down the datastructure

The screen below (Fig. 8.6) shows the result of running sudo to verify the status of the MySQL software in Cloudera. This means that MySQL is active in our system. It should be noted that it is installed by default with the Cloudera sandbox installation. To access the MySQL prompt, use the command: MySQL -u root -h localhost -p.

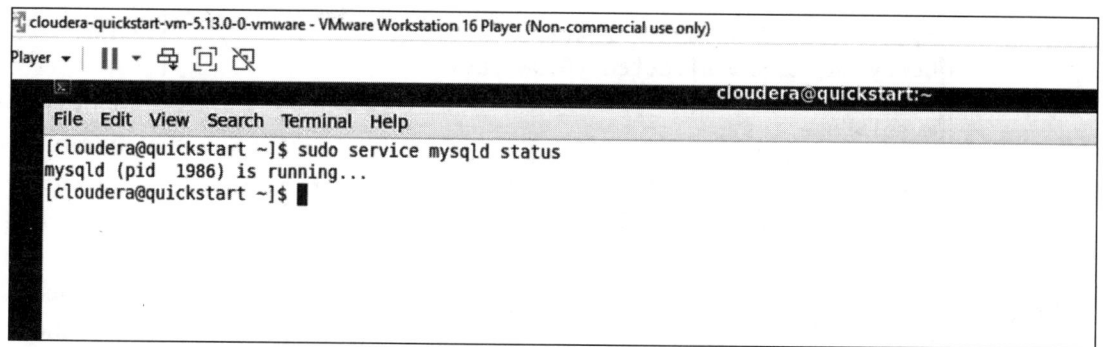

Figure 8.6 MySQL status check in Cloudera quick start

We enter the command show databases in the mysql command line (Fig. 8.7). It lists 12 distinct databases (information schema, cm, firehose, hue, metastore, mysql, nav, navms, oozie, retail db, rman, sentry) as follows:

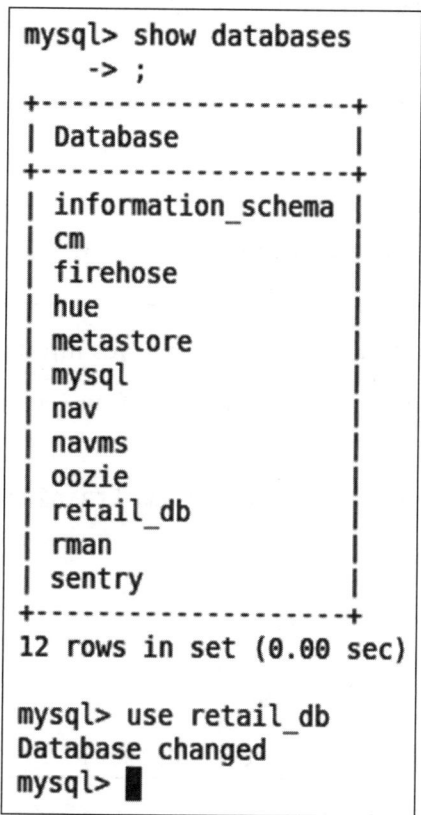

Figure 8.7 MySQL show databases command and use database command

We created a new database called "test". We also created a table called "Training" with two fields – id and name, as shown in Fig. 8.8.

```
mysql> create database test;
Query OK, 1 row affected (0.00 sec)

mysql> use test;
Database changed
mysql> create table training(id int, name varchar(10));
Query OK, 0 rows affected (0.02 sec)
```

Figure 8.8 MySQL creating a database called "test" and a table called "training"

We inserted three records into the table "training" as shown in Fig. 8.9, using insert into training command.

```
mysql> use test;
Database changed
mysql> create table training(id int, name varchar(10));
Query OK, 0 rows affected (0.02 sec)

mysql> insert into training values (1,'raj');
Query OK, 1 row affected (0.01 sec)

mysql> insert into training values (2, 'asha');
Query OK, 1 row affected (0.00 sec)

mysql> insert into training values (3, 'jack');
Query OK, 1 row affected (0.00 sec)
```

Figure 8.9 MySQL inserting three records into the table "training"

We used "select * from training;" command to ensure all the three records are there within the table "training" as shown in Fig. 8.10.

```
mysql> select * from training;
+------+------+
| id   | name |
+------+------+
|    1 | raj  |
|    2 | asha |
|    3 | jack |
+------+------+
3 rows in set (0.00 sec)
```

Figure 8.10 MySQL displaying the records of the table "training"

8.7 BASIC SQOOP COMMANDS FROM CLOUDERA COMMAND PROMPT

Table 8.2 give the basic Sqoop commands that can be used from the Cloudera command prompt.

Table 8.2 Basic Sqoop commands

Basic Sqoop Commands (to be given in Cloudera command Prompt)	
`sqoop version`	To see the version of the Sqoop tool installed.
`sqoop list-databases --connect jdbc:mysql ://localhost/test \--username root -P`	To list all the databases. When it prompts for password give "cloudera".
`sqoop list-tables--connect jdbc :mysql ://localhost/test \--username root -P`	To list all the tables.
`sqoop eval --connect jdbc:mysql:// localhost/test \--username root -P \-- query "select * from training limit 10;"`	This lists down the records of the table training.
`sqoop import-all-tables --connect "jdbc:mysql ://localhost/test \ --username root -P \ --warehouse-dir /user/training/sqoop_ import1 -m 1`	This imports all the table of the database "test" to the warehouse (HDFS) directory mentioned, m1 indicates one mapper will be used for this action.
`hadoop fs -Is /user/training/sqoop_ import/training`	This command list down all the files/ directories in the path given.
`hadoop fs -cat /user/training/sqoop_ import1 /training/part-m-00000`	It displays records of the table training which was imported.
`sqoop import \ --connect jdbc :mysql ://localhost/test \--username root -P \--table movies\--as-textfile \--target- dir/user/training/squoop_file_import2`	This imports the table "movies" of the database "test" to the target directory mentioned as TEXT File.
`hadoop fs -Is /user/training/squoop_file_ import2`	This command lists down all the files/ directories in the path given.
`sqoop import \ --connect jdbc:mysql ://localhost/test \--username root -P \--table movies2 \--as-seq uencefile \--target-di r/user/training/sq uoop_ file_import2`	This imports the table "movies2" of the database "test" to the target directory mentioned as Sequence File.
`sqoop import \ --connect jdbc :mysql ://localhost/test \--username root -P \- where "name like 1%A%111 \--table movies3 -m 6 \--as-avrodatafile \`	This imports the table "movies3" of the database "test" to the target directory mentioned as Avrodata File. (This imports only the records containing name with the character "A").
`sqoop export \ --connect "jdbc:mysql :// localhost/test \--username root -P \ --table training3 \--export-di r/user/ train ing/sqoop_import1/trai ning/ part-m- 00000`	This command exports the data from the directory given to the table given (training3). Ensure the table training3 exists in mysql. Go to sql and check whether table training3 has exported records.

We typed exit command to come out of the sql prompt and get into the Cloudera command prompt once again. The following command (Fig. 8.11) was given from the Cloudera command prompt to connect to the SQL and list down all the databases.

```
[cloudera@quickstart ~]$ sqoop list-databases --connect jdbc:mysql://localhost/test \--username root -P
Warning: /usr/lib/sqoop/../accumulo does not exist! Accumulo imports will fail.
Please set $ACCUMULO_HOME to the root of your Accumulo installation.
22/05/11 03:41:02 INFO sqoop.Sqoop: Running Sqoop version: 1.4.6-cdh5.13.0
Enter password:
22/05/11 03:41:09 INFO manager.MySQLManager: Preparing to use a MySQL streaming resultset.
information_schema
cm
firehose
hue
metastore
mysql
nav
navms
oozie
retail_db
rman
sentry
test
```

Figure 8.11 Connecting SQL from Sqoop listing down all the tables of SQL

The following command (Fig. 8.12) was given from the Cloudera command prompt to connect to the SQL and list down all the records of the table "training". It displays 3 records which we inserted earlier into SQL through SQL prompt.

```
[cloudera@quickstart ~]$ sqoop eval --connect jdbc:mysql://localhost/test \--username root -P \--query "select * from training;"
Warning: /usr/lib/sqoop/../accumulo does not exist! Accumulo imports will fail.
Please set $ACCUMULO_HOME to the root of your Accumulo installation.
22/05/11 03:49:39 INFO sqoop.Sqoop: Running Sqoop version: 1.4.6-cdh5.13.0
Enter password:
22/05/11 03:49:46 INFO manager.MySQLManager: Preparing to use a MySQL streaming resultset.
------------------------
| id        | name     |
------------------------
| 1         | raj      |
| 2         | asha     |
| 3         | jack     |
------------------------
```

Figure 8.12 Connecting SQL from Sqoop displaying all the contents of the table training

8.8 SQOOP IMPORTING

Using this approach, individual tables from a relational database are imported into the Hadoop Distributed File System (HDFS). A table row is handled as a record to transfer in HDFS. The recorded data is preserved in text files as text or binary data in Sequence and Avro files. We can build, load and partition in Hive while importing data.

It parses user-supplied parameters via the command-line interface before passing them to a stage where arguments are induced for Map-only tasks. When the Map receives parameters, it delivers a command to release as many mappers as the user specifies in the command-line interface. When these jobs are ready for the Import command, each mapper task is assigned a specific piece of data to import, based on the key entered into the command-line interface by the user. Sqoop is a parallel processing technique that divides data equally across all mappers to increase process efficiency. Following the import, each mapper connects to the database using the Java database connection model and retrieves the data given by Sqoop.

Following data retrieval, it is written to HDFS, HBase, or Hive, dependent on the command-line options. As a consequence, the Sqoop import is finished. Importing is divided into two stages. First, the database gathers the metadata required for data import. In the second stage, Sqoop sends a map-only Hadoop task to the cluster. Finally, the actual data is sent with the help of the information acquired in this activity (Fig. 8.13).

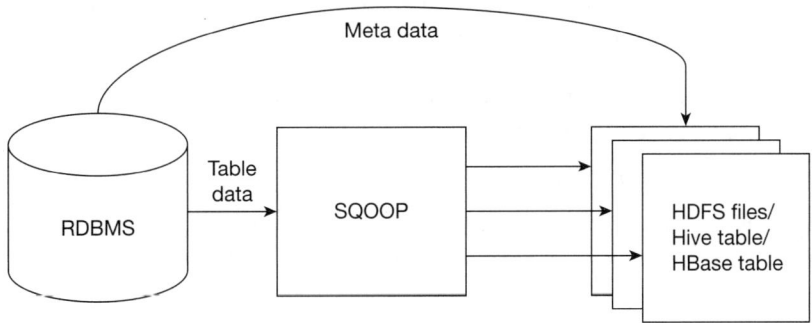

Figure 8.13 Sqoop importing basic structure

The data is stored in an HDFS directory based on the imported table. If required, Sqoop allows the user to choose an alternative directory where the file shall be populated. In this file, which includes comma-delimited fields, entries are separated by new lines. You can manually adjust the format through which the data is transmitted by defining the record terminator character and the field separator.

It is possible to import Sqoop data into Hive. Hive allows you to construct and load divisions or tables when importing data. The right type of mapping between data and details should be conducted when done manually. To operate for loading and splitting the table, metadata can be added to the Hive meta store. It is a data transportation tool with a connector architecture that allows you to connect to new external systems by adding plugins. Figure 8.14 shows for the various Sqoop components.

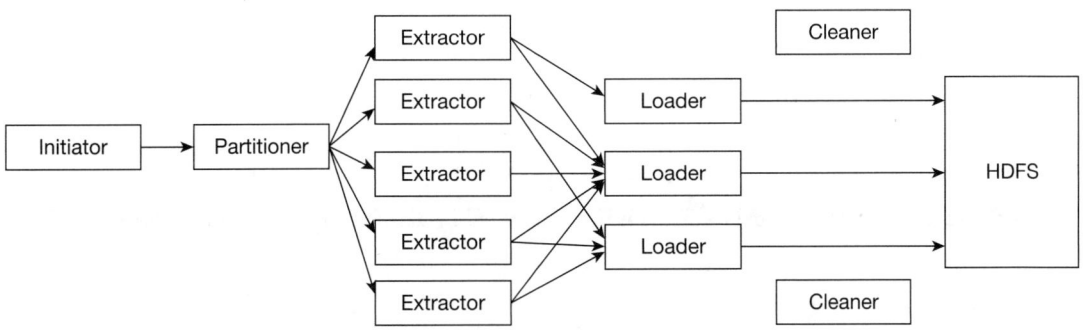

Figure 8.14 Sqoop components

Initiator: The client sends a job to the Sqoop server to load data from one location to another (i.e., RDBMS to HDFS, in this case). The connection pool, schema, and metadata validation are now complete.

Partitioner: It is time to start extracting data. For example, a 1 TB database cannot be handled as a single block of data. As a consequence, we have a partitioner that separates the data into digestible chunks/blocks that may be extracted simultaneously. Please keep in mind that no information is kept here.

Extractor: In this system portion, data is carried from the source in exact chunks/blocks. It is important to note that not all data is saved in memory simultaneously for extraction. It is similar to micro-batch processing. Once again, no data is stored.

Loader: The extracted data is transferred to the destination using the framework's Loader phase. The data has now been wholly saved.

Cleaner: This is simply a de-cluttering procedure to free up previously used resources.

The following command (Fig. 8.15) was given in the Cloudera command prompt in order to import all the tables of the database "test" into HDFS directory "/user/training/sqoop_import1". We have created only one table with the name "training" and hence it will create a directory called "training" within the given folder and will import all the records.

```
sqoop import-all-tables --connect "jdbc:mysql://localhost/test \--username root -P \--warehouse-dir /user/training/sqoop_import1 -m 1
```

Figure 8.15 Sqoop Import of all tables into HDFS directory

The following command (Fig. 8.16) was given in the Cloudera command prompt to list down all the files and directories of "/user/training/sqoop_import1/training"

```
[cloudera@quickstart ~]$ hadoop fs -ls  /user/training/sqoop_import1/training
Found 2 items
-rw-r--r--   1 cloudera supergroup          0 2022-05-11 04:00 /user/training/sqoop_import1/training/_SUCCESS
-rw-r--r--   1 cloudera supergroup         20 2022-05-11 04:00 /user/training/sqoop_import1/training/part-m-00000
[cloudera@quickstart ~]$
```

Figure 8.16 Hadoop FS listing files of HDFS directory

To see the content of the file, part-m-00000, generated in the folder "/user/training/sqoop import1/training," use the following command (Fig. 8.17) in the Cloudera command prompt. It displays three records that we had previously entered into SQL. This means that the table training records were imported into the HDFS Directory.

```
[cloudera@quickstart ~]$ hadoop fs -cat  /user/training/sqoop_import1/training/part-m-00000
1,raj
2,asha
3,jack
[cloudera@quickstart ~]$
```

Figure 8.17 Hadoop FS listing the contents of HDFS file

8.9 SQOOP INCREMENTAL IMPORT

Sqoop offers an incremental import mode that allows you to get just rows that are newer than the previous batch. Sqoop supports append and the latest modified incremental imports. The -incremental argument allows you to specify the incremental import type. For example, you should utilize append mode when importing a table with new rows being added all the time and rising row id values. The check column provides the column that contains the row id. Sqoop imports rows with a check column value greater than the specified -last-value- value. Sqoop provides an alternative table updating approach called the latest modified mode. When rows in the source table may be altered, and each update updates the value of a last-modified column to the current timestamp, this is the best option.

8.10 SQOOP EXPORT

Using the export command, we may move data from the Hadoop database file system to the relational database management system. For example, Sqoop export moves data from HDFS to RDBMS. The records that are considered rows in the table would be the Sqoop file's input. This data is read, processed into records, and then utilized using the delimiter given by the user. The data export process is divided into two steps: the first includes searching the database for metadata, and the second involves data movement (Fig. 8.18).

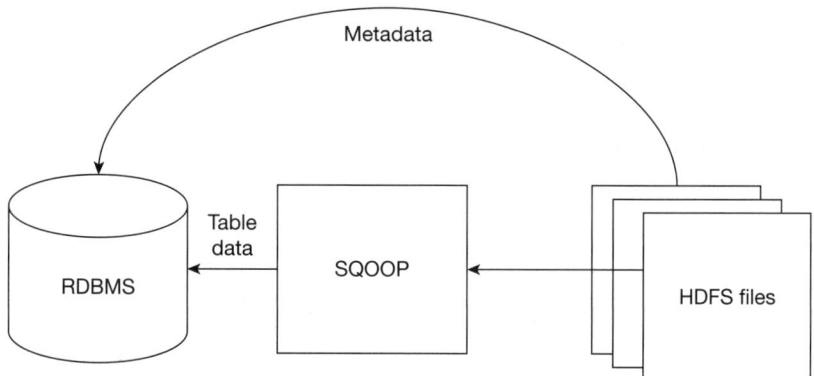

Figure 8.18 Sqoop export basic structure

The files given as input during this process are called records. After that, when a job is submitted, it is mapped into Map Task (Fig. 8.19) that brings the files of the data from Hadoop data storage.

These files may be exported to any structured data destination, such as a relational database management system like MySQL, SQL Server, or Oracle.

Map tasks are used to push Sqoop data into the database once it has been divided into several splits. Occasionally, Hadoop pipelines may be necessary to process data into the

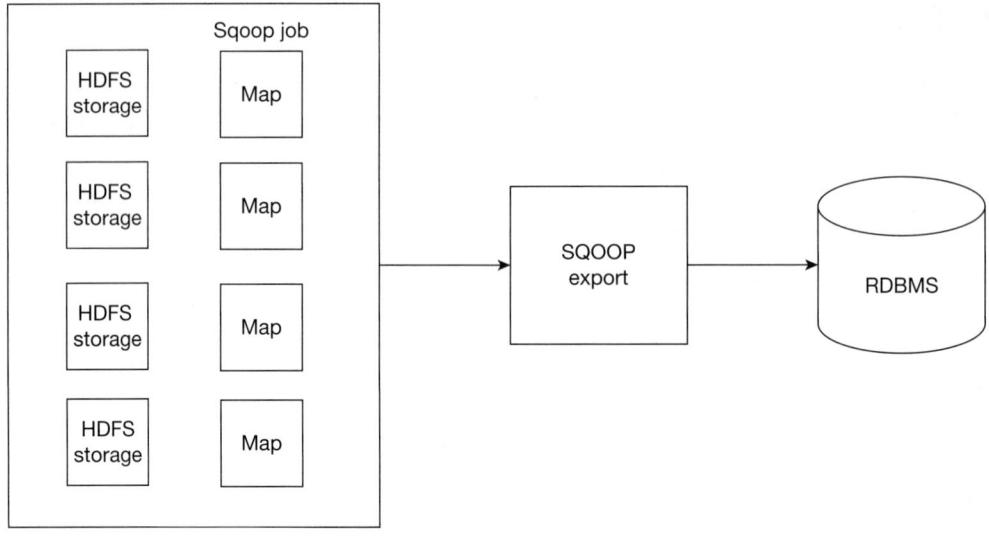

Figure 8.19 Sqoop export basic structure: with Map

production system and perform critical business operations. Sqoop may also be used to export data to any external datastore as necessary. You can use customized connections to external systems that have optimized import and export. The following command (Fig. 8.20) is given in the Cloudera command prompt to export the table data (HDFS) from the export directory to the table "training3" of the database "test".

```
[cloudera@quickstart ~]$ sqoop export \--connect jdbc:mysql://localhost/test \--username root -P \--table training3 \--export-dir /user/
training/sqoop_import1/training/part-m-00000
Warning: /usr/lib/sqoop/../accumulo does not exist! Accumulo imports will fail.
Please set $ACCUMULO_HOME to the root of your Accumulo installation.
22/05/12 09:48:13 INFO sqoop.Sqoop: Running Sqoop version: 1.4.6-cdh5.13.0
Enter password:
22/05/12 09:48:26 INFO manager.MySQLManager: Preparing to use a MySQL streaming resultset.
22/05/12 09:48:26 INFO tool.CodeGenTool: Beginning code generation
22/05/12 09:48:27 INFO manager.SqlManager: Executing SQL statement: SELECT t.* FROM `training3` AS t LIMIT 1
22/05/12 09:48:27 INFO manager.SqlManager: Executing SQL statement: SELECT t.* FROM `training3` AS t LIMIT 1
```

Figure 8.20 Sqoop export command

We get the below message (Fig. 8.21) stating how many records got exported from HDFS to the SQL.

```
            Bytes Written=0
22/05/12 09:50:26 INFO mapreduce.ExportJobBase: Transferred 710 bytes in 113.1884 seconds (6.2727 bytes/sec)
22/05/12 09:50:26 INFO mapreduce.ExportJobBase: Exported 3 records.
[cloudera@quickstart ~]$
```

Figure 8.21 Sqoop export command output

Now, we can login to SQL and display the contents of the table "training3" (Fig. 8.22). It displays 6 records (rows), as the export command was executed twice. This indicates that the export happened successfully and is reflecting in the SQL.

```
[cloudera@quickstart ~]$ mysql -u root -h localhost -p
Enter password:
Welcome to the MySQL monitor.  Commands end with ; or \g.
Your MySQL connection id is 44
Server version: 5.1.73 Source distribution

Copyright (c) 2000, 2013, Oracle and/or its affiliates. All rights reserved.

Oracle is a registered trademark of Oracle Corporation and/or its
affiliates. Other names may be trademarks of their respective
owners.

Type 'help;' or '\h' for help. Type '\c' to clear the current input statement.

mysql> use test;
Reading table information for completion of table and column names
You can turn off this feature to get a quicker startup with -A

Database changed
mysql> select * from training3;
+------+------+
| id   | name |
+------+------+
|    1 | raj  |
|    2 | asha |
|    3 | jack |
|    1 | raj  |
|    2 | asha |
|    3 | jack |
+------+------+
6 rows in set (0.00 sec)
```

Figure 8.22   Listing down the table from SQL to check Sqoop export

8.11 Advantages of Sqoop

In Apache Sqoop, a single action can load the whole table. You may also load all the tables from a database with a single command. You may also utilize Apache Sqoop's incremental load capability to load table portions as they update. Sqoop uses the YARN framework to import and export data, providing fault tolerance to parallelism. Sqoop's operations use the MapReduce algorithm, which includes fault tolerance. HDFS may also be used to import the results of an SQL query. You may use the deflate(gzip) algorithm with the -compress option or the -compression-codec argument to compress your data. You may also load compressed tables with Apache Hive. Apache Sqoop provides connectors for various RDBMS databases, covering nearly the whole circle. Kerberos is a computer network authentication system that employs 'tickets' to allow nodes to securely confirm their identity with one another across an unsecured network. Sqoop supports Kerberos authentication. Data may be imported into Apache Hive for analysis and dumped into

HBase, a NoSQL database. You may instruct Sqoop to import the table into Accumulo rather than an HDFS directory. Sqoop may transport data across structured data stores such as Oracle and Teradata. It also helps us to do ETL operations in a timely and cost-effective manner. It enables the movement of data from several structured data sources, such as Oracle and Postgres. Sqoop allows the automation of many such operations, resulting in increased productivity. It is a powerful tool with a large community of users and is updated frequently because of its ongoing contributions and progress.

8.12 Disadvantages of Sqoop

We cannot stop the procedures of Sqoop in case of any errors. Sqoop connects to the relational database management system through a JDBC connection and this leads to less-than-optimal performance. The hardware configuration of the relational database management system determines Sqoop export performance. The traditional approach of putting data into Hadoop using scripts is inefficient and time-consuming for large data loads. Giving map-reduce programs direct access to data stored on other systems (rather than putting it into Hadoop) complicates things. As a result, the Sqoop method is no longer feasible on Hadoop. Hadoop can handle data in a variety of forms as well as massive volumes of data.

8.13 Need for Apache Flume

To transport data from the sources to HDFS, we may use Hadoop's Put command. However, we can only transfer one file at a time using the Put command, while the data generators generate data quicker. We need a technology that can provide real-time data since older data analysis is less trustworthy. If we use the Put command, we must first pack and prepare the data for upload. It is a difficult task since web servers generate data frequently. We want solutions that can overcome the restrictions of the Put command and transfer "streaming data" with low latency from data producers to centralized storage (especially HDFS). In HDFS, the file will be regarded as a directory entry, with a length of 0 until it is closed. As a result, we need a system that is trustworthy, versatile, and easy to manage for uploading log data into HDFS.

Millions of services/applications run on several servers, creating massive amounts of log data. Companies must review this information to get insights and better understand customer behavior. Businesses require an extensible, scalable, and dependable distributed data collection service to manage logs. The service must be capable of moving unstructured data from the source to the system where it will be processed (such as in Hadoop Distributed FileSystem). Apache Flume is a data ingestion system that gathers, aggregates, and transfers vast amounts of streaming data from various application sources such as log files and events to a centralized data store such as HDFS or HBase. A flume is a versatile, trustworthy, dispersed, and adaptable equipment. Its principal function is to move streaming data (log data) from several web servers to HDFS. Its recovery mechanisms are customizable, and its design is simple and user-friendly. It can gather data in both batch and streaming modes.

Apache Flume, in a nutshell, is an open-source tool for collecting, aggregating, and delivering vast amounts of data from external web servers to central storage. It is a trustworthy and easy-to-use solution. Using Apache Flume, data from several apps may be consumed on HDFS. For example, it might be used to investigate client behavior on various e-commerce sites.

8.14 APACHE FLUME ARCHITECTURE

Apache Flume streams data from many data sources to Hadoop HDFS or Hive. Apache Flume's architecture is straightforward and centred on streaming data flows. The design goal of Flume Architecture is to provide dependability, flexibility, controllability, and flexibility. First, data generators generate large volumes of data collected by individual Flume agents. For example, data is generated by Facebook, Twitter, e-commerce sites, and other sources. Afterward, a data collector (also an agent) takes the data from the agents, aggregates it, and stores it in centralized storage such as HDFS or HBase.

A Flume event is the fundamental unit of data transfer inside the Flume. A Flume event is a basic unit of data that must be transmitted from one location to another. It has a byte array payload that must be delivered from the source to the destination and optional headers. The following is the structure of a typical Flume event. Real-time streaming data is generated via data generators (Fig. 8.23). Individual Flume agents operating on them collect the data provided by data generators. Facebook, Twitter, and other social media platforms are typical data providers.

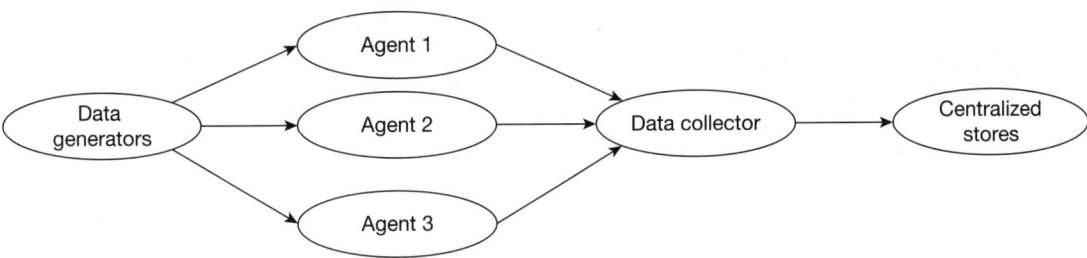

Figure 8.23 Apache Flume basic structure

In Apache Flume, an agent is a standalone daemon process (JVM). It accepts data (events) from customers or other agents and routes it to the appropriate destination (sink or agent). A flume may contain many agents made up of three primary parts. They are the source, the channel, and the sink, respectively (Fig. 8.24).

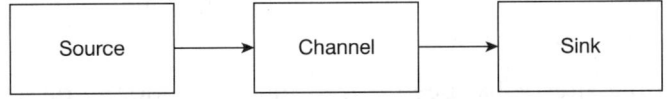

Figure 8.24 Apache Flume Source, Channel and Sink: Structure 1

A source is the part of an Agent that takes data from data generators (such as webservers) and sends it to one or more channels as Flume events. The data generator provides events (data) to Flume so that the target Flume source understands. Apache Flume has a variety of sources, each of which gets events from a different data generator. Examples – Exec source, Avro source, Thrift source, twitter 1% source, NetCat source, HTTP source, Scribe source.

The external Avro client stream sends events to the Avro source. It listens for the Avro source events by using the Avro port number. When an Avro source is used with a Flume agent's built-in Avro Sink, it might result in fatigued collection topologies. The external Thrift client sends events to Thrift Source. The Avro client hears the events through the Thrift port. A Thrift source combined with the Flume agents' built-in Thrift Sink might result in tiered collection topologies. We can configure the Thrift source to start in a secure mode by enabling Kerberos authentication. The thrift source uses two properties, the agent-principal, and agent-key tab, to authenticate to the Kerberos KDC. The Apache Flume source Exec, on start-up, runs a given Unix command. It expects that process to produce data on stdout continuously. Unless the property logStdErr is set to true, stderr is discarded. If for any reason, the process exits, then the source also exits and will not produce any further data. Thus configurations such as cat [named pipe] or tail -F [file] will produce the desired results. These two commands create streams of data. On the other hand, the date will probably not produce the desired result. It produces a single event and exits.

JMS source reads messages from a JMS destination (queue or topic). Because of being a JMS application, this source should work with any JMS provider. But it has only been tested with ActiveMQ. JMS source provides configurable user/pass, batch size, message selector, and message to the flume event converter. The JMS jar provided by the vendor should be included in the Flume classpath. It can be included using any of the following three ways:

(a) plugins.d directory (preferred)
(b) -classpath on the command line
(c) FLUME_CLASSPATH variable in flume-env.sh

Spooling Directory Source allows us to ingest data by placing files that are to be ingested into a "spooling" directory on disk. The Spooling Directory source will look at the specified directory for new files. This source will parse data out of new files as they appear. The data parsing logic is pluggable. When a given file is fully read into the channel, then by default the completion is indicated either by renaming the file or deleting the file. The trackerDir is used for keeping track of processed files. Spooling Directory Source is reliable and does not lead to data loss even if the Apache Flume is restarted or killed.

Some of the condition when it fails is:

(a) If we write a file after it has been placed into the spooling directory, then Apache Flume will print an error to its log file and stop processing.
(b) At a later time, if a file name is reused, then Apache Flume will print an error to its log file and stop processing.

These issues can be resolved by adding a unique identifier like timestamp to log file names when we are moving them into the spooling directory.

Kafka source is an Apache Kafka consumer who reads messages from Kafka topics. If we are having multiple Kafka sources, then we can configure them with the same Consumer Group. This will ensure that each Kafka consumer will read a unique partition set for the topics.

A channel is a transitory storage that collects data and events from a source and buffers them until the sinks consume them. It serves as a link between the sinks and the sources. It is a temporary shop. Flume sources and sinks are connected by Channel. These channels are transactional in nature and can handle any number of sources and sinks.

Examples: Custom Channel, JDBC channel, File system channel, Memory channel, etc.

Sink: A sink saves data to centralized databases such as HBase and HDFS (Fig. 8.25). It consumes data (events) from the channels and sends it to the specified location. A flume agent can have multiple sources, sinks and channels. Another Flume agent or the central storage might be the sink's final destination. Example: HDFS sink

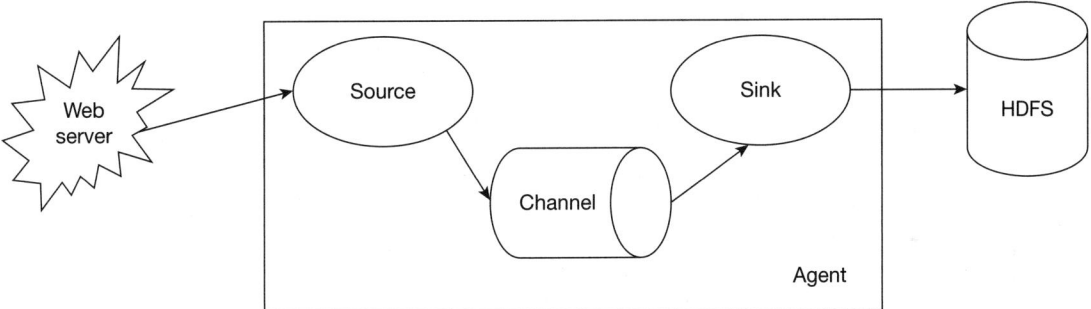

Figure 8.25   Apache Flume Source, Channel and Sink: Structure 2

Additional Components of Flume Agent

The elementary components of the agent have been described previously. In addition, a few other components are critical in the transfer of events from the data generator to the centralized databases. Interceptors change or check flume events as they pass between the source and the channel. In the event of several channels, channel selectors are used to identify which channel should be utilized to convey data. Channel selections are divided into two categories. They are Default channel selectors and Multiplexing channel selectors. Default channel selectors are also known as replicating channel selectors; these selections duplicate all events in each channel. Multiplexing channel selectors determine the channel to which an event should be sent depending on the address in the event's header. Sink Processors are used to call up a specific sink from a set of sinks. These are used to construct sink failover pathways or load balance events over several sinks from a channel.

8.15 Features of Apache Flume

Because Apache Flume is an open-source program, it is free to use. Apache Flume is a highly available, fault-tolerant, and resilient service. It is a distributed system with programmable fail-over and recovery capabilities. It offers many levels of dependability, including best effort and end-to-end delivery:

1. The sources in Apache flume send events across the channel.
2. The flume source sends events to the channel, which the sink consumes.
3. The sink sends the event to the following agent or the terminal repository (like HDFS) only after the events in the flume channel are placed in the next agent channel, or the terminal storage area is erased.

Flume employs a transactional technique to ensure that flume events are delivered reliably. Apache Flume can scale horizontally. Multi-hop flows, fan-in flows, and fan-out flows are all supported by Apache Flume. It also promotes unsuccessful hops, contextual routing and backup (fail-over) routes. Apache Flume can handle a high number of sources, channels, and sinks. Apache Flume can consume log data from several servers into a centralized repository quickly and effectively.

Flume allows us to collect data in real time and batch mode from several web servers. Using Apache Flume, we can ingest enormous amounts of data created by social networking and e-commerce sites into Hadoop DFS. Flume has low latency and excellent throughput. Flumes may be customized for various sources and sinks. Each flume agent has a flume channel, where the flume activities are staged, thus ensuring recovery from failure. Apache Flume supports a durable File channel. The local file system can back up file channels.

Apache Flume maintains a constant data flow across reading and writing tasks. When the data arrival velocity exceeds the data writing rate to the destination, Apache Flume acts as a bridge between data producers and centralized storage. As a result, data is constantly flowing between them. Flume enables us to stream data from many web servers and store it in centralized stores such as HBase and Hadoop HDFS. All transactions in Apache Flume are channel-based. Each communication has two transactions: one for the sender and one for the receiver, which ensures that messages are delivered correctly.

Along with log files, Apache Flume may be used to import massive amounts of data from e-commerce sites like Flipkart and Amazon and social media sites like Twitter and Facebook. Apache Flume provides a dependable method for ingesting online streaming data into HDFS from many sources (email messages, network traffic, log files, social media). In addition, Apache Flume has a highly declarative setup. Flume includes comprehensive documentation, including several examples and patterns, to assist users in learning how to use and set up Flume.

8.16 DATA FLOW IN FLUME

Flume quickly collects log data from several web servers and stores it in a single storage system (HDFS, HBase). Using Flume, we can swiftly extract data from various servers into Hadoop. Flume can also integrate enormous volumes of event data from social networking sites like Facebook and Twitter and e-commerce sites like Amazon and Flipkart

Flume is capable of dealing with a wide range of sources and destinations. Flume can deal with multi-hop flows, fan-in–fan-out flows, and contextual routing. Flume may be scaled horizontally. Flume is a framework for logging data into HDFS. Log servers usually generate events and log data, and Flume agents are placed on these servers. These agents receive data from data producers. The collector, an intermediate node, will collect the data in these agents. Flume can have numerous collectors, just like it may have several agents. Finally, the collected data will be consolidated and transmitted to a centralized storage system such as HBase or HDFS.

Multi-hop Flow: Flume can have numerous agents, and an event may pass through multiple agents before arriving at its final destination. This is referred to as 'multi-hop flow' (Fig. 8.26).

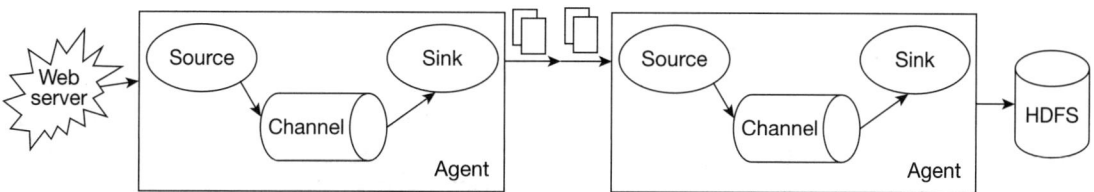

Figure 8.26 Apache Flume Multi-hop flow

Fan-out Flow: Fan-out flow refers to the dataflow from a single source to several channels. This is of two types (Fig. 8.27).

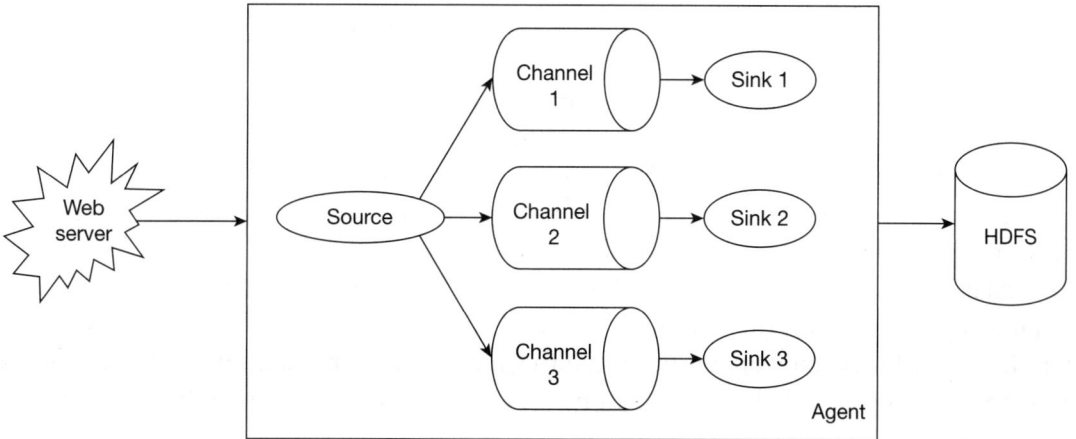

Figure 8.27 Apache Flume Fan-out structure

Fan-in Flow: Fan-in flow is a data flow in which data is transported from several sources to a single channel (Fig. 8.28).

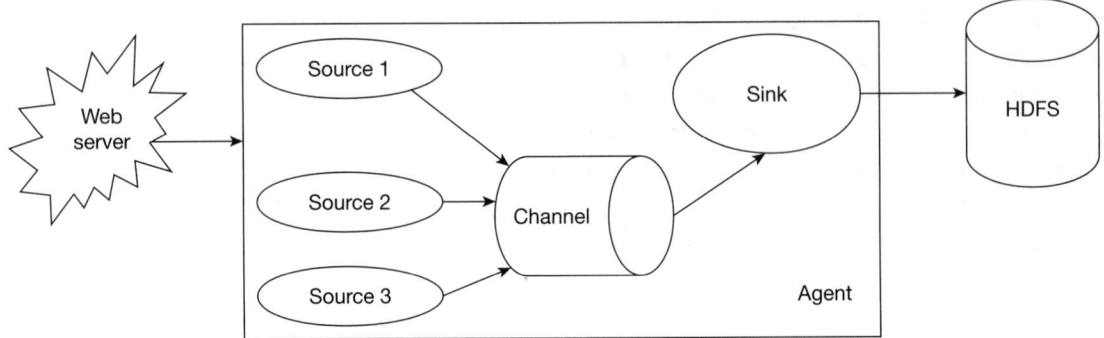

Figure 8.28 Apache Flume Fan-in flow

Data Replication: This refers to the process of replicating data across all specified channels. Multiplexing is a data flow in which data is routed to a specific channel that is listed in the event header.

8.17 Failure Handling in Flume

In Flume, for each event, two transactions take place: one at the sender and one at the receiver. The sender sends events to the receiver. Soon after receiving the data, the receiver commits its own transaction and sends a "received" signal to the sender. After receiving the signal, the sender commits its transaction. (Sender will not commit its transaction till it receives a signal from the receiver).

8.18 Flume Disadvantages

Considering faster data transfer and lower-cost fault tolerance, Apache Flume delivers fewer guarantees than competing systems such as message queues. In Apache Flume's end-to-end dependability mode, the flume events are dispatched at least once, but there are no ordering guarantees. Apache Flume cannot guarantee that each message is unique. Duplicate messages might emerge in a variety of contexts. Flume scalability is generally constrained since scaling the hardware of a conventional Apache Flume may be challenging for any company, and trial-and-error is usually necessary. As a result, the scalability of Flume is frequently overlooked. The throughput that Apache Flume can manage depends on the channel's backing store. If the backup storage is not chosen carefully, scalability and reliability difficulties may arise. It has a complicated topology, making reconfiguration difficult. Despite its drawbacks, Flume's benefits outweigh its weaknesses.

8.19 APACHE FLUME APPLICATIONS

E-commerce enterprises utilize Apache Flume to evaluate client activity from a specific location. We may use Apache Flume to accelerate the transfer of large volumes of data generated by application servers into the Hadoop Distributed File System. For fraud detection, Apache Flume is employed. Apache Flume may be used in IoT applications. Apache Flume may be used to aggregate data supplied by machines and sensors. We may utilize Apache Flume in Security Information and Event Management (SIEM).

8.20 APACHE FLUME INSTALLATION IN WINDOWS 10

Hadoop, SDK Java and Twitter development account are the prerequisites for installing Apache Flume. We assume it is already installed in your machine. The first step is to download Apache Flume binary(tar.gz) from the https://flume.apache.org as below (Fig. 8.29):

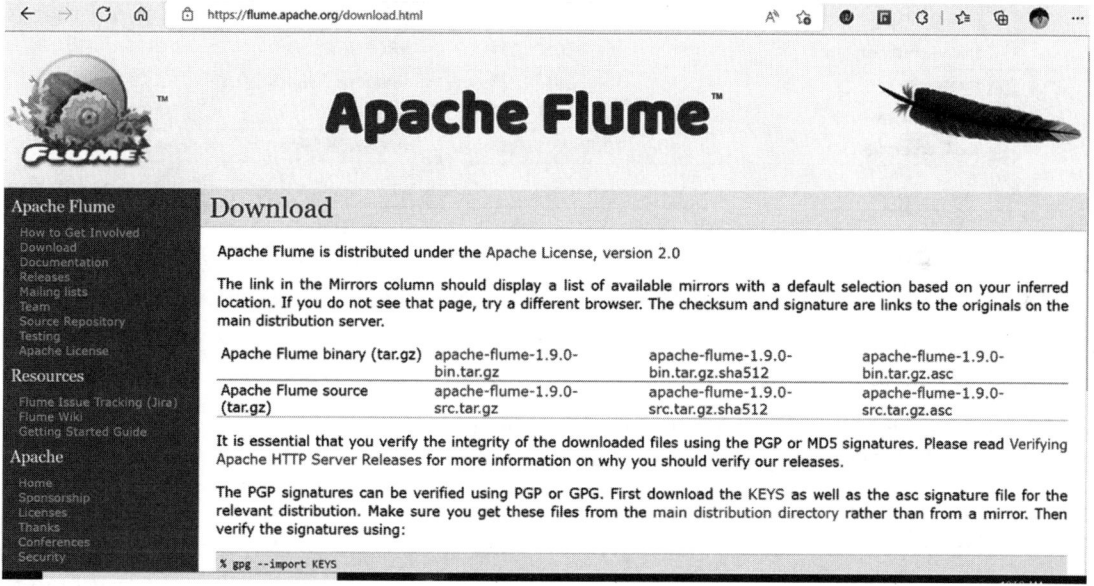

Figure 8.29 Apache Flume download page

After downloading the tar bin file, extract the files into a Folder (C:/). Go to "conf" directory within the installed folder. Remove ". template" extension for these files (Fig. 8.30).

Name	Date modified	Type	Size
flume-conf.properties.template	16-11-2017 17:24	TEMPLATE File	2 KB
flume-env.ps1.template	16-11-2017 17:24	TEMPLATE File	2 KB
flume-env.sh.template	30-08-2018 17:01	TEMPLATE File	2 KB
log4j.properties	10-12-2018 08:53	PROPERTIES File	4 KB

Figure 8.30 Apache Flume downloaded configuration files (Template files)

After removing the ".template" extension, the files will look as shown in Fig. 8.31.

Name	Date modified	Type	Size
flume-conf.properties	16-11-2017 17:24	PROPERTIES File	2 KB
flume-env	16-11-2017 17:24	Windows PowerS...	2 KB
flume-env.sh	30-08-2018 17:01	SH File	2 KB
log4j.properties	10-12-2018 08:53	PROPERTIES File	4 KB

Figure 8.31 Apache Flume downloaded configuration files after removing template extension

Open "flume-env" file and enable the export command for Java (Fig. 8.32):

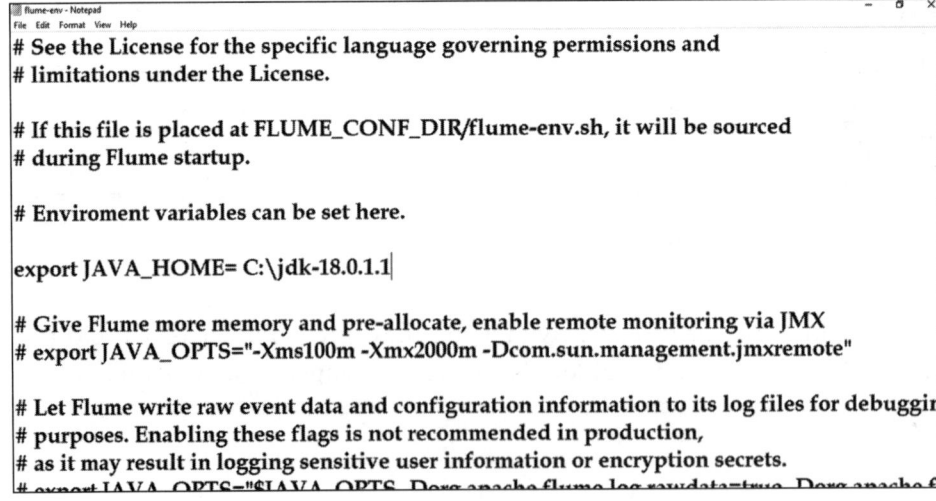

Figure 8.32 Apache Flume environment file: setting Java path

Now, go to the system environment setting and set "FLUME_HOME" variable (Fig. 8.33).

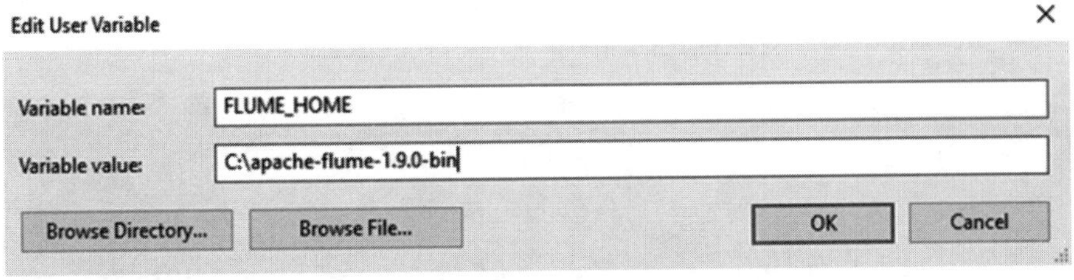

Figure 8.33 Apache FLUME_HOME environment setting

Set "CLASSPATH" for Apache Flume lib directory (Fig. 8.34).

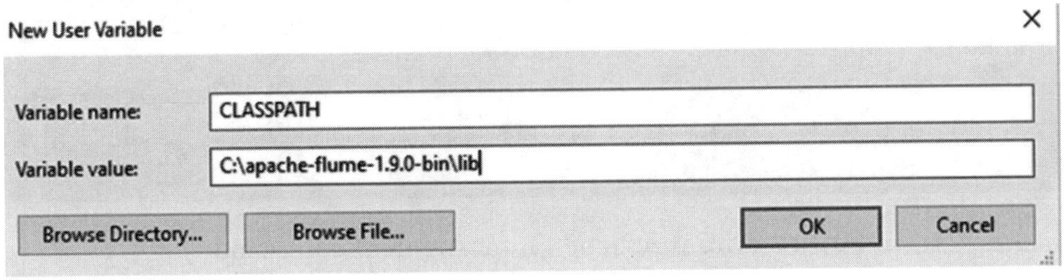

Figure 8.34 Apache CLASSPATH environment setting for Flume bin directory

Add the path for the bin directory of Apache Flume (Fig. 8.35).

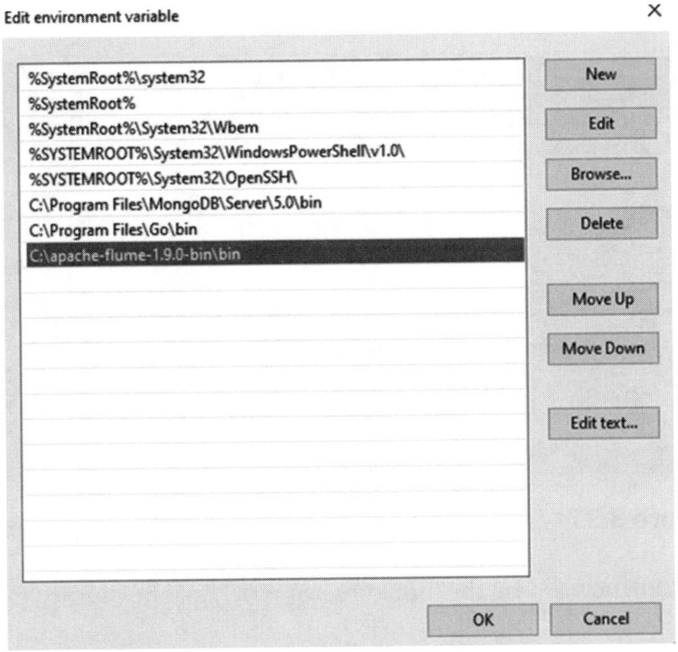

Figure 8.35 Apache Flume Path setting

To check on whether Apache Flume got installed properly, get into the command prompt (CMD), go the Flume installed folder and then get into the bin folder as below. Give the command "flume-ng help". If it displays the help commands (Fig. 8.36), it indicates that the Flume got installed in the specified path.

```
C:\apache-flume-1.9.0-bin\bin>flume-ng help

C:\apache-flume-1.9.0-bin\bin>powershell.exe -NoProfile -InputFormat none -ExecutionPolicy unrestricted -File C:\apach
flume-1.9.0-bin\bin\flume-ng.ps1 help

Usage: flume-ng <command> [options]...

commands:
  help                  display this help text
  agent                 run a Flume agent
  avro-client           run an avro Flume client
  version               show Flume version info

global options:
  -conf <conf>                              use configs in <conf> directory
  -classpath,-C   "value1;value2; .."       append to the classpath
  -property "name1=val;name2=val; .."       sets a JDK system property value
  -dryrun,-d                                do not actually start Flume (test)
  -plugins-path "dir1;dir2"                 semi-colon-separated list of plugins.d directories. See the
                                            plugins.d section in the user guide for more details.
                                            Default: \/plugins.d

agent options:
```

Figure 8.36 Apache Flume-ng help command

To double check on which version of Apache Flume got installed, get into the command prompt (CMD), go the Flume installed folder and then get into the bin folder. Give the command "flume-ng version" and check if it displays current version of the flume installed. In our case the version 1.8.0 got installed as shown in the screen below (Fig. 8.37).

```
C:\apache-flume-1.9.0-bin\bin>flume-ng version

C:\apache-flume-1.9.0-bin\bin>powershell.exe -NoProfile -InputFormat none -ExecutionPolicy unrestricted -File C:\apach
flume-1.9.0-bin\bin\flume-ng.ps1 version
WARN: Config directory not set. Defaulting to C:\apache-flume-1.9.0-bin\conf
Sourcing environment configuration script C:\apache-flume-1.9.0-bin\conf\flume-env.ps1
WARN: Did not find C:\apache-flume-1.9.0-bin\conf\flume-env.ps1
WARN: HADOOP_PREFIX or HADOOP_HOME not found
WARN: HADOOP_PREFIX not set. Unable to include Hadoop's classpath & java.library.path
WARN: HBASE_HOME not found
WARN: HIVE_HOME not found

Running FLUME version :
    class: org.apache.flume.tools.VersionInfo
    arguments:

Flume 1.9.0
Source code repository: https://git-wip-us.apache.org/repos/asf/flume.git
Revision: d4fcab4f501d41597bc616921329a4339f73585e
Compiled by fszabo on Mon Dec 17 20:45:25 CET 2018
From source with checksum 35db629a3bda49d23e9b3690c80737f9
```

Figure 8.37 Apache Flume-ng version checking command

Flume working command: In the bin directory of Apache flume, execute the below command:

flume-ng agent –conf %FLUME_CONF% –conf-file %FLUME_CONF%/flume-conf.properties –name agent

After this, format the namenode of HDFS (hdfs namenode -format), which is installed in the same directory. Go to the Hadoop directory and then get into sbin directory. Give the command to start all the HDFS services (start-dfs). And once it starts, give the command start-yarn to start the Yarn service. Now to go to Hadoop local host (localchost:9000), it indicates Hadoop HDFS services are started.

Create "twitter.conf" file with the below content and place it inside the "conf" directory of the Apache Flume (Fig. 8.38).

```
# Naming the components on the current agent.
TwitterAgent.sources = Twitter
TwitterAgent.channels = MemChannel
TwitterAgent.sinks = HDFS

# Describing/Configuring the source
TwitterAgent.sources.Twitter.type = org.apache.flume.source.twitter.TwitterSource
TwitterAgent.sources.Twitter.consumerKey = Your OAuth consumer key
TwitterAgent.sources.Twitter.consumerSecret = Your OAuth consumer secret
TwitterAgent.sources.Twitter.accessToken = Your OAuth consumer key access token
TwitterAgent.sources.Twitter.accessTokenSecret = Your OAuth consumer key access token secret
TwitterAgent.sources.Twitter.keywords = tutorials point,java, bigdata, mapreduce, mahout, hbase, nosql

# Describing/Configuring the sink

TwitterAgent.sinks.HDFS.type = hdfs
TwitterAgent.sinks.HDFS.hdfs.path = hdfs://localhost:9000/user/Hadoop/twitter_data/
TwitterAgent.sinks.HDFS.hdfs.fileType = DataStream
TwitterAgent.sinks.HDFS.hdfs.writeFormat = Text
TwitterAgent.sinks.HDFS.hdfs.batchSize = 1000
TwitterAgent.sinks.HDFS.hdfs.rollSize = 0
TwitterAgent.sinks.HDFS.hdfs.rollCount = 10000

# Describing/Configuring the channel
TwitterAgent.channels.MemChannel.type = memory
TwitterAgent.channels.MemChannel.capacity = 10000
TwitterAgent.channels.MemChannel.transactionCapacity = 100

# Binding the source and sink to the channel
TwitterAgent.sources.Twitter.channels = MemChannel
TwitterAgent.sinks.HDFS.channel = MemChannel
```

Figure 8.38 Apache Flume conf: Twitter configuration file

Now, Go to the Apache Flume directory in the Command Prompt. Go the bin directory of the Apache Flume. Give the command as in Fig. 8.39.

```
flume-ng agent --conf ./conf/ -f C:\apache-flume-1.9.0-bin/conf/twitter.conf
Dflume.root.logger=DEBUG,console -n TwitterAgent
```

Figure 8.39 Apache Flume Twitter configuration command

Flume creates twitter_data directory and put various log files in it.

8.21 MESSAGING SYSTEM

A messaging system is a simple way for two or more people, devices, or other entities to exchange messages. A messaging system is in charge of sending data from one application to another, allowing programs to focus on their data rather than on how to exchange it. The notion of dependable message queuing underpins distributed messaging. Client applications and the messaging system queue messages asynchronously. There are two messaging patterns available: point-to-point (P2P) and publish-subscribe (pub-sub) messaging systems. Messages in a point-to-point system are stored in a queue. One or more consumers can consume the messages in the queue (Fig. 8.40), but one consumer can only consume one message at a time.

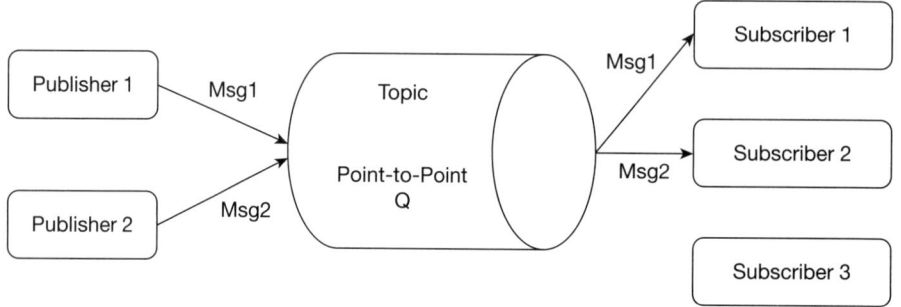

Figure 8.40 Point-to-point messaging system

When a consumer (subscriber) reads a message in the queue, the message is removed from the queue. An Order Processing System is a typical example of this system, in which a single Order Processor handles each order. However, several Order Processors can work at the same time.

Most message patterns are pub-sub (Fig. 8.41). A publish-subscribe messaging system lets a sender send/write a message while a receiver reads it. In Apache Kafka (discussed in the next section), the sender is the producer and the receiver is a consumer who consumes the message by subscribing to it. Messages are saved in a topic in the publish-subscribe system. Consumers can subscribe to one or more topics and consume all of the communications on that subject, unlike a point-to-point system.

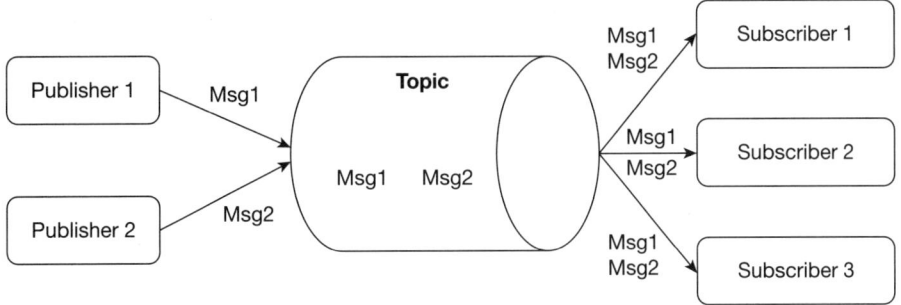

Figure 8.41 Publish-Subscribe (pub-sub) messaging system

Message creators are known as publishers, while message consumers are subscribers in the Publish-Subscribe system. Dish TV, for example, broadcasts various channels such as sports, movies, and music, and everybody may subscribe to their own set of channels and receive them anytime their subscription channels are accessible.

A streaming process is the simultaneous processing of data by several systems. This procedure allows various applications to limit the concurrent data processing, allowing one record to run without waiting for the prior record's output. As a result, a distributed streaming platform allows the user to streamline and execute the streaming process in parallel. As a result, a Kafka streaming platform includes the following critical capabilities: 1. It analyses the streams of records as soon as they appear. 2. It functions similar to a corporate messaging system, publishing and subscribing to record streams. 3. It keeps the record streams fault-tolerant and long-lasting.

8.22 APACHE KAFKA

Apache Kafka is a distributed stream-processing software platform. It is a publish-subscribe messaging system that allows data to be shared among apps, servers, and processors. LinkedIn initially created Apache Kafka, which was eventually contributed to the Apache Software Foundation. Confluent is currently maintaining it under the Apache Software Foundation. Apache Kafka has overcome the problem of sluggishness in data transfer between a sender and a receiver. Apache Kafka is a publish-subscribe messaging system and a full queue that can manage a large amount of data allows messages to be sent from one end-point to another. Both offline and online message consumption is possible with Kafka. Kafka messages are stored on a disk and duplicated throughout the cluster to prevent data loss. Kafka is based on the synchronization service ZooKeeper. It works well with Apache Storm and Spark for real-time streaming data processing. Apache Kafka can process millions of messages or data per second. Between the source and target systems, Apache Kafka acts as a mediator. As a result, data from the source system (producer) is transferred to Apache Kafka, which decouples the data before being consumed by the destination system (consumer). Apache Kafka has excellent performance, with a latency value of less than 10ms, demonstrating a well-versed program. The robust design of Apache Kafka has overcome unexpected data-sharing issues. Apache Kafka is used by companies like Netflix, Uber, and Walmart. In addition, the fault-tolerance of Apache Kafka can be maintained. Fault tolerance refers to the fact that a consumer can occasionally successfully consume the message sent by the producer. However, the consumer cannot execute the message due to a backend database failure or a flaw in the consumer code. As a result, the consumer cannot consume the message again in this case. Apache Kafka was able to remedy this issue by reprocessing the data.

8.22.1 Features of Kafka

Kafka is fault-tolerant, partitioned, replicated, and distributed system. As a result, the Kafka communications system scales up and down quickly. Kafka uses a distributed commit log, meaning messages are sent to the disk as soon as possible and are therefore persistent. For both publishing and subscribing to messages, Kafka has a high throughput. Even when many TB of messages is stored, it maintains consistent performance. As a result, Kafka is speedy and ensures that there will be no downtime or data loss.

8.22.2 Need for Kafka

Kafka is a centralized platform for processing all real-time data sources. Kafka allows for low-latency message delivery while also ensuring fault tolerance in case of machine failure. It can manage a large number of different types of customers. Kafka is speedy, with 2 million writes per second. It publishes all data to disk, which effectively implies that all writes go to the operating system's page cache (RAM). This makes data flow from the page cache to a network socket incredibly efficient.

8.22.3 Kafka Use Cases

Kafka may be utilized in a variety of scenarios. It is frequently used for operational data monitoring. This entails compiling statistics from scattered apps into centralized operational data streams. Kafka may be used to collect logs from many systems and make them available in a consistent format to multiple consumers throughout an organization. Storm and Spark Streaming are popular frameworks that take data from a topic, process it, and write the processed data to a new topic where it is available to users and applications. The high durability of Kafka is also highly valuable in stream processing.

8.23 KAFKA ARCHITECTURE AND TERMINOLOGIES

Before diving into Kafka, familiarize yourself with critical terms like Topics, Partitions, Replicas, Brokers, Clusters, ZooKeeper, producers, consumers, Consumers group, Leader, and Follower (Fig. 8.42).

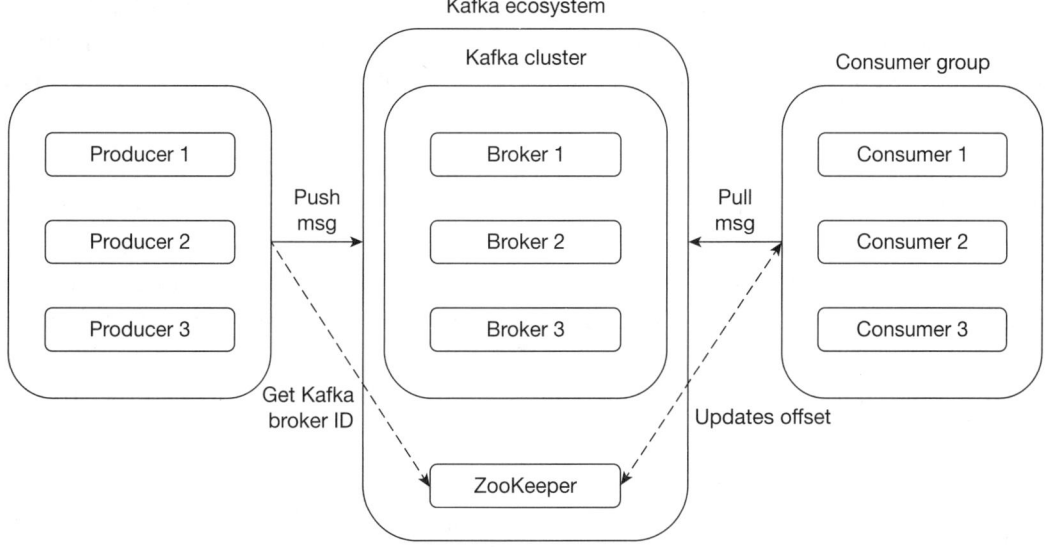

Figure 8.42 Kafka architecture terminologies

The above diagram explains Kafka architecture in a simple way.

Topics: A topic is a general term for a heading or a label given to a group of closely linked concepts. In Kafka, a topic is a category or a common name for storing and publishing a specific data stream. Topics are used to organize data. In Kafka, topics are comparable to database tables. However, they don't have the limitations of database tables.

Partitions: Topics are divided into Partitions. Kafka preserves a minimum of one partition for each subject. Each of these partitions holds messages in an immutable order. A partition is made up of a series of equal-sized segment files. These divisions are arranged in a particular order. Within the subject (topic), the data content is saved in partitions (Fig. 8.43).

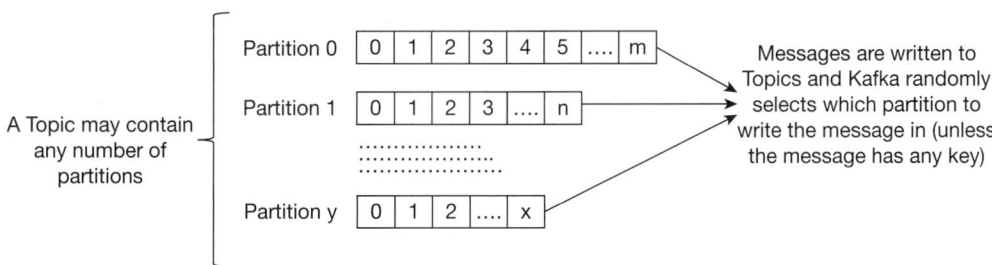

Figure 8.43 Kafka Topic and Partitions structure

As a result, we must indicate the number of divisions when establishing a topic (the number is arbitrary and can be changed later). Each topic is divided into parts and assigned an incremental id called the Offset value. The offset value's order is guaranteed only within the partition, not between partitions. A partition's offsets are unlimited. Kafka is nothing more than a set of subjects (topics) divided into one or more divisions (partitions).

A Kafka partition is a message sequence that is linearly organized and identifiable by its index (called an offset). Data is usually written in chronological order. With unlimited offset values, we may have an endless number of partitions. However, we cannot predict which topic will be written to which partition.

Cluster: Kafka clusters are defined as Kafka instances with multiple brokers. A Kafka cluster may grow without causing any downtime. These clusters are responsible for message data durability and replication. A Kafka cluster comprises one or more brokers (also known as Kafka brokers) who work together to process data. An integer id solely recognizes the cluster's brokers. Because connecting to any one broker means connecting to the entire cluster, Kafka brokers are also known as Bootstrap brokers. Even though a broker does not have all of the data, each broker in the cluster is aware of all other brokers, partitions, and subjects.

Replicas: Replicas are nothing more than backups of a partition. Data is never read or written on replicas. Instead, they are utilized to keep data safe. We can create as many topics as we like in Kafka. It is recognizable by its name, which the user determines. A producer publishes data to the subjects, and a consumer subscribes to the topic to access the data.

Brokers: Brokers are a basic system that keeps track of published data. Per topic, each broker may have zero or more divisions (partitions). Assume that a topic has N partitions and there are N brokers. Each broker will have one partition. If a subject has N partitions and more than N brokers (N + M), the first N brokers will have one partition, and the subsequent M brokers will not have any partitions for that topic. If a topic has N partitions and less than N brokers (N − M), each broker will share one or more partitions. Due to unbalanced load distribution across the brokers, this scenario is not advised. All messages are stored in the partitions set for that subject by the Kafka broker. It guarantees that messages are distributed evenly across partitions. For example, Kafka will store one message in the first partition and the second message in the second partition if the producer sends two messages and there are two partitions.

ZooKeeper: The Kafka broker is managed and coordinated using ZooKeeper. The ZooKeeper service is primarily used to alert producers and consumers of any new brokers in the Kafka system and any broker failures. When the ZooKeeper receives news of the existence or failure of a broker, the producer and consumer make a decision and begin coordinating their tasks with another broker. Apache ZooKeeper, a distributed configuration and synchronization service, is an essential requirement of Apache Kafka. A ZooKeeper cluster connects the Kafka servers and shares information. Kafka holds basic metadata in ZooKeeper, such as topics, brokers, and consumer offsets (queue readers). The failure of the Kafka broker/ZooKeeper has no impact on the status of the Kafka cluster since all vital information is kept in the ZooKeeper, and it routinely replicates this data across its ensemble. Once the ZooKeeper resumes, Kafka will restore the state. Kafka will be available at all times. In the case of a leader failure, ZooKeeper is used to pick a new leader from among the Kafka brokers. The ZooKeeper notifies Apache Kafka whenever something happens, such as a broker dying or new topics being created. A ZooKeeper is intended to work with an odd number of Kafka servers. All writes are handled by the leader server, while the followers handle all reads. A ZooKeeper server is required for any Kafka server to execute and it must be running at all times.

Producers: Producers are the people who send messages on one or more Kafka topics. Kafka brokers receive data from producers. When a producer sends a message to a broker, the broker simply appends it to the previous segment file. The message will be added to a partition. A producer can also deliver messages to a specific partition. When the new broker is launched, all producers instantly look for it and send a message to the new broker. A Kafka producer does not wait for broker acknowledgments and transmits messages as quickly as the broker can handle them.

Consumers: Consumers read broker data. A consumer subscribes to a specific topic. By obtaining data from the brokers, consumers subscribe to one or more subjects and consume published messages. Because Kafka brokers are stateless, the consumer must use partition offset to track the number of messages that have been consumed. When a consumer subscribes to a topic, Kafka gives the consumer the subject's current offset and preserves the offset in the ZooKeeper ensemble. Consumers will poll Kafka for new messages at regular intervals (100 milliseconds). When Kafka gets messages from producers, it passes them on to the consumers. The message will be received and processed by the consumer. The consumer will send an acknowledgment to the Kafka broker after the messages have been digested. When a consumer recognizes a message offset, the consumer has digested all previous messages. To have a buffer of bytes ready to consume, the consumer sends an asynchronous pull request to the broker. Customers may simply specify an offset value to rewind or skip to any point in a partition. ZooKeeper notifies the consumer offset value.

Consumer Group: Instead of a single consumer, a group of consumers with the same Group ID will subscribe to a subject in a queue messaging system. Customers who subscribe to the same topic and have the same Group ID are treated as a single group, and topics are shared among them. Producers periodically submit messages to a topic. Kafka stores all topics in the partitions defined for that topic. A single customer subscribes to a single topic, such as Topic-01, with Group ID Group-1. Until a new consumer subscribes to the same topic, Topic-01, with the same Group ID as Group-1, Kafka communicates with the consumer as in Pub-Sub Messaging. Kafka changes to share mode and distributes the data between the two consumers whenever the new consumer arrives. This sharing will continue until the number of consumers reaches the defined number of partitions for that subject. When the number of subscribers exceeds the number of partitions, the new subscriber will not get any more messages until one of the existing subscribers unsubscribes. This scenario emerges because each Kafka consumer will be allotted at least one partition, and new consumers will have to wait until all partitions have been assigned to current consumers. This feature is also called Consumer Group. In the same way, Kafka will provide the best of both systems in an effortless and efficient manner.

Leader and Follower: The leader is the node that is in charge of all reads and writes for the partition. One server serves as the leader of each division. A follower is a node that follows the commands of the leader. If the leader fails, one of the followers takes over as the new leader. A follower behaves like any other consumer, retrieving messages and updating its own data store.

8.24 KAFKA REPLICATION

In the Big Data realm, Apache Kafka is a distributed software system. As a result, duplicates of the stored data are required for such a system. Each broker in Kafka holds some kind of data. But what happens if the broker or computer goes down? The information will be gone. As a precaution, Apache Kafka has a replication capability (Fig. 8.44) that prevents data loss even if a broker fails. A replication factor is generated for each broker's subjects (topics) in order to do this. Replication factor is the number of copies of data over multiple brokers. The replication factor value should always be greater than 1 (say 2 or 3).

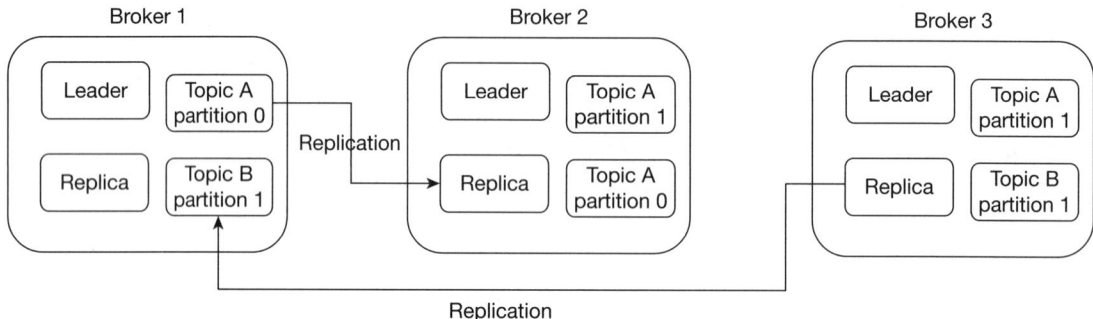

Figure 8.44 Kafka Replication mechanisms

This helps to store a replica of the data in another broker from where the user can access it. For example, suppose we have a cluster containing three brokers say Broker 1, Broker 2, and Broker 3. A topic, namely Topic A, is split into Partition 0 and Partition 1 with a replication factor of 2. Thus, we can see that Partition 0 of Topic A is having its replicas in Broker 1 and Broker 2. Also, Partition1 of Topic B is having its replication in Broker 1 and Broker 3.

It is natural to have confusion when both the actual data and its replicas are present. The cluster may get confused about which broker should serve the client request. To remove such confusion, the following task is done by Kafka: It selects one of the broker's partitions as the leader, and the others become its followers. The data will be synchronized by the followers (brokers). The synchronized data copies are referred to as in-sync replica (ISR). When a leader is present, however, none of the followers are permitted to service the client's request. Apache Kafka provides multiple ISR for the data. However, only the leader is permitted to fulfil the client's request. The leader is in charge of all data read and write activities for the partitions. The ZooKeeper chooses the leader and his or her followers. If the broker holding the leader for the partition fails to serve the data due to any failure, one of its respective ISR replicas will take over the leadership. Afterward, if the previous leader returns, it tries to acquire its leadership again. Let us see an example to understand the concept of leader and its followers.

Consider a cluster with the following three brokers 1, 2, and 3. A topic A is present having two partitions and with replication factor = 2. So, to remove the confusion, Partition-0 under Broker 1 is provided with the leadership. Thus, it is the leader and Partition 0 under Broker 2 will become its replica or ISR. Similarly, Partition 1 under Broker 2 is the leader and Partition 1 under Broker 3 is its replica or ISR. In case Broker 1 fails to serve, Broker 2 with Partition 0 replica will become the leader.

8.25 KAFKA PRODUCERS

A producer is the one which publishes or writes data to the topics within different partitions. Producers are aware of which data should be written to which partition and they broker automatically. The broker and partition do not need to be specified by the user. The key notion in Apache Kafka allows you to transmit messages in a predefined sequence. The key gives the producer two options: automatically transmit data to all partitions or manually send data to a specified partition. The message keys can be used to send data to certain partitions. If the data is keyed by the producers, the data will always be transmitted to the same partition. However, if the producer fails to apply the key when writing the data (Fig. 8.45), it will be delivered in a round-robin fashion. This procedure is termed load balancing. When a producer submits data to a Kafka topic without giving a key, Kafka distributes small bits of data to each partition, resulting in load balancing.

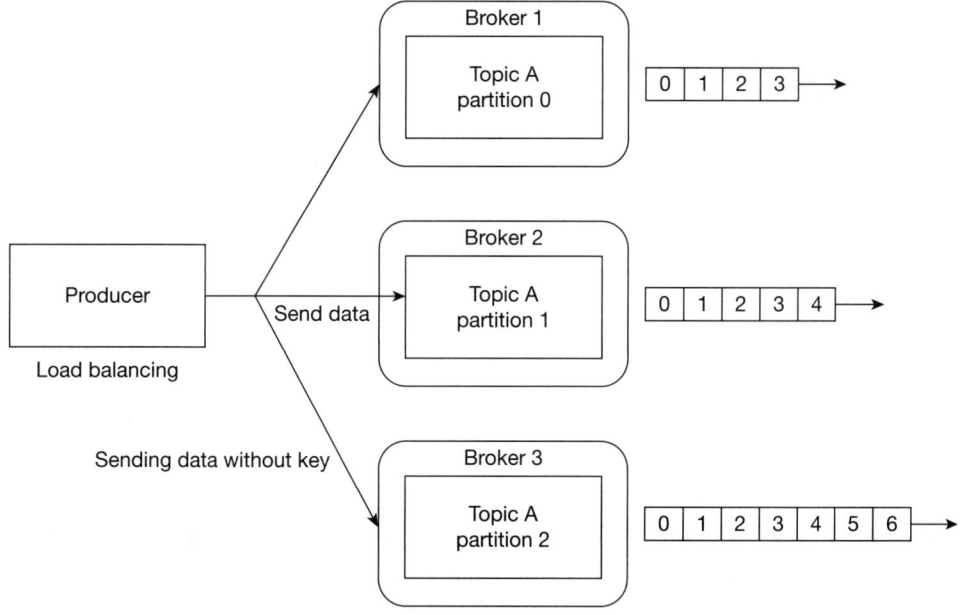

Figure 8.45 Kafka sending data without Key

As a result, a message key can be any string, numeric, or character. There are two methods for determining whether data is delivered with or without a key: When the value of key is NULL, the data is transmitted without a key. As a result, it will be distributed in round-robin style (i.e., distributed to each partition). If the key!=NULL, it signifies the key is associated with the data, and all messages will be delivered to the same partition. Consider the case where a producer publishes data to a Kafka cluster without specifying the key. As a result, the data is spread across each Topic A partition under each broker (Broker 1, Broker 2, and Broker 3).

Consider the case when a producer gives Prod_id as a key (Fig. 8.46). As a result, data from Prod_id 1 will always be sent to Broker 1's partition 0 while data from Prod_id 2 will always be sent to Broker 2's partition 1. As a result, after applying the key, the data will not be dispersed to each division.

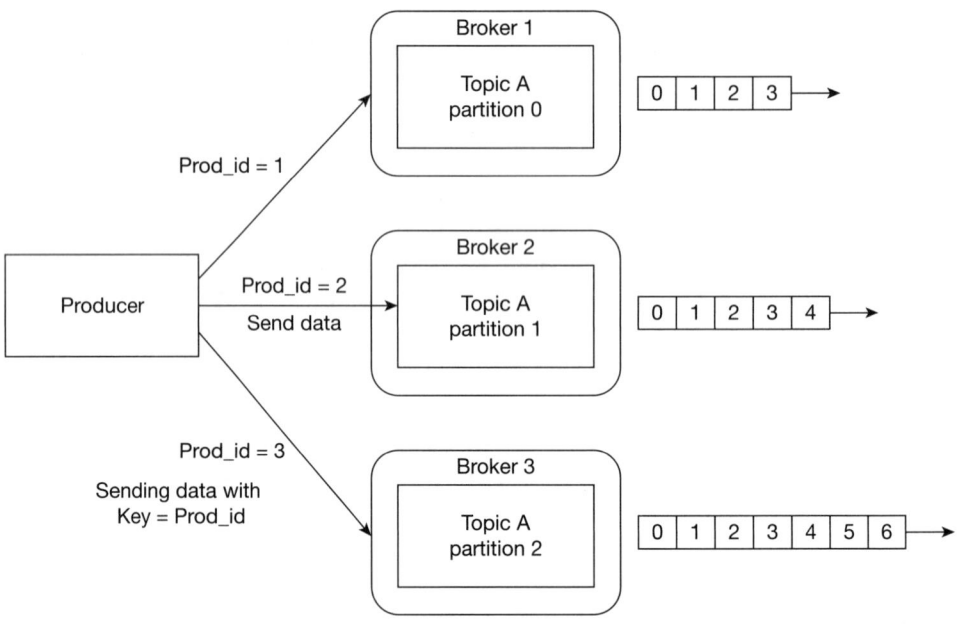

Figure 8.46 Kafka sending data with Key

The producer has additional option for acknowledgment when writing data to the Kafka cluster. It means that the producer can receive confirmation of his or her data writes by obtaining the following acknowledgements.

acks=0: This indicates that the producer transmits the data to the broker without waiting for a response (Fig. 8.47). This may result in data loss since the producer sends another data packet without verifying whether the earlier data was successfully sent to the broker or that the broker is down.

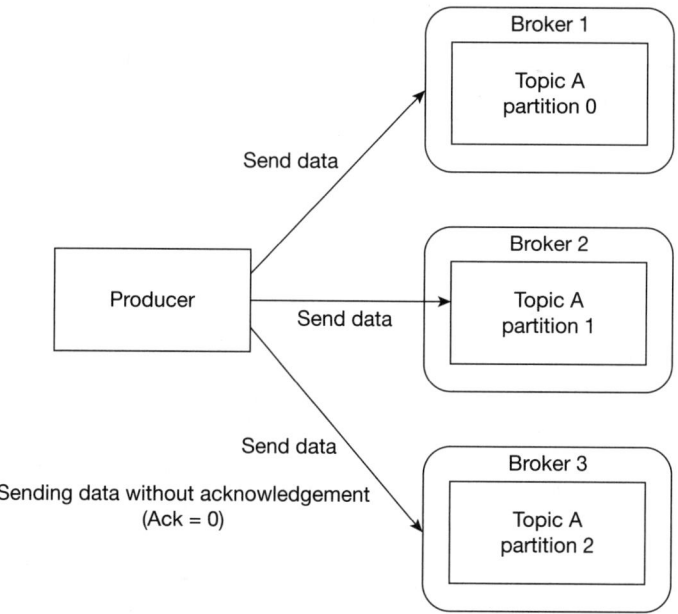

Figure 8.47 Kafka sending data with Ack=0

acks=1: This indicates that the producer will await confirmation from the leader (Fig. 8.48). The leader checks with the broker to see if the data was successfully received before providing feedback to the producer. Only a little amount of data is lost in this situation.

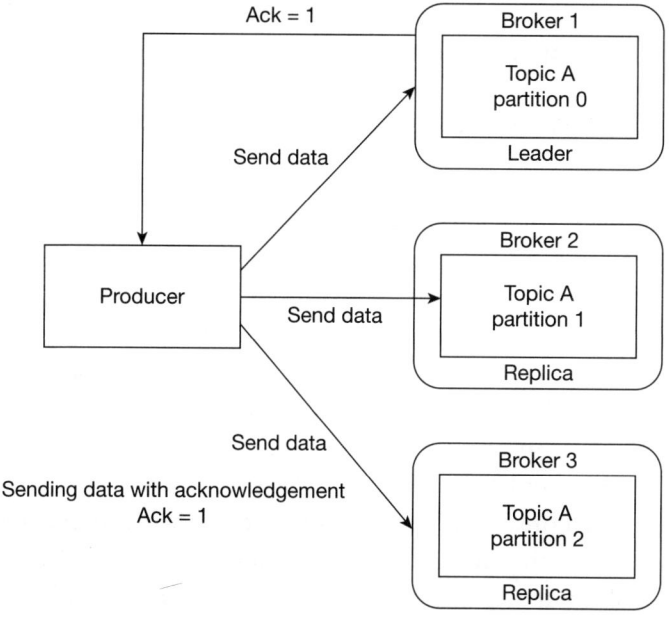

Figure 8.48 Kafka sending data with Ack=1

acks=all **:** Both the leader and the followers acknowledge each other here (Fig. 8.49). The data is effectively received when they successfully acknowledge the data. There is no data loss in this situation.

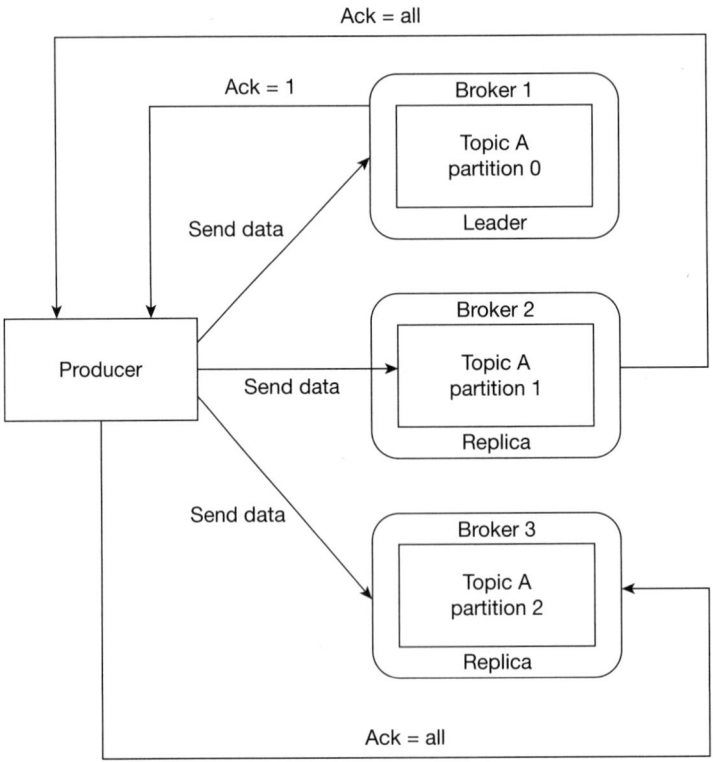

Figure 8.49 Kafka sending data with Ack=all

8.26 Kafka: Consumer and Consumer Groups

A consumer is someone who uses a topic to consume or read data from a Kafka cluster. A consumer also understands from which broker the data should be obtained. The data within each partition is read in a sequential order by the consumer. This indicates that the consumer should not receive data from offset 1 before reading data from offset 0. A consumer can also readily read data from numerous brokers at once. For example: Two customers, Consumer 1 and Consumer 2, are reading data. Consumer 1 is sequentially reading data from Broker 1. Consumer 2, on the other hand, is simultaneously reading data from Brokers 2 and 3, in order.

A consumer group is a collection of consumers (Fig. 8.50) who share similar interests in an application. Each consumer in a group reads data from the exclusive partitions directly. In the event that the number of consumers exceeds the number of partitions, certain consumers will be inactive. If one of the active consumers in the group becomes inactive, the other inactive consumer can take over and become active to read the data. But how can you choose which consumer should read data from which partition first?

Consumers in a group utilize a 'Group Coordinator' and a 'Consumer Coordinator', which allocates a consumer to a partition, to make such choices. This capability is already present in Kafka.

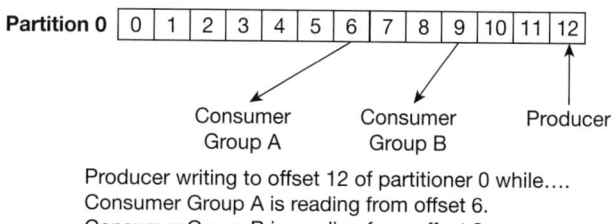

Figure 8.50 Kafka consumer group

Consumer Offsets

The option to preserve an offset value for a consumer group is available in Kafka. By keeping an offset value, it keeps track of the partition from which the consumer group is reading data. When a consumer in a group consumes data, Kafka automatically commits the offsets, or it may be programmed to do so. The consumer offsets topic commits these offsets to real-time. This feature is provided to cover cases of machine breakdown and a consumer's incapacity to access the data. The consumer will be able to resume reading where they left off because of the offset's assurance.

Delivery Semantics

The consumer's option of commitment is determined by when the consumer decides to commit the offsets. An offset is similar to a bookmark used by a reader when reading a book or novel. In Kafka, there are following three delivery semantics used (Fig. 8.51).

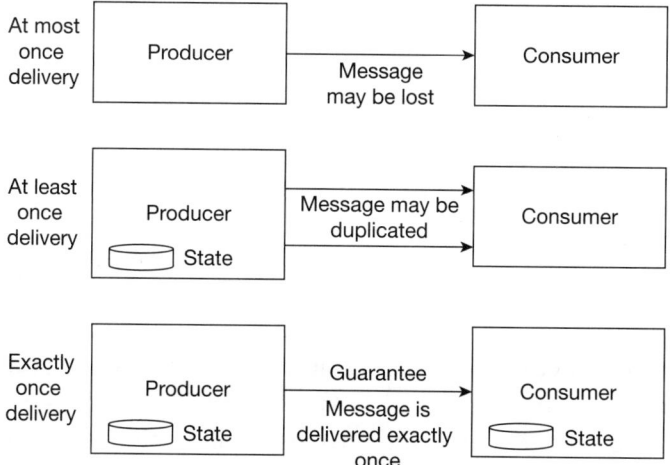

Figure 8.51 Kafka delivery semantics

At Most Once: When the consumer gets the message, the offsets are committed. However, if the message is incorrectly processed, the consumer will be unable to continue reading. As a result, this is the least favoured semantic.

At Least Once: After processing the message, the offsets are committed. The consumer will reread the message if the processing fails. As a result, this is the most common application. Because a consumer can view the same message twice, the messages are processed twice. As a result, an idempotent system is required.

Exactly Once: Only the Kafka Streams API may be used to obtain offsets for Kafka to Kafka workflows. We need to employ an idempotent consumer to achieve Kafka to external system offset.

8.27 QUICK INTRODUCTION TO IMPALA

Unlike typical storage systems, Apache Impala does not have a storage engine. Impala daemon, Impala state store, and Impala catalog services are the three essential components of Apache Impala. We may utilize the three query processing interfaces to connect with Apache Impala: Impala Shell, Hue browser, and JDBC/ODBC driver (Fig. 8.52).

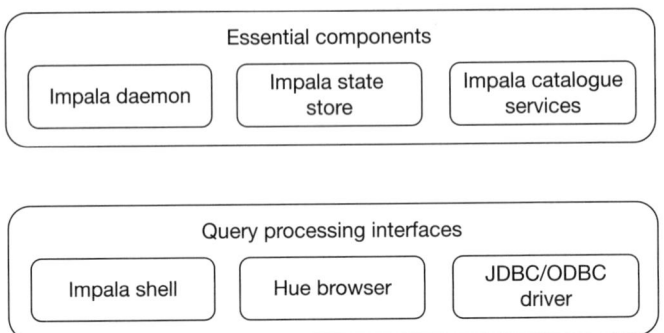

Figure 8.52 Essential components of Impala

It provides low-latency SQL queries with good speed. Impala is the best solution when working with medium-sized datasets and expecting real-time responses from our queries. Impala also comes with its execution engine. Essentially, the intermediate findings are saved in memory. As a result, compared to other MapReduce-based tools, its query execution is lightning-quick. Before Impala, business intelligence data was often reduced into a digestible amount of high-value data. This procedure is also speeded up using Impala. The data arrives in Hadoop after fewer stages, whereas Impala queries it instantaneously. A Hadoop cluster's high-capacity and high-speed storage system also allow you to bring in all data. Furthermore, because Impala can query raw data files, we can bypass the time-consuming procedures of importing and rearranging data. Impala is a very familiar SQL interface, especially to data scientists and analysts. It also offers the ability to query high volumes of data (Big Data) in Apache Hadoop. Also, it provides distributed queries for convenient scaling in a cluster environment. Moreover, it offers the use of cost-effective commodity hardware. Using Impala makes it possible to share data files between different components with no copy or export/import step. It is a single system for Big Data processing and analytics. Hence, customers can avoid costly modelling and ETL just for analytics, through this.

8.28 QUICK INTRODUCTION TO APACHE NiFi

Apache NiFi is a data flow management system based on the ideas of flow-based programming. It provides sophisticated and scalable directed graphs of data routing, transformation, and system mediation logic. NiFi offers a web-based user interface for creating, controlling, providing feedback, and monitoring data flow. It is a platform for data logistics that automates data transportation across several platforms. It offers a variety of quality-of-service choices, such as loss-tolerant vs. guaranteed delivery, low latency vs. high throughput, and priority-based queuing. It is simple to govern data transportation between any source and destination since it enables real-time control. Custom components may be added to Apache NiFi to make it more flexible. It allows you to bring data into NiFi from various sources and generate flow files using data ingestion. It provides real-time control, allowing you to regulate data transit between any source and destination. At the corporate level, it helps visualize dataflow and makes standard tools and extensions available. NiFi makes it possible to use current libraries and Java ecosystem features. It aids organizations in integrating NiFi into their existing infrastructure. NiFi is built to scale out in clusters and provide assured data transmission. Moreover, it helps the user to visualize and monitor track performance and behaviour on a flow chart that provides insight and documentation in real-time. It allows the user to start and stop components individually or in groups. It also enables the user to listen, retrieve, divide, aggregate, route, alter, and drag and drop Dataflow.

SUMMARY

Data ingestion tools are software applications that automatically harvest data from a range of sources and streamline the transmission of different data streams to a single storage location. In addition to data extraction and transmission, data ingestion solutions may help with data processing, modification, and formatting, helping businesses complete analytics tasks faster.

Data Ingestion Types

Data ingestion may be done in three ways: real-time, batches, or a hybrid of the two in a system known as lambda architecture.

    1) Real time data ingestion (RTDI): The practice of gathering and sending data from source systems in real time utilizing methods such as change data capture is known as real-time data ingestion. 2) Batch based data ingestion (BBDI): The technique of gathering and sending data in batches at regular times is known as batch-based data intake. 3) Lambda Architecture data ingestion (LADI): Lambda architecture is a data intake system

that combines real-time and batch processing. Batch, serving, and speed layers constitute the setup.

Benefits of Data Ingestion: Data ingestion technology has several advantages that help teams manage data more efficiently and acquire a competitive advantage. Data intake automates some of the activities that engineers previously had to perform manually, allowing them to focus on more important work. Advanced data intake pipelines, when used in conjunction with ETL systems, may transform diverse types of data into pre-set forms and then send it to a data warehouse. Real-time data input enables organizations to spot problems and opportunities more rapidly and make better decisions.

Some of the famous Hadoop ecosystem ingestion layer tools are Apache Sqoop (RDBMS Connector), Apache Flume (Data Collection), Apache Kafka (Streaming), Apache Impala, Apache NiFi, Storm (Streaming), and Change Data Capture (CDC).

Sqoop may be installed with the use of plugins that are part of the Sqoop extension framework. These connections are fast and effective in transferring data. The JDBC connection, which is accessed via JDBC, is one of them. Depending on the number of mappers specified by the user, the map task will start numerous mappers.

Sqoop has connectors for working with a range of popular databases, including Oracle, Postgres and DB2. There is also a generic JDBC connector for connecting to any database that supports Java's JDBC protocol. Sqoop in Big Data offers a variety of third-party data store interfaces, ranging from Netezza, Teradata, and Oracle to NoSQL stores.

Sqoop uses the MapReduce architecture for importing and exporting data. It is also used to load data into Hadoop ecosystem products like Hive and HBase. Sqoop was created and maintained by Cloudera at first. Apache later fostered it on July 23, 2011.

Sqoop is currently widely used for moving data from RDBMS files to Hadoop for MapReduce processing and other purposes. Sqoop allows us to compress data after it has been processed. It imports and exports data using the YARN architecture, adding fault tolerance to parallelism.

Flume: This architecture's design objective is to meet Dependability, Controllability, and Flexibility. A channel is a transitory storage that collects data and events from a source and buffers them until sinks consume them. It serves as a link between the sinks and the sources. A sink saves data to centralized databases such as HBase and HDFS. It consumes data (events) from the channels and sends it to the specified location.

Flume efficiently ingests log data from numerous web servers into a centralized storage system (HDFS, HBase). We can quickly pull data from multiple servers into Hadoop using Flume. Flume is also used to import massive amounts of event data from social networking sites such as Facebook and Twitter and e-commerce sites such as Amazon and Flipkart.

In Flume, for each event, two transactions take place: one at the sender and one at the receiver. The sender sends events to the receiver. Soon after receiving the data, the receiver commits its own transaction and sends a "received" signal to the sender. After receiving the signal, the sender commits its transaction. The sender will not commit its transaction till it receives a signal from the receiver.

Apache Flume Applications: E-commerce enterprises utilize Apache Flume to evaluate client activity from a specific location. We may use Apache Flume to accelerate the transfer of large volumes of data generated by application servers into the Hadoop Distributed File System.

A messaging system is a simple way for two or more people, devices, or other entities to exchange messages. There are two messaging patterns available: point-to-point (P2P) and publish-subscribe (pub-sub) messaging systems. Messages in a point-to-point system are stored in a queue. One or more consumers can consume the messages in the queue, but one consumer can only consume one message at a time. A publish-subscribe messaging system lets a sender send/write a message while a receiver reads it. A sender is a producer in Apache Kafka, and a receiver is a consumer in Apache Kafka who consumes the message by subscribing to it.

Kafka is a centralized platform for processing all real-time data sources. Kafka allows for low-latency message delivery while also ensuring fault tolerance in case of machine failure. It can manage a large number of different types of customers.

Features of Kafka: Kafka is fault-tolerant, partitioned, replicated, and distributed. As a result, the Kafka communications system scales up and down quickly. Kafka uses a distributed commit log, meaning messages are sent to the disk as soon as possible and are therefore persistent. For both publishing and subscribing to messages, Kafka has a high throughput. Even when many TB of messages is stored, it maintains consistent performance. As a result, Kafka is speedy and ensures that there will be no downtime or data loss.

ZooKeeper: The Kafka broker is managed and coordinated using ZooKeeper. The ZooKeeper service is primarily used to alert producers and consumers of any new brokers in the Kafka system and any broker failures. When the ZooKeeper receives news of the existence or failure of a broker, the producer and consumer make a decision and begin coordinating their tasks with another broker.

Producers are the people who send messages on one or more Kafka topics. Consumers read broker data. A consumer subscribes to a specific topic. Instead of a single consumer, a group of consumers with the same Group ID will subscribe to a subject in a queue messaging system. The leader is the node that is in charge of all reads and writes for the partition. One server serves as the leader of each division. A follower is a node that follows the commands of the leader. If the leader fails, one of the followers takes over as the new leader.

Apache Impala does not have a storage engine. Impala daemon, Impala state store, and Impala catalogue services are the three essential components of Apache Impala. We may utilize three query processing interfaces to connect with Apache Impala: Impala Shell, Hue browser, and JDBC/ODBC driver. Apache Impala provides low-latency SQL queries with good speed. Impala is the best solution when working with medium-sized datasets and expecting real-time responses from our queries.

Apache NiFi: Apache NiFi is a data flow management system built on flow-based programming principles. It offers directed graphs of data routing, transformation, and system mediation logic that are powerful and scalable. NiFi provides a web-based user interface to create, control, providing feedback, and monitoring data flow. It is a data logistics platform that automates data movement across several platforms. It has a wide range of quality-of-service options, including loss-tolerant vs. assured delivery, low latency vs. high throughput, and priority-based queuing.

EXERCISES

Multiple Choice Questions

1. **Another name of hybrid ingestion type is:**
   A. Real-time
   B. Batch
   C. Lambda
   D. Pseudo-real
   Answer: C
   Explanation: Data ingestion may be done in three ways: real-time, batches, or a hybrid of the two in a system known as lambda architecture. Depending on their business goals, IT infrastructure and financial constraints, companies might choose one of these categories.

2. **The practice of gathering and sending data from source systems utilizing methods such as change data capture is known as:**
   A. Real-time data ingestion
   B. Batch data ingestion
   C. Lambda ingestion
   D. Pseudo-real ingestion
   Answer: A
   Explanation: The practice of gathering and sending data from source systems in real time utilizing methods such as change data capture is known as real-time data ingestion. CDC watches transaction or redo logs in real time and transports altered data without interfering with database operations.

3. **This type of ingestion is critical for time-sensitive use cases, such as stock market trading:**
   A. Real-time data ingestion
   B. Batch data ingestion
   C. Lambda ingestion
   D. Pseudo-real ingestion
   Answer: A
   Explanation: For time-sensitive use cases such as stock market trading or power grid monitoring, where companies must respond quickly to new information, real-time ingestion is critical.

4. **The technique of gathering and sending data in batches at regular times is known as:**
   A. Real-time data ingestion
   B. Batch data ingestion
   C. Lambda ingestion
   D. Pseudo-real ingestion
   Answer: B
   Explanation: The technique of gathering and sending data in batches at regular times is known as batch-based data intake. Simple schedules, trigger events, or any other logical ordering can be used by the ingestion layer to gather data.

5. **Apache Sqoop and Kafka are examples of _____.**
   A. Ingestion Layer
   B. Storage Layer
   C. Processing Layer
   D. Analysis Layer
   Answer: A
   Explanation: Some of the famous Hadoop ecosystem ingestion layer tools are Apache Sqoop (RDBMS Connector), Apache Flume (Data Collection), Apache Kafka (Streaming), Apache Impala, Apache NiFi, Storm (Streaming), and Change Data Capture (CDC).

6. **Which of the following is not an example of corporate data warehouses?**
   A. Netezza
   B. Teradata
   C. Oracle
   D. Couchbase
   Answer: D
   Explanation: Sqoop in Big Data supports a wide range of third-party data store interfaces, including corporate data warehouses (such as Netezza, Teradata, and Oracle) and NoSQL stores (such as Couchbase). However, these connectors are not included in the Sqoop package and must be downloaded separately and attached to an existing Sqoop installation.

7. **Sqoop performs data security activities with the help of _____.**
   A. Hashing
   B. Kerberos
   C. Masking
   D. Encryption
   Answer: B
   Explanation: Sqoop performs data security activities with the help of Kerberos.

8. **Sqoop internally turns the command into _____, which are then executed in _____.**
   A. SQL, HDFS
   B. HDFS, SQL
   C. MapReduce, HDFS
   D. MapReduce, Hive
   Answer: C
   Explanation: Sqoop internally turns the command into MapReduce jobs, which are then executed on HDFS.

9. **Sqoop uses this architecture to import and export data:**
   A. Flume
   B. YARN
   C. MapReduce
   D. SQL

Answer: B

Explanation: Sqoop can only import and export data in response to user requests and cannot aggregate data. It simplifies the import and export of data. It uses the YARN architecture to import and export data, providing fault tolerance to parallelism.

10. **In this Sqoop component, the extracted data is transferred to the destination:**
    A. Partitioner   B. Extractor
    C. Loader   D. Cleaner
    Answer: C

    Explanation: The extracted data is transferred to the destination using the framework's Loader phase. The data is wholly saved. Cleaner is simply a de-cluttering procedure to free up previously used resources.

11. **This component of Sqoop separates the data into digestible chunks/blocks that may be extracted simultaneously:**
    A. Partitioner   B. Extractor
    C. Loader   D. Cleaner
    Answer: A

    Explanation: Partitioner is used for extracting data. For example, a 1 TB database cannot be handled as a single block of data. The partitioner separates the data into digestible chunks/blocks that may be extracted simultaneously.

12. **The connection pool, schema, and metadata validation are complete in this component of Sqoop:**
    A. Initiator   B. Extractor
    C. Loader   D. Cleaner
    Answer: A

    Explanation: In the Initiator component, the client sends a job to the Sqoop server to load data from one location to another (i.e., RDBMS to HDFS, in this case). The connection pool, schema, and metadata validation are now complete.

13. **In this Kafka delivery semantics, if the message is incorrectly processed, the consumer will be unable to continue reading:**
    A. Multi-semantics   B. Exactly once
    C. Atleast once   D. Atmost once
    Answer: D

    Explanation

    Atmost once: When the consumer gets the message, the offsets are committed. However, if the message is incorrectly processed, the consumer will be unable to continue reading. As a result, this is the least favoured semantic.

14. **This Kafka delivery semantics is the least favoured semantic:**
    A. Multi-semantics   B. Exactly once
    C. Atleast once   D. Atmost once

Answer: D
Explanation: Same as that for Question 13.

15. **This Kafka delivery semantics is the most favoured semantic:**
    A. Multi-semantics B. Exactly once
    C. Atleast once D. Atmost once
    Answer: C
    Explanation
    Atleast once: After processing the message, the offsets are committed. The consumer will reread the message if the processing fails. As a result, this is the most common application. Because a consumer can view the same message twice, the messages are processed twice. As a result, an idempotent system is required.

Short-answer Questions

1. **Write short notes on Real-time Data Ingestion.**
   The practice of gathering and sending data from source systems in real time utilizing methods such as change data capture (CDC) is known as real-time data ingestion. CDC watches transaction or redo logs in real time and transports altered data without interfering with database operations. A company may gain a better knowledge of their business by combining and analyzing data from both on-premises and cloud settings. For time-sensitive use cases such as stock market trading or power grid monitoring, where companies must respond quickly to new information, real-time ingestion is critical.

2. **Write short notes on Batch-based Data Ingestion.**
   The technique of gathering and sending data in batches at regular times is known as batch-based data intake. Simple schedules, trigger events, or any other logical ordering can be used by the ingestion layer to gather data. When firms need to collect certain data points daily or simply don't need data for real-time decision-making, batch-based ingestion is beneficial. Traditional batch approaches impose unpleasant delays when moving data. The data is already out of date by the time it is gathered and provided. Therefore it cannot be used to make real-time operational decisions.

3. **Write short notes on Lambda Architecture Data Ingestion (LADI).**
   Lambda architecture is a data intake system that combines real-time and batch processing. Batch serving, and speed layers constitute the setup. The first two levels index data in batches, but the speed layer indexes data that hasn't been picked up by the slower batch and serving layers. Data is available for querying with low latency, thanks to this continuous hand-off between levels.

4. **What are the benefits of data ingestion?**
   Data ingestion technology has various benefits that enable teams to manage data more efficiently and gain a competitive advantage. Businesses may collect data from several

places and bring it to a single environment for rapid access and analysis through data ingestion. Data intake automates some of the tasks done manually by engineers earlier, allowing them to focus on more critical tasks. In addition, data engineers may use data ingestion technologies to ensure that their apps and software tools send data quickly and provide a more significant user experience.

5. **Give some examples of Hadoop ecosystem ingestion layer tools.**
   Apache Sqoop (RDBMS Connector), Apache Flume (Data Collection), Apache Kafka (Streaming), Apache Impala, Apache NiFi, Storm (Streaming), and Change Data Capture (CDC).

6. **What is the difference between Data ingestion and ETL systems?**
   While data input methods appear to work similarly to ETL systems, there are significant differences. Data ingestion entails getting data from the source and transferring it to the target site. ETL, on the other hand, is a data ingestion technique that comprises data extraction and transfer and data transformation before it is delivered to the intended destination.

7. **What is Apache Sqoop?**
   Apache Sqoop is a Hadoop tool that transfers data between HDFS (Hadoop storage) and relational database servers, including MySQL, Oracle RDB, SQLite, Teradata, Netezza, and Postgres. Sqoop is a command-line interface that allows data to be moved from relational databases to Hadoop.

8. **What is the primary difference between Flume and Sqoop?**
   Flume exclusively ingests unstructured or semi-structured data into HDFS. Sqoop, on the other hand, can import and export structured data from RDBMS and Enterprise data warehouses to HDFS and vice-versa.

9. **How did Sqoop get its name?**
   Sqoop got its name from the phrase "SQL to Hadoop & Hadoop to SQL." Because the data is transferred and stored in Hadoop, Sqoop allows us to offload part of the ETL (Extract, Load, and Transform) processing onto low-cost, fast, and efficient Hadoop processes.

10. **Write short notes on Sqoop Incremental Import.**
    Sqoop offers an incremental import mode that allows you to get rows that are newer than the previous batch. Sqoop supports append and the latest modified incremental imports. The -incremental argument allows you to specify the incremental import type. The check column provides the column that contains the row id. Sqoop imports rows with a check column value greater than the specified -last-value- value.

11. **Describe the disadvantages of Sqoop.**
    The hardware configuration of the relational database management system determines Sqoop export performance. The traditional approach of putting data into Hadoop using scripts is inefficient and time-consuming for large data loads. Giving map-reduce

programs direct access to data stored on other systems (rather than putting it into Hadoop) complicates things. As a result, this method is no longer feasible.

12. **What are the disadvantages of Flume?**
    Considering faster data transfer and lower-cost fault tolerance, Apache Flume delivers fewer guarantees than competing systems such as message queues. In Apache Flume's end-to-end dependability mode, the flume events are dispatched at least once, but there are no ordering guarantees. Apache Flume cannot guarantee that each message is unique. Duplicate messages might emerge in a variety of contexts. Flume scalability is generally constrained since scaling the hardware of a conventional Apache Flume may be challenging for any company, and trial-and-error is usually necessary.

13. **What are the applications of Apache Flume?**
    E-commerce enterprises utilize Apache Flume to evaluate client activity from a specific location. We may use Apache Flume to accelerate the transfer of large volumes of data generated by application servers into the Hadoop Distributed File System. Apache Flume is employed for fraud detection and may also be used in IoT applications. Apache Flume may be used to aggregate data supplied by machines and sensors. We may utilize Apache Flume in Security Information and Event Management (SIEM).

14. **Why do we need Kafka?**
    Kafka is a centralized platform for processing all real-time data sources. Kafka allows for low-latency message delivery while also ensuring fault tolerance in case of machine failure. It can manage a large number of different types of customers. Kafka is speedy, with 2 million writes per second. It publishes all data to disk, which effectively implies that all writes go to the operating system's page cache (RAM). This makes data flow from the page cache to a network socket incredibly efficient.

15. **What are the features of Kafka?**
    Kafka is fault-tolerant, partitioned, replicated, and distributed. As a result, the Kafka communications system scales up and down quickly. Kafka uses a distributed commit log, meaning messages are sent to the disk as soon as possible and are therefore persistent. For both publishing and subscribing to messages, Kafka has a high throughput. Even when many TB of messages is stored, it maintains consistent performance. As a result, Kafka is speedy and ensures that there will be no downtime or data loss.

16. **Write short notes on Kafka Clusters.**
    Kafka clusters are defined as Kafka instances with multiple brokers. A Kafka cluster may grow without causing any downtime. These clusters are responsible for message data durability and replication. A Kafka cluster comprises one or more brokers (also known as Kafka brokers) who work together to process data. An integer id solely recognizes the cluster's brokers. Because connecting to any one broker means connecting to the entire cluster, Kafka brokers are also known as Bootstrap brokers.

Even though a broker does not have all of the data, each broker in the cluster is aware of all other brokers, partitions, and subjects.

17. **Write short notes on Kafka Brokers.**
    Brokers are a basic system that keeps track of published data. Per topic, each broker may have zero or more divisions (partitions). Assume that a topic has N partitions and there are N brokers. Each broker will have one partition. If a subject has N partitions and more than N brokers (N + M), the first N brokers will have one partition, and the subsequent M brokers will not have any partitions for that topic. If a topic has N partitions and less than N brokers (N − M), each broker will share one or more partitions.

18. **Write short notes on Kafka Producers.**
    Producers are the people who send messages on one or more Kafka topics. Kafka brokers receive data from producers. When a producer sends a message to a broker, the broker simply appends it to the previous segment file. The message will be added to a partition. A producer can also deliver messages to a specific partition. When the new broker is launched, all producers instantly look for it and send a message to the new broker. A Kafka producer does not wait for broker acknowledgments and transmits messages as quickly as the broker can handle them.

Essay-type Questions

1. Explain the different Data Ingestion types in detail.
2. Describe the various features of Sqoop.
3. What are the various Sqoop components?
4. Describe the advantages of Sqoop.
5. What is the need for Apache Flume?
6. What are the features of Apache Flume?
7. Write an essay on Kafka Replication.
8. Write an essay on Kafka Consumer and Consumer Groups.
9. Write an essay on Impala.
10. Write an essay on Apache NiFi.

CHAPTER 9

Hive

LEARNING OBJECTIVES

In the previous chapters, we discussed Big Data and Hadoop fundamentals. This chapter focuses on Hive configuration and installation, internal and external tables in Hive, partitioning and bucketing using Hive, and the various joins we can perform. Hive provides many advantages to Hadoop users, and we take you through a step-by-step process for learning Hive.

9.1 Introduction to Hive

In the previous chapters, we saw how the Hadoop ecosystem offers a low-cost platform for achieving distributed processing and working with large datasets. We have also learned how the programming paradigm MapReduce divides terabytes of data tasks into chunks, resulting in cost-effective solutions. Now, let us look at the data warehouse built on top of Hadoop, which makes summarizing and querying large amounts of data more accessible.

9.2 Need for Hive

So far, all of our infrastructure is built on traditional relational databases and the structured query language (SQL). So, how do we migrate the existing infrastructure to Hadoop? The Apache Hive data warehouse software provides a solution, the "Hive Query Language," to process structured data in Hadoop. Hive was initially developed by Facebook to help the company handle massive amounts of new data. Hive supports data summarization and data querying and has a declarative language with very similar commands to SQL. As a result, it is known as the Hive Query Language (HQL). Furthermore, Hive converts queries into MapReduce programs, making simple operations such as data encapsulation. As a result, it aids developers in analyzing structured and semi-structured data.

Hive provides the option to operate in two modes based on the number and size of the data nodes—(i) Local mode and (ii) MapReduce Mode.

(i) When the data size is small and is restricted to one machine, the local mode is used. For example, the local mode works well when Hadoop has only one data node, which is small.

(ii) The MapReduce mode is used for large datasets when the data in Hadoop is spread across multiple data nodes.

We can specify the mode in which Hive can operate by setting the property. By default, it operates in MapReduce mode; the Hive is configured to operate in local mode using `SET mapred.job.tracker=local;`

9.3 FEATURES OF HIVE

Apache Hive is a free and open-source, Hadoop-based data warehouse tool for extracting meaningful information from data (Fig. 9.1). Data warehousing is the process of storing all types of data generated from various sources in a single location. Client applications written in PHP, Python, Java, C++, and Ruby can be supported by Hive. Data is typically available in three formats: structured (SQL database), semi-structured (XML or JSON), and unstructured (music or video) formats. We use Hive on top of Hadoop to process structured data in tabular format. Hive can efficiently query Petabytes (PB) of data. Since writing code in Java is more complex than writing code in Hive, using Hive makes it easier to query structured data.

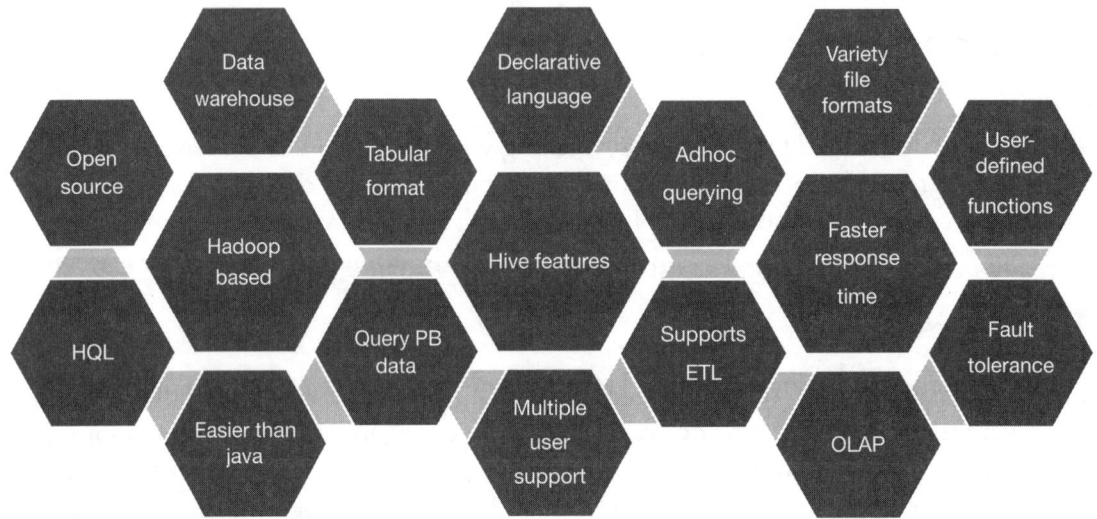

Figure 9.1 Features of Hive

Apache Hive offers a simple query model (HQL) that requires lesser coding than MapReduce and has a very similar syntax to the Structured Query Language (SQL). HQL, like SQL, is a declarative language, which means it is non-procedural. The table's structure is similar to that of an RDBMS. It also supports partitioning and bucketing. With HQL, we can reduce 100 lines of Java code to query structured data, to just four. In addition, Hive Query Language (HQL) allows multiple users to query the data simultaneously.

We can easily integrate custom MapReduce code with Hive to process unstructured data. Hive supports three data structures: partitions, buckets, and tables. As a result, Hive can help us with data mining, predictive modeling, and document indexing.

Hive is a reliable batch-processing framework that can be used as a data warehouse and is built on top of the HDFS. Hive supports ad-hoc querying data on HDFS. It enables us to run ad-hoc queries, which are loosely typed commands or queries whose value is dependent on some variable for data analysis.

Hive has a well-defined architecture supporting metadata management and query optimizations. ETL, or Extract, Transform, and Load, are supported by Apache Hive.

HQL provides many functions that simplify data analytics and faster response time when working with large datasets. Hive allows users to access files from HDFS, Apache HBase, Amazon S3, and other storage systems. It supports very large datasets in the Petabyte range.

Apache Hive supports different computing frameworks and allows users to read data in arbitrary formats. Hive supports various file formats, including textFile, ORC, Avro Files, SequenceFile, Parquet, RCFile, LZO Compression, and others. Apache Hive supports scripting from version **Hive 0.9.0** and a customized I/O that can be extended to various data types. It also includes several built-in functions and supports User-Defined Functions (UDFs) for data cleansing and filtering tasks. UDFs can be defined based on our needs. Hive also receives a lot of support from developers working on Hadoop, who help novice users by giving them the necessary support. Hadoop provides fault tolerance because we store Hive data on HDFS. Apache Hive also supports external tables; this enables us to process data without storing it in HDFS. Hive is intended for OLAP applications (Online Analytical Processing) and can be used to visualize data. Integrating Hive with Apache Tez will allow for real-time processing.

9.4 LIMITATIONS OF HIVE

Hive is not a complete database and does not have the necessary features for Online Transaction Processing (OLTP). However, Hive can build a data warehouse package on top of Hadoop. Therefore, it is suitable for static data analysis, and a fast response time is not required.

The design constraints that impose limits in Hadoop and HDFS also constrain what Hive can do. For example, the most significant limitation reported by users is that it does not perform record-level update, insert and delete. Hive does not support table update and deletion operations and does not support subqueries. However, the update is now available in newer versions.

Another disadvantage faced is that queries generated using Hive have high latency because Hadoop supports batch-processing. Hive is not used to query data in real-time.

In addition, transaction processing is not supported by HQL. Another limitation of Hive is, it always partitions from the last column.

9.5 Hive Architecture

The Apache Hive warehouse solution provides the following components: Hive Clients, Hive Services, and Hive Storage (Fig. 9.2).

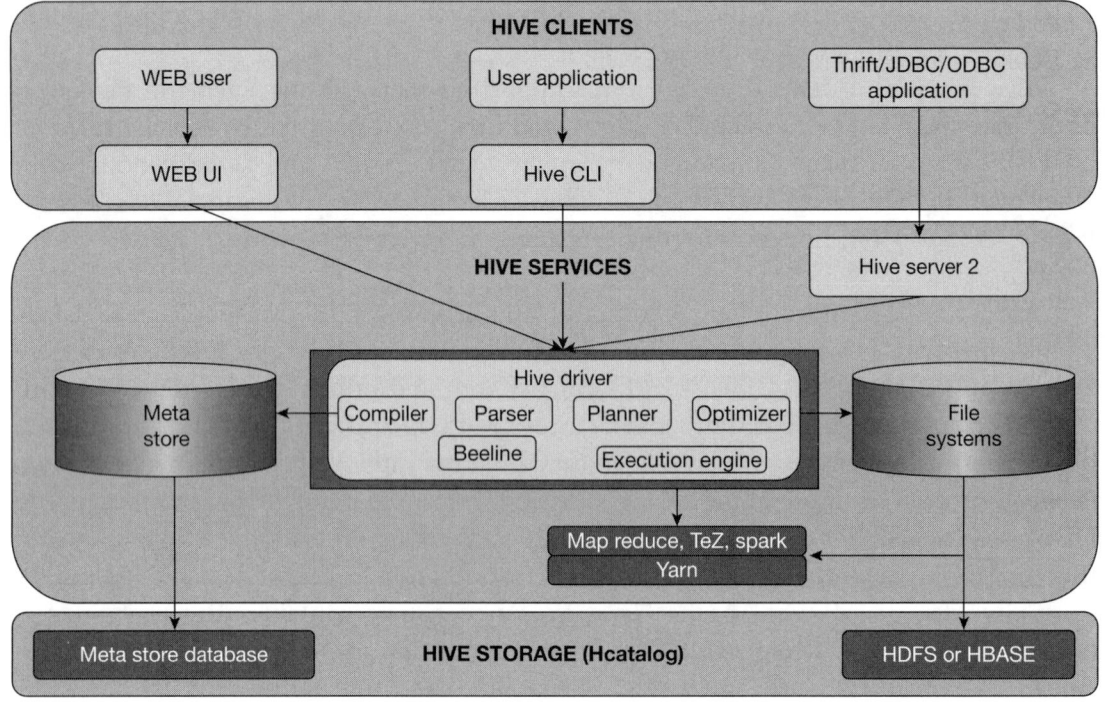

Figure 9.2 Hive architecture

9.5.1 Hive Clients

The Hive client provides different drivers for different applications and is categorized into three types (i) Thrift clients (ii) JDBC clients (iii) ODBC clients.

Thrift clients can run from different programming languages, and Thrift bindings are provided for Java, Python, and Ruby. JDBC client offers a high connectivity solution for JDBC applications and can be defined using the `class org.apache.Hadoop.hive.jdbc.HiveDriver`. ODBC Client constitutes the software library that enables ODBC applications to interact with Hive.

9.5.2 Hive Services

The client interacts with Hive through Hive Services. When the Hive client performs any operation, it communicates with the Hive Services. The default and common way of interacting is through the Hive shell (Command Line Interface). It is a well-known user interface. When running the CLI on a Hadoop cluster, Hive runs in local mode, using local storage instead of HDFS. Hive can also be accessed through a web browser (Hive Web Interface).

Hive offers other services like (i) Beeline (ii) Hive Server2 (iii) Hive Driver (iv) Hive Compiler (v) Optimizer (vi) Execution Engine (vii) Metastore (viii) HCatalog.

The Beeline is a command shell JDBC client supported by HiveServer2. To start Beeline, we need to run the Beeline shell, which is present in the $HIVE_HOME/bin directory. The Beeline server can be run both in the remote and embedded mode.

HiveServer2 is the server interface that enables clients to execute queries. HiveServer2 is the replacement for HiveServer1. HiveServer2 allows clients to run queries against Hive. It will allow multiple clients to send queries to Hive and retrieve the results. It is primarily intended to provide the best possible support for open API clients like JDBC and ODBC. HiveServer1, also known as a Thrift server, was built on the Apache Thrift protocol to handle cross-platform communication with Hive. It enabled various client applications to send queries to Hive and retrieve the results.

However, it could not handle concurrent requests from more than one client. Hence, it was superseded by HiveServer2. By default, the HiveServer2 runs on port 10000, and it provides the best support for open API clients like JDBC and ODBC.

The Hive Driver represents the main driver and communicates with all types of JDBC, ODBC, and other client-specific applications. The driver communicates with all types of JDBC and ODBC client applications to process requests submitted by the user through the command shell. First, the Hive driver receives the HiveQL statements entered into the command shell by the user. Then, it generates session handles for the query and sends them to the compiler. During compilation, optimization, and execution, it manages the lifecycle of a HiveQL statement.

The Hive Compiler gets the metadata from the metastore to parse queries. It generates an execution plan after performing semantic analysis and type-checking on the various query blocks and query expressions stored in the metastore. The Hive compiler translates HiveQL statements and works like the traditional database compiler by performing semantic analysis, type-checking, etc. The execution plan generated by the compiler is a DAG (Directed Acyclic Graph), with each stage representing a map/reduce job, an HDFS operation, and a metadata operation.

The Optimizer performs the transformation operations like column pruning, reordering on the execution plan, and improving efficiency and scalability. To provide optimized DAG, it performs various transformations on the execution plan. For improved performance, it aggregates the transformations, such as converting a pipeline of joins to a single join. To improve performance, the optimizer can also split tasks, such as transforming data before performing a reduce operation.

The Execution Engine executes the execution plan created by the compiler in the order of their dependencies using Hadoop after compilation and optimization. The execution engine processes the query, and the results are generated in the same way that MapReduce results are. It employs the MapReduce flavor.

Metadata means data about data. The metastore is a system catalog. The metastore stores information about the tables and views that you create in Hive and other details such as permissions, schema, and file locations. We have a thrift API on top of Metastore to query the database using JDBC/ODBC connections. Hive Metastore is typically an RDBMS system that can query the schema more quickly without accessing the data. Hive ships with a **Derby** metastore by default, but it is simple to switch to an SQL metastore. The limitation of a Derby store is that only one user can interact with the database at any given time. To initialize the metastore, we run the **schema tool** command and then use derby as **DB type**.

Usually, metastore can be configured in three modes: (i) Remote (ii) Embedded and (iii) Local.

A remotely running MySQL server would be a simple step up (Fig. 9.3). This would enable the use of a separate system to manage the metastore. The metastore is helpful for non-Java applications in remote mode, and the metastore runs in its JVM, not the Hive service JVM. To communicate with the metastore server in the remote mode, the Thrift Network APIs are used.

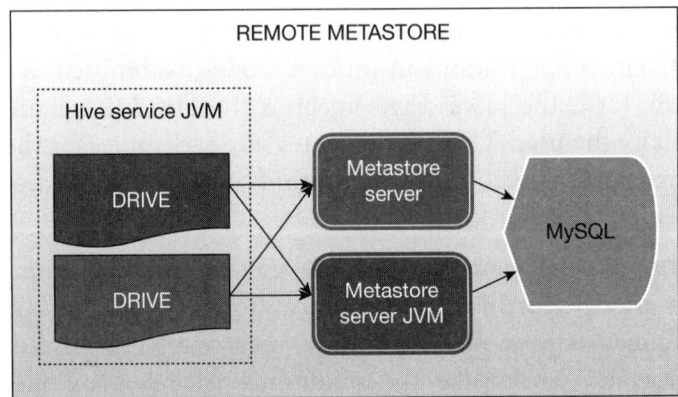

Figure 9.3 Remote metastore

Embedded Metastore The Derby metastore is Hive's default embedded metastore (Fig. 9.4). This is the simplest, but it also has its own set of issues. First, it can only be used by one command-line interface at a time. This is especially aggravating when you close your terminal by accident, since the Hive metastore remains locked. While operating in the embedded mode, the metastore uses the same Java Virtual Machine as the Hive service.

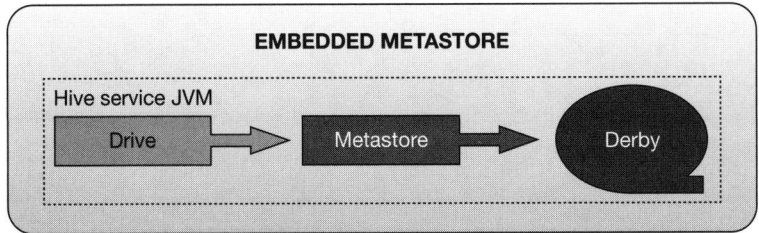

Figure 9.4 Embedded metastore

Finally, the Local metastore (Fig. 9.5) allows us to have many Hive sessions compared to the embedded metastore and allows many users to use the metastore simultaneously. You can swap your Derby metastore for a MySQL one. It is as simple as providing Hive with a connection string. The most basic version would be to have a MySQL database running locally.

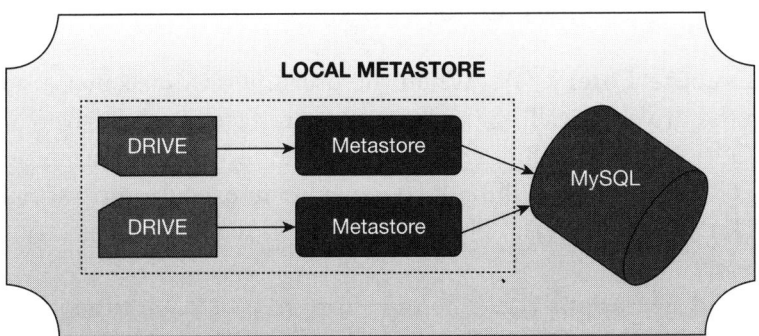

Figure 9.5 Local metastore

Hive Storage and Computing

The storage layer in Hadoop is called HCatalog and helps users with different data processing tools to easily read and write data. HCatalog is Hadoop's table and storage management layer. It allows users to read and write data on the grid using various data processing tools such as Pig, MapReduce, and others. It is built on top of Hive metastore and exposes Hive metastore tabular data to other data processing tools.

9.6 WORKFLOW IN HIVE

Hive can operate in two modes: interactive mode and non-interactive mode. The former mode directs all Hive commands to the Hive shell, whereas the latter type executes the code in console mode. Data is divided into partitions, which are further subdivided into buckets. Aggregation and data skew are used to inform execution plans. Another advantage of using Hive is that it can easily process large amounts of data and has more user interfaces. The workflow in Hive follows the sequence shown in Fig. 9.6.

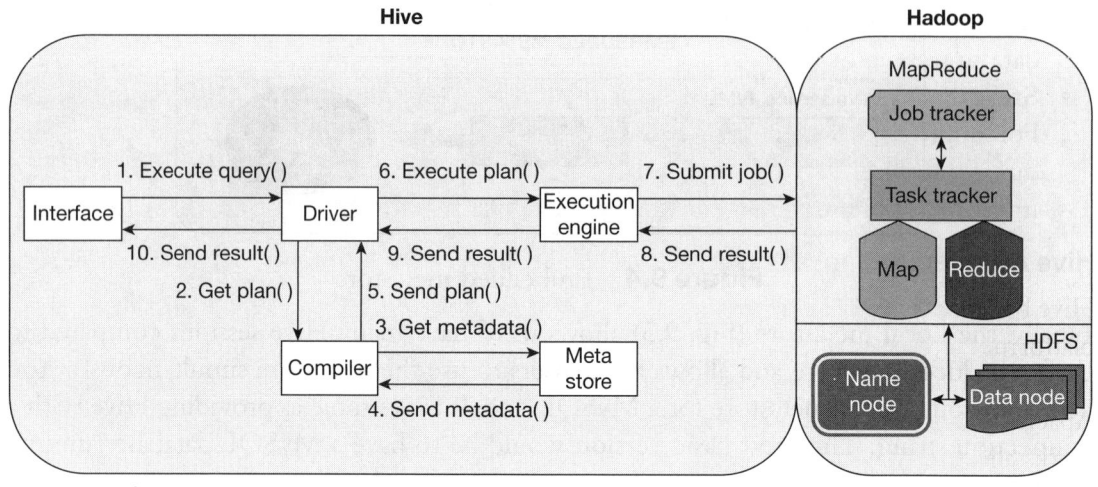

Figure 9.6 Workflow in Hive

- **Step 1 (Execute Query ()):** When the user interface executes a query, it sends a request to the driver by calling the "execute interface" of the driver.
- **Step 2 (Get Plan ()):** The driver creates a session to handle the query and sends the query to the compiler, asking it to generate an execution plan.
- **Step 3 (Get Metadata ()):** The compiler then seeks the necessary metadata from the metastore.
- **Step 4 (Send Metadata ()):** The metastore responds with the metadata necessary to type-check the expressions in the query tree. The compiler uses this metadata to perform type-checking and semantic analysis on the query tree expression; then it creates the execution plan (Directed Acyclic Graph). For example, the plan for MapReduce jobs includes map operator trees (operator trees that are executed on the mapper) and reduce operator trees (operator trees which are executed on the reducer).
- **Step 5 (Send Plan()):** The compiler generates the plan, gathers this information, and sends the plan back to the driver. The plan is a DAG of stages, with each stage being either a map/reduce job or an operation on HDFS.
- **Step 6 (Execute Plan()):** The driver sends the execution plan to the execution engine.
- **Step 7 (Submit Job()):** The execution engine interacts with Hive and Hadoop and processes the query. In addition, the execution engine also communicates bidirectionally with the metastore to perform various operations. Finally, there is bidirectional communication with the client.

To read rows from HDFS files, the deserializer associated with a table or intermediate output is used for each task (either mapper or reducer). These are then processed by the operator tree associated with them. Once the output is generated, it is serialized

and written in the HDFS temporary file. These temporary files are used to supply data to the plan's subsequent map/reduce stages.
- **Steps 8, 9, 10 (Send Result()):** The result is communicated back to the interface. For queries, the execution engine now reads the contents of the temporary files directly from HDFS as part of a driver fetch call. The results are then sent to the Hive interface by the driver.

Hive Architecture and Its Workflow

Hive basically handles Petabytes of data and is thus a data warehouse package on the Hadoop platform. Because Hive is a good choice for handling large amounts of data, it aids in data preparation with the help of an SQL interface to solve MapReduce issues. In addition, Apache Hive is an ETL tool for structured data processing. Knowing how Hive architecture works allows corporate employees to understand Hive's basic operation and get a head start on Hive programming.

9.7 HIVE VS. TRADITIONAL DATABASE

The traditional relational databases are of "Schema on Reading and Schema on Write," which means we must create a table and insert data into the particular table. The main difference between Hive and traditional relational databases is in performing functions like insert, update and modify. While the relational databases allow all these functions to be easily performed, Hive is "Schema on READ only," which means that functions like the update, modifications, etc., cannot be done. (However, newer versions allow updates now). The main differences between Hive and RDBMS database are listed in Table 9.1.

Table 9.1 Difference between Hive and RDBMS

S. No.	Hive	RDBMS
1	Hive is analytics-focused	Traditional RDBMS is focused on online or analytics
2	Transactions are supported by RDBMS	Transactions are not endorsed by Hive (it supports limited transactions)
3	The distributed process in Hive occurs via MapReduce	It varies by RDBMS vendor
4	Hive scales easily to hundreds of nodes	RDBMS rarely scales beyond 20 nodes
5	Hive is designed for commodity hardware	RDBMS is designed for proprietary hardware
6	Hive can handle Petabytes of data at a low cost	RDBMS cannot handle Petabytes of data
7	Hive only supports limited indexing	RDBMS supports full indexing

(Continued)

Table 9.1 (*Continued*)

S. No.	Hive	RDBMS
8	Triggers are not supported in Hive	They are supported in traditional RDBMS
9	Hive has a long latency (minutes)	Conventional RDBMS have a short latency (seconds)
10	Scalability is horizontal in Hive and easily scalable to low cost	Scalability is usually vertical in RDBMS
11	Hive supports OLAP	RDBMS supports both OLAP and OLTP
12	Row-level inserts are not supported in Hive	Row-level inserts are supported in RDBMS

9.8 INSTALLING AND CONFIGURING HADOOP ON UBUNTU

Hadoop is a framework for distributed computing and Big Data comprised of (Hadoop Distributed File System) HDFS and MapReduce (Programming framework). In the earlier versions, Hadoop was meant only for batch computations, and the user could only run the map-reduce programs. Later versions of Hadoop (from version 2) have Hadoop YARN, which provides an API for requesting and allocating resources in the cluster. A single Hadoop cluster consists of a single master node and multiple worker nodes. For configuring Hadoop, the machine must have 4 GB RAM and a minimum 60 GB hard disk to get better performance. Check the Java version.

The below command is used to install default-JDK and check the Java version. Hadoop requires a JRE of 1.6 or higher. It is recommended to install Oracle Java 8.

```
$ sudo apt-get install default-JDK
To check the version of java, we are using the following command.
$ java -version
```

- **Step 1**: Download the Hadoop package 2.8.x and extract Hadoop.

```
Go to http://www.apache.org/dist/hadoop/common/hadoop-2.8.2/
Extract the tar file
$tar xzfHadoop-2.8.2.tar.gz
```

Using the above link, we can download the stable version of Hadoop 2.8.x from Apache mirrors and extract the package to the home directory.

- **Step 2**: Creating Hadoop Group and hduser.

  ```
  $ sudo addgroup Hadoop
  $ sudo adduser --ingroup hadoop hduser
  Adding user `hduser' ...
  Adding new user `hduser' (1001) with group `hadoop' ...
  Creating home directory `/home/hduser' ...
  Copying files from `/etc/skel' ...
  Enter new UNIX password:
  Retype new UNIX password:
  passwd: password updated successfully
  Changing the user information for hduser
  Enter the new value, or press ENTER for the default
          Full Name []:
          Room Number []:
          Work Phone []:
          Home Phone []:
          Other []:
  Is the information correct? [Y/n]
  Then,
  $sudp usermod-a -G sudo hduser
  ```

- **Step 3**: Installing SSH Server and SSH Client
  The standard startup and shutdown require that the secure shell (SSH) be installed.

  ```
  $ sudo apt-get install ssh
  CHECK ssh and sshd
  $ which ssh
  $ which sshd
  ```

- **Step 4**: Generating public and private key pairs
  - To switch the user

  ```
  $ su hduser
  Password:
  ```

  - Generating public/private RSA key pair

  ```
  $ ssh-keygen -t rsa -P ""
  ```

- Key transfer

```
$ cat/home/hduser/.ssh/id_rsa.pub>> /home/hduser/.ssh/authorized_keys
```

The second command adds the newly generated key to the list of authorized keys, allowing Hadoop to use SSH without a password.

Now, to check if SSH works:

```
$ ssh localhost
```

- **Step 5:** Configuring Hadoop

  Hadoop's Java configuration has two important configuration files:

  - The default configuration (which is only read-only) includes core-default.xml, hdfs-default.xml, yarn-default.xml, and mapred-default.xml.
  - The site-specific configuration includes etc/hadoop/core-site.xml, etc/hadoop/hdfs-site.xml, etc/hadoop/yarn-site.xml, and etc/hadoop/mapred-site.xml.

The Hadoop scripts are found in the /bin directory.

These values can be controlled by setting the etc/Hadoop/Hadoop-env.sh, etc/Hadoop/yarn-env.sh.

Hadoop Cluster Setup

The primary step to configure a Hadoop cluster is setting the environment variables and configuration parameters for the Hadoop daemons. Hadoop can be installed in a single-node cluster or a multi-node cluster. The main difference is that in a single-node cluster, there is only one data node on a single machine, whereas, in a multi-node cluster, more data nodes are running, each on a different device.

- HDFS daemons are NameNode, SecondaryNameNode, and DataNode.
- YARN daemons are ResourceManager, NodeManager, and WebAppProxy.

The Job History server also will run if we are using map-reduce programs.

- To add hduser to sudo

```
$ sudo adduser hduser sudo
```

- To move files to /usr/local/Hadoop

```
$ sudo mv*/usr/local/hadoop/
```

- To grant Privileges

```
$ sudo chown -R hduser:hadoop /usr/local/hadoop/
```

- To check Java and Install the updates

    ```
    $ update-alternatives --config java
    ```

- **Step 6**: Setting up the environment variables in Hadoop
  - Edit the bashrc and add Hadoop in the path
  $ nano ~/.bashrc
  For Version 3.0

    ```
    #HADOOP VARIABLES START
    export JAVA_HOME=/usr/lib/jvm/java-8-openjdk-amd64
    export HADOOP_PREFIX=/usr/local/hadoop
    export PATH=$PATH:$HADOOP_PREFIX/bin
    export PATH=$PATH:$HADOOP_PREFIX/sbin
    export HADOOP_MAPRED_HOME=$HADOOP_PREFIX
    export HADOOP_COMMON_HOME=$HADOOP_PREFIX
    export HADOOP_HDFS_HOME=$HADOOP_PREFIX
    export YARN_HOME=$HADOOP_PREFIX
    export HADOOP_COMMON_LIB_NATIVE_DIR=$HADOOP_PREFIX/lib/native
    export HADOOP_OPTS="-Djava.library.path=$HADOOP_PREFIX/lib"
    #HADOOP VARIABLES END
    ```

  - Then source .bashrc in current login session in terminal.
    $ source ~/.bashrc
- **Step 7**: Edit the Hadoop configuration file
  The next step to configure Hadoop is editing Hadoop-env.sh.
  /usr/local/hadoop/etc/hadoop/hadoop-env.sh
  To modify the Hadoop-env.sh file, we need to set JAVA_HOME.

    ```
    export JAVA_HOME=/usr/lib/jvm/java-8-openjdk-amd64
    ```

  Adding the above statement in the Hadoop-env. sh file ensures that the value of the JAVA_HOME variable will be available to Hadoop whenever it is started up.
  FOR VERSION HADOOP 3.1 and JAVA 10 on UBUNTU 18
  Include

    ```
    export HADOOP_OPTS="--add-modules java.activation"
    ```

  (after case Hadoop opts - 3 lines)

Editing coresite.xml:

> The /usr/local/hadoop/etc/hadoop/core-site.xml file contains configuration properties that Hadoop uses when starting up.
>
> This file can be used to override the default settings that Hadoop starts with.
>
> hduser@laptop:~$ Sudo mkdir -p /app/Hadoop/tmp
>
> hduser@laptop:~$ sudo chown hduser:Hadoop /app/Hadoop/tmp
>
> Open the file and enter the following in between the <configuration></configuration> tag:
>
> hduser@laptop:~$ vi /usr/local/hadoop/etc/hadoop/core-site.xml

> <configuration>
>
> <property>
>
> <name>hadoop.tmp.dir</name>
>
> <value>/app/hadoop/tmp</value>
>
> <description>A base for other temporary directories.</description>
>
> </property>
>
> <property>
>
> <name>fs.default.name</name>
>
> <value>hdfs://localhost:54310</value>
>
> <description>The name of the default file system. A URI whose scheme and authority determine the FileSystem implementation. The URL's scheme determines the config property (fs.SCHEME.impl) naming the FileSystem implementation class. The URL's authority is used to determine the host, port, etc. for a filesystem.</description>
>
> </property>
>
> </configuration>

Editing mapred-site.xml:

> By default, the /usr/local/hadoop/etc/hadoop/ folder contains /usr/local/hadoop/etc/hadoop/mapred-site.xml.template file which has to be renamed/copied with the name mapred-site.xml:
>
> hduser@laptop:~$ cp /usr/local/hadoop/etc/hadoop/mapred-site.xml.template /usr/local/hadoop/etc/hadoop/mapred-site.xml

The mapred-site.xml file specifies which framework is used for MapReduce.

```xml
<configuration>
<property>
<name>mapred.job.tracker</name>
<value>localhost:54311</value>
<description>The host and port that the MapReduce job tracker runs
at.  If "local", then jobs are run in-process as a single map
and reduce task.
</description>
</property>
</configuration>
```

Editing hdfs-site.xml:

The /usr/local/hadoop/etc/hadoop/hdfs-site.xmlfilespecifies the directories used as the name node and the data node and has to be configured for each host in the cluster. Before editing this file, the directories that will contain the name node and the datanode should be created. To do that, use the following commands:

hduser@laptop:~$ Sudo mkdir-p /usr/local/hadoop_store/hdfs/namenode
hduser@laptop:~$ Sudo mkdir-p /usr/local/hadoop_store/hdfs/datanode
hduser@laptop:~$ Sudo chown-R hduser:Hadoop/usr/local/hadoop_store

We need to open the file and enter the following content in between the <configuration></configuration> tag:
hduser@laptop:~$ nano /usr/local/hadoop/etc/hadoop/hdfs-site.xml

```xml
<configuration>
<property>
 <name>dfs.replication</name>
 <value>1</value>
 <description>Default block replication.
The actual number of replications can be specified when the file is created.
The default is used if replication is not specified in create time.
 </description>
</property>
<property>
  <name>dfs.namenode.name.dir</name>
  <value>file:/usr/local/hadoop_store/hdfs/namenode</value>
</property>
<property>
  <name>dfs.datanode.data.dir</name>
  <value>file:/usr/local/hadoop_store/hdfs/datanode</value>
</property>
</configuration>
```

Save the changes and restart Hadoop daemons.

To begin using the Hadoop file system, it must first be formatted. Since Hadoop creates the current directory under the /usr/local/hadoop store/hdfs/namenode folder, the format command requires write permission:

hduser@laptop:~$ Hadoop namenode –format

- **Step 8**: Now, it is time to start the newly installed single-node cluster.

```
We can use start-all.sh or (start-dfs.sh and start-yarn.sh)

$ cd /usr/local/hadoop/sbin
$ ls
$ sudo su hduser
$ start-all.sh
$ jps

It shows that the following are up and running. Now we have successfully
installed Hadoop on our system.

9026 NodeManager
f7348 NameNode
9766 Jps
8887 ResourceManager
7507 DataNode
```

The Web interface for Hadoop:

```
Version 2.8: localhost:50070
Version 3.0: localhost:9870
```

9.9 Installing and Configuring Hive

Apache Hive is an open-source data warehouse project for interactive SQL queries on Petabytes of Hadoop data. While Hadoop can organize and store massive amounts of data in various shapes, sizes, and formats, Hive is used to query, summarize, explore, and analyze that data.

We can access Hive here: https://hive.apache.org/downloads.html.

Steps to install Hive 2.3.9 on Ubuntu

```
hduser@laptop:/tmp$ wget http://www-us.apache.org/dist/hive/hive-2.3.9/apache-hive-2.3.9-bin.tar.gz
```

- **Step 1**

```
Download Hive. Once downloaded, locate the apache-hive-2.3.9-bin.tar.gz file in your system and extract it.
hduser@laptop:/tmp$ sudo tar xvzf apache-hive-2.1.0-bin.tar.gz-C /usr/local
```

- **Step 2**
  Configure the Hive files by placing the Hive PATH in the .bashrc file and setting the environment variable **HIVE_HOME.** For opening the .bashrc file, go to the nano editor. Edit your Hive file's correct path and name and save the changes. CTRL + O saves the changes and CTRL+ D exits the editor. Next, open **~/.bashrc** and set the environment variable **HIVE_HOME** to point to the installation directory and PATH:

  ```
  export HIVE_HOME=/usr/local/apache-hive-2.3.9-bin
  export HIVE_CONF_DIR=/usr/local/apache-hive-2.3.9-bin/conf
  export PATH=$HIVE_HOME/bin:$PATH
  export CLASSPATH=$CLASSPATH:/usr/local/hadoop/lib/*:.
  export CLASSPATH=$CLASSPATH:/usr/local/apache-hive-2.3.9-bin/lib/*:.
  ```

  Activating the new setting for Hive:

  ```
  hduser@laptop:/usr/local/apache-hive-2.3.9-bin$ source ~/.bashrc
  ```

  Creating Hive warehouse directory:

  > Hive uses Hadoop, so we must have Hadoop in our path:
  >
  > $ echo $HADOOP_HOME/usr/local/Hadoop
  >
  > In addition, we must use below HDFS commands to create **/tmp** and **/user/hive/warehouse (aka Hive.metastore.warehouse.dir)** and set them **chmod g+w** before we can create a table in Hive:

  ```
  hduser@laptop:~$ hdfs dfs -ls /
  ```

drwxr-xr-x	- hduser supergroup	0 2021-11-23 11:17	/hbase
drwx------	- hduser supergroup	0 2021-11-18 16:04	/tmp
drwxr-xr-x	- hduser supergroup	0 2021-11-18 09:13	/user

- **Step 4**
  Create a 'tmp' directory in HDFS. Use the following commands to create the directory 'warehouse' within the 'hive' directory, which is located in the 'user' directory. The warehouse is where Hive-related data or tables are stored.

  ```
  $hadoop fs -mkdir /user
  $hadoop fs -mkdir /user/hive
  $hadoop fs -mkdir /user/hive/warehouse
  hduser@laptop:~$ hdfs dfs -mkdir -p /tmp
  ```

Use the command to give the write permission to the 'tmp' filegroup members and the warehouse directory.

```
hduser@laptop:~$ hdfs dfs -chmod g+w /tmp
hduser@laptop:~$ hdfs dfs -chmod g+w /user/hive/warehouse
hduser@laptop:~$ hdfs dfs -ls /
```

```
drwxr-xr-x   - hduser supergroup      0 2021-11-23 11:17 /hbase
drwx-w----   - hduser supergroup      0 2021-11-18 16:04 /tmp
drwxr-xr-x   - hduser supergroup      0 2021-11-23 17:18 /user

hduser@laptop:~$ hdfs dfs -ls /user
drwxr-xr-x   - hduser supergroup      0 2021-11-18 23:17 /user/hduser
drwxr-xr-x   - hduser supergroup      0 2021-11-23 17:18 /user/hive
```

Hive data that is stored in the **warehouse** directory is located under **user/hive/warehouse**. The intermediate data for each process is stored in the temporary directory **tmp**.

- **Step 5**

  Open the core-site.xml file in the nano editor. The file is located in home/Hadoop-3.3.1/etc/Hadoop/ (Hadoop Configuration Directory) and adds the following configuration property in the core-site.xml file. To configure **metastore**, we must specify where the database is stored to Hive. This is done by editing the **hive-site.xml** file in the **HIVE_HOME/conf** directory.

```
hduser@laptop:~$ cd $HIVE_HOME/conf
hduser@laptop:/usr/local/apache-hive-2.1.0-bin/conf$ sudo cp hive-default.xml.template hive-site.xml
```

```
<property>
    <name>javax.jdo.option.ConnectionURL</name>
    <value>jdbc:derby:;databaseName=metastore_db;create=true</value>
    <description>
    JDBC connect string for a JDBC metastore.
    To use SSL to encrypt/authenticate the connection, provide database-specific SSL flag in the connection URL.
    For example, jdbc:postgresql://myhost/db?ssl=true for postgres database.
    </description>
</property>
```

Make a file called **jpox. properties** and copy-paste the following code into it:

```
javax.jdo.PersistenceManagerFactoryClass =
org.jpox.PersistenceManagerFactoryImpl
org.jpox.autoCreateSchema = false
org.jpox.validateTables = false
org.jpox.validateColumns = false
org.jpox.validateConstraints = false
org.jpox.storeManagerType = rdbms
org.jpox.autoCreateSchema = true
org.jpox.autoStartMechanismMode = checked
org.jpox.transactionIsolation = read_committed
javax.jdo.option.DetachAllOnCommit = true
javax.jdo.option.NontransactionalRead = true
javax.jdo.option.ConnectionDriverName =
org.apache.derby.jdbc.ClientDriver
javax.jdo.option.ConnectionURL =
jdbc:derby://hadoop1:1527/metastore_db;create = true
javax.jdo.option.ConnectionUserName = APP
javax.jdo.option.ConnectionPassword = mine
```

We need to set permission to the Hive folder:
hduser@laptop:/usr/local$ Sudo chown -R hduser:Hadoop apache-hive-2.3.9-bin.

- **Step 6: Configure HiveServer2**
  To configure Hive with Hadoop, the **hive-env.sh** file placed in the **$HIVE_HOME/conf** directory has to be edited. The following commands navigate to the Hive **conf** folder and add the following lines to the hive-env.sh template file:

  ```
  hduser@laptop:~$ cd $HIVE_HOME/conf
  hduser@laptop:/usr/local/apache-hive-2.1.0-bin/conf

  $ sudo cp hive-env.sh.template hive-env.sh

  Edit the hive-env.sh file by appending the following line:
  export HADOOP_HOME=/usr/local/Hadoop
  ```

We have successfully installed Apache Hive 2.3.9 on Hadoop 3.1.2 on Ubuntu.
Starting HDFS, Hive Server, CLI
We use **Apache Derby 9.15.2.0** database. By default, Hadoop initializes it.

Downloading the external **Apache Derby**:

```
$ cd /tmp
$ wget http://archive.apache.org/dist/db/derby/db-derby-10.15.2.0/db-derby-10.15.2.0-bin.tar.gz
$ sudo tar xvzf db-derby-10.15.2.0-bin.tar.gz -C /usr/local


export DERBY_HOME= /usr/local/db-derby-10.15.2.0-bin
export PATH=$PATH:$DERBY_HOME/bin
export CLASSPATH=$CLASSPATH:$DERBY_HOME/lib/derby.jar:$DERBY_HOME/lib/derbytools.jar
```

Create a directory **"data"** in **the $DERBY_HOME** directory to store metastore data.
$ sudo mkdir $DERBY_HOME/data

We need to run the **schema tool** command below as an initialization step. In our case, we use **derby** as **DB type**:

bin/schematool -dbType derby -initSchema

When we get the following output, we know that our metastore has been initialized, and our schema toll runs.

```
Starting metastore schema initialization to 2.3.9
Initialization script hive-schema-2.3.9.derby.sql
Initialization script completed
schemaTool completed
```

Now start the HiveServer2 using the below command:

```
bin/hiveserver2
```

Next, type the command to launch the beeline command shell on a different tab.

```
bin/beeline -n cirf -u jdbc:hive2://localhost:10000
```

9.10 CREATING AND USING A DATABASE IN HIVE

We shall now discuss the creation and usage of databases. Hive has different types of data types that are used to create databases.

9.10.1 Introduction to Hive Data Types

These various data types and formats in Hive, process and retrieve the data (Fig. 9.7).

- **(i) Primitive Data Types**: are further divided into
  - Numeric data type: Like integer, float, decimal
  - Date/Time data type: timestamp, date, interval

- String data type: char, string
- Miscellaneous data type: Boolean, Binary

(ii) **Complex Data Types**: are further divided into
- Arrays
- Structs
- Maps
- Units

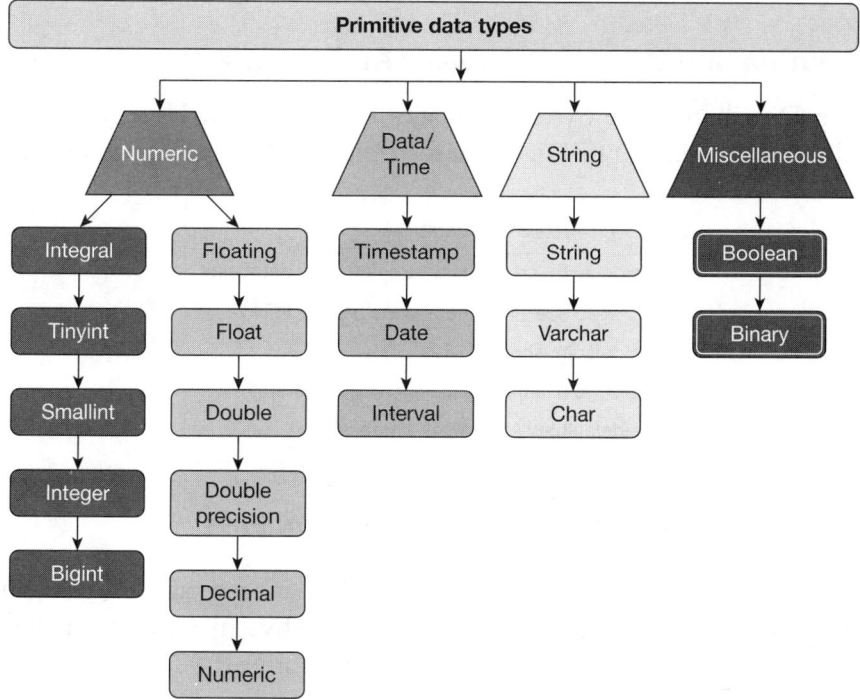

Figure 9.7 Primitive data types in Hive

9.10.2 Categorization of Data in Hive

The data in Hive is categorized into:

Tables: When creating Hive tables, the metadata about the Table is stored in Hive metastore, and the table's data is stored as files in the HDFS. The Hive tables are of two types: (i) Internal Table/ Managed Table (ii) External Table. The default table type in Hive is an internal table unless mentioned otherwise. The difference between an internal table and an external table in Hive is that if an internal table is dropped, both the data in the table/partition and metadata will be deleted. In contrast, only the metadata will be deleted in an external table.

A few of the operations performed on the Hive tables are:

- Filter
- Project
- Join
- Union

Partitions: We go in for partitions to split a large table into small logical tables. Partitions group similar types of data based on the partition key. Partition keys determine how the data is stored, and each unique value (e.g., date) defines a separate partition. For example, Apache Hive organizes the table into partitions for faster access.

Buckets: Partitioned data can be subdivided into buckets for more efficient querying. Buckets are a data organization technique that adds structure to data to be used for efficient queries. The bucketing range is determined by the hash value of one or more columns.

9.10.3 Creating and Using a Database: An Example

The Hadoop Distributed File System manages the queries in Hive. Here, we create a student table with Student ID (SID), SName, SGender, SYear, SDept as an external table.

```
Step 1: Create a new database
hive(default)> create database name_of_database;
Step 2: To see all the databases present in Hive
hive(default)>show databases
Step 3: To use the database created in step 1
hive(default)>use name_of_database;
```

9.11 CREATING AN INTERNAL/MANAGED TABLE IN HIVE

The default table in Hive is internal. In an internal/managed table, when you drop the table, both the metadata and data will be deleted as Hive manages both the table data and schema. The table data will be in a folder named after the table in the HDFS. The default location for an internal/managed table is /user/hive/warehouse. In contrast, in an external table, only the metadata gets deleted.

Example

```
CREATE TABLE IF NOT EXISTS stu.student(
SID int,
name string,
SGender string,
SYear int,
SDept string
)
COMMENT 'Student Details Table'
ROW FORMAT DELIMITED
FIELDS TERMINATED BY ','
```

9.12 Loading Data into a Table

The default location when we load data is /user/hive/warehouse. The Hive Load command moves the data from LOCAL or the HDFS location to the Hive data warehouse or any custom location without any transformations.

Hive Load CSV From HDFS

The Hive Load Data statement is used to load either a text file, a CSV, or an ORC file into the created table. The Hive Load statement performs the same regardless of the table being an Internal/ Managed table or an external table.

> LOAD DATA INPATH '/user/hive/warehouse/studentdetails.csv'
> INTO TABLE Stu. Student;

Once the data is loaded, the source file gets deleted from the source location. Then, the CSV file gets loaded into the Hive data warehouse location, or the custom location specified when the table is created.

Hive Load CSV From Local filesystem

Another way of loading a CSV file from the local filesystem is by using the LOCAL clause. In this case, the source file from the LOCAL file system will not be removed.

> LOAD DATA LOCAL INPATH '/user/hive/warehouse/studentdetails.csv'
> INTO TABLE stu. student;

Clauses that can be used when we load a file:

1. Using OVERWRITE: The use of OVERWRITE with the LOAD command to delete the contents of the target table and replace it with the records from the file referred is optional.
   LOAD DATA LOCAL INPATH '/user/hive/warehouse/studentdetails.csv' OVERWRITE INTO TABLE Stu. student
2. Using PARTITION: We can also use the PARTITION clause to load data into specific partitions of the table. We use it along with OVERWRITE to remove the partition's contents and re-load.
   LOAD DATA LOCAL INPATH '/home/hive/studentdetails.csv' OVERWRITE INTO TABLE stu.student PARTITION(SYear=2).
3. Using INSERT INTO: Like SQL, the Hive query language also allows us to insert rows into the Hive table. We shall see the use of INSERT INTO in Section 9.12.2.

9.12.1 Creating a Table Using LIKE

When we want to create a table like another table, we can use the syntax below:

> CREATE TABLE student_dupl LIKE student;

9.12.2 Adding Data Using INSERT INTO Table

Hive first introduced INSERT INTO starting version 0.8, and it does not modify the existing data. The Hive INSERT INTO syntax will be as follows:

```
INSERT INTO TABLE tablename
[PARTITION(partcol1=val1,partcol2=val2...)]
select_statement1 FROM statement;
Example:
INSERT INTO stu.student VALUES(7, 'Giny', 'F', 2002, 'ECE')
```

9.12.3 Adding Data Using INSERT OVERWRITE

The INSERT USING OVERWRITE command in Hive helps overwrite the table's existing data. The INSERT OVERWRITE inserts the row specified with the VALUES and deletes all the data from the Hive table.

```
INSERT OVERWRITE TABLE tablename [PARTITION (partcol1=val1, partcol2=val2 ...) [IF NOT EXISTS]]
select select_statement FROM from_statement;
```

Example

```
INSERT OVERWRITE TABLE stu.student VALUES(8, 'Reona', 'F', 2003, 'IT')
```

9.13 ALTERING, TRUNCATING AND DROPPING A TABLE

Let us see the use of DROP, ALTER and TRUNCATE now.

DROP TABLE : The DROP TABLE statement deletes the data for a particular table, and all the metadata associated with it is removed from the Hive metastore. If PURGE is not specified, the data is moved to the —trash/current directory. Data will be lost if PURGE is also set with the DROP.

```
DROP TABLE[ IF EXISTS] table_name [PURGE];
DROP TABLE [ IF EXISTS] professor[PURGE];
```

ALTER TABLE : The ALTER TABLE statement enables you to change the structure of an existing table in Hive. The ALTER TABLE statement can change the table, add columns, change the table properties, etc.

```
ALTER TABLE table_name RENAME TO new_table_name;
ALTER TABLE stu.student RENAME TO new_stu.students;
```

We can also add 'Stu_DOB' and 'Stu_Contact' in the 'new_stu.students' table using the ALTER command.

> ALTER TABLE new_stu.students ADD COLUMNS(Stu_DOB STRING,stu_contact STRING);

TRUNCATE TABLE : The TRUNCATE TABLE statement removes all the rows from the table or partition in Hive. So we TRUNCATE the old table named Stu. Student.

> TRUNCATE TABLE stu. student;

9.14 Creating an External Table

Using the EXTERNAL command, we can create an external table. Hive does not manage the external table, so unlike an internal table, only the table metadata from the metastore will be removed when an external table is dropped. The underlying files will not be removed, they can be accessed via HDFS commands or other Hadoop-compatible tools.

> CREATE EXTERNAL TABLE stu.student_external(
> sid int,
> sname string,
> sgender string,
> dept string)
> ROW FORMAT DELIMITED
> FIELDS TERMINATED BY','
> LOCATION '/user/hive/warehouse/student_external';
>
> This will create a folder /user/hive/warehouse/student_external/ on HDFS.

9.15 MapReduce Programs Through Hive

MapReduce has become the standard framework for performing batch processing on commodity hardware with Big Data applications. However, MapReduce code is difficult for developers, data scientists, and administrators to write and understand. Here Hive proves to be an advantage. Hive runs on top of Hadoop and provides an SQL abstraction for MapReduce applications. This allows Hive to interpret any SQL query into a series of MapReduce jobs. Thus, data analysts now need not learn MapReduce to work with Big Data and write MapReduce applications.

Using Catalog to Run MapReduce on Hive Table

HCatalog is a tool that connects Hive metastore tables with MapReduce, Spark, and Pig users to read and write data to Hive's warehouse. HCatalog supports file formats like CSV, JSON, ORC, SequenceFile, and RCFile.

Users of HCatalog also have a relational view of the data in the HDFS and need not worry about how/where the data is stored. Another advantage of HCatalog is that it has a notification service that notifies workflow tools when new data is added to the warehouse.

HCatalog is a storage and management layer for Hadoop that provides the HCatInputFormat and HCatOutputFormat interfaces for MapReduce, Spark and Pig users to read/write data in Hive's data warehouse. In addition, it allows users to read from the partitions of tables and columns and provides the records in a convenient list format to not parse them.

9.16 Hive Commands – Loading, Filtering, Grouping

The Hive Query language (HiveQL) is similar to SQL and allows the user to create tables and databases. Hive also supports the use of various queries like GROUP BY, ORDER BY, SORT BY, CLUSTER BY, DISTRIBUTE BY in Hive.

Order by

By default, the data sorting in Hive is in ascending order. Still, we can use the `order by` clause with the "SELECT" statement to sort data either in ascending order/descending order. The `order by` clause uses the table column for sorting particular column values mentioned with `order by`. Based on the column name we define, the `order by` clause query will select and display the results of the specific column values. Let us use the student table for this.

```
SELECT * FROM stu.student ORDER BY SDept;
```

Group by

The `group by` clause is used in columns for grouping particular column values. For example, for the column name we define as the "group by" clause, the query will select and display results by grouping the specific column values.

```
SELECT Department, count(*) FROM stu.student GROUP BY SDept;
```

Sort by

The `sort by` clause is performed on the columns in Hive tables. The sorting depends on the column names and types. If the columns are *numeric*, the sorting will be in numeric order; if the columns are *string type*, the sorting will be in lexicographic order. The Hive table can be sorted in descending order using DESC and in ascending order using ASC.

```
SELECT * from stu.student SORT BY sid DESC;
```

Cluster by

The `cluster by` clause is used as an alternative to using both `distribute by` and `sort by` clauses and distributes the data based on the key column and then sorts the output data by putting the column values with the same key adjacent to each other. The `cluster` by clause is performed on the reducer side, and so we get N number of sorted output files (N is the number of reducers used in query processing).

```
SELECT SID, SName from stu.student CLUSTER BY sid;
```

Distribute by

On Hive tables, the `distribute` by clause can be used, and all columns/rows that have the same key will be routed to the same reducer.

```
SELECT SID, SName from stu. student DISTRIBUTE BY SID;
```

9.17 DATA TYPES, OPERATORS

Hive provides built-in operators (Fig. 9.8), and these operators can be used to perform mathematical operations on operands.

Built-in operators available in HiveQL:
- Relational operators
- Arithmetic operators
- Logical operators
- Operators on complex types

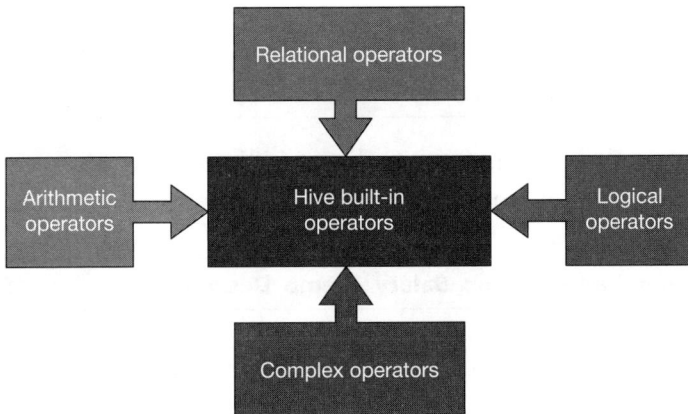

Figure 9.8 Hive data types, operators

9.18 RELATIONAL OPERATORS IN HIVE QL

We use relational operators for relationship comparisons between two operands. The common operators and their meaning are given in Table 9.2.

Table 9.2 Hive relational operators and their meaning

Hive relational operators	Meaning
A=B	If expression A is equivalent to expression B, the result is TRUE; otherwise FALSE.
A != B	If expression A is not equivalent to expression B, it returns a TRUE; otherwise FALSE.
A<B	If expression A is less than expression B, it returns a TRUE; otherwise FALSE.
A<=B	If expression A is less than or equal to expression B, it returns a TRUE; otherwise FALSE.
A>B	If expression A is greater than expression B, the result is TRUE; otherwise FALSE.
A>= B	If expression A is greater than or equal to expression B, the result is TRUE; otherwise FALSE.
A IS NULL	If expression A evaluates to NULL, the result is TRUE; otherwise FALSE.
A IS NOT NULL	If expression A evaluates to NULL, the result is FALSE; otherwise TRUE.
A LIKE B	If string pattern A matches B, the result is TRUE; otherwise FALSE.
A RLIKE B	If A or B is NULL, the result is TRUE; if any substring of A matches B's regular expression; otherwise FALSE.
A REGEXP B	Same as A RLIKE B.

Let us assume the employee table is an Online Children's Toys Shop composed of fields named emp_Id, emp_Name, emp_Salary, emp_Designation, and emp_Dept, as shown below.

emp_Id	emp_Name	emp_Salary	emp_Designation	emp_Dept
1201	James	45000	Dept Manager	Admin
1210	Gabriel	35000	Content Writer	Advertising
1231	Lisa	25000	HR Admin	HR
1205	Joey	15000	Billing	Cash

Let us create a query to retrieve the employee details whose emp_Id is 1205.

```
hive> SELECT * FROM employee WHERE emp_Id=1205
```

emp_Id	emp_Name	emp_Salary	emp_Designation	emp_Dept
1205	Joey	15000	Billing	Cash

Let us create a query to retrieve the employee details whose salary is more than or equal to ₹20000.

```
hive > SELECT * FROM employee WHERE emp_Salary >20000
```

emp_Id	emp_Name	emp_Salary	emp_Designation	emp_Dept
1201	James	45000	Dept Manager	Admin
1210	Gabriel	35000	Content Writer	Advertising
1231	Lisa	25000	HR Admin	HR

9.19 Arithmetic Operators in Hive QL

Arithmetic operators in Hive support a variety of arithmetic operations on the operands. They all return different number types. Table 9.3 describes the arithmetic operators available in Hive.

Table 9.3 Arithmetic operators on Hive

Hive Arithmetic Operators	Meaning
A+B	The addition of A and B is done, and the result is given.
A – 8	Subtraction of B from A is done, and the result is shown.
A*B	Multiplications A and B are done, and the result is given.
A/8	Division of B from A is done, and the result is given.
A%B	The result is the remainder resulting from dividing A by B.
A&B	The result is the bitwise AND of A and B.
A|B	The result is the bitwise OR of A and B.
A^B	The result is the bitwise XOR of A and B.
~A	The result is the bitwise NOT of A.

```
Generate a query that adds two numbers, 15 and 20.
hive> SELECT 15+20 ADD FROM temp;
```

On successful execution, we will get the result:

ADD
35

9.20 Hive Logical Operators

Hive's logical operators enable the creation of logical expressions. Depending on the boolean values of the operands, all return TRUE, FALSE, or NULL. In this case, NULL acts as an "unknown" flag, which means that if the result is dependent on an unknown state, the result itself is unknown.

Hive Logical Operators	Meaning
A AND B	If both A and B are TRUE, the result is TRUE; otherwise, FALSE.
A && B	The result is the same as A AND B.
A OR B	If either A or B is TRUE, the result is TRUE; otherwise FALSE.
A || B	This result will return A OR B.
NOT A	If A is FALSE, it returns a TRUE; otherwise FALSE.
!A	This works in the same way as NOT A.

The following query is used to get the employee details whose Emp_Dept is HR and emp_Salary is more than Rs 20000

```
hive > SELECT * FROM employee WHERE emp_Salary >20000 AND Emp_Dept = "HR"
```

| 1231 | Lisa | 25000 | HR Admin | HR |

9.21 Hive Complex Operators

Hive Complex Operator	Meaning
A[n]	The result returns the nth element in array A. Therefore, the first element has an index of 0.
M[key]	The result returns the value corresponding to the key in the map.
S.x	The result returns the x field of S.

9.22 Joins, Groups

JOIN is a clause used in Apache Hive to combine specific fields from two tables by using a common value in both. But first, let us explore the various types of joins supported by Hive.

Examples: We create two tables, the CUSTOMER table and the ORDER table.

Customer table

CUST_ID	CUST_NAME	Age	Address	Salary
101	Preetha	32	Anna Nagar, Chennai	25,000
102	Sam	23	Kilpauk, Chennai	18,000
103	Joy	27	Saidapet, Chennai	21,000

Order table

ORDER_ID	PRODUCT	PRICE	CUST_ID
100011	SONY TV	14,000	101
100012	FRIDGE	15,000	102
100013	SAMSUNG MOBILE	7,000	103

Let us explore the four types of joins in Hive:

1. Inner join
2. Left outer join
3. Right outer join
4. Full outer join

Inner Join

> hive > SELECT CUST_ID, CUST_NAME, ORDER_ID FROM CUSTOMERS C JOIN ORDERS O ON(c.CUST_ID=O.CUST_ID)

Inner Join repeats the matching record (Fig. 9.9) from the left-hand side table multiple times for each matching record on the right-hand side.

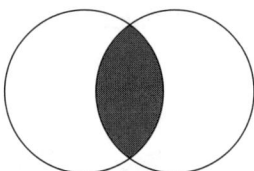

Figure 9.9 Hive inner join

Left Outer Join

The left Outer Join (Fig. 9.10) returns all rows from the left Table (even if there are no matches in the right table).

> hive> SELECT C.CUST_ID,C.CUST_NAME, O.PRICE FROM CUSTOMERS C LEFT OUTER JOIN ORDERS O ON(C.CUST_ID=O.CUST_ID)

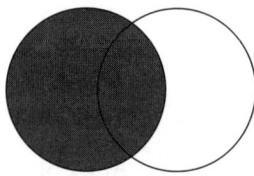

Figure 9.10 Hive left outer join

Right Outer Join

The Hive query language Right Outer Join returns all entries from the right table, even in the case of no matching entry in the left table (Fig. 9.11).

```
hive>SELECT C.CUST_ID, C.CUST_NAME, O.PRICE FROM CUSTOMERS C RIGHT OUTER JOIN
ORDERS O ON(C.CUST_ID=O.CUST_ID);
```

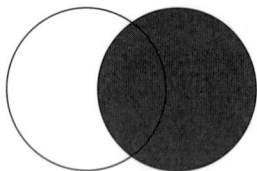

Figure 9.11 Hive right outer join

Full Outer Join

The primary goal of this HiveQL full outer join (Fig. 9.12) is to combine the records from both the left and right outer tables, which fulfil the Hive Join condition. Furthermore, this joined table contains all of the records from both tables or fills in NULL values for any missing matches on either side.

```
hive>SELECT C.CUST_ID, C.CUST_NAME, O.PRICE FROM CUSTOMERS C RIGHT OUTER JOIN
ORDERS O ON(C.CUST_ID=O.CUST_ID);
```

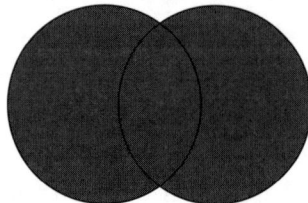

Figure 9.12 Hive full outer join

9.23 Map Join

Apache Hive Map Join (Fig. 9.13) is also known as Auto Map Join, Map Side Join, or Broadcast Join.

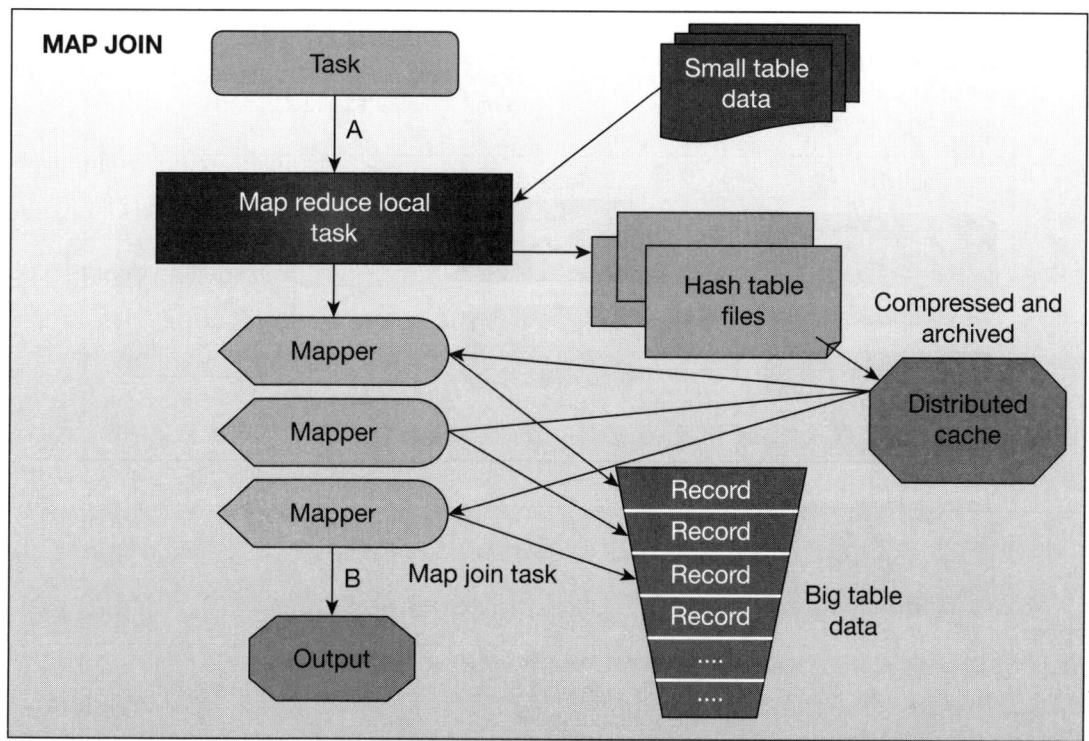

Figure 9.13 Hive MAP join

9.23.1 Parameters of Hive Map Side Join

a. **hive.auto.convert.join:** By default, this option value is set to true. Moreover, when a table size is less than 25 MB (Hive. map join. small Table. filesize) is enabled, and the joins are converted to map-based joins.

b. **Hive.auto.convert.join.noconditionaltask:** Hive generates three or more map-side joins using Hive.auto.convert.join when three or more tables need to be joined, assuming that all tables are small.

If the size of the n−1 table is less than 10 MB, you can combine three or more map-side joins into a single map-side join. We can use Hive.auto.convert.join.noconditionaltask.
SELECT /*+ MAPJOIN(c) */ * FROM orders o JOIN cities c ON (o.city_id = c.id);

9.24 BUCKET JOIN

The below figure talks about the bucket map join (Fig. 9.14).

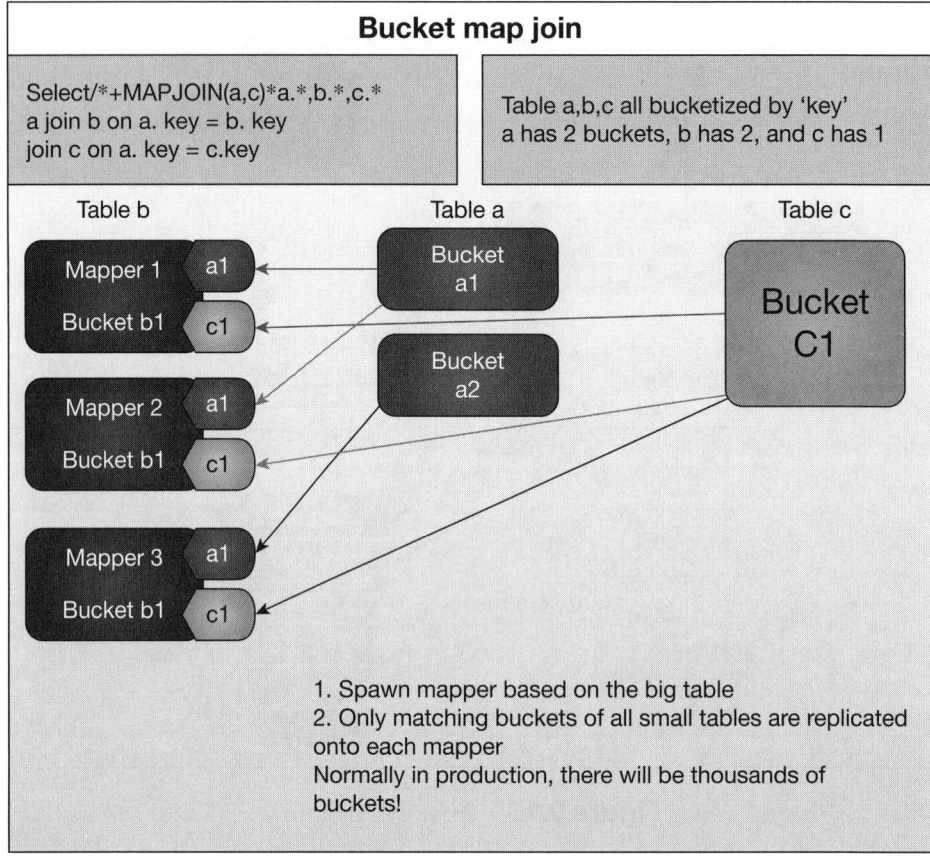

Figure 9.14 Bucket MAP join

9.24.1 Real-estate Example

1. **Creation of real-estate table**
   Create table realest (street string,city string,zip int,state string,beds int,baths int,sqft int,type string,price int) row format delimited fields terminated by ',' or ';'.

2. **Loading data into table**
   Load data local inpath '/home/rachel/Documents/real_state.csv' into table realest;
   Loading data to table states. realest
   OK
   Time taken: 0.454 seconds

3. **Viewing data**
   hive> select * from realest limit 09;
   OK

3526 HIGH ST	SACRAMENTO	95828	CA	2	2	835	Residential	59222
50 OMAHA CT	SACRAMENTO	95813	CA	3	1	1166	Residential	68212
2786 BRANCH ST	SACRAMENTO	95805	CA	2	2	786	Residential	68880
2705 JANETTE WAY	SACRAMENTO	95805	CA	2	1	842	Residential	69307
6101 MCMAHON DR	SACRAMENTO	95814	CA	2	2	787	Residential	81900
5728 PEPPERMILL CT	SACRAMENTO	95831	CA	3	1	1112	Condo	89921
6148 16TH AVE	SACRAMENTO	95832	CA	3	2	1103	Residential	90895
2461 19TH AVE	SACRAMENTO	95810	CA	3	1	1167	Residential	91002
11050 TRINITY RIVER	RANCHO	5660	CA	2	2	831	Condo	94905

Time taken: 0.322 seconds, Fetched: 09 row(s)

4. **Setting bucket**

```
hive> set hive.exec.dynamic.partition=true;

hive> set hive.exec.dynamic.partition.mode=nonstrict;

hive> set hive.exec.max.dynamic.partitions=20000;

hive> set hive.exec.max.dynamic.partitions.pernode=20000;

hive> set hive.enforce.bucketing=true;
```

5. **Structure of table**
   hive> desc realest;
   OK

street	string
city	string
zip	int
state	string
beds	int
baths	int
sqft	int
type	string
price	int

Time taken: 0.093 seconds, Fetched: 9 row(s)

6. Creation of bucket table

hive> create table buest(street string,zip int,state string,b57-eds int,baths int,sqft int,type string,price int) partitioned by (city string) clustered by (street) into 4 buckets row format delimited fields terminated by ',';

OK
Time taken: 0.225 seconds

7. Inserting a value into bucketing table

hive> insert into table best partition(city) select street,zip,state,beds,baths,sqft,type,price,city from realest;

Hive requires the user to manually enable the bucket map to join using the following instruction:

hive>SET HIVE.OPTIMIZE.BUCKETMAPJOIN = TRUE;

This is because bucketing itself is not done automatically, and the user has to ensure that the table is bucketed.

SUMMARY

This chapter covers all the basic concepts of Hive as well as HiveQL and delineates the difference between relational databases and the Hive data warehouse infrastructure. As Hive is built on top of Apache Hadoop, it is ideal for users to perform ad-hoc querying and analysis of large datasets stored in the HDFS (Hadoop Distributed Framework System). As the user does not need to know the specifics of map-reduce to understand Hive, it can be used by even basic programmers and analysts. The chapter explains how to use Hive to query, process, and analyze data. It also deals with advanced concepts like joins, Hive partitions, and bucketing. Once the user gets familiar with HiveQL, he can easily create, alter and drop databases, tables, views, functions, and indexes.

The Apache Hive data warehouse software provides a solution, the "Hive Query Language", to process structured data in Hadoop. It supports data summarization and data querying and has a declarative language with very similar commands to SQL. By default, it operates in MapReduce mode; the Hive is configured to operate in local mode.

Apache Hive is a free and open-source, Hadoop-based data warehouse tool for extracting meaningful information from data. Because writing code in Java is more complex than writing code in Hive, using Hive makes it easier to query structured data. Apache Hive offers a simpler query model that requires less coding than MapReduce and has a very similar syntax to the Structured Query Language (SQL). The query language that we use to work with the Hive is HQL or HIVEQL, making Hive very easy to use. We can easily embed custom MapReduce code with Hive to process unstructured data. In addition, Hive can help us with data mining, predictive modelling, and document indexing. Hive is a reliable batch-processing framework that can be used as a data warehouse. It includes several built-in functions and also supports User-Defined Functions (UDFs) for data cleansing and filtering tasks.

Hive isn't a complete database and does not have the necessary features for Online Transaction Processing (OLTP). However, Hive can build a data warehouse package on top of Hadoop. Therefore, it is suitable for static data analysis, and a fast response time is not required. However, the design constraints that impose limits on Hadoop and HDFS also constrain what Hive can do. Another disadvantage of Hive is queries generated using Hive have high latency because Hadoop supports batch-processing.

The Hive Driver represents the main driver and communicates with JDBC, ODBC, and other client-specific applications. The Hive driver receives the HiveQL statements entered into the command shell by the user. The execution engine processes the query, and the results are generated in the same way that MapReduce results are. The Derby metastore is Hives' default embedded metastore. However, users can swap their Derby metastore for a MySQL one.

Aggregation and data skew are used to inform execution plans. Hive can easily process large amounts of data and has more user interfaces. It is an ETL tool for structured data processing.

The main difference between Hive and traditional relational databases is in performing functions like insert, update and modify. While the relational databases allow all these functions to be easily performed, Hive is "Schema on READ only," which means that functions like the update, modifications, etc. cannot be done. Hive is analytics-focused, whereas traditional RDBMS are focused on online or analytics. HIVE can handle Petabytes of data at a low cost, whereas RDBMS cannot handle Petabytes of data. Scalability is usually vertical in RDBMS; it is horizontal in HIVE and easily scalable to low cost.

The data in Hive is categorized into tables. When creating Hive tables, the metadata about the table is stored in Hive metastore, and the table's data is stored as files in the HDFS. The Hive tables are of two types (i) Internal table/Managed table (ii) External table. The difference between an internal table and an external table in Hive is that if an internal table is dropped, both the data in the table/partition and metadata will be deleted. A few of the operations performed on the Hive tables are Filter, Project, Join, Union, and Partitions. We use partitions to split a large table into small logical tables. For example, Apache Hive organizes the table into partitions for faster access and categorizations. There are four types of joins in Hive: Inner Join, Left outer join, Right Outer Join, Full Outer join.

EXERCISES

Multiple Choice Questions

1. **HQL stands for?**
   A. HDFS Query Language
   B. Hive Query Language
   C. Hadoop Query Language
   D. HBase Query Language
   Answer: B
   Explanation: The Apache Hive data warehouse software provides a solution, the "Hive Query Language," to process structured data in Hadoop. It supports data

summarization and data querying and has a declarative language with very similar commands to SQL. As a result, it is known as the Hive Query Language (HQL). Furthermore, Hive converts queries into MapReduce programs, making simple operations such as data encapsulation. As a result, it aids developers in analyzing structured and semi-structured data.

2. **Hive provides the option to operate in 2 modes. They are:**
   A. Local mode and MapReduce mode
   B. HDFS mode and MapReduce mode
   C. Name mode and Data mode
   D. Client mode and Server mode
   Answer: A
   Explanation: Hive provides the option to operate in two modes based on the number and size of the data nodes.
   (i) Local mode (ii) MapReduce Mode
   (i) When your data size is small and is restricted to one machine, the local mode is used. For example, the local mode works well when Hadoop has only one data node, which is small.
   (ii) The MapReduce mode is used for large datasets when the data in Hadoop is spread across multiple data nodes.

3. **With HQL, we can reduce 100 lines of Java code to query structured data to just four.**
   A. True   B. False
   Answer: A
   Explanation: With HQL, we can reduce 100 lines of Java code to query structured data to just four. In addition, Hive Query Language (HQL) allows multiple users to query the data simultaneously.

4. **Hive supports all the below data structures, except:**
   A. Jar   B. Partitions
   C. Buckets   D. Tables
   Answer: A
   Explanation: Hive supports three data structures: partitions, buckets, and tables. As a result, Hive can help us with data mining, predictive modelling, and document indexing.

5. **Hive supports both ETL and ELT.**
   A. True   B. False
   Answer: B
   Explanation: Hive has a well-defined architecture supporting metadata management and query optimizations. ETL, or Extract, Transform, and Load, is supported by Apache Hive.

6. **Hive supports only internal table.**
   A. True   B. False
   Answer: B
   Explanation: Apache Hive also supports external tables. This enables us to process data without storing it in HDFS. Hive is intended for OLAP applications (Online Analytical Processing). Hive can be used to visualize data. Integrating Hive with Apache Tez will allow for real-time processing.

7. **Hive is not a complete database and does not have the necessary features for Online Transaction Processing (OLTP).**
   A. True   B. False
   Answer: A
   Explanation: Hive is not a complete database and does not have the necessary features for Online Transaction Processing (OLTP). However, Hive can build a data warehouse package on top of Hadoop. Therefore, it is suitable for static data analysis, and a fast response time is not required.

8. **The Hive Client provides different drivers for different applications. This client constitutes the software library that enables ODBC applications to interact with Hive _____.**
   A. Native client   B. ODBC client
   C. JDBC client   D. Thrift client
   Answer: B
   Explanation: The Hive client provides different drivers for different applications and is categorized into three types (i) Thrift clients (ii) JDBC clients and (iii) ODBC clients. Thrift clients can run from different programming languages. Thrift bindings are provided for Java, Python, and Ruby. JDBC Client offers a high connectivity solution for JDBC applications and can be defined using the class org. apache.Hadoop.hive. jdbc.HiveDriver. ODBC client constitutes the software library that enables ODBC applications to interact with Hive.

9. **The client interacts with Hive through?**
   A. Hive clients   B. Hive servers
   C. Hive storage   D. Hive services
   Answer: D
   Explanation: The client interacts with Hive through Hive services. When the Hive client performs any operation, it communicates with the Hive services. The default and common way of interacting are through the Hive shell (command-line interface). It is a well-known user interface.

10. **Hive offers all of the services below, except:**
    A. Hiver interpreter   B. Hive driver
    C. Hive optimizer   D. Metastore
    Answer: A

Explanation: The default and common way of interacting are through the Hive shell (command-line interface). It is a well-known user interface. When running the CLI on a Hadoop cluster, Hive runs in local mode, using local storage instead of HDFS. Hive can also be accessed through a web browser (Hive Web Interface).

Hive offers other services like (i) Beeline (ii) Hive Server2 (iii) Hive driver (iv) Hive compiler (v) Optimizer (vi) Execution engine (vii) Metastore (viii) HCatalog.

11. **This is a command shell JDBC client supported by HiverServer2. It can be run both in the remote and embedded mode.**
    A. Optimizer
    B. Beeline
    C. Hive driver
    D. Hive compiler
    Answer: B
    Explanation: Hive offers other services like (i) Beeline (ii) Hive Server2 (iii) Hive driver (iv) Hive compiler (v) Optimizer (vi) Execution engine (vii) Metastore (viii) HCatalog.
    The Beeline is a command shell JDBC client supported by HiveServer2. Beeline is a JDBC client, and to start it, we need to run the Beeline shell, which is present in the $HIVE_HOME/bin directory. The Beeline server can be run both in the remote and embedded mode.

12. **This is the server interface that enables clients to execute queries. This allows clients to run queries against Hive. It will allow multiple clients to send queries to Hive and retrieve the results.**
    A. Optimizer
    B. Beeline
    C. HiveServer2
    D. Hive compiler
    Answer: C
    Explanation: HiveServer2 is the server interface that enables clients to execute queries. HiveServer2 is the replacement for HiveServer1. HiveServer2 allows clients to run queries against Hive. It will allow multiple clients to send queries to Hive and retrieve the results. It is primarily intended to provide the best possible support for open API clients like JDBC and ODBC. HiveServer1, also known as a Thrift server, is built on the Apache Thrift protocol to handle cross-platform communication with Hive. It enables various client applications to send queries to Hive and retrieve the results.

13. **This communicates with all types of JDBC, ODBC client applications to process requests submitted by the user through the command shell:**
    A. Hive driver
    B. Beeline
    C. HiveServer2
    D. Hive compiler
    Answer: A
    Explanation: The Hive driver represents the main driver and communicates with all types of JDBC, ODBC, and other client-specific applications. The driver communicates with all types of JDBC, ODBC client applications to process requests submitted by the user through the command shell. First, the Hive driver receives the

HiveQL statements entered into the command shell by the user. Then, it generates session handles for the query and sends them to the compiler. During compilation, optimization, and execution, it manages the lifecycle of a HiveQL statement.

14. **This gets the metadata from the metastore to parse queries. It generates an execution plan after performing semantic analysis and type-checking on the various query blocks and query expressions stored in the metastore:**
    A. Hive driver
    B. Beeline
    C. HiveServer2
    D. Hive compiler
    Answer: D
    Explanation: The Hive compiler gets the metadata from the metastore to parse queries. It generates an execution plan after performing semantic analysis and type-checking on the various query blocks and query expressions stored in the metastore. The Hive compiler translates HiveQL statements and works like the traditional database compiler by performing semantic analysis, type-checking, etc. The execution plan generated by the compiler is a DAG (Directed Acyclic Graph), with each stage representing a map/reduce job, an HDFS operation, and a metadata operation.

15. **This performs the transformation operations like column pruning, reordering on the execution plan, and improving efficiency and scalability:**
    A. Hive driver
    B. Hive optimizer
    C. HiveServer2
    D. Hive compiler
    Answer: B
    Explanation: The optimizer performs the transformation operations like column pruning, reordering on the execution plan, and improving efficiency and scalability. To provide optimized DAG, it performs various transformations on the execution plan. For improved performance, it aggregates the transformations, such as converting a pipeline of joins to a single join. To improve performance, the optimizer can also split tasks, such as transforming data before performing a reduced operation.

16. **This processes the query, and the results are generated in the same way that MapReduce results are. It employs the MapReduce flavor.**
    A. Hive driver
    B. Hive optimizer
    C. HiveServer2
    D. Execution engine
    Answer: D
    Explanation: The execution engine executes the execution plan created by the compiler in the order of their dependencies using Hadoop after compilation and optimization. The execution engine processes the query, and the results are generated in the same way that MapReduce results are. It employs the MapReduce flavor.

17. **This stores the information about the tables and views that you create in Hive and other details such as permissions, schema, and file locations:**
    A. Hive driver
    B. Metastore
    C. HiveServer2
    D. Execution engine

Answer: B
Explanation: Metadata means data about data. The metastore is a system catalog. The metastore stores information about the tables and views that you create in Hive and other details such as permissions, schema, and file locations. We have a thrift API on top of Metastore to query the database using JDBC/ODBC connections. Hive Metastore is typically an RDBMS system that can query the schema more quickly without accessing the data.

18. **Hive ships with this metastore by default:**
    A. Derby
    B. HDFS
    C. SQL
    D. MongoDB
    Answer: A
    Explanation: Hive ships with a Derby metastore by default, but it is simple to switch to an SQL metastore. The limitation of a derby store is that only one user can interact with the database at any given time. To initialize the metastore, we run the schema tool command and then use Derby as DB type.

19. **The storage layer in Hive is called as:**
    A. HCatalog
    B. Hive DB
    C. HBASE
    D. HDFS
    Answer: A
    Explanation: The storage layer in Hive is called HCatalog and helps users with different data processing tools to easily read and write data. HCatalog is Hive's table and storage management layer. It allows users to read and write data on the grid using various data processing tools such as Pig, MapReduce, and others. It is built on top of Hive metastore and exposes Hive metastore tabular data to other data processing tools.

20. **Hive can operate in two modes: interactive mode and non-interactive mode.**
    A. True
    B. False
    Answer: A
    Explanation: Hive can operate in two modes: interactive mode and non-interactive mode. The former mode directs all Hive commands to the Hive shell, whereas the latter type executes the code in console mode. Data is divided into partitions, which are further subdivided into buckets. Aggregation and data skew are used to inform execution plans.

21. **Which of the following is false about Hive?**
    A. Hive is analytics-focused, whereas traditional RDBMS are focused on online or analytics.
    B. Transactions are supported by RDBMS but are not endorsed by HIVE. (It supports limited transactions.)

C. HIVE is designed for commodity hardware, whereas RDBMS is designed for proprietary hardware.
D. HIVE scales rarely beyond 20 nodes, whereas RDBMS easily scale to hundreds of nodes.

Answer: D

Explanation: Hive is analytics-focused, whereas traditional RDBMS are focused on online or analytics. Transactions are supported by RDBMS but are not endorsed by HIVE. (It supports limited transactions.) The distributed process in HIVE occurs via MapReduce, whereas it varies by RDBMS vendor. HIVE scales easily to hundreds of nodes, whereas RDBMS rarely scales beyond 20 nodes. HIVE is designed for commodity hardware, whereas RDBMS is designed for proprietary hardware.

22. **When creating Hive tables, the metadata about the table is stored in the HDFS.**
    A. True
    B. False

    Answer: B

    Explanation: When creating Hive tables, the metadata about the table is stored in Hive metastore, and the table's data is stored as files in the HDFS. The Hive tables are of two types (i) Internal Table/Managed table (ii) External table. The default table type in Hive is an internal table unless mentioned otherwise. The difference between an internal table and an external table in Hive is that if an internal table is dropped, both the data in the table/partition and the metadata will be deleted. In contrast, only the metadata will be deleted in an external table.

23. **We go in for this to split a large table into small logical tables:**
    A. Partitions
    B. Buckets
    C. Map
    D. Union

    Answer: A

    Explanation: We use partitions to split a large table into small logical tables. Partitions group similar types of data based on the partition key. Partition keys determine how the data is stored, and each unique value (e.g., date) defines a separate partition. For example, Apache Hive organizes the table into partitions for faster access.

24. **Partitioned data can be subdivided into this for more efficient querying:**
    A. Partitions
    B. Buckets
    C. Pipe
    D. Union

    Answer: B

    Explanation: Partitioned data can be subdivided into buckets for more efficient querying. Buckets are a data organization technique that adds structure to data to be used for efficient queries. The bucketing range is determined by the hash value of one or more columns.

Short-answer Questions

1. **Write short notes on Hive.**
   Apache Hive is a free and open-source, Hadoop-based data warehouse tool for extracting meaningful information from data. Since writing code in Java is more complex than writing code in Hive, using Hive makes it easier to query structured data. Apache Hive offers a simpler query model that requires less coding than MapReduce and has a syntax very similar to the Structured Query Language (SQL). The query language that we use to work with the Hive is HQL or HIVEQL, making Hive very easy to use. We can easily embed custom MapReduce code with Hive to process unstructured data.

2. **Write short notes on Hive driver.**
   The Hive driver represents the main driver and communicates with JDBC, ODBC, and other client-specific applications. The Hive driver receives the HiveQL statements entered into the command shell by the user. The execution engine processes the query, and the results are generated in the same way that MapReduce results are. The Derby metastore is Hives' default embedded metastore. However, users can swap the Derby metastore for a MySQL one.

3. **What are the main differences between Hive and relational databases?**
   The main difference between Hive and traditional relational databases is in performing functions like insert, update and modify. While the relational databases allow all these functions to be easily performed, Hive is "Schema on READ only," which means functions like the update, modifications, etc. cannot be done on Hive. Hive is analytics-focused, whereas traditional RDBMS are focused on online or analytics. Hive can handle Petabytes of data at a low cost, whereas RDBMS cannot handle Petabytes of data. Scalability is usually vertical in RDBMS; it is horizontal in Hive and easily scalable to low cost.

4. **Write short notes on Hive table and its types.**
   The data in Hive is categorized into tables. When creating Hive tables, the metadata about the table is stored in Hive metastore, and the table's data is stored as files in the HDFS. The Hive tables are of two types (i) Internal table/Managed table (ii) External table. The difference between an internal table and an external table in Hive is that if an internal table is dropped, both the data in the table/partition and metadata will be deleted. A few of the operations performed on the Hive tables are Filter, Project, Join, Union, and Partitions. We use partitions to split a large table into small logical tables. For example, Apache Hive organizes the table into partitions for faster access and categorizations.

5. **How is metastore configured in Remote way?**
   Usually, metastore can be configured in three modes: (i) Remote (ii) Embedded and (iii) Local.
   A remotely running MySQL server would be a simple step up. This would enable the use of a separate system to manage the metastore. The metastore is helpful for non-Java applications in remote mode, and the metastore runs in its JVM, not the Hive service JVM. To communicate with the metastore server in the remote mode, the Thrift network APIs are used.

6. **How is metastore configured in Embedded way?**
   Usually, metastore can be configured in three modes: (i) Remote (ii) Embedded and (iii) Local. The Derby metastore is Hive's default embedded metastore. This is the simplest, but it also has its own set of issues. First, it can only be used by one command-line interface at a time. This is especially aggravating when you close your terminal by accident, since the Hive metastore remains locked. While operating in the embedded mode, the metastore uses the same Java Virtual Machine as the Hive service.

7. **How is metastore configured in Local way?**
   Usually, Metastore can be configured in three modes: (i) Remote (ii) Embedded and (iii) Local. The Local metastore allows us to have many Hive sessions compared to the embedded metastore and allows many users to use the metastore simultaneously. You can swap your Derby metastore for a MySQL one. It is as simple as providing Hive with a connection string. The most basic version would be to have a MySQL database running locally.

8. **Write short notes on HCatalog.**
   The storage layer in Hadoop is called HCatalog and helps users with different data processing tools to easily read and write data. HCatalog is Hadoop's table and storage management layer. It allows users to read and write data on the grid using various data processing tools such as Pig, MapReduce, and others. It is built on top of Hive metastore and exposes Hive metastore tabular data to other data processing tools.

9. **What are the primitive Data Types in Hive?**
   - Numeric data type: integer, float, decimal
   - Date/Time data type: timestamp, date, interval
   - String data type: char, string
   - Miscellaneous data type: Boolean, binary

10. **What are the types of complex data types in Hive?**
    - Array
    - Structs
    - Maps
    - Units

Essay-type Questions

1. What is the need for Hive into the Hadoop System?
2. What are the features of Hive?
3. What are the limitations of Hive?
4. Explain Hive architecture in detail.
5. Explain Hive metastore in detail.
6. Explain the workflow in Hive.
7. Compare Hive with the traditional database.
8. What are the different Hive data types? Explain in detail.
9. How is data categorized in Hive?
10. How is an internal/managed table created in Hive? How data is loaded into a Hive table?
11. How are MapReduce programs executed through Hive?
12. How do GROUP BY, ORDER BY, SORT BY, CLUSTER BY, DISTRIBUTE BY work in Hive?
13. How do the four types of joins work in Hive?

CHAPTER 10

HBase

LEARNING OBJECTIVES

In this chapter, we introduce a distributed non-relational database management system, HBase, which is an open-source project and built on the Hadoop file system. The chapter helps the user set up the HBase environment and perform Create, Read, Update and Delete (CRUD) commands. It also teaches the user how can integrate Hive with HBase through Sqoop. Secondary indexing and security are also discussed towards the end of the chapter.

10.1 INTRODUCTION

HBase is a distributed non-relational database management system built on the Hadoop file system. It is an open-source project and can process large volumes of data. Google Bigtable (a paper published in Nov 2006) is the inspiration behind HBase (the initial prototype version released in Feb 2007). Google Bigtable is a compressed, high-performance, proprietary data store built on the Google file system. HBase was created as a Hadoop subproject to allow structured data storage that can be used with most distributed file systems (typically, the Hadoop Distributed File System known as HDFS). HBase is written in Java and supports writing applications in Apache Avro, REST, and Thrift. HBase is a database that sits atop the Hadoop File System, providing read and write access to store data directly in HDFS or through HBase. The HBase system functions linearly and consists of tables like the traditional database. In addition, a ZooKeeper is built into HBase to give high-performance coordination. HBase also works well with Hive to provide fault-tolerant Big Data applications.

Facebook, Netflix, Yahoo, Adobe, and Twitter are just a few firms that utilize HBase as their central database. HBase's purpose is to host big tables with billions of rows and millions of columns on commodity hardware clusters.

10.2 FEATURES OF HBASE

Apache HBase has several unique characteristics including consistency, high availability, Scalability, automatic failover, and many more (Fig. 10.1).

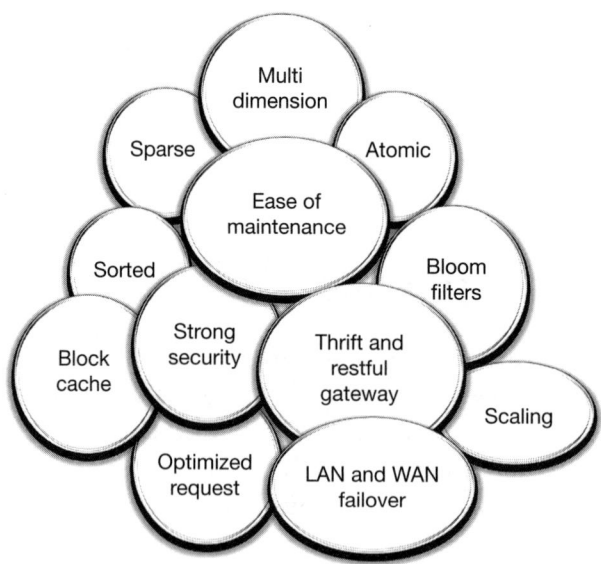

Figure 10.1 Features of HBase

HBase is a map-based database that allows several copies of the same information and is sparse, multi-dimensional, and sorted. We may use the HBase feature for high-speed applications since it provides consistent reads and writes. All other processes are barred from executing any read or write operations during a particular read and write function, called atomic read and write. HBase provides nuclear (atomic) read and write functions at the row level. Therefore, it is possible to create a request that is optimized. For example, because searching is done on a range of rows, and HBase maintains row-keys in lexicographical order, we may create an efficient request by combining these sorted row-keys with the date.

HBase features block cache and Bloom filters that enable real-time query processing. HBase employs Hash tables internally for speedier lookups and provides random access to stored data and means for storing data in indexed HDFS files. HBase provides exceptional write throughput because of its strong security and ease of maintenance.

HBase allows scaling in both linear and modular forms. We may also remark that it is linearly scalable, meaning we can add any number of nodes anytime. HBase scaling is not scale-up but scale-out, which means we don't need to upgrade servers; we only have to add additional machines to the cluster. On the fly, we may add new nodes to the cluster. The cluster may begin rebalancing as soon as a new Region Server node is up and running. Start the Region Server on the new node, and the cluster is scaled up.

HBase not only provides a thrift and restful gateway but also web service gateways for integrating and accessing Java code (HBase Java APIs) for accessing and working with HBase.

HDFS is internally distributed and automatically recovered via multiple block allocation and replications, and HBase operates on top of HDFS; thus, it is also automatically retrieved. This failover is also made easier by utilizing Region Server replication. HBase also has LAN and WAN failover and recovery capabilities. A master server responsible for monitoring the region servers and the cluster's metadata is at the heart of the system. HBase provides automatic failover; so, a system admin can automatically switch data handling to a standby system if a system is compromised.

A key is used to identify value. Binary forms may be stored because the keys and the values are Byte Arrays. Key orders are used to store values. We may conveniently obtain the keys to the values.

In contrast to typical relational databases which employ stores or row-based storage, HBase saves each column independently. As a result, in HBase, columns are saved sequentially rather than in rows. HBase is integrated with Hadoop and the MapReduce framework. It has an easy-to-use Java API for client access and an extensible JRUBY (JIRD) based shell.

10.3 Architecture of HBase

The HBase architecture has three main components: 1. HMaster, 2. Region Server, 3. ZooKeeper (Fig. 10.2).

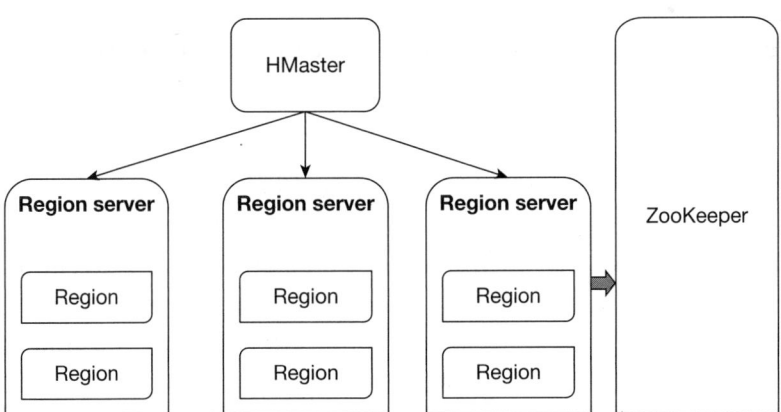

Figure 10.2 Basic architecture of HBase

The client contacts the HMaster. The HMaster allocates regions and load balancing. The Region Server serves the data to read and write by interacting with HDFS, and the Apache ZooKeeper monitors the system. Figure 10.3 shows the HBase architecture diagram after including the client and HDFS. As can be seen from the diagram, the HBase Physical Architecture consists of servers in a Master relationship. The HBase cluster typically consists of one Master node (HMaster) and many Region Servers.

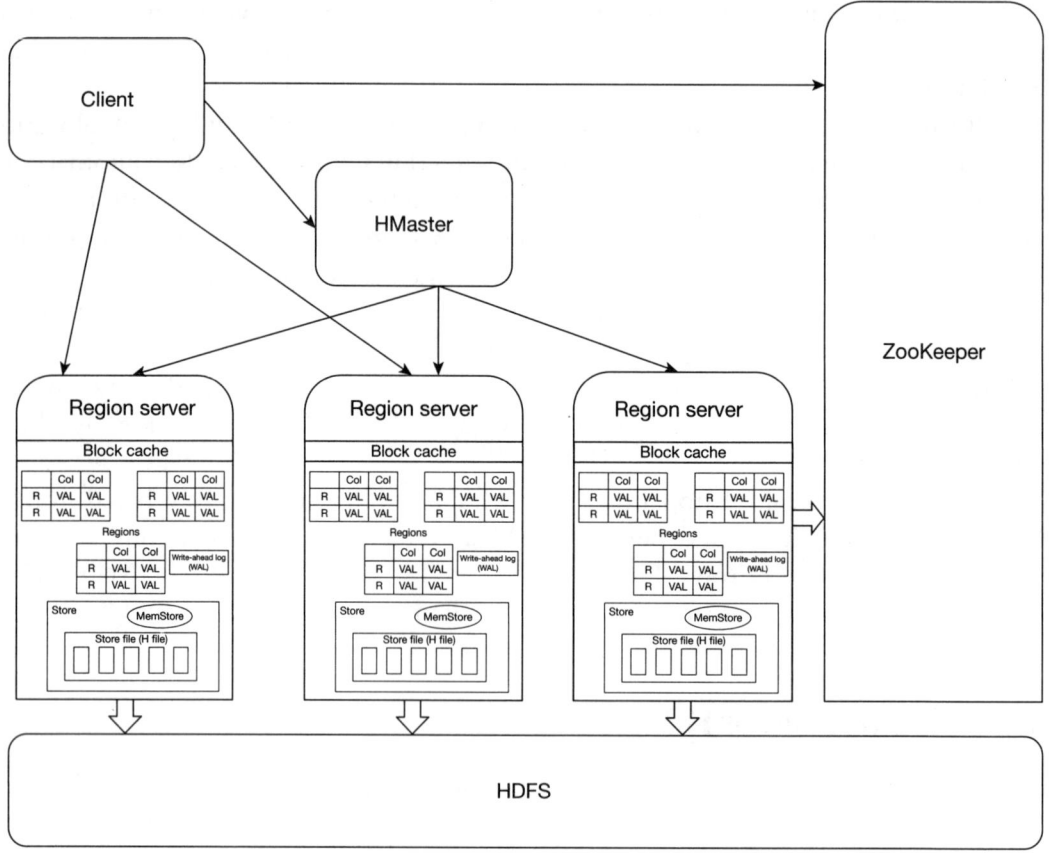

Figure 10.3 Basic architecture of HBase with Region Servers and HDFS

10.3.1 HMaster

The Master's responsibilities include coordinating the servers in the region, allocating regions during launch, reassigning regions for recovery, and load balancing. In addition, the Master monitors All-Region Server instances in the cluster (listens for notifications from ZooKeeper). It moves the regions to less crowded servers after unloading the congested servers. In addition, the Master serves as an interface for creating, deleting, and updating tables (DDL operations). HMaster acts as an interface for all metadata changes and takes responsibility for metadata operations. Negotiating load balancing keeps the cluster in good shape. HMaster is also in charge of schema modifications and other metadata actions like table and column family formation.

10.3.2 Region Server

The Region Server (Refer Figs 10.3 and 10.4) comprises all the Hadoop cluster's machines. The Region Server has minor components such as The Region, Hlog (H File), Store, MemStore, WAL, and various other files.

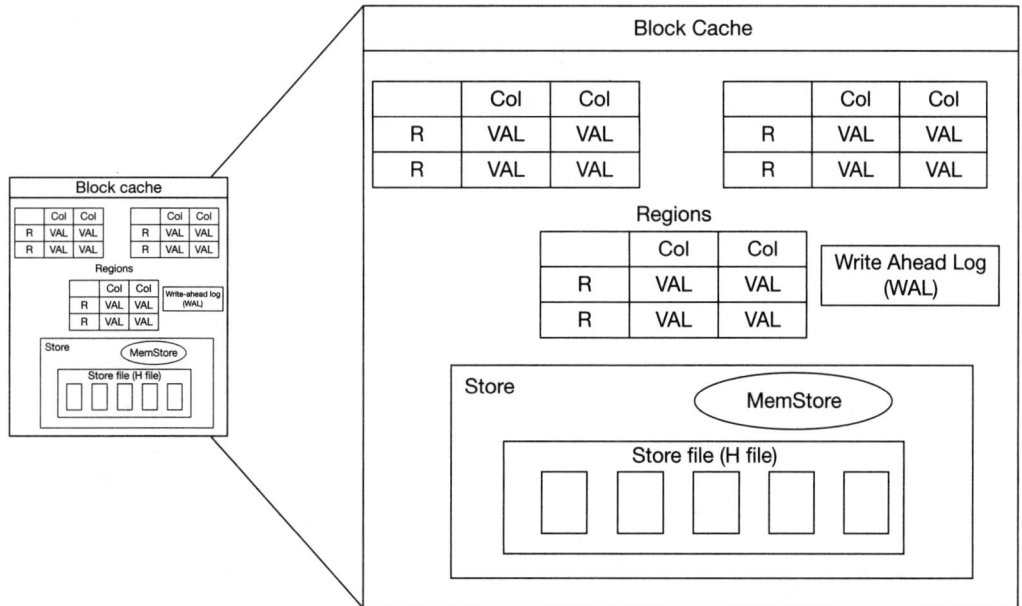

Figure 10.4 Inside Region Server

Regions

HBase uses regions as a database, and it uses WAL (Write-Ahead Log) as a technique to store Logs. In HBase, Data is saved in Tables and stored in Regions. When a Table is too large, it is divided into many Regions. Region Servers are assigned to these Regions across the cluster. The number of regions hosted by each Region Server is nearly the same. Regions have a default size of 256 MB. The Region Server maintains various regions running on HDFS and manages and executes reads and writes on regions.

WAL

Write-Ahead Log (WAL) are files attached to every Region Server (Fig. 10.5) that store the new data that hasn't been committed to permanent storage. WAL files are used to recover data in case of failure.

WAL's most significant function is catastrophe recovery. It keeps track of all data changes in the same way as MySQL's BIN log does. We may recover the data before the crash by replaying the log after the Server has crashed. If writing to WAL fails, the entire operation is deemed a failure. The data will be asynchronously written to the file system when MemStore reaches a specific size or after some time. The data between the two writes to the file system, on the other hand, is maintained in memory.

Block Cache

Block Cache (Fig. 10.6) resides on the Region Server and stores the frequently read data in the memory. If the data in Block Cache has not been recently used, then it is removed from Block Cache. A region server has just one Block Cache instance, which implies that data from all regions hosted by that Server is cached in the same pool. The Block Cache

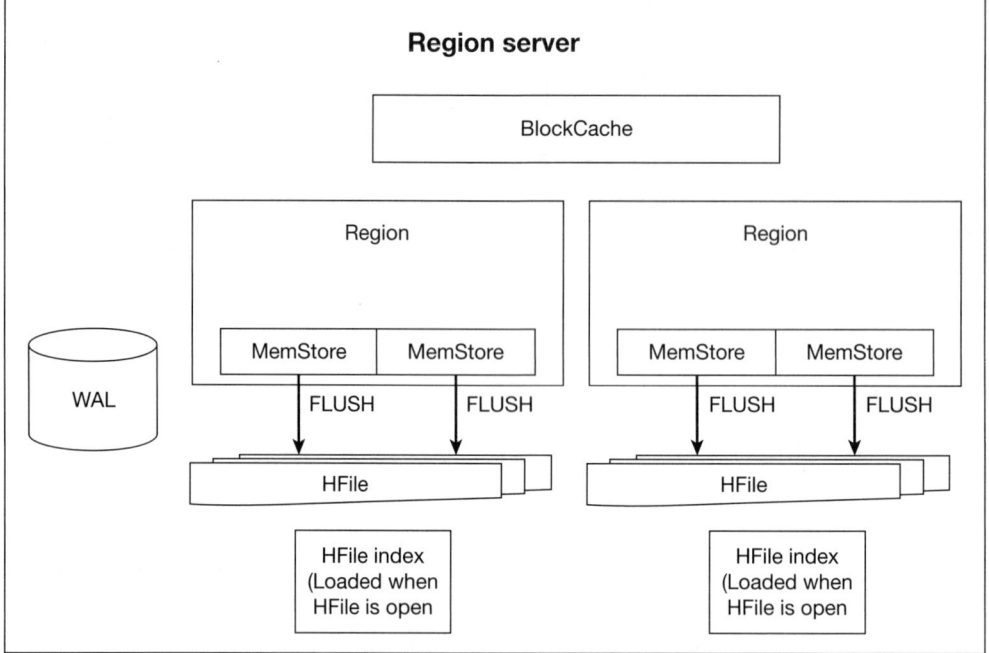

Figure 10.5 Write-Ahead Log (WAL)

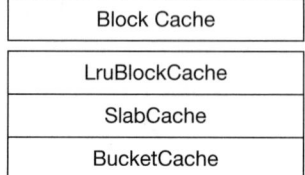

Figure 10.6 Three types of Block Cache

is created when the area server starts up and is kept for the duration of the operation. In the past, HBase only had one Block Cache implementation: the LruBlockCache. However, it now has two additional Block Cache implementations, including SlabCache and BucketCache.

LruBlockCache: This default implementation caches the data blocks in the JVM heap. Single-access, multi-access, and in-memory are the three categories. The sizes of the areas are 25%, 50%, and 25% of the total BlockCache size, respectively. The single-access area is populated using a block read from HDFS. Consecutive accesses advance a block to the multi-access zone. The in-memory region is reserved for blocks loaded from IN MEMORY column families. Finally, old blocks are evicted to create a place for new blocks, regardless of area, using the Least-Recently-Used method, hence the "Lru" in "LruBlockCache".

SlabCache: Using DirectByteBuffers, this approach allocates memory outside the JVM heap (Fig. 10.7). The region in which a specific block will be put is determined by its size. Two sections are allocated by default, occupying 80% and 20% respectively, of the total off-heap cache capacity. The former is used to cache blocks around the same size as the target block. The latter stores blocks that are roughly twice the size of the target block. A block is crammed into the tiniest possible space. If the cache comes across a block that is too large to fit in either region, it will not be stored.

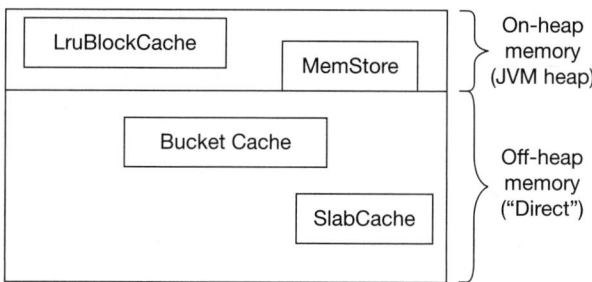

Figure 10.7 On-heap and Off-heap memories

BucketCache: This implementation may be set to one of three modes: heap, off-heap, or file. The BucketCache handles "buckets" of memory for storing cached blocks, regardless of operating mode. A target block size is set for each bucket. The heap implementation produces the buckets on the JVM heap; the off-heap performance manages buckets outside the JVM heap using DirectByteByffers. The file mode demands a path to a file on the disc where the buckets are produced. File mode was designed to work with a low-latency backing store, such as an in-memory filesystem or a file on SSD storage. Bucket Cache produces 14 buckets of various sizes regardless of mode. As with LruBlockCache, it utilizes the frequency of block access to determine usage.

MemStore

MemStore is the write cache that stores all the incoming data (Fig. 10.8) before committing it to the disk or permanent memory. MemStore stores recently added data and acts as an in-memory cache by storing recently added data. Also, there are occasions when it is more advantageous to access recently written data rather than older data. There is one MemStore for each column family in a region, and there are multiple MemStores for a region because each region contains various column families. The data in the MemStore is sorted in lexicographical order before committing to the disk. Also, every MemStore flush creates one HFile per Column Family, which is a fantastic feature.

HFile: When the MemStore has acquired enough data, the complete ordered dataset is written to a new HDFS HFile file. For each Column Family, HBase produces an HFile to contain the details of Cell Key-Value data. Because Key-Value is regularly moved from the MemStore to the hard drive, HFiles will continue to occur over time. This data structure supports random read and write operations on the table. The key will be used to update

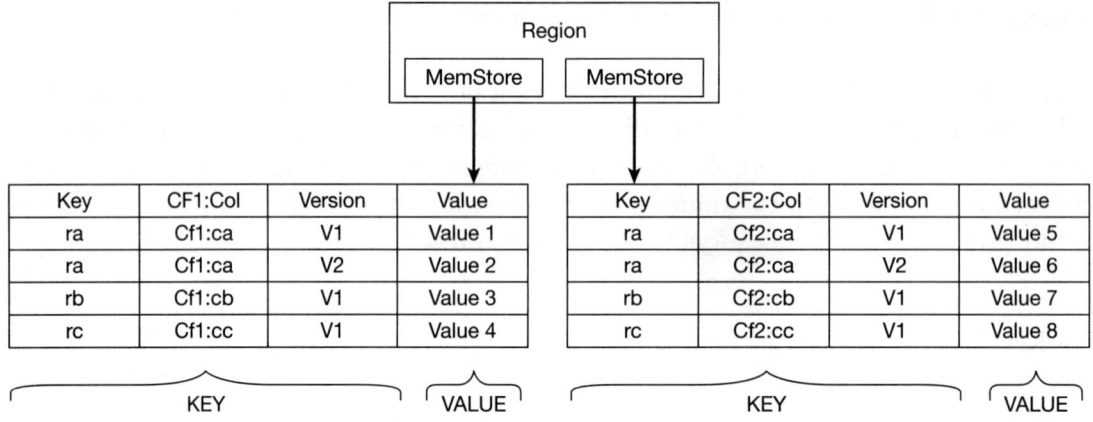

Figure 10.8 MemStore

the table's data, giving us real-time data. Updating a vast data collection is simple by using HFile, which is in the region server. It will save only one region's data, and only one file will be available to house that region's chuck piece (i.e., a large portion or amount) of data. The use of HFile in HBase allows for real-time data storage and updating. When the HFile is opened, the index is loaded and stored in Block Cache memory (Fig. 10.9). The HBase system can perform lookups with just a single disc seek. HBase needs to limit the number of Column Families available. Each Column Family has a MemStore; if one of the MemStores is complete, the whole Column Family is written to the hard drive. It also keeps track of the

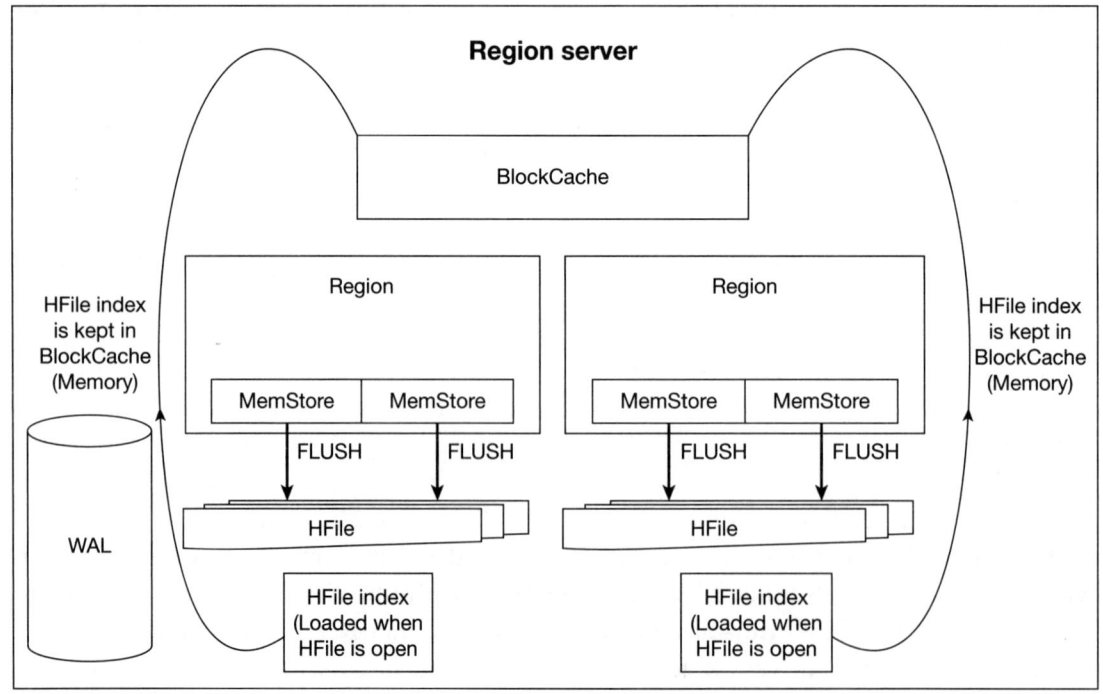

Figure 10.9 HFile index and Block Cache synch

most recent data written. The maximum serial number (sequence number) that can be used is for the system to know as it keeps a check on which data has been saved thus far.

ZooKeeper

ZooKeeper is a distributed coordinator in HBase for region assignments and is used to recover any region server crashes by loading them onto functional region servers. It helps maintain the server state inside the cluster. It keeps track of settings and synchronizes data across several machines.

The HMaster Server sends continuous heartbeats (Fig. 10.10) at regular intervals to ZooKeeper and checks which server is alive. It also provides services like maintaining configuration information, naming, distributing synchronization, server failure notification, etc. In addition, ZooKeeper helps find the path of the Region Server by maintaining the META Server's path. If a client wishes to connect with regions, it must first contact ZooKeeper. The ZooKeeper service keeps track of all the region servers in an HBase cluster, including how many region servers are there and which region servers are hosting which DataNode. HMaster communicates with ZooKeeper to obtain information about region servers. The session with ZooKeeper will terminate, the ephemeral node will be removed, and the listener will get the notification if a Region Server or HMaster fails or the transmitting heartbeat fails for different reasons. Active HMaster monitors for messages sent by region servers that have gone offline and then recovers the failed region server and the region data. On the other hand, inactive HMaster is worried about the news of active HMaster going offline, and then the competition becoming active HMaster.

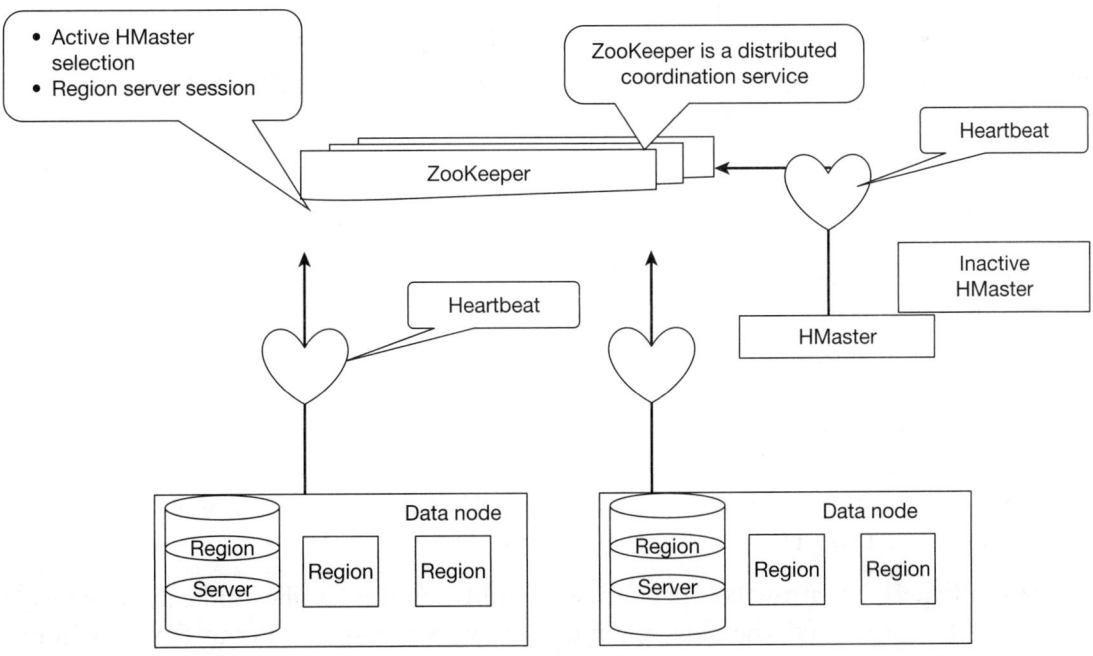

Figure 10.10 Heartbeats and ZooKeeper

10.4 Managing Large Datasets with HBase

Big Data describes an enormous volume of structured and unstructured data that traditional methods cannot process. Traditional databases find it hard to process the data because it is dynamic and changes too fast, making it unsuitable for processing by existing applications. To make use of this data, appropriate technological infrastructure is needed. Doug Laney describes Big Data by defining the three V's: volume, velocity, and variety of data. In recent times, Value and Veracity have been added as the fourth and fifth characteristics of Big Data. In practice, Big Data is not something new, and people have been trying to plan and make decisions for many years with gathered data. However, "Big Data" has gained popularity in recent years because of technological development. Big Data can be divided into three phases based on the type of Data: A database management system (DBMS) that stores and manages (1) Structured data; (2) Web-based non-structured data; (3) Data that comes from mobile devices and sensors. For Big Data to be valuable, storage, processing, and analyzing tools are needed to derive real insight from the data. Relational databases are not suitable for handling Big Data, and this gave way to the need for a NoSQL database. HBase is a distributed and scalable environment that can work with Big Data. The NoSQL database runs on top of Hadoop. It can leverage the Hadoop Distributed File System (HDFS) and benefit from Hadoop's MapReduce programming model. It can host large tables with billions of rows with potentially millions of columns and runs on commodity hardware. HBase is a robust database that blends real-time querying capabilities and batch processing through MapReduce. The advantage of using HBase is that we can query records and derive aggregate analytic reports across massive data.

HBase works with both structured and unstructured data. Although HBase is not a relational database, it requires an approach that is different from modeling data. HBase defines a four-dimensional data model to model the data:

- **Row-key:** This can be seen as the row identifier, and each row has a unique row-key. However, the row-key does not have a data type and is treated internally as a byte array.
- **Column family:** Data within a row is organized into column families. The column family follows the row-key, and each row has the same set of column families; however, the same column families do not require the same column qualifiers across rows.
- **Column qualifier:** The column qualifiers define actual columns and can be seen as column identifiers.
- **Version:** Each column can have a customizable number of versions and access data for a specific version of a column qualifier.

As seen in Fig. 10.11, a row comprises one or more column families and can be accessed by its row-key. To access the data, we must know its row-key, column family, column qualifier, and version.

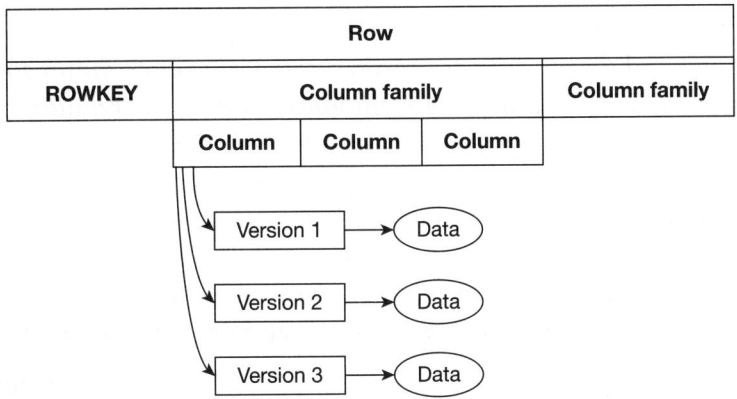

Figure 10.11 Row-column families

The HBase data model helps us understand how to access the data. It can access the data in HBSE in two ways:

- Through the row-key or a table scan of the entire range of row-keys
- In a batch manner, using MapReduce

HBase makes this approach to data access particularly powerful. However, storing data in Hadoop makes it suitable for offline or batch analysis but not for real-time access. HBase addresses this issue using a key-value store for real-time analysis and supporting MapReduce for batch analysis.

Real-time access is depicted as a key-value store in Fig. 10.12.

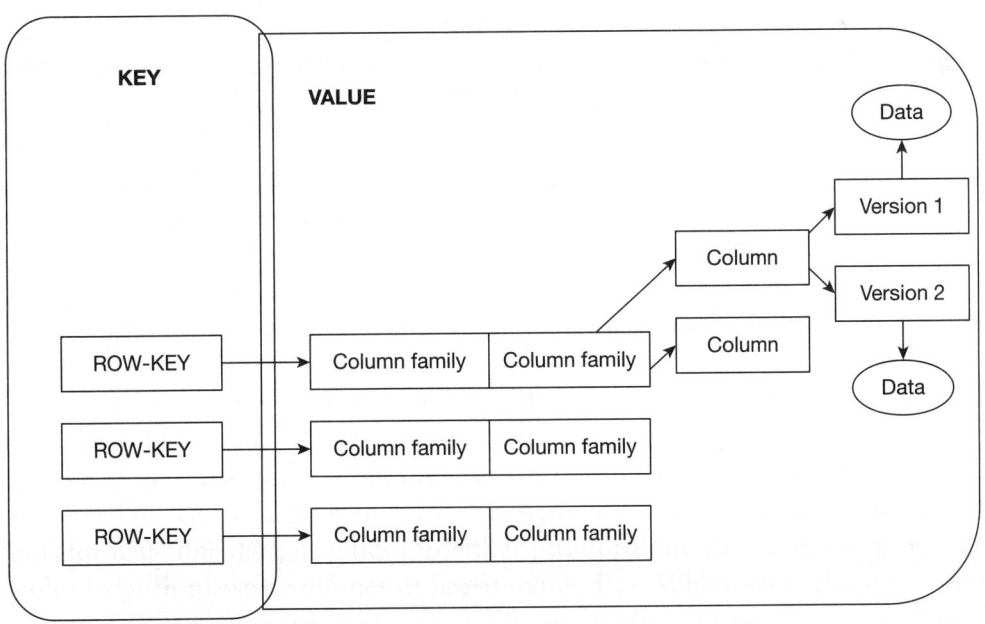

Figure 10.12 Real-time access as a key-value store

We can use the key to retrieve the value associated with that key; in other words, by providing the starting row-key and ending row-key, we may "obtain" the row associated with a row-key. This is referred to as a table scan in HBase. However, it cannot query values in columns in a real-time query. Thus, row-key design is an important issue.

The design of the row-key is vital for two reasons:

- First, table scans operate against the row-key, so it is critical to design the row-key properly to control how much real-time direct access we can perform against HBase.
- HBase runs in a production environment on top of the Hadoop Distributed File System (HDFS), and the data gets distributed across the HDFS based on the row-key. For example, if all our row-keys start with "XXXX", then we have to isolate most of our data to a single node. Hence, the row-key design should be different enough to be distributed across the entire deployment.

So, to access rows efficiently, we must pay attention to row-key design. If data is stored on a per-user basis, the row-keys are ultimately stored as byte arrays in HBase. To get to the rows, we must first build a hash of the user ID (such as an MD5 or SHA-1 hash code) and then append the time to the hash. The advantage of using a hash is two-fold: (1) it distributes values to distribute the data across the cluster, and (2) it ensures that the length of the key is consistent, making it easier to use in table scans.

10.5 HBASE COMPACTION

An HBase table has the following physical storage structure. It is divided into many regions (Fig. 10.13). Even though a region may have several Stores, each only has one column family. An edit initially writes to the MemStore in-memory space of the hosting region store. MemStore is flushed to Store Files on HDFS when its size hits a certain threshold. Because Apache HBase is a distributed data store based on a log-structured

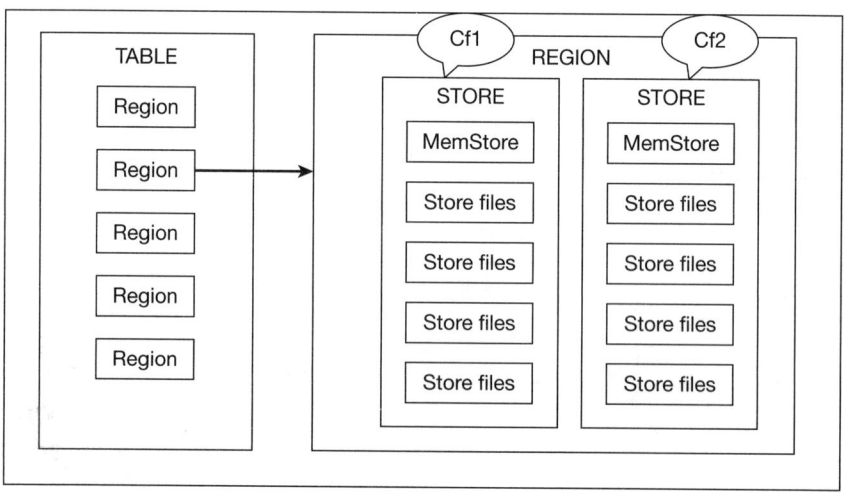

Figure 10.13 Inside the HBase region

merge tree, having only one file per store would provide the best-read speed (Column Family). However, it is impossible to achieve this ideal solution during moments of heavy burst writes. So instead, HBase will attempt to aggregate (merge) HFiles to decrease the number of disc searches required for a read. Compaction is the term given for this procedure.

Compactions choose and aggregate (merge) files from single storage in an area. This procedure entails reading key values from input files and writing out any key values that have not been erased, and ensuring that they are within the time to live (TTL) and do not exceed the number of versions. The newly formed combined file then takes the place of the region's input files. When a client requests data, HBase recognizes that the data from the input files are stored in a single continuous file on a disk, requiring just one seek rather than one for each file as in the unaggregated case. However, the disc IO is not free, and rewriting data again and over might result in significant network and disc over-subscription if not done carefully. Compaction, in other terms, is the process of exchanging some disc IO now for fewer seeks later.

HBase supports two types of compactions: minor and major.

10.5.1 Minor Compaction

Minor compaction is always active (Fig. 10.14) and focuses on newly written files. These files are tiny because they are fresh, and they may include deleting markers for data in earlier files. This compaction does not affect or erase data from older files since it only looks at the newer files. This means that until another compaction type comes along and deletes older data, this compaction type will be unable to remove the erase markers from newer files; otherwise, those previously deleted key values will reappear. Minor compactions are essential as reading a particular row can require many disk reads and cause slow performance. Minor compaction is similar to a merge sort in that rewriting smaller files into fewer but larger ones minimizes the number of storage files.

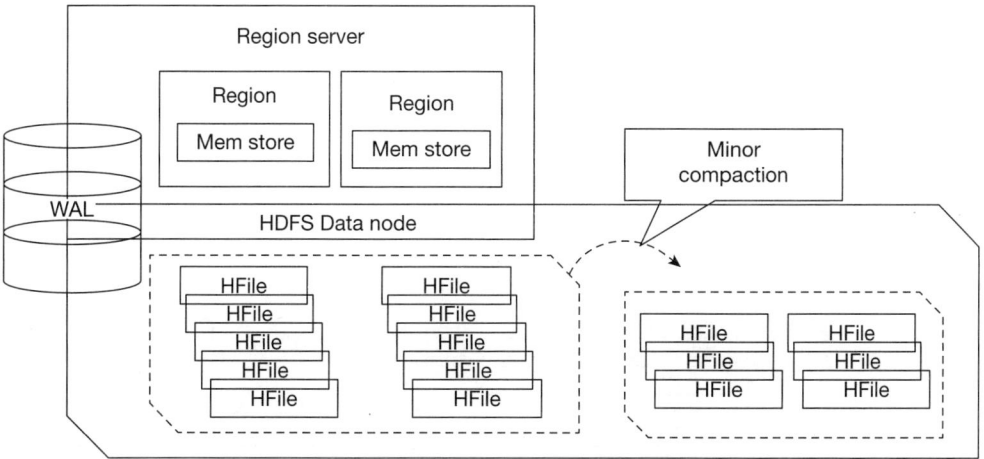

Figure 10.14 HBase minor compaction

As a result, there are two outcomes:

1. The potential to affect data locality is quite limited since the touched files are comparatively younger and smaller. A region server usually tries to write the primary replica of data on the local HDFS data node anyway during a write operation. As a result, minor compaction seldom adds much to data locality.
2. Some performance will be lost because the delete marks are not deleted. On the other hand, minor compactions are crucial for HBase read performance because they keep the total file count under control, which may be a major performance bottleneck if left uncontrolled, especially on spinning drives.

10.5.2 Major Compaction

Major compactions merge all HFiles into one huge HFile (Fig. 10.15), whereas minor compactions combine a customizable number of smaller HFiles into one larger HFile. Major compactions do the cleanup work after a user deletes a record. When a user performs a Delete call, the HBase system places a marker in the key-value pair to be permanently removed during the subsequent major compaction. Major compactions are usually scheduled to run automatically. This compaction is seldom performed (once a week by default) and focuses on a store's comprehensive cleaning (one column family inside one region). Major compaction makes data files that are remote local to the region server. Major compactions read all of a region's Store files and write them all to a single Store file. Significant compaction produces a single file for each storage. Because major compaction rewrites all of the data in a store, it can erase both the delete markers and the older key values that the delete markers have tagged as destroyed. As a result, there are two consequences:

1. File sizes are drastically decreased because delete markers and deleted data are physically erased, especially in a system that receives many delete operations. In a delete-heavy environment, this can result in a significant boost in performance.

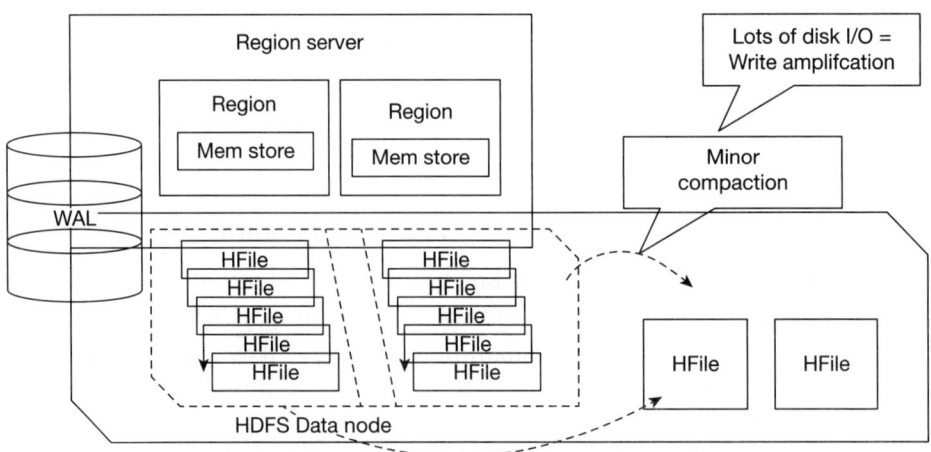

Figure 10.15 HBase major compaction

2. Because a store's whole data is being rebuilt, there is an opportunity to restore data locality for older (and bigger) files where drift may have occurred owing to restarts and rebalances, as mentioned earlier. This activity results in improved read IO performance.

We will get incredible write speed if HBase gathers several HFiles without compacting them (the data is rewritten less frequently). On the other hand, if we tell HBase to compress multiple HFiles sooner, we will get faster read performance, but the same data will be read and rewritten more frequently. To guarantee appropriate read speed, HBase allows us to choose when to start compacting HFiles and what is deemed the maximum limit of HFiles. Flushes and compaction can usually start at the same time. However, when clients write to HBase faster than the system can absorb it, i.e., faster than compactions can lower the number of HFiles, an ever-increasing quantity of HFiles can be compacted until the predefined limit is reached. When this happens, the memstores can continue to buffer the incoming data, but they won't expand endlessly since RAM is limited; thus, the only choice is to disable writes, which HBase does. Many factors that influence this phenomenon are found on Hbase-site.xml.

10.6 SCHEMA DESIGN

NoSQL schema design differs significantly from RDBMS schema design. We could find ourselves looking blankly at a shell after getting something like HBase up and running, thinking about the possibilities of generating our first table. The Apache HBase Shell or the Java API's Admin can build or alter HBase schemas. An HBase table can scale up to billions of rows and many columns based on requirements. Therefore, this table allows the advantage of storing terabytes of data in it. In addition, the HBase table supports high read and write throughput at low latency.

10.6.1 Table Schema

The HBase schema design differs from the relational database schema design. There are several datasets, each with its own set of access patterns and service requirements. As a result, these general guidelines are merely a starting point. Below are the general concepts that need to be followed while designing table schema in HBase:

1. **Row-key:** Each table in an HBase table is indexed based on the row-key, and data is sorted lexicographically by the row-key. There are no secondary indices available on the HBase table.
2. **Automaticity:** All operations on HBase rows are atomic at the row level.
3. **Even distribution:** Reads and writes should be uniformly distributed across all nodes in the cluster. Design the row-key to store related entities in adjacent rows to increase read efficiency.

Consider the size limit as given below, when designing a schema in HBase:

1. Region size: 10 to 50 GB
2. Individual values: Cells not larger than 10 MB (50 MB for Mob)
3. All values in a single row: max 10 MB
4. 1 and 3 column families per table
5. 50–100 regions is a good number for a table with 1 or 2 column families
6. Keep your column family names as short as possible
7. Be aware of write patterns when allocating resources
8. Row keys: 4 KB per key
9. Column qualifiers: 16 KB per qualifier.

10.6.2 HBase Row-key Design

In light of the facts regarding the HBase Key and its role in data scalability and dissemination, there are three design guidelines to consider when deciding on an HBase key for a table: Conciseness, Uniqueness, Data distribution.

Conciseness

Short names for column family and column qualifier are suggested since every data value in HBase is saved as a Key-Value pair. A single byte representing an English alphabet may be chosen as a name for a column family. Still, the number of column qualifiers can be determined by the number of bytes used. In addition, we should create the HBase key's row-key component compactly. Instead of using value strings, we should transform large integer values in the row-keys to bytes. Because the timestamp is implicitly included in HBase Key, do not explicitly put it in the row-key. If a good mapper function can uniquely convert huge data string values to tiny ones, don't include them in the row-key. In addition, if there is a restricted number of large data string values, a lookup table at runtime can reference the original large data strings from the tiny ones.

Uniqueness

It is essential to double-check that the row-key element of the HBase Key uniquely identifies your dataset. If you construct a non-unique row-key you may mistakenly write your separate datasets against the same row-key. If the same is permitted for the table and each write differs in the HBase Key timestamp, they will be saved as several versions. Non-unique row-key, on the other hand, causes users to overwrite distinct datasets against the same row-key if only one version is authorized. You may achieve row-key uniqueness by choosing a collection of columns (or data dimensions) from your dataset that uniquely identifies each of your multiple datasets. There may be several such sets; nevertheless, the optimal set should be short in length and allow users to get data quickly. In addition, many users utilize a variety of hash functions in row-key design to ensure equal data distribution. However, these functions are not one-to-one; thus, depending on them exclusively might compromise the uniqueness of the row-keys.

Data Distribution

Data is distributed across the HBase cluster based on row-key. Our row-key architecture must permit data to be distributed across the cluster. If we do not distribute the data uniformly across the cluster, scalability and performance would be harmed, as just a few nodes in the cluster would have the data. Read/write activities are focused on only a few parts of the tables (hosted on a few nodes) due to poor table row-key design, a phenomenon known as 'Hot-spotting'.

Hot-spotting

As we know, rows in HBase are sorted lexicographically by row-key. This row-key design is optimized for scans, allowing the user to store related rows or rows that need to be read together, near each other. On the other hand, poorly constructed row-keys are a common source of hot-spotting. When a massive quantity of client traffic is routed to one node, or only a few nodes of a cluster, this is known as hot-spotting. This traffic can be caused by reads, writes, or other operations. Write hot-spotting would occur if sequential write operations result in monotonically growing row-keys; since monotonically increasing row-keys would only target one region at a time. Monotonical increase means it either increases or remains constant; it will not decrease. Read hot-spotting occurs when a huge data collection is read from only a few areas. As a result, the read/write throughput and parallelism aspects of Hadoop computing jobs running on the table suffer significantly due to hot-spotting. The traffic leads to performance degradation of the single machine responsible for hosting that region, leading eventually to region unavailability. This traffic can also adversely affect other regions hosted by the same server as the host cannot service the requested load. Therefore, it is essential to design data access patterns to fully and evenly utilize the cluster. To get the best performance of the HBase cluster, row-keys should be designed in such a way as to allow the system to write evenly across all the nodes.

Hot-spotting can be avoided in multiple ways, as discussed hereunder.

Reverse Row-Key: Reversing the row-key of a fixed length or number format is a way to avoid hot spots. This reversing permits the often-modified component of the row-key (the least essential element) to be placed first. This method effectively randomizes the row-key, albeit at the cost of the row-key's orderliness.

Salting: In this context, salting (Fig. 10.16) refers to adding random data to the beginning of a row-key, which has nothing to do with cryptography. Salting refers to adding a randomly assigned prefix to the row-key to make it sort in a different way than it would otherwise. The number of prefixes available is proportional to the number of areas that wish to distribute the data. Salting can assist if we have a few "hot" row-key patterns that repeatedly appear amongst other more uniformly distributed rows. In Fig. 10.16, we used the random numbers (0_, 1_, 2_) as prefixes to the row id, which moved the row ids to the corresponding regions.

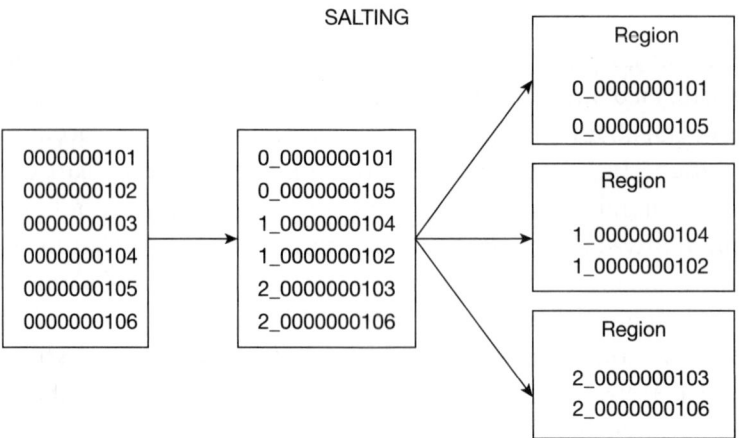

Figure 10.16 HBase Salting

Hashing: When we have the data represented by a string identifier, that is a good choice for hashing the string identifier of the HBase table row-key. For example, if the table stores user data identified by user IDs, hashing is good for the row-key (Fig. 10.17). Instead of using a random assignment, we may also use a one-way hash that causes a particular row to always be "salted" with the same prefix, distributing the load across the Region Servers while maintaining predictability during reads. A deterministic hash allows the client to reassemble the whole row-key and obtain the row using a Get operation.

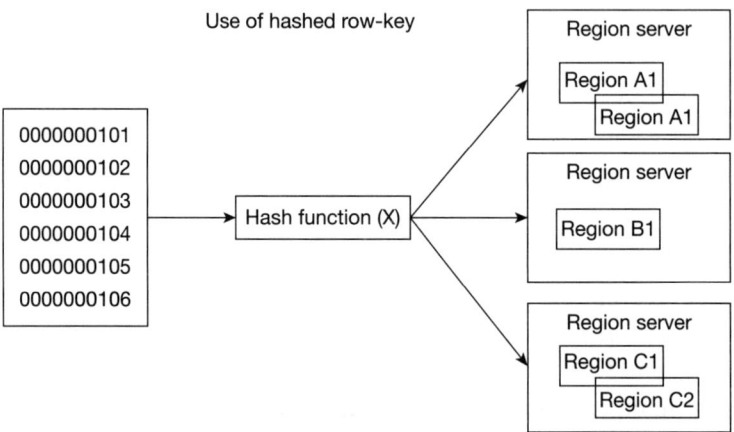

Figure 10.17 HBase Hashed Row-Key

Timestamps: The timestamp of the row-key can be used to retrieve data based on the time stored. If data is saved in a machine log identifiable by a machine number, for example, when constructing a row-key, attach the timestamp to the machine number, for example, machine001#1644404701000.

Combined Row-Key: Combining multiple keys to design a row-key for our HBase table is another option based on our requirements. Scanning for consecutive blocks is the most effective way to read back rows. For example, assume we have a table with a customer-date-user row-key. The prefix customer-first part-of-date makes it easy to read back all the data for a specific customer and date range, but it makes it challenging to read backdate ranges for all users at once without scanning all the rows. The problem is reversed if we use customer-user-date instead of the row-key. Therefore, we should consider our significant read pattern when creating our keys.

Accessibility: Row-keys should be constructed so that data is easily available to users in the most efficient manner possible. When a row-key prefix is used in a search query, the number of HBase regions (and the number of data storage files inside a region) that must be examined for output data is reduced to the minimum. If stored data is to be searched against a specific type of data, the row-key's first and foremost value should be that particular data type. Additional data types can then follow this ubiquitous data type in their frequency of presence throughout all search queries.

Tall vs. Wide Tables: The user's HBase table design impacts row-key design. The row-key includes more data values than a broad table when a tall table is used. Because the HBase region (unit of distribution) is separated across row-key borders, more data in a row-key leads to more row-keys, which leads to more data disseminated over the HBase cluster. On the other hand, fewer data in the row-key means more data is stored against columns, resulting in a smaller data distribution while ensuring atomicity across a larger dataset.

10.6.3 Schema of Column Families

HBase currently does not perform with more than two- or three-column families, so it is good to keep the number of column families low. On a per-Region basis, flushing and compactions are performed, so if one column family carries the bulk of the data, adjacent families will also be flushed, leading to needless I/O. To prevent this, the user can introduce a second and third column family where data access is based on columns.

Multiple-column families exist in a single table; however, it is also good to be aware of the cardinality (i.e., number of rows). For example, two-column families A and B, have 1 million and 1 billion rows, respectively. It is more likely that Column Family A's data will be spread across more regions and region servers, making the overall scans for Column Family A less efficient. So, if a row contains multiple related values, it should be placed in the same family name. Also, the names of the column families should be short as they will also be included in the transferred data for each request.

As we can create as many column qualifiers as needed in each row, the empty cells in the row do not consume any space. The names of column qualifiers should also be short since they are included in the transferred data for each request.

10.7 Other Factors in HBase Schema Design

10.7.1 Region Split

HBase region size is essential when accessing HBase data because in map-reduce, the data split is done by splitting regions (Fig. 10.18). There will not be enough parallelism in the MapReduce jobs if the area size is too large and it splits into two child regions. Each table is in one region at first. A region divides into two child regions when it becomes too large.

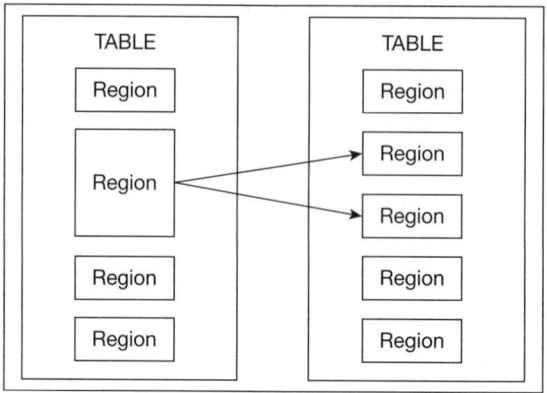

Figure 10.18 HBase region split – Overall view

Both child regions then represent one-half of the original region on the same region server, and each split is reported to the Master Server or HMaster. On the other hand, if the region size is too small, there are many wasted cycles in creating and deleting the MapReduce tasks. Therefore, the optimal size for a region depends on the workload and the cluster configuration. Initially, there is one region per table. However, the HMaster may schedule new regions to be moved to other servers for load balancing reasons (Fig. 10.19).

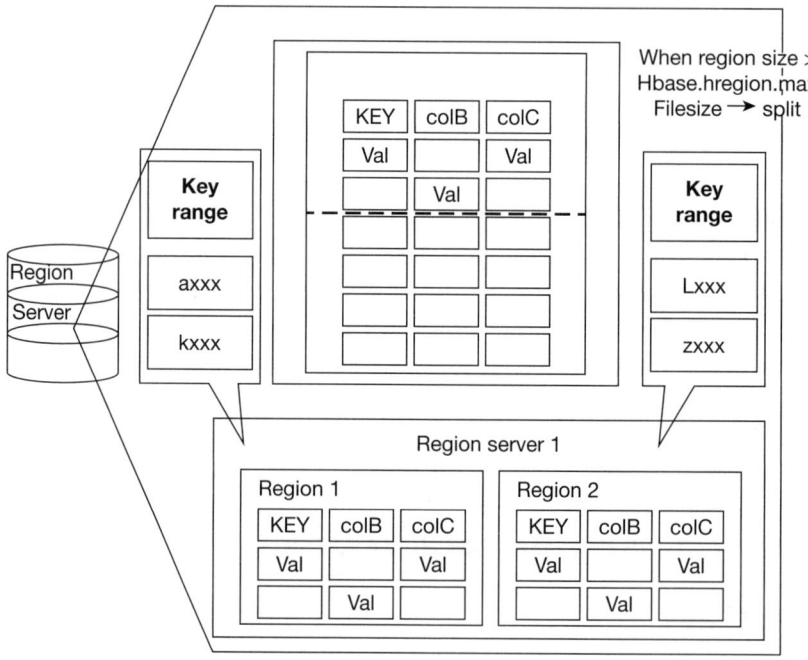

Figure 10.19 HBase region split – Detailed view

10.7.2 Load Balancing

Splitting happens on the same region server, but the HMaster may schedule new regions to be moved off to other servers for help in load balancing. This action causes the new region server to serve data from a remote HDFS node until major compaction moves the data to the region server's local node. HBase data is local when written (Fig. 10.20), but when a region is moved (for load balancing or recovery), the data will not be local to HDFS until the subsequent major compaction.

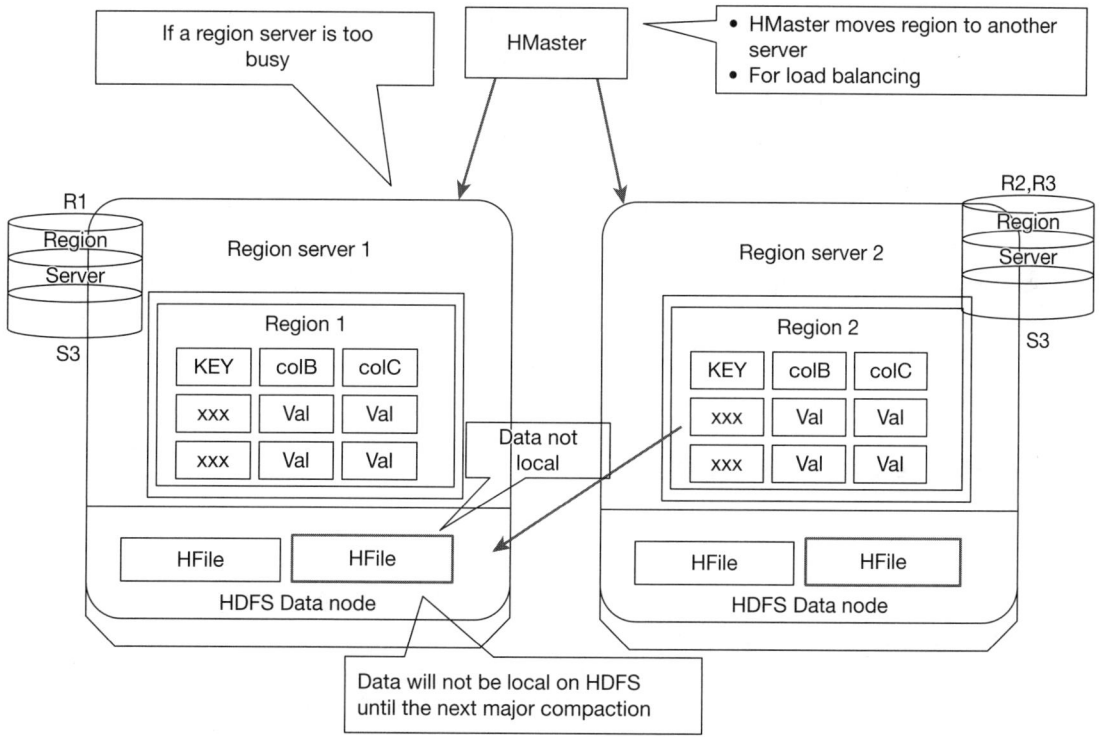

Figure 10.20 HBase Load Balancing

10.7.3 Data Replication

HBase relies on HDFS to provide data safety for the stored files. Data is written to HDFS locally first, then duplicated to a secondary node, and finally to a tertiary node. HDFS replicates all writes and reads to/from the primary node to the WAL and HFile blocks. HFile block replication happens automatically.

HBase replication is a technique for copying data across HBase instances. It may be used as a disaster recovery solution and can help to increase HBase layer availability. It is used for more practical purposes, such as copying updates from a web-facing cluster to a "MapReduce" cluster that automatically processes old and new data and returns the results. The basic architecture pattern for HBase replication is (HBase cluster) master-push; it is much easier to keep track of what is currently being replicated because each region server has its write-ahead log (also known as WAL or HLog). Each area server will participate in replicating its stream of modifications, and one master cluster can copy to any number of slave clusters.

The replication is done asynchronously, which means the clusters can be geographically separated. The links between them can be down for an extended time, and rows inserted on the master cluster will not be accessible on the slave clusters simultaneously (eventual consistency). This design's replication format is essentially similar to MySQL's statement-based replication. However, to preserve atomicity, whole WALEdits (containing multiple cell-inserts from the clients' Put and Delete) are duplicated instead of SQL statements.

Each region server's HLogs are the foundation of HBase replication, and they must be stored in HDFS for as long as they are required to replicate data to any slave cluster. To make failure recovery easier, each Repository Server (RS) reads from the oldest log it needs to duplicate and saves the current position within ZooKeeper. The Save location can be different for each slave cluster, and the queue of HLogs to process can also be varied. The replication clusters can be unequal in size, and the master cluster will use randomness to balance the replication stream on the slave clusters. HBase now supports master/master and cyclic replication and copy-to-many slaves, as of version 0.92.

The WAL file and HFile are both replicated and persisted on disc, but how can HBase recover MemStore updates that did not persist to HFiles?

10.7.4 HBase Crash Recovery

When a Region Server fails, the crashed regions become unavailable until detection and recovery have taken place. ZooKeeper detects node failure when it stops receiving region server heartbeats. After that, the HMaster will be informed that the Region Server has failed, reassigning the regions from that Server to other region servers that are still up and running (Fig. 10.21). Next, HMaster splits the WAL files from the crashed region server and stores the split files in the new region servers' data nodes. To rebuild the MemStore for that particular region, the Region Server will replicate the WAL from the respective split WAL.

10.7.5 Data Recovery

When a region server crashes, the regions it controls are unavailable until the crash is discovered and the failure recovery process is finished. ZooKeeper uses heartbeat detection to identify node failures, and subsequently, HMaster is notified of region server failures.

HMaster allocates the regions handled by the region server to other healthy region servers when it detects a region server failure. HMaster separates the WAL into many files and saves them on the new region server to retrieve data that has not been persisted to HFile in the MemStore of the failed region server. Each region server then recreates a MemStore for the new area allocated by replaying the data in the WAL fragments it retrieved (Fig. 10.22).

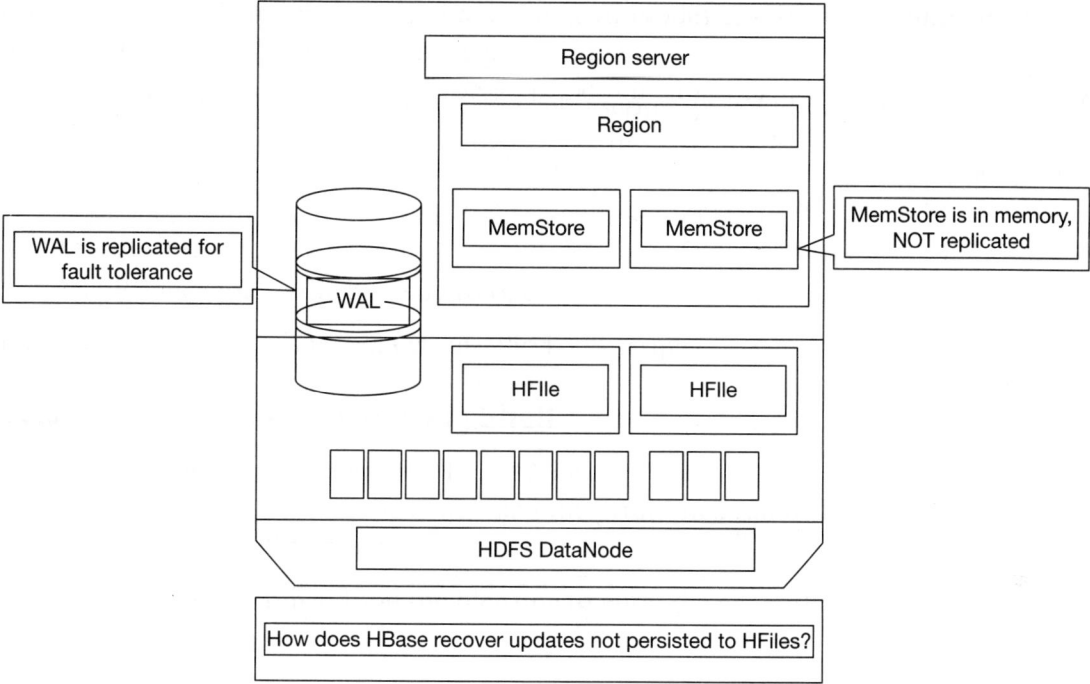

Figure 10.21 HBase crash recovery

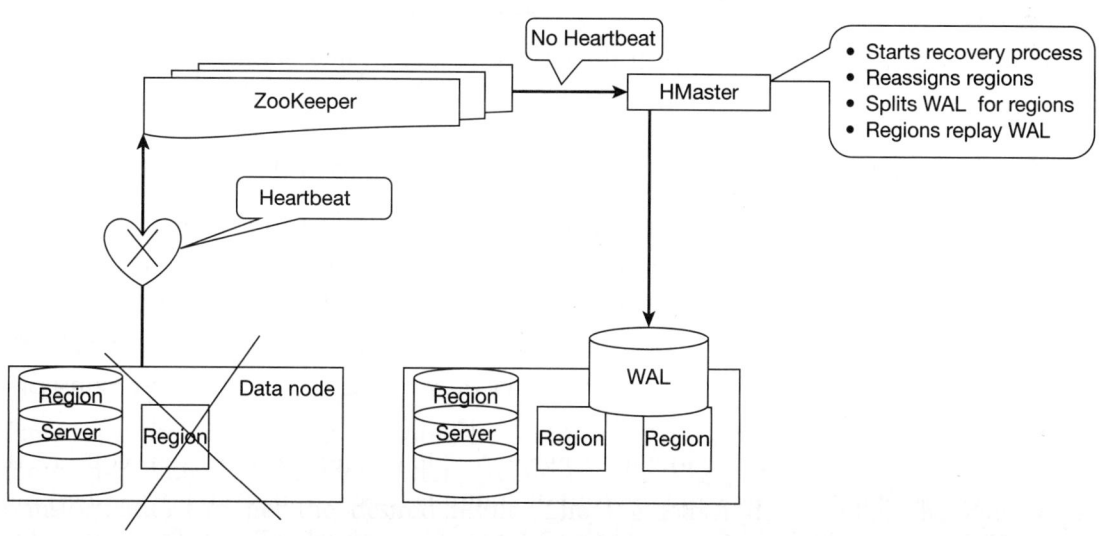

Figure 10.22 HBase data recovery

Write-Ahead Log (WAL) files contain a list of edits, where each edit represents a single put or delete. Edits are written chronologically, so the WAL file is added to the end to maintain persistence. If a failure occurs when the data is still in memory and has not persisted to an HFile, the WAL file is replayed to read the WAL, and add and sort the contained edits to the current MemStore. Finally, the MemStore is flushed to write changes to an HFile (Fig. 10.23).

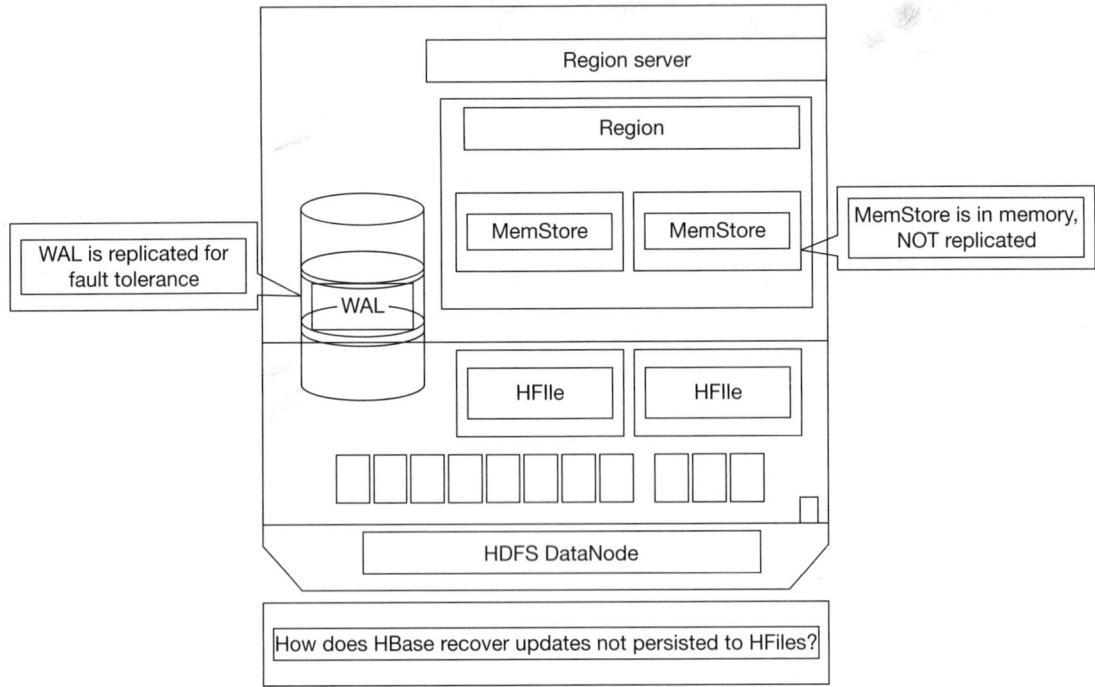

Figure 10.23 HBase Data Recovery: MemStore vs. HFile

10.8 HBase Coprocessor

The Coprocessor is a framework that makes running custom code on Region Server simple. We retrieve data from any data store (such as RDBMS or HBase) while dealing with it (in the case of RDBMS we may use query; and in the case of HBase, we use either Get or Scan). Filtering data (in RDBMS, criteria are inserted in the 'WHERE' clause; in HBase, filters are used) allows us to get only relevant data. After retrieving the relevant data, we may use it to complete our business calculations. This situation is ideal for "small data", such as a few thousand rows with a few columns. However, consider a situation where billions of rows and millions of columns exist. Then, even if we only want a few columns, we must still collect all the rows. In this case, it is preferable to relocate the processing to the data itself, much like a stored procedure (a better analogy is the MapReduce model). We can do this with the aid of a coprocessor.

HBase coprocessor is a framework that offers a library and runtime environment for executing user code within the HBase region server and master processes. It is based on Bigtable coprocessors. System coprocessors may be loaded globally on all tables and regions hosted by the region server. Table coprocessors allow the administrator to define which coprocessors should be loaded on all regions for a table on a per-table basis. The framework supports two separate extension elements to enable adequate flexibility for various coprocessor behaviors. The observer is similar to triggers in traditional databases and the endpoints.

Observers: The concept behind observers is that we can incorporate user code by customizing the coprocessor framework's upcall functions. The callback routines are performed from the core HBase code when specific events occur. The coprocessor framework takes care of activating callbacks during different HBase activities. The coprocessor merely needs to offer the appropriate additional or alternative functionality. Observers can perform authority management, priority setting, monitoring, and secondary index.

We now have three observer interfaces in HBase:

1. **Region Observer:** Hooks for data modification events like Get, Put, Delete, Scan, and so on are provided by Region Observer. Every table area has its instance of the region observer coprocessor, and their observations are limited to that region.
2. **WAL Observer:** It provides hooks for actions using the write-ahead log (WAL). This allows us to watch or listen to WAL writing and rebuilding events. In the context of WAL processing, a WAL Observer is used. Each region server has one of these contexts.
3. **Master Observer:** Hooks for DDL-type operations, such as table creation, deletion, and modification are provided by Master Observer. The Master Observer operates in the HBase master's context.

Endpoint: As previously stated, observers are similar to database triggers. On the other hand, endpoints are more powerful than stored procedures and are identical. A client can call the endpoint at any time. The endpoint implementation will then be carried out remotely in the target region or regions, with the results being sent to the client. The endpoint is a dynamic RPC extension interface. The endpoint implementation is installed on the server. The HBase RPC may then be used to call it. The client library provides convenient methods for calling such dynamic interfaces.

The observer enables clusters to act differently during client operations. Endpoints allow clusters to expand their capabilities and open new operation commands to client applications. The observer is similar to a trigger in an RDBMS and works primarily on the server side. The endpoint is identical to a stored procedure in an RDBMS and works mainly on the client side.

10.9 Setting HBase Environment

We can download HBase directly from the Apache website (http://www.apache.org/dyn/closer.cgi/hbase/). After we have downloaded the file, we have to decompress it to our hard drive. The HBase team recommends that HBase be installed on a UNIX/Linux environment; so if we use Windows, we need to download and install Cygwin and then run HBase.

```
hduser@laptop:~$ wget http://www-us.apache.org/dist/hbase/stable/hbase-1.2.4-bin.tar.gz
hduser@laptop:~$ tar xvzf hbase-1.2.4-bin.tar.gz
hduser@laptop:~$ sudo mv hbase-1.2.4 /usr/local/hbase/
```

To launch HBase, install Java from Oracle's website. Next, define an environment variable named "HBASE_HOME" that points to the root directory where we have decompressed HBase, and then execute the start-hbase.sh script from the HBase's bin directory.

```
~/.bashrc
export HBASE_HOME=/usr/local/hbase
export PATH=$PATH:$HBASE_HOME/bin
```

We need to run the file:

```
hduser@laptop:~$ source ~/.bashrc
```

It (HBase) will log output to the following directory:

```
$HBASE_HOME/logs/
```

Steps to configure Hive and HBase

```
-Install ZooKeeper, HBase, and Hive through Ambari.
-Install the required version of Hadoop.
Add all the required jars: Hive-hbase-handler.jar files are
available on the Hive client path.
-ZooKeeper jar
-Hbase server jar
-Hbase client jar
```

The Hortonworks Data Platform (HDP) can perform Hive and HBase integration. Once HBase is integrated with Hive using the StorageHandler, we can perform READ and WRITE operations on the HBase tables and access the data from both Hive and HBase. For this, first modify the hive-site.xml configuration file. Next, add the required path to the JARs. The complete list of JARs can be seen by running the command HBase MapReduce on the command line.

Note: The HDP version is included in each JAR name. The list of JARs will not work across the various HDP releases but can readily regenerate them.

```xml
<property>
<name>hive.aux.jars.path</name>
<value>
file:///usr/hdp/3.0.1.0-61/hbase/lib/commons-lang3-3.6.jar,
file:///usr/hdp/3.0.1.0-61/hbase/lib/hbase-zookeeper-2.0.0.3.0.1.0-61.jar,
file:///usr/hdp/3.0.1.0-61/hbase/lib/hbase-mapreduce-2.0.0.3.0.1.0-61.jar,
file:///usr/hdp/3.0.1.0-61/hbase/lib/jackson-annotations-2.9.5.jar,
file:///usr/hdp/3.0.1.0-61/hbase/lib/hbase-shaded-miscellaneous-2.1.0.jar,
file:///usr/hdp/3.0.1.0-61/hbase/lib/jackson-databind-2.9.5.jar,
file:///usr/hdp/3.0.1.0-61/hbase/lib/hbase-hadoop-compat-2.0.0.3.0.1.0-61.jar,
file:///usr/hdp/3.0.1.0-61/hbase/lib/hbase-metrics-2.0.0.3.0.1.0-61.jar,
file:///usr/hdp/3.0.1.0-61/hbase/lib/hbase-client-2.0.0.3.0.1.0-61.jar,
file:///usr/hdp/3.0.1.0-61/hbase/lib/hbase-protocol-shaded-2.0.0.3.0.1.0-61.jar,
file:///usr/hdp/3.0.1.0-61/hbase/lib/jackson-core-2.9.5.jar,
file:///usr/hdp/3.0.1.0-61/hbase/lib/protobuf-java-2.5.0.jar,
file:///usr/hdp/3.0.1.0-61/hbase/lib/hbase-shaded-netty-2.1.0.jar,
file:///usr/hdp/3.0.1.0-61/hbase/lib/metrics-core-3.2.1.jar,
file:///usr/hdp/3.0.1.0-61/hbase/lib/hbase-server-2.0.0.3.0.1.0-61.jar,
file:///usr/hdp/3.0.1.0-61/hbase/lib/hbase-hadoop2-compat-2.0.0.3.0.1.0-61.jar,
file:///usr/hdp/3.0.1.0-61/hbase/lib/hbase-metrics-api-2.0.0.3.0.1.0-61.jar,
file:///usr/hdp/3.0.1.0-61/hbase/lib/hbase-common-2.0.0.3.0.1.0-61.jar,
file:///usr/hdp/3.0.1.0-61/hbase/lib/hbase-protocol-2.0.0.3.0.1.0-61.jar,
file:///usr/hdp/3.0.1.0-61/hbase/lib/hbase-shaded-protobuf-2.1.0.jar,
file:///usr/hdp/3.0.1.0-61/hbase/lib/htrace-core4-4.2.0-incubating.jar,
file:///usr/hdp/3.0.1.0-61/zookeeper/zookeeper-3.4.6.3.0.1.0-61.jar
</value>
</property>
```

Starting the HBase and HBase Shell

After HBase has been started, it can interactively access the HBase Shell database, acting as a command interpreter for HBase. It is written in Ruby. Therefore, it is good practice if HBase administrative commands such as the HBase Shell, hbck, or bulk-load commands are run by the HBase user (typically HBase).

```
$hbase shell
```

HBase employs Hadoop files as a storage mechanism to store massive volumes of data. Master Servers and Regions Servers make up HBase. The data that will be stored in HBase will be organized into regions. These regions will also be divided up and kept on servers in different regions.

The programmer may create table schemas and data operations utilizing complete shell mode interaction with these shell commands. Whatever command we use will be reflected in the HBase data model. We employ HBase shell commands in operating system script interpreters like a Bash shell, the command interpreter for most Linux and Unix operating systems. Advanced versions of HBase provide shell commands and JRuby-style object-oriented table references. After successfully installing HBase on Hadoop, we get an interactive shell to execute various commands and perform several operations. Using these commands, we can perform multiple functions (Table 10.1) on data tables that give the client better data storage efficiencies and flexible interaction.

Table 10.1 HBase Data definition language

S.No	Command	Description
1	create	Creates a table
2	list	Lists all the tables in HBase
3	disable	Disables a table
4	is_disabled	Verifies whether a table is disabled
5	enable	Enables a table
6	is_enabled	Verifies whether a table is enabled
7	describe	Provides the description of a table
8	alter	Alters a table
9	exists	Verifies whether a table exists
10	drop	Drops a table from HBase
11	drop_all	Drops the tables matching the 'regex' given in the command

10.10 CREATING HBASE TABLES

HBase tables are different from relational database tables. HBase organizes all its data into tables where the table names are Strings. The create command in HBase is used to build a table. The table name and column family name are required fields when creating a table. Column families are used to group all the columns in HBase.

```
create '<table_name>', '<column_family_name>'
```

Example: Creating an HBase table

```
hbase(main):031:0> create 'students','students_data'
0 row(s) in 2.4850 seconds
=> Hbase::Table - students
```

10.11 LISTING ALL TABLES

Example: To list all tables created in HBase

```
hbase(main):003:0> list
TABLE
students
```

When you type this command into the HBase prompt, it displays a list of all HBase tables. The "List" command displays all of HBase's tables, both existing and newly constructed. The result in the above screen image presently displays the existing tables in HBase. We may filter the output values by supplying optional regular expression arguments to tables (Table 10.2).

Table 10.2 HBase data manipulation language

S.No	Command	Description
1	put	Puts a cell value at a specified column in a specified row in a particular table
2	get	Fetches the contents of a row or a cell
3	delete	Deletes a cell value in a table
4	deleteall	Deletes all the cells in a given row
5	scan	Scans and returns the table data
6	count	Counts and returns the number of rows in a table
7	truncate	Disables, drops, and recreates a specified table

10.12 Adding Data to a Table

Let us put the values of the first row into the student's table, as shown below.

```
put 'table name','row ','Column family:column name','new value'
```

Example: Adding data to a table

```
hbase(main):037:0> put 'students',1,'students_data:name','Joseph'
0 row(s) in 0.0240 seconds
hbase(main):038:0> put 'students',1,'students_data:city','Bengaluru'
0 row(s) in 0.0060 seconds
hbase(main):039:0> put 'students',1,'students_data:age','25'
0 row(s) in 0.0040 seconds
```

10.13 Getting a Row of Data

We can use the `get` command to acquire a single row of data at a time. The additional parameters include TIMERANGE, TIMESTAMP, VERSIONS, and FILTERS.

```
Syntax: get <'tablename'>, <'rowname'>, {< Additional parameters>}
```

Example:

```
hbase(main):008:0> get 'students', 'row1'
COLUMN                  CELL
 cf:a                   timestamp=1645181878, value=value1
1 row(s) in 0.1300 seconds
```

10.14 Scanning a Table

We can get data from HBase using a scan. The HBase Scan command can be executed with various other options or attributes such as TIMERANGE, FILTER, TIMESTAMP, LIMIT, MAXLENGTH, COLUMNS, CACHE, STARTROW, and STOPROW.
Example:

```
hbase(main):007:0> scan 'students'
ROW                    COLUMN+CELL
row1                   column=cf:a, timestamp=1609999899001, value=value1
row2                   column=cf:b, timestamp=1609999899001, value=value2
row3                   column=cf:c, timestamp=1609999899197, value=value3
3 row(s) in 0.1960 seconds
```

10.15 Counting the Number of Rows in a Table

We use the count command to see the total number of rows in a table.
Example:

```
hbase(main):007:0>count 'students'
3 row(s)
Took 0.67 seconds
```

10.16 Altering a Table

To make modifications to an existing table, use the `Alter` command. For example, this command can change the maximum number of cells in a column family, set and delete table scope operators, and delete a column family from a table.
Example: Altering the table by adding column

```
hbase(main):005:0> alter 'test_table', {NAME=> 'colFam2'}
Updating all regions with the new schema...
1/1 regions updated.
Done.
0 row(s) in 2.5210 seconds
```

Example: Altering a table by deleting column

```
hbase(main):013:0> alter 'test_table', 'delete'=> 'colFam2'
Updating all regions with the new schema...
1/1 regions updated.
Done.
0 row(s) in 2.4470 seconds
```

Example: Altering a table to add versions

```
hbase(main):013:0> alter 'test_table', 'delete'=> 'colFam2'
Updating all regions with the new schema...
1/1 regions updated.
Done.
0 row(s) in 2.4470 seconds
```

Example: Altering an HBase table to add Time To Live (TTL)

```
hbase(main):016:0> alter 'test_table', {NAME=> 'colFam1',TTL => 2000 }
Updating all regions with the new schema...
1/1 regions updated.
Done.
0 row(s) in 2.2140 seconds
```

Example: Altering an HBase table to enable Snappy COMPRESSION

```
hbase(main):017:0> alter 'test_table', {NAME=> 'colFam1',COMPRESSION=>'snappy'}
Updating all regions with the new schema...
1/1 regions updated.
Done.
0 row(s) in 2.2530 seconds
```

10.17 DELETING A TABLE ROW, COLUMN

```
hbase(main):006:0> delete 'students', '1', 'students_data:city',
1645182772
0 row(s) in 0.0060 seconds
```

Another command is the `deleteall` to delete all the cells in a row. The example shows how all elements of row 1 in table Personal is deleted.

```
hbase(main):006:0> delete 'students', '1', 'students_data:city',
1645182772
0 row(s) in 0.0060 seconds
```

10.18 DISABLING AND ENABLING A TABLE

Before we delete a table or change its settings, we need to disable the table first, using the `disable` command. Then, it is possible to re-enable it again using the `enable` command. There are two commands to disable a table in HBase: `disable` and `disable_all`. The command `disable` will only disable that table whose table name is mentioned, whereas `disable_all` will disable all the tables matching that regex. In the below example, the command `disable_all` will disable all the tables starting with p. So, if we have three tables like personal, payments, and passwords, all will get disabled.

```
hbase(main):009:0> disable 'students'
0 row(s) in 4.8950 seconds

Syntax: disable_all<"matching regex"
hbase(main):009:0> disable_all 'p.*'
0 row(s) in 1.235 seconds
```

To enable a table that was disabled, we use the `enable` command. Another variant is the `enable_all` command which enables all tables by matching the given regex.

```
hbase(main):010:0> enable 'students'
0 row(s) in 2.4350 seconds

Syntax:enable_all<"matching regex"
hbase(main):010:0> enable_all 'p.*'
```

10.19 Truncating and Dropping a Table

The `drop` command is used to truncate or drop a table in HBase. Before dropping a table in HBase, we first need to disable it. To drop or delete an HBase table, use the following commands: `drop` and `drop_all`.

Example:

```
is_disabled 'students'
true
0 row(s) in 0.0340 seconds
```

Then we can safely drop the table.

```
hbase(main):010:0>drop 'students'
0 row(s) in 1.03 seconds
```

Another command is the `drop_all`, which can be used to drop all tables matching the regex,

```
hbase> drop_all 't.*'
```

The `truncate` command is slightly different. This command disables the table, then drops it, and finally recreates the specified table.

```
hbase(main):011:0> truncate 'students'
Truncating 'one' table (it may take a while):
 - Disabling table...
 - Truncating table...
0 row(s) in 1.4742 seconds
```

To check if the table has been truncated, we can use the scan command again, to verify. Furthermore, we will get a table with zero rows.

```
hbase(main):017:0> scan 'students'
ROW              COLUMN + CELL
0 row(s) in 0.2010 seconds
```

10.20 Determining if Table Exists

Use the `if table exists` command to verify if the table is present in the database. Let us see the syntax usage with an example.

Example:

```
hbase(main):009:0> exists 'students'
Took 0.0711 seconds
=>true
```

10.21 Creating a Hive External Table Stored by HBase

The architecture of HBase allows us to read cells from specific rows and columns quickly, but it has a semi-structured nature that makes it challenging to work with. By mapping HBase tables as Hive tables, we can get the benefits of HiveQL (structured nature that we can query) and the speed benefits of HBase.

In HBase, the data is stored as rows inside tables. All rows have a row-key which is a unique identifier. In addition, all tables have one or more column families which contain different columns for different rows in the same table. The column families are dynamic in structure.

Hive allows us to create a table on HBase consisting of specific columns within a column family or as whole column families of a MAP column represented as key-value pairs. As with HDFS, Hive does not import the data from HBase. When a user queries an HBase table with Hive, it will be executed as a MapReduce job, and tasks will be performed using the HBase Java API. The combination of HBase and Hive offers significant advantages over using HBase alone. Querying in HBase can be difficult as HBase does not provide indexes. So, the user needs to query tables by their row-key, which is a slow process. Using Hive, the user can create an index over any column in an HBase table and efficiently query HBase on fields other than the row-key.

10.21.1 Defining an External Table over HBase Tables

Tables in Hive that use HBase as storage are defined as external tables. They use the same syntax as HDFS-stored tables. The data format need not be specified with HBase because Hive uses the HBase API to access data, and the internal data format need not be known. However, HBase tables must be declared using a specific storage handler that includes properties to identify the HBase table name. The below example shows a `create table` statement for accessing data in the HBase table called personal-events.

> CREATE EXTERNAL TABLE personal_events(rowkey STRING, data STRING)
> STORED BY 'org.apache.hadoop.hive.hbase.HBaseStorageHandler'
> WITH SERDEPROPERTIES ('hbase.columns.mapping' = ':key,cf1:data')
> TBLPROPERTIES ('hbase.table.name' = 'personal-events');

In the example, the row-key is mapped from the HBase table and one column from one-column family. The storage handler provides the key column for all HBase tables, and cf1:data indicates the data column in the cf1 column family. The clauses that need to be specified for external HBase tables are shown in Table 10.3.

Table 10.3 Defining an external table

STORED BY	This is a fixed value specified by org.apache.hadoop.Hive.hbase.HBaseStorageHandler for all HBase tables.
WITH SERDEPROPERTIES	The source columns from HBase have been specified in the hbase.columns.mapping property. They are positional, which means that the first column in the table definition is mapped to the first column in the property list.
TBLPROPERTIES	The source table name is in the hbase.table.name property. The user can provide a schema name.

HBase stores all data as byte arrays. So, it is the user's job to decode the arrays into a suitable format. When the data types for columns are declared in Hive, the encoded byte array must be interpreted in HBase to the type specified.

10.21.2 Mapping Specific HBase Columns and Column Families

To minimize storage and maximize access performance, tables in HBase should include just one- or two-column families with short names. But in Hive, we can map individual columns within column families as primitive data types or map the entire column family as a MAP. For example, we use two-column families in my personal-events table in HBase, where − ed specifies the event data, and mp defines the metadata properties.

```
CREATE EXTERNAL TABLE personal_events(rowkey STRING, eventName STRING, receivedAt STRING, payload STRING, metadata MAP<string, string>)
STORED BY 'org.apache.hadoop.hive.hbase.HBaseStorageHandler'
WITH SERDEPROPERTIES ('hbase.columns.mapping' = ':key,ed:n,ed:t,ed:p,mp:')
TBLPROPERTIES ('hbase.table.name' = 'personal-events');
```

Column mappings are supplied as a comma-separated string in which columns are named using the {column family}:{column name} syntax, and whole families are named using the {column family}: syntax.

Table 10.4 shows the HBase source for each of the Hive columns.

Table 10.4 HBase Source for each of the Hive columns

Hive Column	HBase Column Family	HBase Column
row key	–	–
eventName	ed	n
timestamp	ed	t
payload	de	p
metadata	mp	–

Using this mapping, the user can read HBase data in Hive in a more structured format and utilize the higher-level HiveQL functionality to derive more meaningful and valuable information from the data. For example, the table below shows how raw data looks in HBase while using the HBase Shell to read all the cells with row-key rk1 in the table personal-events.

The timestamps shown are internal fields that record the last modification time of the cell value in HBase. The cell values are all stored as strings, simplifying interoperability between HBase and other tools. For example, the table below shows the same row fetched through Hive.

```
hbase(main):011:0> get 'personal-events', 'rk1'
COLUMN              CELL
ed:n                timestamp=1643355250, value=power.on
ed:p                timestamp=1643355318, value={"some":"json"}
ed:t                timestamp=1643355355, value=1453562878
mp:d                timestamp=1643355337, value=device-id
mp:u                timestamp=1643355356, value=elton
mp:v                timestamp=1643355347, , value=1.0.0
```

10.21.3 Working Hive with HBase (Integration)

The fundamental distinction is that HBase handles CRUD and search queries, whereas Hive handles analytical queries. However, both technologies complement each other as they are strongly interconnected with HDFS and are frequently used with Hadoop.

Sqoop Exports and Imports: Sqoop is one such tool that lets the user automate importing and exporting data from a database. As Sqoop works on the MapReduce framework, it provides a parallel fault-tolerant mechanism. We can also use Sqoop to import data directly into Hive or into a table in HBase, as it supports HBase.

Importing to HBase: All data imported to HBase is converted to string format in the UTF-8 format. There are two mandatory options we must specify when using the Sqoop import command to import data into HBase using Sqoop:

- **hbase-table:** Specifies the table's name in HBase to import the data.
- **column-family:** Specifies which column family Sqoop imports the data from the table.

The example shows how you can import the table 'personal' into an already existing HBase table with the same name and the column family:

```
sqoop import --connect jdbc:mysql://mysql.example.com/sqoop --username sqoop --password sqoop --table personal --hbase-table personal --column-family
```

If the target table and column family do not exist, the Sqoop job will exit with an error. The target table and column family must be created before running an import. The user should specify `–hbase-create-table` so that Sqoop creates the target table and column family if they do not exist, using the default parameters from the HBase configuration.

Sqoop needs to identify which RDBMS column is used as a row-key column in the HBase table. There are three ways to determine the row-key column in the HBase table:

1. The column name is specified by default in the --split-by option.
2. By using the primary key of the table, if it is available.
3. The --hbase-row-key parameter overrides both the --split-by option and the table's primary key.

10.22 ADVANCED INDEXING IN HBASE

In HBase, there are no indexes. The row-key, column family, and column qualifier are all stored in sorted order for byte arrays. Implementing a secondary index for a distributed system like HBase is not a straightforward task. Let us look at two approaches to designing a secondary index.

1. **Client-side implementation**: Here, the client separately handles the index metadata. During writing, the index metadata is created and written with actual data. During the scan, the metadata is first to read to the client-side, and then the actual data is read back from the table.
2. **Server-side implementation**: Here, the server only handles the index metadata during writes and reads.

10.23 HIndex

Recently Huawei released an open-source implementation for HBase secondary indexing [https://github.com/Huawei-Hadoop/hindex. Also, see the issue HBASE-9203]. Huawei used the approach of server-side implementation and also HBase's Co-processor (CP) feature, so the implementation is 100% pluggable with minimal changes to HBase. First, the index metadata is stored in an HBase table, and the metatable is created using the Coprocessor (CP) hooks at the HMaster side. Then, the metadata is written to the index table using the CP hooks at the region server side. Finally, the CP hooks extract the table data and create the metadata for the index table.

When an index table is created, it has regions that have been balanced across the cluster. When the CP hook has to write/read index data, it will be inefficient to read/write it across servers. So, performing an RPC call from a CP hook (which executes along with an RPC) as an anti-pattern is usually discouraged. If we read/write index data into the same Region Server, we can avoid the extra RPC cost. In other words, if we can make a relation between the regions in the main table and index table, and if we can put these regions in the same Region Server, then it is good. HIndex implementation allows us to achieve this.

HIndex maintains a per-region index and will create an index table with the same number of regions as the actual table and having the same Row-Key (RK) range. It uses a custom load balancer on top of the HBase load balancer to maintain the regions. A split or movement for the actual table regions will take similar action for the index regions (CP hooks). There will be only one index table per actual table, irrespective of the number of indices on it, and all indexed metadata will be stored in this single index table.

10.23.1 Writing Data with Index

The Coprocessor (CP) creates the index table Row-Key (RK):

Index table rowkey (RK) = region start key + index name + indexed column(s) value(s) + user table Row Key (RK).

The actual table Row-Key (RK) is added to the index table Row-Key (RK). The indexed column value(s) come(s) first to fetch only the needed data from the index table during a scan with the indexed column value/value range. Then, it stores the entire index metadata in a single index table. It adds the index name as part of the Row-Key (RK).

The Row-Key (RK) starts with the region start key, and when the index is on more than one column, all those column values are appended to the Row-Key (RK). The Put object will normally be created using the HBase client APIs. The CP implementation will decide what index metadata to store and create and store.

10.23.2 Reading Data with Index

A scan on the user table would also create a scanner on the index table. Based on the condition on the indexed column, the user can fetch the required data from the index table. The actual table Row-Key (RK) will be extracted from the index data, and the CP will exact rows in the actual table. This action avoids the read of each row from the actual table and filtering is done based on the condition. HIndex is intelligent enough to decide whether to use index data for a particular scan. If multiple indices are on the table, it can determine what index(es) to use for a specific scan. The scan object at the client-side can be normal as before. The CP hooks inspect the SingleColumnValueFilter(s) passed in Scan to decide the index(es).

10.23.3 HIndex Features

- Multiple indexes on the table
- Multi-column index
- Index on the part of a column value
- Usage of the index on user table scan with column value/range of values on indexed columns
- Bulk loading data to an indexed table.

```
<property>
<name>hbase.coprocessor.master.classes</name>
<value>org.apache.hadoop.hbase.index.coprocessor.master.IndexMasterObserver</value>
</property>
<property>
<name>hbase.coprocessor.region.classes</name>
<value>org.apache.hadoop.hbase.index.coprocessor.regionserver.IndexRegionObserver</value>
</property>
<property>
<name>hbase.coprocessor.wal.classes</name>
<value>org.apache.hadoop.hbase.index.coprocessor.wal.IndexWALObserver</value>
</property>
```

10.24 HBase Admin API

A class that represents the Admin (Table 10.5) in HBase is HBaseAdmin. It is associated with the org.apache. For example, Hadoop.hbase.client package performs an administrator's task using this class.

Table 10.5 Methods in HBase Admin API

1. void createTable(HTableDescriptor desc)	This method is used to create a new table.
2. void createTable(HTableDescriptor desc, byte[][] splitKeys)	This method creates a new table with an initial set of empty regions defined by the specified split keys.
3. void delete column(byte[] tableName, String columnName)	This method is used to delete a column from a table.
4. void deleteColumn(String tableName, String columnName)	This method is also used to delete a column from a table.
5. void deleteTable(String tableName)	The method deletes a table.

10.25 HBase Client API

This section elaborates on utilizing the HBase Java client API to execute CRUD operations on HBase tables. HBase is a Java-based database with a Java Native API. As a result, Data Manipulation Language may be accessed programmatically (DML).

10.25.1 Put Method

This belongs to the org.apache.Hadoop.hbase.client package and is used to insert data into rows and columns in an HBase table.

```
put '<name_space:table_name>', '<row_key>' '<cf:column_name>', '<value>'
```

10.25.2 Get Method

This belongs to the org.apache.Hadoop.hbase. The client package is used to read and retrieve data from the HBase table.

```
Syntax: get '<namespace>:<table_name>', '<row_key>', '<column_key>'
```

10.26 Using HBase in Hadoop Applications

HBase technology has found applications in high-performance and high-reliability distributed systems. The goal of HBase is to build large-scale structured storage clusters consisting of thousands of rows and columns on inexpensive PC Servers. It is different from MapReduce's batch computing framework, which works offline. HBase provides random-access storage and retrieval data platform and overcomes the shortcomings of HDFS, which cannot access data randomly.

In Fig. 10.24, the various layers of the Hadoop 2.0 ecosystem are shown. HBase is located on top of the structured storage layer HDFS, which provides high-reliability storage support for HBase. The MapReduce environment (Fig. 10.25) provides high-performance batch processing for HBase. At the same time, ZooKeeper provides a failover mechanism for HBase. Pig and Hive provide HBase high-level language support for data processing. Finally, Sqoop provides an RDBMS data import function, making it convenient to migrate business data from a traditional database to HBase.

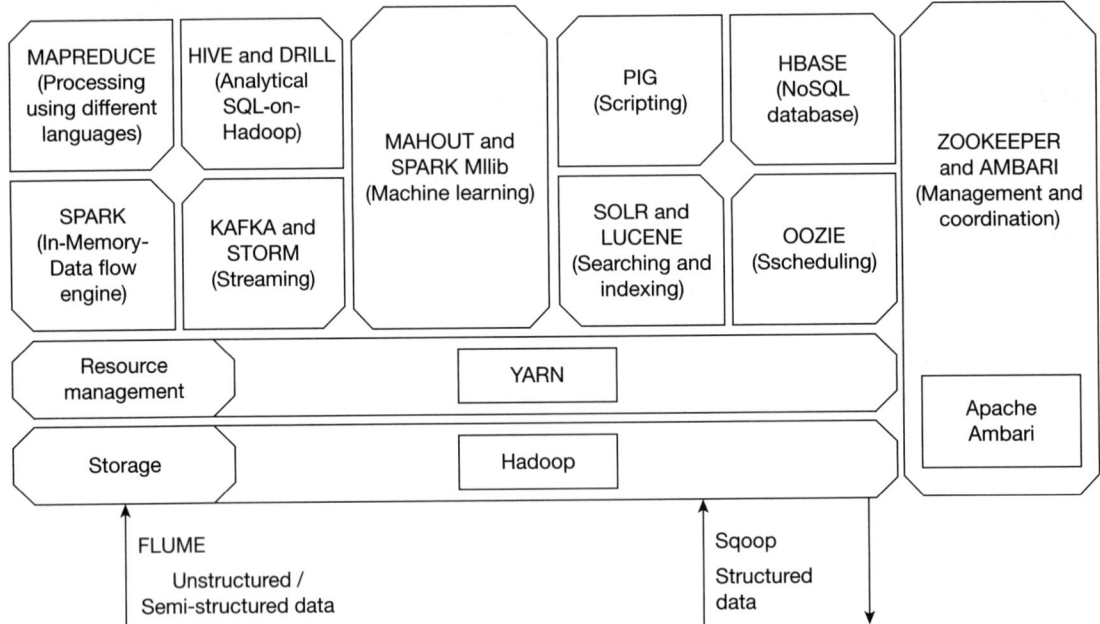

Figure 10.24 Various layers of Hadoop 2.0 ecosystem

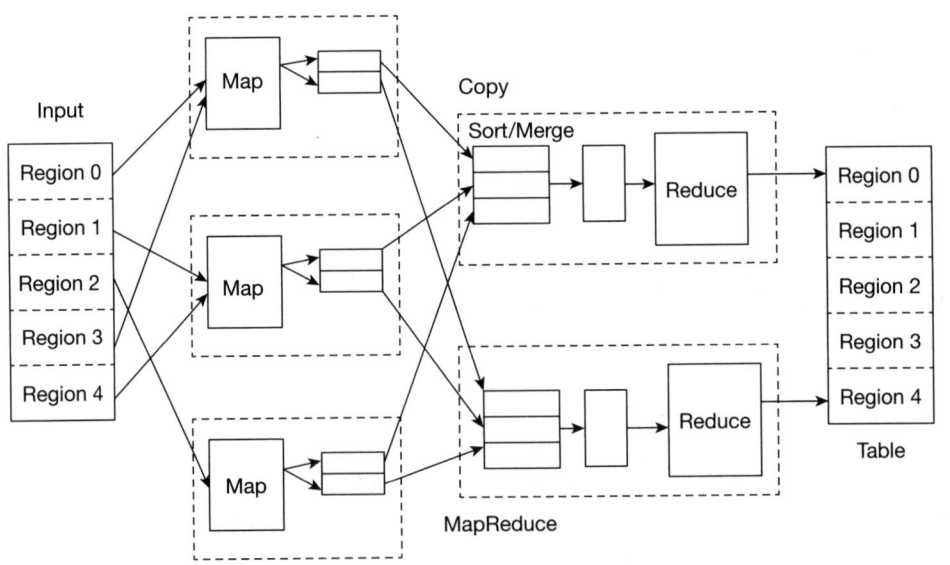

Figure 10.25 MapReduce and HBase

When comparing HBase and HDFS, we can see that the relationship between Table and Region in HBase is comparable to that between File and Block in HDFS. TableInputFormat and TableOutputFormat are HBase APIs for dealing with MapReduce. With HBase, data tables can be directly used as input and output for Hadoop MapReduce, which helps develop MapReduce applications. Thus, HBase users can pay attention to the processing instead of focusing on minor details.

10.27 HBase Advanced Usage

10.27.1 Filters

HBase filters (Fig. 10.26) can significantly enhance working with data stored in tables. The two essential read functions for HBase are `get()` and `scan()`. Both functions support direct access to data or a start and end key, respectively. In addition, the user can limit the data retrieved by progressively adding limiting selectors such as column families, column qualifiers, timestamps, ranges, or version numbers to the query.

Figure 10.26 shows how the filters are configured, then serialized over the network, and then applied to the Server.

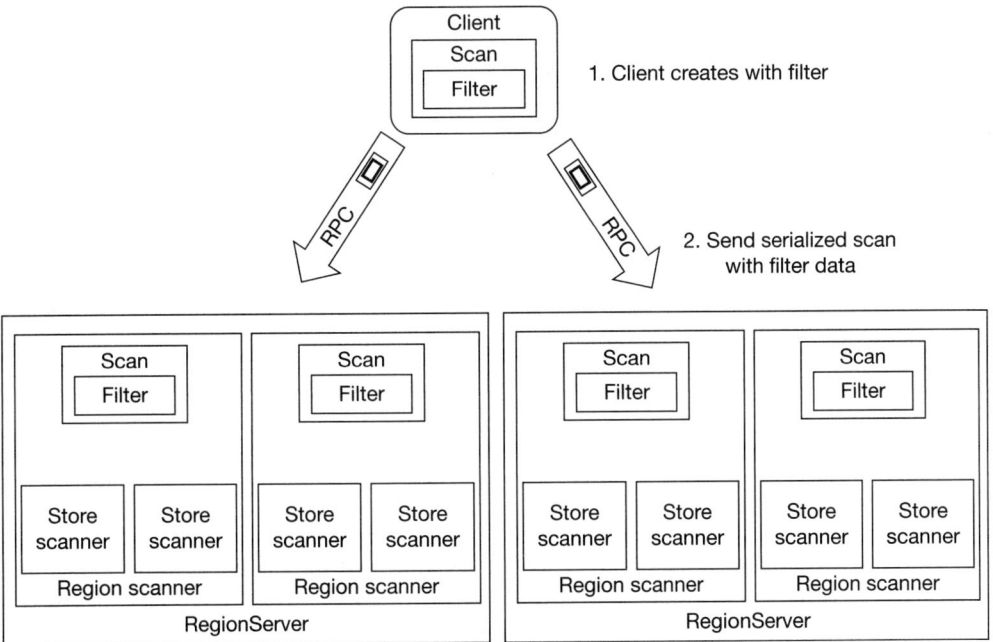

Figure 10.26 HBase filter

10.27.2 The Filter Hierarchy

Filters are commonly used from the HBase Shell for testing and debugging. In parenthesis, HBase filters accept zero or more arguments. If the argument is a string, it is surrounded by single quotes ('string'). Boilerplate code, or simply boilerplate, in computer programming refers to sections of code that are repeatedly used with little or no variation. To avoid repeating boilerplate code in each of the actual filter classes, the abstract Filter Base class implements an empty shell or skeleton. Although most concrete filter classes are direct descendants of FilterBase, a few require an intermediary ancestor class. However, they all operate in the same manner by creating a new instance of the filter and handing it to the Get or Scan instances, using:

> setFilter(filter)

While the filter instance initializes itself, the parameters for whatever the filter is designed to do, need to be supplied. A particular subset of filters, based on CompareFilter, asks the user for at least two specific parameters since the base class uses them to perform its task.

10.27.3 Comparison Operators

A Compare Filter (Table 10.6) first adds one more feature to the base FilterBase class using a comparison operator. Therefore, this filter needs a user-supplied operator, namely the compare(), defining how the comparison result is interpreted.

Table 10.6 HBase comparative operators

Operator	Description
LESS	Match values less than the provided one
LESS_OR_EQUAL	Match values less than or equal to the provided one
EQUAL	Do an exact match on the value and the provided one
NOT_EQUAL	Includes everything that does not match the provided one
GREATER_OR_EQUAL	Match values that are equal or greater than the provided one
GREATER	Only include values greater than the provided one
NO OP	Exclude everything

10.27.4 Comparators

The second type that needs to be added to the CompareFilter-related classes is a comparator to compare the various values and keys differently. They are derived from WritableByteArrayComparable, which implements Writable and Comparable.

10.27.5 Comparison Filters

The first type of filter implementation is the comparison filter. They take the comparison operator and comparator instance described earlier.

> CompareFilter(CompareOp valueCompareOp, WritableByteArrayComparable valueComparator)

- **RowFilter:** This filter gives the user the ability to filter data based on row-keys.
- **FamilyFilter:** This filter is similar to the RowFilter, and compares the column families available in a row instead of the row-key. Using the many operators and comparators provided, the user can filter what is included in the retrieved data at the column-family level.
- **QualifierFilter:** This filter allows the user to filter specific columns from the table.
- **ValueFilter:** The ValueFilter includes only columns that have a specific value. When the ValueFilter is combined with the RegexStringComparator, it can filter using powerful expression syntax.
- **DependentColumnFilter:** The DependentColumn filter is a reference column and controls how other columns are filtered. The timestamp of the reference column is used, and it includes all other columns that have the same timestamp.

10.28 Dedicated Filters

The second type of filter is directly on FilterBase, and because these filters filter out complete rows; they are only helpful when doing scan operations. The `Forget()` calls filter is too restrictive and would result in a very harsh filter approach that includes the whole row or nothing.

SingleColumnValueFilter: This filter is used when we have exactly one column that decides if an entire row should be returned or not.

SingleColumnValueExcludeFilter: The SingleColumnValueFilter is extended to provide a slightly different semantics: the reference column is handed into the constructor and is omitted from the result.

PrefixFilter: The PrefixFilter will return all rows that match this prefix to the user. The prefix needs to be specified when instantiating the filter instance.

PageFilter: It is possible to paginate through rows by employing this filter. When the instance is created, the user must specify a PageSize parameter, which controls how many rows per page should be returned.

KeyOnlyFilter: The KeyOnlyFilter works by applying the filter's ability to modify the processed columns and cells as they pass through. The filter applies the KeyValue.convertToKeyOnly(boolean) call.

FirstKeyOnlyFilter: This filter will allow the user to access the first column as sorted implicitly by HBase in each row.

InclusiveStopFilter: The start row's row borders are inclusive, whereas the stop row's row bounds are exclusive. Therefore, the user can use this filter to overcome the stop row semantics, including the specified stop row.

TimestampsFilter: This filter provides the means when the user needs fine-grained control over what versions are included in the scan result.

ColumnCountGetFilter: We can use this filter only to retrieve a specific maximum number of columns per row. The filter's function Object() { [native code] } can be used to specify the number of columns per row.

ColumnPaginationFilter: This filter is similar to the PageFilter but it can page through rows. It skips all columns until the offset number is reached and includes limit columns. Its constructor has two parameters, namely, limit and offset.

ColumnPrefixFilter: This filter is similar to the PrefixFilter. While the PrefixFilter filters the row-key prefixes, this filter does the same for columns. The output includes all columns with the specified prefix.

RandomRowFilter: This filter allows the user to include random rows in the result. The RandomRowFilter uses a constructor named chance, which represents a value between 0.0 and 1.0.

10.29 DECORATING FILTERS

These filters can help modify or extend the behavior of a filter to gain additional control over the returned data.

SkipFilter: This filter wraps and extends a given filter to exclude a whole row. So, when the filter indicates that a column in a row is omitted, the entire row is skipped.

WhileMatchFilter: This decorating filter works like the previous one but aborts the entire scan once a piece of information is filtered. It works by checking the wrapped filter, seeing that it skips a row by its key or a column of a row.

Filter List: The filter list is used to have several filters in the user application. As a result, it reduces the data returned.

Custom Filters: The user can also implement his filter and the above-supplied filters in HBase.

We can implement the Filter interface or extend the provided FilterBase class. Extending the FilterBase class allows default implementations for all method members of the interface.

10.30 COUNTERS

Many applications that collect statistics (such as clicks or views in online advertising) store the data in log files which would later be analyzed. Using counters allows switching to live accounting preceding the delayed batch processing step. HBase has a mechanism to treat columns as counters where users need not initialize counters. When we use a new counter for the first time, the columns are assumed to be zero (a column qualifier does not yet exist). If we specify one as the result of the first increment call to a new counter, it will return one or the increment of the counter value.

10.30.1 Single Counters

The first type of increment call is for single counters only, where the user needs to specify the exact column to be used.

```
HTable table = new HTable(conf, "counters");   1
long cnt1 =
table.incrementColumnValue(Bytes.toBytes("20110101"),
Bytes.toBytes("daily"), Bytes.toBytes("hits"), 1);   2
long cnt2 =
table.incrementColumnValue(Bytes.toBytes("20110101"),
Bytes.toBytes("daily"), Bytes.toBytes("hits"), 1);   3
long current =
table.incrementColumnValue(Bytes.toBytes("20110101"),
Bytes.toBytes("daily"), Bytes.toBytes("hits"), 0);   4
long cnt3 =
table.incrementColumnValue(Bytes.toBytes("20110101"),
Bytes.toBytes("daily"), Bytes.toBytes("hits"), -1);
```

10.30.2 Multiple Counters

We can also use multiple counters to increment counters using the `increment()` call of HTable, which works similar to the CRUD-type operations.

Result increment (Increment class) throws IOException.

We must also create an instance of the Increment class and fill it with the relevant details like counter coordinates. The constructors provided by this class are:

```
Increment() {}

Increment(byte[] row)

Increment(byte[] row, RowLock rowLock)
```

When instantiating an increment, we must specify the row. This creates a row containing all the counters that will be incremented by the next call to `increase()`. In addition, rowLock is an optional argument that defines a custom row lock instance, providing the user complete control over the function (for example, if the user wants to make a few changes to the same row while protecting it from other authors' revisions).

10.31 COPROCESSORS

The HBase coprocessor feature (Fig. 10.27) allows the user to move part of the computation to where the data lives. A coprocessor enables the user to run an arbitrary code directly on each region server. It runs the code for each location separately, giving the user a trigger-like functionality similar to stored procedures in RDBMS. The user does not have to take specific actions from the client-side, as the framework handles the distributed nature transparently.

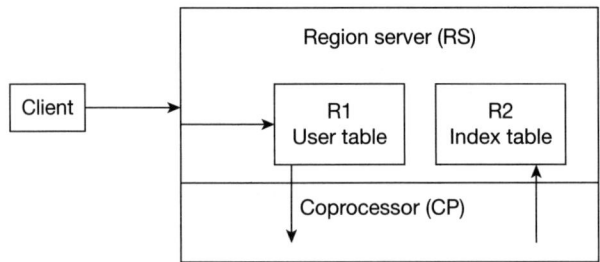

Figure 10.27 HBase coprocessor

10.31.1 The Coprocessor Class

All coprocessor classes are based on this interface, which defines the primary contract and facilitates management by the framework itself. The interface provides two enumerations, namely, priority and state, used throughout the framework. In addition, the coprocessor interface offers two calls – start and stop.

```
void start(CoprocessorEnvironment env) throws IOException;
void stop(CoprocessorEnvironment env) throws IOException;
```

The coprocessor interface calls the two methods `start()` and `stop()` when the coprocessor class is started and eventually when it is stopped. The CoprocessorEnvironment instance retains the state across the lifespan of the coprocessor instance.

10.31.2 Coprocessor Loading

Coprocessors can be loaded in several different methods. First, the user can specify whether coprocessors should be loaded statically or dynamically while the cluster is running. The static approach uses the configuration files and table schemas (Fig. 10.28).

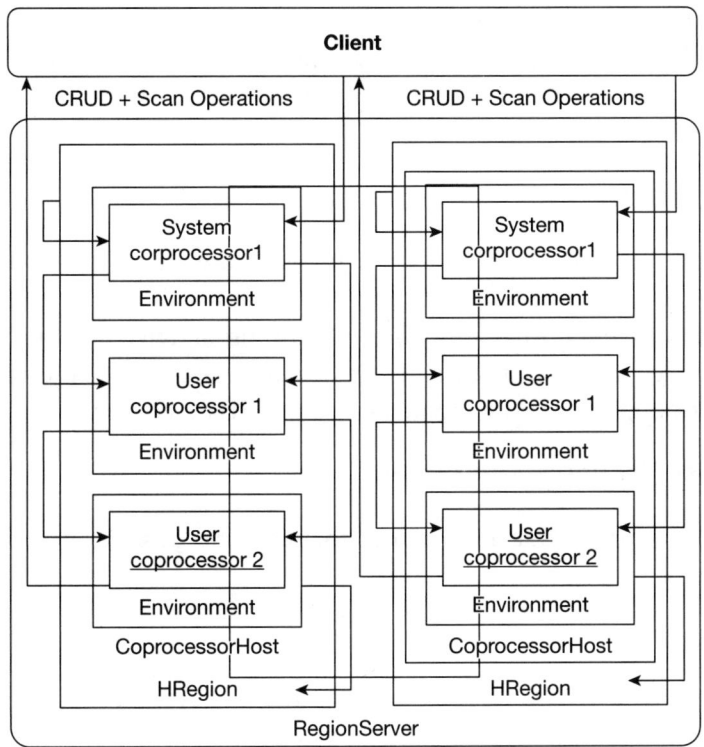

Figure 10.28 HBase CRUD and Scan operation

10.31.3 Loading from the Configuration

The user can also configure globally which coprocessors are loaded when HBase starts, by adding one or more coprocessors to the hbase-site.xml configuration file:

```
<property>
<name>hbase.coprocessor.region.classes</name>
<value>coprocessor.RegionObserverExample,
coprocessor.AnotherCoprocessor</value>
</property>
<property>
<name>hbase.coprocessor.master.classes</name>
<value>coprocessor.MasterObserverExample</value>
</property>
<property>
<name>hbase.coprocessor.wal.classes</name>
<value>coprocessor.WALObserverExample,
bar.foo.MyWALObserver</value>
</property>
```

The table descriptor is used to define what coprocessors are to be loaded. Here, the coprocessors are loaded for table regions (i.e., by region servers). Thus, we can use the approach to load using the table descriptor only for region-related coprocessors and not for Master or WAL-related ones.

10.32 HTABLEPOOL

Rather than establishing an HTable instance for each user request, it is more efficient to construct one once and utilize it. The main reason for this is that building an HTable instance is a relatively expensive and time-consuming activity. Instead, we can use the HTablePool class to construct the instance at startup and use it for the duration. It serves the purpose of pooling client API instances into an HBase cluster.

10.33 HBASE SECURITY AND GRANT

There are three commands that HBase uses for security: `grant`, `revoke`, and `user_permission`.

10.33.1 `grant`

The `grant` command grants specific rights such as reading, writing, executing and administering a table to a particular user. We can grant zero or more privileges to a user from the set of RWXCA, where

    R - represents read privilege.
    W - represents write privilege.
    X - represents execute privilege.
    C - represents creating privilege.
    A - represents admin privilege.

Example:

```
hbase(main):018:0> grant 'Hbuser1', 'RWXCA'
```

10.33.2 `revoke`

Use the `revoke` command to revoke a user's access permissions to a table. Its syntax is as follows:

```
hbase(main):006:0> revoke 'Hbuser1'
```

10.33.3 `user_permission`

This command displays a list of all permissions for a specific table. The syntax of `user_permission` is as follows:

```
hbase>user_permission 'table name'
```

10.34 HBASE VS. HDFS

Table 10.7 compares HBase with HDFS.

Table 10.7 HBase vs. HDFS

S.No	Hadoop Distributed File System (HDFS)	HBase
1.	HDFS is a distributed file system that follows a master-slave architecture and stores data across the cluster.	HBase (Hadoop Database) is a non-relational database built on the HDFS.
2.	HDFS components are master nodes and slave nodes.	HBase has an HBase Master, Region Server, Region, and ZooKeeper.
3.	It provides high latency batch processing.	It offers low-latency random access to single rows from billions of records.
4.	It provides only sequential access to data.	HBase uses Hash tables internally, and it stores the data in an indexed HDFS file.

10.35 APPLICATIONS OF HBASE

- RDBMS becomes slow when the data becomes large. On the other hand, HBase can store vast amounts of data that require fast reads and writes.
- HBase can be used where regular, consistent insertion and overwriting of data is needed. For example, they can use HBase for banking applications that require real-time data updates in ATMs.
- Facebook uses HBase because it needs a system to handle an ever-growing, rarely accessed dataset or a dataset that is highly volatile. HBase also provides the advantage of storing millions of rows and columns on top of clusters of commodity hardware.

SUMMARY

HBase is a distributed non-relational database management system built on the Hadoop file system. It is an open-source project and can process large volumes of data. HBase is written in Java and supports writing applications in Apache Avro, REST, and Thrift. HBase is a database that sits atop the Hadoop File System, providing read and write access to store data directly in HDFS or through HBase.

HBase allows scaling in both linear and modular forms. It provides a thrift and restful gateway and web service gateways for integrating and accessing HBase, besides Java code (HBase Java APIs) for accessing and working with HBase.

HDFS is internally distributed and automatically recovered via multiple block allocation and replications. HBase operates on top of HDFS; thus, it is also automatically retrieved.

The HBase architecture has three main components: 1. HMaster, 2. Region Server, 3. ZooKeeper.

The client contacts the HMaster. The HMaster allocates regions and load balancing. The Region Server serves the data to read and write by interacting with HDFS, and the Apache ZooKeeper monitors the system.

HMaster: The master's responsibilities include post-coordinating with the servers in the region. Its responsibilities include allocating regions during launch, reassigning regions for recovery, and load balancing.

Region Server: The Region Server comprises all the Hadoop cluster's machines. The Region Server has various minor components such as the region, Hlog (H File), Store, MemStore, WAL, and various other files.

Regions: HBase uses regions as a database, and it uses WAL (Write-Ahead Log) as a technique to store logs. WAL's most significant function is catastrophe recovery.

Block Cache: Block Cache resides on the Region Server and stores the frequently read data in the memory.

LruBlockCache: This default implementation caches the data blocks in the JVM heap. Single-access, multi-access, and in-memory are the three categories.

SlabCache: Using DirectByteBuffers, this approach allocates memory outside the JVM heap. The region in which a specific block will be put is determined by its size. Two sections are allocated by default, occupying 80% and 20% respectively, of the total off-heap cache capacity.

BucketCache: This implementation may be set to one of three modes: heap, off-heap, or file. The BucketCache handles "buckets" of memory for storing cached blocks, regardless of the operating mode.

MemStore is the write cache that stores all the incoming data before committing it to the disk or permanent memory. MemStore stores recently added data and acts as an in-memory cache by storing recently added data.

HFile: When the MemStore has acquired enough data, the complete ordered dataset is written to a new HDFS HFile file. For each Column Family, HBase produces an HFile to contain the details of Cell Key-Value data. Because Key-Value is regularly moved from the MemStore to the hard drive, HFiles will continue to occur over time.

ZooKeeper is a distributed coordinator in HBase for region assignments and is used to recover any region server crashes by loading them onto functional region servers. It helps maintain the server state inside the cluster. It keeps track of settings and synchronizes data across several machines.

HBase is a distributed and scalable environment that can work with Big Data. The NoSQL database runs on top of Hadoop. It can leverage the Hadoop Distributed File System (HDFS) and benefit from Hadoop's MapReduce programming model. It can host large tables with billions of rows with potentially millions of columns and runs on commodity hardware.

HBase is a robust database that blends real-time querying capabilities and batch processing through MapReduce. The advantage of using HBase is that we can query records and derive aggregate analytic reports across massive data.

An HBase table can scale up to billions of rows and many columns based on requirements. Therefore, this table allows the advantage of storing terabytes of data in it. In addition, the HBase table supports high read and write throughput at low latency.

There are three design guidelines (Conciseness, Uniqueness, Data distribution) to consider when deciding on an HBase key for a table:

Conciseness: Because every data value in HBase is saved as a Key-Value Pair, short names for column family and column qualifier are suggested. A single byte representing an English alphabet may be chosen as a name for a column family. However, the number of column qualifiers can be determined by the number of bytes used. In addition, we should create the HBase key's row-key component compactly.

Uniqueness: It is essential to double-check that the row-key element of the HBase Key uniquely identifies your dataset.

Data distribution: Data is distributed across the HBase cluster based on row-key. Our row-key architecture must permit data to be distributed across the cluster. If we do not distribute the data uniformly across the cluster, scalability and performance would be harmed, as just a few nodes in the cluster would have the data.

Hot-spotting: We know that rows in HBase are sorted lexicographically by row-key. This row-key design is optimized for scans, allowing the user to store related rows or rows that need to be read together, near each other. On the other hand, poorly constructed row-keys are a common source of hot-spotting. When a massive quantity of client traffic is routed to one node or only a few nodes of a cluster, this is known as hot-spotting.

Salting refers to adding random data to the beginning of a row-key. It has nothing to do with cryptography. Instead, salting refers to adding a randomly assigned prefix to the row-key to make it sort differently than it would otherwise.

Hashing: When we have the data represented by the string identifier, it is better to hash the string identifier of the HBase table row-key. A deterministic hash allows the client to reassemble the whole row-key and obtain the relevant row using a `Get` operation.

HBase replication is a technique for copying data across HBase instances. It may be used as a disaster recovery solution and can help to increase HBase layer availability.

When a Region Server fails, the crashed regions become unavailable until detection and recovery have taken place. ZooKeeper detects node failure when it stops receiving region server heartbeats.

HBase coprocessor is a framework that offers a library and runtime environment for executing user code within the HBase region server and master processes. It is based on Bigtable coprocessors.

The concept behind observers is that we can incorporate user code by customizing the coprocessor framework's upcall functions. The callback routines are performed from the core HBase code when specific events occur.

Region Observer: Hooks for data modification events like Get, Put, Delete, Scan, and so on are provided by Region Observer. Every table area has its instance of the Region Observer coprocessor, and their observations are limited to that region.

WAL Observer: Provides hooks for actions using the write-ahead log (WAL). This allows us to watch or listen to WAL writing and rebuilding events. WAL Observer is used in the context of WAL processing. Each region server has one of these contexts.

Master Observer: Provides hooks for DDL-type operations, such as table creation, deletion, and modification. The Master Observer operates in the HBase master's context.

Endpoints are more powerful than stored procedures and are identical. A client can call the endpoint at any time. The endpoint implementation will then be carried out remotely in the target region or regions, with the results being sent to the client.

Observer enables clusters to act differently during client operations. Endpoints allow clusters to expand their capabilities and open new operation commands to client applications. The observer is similar to a trigger in an RDBMS and works primarily on the server-side. The endpoint is identical to a stored procedure in an RDBMS and works mainly on the client-side.

HBase employs Hadoop files as a storage mechanism to store massive volumes of data. Master Servers and Regions Servers make up HBase. The data stored in HBase is organized into regions. These regions are also divided and kept on different region servers.

HBase tables are different from relational database tables. HBase organizes all its data into tables where the table names are Strings. The `create` command in HBase is used to build a table. The table name and column family name are required fields when creating a table. Column families are used to group all the columns in HBase.

The architecture of HBase allows us to read cells from specific rows and columns quickly, but it has a semi-structured nature that makes it challenging to work with. By mapping HBase tables as Hive tables, we can get the benefits of HiveQL (structured nature that we can query) and the speed benefits of HBase.

Tables in Hive that use HBase as storage are defined as external tables. They use the same syntax as HDFS-stored tables. The data format or SerDe need not be specified with HBase because Hive uses the HBase API to access data, and the internal data format need not be known. However, HBase tables must be declared using a specific storage handler that includes properties to identify the HBase table name.

To minimize storage and maximize access performance, tables in HBase should include just one-or two-column families with short names. But in Hive, we can map individual columns within column families as primitive data types or map the entire column family as a MAP. For example, we use two-column families in my personal-events table in HBase, where – ed specifies the event data, and mp defines the metadata properties.

In HBase, there are no indexes. The row-key, column family, and column qualifier are all stored in sorted order for byte arrays. Implementing a secondary index for a distributed system like HBase is not a straightforward task. There are two approaches to designing a secondary index.

1. **Client-side implementation:** The client handles the index metadata separately. During writing, the index metadata is created and written with actual data. During the scan, the metadata is first read to the client-side, and then the actual data is read back from the table.
2. **Server-side implementation:** Here, the server only handles the index metadata during writes and reads.

HIndex maintains a per-region index and creates an index table with the same number of regions as the actual table and having the same Row-Key (RK) range. It uses a custom load balancer on top of the HBase load balancer to maintain the regions. A split or movement for the actual table regions will take similar action for the index regions (CP hooks). There will be only one index table per actual table, irrespective of the number of indices on it, and all indexed metadata will be stored in this single index table.

MapReduce and HBase: When comparing HBase and HDFS, we can see that the relationship between Table and Region in HBase is comparable to that between File and Block in HDFS. TableInputFormat and TableOutputFormat are HBase APIs for dealing with MapReduce. With HBase, data tables can be directly used as input and output for Hadoop MapReduce, which helps develop MapReduce applications. HBase users can pay attention to the processing instead of focusing on minor details.

Counters: Many applications that collect statistics (such as clicks or views in online advertising) store the data in log files which would be later analyzed. Using counters allows switching to live accounting preceding the delayed batch processing step. HBase has a mechanism to treat columns as counters where users need not initialize counters. When we use a new counter for the first time, the columns are assumed to be zero (a column qualifier does not yet exist). If we specify one as the result of the first increment call to a new counter, it will return one or the increment of the counter value.

The coprocessor feature in HBase allows the user to move part of the computation to where the data lives. A coprocessor enables the user to run arbitrary code directly on each region server. It runs the code for each location separately, giving the user a trigger-like functionality similar to stored procedures in RDBMS. The user does not have to take specific actions from the client-side, as the framework handles the distributed nature transparently.

Rather than establishing an HTable instance for each user's request, it is more efficient to construct one once and utilize it. The main reason for this is that building an HTable instance is a relatively expensive and time-consuming activity. Instead, we can use the HTablePool class to construct the instance at startup and use it for the duration. It serves the purpose of pooling client API instances into an HBase cluster.

EXERCISES

Multiple Choice Questions

1. **Apache HBase is written in which language?**
   A. Scala
   B. C++
   C. Java
   D. Python
   Answer: C
   Explanation: HBase is a distributed non-relational database management system built on the Hadoop file system. It is an open-source project and can process large volumes of data. HBase is written in Java and supports writing applications in Apache Avro, REST, and Thrift.

2. **HBase allows scaling in both linear and modular forms.**
   A. True
   B. False
   Answer: A
   Explanation: HBase allows scaling in both linear and modular forms.

3. **Which of the following is not the main component of HBase?**
   A. HMaster
   B. Data Node
   C. Region Server
   D. ZooKeeper
   Answer: B
   Explanation: The HBase architecture has three main components: 1. HMaster, 2. Region Server, 3. ZooKeeper.

4. **This is responsible for allocating regions during launch, reassigning regions for recovery:**
   A. HMaster
   B. Data Node
   C. Region Server
   D. ZooKeeper
   Answer: A
   Explanation: The Client contacts the HMaster. The Master allocates regions and load balancing. The Region Server serves the data to read and write by interacting with HDFS, and the Apache ZooKeeper monitors the system. The HMaster's responsibilities include post-coordinating the servers in the region. The responsibilities include allocating regions during launch, reassigning regions for recovery, and load balancing.

5. **This comprises all the Hadoop cluster's machines:**
   A. HMaster
   B. Data Node
   C. Region Server
   D. ZooKeeper
   Answer: C
   Explanation: The Region Server comprises all the Hadoop cluster's machines. In addition, the Region Server has various minor components such as The Region, Blog (H File), Store, MemStore, WAL, and multiple files.

6. **HBase uses this as a database:**
   A. HMaster
   B. Data Node
   C. Region
   D. ZooKeeper
   Answer: C
   Explanation: HBase uses Region as a database, and it uses WAL (Write-Ahead Log) as a technique to store logs. WAL's most significant function is catastrophe recovery.

7. **Block Cache resides here and stores the frequently read data in the memory:**
   A. HMaster
   B. Data Node
   C. Region Server
   D. ZooKeeper
   Answer: C
   Explanation: Block Cache resides on the Region Server and stores the frequently read data in the memory.

8. **This default implementation caches the data blocks in the JVM heap:**
   A. LruBlockCache
   B. SlabCache
   C. BucketCache
   D. MemStore
   Answer: A
   Explanation
   LruBlockCache: This default implementation caches the data blocks in the JVM heap. Single-access, multi-access, and in-memory are the three categories.

8. **This approach allocates memory outside of the JVM heap:**
   A. LruBlockCache
   B. SlabCache
   C. BucketCache
   D. MemStore
   Answer: B
   Explanation
   SlabCache: Using DirectByteBuffers, this approach allocates memory outside the JVM heap. The region in which a specific block will be put is determined by its size. Two sections are allocated by default, occupying 80% and 20% respectively, of the total off-heap cache capacity.

9. **This stores recently added data and acts as an in-memory cache by storing recently added data:**
   A. LruBlockCache
   B. SlabCache
   C. BucketCache
   D. MemStore
   Answer: D
   Explanation: MemStore is the write cache that stores all the incoming data before committing it to the disk or permanent memory. MemStore stores recently added data and acts as an in-memory cache by storing recently added data.

10. **When the MemStore has acquired enough data, the complete ordered dataset is written to _____.**
    A. LruBlockCache
    B. SlabCache
    C. BucketCache
    D. HFile

Answer: D

Explanation: When the MemStore has acquired enough data, the complete ordered dataset is written to a new HDFS HFile file. For each Column Family, HBase produces an HFile to contain the details of Cell Key-Value data. Because Key-Value is regularly moved from the MemStore to the hard drive, HFiles will continue to occur over time.

11. **During moments of high incoming writes, HBase will attempt to aggregate (merge) HFiles. This is called _____.**
    A. Compacting   B. Conciseness
    C. Uniqueness   D. Hot-spotting
    Answer: A
    Explanation: Because Apache HBase is a distributed data store based on a log-structured merge tree, having only one file per store would provide the best-read speed (Column Family). However, this ideal solution is impossible to achieve during moments of high incoming writes. So instead, HBase will attempt to aggregate (merge) HFiles to decrease the number of disc searches required for a read. Compaction is the term given for this procedure. HBase supports two types of compactions: minor and major.

12. **A design guideline that states that a single byte representing an English alphabet may be chosen as a name for a column family is called as _____.**
    A. Compacting   B. Conciseness
    C. Uniqueness   D. Hot-spotting
    Answer: B
    Explanation: Considering the role played by HBase Key and in data scalability and dissemination, there are three design guidelines (Conciseness, Uniqueness, Data distribution) provided for deciding on an HBase key for a table.
    Conciseness: Because every data value in HBase is saved as a Key-Value Pair, short names for column family and column qualifier are suggested. A single byte representing an English alphabet may be chosen as a name for a column family. Still, the number of column qualifiers can be determined by the number of bytes used.

13. **It is essential to double-check that the row-key element of the HBase Key uniquely identifies your dataset. This is an example of _____.**
    A. Compacting   B. Conciseness
    C. Uniqueness   D. Hot-spotting
    Answer: C
    Explanation: It is essential to double-check that the row-key element of the HBase Key uniquely identifies your dataset.

14. **When a massive quantity of client traffic is routed to one node, this is known as _____.**
    A. Compacting   B. Conciseness
    C. Uniqueness   D. Hot-spotting

Answer: D
Explanation: We know that rows in HBase are sorted lexicographically by row-key. The row-key design is optimized for scans, allowing the user to store related rows or rows that need to be read together, near each other. On the other hand, poorly constructed row-keys are a common source of hot-spotting. When a massive quantity of client traffic is routed to one node or only a few nodes of a cluster, this is known as hot-spotting,

15. **This refers to adding a randomly assigned prefix to the row-key to make it sort differently than it would otherwise:**
    A. Compacting   B. Conciseness
    C. Salting   D. Hot-spotting
    Answer: C
    Explanation: Salting refers to adding random data to the beginning of a row-key. It has nothing to do with cryptography. Instead, salting refers to adding a randomly assigned prefix to the row-key to make it sort differently than it would otherwise.

16. **This is a framework that offers a library and runtime environment for executing user code within the HBase Region Server and Master Processes:**
    A. HBase Coprocessor   B. Region Observer
    C. WAL Observer   D. Master Observer
    Answer: A
    Explanation: HBase Coprocessor is a framework that offers a library and runtime environment for executing user code within the HBase Region Server and Master Processes. It is based on Bigtable coprocessors.

Short-answer Questions

1. **Write a short note on HBase.**
   HBase is a distributed non-relational database management system built on the Hadoop file system. It is an open-source project and can process large volumes of data. Google Bigtable (a paper published in Nov 2006) is the inspiration behind HBase (the initial prototype version released in Feb 2007). Google Bigtable is a compressed, high-performance, proprietary data store built on the Google file system. HBase is written in Java and supports writing applications in Apache Avro, REST, and Thrift. HBase is a database that sits atop the Hadoop File System, providing read and write access to store data directly in HDFS or through HBase.

2. **List down a few companies that use HBase.**
   Facebook, Netflix, Yahoo, Adobe, and Twitter are just a few firms that utilize HBase as their central database. HBase's purpose is to host big tables with billions of rows and millions of columns on commodity hardware clusters.

3. **List down a few critical features of HBase.**
   Apache HBase has several unique characteristics including consistency, high availability, scalability, automatic failover, and many more. HBase is a map-based database that allows several copies of the same information and is sparse, multidimensional, and sorted. It provides consistent reads and writes. HBase provides nuclear (atomic) read and writes at the row level. HBase allows scaling in both linear and modular forms.

4. **List down three main components of HBase architecture.**
   The HBase architecture has three main components: 1. HMaster, 2. Region Server, 3. ZooKeeper.
   Client contacts the HMaster. The Master allocates regions and load balancing. The Region Server serves the data to read and write by interacting with HDFS, and the Apache ZooKeeper monitors the system. The HBase cluster typically consists of one Master node (HMaster) and many Region servers.

5. **Write short notes on HMaster of HBase architecture.**
   The Master responsibilities include allocating regions during launch, reassigning regions for recovery, and load balancing. All-Region Server instances in the cluster are monitored (listened to for notifications from ZooKeeper). It moves the regions to less crowded servers after unloading the congested servers. In addition, the Master serves as an interface for creating, deleting, and updating tables (DDL operations).

6. **Write short notes on Region Servers.**
   The Region Server comprises all the Hadoop cluster's machines. In addition, the Region Server has various minor components such as The Region, Blog (H File), Store, MemStore, WAL, and multiple files.

7. **What are Regions in HBase architecture?**
   HBase uses Regions as a database, and it uses WAL (Write-Ahead Log) as a technique to store logs. In HBase, data is saved in tables, stored in Regions. When a table is too large, it is divided into many regions. Region Servers are assigned to these regions across the cluster. The number of regions hosted by each Region Server is nearly the same. Regions have a default size of 256 MB. The Region Server maintains various regions running on HDFS and manages and executes reads and writes on them.

8. **What is WAL in HBase architecture?**
   WAL: Write-Ahead Logs (WAL) are files attached to every Region Server, which store the new data that has not been committed to the permanent storage. WAL files are used to recover data in case of failure. WAL's most significant function is catastrophe recovery. It keeps track of all data changes in the same way as MySQL's BIN log does. We may recover the data before the crash by replaying the log after the server has crashed. If writing to WAL fails, the entire operation is deemed a failure. The data will be asynchronously written to the file system when MemStore reaches a specific size or after some time. The data between the two writes to the file system, on the other hand, is maintained in memory.

9. **What is Block Cache in HBase?**
   Block Cache: Block Cache resides on the Region Server and stores the frequently read data in the memory. If the data in Block Cache has not been recently used, then it is removed from Block Cache. A region server has just one Block Cache instance, which implies that all data from all regions hosted by that Server, is cached in the same pool. The Block Cache is created when the area server starts up and is kept for the duration of the operation. In the past, HBase only had one Block Cache implementation: the LruBlockCache. However, it now has two additional Block Cache implementations, including SlabCache and the BucketCache.

10. **Write short notes on LruBlockCache of HBase.**
    LruBlockCache: This default implementation caches the data blocks in the JVM heap. Single-access, multi-access, and in-memory are the three categories. The sizes of the areas are 25%, 50%, and 25% of the total BlockCache size, respectively. The single-access area is populated using a block read from HDFS. Consecutive accesses advance a block to the multi-access zone. The in-memory region is reserved for blocks loaded from IN MEMORY column families. Finally, old blocks are evicted to create a place for new blocks, regardless of area, using the Least-Recently-Used method, hence the "Lru" in "LruBlockCache."

11. **Write notes on SlabCache of HBase.**
    SlabCache: Using DirectByteBuffers, this approach allocates memory outside the JVM heap. The region in which a specific block will be put is determined by its size. Two sections are assigned by default, occupying 80% and 20% respectively, of the total off-heap cache capacity. The former is used to cache blocks around the same size as the target block. The latter stores blocks that are roughly twice the size of the target block. A block is crammed into the smallest possible space. If the cache comes across a block too large to fit in either region, it will not be stored.

12. **What is BucketCache in HBase?**
    BucketCache: This implementation may be set to one of three modes: heap, off-heap, or file. The BucketCache handles "buckets" of memory for storing cached blocks, regardless of the operating mode. A target block size is set for each bucket. The heap implementation produces the buckets on the JVM heap; the off-heap performance manages buckets outside the JVM heap using DirectByteByffers. The file mode demands a path to a file on the disc where the buckets are produced. File mode is designed to work with a low-latency backing store, such as an in-memory filesystem or a file on SSD storage. Bucket Cache produces 14 buckets of various sizes regardless of the mode. As with LruBlockCache, it utilizes the frequency of block access to determine usage.

13. **What is MemStore in HBase?**
    MemStore: is the write cache that stores all the incoming data before committing it to the disk or permanent memory. MemStore stores recently added data and acts

as an in-memory cache by storing recently added data. Also, there are occasions when it is more advantageous to access recently written data rather than older data. There is one MemStore for each column family in a region, and there are multiple MemStores for a region because each region contains various column families. The data in the MemStore is sorted in lexicographical order before committing to the disk. Also, every MemStore flush creates one HFile per Column Family, which is a fantastic feature.

14. **Write short notes on HFlie in HBase.**
    HFile: When the MemStore has acquired enough data, the complete ordered dataset is written to a new HDFS HFile file. For each Column Family, HBase produces an HFile to contain the details of Cell Key-Value data. Because Key-Value is regularly moved from the MemStore to the hard drive, HFiles will continue to occur over time. This data structure supports random read and writes operations on the table.

15. **What is HBase Compaction?**
    During moments of high incoming writes, HBase will attempt to aggregate (merge) HFiles to decrease the number of disc searches required for a read. Compaction is the term given for this procedure. Compactions choose and aggregate (merge) files from single storage in an area.

16. **What is Minor Compaction in HBase?**
    Minor Compaction: This compaction is always active and focuses on newly written files. These files are tiny because they are fresh, and they may include deleting markers for data in earlier files. This compaction does not affect or erase data from older files since it only looks at newer files. This means that until another compaction type comes along and deletes older data, this compaction type will be unable to remove the erase markers from newer files; otherwise, those previously deleted Key Values will reappear. Minor compactions are essential as reading a particular row can require many disk-reads and cause slow performance. Minor compaction is similar to a merge sort in that rewriting smaller files into fewer but larger ones minimizes the number of storage files.

17. **What are the potential outcomes of minor compaction in HBase?**
    The potential to affect data locality is quite limited since the touched files are comparatively younger and smaller. A region server usually tries to write the primary replica of data on the local HDFS data node anyway during a write operation. As a result, a minor compaction seldom adds much to data locality.
    Some performance will be lost because the delete marks are not deleted. On the other hand, minor compactions are crucial for HBase read performance because they keep the total file count under control, which may be a significant performance bottleneck if left uncontrolled, especially on spinning drives.

18. What is Major Compaction in HBase?

Major compactions merge all HFiles into one huge HFile, whereas Minor compactions combine a customizable number of smaller HFiles into one larger HFile. Major compactions do the cleanup work after a user deletes a record. When a user performs a Delete call, the HBase system places a marker in the key-value pair to be permanently removed during the subsequent major compaction. Major compactions are usually scheduled to run automatically. However, this compaction is seldom performed (once a week by default), with focus on a store's comprehensive cleaning (one Column family inside one Region).

19. What general concepts need to be followed while designing a table schema in HBase?

1. **Row-key**: Each table in an HBase table is indexed based on the row-key, and data is sorted lexicographically by the row-key. There are no secondary indices available on the HBase table.
2. **Automaticity**: All operations on HBase rows are atomic at the row level.
3. **Even distribution**: Reads and writes should be uniformly distributed across all nodes in the cluster. The row-key should be designed to store related entities in adjacent rows to increase read efficiency.

20. What is Hot-spotting in HBase?

Hot-spotting: As we know, rows in HBase are sorted lexicographically by the row-key. This row-key design is optimized for scans, allowing the user to store related rows or rows that need to be read together, near each other. On the other hand, poorly constructed row-keys are a common source of hot-spotting. When a massive quantity of client traffic is routed to one node or only a few nodes, this is known as hot-spotting.

21. What is Write Hot-spotting and Read Hot-spotting in HBase?

Write Hot-spotting would occur if sequential write operations result in monotonically growing row-keys, since monotonically increasing row-keys would only target one Region at a time. Read Hot-spotting occurs when a vast data collection is read from only a few areas. As a result, the read/write throughput and parallelism aspects of Hadoop computing jobs running on the table suffer significantly due to hot-spotting.

22. How can hot-spotting be avoided using Reverse Row-Key in HBase?

Reverse Row-Key: Reversing the row-key of a fixed length or number format is a way to avoid hot spots. This reversing permits the often-modified component of the row-key (the least essential element) to be placed first. This method effectively randomizes the row-key, albeit at the cost of the row-key's orderliness.

23. How can hot-spotting be avoided using the Salting method in HBase?

Salting: Salting refers to adding random data to the beginning of a row-key. It has nothing to do with cryptography. Salting refers to adding a randomly assigned prefix to the row-key to make it sort in a different way than it would otherwise. The number of prefixes available is proportional to the number of areas that wish to distribute the data. If we have a few "hot" row-key patterns that appear repeatedly amongst other more uniformly distributed rows, salting can be helpful.

24. **How can hot-spotting be avoided using the Hashing method in HBase?**
When we have the data represented by the string identifier, that is a good choice for hashing the string identifier of the HBase table row-key. For example, if the table stores user data identified by user IDs, hashing is good for the row-key. Instead of using a random assignment, we might use a one-way hash that causes a particular row to always be "salted" with the same prefix, distributing the load across the Region Servers while maintaining predictability during reads. A deterministic hash allows the client to reassemble the whole row-key and obtain that row using a `Get` operation.

25. **How can hot-spotting be avoided using the Timestamp method in HBase?**
Timestamps: The timestamp of the row-key can be used to retrieve data based on the time stored. If data is saved in a machine log identifiable by a machine number, for example, when constructing a row-key, attach the timestamp to the machine number, for example, machine001#1644404701000.

26. **How can hot-spotting be avoided using Combine Row-Key?**
Combining multiple keys to design a row-key for our HBase table is another option based on our requirements. Scanning for consecutive blocks is the most effective way to read back rows. For example, assume we have a table with a customer-date user row-key. The prefix customer-first part-of-date makes it easy to read back all the data for a specific customer and date range, but it makes it challenging to read backdate ranges for all users at once without scanning all the rows. The problem is reversed if we use customer user-date instead of the row-key. Therefore, we should consider our significant read pattern when creating our keys.

27. **How can hot-spotting be avoided using accessibility?**
Row-Keys should be constructed so that data is readily available to users in the most efficient manner possible. When a row-key prefix is used in a search query, the number of HBase regions (and the number of data storage files inside a region) that must be examined for output data is reduced to the minimum. If stored data is to be searched against a specific type of data, the row-key's first and foremost value should be that particular data type. Additional data types can then follow this ubiquitous data type in their frequency of presence throughout all search queries.

28. **Compare the use of tall vs. wide tables to avoid hot-spotting.**
The user's HBase table design impacts row-key design. For example, the row-key includes more data values than a broad table when a tall table is used. Because the HBase region (unit of distribution) is separated across row-key borders, more data in a row-key leads to more row-keys, which leads to more data being disseminated

over the HBase cluster. On the other hand, fewer data in the row-key means more data is stored against columns, resulting in a smaller data distribution while ensuring atomicity across a larger dataset.

29. **What is Region Split in HBase?**
HBase region size is essential when accessing HBase data because in MapReduce, the data split is done by splitting regions. There will not be enough parallelism in the MapReduce jobs if the area size is too large and it splits into two child regions. Each table is in one region at first. A region divides into two child regions when it becomes too large. Both child regions represent one-half of the original region on the same Region server, and each split is reported to the Master Server or HMaster.

30. **How does Load Balancing happen in HBase?**
Splitting happens on the same region server, but the HMaster may schedule new regions to be moved off to other servers for help in load balancing. This action causes the new Region server to serve data from a remote HDFS node until major compaction moves the data to the Region server's local node. HBase data is local when written, but when a region is moved (for load balancing or recovery), the data will not be local to HDFS until the subsequent major compaction.

31. **How does Crash Recovery happen in HBase?**
When a Region Server fails, crashed Regions become unavailable until detection and recovery have taken place. ZooKeeper detects Node failure when it stops receiving region server heartbeats. After that, the HMaster will be informed that the Region Server has failed, and the regions from that server will be reassigned to other region servers that are still up and running. Next, HMaster splits the WAL files from the crashed Region Server and stores the split files in the new region servers' data nodes. To rebuild the MemStore for that particular region, the Region Server will replicate the WAL from the respective split WAL.

32. **How does Data Recovery happen in HBase?**
When a region server crashes, the regions it controls are unavailable until the crash is discovered and the failure recovery process is finished. ZooKeeper uses heartbeat detection to identify node failures, and subsequently, HMaster is notified of region server failures. HMaster allocates the regions handled by the region server to other healthy region servers when it detects a region server failure. HMaster separates the WAL into many files and saves them on the new region server to retrieve data that has not been persisted to HFile in the MemStore of the failed region server. Each Region Server then recreates a MemStore for the new area allocated by replaying the data in the WAL fragments it has retrieved.

33. **Write short notes on HBase Coprocessor.**
HBase coprocessor is a framework that offers a library and runtime environment for executing user code within the HBase region server and master processes. It is based

on Bigtable coprocessors. System coprocessors may be loaded globally on all tables and regions hosted by the region server. Table coprocessors allow the administrator to define which coprocessors should be loaded on all regions for a table on a per-table basis. The framework supports two separate extension elements to enable adequate flexibility for various coprocessor behaviors. The observer is similar to triggers in traditional databases, and the endpoints.

34. **What is an observer in HBase?**
    Observers: The concept behind observers is that we can incorporate user code by customizing the coprocessor framework's upcall functions. The callback routines are performed from the core HBase code when specific events occur. The coprocessor framework takes care of activating callbacks during different base HBase activities. The coprocessor merely needs to offer the appropriate additional or alternative functionality. Observers can perform authority management, priority setting, monitoring, and secondary index.

35. **How many observers are there in HBase?**
    We have three observer interfaces in HBase:
    Region Observer: Hooks for data modification events like `Get`, `Put`, `Delete`, `Scan`, and so on are provided by Region Observer. Every table area has its instance of the Region Observer coprocessor, and their observations are limited to that Region.
    WAL Observer: Provides hooks for actions using the write-ahead log (WAL). This allows us to watch or listen to WAL writing and rebuilding events. A WAL Observer is used in the context of WAL processing. Each region server has one of these contexts.
    Master Observer: Provides hooks for DDL-type operations, such as table creation, deletion, and modification. The Master Observer operates in the HBase master's context.

36. **What is an endpoint in HBase?**
    Observers are similar to database triggers. On the other hand, endpoints are more potent than stored procedures and are identical. A client can call the endpoint at any time. The endpoint implementation will then be carried out remotely in the target region or regions, with the results being sent to the client. The endpoint is a dynamic RPC extension interface. The endpoint implementation is installed on the Server and it may then use HBase RPC to call it. For calling such dynamic interfaces, the client library provides convenient methods.

37. **How does indexing take place in HBase?**
    In HBase, there are no indexes. The row-key, column family, and column qualifier are all stored in sorted order for byte arrays. Implementing a secondary index for a distributed system like HBase is not a straightforward task. Let us look at two approaches to design a secondary index.

1. **Client-side implementation**: The Client handles the index metadata separately. During writing, the index metadata is created and written with actual data. The metadata is first read to the client-side during the scan, and then the actual data is read back from the table.
2. **Server-side implementation**: Here, the Server only handles the index metadata during writes and reads.

38. **List down a few applications of HBase.**
    - RDBMS becomes slow when the data becomes large. On the other hand, HBase can store vast amounts of data that require fast reads and writes.
    - HBase can be used where regular, consistent insertion and overwriting of data is needed. For example, they can use HBase for banking applications that require real-time data updates in ATMs.
    - Facebook uses HBase because it needs a system to handle an ever-growing, rarely accessed or highly volatile dataset. HBase also provides the advantage of storing millions of rows and columns on top of clusters of commodity hardware.

Essay-type Questions

1. Write an essay on the different features of HBase.
2. Explain the architecture of HBase in detail.
3. How does HBase manage a large dataset?
4. Write an essay on HBase compaction and its types.
5. Write an essay on HBase Row-Key Design.
6. How can hot-spotting be avoided?
7. Write an essay on Region Split and Load Balancing in HBase.
8. How does data replication, crash recovery, and data recovery happen in HBase?
9. Write an essay on HBase Coprocessor.

CHAPTER 11

Hadoop Streaming

LEARNING OBJECTIVES

The main objective of this chapter is to discuss real-time analytics, and help the user choose the proper tool for real-time analytics, such as Apache Spark Streaming, Apache Samza, Thread pooling, and Hadoop streaming. We also discuss various subjects related to the streaming.

11.1 INTRODUCTION

Big Data stores and processes Big Data sets, which are complex datasets that can be structured or unstructured and are so large that typical analytical methods cannot handle them. The unpredictability of the Data Management Landscape was one of the critical issues of traditional systems. Big Data is continually evolving, with new businesses and technology emerging daily. Businesses face huge challenges in determining which technology is best for them without introducing additional risks and obstacles. Organizations realize the importance of Big Data Analytics these days, and as a result, they are using Big Data tools and procedures to increase efficiency.

11.2 REAL-TIME ANALYTICS

Businesses may obtain insights and act on data as soon as it enters the system with real-time analytics. Inquiries are answered in seconds using real-time data. They deal with massive amounts of data at a high rate and respond quickly. For example, real-time Big Data Analytics uses data from a financial database to drive trading decisions. On-demand or continuous analytics are both possible. When a user queries for anything, the results are delivered on-demand. If users are given constant updates as events occur, they can be programmed to respond automatically to certain situations. Real-time web analytics, for example, may inform an administrator if page-load performance deviates from established standards. The following are some real-time examples of customer analytics: Orders may be viewed in real-time for better tracking and trend detection. To better analyze user behavior, consumer activities like page views and shopping cart usage are tracked. Customers are targeted with promos while shopping, impacting their decisions in real-time.

11.2.1 Choosing the Proper Tool for Real-time Analytics

To handle streaming data, a system must be able to analyze and offer real-time outcomes. Data processing in real-time isn't just a fad: it is an essential component of the Lambda Architecture. Streaming data processing accounts for the "speed layer" in such a system, enabling a real-time view of occurrences. Furthermore, in the event of data loss, to fill in missing data points (which is prevalent in real-time systems), a batch-oriented Big Data processing pipeline is run in parallel.

Traditional MapReduce-style Big Data jobs, on the other hand, are insufficient for real-time data processing. Hadoop has a lot of useful tools (like the distributed HDFS file system, or Hive, which allows you to access SQL queries on HDFS), but it is not designed for real-time data processing. Hadoop Streaming is a utility for running non-Hadoop applications in the processing pipeline despite its misleading name. There are Big Data frameworks explicitly designed for real-time data sources, such as Apache Storm, Apache Flink, Apache Samza, and Apache Spark Streaming (Fig. 11.1).

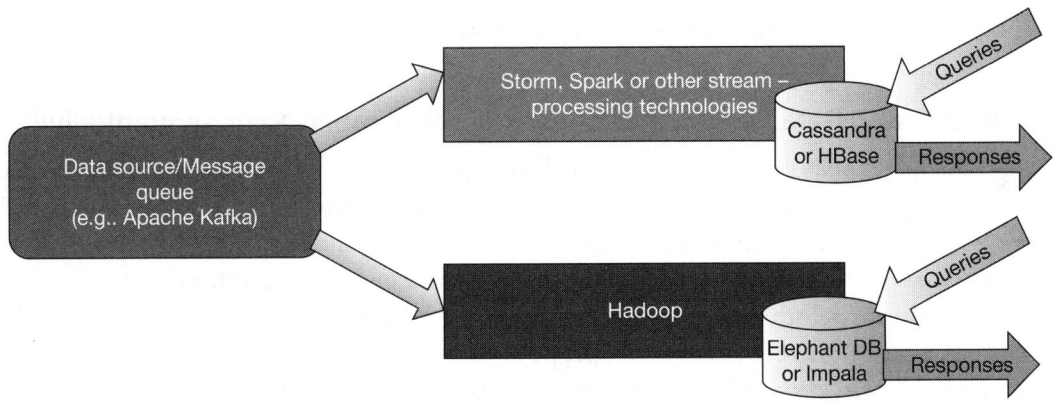

Figure 11.1 Data Source: Choosing proper real-time analytics tool

11.2.2 Apache Spark Streaming

Despite having a straightforward Spark API for communicating changes, Spark Streaming's handling of streaming data is inefficient. Attaining resilience and low-latency message handling takes a lot of work in Spark.

Latency Issues

Apache Spark works in micro-batches, which means it fetches a specific number of messages at a predetermined period. When the buffer is full, Spark will begin processing these messages. Unfortunately, this is incompatible with the nature of processing streaming data. Other frameworks such as Apache Storm are also available, processing messages in real-time rather than batching or buffering them. As a result, in Spark, data processing will not be real-time, even though RDDs, Spark's underlying data structure, provide a fault-tolerant architecture. Windowing techniques are likewise impossible with micro-batching since only a window containing multiple batches is available to be maintained. Furthermore, if a batch's processing duration exceeds the batch interval, more and more waiting micro-batches will be stacked, effectively slowing the stream processing.

State Management Is Not Robust Enough

Because state management is insufficient, Spark Streaming requires a checkpoint directory to save its state and offset the most recently processed message (so that it understands where to go next in the micro-batch). If one of the nodes fails, this is utilized to restore stream processing. Although it seemed like a good idea at the time, it has proven to be problematic: issues such as running out of disk space (which is common these days) when running software in tiny containers such as Docker, which comes with 10GB of disc space by default, deploying a new version of the application that is incompatible with the state before it, and so on.

11.2.3 Apache Samza

Although Samza was designed from the ground–up to interact with Apache Kafka, it can also process data from other streaming sources. Although it is far more capable of handling streaming data than Spark, it still falls short of a certain flexibility.

Serialization and Data Transformation Do Not Necessarily Occur Sequentially

Samza anticipates that communications will be converted as soon as they are consumed, with modifications occurring afterward. On paper, it sounds incredible, but it has little to do with real-world applications, much like Spark's state management. During the serialization step, message keys are inaccessible. Some transformations have to be executed on raw byte data before the message could be deserialized. For this, message keys are needed. As a result, there is no choice except to provide the data in a serialized way, which Samza forbids. This compelled workflow isn't always appropriate.

Programming with Configurations Is Not Feasible

A Java properties file is used to define Samza jobs. This is inefficient and prone to mistakes (think Spring Framework's application.xml files.) Furthermore, this means that every SerDe (serializer–deserializer, as defined by Samza) and transformation must be stated here; thus, any naming or other issues only become apparent during runtime. (It would be more productive to find errors in compilation time.)

Cluster Mode Is Only Compatible with YARN

Although YARN is a reliable solution for Hadoop MapReduce or Spark Batch operations, allowing you to establish a Hadoop cluster and run a cluster quickly (distributed and robust), running cluster mode in the Samza process is somewhat complicated.

11.2.4 What Would a Perfect Solution Entail?

We understand the challenges of real-time data processing and the limitations of some current solutions. The following characteristics should be included in an ideal streaming data processing solution:

1. It should rely on a cluster of machines sharing nothing (or as little as feasible) to simplify the design and prevent failure scenarios caused by node loss.
2. Streaming data should be saved locally on each machine rather than being distributed across all nodes. This local machine should be the first point of interaction when updating or querying a state.
3. It also commits the state to a shared state store accessible to all nodes for robustness, allowing new nodes to obtain from this typical state store to get their current state.
4. It makes use of an internal state/offset storage that isn't prone to resource restrictions, such as disk space.
5. It has a user-friendly, test-friendly API. It's good if you can declare pipelines with updates that are chained together.
6. Support for functional programming paradigms is also beneficial.

Kafka Streams is a framework that meets these requirements. It was developed by the same team that developed Apache Kafka. As a result, our streaming data platform is limited to using Kafka as its backbone. This isn't a significant compromise because most teams/companies utilize Kafka as their primary message broker for real-time data. The Spark Streaming application for Kafka Streams that manage large data loads was built to address the concerns raised above. Figure 11.2 compares how the two applications stack up in terms of production load.

It can be seen that Kafka Streams outperforms Spark Streaming in real-time data processing since it necessitates less CPU processing and memory while retaining the same pace. Reduced costs can be significant as a result of this. Kafka Streams also fixes some of Spark Streaming's state management difficulties.

11.2.5 Challenges to Be Solved

IT teams need to face the following challenges while moving to streaming solutions:

1. **Scalability:** Example for scalability includes increased sales, addition of more staff, or a new product showing a lot of potential in the market. It may also be a mix of all three. The business frequently has high expectations that IT would swiftly set up a "remote office" with everything; users will need to roll out a program to a new team. This is especially true, now that SaaS apps and cloud-based services fuel organizations. It is not as straightforward as a few mouse clicks or a phone call to a supplier. The most common stumbling problem is IT teams attempting to scale up in remote, SaaS-based settings.

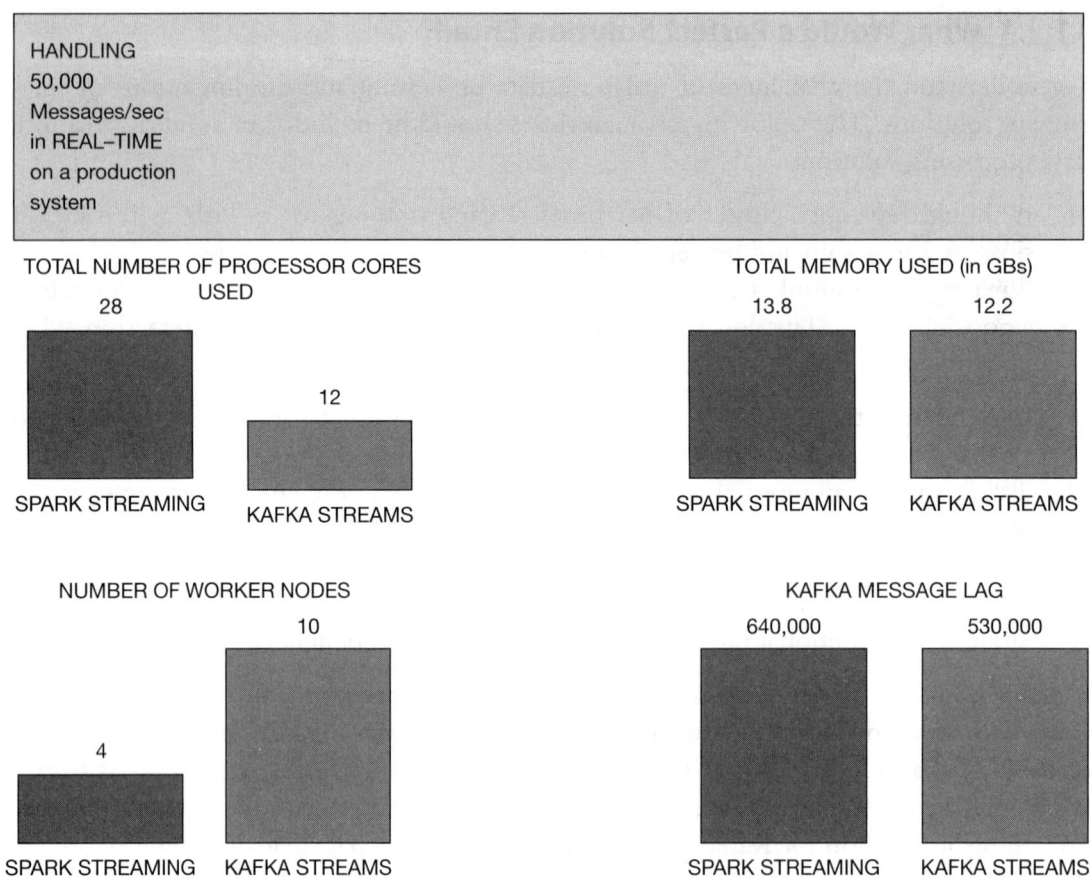

Figure 11.2 Spark streaming vs. Kafka streaming – Comparison

2. **Application Dimensions:** There are two well-known factors in in-house app management: First, the number of people who use them at the host company keeps increasing, and second, the company does not own them all. Thanks to distributed budgeting and easy "SaaS availability", new software can be downloaded and used by any team without consulting IT, thanks to distributed budgeting and easy "SaaS availability". While this is helpful for non-technical use, we know that the moment the app becomes slow it impedes the overall performance. The problem arises if the network is not kept inbound.

3. **Reliability and Performance:** Apps are rarely down these days. Your key application providers may experience unscheduled downtime "occasionally, once or twice a year". It can also be a non-event if it happens during off-peak hours. Today's company personnel have a problem with sluggish applications. Because of performance and reliability difficulties, apps might get a negative representation on the sales floor and hamper your marketing department.

4. **Identity Access Control (IAC):** A host of challenges develop when legacy systems are working together with new performance and application requirements. They could be expensive to maintain and operate throughout an organization's infrastructure. As a result, in recent years, firms such as Last Pass have had success attacking the problem with SSO and SaaS solutions. When your firm has 50 employees in two locations, IAC is simple, but you must optimize your provisioning processes with 500 employees in 20 locations. You can't rely on random work or scripts, and you'll need to evolve to incorporate more modern solutions.

5. **Support for "Hybrid Cloud":** Today's business infrastructure mixes your legacy infrastructure and cloud-based technology. The balance could shift depending on your company's specific journey, but providers increasingly own devices and links. While scalability is desirable, IT will need to discover new ways to monitor and notify network and application performance as they lose sight and control of these devices. In addition, because there are fewer physical devices to manage, smaller centralized teams are becoming more common.

6. **Cost Pressures:** IT departments aren't necessarily making more money as they shift to a decentralized, cloud-based model. Furthermore, there is pressure to cut costs across the board and pressure on IT to prove its worth by increasing the company's bottom line. As a result, IT must become more cost-effective while boosting performance and reliability. This significantly impacts scalability, especially considering how fast the business changes. It is simple to add more seats to a SaaS subscription, but it is not inexpensive. When IT makes modifications or additions, the complexity of SaaS pricing and licensing can cause confusion and unexpected billing surprises.

11.3 THREAD POOLING

A thread pool is a software architecture paradigm for creating concurrent execution in a computer program. For example, the worker-crew concept, often known as replicated workers, is a thread pool that keeps several threads waiting for the supervisory program to allocate tasks for concurrent execution. The notion enhances speed by retaining a pool of threads and avoids the frequent production and destruction of threads for short-lived processes that cause execution delays. The computing resources available to the application, such as a parallel task queue, define the number of threads accessible. The size of a thread pool is the number of threads kept in reserve for task execution. It is usually a programmable application parameter that can be tweaked to improve program performance. Choosing the right thread pool size is critical to getting the best results. The overhead of thread generation and destruction is restricted to the pool's initial formation, which could lead to better speed and system stability than starting a new thread for each task. Creating and deleting a thread and its associated resources might take a long time. On the other hand, many reserve threads waste resources, and performance is degraded by context switching across runnable threads. By linking a socket connection to another network host with a thread that survives through numerous network transactions, a network socket that connects to another host can be maintained efficiently. Using a thread pool may be helpful even when thread launch time is considered. Thread pools make it easier to queue work, control concurrency, and sync threads at a higher level than with manual thread management. However, the performance benefits of utilization may be secondary in other instances. For example, a single machine is usually used to run a thread pool. On the other hand, thread pools are like server farms; they distribute jobs to worker processes across multiple computers to boost total throughput. This approach works well with embarrassingly parallel problems.

The number of threads in an application can be dynamically altered over time, and is dependent on the number of waiting jobs. For example, if many web page requests are received, a web server can add threads and when the number of such requests decreases, the server can remove threads. However, having a more significant thread pool comes at the cost of increased resource utilization.

The algorithm for deciding when to establish or remove threads has to consider the overall performance impact. Having too many threads wastes resources and time in creating the ones that aren't needed. Destroying many threads is also not advisable since it takes longer to recreate them later. Slowly creating threads could lead to poor client performance (long wait times). Destroying threads too slowly can cause problems by depleting the resources available to other processes.

11.4 STREAM COMPUTING

Streaming data is available to businesses from various sources like the web, social networks, clickstreams, sensors, the cloud, machines and devices, and so on. The demand for real-time data and customer insights has accelerated the proliferation of this type of data and the requirement to extract business intelligence from it. However, gathering and analyzing streaming data has its drawbacks.

Data Streaming Is a Difficult Task

Streaming data is particularly tough to handle since it is constantly generated by a range of sources and devices and given in various formats. Because so few developers have the abilities and expertise needed to work with live data, it is practically impossible for businesses to provide real-time access to employees who are anxious to get their hands on it. The Internet of Things (IoT) is an excellent example of how complex streaming data can be. Data from IoT devices is continuously available; there is no beginning or finish; it just keeps building up. A traditional batch processing strategy does not work because of the constant flow of data and the diversity of data kinds that IoT data contains. For example, consider a single wind turbine, there could be hundreds of devices and sensors. Every device serves a specific purpose: measuring oil level, turbine position, tower sway, blade pressure, and temperatures. Because different businesses frequently manufacture these devices, the data they produce might be pretty varied. In this heterogeneous devices and sensor data context, the data format can change unexpectedly, possibly disrupting data pipelines.

Data Is in High Demand, but IT Can't Keep Up

Many firms are returning to the much-maligned business–IT divide due to the challenges of integrating and accessing streaming data. The IT department has trouble expanding its capabilities to provide data to the business department. The business team urgently requires the data to respond to commercial requests and provide timely new business potential with analytics. The issues arise when the business team, desperate for access to the streaming data, bypasses IT and uses an ad-hoc solution or plan to get it. The business personnel's methods and processes for obtaining data access go against IT protocol, resulting in unwanted new data silos and a significant data governance risk.

Create Real-time Data Pipelines as a Solution

The dangers of streaming data are pretty acute for data-driven businesses and there is a growing disconnect between business and technology that produces new issues. Talend Data Streams, a cloud-based free program that can be downloaded and installed in minutes via the Amazon Web Services (AWS) Marketplace, was created to address these issues. The winner is Self-Service Streaming Data.

Talend Data Streams is a self-service online UI for streaming data integration that is easy and accessible to many data professionals, including data scientists, expert data analysts, and ad-hoc integrators. Talend Data Streams brings together the automation and deployment capabilities of Talend that businesses want with easy tools that can be tailored to meet specific requirements. One Unified Interface is the winner. Using Apache Beam, a unified programming paradigm that provides an abstraction layer for numerous run profiles that are extremely efficient and trustworthy, can develop streaming and batch pipelines using a single interface. With Talend Data Streams, everything is considered a stream, with streaming data having an unbounded source and batch data having a bounded source. The pipelines are highly portable because Apache Beam supports many frameworks. Instead of migrating your data to a specific processing framework such as Apache Spark, Apache Flink, or Google Cloud, Apache Beam allows you to process your data wherever it is.

Schema-on-read is a feature of Talend Data Streams that allows your data schema to be discovered automatically. The program can handle any schema at any moment, and it can even patch around columns it doesn't recognize so that it can focus on the scripting columns. This means that any changes to the source schema do not affect the pipeline's real-time data flow.

11.5 THE FUTURE OF DATA STREAMING

Talend Cloud also includes Talend Data Streams, transforming the Talend Cloud applications into a truly collaborative platform for all types of data users. Data pipelines, metadata, and datasets may all be accessed from anywhere on the platform. Data experts such as analysts and data scientists can use Data Streams to perform data ingestion and lightweight Extract, Transform, and Load (ETL) procedures without consulting IT, all while capturing metadata. Within hours or minutes, data engineers may prepare streaming data using the Talend Data Streams UI, integrate a data quality recipe from Talend Data Preparation in the pipeline, and distribute datasets throughout the platform. To share datasets across the platform in hours or minutes, a high-quality Talend Data Preparation template may be used in the pipeline. Talend Data Streams' unique Live Preview capability gives data engineers quick gratification by revealing the progress of data transformation at every step. This real-time, up-front perspective also speeds up testing and troubleshooting. Companies can also use Talend Data Streams' Python component to customize their transformations using Python code or existing scripts. The Talend Data Streams app is now available on the Amazon Marketplace as free single-user software. Additional features are to be added to Talend Data Streams shortly. Through Talend Cloud, the software will be commercially offered as Software-as-a-Service (SaaS), a fully managed service. Future versions will have more significant data preparation capabilities and in-flight data quality checks on data before it reaches the data lake to maintain high quality.

11.6 Stream Computing's Advantages in the Big Data world

Using the support staff of a hosted cloud provider saves money. All basic cloud environment tasks are maintained by the hosted cloud provider, which includes qualified specialists in charge of data backups, restores, and hardware and storage services, without requiring additional subscribed support services. Adding the capacity to stream large amounts of data to a system's infrastructure usually requires existing employees to be trained (or hiring new people) to handle the new technologies. On the other hand, the offer of knowledge comes as standard with hosted cloud provider services. Data backups and restore requests are handled automatically, giving businesses a smooth way to keep their data safe in the cloud.

Furthermore, upgrades, bug fixes, and hardware part replacements are provided at no additional cost to consumers by the hosted cloud provider, ensuring that the cloud environment is up to date and cutting-edge. Leased Cloud Infrastructures, Software, Platforms, and Services result in lower costs. The "pay-as-you-go" service is a novel concept that allows businesses to "lease" whatever software program, platforms, or other services they desire. This can be done on a month-to-month basis in some circumstances. Businesses can stop using a service or function if they no longer want it, rather than paying a predetermined fee for a collection of packaged services they may never use. Also, because of the hosted cloud provider's expertise, the processes for massive data migrations, new hardware installations, and the addition of software applications and services are rapid and efficient.

Scalability

The provision of future storage, memory, processor capacity, and the system availability required to accommodate massive amounts of expansion is a recurring worry in infrastructure and IT service budget planning. Businesses plan for expansion, which is necessary to succeed in a competitive economy. As a result, the cloud environment must have sufficient capacity, performance and scalability to meet modest and rapid business development. In addition, the cloud infrastructure allows for practically infinite scalability. As a result, businesses may generate as much Big Data and demand as they want without fear of outgrowing their capabilities to meet these demands.

Real-time Analytics

Users may see, analyze, and recognize data as it enters a system with real-time data analytics. The data is infused with logic and calculations to give consumers the perception that they need to make real-time decisions.

Apache Spark Streaming is a Big Data platform for real-time data stream analytics. Cisco Connected Streaming Analytics (CSA) is a platform that provides rapid actionable insights from high-velocity streams of live data from numerous sources.

Oracle Stream Analytics (OSA) is a platform that gives "Fast Data", a graphical interface. SAP HANA is a real-time analytics and streaming analytics platform. SQL (Structured Query Language) Stream Blaze is an analytics platform that provides developers and analysts with a real-time, easy-to-use, and powerful visual programming environment. TIBCO Stream Base is a streaming analytics platform that allows developers to build apps quickly. Informatica is a real-time data streaming tool that turns a deluge of small messages and events into unrivaled business opportunity.

Firms can get the awareness of data and act on it as soon as it enters their system via real-time analytics. Real-time app analytics questions are answered in seconds. They can process a vast volume of data quickly and with a short reaction time. For example, real-time Big Data Analytics analyses data from financial databases to help traders make better judgments. On-demand and continuous analytics are both possible. When a user wants results, on-demand analytics notifies them. Continuous refurbishment users can be configured to respond automatically to situations as they occur. Real-time web analytics, for example, may re-energize an administrator if the page load presentation exceeds the current limit.

Examples of real-time customer analytics include orders that are viewed in real-time for enhanced traceability and fashion identification. To understand user etiquette, customer activity like page views and shopping cart utilization are modernized continuously. Customers can be selected as they shop for things in a store, influencing real-time decisions.

Tools for real-time data analytics can either push or draw data. Streaming necessitates the faculty to push massive volumes of fast-moving data. When streaming consumes too many assets, data can be transmitted at intervals ranging from seconds to hours depending on the company needs. However, this necessitates budgeting to avoid disrupting operations.

The reaction time of real-time analytics might range from instantaneous to a few seconds or minutes. The following are the elements of real-time data analytics.

- Aggregator
- Broker
- Analytics engine
- Stream processor

The main benefit of real-time data analytics is momentum. The less time a firm waits between receiving data and analyzing it, the more data insights it may use to make changes and act on a critical decision. Similarly, real-time data analytics tools allow businesses to monitor how people interact with a product immediately after it is released, allowing them to make necessary adjustments without delay. Other advantages and uses include managing location data, detecting abnormalities, and better marketing.

11.7 How Streaming Works

Sensors from the Internet of Things, servers, security logs, applications, and internal/external systems are just a handful of today's data sources. Controlling the volume and velocity of data generated, much alone the structure, is practically impossible. Traditional systems are built to collect, process, and structure data before it can be acted upon. In contrast, streaming data architecture allows users to consume, persist in storage, enrich, and analyze the streaming data. As a result, data stream applications will always require two primary functions: storage and processing. Storage must record large amounts of data consistently and sequentially. Processing must be able to communicate with storage, ingest data, analyze it, and compute with it. This adds to the problems and considerations when working with legacy databases or systems. Streaming data applications can now be built using a variety of platforms and tools. Streaming data is used in real-time stock exchanges, real-time retail inventory management, social media feeds, multiplayer gaming engagements, and ride-sharing apps, to name a few examples. For example, when a passenger calls Uber, real-time data streams combine to create a seamless customer experience. The software combines real-time position monitoring, traffic statistics, pricing, and traffic data to match the rider with the best possible driver, compute a fee, and anticipate journey time based on real-time and historical data. Streaming data, in this sense, is the initial step for every data-driven organization, allowing for massive data acquisition, integration, and real-time analytics.

11.8 Real-time Streams vs. Batch Processing

Data must be downloaded in batches before processing, storing, or analyzing it, in batch data processing methods. In contrast, streaming data is continuously received, allowing it to be treated in real-time, the second it is generated. Streaming data is delivered in the form of unending streams of events. This data comes in a range of sizes and forms, and it comes from a variety of places, including the cloud, on-premises, and hybrid cloud. Due to the complexity of today's modern requirements, legacy data processing technologies have become useless for most use cases. They can only process data as groups of transactions gathered over time. Before data goes stale, modern businesses must act on updated data every millisecond. This continuous data delivers a host of advantages that change the way businesses function.

11.9 HADOOP STREAMING

Hadoop Streaming is a feature/utility of the Hadoop ecosystem that allows users to run a MapReduce job as Mapper and Reducer from an executable script. Hadoop Streaming is sometimes mistaken for real-time streaming, although it is merely a tool that executes a script in the MapReduce architecture. For example, the executable script might include a code for real-time data ingestion. The Hadoop Streaming utility's core feature is that it runs the Mapper and Reducer without needing external scripts. It produces a MapReduce job, sends it to the cluster, and watches it until it gets completed.

In Fig. 11.3, the Mapper accepts key–value pairs from the Input Reader/Format, maps them according to code logic, and then sends the data to the Reduce stream, which aggregates the data and releases it to the output.

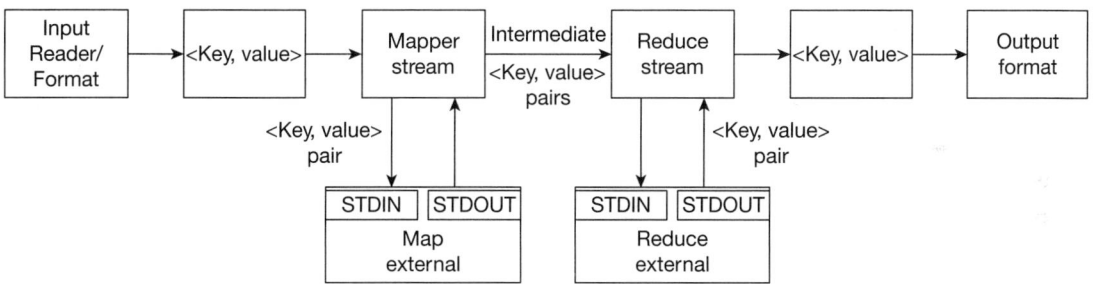

Figure 11.3 Hadoop streaming architecture

The mapper and reducer scripts (in the example above) receive the input from STDIN line by line, and emits the output to STDOUT. The program starts a MapReduce task, sends it to a suitable cluster, and tracks its progress until it is completed. When a script is supplied for mappers, the script is launched as a distinct process for each mapper task when the mapper is initialized. The mapper job translates its inputs (key–value pairs) into lines, which it then pushes to the process's standard input. Meanwhile, the mapper collects the line-oriented outputs from the standard output and turns each line into a key–value pair, which the mapper gathers as a result. When a reducer script is supplied, each reducer job runs the script as a distinct process before initializing the reducer. As the reducer task runs, it turns the key–value pairs in its input into lines and feeds the lines to the process's standard input. Meanwhile, the reducer collects the process's line-oriented outputs from STDOUT and turns each line into a key–value pair, which is subsequently collected as the reducer's result. The prefix of a line until the first tab character is the key for both mapper and reducer, and the remainder of the line is the value except for the tab character. When a line has no tab characters, the entire line is considered a key, and the value is null. This can be changed by using the –input format command option for the mapper and the –output format command option for the reducer.

11.9.1 Hadoop Streaming Characteristics

Hadoop Streaming provides several useful features: On Hadoop clusters, users can run non-Java-programmed MapReduce tasks. Python, Perl, and C++ are among the supported languages. Hadoop Streaming keeps track of the tasks' progress and offers logs of their complete execution for analysis. Hadoop Streaming is based on the MapReduce model, allowing scalability, flexibility, and security. Streaming tasks in Hadoop are simple to create and don't require any code (except for executables). It does not work without Hadoop. As we discussed already, it does not support true streaming. It has no data retention options.

Other open-source tools and utilities for real-time and batch extensive data analysis are available on the market. Choosing the ideal one necessitates a thorough understanding of these technologies. Table 11.1 compares the various popular tools to help you pick the best one for your needs.

Table 11.1 Hadoop streaming vs. others

Tools/Utility	True streaming	Processing framework	Performance	Scalability	Hadoop framework	Data retention	Languages
Hadoop Streaming	No	MapReduce	Relatively low	Scalable	Doesn't run without Hadoop	No	Python, Perl, C++
Spark Streaming	No	In-memory computation	Relatively higher	Scalable	Can work without Hadoop	No	Java, Scala, Python
Kafka	Yes	Java-based	High throughput of data	Scalable	Can work without Hadoop	Configurable	Java, Python

Popular Hadoop Streaming Parameters

Streaming allows you to use both streaming and generic command parameters. Table 11.2 provides a list of standard command-line syntax. Hadoop Streaming supports streaming command parameters as well as generic command options.

The general command line syntax is:

mapred streaming [genericOptions] [streamingOptions]

Table 11.2 Hadoop streaming parameters

Parameters	Desirability	Description
-input	Required	Input directory or file location for the Mapper.
-output	Required	Output directory location for the Reducer.
-mapper	Required	Mapper file (for Python) or Java class name or executable.
-reducer	Required	Reducer file (for Python) or Java Class name or executable.
-inputformat	Optional	The Java class name should return the key-value pair from the input specified other than the text format. Default is TextInputFormat.
-outputformat	Optional	The Java class name should return the key-value pair from the output specified other than the text format. Default is TextOutputFormat.
-partitioner	Optional	The Java class name behaves as a partitioner that partitions the data based on the key.
-combiner	Optional	The Java class combines the output from the Mapper into one stream before sending the data to the Reducer.
-cmdenv name=value	Optional	Passes the environment variable to streaming commands.
-verbose	Optional	Used to get verbose output.
-numReduceTasks	Optional	Specifies the number of reducers to act. Default is 1.
-mapdebug	Optional	An additional script path will be called when the Map task fails.
-reducedebug	Optional	An additional script path will be called when the Reduce task fails.

11.9.2 Specifying Other Plugins for Jobs

Just as with a normal MapReduce job, we can specify other plugins for a streaming job:

```
-inputformat JavaClassName
-outputformat JavaClassName
-partitioner JavaClassName
-combiner streaming Command or JavaClassName
```

The input format class you provide should return key–value pairs of the Text class. If no input format class is specified, TextInputFormat is utilized as the default. The keys will be disregarded since the TextInputFormat delivers keys of the Long Writable class that are not part of the input data; only the values will be routed to the streaming mapper. The output format class you provide should take key–value pairs from the Text class. If no output format class is specified, the TextOutputFormat is utilized by default.

Setting Environment Variables

To set an environment variable in a streaming command, use:

> -cmdenv EXAMPLE_DIR=/home/example/dictionaries/

Generic Command Options [[**H3**]]

Streaming allows you to use both streaming and generic command parameters. The following is a list of standard command-line syntax. **Note**: The command will fail if the generic options are placed before the streaming options. For an example, see Making Archives Available to Tasks.

> bin/hadoop command [genericOptions] [streamingOptions]

The Hadoop generic command options

Table 11.3 lists down various parameters for the Hadoop generic options.

Table 11.3 Hadoop generic command options

Parameter	Desirability	Description
-conf configuration_file	Optional	Specify an application configuration file
-D property=value	Optional	Use value for the given property
-fs host:port or local	Optional	Specify a namenode
-jt host:port or local	Optional	Specify a job tracker
-files	Optional	Specify comma-separated files to be copied to the Map/Reduce cluster
-libjars	Optional	Specify comma-separated jar files to include in the classpath
-archives	Optional	Specify comma-separated archives to be unarchived on the computer machines

SUMMARY

Businesses may obtain insights and act on data as soon as it enters the system with real-time analytics. Inquiries are answered in seconds using real-time data. They deal with massive amounts of data at a high rate and respond quickly.

To handle streaming data, a system must be able to analyze and offer real-time outcomes. Data processing in real-time is an essential component of the Lambda Architecture.

Streaming data processing accounts for the "speed layer" in such a system, enabling a real-time view of occurrences.

Hadoop Streaming is a utility for running non-Hadoop applications in the processing pipeline despite its misleading name. There are also Big Data frameworks explicitly designed for real-time data sources, such as Apache Storm, Apache Flink, Apache Samza, and Apache Spark Streaming.

Apache Spark Streaming: Despite having a straightforward Spark API for communicating changes, Spark Streaming's handling of streaming data is inefficient. Attaining resilience and low-latency message handling takes a lot of work in Spark. It works in micro-batches, which means it fetches a specific number of messages at a predetermined period. When the buffer is full, Spark will begin processing these messages. Unfortunately, this is incompatible with the nature of processing streaming data. Other frameworks, such as Apache Storm are also available, processing messages in real-time rather than batching or buffering them.

Although Samza was designed from the ground-up to interact with Apache Kafka, it can also process data from other streaming sources. Although it is far more capable of handling streaming data than Spark, it still falls short on flexibility. Serialization and data transformation do not necessarily occur sequentially. Samza anticipates that communications will be converted as soon as they are consumed, with modifications occurring afterward. On paper, it sounds incredible, but it has little to do with real-world applications, much like Spark's state management.

A thread pool is a software architecture paradigm for creating concurrent execution in a computer program. For example, the worker-crew concept, often known as replicated workers, is a thread pool that keeps several threads waiting for the supervisory program to allocate tasks for concurrent execution. The notion enhances speed by retaining a pool of threads and avoids the frequent production and destruction of threads for short-lived processes that cause execution delays.

Streaming data pours into businesses from various sources, like the web, social networks, clickstreams, sensors, the cloud, machines, and devices and so on. The demand for real-time data and customer insights has accelerated the proliferation of this type of data and the requirement to extract business intelligence from it. However, gathering and analyzing streaming data has its drawbacks.

Talend Cloud includes Talend Data Streams, transforming the Talend Cloud applications into a truly collaborative platform for all types of data users. Data pipelines, metadata, and datasets may all be accessed from anywhere on the platform. Data experts, such as analysts and data scientists, can use Data Streams to perform data ingestion and lightweight Extract, Transform, and Load (ETL) procedures without consulting IT, all while capturing metadata. Within hours or minutes, data engineers may prepare streaming data using the Talend Data Streams UI, integrate a data quality recipe from Talend Data Preparation in the pipeline, and distribute datasets throughout the platform.

The main benefit of real-time data analytics is momentum. The less time a firm must wait between receiving data and analyzing it, the more data insights it may use to make changes and act on a critical decision. Similarly, real-time data analytics tools allow businesses to monitor how people interact with a product immediately after it is released, allowing them to make necessary adjustments without delay. Other advantages and uses include managing location data, detecting abnormalities, and better marketing.

Hadoop Streaming is a feature/utility of the Hadoop ecosystem that allows users to run a MapReduce job as Mapper and Reducer from an executable script. Hadoop Streaming is sometimes mistaken for real-time streaming, although it is merely a tool that executes a script in the MapReduce architecture. For example, the executable script might include code for real-time data ingestion. The Hadoop Streaming utility's core feature is that it runs the Mapper and Reducer without needing external scripts, produces a MapReduce job, sends it to the cluster, and watches it until it is completed.

Hadoop Streaming provides several useful features: On Hadoop clusters, users can run non-Java-programmed MapReduce tasks. Python, Perl, and C++ are among the supported languages. Hadoop Streaming keeps track of tasks' progress and offers logs of their complete execution for analysis. Hadoop Streaming is based on the MapReduce model, allowing scalability, flexibility, and security. Streaming tasks in Hadoop are simple to create and don't require any code (except for executables). However, they do not work without Hadoop.

EXERCISES

Multiple Choice Questions

1. **This is a utility for running non-Hadoop Applications:**
   A. Hadoop Streaming
   B. Apache Spark Streaming
   C. Apache Samza
   D. Thread Pool
   Answer: A
   Explanation: Hadoop Streaming is a utility for running non-Hadoop applications in the processing pipeline despite its misleading name. There are also Big Data frameworks explicitly designed for real-time data sources, such as Apache Storm, Apache Flink, Apache Samza, and Apache Spark Streaming.

2. **This is designed from the ground–up to interact with Apache Kafka:**
   A. Hadoop Streaming
   B. Apache Spark Streaming
   C. Apache Samza
   D. Thread Pool
   Answer: C
   Explanation: Although Samza was designed from the ground–up to interact with Apache Kafka, it can also process data from other streaming sources. Although it is far more capable of handling streaming data than Spark, it still falls short on flexibility. Serialization and data transformation do not necessarily occur sequentially. Samza

anticipates that communications will be converted as soon as they are consumed, with modifications occurring afterward. Theoretically, it sounds incredible, but it has little to do with real-world applications, much like Spark's state management.

3. **This is a software architecture paradigm for creating concurrent execution in a computer program:**
   A. Hadoop Streaming
   B. Apache Spark Streaming
   C. Apache Samza
   D. Thread Pool
   Answer: D
   Explanation: A thread pool is a software architecture paradigm for creating concurrent execution in a computer program. For example, the worker-crew concept, often known as replicated workers, is a thread pool that keeps several threads waiting for the supervisory program to allocate tasks for concurrent execution. The notion enhances speed by retaining a pool of threads and avoids the frequent production and destruction of threads for short-lived processes that cause execution delays.

Short-answer Questions

1. **What are the advantages of the Real-time Analytics? Give some examples.**
   Businesses may obtain insights and act on data as soon as it enters the system with real-time analytics. Inquiries are answered in seconds using real-time data. They deal with massive amounts of data at a high rate and respond quickly. The following are some real-time customer analytics examples: Orders may be viewed in real-time for better tracking and trend detection. To better analyze user behavior, consumer activities like page views and shopping cart usage can be tracked. Similarly, customers can be targeted with promos while shopping, impacting their decisions in real-time.

2. **What are the characteristics of a perfect solution for real-time analytics?**
   The following characteristics should be included in an ideal streaming data processing solution: It should rely on a cluster of machines that share nothing (or as little as feasible) to simplify the design and prevent failure scenarios caused by node loss. It should also save the state locally on each machine rather than distributing it across all nodes. This is the first point of interaction when updating or querying a state. It also has to commit the state to a shared state store, accessible to all nodes for robustness, allowing new nodes to be obtained from this typical state store to get their current state. It makes use of an internal state/offset storage that isn't prone to resource restrictions, such as disk space. It has a user-friendly, test-friendly API. It is good if you can declare pipelines with updates that are chained together. Support for functional programming paradigms is also beneficial.

3. **What are the advantages of real-time analytics?**
   The main benefit of real-time data analytics is momentum. The less time a firm must wait between receiving data and analyzing it, the more data insights it may use to make changes and act on a critical decision. Similarly, real-time data analytics tools

allow businesses to monitor how people interact with a product immediately after it is released, allowing them to make necessary adjustments without delay. Other advantages and uses include managing location data, detecting abnormalities, and better marketing.

4. **Differentiate between real-time streams and batch processing.**
   Data must be downloaded in batches before processing, storing, or analyzing in batch data-processing methods. In contrast, streaming data is continuously received, allowing it to be treated in real-time the second it is generated. Data is now delivered in the form of unending streams of events. This data comes in a range of sizes and forms, and it comes from a variety of places, including the cloud, on-premises, and hybrid cloud. Due to the complexity of today's modern requirements, legacy data processing technologies have become useless for most use cases. They can only process data as groups of transactions gathered over time. Before data goes stale, modern businesses must act on updated data every millisecond. This continuous data delivers a host of advantages that change the way businesses function.

Essay-type Questions

1. Write an essay on Apache Spark Streaming. What are the different issues associated with this process?
2. Write an essay on Apache Samza Streaming. What are the different issues faced by this framework?
3. What are the challenges to be solved in an application which does real-time data analytics?
4. Write an essay on Thread Pooling.
5. What are the difficulties in data streaming?
6. Write an essay on the future of data streaming.
7. What are the advantages of stream computing in the Big Data world?
8. How does streaming technology work?
9. Write an essay on Hadoop Streaming.

CHAPTER 12

Pig Latin

> **LEARNING OBJECTIVES**
>
> In this chapter, we discuss Pig Latin, a dataflow language. It examines the configuration and installation of Pig to help us get started with Pig for Big Data processing. Then the chapter discusses how to write Pig Latin scripts, the various data types, operators, and commands, grunt shell and the basic operators used in Pig, built-in functions of Pig, write, load, and store functions. Finally, the chapter explains the Pig Latin script optimization. It compares Pig language with MapReduce and Hive.

12.1 Introduction

Apache Hadoop, in the year 2008, released a high-level platform called **Apache Pig** supported by Yahoo's researchers, to analyze large datasets. **Pig Latin (Apache Pig)** is a high-level language for data analysis programs.

Apache Pig is a platform for studying huge datasets that includes a high-level language for defining data analysis algorithms as well as infrastructure for assessing them. It has a lot of relational capabilities that make it simple to join, organize, and aggregate data.

Pig provided the advantage of executing MapReduce, Apache Spark, and Apache Tez jobs. The salient properties of Pig programs are that their structure supports substantial parallelization of data analysis tasks, optimizes execution automatically, and allows users to create their function for special-purpose processing. For example, in MapReduce, the development cycle is very long, and the time between job submission and getting the output for a "Big Data job" is very long.

Apache Pig is a procedural language that supports a multi-query approach. While it keeps the scalability and reliability of Apache Hadoop, Apache Pig simplifies the programming. Most languages require users to have a basic knowledge of programming, but Pig is similar to SQL and easy for anyone to learn.

Pig has a lot in common with ETL, primarily if the ETL tools are used on several servers simultaneously. The Hadoop ecosystem includes Apache Pig. Hive and Pig are designed to load and transform unstructured, structured, and semi-structured data into HDFS, unlike many standard ETL solutions that are good at structuring data.

Pig is a high-level tool that requires you to understand Pig Latin, its advanced language. Pig Latin is a programming language that aids in creating data analysis tools. Using this language, you can write, read, and process data while designing particular functions for these tasks.

Pig Latin scripts will be automatically converted to MapReduce operations. The Pig Engine (also known as Apache Pig) assists in converting the written scripts into MapReduce operations and is of significant help in doing Big Data Analytics. It is a fast-programming language that streamlines several operations and helps to save time. While there is a learning curve, once you get beyond it, you will find it as one of the most accessible tools to deal with.

12.2 Basic Features of Apache Pig

Apache Pig supports relational style operations like filter, union, group, join, sort, etc. Apache Pig is extensible, allowing users to write their user-defined functions and processes. It implements a subset of relational algebra, and hence it is easy to learn for SQL programmers. Apache Pig allows users to insert their code anywhere in the data pipeline. The data structure of Apache Pig is multivalued, nested, and richer. Apache Pig is more suited for Big Data because it can handle both structured and unstructured data analysis. Pig contains a lot of operators that you may utilize to make your programming activities easier. It allows you to customize your functions to meet your individual needs (User-Defined Functions, or UDFs), and they may be written in any programming language, including Python, JRuby, Jave, and others. Pig optimizes your actions automatically before conducting them. It allows you to focus on the overall project rather than worry about individual Map and Reduce functions.

You don't need to know Java to use MapReduce and complete its tasks. Pig allows you to do basic operations with fewer lines of code. For example, when you use Pig to conduct MapReduce tasks, you write 20 times less code than if you didn't use Pig. Pig may save you a lot of time working on MapReduce applications. It has a wide variety of operations, including Join, Extract, Filters, etc. Pig has a lot of data types in its model that MapReduce doesn't have. For example, bags, tuples, and a few more things fall under this category.

12.3 Apache Pig Architecture

Apache Pig provides the scalability of Hadoop and hence can process the large volume of data present in the Hadoop File system. Apache Pig proves useful where time-sensitive data loads and analytical insights are required. The two modes in which Pig can be executed are Local Mode and MapReduce Mode.

- **Local Mode:** In Local mode, the Pig Latin scripts execute from the local host/local file system. The advantage of running Pig in the local mode is that the user does not need to worry about Hadoop or HDFS. Pig commands will be run locally in the JVM, and this mode is usually helpful in the testing phase.
- **MapReduce Mode:** In MapReduce mode, the script will automatically invoke a MapReduce job in the backend to operate on the data that exists in the HDFS.

Either of these mechanisms can execute Pig Latin scripts.

12.3.1 Using the Interactive Pig Shell

The user can interactively enter Pig Latin scripts and see the output using the interactive Grunt shell in Pig. Executing the code using the grunt shell can be helpful when the user is in the initial stage of development.

Use the "pig" command and the filename to enter the grunt shell. To enter the grunt shell in Local mode

```
pig -x local
```
Entering the grunt shell in local mode

To enter the grunt shell in MapReduce mode

```
pig -x mapreduce
```
Entering the grunt shell in MapReduce mode

The MapReduce mode will be chosen by default if the pig command is passed without arguments.

12.3.2 Using Batch Processing

Pig Latin scripts contain files that are saved as .Pig. The Pig optimizer will decide the order of execution of the Pig scripts. User-defined functions can be executed with Java, Python or JavaScript. Let us now look at the architectural components of Apache Pig in detail (Fig. 12.1).

Pig Parser

Pig scripts are written and executed by any one of the execution mechanisms (batch/interactive/embedded mode). After execution, the Pig parser will apply a series of transformations to get the desired result. The Pig Parser does syntax checking, type checking, and other miscellaneous checks, and the output is generated as a DAG (Directed Acyclic Graph). In the directed acyclic graph (DAG) output, the logical operators will be represented as nodes and flow as edges. The parsed output is then given to the optimizer.

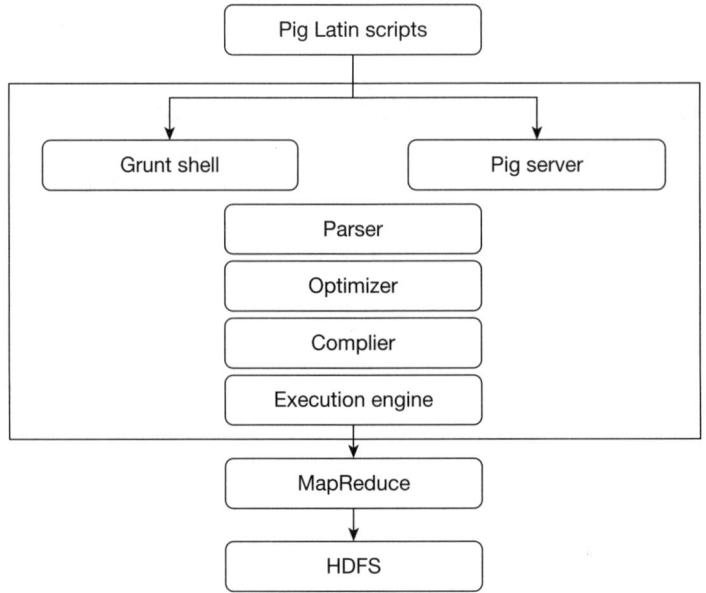

Figure 12.1   Pig architecture

Pig Optimizer

The Pig Optimizer performs logical optimization of the DAG such as splitting, merging, projection, pushdown, transformation, and reordering. The Pig optimizer processes the extracted data and improves query performance. The optimizer's primary goal is to lower the quantity of data in the pipeline at any given moment while processing the extracted data, and it accomplishes this by doing tasks such as:

1. **PushUpFilter:** If the filter has many conditions and may be divided, Pig divides the conditions and pushes each condition up independently. Choosing these parameters earlier in the process helps to reduce the number of records still in the pipeline.
2. **PushDownForEachFlatten:** Applying flattens as late as feasible in the plan provides a cross product between a complicated type such as a tuple or a bag and the other fields in the record. As a result, the quantity of records in the pipeline is kept low.
3. **ColumnPruner:** The optimizer's primary goal is to lower the quantity of data in the pipeline at any given moment while processing the extracted data. It reduces the size of a record by omitting columns that are never used or are no longer needed. After each operator, this can be used to trim the fields as aggressively as feasible.
4. **MapKeyPruner:** Reduces the size of the record by removing map keys that are never utilized.
5. **Limit Optimizer:** Pig turns the load or sort operator into a limit-sensitive version, which does not need processing the entire dataset if the limit operator is applied immediately after the load or sort operator. The number of records is reduced by applying the restriction early.

Pig Compiler

The Pig compiler compiles the output generated by the optimizer into a series of MapReduce jobs. The optimized logical plan is automatically converted into MapReduce jobs, and the performance is improved by rearranging the execution order of the jobs.

Pig Execution Engine

The Pig Execution engine sends the MapReduce jobs to Hadoop for execution. These MapReduce jobs are executed on the Hadoop platform to produce the desired results. The DUMP statement displays the results on the console/screen. The STORE statement stores the results in HDFS (Hadoop Distributed File System).

12.4 INTERPRETING PIG SCRIPTS

Apache Pig is mainly used for ad-hoc processing, and a Pig Latin script consists of logical, optimized logical, physical, and MapReduce execution plans, as shown in Fig. 12.2.

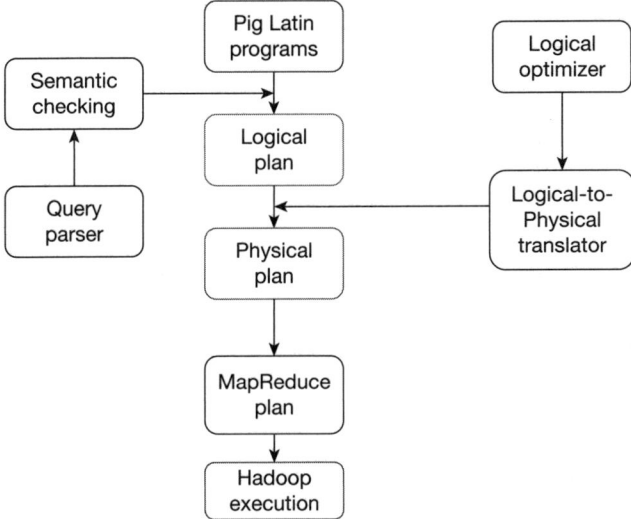

Figure 12.2 Interpreting a Pig script

The logical and physical plans are created during the execution of a Pig script. Apache Pig processes Pig Latin statements in the following manner: Pig performs basic parsing and validates all statements' syntax and semantics. The parser produces a logical plan which describes the logical operators which have been executed, and no data processing is performed during the creation of the logical plan. For each line of the logical plan, syntax checking is performed, and when an error occurs, an exception will be thrown, and program execution will be stopped. Once the logical plan is generated, the script will move to the physical plan that describes the physical operators. Apache Pig will perform limited optimization before execution. When compared to SQL, Apache Pig is a data flow language which means the user will be writing in a sequence of steps.

Although Pig has very few BI tools integrated into it, the recent good news is that Pig can be integrated with Apache Zeppelin 0.7; so now users can write Pig Latin scripts and visualize the result.

12.5 APACHE PIG INSTALLATION ON UBUNTU

The user should have installed Apache Hadoop and Java JDK to install Pig. In the previous chapters, we have discussed the installation and configuration of Apache Hadoop. You can download Pig from the link below:

Installation link for Pig

```
https://pig.apache.org/releases.html
```

When we click the link, it displays all Apache Pig Releases (Fig. 12.3). We shall choose the latest version.

Apache Pig Releases

- Download
- News
  - 19 June, 2017: release 0.17.0 available
  - 8 June, 2016: release 0.16.0 available
  - 6 June, 2015: release 0.15.0 available
  - 20 November, 2014: release 0.14.0 available
  - 4 July, 2014: release 0.13.0 available
  - 14 April, 2014: release 0.12.1 available
  - 14 October, 2013: release 0.12.0 available
  - 1 April, 2013: release 0.11.1 available
  - 21 February, 2013: release 0.11.0 available
  - 6 January, 2013: release 0.10.1 available
  - 25 April, 2012: release 0.10.0 available
  - 22 January, 2012: release 0.9.2 available
  - 5 October, 2011: release 0.9.1 available
  - 29 July, 2011: release 0.9.0 available
  - 24 April, 2011: release 0.8.1 available
  - 17 December, 2010: release 0.8.0 available
  - 13 May, 2010: release 0.7.0 available
  - 1 March, 2010: release 0.6.0 available
  - 29 October, 2009: release 0.5.0 available
  - 29 September, 2009: release 0.4.0 available
  - 25 June, 2009: release 0.3.0 available
  - 8 April, 2009: release 0.2.0 available
  - 5 December, 2008: release 0.1.1 available
  - 11 September, 2008: release 0.1.0 available

Figure 12.3 The various Apache Pig Releases available

Figure 12.4 indicates the folder structure for downloading PIG. Download the latest file. Move the downloaded tar file (pig-0.17.0.tar.gz) to the same directory where Hadoop is installed. Then untar the file (pig-0.17.0.tar.gz) using the command given in the code snippet below. In the below tar command, x extracts an archived file, z means file wget, and f refers to the filename of the archived file.

```
cirf@ubuntu:~$ tar zxf pig-0.17.0.tar.gz
```
Tar command

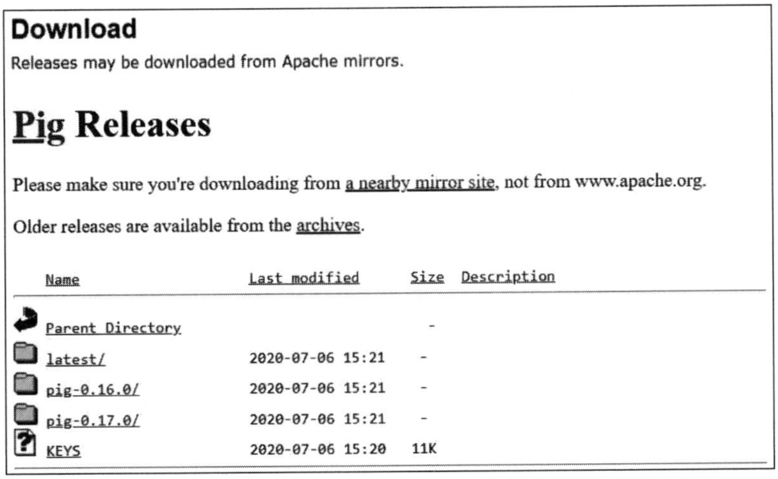

```
Download
Releases may be downloaded from Apache mirrors.
```

Pig Releases

```
Please make sure you're downloading from a nearby mirror site, not from www.apache.org.

Older releases are available from the archives.

  Name              Last modified      Size  Description

  Parent Directory                       -
  latest/           2020-07-06 15:21     -
  pig-0.16.0/       2020-07-06 15:21     -
  pig-0.17.0/       2020-07-06 15:21     -
  KEYS              2020-07-06 15:20    11K
```

Figure 12.4   Latest Release (0.17.0)

Then, we need to edit the ".bashrc" file. To edit this file, execute the below command:

```
cirf@ubuntu:~$ nano .bashrc
```
Editing the bashrc file

And in this file, we need to add the following:

```
export PATH= $PATH:/home/cirf/pig-
0.17.0/bin export PIG_HOME=
/home/cirf/pig-0.17.0 export
PIG_CLASSPATH=
$HADOOP_HOME/conf
```
Setting Apache Pig environment variables

Run the below command to update the changes in the same terminal.

```
$source .bashrc
```
bashrc command to initialize the shell

Then we can test if Apache Pig was installed correctly using the command below.

```
Command: $pig -version
```
Checking the Pig version

12.6   GRUNT SHELL COMMANDS

Grunt is the interactive shell in Pig that enables the user to interact with HDFS. The grunt shell has some basic utility commands (Table 12.1) and file-related commands. File related commands are similar to Linux/HDFS (CopyFromLocal, CopyToLocal, mv, rm etc.) related commands.

Table 12.1 Grunt utility and file commands

S. No	Type	Command
1.	Utility commands	Help, Quit, Kill jobid, Set debug[ON|OFF], Set job.name 'jobname'.
2.	File commands	Cat, Cd, CopyFromLocal, copyToLocal, cp, ls, mkdir, mv, pwd, rm, rmf, exec, run.

`Exec` and `Run` are two new file commands that will run inside the Grunt shell and help debug Pig scripts. The difference between `exec` and `run` is that `exec` will execute in a separate space from the Grunt shell while `run` will execute in the same space as Grunt (interactive mode).

sh

The user can invoke any shell commands using the 'sh' command. However, shell environment commands cannot be executed using the 'sh' (except -cd command) from the grunt shell. For example, all the files and directories will be listed when sh ls is executed.

```
grunt> sh ls
```
sh command

fs

`fs` is a shell command and using the 'fs', the user can get a list of available files from the HDFS, create a directory and move data, etc.

```
grunt>fs -ls
grunt>fs -mkdir/tempdata
```

The user can clear the screen and output the executions using the clear command.

```
grunt> clear
```
clear command

Help

The list of Pig commands or Pig properties can be printed using the `help` command.

```
grunt> help
```
help command

History

The `history` command will display a list of statements since the Grunt shell was invoked.

```
grunt>history
```
History command

SET

The SET command, when executed, will assign values to keys that are case-sensitive in Pig.

```
grunt> SET debug 'off'
grunt> SET job.name
'hello'
grunt>SET default_parallel 100
```
SET command

Table 12.2 lists the various parameters (key) possible with SET command.

Table 12.2 List of values for SET

Key	Description
default_parallel	The default parallel sets the number of reducers for a map job by passing a whole number (integer) as a value to the key.
debug	The debugging feature in Apache Pig is passed on/off to this key. (Example: SET debug 'on')
job.name	The job.name can set the Job name by passing a string value to this key.
job.priority	The priority of a job can be set by passing one of the following values to this key – • very_low • low • normal • high • very_high
stream.skippath	The stream.skippath is used for streaming and passes the path in the form of a string.

Command Quit

The user can exit/quit from the Grunt shell using this command.

```
grunt>quit
```

12.7 Pig Data Model

Pig Latin's data model allows it to handle a wide range of data (Fig. 12.5) including Bag and Tuple. Pig Latin is capable of handling both atomic data types such as int, float, long, and double, and complicated data types such as tuple, bag, and map. It is a very powerful language and flexible in how Pig processes the data. It provides good support for user-defined functions. Pig Latin programs can be written as a sequence of steps where each step in the program will be a high-level data transformation and support operation like filter, join, union and group. Table 12.3 represents various data types and their corresponding PIG class for the reference.

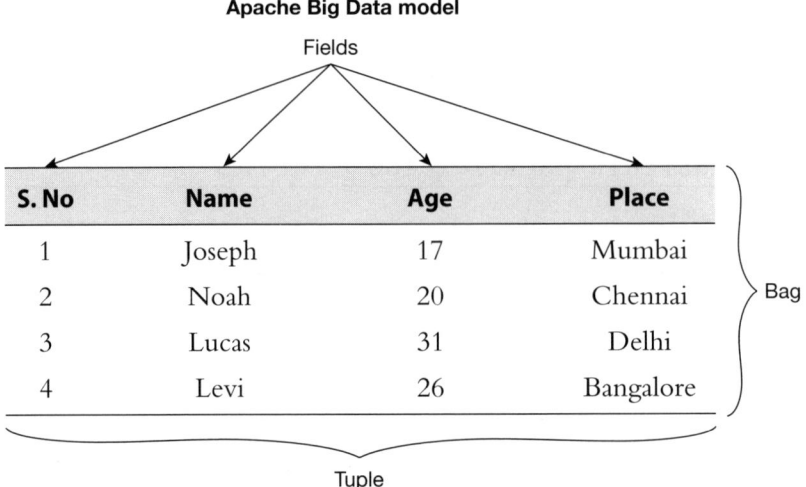

Figure 12.5   Pig data model representation

Table 12.3   Pig data types and their implementation class

S. No	Pig Data Type	Implementing Class
01	Bag	Org.apache.pig.data.DataBag
02	Tuple	Org.apache.pig.data.Tuple
03	Map	java.Util.Map <Object, Object>
04	Integer	java.lang.Integer
05	Long	Java.lang.Long
06	Float	java.lang.Float
07	Double	java.lang.Double
08	Chararray	java.lang.String
09	Bytearray	byte[]

12.7.1 Pig Data Types

There is a famous saying, "Pigs eat anything". The name "Pig" for the data type platform is symbolic of saying that the input data can be in any form. Pig's data types comprise the data model and consist of scalar or complex data types (bags/tuples/maps). Pig can operate on any form of data (nested/relational/semi-structured/structured). With Pig, the data model is specified when you load the data. Any data loaded from disk into Pig will have a specific schema and structure, and Pig needs to understand the structure. Also, the Pig data model allows the user to manage table-like structures and nested hierarchical data structures to support the diversity of data. Scalar types contain a single value, while complex types include other values, such as Tuple, Container, and Map. Figure 12.6 shows the two data types that Pig's data model supports.

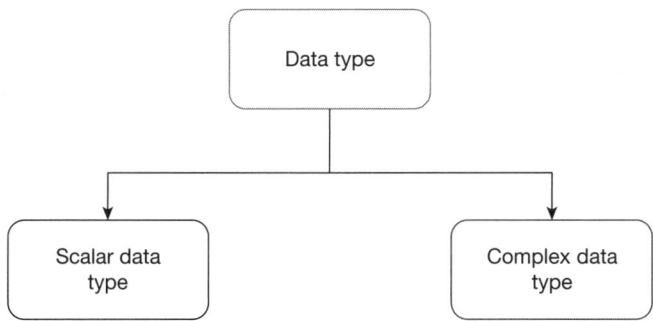

Figure 12.6 Data types in Pig

Scalar Data Type

The basic data types in Pig Latin are atomic, also known as scalar data types (Table 12.4), which are utilized in all kinds such as string, float, int, double, long, char[], and byte[]. Primitive data types are another name for atomic data types. For example, in a field (column), each cell value is an atomic data type.

Pig Latin has atomic values that are scalar. An atomic value is a single value stored in a string form and can be used as a number, string, or binary object. Typecasting is supported in Pig. If the data type is not specified, it defaults to a byte array.

Table 12.4 Scalar data types

S. No	Data Type	Description
1.	int	This scalar data type is a signed 32-bit integer.
2.	long	This scalar data type is a signed 64-bit integer.
3.	float	This scalar data type is a signed 32-bit decimal.
4.	double	This scalar data type represents a 64-bit floating-point.
5.	chararray	This scalar data type represents a character array(string) in Unicode UTF-8 format.
6.	bytearray	This scalar data type is a byte array/binary object.
7.	boolean	This scalar data type represents a boolean value.
8.	datetime	This scalar data type represents a date/time.
9.	Biginteger	This scalar data type represents a JAVA Big Integer.
10.	Bigdecimal	This scalar data type represents a JAVA Big Decimal.

Complex Data Type

A complex data type is frequently made up of several different data types. You could, for example, design a complicated data type with built-in types, opaque types, and other complex types as components. Pig Latin has three complex data types namely: Tuple, Bag and Map (Table 12.5).

Table 12.5 Complex data types

S. No	Data Type	Description
1.	Tuple	A tuple is a complex data type that contains an ordered set of fields (any type). The tuple is used in a row in a relation. A relation represents the complete database, and a bag of tuples is called a relation.
2.	Bag	A Bag is a complex data type and is an unordered collection of tuples. In a bag, each tuple in the set can contain an arbitrary number of fields of any type. It is represented by tuples separated by commas and enclosed within curly brackets.
3.	Map	A key-value pair [key#value] is known as a map. It is a complex data type. While the key must be unique and of a char array type, the value can be stored in any type. Maps help process semi-structured data such as JSON and XML.

12.7.2 Pig Latin Statements

Pig statements are the basic constructs that work with relations and include expressions and schemas. Every statement in Pig ends with a semicolon (;). The Pig can take a relation as input and produce another as output except for the LOAD and STORE statements.

Example

```
grunt> Student_details = LOAD 'student_details.txt' USING
PigStorage(',')as
( id:int, firstname:chararray, lastname:chararray,
phone:chararray, city:chararray );
```

Pig provides a platform to users that cannot code in Java where each processing step results in a new dataset or relation.

Consider the example,

```
X = load 'stu';
```

Here, "X" is the name of a relation or new dataset fed while loading the dataset "stu". "X" is not a variable even though it acts as a variable. So once the assignment is done, "X" will be permanent, and the relation's name can be reused in other steps.

Example

```
X = load 'stu';
X = filter X by age > 18.0;
X = foreach X generate stuname;
```

A new dataset is created, although the reassignment is not done for "X" in every step. Pig Latin also has a concept of fields called columns. In the above example, "age" and "stuname" are called fields or columns. The user can relax while defining keywords in Apache Pig Latin because they are not case-sensitive. It is important to note that the relations and column names are case-sensitive. For example, X = load 'stu'; is not equivalent to x = load 'stu'; Commenting for Pig statements is simple: For multi-line comments in the Apache pig scripts, we use "/* … */" and for single-line comments we use "–".

12.7.3 Pig Arithmetic Operators

The four basic arithmetic operations are addition, subtraction, multiplication, and division. For example, "+" (Plus), "–" (Minus), "*" (Subtraction), "/" (Division), and "%" (Remainder) are arithmetic operators that execute operations on numbers. An operator does something with one or more operands. Operators are basic mathematical operators. Table 12.6 describes the arithmetic operators of Pig Latin. Suppose a = 20 and b = 30.

Table 12.6 Arithmetic operators

S. No	Operator	Description	Example (a = 20 and b=30)
1	+	Adds values on either side of the operators	a + b will give the value of 30
2	-	Subtracts right-hand operand from left-hand operand	a – b will give the value of −10
3	*	Multiplies values on either side of the operator	a*b will give the value of 600
4	/	Divides left-hand operand by right-hand operand	b/a will give the value of 1.5
5	%	Divides left-hand operand by right-hand operand and returns remainder	b % a will give the value of 10
6	?:	Bincond: Evaluates the Boolean operators. It has three operands as shown: variable x = (expression) ? value1 if true : value2 if false.	b = (a == 1)? 05: 10; if a = 1 the value of b is 05. if a!=1 the value of b is 10
7.	CASE WHEN THEN ELSE END	The case operator is equivalent to nested bincond operator.	CASE b % 2 WHEN 0 THEN 'even' WHEN 1 THEN 'odd' END

The following is a sample data:

> **File Name: test.csv**
>
> 6729, DIANA,CHAIRMAN, 0,11/Dec/2000, 5000, 0, 10
> 6398, LESSLY, DIRECTOR, 6729, 11/June/2001, 2850, 0, 10
> 6217, CRONJE, DIRECTOR, 6729, 26/Aug/2002, 2450, 0, 20
> 6826, JACOB, DIRECTOR, 6729, 14/Jan/2009, 2975, 0, 30
> 6935, SCOTT, MANAGER, 6398, 19/Jan/2020, 3000, 0, 10
> 6044, HONDA, ANALYST, 6935, 14/Feb/2019, 3000, 0, 10
> 6353, ASHA, CLERK, 6044, 07/Mar/2022, 800, 0, 10
> 6162, DOREEN, SALESMAN, 6217, 21/Apr/2017, 1600, 300, 20
> 6671, JASMINE, SALESMAN, 6826, 12/Apr/2017, 1250, 500, 30

Let us try to load the data inside test.csv into a table titled "emp" with the command as shown below:

> **Loading the data into a relation**
> Execute the below in a single line to avoid each line execution.
>
> emp = LOAD 'Desktop/test.csv' USING PigStorage(',') AS
>   (empno:int,
>   ename:chararray,
>   job:chararray,
>   mgr:int,
>   hiredate:chararray,
>   sal:double,
>   comm:double,
>   deptno:int);

Let us group the relation "emp" using the Group operator and save the result in the relation "empgroup", as shown below.

> empgroup = GROUP emp BY deptno;
>
> The below command will show how the data has been grouped.
> dump empgroup;

The resultant data grouped by the deptno is shown below.

> 6729, DIANA,CHAIRMAN, 0,11/Dec/2000, 5000, 0, 10
> 6398, LESSLY, DIRECTOR, 6729, 11/June/2001, 2850, 0, 10
> 6935, SCOTT, MANAGER, 6398, 19/Jan/2020, 3000, 0, 10
> 6044, HONDA, ANALYST, 6935, 14/Feb/2019, 3000, 0, 10
> 6353, ASHA, CLERK, 6044, 07/Mar/2022, 800, 0, 10
> 6217, CRONJE, DIRECTOR, 6729, 26/Aug/2002, 2450, 0, 20
> 6162, DOREEN, SALESMAN, 6217, 21/Apr/2017, 1600, 300, 20
> 6826, JACOB, DIRECTOR, 6729, 14/Jan/2009, 2975, 0, 30
> 6671, JASMINE, SALESMAN, 6826, 12/Apr/2017, 1250, 500, 30

12.7.4 Pig Comparison Operators

Table 12.7 describes the comparison operators of Pig Latin.

Table 12.7 Pig comparison

S. No	Operator	Description
1.	==	The == is a comparison operator that will check if the values of two operands are equal or not.
2	!=	A != is a comparison operator that will check if the values of two operands are equal or not.
3	>	A > (Greater than) is a comparison operator that will check if the value of the left operand is greater than the value of the right operand.
4	<	A < (Less than) comparison operator will check if the value of the left operand is less than the value of the right operand.
5	>=	A >=(Greater than or equal to) is a comparison operator that will check if the value of the left operand is greater than or equal to the value of the right operand.
6	<=	A <= (Less than or equal to) is a comparison operator that will check if the left value is less than or equal to the value on the right.
7	Pattern match (x matches regex)	A comparison operator performs regular expression (regex) matching of a string x by checking if the string on the left matches the constant on the right. It uses the Java regular expression classes available under java.util.regex.pattern class to specify the regular expression and perform pattern matching.

12.7.5 Pig Type Construction Operators

Table 12.8 explains Type construction operators of Pig.

Table 12.8 Type construction operators

S. No	Operator	Description
1.	()	The Tuple constructor operator is a typical construction operator for constructing a tuple. E.g.:(Hannah, 9)
2.	{}	The Bag constructor operator is a typical construction operator for constructing a bag. E.g.: {(Hannah,9),(Divya,10)
3.	[]	The Map constructor operator is a typical construction operator for constructing a tuple.[name#Hannah,age#10]

12.7.6 Pig Relational Operators

Pig provides relational operators to operate on the data and perform operations like sorting, joining and filtering the data. Table 12.9 describes various relational operators of Pig.

Table 12.9 Relational operators

Operator	Description
	Relational Operator for Loading and Storing
LOAD	LOAD is a Pig relational operator to load the data from the local file system LOCAL or HDFS.
STORE	STORE is a Pig relational operator that saves to the local file system LOCAL or HDFS.
	Relational Operator for Filtering
FILTER	FILTER is a Pig relational operator that will remove unwanted rows from a relation and select which records will be retained in the data pipeline.
DISTINCT	DISTINCT is a Pig relational operator that will remove duplicate rows from a relation.
FOREACH, GENERATE	GENERATE is a Pig relational operator that generates data transformations based on the columns of data. A simple version of FOREACH will also work as a relational operator for project-specific columns of a relation to the output.
STREAM	STREAM is a Pig relational operator that transforms a relation using an external program.
	Relational Operator for Grouping and Joining
JOIN	JOIN is a Pig relational operator to join two or more relations. When a join is performed, Apache Pig will store all relations in memory for faster processing after the first one.
COGROUP	COGROUP is a Pig relational operator to group the data in two or more relations.
GROUP	GROUP is a Pig relational operator to group the data in a single relation. Apache Pig groups together two or more relations with common group values.
CROSS	CROSS is a Pig relational operator that will collect together records with the same key to create the flat cross product of two or more relations. However, the CROSS relational operator is expensive, and it is better to avoid it.
	Relational Operator for Sorting
ORDER	ORDER is a Pig relational operator to arrange a relation in sorted order based on one or more fields (i.e., ascending or descending).
LIMIT	LIMIT is a Pig relational operator to get a limited number of tuples from a relation.
	Relational Operator for Combining and Splitting
UNION	UNION is a Pig relational operator that combines two or more relations into a single relation but does not guarantee the order of tuples and allows duplicates. Furthermore, the UNION operator in Pig doesn't require the relations to have the same number of schemas or even the same number of fields.

(Continued)

Table 12.9 *(Continued)*

Operator	Description
SPLIT	SPLIT is a Pig relational operator that will split a single relation into two or more relations based on the given Boolean expression.
<td colspan="2" align="center">**Diagnostic Operators** The load statement is used in Pig to load the data into the specified relation. In addition, there are four diagnostic operators in Pig, namely Dump, Describe, Explain and Illustrate.</td>
DUMP	DUMP is a Pig diagnostic operator that will run/execute the Pig Latin statements and print the contents of a relation on the screen. The DUMP operator is meant for working in interactive mode, and the results are not saved/persisted. The user can also use the DUMP operator as a debugging tool to ensure the results the user expects are generated.
DESCRIBE	DESCRIBE is a Pig diagnostic operator to describe the schema of a relation.
EXPLAIN[–script pigscript] [–out path] [–brief] [–dot] [–param param_name = param_value] [–param_file file_name] alias;	EXPLAIN is a Pig diagnostic operator to display execution plans. So the user can view the logical, physical, or MapReduce execution plans to compute a relation. When no script is given, the logical plan will show a pipeline of operators to be executed to build a relation. The physical plan will show how the logical operators are translated to backend-specific physical operators. The MapReduce will show how the physical plan will be grouped to MapReduce jobs.
ILLUSTRATE {alias | - script scriptfile};	ILLUSTRATE is a Pig diagnostic operator to review how the data will be transformed through a series of statements.

The functions STARTSWITH and ENDSWITH check inputs to see if the first parameter finishes with the second argument's string. Here, we'll talk about the word "ENDSWITH".

First, let us create a CSV (test1.csv) file as below and store it in the desktop.

```
File Name: test1.csv

2021_Spider-Man
2021_Eternals
2021_Black Widow
2020-Bad Boys for Life
2020_Sonic the Hedgehog
2020_The Invisible Man
2018_Avengers
2018_Jurassic World
```

Let us load the CSV file into a relation (csvdata) and then split the data using ENDSWITH function as below:

```
Loading data into csvdata:
csvdata = LOAD 'Desktop/test1.csv' USING PigStorage() as (data:chararray);

Splitting the data using ENDSWITH function.
displaydata = FOREACH csvdata GENERATE ENDSWITH(data, 'Life');

Retrieve data.
DUMP displaydata;
```

The below is the resultant retrieved data. If we look at the data and output below, we'll see that one out of eight rows is TRUE, indicating that the requested phrase was found there. This function is helpful in situations where we are faced with a significant example or criteria in real-time.

```
(false)
(false)
(false)
(true)
(false)
(false)
(false)
(false)
```

12.8 ADVANCED PIG LATIN

Pig consists of two functions, as shown in Fig. 12.7: 1. Built-in functions, and 2. User-defined functions. At the same time, there is a wide range of built-in functions. To perform specific functions, users will need to write their functions to fulfill their requirement. Such functions are known as user-defined functions (UDF).

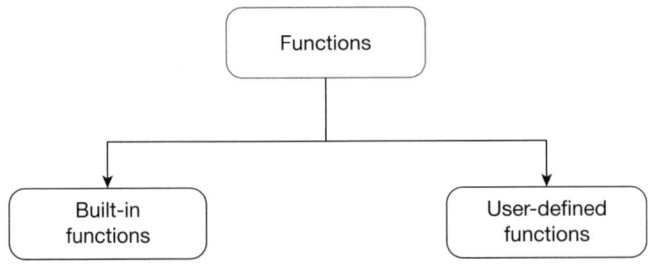

Figure 12.7 Functions in Pig Latin

12.8.1 Built-in Functions in Pig

Apache Pig provides various built-in functions: `eval`, `load`, `store`, `math`, `string`, `date-time`, `bag`, and `tuple`.

Apache Pig Built-in `Eval` Functions

Table 12.10 shows the built-in eval functions of Pig.

Table 12.10 Built-in `Eval` functions

S. No	Function	Description
1.	AVG()	An AVG() function computes the average of the numerical values within a single-column bag.
2.	BagToString()	A BagToString() function concatenates the elements of a bag into a string. While concatenating, a delimiter can be placed between these values (optional).
3.	CONCAT()	A CONCAT() function concatenates two or more expressions of the same type. CONCAT() can concatenate either two strings (char array) or two-byte strings.
4.	COUNT()	A COUNT() function calculates the number of elements in a bag.
5.	DIFF()	This DIFF() function compares two bags (fields) in a tuple and will return the tuples in one bag but not in the other.
6.	IsEmpty()	This IsEmpty() function checks if a bag or map is empty.
7.	MAX()	This MAX() function calculates the highest value for a column in a single-column bag. The column must be a numeric type or a char array.
8.	MIN()	This MIN() function is used to get the minimum (lowest) value in a single-column bag. The column must be a numeric type or a char array.
9.	SIZE()	The SIZE() function calculates the number of elements. For numeric scalar data types, it returns 1. For example, for a bag, it counts the number of tuples. A char array counts the number of characters, and a byte array counts the number of bytes.
10.	SUM()	This SUM() function is used to get the total of the numeric values in a single-column bag.
11.	TOKENIZE()	This TOKENIZE() function is used to split a string (which contains a group of words) into a bag of words. The recognized word separators are space, double quote("),comma, parenthesis and asterisk(*).

Apache Pig `Load` and `Store` Functions

The Load and Store functions in Apache Pig determine how the data goes in and comes out of Pig. Table 12.11 shows the list of load and store functions available in Pig. In Pig, it is also possible to store and load compressed data.

Table 12.11 `Load` and `Store` functions

S. No	Function	Description
1.	PigStorage()	The PigStorage() function is used to load and store structured files.
2.	TextLoader()	The TextLoader() function is used to load unstructured data into Pig.
3.	BinStorage()	The BinStorage() function is used to load and store data.

Table 12.12 describes various Bag and Tuple Functions.

Table 12.12 Bag and Tuple functions

S. No	Function	Description
1.	ToBag()	The ToBag() function converts two or more expressions into a bag.
2.	Top()	The Top() function is used to get the top N tuples of a relation.
3.	ToTuple()	The ToTuple() function converts one or more expressions into a tuple.
4.	ToMap()	The ToMap() function is used to convert the key-value pairs into a Map.

Apache Pig String Functions

In Apache Pig, many string functions work on a sequence of characters. Let us look at a few String functions with examples.

The upper function allows char array data and will convert the string into uppercase.

```
grunt>uppdata=FOREACH student GENERATE UPPER(stuname);
grunt>subdata=FOREACH stuexample GENERATE (firstname),
SUBSTRING (firstname,0,2);
```

Example: String Function

The substring function returns a substring of the given string when the input string, start index, and stop index are given. In the example, the substring function will start at position 0 and end at position 2.

Apache Pig Date-time Functions

The Pig date-time functions are dependent on the Java Date API and the JODATIME API. The packages under the JODATIME API version 2.10.14 provide support for dates, times, durations, intervals, etc. There are seven packages namely time, time.base, time.chrono, time.convert, time.field, time.format and time.tz.

```
grunt>ToDate(milliseconds)
grunt>ToDate(IOS string)
grunt>ToDate(userstring,format)
```

```
grunt>ToDate(userstring,format,timezone)
```

Date Time Functions

The ToDate(milliseconds) function will return the date-time object in milliseconds. Other variations of the ToDate include taking the input as an IOS string or as the user string and format, or user string format, and time zone. For example, Pig has similar functions to get the day, get the hour, etc.

12.8.2 Apache Pig User-Defined Functions (UDF)

Apart from a wide range of built-in functions, Apache Pig also supports users by allowing them to create User-Defined Functions (UDFs). Apache Pig is built on Java; so it works efficiently on the Java repository for user-defined functions named Piggy Bank. Developers are encouraged to write and contribute a UDF to the Piggy Bank if they cannot find the function of their choice.

The advantage of Piggy Bank is that the user can contribute their UDF and access the UDFs written by other users. Apart from Java, Pig also supports other programming languages like JavaScript, Jython, Python, Ruby, and Groovy.

Accessing User-defined Functions in the Piggy Bank

Piggy Bank functions are currently distributed in source form, and users need to build the required package for themselves. Apache Pig does not have any binary distributions currently.

> **To build a jar file that contains all available UDFs, follow these steps:**
> Step 1: Checkout UDF code:
> **svn co http://svn.apache.org/repos/asf/pig/trunk/contrib/piggybank**
> Step 2: Add pig.jar to your ClassPath:
> **export CLASSPATH=$CLASSPATH:/path/to/pig.jar**
> Step 3: Build the jar file:
> **from directory trunk/contrib/piggybank/java run ant**. This will generate piggybank.jar in the same directory.

Accessing User-defined Functions in Piggy Bank

A Javadoc description of the functions is obtained by running ant Javadoc from the directory trunk/contrib/piggybank/java. The documentation is generated in the directory trunk/contrib/piggybank/java/build/javadoc.

The user needs to determine to which package it belongs, to use a function. The main packages corresponding to the function types given above are:

> org.apache. Pig. Piggybank Piggybank. comparison -This package is for custom comparator used by ORDER operator
>
> org.apache.pig.piggybank.evaluation - This package is for eval functions like aggregates and column transformations
>
> org.apache.pig.piggybank.filtering - This package is for functions used in FILTER operator org.apache.pig.piggybank.grouping - This package is for grouping functions org.apache.pig.piggybank.storage - This package is for load/store functions

Pig packages

Developing and Testing Pig Latin Scripts Running a Pig Latin Script

Pig Latin Scripts can be executed either in Local (Batch) mode or the MapReduce mode. First, the user must write all the required Pig Latin statements in a single file and save it as a .pig file. Then the Pig Script can be executed from the Linux shell in either way, as shown below:

LOCAL MODE	MAP REDUCE MODE
$ pig -x local Sample_local.pig	$ Pig -x mapreduce Sample_map. Pig

Then the script can be executed from the Grunt shell using the exec command as shown below.

```
grunt>exec /samplescript.pig
```
Exec command

Executing a Pig Script from HDFS

The user can also execute a Pig script that resides in the HDFS, as shown below. Suppose there is a Pig script with the name samplescript.Pig in the HDFS directory named /pig_data/.

```
$ pig -x mapreduce hdfs://localhost:9000/pig_data/samplescript.pig
```
Executing a Pig script from HDFS

Testing: Unit Testing Pig Latin Scripts

PigUnit allows the user to perform three types of testing: Unit testing, regression testing, and rapid prototyping. Testing is needed for the logic when the user makes changes to the script, to the user-defined functions, and to check the compatibility of the version the user is running Pig and Hadoop in. The good thing is that no cluster setup is required to test Pig in local mode.

Let us look at how the user can perform unit testing with Pig Latin Script.

For unit testing of Pig scripts, a Pig Unit library enables the running of Pig scripts using JUnit. The Pig Unit can be run both in Local and MapReduce mode, but Local mode will be used by default. So, when it comes to choosing between the Local mode or the MapReduce mode, the user must note that MapReduce mode requires a Hadoop cluster and the installation of HDFS. However, the Local mode does not require installation of HDFS and will enable the user to use the local file system as a Hadoop cluster,

The minimal setup for the Pig Unit test includes the installation of these four libraries:

1. Hadoop Core is needed for working with the Hadoop File System.
2. Apache Pig Unit refers to the core component for running tests.
3. Jline is needed for reading input.
4. Joda Time is needed for time operations used by Pig Unit.

12.9 MAKING PIGS FLY BY OPTIMIZING PIG SCRIPTS

Performance is an essential aspect of Big Data processing and leads to faster decision-making. Hence it is needed to optimize Pig and decrease the running time of jobs.

12.9.1 Advanced Joins

Joins are performed on the Reducer side and prove to be a costly operation in Pig. So, when it comes to using joins, a user needs to pay extra attention so that performance is not affected. Three types of joins will improve performance, namely, 1. Fragmented Replicated Joins, 2. Shewed Joins, and 3. Merge Joins.

Working with Fragment Replicated Joins

A fragmented replicated join works by fragmenting and replicating the tables to be joined. Fragmenting means partitioning the table, while replicating means duplicating or creating copies of the table. Fragment joins support inner and left outer joins and they work best when one or more of the relations in the table is small enough to fit into the main memory. The keyword "replicated" is used in the join operator and the USING clause is used to perform a replicated join.

Replicated joins work on the map-side and perform faster than regular joins because they do not require the user to perform a Reduce task. The maximum size of a relation that can be put into memory is 1GB and is done by setting the property pig.join.replicated. max.bytes. If this property value is exceeded, the join will fail, and an error will be generated. The following example uses two relations: a significant relation is joined with two more minor relations (namely, medium and small).

```
bigrel = LOAD 'big_data' AS (br1,br2,br3);
mediumrel = LOAD 'medium_data' AS (mr1,mr2,mr3);
smallrel = LOAD 'small_data' AS (sr1,sr2,sr3);
C = JOIN big BY br1, medium BY mr1, small BY sr1 USING 'replicated';
```

Replicated join

```
student_details = load 'student_details.csv' using
PigStorage(',') as (sno:int,sname:chararray,
sage:int,dno:int);
dept_details = load 'department_details.csv' using
PigStorage(',') as (dno:int,dname:chararray); studentjn
= join student_details by dno,dept by dno USING
'replicated';
```

Example: Working with User-defined Joins

To join two datasets, MapReduce copies the output of the two Map tasks to another node, and the join is performed in a Reduce task. For example, to join the 'student.csv' and the 'department.csv' datasets, the output of both the student Map task and the output of the department Map task are sent to the Reduce node, where the join functionality is performed by matching the data from both Map outputs. A replicated join puts one or more datasets into the distributed cache. Then it reads the other dataset from the same

Map node and it does not need to perform a Reduce side task. Performance improves when the reduce side task is avoided.

A Pig Latin script gets compiled as a group of MapReduce jobs, and each MapReduce job adds to the overhead in a query. As the Hadoop MapReduce jobs were built for batch processing, minimizing overheads like job start-up time was not considered. So, when a MapReduce job starts, it takes about 5 and 15 seconds, assuming there is capacity in the cluster to run the job immediately.

When writing user-defined joins, it is good to note that Pig moves data between MapReduce jobs by storing it in the HDFS. The data is read from disk and written to disk at every MapReduce boundary. Every MapReduce job will act as a blocking operator, meaning that the MapReduce job $N + 1$ cannot start until all tasks from MapReduce job N are completed. So, there is an issue of bottlenecks while executing the slower tasks. Hence, to enhance optimization while writing joins, the user can write an "Eval" and consolidate the work of two or more MapReduce jobs into one so that Pig will execute faster. The user will have more control over the joins and will not have any size constraints.

12.9.2 Handling Key Skew

Skew in Join

Skewed joins will work well when the data is sufficiently skewed and extensive data is associated with a given relation. In such skewed data cases, the Reduce node that is processing the key with the big volume of data will have slower performance, and sometimes it might even fail the job. Pig Latin provides an advanced join called a skewed join to address these skewed data cases and improve performance.

Let us discuss how key skew is handled by the JOIN, ORDER BY, and GROUP BY operators.

```
stu = load 'student.csv' using PigStorage(',') as
(stuno:int,stufirstname:chararray,stulastname:chararray,
stuphoenno:int,studeptname:chararray);
dept = load 'department.csv' using PigStorage(',') as
(deptno:int,deptname:chararray); stujn = join stu by
deptno,deptname by deptno using 'skewed';
```

Pig Latin Skewed Join

Skew in ORDER BY

The ORDER BY statement performs a global sort, making sure the output of each partition is sorted. This means that all outputs of each partition N are guaranteed to be less than or equal to the output of partition $N + 1$. Pig deals with key skew by sending all instances of a given key to the same partition. The partitioner will distribute records in a round-robin fashion to balance the load. This allows Pig to split keys with large numbers of records across multiple reducers and avoids imbalance between reducers. Using this method, Pig is generally able to balance the workload.

Skew in GROUP BY

Aggregation operations require that all records with the same key be collected together. This makes the "one key, one reducer" rule, followed by JOIN and ORDER BY, which is not possible for the GROUP BY operation. Pig has several ways to manage the skew, one of which uses aggregate operations.

Let us now look at what we learned in user-defined functions: a function can be decomposed into an initial step, an intermediate step, and a final step. This is an algebraic function, and Apache Pig will run them in the Map, Combine, and Reduce phases. The initial (Map) implementation will be run once per record, the intermediate (Combine) implementation will be run zero or more times per key, and the final (Reduce) implementation will be run once per key. The advantage of using algebraic aggregation functions is that it dramatically reduces the effect of skew. In addition, the amount of data shipped across the network and written to disk can be significantly reduced by performing early aggregation. This results in improving the performance significantly.

The associated combiner will produce one record for a key regardless of the number of records a mapper has with a given key in its input. Also, as part of the Map and Reduce phases, if the number of outputs given to a reducer exceeds a configurable threshold, a merge phase will be invoked. This process avoids inefficient merges with too many input streams during the Reduce phase. In addition, this effectively prevents skew for the reducers in cases where algebraic aggregation functions are used.

12.9.3 "On the Fly" Replanning by the Pig Community

The Apache Pig community initially focused on building various implementations of operators so that Pig users could choose the best operator applicable for their situation. While this allows users a large degree of control, it also pushes a significant burden onto them. Exhaustive testing is needed to determine the best operator, and it is not adaptive in the face of change. Instead, the freedom to make choices to select the correct operator should be enforced.

There is also a lack of statistics for existing data and the limited usability of statistics for longer Pig Latin scripts. Such errors for operators near the end of the data pipeline become intolerable in programming. The availability of statistics on some or all of the input data of the script would help plan the initial phases of execution of the script.

Hence, the Pig community proposed **"on the fly"** replanning to investigate areas and determine the best design.

The Optimal Frequency of Replanning

There is a cost to collect statistics, so replanning at every MapReduce job will introduce a noticeable slowing down. So, the user needs to understand the inflection point between the cost of collecting statistics and replanning, and the excessive error introduced by the number of operators for which estimates are done. Estimating the number of records in a file and the cardinality of a few key fields in those records needs to be done efficiently. On the other hand, estimating the distribution of values in a field (e.g., building a histogram) is more valuable from an optimization standpoint, but it still turns out to be more expensive. So, the user needs to experiment and understand the cost of collecting any particular statistic and decide whether it is worth the planning benefit.

Accuracy of the Statistics

Efficiency is based on how fast the sampling techniques are.

The more errors introduced in collecting the statistics, the less accurate the resulting plans will be, and the user will often need to re-collect and re-plan.

As a simple example, we will write an `Eval` function Fig. 12.8 that performs a join on the student.csv and department.csv using the distributed cache. Take a simple dataset student.csv with the student id, first name, last name, phone, and department (Table 12.13).

Table 12.13 student.csv

Student ID	First Name	Last Name	Phone	Dept. Name
101010	Aarti	Bansal	9841309829	CSE
101012	Ritvik	Roshan	9010208828	IT
101014	Venkat	Kumar	9929100100	ECE
101016	Jincy	Moses	9853562791	MECH
101017	Lavanya	Prakash	9874252729	CIVIL
101019	Joana	Prabhu	9289201021	IT

Consider another dataset called department.csv (Table 12.14).

Table 12.14 department.csv

Dept ID	Dept NAME
100	CSE
200	IT
300	ECE
400	MECH
500	CIVIL

The code below shows how to implement a user-defined `Eval` function in Java using the distributed cache that converts the department name into lowercase. It also returns "OTHERS" as the department name if no department number is in the student table. The distributed cache is a helpful feature for keeping small files on the data nodes and avoiding complex tasks. The 'Exec' method of the `Eval` function helps access the distributed cache.

```
public class CacheJoin extends EvalFunc
{
@Override
    public String exec(Tuple input) throws IOException
    {
        Integer deptno = (Integer) input.get(0); if (deptno != null)
        return getdeptname("./department.csv", dno); else return "OTHERS";
    }
    String getdeptname(String filename, int deptno) throws FileNotFoundException
    {
        Scanner sc = new Scanner(new FileReader(filename)); HashMap map = new HashMap();

    while (sc.hasNext())
    {
        String[] values = sc.nextLine().split(","); map.put(new
        Integer(values[0]), values[1]); } String deptname = map.get(new
        Integer(deptno));
            if (deptname != null)
            {
                deptname = deptname.toLowerCase();
            }
            return dname;
    }
@Override
    public List getCacheFiles()
    {
        ArrayList dsfiles = new ArrayList();
        dsfiles.add("/user/hdfs/department.csv");
        return dsfiles;
    }
}
```

Figure 12.8 Writing `Eval` function using distributed cache

User-Defined EVAL function in Java

There are also other advanced ways to write an EVAL function, such as aggregate, accumulator and filter functions.

12.10 ALGEBRAIC FUNCTION IN PIG

An algebraic interface is derived from EvalFunc and it has three initial, intermediate, and final data methods. The algebraic interface takes bags as input and produces a scalar output. The three stages of the algebraic interface are similar to the map, combine and reduce that we saw when we learned Hadoop and MapReduce (Table 12.15).

Table 12.15 Algebraic interface methods

`getInitial()`	This `getInitial()` algebraic function is invoked once for each input tuple by the map process. This function produces partial results.
`getIntermed()`	This `getIntermed()` algebraic function produces partial results and is invoked once by each combiner.
`getFinal()`	This `getFinal()` algebraic function is invoked once by the reducer and produces the final results.

```
Public interface Algebraic
{
    Public string getInitial();
    Public string getIntermed();
    Public string getFinal();
}
```

Algebraic interface methods

12.11 Accumulator

Not all functions fit into the algebraic interface, and problems in memory usage can occur with Pig. So, in such cases, we can consider using the accumulator interface. Using this interface, Pig guarantees that the data for the same key is passed continuously but in small increments. This interface has three methods as shown in Table 12.16.

Table 12.16 Accumulator interface methods

`accumulate(Tuple b)`	This accumulator function is called one or more times. But, first, the function processes the input tuple.
`getValue()`	This accumulator function is called once all fundamental values are passed to the accumulator.
`getCleanup()`	This `getCleanup()` accumulator function is called after `getValue()` to perform the cleanup operation.

12.12 Writing a Function

12.12.1 Writing a Filter Function

Filter functions are `eval` functions that return a Boolean value and can be used anywhere a Boolean expression is appropriate. The user must extend the **FilterFunc** class and implement the `exec()` method to implement the filter function.

12.12.2 Writing a Load and Store Function

Many load and store functions are available, like PigStorage, TextLoader, etc., in Pig while other user-defined functions are available in Piggy Bank. However, the user might want to write a load and store function for his requirement. Let us see a brief example of how the user can write and implement his load and store function.

Writing a Load Function

To write a load function, the user must first extend the abstract class LoadFunc. The **LoadFunc** in Pig is tightly coupled with Hadoop's **InputFormat** class, So the complexity of reading the data and creating a record will depend on writing the InputFormat class (Table 12.17).

While **LoadFunc** is the main abstract class for implementing a loader, the user needs to override the methods given below

Table 12.17 LoadFunc **methods**

getInputFormat()	The getInputFormat() load method returns the input format class of MapReduce suitable for input files.
setLocation()	The setLocation() load method will set the split ready by Pig. It will be called before the getNext() method.
prepareToRead()	This prepareToRead() load method is used to communicate the load location to the loader.
getNext()	This getNext() load method will return tuples until all are finished.

In addition to **LoadFunc**, three other optional interfaces are available that can provide added functionality. The **LoadMetadata** interface allows the user to load the metadata about data. It has four methods as given below (Table 12.18).

Table 12.18 LoadMetadata **methods**

getSchema()	The getSchema() load method automatically retrieves and defines the schema for a relation.
getPartitionKeys()	The getPartitionKeys() load method returns partition keys if available; if no partition keys are available, it returns null and is helpful to read data from Hive tables.
getStatistics()	The getStatistics() load, method returns the statistics about data to be loaded, otherwise returns null.
setPartitionFilter()	To setPartitionFilter() load method is used to filter the partitions.

LoadPushdown is another interface that improves performance by loading only the required fields. It has two methods (Table 12.19), namely getFeatures() and pushProjection().

Table 12.19 LodPushDown methods

getFeatures()	This getFeatures() load method returns a set of operations that can be pushed down.
pushProjection()	This pushProjection() load method informs the required field names to the loader.

LoadCaster interface is useful when the user needs to convert the data into the appropriate data type. For example, the default data type is a byte array, and LoadCaster is used to convert it into other Pig Latin datatypes.

Writing a Store Function

The user needs to implement a StoreFuncInterface or extend the **StoreFunc** abstract class to interact with metadata systems and write a storage function. To write a Store Function, the user needs to override four methods as given below (Table 12.20).

Table 12.20 StoreFunc methods

getOutputFormat()	The getOutputFormat() store method will be called when the job is launched. This method returns the output format class.
setStoreLocation()	The setStoreLocation() method will set the output location as the user input given in the store command of a Pig script.
prepareToWrite()	The prepareToWrite() store method is the starting point for storing data. The prepareToWrite() is called before the putNext() method.
putNext()	The putNext() store method is responsible for writing data to the output directory after converting to the appropriate data type.

While using the getOutputFormat() method, the user can use the MapReduce output format classes or the Pig output format class. MapReduce output format classes are FileOutputFormat, TextOutputFormat, and SequenceFileOutputFormat. Pig output format class is PigTextOutputFormat. We can implement the interface when the storage function can store both schema and data.

StoreMetaData: In addition to the StoreFunc abstract class, there is an optional interface StoreMetadata to achieve added functionality. For example, the StoreMetadata interface can be used when the user needs to store schema and statistics (Table 12.21).

Table 12.21 StoreMetadata methods

storeSchema()	This storeSchema() is a storeMetadata method that is used for storing metadata into the output directory.
storeStatistics()	The storeStatistics() is a storeMetadata method used to store statistics about data in the output directory.

12.13 COMPARISON OF PIG WITH HIVE AND MAPREDUCE

Hadoop is an open-source framework. Apache Pig is one component of the Hadoop ecosystem that can be used to analyze Big Data. Hive is another component of the Hadoop ecosystem that works on metadata and supports the complete ACID properties of the database. Hive has a language called HiveQL that is similar to SQL for querying and runs on the batch processing system with high latency. MapReduce is a YARN-based system for processing large datasets and enables massive scalability for working in distributed environments.

12.13.1 Apache Pig vs. MapReduce

Pig is a programming language for analyzing massive amounts of data. Pig Latin is a Hadoop extension that provides a high-level data processing language to make Hadoop programming more accessible. We can achieve the functionality by writing only a few lines of code because Pig is a scripting language. MapReduce is a data processing scaling approach. It is a framework for developing distributed data processing applications, not a program. Programs created with the MapReduce architecture have grown to thousands of computers with ease. It is tough to execute join functionality while utilizing Hadoop MapReduce as the coding technique, making complicated business logic difficult and time-consuming to implement. A significant amount of development effort is necessary to determine how various Map and Reduce joins will be performed. There is a potential that Hadoop developers may be unable to map the data into the desired schema format. Table 12.22 compares Apache Pig with MapReduce.

Table 12.22 Apache Pig vs. MapReduce

Apache Pig	MapReduce
Apache Pig is a data flow language with operations such as loops and filters.	MapReduce is a data processing paradigm with mapper and reducer functions and job chaining.
Apache Pig is a high-level language and simplifies Hadoop programming.	MapReduce is low-level and complex as it relies on Java.
It is easy and simple to perform a join operation in Apache Pig. Very little knowledge of SQL is needed to program in Apache Pig.	It is pretty tricky for MapReduce to perform a Join operation between datasets. The user must know Java to work with MapReduce.
Apache Pig uses a multi-query approach and improves efficiency by avoiding redundant evaluation.	MapReduce will require more number of lines to perform the same task.
In Apache Pig, the compiler automatically optimizes the script. The user does not have to tune the program manually. It also provides automatic speed-up.	MapReduce jobs have a lengthy compilation process that involves three stages the map stage, the shuffle stage, and the reduce stage.

12.13.2 Apache Pig vs. Hive

Hive and Pig are two critical components of the Hadoop ecosystem, allowing multiple datasets to be processed and analyzed. However, there are a few key distinctions between the two. The Hive vs. Pig argument is a current subject in the tech sector. Table 12.23 compares Apache Pig with Hive.

Table 12.23 Apache Pig vs. Hive

Apache Pig	Hive
Apache Pig is a high-level platform that uses a language called Pig Latin. It was created at Yahoo.	Hive is a data warehouse infrastructure that uses a language called HiveQL. It was created on Facebook.
Pig Latin is a data flow language where a chain of operations is processed in pipelines. First, the data gets converted to MapReduce jobs.	HiveQL is a query processing language and is similar to SQL.
The Pig can work with real-time data.	Hive is not able to work on real-time data analysis.
Apache Pig can handle structured, unstructured, and semi-structured data.	Hive is mostly for structured data.

SUMMARY

Apache Pig is a platform for studying huge datasets that includes a high-level language for defining data analysis algorithms as well as infrastructure for assessing them. It has a lot of relational capabilities that make it simple to join, organize, and aggregate data.

PIG has a lot in common with ETL, primarily if the ETL tools are used on several servers simultaneously. The Hadoop ecosystem includes Apache Pig. Hive and Pig are designed to load and transform unstructured, structured, and semi-structured data into HDFS, unlike many standard ETL solutions that are good at structuring data.

Apache Pig provides the scalability of Hadoop and hence can process the large volume of data present in the Hadoop File system. Apache Pig proves useful where time-sensitive data loads and analytical insights are required. The two modes in which Pig can be executed are Local mode and MapReduce mode.

- **Pig Parser:** Pig scripts are written and executed by any one of the execution mechanisms (batch/interactive/embedded mode). After execution, the Pig parser will apply a series of transformations to get the desired result. The Pig Parser does syntax checking, type checking, and other miscellaneous checks, and the output is generated as a DAG (Directed Acyclic Graph) graph.
- **Pig Optimizer:** The Pig optimizer performs logical optimization of the DAG such as splitting, merging, projection, pushdown, transformation, and reordering. The Pig optimizer processes the extracted data and improves query performance. The optimizer's primary goal is to lower the quantity of data in the pipeline at any given moment while processing the extracted data.

- **Pig Compiler:** The Pig compiler compiles the output generated by the optimizer into a series of MapReduce jobs. The optimized logical plan is automatically converted into MapReduce jobs, and the performance is improved by rearranging the execution order of the jobs.
- **Pig Execution Engine:** The Pig Execution engine sends the MapReduce jobs to Hadoop for execution. These MapReduce jobs are executed on the Hadoop platform to produce the desired results. The DUMP statement displays the results on the console/screen. The STORE statement stores the results in HDFS (Hadoop Distributed File System).

Pig performs basic parsing and validates all statement syntax and semantics. The parser produces a logical plan which describes the logical operators which have been executed, and no data processing is performed during the creation of the logical plan. For each line of the logical plan, syntax checking is performed, and when an error occurs, an exception will be thrown, and program execution will be stopped. Once the logical plan is generated, the script will move to the physical plan that describes the physical operators. Apache Pig will perform limited optimization before execution. When compared to SQL, Apache Pig is a data flow language which means the user will be writing in a sequence of steps.

Grunt is the interactive shell in Pig that enables the user to interact with HDFS. The grunt shell has some basic utility commands.

The Pig can operate on any form of data (nested/relational/semi-structured/structured). With Pig, the data model is specified when you load the data. Any data loaded from disk into Pig will have a specific schema and structure, and Pig needs to understand the structure. Also, the Pig data model allows the user to manage table-like structures and nested hierarchical data structures to support the diversity of data. Scalar types contain a single value, while complex types include other values, such as Tuple, Container, and Map.

The basic data types in Pig Latin are atomic, also known as scalar data types, which are utilized in all kinds such as `string`, `float`, `int`, `double`, `long`, `char[]`, and `byte[]`. Primitive data types are another name for atomic data types. For example, in a field (column), each cell value is an atomic data type.

A complex data type is frequently made up of several different data types. You could, for example, design a complicated data type with built-in types, opaque types, different kinds, and other complex types as components. Pig Latin has three complex data types namely: Tuple, Bag and Map.

Pig consists of two functions, 1. Built-in functions, and 2. User-Defined Functions. There is a wide range of Built-in functions that can be used to perform specific functions. At the same time, the users will need to write their functions to fulfill their requirement. Such functions are known as User-Defined functions (UDF).

EXERCISES

Multiple Choice Questions

1. **Apache Pig got released in the year _____.**
   A. 2008
   B. 2018
   C. 2020
   D. 2000
   Answer: A
   Explanation: Apache Hadoop, in the year 2008, released a high-level platform supported by Yahoo's researchers called **Apache Pig** to analyze large datasets. **Pig Latin (Apache Pig)** is the high-level language for data analysis programs.

2. **Apache Pig has a lot in common with _____.**
   A. ELT
   B. ETL
   C. Flume
   D. HDFS
   Explanation: PIG has a lot in common with ETL, primarily if the ETL tools are used on several servers simultaneously. The Hadoop ecosystem includes Apache Pig. Hive and Pig are designed to load and transform unstructured, structured, and semi-structured data into HDFS, unlike many standard ETL solutions that are good at structuring data.

3. **This helps to convert Pig Latin into MapReduce _____.**
   A. Pig Optimizer
   B. Pig Compiler
   C. Pig Engine
   D. Pig Interpreter
   Answer: C
   Explanation: Pig Latin scripts will be automatically converted to MapReduce operations. The Pig Engine (also known as Apache Pig) assists in converting the written scripts into MapReduce operations. This tool will significantly assist in doing Big Data Analytics.

4. **What are the two modes of Apache Pig?**
   A. Local mode and Track mode
   B. Local mode and Rack mode
   C. Local mode and Yarn mode
   D. Local mode and MapReduce mode
   Answer: D
   Explanation: Apache Pig provides the scalability of Hadoop and hence it can process the large volume of data present in the Hadoop File system. Apache Pig proves useful where time-sensitive data loads and analytical insights are required. The two modes in which Pig can be executed are Local Mode and MapReduce Mode.

5. **This applies a series of transformations and does syntax checking and type checking:**
   A. Pig Parser
   B. Pig Optimizer
   C. Pig Compiler
   D. Pig Execution Engine

Answer: A
Explanation
Pig Parser: Pig scripts are written and executed by any one of the execution mechanisms (batch/interactive/embedded mode). After execution, the Pig parser will apply a series of transformations to get the desired result. The Pig parser does syntax checking, type checking, and other miscellaneous checks, and the output is generated as a DAG (Directed Acyclic Graph) graph. In the directed acyclic graph (DAG) output, the logical operators will be represented as nodes and flow as edges. The parsed output is then given to the optimizer.

6. **This applies splitting, merging, and pushdown, to lower the quantity of data:**
   A. Pig Parser
   B. Pig Optimizer
   C. Pig Compiler
   D. Pig Execution Engine
   Answer: B
   Explanation
   Pig Optimizer: The Pig Optimizer performs logical optimization of the DAG such as splitting, merging, projection, pushdown, transformation, and reordering. The Pig optimizer processes the extracted data and improves query performance. The optimizer's primary goal is to lower the quantity of data in the pipeline at any given moment while processing the extracted data.

7. **This converts the output generated by the optimizer into a series of MapReduce jobs:**
   A. Pig Parser
   B. Pig Optimizer
   C. Pig Compiler
   D. Pig Execution Engine
   Answer: C
   Explanation
   Pig Compiler: The Pig compiler compiles the output generated by the optimizer into a series of MapReduce jobs. The optimized logical plan is automatically converted into MapReduce jobs, and the performance is improved by rearranging the execution order of the jobs.

8. **This sends the MapReduce jobs to Hadoop for the execution:**
   A. Pig Parser
   B. Pig Optimizer
   C. Pig Compiler
   D. Pig Execution Engine
   Answer: D
   Explanation
   Pig Execution Engine: The Pig Execution Engine sends the MapReduce jobs to Hadoop for execution. These MapReduce jobs are executed on the Hadoop platform to produce the desired results. The DUMP statement displays the results on the console/screen. The STORE statement stores the results in HDFS (Hadoop Distributed File System).

9. **The user can invoke any shell command using this command:**
   A. fs command
   B. help command
   C. sh command
   D. history command
   Answer: C
   Explanation: The user can invoke any shell commands using the sh command. However, shell environment commands cannot be executed using the sh (except -cd command) from the grunt shell. For example, all the files and directories will be listed when sh ls is executed.

Short-answer Questions

1. **Write a short note on Apache Pig.**
   Apache Pig is a procedural language that supports a multi-query approach. The Hadoop ecosystem includes Apache Pig. Hive and Pig are designed to load and transform unstructured, structured, and semi-structured data into HDFS, unlike many standard ETL solutions that are good at structuring data. Pig Latin scripts will be automatically converted to MapReduce operations. The Pig Engine (also known as Apache Pig) assists in converting the written scripts into those operations. This tool will significantly assist in doing Big Data Analytics. It is a fast-programming language that streamlines several operations and helps to save time.

2. **What are the basic features of Apache Pig?**
   Apache Pig supports relational style operations like filter, union, group, join, sort, etc. Apache Pig is extensible, allowing users to write their user-defined functions and processes. Apache Pig implements a subset of relational algebra, and hence it is easy to learn for SQL programmers. Apache Pig allows users to insert their code anywhere in the data pipeline. The data structure of Apache Pig is multivalued, nested, and richer. Apache Pig is more suited for Big Data because it can handle both structured and unstructured data analysis.

3. **What are the two modes in which Pig can be executed?**
   The two modes in which Pig can be executed are Local Mode and MapReduce Mode.
   Local Mode: In Local Mode, the Pig Latin scripts execute from the local host/local file system. The advantage of running Pig in the local mode is that the user does not need to worry about Hadoop or HDFS. Pig commands will be run locally in the JVM, and this mode is usually helpful in the testing phase.
   MapReduce mode: In MapReduce mode, the script will automatically invoke a MapReduce job in the backend to operate on the data that exists in the HDFS.
   Either of these mechanisms can execute Pig Latin scripts.

4. **What is the role of Pig Parser?**
   Pig scripts are written and executed by any one of the execution mechanisms (batch/interactive/embedded mode). After execution, the Pig parser will apply a series of

transformations to get the desired result. The Pig parser does syntax checking, type checking, and other miscellaneous checks, and the output is generated as a DAG (Directed Acyclic Graph) graph. In the directed acyclic graph (DAG) output, the logical operators will be represented as nodes and flow as edges. The parsed output is then given to the optimizer.

5. **What is the role of Pig Optimizer?**
   The Pig optimizer performs logical optimization of the DAG such as splitting, merging, projection, pushdown, transformation, and reordering. The Pig optimizer processes the extracted data and improves query performance. The optimizer's primary goal is to lower the quantity of data in the pipeline at any given moment while processing the extracted data.

6. **What is the role of Pig Compiler and Execution Engine?**
   Pig Compiler: The Pig compiler compiles the output generated by the optimizer into a series of MapReduce jobs. The optimized logical plan is automatically converted into MapReduce jobs, and the performance is improved by rearranging the execution order of the jobs.
   Pig Execution Engine: The Pig execution engine sends the MapReduce jobs to Hadoop for execution. These MapReduce jobs are executed on the Hadoop platform to produce the desired results. The DUMP statement displays the results on the console/screen. The STORE statement stores the results in HDFS (Hadoop Distributed File System).

7. **Can you explain the phrase, "Pigs eat anything", with respect to Pig Programming?**
   The saying, "Pigs eat anything", is symbolic of saying that the input data can be in any form. Pig's data types comprise the data model and consist of scalar or complex data types (bags/tuples/maps). The Pig can operate on any form of data (nested/relational/semi-structured/structured). With Pig, the data model is specified when you load the data. Any data loaded from the disk into Pig will have a specific schema and structure, and Pig needs to understand the structure. Also, the Pig data model allows the user to manage table-like structures and nested hierarchical data structures to support the diversity of data. Scalar types contain a single value, while complex types include other values, such as Tuple, Container and Map.

8. **List down the various scalar data type of Pig language.**
   The basic data types in Pig Latin are atomic. They are also known as scalar data types, which are utilized in all kinds such as `string`, `float`, `int`, `double`, `long`, `char[]`, and `byte[]`. Primitive data types are another name for atomic data types. For example, in a field (column), each cell value is an atomic data type. Pig Latin has atomic values that are scalar. An atomic value is a single value stored in a string form and can be used as a number, string, or binary object. Typecasting is supported in Pig. If the data type is not specified, it defaults to a byte array.

S. No	Data Type	Description
1.	int	This scalar data type is a signed 32-bit integer.
2.	long	This scalar data type is a signed 64-bit integer.
3.	float	This scalar data type is a signed 32-bit decimal.
4.	double	This scalar data type represents a 64-bit- floating-point.
5.	chararray	This scalar data type represents a character array(string) in Unicode UTF-8 format.
6.	bytearray	This scalar data type is a byte array/binary object.
7.	boolean	This scalar data type represents a Boolean value.
8.	datetime	This scalar data type represents a date/time.
9.	Biginteger	This scalar data type represents a JAVA Big Integer.
10.	Bigdecimal	This scalar data type represents a JAVA Big Decimal.

9. **List down the various complex data types in Pig language.**

A complex data type is frequently made up of several different data types. You could, for example, design a complicated data type with built-in types, opaque types, different kinds, and other complex types as components. Pig Latin has three complex data types, namely, Tuple, Bag and Map.

S. No	Data Type	Description
1.	Tuple	A tuple is a complex data type that contains an ordered set of fields (any type). The tuple is used in a row in a relation. A relation represents the complete database, and a bag of tuples is called a relation.
2.	Bag	A bag is a complex data type and is an unordered collection of tuples. In a bag, each tuple in the set can contain an arbitrary number of fields of any type. It is represented by tuples separated by commas and enclosed within curly brackets.
3.	Map	A key-value pair [key#value] is known as a map. It is a complex data type. While the key must be unique and of a char array type, the value can be stored in any type. Maps help process semi-structured data such as JSON and XML.

10. **Give an example of Load Statement in Pig language.**

Pig statements are the basic constructs that work with relations and include expressions and schemas. Every statement in Pig ends with a semicolon (;).

Example

```
grunt> Student_details = LOAD 'student_details.txt' USING
PigStorage(',')as
( id:int, firstname:chararray, lastname:chararray,
phone:chararray, city:chararray );
```

11. **Give examples for Pig Type Construction Operators.**
    The below table explains Type Construction Operators of Pig.

S. No	Operator	Description
1.	()	The Tuple constructor operator is a typical construction operator for constructing a tuple. E.g.:(Hannah, 9)
2.	{}	The Bag constructor operator is a typical construction operator for constructing a bag. E.g.: {(Hannah,9),(Divya,10)
3.	[]	The Map constructor operator is a typical construction operator for constructing a tuple. E.g.: [name#Hannah,age#10]

12. **Explain any five Pig Built-in Eval Functions.**
    The below table represents built-in `eval` functions of Pig.

S. No	Function	Description
1.	AVG()	An AVG() function computes the average of the numerical values within a single-column bag.
2.	BagToString()	A BagToString() function concatenates the elements of a bag into a string. While concatenating, a delimiter can be placed between these values (optional).
3.	CONCAT()	A CONCAT() function concatenates two or more expressions of the same type. CONCAT can concatenate either two strings (char array) or two-byte strings.
4.	COUNT()	A COUNT() function calculates the number of elements in a bag.
5.	DIFF()	This DIFF() function compares two bags (fields) in a tuple and will return the tuples in one bag but not in the other.

13. **Explain Apache Pig date and time functions.**
    The Pig Date Time functions are dependent on the Java Date API and the JODATIME API. The packages under the JODATIME API version 2.10.14 provide support for dates, times, durations, intervals, etc. There are seven packages namely time, time.base, time.chrono, time.convert, time.field, time.format and time.tz. The ToDate (milliseconds) function will return the date-time object in milliseconds. Other variations of the ToDate include taking the input as an IOS string or as the user string and format or user string, format, and timezone. For example, Pig has similar functions to get the day, get the hour, etc.

14. **What is Piggy Bank? What are its advantages?**
    Apart from a wide range of built-in functions, Apache Pig also supports the user by allowing them to create User-Defined Functions (UDFs). Apache Pig is built on Java, so it works efficiently on the Java repository for user-defined functions named Piggy Bank. Developers are encouraged to write and contribute a UDF to the Piggy Bank if they cannot find the function of their choice. The advantage of Piggy Bank is that

the user can contribute their UDF and access the UDFs written by other users. Apart from Java, Pig also supports other programming languages like JavaScript, Jython, Python, Ruby, and Groovy.

15. **How can users perform unit testing with Pig Latin?**
    For unit testing of Pig scripts, a Pig Unit library enables the running of Pig scripts using JUnit. Pig Unit can be run both in Local and MapReduce mode, but Local mode will be used by default. So, when it comes to choosing between the Local mode or the MapReduce mode, the user must note that MapReduce mode requires a Hadoop cluster and the installation of HDFS. The Local mode, on the other hand, doesn't require installation of HDFS and will enable the user to use the local file system as a Hadoop cluster.

16. **What is the minimal setup required for Pig Unit Testing?**
    The minimal setup for the Pig Unit test includes the installation of these four libraries:
    1. Hadoop Core is needed for working with the Hadoop File System.
    2. Apache Pig Unit refers to the core component for running tests.
    3. Jline is needed for reading input.
    4. Joda Time is needed for time operations used by Pig Unit.

17. **Write short notes on Advanced join in the Pig programming.**
    Joins are performed on the Reducer side and prove to be a costly operation in Pig. So, when it comes to using joins, a user needs to pay extra attention so that performance is not affected. Three types of join will improve performance, namely, 1. Fragmented Replicated Joins, 2. Shewed Joins, and 3. Merge Joins.

18. **What are the methods to override to write a store function in Pig Latin?**
    The user needs to implement a StoreFuncInterface or extend the **StoreFunc** abstract class to interact with metadata systems and write a storage function. To write a Store Function, the user needs to override using one of the four methods as given below:

`getOutputFormat()`	The `getOutputFormat()` store method will be called when the job is launched. This method returns the output format class.
`setStoreLocation()`	The `setStoreLocation()` method will set the output location as the user input given in the store command of a Pig script.
`prepareToWrite()`	The `prepareToWrite()` store method is the starting point for storing data. The `prepareToWrite()` is called before the `putNext()` method.
`putNext()`	The `putNext()` store method is responsible for writing data to the output directory after converting to the appropriate data type.

19. **How LoadPushdown interface helps performance in the Pig language?**
    LoadPushdown is an interface that improves performance by loading only the required fields. It has two methods namely getFeatures() and pushProjection().

getFeatures()	This getFeatures() load method returns a set of operations that can be pushed down
pushProjection()	This pushProjection() load method informs the required field names to the loader.

Essay-type Questions

1. Explain the basic features of Apache Pig.
2. Explain Apache Pig Architecture in detail.
3. Write an essay on interpreting Pig Scripts.
4. What is Grunt shell in Pig? Explain any five grunt shell commands in detail along with code snippet.
5. Explain two Pig data types in detail.
6. Explain Pig Latin statement Load in detail and provide examples.
7. Explain Pig Arithmetic Operators in detail along with examples.
8. Explain the various Pig relational operators in detail.
9. Compare Pig with MapReduce and Hive.

CHAPTER 13

Fundamentals of Spark

> **LEARNING OBJECTIVES**
>
> The main objective of this chapter is to discuss the fundamentals of Apache Spark. This is an open-source software that is used for processing Big Data. The key benefit of utilizing this program is that it allows you to stream data. In addition, Apache Spark supports the APIs of many languages, and it has plenty of libraries to do processing in a faster way.

13.1 INTRODUCTION

Apache Spark is a lightning-fast, open-source, distributed data analytical engine used to quickly and efficiently process Big Data. It is based on a cluster computing framework where a set of systems are loosely or tightly connected and work together, giving the appearance of a single system. Spark provides data parallelism and fault tolerance by distributing the task across the various distributed systems. Doing so augments the computational power of the system to handle large datasets.

It can process practically any form of data at lightning speed, regardless of its structure or size. Spark may be immediately integrated into Hadoop's HDFS and used as a powerful data processing tool. When combined with YARN, it can operate on the same cluster as MapReduce Jobs. Learning Spark has become a worldwide standard, as the field of Big Data Analytics has risen to new heights thanks to Apache Spark. Spark earned a spot among the top-level Apache Projects because of its lightning-fast speed and its In-Memory Processing Capability.

Spark supports top-tier programming languages such as Scala, Java, and Python through its simple and quicker programming interface. Consequently, Spark became the leading legend in the Production Environment, which caused a considerable increase in its demand. Spark is favored by several top MNCs, like Adobe, Yahoo, NASA, and others, due to its unmatched capabilities and dependability. Similarly, the need for Spark Developers is on the rise.

13.2 APACHE SPARK IN HADOOP ECOSYSTEM

Data science is a new subject that focuses on data analysis and has come up in recent years. Spark can be considered to fit into the processing stage of the Hadoop ecosystem. However, Spark SQL and Spark GraphX fit into the ecosystem's Analysis (Fig. 13.1).

Hadoop ecosystem				
Ingestion	Storage	Processing	Analysis	Management and coordination
Apache Sqoop (RDBMS connector)	HDFS (Structured data)	MapReduce (Data processing)	Pig (Scripting)	ZooKeeper Apache Ambari Cloudera manager Map R control system Hortonworks Oozie (Workflow monitoring)
Apache Flume (Data collection)	HBASE (Unstructured, columnar store)	Yarn (Cluster resource mgmt)	Hive (SQL query)	
Apache Kafka (Streaming)	MongoDB	Spark	Spark SQL	
Apache Impala	Apache Cassandra		Spark GraphX	
Apache NiFi			Apache Mahout (Machine learning)	
Storm (Streaming)			Tableau (Visualization)	
Change data capture (CDC)			Drill (Interactive analytics)	

Figure 13.1 Hadoop ecosystem

Spark discloses development APIs, allowing data workers to complete streaming, machine learning, or SQL tasks that require frequent data access. Spark is capable of batch as well as stream processing. Batch processing is when a previously gathered work is processed in a single batch. On the other hand, stream processing refers to dealing with Spark flowing data. It works with all Big Data tools. Like any other Hadoop data source, Spark can run on Hadoop clusters. Apache Spark also takes Hadoop MapReduce to the next level in terms of processing speed, data cashing, performing iterative jobs, and Machine Learning Applications as shown in Table 13.1.

A common misconception about Spark is that it is a Hadoop extension. However, this is not the case. Spark is not dependent on Hadoop because it has its own cluster management mechanism. Essentially, Hadoop is solely used for storage while using Spark. Spark implements data processing 10–100x quicker than Hadoop MapReduce because of in-memory processing. For any of the data processing jobs, MapReduce, on the other hand, uses persistent storage. Unlike Hadoop, Spark has built-in libraries for batch processing, streaming, Machine Learning, and interactive SQL queries, among other things. Hadoop,

Table 13.1 MapReduce vs. Spark

Criteria	MapReduce	Spark
Processing speed	Good	Excellent (up to 100 times faster)
Data caching	Hard disk	In-memory
Performing iterative jobs	Average	Excellent
Dependency on Hadoop	Yes	No
Machine Learning applications	Average	Excellent

on the other hand, only allows batch processing. Hadoop is heavily reliant on disks, but Spark encourages caching and data storage in memory. Iterative computing is the ability of Spark to conduct calculations on the same dataset many times. Hadoop, on the other hand, does not support iterative computation.

Apache Spark may be utilized by accessing high-level APIs like Java, Scala, Python, and R. Most crucially, Spark is 100 times quicker than Hadoop In-Memory mode and ten times faster than Hadoop On-Disk mode.

13.3 HISTORY OF SPARK

The story started in 2009 when a research project was given in UC Berkeley AMP-Lab to develop a framework for cluster management with MESOS. Once MESOS was created, the need for scaling machine learning on top of Hadoop was felt as Hadoop was slow for Machine Learning. This paved the path for Apache Spark's existence. Matei Zachariah was the one who started Spark initially. The primary paper entitled "Spark: Cluster Computing with Working Sets" was published in June 2010. In early 2010, Spark was open-sourced under a BSD license (Fig. 13.2).

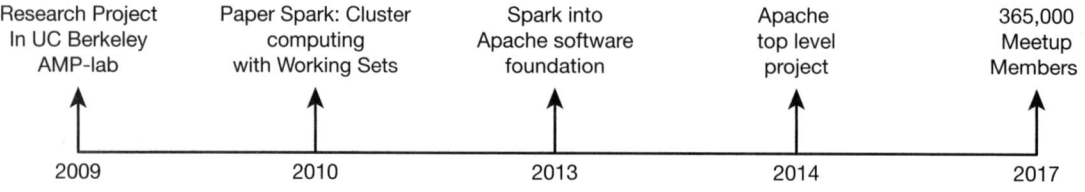

Figure 13.2 History of Spark

In its nurturing phase, Spark paved its way into the Apache Software Foundation (ASF) in June 2013. Later it got established as an Apache Top-level Project in February 2013. From its humble beginning in 2009, Apache Spark has become the most crucial framework for Big Data distributed processing, globally. Today, many organizations are espousing Apache Spark and Hadoop to handle their large datasets. In 2017, Spark had nearly 365,000 meetup members who contributed a lot to the development of Spark. Many research papers were also presented over the years with many ideas.

13.4 VERSIONS OF SPARK

After Apache Spark became open-source, many changes and enhancements were made, leading to the release of various versions of Apache Spark. Each version comes with new features and added functions. Table 13.2 gives a clear idea of the multiple versions of Apache Spark with their release date and the added features.

Table 13.2 Versions of Apache Spark

Version	Release date	Added features	Latest version
0.5	12.06.2012	1. New operators like sortBykey	0.5.1
0.6	13.10.2012	1. Standalone deploy mode 2. `Persist()` method over RDD 3. Many join operators	0.6.2
0.7	27.02.2013	1. Python API Pyspark 2. Shuffle operations and performance improvements	0.7.3
0.8	25.09.2013	1. Monitoring UI and dashboards 2. Machine Learning Library	0.8.1
0.9	02.02.2014	1. Updates Spark over Scala 2.10 2. The first version of Graph X 3. Streaming listeners	0.9.2
1.0	26.05.2014	1. Added SPARK SQL 2. Extended JAVA and PYTHON support	1.0.2
1.1	11.09.2014	1. Added JDBC/ODBC servers to connect to SPARK SQL 2. Support for JSON	1.1.1
1.2	18.12.2014	1. Improvements in performance and usage over Spark core engine 2. Upgradation of shuffling mechanism	1.2.2
1.3	13.03.2015	1. Introduction of DataFrame API, multiple-level aggregation trees 2. Introduction of Kafka docs	1.3.1
1.4	11.06.2015	1. Introduction of package SparkR Expansion of MLlib 2. Visualization of SparkDAGs 3. Docker support in Mesos	1.4.1
1.5	09.09.2015	1. Improvement of API like RDD, DataFrame 2. Handled memory management	1.5.2
1.6	04.01.2016	1. Reading of non-standard JSON files 2. New Spark API to work with custom objects	1.6.3

(Continued)

Table 13.2 (Continued)

Version	Release date	Added features	Latest version
2.0	26.07.2016	1. Hive style bucketing 2. Improvements in performance and SQL 3. Introduction of Native SQL Parser 4. New functionalities like apply, etc., were added to R	2.0.2
2.1	28.12.2016	1. Improvement in Spark streaming with Kafka support 2. Introduction of JSON parser 3. Introduction of pager ranks in R 4. Introduction of faster regression features	2.1.3
2.2	11.07.2017	1. Support for creating Hive tables with DataFrame writer and catalog 2. Introduction of broadcast joins and map joins for SQL queries 3. Introduction of parsing of multiple JSON files	2.2.3
2.3	28.02.2018	1. Introduction of Spark over Kubernetes, history server, and dynamic partitioning in Hive 2. Performance improvement over pyspark	2.3.4
2.4	02.11.2018	1. Additional support to Scala 2.12 2. Introduction of Built-in Avro Data Source 3. Introduction of coalescing and repartitions for SQL queries	2.4.7
3.0	18.06.2020	1. Adaptive query execution 2. Dynamic partition pruning 3. ANSI SQL compliance 4. New UI for structured streaming	3.0.1

13.4.1 Spark 3.0

The Spark ecosystem gained several new features, performance improvements, and compatibility with this version. This is a result of the open-source community's outstanding efforts. Over 3,400 JIRA tickets were resolved. Spark 3.0 introduces several new features and performance enhancements. The following are the most promising:

Enhancements to Adaptive Query Execution (AQE)

Unlike other technologies, Spark's runtime adaptivity is critical since it optimizes execution plans depending on the input data. Broadcasting is an excellent example of the significance of dynamic adaptation of execution strategies. If the table size permits it, the adaptive execution mode can change a shuffle join to a broadcast join (i.e., if its size does not exceed the broadcast limit). This may be possible for some data inputs, but it may not be possible for others. Data skewness is another excellent example of the relevance of AQE. The partitions utilized in future modifications can be dynamically changed when the Adaptive Query Execution option is enabled.

ANSI SQL Compliance

Migration of workloads from other SQL engines to Spark SQL requires ANSI SQL compliance. To increase compliance, this edition uses the Proleptic Gregorian calendar and allows users to prevent the usage of ANSI SQL reserved keywords as identifiers. Furthermore, runtime overflow checking in numeric operations and compile-time type enforcement when putting data into a table with a predetermined schema have been included. These new validations improve the data quality.

Pandas UDF API Improvements

Pandas UDFs (User-Defined Functions) are among the most critical additions since version 2.3, allowing users to use the pandas API in Apache Spark. Pandas UDFs with Python-type hints have a new interface in Apache Spark's latest edition. Panda UDFs were inconsistent and difficult to follow and utilize in their early iterations. In this regard, the type indications included in version 3.0 will undoubtedly assist developers in avoiding misunderstandings.

New built-in Features

Bit counts, hyperbolic functions (e.g., hyperbolic sin/cos/tan), and csv operations are among the new built-in functions in Spark 3.0.

Dynamic Partition Pruning

When the optimizer cannot determine the partitions, it may skip at build time, and Dynamic Partition Pruning is used here. This is typical in star schemas, which include one or more fact tables that relate to any number of dimension tables. We can prune the partitions read from a fact table in such join operations by finding the partitions that come from filtering the dimension tables. In a TPC-DS test, 60 out of 102 queries showed a substantial speed increase of 2 to 18 times.

Improvements in Deep Learning using Hydrogen

It is commonly understood that to construct AI/ML models that function exceptionally well, vast data must be used to train them. One of the key difficulties has been compatibility between data processing frameworks (such as Spark) and distributed deep learning frameworks. While Spark jobs are separated into numerous distinct tasks, most Deep Learning frameworks have a completely different execution methodology (e.g., tasks are dependent on each other). Project Hydrogen is a Spark effort that attempts to combine extensive data processing and machine learning model training. It is divided into three sections: Mode of barrier execution, Data exchange optimization, and Scheduling with consideration for accelerators.

13.5 SPARK ECOSYSTEM

Spark is an open-source processing engine that competes with Hadoop. It was founded on fast speed, ease of use, and higher developer productivity at first. Machine learning, real-time stream processing, and graph calculations are also supported. In addition, Spark has in-memory computing capabilities. It also promotes APIs like R, SQL, Scala, Python, and Java to make development easier (Fig. 13.3).

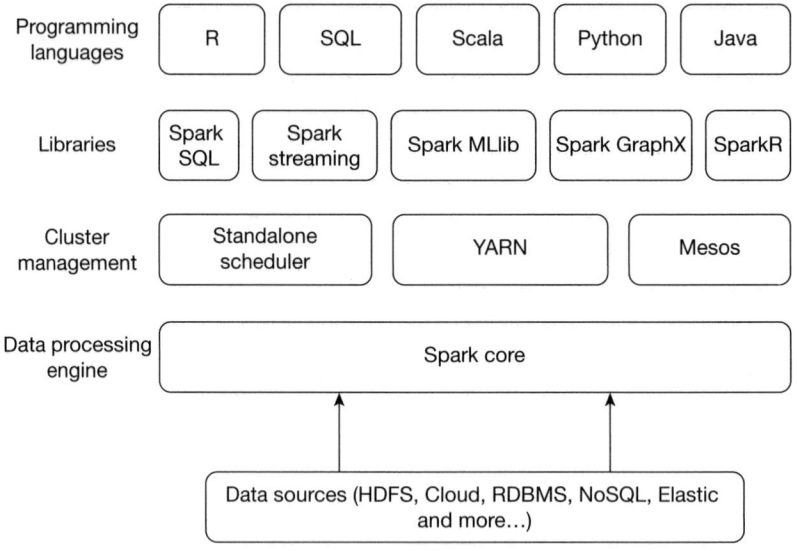

Figure 13.3 Spark ecosystem

Spark hides the complexities of distributed systems programming, network connection, and fault tolerance for engineers, providing a straightforward solution to parallelize these applications across clusters. They have enough control over the system to monitor, inspect, and tune programs while quickly accomplishing routine tasks. In addition, because the API is modular (based on sending dispersed collections of objects), it is simple to group, work into reusable libraries and test locally.

13.5.1 Spark Ecosystem: Supporting Languages

Data scientists apply their knowledge to analyze data to answer a query or uncover new information. Because their workflow frequently involves ad hoc analysis, they prefer to use interactive shells rather than complicated apps that allow them to examine the results of searches and code snippets in the shortest amount of time. Spark's speed and straightforward APIs are ideal for this, and its built-in libraries provide access to a wide range of algorithms right out of the box. The engineer persona can be used to characterize the other critical use case of Spark. Engineers, for our purposes, are a broad category of software professionals who use Spark to create production data processing systems. These programmers are usually familiar with encapsulation, interface design, and object-oriented software engineering techniques. They often hold a computer science degree. They create and build software solutions that implement a commercial use case using their engineering skills. Spark is used for their data processing applications because it has an extensive range of features, is simple to learn and use, and is mature and trustworthy.

R Programming language provides a robust framework for statistical analysis and machine learning. It enhances the developer's productivity as well. We can utilize the R language in conjunction with SparkR to manage processing on a single machine.

Spark is based on the Scala programming language. As a result, it gives you access to some of Spark's best features. Other languages that support Spark might not have those features.

Python is a language that comes with several useful libraries for data analysis. However, in comparison to Scala, Python is a little slower.

Java is another language that Spark supports. Java is an excellent choice for developers with a Java + Hadoop background.

13.5.2 Spark Ecosystem: Spark Core

Spark Core is the heart of the program. It essentially serves as an execution platform for all Spark applications. Spark also provides a generic platform to handle a wide range of applications. In addition, it achieves performance by allowing for in-memory computing. As a result, Spark Core serves as the foundation for parallel and distributed data processing.

Some of Apache Spark Core's essential features are:

- It is in charge of the most critical I/O functions.
- Significant in terms of programming and observing the Spark cluster's role
- Dispatching of tasks
- Recovery from a fault.

Spark has many components that help with various data science jobs. The Spark shell makes interactive data processing with Python or Scala. Spark SQL additionally comes with a distinct SQL shell that can be used to perform SQL data exploration, or it may be utilized as a part of a conventional Spark program or used in the Spark shell. The MLLib libraries help with machine learning and data analysis. There is also support for calling out to external Matlab or R programs. Spark allows data scientists to work on problems with larger datasets than they could with R or Python earlier.

Datasets are Spark data structures (available from version 1.6) that combine the JVM object features of RDDs (the ability to alter data using lambda functions) with a Spark SQL-optimized execution engine.

13.5.3 Spark Ecosystem: Spark SQL

Spark SQL is a layer on top of Spark that allows users to perform SQL/HQL queries. Using Spark SQL, we can handle both structured and semi-structured data. It also promises to speed up current deployments by up to 100 times by running unmodified queries. Apache Spark SQL component provides a distributed data processing framework for structured data. Spark receives more information about the data structure and computation by using Spark SQL. Spark can use this information to do additional optimizations. It computes an output using the same execution engine. The calculation is not dependent on an API or language. Spark SQL can access both structured and semi-structured data. It also allows for complex, interactive, and analytical live and historical data applications. Spark SQL is a structured data processing module for Spark. As a result, it performs the function of a distributed SQL query engine.

Features of Spark SQL

Cost-based Optimizer: The practice of altering a system to run more efficiently or use fewer resources is optimization. The most technically challenging component of Apache Spark is Spark SQL. Spark SQL handles both SQL queries and the DataFrame API.

Catalyst Optimization: A catalyst optimizer is hidden deep within Spark SQL.

It provides several advanced programming language capabilities that enable us to create an expandable query optimizer. To integrate Spark SQL, a new extensible optimizer named Catalyst was developed. This optimizer is built using Scala's functional programming constructs (Fig. 13.4).

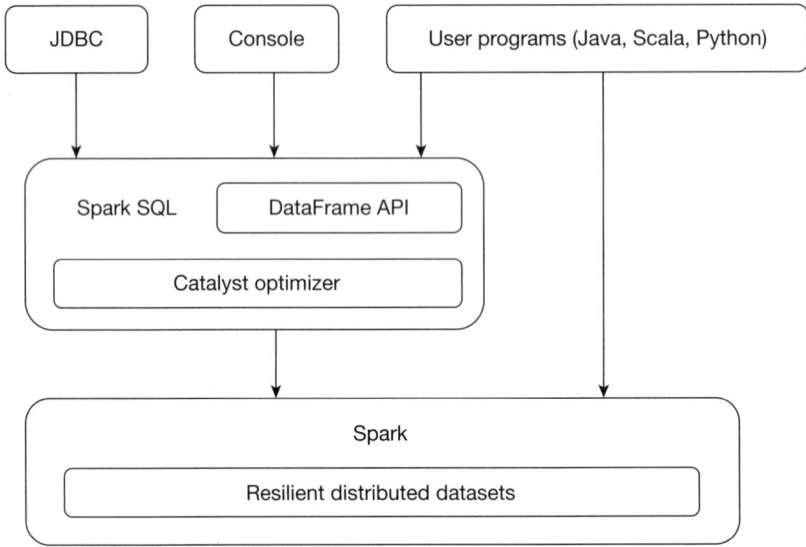

Figure 13.4 Catalyst optimizer

Catalyst optimizer supports both rule-based and cost-based optimization. The rule-based optimizer uses a collection of rules to determine how to execute the query in rule-based optimization. On the other hand, cost-based optimization discovers the most efficient way to execute SQL statements. Multiple plans are developed using rules in cost-based optimization, and then their costs are determined.

Using the Spark engine to scale thousands of nodes and multi-hour queries allows for fault tolerance in the middle of a query. The data application is scheduled, distributed, and monitored throughout the cluster via a Spark engine. In Hadoop clusters, Spark engine is utilized to perform mappings. It contains Spark SQL batch and ETL tasks, streaming data from sensors, IoT and machine learning, among other things.

Complete Interoperability with Current Hive Data: DataFrames and SQL provide a standard interface for interacting with various data sources such as Hive, Avro, Parquet, ORC, JSON, and JDBC. These data sources have the ability to transport structured data within Spark programs via SQL or a familiar DataFrame API.

Scalable, High-throughput, Fault-tolerant: Apache Spark Streaming adds to the main Spark API that provides scalable, fault-tolerant live data stream processing. Spark can read data from Kafka, Flume, Kinesis, and TCP sockets, among other sources. In addition, it can work with a variety of algorithms. Finally, the Data is saved to a file system, databases, and real-time dashboards. For real-time streaming, Spark employs micro-batching.

Micro-batching: Micro-batching is a technique for treating a stream as a series of small batches of data by a process or task (Fig. 13.5).

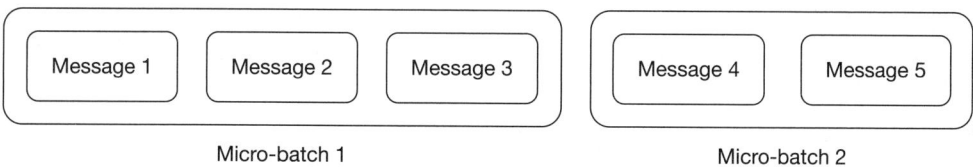

Figure 13.5 Micro-batching

As a result, Spark Streaming divides live data into discrete batches. After that, it sends the data to the batch system to be processed. It has fault tolerance properties as well.

13.5.4 Spark Streaming

Spark Streaming is divided into three phases: Gathering, Processing, and Data Storage.

Gathering: There are two types of built-in streaming sources in Spark Streaming. Primary sources are the sources that the Streaming Context API supports. File systems and socket connections are two examples of essential sources. Advanced sources are extra utility classes that provide access to Kafka, Flume, and Kinesis. As a result, Spark can access data from various sources, including Kafka, Flume, Kinesis, and TCP connections (Fig. 13.6).

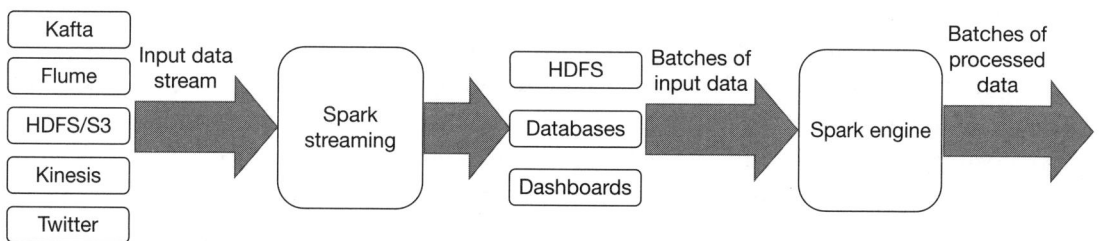

Figure 13.6 Spark streaming and Spark engine

Processing: Complex algorithms written as a high-level function are used to process the acquired data. Map, reduce, join, and window are just a few examples.

Data Storage: When processed, data is pushed out to file systems, databases, and live dashboards.

Spark Streaming also provides high-level abstraction. It is called DStream or the discretized stream. In Spark, DStream denotes a continuous data stream (Fig. 13.7).

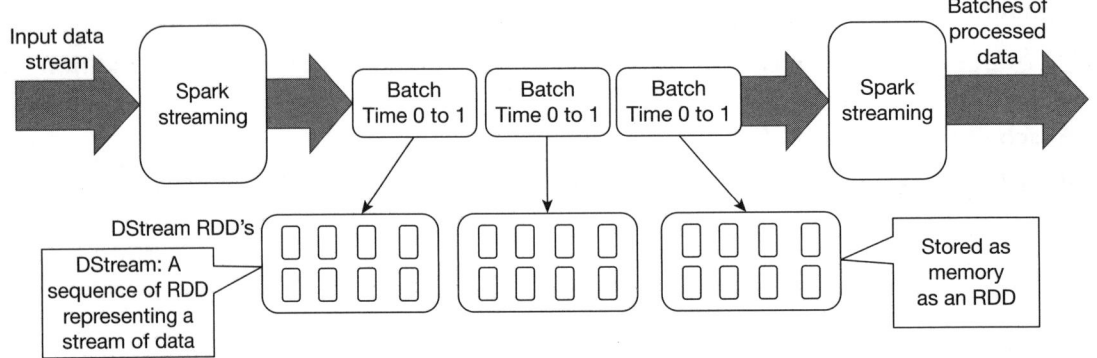

Figure 13.7 Spark DStream

DStream can be created in two ways: from Kafka, Flume, or Kinesis sources or by performing high-level operations on other DStreams. As a result, DStream is a succession of RDDs on the inside.

13.5.5 Spark MLlib

Apache Spark MLlib is a library that considers high-quality machine learning algorithms and fast performance. The goal of MLlib is to make machine learning more scalable and accessible. It includes machine learning libraries with several machine learning methods implemented. Clustering, regression, classification, and collaborative filtering are just a few examples. MLlib also includes several lower-level machine learning primitives, such as the general gradient descent optimization technique.

The RDD-based API in the Spark.mllib package went into maintenance mode in Spark Version 2.0. In this edition, the DataFrame-based API is the primary Machine Learning API for Spark. As a result, MLlib will not add any new features to the RDD-based API in the future. The move to a DataFrame-based API by MLlib is because it is more user-friendly than RDD. DataFrames contain Spark Data sources, SQL DataFrame queries, Tungsten and Catalyst optimizations, and uniform APIs across languages, to name a few advantages. Breeze, a linear algebra package, is also used by MLlib. Breeze is a set of numerical computing and machine learning libraries.

13.5.6 Spark GraphX

Apache Spark GraphX is an API for graphs and parallel graph execution. It is a data repository and network graph analytics engine. Graphs can be used for clustering, classification, traversal, searching, and pathfinding. GraphX further adds to Spark RDD's capabilities by introducing a new Graph abstraction: a directed multigraph with characteristics associated with each vertex and edge.

GraphX additionally improves the representation of vertex and edge data types when they are primitive data types. It includes core operators (such as subgraph, join Vertices, and aggregate Messages) and an optimized version of the Pregel API to facilitate graph computing.

13.5.7 SparkR

Apache Spark 1.4 was released as SparkR. SparkR DataFrame is the most critical part of SparkR. In R, DataFrames are a fundamental data structure for data processing. With libraries like Pandas and others, the concept of DataFrames has been extended to other languages. R also includes tools for data handling, calculation, and graphical presentation. As a result, the primary goal of SparkR is to test various strategies for combining R's usability with Spark's scalability. It is an R package that provides a simple client using Apache Spark from R.

Advantages of SparkR

SparkR can read data from various sources by tapping into Spark SQL's data sources API such as Hive tables, JSON files and Parquet files. Many additional data processing tools support Parquet as a columnar format file. Spark SQL reads and writes Parquet files and considers it as one of the best Big Data Analytics formats available. SparkR DataFrames inherit the computation engine's code generation and memory management optimizations. SparkR DataFrame operations are distributed over all cores and machines in the Spark cluster. As a result, SparkR DataFrames can handle terabytes of data and thousands of workstations in clusters.

13.5.8 Cluster Management

The cluster manager is a platform for running Spark in cluster mode. It allocates resources to all worker nodes as needed and manages all nodes. We may state that master and worker nodes exist in a cluster. Worker nodes benefit from the efficient working environment provided by master nodes. Spark cluster managers come in three flavors. These cluster managers are supported by Spark: 1. Standalone cluster manager 2. Hadoop Yarn and 3. Apache Mesos. Apache Spark also supports pluggable cluster management. The cluster manager's primary responsibility is to provide resources to all applications. It may be described as an external service for getting cluster resources.

Let us look at each of these cluster managers in more detail:

Standalone Cluster Manager

It is included in the Spark distribution and serves as a primary cluster manager. The essence of the standalone cluster manager is that it is resilient to work failures. It can manage resources according to application requirements. It runs smoothly on Linux,

Windows, and Mac. HDFS (Hadoop Distributed File System) data is also accessible. This is the most straightforward method of running Apache Spark on this cluster. It also has a high master availability. It has a master and several workers in cluster management. It contains available resources such as RAM and CPU cores that are configurable. Mode Spark provides resources in this cluster based on its core. By default, an application can use all of the cores available in the cluster. If our master crashes, the ZooKeeper quorum can assist. It uses a standby master to retrieve the master. Several file systems can also be used to retrieve the master. These programs have a web user interface that serves as a watchdog for the cluster and task statistics. It aids in providing a variety of data on memory or ongoing processes. Every task done by this cluster management provides a full log output. Even after the program has exited, Web UI may recreate the application's UI.

Hadoop Yarn

It is a distributed computing framework that works with Hadoop. It also keeps track of task scheduling and resource management. The masters and slaves in this cluster are pretty accessible to us. We also have executors and a pluggable scheduler accessible. It may also be used on Linux and Windows. MapReduce 2.0 is another name for Hadoop Yarn. It also separates the functions of resource management and task scheduling. A job request is sent to YARN Resource Manager, which then works on the request based on the number of resources available. The Yarn system is an enormous plan. It chooses the location where the resources are employed. This is the next level in the MapReduce framework's development. Yarn functions as a resource manager component and was created in response to the requirement to expand Hadoop tasks. With the aid of Yarn, we can optimize Hadoop tasks. For brief and quick Spark works, the Yarn is the goal. However, Yarn is not suitable for both long-running services and short-term inquiries. Thus, it is not described as a perfect system. The Yarn is ideal for projects that can be readily restarted if they fail. Yarn does not work with databases or distributed file systems.

On the other hand, the huge Yarn scheduler supports a variety of workloads. The Yarn is not designed to be light. It cannot accommodate the expanding number of contemporary algorithms.

Apache Mesos

It is a cluster manager that is distributed. It, like Yarn, is widely available to both masters and slaves. It may also manage resources for each application separately. Spark jobs, Hadoop MapReduce, and other service applications may be readily run. Apache provides APIs for Java, Python, and C++. Mesos may also be run on Linux or Mac OSX. Now let us take a look at the working of Mesos. At first, it influences the availability of resources. Then it returns the offer to its framework. There is a possibility that such bids will be rejected or approved by the framework. This is a two-level scheduler concept with pluggable scheduling. This system is also classified as non-monolithic. It can schedule an endless number of algorithms and is feasible only because it can turn down offers. As a result, it can support thousands of schedules on the same cluster. It enables two-level scheduling as mentioned earlier, and as a result, it chooses the algorithm to employ for scheduling the jobs it needs to do. This technique is similar to using a laptop or smartphone to run many programs simultaneously. Mesos is the natural arbiter. It has complete control over all apps. Years of operating system experience are one of this idea's most remarkable parts.

We can compare all three cluster managers based on the following points:

High Availability (HA): Automatic recovery is available in the standalone manager. The master can be quorum-recovered using standby masters in ZooKeeper. This cluster is robust; therefore, we can recover the master manually using the file system. Whether master recovery is enabled or not, it aids worker failures. The Mesos cluster management also assists ZooKeeper with master recovery. It also allows the master's rescue. In the case of a failure, tasks that are presently running can continue to run. Apache Hadoop YARN provides manual and automated recovery through the ZooKeeper resource management. It uses a command-line utility for manual recovery. There is no need to operate a separate ZooKeeper controller, as there is with Mesos and a standalone manager. ZooKeeper is used in this system to keep track of the resource managers' status.

Security: These cluster managers, including Apache Spark, enable shared secret authentication. The user must set up each node with the authentication only in the standalone manager. We employ SSL (Secure Sockets Layer) to encrypt data for communication protocols. SASL (Simple Authentication and Security Layer) encryption is available for block transfers. We also have various data encryption alternatives. Access control lists may be used to access Spark apps through the web user interface. Mesos enables authentication for every entity communicating with the cluster. This comprises slaves and the master, cluster applications, and operators. The user can choose whether to permit these entities to utilize authentication or not. Access control lists are used in Mesos to grant access to services. Mesos already has unencrypted communication between modules. SSL (Secure Sockets Layer) can be used to encrypt this conversation. Authentication, service authorization, and web and data security are all possible with Hadoop Yarn. Kerberos is used for authenticating each user and service in Hadoop and is useful for distributed service level access. We can use access control lists to manage who has access to Hadoop services. SSL allows us to encrypt data and communication between clients and services. It uses HTTPS to encrypt data sent between the web interface and clients.

Monitoring: We have a web UI for each Apache Spark application that allows us to track it. This online interface displays tasks, jobs, executors, and storage data. We can access the detailed log output for Spark's standalone cluster management tasks. The output can also provide job statistics and look at clusters via the web interface. We may reach master and slave nodes in Apache Mesos using URLs that contain metrics supplied by Mesos. We have a Web interface for resource managers and node managers in Hadoop YARN. Each node receives information from the node management. It gives metrics for the cluster in a resource manager.

Thus, it can be seen that Standalone is the easiest to set up of all the Spark cluster administrators. Additionally, it has the same functionality as other Spark cluster administrators. If we need to schedule many resources, we may use YARN and Mesos managers. Yarn is pre-installed on Hadoop platforms, which is one of its advantages. One advantage of Mesos over others is that it allows for fine-grained sharing. Finally, Apache Spark is platform-independent. So, the choice of the manager to be used is determined by our needs and objectives.

13.6 Design Principles of Apache Spark

The industry lacked a general-purpose cluster computing solution before Spark. As a result, we required a variety of technologies alongside Hadoop to meet various criteria such as batch processing, which necessitated the use of Hadoop MapReduce.

Stream processing is done with Apache Storm / S4. We utilize Apache Impala / Apache Tez for interactive processing. For graph processing, we need Neo4j and Apache Giraph (Fig. 13.8).

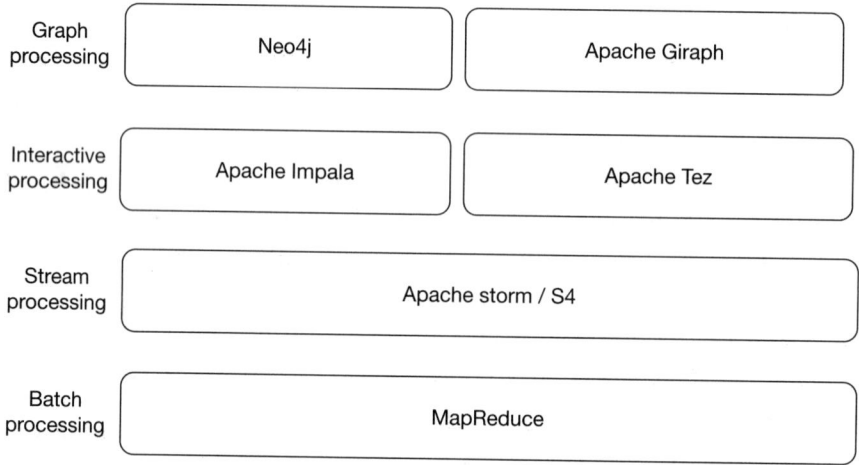

Figure 13.8 Design principles of Apache Spark

As a result, the sector has a high demand for a strong engine. It can process data in both real-time (streaming) and batch mode. We also need an engine that could respond in under a second and do in-memory processing. Thus, Spark is indispensable for all the design principles.

A Unified Engine

Apache Spark uses high-level libraries and offers SQL queries and streaming data capabilities. Furthermore, machine learning and graph processing are simple to implement. These standard libraries essentially increase developer productivity. Finally, the requirement for the unified engine is met by Apache Spark, which has various tools for processing the requests quickly and easily. Spark has evolved into a formidable open-source engine. It allows us to do both real-time and interactive stream processing. We may also utilize it simultaneously for graph, in-memory, and batch processing. The most attractive feature of this system is that we can use it all simultaneously. Users will also benefit from the convenience of use and standard interface.

13.7 Advantages of Spark

Apache Spark is a boon to the industry which is processing Big Data. It has met the expectations of the developers when it comes to querying, processing, and analysis in a better way. Moreover, Apache Spark, with its diversified benefits (Fig. 13.9), has made it more attractive in the Big Data Platform. Here are the advantages of Apache Spark:

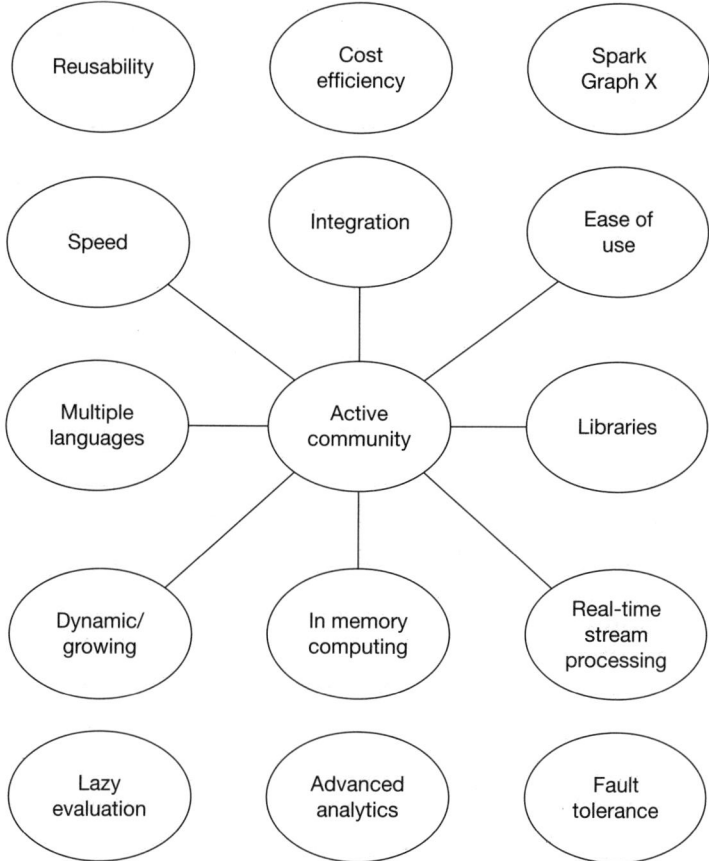

Figure 13.9 Apache Spark advantages

Speed: Every organization has started to process large-scale data every day. When processing this Big Data, speed becomes the most critical factor to be considered. Apache Spark has gained popularity among developers because of its processing speed. Spark uses an in-memory computing technique wherein the data is processed in the RAM rather than in the local disks, which are slower. This increases the computational speed significantly.

One of the essential features of Spark is its matchless speed. As a result, Spark is the most sought-after technology in Big Data. High-speed processing is needed when Big Data is considered as volume, veracity, value, variety, and velocity are the characteristics of Big Data. The capacity of Spark is so high that it can handle several petabytes of clustered Data concurrently from more than 8000 nodes. Compared to Hadoop, Spark is 100x faster when processing Big Data. This feature of fast processing of Big Data has made Spark more popular among data scientists. Spark achieves this processing speed by reducing the time taken for the reading and writing operations using Resilient Distributed Datasets (RDD)s. As a result, Spark runs 100 times faster in memory and ten times faster on disk when it runs an application in the environment of Hadoop.

Integrated with Hadoop: Apache Spark is fabricated on top of HDFS, a distributed file system that can handle Big Data. So, Spark is a fast-processing engine compatible with Hadoop data. It can process data available on HDFS, Cassandra, and Hive (Fig. 13.10).

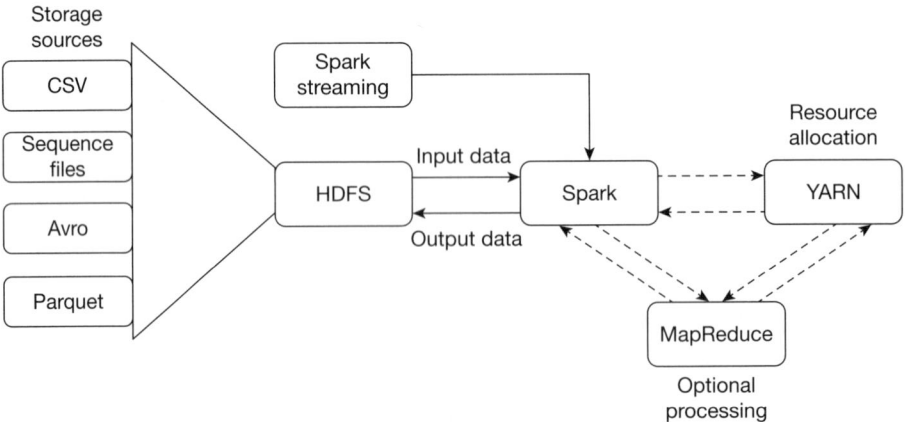

Figure 13.10 Apache Spark Hadoop integration

Spark can run independently and on Apache YARN (Yet Another Resource Negotiator). Thus, Spark integrates well with HDFS. Spark also supports multiple file formats like JSON, CSV, ORC, Avro, etc. This provides Spark users flexibility.

Ease of use: Apache Spark comes with a rich package of Application Programming Interfaces (API), which helps perform various operations on massive datasets. An API, in simple words, acts as an intermediate between applications. Spark API tools are developer-friendly; and with a simple method call, complex distributions can be handled. Furthermore, Apache Spark provides more than 80 high-level operators, which helps build applications in parallel. Moreover, Spark is easy to use as it allows for bindings for languages like Java, Scala, Python, R, etc. Hence the application developers and data scientists rely on this tool for better performance and computational speed without digging into more levels of detail.

Better Access to Big Data: Apache Spark is emerging with new opportunities in extensive data work. A survey conducted by IBM reveals that more than a million people will be trained on Apache Spark to become data engineers and scientists.

Support for Multiple Languages: Spark allows developers to write applications in different languages like Java, R, Scala, Python, etc. Consequently, it gives dynamicity and overcomes one of the disadvantages of Hadoop, as applications can be written only in Java in Hadoop. Furthermore, Spark offers built-in APIs in languages like Java, Python, and Scala, making it easier to work in Spark.

Plethora of Libraries: Apache Spark comes with a bundle of libraries. It not only supports maps and reduces, but also provides libraries to support machine learning, queries, data streaming, and analysis of graphs. Machine learning includes a framework to support feature selection, transformations, and extraction for the structured dataset. This is an added advantage to Spark, making it a sought-after tool by developers.

Dynamic in Nature: Spark is highly active as it provides 80 high-level operators that support interactive querying. Applications can also be developed in parallel with the help of these operators. Hence it is considered to be a rich tool in this aspect. Spark allows the developers to build applications using different languages, providing greater flexibility than other tools used in the Big Data environment. Spark can run on various tools like Hadoop Yarn, Mesos, and even in a cloud environment. In cluster mode, it can also run independently. Spark can run on one environment and read data from another source. For example, it can run on the YARN cluster manager and read Hadoop data from HBase, Hive, Cassandra, etc.,

In-memory Computing: The speed of analysis is higher in Spark as it implements in-memory processing. Unlike Hadoop, Spark stores data in the Random Access Memory of the servers. Hence there is no need to transfer data in and out of the cluster as done in Hadoop. Furthermore, as the data is cached in the main memory, it is not necessary to fetch data from the disk whenever the data is needed for executing applications. Hence, the accessing speed of the data is reduced, thereby accelerating the speed of processing. This is one of the reasons why Spark can handle data faster. Furthermore, the in-memory computation is facilitated in Spark with the use of a DAG execution engine, which enables acyclic data flow, thereby resulting in higher speed.

Real-time Stream Processing: Real-time data streaming is a process in which the data is processed as it is received. This helps in taking actions immediately based on the changing conditions in real-time. The generation of real-time data is rising exponentially every second as the usage of applications is growing continuously. This data have to be processed and manipulated in live streams to help the firms identify fraudulent activities and threats and enhance their organization's performance by analyzing the generated data. Apache Spark provides smooth streaming of real-time data using the state-of-art methods to write streaming codes and maintain the same. This feature of Spark is one of the most important advantages which makes Spark popular among data analysts and developers. Since Spark processes real-time data, the outcomes are instant, and they can be obtained within a few nanoseconds or mins. Furthermore, unlike other tools for streaming data, Spark can recover the lost data without writing any extra code, which makes it more sophisticated.

Advanced Analytics: Apache Spark has a rich store of functions for processing Big Data Analytics and Machine Learning. Spark comes with dedicated tools for processing interactive and declarative SQL queries, real-time streaming data, MapReduce functions, machine learning algorithms, and graph algorithms.

Fault Tolerance: Spark's fault tolerance level is high compared to Hadoop. Spark achieves fault tolerance in storage and computation by backing up the data to another node. It handles the failure of a working node with the help of the Spark Abstraction RDD, which ensures that data loss is zero. The Apache Spark fault tolerance feature indicates that RDD can manage any loss. It is capable of recovering the defect, where fault refers to failure. RDD provides the capacity to fix any bugs or recover the discovered losses. To recover the deleted data, we'll require a redundant element. In the self-recovery process, redundant data is crucial since it can be used finally to retrieve lost data.

Furthermore, while working with Spark, we may apply several transformations to RDDs. This results in a sensible execution strategy for all jobs. Lineage graph is another name for this logical execution strategy.

Lazy Evaluation: Spark increases the system's efficiency by a lazy evaluation which reduces the work it has to do. This occurs during Spark transformation. Lazy evaluation means that the data residing in RDD will not get executed unless there is an action trigger. It waits for the completion of the code and then efficiently processes the instruction. Spark's ability helps to optimize the decisions as everything is transparent to the Spark engine even before an action is triggered. Spark acts on data in an intelligent fashion. When you tell Spark to do anything with a dataset, it follows your instructions and takes a note of it so it does not forget – but it does not do anything until you ask for the outcome. The action is not executed immediately when a transformation like a `map()` is called on an RDD. Spark does not analyze transformations until you make an action. This helps to improve the overall data processing workflow.

Reusability: Spark codes can be used for joining stream data with historical data, batch-processing, and for running ad-hoc queries on streaming data.

Cost Efficiency: Apache Spark is open-source software, and hence the user does not need to pay for licensing. It comes with in-built functions for machine learning, streaming applications, and graph processing, thereby reducing the cost for organizations that use Spark according to their requirements.

Spark GraphX: Spark has an exclusive GraphX component for graph and graph-parallel computations. This has a collection of algorithms and builders to simplify the tasks related to Graph analytics. Web analytics is a developing field when Big Data is considered.

E-commerce has taken over the corporate sector. The driving force for the entire e-commerce world is graph analytics. Graph processing helps to identify the relationship between entities in data and is mapped to analyze social media and advertisement data. This, in turn, aids in providing suggestions, ranking, viewing items, etc. The recent progress in machine learning and data mining is based on graph processing, which helps organizations expand their territory and improve their business. Hence solving graph problems and designing graph models have gained more interest. Apache Spark supports real-time data stream processing, but it also supports graph processing. It has come up with many graph algorithms and constructors that help simplify graph analytics.

Spark is Potential: In this age of fast-growing technology, companies need to manage two different systems to handle the Big Data that is getting generated. One application has to be developed for publishing and storing real-time data, and a separate application has to be designed to manipulate and analyze the data. This demands a lot of computational time and space for storing this data. Apache Spark provides concurrent batch and stream processing of data, which helps the organizations to make their designing, deployment, and maintenance issues easier. Spark allows the developers to create parallel applications in different languages with the help of the operators. The availability of well-built libraries for graph processing and machine learning makes it more sophisticated. The in-memory computing for processing data and low latency in Apache Spark helps handle the challenges faced in advanced data analytics. This has made Spark a powerful tool.

Demand for Spark Developers: Spark is gaining popularity as it has many advantages. The attractive and extensive data framework, in-memory computing techniques, iterative computing, real-time data streaming, and graph processing have made it more appealing. Spark developers are in great demand as many big companies use Spark to process their data. Apache Spark engineers receive handsome remuneration packages.

Active Spark Community: Since 2009, more than 1200 developers from nearly 300 companies have contributed to the development of Apache Spark. These community developers are extending their support continuously for the enhancement and upgradation of Spark. Mailing lists can be used to post queries, while Spark conferences and meetup groups are useful for people to discuss more on Spark. Apache has a colossal open-source community working behind it to make it more powerful. Different versions are released with updated coding to overcome some of the limitations in Spark. This is the greatest strength of Apache Spark.

13.8 DISADVANTAGES OF APACHE SPARK

Every technology needs continuous improvement, and Apache Spark is not an exception (Fig. 13.11). Though Spark was developed to perform fast computing using cluster computing technology, developers who work on Big Data using Spark still face specific challenges. The following are the limitations of Apache Spark:

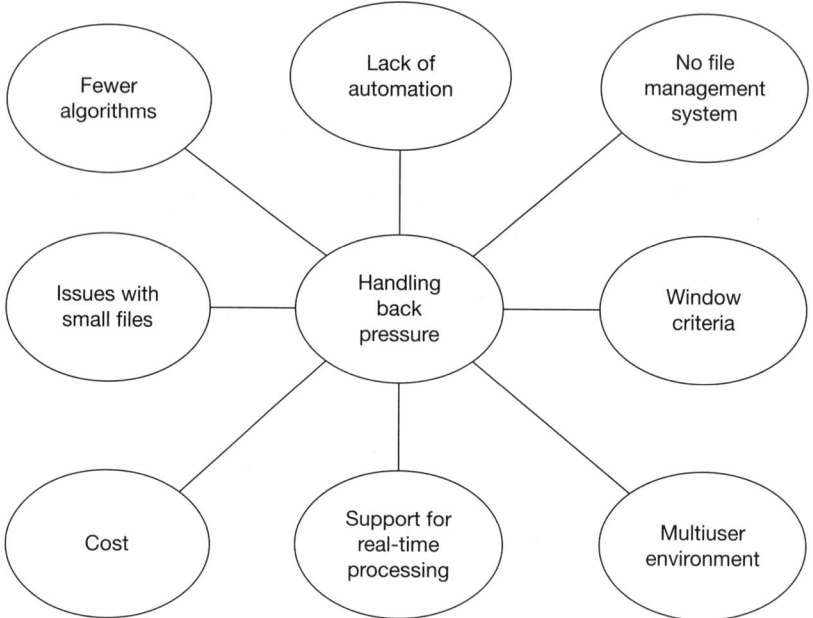

Figure 13.11 Apache Spark disadvantages

Lack of Automatic Optimization Process: Optimization is adapted to use resources and increase job execution speed effectively. Any unit of work is known as a job. The datasets and jobs must be optimized manually when working with Apache Spark. The users can state the number of partitions if they want to make partitions. To fix the number of required partitions on their own, the user must pass the number of partitions as a second parameter in the parallelize method. The Resilient Distributed Datasets are formed in Apache Spark using the parallelizing method, from the existing collection present in the driver. Any operation can be done in parallel with the elements present in the collection. These partitions must be controlled manually to get the correct partition and cache. When automation is done in most platforms and techniques, Spark's lack of an automatic optimization process proves to be a disadvantage.

No File Management System: One of the significant issues of Apache Spark is that it does not have a file management system of its own. File management must be integrated with other platforms. Therefore, it depends on Hadoop Distributed File System or any other cloud-based platform for the file management system.

Fewer Number of Algorithms: Machine Learning Algorithms are stored in the Spark MLlib library within the Apache Spark framework. However, this Spark library does not have many machine learning algorithms. Hence there is a lag in terms of available algorithms like Tanimoto distance. As the number of available algorithms is limited, it is considered as one of the disadvantages of Spark.

Issues with Small Files: The problem of small files arises when developers use Apache Spark with Hadoop. Limited large files are made available by Hadoop instead of small files and this becomes a problem when Spark is used with Hadoop since there are many small files when Apache Spark is used with Hadoop. However, Spark stores all these files as zipped files in S3 (Simple Storage Service). This looks acceptable, except that there are many small gzipped files. When these files are unzipped to retrieve the data, Spark has to decompress these files by keeping these files over the network. The entire file must be in one core to decompress these zipped files. So, much time is consumed to burn cores and unzip the files in sequence. This time-consuming procedure, in turn, affects the processing of data. Once the files are unzipped, there will be many tiny partitions within an RDD as each file will become a partition in the resulting RDD. To enhance processing efficiency, repartitioning of RDDs has to take place to make them manageable. Extensive shuffling over the network has to be done to improve the processing efficiency. So, this has become an issue when Apache Spark is used with Hadoop.

Window Criteria: In Apache Spark Streaming, the data is divided into small batches based on a pre-defined time interval. So, it supports a time-based window (Fig. 13.12) and does not support a record-based window like Flink. Sliding Window manages data packet delivery between several computer networks.

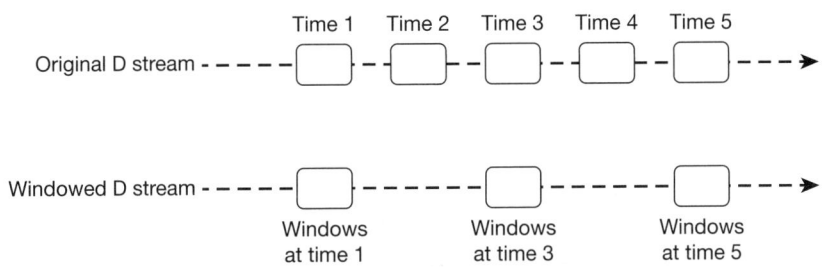

Figure 13.12 Windows DStream

The Spark Streaming library supports windowed computations, which apply RDD transformations to a sliding data window. When the window slides, the RDDs that fall within that window are merged and processed to create new RDDs for the windowed DStream.

Cost-effectiveness: The in-memory computing capability of Apache Spark is highly effective when it comes to machine learning and batch-processing. In-memory indicates that the data to be processed is kept in Random Access Memory (RAM) instead of disks so that the processing can be done in parallel. This, in turn, will enhance the computational speed. The in-memory computing of Apache Spark has made it famous for Big Data processing. However, though the computational speed is very high in Apache Spark, it is not user-friendly as it needs RAM with a considerable capacity to process the in-memory data. Hence it becomes a costly affair. Compared to Hadoop MapReduce, which has low-cost disk space, Spark is very expensive. This is also one of the disadvantages of Apache Spark.

Lack of Full Support for Real-time Processing: Apache Spark Streaming is one of the essential features of Spark, which results in low latency. In Spark streaming, the data received live from the data sources are divided into batches in a pre-defined interval. Each batch or partition is handled like a Spark Resilient Distributed Database (RDD), and each partition is processed using various operations like join, map, reduce, etc. Once the processing is done, the results of these operations are converted into batches again. This clearly shows that Spark streaming is micro-batch processing with near real-time processing of live data and not complete real-time processing.

Iterative Processing: Iterative processing indicates that the results obtained in transition are used repeatedly. However, as Apache Spark iterates the data in batches, every iteration has to be scheduled separately and executed one after the other. Hence this becomes a disadvantage when using Apache Spark. The time between an action and the reaction to that necessary procedure is known as latency. If the latency is high, the throughput (unit of information processed in a given time) will be low. Hence latency and throughput are inversely proportional. The latency of Apache Spark is less when compared to Hadoop, but it is high compared to Apache Flink. This makes Flink look better than Apache Spark as it has lower latency and hence gives higher throughput.

Handling Backpressure: Apache Spark can process a massive amount of data. As data grows, handling the flow of data becomes an issue. Buffer is used for storing data temporarily when it moves from one place to another. When the buffer is complete, it cannot receive the incoming data, and the data gets built up at the input/output switches. Transfer of data cannot take place till the buffer is emptied. This is known as backpressure. Apache Spark fails to handle this backpressure implicitly. This backpressure has to be relieved manually – a disadvantage for developers who use Apache Spark.

Not Suitable for a Multi-user Environment: A multi-user environment is a workspace where many users can log in and work concurrently. Unfortunately, Apache Spark cannot handle many users concurrently, and hence it is not suitable for a multi-user environment.

Though Apache Spark has certain limitations, its demand in the market has never been in decline. Many companies still prefer it for handling and processing Big Data. Moreover, the Apache Spark community has never failed to attract the market with its enhanced versions to overcome these disadvantages.

13.9 INSTALLATION OF APACHE SPARK ON WINDOWS

For new users, installing Apache Spark on Windows 10 may seem complicated, but it will be up and running in no time if the given instructions are followed.

Step 1: The first step to initiate the installation of Spark is to download the Apache Spark tar file. Figure 13.13 shows the first screen when you click the following link for downloading Spark.
https://spark.apache.org/downloads.html

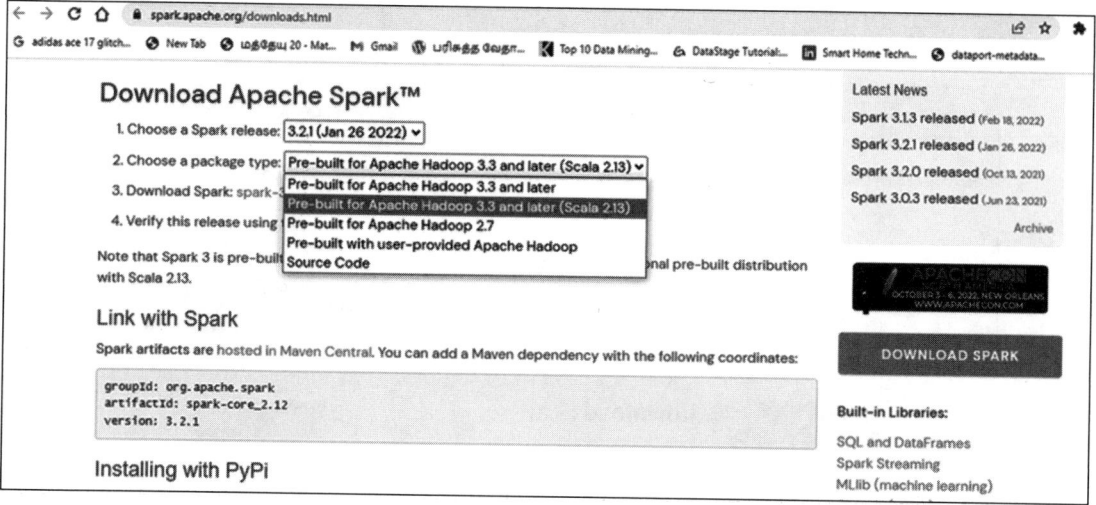

Figure 13.13 Downloading options for installing Spark

Step 2: After downloading the tar file, unzip the file. Figure 13.14 shows the extraction of the Spark tar file.

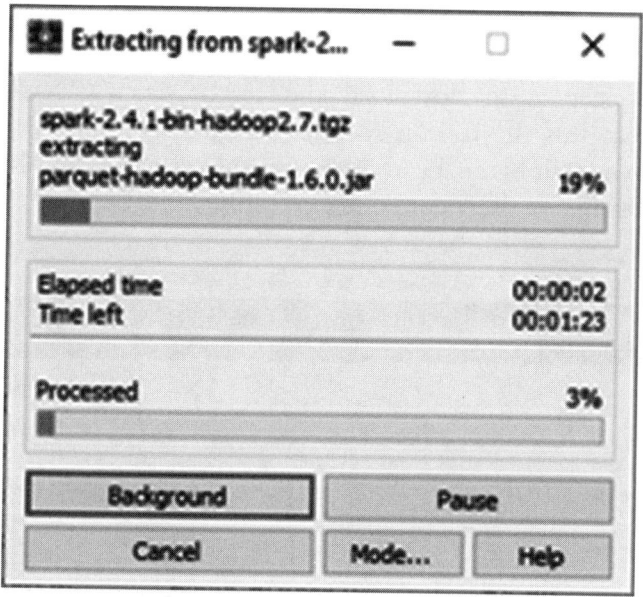

Figure 13.14 Extracting files from the downloaded Spark tar file

Step 3: If the machine already has Java Development Kit Version 8, you may skip this step. This version of JDK is recommended as it includes lambda expressions that support Spark's API to support these expressions. If the system does not have JDK version 8, it can be downloaded using the following link: https://filehippo.com/download_java-development-kit-64/. Figure 13.15 shows the screen for downloading JDK version 8.

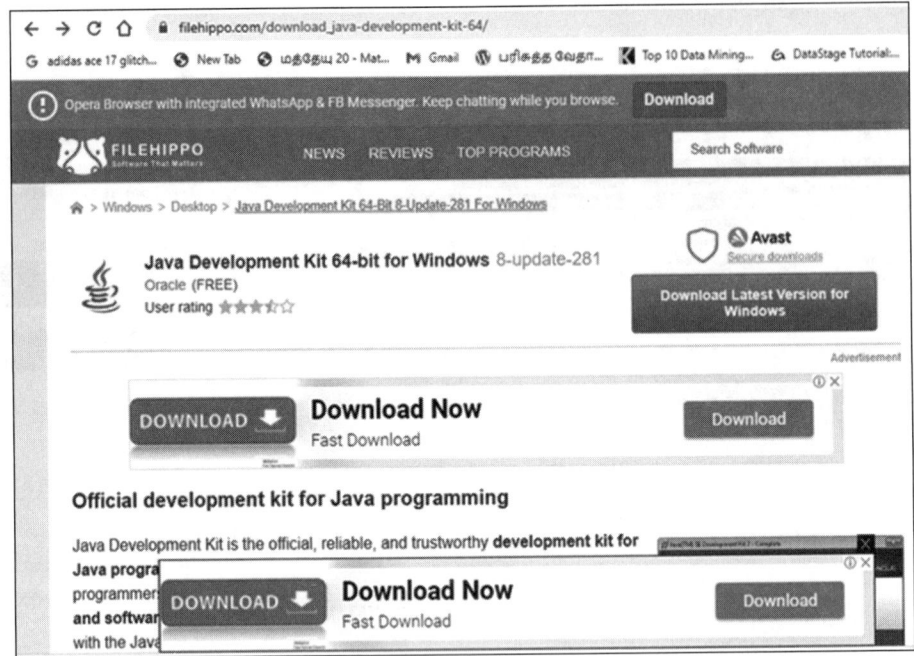

Figure 13.15 Option for downloading JDK version 8

Step 4: The next step is to download the HADOOP WINUTILS file. Apache Spark needs this file to run locally. Figure 13.16 shows the list of winutils. The following link can be used to download the winutils file from Github: https://github.com/steveloughran/winutils.

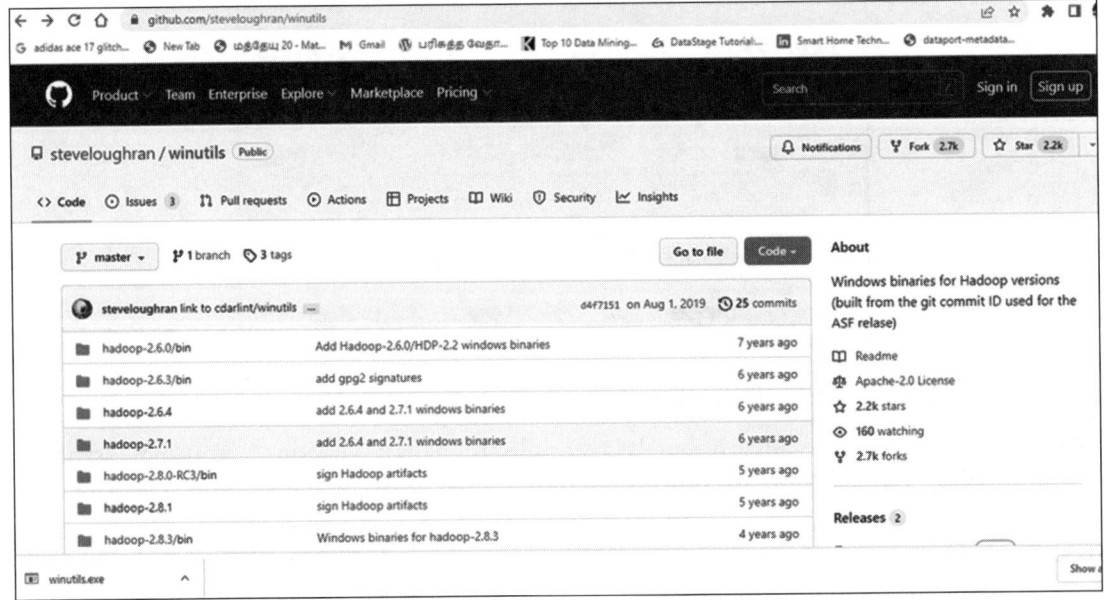

Figure 13.16 Hadoop Winutils options

Step 5: From the Hadoop Winutils option, select Hadoop 2.7.1. Figure 13.17 shows the bin and readme file seen once the Hadoop 2.7.1 is selected from winutils.

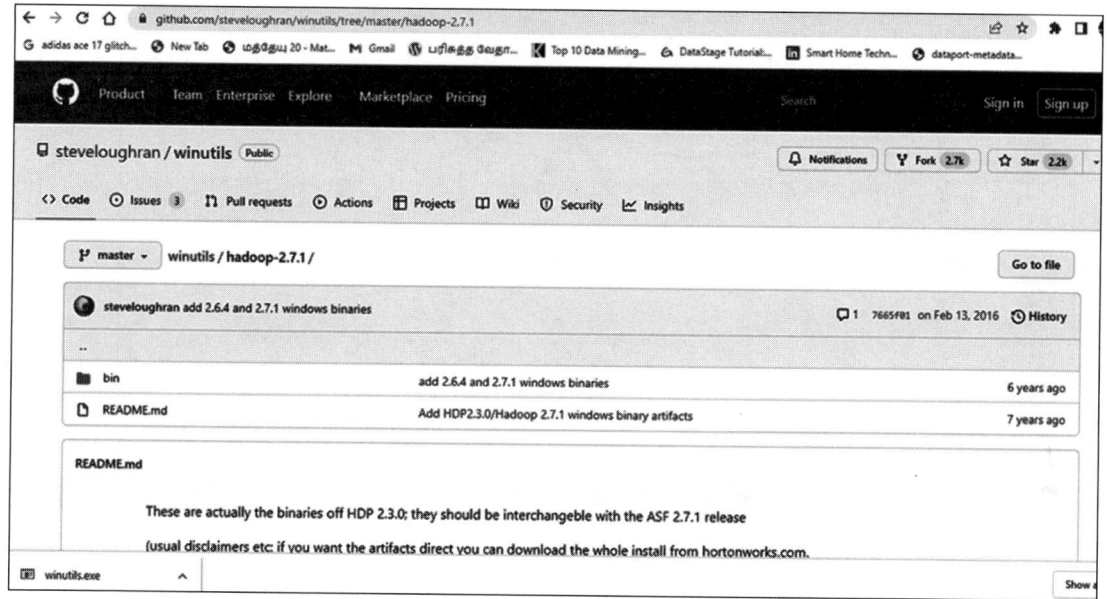

Figure 13.17 The files in Hadoop 2.7.1

Step 6: Choose the bin, which is shown in Fig. 13.18. After choosing the bin, click on the WINUTILS file and download it.

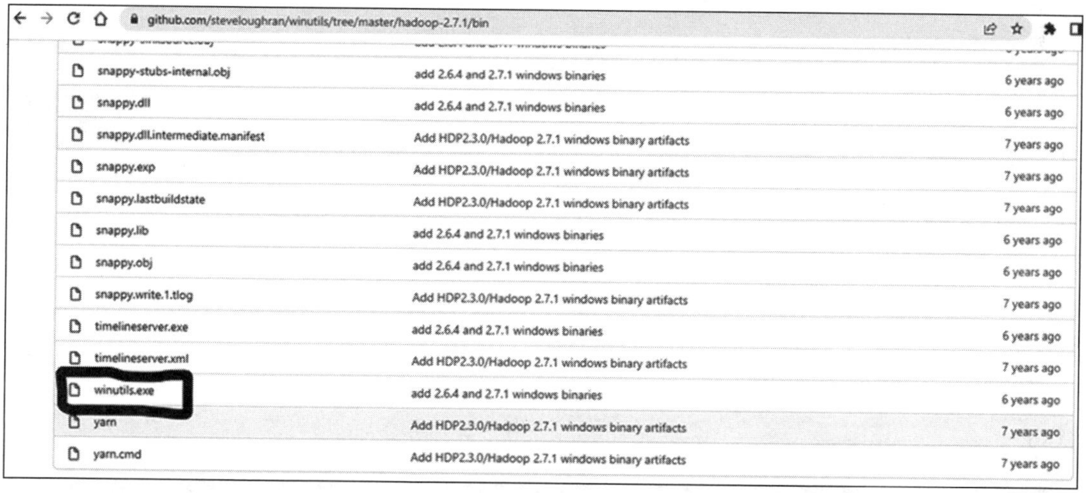

Figure 13.18 Selecting the winutils from the bin folder

Step 7: Once the Spark and Java are installed, paste these folders into the local disk C. Figure 13.19 shows the Spark and Java folders in the local disk C.

674 • Big Data Analytics

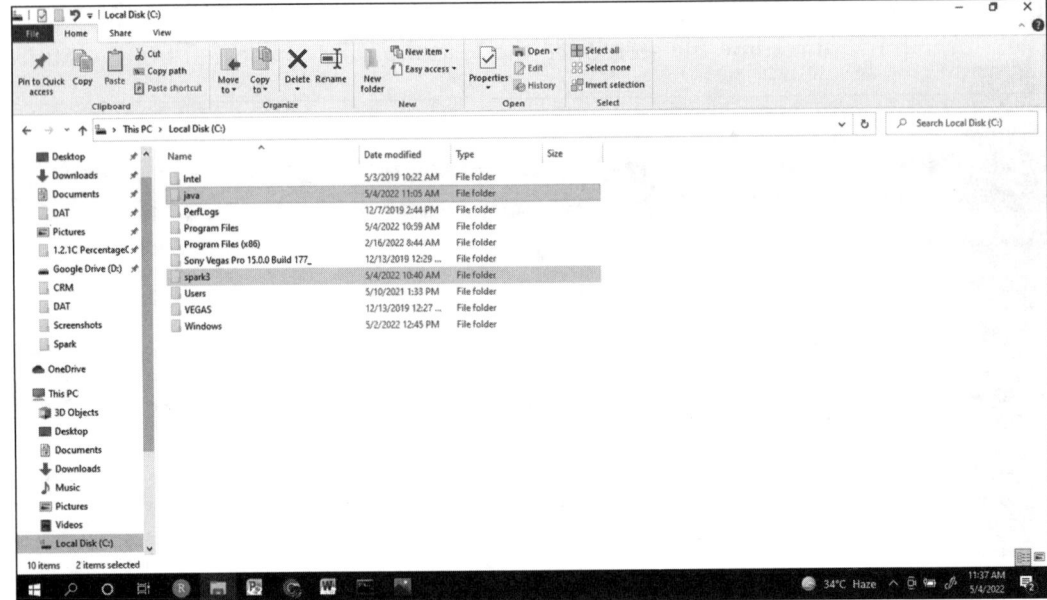

Figure 13.19 Java and Spark folders in local disk C

Step 8: Now paste the WINUTILS into the bin folder of Spark's root directory. This is shown in Fig. 13.20.

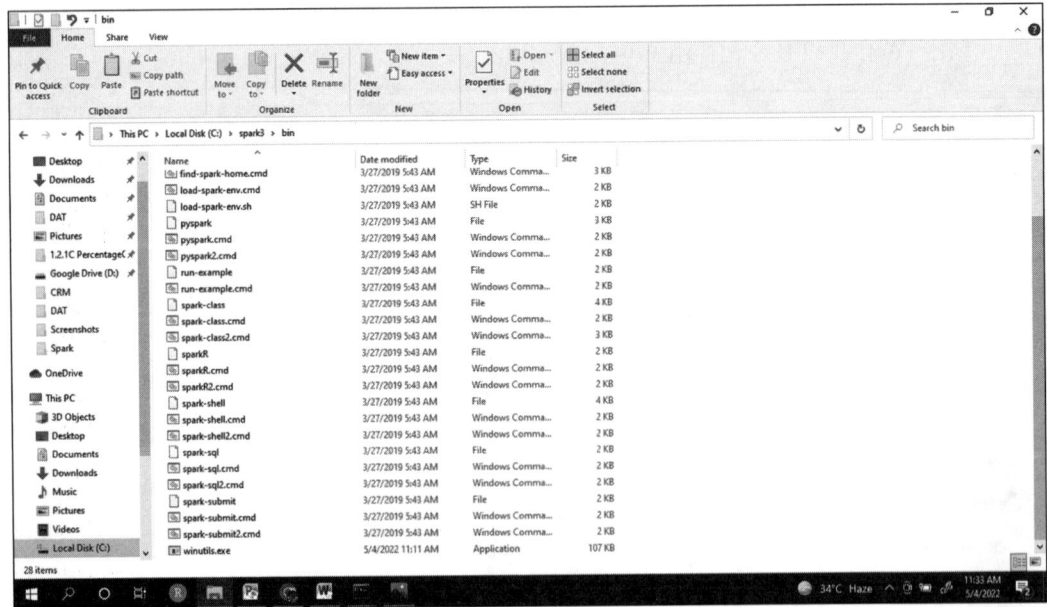

Figure 13.20 Winutils pasted in the bin folder of the Spark's Root Directory

Step 9: As a next step, the path has to be set for JDK and Spark. To perform this, in the search bar, type env and choose the option environment variables for your account. This is clearly shown in Fig. 13.21.

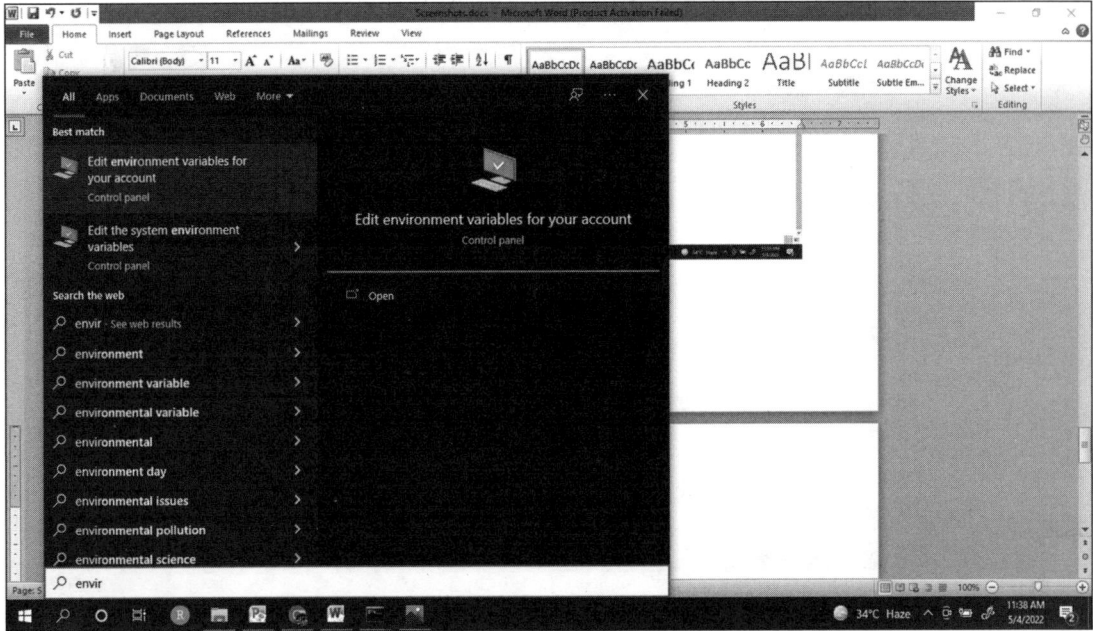

Figure 13.21 Selection of the environment variables for the account

Step 10: The next step is to set the path in the path folder for JAVA_HOME, JAVA_PATH, HADOOP_HOME, and SPARK_HOME. To perform this, click on New and set the path. Figure 13.22 shows how to set a path in the path folder.

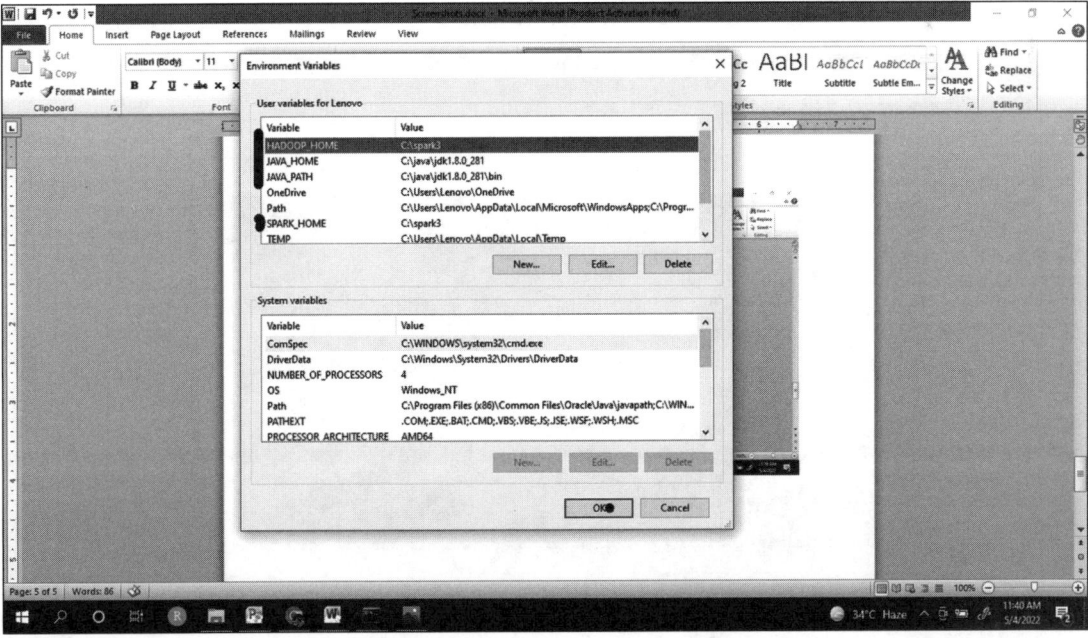

Figure 13.22 New option to create path folder

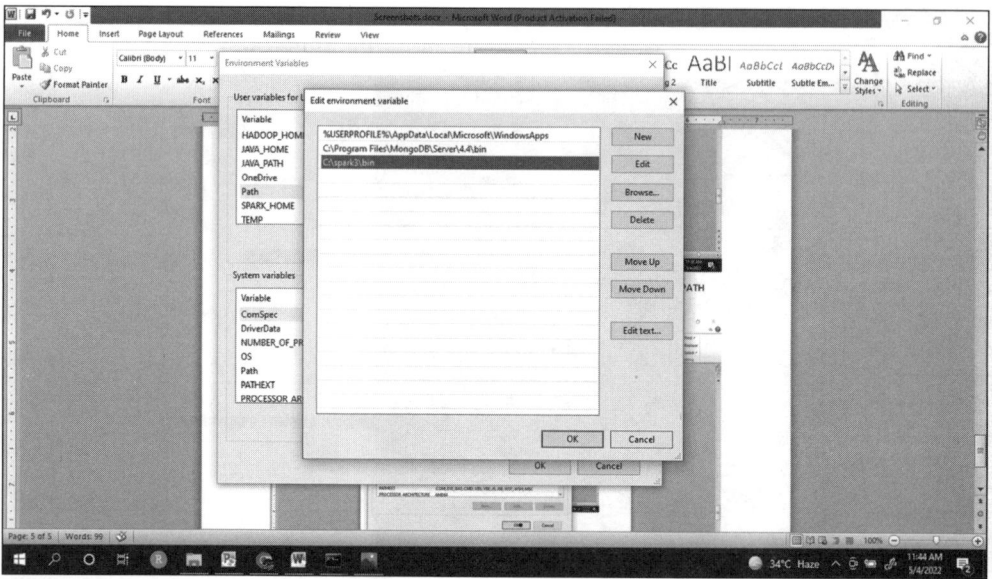

Figure 13.23 Path folder in Spark's bin folder

Step 11: Now Spark is ready to be used. To run Spark, go to the command prompt. To do this, just press Windows + R and type cmd. Once the working environment gets opened, just type the command **spark-shell.** This is shown in Fig. 13.24. Once the enter key is pressed, it shows a screen, as seen in Fig. 13.25, indicating that Spark is installed and ready to use in Scala. This is how the installation of Spark is done. Though it looks extensive, installing Spark does not take much time.

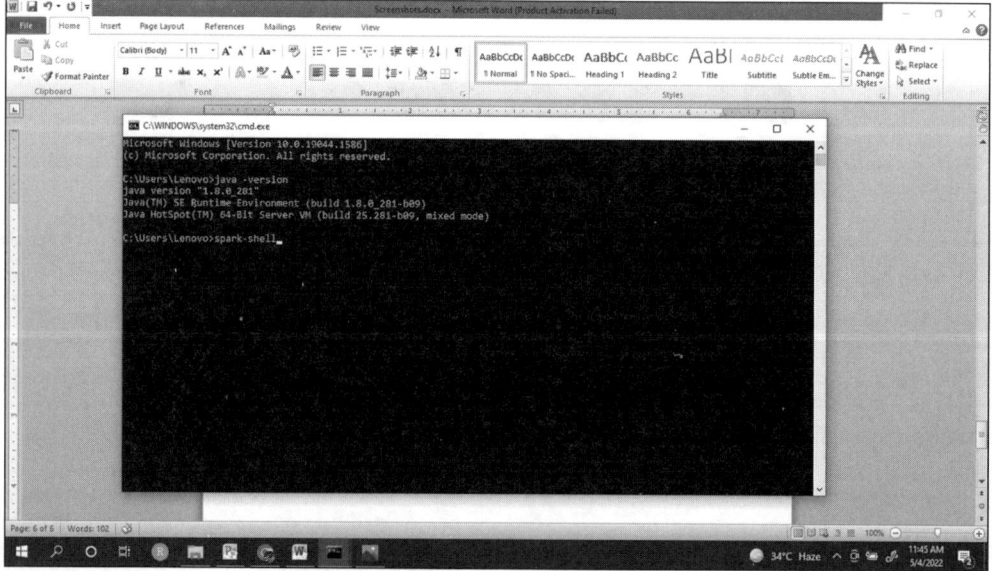

Figure 13.24 Command spark-shell typed in the working environment

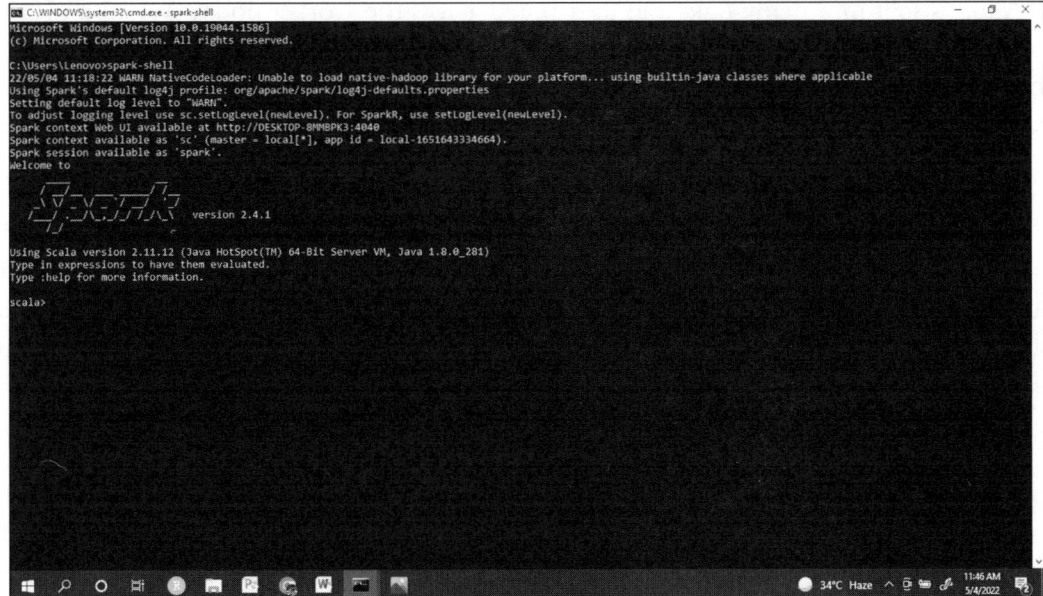

Figure 13.25 Spark is installed and ready to work in Scala

13.10 APACHE SPARK PHYSICAL ARCHITECTURE

Figure 13.26 depicts the basic architectural overview of Apache Spark. It consists of Master Node, Driver Program, Spark Context, Cluster manager and Executors (Worker), Task, and Cache.

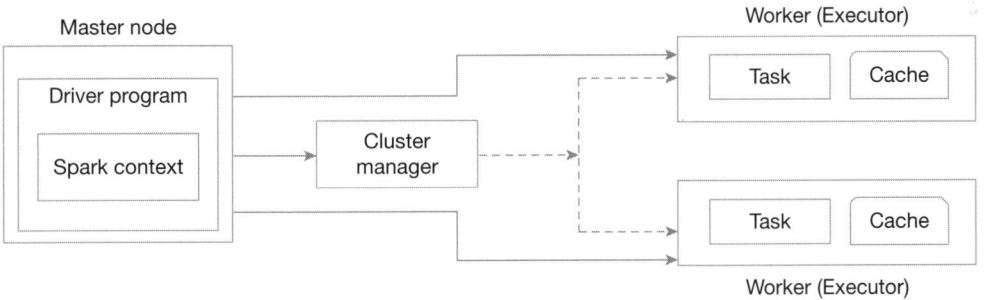

Figure 13.26 Spark – Physical architecture

The driver program, which powers our application, is located in the master node. The code we are creating acts as a driver program. The interactive shell functions will also act as the driver program. The driver program first builds a Spark Context. Assume that the Spark context is a gateway to all the Spark functions. It is similar to how you connect to your database. Any database command you issue travels through the database connection.

Similarly, everything you do on Spark is filtered by Spark context. This Spark context now manages numerous jobs in conjunction with the cluster manager. The driver application and Spark context handle the task execution within the cluster.

A job is split into many tasks and distributed across the worker nodes. When an RDD is formed in the Spark context, it may be spread and cached over several nodes. Broadcast variables are also obtained via RDD. Broadcast variables are read-only variables that allow the programmer to cache them and access them on each computer rather than delivering copies with tasks. We can also use Spark Context to generate an accumulator. It allows us to access Spark services and assists us in running jobs till we manually terminate Spark Context.

Additionally, Spark Context provides access to Spark Cluster Manager, Spark Standalone, YARN, and Apache Mesos, which can be chosen as a cluster manager. It may be possible to assign containers for executors using YARN (head node) and node management (worker node). It will allocate memory and cores when resources become available.

Worker nodes are slave nodes whose sole purpose is to carry out tasks. These tasks are then run on the worker node's partitioned RDDs, returning the result to the Spark Context. Spark Context takes the job, divides it into tasks, and then distributes it to the worker nodes. These tasks operate on the partitioned RDD, gather results, and return to the main Spark Context.

Making Sparkconf is the primary entry point to Spark functionality. We have a few setting options. These arguments are passed to Spark context via the Spark driver application to describe the application's characteristics. We choose the settings based on the functions we require. Some of them are used by executors to allocate resources in a cluster. Cluster resources include the number, memory capacity, and CPUs. It also simplifies our access to the Spark cluster. We can utilize textfile, sequence files, and parallelize thanks to Spark context objects, which can execute in the following contexts: local, yarn-client, Mesos URL, and Spark URL. As previously discussed, we may use it to generate RDDs, broadcast variables, accumulators, and perform tasks. We can carry most of these items till we cease Spark Context.

You can divide jobs into additional divisions and run them in parallel across several computers as the number of employees grows. So, it will be much quicker. In addition, as the number of workers increases, so does the amount of memory available, and you may cache tasks to make them run fast.

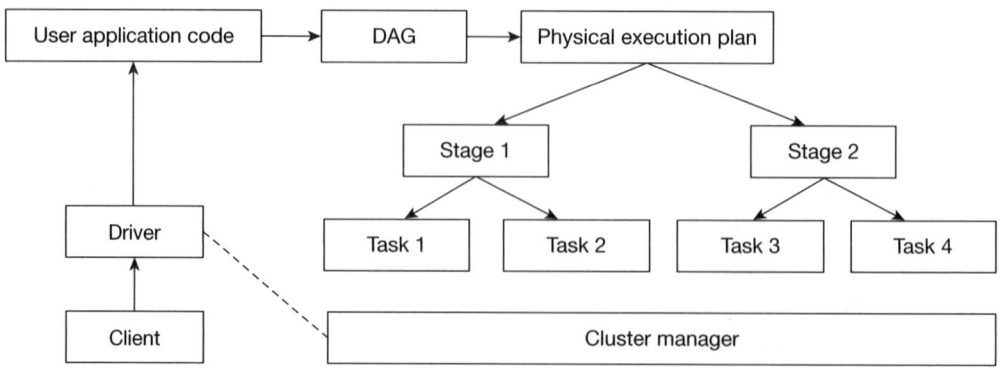

Figure 13.27 Spark – Physical execution plan

Step 1: The customer (client) provides the code for the Spark user application (Fig. 13.27). When user code, including transformations and actions, is given, the driver implicitly turns it into a DAG (logically directed acyclic graph). It also does optimizations like pipelining transformations at this level.

Step 2: The DAG logical graph turns into a physical execution plan with several steps. It creates physical execution units called tasks under each stage after converting them to a physical execution plan. The jobs are then grouped and submitted to the cluster.

Step 3: The driver now communicates with the cluster manager and negotiates resource allocation. The cluster manager starts executors in worker nodes on behalf of the driver. Depending on the data placement, the driver will now deliver tasks to the executors. When executors first startup, they register with drivers. As a result, the driver will have a comprehensive picture of the job executors.

Step 4: The driver application will monitor the executors that run during task execution. Future jobs are also scheduled by the driver node depending on data placement.

In Apache Spark, a stage is a logical unit of execution. It is a phase in a physical execution plan. In Spark, there are two stages: ShuffleMapstage and ResultStage. It is a collection of parallel jobs, one for each division.

In other words, each work is broken into smaller groups of tasks, referred to as phases. It is extremely similar to the map and reduce phases of MapReduce in terms of dependencies. For example, a Spark job is just a calculation that has been divided into Stages/Phases (Fig. 13.28).

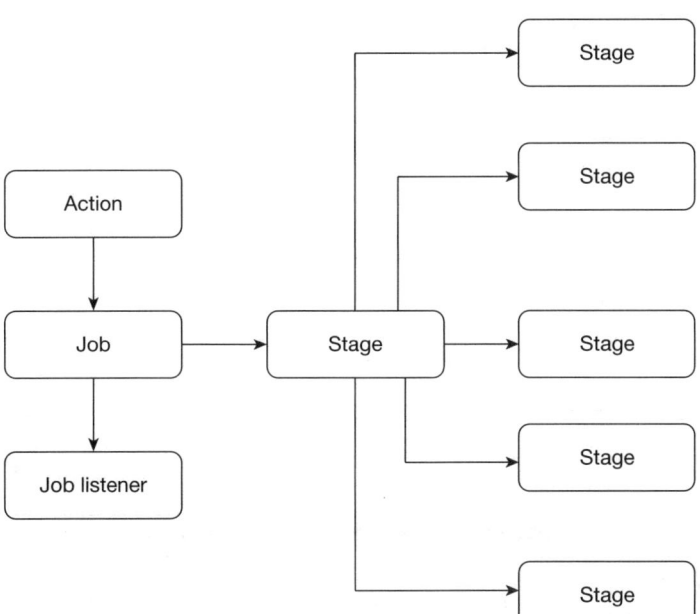

Figure 13.28 Spark Job and Stage

With the use of its id, we may uniquely identify a stage. DAGScheduler advances the internal counter nextstageId, whenever it adds a stage. It assists in keeping track of the number of stage submissions. Many more dependent parent stages can be linked to one stage because the stage can only function on a single RDD's partitions even when shuffle dependencies signal a stage's conclusion. Following that, stage submission causes a succession of dependent parent stages to run. Finally, every stage has a first JobId, which is the id of the work that is being submitted.

ShuffleMapStage: In the physical execution of a DAG, ShuffleMapStage is an intermediate stage. It generates data for the subsequent step(s). It also creates shuffle map output files. It may also be the last step in an adaptive query planning/scheduling project. We can also submit it individually as a Spark task for adaptive query planning. When ShuffleMapStage is run, it stores map output files. Reduce tasks can subsequently retrieve those files. When all map outputs are accessible, the ShuffleMapStage is deemed complete. Sometimes output locations are missing, which implies partitions are not computed or destroyed.

The internal registry outputLocs and _numAvailableOutputs can be used to keep track of how many shuffle map outputs are available. ShuffleMapStage is an input for the next stages in the DAG of stages. It is called the map side of shuffle dependence. Before the shuffle process, there might be numerous pipeline activities, such as map and filter in ShuffleMapStage. A single ShuffleMapStage can also be shared across many workloads.

Result Stage: The Result Stage (Fig. 13.29) runs a function on an RDD to conduct a Spark action in a user application. In general, we think of it as the last step. In other words, it is the final stage of a task where a function is applied to one or more partitions of the target RDD. It also aids in the computation of an action's outcome.

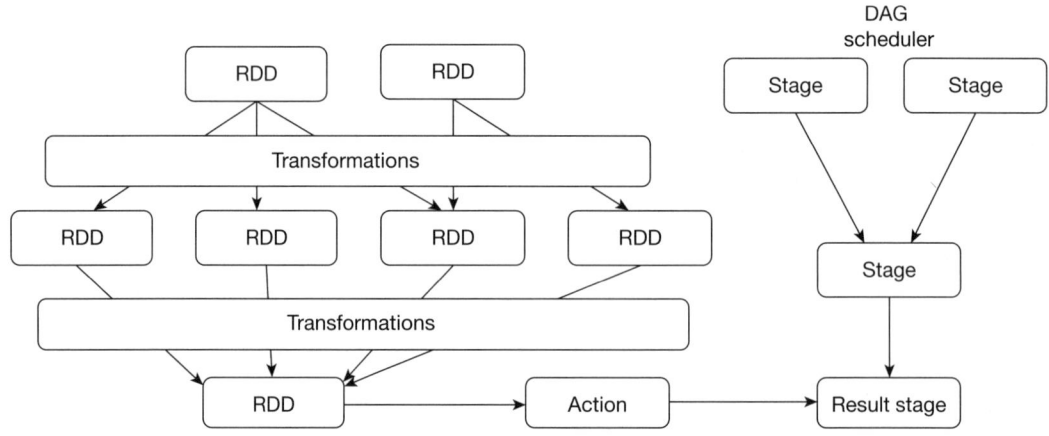

Figure 13.29 Spark Result Stage

Spark Executors

Spark has some distributed agents that are responsible for job execution. Executors are the dispersed agents. To put it another way, a worker node processes an application.

It also performs jobs and stores data on a disk or in memory, among other things. Each application, in essence, has its executor.

Furthermore, it sends partial metrics for current jobs to the driver's receiver. It provides RDDs with in-memory storage. Finally, the block manager caches them in spark programs. Streaming Receivers are Apache Spark objects whose main job is to consume data from various sources and send it to Spark. Streaming contexts, as long-running jobs on various executors, can be used to generate receiver objects. There are two different kinds of receivers. They are:

Reliable Receiver: When data is received and appropriately copied in Apache Spark Storage, the receiver acknowledges data sources.

Unreliable Receiver: Certain receivers fail to detect data sources while receiving or duplicating data in Apache Spark Storage.

While initiating, an executor registers with the driver. It also communicates directly to carry out duties. Executor offers are specified by executor id and the host on which an executor executes. It can perform various jobs throughout its lifespan, both sequentially and concurrently. In addition, the internal register keeps track of running tasks via the task ids. Executors employ an executor task launch worker thread pool to launch tasks. It also uses the Heartbeat Sender Thread to deliver metrics and heartbeats. The cluster mode lets you have as many Spark executors as data nodes and as many cores as you like. Executors may be identified by their id, hostname, environment (SparkEnv), and classpath.

Note: Executor backends exclusively manage executors.

13.11 APACHE SPARK LAYERED ARCHITECTURE

The architecture of Apache Spark has well-defined layers with various Spark components. Spark's layers and components are loosely coupled, which means that they are disconnected from each other. Many libraries and extensions are integrated into the architecture of Spark. The layered architecture of Spark is based on the following two abstractions:

1. Resilient Distributed Dataset (RDD)
2. Directed Acyclic Graph (DAG)

13.11.1 Resilient Distributed Dataset (RDD)

RDD is Apache Spark's core data structure. RDDs serve as the foundation for all Spark applications. RDDs is an acronym denoting **R**esilient **D**istributed **D**ataset. Resilient means it is fault-tolerant and capable of data reconstruction in case of a failure. Distributed means, data is distributed among numerous nodes in a cluster. Dataset means, a set of values for partitioned data (Fig. 13.30).

RDD in Spark is an immutable (read-only) collection of objects, indicating that the original RDD cannot be changed. The objects in RDD can be of any type (Python, Java, or Scala), and they can be of user-defined classes. The objects are stored on the disks or in

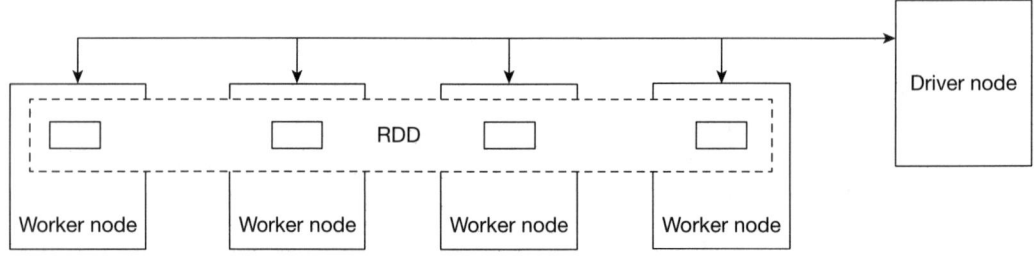

Figure 13.30 Spark RDD

the memory of different machines in the cluster. An RDD can be split into many logical partitions (Fig. 13.31) that can be stored and processed on various machines present in a cluster.

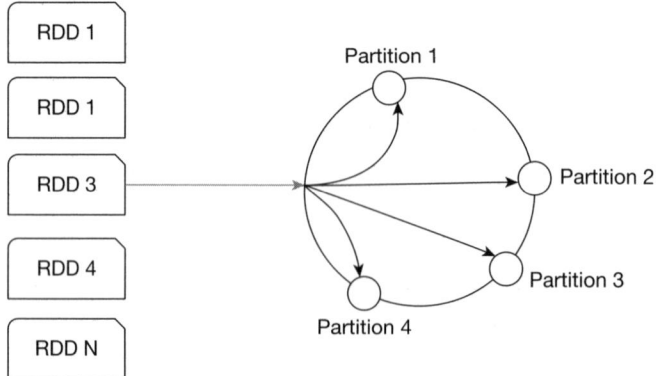

Figure 13.31 Spark RDD partition

It is a data abstraction layer on top of the distributed collection. It is immutable and follows lazy transformations. An RDD's data is divided into chunks based on a key. RDDs are highly robust, as the same data chunks are duplicated over numerous executor nodes, allowing them to recover from any problems swiftly. As a result, even if one executor node fails, another will still process the data. By combining the power of several nodes, you can run functional computations against your dataset very rapidly. Resilient means fault-tolerant. Spark RDD is resilient as it can rebuild the missing or lost data due to node failure by keeping track of the lineage graph (DAG). In addition, RDD rebuilds itself by remembering how it is created from other datasets. They are distributed as the data is disseminated on several nodes. Dataset indicates the records of data that is worked with. The external data, either a CSV file, JSON file, text file, or database from JDBC, can be loaded by the user without any specific data structure. When it comes to the distributed environment, each RDD dataset is separated into logical divisions that may be calculated on multiple cluster nodes. As a result, you may conduct concurrent transformations or actions on the whole dataset (Fig. 13.32). You will not have to worry about distribution since Spark will take care of it.

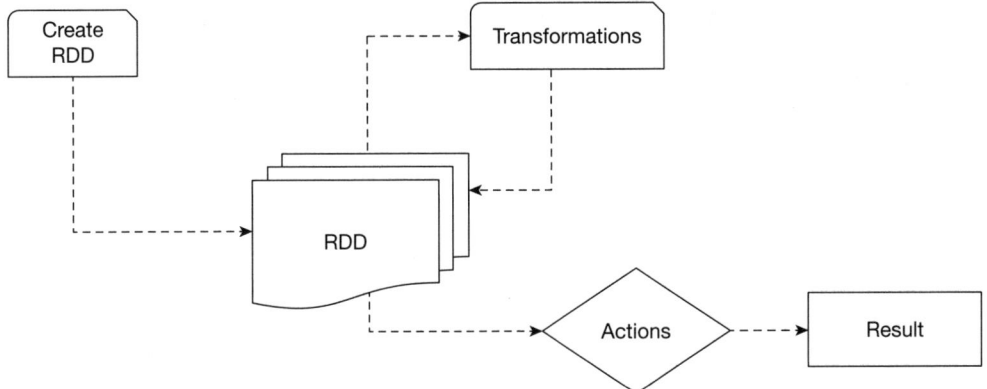

Figure 13.32 Workflow of RDD

13.11.2 Directed Acyclic Graph (DAG)

In graph theory, a graph consists of edges and vertices. Vertices are any points or nodes that can be connected with the help of edges. DAG (Directed Acyclic Graph) is a finite direct graph with no directed cycles. There are a limited number of vertices and edges, each of which leads from one vertex to the next. It consists of a series of vertices with each edge pointing from one to the next in the sequence.

In Apache Spark, a DAG is a collection of Vertices and Edges, where the vertices represent RDDs and the edges indicate RDD operations (Fig. 13.33). Every edge in a Spark DAG points from earlier to later in the sequence. When Action is called, the newly generated DAG is submitted to DAG Scheduler, which divides the graph into task phases. It is a strict extension of the MapReduce model. DAG operations outperform other systems like MapReduce in terms of global optimization. In more sophisticated jobs, the picture of DAG gets clearer.

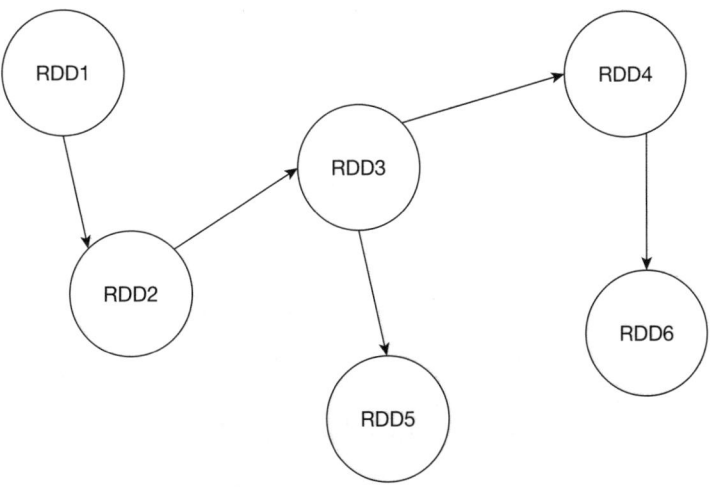

Figure 13.33 DAG vs. RDDs

13.12 WAYS TO CREATE RDD IN SPARK

The Resilient Distributed Dataset can be created using different methods (Fig. 13.34).

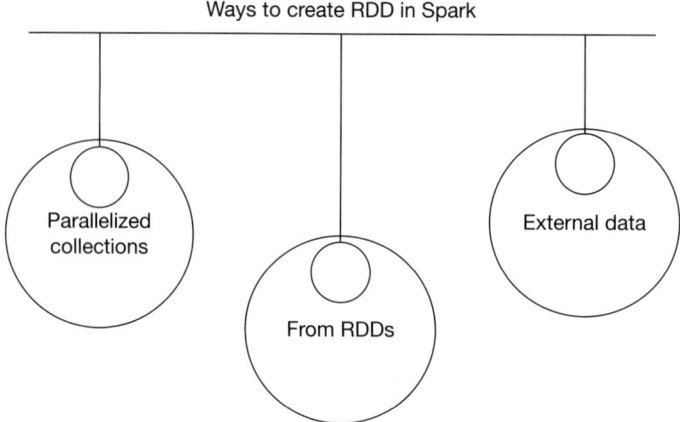

Figure 13.34 Ways to create RDDs

The first method used to create RDD is using Parallelized Collection. In general, RDDs can be created by the method of parallelizing. This is the simplest and basic way to create RDD in the initial stages of Spark. RDD is created very quickly by using this method. Parallelizing is feasible by taking the existing collection from the driver program like Python, Scala, and Java and invoking the Spark context's `parallelize()` method. The entire dataset should reside on one machine, and hence this process is mainly used in testing and prototyping. Usually, this method is used by users to create a dataset.

The second method for creating RDD is from the external datasets. RDDs can be developed from any external storage sources supported by Hadoop, like HDFS, Cassandra, HBase, and even the local file system. For example, Apache Spark supports text files, Hadoop input format, and sequence files. RDD textfile can be created by calling the spark contexts `textfile()` method. The URL of the file is used by this method. The URL can be a local path on the machine, a database, or a HDFS; the worker node and the local path should be the same. A database reader interface can read a dataset from external storage.

The following commands are used to load the dataset which are stored in different formats.

(i) To load a dataset which is in the CSV format:
val dataRDD = spark.read.csv("path/of/csv/file").rdd
.rdd method is used to convert the dataset into RDD.
(ii) To load a JSON file:
val dataRDD = spark.read.json("path/of/json/file").rdd
(iii) To load a textfile:
val dataRDD = spark.read.textFile("path/of/text/file").rdd

The third method for creating RDD is from the existing RDD. One of the characteristics of RDD is that it is immutable. Hence nothing can be changed. So, a new RDD can be created from the existing RDD. Creating a new dataset from the existing dataset is called transformation. So, new RDDs are created whenever transformation takes place. Since no changes can be done on the created RDD, consistency over the cluster is maintained.

13.13 PAIRED RDD

User-defined classes can be included in Spark RDDs. Any type of Scala, Python, or Java object is also included. It is a partitioned, read-only collection of records. Spark RDDs are a fault-tolerant group of components that may be used in parallel. Spark RDDs may be created in one of three methods: with other RDDs, data in stable storage, and parallelizing existing collection in the driver program. It is feasible to perform quicker and more efficient MapReduce operations by employing RDD.

A Spark Paired RDD (Fig. 13.35) is an RDD that has a key-value pair. A key-value pair contains two connected data items (KVP). The identification is the key, and the value is the data corresponding to the key value.

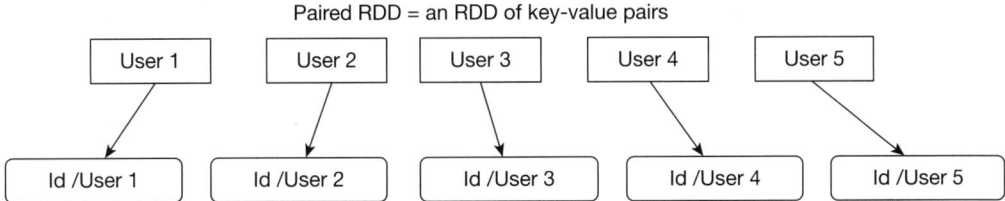

Figure 13.35 Paired RDDs

Furthermore, most Spark operations operate with RDDs holding any sort of object. A few specific procedures are available on RDDs of key-value pairs. Distributed "shuffle" actions, such as grouping or aggregating elements by a key, are an example. In Scala, these procedures are accessible automatically on RDDs holding Tuple2 objects. The key-value pair operations are accessible in the Pair RDD functions class. This wraps around a tuple RDD.

13.14 FEATURES OF SPARK RDD

Spark RDD has some remarkable features that help Spark execute Big Data quickly.

One of the essential features of Spark RDD is its **in-memory computation** (Fig. 13.36). Data can be stored in RDD as long as the user needs it. This storage of data is independent of size and quantity. Any amount of data with different sizes can be stored. In-memory computation indicates that information evaluation can be done in the random-access memory. Therefore, keeping the data in memory elevates the performance on a large scale. In-memory processing refers to the rapid access of data from physical memory.

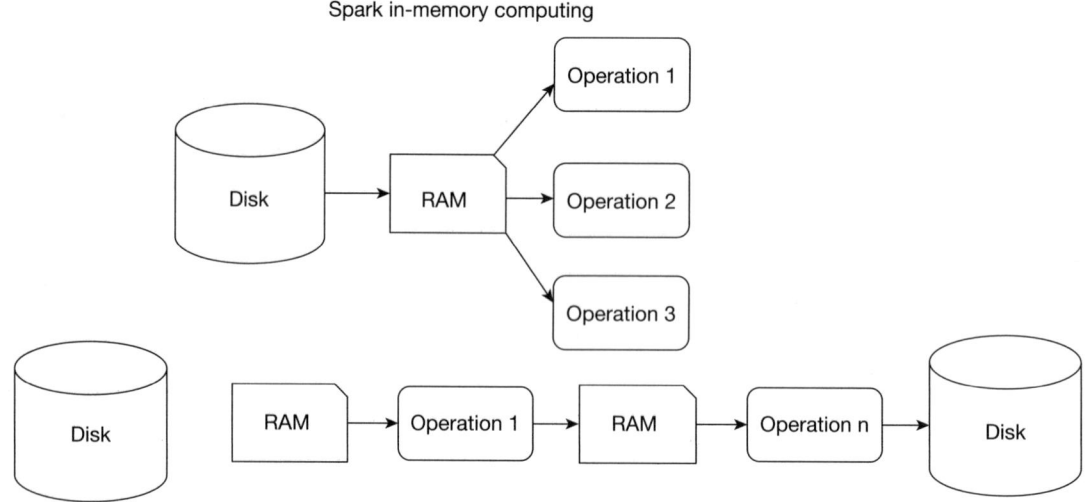

Figure 13.36 Spark in-memory computing

Lazy evaluation is a feature that helps in reducing the amount of work to be done. It indicates that the execution of a process does not start immediately when an operation is called. Instead, action is necessary to trigger the execution of an operation. Till the action is triggered, the data in the RDD will not be available or transformed. This helps in reducing the amount of work it has to do. Spark does the maintenance of every operation with the help of DAG.

Another feature that makes Spark unique is its ability for **fault tolerance**. If a failure is encountered in the worker node, RDD can recover itself with the help of the lineage of operations. Although different transformations are applied to RDD, it creates a logical execution plan known as the lineage graph. If any data in the RDD is lost because of any fault in the working node, it can be recomputed by applying the exact computation on the node of the lineage graph. This helps in increasing fault tolerance. Because Spark doesn't provide data replication in memory, any lost data is recreated via RDD lineage. RDD lineage is a method for reassembling lost data partitions. The finest part is that RDDs never forget how to construct from other datasets.

One of the features of RDD which makes it consistent is **immutability**. Once RDDs are created, they cannot be manipulated, i.e., they are read-only. Furthermore, since RDDs cannot be changed, new RDDs can be made through transformation processes.

Persistence is another feature that Spark RDD exhibits. Data can be stored in persistent storage, disk, and memory. RDD is frequently stored in memory and data can be directly retrieved from memory without going to disk. This helps in enhancing the speed of computation to a large extent. Furthermore, multiple operations can be performed on the same data by storing the data explicitly in memory using the `cache()` or `persist()` functions (dealt with later in this chapter). This is helpful in reducing the time as it enables reusability of data.

Partitioning is one of the critical features exhibited by Spark RDD. Partitions in RDD are logical, and the data is distributed across various nodes in the cluster. Furthermore, logic indicates that the divisions are only for enhancing processing, and there is no division internally. Hence, whenever any operation is performed, parallelism is achieved.

Parallelism is yet another feature of Spark RDD. RDDs are logically partitioned, as discussed previously, and hence when any operation is performed, it executes parallelly on the entire data across the cluster.

Location Stickiness is also a feature of RDD. RDDs support the computation of partitions by defining placement preferences. This indicates the information about the location of RDD. The DAG Scheduler places the partition so that the data is closer to the task to increase operational efficiency. By doing so, the speed of computations is increased to a greater extent.

RDDs support **coarse-grained operations**. This means that the operation applies to the entire cluster in the RDD and not to an individual element in the dataset.

Types is one of the features of RDD. RDDs are of different types like RDD[long], RDD[String], and RDD[Int].

Another feature of Spark RDD which makes it remarkable is that there are **no limitations** on the number of RDDs.

There can be as many RDDs as required, and it depends totally on the size of the memory and the disk. Thus, using RDD, the limitations in the usage of Hadoop MapReduce are overcome, and a large volume of data is handled with less time complexity. Hence, Spark RDD's salient features help increase the computational speed and, thereby, the system's performance.

13.15 Persistence and Caching Mechanisms in Apache Spark

Persistence and caching are optimization techniques of Spark RDD that may be used for iterative and interactive computations of Spark. Iterative computations indicate the reuse of results in numerous computations when multistage applications are considered, whereas interactive computations allow the data to flow in two ways. First, these techniques help store the intermediate result in the upcoming stages. By doing so, the computation overhead can be reduced. Second, RDD can be cached and persisted through `cache()` and `persist()` methods.

Mechanism of RDD Persistence

As discussed earlier, by default, RDDs are re-computable on each action. To overcome this, RDDs can be persisted so that every time an action occurs in an RDD, no re-computation takes place. When the `persist()` method is invoked, the RDD stores the computation results in the partition.

Apache Spark can be used with the help of coding with Scala, Python, Java, etc. When working with Java and Scala, the `persist()` method stores the data in the Java Virtual Machine as an un-serialized object. Likewise, when the `persist()` method is called in Python, it will serialize the data before persisting. Serialize means that the data is converted into a one-byte array per partition. Spark allows various storage options like memory or disk. Therefore, whenever the `persist()` method is applied, the RDDs obtained can be stored in different storage levels. Once the level for storing RDD is assigned, it cannot be changed.

Mechanism of RDD Caching

When applications access the same RDDs several times, a cache mechanism increases the speed. The cache is persistent with the default storage at the memory level only. The following are the situations when the cache method is used:

(i) When RDD is reused in interactive machine learning applications.
(ii) When RDD is reused in standalone spark applications.
(iii) When the computations of RDD are expensive, this helps in reducing the recovery cost.
(iv) Whenever a failure occurs in an executor.

Difference between Spark RDD Cache and Persistence

Though the functionalities of Spark Cache and Persistence are the same, these methods differ syntactically. The only difference between `cache()` and `persist()` methods is storage. When the `cache()` method is applied, the resultant RDD is stored at the default level, which is the MEMORY_ONLY, while `persist()` method allows RDDs to be held in different storage levels as explained below.

Need for Persistence in Apache Spark

Apache Spark allows the use of the exact RDD multiple times. However, when the RDD is used or evaluated many times, action is called to execute the information. This consumes memory space and time exceptionally when iterative algorithms are implemented and data is referred to multiple times. The persistence technique is introduced just to overcome this problem of repeated computation.

Benefits of RDD Persistence in Apache Spark

The RDD persistence methods in Apache Spark have many advantages that enhance the entire system's efficiency. Here are some of the benefits of RDD persistence:

(i) First, the performance speed of applications is enhanced.
(ii) Second, time consumption is reduced, which in turn increases work efficiency.
(iii) Third, it is cost-effective.
(iv) Finally, the execution time of the process is lessened.

Storage Levels of Persisted RDDs

Various storage levels can be used in Apache Spark to store persisted RDDs using the `Persist()` method. For example, the following are the different storage levels of persisted RDDs:

(i) **MEMORY_ONLY:** This is the default storage level. RDD is stored as a deserialized Java object in the Java Virtual Machine at this level. If the size of the RDD is greater than the memory, some of the data partitions are not cached but recomputed whenever they are needed. At this level, the data storage space is very high, and the computation time of the CPU is meager. Therefore, data is stored only in memory, and a disk is not used for storage.

(ii) **MEMORY_AND_DISK:** The RDD is stored as a deserialized Java object in the Java Virtual Machine at this storage level. If the size of the RDD does not fit the memory cluster, the excess partition is stored in the disk and retrieved from the disk whenever needed. At this storage level, the data storage space is high, and the computation time of the CPU is medium. Therefore, data is stored both in memory and disk.

(iii) **MEMORY_ONLY_SER:** In this level, the RDD is stored in the memory as a serialized Java object (one-byte array per partition). This is much more space-efficient when compared to deserialized objects, especially when a fast serializer is used. Because of this, some of the data partitions may not be cached, and it is calculated only when required. However, the storage space is low at this storage level, and the CPU computation time is high. Therefore, data is stored in memory only.

(iv) **MEMORY_AND_DISK_SER:** This storage level is very similar to MEMORY_ONLY_SER, except that it stores the left-over partition in the disk, and not in the memory. At this level, the space used for storage is low, and the computation time of the CPU is high. Therefore, data is stored both in-memory and on-disk storage.

(v) **DISK_ONL:** At this level, the storage of RDD is only on the disk. Here the space used for storage is low, and the computation time of the CPU is high. Therefore, data is stored only on a disk.

How to un-persist RDD in Spark?

Apache Spark keeps track of the cache of each node. Spark expels the old data partition automatically using the LRU (Least Recently Used) algorithm when the cached data in a node exceeds the storage limit. This algorithm categorizes the data as less used and frequently used and spills out the less-used data. This can also be accomplished manually with the help of the `RDD.unpersist()` method.

13.16 OPERATIONS OF APACHE SPARK RDD

There are two types of operations supported by Apache Spark RDD (Fig. 13.37): Transformations and Actions.

Transformations are functions that are applied to RDDs to produce a new RDD. It does not do anything unless something happens. Transformations include functions like `map()` and `filer()`. The `map()` method iterates over every line in the RDD and separates it into a new RDD. The `filter()` method builds a new RDD by choosing elements from the current RDD sent as an input to the function.

Actions are Spark procedures that assist in working with the actual dataset. They aid in the flow of data from the executor to the driver. An action in Spark is used to return data from an RDD to the local computer. RDD operations return non-RDD values instead of transformations, which exclusively produce RDD. For example, the `reduce()` method is a loop that is repeated until only one value remains. The `take()` action copies all of an RDD's values to the local node.

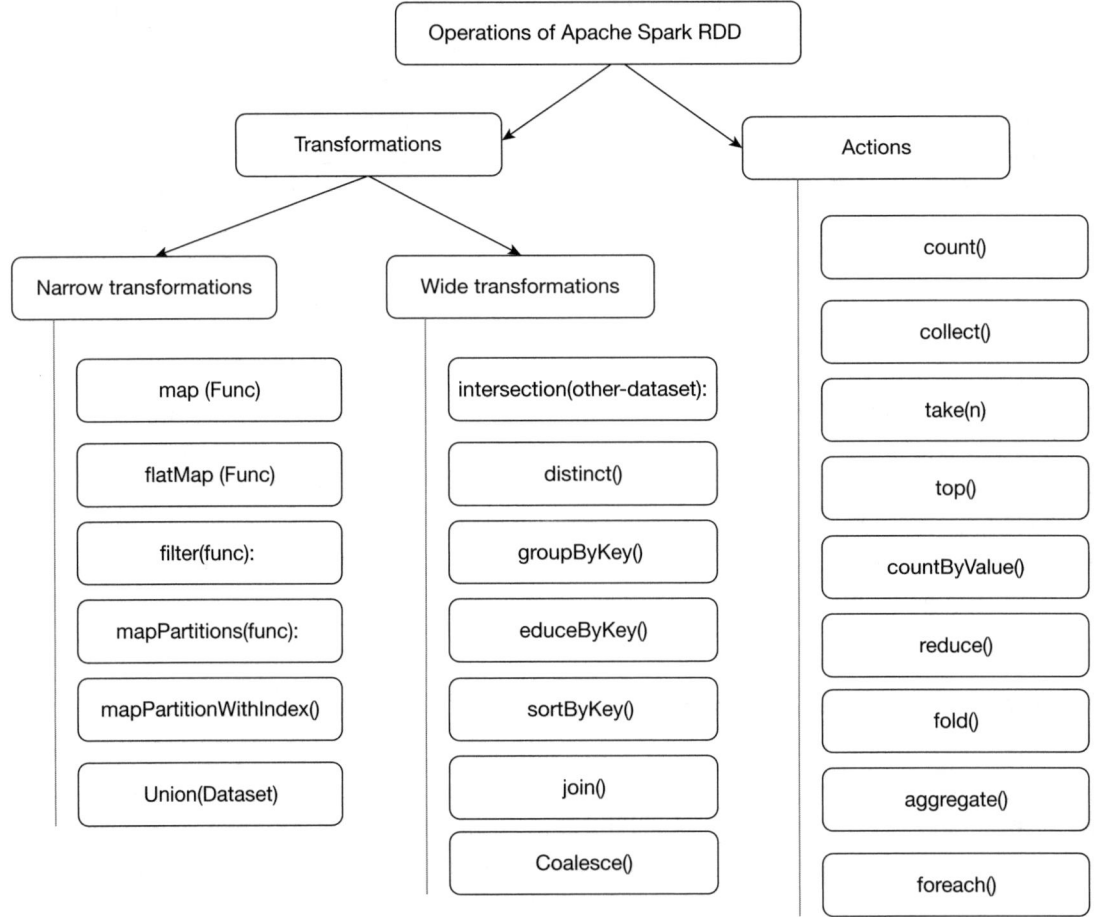

Figure 13.37 Transformations and Actions

13.16.1 Transformations

Apache Spark transformation is the operation that creates a new RDD from the existing RDD. One RDD is taken as the input, and one or more RDDs are produced. Whenever transformation is applied, a new RDD is created, proving that RDDs are immutable. Transformations are lazy, which means that the RDD will be logged in but not executed when an operation is applied. The result or exception will be obtained only when an action is triggered. After the transformation, the original RDD will always be different from the parent RDD. The new RDD created may be more minor, more significant, or the same size as the parent.

Types of Transformations

Transformations may be Narrow or Wide.

In narrow transformations, all the data required to process the records in the single partition is present in the single partition of the parent RDD. Therefore, the result is calculated by using a subset of the partition.

Some examples of Narrow transformations are given below:

(a) **map(func):** when using the map() transformation, any function is taken and applied to every element of the RDD. The flexibility in using this map() function is that the return type of the RDD need not be the same as the input RDD. For example, if the input RDD is of integer type, after applying the map() function, the resultant RDD can be of Boolean type.

(b) **flatMap(func):** This function is applied to every element in the RDD and it returns zero or more elements in the output RDD. Functions map() and flatMap() are similar in taking a line from the input RDD and applying the function on the same line. The major difference between map() and flatMap() is that map() function returns only one element whereas flatMap() returns zero or more elements.

(c) **Filter (func):** The name itself indicates that the function filter() is used to filter the needed data from a collection of data. This function is a narrow transformation as the data is not shuffled from one partition to the other partitions.

(d) **mapPartitions(func):** The mapPartitions() transformation converts each input RDD partition into any number of elements in the result. mapPartition() can be an alternative for map() applied simultaneously on every partition. The difference is that the mapPartition() function runs separately on each block partition.

(e) **mapPartitionWithIndex():** This transformation function is similar to mapPartitions() and it also provides an integer as an index value representing the partition. map() function is applied on partitions one after the other based on the index value.

(f) **Union(Dataset):** The union() transformation is used to combine two RDDs and it returns a dataset containing all the elements of both the RDDs. It should be noted that the two RDDs should be of the same data type.

In comprehensive transformations, all the data required to execute a process in the single partition is present on multiple partitions of the parent RDD.

The following are the examples of wide transformations:

(a) **intersection(other-dataset:** The intersection() transformation function creates a new RDD with the common elements from both the RDDs. The main rule for this function is that both the RDDs should be of the same data type.

(b) **`distinct()`:** This function is used to remove duplicate data elements. The resultant dataset contains distinct elements from the source dataset.
(c) **`groupByKey()`:** This transformation, when used on a dataset with (K, V) pairs, shuffles the data based on the key-value K in another RDD. This transformation function paves the way for unnecessary data transfer over the network.
(d) **`reduceByKey(fun, [numTasks])`:** When this transformation is used on a dataset with a (K, V) pair, the pairs with the same key on the same machine are combined before the data is shuffled.
(e) **`sortByKey()`:** This function, when applied on a dataset with (K, V) pairs, sorts the data in another RDD according to the key K value.
(f) **`join()`:** In Spark transformation, `join()` function is defined on pair-wise RDD. This is used to combine two tables using common values. For example, when this function is used on datasets of type (K, V) and (K, W) pairs, the resultant dataset will be (K, (V, W)) pairs with all the element pairs for each key.
(g) **`Coalesce ()`:** The `coalesce()` function avoids real shuffling using the existing partition. The source RDD's number of partitions can also be lowered to numPartitions using this transformation function.

13.16.2 Actions

In Apache Spark, actions are triggered to perform computations on the dataset and give the result or exception to the driver of the RDD. However, new RDDs are not formed as in transformations. Hence, RDD actions will give non-RDD values only.

List of actions that are used often in Spark:

(a) **`count()`:** This action returns the number of elements present in an RDD.
(b) **`collect()`:** This is the simplest and most common operation that displays an RDD's content. The entire RDD is expected to fit in the memory when this function is used.
(c) **`take(n)`:** This action is similar to the `collect()` action, and the only difference is that the `take()` action can print any number of rows based on the selection criteria given by the user. This returns n number of elements from RDD. Here, the order of the elements cannot be presumed. This action tries to cut the number of partitions accessed, and hence the collection is biased.
(d) **`top()`:** This action retrieves the top elements from the RDD if ordering is seen; else, default data order is taken.
(e) **`countByValue`:** This action of Spark returns the number of times an element occurs in an RDD.
(f) **`reduce()`:** The `reduce()` action is used to produce an output taking two elements from the RDD. The output type is similar to the input data type. The addition is the simplest form of this action. The argument accepts cumulative and associative operations so that computations can be carried out correctly in parallel.
(g) **`fold()`:** This action is similar to `reduce()`. Also, a zero value is taken as an input for the initial call on every partition. The main difference between `fold()`

and `reduce()` action is that when there is an empty collection, `reduce()` action throws an exception, but the `fold()` action defines the empty collection.

(h) **`aggregate()`:** This action allows the resultant data type to be different from the input. It takes two functions to produce the result. One function is applied to combine the element from the RDD to the accumulator, and the other function is used to combine the accumulator.

(i) **`foreach()`:** This action is used when an operation is applied to every element in the RDD without returning a value to the driver.

13.17 Limitations of Apache Spark RDD and Ways to Overcome It

Spark RDD lacks an input optimization engine. Apache Spark uses many advanced optimizers such as catalyst optimizer and Tungsten execution engine. However, RDDs cannot use these optimizers, so optimization cannot be done automatically. So, optimization of RDD is done manually on each RDD. This problem is solved in datasets and dataframes that use a catalyst to generate optimized logical and physical query plans. The same optimizer code can be used for the dataset/data frame APIs of R, Java, Scala, and Python. A DataFrame (Fig. 13.38) is a dataset that has been structured into SQL-like columns. DataFrame is similar to a data table in a relational database. Spark DataFrames are geared toward Big Data.

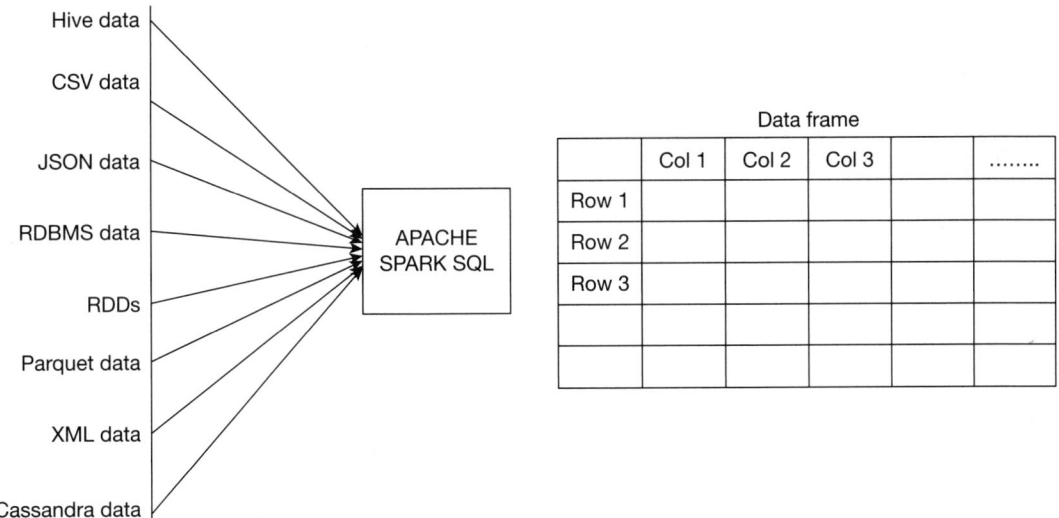

Figure 13.38 Apache Spark SQL: DataFrame

RDD does not have runtime type safety and static typing. This means that error checking is not allowed at runtime. This limitation is overcome by providing compile-time type safety by datasets to build complex data workflows. Compile-time type safety means that a compile-time error will be thrown whenever any other type of data element is added to the list. This helps in identifying the error and keeping the code safe.

One of the limitations of RDD is that it degrades when memory is not enough. This problem is related to the storage issue and arises when there is no space in memory or disk to store the RDD. Degradation of RDD occurs because of this issue. However, even though the partitions that do not find space in memory are stored in the disk, there is no change in the performance level. This problem can be solved by increasing the RAM and disk size.

Other limitations of RDD are its performance limitation, overhead serialization, and garbage collection. In-memory RDD is stored as Java Virtual Machine objects. This encompasses the overhead of Java Serialization and Garbage collection and becomes more expensive as the size of the data increases. Furthermore, the cost of garbage collection depends totally on the number of Java objects. Therefore, as the number increases, the cost also increases. Using a data structure, this limitation can be overcome with lesser objects, reducing the cost, and the object can be persisted in serialized form.

RDD is not very suitable for handling structured data. Any data stored in a predefined format is known as structured data. However, Apache Spark does not infer any data schema like other APIs. Hence handling structured data is not possible. Instead, DataSet (Fig. 13.39) and DataFrame are distributed collections of data organized into columns and they provide the schema view for the data. Thus, the structured data is handled.

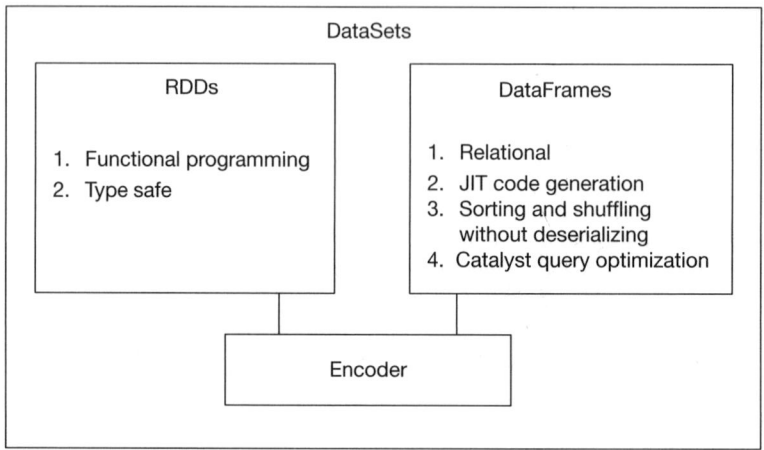

Figure 13.39 Apache Spark DataSets

DataFrames are analogous to tables in relational databases or R/Python DataFrames. It is a relational table with excellent optimization techniques. DataFrame's concept is that it enables the processing of enormous amounts of structured data. The rows in the DataFrame have Schema. The Schema is a representation of data structure. DataFrame in Apache Spark is superior to RDD, yet it also has RDD characteristics. Immutability, in-memory processing, robustness, and distributed computing capabilities are all traits shared by RDD and DataFrame. It enables the user to impose a structure on a dispersed dataset. As a result, higher-level abstraction is provided.

13.18 DIRECTED ACYCLIC GRAPH (DAG)

RDD is dealt with in detail in the previous sections. In this section, we shall discuss the next abstraction of Spark, the DAG. In graph theory, a graph consists of edges and vertices. Vertices are any points or nodes that can be connected with the help of edges. A directed acyclic graph (DAG) is a finite direct graph that has no directed cycles. There are a finite number of vertices and edges, each of which leads from one vertex to the next. It consists of a series of vertices with each edge pointing from one to the next in the sequence.

In Apache Spark, a DAG is a collection of vertices and edges, where the vertices represent RDDs and the edges indicate RDD operations. Every edge in a Spark DAG points from earlier to later in the sequence. When Action is called, the newly generated DAG is submitted to DAG Scheduler, which divides the graph into task phases. It is a strict extension of the MapReduce model. DAG operations outperform other systems like MapReduce in terms of global optimization. In more sophisticated jobs, the picture of DAG gets clearer.

13.19 DAG IN APACHE SPARK

The Apache Spark DAG allows the user to delve deeper into a stage and expand on any stage's details. The details of all RDDs relating to that stage are extended in the stage view. The Spark RDD is divided into phases by the Scheduler based on the transformations that have been applied.

Each stage is made up of tasks that are based on the RDD's partitions and they conduct the same calculation in parallel. The graph depicts navigation, with directed and acyclic referring to how it is carried out.

13.19.1 Need for DAG in Apache Spark

The constraints of Hadoop MapReduce became a significant motivator for Spark to implement DAG. The computation is done in three phases using MapReduce:

- The information is retrieved from HDFS.
- After that, Map and Reduce operations are performed.
- The computed result is stored in HDFS.

Each MapReduce operation is distinct from the others, and Hadoop does not know which MapReduce action will be executed next. Therefore, it is not always necessary to read and send back the immediate result between two map-reduce operations for iterations. As a result, memory in stable storage (HDFS) or disc memory is wasted.

In a multiple-step process, all jobs are blocked until the preceding one is completed. As a result, complicated computations with tiny data volumes can take longer.

Spark creates a DAG (Directed Acyclic Graph) of sequential computing phases. This allows us to optimize the execution strategy; for example, by reducing data scrambling. In MapReduce, however, it is done manually by tweaking each MapReduce phase.

13.19.2 Working Principle of DAG in Spark

The interpreter is the initial layer. Next, Spark interprets the code with certain modifications using a Scala interpreter.

When the code is typed into the Spark console, it constructs an operator graph. This operator graph is submitted to the DAG Scheduler (Fig. 13.40) when a call of Action on Spark RDD is at a high level.

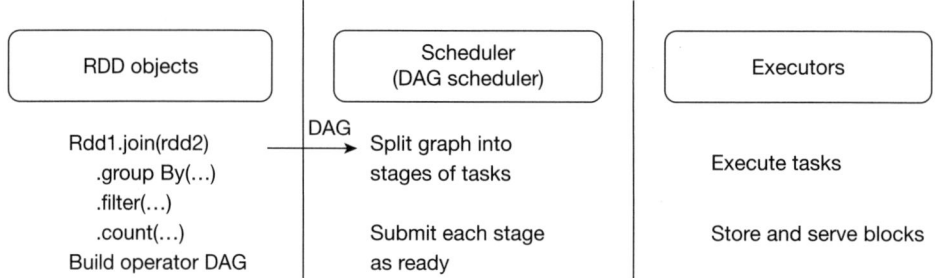

Figure 13.40   DAG Scheduler

In the DAG Scheduler, the operators are divided into job stages. A stage contains tasks based on the input data's partitioning. The DAG scheduler connects operators in a pipeline. Map operators, for example, schedule in a single step. The Task Scheduler receives the stages. Then, it starts a task using the cluster manager. The task scheduler is unaware of the stage dependencies. On the slave, the workers carry out the work.

Achieving Fault Tolerance using DAG in Spark

RDD divides into partitions, and each node operates on one of them at any given time. In this case, a set of Scala functions is run on an RDD partition. These operations combine to form a DAG, which the Spark execution engine recognizes. Let us say a node collapses in the middle of an operation, such as n3, which is dependent on operation n2, which, in turn, is dependent on operation n1. When the cluster management discovers that a node has died, another node is assigned to continue processing. This node will work on the RDD's specific partition and the sequence of operations it must complete (n1→n2→n3). There will no longer be any data loss.

Working on the DAG Optimizer in Spark

In Apache Spark, the DAG is optimized by reordering and combining operators. For example, when a Spark task is submitted that includes a map() and a filter operation, the DAG optimizer will change the order of the operations as filtering reduces the number of records that must be mapped.

DAG's Benefits in Spark

The Directed Acyclic Graph can be used to retrieve the lost RDD. There are only two queries in MapReduce: map and reduce. However, in DAG, there are several levels. As a result, DAG is more versatile for SQL query execution. Furthermore, DAG aids in the attainment of fault tolerance. As a result, we will be able to recover the data that has been lost. It can perform better global optimization than a Hadoop MapReduce system.

13.20 APPLICATIONS OF APACHE SPARK

Every organization tries its best to stand tall among other organizations in this competitive world. Each organization generates volumes of data and tries to process it according to its requirements. Every engine works has its use cases, and organizations are trying to use a combination of these tools to meet their desired needs.

Since its inception in 2009, the Apache Spark framework has captured the eyes of professionals worldwide who are working in Big Data frameworks. Spark has enormous features like speed, in-memory computing, graph processing, real-time data streaming, etc., which has made it an efficient tool for Big Data. According to the latest statistics, it is forecasted that Spark is expected to grow in Asia-Pacific with a CAGR of 33.95% between the periods 2018–2025. Many top companies like Apple, Google, and Facebook use Spark to process their data.

13.20.1 Streaming Data

One of the critical use cases of Apache Spark is its capability to process streaming data. Massive amount of data is being generated from all over the world, each second. This has forced companies to process and analyze vast amounts of data. Spark allows the developers to use a single framework to enhance the capability of data processing and other needs. The following are a few ways in which companies use streaming for their business prospectives.

Streaming Extract Transform Load (ETL)

When traditional ETL tools are used for batch processing in a database environment, the data must be read first, and then converted into a compatible database format. Finally, it has to be stored in the target database. However, in Spark's streaming, the data is cleaned and aggregated continuously before moving it into the data repositories.

Data Enrichment

Data enrichment enhances the collected data by combining it with other relevant data for better processing and analysis. Apache Spark does this by combining the real-time data with static data to perform analysis. For example, online marketing companies conglomerate customers' live behavioral data with the customers' historical data to target the customer with customized advertisements and deliverables.

Trigger Event Detection

Event detection aims to identify events by identifying the patterns. Spark streaming helps organizations quickly identify unusual ways that threaten the smooth functioning of the system. Many organizations use triggers to enable them to detect unique events. For example, finance companies see fraudulent transactions and take immediate actions to avoid loss. In hospitals, triggers monitor patients and alert the care-takers if any abnormal health changes are noticed. Thus, event detection plays a vital role in many organizations.

Complex Session Analysis

Using Apache Spark's streaming, live session events can be grouped and analyzed. Events like user activity after logging into an application or website, the duration of the session, and other session information can be analyzed continuously by using the machine learning models. For example, Netflix uses this session analysis to get a deep insight into the number of users using this site and the type of shows or movies they are interested in. By knowing this, recommendations can be made based on the user's interest.

Machine Learning

The subsequent use case of Apache Spark is its creditable machine learning competency. Spark has a rich framework that enables the users to run repeated queries on different datasets to perform advanced analytics. Spark's MLlib is widely used as it has algorithms for supporting data mining techniques like clustering, classification, and segmentation. With the help of this feature, the marketing industry can segment customers and target them to promote their products. In addition, many companies use recommendation engines to perform their jobs faster. Machine learning ability also proves good for network security in the business. Security providers use the components in the Spark Stack to examine the data packets in the network and track known malicious packets before storing them in the data repositories. Once the packets arrive in storage, they are further analyzed by other Spark components to identify new threats to protect the data from hackers and ensure protection to the clients in real-time.

Interactive Analysis

Another great application of Spark is its ability to support interactive analytics. Compared with other tools that handle batch processing, Spark is much faster. Without sampling, Spark can process exploratory queries. Spark can process complex datasets and provide interactive visualization when combined with visualization tools. Machine learning algorithms can process interactive queries against live data using Spark. This helps the users to run queries during the current session. In this situation, old data will be used to train the algorithms and integrated into new data to learn from it as it enters the memory.

Fog Computing

Though Big Data Analytics is gaining much attention, the concept which is kindling the imagination of many in today's tech community is the Internet of Things (IoT). The IoT embeds many intelligent devices with sensors that can communicate among themselves and the users by creating an entirely interconnected world between devices and users. They provide applications to people which can be used in their day-to-day life. As the number of users who adapt to IoT platforms increases continuously, the amount of data collected is growing beyond comprehension. These data have to be processed and delivered appropriately. There is a need for massively parallel processing to efficiently perform this processing of various data generated from devices. Such parallel processing has become hard to manage in the current scenario when analytics is done in the cloud as it requires distributed massive parallel processing. Here arises the need for fog computing.

Fog computing uses the decentralization technique to place storage and processing components at the edge of the cloud. However, some challenges accompany fog computing as it needs low latency and massively parallel machine learning processing. It also needs complex algorithms to analyze graphs. Apache Spark comes as a solution to meet these challenges in fog computing by providing the required stack components such as Shark for interactive querying, Machine Learning library (MLlib) for algorithms, GraphX for graphical analysis, and spark streaming.

13.21 Spark in Real-world

As discussed in the previous sections, Apache Spark is used by many companies to process the generated data from various sources. For example, E-commerce companies and online advertising companies like Netflix use Spark to get insights into the data to attract more users. Some of the other well-known companies that use Spark are discussed in this section:

Alibaba's online shopping has millions of users who use the platform every day for searching and placing orders. As a result, hundreds of petabytes of data are generated every day. Graphical representation is needed for these user interactions, and machine learning algorithms are required for complex data analytics. Alibaba relies on Spark to process its data to satisfy its customers by providing suggestions on products based on their choice, trend, and other criteria, to make their shopping experience satisfactory.

In the travel and tourism industry, the name TripAdvisor is very familiar. If a person plans to go for a personal or official trip, TripAdvisor helps them. A considerable amount of data is generated as many users around the globe are using it every day. Apache Spark offers recommendations for planning the trip based on the user's choice of destination and other preferences. It guides to travel, lodging, restaurants, and sightseeing places. It also ranks the tourist places based on user feedback and reviews. TripAdvisor uses Apache Spark for all this massive processing.

Yahoo is contributing a lot to the development of Big Data. It is one of the giant Hadoop Cluster and uses Apache Spark to identify the topics of interest with the help of machine learning capabilities. This is very similar to hashtags trending on Twitter and Facebook. In earlier days, these functionalities were done by writing algorithms with more than a thousand lines of code in C or C++ language. However, now, with Apache Spark and Scala, these algorithms are executed with very few hundred lines of code. This has made a significant impact in the programming world by changing the perspective on coding and maintenance. Apache Spark takes the credit for making this possible.

MyFitnessPal is a fitness portal that has over 80 million active users. This portal helps the users to lead a healthy lifestyle by offering them the fitness regime to be followed and suggesting to them the proper diet that has to be taken. The portal receives the data like their food habits, exercises, and lifestyle and uses this data to offer them suggestions. Apache Spark is used to scan the entire data, both structured and unstructured. Any data stored in a pre-defined format, such as customer data, call history, etc., are said to be structured data. Unstructured data are stored in the native format. For example, images, audio, and video files. As this portal suggests exercises and diet; it processes these data types to offer the best recommendations for its users.

Uber is a multinational company that helps customers to book online taxis. It handles lakhs of drivers to commute users within a city or a town. This taxi dispatching company generates terabytes of data through its users. Uber uses Spark streaming, HDFS, and Kafka to construct a pipeline for extraction, transformation, and data loading. First, Uber converts the unstructured event data into structured data as it is published, and then it uses the tools to perform complex analytics.

Pinterest is an image sharing and social media service that allows users to save and discover material on the internet through pinboards made up of photographs, animated GIFs, and videos. Using a similar ETL process, Pinterest uses Spark Streaming to get real-time insights into how people worldwide interact with Pins. As a result, as consumers traverse the site and see similar pins, Pinterest may provide more relevant recommendations to help them choose recipes, decide which things to buy, and plan trips to various destinations.

Conviva, a streaming video provider, is second only to YouTube, with an average of around 4 million video feeds monthly. Conviva uses Spark to lower customer churn by optimizing video streams and managing live video traffic, ensuring a smooth, high-quality watching experience.

13.22 USE CASES OF SPARK

Finance

Spark is utilized in various functional and technological domains in the finance business. Building a Data Warehouse for batch processing systems and daily reporting is an everyday use case. The Spark DataFrames abstraction has been utilized as a general ingestion platform that can ingest data in various forms from many sources. Financial sector firms also utilize Apache Spark MLlib to build and train fraud detection models. Some banks have begun to use Spark to classify text in money transfers. Some firms use Apache Spark to gather, analyze, and detect.

Healthcare

The healthcare industry is the most recent to embrace innovative technologies such as Big Data and machine learning to give cutting-edge services to its patients. Hospitals use Spark-enabled healthcare applications to assess patients' medical histories and indicate potential health issues based on learning and history. Furthermore, with the healthcare segment generating large volumes of data, processing that data promptly and providing insights based on it posed a difficulty, which was easily solved by Apache Spark.

Airline Sector

Due to the complexity of customer behavior, airline customer segmentation is a complex topic to grasp. However, IT solutions providers for the aviation sector have the tools and infrastructure to manage all ticketing and booking data and a thorough awareness of airline requirements and market specifications. In addition, they use unsupervised machine learning approaches to improve our understanding of customer behavior by merging multiple data sources supplied by different airline systems. Traditional segmentation methods relied on business insights and the human creation of criteria. However, these approaches have limitations and preconceptions that can be fatal to a company's bottomline.

On the other hand, the data-driven strategy is resistant to turnover, preconceptions, and market shifts. The model can extract meaningful insights about typical customer behavior and intents utilizing a data-driven approach with Spark and MLlib. Spark MLlib approaches for supervised and unsupervised learning are employed at scale to train models for prediction. The customer is then assisted in implementing the gained insights in day-to-day operations.

Media

Netflix, Hotstar, and other media organizations use Apache Spark as the brains behind their technology engines. When a Netflix subscriber turns on the service, the user's favorite content begins to play automatically. Recommendation engines based on machine learning methods like Spark MLlib are used to accomplish this. Netflix leverages historical data from user content selection to train its machine learning algorithms; then it tests them offline before deploying them live and ensuring that they operate in Production.

Netflix has a Time Travel engine that uses Apache Spark and other Big Data technologies to Snapshot online services. It also uses the snapshot data offline to produce features and communicate facts and features between experiments without calling live systems.

Energy

Apache Spark is gaining attention around the world. Apps are operating or extracting data from the home environment. It is processed by Spark to make life easier and better. An average person who is not involved in the software industry may not be aware of this. Companies that provide energy aim to predict electricity and gas consumption trends in homes and give the users information to better use their equipment, minimize energy consumption, and save money and energy. Machine learning is applied to these data using Apache Spark MLlib for disaggregation, home comparison, and indirect techniques for non-smart clients. By displaying patterns from intelligent consumers and smart meters, the analytics engine can show customers how they have spent energy, their top three spends and how they can reduce their energy usage. This provides clients with a wealth of information and teaches them how to use energy efficiently in their homes.

Gaming

The Online Gaming industry is another beneficiary of the Apache Spark technology. For example, Riot Games uses Spark to combat abusive language in chat in team games. It faced many challenges as many players used toxic words. To overcome this, game designers attempted to predict the terms gamers would use in a game or situation. They employed a neural model called "Word2Vec" with 256 dimensions and contained months of chat records. Spaces and lowercase letters separated each word in the chat. The model was trained on natural language processing (NLP) for acronyms, short forms, and colloquial phrases, among other things and the variations were significant. The researchers developed a model that could predict harmful or poisonous words. The gaming corporation has around 100 million monthly users; therefore, the data is massive. They use Spark MLlib to train their models, which include Logistic Regression Random Forest Gradient Boosted Trees as one of the techniques. As they fine-tuned their models with more precision, the results are seen to be astonishing.

13.23 SPARK VS. HADOOP

In this section, we compare compare and contrast the significant differences and similarities between the two frameworks, Apache Spark and Hadoop, from several perspectives. Cost, performance, security, and convenience of use are just a few.

Performance: When considering the performance of Hadoop and Spark in terms of data processing, it may not seem natural to compare the two frameworks. However, we can draw a line and see clearly which tool is faster. Hadoop improves the overall performance by accessing data stored locally on HDFS. Spark's in-memory processing, on the other hand, is not a match. According to Apache, Spark appears to be 100x quicker than Hadoop with MapReduce when calculating RAM. However, sorting data on discs maintained its dominance. To handle 100 TB of data on HDFS, Spark was 3x faster and required 10x fewer nodes. In 2014, this standard was sufficient to set the world record. The fundamental reason for Spark's dominance is that it does not read or write intermediate data to drives; instead, it relies on RAM. On the other hand, Hadoop collects data from various sources and uses MapReduce to process it in batches.

Cost: When comparing Hadoop with Spark in terms of cost, we need to look beyond the software's price. This is because both platforms are free and open-source. However, the infrastructure, maintenance, and development expenditures must be factored in to arrive at a reasonable Total Cost of Ownership estimate (TCO).

The underlying hardware required to operate these tools is the most significant cost component. On the other hand, Hadoop's cost of operation is minimal because it uses any sort of disc storage for data processing.

For real-time data processing, Spark, on the other hand, relies on in-memory computations. As a result, spinning up nodes with a lot of RAM significantly raises the total cost of ownership.

The creation of applications is also a concern. However, Hadoop has been around for longer than Spark, and finding software engineers who work with Hadoop is easier.

Thus, Hadoop infrastructure is more cost-effective. While this assertion is valid, it is essential to note that Spark processes data significantly more quickly. As a result, fewer machines are required to do the same activity.

Data Processing: Both of these paradigms approach data in very different ways. For example, although both Hadoop and Spark use MapReduce to process data in a distributed setting, Hadoop is better suited for batch processing. Spark, on the other hand, excels at real-time processing.

The purpose of Hadoop is to store data on discs and then analyze it in batches in a distributed setting. To handle enormous amounts of data, MapReduce does not require a lot of RAM. Hadoop stores data on standard hardware and is best suited for linear data processing.

Apache Spark works with durable datasets (RDDs), a distributed set of elements stored on nodes across the cluster in partitions. An RDD is frequently too big for a single node to handle. As a result, Spark splits the RDDs and conducts the operations in parallel on the closest nodes. The system uses a Directed Acyclic Graph to track all activities performed on an RDD (DAG).

Spark easily handles live streams of unstructured data, thanks to its in-memory computations and high-level APIs. In addition, the data is divided into several partitions. A node can have as many partitions as it needs, but none can expand to another node.

Fault Tolerance: Regarding fault-tolerance, we can claim that both Hadoop and Spark provide an acceptable level of failure handling. However, we can also say that their approaches to fault tolerance differ.

Fault tolerance is at the heart of Hadoop's operation. Data is replicated multiple times among the nodes. In case of a problem, the system resumes work by generating the missing blocks from other locations. The master nodes track all slave nodes. Finally, if a slave node fails to respond to a master's pings, the master transfers the pending work to another slave node.

To accomplish fault tolerance, Spark employs RDD blocks. The system keeps track of the process of creating the immutable dataset. When there is a difficulty, it can restart the process. In addition, Spark can rebuild data in a cluster using DAG workflow tracking. Spark can withstand errors in a distributed data processing ecosystem because of this data structure.

Scalability: As for scalability, the distinction between Hadoop and Spark becomes hazier. To deal with large amounts of data, Hadoop employs HDFS. As a result, Hadoop can swiftly scale to meet demand as the volume of data grows dramatically. On the other hand, because Spark lacks its file system, it must rely on HDFS to handle massive data. The clusters may expand and improve computational capability by adding more servers to the network. As a result, both frameworks can have tens of thousands of nodes. As a result, the vast volume of data that can be handled and the number of computers added to each cluster are limitless. Eight thousand machines in a Spark environment with petabytes of data are verifiable. Hadoop clusters are well recognized for having tens of thousands of servers.

Ease of Use and Programming Language Support: Spark is a newer framework with fewer specialists than Hadoop, which is more user-friendly. On the other hand, Spark supports various languages in addition to its native language (Scala): Java, Python, R, and Spark SQL. This allows programmers to utilize their preferred programming language.

Hadoop is a Java-based framework. Therefore, Hadoop lacks an interactive method to assist users. It does, however, connect with the Pig and Hive tools to make developing sophisticated MapReduce applications easier.

Spark wins in the ease-of-use category with its interactive mode and support for APIs in many languages. For example, the Spark shell can analyze data interactively with Scala or Python. Furthermore, Spark is easier to use than Hadoop MapReduce since the shell quickly replies to queries.

Spark also has the advantage of allowing programmers to reuse the existing code, where possible. As a result, developers can shorten their time to create an application. This procedure can be improved by combining historical and real-time data.

Security: When it comes to Hadoop vs. Spark security, Hadoop wins, hands down. Spark's security is turned off by default. If this problem is not addressed, the setup will be revealed. Authentication by shared secret or event recording can be used to increase Spark's security. However, for production workloads, this is insufficient.

On the other hand, Hadoop uses a variety of authentication and access control mechanisms. Kerberos authentication is the most complicated to implement. Hadoop supports Ranger, LDAP, ACLs, inter-node encryption, conventional file permissions on HDFS, and Service Level Authorization, if Kerberos is too much for the user. On the other hand, Spark can achieve a sufficient level of security by integrating with Hadoop. Spark will be able to leverage both Hadoop and HDFS techniques. Additionally, when Spark is run on YARN, the earlier advantages can be taken as additional authentication mechanisms.

Machine Learning: In-memory computing is great for machine learning because it is an iterative process. As a result, Spark has been shown to be a more efficient option in this area. This is because Hadoop MapReduce divides jobs into concurrent tasks that may be too massive for machine learning algorithms to handle. In Hadoop applications, this approach causes I/O performance difficulties. In Hadoop clusters, the Mahout library is the primary machine learning platform. Mahout uses MapReduce for clustering, classification, and recommendation. Samsara began to displace this effort. MLlib, Spark's default machine learning library, is included. This library conducts in-memory iterative machine learning computations. It has tools for regression, classification, persistence, pipeline construction, and evaluation, among other things. Spark with MLlib is 9x quicker than Apache Mahout in a Hadoop disk-based context. Spark is a superior alternative for Machine Learning when more efficient results are required results than what Hadoop can provide.

Scheduling and Resource Management: Hadoop does not provide a scheduler. Resource management and scheduling rely on third-party software. YARN is in charge of resource management in a Hadoop cluster, thanks to Resource Manager and NodeManager. Oozie is one of the workflow scheduling solutions available. Individual application state management is not handled by YARN. It only uses the available computing power. Plug-ins like Capacity Scheduler and Fair Scheduler are used with Hadoop Map Reduce. These schedulers ensure that applications have access to the resources they require while maintaining the cluster's efficiency. For example, the Fair Scheduler allocates the required resources to the apps while ensuring that all applications receive the same resource allocation. The DAG scheduler is in charge of breaking down operators into phases.

DAG scheduling and Spark must execute numerous jobs at each stage. The Spark Scheduler and Block Manager manage job and task scheduling, monitoring, and resource distribution in a cluster. By comparing both frameworks, it is seen that in large data applications, both frameworks are critical. While Spark appears to be the go-to platform due to its speed and user-friendly mode, some use cases necessitate the use of Hadoop. This is true when a large volume of data needs to be analyzed. Spark has a higher maintenance budget than Hadoop, but it also requires less hardware to execute the same tasks. It is important to note that both frameworks have their advantages and disadvantages. They operate at their best when they work together.

13.24 SAMPLE PROGRAM

To start programming with Spark, word count is used as an example program.

1. A text file containing the words should be created to start the program. Here data is the text file. Once the file is created, the variable is declared by giving the path of the text file for which word count has to be found. The following is the command
   `scala> val text = sc.textFile("c:/data.txt")`

   Output
   text: org.apache.spark.rdd.RDD[String] = c:/data.txt MapPartitionsRDD[1] at textFile at <console>:24

   Figure 13.41 shows the output that is obtained by executing the above command.

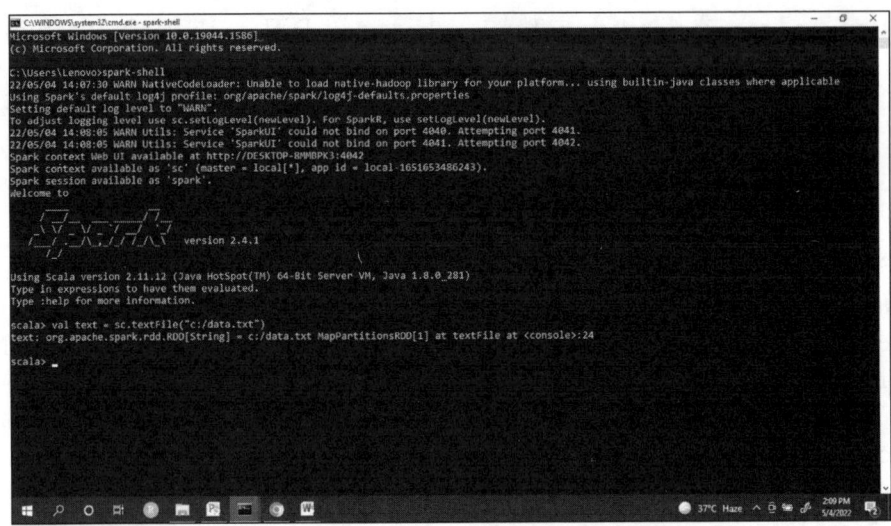

Figure 13.41 Output of the variable declaration command

2. The next command is the text.collect, used to collect the text.
   scala> text.collect

   Output
   res0: Array[String] = Array(Hi how are you, keep hit hat hut, creeper jack and jill, humpty dumpty)

   Figure 13.42 shows the output of the text collect command.

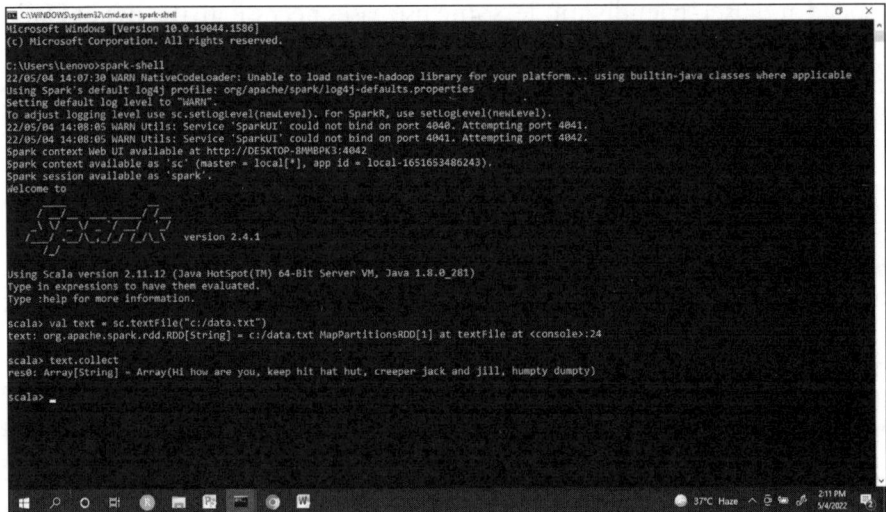

Figure 13.42 Output of the text collect command

3. The command for splitting the words by comma is as follows and the output of this command is shown in Fig. 13.43.
   scala> val counts= text.flatMap(line => line.split(""))

Output

counts: org.apache.spark.rdd.RDD[String] = MapPartitionsRDD[2] at flatMap at <console>:25

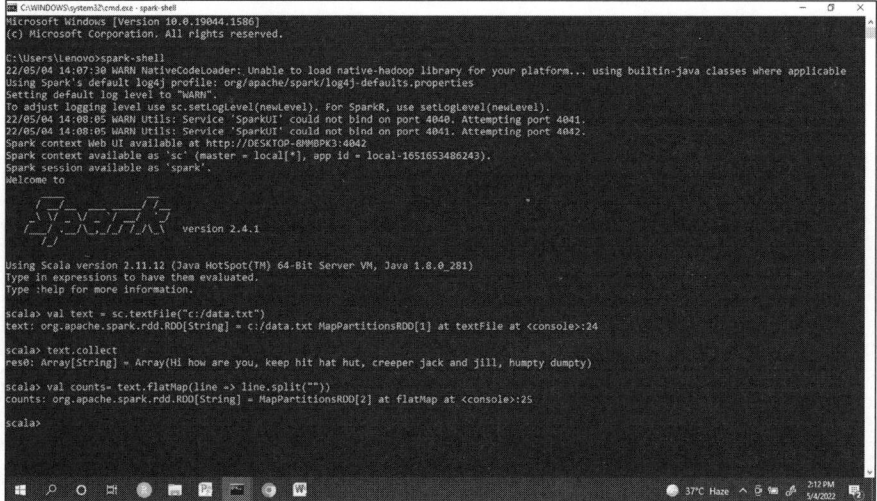

Figure 13.43 Output of the command to split words by comma

4. `scala> counts.collect`

   The above command is used to create an array of the letters in the text file. The output of this command after execution is shown in Fig. 13.44.

Output

res1: Array[String] = Array(H, i, " ", h, o, w, " ", a, r, e, " ", y, o, u, k, e, e, p, " ", h, i, t, " ", h, a, t, " ", h, u, t, c, r, e, e, p, e, r, " ", j, a, c, k, " ", a, n, d, " ", j, i, l, l, h, u, m, p, t, y, " ", d, u, m, p, t, y)

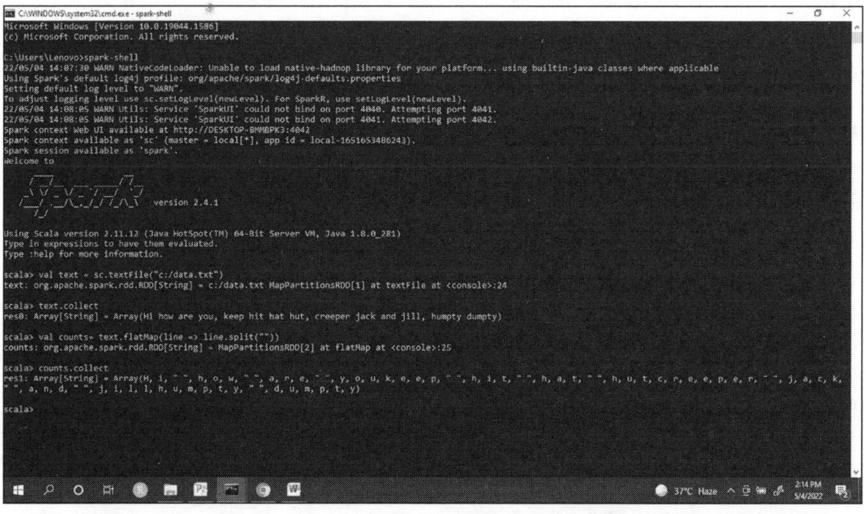

Figure 13.44 Output of the counts.collect command

5. Use the following command to place the `key(1)` for every word. The output is shown in Fig. 13.45.

   ```
   scala> val mapf=counts.map(word=>(word,1))
   ```

   Output

   mapf: org.apache.spark.rdd.RDD[(String, Int)] = MapPartitionsRDD[3] at map at <console>:25

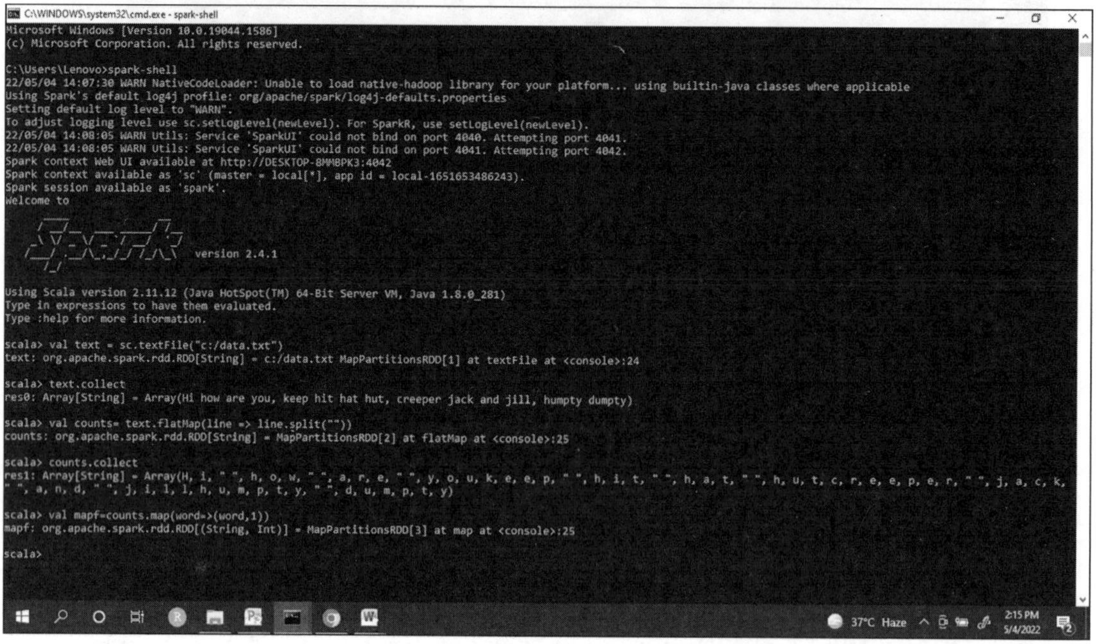

   Figure 13.45 Output of the command to place the `key(1)` to every word

6. `scala> mapf.collect`

   The above command is executed to get the map with the key specified, and the output screen of this command after execution is shown in Fig. 13.46.

   Output

   res2: Array[(String, Int)] = Array((H,1), (i,1), (" ",1), (h,1), (o,1), (w,1), (" ",1), (a,1), (r,1), (e,1), (" ",1), (y,1), (o,1), (u,1), (k,1), (e,1), (e,1), (p,1), (" ",1), (h,1), (i,1), (t,1), (" ",1), (h,1), (a,1), (t,1), (" ",1), (h,1), (u,1), (t,1), (c,1), (r,1), (e,1), (e,1), (p,1), (e,1), (r,1), (" ",1), (j,1), (a,1), (c,1), (k,1), (" ",1), (a,1), (n,1), (d,1), (" ",1), (j,1), (i,1), (l,1), (l,1), (h,1), (u,1), (m,1), (p,1), (t,1), (y,1), (" ",1), (d,1), (u,1), (m,1), (p,1), (t,1), (y,1))

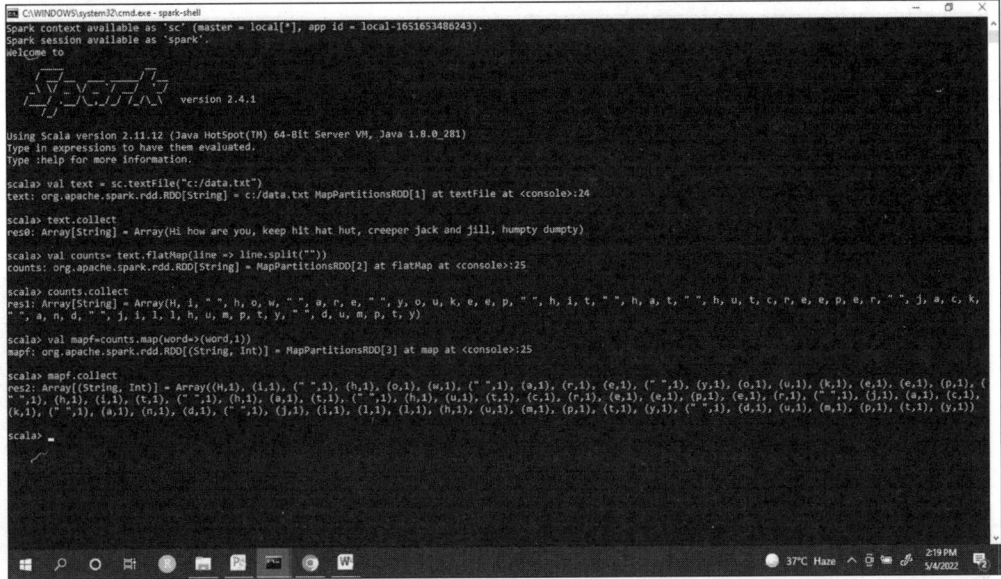

Figure 13.46 Output of the mapf.collect command

7. The following command is used to add the keys of same words and the output is depicted in Fig. 13.47.

    ```
    scala> val reducef=mapf.reduceByKey(_+_)
    ```

    Output
    reducef: org.apache.spark.rdd.RDD[(String, Int)] = ShuffledRDD[4] at reduceByKey at <console>:25

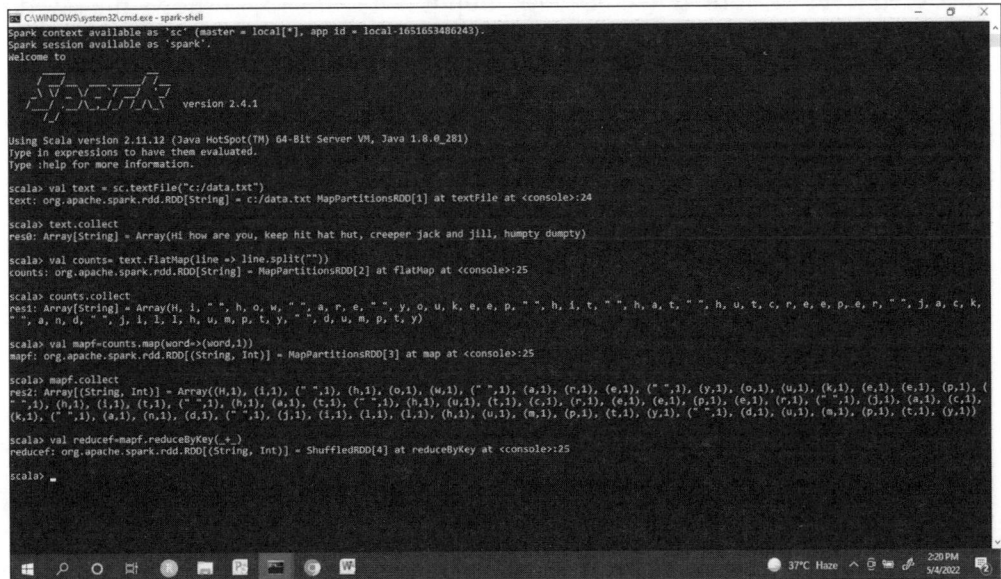

Figure 13.47 Output of the command to add the keys of the exact words

8. `scala> reducef.collect`
   The above command is used to find the number of times an alphabet is located in the text file. The screenshot of the output of this command is given in Fig. 13.48.

   Output
   res3: Array[(String, Int)] = Array((d,2), (p,4), (t,5), (h,5), (" ",10), (n,1), (j,2), (H,1), (r,3), (l,2), (w,1), (e,6), (a,4), (i,3), (k,2), (y,3), (u,4), (o,2), (m,2), (c,2))

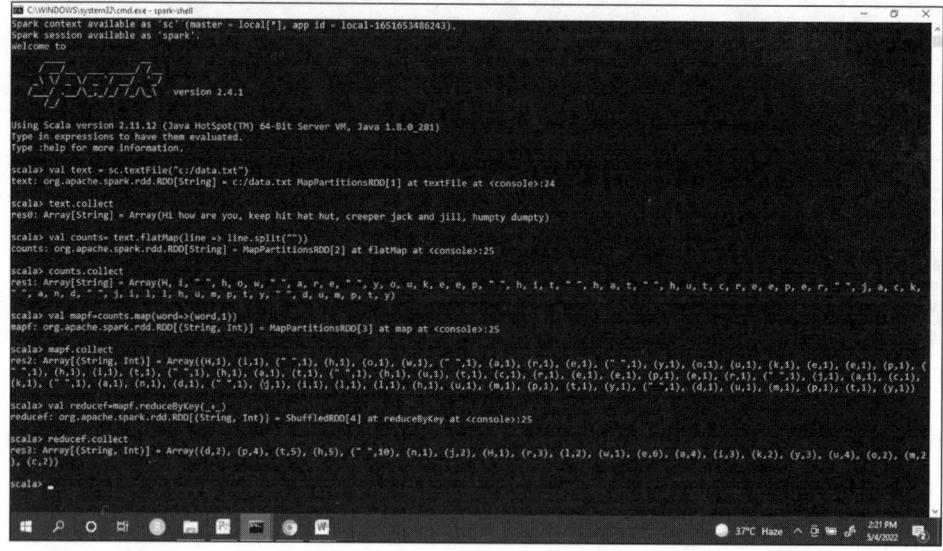

Figure 13.48 Output of the command reducef.collect

9. Use the following command to save the output files in your C drive:
   scala> reducef.saveAsTextFile("c:/spark_ouput"). Figure 13.49 shows the saved files in the Spark output file in the C drive.

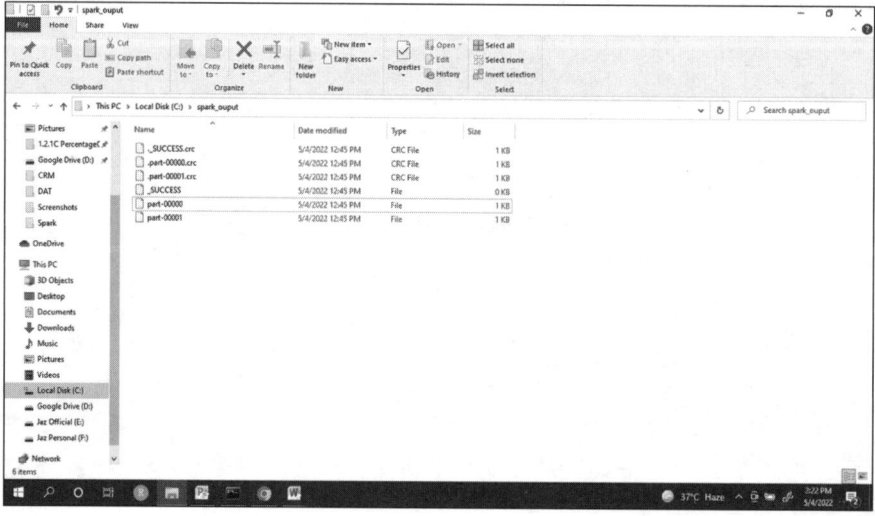

Figure 13.49 Files saved in the Spark output folder

10. The saved output folder can be viewed by right-clicking the file and opening it with a notepad. This is shown in Figure 13.50, and the content of the stored file is shown in Figure 13.51.

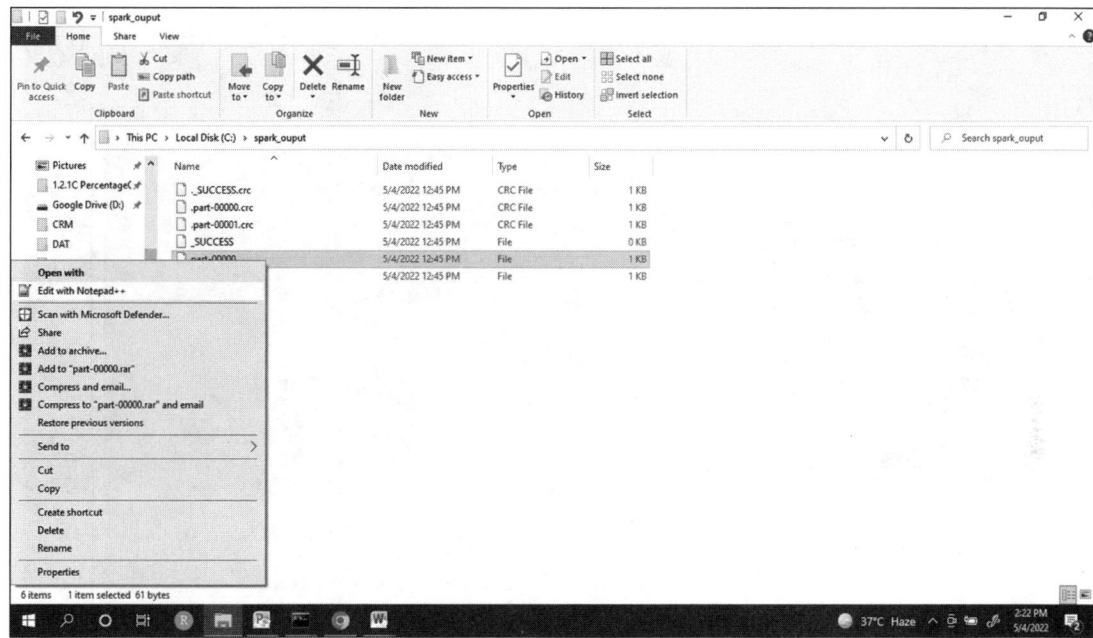

Figure 13.50   Screenshot showing the opening of the saved file

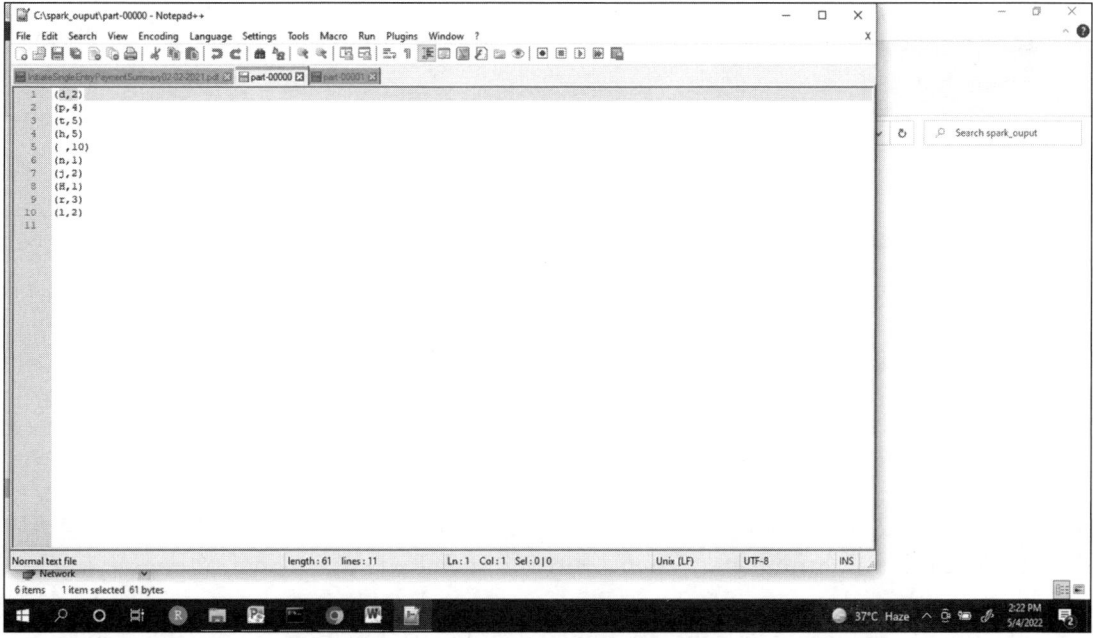

Figure 13.51   Content in the saved file

11. To check the creation of the user interface, copy the highlighted URL in the browser. The highlighted URL is shown in Figure 13.52, and the details after pasting the URL in the browser are shown in Figure 13.53.

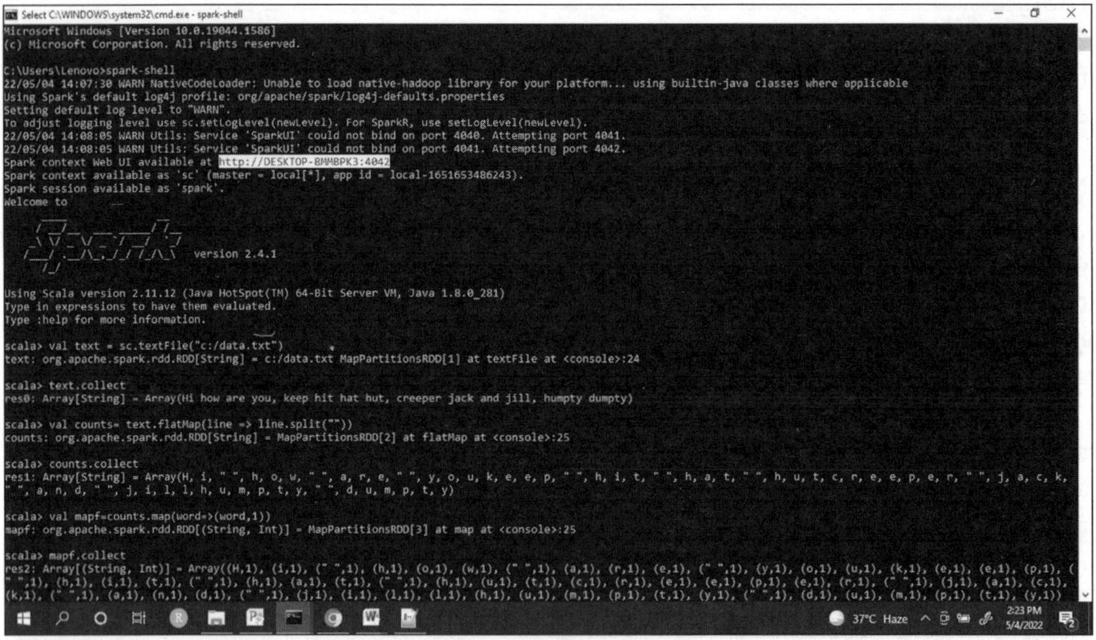

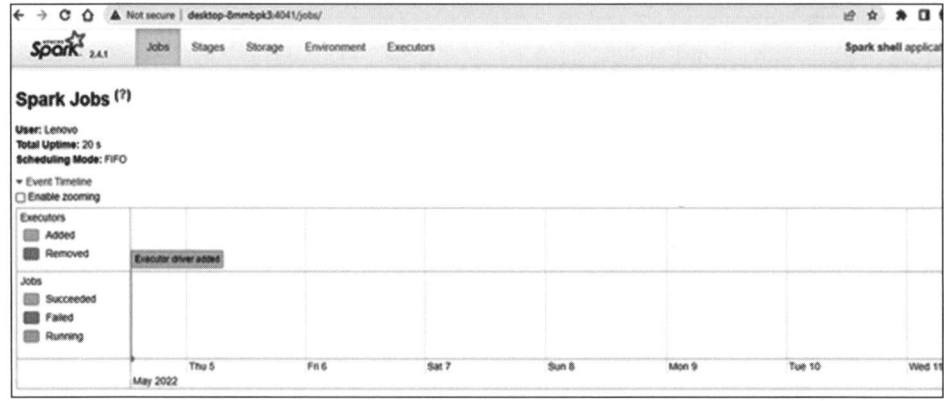

Figure 13.52   Highlighted URL to be copied in the browser

Figure 13.53   Screenshot of the created UI

SUMMARY

Apache Spark is a lightning-fast, open-source, distributed data analytical engine used to quickly and efficiently process Big Data. It is based on a cluster computing framework where a set of systems are loosely or tightly connected and work together, giving the appearance of a single system. Spark provides data parallelism and fault tolerance by distributing the task across the various distributed systems. Doing so augments the computational power of the system to handle large datasets.

In its nurturing phase, Spark paved its way into the Apache Software Foundation (ASF) in June 2013. Later it got established as an Apache Top-level Project in February 2013. From its humble beginning in 2009, Apache Spark has become the most crucial framework for Big Data distributed processing, globally. Today, many organizations are espousing Apache Spark and Hadoop to handle their large datasets. In 2017, Spark had nearly 365,000 meetup members who contributed a lot to the development of Spark. Many research papers are also presented over the years with many ideas.

Spark is an open-source processing engine that competes with Hadoop. It was founded on fast speed, ease of use, and higher developer productivity at first. Machine learning, real-time stream processing, and graph calculations are also supported. In addition, Spark has in-memory computing capabilities. It also promotes APIs like R, SQL, Scala, Python, and Java to make development easier.

Spark hides the complexities of distributed systems programming, network connection, and fault tolerance for engineers, providing a straightforward solution to parallelize these applications across clusters. They have enough control over the system to monitor, inspect, and tune programs while quickly accomplishing routine tasks. In addition, because the API is modular (based on sending dispersed collections of objects), it is simple to group work into reusable libraries and test it locally.

R Programming language provides a robust framework for statistical analysis and machine learning. It enhances the developer's productivity as well. We can utilize the R language in conjunction with SparkR to manage processing on a single machine.

Spark is based on the Scala programming language. As a result, it gives you access to some of Spark's best features. Other languages that support Spark might not have those features.

Python is a language that comes with several useful libraries for data analysis. However, compared to Scala, Python is a little slower. Java is another language supported by Spark. Thus, Java is an excellent choice for developers with a Java + Hadoop background.

Spark Core is the heart of the program. It essentially serves as an execution platform for all Spark applications. Spark also provides a generic platform to handle a wide range of applications. In addition, it achieves performance by allowing for in-memory computing. As a result, Spark Core serves as the foundation for parallel and distributed data processing.

Datasets are Spark data structures (available from version 1.6) that combine the JVM object features of RDDs (the ability to alter data using lambda functions) with a Spark SQL-optimized execution engine.

Spark SQL is a layer on top of Spark that allows users to perform SQL/HQL queries. Using Spark SQL, we can handle both structured and semi-structured data.

Catalyst Optimizer supports both rule-based and cost-based optimization. The rule-based optimizer uses a collection of rules to determine how to execute the query in rule-based optimization. On the other hand, cost-based optimization discovers the most efficient way to execute SQL statements. Multiple plans are developed using rules in cost-based optimization, and then their costs are determined.

Spark Streaming is divided into three phases: Gathering, Processing, and Data Storage.

DStream can be created in two ways: from Kafka, Flume, or Kinesis sources or by performing high-level operations on other DStreams. As a result, DStream is a succession of RDDs on the inside.

Apache Spark MLlib is a library that considers high-quality machine learning algorithms and fast performance. The goal of MLlib is to make machine learning more scalable and accessible. It includes machine learning libraries with several machine learning methods implemented.

Apache Spark GraphX is an API for graphs and parallel graph execution. It is a data repository and network graph analytics engine. Graphs can be used for clustering, classification, traversal, searching, and pathfinding. GraphX further adds to Spark RDD's capabilities by introducing a new Graph abstraction: a directed multigraph with characteristics associated with each vertex and edge.

Apache Spark 1.4 was released as SparkR. SparkR Data Frame is an essential part of SparkR. In R, DataFrames are a fundamental data structure for data processing. With libraries like Pandas and others, the concept of DataFrames has been extended to other languages.

The cluster manager is a platform for running Spark in cluster mode. It allocates resources to all worker nodes as needed and manages all nodes. We may state that master and worker nodes exist in a cluster. Worker nodes benefit from the efficient working environment provided by master nodes. Spark cluster managers come in three flavors.

Hadoop Yarn is a distributed computing framework that works with Hadoop. It also keeps track of task scheduling and resource management. The masters and slaves in this cluster are pretty accessible to the user. They also have executors and a pluggable scheduler.

Apache Mesos is a distributed cluster manager. Like Yarn, it is widely available to both masters and slaves. It may also manage resources for each application separately. Spark jobs, Hadoop MapReduce, and other service applications may be readily run.

Apache Spark is a boon to the industry which is processing Big Data. It has met the expectations of the developers when it comes to querying, processing, and analysis in a better way. Here are the advantages of Apache Spark:

1. One of the essential features of Spark is its matchless speed. As a result, Spark is the most sought-after technology in Big Data.
2. It can be easily integrated with Hadoop: Apache Spark is fabricated on top of HDFS, a distributed file system that can handle Big Data. So, Spark is a fast-processing engine compatible with Hadoop data. It can process data available on HDFS, Cassandra, Hive, etc.
3. Spark can operate independently and on Apache Yarn, allowing its processing engines to run and process data stored in HDFS.
4. Spark allows developers to write applications in languages like Java, R, Scala, Python, etc.

5. Apache Spark comes with a bundle of libraries. It supports maps and reduces, and also provides libraries to support machine learning, queries, data streaming, and analysis of graphs. This makes it a sought-after tool by developers.
6. The speed in the analysis is higher in Spark as it implements in-memory processing. Unlike Hadoop, Spark stores data in the Random Access Memory of the servers. Hence there is no need to transfer data in and out of the cluster as is done in Hadoop.
7. Spark facilitates real-time data streaming, where the data is processed as it is received. This helps in taking actions immediately based on the changing conditions in real-time.
8. Apache Spark has a rich store of functions for processing Big Data Analytics and Machine Learning.
9. Spark increases the system's efficiency by a lazy evaluation which reduces the work it has to do. Lazy evaluation indicates that the data residing in RDD will not get executed unless there is an action trigger.

Following are the limitations of Spark:

1. One of the significant issues of Apache Spark is that it does not have a file management system on its own. As Apache Spark does not have a file management system, it must be integrated with other platforms. Therefore, it depends on Hadoop Distributed File System or any other cloud-based platform for the file management system.
2. **Fewer Numbers of Algorithms:** The Machine Learning Algorithms are stored in the Spark MLlib library. However, this Spark library does not have many machine learning algorithms. Hence there is a lag in terms of available algorithms like Tanimoto distance. As the number of available algorithms is few, it is considered a limitation of Spark.
3. **Issues with Small Files:** The problem of small files arises when developers use Apache Spark with Hadoop. Limited large files are made available by Hadoop instead of small files. This problem continues even when Spark is used with Hadoop.
4. **Window Criteria:** In Apache Spark Streaming, the data is divided into small batches based on a pre-defined time interval. So, it supports a time-based window and does not support a record-based window like Flink. Sliding Window manages data packet delivery between several computer networks.
5. **Iterative Processing:** Iterative processing indicates that the results obtained in transition are used repeatedly. However, as Apache Spark iterates the data in batches, every iteration has to be scheduled separately and executed one after the other. Hence, this becomes a disadvantage when using Apache Spark.
6. **Not suitable for a multi-user environment:** A multi-user environment is a workspace where many users can log in and work concurrently. Unfortunately, Apache Spark cannot handle many users together, and hence it is not suitable for a multi-user environment.

Though Apache Spark has the above-mentioned limitations, its demand in the market has never been in the decline. Many companies still prefer it for handling and processing Big Data. Moreover, the Apache Spark community has never failed to attract the market with its enhanced versions to overcome these disadvantages.

Spark Executors: Spark has some distributed agents responsible for job execution. Executors are the dispersed agents. To put it another way, a worker node processes an application. It also performs jobs and stores data on a disk or in memory, among other things. So, each application, in essence, has its executor.

The architecture of Apache Spark has well-defined layers with various Spark components. Spark's layers and components are loosely coupled, which indicates that they are disconnected from each other. Many libraries and extensions are integrated into the architecture of Spark. The layered architecture of Spark is based on the following two abstractions:

1. Resilient Distributed Dataset (RDD)   2. Directed Acyclic Graph (DAG).

RDD is Apache Spark's core data structure. RDDs serve as the foundation for all Spark applications.

In Apache Spark, a DAG is a collection of Vertices and Edges, where the vertices represent RDDs and the edges indicate RDD operations. Every edge in a Spark DAG points from earlier to later in the sequence. When Action is called, the newly generated DAG is submitted to DAG Scheduler, which divides the graph into task phases.

Paired RDD: A Spark-paired RDD is an RDD that has a key-value pair. A key-value pair contains two connected data items (KVP). The identification is the key, and the value is the data that corresponds to the key value.

One of the features of RDD which makes it consistent is immutability. Once RDDs are created, they cannot be manipulated, i.e., they are read-only. Since RDDs cannot be changed, new RDDs can be created by doing transformation processes.

Persistence is another feature that Spark RDD exhibits. Data can be stored in persistent storage, disk, and memory. RDD is frequently stored in memory to retrieve data directly from memory, without going to the disk.

Partitioning is one of the critical features exhibited by Spark RDD. Partitions in RDD are logical, and the data is distributed across various nodes in the cluster. Furthermore, logic indicates that the divisions are only for enhancing processing, and there is no division internally. Hence, whenever any operation is performed, parallelism is achieved.

Parallelism is yet another feature of Spark RDD. RDDs are logically partitioned and hence when any operation is performed, it executes parallelly on the entire data across the cluster.

Location Stickiness is also a feature of RDD. RDDs support the computation of partitions by defining placement preferences. This indicates the information about the location of RDD. The DAG Scheduler places the partition so that the data is closer to the task to increase operational efficiency. By doing so, the speed of computations is increased to a greater extent.

Persistence and Caching are optimization techniques of Spark RDD that may be used for iterative and interactive computations of Spark. Iterative computations indicate the reuse of results in numerous computations when multistage applications are considered, whereas interactive computations allow the data to flow in two ways. First, these techniques help store the intermediate result in the upcoming stages. By doing so, the computation overhead can be reduced. Second, RDD can be cached and persisted through `cache()` and `persist()` methods.

There are two types of operations supported by Apache Spark RDD: Transformations and Actions.

Transformations are functions that are applied to RDDs to produce a new RDD. Transformations include functions like `map()` and `filter()`. The `map()` method iterates over every line in the RDD and separates it into a new RDD. The `filter()` method builds a new RDD by choosing elements from the current RDD sent as an input to the function.

Actions are Spark procedures that assist in working with the actual dataset. They aid in the flow of data from the executor to the driver. An action in Spark is used to return data from an RDD to the local computer. RDD operations return non-RDD values instead of transformations, which exclusively produce RDD. For example, the `reduce()` method is a loop that is repeated until only one value remains. The `take()` action copies all of an RDD's values to the local node.

Types of transformations: Narrow Transformations and Wide Transformations are two types of transformations.

In narrow transformations, all the data required to process the records in the single partition is present in the single partition of the parent RDD. Therefore, the result is calculated by using a subset of the partition.

RDD does not have runtime type safety or static typing. This means that error checking is not allowed at runtime. This limitation is overcome by providing compile-time type safety by datasets to build complex data workflows. Compile-time type safety means that a compile-time error will be thrown whenever any other type of data element is added to the list. This helps in identifying the error and keeping the code safe.

One of the limitations of RDD is that it degrades when memory is not enough. This problem is related to the storage issue and arises when there is no space in memory or disk to store the RDD. Degradation of RDD occurs because of this issue. However, even though the partitions that do not find space in memory are stored in the disk, there is no change in the performance level. This problem can be solved by increasing the RAM and disk size.

Other limitations of RDD are its performance limitation, overhead serialization, and garbage collection. In-memory RDD is stored as Java Virtual Machine objects. This encompasses the overhead of Java Serialization and Garbage Collection and becomes more expensive as the size of the data increases. Furthermore, the cost of garbage collection depends totally on the number of Java objects. Therefore, as the number increases, the cost also increases. Using a data structure, this limitation can be overcome with lesser objects, reducing the cost, and the object can be persisted in serialized form.

RDD is not very suitable for handling structured data. Any data stored in a predefined format is known as structured data. However, Apache Spark does not infer any data schema like other APIs. Hence handling structured data is not possible. Instead, DataSet and DataFrame are distributed collections of data organized into columns and they provide the schema view for the data. Thus, the structured data is handled.

In the DAG Scheduler, the operators are divided into job stages. A stage contains tasks based on the input data's partitioning. The DAG scheduler connects operators in a pipeline.

The Directed Acyclic Graph can be used to retrieve the lost RDD. There are only two queries in MapReduce: map and reduce; however, in DAG, there are several levels. As a result, DAG is more versatile for SQL query execution. Furthermore, DAG aids in the attainment of fault tolerance. As a result, we will be able to recover the data that has been lost. It can perform better global optimization than a Hadoop MapReduce system.

Alibaba's online shopping has millions of users who use the platform every day for searching and placing orders. As a result, hundreds of petabytes of data are generated every day. Graphical representation is needed for these user interactions, and machine learning algorithms are needed for complex data analytics. Alibaba relies on Spark to process its data to satisfy its customers by providing suggestions on products based on their choice, trend, and other criteria, to make their shopping experience satisfactory.

Uber is a multinational company that helps customers to book online taxis. This taxi dispatching company handles lakhs of drivers to commute users within a city or a town and generates terabytes of data through its users. Uber uses Spark streaming, HDFS, and Kafka to construct a pipeline for extraction, transformation, and data loading. First, Uber converts the unstructured event data into structured data as it is published, and then it uses the tools to perform complex analytics.

Hadoop improves the overall performance by accessing data stored locally on HDFS. Spark's in-memory processing, on the other hand, is not a match. According to Apache, Spark appears to be 100x quicker than Hadoop with MapReduce, when calculating RAM.

Spark easily handles live streams of unstructured data, thanks to its in-memory computations and high-level APIs. In addition, the data is divided into several partitions. A node can have as many partitions as it needs, but none can expand to another node.

EXERCISES

Multiple Choice Questions

1. **Spark Engine is written in which language?**
   A. C++
   B. Scala
   C. Java
   D. Python
   Answer: B
   Explanation: Spark is based on the Scala programming language. As a result, it gives you access to some of Spark's best features. Other languages that support Spark might

not have these features. For example, Python is a language that comes with several useful libraries for data analysis. However, in comparison to Scala, Python is a little slower. Java is another language that Spark supports.

2. **This is the execution platform for all Spark Applications:**
   A. Spark Core
   B. Cluster Management
   C. Libraries
   D. Programming languages
   Answer: A
   Explanation: Spark Core is the heart of the program. It essentially serves as an execution platform for all Spark applications. Spark also provides a generic platform to handle a wide range of applications. In addition, it achieves performance by allowing for in-memory computing. As a result, Spark Core serves as the foundation for parallel and distributed data processing.

3. **Which of the following is not a core feature of Apache Spark Core?**
   A. It is in charge of the most critical I/O functions.
   B. Dispatching of tasks
   C. Recovery from a fault
   D. Managing all nodes
   Answer: D
   Explanation: Some of Apache Spark Core's essential features are: It is in charge of the most important I/O functions. It is significant in terms of programming and observing the Spark cluster's role. It controls the dispatching of tasks and recovery from a fault. The cluster manager manages all nodes.

4. **Using Spark SQL, we can handle both structured and semi-structured data.**
   A. True
   B. False
   Answer: A
   Explanation: Spark SQL is a layer on top of Spark that allows users to perform SQL/HQL queries. Using Spark SQL, we can handle both structured and semi-structured data. It also promises to speed up current deployments by up to 100 times by running unmodified queries.

5. **Which of the following is true about the Catalyst Optimizer of Spark SQL?**
   A. It supports only cost-based optimization.
   B. It supports only rule-based optimization.
   C. It supports both rule-based and cost-based optimization.
   D. It supports neither rule-based nor cost-based optimization.
   Answer: C
   Explanation: Catalyst Optimizer supports both rule-based and cost-based optimization. The rule-based optimizer uses a collection of rules to determine how to execute the query in rule-based optimization. On the other hand, cost-based optimization discovers the most efficient way to execute SQL statements. Multiple plans are developed using rules in cost-based optimization, and then their costs are determined.

6. **Three phases of Spark Streaming in the correct order are:**
   A. Processing, Data Storage, and Gathering
   B. Processing, Gathering, and Data Storage
   C. Gathering, Data Storage, and Processing
   D. Gathering, Processing, and Data Storage
   Answer: D
   Explanation: Spark Streaming is divided into three phases: Gathering, Processing, and Data Storage.

7. **Which of the following is the Machine Learning library of Spark?**
   A. Spark GraphX   B. SparkR
   C. Spark MLlib   D. Spark SQL
   Answer: C
   Explanation: Apache Spark MLlib is a scalable Machine Learning library that considers high-quality algorithms and fast performance. The goal of MLlib is to make machine learning more scalable and accessible. It includes machine learning libraries with several machine learning methods implemented.

8. **This is an API for graphs and parallel graph execution:**
   A. Spark GraphX   B. SparkR
   C. Spark MLlib   D. Spark SQL
   Answer: A
   Explanation: Apache Spark GraphX is an API for graphs and parallel graph execution. It is a data repository and network graph analytics engine. Graphs can be used for clustering, classification, traversal, searching, and pathfinding. GraphX further adds to Spark RDD's capabilities by introducing a new Graph abstraction: a directed multigraph with characteristics associated with each vertex and edge.

9. **This version of Spark was released as SparkR:**
   A. Version 1.0   B. Version 1.4
   C. Version 2.0   D. Version 3.0
   Answer: B
   Explanation: Apache Spark 1.4 was released as SparkR. SparkR DataFrame is the most important part of SparkR. In R, DataFrames are a fundamental data structure for data processing. With libraries like Pandas and others, the concept of DataFrames has been extended to other languages. R also includes tools for data handling, calculation, and graphical presentation.

10. **Which of the following is not a flavor of Spark Cluster Manager?**
    A. Standalone Cluster manager   B. Pseudo-Cluster Manager
    C. Hadoop yarn   D. Apache Mesos
    Answer: B
    Explanation: Spark cluster managers come in three flavors. These cluster managers are supported by Spark: 1. Standalone Cluster Manager 2. Hadoop Yarn 3. Apache

Mesos. Apache Spark also supports pluggable cluster management. The cluster manager's primary responsibility is to provide resources to all applications. It may be described as an external service for getting cluster resources.

11. **Which of the following is pre-installed on Hadoop platforms?**
    A. Standalone Cluster Manager   B. Pseudo Cluster Manager
    C. Hadoop YARN   D. Apache Mesos
    Answer: C
    Explanation: Standalone is the easiest to set up of all the Spark cluster administrators. Additionally, it has the same functionality as other Spark cluster administrators. If we need to schedule many resources, we may use YARN and Mesos managers. YARN is pre-installed on Hadoop platforms, which is one of its advantages. One advantage of Mesos over others is that it allows for fine-grained sharing. Finally, Apache Spark is platform-independent. So, the choice of the manager to be used is determined by our needs and objectives.

12. **Which of the following use fine-grained sharing?**
    A. Standalone Cluster Manager   B. Pseudo Cluster Manager
    C. Hadoop YARN   D. Apache Mesos
    Answer: D
    Explanation: Same as that for Question 11.

13. **Before Spark, this was used for Batch Processing:**
    A. Impala   B. MapReduce
    C. Apache Storm   D. Neo4j
    Answer: B
    Explanation: The industry lacked a general-purpose cluster computing solution before Spark. As a result, we required a variety of technologies at Hadoop to meet various criteria, such as batch processing necessitating the use of Hadoop MapReduce.
    Stream processing is done with Apache Storm/S4. We utilize Apache Impala/Apache Tez for interactive processing. For graph processing, we need Neo4j and Apache Giraph.

14. **Before Spark, this was used for Stream Processing:**
    A. Impala   B. MapReduce
    C. Apache Storm   D. Neo4j
    Answer: C
    Explanation: Same as that for Question 13.

15. **Before Spark, this was used for Interactive Processing:**
    A. Impala   B. MapReduce
    C. Apache Storm   D. Neo4j
    Answer: A
    Explanation: Same as that for Question 13.

16. **Apache Spark has gained popularity among developers because of its:**
    A. Ease of use
    B. Speed
    C. Fault tolerance
    D. Lazy evaluation
    Answer: B
    Explanation: All organizations have started to process large-scale data these days. When processing this Big Data, speed becomes the most critical factor to be considered. Apache Spark has gained popularity among developers because of its processing speed. Spark uses an in-memory computing technique wherein the data is processed in the RAM rather than in the local disks, which are slower. This increases the computational speed significantly.

17. **Spark can handle several petabytes of clustered data concurrently from more than:**
    A. 8 nodes
    B. 80 nodes
    C. 800 nodes
    D. 8000 nodes
    Answer: D
    Explanation: One of the essential features of Spark is its matchless speed. As a result, Spark is the most sought-after technology in Big Data. High-speed processing is needed when Big Data is considered, as volume, veracity, value, variety, and velocity are the characteristics of Big Data. Furthermore, the capacity of Spark is so high that it can handle several petabytes of clustered data concurrently from more than 8000 nodes.

18. **Compared to Hadoop, Spark is _____ faster when the processing of Big Data comes into the picture:**
    A. 2x
    B. 10x
    C. 100x
    D. 1000x
    Answer: C
    Explanation: Compared to Hadoop, Spark is 100x faster when the processing of Big Data comes into the picture. This feature of fast processing of Big Data has made Spark more popular among data scientists. Spark achieves this processing speed by reducing the time taken for the reading and writing operations using Resilient Distributed Datasets (RDD)s. As a result, Spark runs 100 times faster in memory and ten times faster on disk when it runs an application in the environment of Hadoop.

19. **Apache Spark provides more than _____ number of high-level operators.**
    A. 10
    B. 80
    C. 200
    D. 1000
    Answer: B
    Explanation: Apache Spark provides more than 80 high-level operators, which helps build applications in parallel. Moreover, Spark is easy to use as it allows for bindings for languages like Java, Scala, Python, R, etc. Hence the application developers and data scientists rely on this tool for better performance and computational speed without digging into more levels of detail.

20. **This indicates that the data residing in Spark RDD will not get executed unless there is an action trigger:**
    A. Delayed Evaluation
    B. Standard Evaluation
    C. Lazy Evaluation
    D. Blocked Evaluation
    Answer: C
    Explanation: Spark increases the system's efficiency by a lazy evaluation, which reduces the work it has to do. This occurs during Spark transformation. Lazy evaluation indicates that the data residing in RDD will not get executed unless there is an action trigger. It waits for the completion of the code and then efficiently processes the instruction.

21. **Which of the following is a disadvantage of Spark?**
    A. Lazy Evaluation
    B. Ease of Use
    C. Fault Tolerance
    D. Auto Optimization
    Answer: D
    Explanation:
    Lack of Automatic Optimization Process: The datasets and jobs must be optimized manually when working with Apache Spark. The users can state the number of partitions if they want to make partitions. However, to fix the number of required partitions independently, the user must pass the number of partitions as a second parameter in the parallelize method.

22. **Apache Spark has a state-of-the-art file management system:**
    A. True
    B. False
    Answer: B
    Explanation: One of the significant issues of Apache Spark is that it does not have a file management system of its own. As Apache Spark does not have a file management system, it has to get integrated with other platforms. Therefore, it depends on Hadoop Distributed File System or any other cloud-based platform for the file management system.

23. **This presents in the master node of Spark physical architecture:**
    A. Driver Program
    B. Cluster Manager
    C. Tasks
    D. Cache
    Answer: A
    Explanation: The driver program, which powers the Spark application, is located in the master node. The code we are creating acts as a driver program. The interactive shell functions will also act as the driver program. The driver program first builds a Spark Context.

24. **This is a gateway to all the Spark functions. It is similar to how we connect to our database through connection.**
    A. Worker
    B. Spark Context
    C. Driver Program
    D. Task

Answer: B

Explanation: Assume that the Spark context is a gateway to all the Spark functions. It is similar to how you connect to your database. Any database command you issue travels through the database connection. Similarly, everything you do on Spark is filtered by Spark context. This Spark context now manages numerous jobs in conjunction with the cluster manager. The driver application and Spark context handle the task execution within the cluster.

25. **These are slave nodes whose sole purpose is to carry out tasks in Spark:**
    A. Worker Node   B. Master Node
    C. Driver Program   D. Spark Context
    Answer: A
    Explanation: Worker nodes are slave nodes whose sole purpose is to carry out tasks. These tasks are then run on the worker node's partitioned RDDs, returning the result to the Spark Context. Spark Context takes the job, divides it into tasks, and then distributes it to the worker nodes. These tasks operate on the partitioned RDD, gather results, and return to the main Spark Context.

26. **DAG in Spark stands for:**
    A. Distributed Acyclic Graph   B. Directed Analysis Graph
    C. Directed Acyclic Graph   D. Directed Activity Graph
    Answer: C
    Explanation: The layered architecture of Spark is based on the following two abstractions:
    1. Resilient Distributed Dataset (RDD)
    2. Directed Acyclic Graph (DAG)

27. **Once RDDs are created, they cannot be manipulated. This is represented by:**
    A. Immutability   B. Persistence
    C. Partitioning   D. Parallelism
    Answer: A
    Explanation: One of the features of RDD which makes it consistent is immutability. Once RDDs are created, they cannot be manipulated, i.e., it is read-only. Since RDDs cannot be changed, new RDDs can be created by doing transformation processes.

28. **RDD is frequently stored in memory to retrieve data directly from memory without going to the disk. This is known as:**
    A. Immutability   B. Persistence
    C. Partitioning   D. Parallelism
    Answer: B
    Explanation: Persistence is another feature that Spark RDD exhibits. Data can be stored in persistent storage, disk, and memory. RDD is frequently stored in memory to retrieve data directly from memory without going to the disk.

29. **Whenever any operation is performed in RDD, this is achieved:**
    A. Immutability
    B. Persistence
    C. Partitioning
    D. Parallelism
    Answer: D
    Explanation: Partitioning is one of the important features exhibited by Spark RDD. Partitions in RDD are logical, and the data is distributed across various nodes in the cluster. Furthermore, logic indicates that the divisions are only for enhancing processing, and there is no division internally. Hence, whenever any operation is performed, parallelism is achieved.

Short-answer Questions

1. **Write short notes on Apache Spark.**
   Apache Spark is a lightning-fast, open-source, distributed data analytical engine used to quickly and efficiently process Big Data. It is based on a cluster computing framework where a set of systems are loosely or tightly connected and work together, giving the appearance of a single system. Spark provides data parallelism and fault tolerance by distributing the task across the various distributed systems. Doing so augments the computational power of the system to handle large datasets. Spark may be immediately integrated into Hadoop's HDFS and used as a powerful data processing tool. When combined with YARN, it can operate on the same cluster as MapReduce Jobs.

2. **What are the programming languages supported by Spark? List down a few companies using Spark.**
   Spark supports top-tier programming languages such as Scala, Java, and Python through its simple and quicker programming interface. As a result, a significant spike in demand propelled Spark to become the leading legend in the Production Environment. Spark is favored by several top MNCs such as Adobe, Yahoo, NASA, and others, due to its unmatched capabilities and dependability. Similarly, the need for Spark Developers is on the rise.

3. **Quickly compare Hadoop MapReduce with Spark.**
   Spark is not dependent on Hadoop because it has its cluster management mechanism. Essentially, Hadoop is solely used for storage while using Spark. Spark implements data processing 10–100x quicker than Hadoop MapReduce because of in-memory processing. MapReduce, on the other hand, uses persistent storage. Unlike Hadoop, Spark has built-in libraries for batch processing, streaming, Machine Learning, and interactive SQL queries, among other things. Hadoop, on the other hand, only allows batch processing. Hadoop is heavily reliant on disks, but Spark encourages caching and data storage in memory. Iterative computing is the ability of Spark to conduct calculations on the same dataset many times. Hadoop, on the other hand, does not support iterative computation.

4. **How does Spark 3.0 support enhancements to Adaptive Query Execution?**
   Unlike other technologies, Spark's runtime adaptivity is critical since it optimizes execution plans depending on the input data. Broadcasting is an excellent example of the significance of dynamic adaptation of execution strategies. If the table size permits it, the adaptive execution mode can change a shuffle join to a broadcast join (i.e., if its size does not exceed the broadcast limit). This may be possible for some data inputs, but it may not be possible for others. Data skewness is another excellent example of the relevance of AQE. The partitions utilized in future modifications can be dynamically changed when the Adaptive Query Execution option is enabled.

5. **How does Spark 3.0 support ANSI SQL Compliance?**
   Migration of workloads from other SQL engines to Spark SQL requires ANSI SQL compliance. To increase compliance, this edition uses the Proleptic Gregorian calendar and allows users to prevent the usage of ANSI SQL reserved keywords as identifiers. Furthermore, runtime overflow checking in numeric operations and compile-time type enforcement when putting data into a table with a predetermined schema have been included. These new validations improve the data quality.

6. **How does Spark 3.0 support Dynamic Partition Pruning?**
   When the optimizer cannot determine the partitions, it may skip at build time, and dynamic partition pruning is used here. This is typical in star schemas, which include one or more fact tables that relate to any number of dimension tables. We can prune the partitions read from a fact table in such join operations by finding the partitions that come from filtering the dimension tables. In a TPC-DS test, 60 out of 102 queries showed a substantial speedup of 2 to 18 times.

7. **Write short notes on Spark Core.**
   Spark Core is the heart of the program. It essentially serves as an execution platform for all Spark applications. Spark also provides a generic platform to handle a wide range of applications. In addition, it achieves performance by allowing for in-memory computing. As a result, Spark Core serves as the foundation for parallel and distributed data processing.

8. **List some of the important features of Apache Spark Core.**
   - It is in charge of the most important I/O functions.
   - It is significant in terms of programming and observing the Spark cluster's role.
   - Dispatching of tasks.
   - Recovery from a fault.

9. **Write short notes on Spark SQL.**
   Spark SQL, Spark Streaming, Spark MLlib, Spark GraphX, and SparkR are the components of the Apache Spark Ecosystem that enable Apache Spark. Spark SQL is a layer on top of Spark that allows users to perform SQL/HQL queries. Using Spark SQL, we can handle both structured and semi-structured data. It also promises to speed up current deployments by up to 100 times by running unmodified queries.

10. **What is Catalyst optimization in Spark SQL?**
    A catalyst optimizer is hidden deep within Spark SQL. It provides several advanced programming language capabilities that enable us to create an expandable query optimizer. To integrate Spark SQL, a new extensible optimizer named Catalyst was created. This optimizer was built using Scala's functional programming constructs.

11. **How is fault-tolerance in the middle of a query taken care of in Spark SQL?**
    Fault tolerance is achieved by employing the Spark engine to scale thousands of nodes and multi-hour queries. The data application is scheduled, distributed, and monitored throughout the cluster via a Spark engine. In Hadoop clusters, Spark Engine is utilized to perform mappings. It may be used in a variety of situations. It contains Spark SQL batch and ETL tasks, streaming data from sensors, IoT, and machine learning, among other things.

12. **What is Micro-batching in Spark SQL?**
    Micro-batching is a technique for treating a stream as a series of small batches of data by a process or task. As a result, Spark Streaming divides live data into discrete batches. After that, it sends the data to the batch system to be processed. It has fault tolerance properties as well.

13. **Write short notes on the Gathering Phase of Spark Stream.**
    There are two types of built-in streaming sources in Spark Streaming. Basic sources are the sources that the Streaming Context API supports. File systems and socket connections are two examples of basic sources. Advanced sources are extra utility classes that provide access to advanced sources such as Kafka, Flume, and Kinesis. As a result, Spark can access data from various sources, including Kafka, Flume, Kinesis, and TCP connections.

14. **Write short notes on Spark MLlib.**
    Apache Spark MLlib is a scalable Machine Learning library that considers high-quality algorithms and fast performance. The goal of MLlib is to make machine learning more scalable and accessible. It includes machine learning libraries with several machine learning methods implemented. Clustering, regression, classification, and collaborative filtering are just a few examples. MLlib also includes several lower-level machine learning primitives, such as the general gradient descent optimization technique.

15. **Write short notes on Spark GraphX.**
    Apache Spark GraphX is an API for graphs and parallel graph execution. It is a data repository and network graph analytics engine. Graphs can be used for clustering, classification, traversal, searching, and pathfinding. GraphX further adds to Spark RDD's capabilities by introducing a new Graph abstraction: a directed multigraph with characteristics associated with each vertex and edge.

16. **Write short notes on SparkR.**
    Apache Spark 1.4 was released as SparkR. SparkR DataFrame is the most important part of SparkR. In R, DataFrames are a basic data structure for data processing. With libraries like Pandas and others, the concept of DataFrames has been extended to other languages. R also includes tools for data handling, calculation, and graphical presentation. As a result, the major goal of SparkR was to test various strategies for combining R's usability with Spark's scalability. It is an R package that provides a simple client using Apache Spark.

17. **What are the advantages of SparkR?**
    SparkR can read data from various sources by tapping into Spark SQL's data sources API such as Hive tables, JSON files and Parquet files. Many additional data processing tools support Parquet as a columnar format file. Spark SQL reads and writes Parquet files and considers it as one of the best Big Data Analytics formats available. SparkR DataFrames inherit the computation engine's code generation and memory management optimizations. SparkR DataFrame operations are distributed over all cores and machines in the Spark cluster. As a result, SparkR DataFrames can handle terabytes of data and thousands of workstations in clusters.

18. **Write short notes on the Cluster Manager of Spark.**
    Cluster manager is a platform for running Spark in cluster mode. It allocates resources to all worker nodes as needed and manages all nodes. We may state that master and worker nodes exist in a cluster. Worker nodes benefit from the efficient working environment provided by master nodes.

19. **What are the different flavors of Spark Cluster Manager?**
    Spark cluster managers come in three flavors. These cluster managers are supported by Spark: 1. Standalone cluster manager 2. Hadoop YARN and 3. Apache Mesos. Apache Spark also supports pluggable cluster management. The cluster manager's primary responsibility is to provide resources to all applications. It may be described as an external service for getting cluster resources.

20. **Write short notes on Standalone Cluster Manager of Spark.**
    Standalone Cluster Manager is included in the Spark distribution and serves as a primary cluster manager. The essence of the standalone cluster manager is that it is resilient to work failures. It can manage resources according to application requirements. It runs smoothly on Linux, Windows, and Mac. HDFS (Hadoop Distributed File System) data is also accessible. This is the most straightforward method of running Apache Spark on this cluster. It also has a high master availability. It has a master and several workers in cluster management.

21. **Write short notes on the Hadoop YARN cluster manager of Spark.**
    Hadoop YARN is a distributed computing framework that works with Hadoop. It also keeps track of task scheduling and resource management. The masters and slaves in this cluster are pretty accessible to the user. They also have executors and

a pluggable scheduler accessible, and may also be used on Linux and Windows. MapReduce 2.0 is another name for Hadoop YARN. It also separates the functions of resource management and task scheduling.

22. **Write short notes on Apache Mesos cluster manager of Spark.**
    It is a cluster manager that is distributed. It, like YARN, is widely available to both masters and slaves. It may also manage resources for each application separately. Spark jobs, Hadoop MapReduce, and other service applications may be readily run. Apache provides APIs for Java, Python, and C++. Mesos may also be run on Linux or Mac OSX.

23. **What are the design principles for Apache Spark?**
    The industry lacked a general-purpose cluster computing solution before Spark. As a result, a variety of technologies was required at Hadoop to meet diverse criteria such as batch processing, necessitating the use of Hadoop MapReduce.
    Stream processing is done with Apache Storm/S4. We utilize Apache Impala/Apache Tez for interactive processing. For graph processing, we need Neo4j and Apache Giraph. As a result, the sector had a high demand for a strong engine that could process data in both real-time (streaming) and batch mode. We also needed an engine that could respond in under a second and do in-memory processing. Apache Spark was designed to address these concerns.

24. **Write short notes on the speed of Spark.**
    Spark uses an in-memory computing technique wherein the data is processed in the RAM rather than in the local disks, which are slower. This increases the computational speed significantly. The capacity of Spark is so high that it can handle several petabytes of clustered data concurrently from more than 8000 nodes. Compared to Hadoop, Spark is 100x faster in the processing of Big Data. Spark achieves this processing speed by reducing the time taken for the reading and writing operations using Resilient Distributed Datasets (RDD)s. As a result, Spark runs 100 times faster in memory and ten times faster on disk when it runs an application in the environment of Hadoop.

25. **Write short notes on the ease of use of Spark.**
    Apache Spark comes with a rich package of Application Programming Interfaces (API), which helps perform various operations on massive datasets. An API, in simple words, acts as an intermediate between applications. Spark API tools are developer-friendly, and with a simple method call, complex distributions can be handled. Furthermore, Apache Spark provides more than 80 high-level operators, which helps build applications in parallel. Moreover, Spark is easy to use as it provides bindings for languages like Java, Scala, Python, R, etc.

26. **Write short notes on the dynamic nature of Spark.**
    Spark is highly dynamic as it provides 80 high-level operators who support interactive querying. Applications can also be developed in parallel with the help of

these operators. Hence it is considered to be a rich tool in this aspect. Spark allows the developers to develop applications using different languages, providing greater flexibility than other tools used in the Big Data environment. Spark can run on various tools like Hadoop Yarn, Mesos, and even in a cloud environment. In cluster mode, it can also run independently. Spark can run on one environment and read data from another source. For example, it can run on the YARN cluster manager and read Hadoop data from HBase, Hive, Cassandra, etc.

27. **Write short notes on the in-memory computing of Spark.**
    Spark's speed in the analysis is higher as it implements in-memory processing. Hence there is no need to transfer data in and out of the cluster as done in Hadoop. Furthermore, as the data is cached in the main memory, it is not necessary to fetch data from the disk whenever needed for executing applications. This reduces the accessing speed of the data, thereby accelerating the speed of processing. Furthermore, the in-memory computation is facilitated in Spark with the use of a DAG execution engine which enables acyclic data flow, thereby resulting in higher speed.

28. **Write short notes on the real-time stream processing of Spark.**
    Real-time data streaming is a process in which the data is processed as it is received. This helps in taking actions immediately based on the changing conditions in real-time. The generation of real-time data is rising exponentially every second as the usage of applications is growing continuously. Apache Spark provides smooth streaming of real-time data using the state-of-art methods to write streaming codes and maintain the same. Furthermore, unlike other tools for streaming data processing, Spark can recover the lost data without writing any extra code, which makes it more sophisticated.

29. **Write short notes on the fault tolerance nature of Spark.**
    Spark achieves fault tolerance in Storage and computation by backing up the data to another node. It handles the failure of a working node with the help of the Spark Abstraction RDD, which ensures that data loss is zero. In addition, RDD provides the capacity to recover any bugs or losses discovered. To recover the deleted data, we shall require a redundant element. In the self-recovery process, redundant data is crucial. Finally, redundant data can be used to retrieve lost data.

30. **Write notes on Lazy Evaluation of Spark.**
    Spark increases the system's efficiency by a lazy evaluation which reduces the work it has to do. Lazy evaluation indicates that the data residing in RDD will not get executed unless there is an action trigger. It waits for the completion of the code and then efficiently processes the instruction. When you tell Spark to do anything with a dataset, it follows your instructions and takes a note of it so it doesn't forget – but it doesn't do anything until you ask for the outcome. The action is not executed immediately when a transformation like a `map()` is called on an RDD.

31. **Write short notes on the Cost Efficiency of using Spark.**
    Apache Spark is open-source software, and hence the user need not pay for licensing. In addition, it comes with in-built functions for machine learning, streaming applications, and graph processing, thereby reducing the cost for organizations that use Spark according to their requirements.

32. **Write short notes on the Active Spark community.**
    Since 2009, more than 1200 developers from nearly 300 companies have contributed to the development of Apache Spark. These active community developers are extending their support continuously for the enhancement and up-gradation of Spark. Mailing lists can be used to post queries, and Spark conferences and meetup groups are there for people to discuss more on Spark. Apache has a colossal open-source community working behind it to make it more powerful. Different versions are released with updated coding to overcome some of the limitations in Spark. This is the greatest strength when Apache Spark is considered.

33. **Write short notes on the lack of an Automatic Optimization Process in Spark.**
    Optimization is a technique adapted to effectively use resources and increase job execution speed. The datasets and jobs must be optimized manually when working with Apache Spark. To fix the number of required partitions on their own, the user must pass the number of partitions as a second parameter in the parallelize method. The Resilient Distributed Datasets (RDD)s are formed in Apache Spark using the parallelizing method from the existing collection present in the driver. Any operation can be done in parallel with the elements present in the collection. These partitions must be controlled manually to get the correct partition and cache. When automation is done in most platforms and techniques, Spark's lack of an automatic optimization process proves to be a disadvantage.

34. **What are Window Criteria in Spark?**
    In Apache Spark Streaming, the data is divided into small batches based on a pre-defined time interval. So, it supports a time-based window and does not support a record-based window like Flink. Sliding Window manages data packet delivery between several computer networks. The Spark Streaming library supports windowed computations, which apply RDD transformations to a sliding data window. When the window slides, the RDDs that fall within the window are merged and processed to create new RDDs for the windowed DStream.

35. **What is backpressure in Spark?**
    Apache Spark can process a massive amount of data. As data grows, handling the flow of data becomes an issue. Buffer is used to storing data temporarily when it moves from one place to another. When the buffer is complete, it cannot receive the incoming data, and the data gets built up at the input/output switches. Transfer of data cannot take place till the buffer is emptied. This is known as backpressure.

Apache Spark fails to handle this backpressure implicitly. It has to be done manually – a disadvantage for developers who use Apache Spark.

36. **Why is Spark not suitable for a multi-user environment?**
    A multi-user environment is a workspace where many users can log in and work concurrently. Unfortunately, Apache Spark cannot handle many users concurrently, and hence it is not suitable for a multi-user environment. However, in spite of this limitation, the demand for Apache Spark in the market has never been in decline. Many companies still prefer it for handling and processing Big Data. Apache Spark community has never failed to attract the market with its enhanced versions to overcome these disadvantages.

37. **How does the driver program help in Spark?**
    The driver program, which powers the Spark application, is located in the master node. The code we are creating acts as a driver program. The interactive shell functions will also act as the driver program. The driver program first builds a Spark Context. Assume that the Spark context is a gateway to all the Spark functions. It is similar to how you connect to your database. Any database command you issue travels through the database connection.
    Similarly, everything you do on Spark is filtered by Spark context. This Spark context now manages numerous jobs in conjunction with the cluster manager. The driver application and Spark context handle the task execution within the cluster.

38. **What is Spark Executors?**
    Spark has some distributed agents that are responsible for job execution. Executors are the dispersed agents. To put it another way, a worker node processes an application. It also performs jobs and stores data on a disk or in memory, among other things. Each application, in essence, has its executor.
    Furthermore, it sends partial metrics for current jobs to the driver's receiver. It also provides RDDs with in-memory storage. Finally, the block manager caches them in Spark programs.

39. **What is Resilient Distributed Dataset in Spark?**
    RDD is the primary data structure of Apache Spark. RDDs serve as the foundation for all Spark applications. RDD is an acronym denoting: Resilient Distributed Dataset. Resilient means it is fault-tolerant and capable of data reconstruction in a failure. Distributed means that Data is distributed among numerous nodes in a cluster. Dataset means a set of values for partitioned data.

40. **What is Directed Acyclic Graph in Spark?**
    In Apache Spark, a DAG is a collection of Vertices and Edges, where the vertices represent RDDs and the edges indicate RDD operations. Every edge in a Spark DAG points from earlier to later in the sequence. When Action is called, the newly generated DAG is submitted to DAG Scheduler, which divides the graph into task phases. It is a strict extension of the MapReduce model. DAG operations outperform

other systems like MapReduce in terms of global optimization. In more sophisticated jobs, the picture of DAG gets clearer.

41. **How does Spark streaming Extract Transform Load (ETL) happen?**
    When traditional ETL tools are used for batch processing in a database environment, the data must be read first, and then converted into a compatible database format. Finally, it has to be stored in the target database. However, in Spark's streaming, the data is cleaned and aggregated continuously before moving it into the data repositories.

42. **How is fog computing taken care of in Spark?**
    Fog computing uses the decentralization technique to place storage and processing components at the edge of the cloud. However, some challenges accompany fog computing as it needs low latency and massively parallel machine learning processing. It also needs complex algorithms to analyze graphs. Apache Spark comes as a solution to meet these challenges in fog computing by providing the needed stack components like Shark for interactive querying, a machine learning library (MLlib) for algorithms, GraphX for graphical analysis, and Spark streaming.

43. **How does Spark supports interactive analysis?**
    Another great application of Spark is its ability to support interactive analytics. Compared with other tools that handle batch processing, Spark is much faster. Without sampling, Spark can process exploratory queries. Spark can process complex datasets and provide interactive visualization when combined with visualization tools. Machine learning algorithms can process interactive queries against live data using Spark. This helps the users to run queries during the current session. In this situation, old data will be used to train the algorithms and integrated into new data to learn from it as it enters the memory.

44. **Write notes on achieving fault tolerance using DAG in Spark.**
    RDD divides into partitions, and each node operates on one of them at any given time. In this case, a set of Scala functions is run on an RDD partition. These operations combine to form a DAG, which the Spark execution engine recognizes. Let us say a node collapses in the middle of an operation, such as n3, which is dependent on operation n2, which, in turn, is dependent on operation n1. When the cluster management discovers that a node has died, another node is assigned to continue processing. This node will work on the RDD's specific partition and the sequence of operations it must complete (n1→n2→n3). There will no longer be any data loss.

Essay-type Questions

1. Write an essay on the history of Spark.
2. What are the highlights of Spark 3.0?
3. Write an essay on Spark Ecosystem: Supporting Languages.

4. Write an essay on Spark Ecosystem: Spark Core.
5. Write an essay on Spark Ecosystem: Spark SQL.
6. Write an essay on Spark Streaming.
7. Write an essay on Spark MLlib and Spark GraphX.
8. What is SparkR, and what are its advantages?
9. Write an essay on Cluster Management in Spark.
10. Compare the three types of cluster management in Spark.
11. Write an essay on the design principles for Apache Spark.
12. Explain the top advantages of Spark.
13. What are the key disadvantages of Spark?
14. Explain Apache Spark Physical Architecture.
15. Explain Apache Spark Layered Architecture in detail.
16. What are the ways to create RDD in Spark?
17. What are the predominant features of Spark RDD?
18. Write an essay on RDD Persistence and RDD Caching Mechanisms in Apache Spark.
19. Compare and contrast Spark vs. Hadoop.

CHAPTER **14**

Introduction to NoSQL Database Concepts

> **LEARNING OBJECTIVES**
>
> When starting new in the Big Data arena, many users find it hard to understand the philosophy of NoSQL. This chapter intends to give such beginners a starting point in their journey to the NoSQL landscape. It starts with a simple definition of NoSQL and explains how it differs from RDBMS concepts, before proceeding to discuss the types of NoSQL, the advantages of NoSQL, and concludes with an overview of Cassandra, MongoDB, and HBase.

14.1 INTRODUCTION

When using RDBMS for massive data, the system response time becomes slow. To address this issue, we could "scale up" our systems by upgrading our existing hardware. However, this is an expensive procedure of RDBMS. The alternative is to distribute the database load across multiple hosts. This is known as "scaling out." NoSQL is based on this scale-out principle. Because NoSQL databases are non-relational, they scale out better than relational databases designed for web applications. The concept of NoSQL databases became popular among Internet powerhouses such as Google, Facebook, and Amazon, which deal with massive amounts of data.

14.2 RELATIONAL DATABASES

Relational DBMS (database management systems) were created in the era of mainframes and business applications, long before the Internet, cloud, Big Data, mobile, and today's massively interactive enterprise. These databases were created to be run on a single server – the larger, the better. To scale up, the only way to increase the capacity of these databases was to upgrade the servers (processors, memory, and storage). For decades, relational databases have stored what we call structured data. Tables are data groupings that have been subdivided.

The tables have well-defined data units in type, size, and other constraints.

Refer to Fig. 14.1 for the relational table representation. A homogenous (same type) dataset is represented using the same color. For example, a filled-in table may appear as shown in Fig. 14.2.

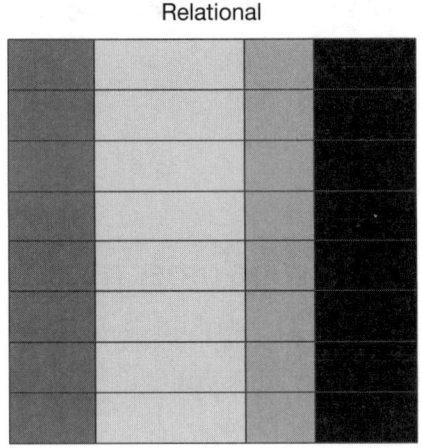

Figure 14.1   Relational table representation

Roll_Number	Student_Name	Age	Weight_Kg	CGPA
1001	Liam	11	35	4
1002	Noah	11	37	3
1003	Oliver	10	38	4.1
1004	Elijah	10	39	3.1
1005	Olivia	11	35	3.3
1006	Charlotte	11	37	3.7
1007	Ava	10	36	3.65

Figure 14.2   Example of a table (Student data)

Each group unit is referred to as a row (Fig. 14.3), and each data unit is referred to as a column (Fig. 14.4). Relational databases get their name because the columns can have relationships between them, such as parent-child.

	Roll_Number	Student_Name	Age	Weight_Kg	CGPA
ROW →	1001	Liam	11	35	4

Figure 14.3   Example of a table (Student data): Row

Scaling horizontally is difficult because consistency is one of the most critical factors.

COLUMN

Roll_ Number	Student_ Name
1001	Liam
1002	Noah
1003	Oliver
1004	Elijah
1005	Olivia
1006	Charlotte
1007	Ava

Figure 14.4 Example of a table (Student data): Column

14.3 NoSQL Definition

NoSQL does not have a rigid definition. However, several observations can be made, such as that it does not employ relational model, and that it is open-source, schema-less, and meant for unstructured data storage and retrieval. Moreover, NoSQL offers a variety of options for data organization. For example, NoSQL may be used in data analytics, extensive data management, social networks, and mobile app development by providing varied data formats.

NoSQL ("Not only SQL") became popular in the mid-2000s due to the rise of cloud computing, Big Data, and web and mobile applications. It is now the preferred database due to its high performance, scalability, and ease of use.

14.4 Types of NoSQL Databases

The four primary NoSQL variations (Fig. 14.5) are column-oriented database, key-value store, document store, and graph database. Each type addresses an issue that relational databases are unable to handle.

14.4.1 Column Family Databases

Column family databases (column-oriented databases) store data as rows with several columns linked by a row key (Fig. 14.6). Column families are collections of data that are often accessed together.

HBase, Hyper table, and Amazon DynamoDB are prominent column family databases. Traditional relational databases are row-oriented, with each row having its row-id and each field inside each row being kept in its table (Fig. 14.7). Every row in a row-oriented database is examined every time you look something up, regardless of the columns you

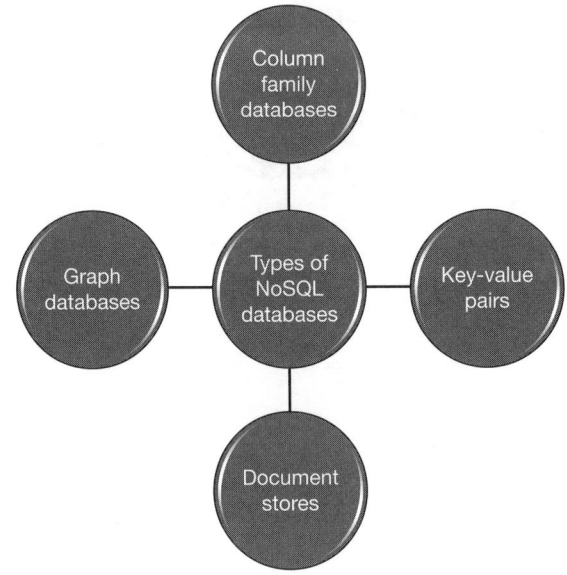

Figure 14.5 Types of NoSQL databases

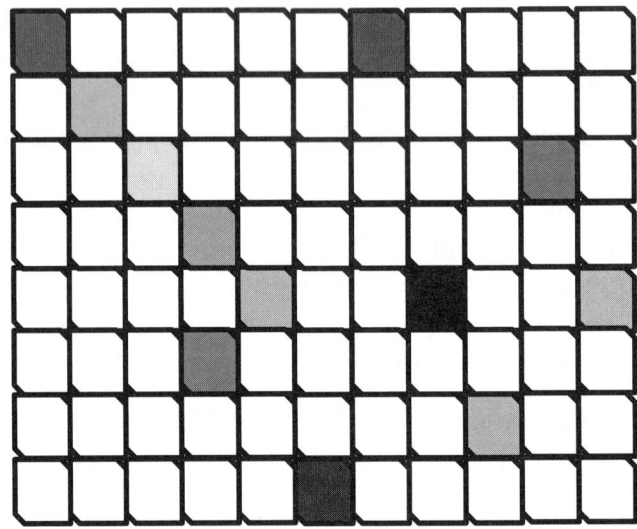

Figure 14.6 Column family representation

need. On the other hand, column databases store each column separately, allowing for faster scans when only a few columns are involved.

These databases store data in columns, allowing users to access only the columns they want without wasting RAM on non-essential data. This database seeks to overcome the shortcomings of key-value and document stores; however, it is not recommended for newer teams or projects due to its complexity. Wide-column databases such as Apache HBase and Apache Cassandra are open-source options. Apache HBase is based on the

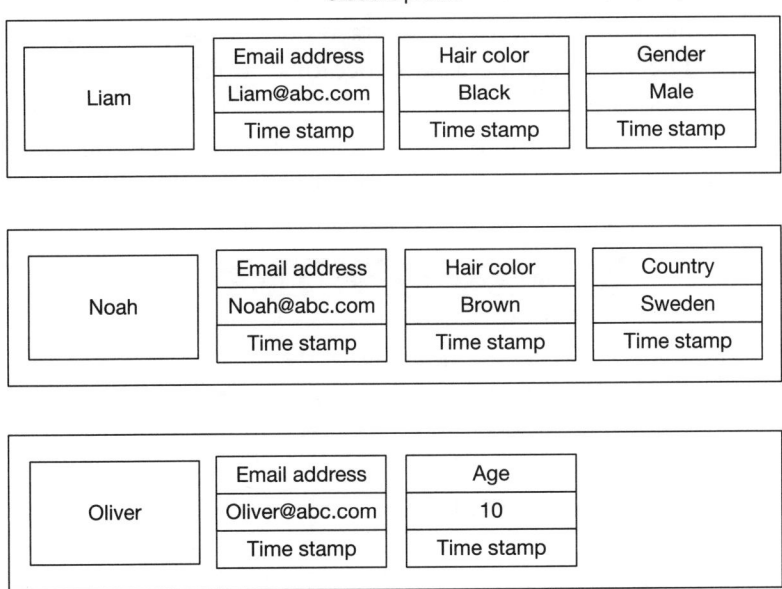

Figure 14.7 Column family: Example

Hadoop Distributed File System, which allows for the storage of sparse datasets prevalent in many Big Data applications. On the other hand, Apache Cassandra was built to handle enormous volumes of data across several servers and clusters over different data centers. As a result, it has been applied to many applications, including social networking sites and real-time data analytics.

14.4.2 Key-Value Pair Database

Key-value pairs (Key-value store): Key-value pair database (Fig. 14.8) is one of the most straightforward NoSQL data stores to use from an Application Programming Interface (API) perspective. Examples of key-value databases are Riak, Redis, Berkley DB, Amazon DynamoDB, and Couchbase. The simplest of the NoSQL databases are key-value stores. As the name implies, they are a collection of key-value pairs, and their simplicity makes them the most scalable of the NoSQL database types capable of holding massive quantities of data.

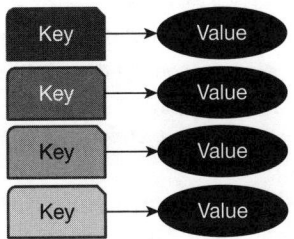

Figure 14.8 Key-Value representation

This is commonly thought of as the most basic sort of NoSQL database. Each item has a key and a value in this schema-free data model, which is set up as a dictionary of key-value pairs. The value can be a sequence of data representing each item on the user's shopping cart, and the key can be the same as the shopping card ID from the SQL database (Fig. 14.9). It is frequently used to save and store user session data like shopping cards. It is not optimum to extract numerous records at once, even if you need to do so. Open-source key-value databases include Redis and Memcached.

Key	Value
Customer 1	Liam
Customer 2	Noha
Order 1	Liam, Tshirt, Black, XL, $100
Order 2	Noha, Jeans, L, $200

Figure 14.9 Key-Value example

14.4.3 Document Store

Documents are the central concept in document databases. It stores the data in JSON-like documents having key-value pairs. As the name implies, the document stores and organizes data in a document (Fig. 14.10). Tables, rows, and columns are not present. Instead, a single document contains all the information on a single entity or aggregate unit. As a result, we obtain all the information when we query for that item, preferably without the need for numerous references or joins.

Table

Roll_Number	Student_Name	Age	Weight_Kg	CGPA
1001	Liam	11	35	4
1002	Noah	11	37	3
1003	Oliver	10	38	4.1

Document 1
"Roll_Number": "1001"
"Student_Name": "Liam"
"Age": "11"
"Weight_Kg": "35"
"CGPA": "4"

Document 2
"Roll_Number": "1002"
"Student_FullName": "Noah James"
"Age": "11"
"Weight_Kg": "37"
"CGPA": "3"

Document 3
"Roll_Number": "1003"
"Student_First_Name": "Oliver"
"Student_last_Name": "Lehman"
"Age": "10"
"Weight_Kg": "38"
"CGPA": "4.1"

Figure 14.10 Document store example

Document databases contain data in documents, as the name indicates. As a result, they can frequently assist in managing semi-configured data in JSON, XML, or BSON forms.

When used in apps, it maintains data together, reducing the amount of translation necessary. Data formats that provide developers more freedom (e.g., name and first name) do not have to match across documents. However, this might be problematic for complicated transactions, resulting in data corruption. Document databases (Fig. 14.11) are commonly used in content management systems and user profiles. MongoDB, the MEAN stack's database component, is an example of a document-oriented database.

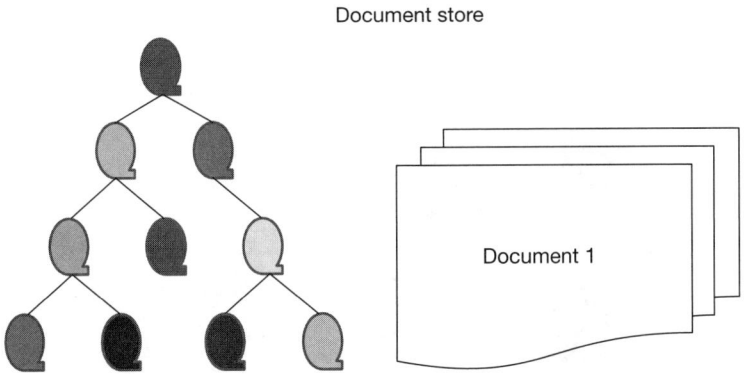

Figure 14.11   Document store representation

For example, MongoDB is a document database that stores data as a hierarchy of key-value pairs, allowing branching at different levels (a maximum of three levels). Some popular document databases are MongoDB, CouchDB, Terrastore, OrientDB, RavenDB, and Lotus Notes that use document storage.

Document databases such as MongoDB provide a rich query language, and constructs such as database and indexes allow for an easier transition from relational databases. Also, MongoDB stores data in JSON-like .BSON files having the structure of the document as given below:

```
{
"First_name": "Rakesh",
"Middle_name": "Kumar",
"Last_name": "Gaikwad",
"Age": 40,
"Address: "{
        "Street": "Gandhi Colony",
        "City": "Solapur"
    },
}
```

14.4.4 Graph Database

These databases store entities and relationships between these entities. Entities are also known as nodes with properties, and relations are known as edges that can have properties. Many graph databases such as Neo4J, Infinite Graph, OrientDB, or FlockDB are examples. This database type is designed to store relationships between entities efficiently.

Graph databases (Fig. 14.12) are the solution for densely interconnected data, such as social networks, scientific publication citations, or capital asset clusters. This type of database is commonly used to store data from a knowledge graph. Data components are stored using nodes (vertices), edges, and attributes (properties).

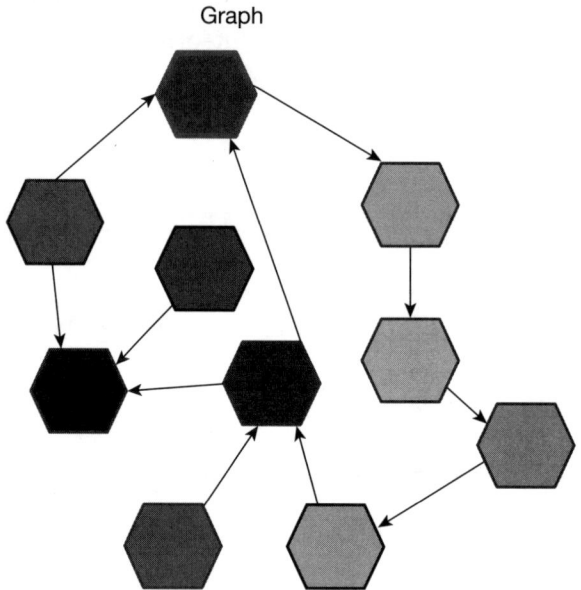

Figure 14.12 Graph store representation

A node can be anything, including a person or location. An edge defines the connection between nodes. For example, a client like IBM or an agency like Ogilvy may be a node (Fig. 14.13). Therefore, the alliance of IBM and Ogilvy can be classified as a customer relationship, which gives them a competitive advantage. The entities themselves are referred to as nodes. This might also be a person in a social network. The relationship between two entities is referred to as an edge. A line symbolizes this connection, and it has its own set of features. Given enough relation and entity types, graphs can grow quite complicated.

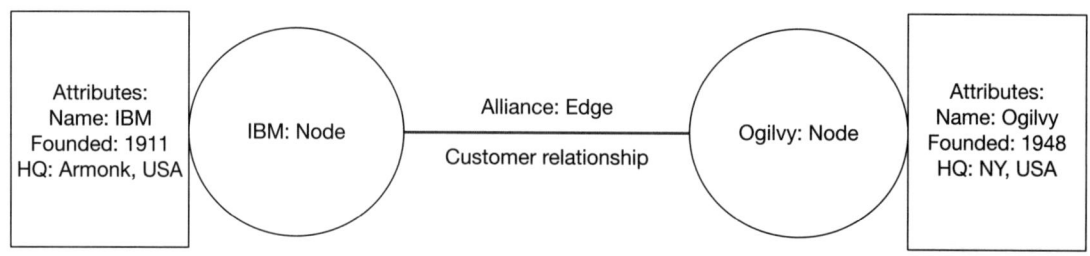

Figure 14.13 Graph store example

The network of connections between the members of a graph is stored and managed using graph databases. Neo4j (link outside IBM) is a Java-based graph-based database service that comes in two flavors: an open-source community edition with online backup and high availability extensions and a pre-packaged licensed version with backup and extensions.

Data is stored in the main memory (*in-memory store*) rather than on the disc in this form of database (such as IBM solid DB), making data access quicker than traditional disk-based databases.

14.5 Examples of NoSQL Databases

Many businesses have joined the NoSQL market (Table 14.1). There are several popular NoSQL databases: Apache CouchDB is an open-source JSON document-based database that uses JavaScript as its query language. Elasticsearch is a document-based database built into the full-text search engine. Finally, Couchbase is a key-value and document database that allows developers to create a cloud, mobile, and edge computing applications that are responsive and adaptable.

Table 14.1 NoSQL examples

Key Value Store	Document Databases	Column Databases	Graph Databases
Redis	MongoDB	HBase	Neo4J
Riak	ChuchDB	Cassandra	Infinite Graph
SimpleDB	Elastic Search	DynamoDB	Orient DB
CouchBase	Terrastore, OrientDB, RavenDB, and Lotus Notes	BigTable	Flock DB

14.6 Advantages of NoSQL Databases

Data replication is one of NoSQL's capabilities. Essentially, it mirrors data to other nodes in the cluster. Replication can be random or targeted to maximize data protection, such as placing a node in a different data center. The partitioning policy is another feature of NoSQL. The partitioning policy determines where the key is placed on each node. This can also be done at random or in order. NoSQL can strike a balance between load balancing and query performance optimization when using both types of partitioning policies.

Despite significant advancements in the RDBMS domain over the years, relational databases rely on database administrators, also known as DBAs. On the other hand, NoSQL databases are typically built from the ground-up, to eliminate unnecessary management, automate repair data distribution, and simplify data models, resulting in lower administration and performance requirements.

Over the last decade, transaction rates have increased rapidly, as have the volumes of data that must be stored, leading to "Big Data", as well as the "data industrial revolution".

As a result, RDBMS capacity grew to meet the demands of the new data volumes, but, as with transaction rates, there is a practical limit to how much data volume can be managed by a single RDBMS. So instead, many people are turning to NoSQL systems like Hadoop to handle their Big Data volumes, as these outperform the capabilities of the most popular RDBMS.

NoSQL databases are frequently more scalable and, at the same time, provide superior performance when compared to relational databases. Furthermore, when compared to the relational model, the flexibility and ease of use of their data models can speed development, particularly in the cloud computing environment. NoSQL databases were developed during the Internet and cloud computing eras when it was easier to implement a scale-out architecture. Scalability is achieved in a scale-out architecture by distributing data storage and processing work across a large cluster of computers. This scale-out architecture is especially easy to implement in cloud computing environments, where new computers and storage can be added to a cluster with relative ease. When data volume or traffic increases, the scale-out architecture of NoSQL systems provides a clear path to scalability. Achieving the same level of scalability with SQL databases can be costly, time-consuming, or impossible.

NoSQL databases are intended to manage the ever-increasing transaction and data volumes by utilizing low-cost commodity server clusters. On the other hand, RDBMSs necessitate expensive storage systems and patented servers, resulting in a higher cost per volume of data stored. This means that you can store and process a greater volume of data at a much lower cost.

The adoption of NoSQL databases has been primarily driven by developers who find it easier to create various applications with NoSQL databases than with relational databases. Furthermore, NoSQL databases store data in forms similar to the types of data objects used in applications, requiring fewer transformations when moving data in and out of the databases.

Data in native formats can be stored in NoSQL databases, which eliminates the need for developers to adapt the data to the store. In addition, storing data "as is" eliminates the need for a front-end ETL system to convert semi-structured data into the row-and-column formats. It also ensures that fewer applications need to be developed or purchased to launch a new database.

A large developer community supports most NoSQL databases. This means that there is a tool ecosystem and a community of other developers to connect with. NoSQL databases support widely used data formats, such as text data, JSON file format, simple binary values, sparse data, and graph database. Text data and time series data are both examples of Big Data that has the ability to deal with change throughout time. The capacity to manage unstructured text significantly increases the quantity of data accessible and can help businesses make better decisions. JSON files are nested human-readable files made up of name and value pairs. This format can store extremely complex parent-child hierarchical structures in document databases. Simple binary values, lists, maps, and strings can be processed quickly in key-value stores. Sparse data can be stored efficiently in columnar databases, where null values take up no space. They are also helpful for storing not-frequently changing data (nonvolatile data). Graph databases can store networks of related information.

RDBMSs, particularly large ones, are a nightmare when it comes to change management. Even minor changes must be monitored closely because it may result in downtime or reduced service levels. Furthermore, NoSQL databases frequently allow developers to directly change the data structure. To begin with, document databases do not have a fixed data structure. As a result, a new document type can be stored in the same way that the current one. New values and columns can be added to key-value and column-oriented stores without disrupting the current structure. In response to new data types, graph database developers add nodes with new properties and arcs with new meanings. Changes to applications or database schema, for example, do not have to be managed as a single change unit, making the process much simpler.

Rather than requiring a relational model within the underlying database, NoSQL databases allow access languages that may comprehend the stored data. As a result, NoSQL databases can accommodate many data architectures.

As more customer interactions occur online through Web and mobile apps, availability becomes a major, if not primary, concern. These mission-critical applications must be accessible 24 hours a day, seven days a week, with no exceptions. Relational databases deployed on a single physical server or those that rely on clustering with shared storage, face a challenge in providing 24×7 availability. The database becomes unavailable if deployed as a single server and fails; or as a cluster, and the shared storage fails. In contrast to relational technology, a distributed NoSQL database partitions and distributes data to multiple database instances with no shared resources.

Furthermore, for high availability, the data can be replicated to one or more instances (inter-cluster replication). While relational databases such as Oracle require additional software for replication (e.g., Oracle Active Data Guard), NoSQL databases do not – it is built-in and automatic. Furthermore, automatic failover ensures that if one of the nodes fails, the database can continue to perform reads and writes by routing the requests to a different node.

14.7 NoSQL Usage

A NoSQL database is most commonly used for distributed data repositories with enormous storage requirements. However, NoSQL is also used in extensive data and real-time web apps.

Session Store: Using the relevant database to manage session data is difficult, especially in over-developed applications. In such cases, using a global session store that manages session information for each user who visits the site is the best approach. However, NoSQL is well-suited for storing large amounts of web application session data. Additionally, since session data is not structured, storing it as definitive documents instead of database entries is trivial.

User Profile Store: Keeping the user profile via Web and mobile applications enables online transactions, user preferences, authentication, and other features. Users of Web and mobile apps have increased dramatically in recent years. Because it is constrained to a single server, the relational database cannot properly manage such a vast number of user profile data. Scaling is cost-effective when using NoSQL since capacity may be readily expanded by adding a server.

Content and Metadata Store: Many businesses, such as publishing companies, need space to combine multiple learning tools into one site and store vast amounts of data, such as articles, digital material, and e-books. In addition, content-based applications receive more traffic, thus requiring a longer response time for their metadata. NoSQL allows for quick data access and storage of various products when creating content-based applications.

Mobile Applications: Because smartphone users are continually expanding, mobile applications are experiencing growth and volume issues. Using a NoSQL database, you may begin developing mobile applications at a modest scale. It is simple to scale up with NoSQL as users grow, which is more complicated with relational databases. In addition, because NoSQL databases store data without schema, application developers can update programs without requiring substantial changes to the database. Mobile app firms use NoSQL like Kobo and Playtika, which serve millions of customers globally.

Third-Party Data Aggregation: It is common for a company to require access to data produced by a third party. A consumer-packaged products company, for example, may want store sales data as well as shopper purchase history. NoSQL databases are helpful in such situations because they can handle massive volumes of data produced at high rates from numerous data sources.

Internet of Things: Today, billions of gadgets, including smartphones, tablets, household appliances, and systems deployed in hospitals, automobiles, and warehouses, are linked to the Internet. As a result, such gadgets create and develop a significant amount and variety of data. Relational databases, however, are incapable of storing such information. NoSQL enables enterprises to increase concurrent access to data from billions of linked devices and systems, store massive volumes of data, and fulfill performance requirements.

E-Commerce: E-commerce companies use NoSQL to store a massive volume of data and large amounts of requests from the user.

Social Gaming: Data-intensive apps such as social games can reach millions of users. Such an increase in the number of users and the volume of data necessitates deploying a database system that can store such data and be expanded to accommodate the increasing number of users. NoSQL is appropriate for such applications. Some mobile game businesses, like Electronic Arts, Zynga, and Tencent, have adopted NoSQL.

Ad Targeting: Displaying advertising or offers on the current web page is a money-making decision. Platforms collect behavioral and demographic details of users to select which set of people to target and which web page to display advertisements on. A NoSQL database allows ad agencies to track user details and deploy them rapidly, boosting the likelihood of clicks. Ad targeting firms use NoSQL like AOL, Mediamind, and PayPal.

14.8 SQL vs. NoSQL

Table 14.2 summarizes the main distinctions between SQL and NoSQL databases.

Table 14.2 SQL vs. NoSQL

	SQL Databases	NoSQL Databases
Model for data storage	Fixed-row and fixed-column tables	Documents in JSON format, Key-value pairs are key-value pairs. Tables with rows and dynamic columns that are wide-column. Nodes and edges in a graph
History of development	It was created in the 1970s to avoid data duplication.	Developed in the late 2000s, focuses on scale and quick application, change enabled by agile and DevOps approaches.
Examples	Oracle, MySQL, Microsoft SQL Server, and PostgreSQL	Document: MongoDB and CouchDB, Key-value: Redis and DynamoDB, Wide-column: Cassandra and HBase, Graph: Neo4j and Amazon Neptune
Primary purpose	General-purpose	General-purpose document. Key-value: vast volumes of data may be accessed using simple lookup queries. Wide-column: vast volumes of data with predictable query patterns. Graph: the analysis and traversal of relationships between corresponding data.
Schemas	Rigid	Flexible
Scaling	Vertical (scale-up with a larger server)	Horizontal (scale-out across commodity servers)
Multi-record ACID Transactions	Supported	The majority of them do not allow multi-record ACID transactions. However, some, such as MongoDB, do.
Joins	Usually, necessary	Typically, this is not necessary.
Data-to-object mapping	ORM is required (object-relational mapping)	Many applications do not necessitate ORMs. On the other hand, MongoDB documents map directly to data structures in most popular programming languages.

14.9 NewSQL

NewSQL is a database language that combines and expands on Structured Query Language (SQL) and NoSQL concepts and principles. It is "a DBMS that provides the scalability and flexibility promised by NoSQL while still supporting SQL queries and/or ACID, or that which improves performance for appropriate workloads".

NuoDB is a distributed database designed with SQL service that has all the properties of ACID transactions, standard SQL language support, and relational logic. It is one example of a NewSQL database. NuoDB is a web-scale distributed database that provides a rich SQL implementation and confirmed ACID transactions. It is a distributed system that scales up according to cloud service requirement, ensuring high availability and resilience. Unlike traditional shared-disk or shared-nothing architectures, NuoDB provides a new type of peer-to-peer, on-demand independence that results in high availability, low latency, and an easy-to-manage deployment model. ClustrixDB's massively parallel processing enables real-time analytics on your live operational data. VoltDB is a lightning-fast in-memory database with insanely fast read and write speeds. This NewSQL database supports JSON and event-level transactions. Xeround solution by Crunchbase provides elastic cloud computing infrastructure that is scalable for elastic data management and data federation within and across clouds. MemSQL is a real-time analytics platform that enables businesses to quickly query large amounts of data and adapt to changing business conditions.

14.10 ACID

The ACID properties (Fig. 14.14) are a collection of standards that transactions must follow. The abbreviation ACID stands for Atomicity, Consistency, Isolation, and Durability, four interdependent qualities. These principles underpin most of any current relational database system.

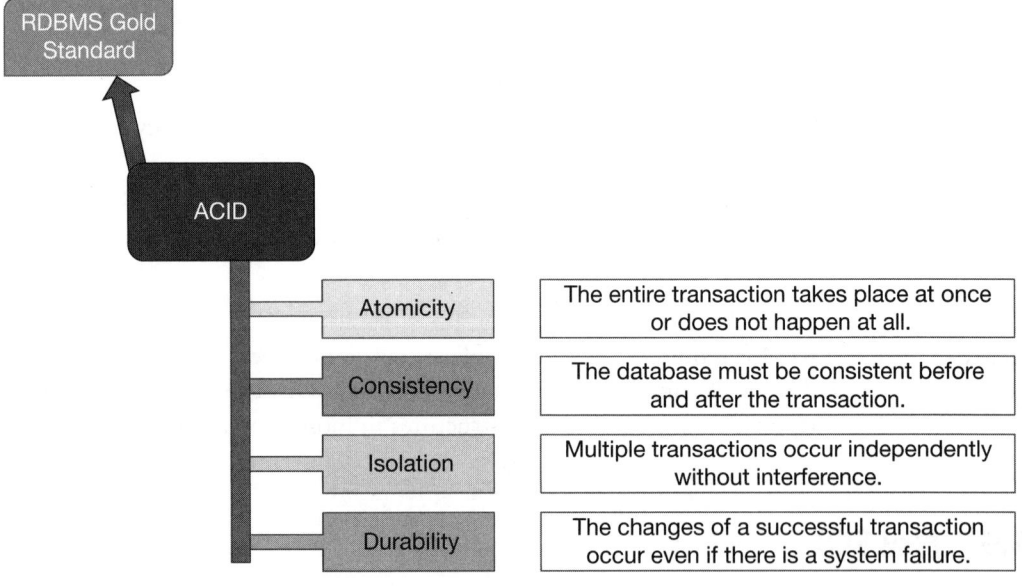

Figure 14.14 ACID properties

14.10.1 Atomicity

A transaction must be Atomic, which means that all changes made by it must be performed as a single unit, or it will not be performed at all (Fig. 14.15). The atomic property is violated if a partial transaction is committed and the database is left in an inconsistent state. As a result, atomicity requires the capacity to commit or rollback transactions. *Atomic* means "all or nothing". When a statement is executed, every transaction must be successful for it to be considered successful. When one update succeeds and another fails, it will not be considered because there is no such thing as a partial success or partial failure.

An excellent example of this is money transfer at an ATM: Transfer involves taking money from one account (Account A) and depositing it in another (Account B). This procedure cannot be divided into two parts. Both (credit and debit) must be successful at the same time to call the overall transaction successful. Or, if it fails, both (credit and debit) must fail simultaneously.

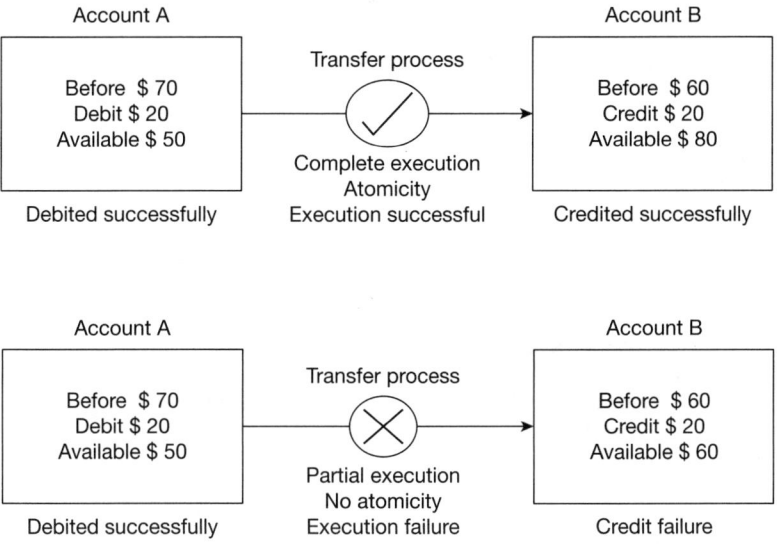

Figure 14.15 ACID properties: Atomicity

14.10.2 Consistency

The transaction must maintain database Consistency (Fig. 14.16), which implies that the database must start the transaction in a state of Consistency and end the transaction in a state of Consistency. *Consistent* data indicates that it travels from one legitimate state to another without having different values.

For example, if a transaction tries to remove a customer and her order history, it cannot leave the order rows that reference the deleted customer's primary key; this is an unpredictable condition that would result in problems if someone tried to read the order records. The below example (Fig. 14.17) indicates another example of Consistency while reading records.

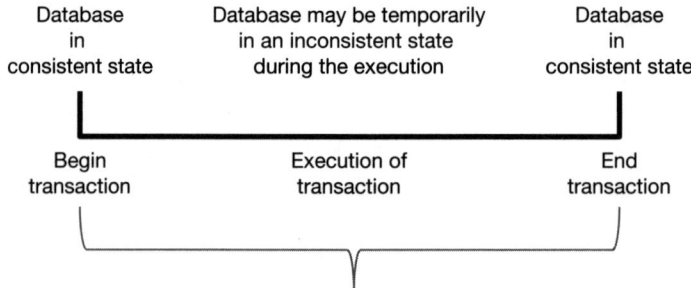

Figure 14.16 ACID properties: Consistent state

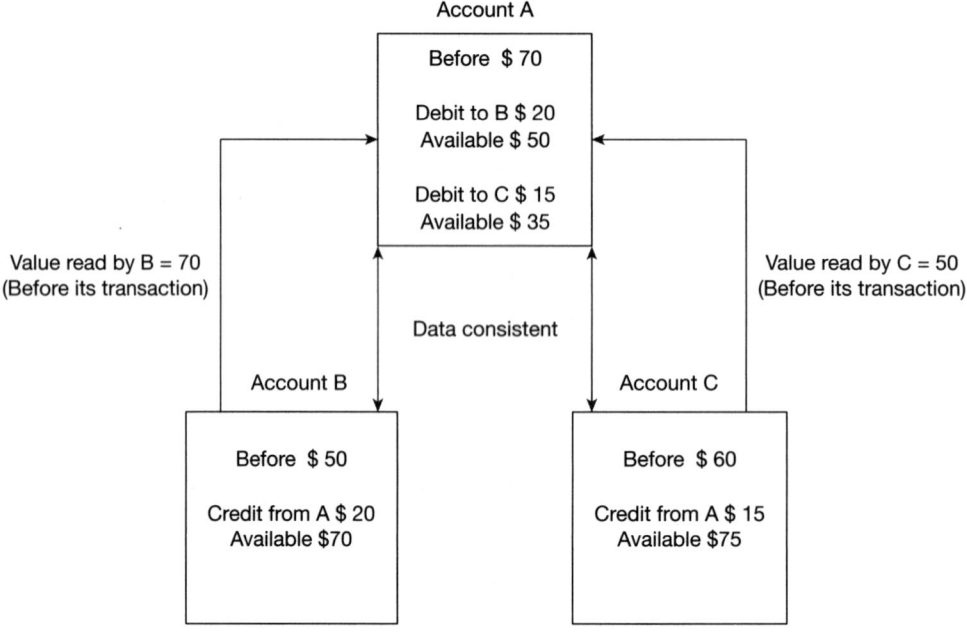

Figure 14.17 ACID properties: Consistency

14.10.3 Isolation

Isolated transactions are called "serializable" because they do not occur all at once. *Isolated* means that concurrently running transactions will not become entangled; they will each run in their area (independently). If two transactions attempt to change the same data simultaneously, one of them must wait for the other to complete its transaction.

Each transaction is ranked globally to ensure that all the previous transactions are completed before the next transaction begins (Fig. 14.18). This does not mean that two operations cannot take place at the same time. Multiple transactions are permitted as long as none of them can affect the other transactions simultaneously.

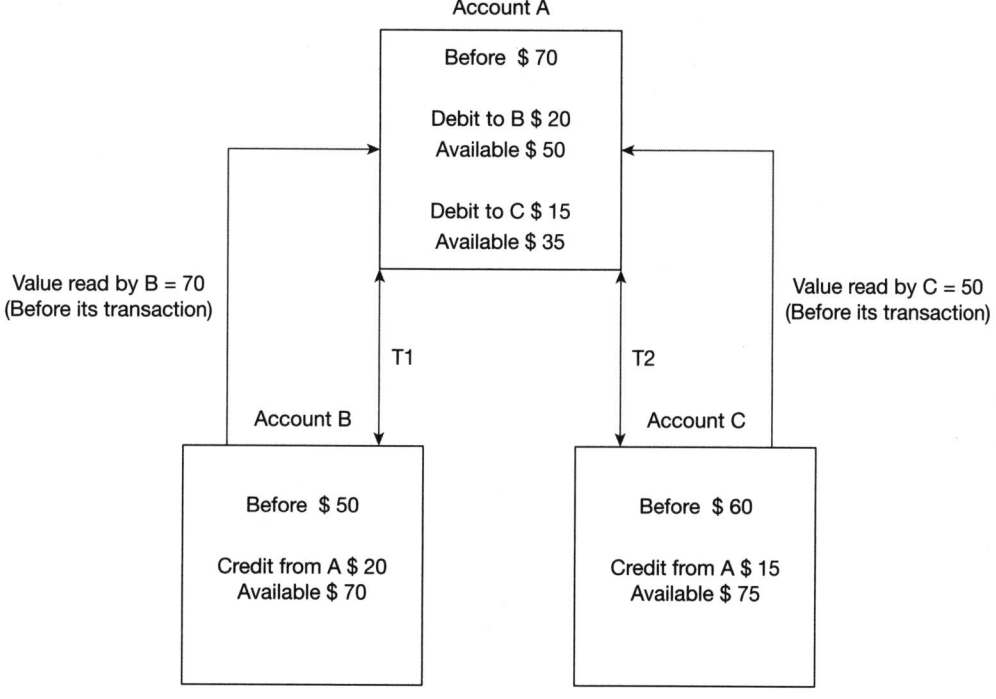

Figure 14.18 ACID properties: Independent state

14.10.4 Durability

Durability is the final component of the ACID method. Even if the system fails, durability ensures that appropriately committed database changes (transactions) are retained permanently. *Durable* changes made after the transaction will not be lost.

On the surface, these qualities appear to be so appealing that they don't seem deserving of discussion. For example, no one running a database would presumably advise that data changes don't have to last a long time; after all, the point of making updates is that they are there for others to read. But, on the other hand, an in-depth investigation may cause us to wish to find a means to fine-tune and regulate these qualities. This guarantees that the database's data is not tampered with by:

- Service interruptions
- Crashes
- Other sources of failure.

It is a common misconception that NoSQL databases do not handle ACID transactions, putting Consistency at risk. This is a rather broad simplification. It is true, in general, that aggregate-oriented. ACID transactions that span many aggregates do not exist in databases. Instead, they allow for one-at-a-time atomic manipulation of a single total.

Of course, if we need to atomically alter many aggregates, we will have to do it ourselves in the application code. However, in reality, we find that we can usually keep our Atomicity requirements inside a single aggregate; in fact, this is one of the factors we examine when selecting how to partition our data into aggregates.

Transactions become more complicated when there is a lot of traffic. When a relational database is horizontally scaled, it becomes distributed, and transactions are disseminated over numerous systems rather than within a single table or database. The transaction manager must coordinate among the different nodes to maintain the ACID features of transactions.

14.11 BASE

With the emergence of NoSQL databases, data manipulation became more flexible and fluid. As a result, a new database model matching these attributes was created.

The BASE is a little more difficult to remember than ACID. But, on the other hand, the words underlying it hints at how the BASE model differs. The BASE (Fig. 14.19) stands for:

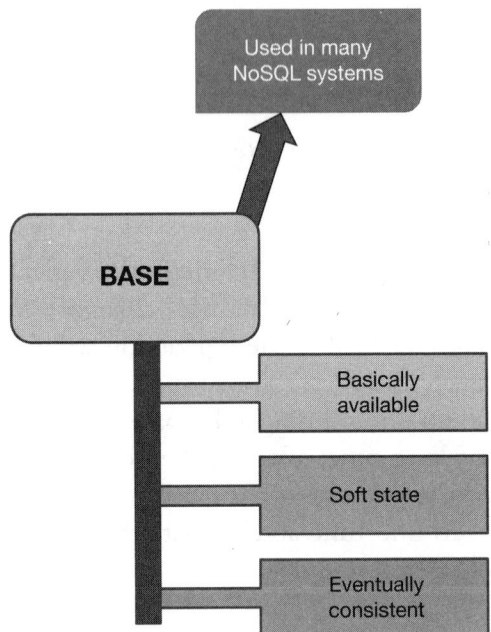

Figure 14.19 BASE properties

Basically Available This constraint states that the system guarantees the availability of the data in terms of the CAP Theorem; any request will be responded to. However, that response could still be 'failure' to obtain the requested data, or the data could be inconsistent or changing, similar to waiting for a cheque to clear in your bank account.

In contrast to relational technology, a distributed NoSQL database partitions and distributes data to multiple database instances with no shared resources. Furthermore, for high availability, the data can be replicated to one or more instances (inter-cluster replication). While relational databases such as Oracle require additional software for replication (e.g., Oracle Active Data Guard), NoSQL databases do not – it is built-in and automatic. Furthermore, automatic failover ensures that if one of the nodes fails, the database can continue to perform reads and writes by routing the requests to a different node.

Soft State Data values may fluctuate over time due to a lack of immediate Consistency. The system's state may change over time; so changes may occur due to 'eventual consistency even when there is no input'. Hence, the system's state is always 'soft'. As a result, the BASE model abandons the idea of a database that ensures sustainability and instead assigns that responsibility to developers.

Eventually Consistent Just because the BASE does not implement instant Consistency, it does not mean that Consistency will not be achieved in the end. When the system no longer receives input, it will eventually become consistent. The data will eventually reach its destination, but the system will accept input. However, it will not check the Consistency of each transaction before moving on to the next one. Google's Bigtable, Amazon's Dynamo, and Facebook's Cassandra are a few examples of large-scale distributed data systems that deal with the loss of Consistency while maintaining system reliability.

14.12 Two-phase Commit

The concept of a two-phase commit (often known as "2PC") is introduced to account for the successful completion of transactions involving many hosts (servers). However, because a two-phase commit locks all associated resources, it is only appropriate for activities that can be completed in a short period. A two-phase commit is a predefined protocol that ensures that a database commit is applied when a commit operation must be split into two parts (Prepare, Commit). In database management, saving data changes is referred to as committing, and undoing changes is referred to as rolling back. The process can become more difficult when the data is spread across geographically diverse servers in distributed computing (i.e., each server is an independent entity with separate log records).

A consensus method lies at the heart of any distributed system. A coordinator is required for this protocol (consensus method). The client first contacts the coordinator. In two phases, the coordinator strives to reach an agreement among a group of processes (also known as Participants), thus the name (Two-phase Commit).

A coordinator (typically the process that started the commit) receives approval or rejection to commit the data modifications of interested processes in the first phase of the protocol, known as the "commit-request phase" or the "voting phase". After that, the coordinator will only commit if the participants/subscribers agree. Otherwise, it will abort the process.

The coordinator tells the outcome participants (a commit phase). Then, the entire transaction is rolled back, all sub-transactions are completed, and the momentarily locked resources are freed, depending on the outcome.

The coordinator and the participants exchange the following messages during the two phases:

14.12.1 Commit–request Phase

This phase is also called the pre-commit phase, prepare phase or voting phase. The coordinator sends a query to all participants (Fig. 14.20), asking them to commit a message, and then waits for their responses.

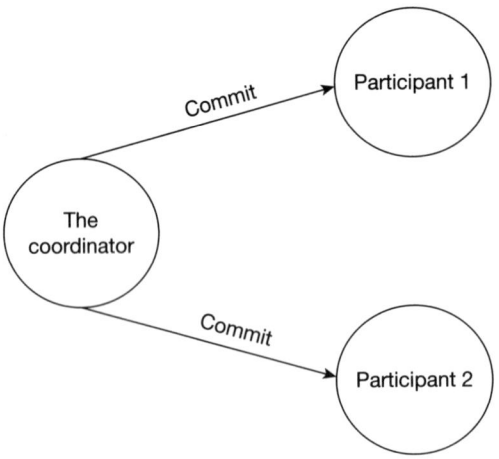

Figure 14.20 Two-phase commit (Commit-request phase: Step 1)

The participants process the transaction, who either commit it or roll it back. Finally, they record their actions in an undo and redo log. If the transaction was successful, participants react to the coordinator with "ready". If the transaction is unsuccessful, they answer with "failed" (Fig. 14.21).

Commit Phase (Post-decision Phase)

If all participants submit "ready" messages to the coordinator, they commit to them (Fig. 14.22).

Participants can finish the transaction and release all locks and resources with a commit. Participants then respond with an acknowledgment (Fig. 14.23). If all parties acknowledge the transaction, the coordinator declares it complete.

In case one of the participants responds with a "failed" message (Fig. 14.24):

- Abort is sent to all participants by the coordinator.
- Participants roll back the transaction (using the undo log) and release all locks and resources at the end.
- The coordinator receives an acknowledgment from the participants.
- After acknowledging all participants, the coordinator will roll back the transaction.

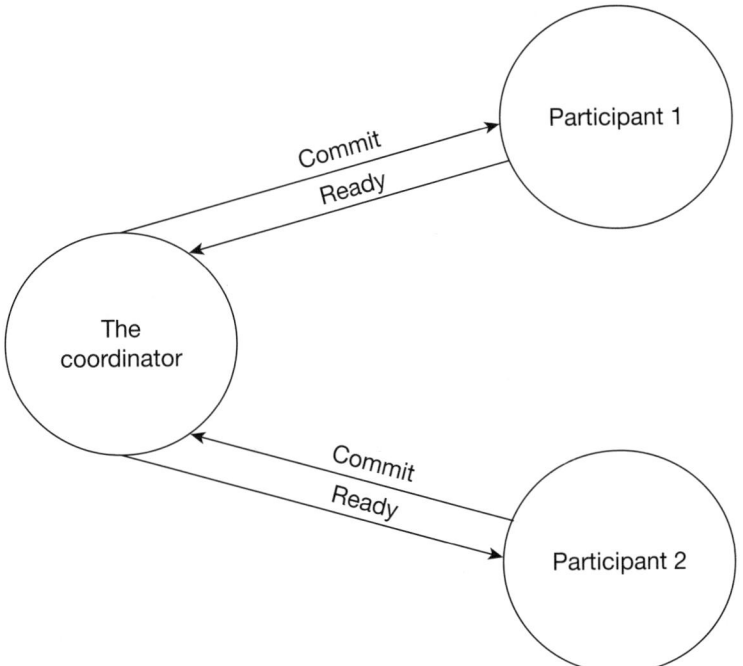

Figure 14.21 Two-phase commit (Commit-request phase: Step 2)

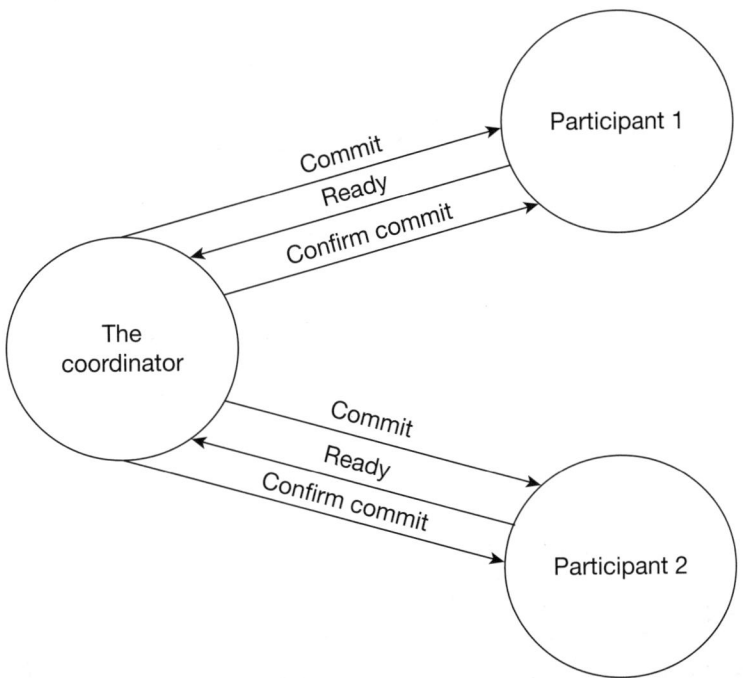

Figure 14.22 Two-phase commit (Commit phase: Step 1)

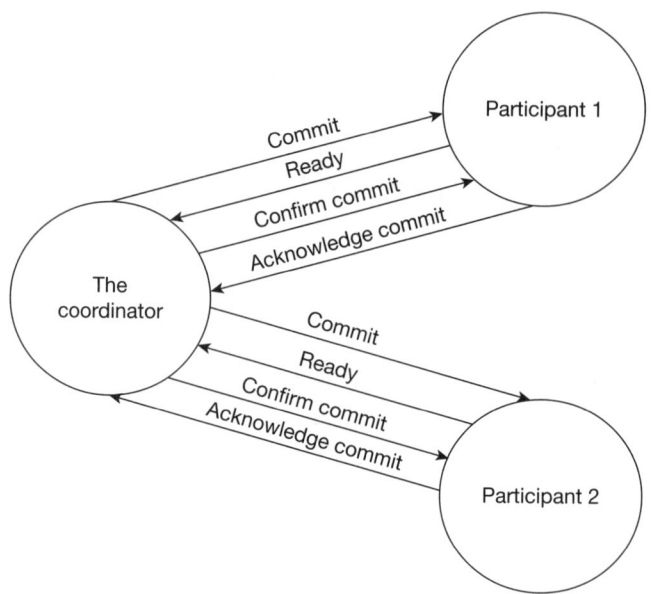

Figure 14.23   Two-phase commit (Commit phase: Step 2)

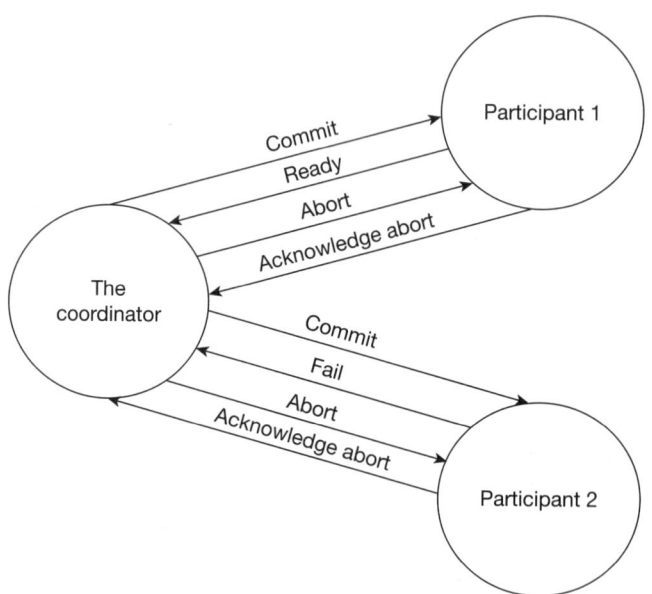

Figure 14.24   Two-phase commit (Commit failure)

14.13   Schema

Schema means the logical structure of data. Creating sophisticated schemas is one of relational database systems' most acclaimed features. A relational model can be used to represent domain objects. To help this endeavor, the database industry has developed expensive tools like the CA Erwin Data Modeler.

A schema for a university database, for example, would call for a Student table and a Course table. However, a join table must be built because of the "many-to-many" relationship (one student can attend several courses simultaneously, and one course can have multiple students), which pushes us to write more complicated SQL queries to connect these tables. In turn, join statements might be slow. Again, in a small system, this is not a significant issue. However, when you have a lot of entries in many tables, sophisticated queries and several joins may slow down the system.

Finally, not all schemas fit the relational model well. For example, a system that has gained popularity in the last decade is the complex event processing system, which expresses state changes in a high-speed stream. It is frequently beneficial to contextualize events during the run against other related events to predict specific outcomes and improve business decision-making. Although event streams can be described in terms of relevant database terms, this is an extension.

An application developer should be acquainted with the various object-relational mapping (ORM) frameworks that have emerged in recent years to assist in the challenging task of mapping application objects to a relevant model.

It does, however, present other issues, such as increased memory needs, and it frequently contaminates application code with more bulky mapping code. Here is an example of a Java function that uses Hibernate to "lighten the load" of writing SQL code:

```
@CollectionOfElements
@JoinTable(name="store_description",
   joinColumns = @JoinColumn(name="store_code"))
@MapKey(columns={@Column(name="for_store",length=3)})
@Column(name="description")
private Map getMap() {
   returnthis.map;
   } //... etc.
```

With some systems such as those that make extensive document exchange, such as services or XML-based applications, there may not always be direct mapping to the associated database. This makes the problem worse.

14.13.1 Sharding and Share Nothing Architecture

Sharding is a mechanism for distributing data over numerous workstations to simulate a program accessing a single database. As implemented by MongoDB, sharding is ideal for the new generation of cloud-based computing platforms since it allows for dynamic, load-sensitive automated scaling, where capacity is used only when needed and turned down when not.

14.13.2 Partitioning Horizontal and Vertical Data

The data partitioning mechanism separates data over numerous separate data stores. These datastores might be local (on the same system) or remote (on separate systems).

Co-resident partitioning is a technique for reducing the size of individual indices and the amount of I/O needed to update data. In addition, remote partitioning aims to increase bandwidth access by utilizing extra network ports and disc data I/O channels.

Partitioning Data Vertically

Vertical partitioning: It is the process of splitting a record along column boundaries (Fig. 14.25) and storing the pieces in different tables or collections. It might be argued that using joined tables with a one-to-one connection in a relational database architecture is a type of co-resident vertical data partitioning.

Original table

Roll_Number	Student_Name	Age	Weight_Kg	CGPA
1001	Liam	11	35	4
1002	Noah	11	37	3
1003	Oliver	10	38	4.1
1004	Elijah	10	39	3.1
1005	Olivia	11	35	3.3
1006	Charlotte	11	37	3.7
1007	Ava	10	36	3.65

Vertical partitions

VP1

Roll_Number	Student_Name	Age
1001	Liam	11
1002	Noah	11
1003	Oliver	10
1004	Elijah	10
1005	Olivia	11
1006	Charlotte	11
1007	Ava	10

VP2

Roll_Number	Weight_Kg	CGPA
1001	35	4
1002	37	3
1003	38	4.1
1004	39	3.1
1005	35	3.3
1006	37	3.7
1007	36	3.65

Figure 14.25 Vertical partition

On the other hand, MongoDB does not lend itself to this type of partitioning since its records (documents) do not fit into the tidy row-and-column model. As a result, properly separating a row-based on its column borders is difficult. MongoDB likewise encourages the usage of embedded documents, although it does not explicitly provide the ability to link together collections.

Partitioning Data Horizontally

In MongoDB, horizontal partitioning (Fig. 14.26) is where the action is, and sharding is a popular kind of horizontal partitioning. Sharding lets you partition a collection over different servers to increase performance in a large-document collection. For example, when a set of user records is split among several servers, this is an example of sharding.

Original table

Roll_Number	Student_Name	Age	Weight_Kg	CGPA
1001	Liam	11	35	4
1002	Noah	11	37	3
1003	Oliver	10	38	4.1
1004	Olivia	11	35	3.3
1005	Charlotte	11	37	3.7
1006	Ava	10	36	3.65

Horizontal partitions

HP1

Roll_Number	Student_Name	Age	Weight_Kg	CGPA
1001	Liam	11	35	4
1002	Noah	11	37	3
1003	Oliver	10	38	4.1

HP2

Roll_Number	Student_Name	Age	Weight_Kg	CGPA
1004	Olivia	11	35	3.3
1005	Charlotte	11	37	3.7
1006	Ava	10	36	3.65

Figure 14.26 Horizontal partition

For example, all records for persons whose roll numbers are lesser than or equal to 1003 are stored on one server (HP1), while others are stored on another (HP2). The sharding key function, also known as the data hashing function, is the rule that separates the data. Simply said, sharding allows you to handle a cloud of shards as if it were a single collection, and an application does not need to be aware that the data is dispersed over different computers. Traditional sharding methods need the application to actively choose the server a specific document is kept on, to route its requests appropriately. Traditionally, an application is connected to a library responsible for storing and accessing data in sharded datasets.

Implementing Sharding with MongoDB

MongoDB (Fig. 14.27) employs a proxy method to facilitate sharding, and the supplied mongos daemon serves as a controller for many MongoDB-based shard servers. The app first connects to the mongos daemon as if it were a single MongoDB database server and then delivers all of its commands (such as updates, queries, and deletes) to that mongos daemon.

Sharding and Shared-nothing Architecture

Introducing Sharding to the design is an approach to scale a relational database. Large websites such as eBay, which handles billions of SQL queries every day, and other Web 2.0 apps, have successfully implemented this. The notion is that instead of storing all of the data on a single server or duplicating all of the data across all the computers in a cluster, you split the data horizontally and host each chunk independently.

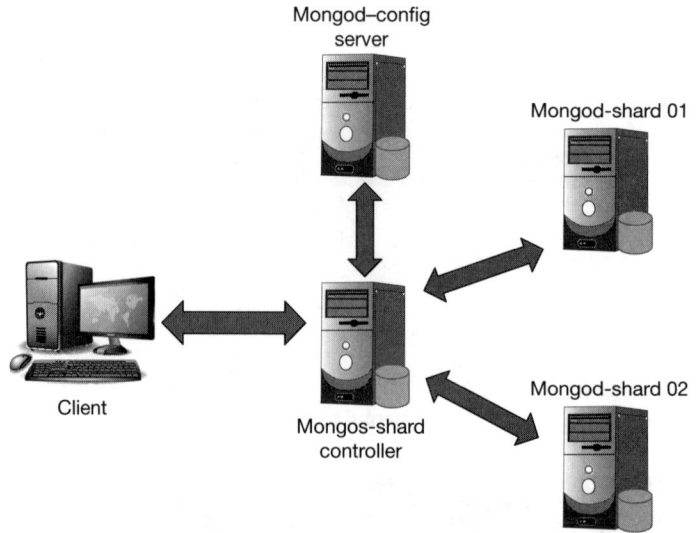

Figure 14.27 Sharding with MongoDB

Consider a vast customer table in a relational database, for example. Vertical scaling by adding CPU, memory, and faster hard drives is the least disruptive option (at least for the development team), but as the number of clients grows, the requirement for more computers grows. Do you simply duplicate the data to be available to all machines? Or do you split the single customer table into multiple databases, each with only a subset of the records and their order preserved? When clients run queries, they only load the computer that holds the record they are looking for, leaving the other machines unloaded. It appears that a good key must be discovered for the records to be shared in the correct order. For example, customers' records from 26 machines may be separated into one for each letter of the alphabet. Each hosting company only keeps a record of customers whose last names begin with the letter. However, this is unlikely to be a smart strategy: there aren't many last names that start with "Q" or "Z", so those computers will stay idle while the records on "J," "M," and "S" machines will rise. Therefore, you might share the computer based on a number, such as a customer's phone number, "member since" date, or the state name. Everything is dependent on how your data will most likely be disseminated.

14.13.3 Four Basic Strategies for Shard Structure

There are four basic strategies for determining shard structure:

Feature-based Shard or Functional Segmentation

Randy Shoup, a distinguished Architect at eBay, used this technique in 2006 when he assisted in the maturation of their architecture to serve billions of inquiries every day. The data is separated using this method not by separating records in a single table (as in the customer example outlined previously) but by splitting characteristics that don't overlap too much into distinct databases. At eBay, for example, users are in one shard while products for sale are in another (Fig. 14.28).

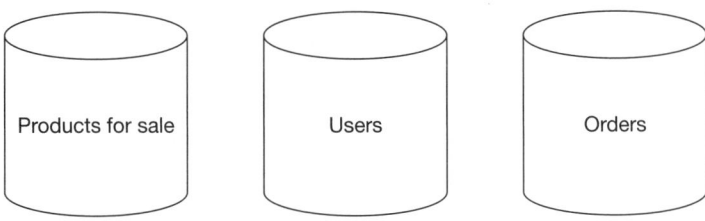

Figure 14.28 Feature-based shard

Likewise, Flixster keeps track of movie ratings in one place and comments in another. But, again, this strategy relies on a thorough grasp of your domain to segregate data cleanly.

Key-based Sharding

Using this method, you locate a key in your data that equally distributes it among shards (Fig. 14.29). Instead of keeping one letter of the alphabet for each server, as in the previous examples, a one-way hash on a critical data piece distributes data among computers based on the hash.

Figure 14.29 Key-based sharding

Key-based sharding, also known as hash-based sharding, entails taking a value from newly written data – such as a customer's ID number, roll number, or other identifiers – and then passing it through a hash function to determine which shard the data should be sent to. A hash function is a function that takes a piece of data (for example, a roll number) as input and returns a discrete value known as a hash value as output. When sharding is used, the hash value is a shard ID used to determine which shard the incoming data will be stored on.

Shard keys, like primary keys, are columns that are used to create a unique identifier for individual rows. A shard key, in general, should be static, which means it should not contain values that change over time. Otherwise, it would increase the work required for update operations, potentially slowing performance.

While key-based sharding is a common sharding architecture, it can be difficult to dynamically add or remove additional servers from a database. As you add servers, each server will require a corresponding hash value. Many, if not all, of your existing entries will need to be remapped to their new, correct hash value before being migrated to the appropriate server. When you start rebalancing the data, neither the new nor the old hashing functions will work. As a result, your server will not write new data during the migration, and your application may experience downtime.

Range-based Sharding

Using this method (Fig. 14.30), you locate a range of values in the data and distribute it among shards. As an example, suppose you have a database that stores student information. You could create a few different shards based on which CGPA range they fall into, like this:

Original table

Roll_Number	Student_Name	Age	Weight_Kg	CGPA
1001	Liam	11	35	4
1002	Noah	11	37	3
1003	Oliver	10	38	4.1
1004	Elijah	10	39	3.1
1005	Olivia	11	35	3.3
1006	Charlotte	11	37	3.7
1007	Ava	10	36	3.65

<3.5

Roll_Number	Student_Name	Age	Weight_Kg	CGPA
1002	Noah	11	37	3
1004	Elijah	10	39	3.1
1005	Olivia	11	35	3.3

3.5 to 4

Roll_Number	Student_Name	Age	Weight_Kg	CGPA
1001	Liam	11	35	4
1006	Charlotte	11	37	3.7
1007	Ava	10	36	3.65

>4

Roll_Number	Student_Name	Age	Weight_Kg	CGPA
1003	Oliver	10	38	4.1

Figure 14.30 Range-based sharding

The main advantage of range-based sharding is its ease of implementation. Each shard contains a unique set of data, but they all have the same schema and the original database. The application code reads the data range and writes it to the corresponding shard. On the other hand, range-based sharding does not protect data from being unevenly distributed, resulting in the database becoming unbalanced due to such uneven distribution. These unevenly distributed databases are called hotspots.

Lookup Table (Directory-based Sharding)

In this technique (Fig. 14.31), one of the cluster nodes acts as a "yellow pages" directory, determining which node holds the data that needs to be accessed. To implement directory-based sharding, a lookup table that uses a shard key to track which shard contains which

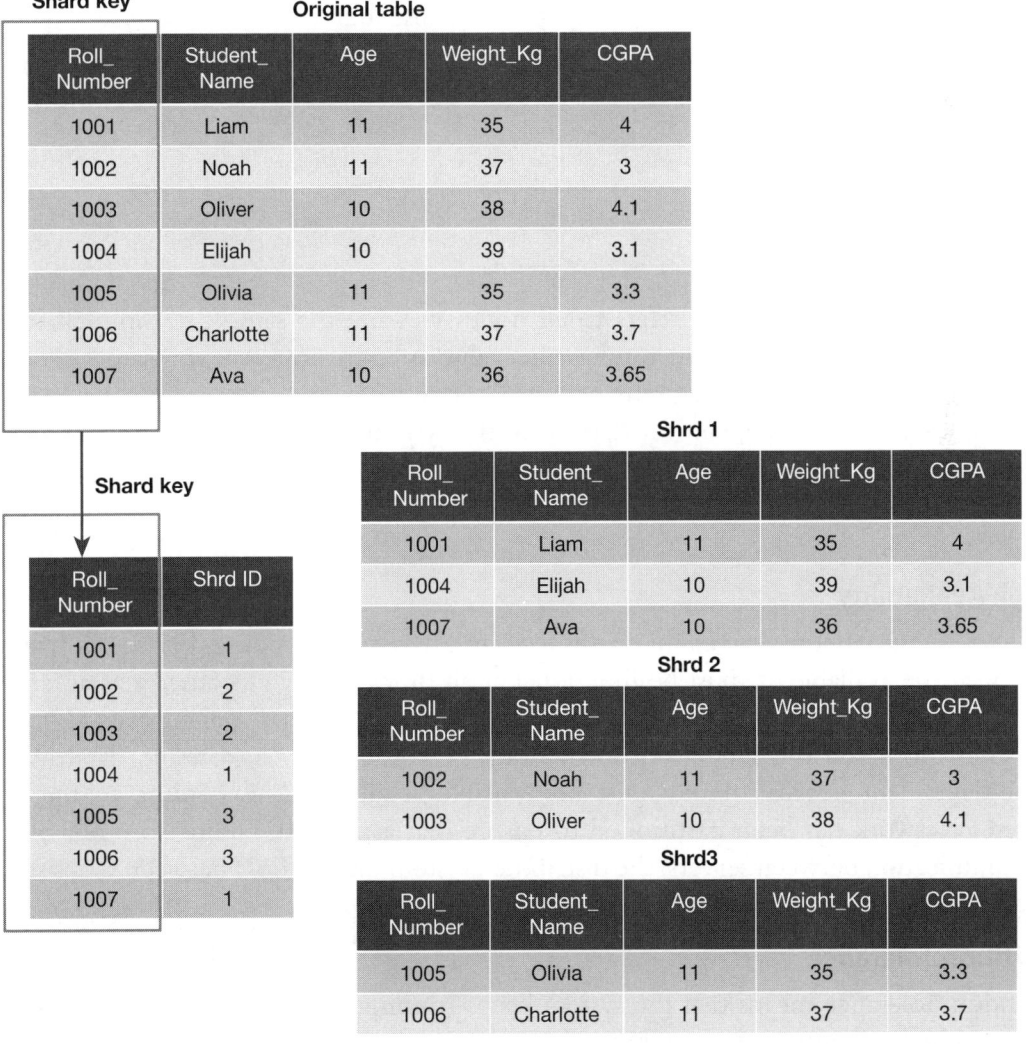

Figure 14.31 Lookup table-based sharding

data must be created and maintained. A lookup table is a table that stores a fixed set of information about where specific data can be found. However, there are two apparent drawbacks to this. The first is that the performance will suffer every time you travel through the lookup table as an additional hop. The second is that the lookup table becomes a single point-of-failure and a bottleneck.

The Roll Number column is designated as a shard key in this case. Data from the shard key is written to the lookup table and the Shard (ID) to which each row should be written. Each key is associated with a unique shard. It differs from key-based sharding in that it does not use a hash function to process the shard key; instead, it checks the key against a lookup table to determine where the data should be written.

14.14 Brewer's CAP Theorem

According to the CAP theorem (Fig. 14.32), a distributed computing system cannot simultaneously guarantee partition tolerance, consistency, and availability. A distributed computing system must choose two of the three options listed below:

- High consistency
- High availability
- Partition tolerance

Consistency

The term "high consistency" refers to all nodes viewing the same data simultaneously. In simple terms, a read action returns the value of the most recent write operation, resulting in identical data being returned by all nodes.

A transaction is consistent if it starts with the system in a consistent state and ends in a consistent state. In this paradigm, a system can be inconsistent throughout a transaction. However, if an error occurs at any point during the process, the entire transaction is rolled back.

High Availability

Every request, whether successful or unsuccessful, receives a response. For the distributed system to be available, it must be functional at all times. Every customer gets an answer regardless of the status of any one node in the system. This is a straightforward statistic for evaluation: you can send/read instructions, or you cannot. As a result, databases are time-dependent because nodes must be available at all times. According to the idea, when a network has been partitioned to ensure that a network failure does not disrupt communication between servers, the distributed system must choose between Consistency and Availability.

Partition Tolerance

Partition Tolerance means that the system keeps running despite the network delaying a large volume of communications between nodes. A partition-tolerant system can tolerate any network failure that does not affect the whole network. To guarantee that the system remains functioning during outages, data records are correctly copied across a range of nodes and networks. Partition Tolerance is not an option when working with current distributed systems. It is a must. As a result, we must choose between Consistency and Availability.

Figure 14.32 captures this:

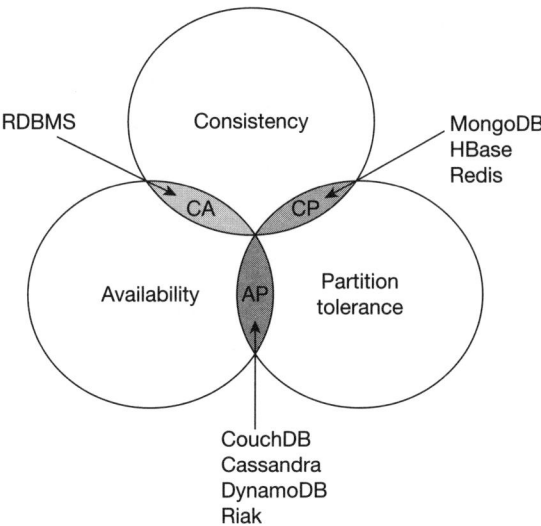

Figure 14.32 CAP Theorem

The CAP theorem has mostly helped **determine database servers' infrastructure and configuration priorities**. However, it is still feasible to attain both Consistency and Availability within acceptable bounds in such a setting. For example, when new writes propagate throughout the system, data may be inconsistent for short periods. Therefore, critical servers that handle client reads/writes may be partitioned so that failures in other areas have no impact on end-user performance.

In comparison to RDBMS transactions that adhere to the ACID (Atomicity, Consistency, Isolation, Durability) theorem, NoSQL DBMS adheres to the CAP (Consistency, Availability, Partition tolerance) theorem, and their transactions also adhere to the BASE principle (Fig. 14.33).

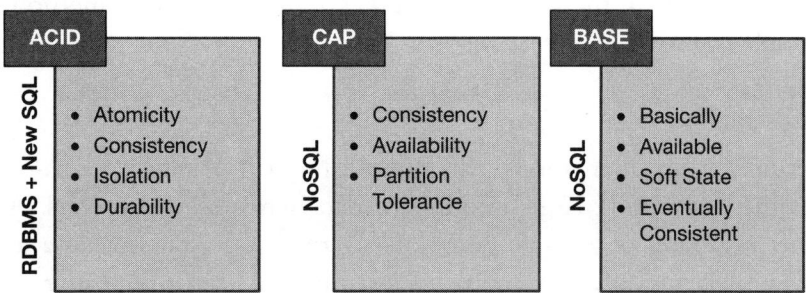

Figure 14.33 ACID vs. CAP vs. BASE

14.15 Cassandra – Definition and Features

14.15.1 Definition

"Apache Cassandra is an open-source, distributed, decentralized, elastically scalable, highly available, fault-tolerant, a tuneable consistent, column-oriented database that is based on Amazon's Dynamo and Google's Bigtable data model". It was developed at Facebook and is now used on some of the most popular websites on the Internet (Fig. 14.34).

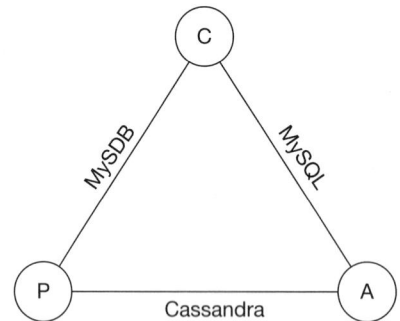

Figure 14.34 Cassandra in CAP

Cassandra is the most popular comprehensive column store database system. Cassandra was developed for Facebook's Inbox Search feature and was made open-source in 2008. On February 17, 2010, it was designated as an Apache top-level project. Its business characteristics, like scalability and high availability, make it perfect for managing enormous amounts of data and offering near-real-time analysis. In addition, Cassandra, which is developed in Java, offers both synchronous and asynchronous replication for each modification. Furthermore, because of its fault tolerance and durability, it is ideal for always-on applications.

Cassandra is a distributed NoSQL database that is peer-to-peer. It uses a cluster of homogeneous nodes to execute. It is designed to manage massive amounts of data. Handling this data should provide a high level of capabilities as well. When it comes to reading and writing operations, Cassandra performs admirably. There are no masters, slaves, or distinct leaders in the Cassandra cluster's architecture. This method ensures that there is no single point-of-failure.

14.15.2 Features

Apache Cassandra is an open-source, distributed NoSQL database management system (DBMS) designed to handle large amounts of data across several servers. As a result, it eliminates the possibility of a single point-of-failure. Cassandra also has a lot of support for clusters that span multiple data centers. Cassandra has several imposing characteristics. Here are a few of the aspects that will be discussed:

MapReduce Support

It supports Hadoop integration as well as MapReduce. Also supported are Apache Hive and Apache Pig.

Query Language

The CQL was created by Cassandra (Cassandra Query Language). Cassandra is accessed with a simple interface. CQL features a simple interface for querying Cassandra, an alternative to standard SQL. CQL also offers an abstraction layer to disguise the structure implementation and gives a native syntax for collections.

The example below demonstrates how to build a keyspace with a column family in CQL 3.0:

```
CREATE KEYSPACE MyKeySpace
WITH REPLICATION = { 'class' : 'SimpleStrategy',
                     'replication_factor' : 3 };

USE MyKeySpace;

CREATE COLUMNFAMILY MyColumns (id text, Last text,
                     First text, PRIMARY KEY(id));
INSERT INTO MyColumns (id, Last, First)
VALUES ('1', 'Doe', 'John');

Query:
SELECT * FROM MyColumns;

Which gives:
id | First | Last
----+-------+------
1  | Ratul | Sarkar
(1 row)
```

Distributed and Decentralized

The cluster's nodes all have the same function. There is no chance of failure, and the data is distributed throughout the cluster, but there is one flaw: the master is not present in each node to process service calls. Cassandra is distributed, which means it can run on multiple machines when it appears to users as an entity.

In the Point-to-Point (P2P) network, otherwise called a Decentralized Environment, the data is stored in each client machine. The distributed database connects several devices on a peer-to-peer (one-to-one) network, where each recreates and saves an exact copy of the database and updates itself independently. The primary advantage of P2P is the lack of central authority. When a database update happens, each computer constructs the new transaction, and then the nodes vote using a consensus algorithm that determines the correct copy. Once a consensus has been arrived at, all the other nodes update themselves with the new replica of the database. This validation and consensus mechanism can ensure verification. It is challenging to change the rules or structure of the database without the consensus of the people who use it.

Running a single Cassandra node is a waste of time. Therefore, much of its architecture and coding was created to function on various computers and maximize performance across numerous data center racks or even for a single Cassandra cluster running across multiple data centers. This allows data to be written to any node in the cluster with confidence that Cassandra will receive it.

When scaling many different data stores (MySQL, Bigtable), you'll need to put up some master nodes to arrange slave nodes. On the other hand, Cassandra is decentralized, which means that each node is identical; no Cassandra node conducts organizing operations separate from those performed by other nodes. Instead, Cassandra employs a peer-to-peer protocol and gossip to track which nodes are alive and which are dead.

Fault Tolerance

For failure tolerance, data is automatically saved and copied. If a node fails, it is replaced as soon as possible. Because Cassandra is decentralized, it has no single point-of-failure. A Cassandra cluster's nodes, all have the same functionality. "Server symmetry" is a term used to describe this.

There cannot be a particular host coordinating operations because they all perform the same thing, as with the master/slave structure seen in MySQL, Bigtable, and many other systems.

Many distributed data solutions use a replication technique to store multiple copies of data on different servers (such as RDBMS clusters), which transfers the data to many machines to serve simultaneous requests and increase performance. This procedure is typically not decentralized, as in Cassandra, but instead defined as a master/slave relationship. The servers in a cluster like this do not all work similarly. This allows you to create a cluster by designating one server as the master and the rest as slaves. The master serves as the authoritative data source and communicates with the slave nodes in a one-way manner, requiring them to synchronize their copies. The entire database is at peril if the master node fails. As a result, one of Cassandra's High Availability pillars is its decentralized architecture. While master/slave replication is most commonly associated with RDBMS, master/slave replication may also be found in NoSQL databases such as MongoDB.

As a result, decentralization has two significant advantages: it is simpler to use than master/slave, and it aids in preventing outages. A decentralized store can be easier to operate and maintain than a master/slave store because all nodes are the same. As a result, scaling does not need any special abilities. To make it function, you only need to make a few changes. The master in a master/slave system can potentially be a single point-of-failure (SPOF). Numerous masters are usually utilized to make the environment more complicated to get around this. Because all Cassandra's copies are identical, service will not be disrupted if a node fails. In brief, Cassandra has no single point-of-failure since it is distributed and decentralized, allowing for high availability.

Supports Replication and Multi Data Center Replication

Cassandra's optimal settings include the replication factor. Cassandra also has a distributed mechanism for deploying numerous nodes across many data centers and other essential capabilities.

Elastic Scalability

It is intended to gradually increase read/write throughput as more machines are added without interfering with existing applications.

Scalability is an architectural attribute of a system that allows it to handle more requests while maintaining performance. To do this, simply add more hardware capacity and memory to your existing machine. As a result, one of Cassandra's High Availability pillars is its decentralized architecture. Horizontal scaling means adding extra machines, each with all or a portion of the data so that no one machine handles all requests. However, the software must have an internal mechanism for keeping its data in sync with the other nodes in the cluster.

Elastic scalability is a type of horizontal scalability that is more flexible. It implies that your cluster may scale up and down in real-time. To do this, the cluster must accept extra nodes that can join by receiving a copy of part or all of the data and begin serving new user requests without causing significant disruption or needing the cluster to be adjusted. There is no need to restart the process, update the application queries, or rebalance the data manually. Instead, Cassandra will track it down and put it to work.

Scaling down entails reducing part of the cluster's processing capability. For example, you may need to do this if you are moving your software components to a new site or if your application loses customers and you start selling hardware.

High Availability and Fault Tolerance

A system's availability is assessed in terms of its capacity to satisfy requests in broad architectural terms. On the other hand, computers can fail in several ways, ranging from hardware component failure to network disruption to corruption.

These kinds of failures can occur on any machine. There are, of course, extremely advanced (and sometimes prohibitively costly) computers that can minimize many of these situations by including internal hardware redundancy and failure warning features. However, anyone may accidentally damage an Ethernet connection, and catastrophic occurrences can afflict a single data center. Therefore, a system must typically consist of many networked computers that are highly available. In addition, the computers must use software that can operate in a cluster and has a method for detecting node failures and routing requests to another area of the system.

Cassandra is very accessible. The cluster's failing nodes may be replaced with no downtime. Furthermore, data may be replicated across multiple data centers to improve local performance and avoid downtime in the case of disasters.

Tunable Consistency

Consistency means that a read returns the most recently written value. For example, consider two clients on an eCommerce site attempting to add identical items to their shopping baskets. If I put the last item in stock in my basket just after you, you should get it, and I should be told it is no longer available for purchase. This is guaranteed to occur when a write state is consistent across all nodes with that data. Growing data storage necessitates making data consistency, node availability, and partition tolerance tradeoffs. Cassandra is usually referred to be "eventually consistent"; however, this is a misnomer. Cassandra compromises on some consistency for absolute availability. Availability out of the box. On the other hand, Cassandra is more correctly described as a "tuneable consistency," allowing you to simply choose the amount of Consistency you desire while keeping the level of Availability (Availability in check).

Cassandra's tuneable Consistency (Fig. 14.35) is derived from the fact that it enables per-operation tradeoffs between Consistency and Availability via consistency levels. The consistency level of an operation specifies how many replicas must respond to the coordinator (the node that receives the client's read/write request) for the operation to be considered successful.

Cassandra consistency levels

The following consistency levels are available:

- **ONE** – Only a single replica must respond.
- **TWO** – Two replicas must respond.
- **THREE** – Three replicas must respond.
- **QUORUM** – A majority (n/2 + 1) of the replicas must respond.
- **ALL** – All of the replicas must respond.
- **LOCAL_QUORUM** – A majority of the replicas in the local datacenter (whichever datacenter the coordinator is in) must respond.
- **EACH_QUORUM** – A majority of the replicas in each datacenter must respond.
- **LOCAL_ONE** – Only a single replica must respond. In a multi-datacenter cluster, this also guarantees that read requests are not sent to replicas in a remote datacenter.
- **ANY** – A single replica may respond, or the coordinator may store a hint. If a hint is stored, the coordinator will later attempt to replay the hint and deliver the mutation to the replicas. This consistency level is only accepted for write operations.
- **SERIAL** – This consistency level is only for use with lightweight transaction. Equivalent to QUORUM.
- **LOCAL_SERIAL** – Same as SERIAL but used to maintain consistency locally (within the single datacenter). Equivalent to LOCAL_QUORUM.

Figure 14.35 Cassandra consistency levels

The word "eventual consistency" has sparked some controversy in the business. As a result, some practitioners are hesitant to utilize an "eventually consistent" approach. For social web apps where data isn't essential, eventual Consistency may be acceptable. But when the information is valuable, it is irrational to allow for eventual Consistency.

They are leaving aside that this approach is used by all of the most prominent web applications (Amazon, Facebook, Google, and Twitter), and there may be something to it. Because data is their core product, it is likely quite significant to the organizations that run these programs. They are multibillion-dollar corporations with billions of consumers to serve in a fiercely competitive environment. It may be conceivable to achieve assured, instantaneous, and flawless Consistency through a heavily frequented system that runs in parallel over many networks. Some detractors contend that some Big Data databases such as Cassandra, have merely eventual Consistency, whereas all other distributed systems have tight Consistency. However, the reality isn't often so black and white, and the binary opposition between consistent and inconsistent isn't always represented in practice. Instead, there exist degrees of Consistency, which are very vulnerable to external factors in the actual world.

Architects have various consistency models to choose from, including Eventual Consistency. Let us look at these models to see how they work and what the tradeoffs are:

Strict Consistency: This is a strict degree of Consistency, often known as sequential Consistency. It demands that any reader always returns the most recently written value. Let us see what "most recently written" implies. It denotes the value that was most recently written on the system. This is not difficult to observe in a single-processor computer because the single clock knows the operation sequence. However, it becomes considerably slicker in a system that runs across many geographically distributed data centers. To do so, you will need a global clock that can timestamp all actions, independent of where the data is stored, who is making the request, and how many (possibly disparate) services are required to respond.

Causal Consistency: This is a weaker variant of the strict Consistency principle. This eliminates the myth of a universal clock, which can synchronize all actions wonderfully without significant interruption. Rather than relying on timestamps, causal Consistency employs a more semantic approach, aiming to discover the reason of events to ensure that their sequence is consistent. It implies that possibly related writes must be read in order. If two independent operations write to the same field simultaneously, it is assumed that the writes are not causally related. However, if one write follows another, we can infer that they are causally related. According to Causal Consistency, causal texts must be read in order.

Weak (eventual) Consistency: Eventually, on the surface, Consistency means that all changes within a distributed system will spread to all copies, although this may take some time. All copies will eventually be uniform.

Row-oriented: Cassandra is sometimes described as a "column-oriented" database, which is accurate. It is not relational, but it does use sparse multi-dimensional hash tables to express its data structures. The term "sparse" means that each row can include one or more columns, but they do not have to be the same as other rows (as in a relational model). Instead, each row has its unique key that may be used to retrieve the data. Although it is not improper to refer to Cassandra as a columnar or column-oriented database, it is probably more practical to consider it in terms of an indexed, row-oriented database. Data orientation is a feature because numerous data models are simple to perceive and utilize in a non-relational model. Assuming that the relational model is always preferable, regardless of application, it is a strange mix of laziness and probably encourages far more effort than required. Cassandra uses a multi-dimensional hash table to store data for the time being. That means you won't have to plan out your data structure or the fields your records will need ahead of time. This is useful if you are in startup mode and often add and delete features. It is especially appealing if you need to support an Agile development process but don't have the time to do a months-long investigation upfront. If your company expands and you need to add or remove fields on the fly without interfering with service, or if your business grows and you need to add or remove fields on the fly without disrupting service, Cassandra allows you to do so. That is not to imply you shouldn't worry about your data. Cassandra, on the other hand, necessitates a shift of perspective. You are allowed to conceive your questions first and then give the data that answers them, rather than developing a perfect data model and then developing queries around it as in RDBMS.

Schema-Free: Cassandra needs you to construct an outer container for column families called a keyspace. Column families and particular configuration attributes are stored in the keyspace, which is a logical namespace. The data names and orders associated with them are column families. Aside from that, the data tables are sparse, so you may start populating them with data and using the columns you want right away; you don't have to declare your columns ahead of time. Cassandra recommends modeling the queries you want and then providing the data around them, rather than modeling data upfront using costly data modeling tools and then constructing searches with complicated join statements.

High Performance: Cassandra was built from scratch to take full advantage of multiprocessor/multicore processors and scale to hundreds of them spread across multiple data centers handling hundreds of terabytes with consistency and ease. Cassandra has been shown to work very well under extreme conditions. A simple commodity workstation can always display a high throughput for writes per second. You can keep all of Cassandra's attractive qualities without losing performance as you add more servers.

Cassandra's architecture comprises nodes, clusters, and data centers. There are other components in addition to these. Cassandra is a database that stores data in rows. Using the CQL, authorized users may connect to any node in any data center.

14.15.3 Key Structures in Cassandra

The following are Cassandra's significant structures (Fig. 14.36).

Node: This is the location where the data is kept. Cassandra would not exist without it. It is similar to having a single server in a rack. In addition, it eliminates the possibility of a single point of failure.

Data Center: A data center is comprised of numerous nodes. This might be a physical or a virtual location. Data centers are separated and chosen based on the workload. The data center is used to determine the replication factor. Data can be written to multiple data centers depending on this replication factor.

Cluster: One or more data centers make up a cluster. Clusters frequently span many physical areas.

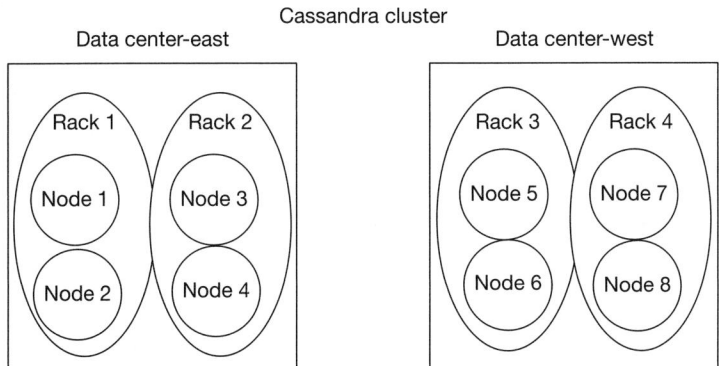

Figure 14.36 Cassandra cluster representation

In the case of write processing (Fig. 14.37), save to memory construction is used after writing to the disk's commit log. Memtable is a partition cache. Cassandra flushes the data by sorting Memtable according to the token and sequentially writing the data to disc. A partition index is created on the desktop that maps the token to a location on the disc. The most recent write flushes to the SS Table. The process of writing is as follows: 1. Write Process 2. Write to the Memtable 3. Write to the commit log 4. Memtable to SS Table Flush.

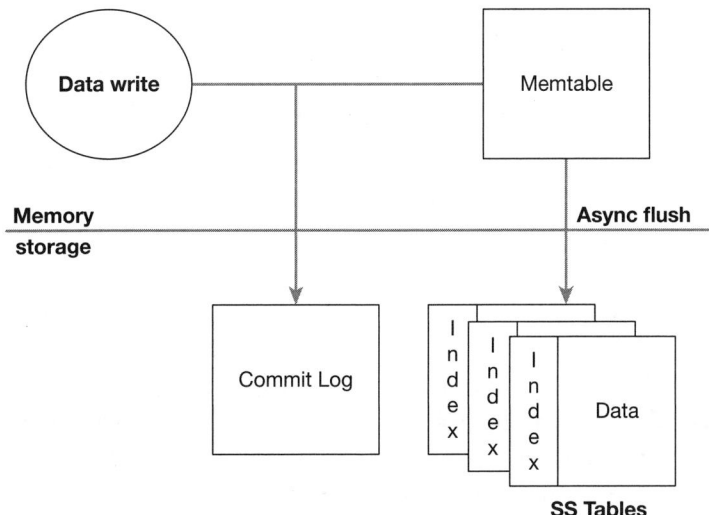

Figure 14.37 Cassandra data writing

There are several processing patterns for reading data (Fig. 14.38):

- Examine the data in the Memtable
- Check the row cache if it is enabled
- Examine the bloom filter
- Check if partition key cache is enabled
- If the partition key cache contains data, move to the offset map
- Examine the partition summary. Partition index access.
- Obtain data from a disc
- Obtain SS Table data from the disc.

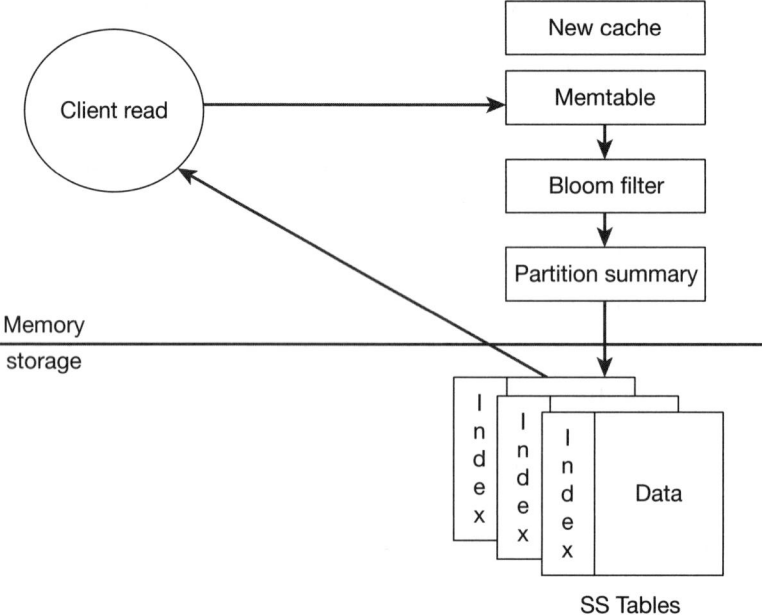

Figure 14.38 Cassandra data reading

In addition to these, several additional components play a role in Cassandra.

1. **Commit Log:** The commit log keeps track of the data committed to ensuring data persistence. The data is first transferred to a sorted string table (SS Table). The commit log can be archived, erased, or recycled after this operation is complete.
2. **SS Table:** This table, as previously said, holds the log or memory tables at regular intervals. It is a data file that can't be changed. SS tables may have a lot of data in a logical order. For each Cassandra table, they insert data and keep information.
3. **CQL Table:** The Cassandra Query table has columns from which data may be retrieved using the primary key.
4. **Bloom Filter:** A primary cache stores non-deterministic algorithms for testing. For example, it determines whether or not an element is a member of the set. These filters are typically accessible after each query is completed.

Critical Components to Configure Cassandra

There are the following components in Cassandra:

Gossip: As the term implies, communication between peers is required to find and communicate the location and status of information about all nodes.

This data/information should be stored locally so that each node may use it as soon as it is required to restart. By sharing information, nodes discover information about other nodes.

This can only be done for three nodes at a time. The data is not distributed to every node in the cluster or data center. Instead, the data is shared with a few nodes, but the state data is gradually spread throughout the cluster.

Partitioner: The partitioner determines which node is responsible for receiving the initial replica of any data. It is also in charge of ensuring that these clones are distributed.

It will determine which node in the cluster should have which replication. Each row of data should have its unique identifier. A primary key or partition key can be used to do this.

The partitioner is a hash function that aids in obtaining a token from any row's main key. A num token value is issued to each node, which may be used as the partitioner.

The created token value is used to determine which node receives the replica of the rows.

Replication Factor: This factor determines the overall number of copies in the cluster. For example, if the replication factor is 1, each row is only replicated once on each node.

In the same way, if the replication factor is 2, two copies are kept, each on a distinct node. As previously stated, Cassandra does not have a master–slave architecture; each copy is vital.

Every data center has its replication factor. This factor should be more significant than one but not greater than the cluster's total number of nodes.

Snitch: Snitch is a replication strategy that assists in determining where replicas for a group of machines in the data center and the rack should be placed. A dynamic layer aids in monitoring performance by selecting the best copy from which data may be read. Only after a cluster is built should snitches be specified. Most installations have default values enabled. In addition, the Cassandra.yml file contains the dynamic snitch threshold for each node where the configuration adjustments may be changed.

Snitch is a component that determines the network topology of the entire Cassandra cluster. It converts the node's IP address to the data center and rack to which it belongs. This ensures that the data is placed so that the cluster can handle outages at the rack/datacenter level. The default snitch is the Simple Snitch. However, we decided to migrate to a more resilient Cassandra cluster called GossipingPropertyFileSnitch (GPFS), which is a recommended snitch for production-grade clusters, to improve data resiliency. Unfortunately, while the latter is a rack and datacenter-aware snitch, the former does not recognize any of this information.

Merkle Tree: Differences in data blocks are possible. The Merkle tree is a type of hash tree that detects differences quickly. The hash tree's leaf nodes carry hashes of individual data blocks, whereas parent nodes store or have knowledge about their children's hashes.

It is easy to identify discrepancies between the nodes present when using this strategy.

Mem Table: This table contains information on caches whose data is not removed and is still in memory. Cassandra is a NoSQL database that can handle large volumes of data. Because it lacks a traditional master-slave design, all nodes are equally essential. Furthermore, the nodes have replicas across the cluster according to the replication factor. This ensures that the data is stable and long-lasting. With all of these options, it's evident that Cassandra is an excellent choice for large data. As a result, Cassandra is long-lasting, fast, and reliable.

14.15.4 Cassandra Advantages and Use Cases

Unlike MongoDB, Cassandra offers a masterless "ring" design, which provides several advantages over traditional systems such as master–slave architecture. Consequently, all nodes in a cluster are treated equally, and a quorum may be obtained by utilizing most nodes. Like any other RDBMS, Cassandra stores data in columns and rows, but it adds flexibility by enabling rows to have alternate columns and modifying the column structure. Aside from that, its query language, Cassandra Query Language (CQL), closely mirrors regular SQL syntax, making it easier to understand for SQL users. This offers it an advantage in any Cassandra vs. HBase comparison.

Cassandra's cluster is extremely available and dependable because of robust repair mechanisms for reading, writing, and entropy (data consistency). Furthermore, provided a quorum of nodes is maintained and the replication factor is calibrated appropriately, the lack of a single point-of-failure can enable a highly available architecture. This provides superior fault tolerance than document stores like MongoDB, which can take up to 40 seconds to recover from a failure. Messaging systems (because of their higher read and write efficiency), real-time sensor data, and e-commerce websites are some of Cassandra's most prominent use cases.

14.16 MongoDB

MongoDB (Fig. 14.39) is the most popular document storage system and one of the most popular database management systems. It was established in 2007 by the team behind DoubleClick (which is now owned by Google) to address the scalability and agility issues that DoubleClick faced when serving Internet advertisements.

MongoDB is offered in two editions: community and enterprise. The enterprise edition includes additional corporate features such as LDAP, Kerberos, auditing, and on-disk encryption.

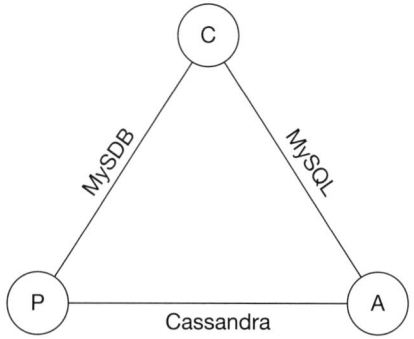

Figure 14.39 MongoDB CAP theorem

14.16.1 Architecture of MongoDB

Figure 14.40 represents MongoDB Architecture.

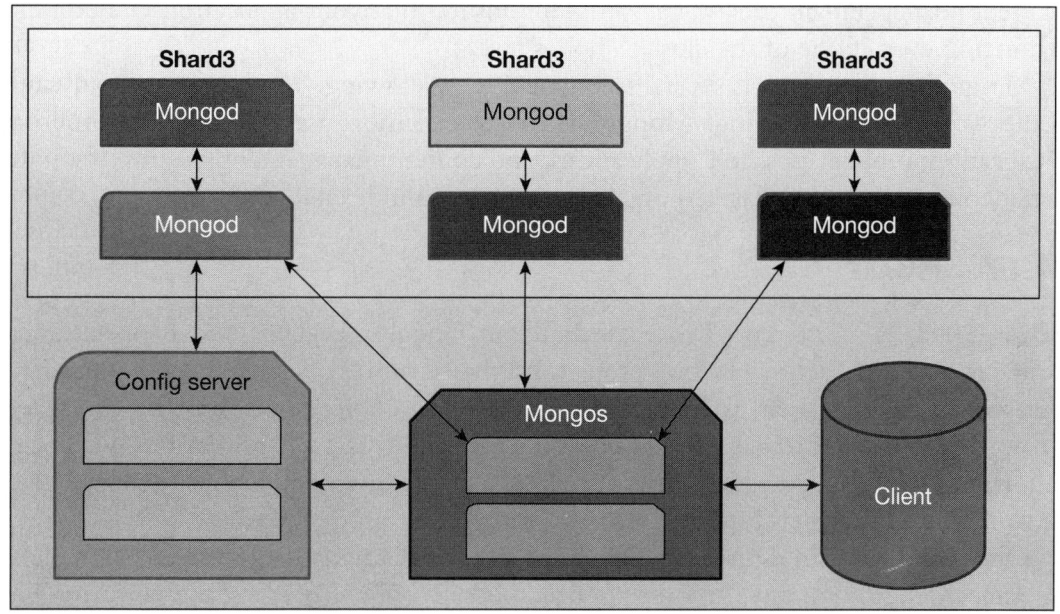

Figure 14.40 MongoDB architecture

Database: To put it another way, it is the physical container for data. With several databases running on a single MongoDB server, each database has its own set of files on the file system.

Collection: A database collection is a grouping of database documents. A table is the RDBMS counterpart of a collection. A single database houses the whole collection. When it comes to collections, there are no schemas. Different documents inside a collection may contain various fields, but they are all intended to serve the same function or accomplish the same goal.

Document: A document is simply a collection of key-value pairs. Dynamic schemas are used to associate documents. The advantage of dynamic schemas is that each document in a collection does not have the same structure or fields. A collection document's standard fields can also include various data types.

14.16.2 MongoDB Advantages and Use Cases

MongoDB is a schema-free database that stores data in JSON-like documents (binary JSON). This enables more flexibility and agility regarding the sort of records that may be retained and the fields that can vary from one document to the next. Furthermore, the integrated documents provide faster queries through indexes, decreasing the I/O overload associated with database systems. Support for schema on write and dynamic schema for quickly changing data structures are also included.

MongoDB also includes several enterprise-level features, like high availability and horizontal scalability. High availability is achieved using replica sets, which incorporate data redundancy and automatic failover. This ensures that your application will continue to function even if one of the cluster's nodes fails.

MongoDB also supports several storage engines, allowing you to tailor your database to the workload it is serving. MongoDB's most common use cases are real-time data visualization, mobile apps, IoT applications, and content management systems. It also has incremental operations, a layered object structure, and indexable array attributes.

14.17 HBase

HBase (2008) is a distributed database built on Google's Bigtable and is open-source, created as part of Apache's Hadoop project. It is based on HDFS and incorporates various Bigtable capabilities such as in-memory operations, compression, and Bloom filters. HBase is a Java-based database that accepts external APIs such as Thrift, Avro, Scala, Jython, and REST. In addition, HBase provides a standalone version of its database, which is mainly utilized for development purposes rather than production.

One of HBase's strengths is its use of HDFS as a distributed file system. This allows the database to store massive amounts of data, perhaps billions of rows, and perform quick analysis. When data grows to gigabytes or petabytes, this sparse data support, along with the fact that it can be housed on commodity server hardware, ensures that the solution is highly cost-effective. Furthermore, it adds to one of the distribution's significant advantages: failover support with automated recovery.

To boost query speed, certain Bigtable technologies, like Bloom filters and block caches, can be used. Furthermore, in any HBase vs. Cassandra comparison, HBase benefits Consistency, as reads and writes comply with instantaneous Consistency, unlike Cassandra's eventual Consistency. Finally, its close relationship with Hadoop projects and MapReduce is an intriguing Hadoop distribution choice.

HBase is often used for online log analytics, Hadoop distributions, write-intensive applications, and data-intensive applications (like Tweets, Facebook posts, etc.).

14.17.1 HBase Architecture

Tables in HBase are divided into regions (Fig. 14.41) and serviced by region servers. Column families split regions vertically into "Stores". In HDFS, stores are stored as files. To describe the storage structure, the term 'store' is used for regions.

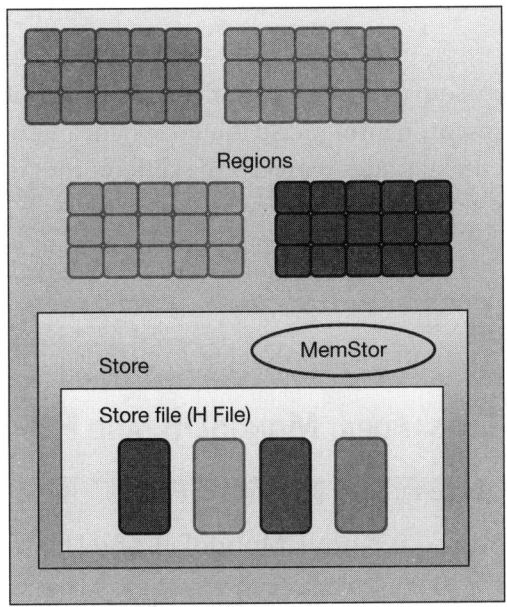

Figure 14.41   HBase architecture

HBase's three main components are client library, master server, and region servers. In addition, servers in other regions can be added or withdrawn as needed.

Master server

The master server –
- assigns regions to region servers, utilizing Apache ZooKeeper for this purpose.
- manages region load balancing across area servers. It moves the regions to less crowded servers after unloading the congested servers.
- negotiates load balancing to keep the cluster in good shape.
- is in charge of schema modifications and other metadata actions such as table and column family creation.

Regions

Regions are only tables split up and spread across the region servers.

Region server

The region servers have regions that –
- handle data-related actions and communicate with the client.
- handle read and write requests for all the areas beneath it.
- follow the region size thresholds to determine the region's size.

When we look at the region server more closely, we can see that it has regions and stores, as illustrated below:

A memory store and HFiles are included in the store. Memstore works similar to cache memory. Everything that is input into HBase is saved initially here. The data is then transported and stored as blocks in H files, and the Memstore is flushed.

ZooKeeper

- ZooKeeper is an open-source project that offers various services, such as configuration information management, naming, distributed synchronization, and so on.
- ZooKeeper has ephemeral nodes representing different region servers. Master servers use these nodes to discover available servers.
- In addition to availability, the nodes are also used to track server failures or network partitions.
- Clients communicate with region servers via ZooKeeper.
- HBase itself will take care of the ZooKeeper in pseudo and standalone modes.

14.18 COMPARING CASSANDRA, MONGODB, AND HBASE

Table 14.3 compares the three famous NoSQL databases.

Table 14.3 Comparison of Cassandra, MongoDB, and HBase

Name	Cassandra	MongoDB	HBase
Architecture	Wide column store	Document store	Wide column store
Server OS	FreeBSD, Linux, OS X, Windows	Linux, OS X, Solaris, Windows	Linux, Unix, Windows
Distributed system consistency	Eventual and immediate consistency	Eventual and immediate consistency	Immediate consistency
Owner and developer	Apache Software Foundation	MongoDB, Inc.	Apache Software Foundation
Replication	Masterless ring	Master–slave replication	Master–slave replication
Programming language (Base code)	Java	C++	Java
Supported programming languages	C#, C++, Clojure, Erlang, Go, Haskell, Java, Node.js, Perl, PHP, Python, Ruby, Scala	C, C#, C++, Erlang, Haskell, Java, JavaScript, Perl, PHP, Python, Ruby, Scala	C, C#, C++, Groovy, Java, PHP, Python, Scala

(Continued)

Table 14.3 (*Continued*)

Name	Cassandra	MongoDB	HBase
Editions	Community with option of third-party support	Community (free) and enterprise	Community
Popular use cases	Sensor data, Messaging systems, E-commerce websites, Always-on applications, Fraud detection in banks	Operational intelligence, Product data management, Content management systems, IoT, Real-time analytics	Online log analytics, Hadoop, Write-heavy applications, MapReduce
DBaaS	Instaclustr Cassandra as a Service, DataStax Database as a Service	MongoDBAtlas, mLab MongoDB, ScaleGridMongoDB Hosting	None
Key customers	eBay, McDonald's, Walmart, Comcast, Facebook, Instagram, GitHub, CERN, Netflix, Reddit	Adobe, eBay, Google, Cisco, SAP, Facebook, Royal Bank of Scotland, Trend Micro	23andMe, Salesforce, Netflix, Bloomberg, Sophos, Adobe, Xiaomi, Yahoo

SUMMARY

In this chapter, we have taken an introductory look at the defining characteristics, history, and significant features of NoSQL. Then, we have seen the types of NoSQL, its advantages, and industry usage. We also examined the sharding architecture and Brewer's CAP Theorem. Finally, we compared the features of NoSQL databases such as Cassandra, HBase, and MongoDB.

NoSQL ("Not Only SQL") became popular in the mid-2000s due to the rise of cloud computing, Big Data, and web and mobile applications. It is now the preferred database due to its high performance, scalability, and ease of use.

No SQL does not employ relational model. It is open-source, schema-less, and meant for unstructured data storage and retrieval. Moreover, NoSQL offers a variety of options for data organization.

The four primary NoSQL variations are column-oriented database, key-value store, document store, and graph database. Each type addresses an issue that relational databases are unable to handle.

HBase, Hyper table, and Amazon DynamoDB are prominent columns family databases.

Examples of key-value databases are Riak, Redis, Berkley DB, Amazon DynamoDB, and Couchbase.

Some popular document databases are MongoDB, CouchDB, Terrastore, OrientDB, RavenDB, and Lotus Notes that use document storage.

Graph databases are Neo4J, Infinite Graph, OrientDB, or FlockDB.

The **advantages of NoSQL databases** include data replication, eliminating unnecessary management, automated repair data distribution, and simpler data models, resulting in lower administration and performance requirements. NoSQL systems like Hadoop handle their Big Data volumes, as these outperform the capabilities of the most popular RDBMS. NoSQL databases are frequently more scalable, and at the same time, provide superior performance when compared to relational databases. NoSQL databases are intended to manage the ever-increasing transaction and data volumes by utilizing low-cost commodity server clusters. Data in native formats can be stored in NoSQL databases, which eliminates the need for developers to adapt the data to the store. As a result, a large developer community supports most NoSQL databases.

Changes to applications or database schema do not have to be managed as a single change unit, making the process simpler.

- **NoSQL usage:** A NoSQL database is most commonly used for distributed data repositories with enormous storage requirements. However, NoSQL is also used in extensive data and real-time web apps such as Session Store, User Profile Store, Content and Metadata Store, Mobile Applications, Third-Party Data Aggregation, Internet of Things, E-Commerce, Social Gaming, and Ad Targeting.
- **New SQL**: NewSQL is a database language that combines and expands on Structured Query Language (SQL) and NoSQL concepts and principles. It is "a DBMS that provides the scalability and flexibility promised by NoSQL while still supporting SQL queries and/or ACID, or that which improves performance for appropriate workloads".

The ACID properties are a collection of standards that transactions must follow. The acronym ACID stands for Atomicity, Consistency, Isolation, and Durability, four interdependent qualities. Atomic means "all or nothing". The transaction must maintain database Consistency, which implies that the database must start the transaction in a state of Consistency and end the transaction in a state of Consistency.

Isolated transactions are called "serializable" because they do not occur all at once. Isolated means that the concurrently running transactions will not become entangled; they will each run in their area (independently). Even if the system fails, Durability ensures that appropriately committed database changes (transactions) are retained permanently. Durable changes made after the transaction will not be lost.

The acronym BASE stands for: Basically Available, Soft State, Eventually Consistent.

The concept of a two-phase commit (often known as "2PC") is introduced to account for the successful completion of transactions involving many hosts (servers). However, because a two-phase commit locks all associated resources, it is only appropriate for activities that can be completed in a short period.

Schema means the logical structure of data. Creating sophisticated schemas is one of relational database systems' most acclaimed features. A relational model can be used to represent domain objects.

Sharding is a mechanism for distributing data over numerous workstations to simulate a program accessing a single database.

- **Vertical partitioning:** It is the process of splitting a record along column boundaries and storing the pieces in different tables or collections.
- **Feature-based shard or functional segmentation:** At eBay, for example, users are in one Shard while products for sale are in another.
- **Key-based sharding:** Using this method, you locate a key in your data that equally distributes it among shards. A one-way hash on a critical data piece distributes data among computers based on the hash.
- **Range-based sharding:** Using this method, you locate a range of values in the data and distribute it among shards.
- **The lookup table (Directory-based sharding):** In this technique, one of the cluster nodes acts as a "yellow pages" directory, determining which node holds the data that needs to be accessed.
- **Brewer's CAP Theorem:** According to the CAP theorem, a distributed computing system cannot guarantee Consistency, Availability and Partition tolerance simultaneously. A distributed computing system must choose two of the three options.

Apache Cassandra is an open-source, distributed, decentralized, elastically scalable, highly available, fault-tolerant, and tuneable consistent, column-oriented database based on Amazon's Dynamo and Google's Bigtable data model. It was developed on Facebook and is now used on some of the most popular websites on the Internet.

The following are Cassandra's significant structures:

- **Node:** This is the location where the data is kept. Cassandra would not exist without it.
- **Data Center:** A data center is comprised of numerous nodes. This might be a physical or a virtual location. Data centers are separated and chosen based on the workload.
- **Cluster:** One or more data centers make up a cluster. Clusters frequently span many physical areas.

MongoDB is the most popular document storage system and one of the most popular database management systems. It was established in 2007 by the team behind DoubleClick (which is now owned by Google) to address the scalability and agility issues that DoubleClick was experiencing when serving Internet advertisements.

HBase (2008) is a distributed database built on Google's Bigtable and is open-source. It is based on HDFS and incorporates various Bigtable capabilities such as in-memory operations, compression, and Bloom filters. HBase is a Java-based database that accepts external APIs such as Thrift, Avro, Scala, Jython, and REST. In addition, HBase provides a standalone version of its database, which is mainly utilized for development purposes rather than production.

EXERCISES

Multiple Choice Questions

1. **All of the following are the characteristics of NoSQL, except:**
   A. High performance
   B. Schema full
   C. Ease of Use
   D. Schema Less
   Answer: B
   Explanation: NoSQL (Not Only SQL) became popular in the mid-2000s due to the rise of cloud computing, Big Data, and web and mobile applications. It is now the preferred database due to its high performance, scalability, and ease of use. NoSQL does not employ relational model, it is open-source, schema-less, and meant for unstructured data storage and retrieval. Also, NoSQL offers a variety of options for data organization.

2. **All of the following are NoSQL variations, except:**
   A. Column-oriented
   B. Key Value Store
   C. Row-oriented
   D. Graph Database
   Answer: C
   Explanation: The four primary NoSQL variations are column-oriented database, key-value store, document store, and graph database. Each type addresses an issue that relational databases are unable to handle.

3. **All of the following are examples of Column Family database, except:**
   A. MongoDB
   B. Hyper table
   C. HBase
   D. Amazon DynamoDB
   Answer: A
   Explanation: HBase, Hyper table, and Amazon DynamoDB are prominent column-family databases. Examples of key-value databases are Riak, Redis, Berkley DB and Couchbase. Some popular document databases are MongoDB, CouchDB, Terrastore, OrientDB, RavenDB, and Lotus Notes that use document storage. Graph databases are Neo4J, Infinite Graph, OrientDB, or FlockDB.

4. **All of the following are the advantages of NoSQL, except:**
   A. Simpler data models
   B. Lower administration
   C. Scalable
   D. Patented Servers
   Answer: D
   Explanation: Data replication, eliminating unnecessary management, automated repair data distribution, and simpler data models, resulting in lower administration and performance requirements, are the advantages of NoSQL databases. NoSQL systems like Hadoop handle their Big Data volumes, as these outperform the capabilities of the most popular RDBMS. NoSQL databases are frequently more scalable and, at the same time, provide superior performance when compared to relational databases.

5. **NewSQL is a database language that combines and expands on Structured Query Language (SQL) and NoSQL concepts and principles.**
   A. True
   B. False
   Answer: A
   Explanation: NewSQL is a database language that combines and expands on Structured Query Language (SQL) and NoSQL concepts and principles. It is "a DBMS that provides the scalability and flexibility promised by NoSQL while still supporting SQL queries and/or ACID, or that which improves performance for appropriate workloads".

6. **In ACID properties, A stands for _____.**
   A. Atomicity
   B. Ambiguity
   C. Availability
   D. Accessibility
   Answer: A
   Explanation: The ACID properties are a collection of standards that transactions must follow. The acronym ACID stands for Atomicity, Consistency, Isolation, and Durability, four interdependent qualities. Atomic means "all or nothing". The atomic property is violated if a partial transaction is committed. When a statement is executed, every transaction must be successful for it to be considered successful.

7. **In ACID properties, C stands for _____.**
   A. Concept
   B. Consistency
   C. Context
   D. Cluster
   Answer: B
   Explanation: The ACID properties are a collection of standards that transactions must follow. The acronym ACID stands for Atomicity, Consistency, Isolation, and Durability, four interdependent qualities. The transaction must maintain database Consistency, which implies that the database must start the transaction in a state of Consistency and end the transaction in a state of Consistency.

8. **In ACID properties, D stands for _____.**
   A. Data Center
   B. Data
   C. Durability
   D. Document Store
   Answer: C
   Explanation: The ACID properties are a collection of standards that transactions must follow. The acronym ACID stands for Atomicity, Consistency, Isolation, and Durability, four interdependent qualities. Durability ensures that appropriately committed database changes (transactions) are retained permanently, even if the system fails. Durable changes made after the transaction will not be lost.

9. **In BASE properties of NoSQL, S stands for _____.**
   A. Schema-less
   B. Sharding
   C. Scalability
   D. Soft State
   Answer: D

Explanation: The acronym BASE stands for: Basically Available, Soft State, Eventually Consistent.

10. It is the process of splitting a record along column boundaries and storing the pieces in different tables or collections.
    A. Vertical Partitioning
    B. Horizontal Partitioning
    C. Straight Partitioning
    D. Boundaries Partitioning
    Answer: A
    Explanation: Vertical partitioning is the process of splitting a record along column boundaries and storing the pieces in different tables or collections.

11. At eBay, users are in one shard while products for sale are in another. This is an example for:
    A. Key-based sharding
    B. Feature-based sharding
    C. Range-based sharding
    D. Directory-based sharding
    Answer: B
    Explanation
    Feature-based Shard or Functional Segmentation: At eBay, for example, users are in one Shard while products for sale are in another.
    Key-based Sharding: Using this method, you locate a key in your data that equally distributes it among shards. A one-way hash on a critical data piece distributes data among computers based on the hash.
    Range-based Sharding: Using this method, you locate a range of values in the data and distribute it among shards.
    The Lookup Table (Directory-based Sharding): In this technique, one of the cluster nodes acts as a "yellow pages" directory, determining which node holds the data that needs to be accessed.

12. Using this method, you locate a key in your data that equally distributes it among shards:
    A. Key-based sharding
    B. Feature-based sharding
    C. Range-based sharding
    D. Directory-based sharding
    Answer: A
    Explanation Same as that for Question 11.

13. In this technique, one of the cluster nodes acts as a "yellow pages" directory, determining which node holds the data that needs to be accessed:
    A. Key-based Sharding
    B. Feature-based Sharding
    C. Range-based Sharding
    D. Directory-based Sharding
    Answer: D
    Explanation: Same as that for Question 11.

Short-answer Questions

1. **What is the meaning of NoSQL?**
   NoSQL does not have a rigid definition. Still, several observations can be made, such as, No SQL does not employ relational model, it is open-source, schema-less, and meant for unstructured data storage and retrieval. Moreover, NoSQL offers a variety of options for data organization. NoSQL ("Not only SQL") turned out to be popular in the mid-2000s due to the rise of cloud computing, Big Data, and web and mobile applications. It is now the preferred database due to its high performance, scalability, and ease of use.

2. **What are the types of NoSQL Databases?**
   The four primary NoSQL variations are column-oriented database, key-value store, document store, and graph database. Each type addresses an issue that relational databases are unable to handle.

3. **Write a short note on column-family databases.**
   Column-family databases (column-oriented databases) store data as rows with several columns linked by a row key. Column families are collections of data that are often accessed together. HBase, Hyper table, and Amazon DynamoDB are prominent columns family databases.

4. **Define Key-Value pair database.**
   Key-value pair database is one of the most straightforward NoSQL data stores to use from an Application Programming Interface (API) perspective. Examples of key-value databases are Riak, Redis, Berkley DB, Amazon DynamoDB, and Couchbase. The simplest of the NoSQL databases are key-value stores. As the name implies, they are a collection of key-value pairs, and their simplicity makes them the most scalable of the NoSQL database types, capable of holding massive quantities of data.

5. **Write a short note on document datastore.**
   Documents are the central concept in document databases. It stores the data in JSON-like documents having key-value pairs. As the name implies, the document stores and organizes data in a document. Tables, rows, and columns are not present. Instead, a single document contains all of the information on a single entity or aggregate unit. As a result, we obtain all of the information when we query for that item, preferably without the need for numerous references or joins.

6. **Write a short note on graph database.**
   Graph databases store entities and relationships between these entities. Entities are also known as nodes with properties, and relations are known as edges that can have properties—many graph databases such as Neo4J, Infinite Graph, OrientDB, or FlockDB are examples. This database type is designed to store relationships between entities efficiently.

7. **Give some examples for NoSQL database.**
   Many businesses have joined the NoSQL market. For example, Apache CouchDB is an open-source JSON document-based database that uses JavaScript as its query language. Elasticsearch is a document-based database built into the full-text search engine. Finally, Couchbase is a key-value and document database that allows developers to create a cloud, mobile, and edge computing applications that are responsive and adaptable.

8. **Write short notes on Sharding and Share Nothing Architecture.**
   Sharding is a mechanism for distributing data over numerous workstations to simulate a program accessing a single database. As implemented by MongoDB, sharding is ideal for the new generation of cloud-based computing platforms since it allows for dynamic, load-sensitive automated scaling, where capacity is used only when needed and turned down when not.

9. **Write short notes on Gossip in Cassandra.**
   As the term implies, communication between peers is required to find and communicate the location and status of information about all nodes.
   This data/information should be stored locally so that each node may use it as soon as it is required to restart. By sharing information, nodes discover information about other nodes.
   This can only be done for three nodes at a time. The data is not distributed to every node in the cluster or data center. Instead, the data is shared with a few nodes, but the state data gradually spreads throughout the cluster.

10. **Write short notes on Partitioner in Cassandra.**
    The partitioner determines which node is responsible for receiving the initial replica of any data. It is also in charge of ensuring that the data clones are distributed.
    It will determine which node in the cluster should have which replication. Each row of data should have its unique identifier. A primary key or partition key can be used to do this.
    The partitioner is a hash function that aids in obtaining a token from any row's main key. A num token value is issued to each node, which may be used as the partitioner. The created token value is used to determine which node receives the replica of the rows.

11. **Write short notes on Replication Factor in Cassandra.**
    Replication Factor determines the overall number of copies in the cluster. For example, if the replication factor is 1, each row is only replicated once on each node. In the same way, if the replication factor is two, two copies are kept, each on a distinct node. As previously stated, Cassandra does not have a master-slave architecture; each copy is vital.
    Every data center has its replication factor. This factor should be more significant than one but not greater than the cluster's total number of nodes.

12. **Write short notes on Snitch in Cassandra.**
    Snitch is a replication strategy that assists in determining where replicas for a group of machines in the data center and the rack should be placed. A dynamic layer aids monitoring and performance by selecting the best copy from which data may be read. Only after a cluster is built should snitches be specified. Most installations have default values enabled. In addition, the Cassandra.yml file contains the dynamic snitch threshold for each node where the configuration adjustments may be changed. Snitch is a component that determines the network topology of the entire Cassandra cluster. It converts the node's IP address to the data center and rack to which it belongs. This ensures that the data is placed so that the cluster can handle outages at the rack/datacenter level. The default snitch is the Simple Snitch. However, we decided to migrate to a more resilient Cassandra cluster called GossipingPropertyFileSnitch (GPFS), which is a recommended snitch for production-grade clusters, to improve data resiliency. Unfortunately, while the latter is a rack and datacenter-aware snitch, the former does not recognize any of this information.

Essay-type Questions

1. Write an essay on Column-family databases.
2. Write an essay on key-value pair database.
3. Write an essay on Document Store database.
4. Write an essay on Graph database.
5. What are the advantages of NoSQL databases?
6. What are the usages of NoSQL databases?
7. Write an essay on New SQL.
8. How are ACID properties taken care of in NoSQL?
9. How are BASE properties taken care of in NoSQL?
10. How is Two-phase Commit taken care of in NoSQL?
11. What is Schema?
12. What is Partitioning? Explain Vertical Partitioning and Horizontal Partitioning.
13. Write an essay on key-based sharding.
14. Write an essay on range-based sharding.
15. Write an essay on directory-based sharding.
16. Write an essay on Brewer's CAP Theorem.
17. Write an essay on Cassandra and its features.

18. Write an essay on Tunable Consistency.
19. Write an essay on Eventual Consistency.
20. Write an essay on Strict Consistency, Causal Consistency and Weak Consistency.
21. Write an essay on Row-oriented and Column-oriented Database.
22. Write an essay on schema-free and high-performance nature of Cassandra.
23. Write an essay on the architecture of Cassandra.
24. How does Write and Read process happen in Cassandra?
25. What are the additional components of Cassandra?
26. What are the advantages of Cassandra and its use cases?
27. What is MongoDB? Describe its basic architecture.
28. What are the advantages of MongoDB and its use cases?
29. What is HBase? Describe its basic architecture.

CHAPTER **15**

Cassandra Data Model

> **LEARNING OBJECTIVES**
>
> Cassandra is an Apache distributed database designed to manage huge volumes of structured data and is very scalable. It ensures high availability and eliminates the possibility of a single point-of-failure. This chapter begins with an overview of Cassandra, then moves on to its architecture, installation, and key classes and interfaces. It then explains how to use CQLSH, examines the data types and collections accessible in CQL and the applications of user-defined data types.

15.1 Introduction

Cassandra is a distributed database management system for conventional servers that can handle massive amounts of structured data. Cassandra is a distributed database that can handle massive volumes of data and it is a type of NoSQL database. Apache HBase and MongoDB also belong to this type of NoSQL database. Data is replicated across several machines, ensuring high availability, and eliminating single points of failure in Cassandra. It is reliable, scalable, and consistent. It is a database with columns. Its data model is built on Google's Bigtable, and its distribution strategy is based on Amazon's Dynamo. It was developed at Facebook and is very different from relational database management systems. Cassandra combines a more sophisticated "column family" data model with a dynamo-style replication strategy with no single point-of-failure. Some of the largest firms like Facebook, Twitter, eBay, Twitter and Netflix, utilize Cassandra. Cassandra was created for an inbox search on Facebook. In July 2008, Facebook made it open-source. Then, in March 2009, Cassandra was approved for the Apache Incubator. In February 2010, it was designated as an Apache top-level project.

Cassandra is highly scalable, allowing for the addition of more hardware to support clients and data as needed. Cassandra has no single point-of-failure and is always accessible for mission-critical applications that cannot afford downtime. Cassandra is linearly scalable, which means that as the number of nodes in the cluster grows, so does the throughput. As a result, it maintains a rapid response time. Cassandra is a flexible data storage system that can handle all types of data, including structured, semi-structured, and unstructured data. In addition, it can dynamically adapt to changes in your data structures based on your requirements. Cassandra's versatility allows data to be deployed anywhere, by duplicating data across various data centers. Atomicity, Consistency, Isolation, and Durability are all qualities that Cassandra (ACID properties). Cassandra was built from the ground-up to run on low-cost commodity hardware. As a result, it has lightning-fast write speeds and can store hundreds of terabytes of data without losing read speed.

15.2 Use Cases of Cassandra

Cassandra is an excellent database that can handle large amounts of data. Therefore, it is suitable for companies that provide mobile phones and messaging services. Cassandra is the best choice because these companies have vast amounts of data. Cassandra can process high-speed data, making it an ideal database for applications that receive data at very high speeds from various devices and sensors. Many merchants rely on Cassandra to provide continuous cart protection and rapid product entry and exit. Cassandra is an excellent database for many online business and social media providers to analyze and recommend to their customers.

15.3 Cassandra Installation in Windows Environment

Cassandra can be installed in two ways: one way is to install Apache Cassandra Datastax community edition and another is to install the Apache Cassandra open edition. We are going to install Apache Cassandra open edition, directly from the Apache Website. Windows is the best platform to use. To install Cassandra into the machine, first we need to have the Java Development Kit (JDK) set up and the Python 2.7.x edition.

15.3.1 Installing Python 2.7.x Edition

First, visit the website of python (python.org). It will display a screen as shown in Fig. 15.1. Click on the Python 2.7.18 version link as shown.

When you Click on the Python 2.7.18 version link, it will take us to the next screen where we need to choose the operating system. Since we are going to install the Windows edition, we need to choose the Windows edition installer as shown in Fig. 15.2.

Once the Windows MSI Installer is downloaded, double click on the execution file to install Python, it will ask for the details. Choose "Install for all users" and click the Next button as shown in Fig. 15.3.

The next screen asks for the details of the folder where the Python version is to be stored. We want to install the same in the folder "E:" and hence we change the folder as shown in Fig. 15.4 and click Next.

Cassandra Data Model • 793

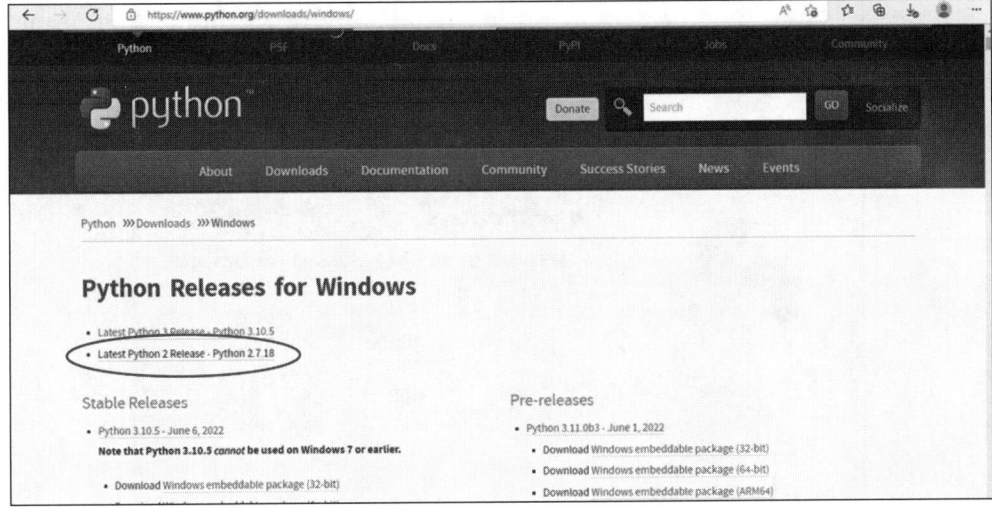

Figure 15.1 Python download: Home page

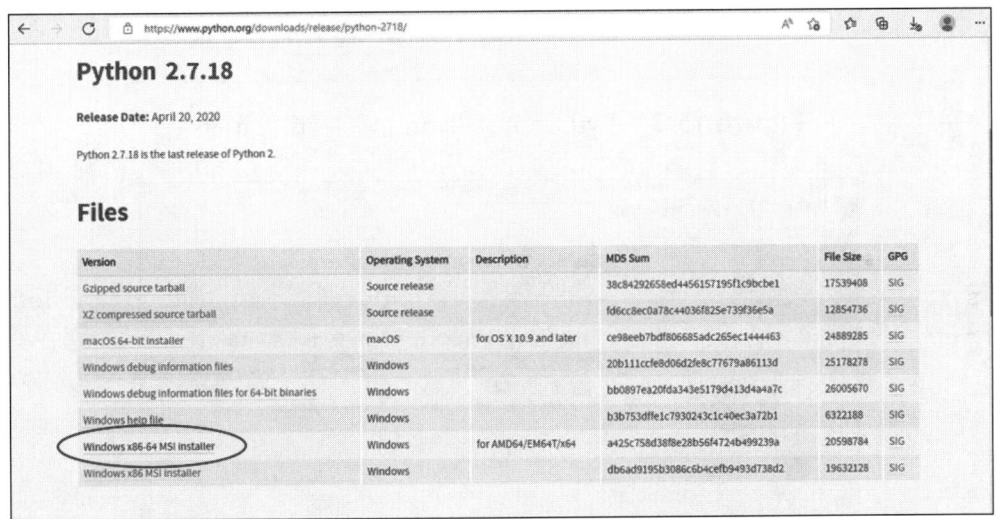

Figure 15.2 Python download: Operating systems

The next screen is as shown in Fig. 15.5, indicating how much disk usage is required for the installations. It shows the Python installations requires 32 MB hard drive space. Click Next as shown in the figure.

The next screen indicates that the installation of Python got completed. Click Finish button as shown in Fig. 15.6, to exit the installer.

After installing the python version, set the environment variable, in particular the path system variable ("path") in the Windows system, in order to complete the installation steps.

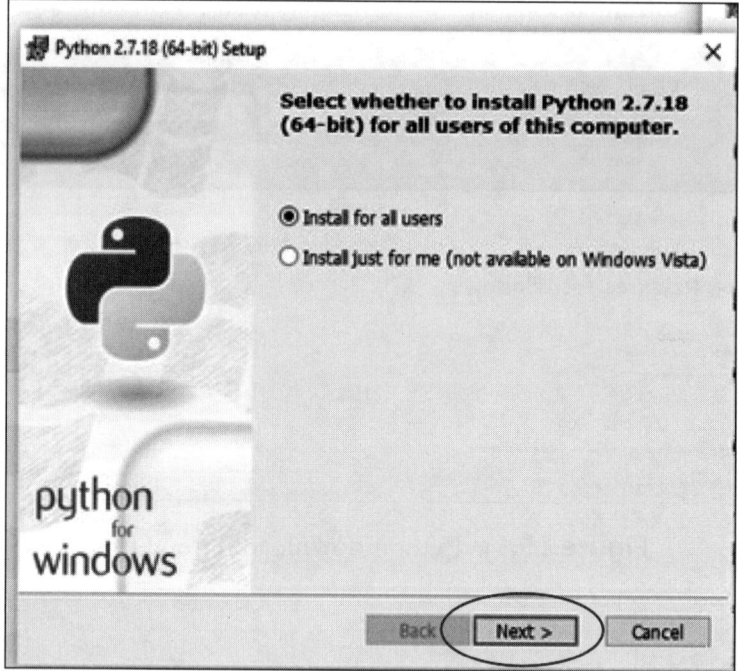

Figure 15.3 Python installation: Selecting users

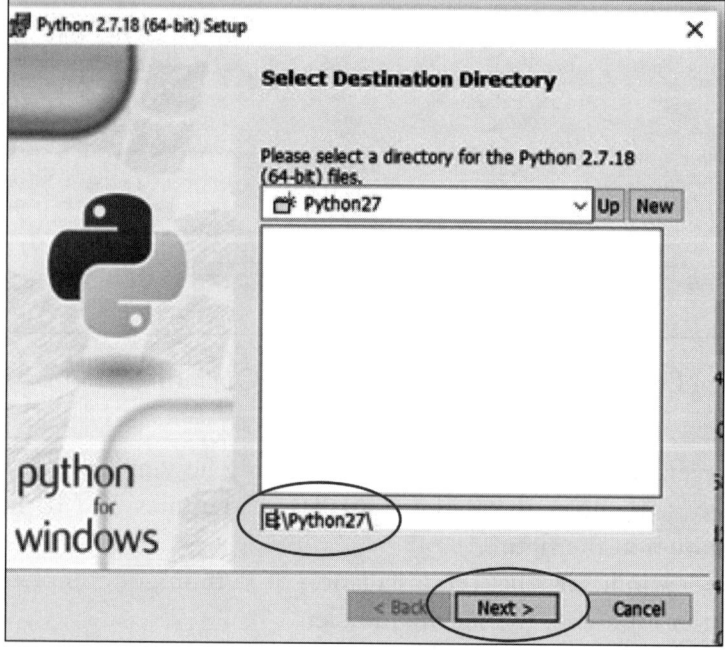

Figure 15.4 Python installation: Selecting the folders

Cassandra Data Model • **795**

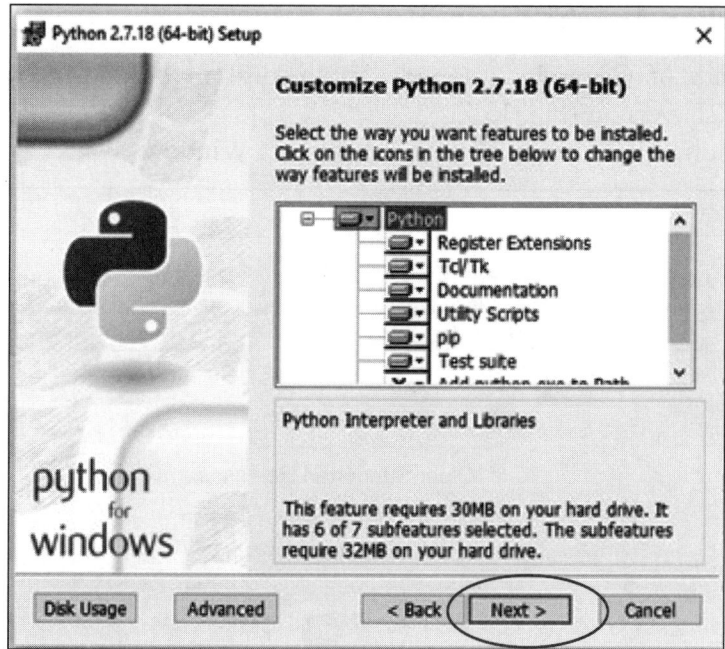

Figure 15.5 Python installation: Disk usage

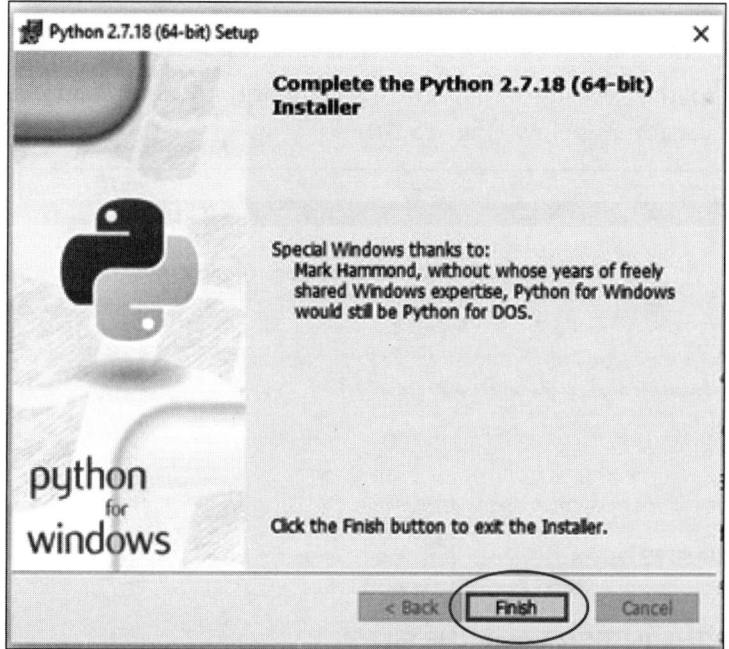

Figure 15.6 Python installation: Finish button

15.3.2 Installing Apache Cassandra

Visit the website of Cassandra (cassandra.apache.org) in order to download Apache Cassandra (3.0.27) version (Fig. 15.7).

Note: Version 4.0 of Cassandra does not support Windows.

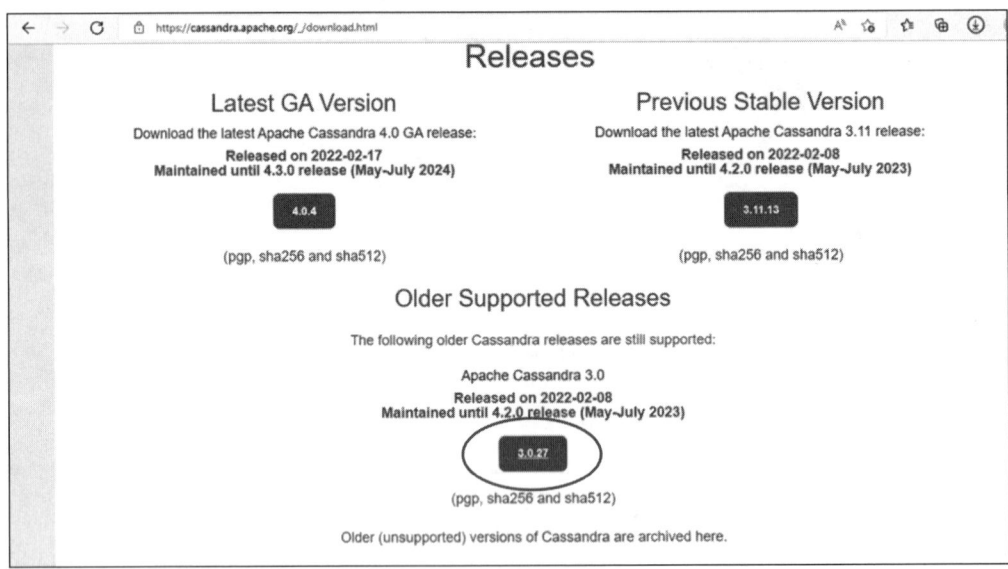

Figure 15.7 Cassandra download: Apache home page

It will take us to the website of Apache (apache.org) to download Apache Cassandra (3.0.27) bin.tar version as below (Fig. 15.8).

Figure 15.8 Cassandra download: Apache Mirror Site download

Using a compression program, unzip the compressed tar.gz folder. The compressed folder was unzipped, and the contents were placed in the "E:/Program Files/apache-cassandra-3.0.27" folder in this example. After this, set the environment variable, in particular the path system variable ("path") in the Windows system, in order to complete the installation steps. Set the "CASSANDRA_HOME" class path (Fig. 15.9) to the directory of the Cassandra ("E:/Program Files/apache-cassandra-3.0.27").

Figure 15.9 Cassandra installation: Setting Cassandra home

Starting Cassandra Server

Go the bin directory of the Cassandra ("E:/Program Files/apache-cassandra-3.0.27/bin") and give the command "Cassandra" to start the Cassandra server. This screen below will be shown, to indicate that the Cassandra server got started (Fig. 15.10).

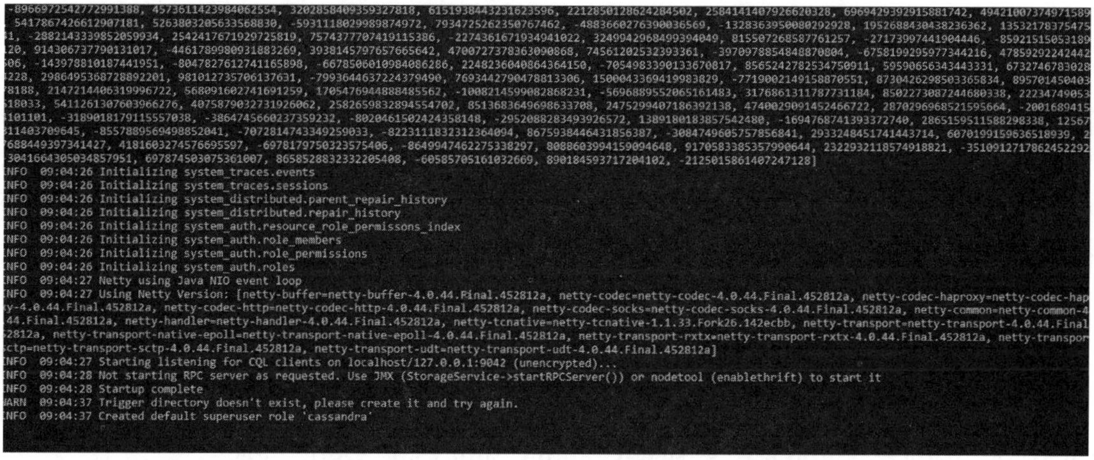

Figure 15.10 Cassandra Server start

Starting the client (cqlsh)

Without closing the sever, open one more command prompt (cmd). Go the bin directory of the Cassandra ("E:/Program Files/apache-cassandra-3.0.27/bin") and give the command "cqlsh" to start the Cassandra client. The Cassandra client gets started and it gives the cqlsh command prompt as shown in the screen (Fig. 15.11).

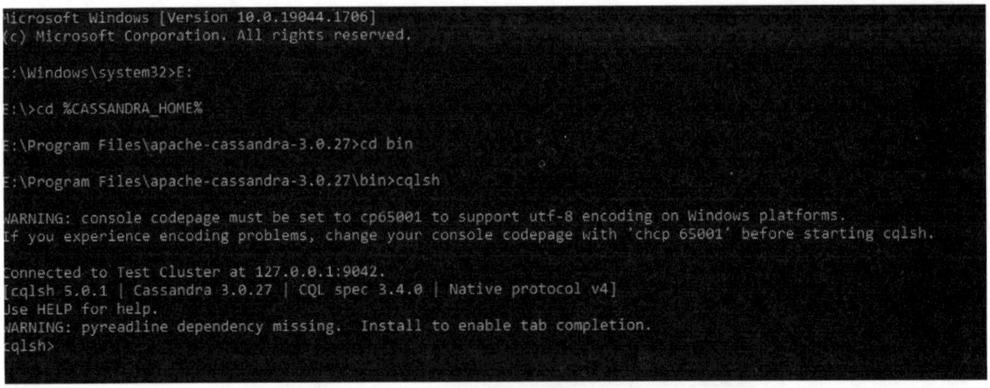

Figure 15.11 Cassandra CQL Shell start

15.4 CASSANDRA BASIC CQL

A query language is the computer language used to execute queries in databases and information systems. For example, the primary query language for connecting with the Apache Cassandra database is the Cassandra query language (CQL). The standard query language for processing relational databases is SQL (Structured Query Language). Relational query languages, such as SQL, are vertically scalable, fixed-schema, table-based databases that handle medium amounts of data. NoSQL query languages like CQL can query horizontally distributed server clusters, are highly scalable, manage unstructured data, do not require a fixed schema, avoid joins, and are easily extensible. Cassandra CQL, a simple alternative to Structured Query Language (SQL), is a declarative language developed to provide abstraction in accessing Apache Cassandra. CQL can be used to create/investigate Cassandra's keyspaces. This section will walk you through some of the often-used CQL commands for connecting to and querying data in a Cassandra cluster.

Cassandra Query Language (CQL)

CQL is a simple interface for querying Cassandra that may also be used to replace regular SQL. CQL offers a native vocabulary for collections and adds an abstraction layer to conceal the implementation of structure. There are four basic Cassandra database related elements, namely: Cluster, Keyspace, Column Family and CQL Table (Fig. 15.12).

The cluster is Cassandra's outer structure. A cluster is a Keyspace container. Cassandra is also known as the ring because it assigns data to cluster nodes by organizing them in a ring. A node stores a replica for a particular set of data. A keyspace (Fig. 15.13) is equivalent to a schema or database in a relational paradigm. It consists of multiple column families (Tables).

A column family is a container containing an ordered group of rows, each of which comprises an ordered group of columns. Depending on your demands, you may add any column to any column family at any moment. When columns are returned to you in a query, the comparator value determines how they will be ordered (Fig. 15.14).

Cassandra Data Model • 799

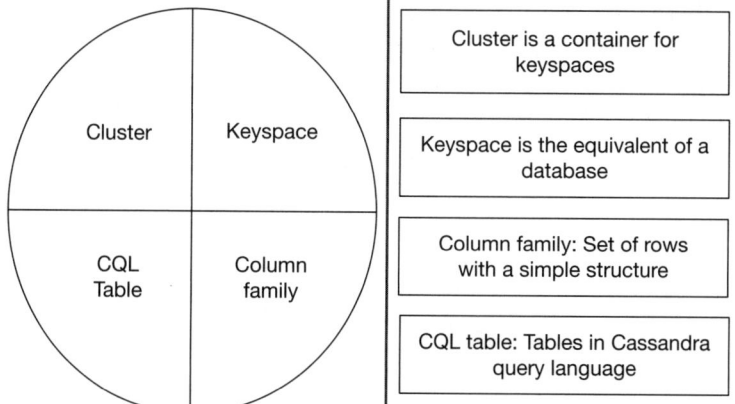

Figure 15.12 Cassandra database related elements

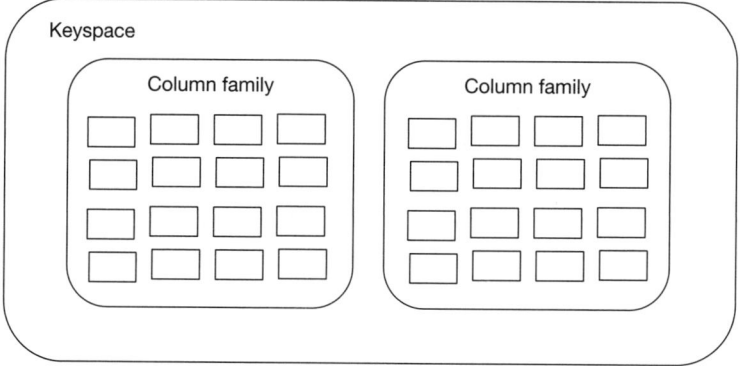

Figure 15.13 Cassandra keyspace and column family

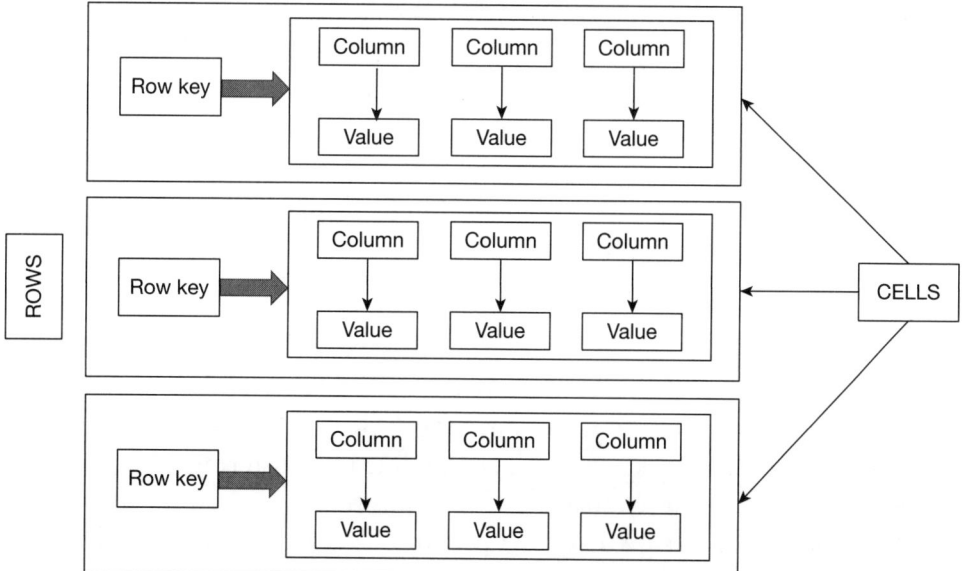

Figure 15.14 Cassandra column family and rows

A row (Fig. 15.15) is a grouping of columns that has been sorted. In Cassandra, it is the smallest unit that contains connected data. Data or information can be stored in any component of a row.

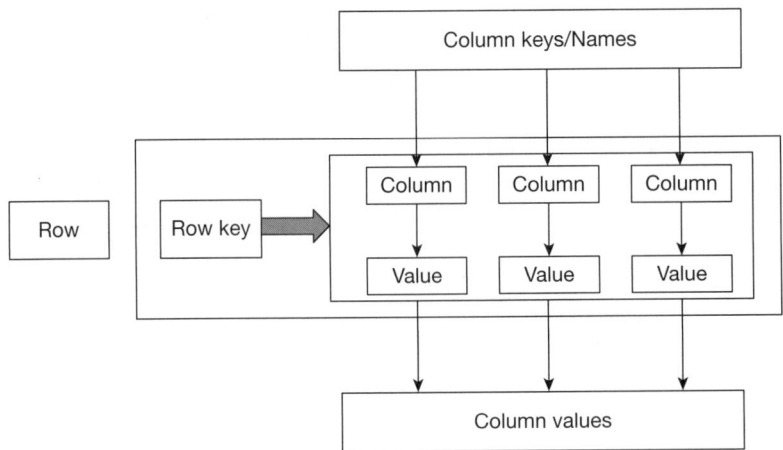

Figure 15.15 Cassandra row structure

Each Cassandra cluster uses a system keyspace to hold system-wide metadata. The replication settings in Keyspace determine how data is distributed and duplicated in clusters. A cluster typically comprises only one Keyspace; however, a cluster may have many keyspaces (Table 15.1).

Table 15.1 Relational Database vs. Cassandra

Relational Database	Cassandra
Database	Key space
Table	Column family
Primary key	Row key
Column name/value	Column name/value

There are three types of Primary Keys: namely: Single Primary Key, Compound Primary Key and Composite Partitioning Key (Fig. 15.16).

Single Primary Key: There is only one Primary Key column in the Single Primary Key. The partitioning key is another name for this column. Based on this column, data is partitioned. The partition key is used to distribute data among various nodes.

Compound Primary Key: Data is partitioned and subsequently clustered in Compound Primary Key. The partitioning key is race name, while the clustering key is race position. Race names are used to split the data, and race positions are used to cluster the data. Clustering is a method of sorting data in a partition. When rows for a partition key are kept in order depending on the clustering column, retrieval of rows is highly efficient.

Composite Partitioning Key: It is used to divide the data into numerous partitions. The composite partition key comprises race year and race name, and data will be partitioned using both columns. The rank will be used to cluster the data. It is utilized when there is too much data on a single partition.

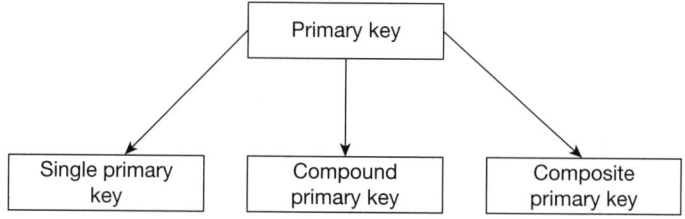

Figure 15.16 Types of primary keys in Cassandra

Metadata is stored in the System Keyspace. The two main metadata stored in the system key space are: Schema definition and Migration data.

Schema definition includes the following: the cluster name, keyspace definition, the node's token, and whether the node is bootstrapped. Migration data includes information on the extent of the system keyspace and whether the keyspace has been updated. Cassandra keeps track of its state in tables called System Keyspace Tables.

15.5 HOW TO CREATE, ALTER, DROP AND USE KEYSPACE IN CASSANDRA

Use the Create KEYSPACE statement to create a Keyspace.
Use the ALTER KEYSPACE statement to modify the Keyspace.
Use the DROP KEYSPACE command to remove Keyspace.
Use the USE KEYSPACE statement to use Keyspace.

15.5.1 Create Keyspace

To create Keyspace in Cassandra, use the "CREATE KEYSPACE" command. CREATE KEYSPACE <identifier> WITH <properties>

The properties used while creating a keyspace are:

- Keyspace Name
- Replication Strategy
- Replication Factor
- Durable Writes

Rules for Keyspace_name
- Maximum of 48 characters
- Must begin with a letter
- The next character may be letters, digits, or underscore
- The operation fails if a keyspace with the same name already exists
- Use the IF NOT EXIST clause to prevent error messages.

Cassandra may be told whether or not to utilize the commit log for updates on the current Keyspace using Durable Writes. This option is not required. TRUE is the default setting for durable writes.

Replication_map

The replication map shows the number of copies (replicas) of data held in the data center. It affects consistency, availability, and speed. A replica is stored on many nodes to provide reliability and fault tolerance. A replication strategy specifies the node where replicas are kept. The replication factor is the total number of replicas in the cluster. A replication factor of 1 indicates that each row is kept on only one node in the cluster. Similarly, a replication factor of 2 indicates that each row contains two copies on two separate nodes. There is no primary or master replica; all replicas are equally important. In general, the replication factor should not exceed the number of nodes in the cluster.

Cassandra Query Language (CQL) allows developers to interact with Cassandra. The syntax of the Cassandra query language is very similar to the syntax of SQL.

A replication strategy: It is established for each Keyspace and is determined when the Keyspace is created. There are two replication strategies, which are as follows:

- Simple Strategy, and
- Network Topology Strategy.

15.5.2 Simple Strategy

In the case of a single data center, a simple technique is applied (Fig. 15.17). The first copy of this technique is installed on the selected node, and subsequent nodes are placed clockwise regardless of the rack or node position in the ring.

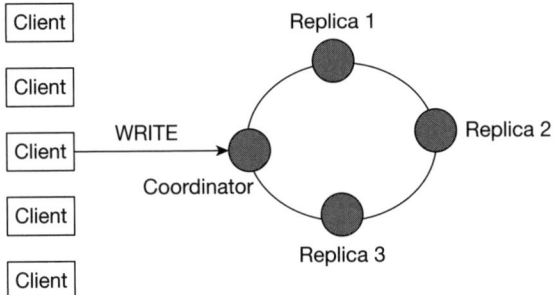

Figure 15.17 Simple strategy

It is exclusively utilized for development, even if you only have one data center. Use Network Topology Strategy if you have more than one data center. Simple Strategy mounts the first replica on the node specified by the partitioner in the Cassandra.YAML file.

Further copies are inserted into the ring of the next node in the clockwise direction, regardless of topology.

The employee keyspace is created with replication factor 3 in the following CQL statement.

```
CREATE KEYSPACE IF NOT EXISTS employee
  WITH REPLICATION = {
    'class' : 'SimpleStrategy',
    'replication_factor' : 3
  };
```

15.5.3 Network Topology Strategy

This strategy is strongly advised because it makes it much easier to scale the cluster to various data centers. It specifies the number of replicas required for each data center. The replica is installed in the same data center and runs clockwise in a ring until it reaches the initial node on another rack. Replication is placed in a different rack because nodes in the same rack (or similar physical group) can fail at the same time due to power, cooling, or network issues. This method is used when you have multiple data centers. This technique requires you to specify the replication factor for each data center individually (Fig. 15.18).

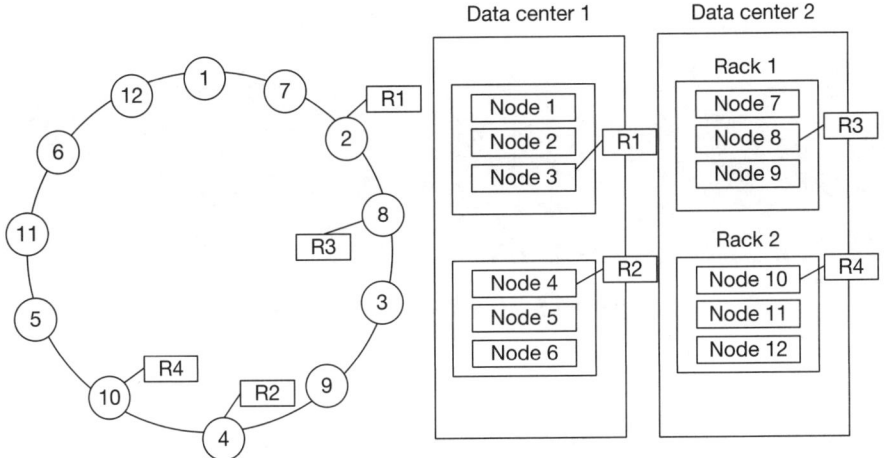

Figure 15.18 Network topology strategy

Create Keyspace

Create Keyspace command can be used to create the keyspace in Cassandra. Keyspace is the equivalent terminology for database. While creating keyspace, we give the class which indicates the strategy and the replication factor. We create a keyspace called "school" with the "SimpleStrategy" and also with the replication factor of 3 as shown in Fig. 15.19.

```
cqlsh> Create keyspace school WITH replication = { 'class': 'SimpleStrategy', 'replication_factor': 3};
cqlsh> Describe keyspaces

school  system_schema  system_auth  system  system_distributed  system_traces

cqlsh>
```

Figure 15.19 Create keyspace

The CQL statement for creating the "Academic" keyspace with two data centers, namely, the Chennai data center with replication factor 3 and the Bangalore data center with replication factor 2, is as follows:

```
CREATE KEYSPACE IF NOT EXISTS Academic
  WITH REPLICATION = {
    'class' : 'NetworkTopologyStrategy',
    'chennai' : 3 , // Datacenter 1
    'bangalore' : 2 , // Datacenter 2
  };
```

Describe Keyspaces

Describe Keyspaces command (Fig. 15.20) can be used to list down all the keyspace names in the Cassandra. **Note**: Semicolon is given at the end of the statement to indicate the end of the statement (or query) that can be executed.

The below screen indicates the list of keyspaces that are available, which includes the newly created keyspace ("school") and other system level keyspaces including: "system_schema", "system_auth", "system", "system_distributed", and "system_traces."

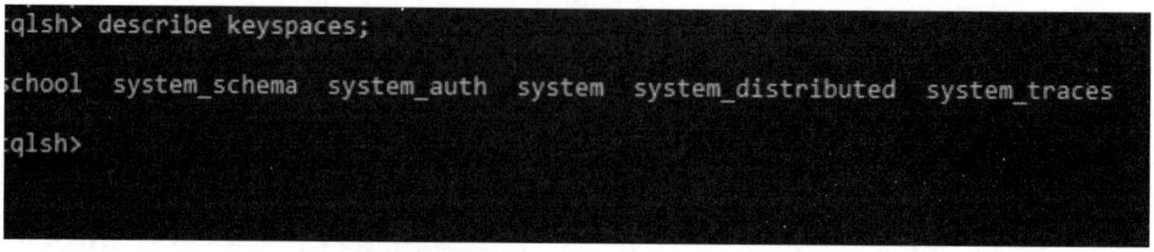

```
qlsh> describe keyspaces;

chool  system_schema  system_auth  system  system_distributed  system_traces

qlsh>
```

Figure 15.20 Describe keyspaces

Alter Keyspace
Syntax
```
ALTER KEYSPACE <identifier> WITH <properties>      Or
ALTER KEYSPACE "KeySpace Name" WITH replication = {'class':
'Strategy name', 'replication_factor' : 'No.Of replicas'};
ALTER KEYSPACE syntax diagram
```

- The keyspace_name cannot be altered.
- Cassandra throws an error message if the Keyspace does not exist.
- A replication map's approach and replication factors can be altered.
  You can change the value of DURABLE_WRITES by changing it to true or false.
  To disregard the error notice, use the IF EXIST clause.

Drop Keyspace
Syntax
```
DROP keyspace KeyspaceName;
```
The DROP KEYSPACE command deletes all keyspace components, including tables, column families, and index data.

- If the keyspace does not exist, Cassandra will throw an error message.
- To disregard the error notice, use the IF EXIST clause.

Use Keyspace Use keyspace command (Fig. 15.21) can be used to utilize the keyspace (database) for the upcoming CQL commands in Cassandra. The below screen indicates the usage of the system-created keyspace titled "system_auth". The command, "describe tables;" further lists down all the tables in the specified keyspace ("system_auth").

```
cqlsh:school> use system_auth;
cqlsh:system_auth> describe tables;

resource_role_permissons_index   role_permissions   role_members   roles

cqlsh:system_auth>
```

Figure 15.21 Use keyspace

15.6 COLUMN FAMILIES

A column family is a logical division that associates comparable data and is analogous to a table in RDBMS (Relational Database Management System). In Cassandra, a Column Family is a row containing ordered columns. They represent the stored data's structure. Keyspace (database) contains these Cassandra Column families. Each keyspace contains at least one column family. Each column's row is made up of several columns. In Cassandra, columns are the fundamental building blocks of the data structure. Three values are kept in each column: name, timestamp, and value are the key or column names. Furthermore, columns in these rows can be added or removed based on the user's needs. Column families in Cassandra, on the other hand, are predetermined and cannot be changed. A super-column family, a table with numerous columns, is also available.

15.6.1 Types of Columns

In the world of RDBMS, a Column Family is equivalent to a table. There are several types of columns.

The names and data formats for static columns are defined in the static column family. As a result, when the column family is created, you have the choice of naming the columns and data types. Because the columns remain static and the number of columns accessible is known, it is called static. The names and data formats for static columns are defined in the static column family. As a result, when the column family is created, you have the choice of naming the column and data types.

Cassandra allows you to name your columns however you want. In Cassandra, columns are the fundamental building blocks of the data structure. Three values are kept in each column. Name, timestamp, and value are the key or column names.

In addition, the columns in these rows can be added or removed according to the user's needs. On the other hand, the Cassandra column families are predetermined and hence cannot be modified. There is also a super-column family, which has a collection of numerous columns. We get large rows when actual data is placed in column names. Wide rows facilitate data ordering and thus efficient filtering because column names are physically ordered (range scans). If necessary, you will be able to quickly lookup a single column within a large row. In Cassandra, comprehensive row-column families are frequently used (with composite columns) to create custom indexes. You can also denormalize a one-to-many relationship as a broad row without duplicating data. However, it should be done only if you have a lot of data to query and you need to improve read performance. A column made up of a map of columns is known as a super-column. It has a name and a value that involves a column map. A column family made up of super-columns is known as a super-column family. A NoSQL object that contains column families is known as a super-column family. It is a tuple (pair) made up of a key-value pair, where the key is mapped to a value that belongs to one of the column families. A super-column family is analogous to a "view" on several tables in relational databases. It may also be viewed as a table map. Having some form of perspective on a lot of tables is essential when creating a data model. The use of a super-column family is comparable to distributed data storage. However, because data stores like Apache Cassandra are non-relational, there are no "joins" between the "tables." For example: User name (Super-column) can have columns like First name and Last name.

A keyspace is a container for application data that must have a name and a set of related attributes, similar to an RDBMS database. The Cassandra keyspace database is a relational database. A keyspace consists of several Column Families/Tables. A Cassandra column family is an SQL table. A Primary Key comprises a Row/Partition Key and a Cluster Key, and allows users to identify internal rows of data uniquely. A Row/Partition Key determines the node on which data is stored. A Cluster Key determines the sort order of data within a row.

15.7 Cassandra Table

In this section, let us look into the details of how to create a table, insert data, and update table.

We can create a table with Cassandra's CREATE TABLE command (Fig. 15.22). Column families, much like RDBMS tables, are utilized to store data here. As a result, the CREATE TABLE command can be used in Cassandra to create a column family. We are creating a table titled "students" within the keyspace database titled "school". The use command is used to utilize the keyspace "school" first, before giving the command to create the table ("students").

```
cqlsh:school>
cqlsh:school>
cqlsh:school> use school;
cqlsh:school> CREATE TABLE students (
          ... stud_id int PRIMARY KEY,
          ... stude_name text
          ... );
cqlsh:school> select * from students;

 stud_id | stude_name
---------+------------

(0 rows)
cqlsh:school>
```

Figure 15.22   Create Table

We can also define a primary key while creating the table. There are two types of primary keys, namely, single primary key and compound primary key. In the above table, "stud_id" is specified as single primary key of the table titled "students". We may verify the table with the command "select * from students". Since no records (rows) are inserted into the table, it only displays the structure of the table.

15.7.1 Inserting and Displaying Data from the Table

Insert command ("INSERT INTO Table name (column names) VALUES (Values)"), can be used to insert the values into the table. Column names and Values are separated by the key word comma. The screen shown in Fig. 15.23 indicates the commands that are used to insert three rows into the table titled "students". After inserting the values into the table, "select * from students" is used to display all the rows of the table as shown below.

```
cqlsh:school> INSERT INTO students (stud_id, stude_name) VALUES(100, 'joseph');
cqlsh:school> INSERT INTO students (stud_id, stude_name) VALUES(110, 'Andrea');
cqlsh:school> INSERT INTO students (stud_id, stude_name) VALUES(120, 'Beckey');
cqlsh:school> select * from students;

 stud_id | stude_name
---------+------------
     110 |     Andrea
     120 |     Beckey
     100 |     joseph

(3 rows)
cqlsh:school>
```

Figure 15.23   Insert Data into Table

15.7.2 Updating the Table Data

Update command ("UPDATE Table name SET column name = value WHERE column name = value") can be used to update the data of the table. Figure 15.24 shows the commands that are used to update the table "students", set the student name (stude_name) as "Jasmine", where the student Id (stude_id) = 120. After updating the values into the table, "select * from students" is used to display all the rows of the table as shown below. It can be seen that the name for the student id (120) got changed to "Jasmine" from "Beckey".

```
cqlsh:school> UPDATE students SET stude_name = 'Jasmine' WHERE stud_id = 120;
cqlsh:school> select * from students;

 stud_id | stude_name
---------+------------
     110 |     Andrea
     120 |    Jasmine
     100 |     joseph

(3 rows)
cqlsh:school>
```

Figure 15.24 Updating the Table data

15.8 DATA TYPES IN CASSANDRA

In the above table (students), we have created two columns for student id (stud_id) and student name (stude_name). Student id is of the type Integer and Student name is of the type Text. Cassandra has a set of date types as shown in Table 15.2.

Table 15.2 Cassandra data types

CQL Type	Constants	Description
ascii	Strings	US-ascii character string
bigint	Integers	64-bit signed long
blob	blobs	Arbitrary bytes in hexadecimal
boolean	Booleans	True or False
counter	Integers	Distributed counter values 64 bit
decimal	Integers, Floats	Variable precision decimal
double	Integers, Floats	64-bit floating point
float	Integers, Floats	32-bit floating point
frozen	Tuples, collections, user defined types	stores cassandra types
inet	Strings	IP address in ipv4 or ipv6 format
int	Integers	32 bit signed integer
list		Collection of elements
map		JSON style collection of elements
set		Collection of elements
text	strings	UTF-8 encoded strings
timestamp	Integers, Strings	ID generated with date plus time

(Continued)

Table 15.2 (Continued)

CQL Type	Constants	Description
timeuuid	uuids	Type 1 uuid
tuple		A group of 2,3 fields
uuid	uuids	Standard uuid
varchar	strings	UTF-8 encoded string
varint	Integers	Arbitrary precision integer

15.8.1 Collection Data Type in Cassandra

Collection data type consists of List, Map and Set. These are special data types.

List Data Type

A list is employed when the order of the items must be maintained. The index of the items in a list data type may be used to access the values of the list data type (Fig. 15.25).

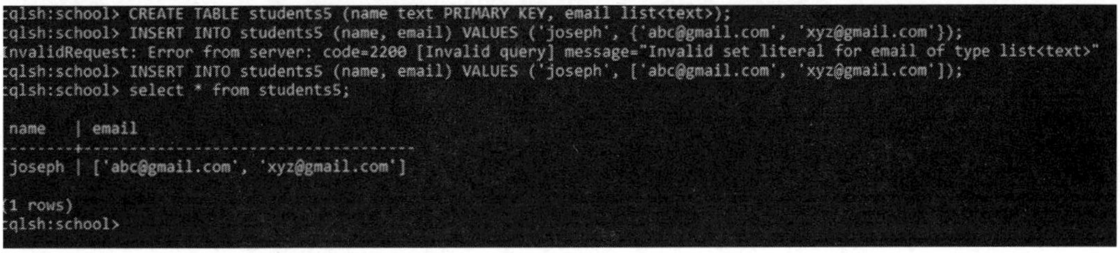

```
cqlsh:school> CREATE TABLE students5 (name text PRIMARY KEY, email list<text>);
cqlsh:school> INSERT INTO students5 (name, email) VALUES ('joseph', {'abc@gmail.com', 'xyz@gmail.com'});
InvalidRequest: Error from server: code=2200 [Invalid query] message="Invalid set literal for email of type list<text>"
cqlsh:school> INSERT INTO students5 (name, email) VALUES ('joseph', ['abc@gmail.com', 'xyz@gmail.com']);
cqlsh:school> select * from students5;

 name   | email
--------+----------------------------------
 joseph | ['abc@gmail.com', 'xyz@gmail.com']

(1 rows)
cqlsh:school>
```

Figure 15.25 Collection data type: List

In Fig. 15.25, we created a table titled "students5" which has two fields, namely, name and email. A single name can have multiple emails and hence email type is created as list. While giving the values of the list, it is given inside the square bracket, separated by the delimiter comma.

In Fig. 15.26, we updated the table titled "students5". We added another email id to the student with the name "joseph". SET command is used to update the email field, WHERE Clause is used to identify the specified set of record to be updated.

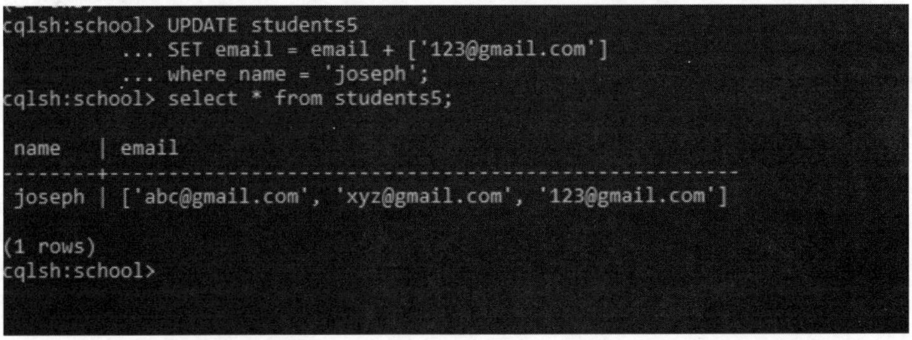

```
cqlsh:school> UPDATE students5
          ... SET email = email + ['123@gmail.com']
          ... where name = 'joseph';
cqlsh:school> select * from students5;

 name   | email
--------+-------------------------------------------------
 joseph | ['abc@gmail.com', 'xyz@gmail.com', '123@gmail.com']

(1 rows)
cqlsh:school>
```

Figure 15.26 Collection data type: List update

Map Data Type

A Map is employed when the key-value pair of elements is to be maintained.

In Fig. 15.27, we created a table titled "students4" which has two fields, namely, name and address. A single name can have multiple address with its identification and value, and hence address type is created as map. While giving the values of the map, it is given inside the braces, separated by the delimiter comma.

```
cqlsh:school> CREATE TABLE students4 (name text PRIMARY KEY, address map<text,text>);
cqlsh:school> INSERT INTO students3 (name, address) VALUES ('joseph', {'home': 'chennai', 'school' : 'chennai2'});
InvalidRequest: Error from server: code=2200 [Invalid query] message="Unable to coerce 'home' to a formatted date (long)"
cqlsh:school> INSERT INTO students3 (name, address) VALUES ('joseph', {'home' : 'chennai', 'school' : 'chennai2'});
InvalidRequest: Error from server: code=2200 [Invalid query] message="Unable to coerce 'home' to a formatted date (long)"
cqlsh:school> INSERT INTO students4 (name, address) VALUES ('joseph', {'home' : 'chennai', 'school' : 'chennai2'});
cqlsh:school> select * from students4;

 name   | address
--------+-------------------------------------------
 joseph | {'home': 'chennai', 'school': 'chennai2'}
```

Figure 15.27 Collection data type: Map

(**Note**: The error in the above screen indicates that we are trying to insert a value into another table students3 instead of students4).

Set data Type

A Set is employed when we want to use a collection of more than one element. Let us say a person can have more than one phone.

In Fig. 15.28, we created a table titled "students2", which has two fields, namely, name and phone (numbers). A single name can have more than one phone number, and hence phone is created as set with variant as type. While giving the values of the set, it is given inside the braces, separated by the delimiter comma.

```
cqlsh:school> CREATE TABLE students2 (name text PRIMARY KEY, phone set<varint>);
cqlsh:school> select * from students2;

 name | phone
------+-------

(0 rows)
cqlsh:school> INSERT INTO students2 (name, phone) VALUES ('joseph', {9940076029, 9841280765});
cqlsh:school> select * from students2;

 name   | phone
--------+--------------------------
 joseph | {9841280765, 9940076029}

(1 rows)
cqlsh:school>
```

Figure 15.28 Collection data type: Set

In Fig. 15.29, we updated the table titled "students2". We added another phone number to the student with the name "joseph". SET command is used to update the phone number, WHERE Clause is used to identify the specified set of records to be updated.

```
cqlsh:school> UPDATE students2
          ... SET phone = phone + {9768761234}
          ... WHERE name = 'joseph';
cqlsh:school> select * from students2;

 name   | phone
--------+--------------------------------------------
 joseph | {9768761234, 9841280765, 9940076029}

(1 rows)
cqlsh:school>
```

Figure 15.29 Collection data type: Set update

User-defined Data Type in Cassandra

CQL allows users to design their data types based on their needs. After defining a data type and fields inside it, the user may modify, validate, and even delete a field or the data type.

In Fig. 15.30, we have created the user-defined datatype called "address" using "CREATE TYPE" syntax. The address data type consists of other data types including Door number indicated by doorno (int), Apartment name indicated by aptname(text), and Street name indicated by streetname (text).

```
cqlsh:school> CREATE TYPE address (
          ... doorno int,
          ... aptname text,
          ... streetname text);
cqlsh:school> Describe TYPE address;

CREATE TYPE school.address (
    doorno int,
    aptname text,
    streetname text
);

cqlsh:school>
```

Figure 15.30 User-defined data type

In Fig. 15.31, we have altered the user-defined datatype called "address" using "ALTER TYPE" syntax. Earlier, the address data type consisted of other data types including Door number indicated by doorno (int), Apartment name indicated by aptname(text), and Street name indicated by streetname (text). Now, we are renaming the streetname to stname. When we use "Describe TYPE address", it clearly indicates that the change is as specified above.

```
cqlsh:school> ALTER TYPE address
          ... RENAME streetname TO stname;
cqlsh:school> Describe TYPE address;

CREATE TYPE school.address (
    doorno int,
    aptname text,
    stname text
);
```

Figure 15.31 User defined data type: Alteration

Sorting

Using ORDER BY, you may simply change the order in which records are returned to you in your query in an RDBMS. The default sort order cannot be changed; the records are returned in the order in which they were written by default. If you wish to change the order, simply change your query and sort by any set of columns. On the other hand, sorting is handled differently in Cassandra; it is a design decision. The sort order available on queries is set in stone and is dictated by the clustering columns you specify in the CREATE TABLE command. The CQL SELECT statement supports the ORDER BY semantics, but only in the order indicated by the clustering columns.

15.9 Cassandra BATCH

BATCH is used in Cassandra to perform many modification statements (insert, update, delete) simultaneously. It comes in handy when you need to update specific columns while also deleting others. First, we display all the values (rows) of the students. It displays five records as shown in Fig. 15.32.

We want to execute one INSERT, one UPDATE, one DELETE statement together in a BATCH Mode. We are inserting another record into the students table with the values of 160 and Wesley. At the same time, we are updating the name of the student with the Id of 140 to "Christina" from "Chris". We are also deleting the full record with the student id = 150. Figure 15.32 shows how the BATCH statement is created and executed. When we display the records of the table "students" again, it clearly displays all the changes executed through the BATCH statement.

15.10 Difference Between Cassandra and RDBMS

Cassandra is a distributed NoSQL database management system with excellent performance and scalability. Cassandra is a database that works with unstructured data and has a high data velocity. The data is written in Cassandra, and it is read from many places. Each row represents a unit of replication, and each column represents a unit of storage. RDBMS

```
qlsh:school> select * from students;

stud_id | stude_name
--------+-----------
    110 |     Andrea
    120 |    Jasmine
    140 |      Chris
    130 |      Robin
    150 |     Lessly

(5 rows)
qlsh:school> BEGIN BATCH
         ... INSERT INTO students (stud_id, stude_name) VALUES (160, 'Wesley');
         ... UPDATE students set stude_name = 'Christina' WHERE stud_id = 140;
         ... DELETE stude_name from students WHERE stud_id = 150;
         ... APPLY BATCH;
qlsh:school> select * from students;

stud_id | stude_name
--------+-----------
    110 |     Andrea
    120 |    Jasmine
    140 |  Christina
    160 |     Wesley
    130 |      Robin
    150 |       null

(6 rows)
qlsh:school>
```

Figure 15.32 BATCH update in Cassandra

(Relational Database Management System) is a database management system or software for relational databases that employs Structured Query Language (SQL) to query and update the database. It works with structured data and is fast at handling incoming input. In a relational database management system (RDBMS), data is primarily written in one place. However, it may also originate from one or a few places, and a row may represent a single record column representing an attribute. Table 15.3 explains the key differences between RDBMS and Cassandra.

Table 15.3 Cassandra vs. RDBMS

Sl. No.	Cassandra	RDBMS
1	Cassandra is a distributed NoSQL database management system with outstanding performance and scalability.	A relational database management system (RDBMS) is a database management system or software developed for relational databases.
2	Cassandra is a NoSQL database.	For querying and updating the database, RDBMS uses SQL.
3	It has a flexible schema.	It has a fixed schema.
4	Cassandra's architecture is peer-to-peer, with no single point of failure.	The master-slave architecture of RDBMS creates a single point of failure.
5	Cassandra is capable of handling large amounts of data in a short amount of time.	RDBMS can manage moderately fast incoming data.

(Continued)

Table 15.3 (Continued)

Sl. No.	Cassandra	RDBMS
6	Cassandra has multiple data sources, meaning data come from one or a few places.	RDBMS has a limited data source, meaning that data comes from various sources.
7	Simple transactions are supported.	Complex and layered transactions are supported.
8	Keyspace is the outermost container in Cassandra.	The database is the outermost container of RDBMS.
9	Cassandra keeps track of distributed deployments.	RDBMS follows centralized deployments.

15.11 DENORMALIZATION

The need for normalization is frequently stressed in relational database architecture. Unfortunately, this is not advantageous when working with Cassandra because it performs best when the data model is denormalized. Denormalization of data in relational databases is a common occurrence in businesses. This can be attributed to one of two factors. The first is in terms of performance. Companies denormalize general queries because they can't obtain the required performance when they have to run so many joins on years' worth of data. This works, but it goes against the grain of how relational databases are supposed to be structured, leaving one to wonder whether utilizing a relational database is the best option in these situations. A business document structure that demands retention is a second reason that relational databases are denormalized on purpose. For example, you have an enclosing table that references several other tables whose data may change over time, but you must keep the enclosing document as a historical snapshot. Invoices are a typical example here.

You already have customer and product tables, so you'd assume you could just create an invoice that references them. In practice, however, this should never be done. Customer or price information could change, causing the invoice document to lose its integrity as it was on the invoice date, violating audits, reports, or laws, and causing other issues. Furthermore, denormalization violates Codd's standard forms in the relational world; thus, you strive to avoid it. Denormalization, on the other hand, is normal in Cassandra. If the data model is simple, it is not required. Denormalization in Cassandra previously required the creation and maintenance of numerous tables. Now, Cassandra has materialized views, which allows you to generate numerous denormalized data views depending on your base table architecture, starting with version 3.0. Cassandra is in charge of maintaining a materialized view on the server and syncing the view with the spreadsheet.

15.12 DESIGN PATTERNS

The term "design pattern" is widely misinterpreted in the software development community. However, it is, in a broad sense, a collection of answers to well-known issues in particular contexts. In the following sections, we shall see how Cassandra's unique features are equipped to solve real-world challenges and examine a few real-life instances of such design patterns.

15.12.1 Coexistence Patterns

Cassandra is a popular NoSQL data storage that resembles a classic RDBMS. Even though the underlying structure of these tables is entirely different, Cassandra column families (also known as Cassandra tables) have a logical similarity to RDBMS-based tables in the eyes of the users. As a result, Cassandra is best-suited for use in conjunction with traditional RDBMS to solve problems that standard RDBMS cannot. The issue here is that, in the eyes of end-users, RDBMS tables and Cassandra column families are very similar; therefore, many users and data modelers try to utilize Cassandra in the same manner as they use RDBMS. Cassandra is a popular NoSQL data storage system that looks similar to a traditional RDBMS. Cassandra column families (also known as Cassandra tables) bear a logical similarity to RDBMS-based tables from the users' perspective, even though their underlying structure is fundamentally different. As a result, Cassandra is best-suited for using traditional RDBMS to solve problems that traditional RDBMS cannot.

Many users and data modelers want to utilize Cassandra in the same way they use RDBMS. Create your data model based on these considerations. In Big Data, applications take precedence over data models, and data models are no longer in charge of application design. Create a data model that meets the requirements of your application. In every organization, new reporting requirements emerge regularly. The underlying data store is the most challenging aspect of creating reports in RDBMS. To generate a simple report, you may need to join numerous tables. You can collect the data you need for your report using RDBMS components like views, stored procedures, and indexes. However, the query plan for generating the report is usually quite complicated. When generating such reports on the fly, the amount of processing power must be considered. Because of this complication, it is typical for reporting requirements to have a separate database that contains the data exported from the transaction table. This is where using Cassandra or another NoSQL database as your report data store is advantageous. Any organization's data aggregation and summarizing needs are standardized. Hence, storing only the summary statistics and shifting the transaction data to the archive helps restrict the expansion of the data. This data is frequently aggregated and summarized for statistical reasons.

15.13 RDBMS Migration Patterns

Switching from RDBMS to Cassandra for all types of technological transitions is not advisable. There are a few things to think about before completing the conversion. First, the transition from RDBMS to Cassandra is identical. New technologies that replace old technologies must, at the very least, coexist peacefully for a brief time. This will enable stakeholders to have more faith in the new technology. Various technical specialists offer various approaches for the RDBMS-to-NoSQL migration strategy. Many of these recommendations are specific to a particular NoSQL data store and concentrate on a single topic. In most situations, the process, not the technology, is summarized. It is not straightforward to switch from RDBMS to Cassandra.

The fundamental reason is that most firms have used and trusted RDBMS-based solutions for a long time. As a result, transitioning from a solid RDBMS-based system to Cassandra is not for the faint of heart. Taking advantage of Cassandra's new or unique capabilities not available in many standard RDBMSs is one of the best ways to achieve this goal. However, this also stops you from utilizing Cassandra in the same way that you would any other RDBMS. Cassandra is one of a kind. Cassandra is not a relational database management system. The strategy of relying on one's qualities applies to the transfer from RDBMS to Cassandra and the transition between paradigms.

You can start your final complete RDBMS migration right now if you use Cassandra's unique capabilities correctly. Collection object modeling in an RDBMS is time-consuming since it necessitates the definition of numerous tables and the usage of joins to retrieve the data. Many RDBMSs support this by allowing users to build custom data types, although there is no industry standard in this area. In real-world applications, collection objects are relatively common. In applications, lists of actions, tuples of linked values, collections of objects, dictionaries, and so on are prevalent. Cassandra is a column family data type, which can be modeled in a complex fashion. Counting is a process that many business operations and applications require. These must be modeled as integers or long numbers in RDBMS, but applications frequently commit significant errors by misusing them. The column family counter data type in Cassandra solves this problem. It is impossible to delete unneeded records from an RDBMS table using an automated approach. If some application events occur, the application program or another mechanism should be used to eliminate them. Many data elements, on the other hand, have a predetermined lifespan. They should vanish without the need for external intervention. Cassandra knows how to get things done.

15.14 CAP Patterns

The number of components in massive Internet applications or online services, also known as the Internet of Things (IoT) applications, is enormous, and their distribution methods are inconceivable. There are hundreds of application servers, data storage nodes, and several additional components throughout the ecosystem. In such a case, executing an atomic transaction with the approval of all the components involved is impossible for all practical purposes. All distributed computing systems must provide three fundamental assurances known as CAP guarantees: consistency, availability, and partition tolerance, even if not all can execute simultaneously. The distribution of application nodes is essential for IoT applications. This means that it is very likely a network partition. Therefore, it is essential to guarantee P. This raises the question of whether to revoke the C or A warranty. At this point, the situation is not as tricky as depicted in the CAP theorem inferred by Eric Brewer. You do not need to set 100%

C and 100% A guarantees for all use-cases, for a particular IoT application. You can adjust the C warranty according to the need for the A warranty. In other words, it is called adjustable consistency. Depending on how the data is taken into Cassandra and consumed by Cassandra, it can be tuned to achieve the best results for the proper read and write needs of the application. The data writing speed is extremely fast in some applications. Cassandra's data collection speed is, in other words, lightning-fast. This is one of the write-intensive applications. In some situations, the ability to scan data will be essential. This is essential in applications requiring a large amount of data processing. This area includes data analytics, batch processing, and other similar applications. These are read-intensive apps. There is now a third group of applications in which both fast writes and quick reads are equally important. These are the types of applications in which there is a continuous input of data and a need for clients to interpret the data for various purposes. These are read-write balanced applications.

The level of consistency required for each of the preceding three types of applications, i.e., read-intensive, write-intensive and read-write applications, is entirely different. There is no one-size-fits-all approach to tune for the requirements of all three types of applications. The consistency levels for each of the three applications must be modified independently. Various design patterns have emerged for applications with fast write, fast read, and medium write and read needs. The usage of Cassandra's changeable integrity parameters is central to all of these design approaches.

15.15 Temporal Patterns

The use of data that changes over time in all applications is called time data, which is very important. Whenever you need to maintain a chronology, you need a temporary date. Numerous applications require a great deal of time-sensitive data storage, retrieval, and processing. The main challenge in working with data stored in data stores is its widespread use for analyzing and retrieving data based on different time sort orders. Therefore, the data store used to collect time data must be able to store the data in strict time series. There are so many usage patterns in the real world that they will show behavior over time. The first is the general time series category – for example, the seasonal variation in weather, such as the cold winter and warm summer months. Another example is stock market trends, where high and low points can be seen over days, weeks, or even years. The second is the log category such as business audit logs, transaction logs, etc. The third is conversation categories, such as conversation messages in chat applications. This classification is helpful because it is often utilized in many applications. Many applications will have different data stores recording this temporal data, and designers may underestimate this element. Finally, many applications will have different data stores capturing this temporal data. An enterprise-wide solution design requires a standard strategy for dealing with temporal data that fall into these three categories. To put it another way, there should be a standard manner of recording temporal data, a standard way of processing temporal data, and a standard set of tools and libraries for managing temporal data. Temporary data is widely used in a wide range of applications. From a Cassandra perspective, data modeling of time data is critical for optimal storage and fast access to data. You can design a very effective and robust time data model by focusing on just a few aspects, such as partition keys, primary keys, clustering columns, and the number of records saved in a large Cassandra series.

SUMMARY

Cassandra is a distributed database management system for conventional servers that can handle massive amounts of structured data and it is a type of NoSQL database. Apache HBase and MongoDB also belong to the type of NoSQL database. Data is replicated across several machines, ensuring high availability, and eliminating single points of failure in Cassandra. It is reliable, scalable, and consistent. It is a database with columns.

Cassandra is an excellent database that can handle large amounts of data. Therefore, it is suitable for companies that provide mobile phones and messaging services. Cassandra is the best choice because these companies have vast amounts of data. Cassandra can process high-speed data, making it an ideal database for applications that receive data at very high speeds from various devices and sensors. Many merchants rely on Cassandra to provide continuous cart protection and rapid product entry and exit. Cassandra is an excellent database for many online business and social media providers to analyze and recommend to their customers.

- **Cassandra Query Language (CQL):** CQL is a simple interface for querying Cassandra that may also be used to replace regular SQL. CQL offers a native vocabulary for collections and adds an abstraction layer to conceal the implementation of structure. There are four basic Cassandra database related elements, namely: Cluster, Keyspace, Column Family and CQL Table.
  A column family is a container that has an ordered group of rows, each of which comprises an ordered group of columns. Depending on your demands, we may add any column to any column family at any moment. When columns are returned to you in a query, the comparator value determines how they will be ordered
  There are three types of Primary Keys: namely: Single Primary Key, Compound Primary Key and Composite Partitioning Key.
- **Single Primary Key:** There is only one Primary Key column in the Single Primary Key. The Partitioning Key is another name for this column. Based on this column, data is partitioned. The partition key is used to distribute data among various nodes.
- **Compound Primary Key:** Data is partitioned and subsequently clustered in Compound Primary Key. The partitioning key is the race name, while the clustering key is the race position. Race names will be used to split the data, and race positions will be used to cluster the data. Clustering is a method of sorting data in a partition.

When rows for a partition key are kept in order depending on the clustering column, retrieval of rows is highly efficient.
- **Composite Partitioning Key:** It is used to divide the data into numerous partitions. The composite partition key comprises race year and race name, and data will be partitioned using both columns. The rank will be used to cluster the data. It is utilized when there is too much data on a single partition.
- **A Replication Strategy:** It is established for each Keyspace and is determined when the Keyspace is created. There are two replication strategies, which are as follows:
  - Simple Strategy, and
  - Network Topology Strategy.
- **Simple Strategy:** In the case of a single data center, a simple technique is applied. The first copy of this technique is installed on the selected node, and subsequent nodes are placed clockwise regardless of the rack or node position in the ring. It is exclusively utilized for development, even if you only have one data center. Use Network Topology Strategy if you have more than one data center. The Simple Strategy mounts the first replica on the node specified by the partitioner in the Cassandra.YAML file.
- **Network Topology Strategy:** This strategy makes it much easier to scale the cluster to various data centers. It specifies the number of replicas required for each data center. The replica is installed in the same data center and runs clockwise in a ring until it reaches the initial node on another rack. Replication is placed in a different rack because nodes in the same rack (or similar physical group) can fail at the same time due to power, cooling, or network issues. This method is used when you have multiple data centers and requires you to specify the replication factor for each data center individually.

BATCH is used in Cassandra to perform many modification statements (insert, update, delete) simultaneously. It comes in handy when you need to update specific columns while also deleting others.

Cassandra is a distributed NoSQL database management system with excellent performance and scalability. Cassandra is a database that works with unstructured data and has a high data velocity. The data is written in Cassandra, and it is read from many places. Each row represents a unit of replication, and each column represents a unit of storage. RDBMS (Relational Database Management System) is a database management system or software for relational databases that employs SQL (Structured Query Language) to query and update the database. It works with structured data and can handle incoming input relatively fast. In a relational database management system (RDBMS), and data is primarily written in one place. However, it may also originate from one or a few places, and a row may represent a single record column representing an attribute.

EXERCISES

Multiple Choice Questions

1. **CQL in Cassandra stands for:**
   A. Cassandra Query Language
   B. Customer Query Language
   C. Cassandra Quote Language
   D. Customized Query Language
   Answer: A
   Explanation: Cassandra Query Language (CQL) is a simple interface for querying Cassandra. It may also be used to replace regular SQL. CQL offers a native vocabulary for collections and adds an abstraction layer to conceal the implementation of structure.

2. **Cassandra's outer structure is called _____.**
   A. Cluster
   B. Keyspace
   C. Column Family
   D. Table
   Answer: A
   Explanation: The cluster is Cassandra's outer structure. A cluster is a Keyspace container. Cassandra is also known as the ring because it assigns data to cluster nodes by organizing them in a ring. A node stores a replica for a particular set of data. A keyspace is equivalent to a schema or database in a relational paradigm. It consists of multiple column family (Tables).

3. **This is equivalent to a schema or database in a relational paradigm:**
   A. Cluster
   B. Keyspace
   C. Column Family
   D. Rows
   Answer: B
   Explanation: Same as that for Question 2.

4. **This is a container containing an ordered group of rows, each of which comprises an ordered group of columns:**
   A. Cluster
   B. Keyspace
   C. Column Family
   D. Rows
   Answer: C
   Explanation: A column family is a container containing an ordered group of rows, each of which comprises an ordered group of columns.

Short-answer Questions

1. **List down a few use-cases of Cassandra**
   Cassandra is an excellent database that can handle large amounts of data. Therefore, it is suitable for companies that provide mobile phones and messaging services. Cassandra is the best choice because these companies have vast amounts of data. Cassandra can process high-speed data, making it an ideal database for applications that receive

data at very high speeds from various devices and sensors. Many merchants rely on Cassandra to provide continuous cart protection and rapid product entry and exit. Cassandra is an excellent database for many online business and social media providers to analyze and recommend to their customers.

2. **What is CQL?**
Cassandra Query Language (CQL) is a simple interface for querying Cassandra that may also be used to replace regular SQL. CQL offers a native vocabulary for collections and adds an abstraction layer to conceal the implementation of structure. There are four basic Cassandra database related elements, namely, Cluster, Keyspace, Column Family and CQL Table.

3. **What is Cluster in Cassandra?**
The cluster is Cassandra's outer structure. A cluster is a Keyspace container. Cassandra is also known as the ring because it assigns data to cluster nodes by organizing them in a ring. A node stores a replica for a particular set of data. A Keyspace is equivalent to a schema or database in a relational paradigm. It consists of multiple column family (Tables).

4. **What is Column Family in Cassandra?**
A column family is a container, which has an ordered group of rows, each of which comprises an ordered group of columns. Depending on our demands, we may add any column to any column family at any moment. When columns are returned in a query, the comparator value determines how they will be ordered.

5. **Differentiate between the key terminologies in Relational Database and Cassandra.**

Relational database	Cassandra
Database	Keyspace
Table	Column family
Primary key	Row key
Column name/value	Column name/value

6. **What are the three types of Primary Keys in Cassandra?**
Single Primary Key: There is only one Primary Key column in the Single Primary Key. It is also called the Partitioning Key. Based on this column, data is partitioned. The partition key is used to distribute data among various nodes.
Compound Primary Key: Data is partitioned and subsequently clustered in Compound Primary Key. The partitioning key is the race name, while the clustering key is the race position. Race names are used to split the data, and race positions are used to cluster the data. Clustering is a method of sorting data in a partition. When rows for a partition key are kept in order depending on the clustering column, retrieval of rows is highly efficient.

Composite Partitioning Key: It is used to divide the data into numerous partitions. The composite partition key comprises race year and race name, and data will be partitioned using both columns. The rank will be used to cluster the data. It is utilized when there is too much data on a single partition.

7. **What are the metadata stored in System Keyspace?**
   Metadata is stored in the System Keyspace. Two mail metadata stored in the system key space are: Schema definition and Migration data. Schema definition includes the cluster name, keyspace definition, the node's token, and whether the node is bootstrapped. Migration data includes information on the extent of the system keyspace and whether the keyspace has been updated. Cassandra keeps track of its state in tables called System keyspace tables.

8. **What are the properties used while creating a keyspace?**
   - Keyspace Name
   - Replication Strategy
   - Replication Factor
   - Durable Writes

9. **What are the rules for Keyspace_name?**
   - Maximum of 48 characters
   - Must begin with a letter
   - The next character may be letters, digits, or underscore
   - The operation fails if a keyspace with the same name already exists.
   - Use the IF NOT EXIST clause to prevent error messages.

10. **What is Replication_map, Replication strategy and Replication factor?**
    The replication map shows the number of copies (replicas) of data held in the data center. It affects consistency, availability, and speed. A replica is stored on many nodes to provide reliability and fault tolerance. A replication strategy specifies the node where replicas are kept. The replication factor is the total number of replicas in the cluster. A replication factor of 1 indicates that each row is kept on only one node in the cluster.

11. **What is Simple Strategy in Cassandra?**
    Simple Strategy: In the case of a single data center, a simple technique is applied. The first copy of this technique is installed on the selected node, and subsequent nodes are placed clockwise regardless of the rack or node position in the ring.

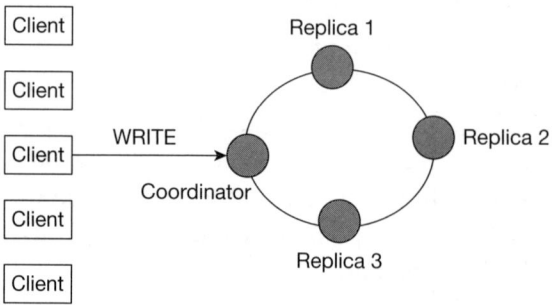

12. **What is Network Topology Strategy?**
    Network Topology Strategy is strongly advised because it makes it much easier to scale the cluster to various data centers. This strategy specifies the number of replicas required for each data center. The replica is installed in the same data center and runs clockwise in a ring until it reaches the initial node on another rack. Replication is placed in a different rack because nodes in the same rack (or similar physical group) can fail at the same time due to power, cooling, or network issues. This method is used when you have multiple data centers. This technique requires you to specify the replication factor for each data center individually.

13. **Write Cassandra syntax for creating a keyspace "school" with simple strategy and replication factor of 3.**

```
cqlsh> Create keyspace school WITH replication = { 'class': 'SimpleStrategy', 'replication_factor': 3};
cqlsh> Describe keyspaces

school  system_schema  system_auth  system  system_distributed  system_traces

cqlsh>
```

14. **Write Cassandra syntax for creating a table titled "students" inside the keyspace title "school".**

```
cqlsh:school>
cqlsh:school>
cqlsh:school> use school;
cqlsh:school> CREATE TABLE students (
          ... stud_id int PRIMARY KEY,
          ... stude_name text
          ... );
cqlsh:school> select * from students;

 stud_id | stude_name
---------+------------

(0 rows)
cqlsh:school>
```

Essay-type Questions

1. Explain types of Replication Strategy of Cassandra in detail.
2. Explain Cassandra table and its related CQL commands in detail.
3. Explain Cassandra Collection data types and its related CQL commands in detail.
4. Explain BATCH command of CASSANDRA in detail with example.
5. Explain the difference between Cassandra and RDBMS in detail.
6. Explain the denormalization concept of Cassandra in detail.
7. Explain coexistence pattern of Cassandra in detail.
8. Explain CAP pattern of Cassandra in detail.
9. Explain temporal pattern of Cassandra in detail.

CHAPTER 16

Cassandra Architecture

> **LEARNING OBJECTIVES**
>
> The main objective of this chapter is to discuss the architecture of Cassandra and elaborate on the peer-to-peer approach followed by its database system.

16.1 Introduction

Cassandra is a distributed NoSQL database that is peer-to-peer and uses a cluster of homogeneous nodes. It can deal with massive amounts of data. It can process this data while also delivering a high level of functionality. When it comes to reading and writing operations, Cassandra performs admirably. There are no masters, slaves, or distinct leaders in the Cassandra cluster's architecture.

16.1.1 Cassandra Architecture

Cassandra's architecture comprises three parts: nodes, clusters, and data centers (Fig. 16.1). There are additional components (commitlog, memtable, SS table, Bloom filer) in addition to these. Cassandra is a database that stores data in rows. Using the CQL, authorized users may connect to any node in any data center.

Node

Cassandra's most fundamental component (node) is the location where the data is kept. It is like having a single server in a rack. It eliminates the possibility of a single point-of-failure.

Data Center

The term "data center" refers to a cluster of nodes. This data center might be a physical or a virtual location, separated and chosen based on the workload. It is used to determine the replication factor. Data can be written to different data centers depending on this replication factor.

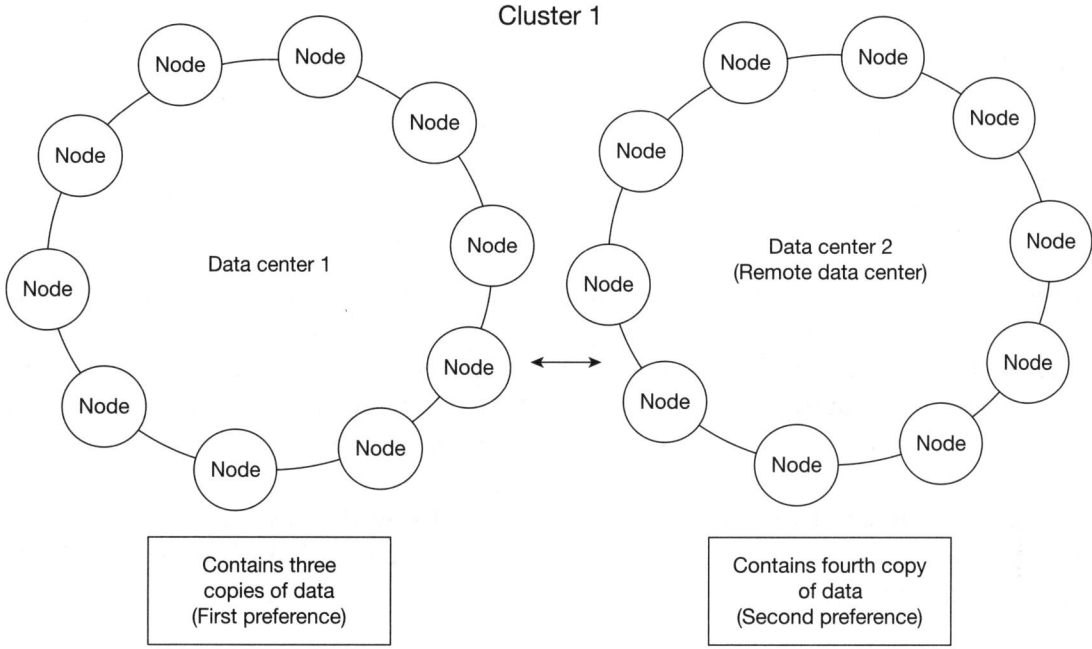

Figure 16.1 Cassandra: Basic architecture

Cluster

A cluster is made up of one or more data centers. Clusters are generally spread over many physical sites.

Cassandra was created to meet a variety of architectural needs. It is built in such a way that there are no master or slave nodes. The most crucial criterion is to eliminate any single point-of-failure. This means that if a cluster has 100 nodes and one of them fails, the cluster should still function. However, in Hadoop, a namenode failure might bring the entire system to a halt. Massive scalability is another necessity, with a cluster capable of holding hundreds or thousands of nodes. Moreover, it should be able to add a new node to a cluster without restarting it. It features a ring-type architecture, which means that its nodes are logically dispersed in a ring shape. Data is disseminated among all nodes automatically. Furthermore, the data is distributed among the cluster nodes using the hash values of the keys, allowing for both processing and data distribution. A hash value is a number that corresponds to a numeric value for each given key. The text 'ABC,' for example, might be mapped to 101, whereas the decimal figure 25.34 could be mapped to 257. An algorithm is used to create a hash value. In addition, significant data read and write speed is needed so that the system may be scaled. Cassandra uses a peer-to-peer distributed architecture with data dispersed across all nodes in a cluster. Data is copied among nodes for redundancy, like HDFS. Data is stored in memory and then written to the disk later. A cluster's nodes, all have the same function. Each node is self-contained while yet being linked to other nodes. Regardless of where the data is stored in the cluster, each node in the cluster can accept read and write requests. When a node fails, other nodes in the network can service read/write requests.

Cassandra architecture also has the following features: The Cassandra architecture supports multiple data centers. Data can be copied from one data center to another. Three copies of data can be kept in one data center, with the fourth copy being kept in a distant data center for remote backup. A local data center is preferred over a faraway data center for data readings.

Cluster nodes communicate with one another for a variety of reasons. The following are some of the components that are employed in this process:

Seeds: Each node has a list of seeds and a collection of other nodes. When a node initially joins a cluster, it is bootstrapped using a seed node. A seed has no other purpose than to germinate and is not a single point-of-failure. After bootstrapping, a node does not require a seed for further restarts. Therefore, it is best to utilize two to three seed nodes per Cassandra data center and maintain the seeds list consistently across all nodes.

Two nodes link to two additional nodes designated as seed nodes at initialization. Seed node information is no longer necessary once all four nodes are linked, as the steady state has been attained (Fig. 16.2).

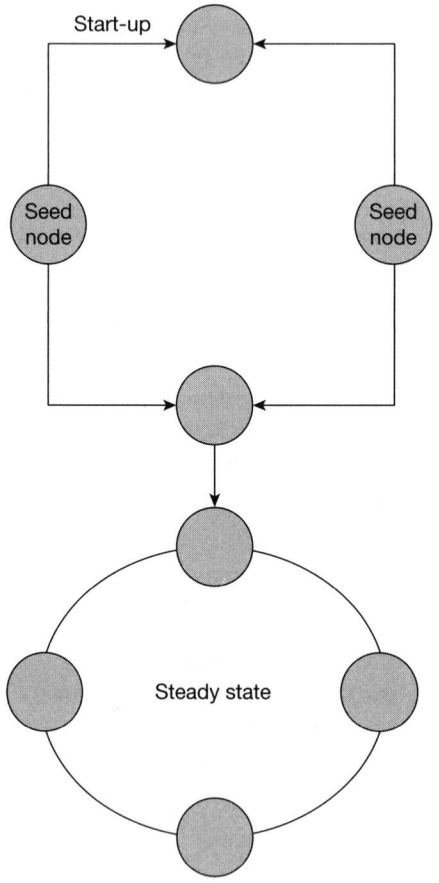

Figure 16.2 Cassandra seed node and steady state

Gossip: Gossip is a peer-to-peer communication mechanism utilized by Cassandra nodes. A node receives gossip about the status of all other nodes. Every second, a node receives gossips from up to three other nodes. The gossip messages adhere to a particular structure and version numbering system to ensure effective communication.

16.1.2 Features of Cassandra

Distributed: Every node in the cluster performs the same function. There is no risk of failure, and the dataset is dispersed throughout the cluster. However, there is one issue: the master is not present in each node to handle service requests. Cassandra makes data distribution simple by allowing you to replicate data across different data centers and distribute it wherever you need it.

Flexible data storage: Cassandra accepts many data types, including structured, semi-structured, and unstructured data. It makes it easier for you to modify your data structures as needed.

Rigid architecture: Cassandra has no single point-of-failure and is always accessible for mission-critical applications that can't afford to go down.

Supports replication and multi-data-center replication: The replication factor comes with the optimal settings in Cassandra. Cassandra is built to be a distributed system that allows for the deployment of a large number of nodes across many data centers, among other things.

Highly scalable: It is meant to increase throughput when more computers are added gradually without interfering with existing applications. Cassandra is highly scalable, allowing you to add more hardware to accommodate more clients and data as needed. Cassandra is designed to grow horizontally as much as you need it to and over as many geographical sites as needed, rather than vertically.

Support for transactions: Atomicity, Consistency, Isolation, and Durability are all supported by Cassandra (ACID).

Tunable consistency: Cassandra provides many performance adjustments in addition to the standard JVM performance tweaking. Table level compression settings, which may be specified when establishing or modifying tables, are enabled by default.

Fault-tolerance: For fault-tolerance, data is automatically saved and replicated. If a node fails, it is replaced as soon as possible. Consider a cluster of four nodes, each holding a copy of the same data. If one node is no longer available, the other three nodes can fill the space.

Hadoop integration with MapReduce support: It has Hadoop integration with MapReduce support. Also supported are Apache Hive and Apache Pig.

Hybrid: Cassandra's architecture is quite robust. At the same time, it is highly adaptable. Because data is stored across several nodes, it has very low latency. No single data loss is possible in a data center of any size. It can work in both public and private clouds with no change in performance.

Writes quickly: Cassandra was built from the ground-up to run on low-cost commodity hardware. As a result, it has lightning-fast write speeds and can store hundreds of terabytes of data without losing read speed. You can simply toss your data into the database at very high speeds since data may come in unstructured.

Sharp security: Cassandra delivers a high level of security across several data centers and nodes.

An audit logging function keeps track of DDL, DML, and DCL processes. It will ensure that the activities have no negative influence on the performance. A feature named fqltool monitors the replaying and recording of workloads. It also does workload analysis.

CQL: Cassandra has introduced the CQL query language (Cassandra Query Language). It is a straightforward interface for interacting with Cassandra. Cassandra is a NoSQL database in which it is easier to move data horizontally across clusters. It has the potential for tremendous scalability, and is not limited by joins or fixed schemas.

Some Facts About Cassandra

- Cassandra was not row-level consistent before the revisions of versions of Cassandra up to Cassandra 1.0, which meant adding and updating the table. As a result, it may inconsistently influence the non-key columns when the same row is processed simultaneously.
- Row-level isolation was used in Cassandra 1.1 to overcome this problem.
- The removal of Tombstone (source Internet) markers has also been linked to performance deterioration with severe consequences.
- Cassandra is a database management system cross between a key-value store and a tabular database.
- Tables can be created, discarded, and changed at any moment throughout the execution of a query or update.
- The table column family represents an RDBMS. A row-key, name, value, timestamp, and so on uniquely identify each row. In Cassandra, a table is a disrupted multi-dimensional map monitored by a key. A super-column family specifies different uses.

16.2 Cassandra's Peer-to-Peer Approach

Cassandra is a distributed peer-to-peer system consisting of a cluster of nodes; each node can accept read or write requests. Using the peer-to-peer gossip communication protocol, each node in the cluster sends state information about itself and other nodes.

The Cassandra storage engine's primary components are as follows:

Commit Log: Each node in the Cassandra cluster maintains a sequential commit log of write activity to disk to ensure data integrity. These writes are indexed and written to a memtable, an in-memory structure.

Memtable: The memtable is similar to the writeback cache in that write I/O is directed to it, and the host immediately verifies its completion. This has the benefit of having low latency and high throughput. By default, the memtable structure is kept in the Java heap. However, as with Cassandra 2.1, you can store memtables outside the Java heap to mitigate garbage collection (GC).

SSTables: When the commit log fills up, a flush occurs, and the contents of the memtable are written to disc in an SSTables data file. The memtable is cleaned, and the commit log is regenerated at the end of this operation. Cassandra automatically divides and replicates these writes across the cluster. Cassandra consolidates SSTables on a regular basis using a process known as "compaction". The frequency of these compactions is determined by numerous factors that are defined in Cassandra's YAML configuration file or Cassandra Query Language (CQL) commands. The Cassandra.yaml file is Cassandra's primary configuration file. It would help if you restarted the node after altering properties in the Cassandra.yaml file for the changes to take effect. For example, Cassandra performs compaction operations by merging keys, combining columns, evicting tombstones (data that has been declared obsolete), consolidating SSTables, and creating new indexes. This is a robust design because the system is naturally available and highly scalable.

16.3 GOSSIP AND FAILURE DETECTION

Cassandra's communication between nodes is often similar to peer-to-peer communication, with each node communicating with one another. In this situation, information exchange happens among all the nodes. The gossip protocol is a means of reducing communication disruption. When one node communicates with another in Cassandra, the node required to answer sends information about its state and the node it previously talked about. This approach minimizes network logs, preserves more information, and increases information retrieval efficiency. The protocol's primary function is to simultaneously give up-to-date information from any node.

The gossip protocol is an internal communication strategy used by cluster nodes to communicate with one another. Gossip is an inter-nodal broadcast technique that is efficient, lightweight, and dependable. It is a decentralized, "epidemic," and fault-tolerant peer-to-peer communication protocol. Cassandra uses gossip to find peers and share metadata.

Every second, each node's gossip process runs and exchanges state messages with up to three other nodes in the cluster. Because the entire process is decentralized, nothing or no one coordinates the gossip between the nodes. Each node will always choose one to three peers to gossip. It will always choose a live peer (if any) in the cluster, a seed node from the cluster, or possibly an unavailable node.

The TCP three-way handshake is quite similar to the gossip messaging. With a conventional broadcast protocol, there might have been only one message per round, and the data could have been allowed to flow gradually throughout the cluster. However, having three messages for each gossip round introduces anti-entropy to the gossip protocol. This method allows for substantially faster "convergence" of data shared by two interacting nodes (Fig. 16.3).

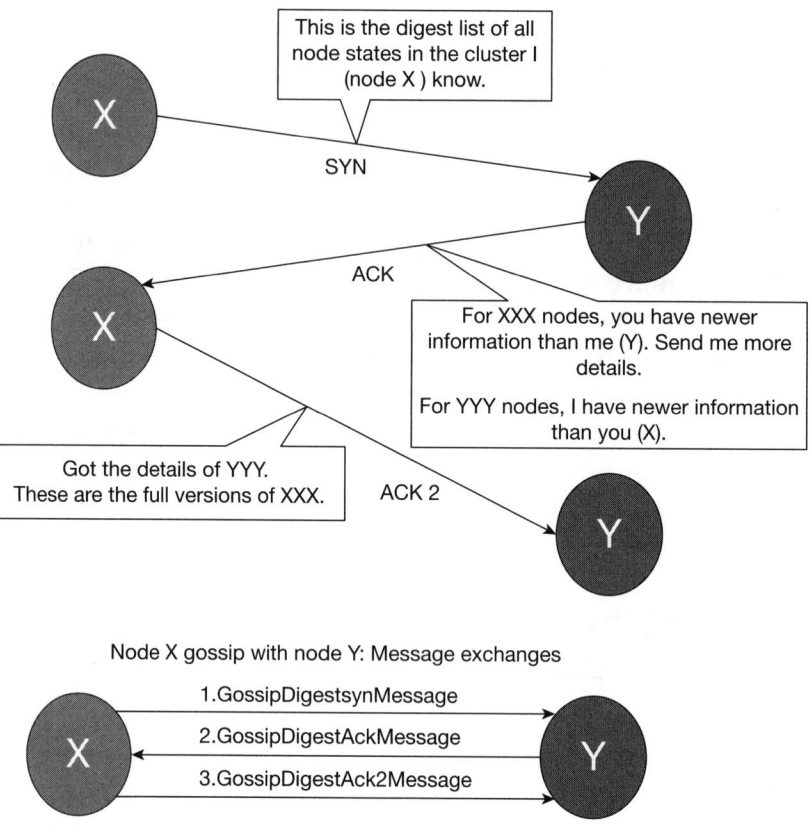

Figure 16.3 Gossip and failure detection in Cassandra

SYN (DigestSynMessage): The initiating node sends the SYN message, which comprises a list of all the nodes in the cluster. It holds tuples containing a cluster node's IP address, generation, and heartbeat version. Host X will send a Gossip Digest Syn Message every second. This includes the largest (latest) version of the local state. When Host Y receives this Message, it sorts the versions and compares them to the local version. Second, it will recognize that the newer local state is more outdated than the remote state (Host X). Then it creates a Message to inform Host X of this information.

ACK (DigestAckMessage): After receiving a SYN message, the peer compares its metadata information to that sent by the initiator and generates a diff. ACK comprises two types of information. The first section contains updated metadata information (AppStates) that the peer has, but the initiator does not; and the second section has a digest of nodes that the initiator has, but the peer does not. Essentially, the digest list contains the status that Host Y requires from Host X. Likewise, the state_map contains the status information that Node X needs.

ACK2 (DigestAck2Message): The initiator receives the ACK from the peer, updates its metadata from the AppStates, and sends back ACK2 with the metadata information required by the peer. The peer receives ACK2, updates its metadata, and the gossip cycle ends. Host Y receives the message and updates the local state with the information from state_map.

It is vital to remember that this messaging protocol will only generate a constant quantity of network traffic. There will be little network spike because the initial digest is only broadcast to three nodes, and data convergence occurs via a fairly continuous ACK and ACK2. However, once a node becomes operational, all nodes may wish to communicate data to the operational peer, resulting in a Gossip Storm.

So how does a new node decide when and with whom to start communicating? Cassandra has many seed provider implementations that provide a list of seed addresses for new nodes and sends gossip to one of them right away. After the first gossip round, the node can get cluster membership information about all other nodes in the cluster and gossip with the other nodes.

How can We Tell if a Node Is UP/DOWN in the Cluster?

The error detector is the only component in Cassandra to do this (only the primary gossip class can mark a node as UP). This heartbeat listener logs the timestamps and intervals at which heartbeat updates are received from each peer. It determines if the peer is UP/DOWN based on the reported data. How do the nodes that are up/down affect the cluster? Write operations are not affected. If the node does not receive an acknowledgment of writing to the peer, the node only saves it as a hint. The nodes will stop sending read requests to a peer in the DOWN state, and gossiping can be attempted because the node is unreachable. All repair stream sessions are also closed when an unavailable node is involved.

What if a Peer Is Responding Very Slowly or Timing Out?

Snitch: Multiple replicas are a very significant element of Cassandra. We define the data center and the number of replicas in the replication strategy. Snitch can use this information to identify the node and the rack it belongs to. Snitch's job in Cassandra is to figure out which data centers and racks it should use to read and write data. By default, all snitches in Cassandra are dynamic. They tell Cassandra about the network topology and enable Cassandra to distribute copies more precisely; the Replication strategy installs replicas depending on the information supplied by the new snitch. Table 16.1 describes the various snitch types in detail.

Cassandra also features the Dynamic Snitch component, which records, and analyses read request latencies to peer nodes. It rates peer latencies in a rolling window, recalculates it every 100ms, then resets the scores every 10 minutes to account for any other activities (such as garbage collection) that delay a peer's response time. As a result, the Dynamic Snitch assists you in identifying slow nodes and avoiding them when indulging in Gossip. Cassandra Gossip feeds back the latest status. So, for example, Host X sends a Gossip

Table 16.1 Snitch types

S. No	Snitch Type	Description
1	Dynamic snitching	Monitors the performance of reads from the various replicas and chooses the best replica based on this history.
2	Simple Snitch	It is used only for single-datacenter deployments.
3	RackInferringSnitch	Determines the location of nodes by rack and datacenter corresponding to the IP addresses.
4	PropertyFileSnitch	Determines the location of nodes by rack and datacenter.
5	GossipingPropertyFileSnitch	Automatically updates all nodes using gossip when adding new nodes and is recommended for production.
6	Ec2Snitch	Use the Ec2Snitch with Amazon EC2 in a single region.
7	Ec2MultiRegionSnitch	Use the Ec2MultiRegionSnitch for deployments on Amazon EC2 where the cluster spans multiple regions.
8	GoogleCloudSnitch	Use the GoogleCloudSnitch for Cassandra deployments on Google Cloud Platform across one or more regions.
9	CloudstackSnitch	Use the CloudstackSnitch for Apache Cloudstack environments.

message to Host Y, and after exchanging the messages, the two hosts are in the same state. Gossip Messages States is a versioned collection of keys/values, so the values have changed if there is a new version. Cassandra Gossip does not broadcast all the states it synchronizes with. It sends a version excerpt and exchanges only the old status.

Failure Detection and Recovery

Gossip forms the basis of ring membership, but the error detector determines whether the node is up or down. Each Cassandra node runs a variant of the Phi Accrual Failure Detector. In this case, each node always makes an independent decision on whether the peer node is available. This decision is primarily based on the state of the heartbeat received. For example, if a node does not recognize an increase in heartbeats from the node for some time, the error detector "slows over" the node, after which Cassandra stops transferring reads to the node. If a node starts to beat again, Cassandra will try to establish a connection and mark the node as available if it can open a communication channel.

16.4 SS Tables and Commit Log

Cassandra persists data on disc via SSTables (Sorted Strings Tables), which are immutable data files. Compactions are triggered by Cassandra when SSTables are flushed to disc from memtables or streamed from other nodes. Compactions merge multiple SSTables into one (Fig. 16.4). The old SSTables can be removed once the new SSTable has been written.

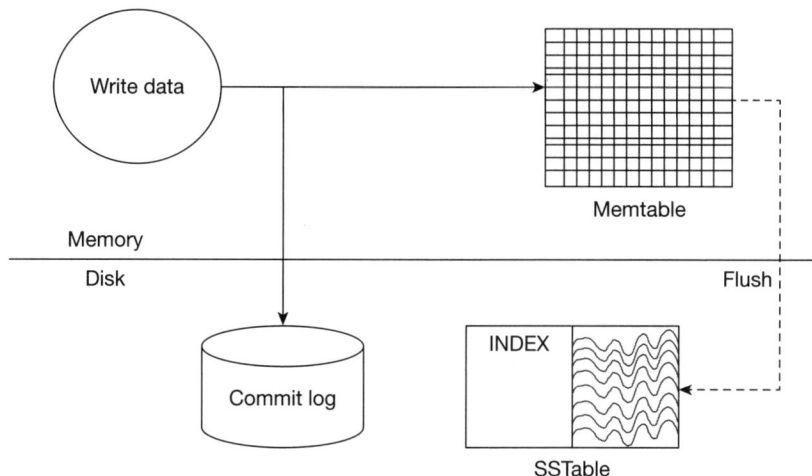

Figure 16.4 SS Table and memtable in Cassandra

Each SSTable is made up of several components (Table 16.2) that are saved in several files:

Table 16.2 SSTable components

S. No	Component	Description
1	Data.db	The real data.
2	Index.db	An index that links partition keys to Data.db file places.
3	Summary.db	By default, each 128th entry in the Index.db database is sampled.
4	CompressionInfo.db	Metadata about the offset and length of the compressed block in the Data.db file.
5	Statistics.db	Metadata about SSTables is stored here, including timestamps, tombstones, clustering keys, compression, repair, compression, TTL, etc.
6	Digest.crc32	CRC32 digest of the Data.db file.
7	contents.txt	A simple text list of SSTable component files.

16.4.1 Partition and Token

These are used for a hash function on each node. The hash function takes a variable-length input and turns it to a fixed-length value. A hashing method (partition) generates an integer value (token) that identifies the location of a partition within a cluster (Fig. 16.5).

Types of Partition

Random Partitioner: Prior to Cassandra 1.2, the default partitioner was Random Partition. It was used in conjunction with vnodes. It has a standardized distribution. Hash values in a range of 0 to 2127−1 are used.

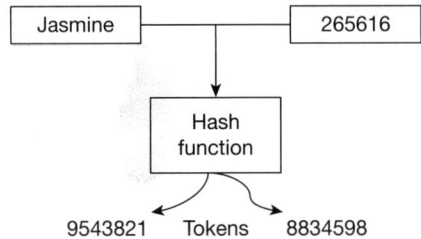

Figure 16.5 Partition and tokens in Cassandra

ByteOrderPartitioner: Ordered scans by the main key are possible by using the ordered partitioner. This implies that we can scan rows as though we were looking through a standard index with a cursor.

Murmur3Partitioner: The default partitioner is Murmur3Partitioner. It outperforms Random Partitioner in terms of both performance and speed. Based on the Murmur Hash function, it distributes data uniformly. The partition key has a 64-bit hash value range of 263 to 263−1.

In the Data.db file, the lines are organized by partition. These partitions are sorted in token order (by the partition key hash if you use the default Murmur3Partitioner). Within the partition, the rows are stored in the order of the cluster keys. SSTable can optionally be compressed using block-based compression.

16.4.2 Compression Offset Map

A pointer to the exact spot on the disc where the desired partition data was discovered, is stored in the compressed offset map. It is kept in off-heap memory and can be accessed by the partition key cache or the partition index. Once the compression offset map has located the disc, the desired compression partition data is extracted from the correct SSTable. The query returns the result set. Within a partition, not all rows are searched at the same time. Querying at the beginning of a partition (the first few rows clustered by a key definition) is slightly cheaper because you don't have to look at the partition-level index. Per compressed terabyte, the compression offset map grows to 13GB. The larger the compression offset table and the more data you compress, the more blocks are compressed. Although it requires CPU resources to iterate the compression offset map, compression is enabled by default. Compression improves the page cache's effectiveness and works in most circumstances in theory.

16.4.3 Cassandra Commit Log

Database "writes" are referred to as "mutations". They are the application's INSERT, UPDATE, and DELETE statements. The term "mutation" is employed since these commands affect the data in the database. The Cassandra Commit Log is an additional dedicated log used to track mutations made to a column family and provide persistence for those mutations. Each mutation is first added to the commit log before being applied to an in-memory writeback cache called memtable. However, if Cassandra suddenly shuts down or crashes, the mutations stored in it can be lost if Memtable is not flushed to the disk to create the SSTable. Therefore, Cassandra replays the commit log at startup to recover any data that was not saved to disk. Mutations can be inserted, updated, or deleted into partitions. Mutations can span single or multiple columns. Each mutation is associated with a partition key and a timestamp. Cassandra will keep the latest one if multiple mutations occur with the same partition key. Memtable combines different mutations in the same partition and groups them into single-row mutations. Commit logs provide a faster way to persist changes applied to memtables before flushing them to disk.

SSTables are stored in separate files for each Column Family. Cassandra can receive mutations to multiple Column families at the same time. If these mutations need to be persisted, Cassandra must issue multiple disks and write one for each mutation applied to a Column family. This will cause more disk seeks and random I/O to disk, which will impact performance. Commit Log provides a way to solve this performance issue. It converts this random I/O to sequential I/O by writing mutations of different Column Families into the same file. Also, it provides batching mutation; so in a single disk write, multiple mutations are synced to disk to reduce disk I/O and make the changes durable. It also helps to buffer mutations of each Column Family into a separate Memtable and flush them to disk using sequential I/O. Commit Log cannot grow forever. It needs to be truncated often to reduce its size so that Cassandra spends less time replaying the unsaved changes the next time it starts from a sudden shutdown.

Cassandra provides a few configuration settings to tune the Commit Log size. Also, mutations in Commit Log are cleaned up when a Memtable is flushed to SSTable. For each Memtable flush, Cassandra maintains the latest offset of the Commit Log called Replay position. When Memtable flush completes successfully, all the mutations for that particular Column Family, stored before the Replay position, are discarded from the Commit Log.

16.5 Cassandra Memtable

The Memtable (storage table) stores the current mutation applied to the column family. They act as writeback caches, providing faster write and faster read performance for recently written data. Mutations are organized into memtables in a sorted order using the Skiplist data structure. Each column family is associated with its memtable.

Memtable Size

There are two types of settings that limit the size of a memtable, depending on whether the memtable is in or out of the heap. Both are displayed in MB.

By default, these settings are commented out in cassandra.yaml.
memtable_heap_space_in_mb: 2048

Cassandra allocates 1/4 of the maximum heap size to the Cassandra process if the memtable size is not set. Example: If the maximum size is 64 GB, the storage size will be 16 GB.

16.5.1 Memtable Allocation Types

The allocation type in Cassandra.yaml determines how Memtable data is stored. The allocation kinds that are supported are as shown in Fig. 16.6.

```
unslabbed_heap_buffers
heap_buffers
offheap_buffers
offheap_objects
```

Figure 16.6 Memtable allocation types in Cassandra

Cassandra is set up to store Memtable data in heap space by default (memtable_allocation_type: heap_buffers). To reduce heap fragmentation, it employs a Slab allocator (Fig. 16.7).

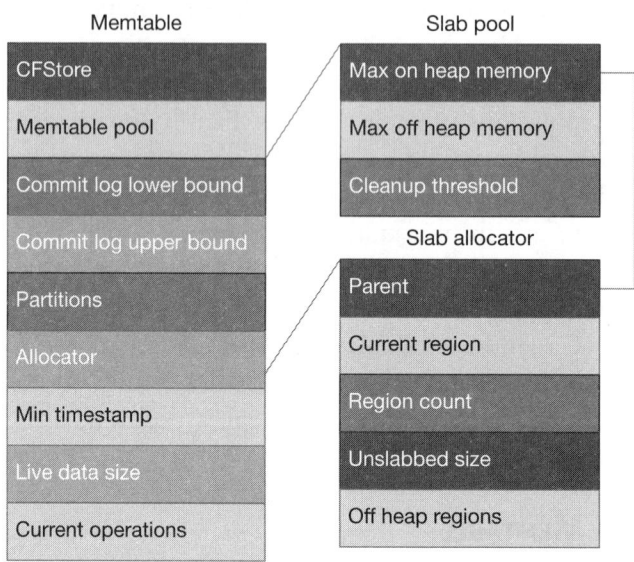

Figure 16.7 Memtable, slab pool and slab allocator in Cassandra

Figure 16.7 shows the mapping between the various components of the memtable. The storage table is created when Cassandra starts. Pools are allocated on the heap or both on and off the heap, based on the memtable memory type configured in Cassandra.yaml. All memtables use the same memtable pool that controls all memtable memory usage. Each memtable has its allocator to handle allocation requests. The allocator object has a reference to the parent memtable pool for the configured limit. The memtable contains its column family, memtable pool, location in the commit log segment where the data is held, and a reference to the mutation. The commit log lower limit is set when memtables are created and points to the location of the active commit log segment that stores the memtable mutations. The upper and lower bounds of the commit log are set to the last mutation position in the commit log. When a memtable is flushed, these two boundaries are used to destroy the commit log segment that stores the mutation in the memtable. Boundaries can refer to either the same commit log or different segments of the commit log. A commit log can contain mutations from multiple memtables, and a memtable can hold mutations from multiple commit log segments.

The field "Minimum.Timestamp" contains the minimum timestamp of all partitions stored in this memory table. Live Data Size stores the size of all mutations applied to this memtable. The partition contains the actual column. Family mutations are applied to this memtable. The Current Operations metric keeps track of the number of columns updated in the saved mutation.

16.5.2 Slab Allocator

To reduce heap fragmentation, the slab allocator tries to aggregate smaller memory allocations of less than 128 KB into a larger block of 1 MB. Allocations larger than 128 KB are allocated straight from the heap of the JVM. When the allocations in a slab region have comparable lifetimes, the main concept is to reclaim more space from previous generations of the JVM heap. For example, when an integer column is modified, a memory space of 4 bytes is required. It will be allocated in the current slab area, and the allocation count will be increased by 4 bytes, and the next free offset pointer will be bumped by 4 bytes. If an application exceeds 128 KB in size, the allocations will spill all over the heap, resulting in heap fragmentation, which will need the JVM to de-fragment the heap space. There will be a slab allocator for each memtable. Multiple memtables are maintained by a single Slab Pool, which has the preset memtable size settings and guarantees that the total amount of data stored in all Memtables does not exceed the threshold.

Partitions

A Skip List data structure is used to manage partitions in a memtable. Each partition keeps track of the mutations applied to a particular row. A mutation is an insert of a zero or more columns, and update or delete action done to a record.

16.5.3 Memtable Flush

Memtables are assigned to each column family. All live mutations to a column family will be appended to the commit log and applied to Memtable. Data from the Memtables and SSTables and the results are merged during the reading. When a memtable heap threshold exceeds or expires or reaches the commit log threshold, it will be flushed to disk to create an SSTable. The expiry is controlled using a flush period setting set as a schema property (memtable_flush_period_in_ms) on the column family definition. By default, the purge time is set to zero.

The condition for exceeding memory space is determined by the memory size limit set and the internally calculated garbage collection threshold. The flash threshold is calculated using memtable_flush_writers. This is two by default for a single Cassandra data dictionary. Therefore, memtable_cleanup_threshold is 0.33.

memtable_cleanup_threshold = 1 / (memtable_flush_writers + 1)

If the configured heap memory limit is 2 GB, the storable size threshold is 2 GB * 0.33333334, which is about 683 MB.

If the combined size of all unemptied memtables reaches 683 MB, the memtable with the most live data will be empty. If the total space used by the commit log exceeds the commitlog_total_space_in_mb configuration value, Cassandra will select the memtable associated with the oldest segment and remove them. If the oldest commit log segment contains data from different column families, the memory tables for those column families will be flushed. The default value for the total space of commit log in MB is 8 MB or 1/4 of the total space in the commit log directory. Other factors such as repair, nodetool drain, or flush may cause memtables to flush to disk. A column family can have multiple memtables if the flash is pending on the previous memtable.

16.5.4 Row Cache

When the majority of the data fits in memory, as it does in most other databases, reads are the fastest. While operating system page caches offer the highest speed, line caches can help with highly read-intensive processes where reads account for 95% of the load. The line cache cannot be utilized for activities that require much writing. A fraction of the partition data recorded on the disc is stored in the SSTable in memory when row cache is enabled. Cassandra 2.2 is stored in off-heap memory, thanks to a new implementation that lowers the JVM's garbage collection strain. For a given period, the subset saved in the row cache uses a configurable amount of memory. When the row cache fills up, LRU (least recently used) eviction is used to reclaim memory. The number of rows to store and the row cache size are both customizable. Configuring the number of rows to be saved is a handy feature that makes reading a "Last 10 Items" query a breeze. If row cache is enabled, the data for the chosen partition is read from the row cache, potentially saving two-disc requests. Row cache rows are frequently accessed rows merged and saved to the row cache as they are accessed from the SSTables. The data is available for later inquiries after it has been stored. There is no write-through in the row cache. If the row receives a write, the cache for that row is invalidated, and the record is not cached again until it is read. Similarly, updating a partition evicts the entire partition from the cache. The Bloom filter is used when the desired partition data is not found in the row cache.

16.5.5 Cassandra Memtable Metrics

Cassandra provides various Memtable metrics (Table 16.3) as part of the column family metrics.

Table 16.3 Cassandra Memtable metrics

Metric	Description
memtableColumnsCount	Number of columns in memtable
memtableOnHeapSize	The amount of data stored in the memtable is allocated to heap memory. This includes the overhead associated with column
memtableOffHeapSize	The amount of data stored outside the heap by this memtable. This includes column-related overhead Live data size
memtableLiveDataSize	Live data size
AllMemtableOnHeapSize	Amount of heap memory used by all memory tables
AllMemtableOffHeapSize	Amount of data stored outside the heap by all memory tables
AllMemtableLiveDataSize	Amount of data stored in the memtable, excluding any data structure overhead
memtableSwitchCount	Number of times a full memtable for this table was swapped for an empty one.

16.6 Hashing to the Rescue

Cassandra achieves easy availability and scalability by using a statistics layout that permits any node within the gadget to realize the area of a selected key in the cluster. This is accomplished through the usage of an allotted hash table (DHT) layout, primarily based on the Amazon Dynamo architecture. Cassandra's topology is organized in a ring, with each node owning a specific range of data. Consistent hashing assigns keys to particular nodes, permitting nodes to be introduced or eliminated while not having to rehash each key based totally on the brand-new range. The partitioner determines which node owns a selected key. Cassandra comes with some partitioner implementations; however, developers can create their personal partitions by imposing a Java interface.

Replication Across the Cluster

Cassandra features an advanced replication system that provides rack and data center awareness. This means that replicas can be configured to maintain availability in catastrophic events such as switch failures, network partitions, or data center failures. Cassandra also includes a mechanism to maintain the replication factor in a node failure.

Replication Across Data Centers

Perhaps Cassandra's unique feature for high availability is a multi-datacenter replication system. This system can be easily configured to replicate data between physical or virtual data centers. This facilitates the placement of geographically dispersed data centers without the need for complex schemes to keep data in sync. We can also create separate data centers for online transactions and large analytics workloads so that data written in one data center can be instantly reflected in other data centers.

The Consistency Continuum

Cassandra is frequently described as an eventually consistent system. This term can cause fear and disappointment for people who have long relied on the powerful integrity features of their favorite relational databases. However, as mentioned above, consistency should be considered continuous, not absolute. Against this background, Cassandra can be described more accurately as an adjustable consistency. In this case, the degree of the same assurance of integrity can be specified at the statement level. This allows application architects to ultimately control the trade-offs between call-level consistency, availability, and performance, rather than imposing a universal strategy on each use case.

16.7 COMPACTION IN CASSANDRA

Cassandra consolidates SSTables on a regular basis using a process known as "compaction". The frequency of these compactions is determined by numerous factors that are defined in Cassandra's YAML configuration file or Cassandra Query Language commands (CQL).

Compaction Strategies

Choosing the optimal compaction strategy for your workload will give the optimum performance for querying and compaction. Table 16.4 describes the various compaction strategies.

Table 16.4 Compaction strategies

S. No	Compaction Strategy	Description
1	Size Tiered Compaction Strategy (STCS)	The standard compaction method. This is a good fallback when alternative tactics don't fit the workload. Most useful for workloads that aren't strictly time series and use spinning discs or when the I/O from LCS is too high.
2	Leveled Compaction Strategy (LCS)	The Leveled Compaction Strategy (LCS) is designed for workloads with many updates and deletes. For immutable time series data, it is not a good option.
3	Time Window Compaction Strategy (TWCS)	Immutable time series data are the focus of the Time Window Compaction Strategy.

Types of Compactions

In Cassandra, the idea of compaction is utilized for a variety of processes; the common thread is that these actions take one or more SSTables and output new SSTables. Table 16.5 provides a few examples of compactions.

Table 16.5 Compaction types

S. No	Compaction Type	Description
1	Minor compaction	In Cassandra, minor compaction is automatically triggered.
2	Major compaction	Occurs when a user performs compaction on all SSTables on the node.
3	User-defined compaction	Occurs when a user initiates compaction on a specific set of SSTables.
4	Scrub	Repairs any broken SSTables. If the data is faulty, this can potentially destroy valid data; if this happens, you will need to execute a complete repair on the node.
5	UpgradeSSTables	This command will upgrade SSTables to the most recent version. After updating to a new major version, run this.
6	Cleanup deletes	This is because the bootstrapped node will inherit some ranges from the neighboring nodes.
7	Secondary Index rebuilds	Rebuilds the node's secondary indexes.
8	Anticompaction	After repair, the mended ranges are separated from the SSTables that existed when repair began.
9	Subrange compression	It is possible only to condense a specific subrange – this could be beneficial if you know of a token that has been misbehaving by accumulating many updates or deletes.

16.8 TOMBSTONES IN CASSANDRA

Information about deleted keys should be saved in an eventually consistent system like Cassandra to avoid accessing deleted data. When a row or column is erased, this information is saved as a tombstone. Tombstones are kept till the grace time for the column family is not exceeded. Only tombstones older than the Garbage Collection (GC) grace period are removed by significant compaction. When repairs are made, tombstones are shared throughout all copies. Repair should be conducted regularly to avoid reviving destroyed data.

A Row tombstone is formed when a row is destroyed, a Column tombstone is created when a specific column from a row is deleted, and a Range tombstone is created when a super-column is deleted. The application's deletion timestamp (MarkedForDeleteAt) and the local deletion timestamp are included in Tombstone (LocalDeletionTime). The start and finish column names are also included in the range tombstone (Fig. 16.8).

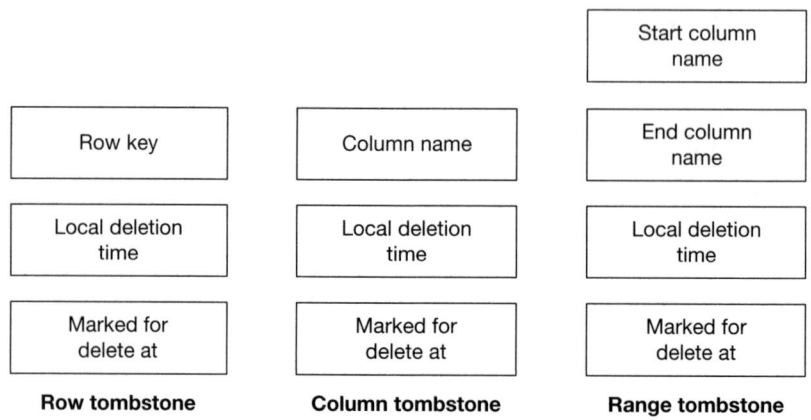

Figure 16.8 Different types of tombstones in Cassandra

A Replication Factor is defined in a Cassandra cluster, and it specifies how many nodes each key and its related columns are written to. The client in Cassandra (as in Dynamo) chooses the number of replicas to block for writes, including removals. In addition, the client can specify a Consistency Level that is smaller than the cluster's Replication Factor, which means that the coordinating server node should report the write as successful even if some replicas are unavailable or otherwise unresponsive to the write.

As a result, the "eventual" in eventual consistency refers to the possibility of seeing outdated data if a client reads from a replica that did not get the update with a low enough Consistency Level. Cassandra reduces the inconsistency window using HintedHandoff, ReadRepair, and AntiEntropy and greater consistency levels like ConstencyLevel.QUORUM.

Another aspect of the difficulty is determining whether it is safe to delete tombstones. Such deletion cannot be done in an entirely distributed system. We could use a coordinator like ZooKeeper, but it would detract from the design's simplicity while also complicating operations since the user will then be monitoring two systems instead of one.

We use GCGraceSeconds as a constant and track tombstone age in each node locally. It can be GC'd during compaction after it has aged past the constant (see MemtableSSTable). This indicates that if a node is offline for more than GCGraceSeconds, it should be treated as a failed node and replaced according to Operations. After users have anti-entropy tuned to their liking, it may be lowered as required. If the user has only one Cassandra node, it can be turned off completely, and tombstones will be GC'd at the first large compaction. Since version 0.6.8, minor compactions have also affected GC tombstones.

Cassandra reduces the inconsistency window using HintedHandoff, ReadRepair, and AntiEntropy.

16.9 Hinted Handoff

Hinted handoff is a Cassandra feature that improves the cluster consistency process and anti-entropy when a replica-owning node is unavailable to accept a replica from a successful write operation owing to network challenges or other concerns. Except when a client application utilizes a consistency level of ANY, hints handoff is not a mechanism that assures successful write operations. In the Cassandra.yaml file, you may allow or disable suggested handoff.

When suggested handoff is enabled, and consistency can be satisfied during a write operation, the coordinator keeps a hint about dead replicas in the local system.hints table in one of the following scenarios:

- A replica node for the row is known to be down ahead of time.
- The write request is not responded to by a replica node.

Cassandra does not record the hint when the cluster fails to fulfill the consistency level requested by the client. The structure of the hint is as follows:

- The location of the downed replica
- Version metadata
- The actual data that is being written.

After a replica fails, hints are kept for 3 hours by default. This is because, a prolonged replica failure can cause the node to go down forever (dead node). This time interval can be configured using the max_hint_window_in_ms property in the Cassandra.yaml file.

If the node recovers after the save time has elapsed, perform a repair to duplicate the data written during the downtime again. After detecting from gossip that the node containing the lead has recovered, the node sends the data stream corresponding to each read to the destination.

In addition, every 10 minutes, the node checks for signs of writes that have timed out during outages that the fault detector is too short of rumoring. For example, in a cluster of two nodes, A and B, with a replication factor (RF) of 1, each row is stored on one node. Suppose node A fails while writing row K to node A at consistency level 1. Then Writes fail because Reads always reflect the last write.

$W + R >$ Replication factor

where W is the number of nodes block for Writes, and R is the number of nodes block for Reads. Cassandra does not write a hint in B. Because Cassandra cannot read the data at any consistency level until A comes back up and B transmits the data to A, Cassandra does not write a hint to B and call the write good.

Each row is kept on two nodes in a key space with a replication factor of two in a cluster of three nodes, A (the coordinator), B, and C. Assume that node C fails. Row K is written to node A by the client. Row K is replicated to node B, and the clue for downed node C is written to node A by the coordinator. Cassandra declares the write good when the consistency level is set to ONE, indicating that Cassandra can read the data on node B. Node A responds to the suggestion when node C is restored by sending data to node C (Fig. 16.9).

Extreme Write Availability: Cassandra supports consistency level ANY for applications that need Cassandra to allow writes even when all of the standard replicas are offline and

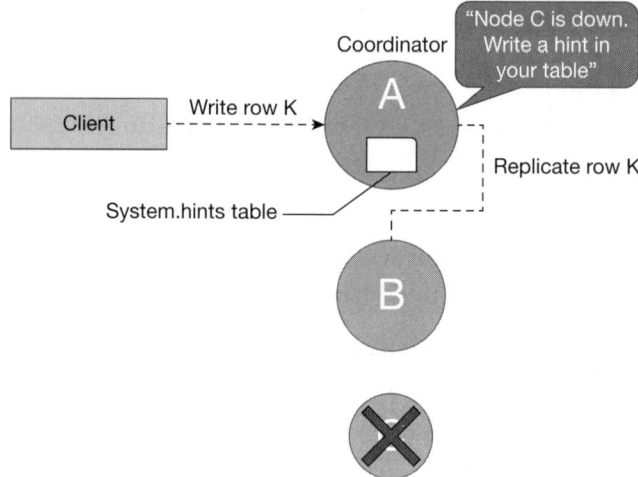

Figure 16.9 Hinted handoff in Cassandra

not even consistency level ONE can be fulfilled. ANY ensures that the writing is persistent and readable once an appropriate replica target is found and the hint reply is received.

Performance: Hinted handoff is designed to force Cassandra to keep completing the same amount of writes even when the cluster's capacity is lowered. It is not a good idea to overload the cluster and leave no room for failures. Hinted handoff is intended to reduce excess stress placed on the cluster.

The repair and fine print: A widespread misconception is that Hinted Handoff allows you to escape without the need for repair securely. This is not the case (as of Cassandra 0.8.x) because Hinted Handoff occurs only when the failure detector detects that a replica is unavailable. That is, there is a window when a node is dead and not receiving writes (for Consistency Level ALL), but no indications are produced for it.

16.10 ANTI-ENTROPY AND READ REPAIR

Anti-entropy and read repair functions are important for every Cassandra cluster. These are used for routine maintenance and when a cluster needs fixing. Frequent data deletions and downed nodes are common causes of data inconsistency, which necessitates repairs for the proper functioning of the cluster.

16.10.1 Anti-entropy

Anti-entropy compares all replicas' data and updates each one to the most recent version. The replica synchronization technique uses anti-entropy to ensure that data on multiple nodes is updated to the most recent version. For anti-entropy correction, Cassandra employs the Merkle tree. A Merkle tree is a hash tree with leaves of individual key values. Data inconsistency is commonly caused by frequent data removals and downed nodes. Run the node tool repair command to perform the anti-entropy repair for routine maintenance and when a cluster requires repair.

Anti-entropy has two phases in the process.

- For each replica, make a Merkle tree.
- To find the difference, compare the Merkle trees.

Merkle trees are binary hash trees with individual key-value hashes as leaves. The hash of a row value is the leaf of a Cassandra Merkle tree. Each parent node in the tree above it is a hash of its children. Casandra can verify each branch independently without requiring the coordinator node to download the complete dataset since higher nodes in the Merkle tree reflect data farther down.

Cassandra utilizes a compact tree variant with a depth of 15 (215 = 32K leaf nodes) for anti-entropy repair. In a node with a million partitions and one broken partition, around 30 partitions are streamed, which is the number of partitions that fall into each tree's leaves. Smaller Merkle trees are used by Cassandra because they need less storage memory and may be sent to other nodes more rapidly during the comparison process.

When a seed node receives a Merkle tree from a participating peer node, it compares each tree to all other trees. When a difference is detected, the different nodes exchange data in the conflict area, and new data are written to the SSTable. The comparison starts at the top node of the Merkle tree. If you do not find any difference, you do not need to repair the data. If a difference is found, the process moves to the child node on the left and then to the child node on the right for comparison. If a node turns out to be different, the data in the area associated with that node will be inconsistent. All data corresponding to the leaves below this Merkle Tree node will be replaced with the new data. For each set of replicas, Cassandra performs validation compression on only one replica at a time. Creating a Merkle tree consumes many resources. It strains the disk I/O and consumes memory. Some of the options described here can help reduce the impact on the performance of your cluster.

Run the node tool repair command on the specified node or all nodes if no node is specified. The Operations Coordinator node is the node that initiates the repair. First, the coordinator node decides which peer nodes have the same data range when constructing the Merkle tree. Next, the main or validation compression is triggered on the peer node. Validation compression reads and generates a hash of each row in the stored column family, adds the result to the Merkle tree, and returns the tree to the start node. The Merkle tree uses a data hash because it is generally smaller than the data itself.

16.10.2 Read repair

Many factors influence cluster stability, including correct configuration, dedicated resources, production load, and the professionalism of the operations team, but the truth remains that the chances of nodes failing and, therefore, data becoming inconsistent are pretty high.

There are, fortunately, a few solutions to the inconsistency problems, as outlined here:

Nodetool Repair

Nodetool is a tool for repairing nodes. This is the most common and default way. It uses the command on a node that was unavailable for all tables or their subsets. However, there is one condition: while performing the command, all nodes should be up.

The default and primary technique for resolving inconsistencies is to utilize the nodetool repair tool; hence, the apparent issue is when and why to employ the read repair method. At some point, our Cassandra cluster may become extremely unstable, and it may take a long time for all of the nodes to recover to the UP state. Then, the nodetool repair tool cannot be used to resolve discrepancies since the data becomes inconsistent. Given these conditions, the best we can do is to use the read repair capability to ensure that the data is consistent at the Quorum level on at least the majority of copies. Read repair is an essential characteristic since it means that the cluster organism is repairing itself during reading requests, or more precisely, it is repairing the proper data copies. If the replicas participating in a read request are out of sync, they are re-aligned. During a read request, read repair is the process of repairing data replicas. If all replicas in a read request are consistent at the chosen read consistency level, the data is sent to the client with no read repair required. However, if the replicas engaged in a read request are not consistent at the provided consistency level, a read repair is done to make the replicas consistent. The client receives the most up-to-date information. The read repair operates in the foreground and does not send a response to the client until the read repair is complete and up-to-date data is produced.

Nodetool Repair

When used against a node, the repair command begins repair for a set of tokens. The range being mended is determined by the settings selected. The default parameters, calls "nodetool repair", and commences repair of the node's whole token range.

Complete Rehab

Full Repairs work on the whole token range of data.

Incremental Repair

This type of repair only fixes data that has been written since the last incremental repair. The default repair type is incremental repair, which can considerably reduce the time and I/O cost of conducting a repair frequently. It divides the data into fixed and unrepaired SSTables, and only fixes the data that has not been mended. Once data has been marked as fixed, an incremental repair will not attempt to repair it again.

16.11 BLOOM FILTERS IN CASSANDRA

16.11.1 Bloom Filter

A primary cache stores non-deterministic algorithms for testing. For example, it determines whether or not an element is a member of the set. These filters are typically accessible after each query is completed.

Cassandra merges the data on disk (in SSTables) with the data in RAM (in Memtables) at the read path. Cassandra uses a Bloom filter data structure to prevent it from examining each SSTable data file for a given partition. The Bloom filter cannot guarantee that the data is in a particular SSTable, but the more RAM you use, the more accurate the Bloom filter.

The developer can fine-tune this behavior on a table-by-table basis by setting bloom_filter_fp_chance to a float between 0 and 1.

The probability of Bloom_filter_fp is 0.1 for Leveled Compaction Strategy tables and 0.01 for all other tables.

Bloom filters are stored in RAM, but the operator should ignore them when choosing the maximum heap size because they are outside the heap. A Bloom filter with Bloom_filter_fp_chance = 0.01 uses about three times as much memory as the same table with bloom_filter_fp_chance = 0.1. The parameters should be adjusted according to the application. Users with more RAM and slower disks may benefit from lowering the Bloom filter's fp chance to a lower value (e.g., 0.01) to avoid unnecessary IO operations. Users with low RAM, dense nodes, or high-speed drives may tolerate the opportunity for a larger Bloom filter fp to save RAM at the expense of additional IO operations. Setting the fp probability of the Bloom filter to a much higher value is suitable for infrequently read workloads or workloads that are read-only by scanning the entire dataset (such as analytical workloads).

16.11.2 Changing Bloom Filter

The possibility of false Bloom filter detection is shown in the DESCRIBE TABLE output as a possible field Bloom filter fp. The ALTER TABLE statement allows the operator to change the value.

ALTER TABLE keyspace.table WITH bloom_filter_fp_chance=0.01

Operators should be aware that this change is not immediate. Bloom filters are computed when a file is saved to disc as an SSTable filter component. When the ALTER TABLE statement is issued, a new file containing the new Bloom filter is computed when a file is saved to disc as an SSTable filter component. If the operator needs to modify and enable bloom_filter_fp_chance, you can use SSTableRewrite with nodetool. Next, trigger a scrub or node tool upgrade from the stables. Both rebuild the stables on your hard drive and regenerate the Bloom filters.

16.12 LOAD BALANCING IN CASSANDRA

A Cassandra cluster is frequently comprised of multiple nodes; the Load Balancing Policy (LBP) is a critical component that determines:

1. which nodes, the driver will communicate with,
2. which coordinator to select for each new query, and
3. which nodes to utilize as failover.

It is specified as follows in the configuration:

```
datastax-java-driver.basic.load-balancing-policy {
   class = DefaultLoadBalancingPolicy
}
```

Node Distance

To define how connections will be created, the policy computes a distance for each node:

The LOCAL and REMOTE distances are both "active," indicating that the driver will keep connections to this node open. Connection pools can be sized independently for each distance.

The value IGNORED means that the driver will never attempt to connect.

---

class cassandra.policies.HostDistance

A measure of how "distant" a node is from the client, which may influence how the load balancer distributes requests and how many connections are opened to the node.

IGNORED = -1
A node with this distance should never be queried or have connections opened to it.

LOCAL = 0
Nodes with LOCAL distance will be preferred for operations under some load balancing policies (such as DCAwareRoundRobinPolicy) and will have a greater number of connections opened against them by default.

This distance is typically used for nodes within the same datacenter as the client.

REMOTE = 1
Nodes with REMOTE distance will be treated as a last resort by some load balancing policies (such as DCAwareRoundRobinPolicy) and will have a smaller number of connections opened against them by default.

This distance is typically used for nodes outside of the datacenter that the client is running in.

Query Plan

When the driver runs a query, it instructs the policy to generate a query plan. The driver then attempts each node in turn, advancing along the plan based on the retry and speculative execution policies. The contents and order of query plans vary depending on the implementation, but policies typically return plans that are different for each query to balance the load across the cluster. The query plan only contain nodes that are identified to be able to process queries.

> class cassandra.policies.LoadBalancingPolicy
> Load balancing policies are used to decide how to distribute requests among all possible coordinator nodes in the cluster.
>
> In particular, they may focus on querying "near" nodes (those in a local datacenter) or on querying nodes that happen to be replicas for the requested data.
>
> You may also use subclasses of LoadBalancingPolicy for custom behavior.
>
> distance(host)
> Returns a measure of how remote a Host is in terms of the HostDistance enums.
>
> populate(cluster, hosts)
> This method is called to initialize the load balancing policy with a set of Host instances before its first use. The cluster parameter is an instance of Cluster.
>
> make_query_plan(working_keyspace=None, query=None)
> Given a Statement instance, return a iterable of Host instances which should be queried in that order. A generator may work well for custom implementations of this method.
>
> Note that the query argument may be None when preparing statements.
>
> working_keyspace should be the string name of the current keyspace, as set through Session.set_keyspace() or with a USE statement.
>
> check_supported()
> This will be called after the cluster Metadata has been initialized. If the load balancing policy implementation cannot be supported for some reason (such as a missing C extension), this is the point at which it should raise an exception.

Default Policy

The driver comes up with a variety of built-in load balancing algorithms that could be stacked into one another to provide even more options. This has proven to be complicated: it is not apparent which policy(ies) to adopt for a particular use case, and nested policies can occasionally affect one another's effects in subtle and difficult-to-predict ways.

Local Only

The default policy "only connects to single data center". The argument is that in a typical multi-region deployment, one or more Cassandra datacenters will be coupled with one or more application instances.

Prior driver versions are allowed to implement application-level failover, such as apps to connect to nodes in DC2 if all Cassandra nodes in DC1 are unavailable (Fig. 16.10). If a data center goes down all at once, it will most likely be due to a catastrophic failure in Region 1, with the application node, down. So instead, cross-region failover should be used (handled by the load balancer in this example). As a result, the default policy does not allow distant nodes; only the LOCAL or IGNORED distance is assigned. In addition, a local data center name must be specified, either in the configuration:

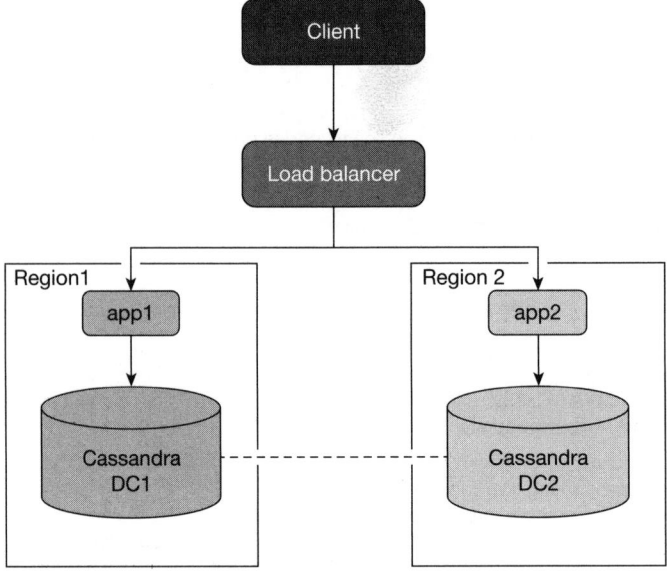

Figure 16.10 Load balancing in Cassandra

```
datastax-java-driver.basic.load-balancing-policy {
      local-datacenter = datacenter1
}
```

Alternatively, while creating the session programmatically:

```
CqlSession session = CqlSession.builder()
      .withLocalDatacenter("datacenter1")
      .build();
```

If neither is provided, the programmed value is utilized.

Policy Behavior

When the policy generates a query plan, it first examines the routing information in the statement. The query plan consists of a basic round-robin shuffle of all linked nodes if none exist. If the statement includes routing information, the policy utilizes it to identify which replicas contain the associated data. The query plan is then returned, with the replicas shuffled in random order, followed by a round-robin shuffle of the remaining nodes.

Optional Node Filtering

Finally, the default policy allows you to implement an optional node filter immediately after testing for inclusion in the local DC. If a node fails this test, it will be marked as IGNORED, and the driver will not try to connect to the node. This is an effective way to exclude nodes based on specific criteria.

You can run the filter with the following settings:

```
datastax-java-driver.basic.load-balancing-policy {
    class = DefaultLoadBalancingPolicy
    local-datacenter = datacenter1
    filter-class = com.acme.MyNodeFilter
}
```

Custom Implementation

You can use your implementation in your configuration by specifying a fully qualified name.

Using Multiple Policies

You can override the load balancing policy in the execution profile.

```
datastax-java-driver {
    basic.load-balancing-policy {
    class = DefaultLoadBalancingPolicy
    }
    profiles {
    custom-lbp {
    basic.load-balancing-policy {
    class = CustomLoadBalancingPolicy
    }
    }
    slow {
    request.timeout = 30 seconds
    }
    }
}
```

The custom-LBP profile uses a specialized policy. The slow profile inherits the default profile. The driver only produces and reuses one DefaultLoadBalancingPolicy.

16.13 CASSANDRA READ PROCESS

Cassandra's read procedure assures quick reads. Parallel reading is placed across all nodes. If a node fails, data is read from the data copy. The replica is given priority based on its distance. The Cassandra reading method includes the following features:

- Data on the same node is prioritized and considered as data local.
- Data on the same rack is given second priority and is regarded as rack local.
- Data on the same data center get third priority and is considered as data center local.
- Finally, data at a different data center is prioritized the least.
- Data in the Memtable and SSTable is verified first to see if it is already in memory to be accessed faster.

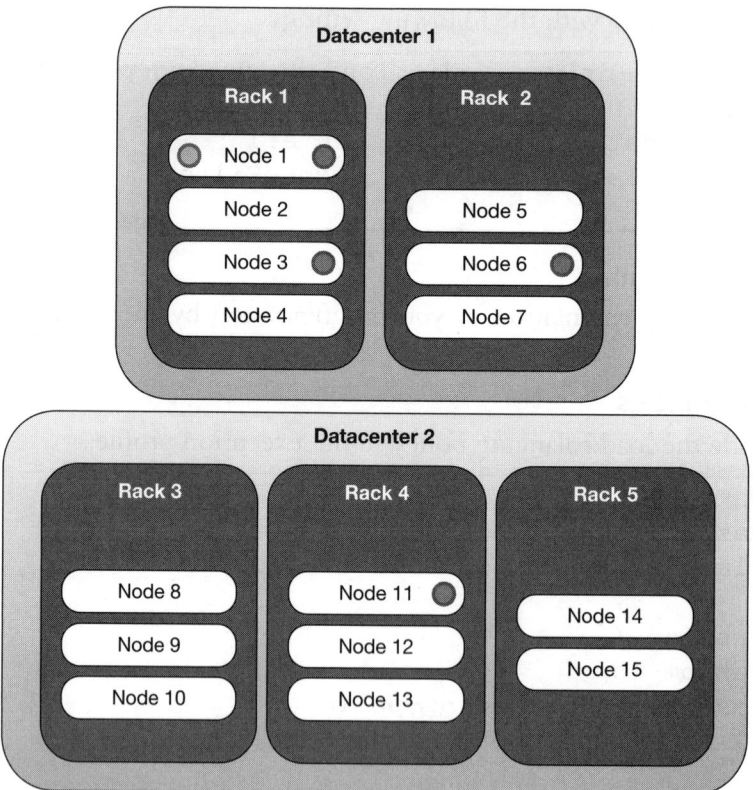

Figure 16.11 Reading in Cassandra: Datacenter structure

The cluster shown in Fig. 16.11 operates two data centers: data center 1 and data center 2. The data center 1 has two racks (Rack 1 and Rack 2) whereas the data center 2 has three racks (Rack 3, Rack 4 and Rack 5). This cluster contains fifteen nodes, with nodes 1 to 4 on Rack 1, nodes 5 to 7 on rack 2, nodes 8 to 10 on Rack 3, nodes 11 to 13 on Rack 4, and nodes 14 and 15 on Rack 5.

16.13.1 Example of Cassandra Read Process

An example of the Cassandra read process is provided in Fig. 16.12. The Cassandra read process is depicted in a cluster of two data centers, five racks, and 15 nodes. Data row 1 is replicated.

    The first copy is kept on node 7.
    Node 5 holds the second copy.
    The third copy is kept on node 3.

These nodes (3, 5 and 7) are all located in data center 1. The fourth copy is kept on the data center 2, on the node 13. If a client process operates on data node 7, and requests access to data row 1 and node 7 (seven), it will be prioritized because the data is local there. The next choice is node 5, where the data is rack local. The next preference is for node 3, where the data is located on a separate rack but within the same data center.

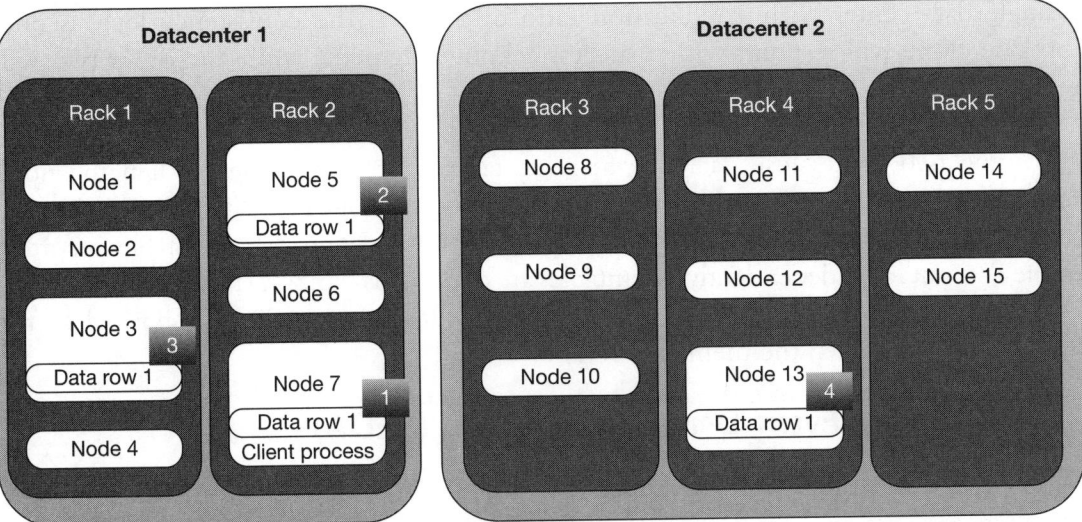

Figure 16.12 Reading in Cassandra: Datacenter structure with replication

Node 13 is given the slightest (low) consideration because it is located in a different data center (Data Center 2). So, in this example, the read process prefers nodes 7, 5, 3, and 13, in that order.

Clients may connect to any node in the cluster to execute readings, making read operations simple. When a client connects to a node that does not have the data it is seeking to read, that node becomes the coordinator node. A coordinator can send three different sorts of reading requests to replicas.

- Direct request
- Digest request
- Read repair request

The read request is sent to one of the replicas by the coordinator node in the direct request procedure. The coordinator then makes the digest request to the number of replicas defined by the consistency level and verifies that the data received is updated. Consistency TWO means that any two nodes in the data center will accept. The coordinator then sends a digest request to all remaining replicas. If data is inconsistent between nodes, a background Read Repair Request is performed, ensuring that the most recent data is available across all nodes.

16.14 Cassandra Write Process

The coordinator sends a write request to replicas. Write requests will be forwarded to all replicas if they are up and running, regardless of their consistency state. The consistency level determines the number of nodes that respond with a success acknowledgment. The node will respond with a success acknowledgment if data is successfully written to the commit log and memtable. Write requests will be delivered as three copies in a single data center with a replication ratio of three. If the consistency level is one, just one clone will respond with a success acknowledgment, while the other two will remain dormant.

Cassandra will use its built-in repair mechanism to make the row consistent if the remaining two copies lose data due to node failures or other issues. When the node receives a write request, it is initially logged in the commit log. The data is then written to the memtable by Cassandra. Each write request publishes data to the memtable, recorded to the commit log independently. Memtables are data that is temporarily saved in memory, whereas Commit logs transaction records for backup purposes. Data is flushed to the SSTable data file when the memtable is full.

16.15 STAGED EVENT-DRIVEN ARCHITECTURE (SEDA)

Facebook used a staged event-driven architecture (SEDA) to combine Amazon's Dynamo distributed storage and replication techniques with Google's Bigtable data and storage engine paradigm to create Apache Cassandra. Both Dynamo and Bigtable were created to answer the growing demand for scalable, dependable, and highly available storage solutions, but they both have flaws.

SEDA is designed to handle high concurrency and make the creation of well-conditioned services easier. Applications in SEDA are made up of a network of event-driven stages linked by explicit queues. When demand exceeds service capacity, this architecture allows services to be well-conditioned to load, preventing resources from being overcommitted. Despite considerable swings in demand, SEDA uses a system of dynamic resource controllers to maintain stages within its operating regime.

Applications in SEDA are built as a network of stages, each with its incoming event queue. Each stage is a reliable building piece that may be individually loaded by thresholding or filtering its event queue. Making event queues explicit also helps programs make smart scheduling and resource-management decisions, such as to request reordering, filtering, and aggregation. In addition, SEDA controls resource allocation and scheduling of application components via dynamic resource throttling, allowing the system to adapt to overload scenarios.

The stage is the most basic processing unit in SEDA. A stage is a self-contained application component that includes an event handler, an incoming event queue, and a thread pool. Each step is controlled by a controller that influences scheduling and thread allocation. Stage threads work by grabbing a batch of events from the incoming event queue and invoking the event handler provided by the application. Each batch of events is processed by the event handler, which then transmits zero or more events by enqueuing them on the event queues of other stages.

SEDA's main objectives are as follows:

- **Massive concurrency should be supported:** SEDA uses event-driven execution to reduce performance reduction caused by threads. However, this also necessitates the system's provision of scalable and efficient I/O primitives.

- **Make the creation of well-conditioned services more straightforward:** SEDA hides application programmers from many of the minutiae of scheduling and resource management, reducing the difficulty of developing Internet services. The architecture also allows for the modularization of these applications and debugging and performance analysis.
- **Allow for introspection:** Applications should be able to inspect the request stream to adapt to changing load circumstances. For example, to enable degraded service under severe demand, the system should be able to prioritize and filter requests.
- **Support self-tuning resource management:** Instead of requiring a priori knowledge of application resource requirements and client load characteristics, the system should dynamically alter resource management parameters to achieve performance goals. For example, the number of threads allotted to a stage can be chosen automatically depending on perceived concurrency demands rather than being hard-coded by the programmer or administrator.

The SEDA model raises new questions in the field of Internet service design. The use of explicit event queues and dynamic resource controllers opens up the possibility of new scheduling and resource management algorithms tailored expressly for services. We want to build a universal flow-control method for communication between stages as part of our future work; under this scheme, each event requires a specific number of credits to enqueue into the destination stage's event queue. Interesting load conditioning rules may be built by allocating a variable number of credits to each event.

16.16 Cassandra Migration

Today, many applications are created with relational database technologies such as PostgreSQL, MySQL, Microsoft SQL Server, and Oracle Database. For at least 20 years, relational technology has served as the dominant database for application development; because of modern systems' availability and scalability needs (coupled with the ability to employ open-source technology to make considerable savings), many organizations are reconsidering their decision and migrating to Cassandra.

16.16.1 Migration Approaches

Cassandra migration, in our experience, has two basic approaches: big-bang migration and parallel execution.

Big-bang migration is an approach that involves suspending the program, migrating data from an existing database to Cassandra, and then resuming the application with a Cassandra-compatible version. The big-bang technique decreases the effort required to design migration tools and application transition versions and the operational effort required to manage the transfer. However, consider the following disadvantages before pursuing the big-bang strategy: Copying data can require significant application downtime. To move data reliably and completely to Cassandra, the application must stop writing to the current database for some time. This process can take hours or days, depending on the amount of data. This downtime may be reduced if you can load a relational database snapshot and ensure a copy of the changes since the snapshot is extracted and loaded as soon as the application is terminated.

Parallel execution modifies the application to write to Cassandra and a relational database simultaneously, verifying that it is working correctly (through regular tuning and performance monitoring) and gradual reading in Cassandra. This strategy often requires additional development work and additional work to operate the system throughout the transition period. However, it can be run without downtime and builds confidence in new solutions in production before the potential for rollbacks disappears. Here are some considerations for this technique: You need a reliable and repeatable mechanism to ensure that your relational and Cassandra databases sync while your application is still being updated. This runs periodically during parallel execution to ensure that everything is working correctly. The ideal method is most likely to be able to perform an exact match against a selected subset or a random sample of data.

Most of the initial loading of a Cassandra database can come from an offline snapshot of a production relational database. As a result, the first application of the synchronization technique is to update Cassandra with changes made to the relational database after the snapshot, when both are online. You can also use the sync process to troubleshoot issues with writing to Cassandra after the first sync.

16.16.2 Partition Key Cache

The partition key cache stores the partition index cache in off-heap memory when enabled. The key cache records the lookup during the read operation on every "hit" and utilizes a modest amount of programmable memory. You can proceed straight to the compression offset map to discover the compressed block on the disc that holds the data if you find the partition key in the cache. When the partition key cache is warmed up, it dramatically improves the efficiency of cold boot readings, especially if it does not yet include or clear the keys stored in the key cache. You can limit the number of partition keys saved in the key cache if your node has very little memory. The partition summary is searched if the partition key is not found in the key cache. The number of partition keys kept in the key cache determines the size of the partition key cache.

16.16.3 Partition Summary

An off-heap memory structure that stores a sample partition index is known as a partition overview. All partition keys are stored in the partition index, and the partition summary samples all X keys and maps their locations in the index file. If the partition summary is set to sample every 20 keys, store the first key's position as the start of the SSTable file, the 20th key's place as the end of the file, and so on. The partition overview isn't as precise as knowing the location of the partition key, but it can help you discover the partition data faster. The partition index is searched when a range of probable partition key values has been discovered. You can exchange memory for performance by selecting the sampling frequency because the more granularity the partition summary has, the more memory it will need. The index interval property in the table definition is used to adjust the sampling frequency. The index summary capacity in the MB attribute specifies a fixed amount of memory, which is set to 5% of the heap size by default.

16.16.4 Partition Index

The index of all partition keys associated with the offset is stored on the disc in the partition index. The search will proceed to the partition index to find the location of the appropriate partition key when a set of partition keys is verified in the partition overview. Over the passing range, a single search and sequential read of the columns is conducted. The partition index then advances to the compression offset map and finds the data containing compression block on the disc using the information it has gathered. You will have to do two-disc searches if you need to look up information in the partition index.

16.16.5 Cache Migration Pattern

Accessing a database from a relational database management system (RDBMS) or any massively distributed NoSQL data store is always an input/output (I/O)-intensive activity. Caching is frequently used, but relatively static data makes sense so that apps that consume it can get it fast. In these situations, it is better to use an in-memory cache rather than repeatedly accessing the database on a request-by-request basis. Using the cache is not always a fun experience. Strange problems often occur, such as data loss, sync loss with the data source, and other data integrity issues. For various reasons, the wrong components often stay in the enterprise solution stack. Overlooking some features and adopting technology with less background work is a very common pitfall. Cache usage is often done in the solution stack to reduce response latency. As soon as the first result is good, more and more data are thrown into the cache. Slowly, it becomes an exercise to see more and more data in the cache, and problems will begin to emerge. Pure in-memory cache solutions are popular with everyone because they can quickly serve data until it begins to be lost. This is due to a system bug and an application and node crash. Caches serve data much faster than other data stores. However, if your cache solution causes data integrity issues, we recommend migrating to a NoSQL data store such as Cassandra. Is Cassandra more efficient than an in-memory cache? No, the answer is self-evident. However, it is not as bad as many people believe, either. Cassandra may be set up for quick reads, with added benefits like high data integrity and extensive replication features. The cache is OK as long as it fulfills its purpose without causing data loss or other issues with data integrity. Regarding data access performance, Cassandra cannot be utilized as a cache replacement. Cassandra, on the other hand, always helps in preserving data integrity, thanks to its customizable integrity capabilities. You may increase your data access to a high level, much better than many other data stores, by regularly optimizing and managing your data with clean, well-written application code.

16.16.6 Estimating a Migration

The actual effort necessary to complete the migration will depend heavily on the specifics of your application and environment. However, many regular, high-level activities will be shared by all migrations. A typical task list would look something like this (ranked roughly from most work to least work):

- Revision and testing of operating procedures
- Performance and absorption to evaluate your application
- Perform conversion trials
- Plan and carry out production migration
- Modifications to the application code
- The application's functional regression test
- Create a migration tool
- Create a reconciliation tool
- Create the Cassandra schema.

The following are some of the factors that will determine the level of effort for each of these items:

- The total number of tables in the source database
- The number of possible table access paths (combinations of columns used in where clauses)
- The chosen migration strategy
- The level of migration preparation.

16.17 STREAMING

Apache Cassandra 4.0 includes several improvements to streaming. The mechanism by which cluster nodes share data in the form of SSTables is known as streaming. SSTables are streamed for a variety of operations, including:

- SSTable repair
- Host replacement
- Range movements
- Bootstrapping
- Rebuild
- Cluster expansion.

16.17.1 Streaming Based on Netty

Cassandra 4.0 streaming is based on non-blocking input/output (NIO) using Netty (CASSANDRA12229). It is intended to replace the single-threaded (or sequential), synchronous, and blocking concepts of streaming messages and file transfers. Non-blocking, asynchronous, and multi-threaded streaming are all supported by Netty. The thread does not wait for a response to the request sent, so it will continue streaming if it is not blocked. You can respond in a different thread. The connection and thread are disconnected, and there is no 1: 1 relationship with asynchronous streaming. Therefore, you can open more connections than threads.

16.17.2 Zero-copy Streaming

Cassandra pre4.0 reifies the SSTables into objects when streaming. Because some SSTables can be sent as a full file rather than separate partitions, this generates unneeded junk and slows down the entire streaming process. Cassandra 4.0 now supports full streaming SSTables (CASSANDRA14556), enabling quicker streaming with ZeroCopy APIs. If this option is set, Cassandra will use ZeroCopy for qualified SSTables, substantially speeding up transfers and increasing throughput. A zero-copy approach avoids bringing data into userspace on both the transmitting and receiving sides. As a result, any streaming-related operations will see an improvement. However, zero-copy streaming is hardware dependent. Therefore, it is limited only by hardware limitations (network and disk IO).

Zero-copy streaming is five times faster than partition-based streaming in benchmark tests. Faster streaming improves availability. The streaming tempo primarily determines cluster recovery time. Cassandra clusters with failed nodes recover significantly faster (5x faster). If the node fails, you need to stream the SSTable to the backup node. During the replacement procedure, the new Cassandra node will stream the SSTable from the surrounding nodes, including a copy of the data associated with the new node's token space. Depending on the amount of data stored, this process can require significant network bandwidth and can be time-consuming. The longer these range movement operations are, the less available the cluster is. If multiple nodes fail, high availability is significantly reduced. The sooner the new node stops streaming data, the faster the traffic will be processed and the more available the cluster will be.

Enabling Zero-copy Streaming

Setting the following option allows zero-copy streaming in Cassandra.yaml.

```
stream_entire_sstables: true
```

By default, zero-copy streaming is enabled and SSTables become eligible for Zero Copy Streaming

Zero-copy streaming is employed if all partitions in the SSTable must be transferred. This is common when utilizing the LeveledCompactionStrategy or token range partitioning of SSTables. All partition keys in the SSTables are iterated over to assess eligibility for zero-copy streaming.

Benefits of Zero-copy Streaming

Cassandra can zero-copy stream a fully qualified SSTable containing all components between nodes, when enabled. This will significantly speed up network transmission. However, network transmissions are affected by the throttle provided by the outbound stream throughput. The GC load is off on both the sending and receiving nodes, when enabled. This feature is automatically removed. When cross-node encryption is enabled, it is currently available for leveling compression.

Configuring for Zero-copy Streaming

Using throttle slows down the streaming speed. The outbound stream throughput feature limits all outbound streaming file transfers on the node to the total throughput per specified Mbps. If not set, the default value is 200 Mbit/s or 24 MiB/s.

```
stream_throughput_outbound: 24MiB/s
```

To run the zero-copy streaming test, set the outbound stream throughput to a very high value. Otherwise, significant throttling will occur, and the benchmark results will be meaningless.

This parameter allows the user to adjust the InterDC stream throughput and adjust all network stream traffic configured with output stream throughput. If this option is not selected, the default speed is 200Mbps or 25MB/s.

```
inter_dc_stream_throughput_outbound: 24MiB/s
```

SSTable components are streamed in their entirety via zero-copy Streaming. Custom components, such as those utilized by a custom compaction strategy may also be provided.

Repair Streaming Preview

Repairing through the use of nodetool restore involves streaming constant SSTables. A restore preview has been provided to offer an approximation of ways a lot of restore streaming could be required. Repair preview (CASSANDRA-13257) is prompted via means of nodetool restore —preview the use of the -prv, —preview options. It decides the degrees and quantity of facts to be broadcast; however, it is now no longer accurate.

16.17.3 Parallelizing of Streaming of Keyspaces

Cassandra 4.0 has parallelized the streaming of distinct keyspaces for bootstrap and rebuild. When the number of replicates in each DC is three or more, Range Streamer selects individual nodes from which data can be streamed (CASSANDRA-4650). Optimization distributes the streaming load across the cluster. Without optimization, some nodes may be selected to transfer more data than others. With this patch, you can select a dedicated node to stream only one area. This improves performance when bootstrapping the node while offloading the data-serving node. This has no effect if N is 3 on each DC, as N only supplies data from 2 nodes.

Stream Operation Types

It is essential to understand the nature or purpose of a particular stream. Version 4.0 contains an enumeration to distinguish between different types of streams. Stream kinds can be found in both stream requests and stream tasks. The different kinds of stream types are:

- Restore replica count
- Unbootstrap
- Relocation
- Bootstrap
- Rebuild
- Bulk Load
- Repair.

SUMMARY

Cassandra is a distributed NoSQL database that is peer-to-peer. It uses a cluster of homogeneous nodes. It can deal with massive amounts of data. It can process this data while also delivering a high level of functionality. When it comes to reading and writing operations, Cassandra performs admirably. There are no masters, slaves, or distinct leaders in the Cassandra cluster's architecture.

Cassandra's architecture comprises three parts: nodes, clusters, and data centers. There are also components (commitlog, memtable, SS table, Bloom filer) in addition to these. Cassandra is a database that stores data in rows. Using the CQL, authorized users may connect to any node in any data center.

- **Node:** Cassandra's most fundamental component (node) is the location where the data is kept. It is like having a single server in a rack. It eliminates the possibility of a single point of failure.
- **Data Center:** The term "data center" refers to a cluster of nodes. This data center might be a physical or a virtual location, separated and chosen based on the workload. The data center is used to determine the replication factor. Data can be written to different data centers depending on this replication factor.
- **Cluster:** A cluster is made up of one or more data centers. Clusters are generally spread over many physical sites.
- **Seeds:** Each node has a list of seeds and a collection of other nodes. When a node initially joins a cluster, it is bootstrapped using a seed node. A seed has no other purpose than to germinate and is not a single point-of-failure. After bootstrapping, a node does not require a seed for further restarts. Therefore, it is best to utilize two to three seed nodes per Cassandra data center and maintain the seeds list consistently across all nodes.
- **Gossip:** Gossip is the peer-to-peer communication mechanism utilized by Cassandra nodes. A node receives gossip about the status of all other nodes. Every second, a node gossips with up to three other nodes. The gossip messages adhere to a particular structure and version numbering system to ensure effective communication.

- **Commit Log:** Each node in the Cassandra cluster maintains a sequential commit log of write activity to disk to ensure data integrity. These writes are indexed and written to a memtable, an in-memory structure.
- **Memtable:** The memtable is similar to the writeback cache in that write I/O is directed to it, and the host immediately verifies its completion. This has the benefit of having low latency and high throughput. By default, the memtable structure is kept in the Java heap. However, as with Cassandra 2.1, you can store memtables outside the Java heap to mitigate garbage collection (GC).
- **SSTables:** When the commit log fills up, a flush occurs, and the contents of the memtable are written to disc in an SSTables data file. The memtable is cleaned, and the commit log is regenerated at the end of this operation. Cassandra automatically divides and replicates these writes across the cluster. Cassandra consolidates SSTables on a regular basis using a process known as "compaction".
- **Snitch:** Multiple replicas are a very significant element of Cassandra. We define the data center and the number of replicas in the replication strategy. Snitch can use this information to identify the node and the rack it belongs to. The snitch's job in Cassandra is to figure out which data centers and racks it should use to read and write data. By default, all snitches in Cassandra are dynamic. They tell Cassandra about the network topology and enable Cassandra to distribute copies more precisely. The replication strategy installs replicas depending on the information supplied by the new snitch.
- **Partition and Token:** These are used for a hash function on each node. The hash function takes a variable-length input and turns it to a fixed-length value. A hashing method (partition) generates an integer value (Token) that identifies the location of a partition within a cluster.
  Database "writes" are referred to as "mutations". They are the application's INSERT, UPDATE, and DELETE statements. Because these commands affect the data in the database, the term "mutation" is employed.
- **Slab Allocator:** To reduce heap fragmentation, the slab allocator tries to aggregate smaller memory allocations of less than 128KB into a larger block of 1MB. Allocations larger than 128KB are allocated straight from the heap of the JVM. When the allocations in a slab region have comparable lifetimes, the main concept is to reclaim more space from previous generations of the JVM heap.
- **Replication across the cluster:** Cassandra features an advanced replication system that provides rack and data center awareness. This means that replicas can be configured to maintain availability in catastrophic events such as switch failures, network partitions, or data center failures. Cassandra also includes a mechanism to maintain the replication factor in a node failure.
- **Replication across data centers:** Perhaps Cassandra's unique feature for high availability is a multi-datacenter replication system. This system can be easily configured to replicate data between physical or virtual data centers. It facilitates the placement of geographically dispersed data centers without the need for complex

schemes to keep data in sync. We can also create separate data centers for online transactions and large analytics workloads so that data written in one data center can be instantly reflected in other data centers.

- **Tombstones in Cassandra:** Information about deleted keys should be saved in an eventually consistent system like Cassandra to avoid accessing deleted data. When a row or column is erased, this information is saved as a tombstone. Tombstones are kept till the Garbage Collection (GC) grace time for the column family is not exceeded. Only tombstones older than the GC grace period are removed by significant compaction. When repairs are made, tombstones are shared throughout all copies. Repair should be conducted regularly to avoid reviving destroyed data.

Hinted handoff is a Cassandra feature that improves the cluster consistency process and anti-entropy when a replica-owning node is unavailable to accept a replica from a successful write operation owing to network challenges or other concerns. Except when a client application utilizes a consistency level of ANY, hints handoff is not a mechanism that assures successful write operations. In the Cassandra.yaml file, you may allow or disable suggested handoff.

Anti-entropy compares all replicas' data and updates each one to the most recent version. The replica synchronization technique uses anti-entropy to ensure that data on multiple nodes is updated to the most recent version. For anti-entropy correction, Cassandra employs the Merkle tree. A Merkle Tree is a hash tree with leaves of individual key values. Data inconsistency is commonly caused by frequent data removals and downed nodes. Run the node tool repair command to perform the anti-entropy repair for routine maintenance and when a cluster requires repair.

- **Nodetool Repair:** When used against a node, the repair command begins repair for a set of tokens. The range being mended is determined by the settings selected. The default parameters, just calling "nodetool repair," commence a repair of the node's whole token range.
- **Complete Rehab:** Full Repairs work on the whole token range of data.
- **Incremental Repair:** This type of repair only fixes data that has been written since the last incremental repair. The default repair type is incremental repairs, which can considerably reduce the time and I/O cost of conducting a repair frequently. It divides the data into fixed and unrepaired SSTables, and only fixes the data that has not been mended. Once data has been marked as fixed, an incremental repair will not attempt to repair it again.
- **Bloom Filter:** A primary cache stores non-deterministic algorithms for testing. For example, it determines whether or not an element is a member of the set. These filters are typically accessible after each query is completed.

Clients may connect to any node in the cluster to execute readings, making read operations simple. When a client connects to a node that does not have the data it

is seeking to read, that node becomes the coordinator node. A coordinator can send three different sorts of reading requests to replicas:
- Direct request
- Digest request
- Read repair request.
- **Staged Event-Driven Architecture (SEDA):** Facebook used a staged event-driven architecture (SEDA) to combine Amazon's Dynamo distributed storage and replication techniques with Google's Bigtable data and storage engine paradigm to create Apache Cassandra. Both Dynamo and Bigtable were created to answer the growing demand for scalable, dependable, and highly available storage solutions.
- **Cassandra Query Language (CQL):** CQL is a simple interface for querying Cassandra, which may also be used to replace regular SQL. CQL offers a native vocabulary for collections and adds an abstraction layer to conceal the implementation of structure. There are four basic Cassandra database-related elements, namely: Cluster, Keyspace, Column Family and CQL Table.

The cluster is Cassandra's outer structure. A cluster is a Keyspace container. Cassandra is also known as the ring because it assigns data to cluster nodes by organizing them in a ring. A node stores a replica for a particular set of data. A keyspace is equivalent to a schema or database in a relational paradigm. It consists of multiple Column families (Tables).

A column family is a container containing an ordered group of rows, each of which comprises an ordered group of columns. Depending on our demands, we may add any column to any column family at any moment. When columns are returned in a query, the comparator value determines how they will be ordered.

A row is a grouping of columns that have been sorted. In Cassandra, it is the smallest unit that contains connected data. Data or information can be stored in any component of a Row.

Each Cassandra cluster uses a system keyspace to hold system-wide metadata. The replication settings in Keyspace determine how data is distributed and duplicated in clusters. A cluster typically comprises only one Keyspace; however, a cluster may have many keyspaces.

- **Simple Strategy:** In the case of a single data center, a simple technique is applied. The first copy of this technique is installed on the selected node, and subsequent nodes are placed clockwise regardless of the rack or node position in the ring.
- **Network Topology Strategy:** It is strongly advised because it makes it much easier to scale the cluster to various data centers. This strategy specifies the number of replicas required for each data center.

EXERCISES

Multiple Choice Questions

1. **Cassandra is a distributed NoSQL database.**
   A. True
   B. False
   Answer: A
   Explanation: Cassandra is a distributed NoSQL database that is peer-to-peer. It uses a cluster of homogeneous nodes. It can deal with massive amounts of data. It can process this data while also delivering a high level of functionality. When it comes to reading and writing operations, Cassandra performs admirably. There are no masters, slaves, or distinct leaders in the Cassandra cluster's architecture.

2. **This is the fundamental component of Cassandra and is the location where the data is kept:**
   A. Node
   B. Data center
   C. Cluster
   D. Coordinator
   Answer: A
   Explanation: Node is Cassandra's most fundamental component. It is the location where the data is kept. It is like having a single server in a rack and eliminates the possibility of a single point-of-failure.

3. **This refers to cluster of nodes. It is used to determine the replication factor:**
   A. Node
   B. Data Center
   C. Cluster
   D. Coordinator
   Answer: B
   Explanation: The term "data center" refers to a cluster of nodes. This data center might be a physical or a virtual location, separated and chosen based on the workload. The data center is used to determine the replication factor. Data can be written to different data centers depending on this replication factor.

4. **These are generally spread over many physical sites:**
   A. Node
   B. Data center
   C. Cluster
   D. Coordinator
   Answer: C
   Explanation: A cluster is made up of one or more data centers. Clusters are generally spread over many physical sites.

5. **This helps for bootstrapping Cassandra:**
   A. Data node
   B. Data center
   C. Cluster
   D. Seeds node
   Answer: D
   Explanation: Each node has a list of seeds and a collection of other nodes. When a node initially joins a cluster, it is bootstrapped using a seed node. A seed has no other

purpose than to germinate and is not a single point-of-failure. After bootstrapping, a node does not require a seed for further restarts. Therefore, it is best to utilize two to three seed nodes per Cassandra data center and maintain the seeds list consistently across all nodes.

6. **Each node in the Cassandra cluster maintains this to ensure data integrity:**
   A. Commit Log
   B. MemTable
   C. SSTables
   D. Hash
   Answer: A
   Explanation: Each node in the Cassandra cluster maintains a sequential Commit Log of write activity to disk to ensure data integrity. These writes are indexed and written to a Memtable, an in-memory structure.

7. **By default, this is kept in the Java heap. However, as with Cassandra 2.1, you can store this outside the Java heap to mitigate garbage collection (GC):**
   A. Commit Log
   B. MemTable
   C. SSTables
   D. Hash
   Answer: B
   Explanation: The MemTable is similar to the writeback cache in that write I/O is directed to it, and the host immediately verifies its completion. This has the benefit of having low latency and high throughput. By default, the memtable structure is kept in the Java heap. However, as with Cassandra 2.1, you can store memtables outside the Java heap to mitigate garbage collection (GC).

8. **Cassandra consolidates this on a regular basis using a process known as "compaction":**
   A. Commit Log
   B. MemTable
   C. SSTables
   D. Hash
   Answer: C
   Explanation: When the commit log fills up, a flush occurs, and the contents of the memtable are written to disc into an SSTable data file. The memtable is cleaned, and the commit log is regenerated at the end of this operation. Cassandra automatically divides and replicates these writes across the cluster. Cassandra consolidates SSTables on a regular basis using a process known as "compaction". The frequency of these compactions is determined by numerous factors that are defined in Cassandra's YAML configuration file or Cassandra Query Language (CQL) commands.

9. **This is Cassandra's primary configuration file:**
   A. node.yaml
   B. Cassandra.yaml
   C. Cassandra.xml
   D. config.xml
   Answer: B
   Explanation: The Cassandra.yaml file is Cassandra's primary configuration file. It would help if you restarted the node after altering properties in the Cassandra.yaml file for the changes to take effect. For example, Cassandra performs compaction

operations by merging keys, combining columns, evicting tombstones (data that has been declared obsolete), consolidating SSTables, and creating new indexes. This is a robust design because the system is naturally available and highly scalable.

10. **This protocol is an internal communication strategy used by Cassandra cluster nodes to communicate:**
    A. TCP
    B. IO
    C. https
    D. Gossip
    Answer: D
    Explanation: The Gossip protocol is an internal communication strategy used by cluster nodes to communicate with one another. Gossip is an inter-nodal broadcast technique that is efficient, lightweight, and dependable. It is a decentralized, "epidemic", and fault-tolerant peer-to-peer communication protocol. Cassandra uses gossip to find peers and share metadata.

11. **The initiating node sends this message, which comprises a list of all the nodes in the cluster:**
    A. SYN
    B. ACK
    C. ACK1
    D. ACK2
    Answer: A
    Explanation
    SYN (DigestSynMessage): The initiating node sends the SYN message, which comprises a list of all the nodes in the cluster. It holds tuples containing a cluster node's IP address, generation, and heartbeat version. Host X will send a Gossip Digest Syn Message every second. This includes the largest (latest) version of the local state. When Host Y receives this message, it sorts the versions and compares them to the local version. Second, it will recognize that the newer local state is more outdated than the remote state (Host X). Then it creates a message to inform Host X of this information.

12. **This comprises two types of information. The first section contains updated metadata information (AppStates) that the peer has, but the initiator does not; and the second section has a digest of nodes that the initiator has, but the peer does not:**
    A. SYN
    B. ACK
    C. ACK1
    D. ACK2
    Answer: B
    Explanation
    ACK (DigestAckMessage): After receiving a SYN message, the peer compares its metadata information to that sent by the initiator and generates a diff. ACK comprises two types of information. The first section contains updated metadata information (AppStates) that the peer has, but the initiator does not; and the second section has a digest of nodes that the initiator has, but the peer does not. Essentially, the digest list contains the status that Host Y requires from Host X. Likewise, the state_map contains the status information that Node X needs.

13. **The peer receives this message, updates its metadata, and the gossip cycle ends:**
    A. SYN
    B. ACK
    C. ACK1
    D. ACK2
    Answer: D
    Explanation
    ACK2 (DigestAck2Message): The initiator receives the ACK from the peer, updates its metadata from the AppStates, and sends back ACK2 with the metadata information required by the peer. The peer receives ACK2, updates its metadata, and the gossip cycle ends. Host Y receives the message and updates the local state with the information from state_map.

14. **In Cassandra, this helps to figure out which data centers and racks it should use to read and write data:**
    A. Partition
    B. Snitch
    C. Token
    D. Commit log
    Answer: B
    Explanation: Multiple replicas are a very significant element of Cassandra. We define the data center and the number of replicas in the replication strategy. Snitch can use this information to identify the node and the rack it belongs to. Snitch's job in Cassandra is to figure out which data centers and racks it should use to read and write data. By default, all snitches in Cassandra are dynamic. They tell Cassandra about the network topology and enable Cassandra to distribute copies more precisely; the replication strategy installs replicas depending on the information supplied by the new snitch.

15. **It is a hash function on each node, which takes a variable length input and turns it to a fixed length value:**
    A. Partition
    B. Snitch
    C. Token
    D. Commit Log
    Answer: A
    Explanation
    Partition and Token: They are used for a hash function on each node. The hash function takes a variable-length input and turns it to a fixed-length value. A hashing method (Partition) generates an integer value (Token) that identifies the location of a partition within a cluster.

16. **Partition generates an integer value that identifies the location of a partition within a cluster:**
    A. Partition number
    B. Snitch
    C. Token
    D. Commit Log
    Answer: C
    Explanation: Same as that for Question 15.

17. **In Cassandra, when a row or column is erased, this information is saved as a _____.**
    A. Partition number B. Snitch
    C. Tombstones D. Commit log
    Answer: C
    Explanation: Information about deleted keys should be saved in an eventually consistent system like Cassandra to avoid accessing deleted data. When a row or column is erased, this information is saved as a tombstone. Tombstones are kept till the Garbage Collection (GC) grace time for the column family is not exceeded. Only tombstones older than the GC grace period are removed by significant compaction. When repairs are made, tombstones are shared throughout all copies. Repair should be conducted regularly to avoid reviving destroyed data.

18. **The replica synchronization technique uses this to ensure that data on multiple nodes is updated to the most recent version:**
    A. Bloom filter B. Commit Log
    C. Compaction D. Anti-entropy
    Answer: D
    Explanation: Anti-entropy compares all replicas' data and updates each one to the most recent version. The replica synchronization technique uses anti-entropy to ensure that data on multiple nodes is updated to the most recent version. For anti-entropy correction, Cassandra employs the Merkle tree.

Short-answer Questions

1. **What are the components of Cassandra architecture?**
   Cassandra's architecture comprises three parts: nodes, clusters, and data centers. There are additional components (commitlog, memtable, SS table, Bloom filer) in addition to these. Cassandra is a database that stores data in rows. Using the CQL, authorized users may connect to any node in any data center.

2. **Define Node, Data Center and Cluster in Cassandra.**
   Node: Cassandra's most fundamental component (node) is the location where the data is kept. It is like having a single server in a rack. It eliminates the possibility of a single point-of-failure.
   Data Canter: The term "data center" refers to a cluster of nodes. This data center might be a physical or a virtual location, separated and chosen based on the workload. The data center is used to determine the replication factor. Data can be written to different data centers depending on this replication factor.
   Cluster: A cluster is made up of one or more data centers. Clusters are generally spread over many physical sites.

3. **Define Seeds in Cassandra.**
   Each node has a list of seeds and a collection of other nodes. When a node initially joins a cluster, it is bootstrapped using a seed node. A seed has no other purpose than to germinate and is not a single point-of-failure. After bootstrapping, a node does not require a seed for further restarts. Therefore, it is best to utilize two to three seed nodes per Cassandra data center and maintain the seeds list consistently across all nodes.

4. **Define Gossip in Cassandra.**
   Gossip is the peer-to-peer communication mechanism utilized by Cassandra nodes. A node receives gossip about the status of all other nodes. Every second, a node gossips with up to three other nodes. The gossip messages adhere to a particular structure and version numbering system to ensure effective communication.

5. **Define Commit Log in Cassandra.**
   Each node in the Cassandra cluster maintains a sequential commit log of write activity to disk to ensure data integrity. These writes are indexed and written to a memtable, an in-memory structure.

6. **Define Memtable in Cassandra.**
   The memtable is similar to the writeback cache in that write I/O is directed to it, and the host immediately verifies its completion. This has the benefit of having low latency and high throughput. By default, the memtable structure is kept in the Java heap. However, as with Cassandra 2.1, you can store memtables outside the Java heap to mitigate garbage collection (GC).

7. **Define SSTables in Cassandra.**
   SSTables: When the commit log fills up, a flush occurs, and the contents of the memtable are written to disc in an SSTable data file. The memtable is cleaned, and the commit log is regenerated at the end of this operation. Cassandra automatically divides and replicates these writes across the cluster. Cassandra consolidates SSTables on a regular basis using a process known as "compaction".

8. **What is Snitch in Cassandra?**
   Snitch: Multiple replicas are a very significant element of Cassandra. We define the data center and the number of replicas in the replication strategy. Snitch can use this information to identify the node and the rack it belongs to. Snitch's job in Cassandra is to figure out which data centers and racks it should use to read and write data. By default, all snitches in Cassandra are dynamic. They tell Cassandra about the network topology and enable Cassandra to distribute copies more precisely; the Replication strategy installs replicas depending on the information supplied by the new snitch.

9. **Define Partition and Token in Cassandra.**
   Partition and Token: These are used for a hash function on each node. The hash function takes a variable-length input and turns it to a fixed-length value. A hashing method (partition) generates an integer value (Token) that identifies the location of a partition within a cluster.

10. **Define mutations in Cassandra.**
    Database "writes" are referred to as "mutations." They are the application's INSERT, UPDATE, and DELETE statements. Because these commands affect the data in the database, the term "mutation" is employed.

11. **What is Slab Allocator?**
    Slab Allocator: To reduce heap fragmentation, the slab allocator tries to aggregate smaller memory allocations of less than 128KB into a larger block of 1MB. Allocations larger than 128KB are allocated straight from the heap of the JVM. When the allocations in a slab region have comparable lifetimes, the main concept is to reclaim more space from previous generations of the JVM heap.

12. **What are Tombstones in Cassandra?**
    Tombstones in Cassandra: Information about deleted keys should be saved in an eventually consistent system like Cassandra to avoid accessing deleted data. When a row or column is erased, this information is saved as a tombstone. Tombstones are kept till the Garbage Collection (GC) grace time for the column family is not exceeded. Only tombstones older than the GC grace period are removed by significant compaction. When repairs are made, tombstones are shared throughout all copies. Repair should be conducted regularly to avoid reviving destroyed data.

13. **What is Hinted Handoff in Cassandra?**
    Hinted handoff is a Cassandra feature that improves the cluster consistency process and anti-entropy when a replica-owning node is unavailable to accept a replica from a successful write operation owing to network challenges or other concerns. Except when a client application utilizes a consistency level of ANY, hints handoff is not a mechanism that assures successful write operations. In the Cassandra.yaml file, you may allow or disable suggested handoff.

14. **What is Anti-entropy in Cassandra?**
    Anti-entropy compares all replicas' data and updates each one to the most recent version. The replica synchronization technique uses anti-entropy to ensure that data on multiple nodes is updated to the most recent version. For anti-entropy correction, Cassandra employs the Merkle tree. A Merkle Tree is a hash tree with leaves of individual key values. Data inconsistency is commonly caused by frequent data removals and downed nodes. Run the node tool repair command to perform the anti-entropy repair for routine maintenance and when a cluster requires repair.

15. **What is Nodetool Repair in Cassandra?**
    Nodetool Repair: When used against a node, the repair command begins repair for a set of tokens. The range being mended is determined by the settings selected. The default parameters, just calling "nodetool repair", commence a repair of the node's whole token range.

16. **What is Bloom Filter in Cassandra?**
    Bloom Filter: A primary cache stores non-deterministic algorithms for testing. For example, it determines whether or not an element is a member of the set. These filters are typically accessible after each query is completed.

17. **What is SEDA in Cassandra?**
    Staged Event-Driven Architecture (SEDA): Facebook used a staged event-driven architecture (SEDA) to combine Amazon's Dynamo distributed storage and replication techniques with Google's Bigtable data and storage engine paradigm to create Apache Cassandra. Both Dynamo and Bigtable were created to answer the growing demand for scalable, dependable, and highly available storage solutions.

18. **What is CQL in Cassandra?**
    Cassandra Query Language (CQL): CQL is a simple interface for querying Cassandra that may also be used to replace regular SQL. CQL offers a native vocabulary for collections and adds an abstraction layer to conceal the implementation of structure. There are four basic Cassandra database-related elements, namely: Cluster, Keyspace, Column Family and CQL Table.

19. **What is Cluster and Column family in Cassandra?**
    The cluster is Cassandra's outer structure. A cluster is a Keyspace container. Cassandra is also known as the ring because it assigns data to cluster nodes by organizing them in a ring. A node stores a replica for a particular set of data. A keyspace is equivalent to a schema or database in a relational paradigm. It consists of multiple column family (Tables).
    A column family is a container containing an ordered group of rows, each of which comprises an ordered group of columns. Depending on our demands, we may add any column to any column family at any moment. When columns are returned in a query, the comparator value determines how they will be ordered.

20. **What is Simple Strategy and Network Topology Strategy in Cassandra?**
    Simple Strategy: In the case of a single data center, a simple technique is applied. The first copy of this technique is installed on the selected node, and subsequent nodes are placed clockwise regardless of the rack or node position in the ring.
    Network Topology Strategy: It is strongly advised because it makes it much easier to scale the cluster to various data centers. This strategy specifies the number of replicas required for each data center. The replica is installed in the same data center and runs clockwise in a ring until it reaches the initial node on another rack.

Replication is placed in a different rack because nodes in the same rack (or similar physical group) can fail at the same time due to power, cooling, or network issues. This method is used when you have multiple data centers. This technique requires you to specify the replication factor for each data center individually.

Essay-type Questions

1. What is the architectural need of Cassandra?
2. What is Cassandra? Explain the architecture components of the Cassandra.
3. What are the features of Cassandra?
4. Explain Cassandra's Peer-to-Peer Approach in detail.
5. Explain Gossip and Failure Detection in Cassandra.
6. Explain Cassandra Commit Log in detail.
7. Explain Cassandra Memtable, Slab Allocator, Partitions in detail.
8. Explain Hashing to the rescue of Cassandra in detail.
9. Explain Tombstones in Cassandra.
10. Explain Hinted Handoff in Cassandra.
11. Explain Anti-entropy of Cassandra in detail.
12. Explain Read repair of Cassandra in detail.
13. Explain Load Balancing in Cassandra.
14. Explain Cassandra Read Process.
15. Explain Cassandra Write Process.
16. Explain Staged Event-Driven Architecture (SEDA).
17. Explain the various Migration possibilities with Cassandra.
18. Explain Streaming process of Cassandra in detail.

CHAPTER 17

MongoDB

> **LEARNING OBJECTIVES**
>
> MongoDB is a web application and internet infrastructure database management system. The data model and persistence mechanisms are designed for high read and write throughput and rapid scaling and failover avoidance. MongoDB provides good performance, whether an application runs with one database node or hundreds of nodes. This chapter will discuss various aspects of MongoDB, including its key features, creation and querying through indexes, principles of schema design, and MongoDB Query Language.

17.1 Introduction

If you have developed an online app in the past several years, you most probably would have utilized a relational database (RDBMS) as the primary data storage. The majority of programmers are conversant with SQL. Most of us can appreciate the elegance of an appropriately normalized data model, as well as the necessity of transactions and the assurance provided by a trustworthy storage engine. Even if we don't like interacting with the relational databases directly, we may use various tools to help us navigate the complexities, from administrative consoles to object-relational mappers. That being said, relational databases are well-established and well-known. As a result, when a small but vocal group of developers begins to advocate for other data stores, issues about their practicality and utility arise, raising questions such as: Are these new data stores relational database systems' replacements? Who is using them in production, and why are they being used? What are the advantages and disadvantages of switching to a non-relational database?

MongoDB is a web application and internet database management system. The data model and persistence mechanisms are designed for high read and write throughput and rapid scaling and failover. MongoDB provides good performance whether an application wants just one database node or hundreds of nodes. However, not everyone requires large-scale operations. So, why would you utilize MongoDB in the first place? MongoDB turns out to be appealing, not because of its scaling technique but its straightforward data model. Because a document-based data model may represent rich, hierarchical data structures, it is generally possible to avoid the time-consuming multi-table joins that relational databases require.

17.2 History of MongoDB

MongoDB was created in early 2007 as part of a project to provide platform-as-a-service (PaaS) application software, similar to Microsoft Azure. A New York-based company named 10gen changed its name to MongoDB Inc. So, the initial development was focused on building a PaaS. Later, in 2009, MongoDB came to the market as an open-source database server. Finally, in March 2010, it launched its first ready product, version 1.4. Version 5.0, which was released on July 13, 2021, is the most recent and stable version of MongoDB. MongoDB replaces the concept of rows in relational data structures with the concept of documents. As a result, it allows developers to change data models with ease. MongoDB allows embedded document arrays and expresses complex hierarchical relationships using a single record because it is document-based. It is also schema-free, which means the document's keys aren't set in stone. As a result, large-scale data migrations are no longer an option.

17.3 MongoDB Environment Setup

First, find and download the latest version of MongoDB, compatible with the computer system. Then use this (http://www.mongodb.org/downloads) link and follow the instruction to install MongoDB on your PC. In this chapter, we shall discuss creating a comprehensive environment for working with MongoDB. The procedure of installing MongoDB on various operating systems is likewise diverse. It can be picked up based on convenience.

17.3.1 Install MongoDB on Windows

MongoDB's website has all the installation instructions, and the database is compatible with Windows, Linux, and Mac OS. However, it is worth noting that MongoDB will not run on Windows XP; upgrade to the latest version of Windows to use it. Let us see how to download and install MongoDB on the Windows 10 operating system. To begin, open the preferred browser and search for MongoDB (Fig. 17.1); the first link on the browser will direct to the MongoDB download page.

After clicking on the link, the MongoDB download center page will open. First, we want to download and install the community server. So, click on the community server and then select Windows, and it displays only one option: windows 64-bit x64. Then click on the Download button to start downloading the MongoDB MSI file (Fig. 17.2).

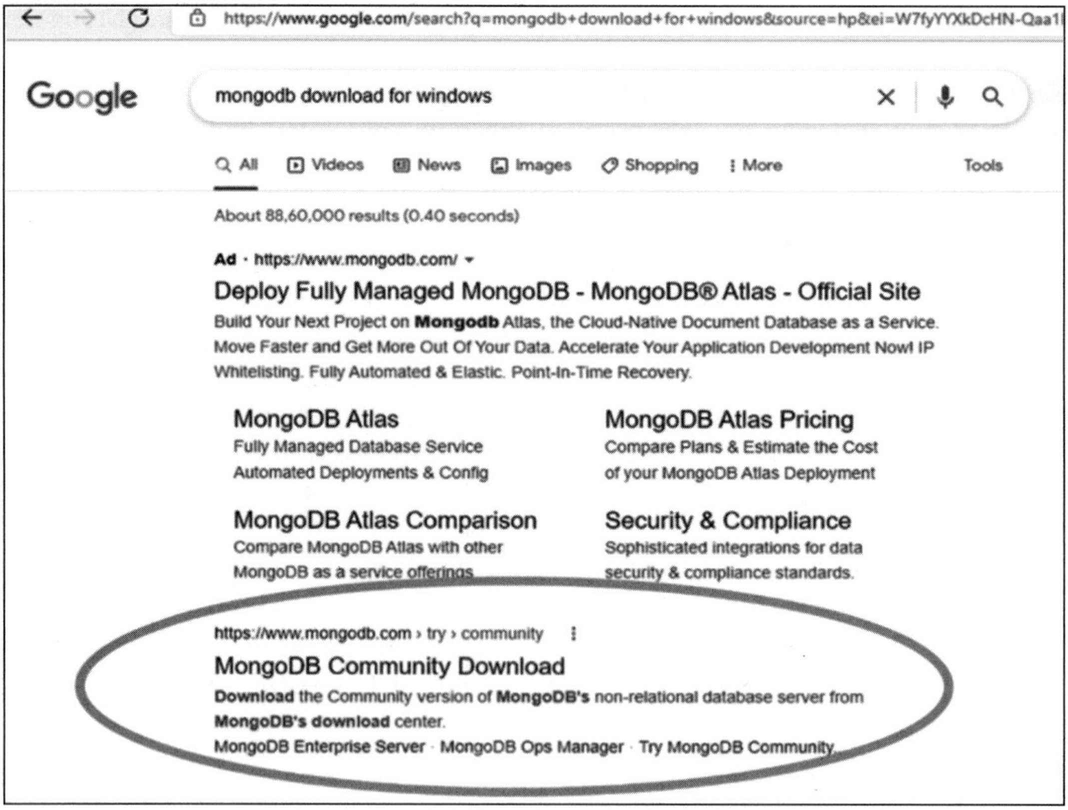

876 ● Big Data Analytics

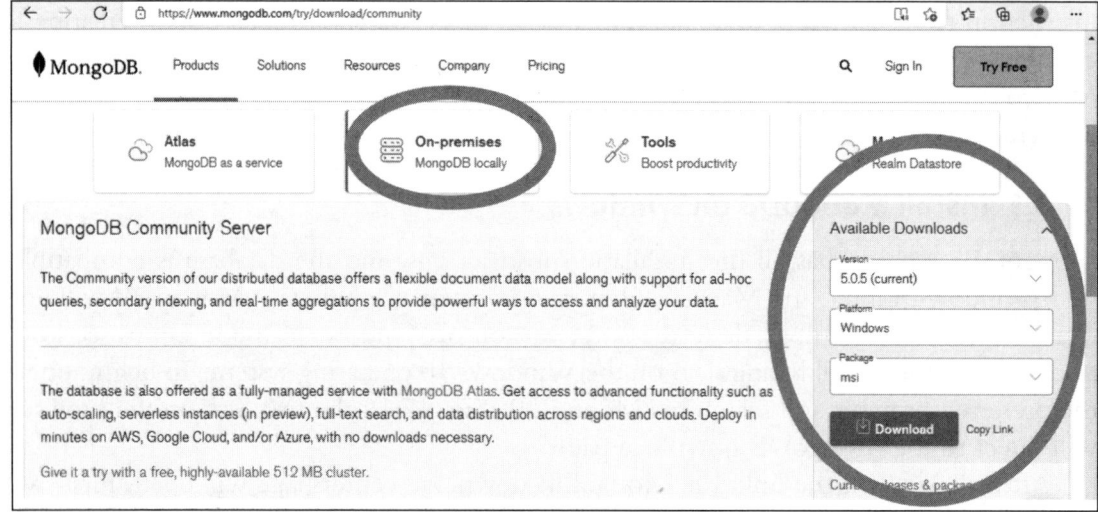

Figure 17.1 MongoDB download link search

Figure 17.2 MongoDB download: Community server: Windows version

Once the MSI file download (Fig. 17.3) is complete, click on the MSI file.

Figure 17.3 MongoDB: Windows version: MSI file

Now it displays the installation wizard (Fig. 17.4). Click Next.

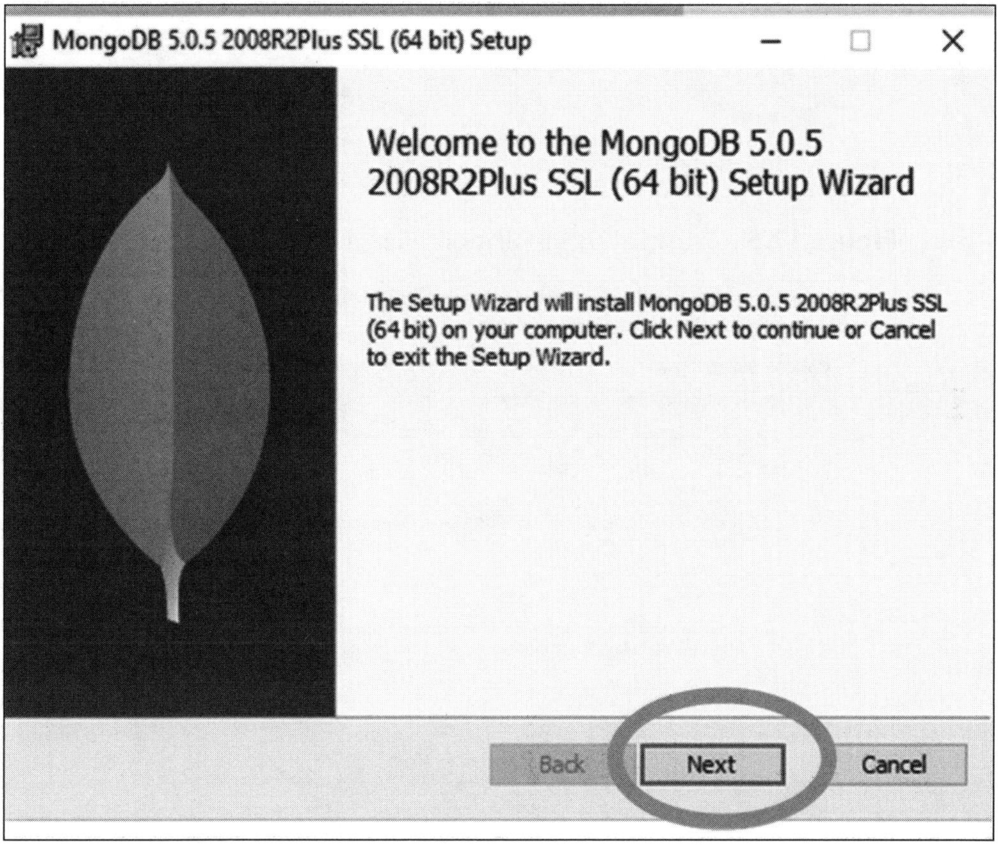

Figure 17.4 MongoDB installation wizard of Windows version

Then accept the license terms and conditions (Fig. 17.5), and then click Next, on this next window.

Two options are shown: Complete, and the other is Custom. We will install the complete version (Fig. 17.6) of MongoDB, which is the recommended option with full features.

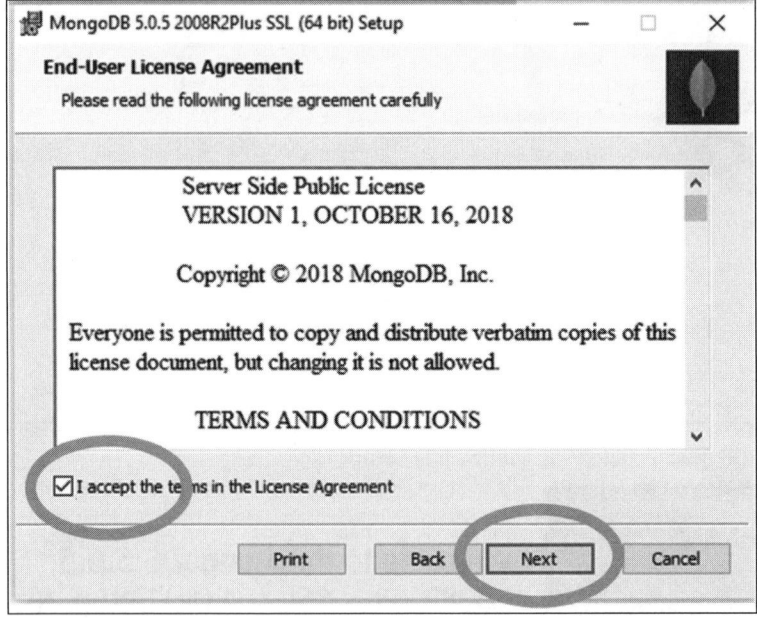

Figure 17.5   MongoDB installation wizard: License agreement

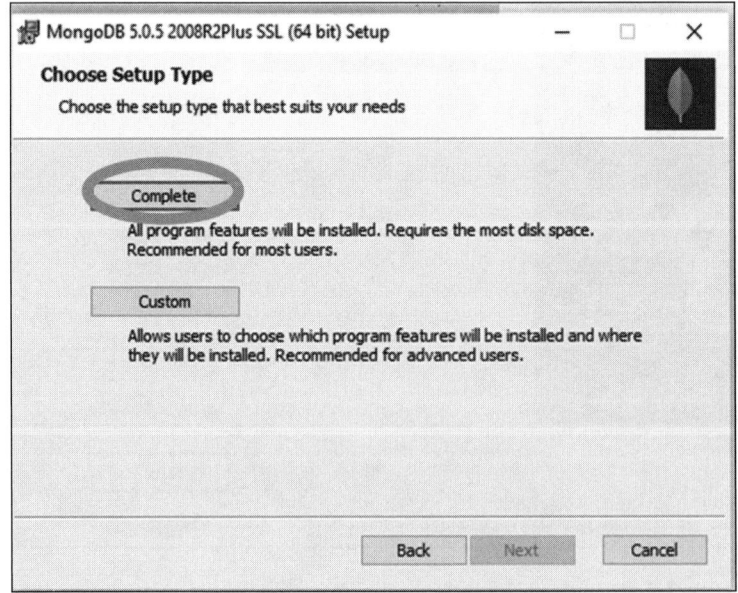

Figure 17.6   MongoDB installation wizard: Setup type

In the next window, an option says install MongoDB as a service. Leave this as default, which says "run service as a network service user," and it creates two directories; one is the data directory, and the other is the log directory at the locations specified. Keep everything as default and click Next (Fig. 17.7).

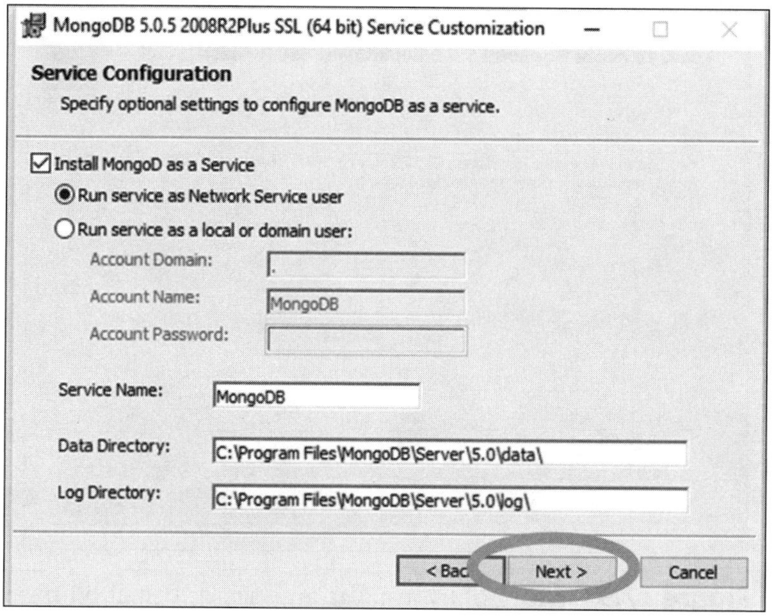

Figure 17.7 MongoDB installation: Wizard service configuration

The following window will ask whether to install a MongoDB compass, the official graphical user interface (GUI) for MongoDB. Leave this checkbox as checked. Click Next (Fig. 17.8).

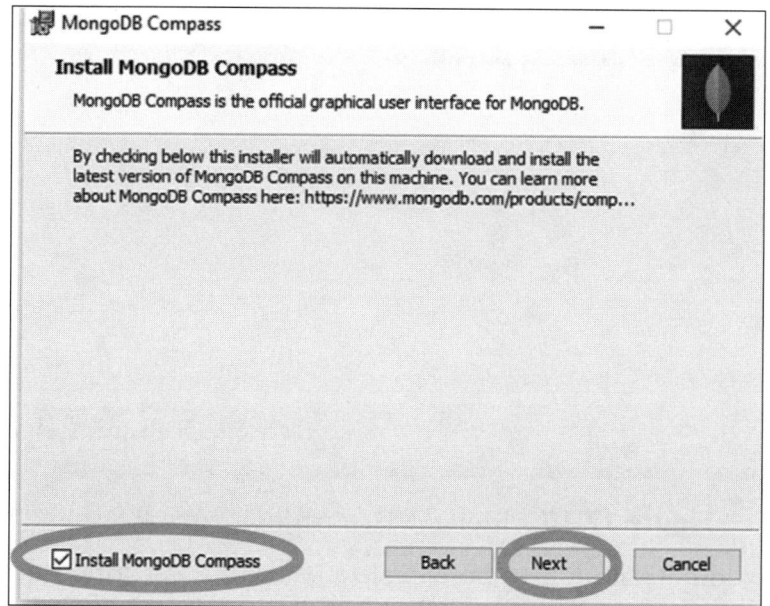

Figure 17.8 MongoDB installation wizard: Install MongoDB compass

Now, click "Install" button (Fig. 17.9).

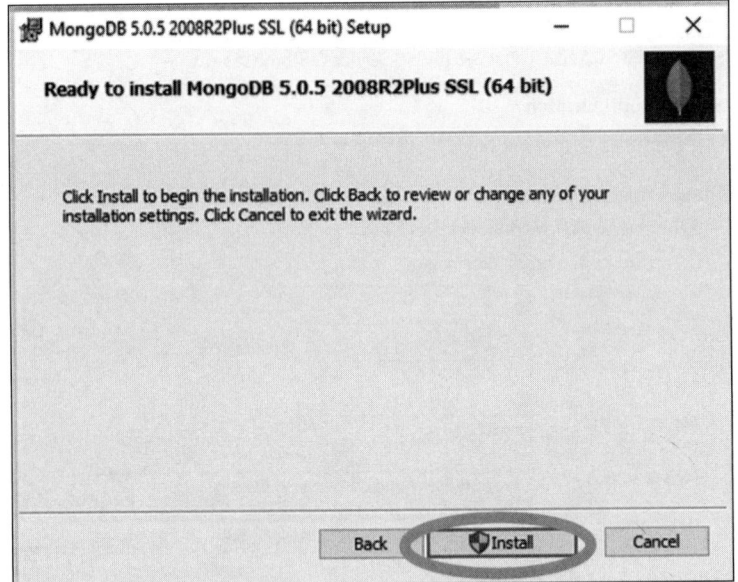

Figure 17.9 MongoDB installation wizard: Install button

The installation of MongoDB will start (Fig. 17.10).

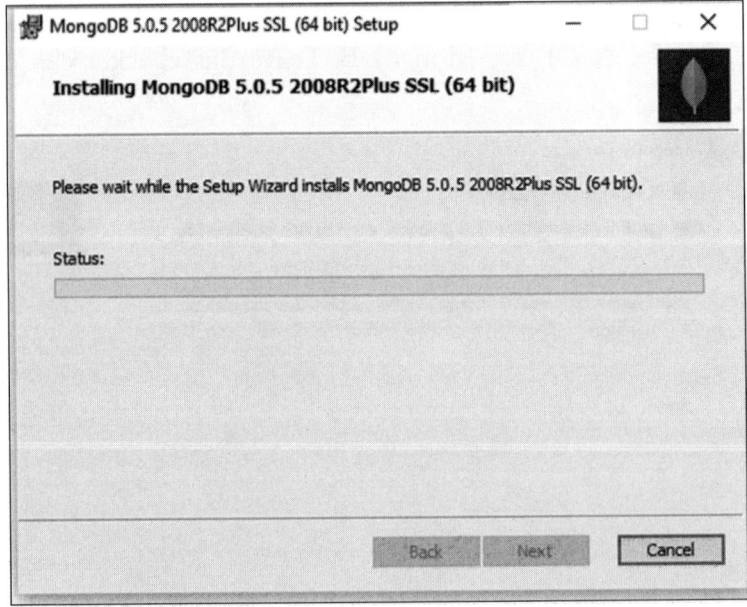

Figure 17.10 MongoDB installation wizard: Status

Let us wait for the installation to be complete. After the installation of MongoDB is successfully finished, the following window will show "Completed". Click the Finish button (Fig. 17.11).

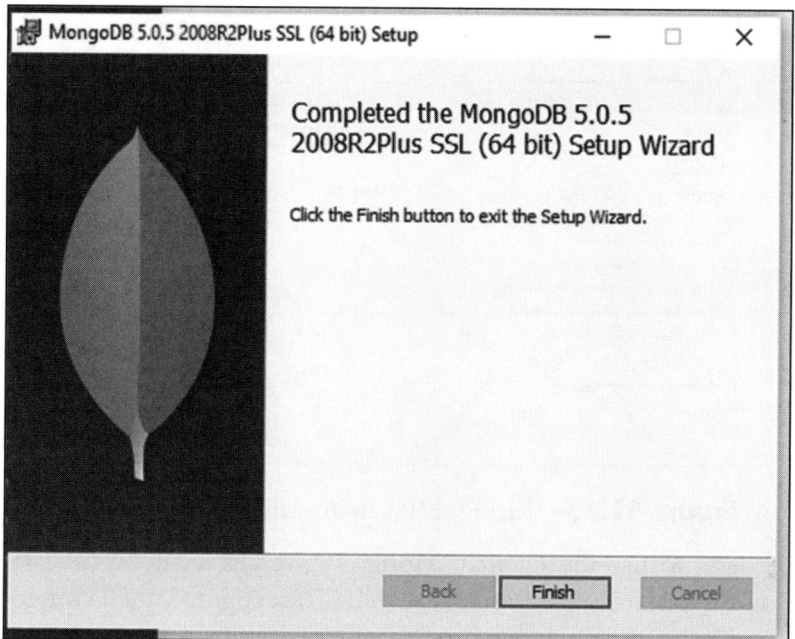

Figure 17.11 MongoDB Installation wizard: Finish button

Once the MongoDB is installed on the Windows operating system, go to the location where MongoDB is installed. Go to the C directory and then Program Files, and we will be able to see this MongoDB folder. And then, click on the server directory and click on whatever version of MongoDB is installed; a folder will be created with that version name. Click on this version name, to see all these files and folders. Now, click on the bin folder to find all the MongoDB-related executable files.

Three applications are available inside the bin directory, namely: mongo, mongod, mongos (Fig. 17.12). The above path needs to be added to the environment variable (Path) to execute bin directory commands from the root directory itself. First, search for "environment var" in the command prompt. Next, open the system environment variable. And then Add the new "Path" as per the above bin directory (Fig. 17.13).

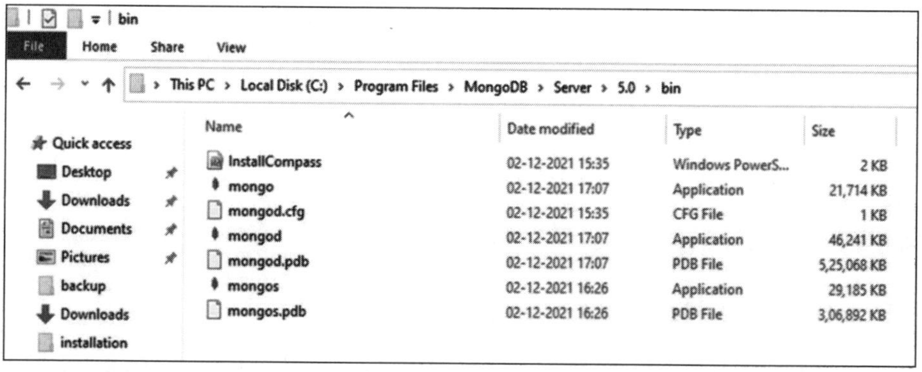

Figure 17.12 MongoDB installation directory structure

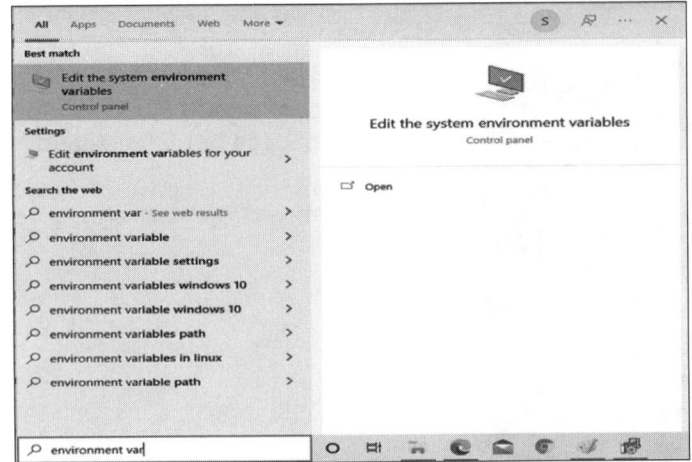

Figure 17.13 MongoDB environment variable setup

Whenever we need to use the client ("Mongo"), we always need to start the daemon ("Mongod") on the other shell command screen. To recognize the "Mongod" command or "Mongo" command from anywhere (any folder), you need to set the environment variable for the Database(dB).

Go to the MongoDB installation folder, "MongoDB," "server," and the "version(5.0)" and then the "bin" directory. Copy the full path of this bin directory. Next, right-click on the windows icon and click on the System option. Once the system window is open, we click advanced system settings and environment variables. First, we need to add the DB path (copied) to the path environment variable. Under system variable, we will find the variable name called "path", double click on it, and then click on "new" and add the path of the bin directory (copied already) of your MongoDB. Once we have pasted this MongoDB path, click OK. Now, we can give the MongoDB commands from any directory of the command prompt (in our case, its "C:\users\acer").

When we ran the MongoDB installation wizard, we have checked a checkbox that says run as a service; for that to take effect, we need to restart the Windows operating system. Once we restart the Windows operating system, the Mongod service will automatically start by itself, and then we do not even need to run Mongod in a different terminal. Instead, we can directly open our terminal (Mongo) and give the command to connect to the server. So, let us restart the Windows operating system. Then we will check whether the Mongod is running automatically or not. Once we have restarted our Windows operating system, we will open the command prompt, give the command (Mongo), and press Enter. We can see the client is connecting to the server without even running the "Mongod" command in the different terminals.

17.3.2 Starting the MongoDB Server

We need to build a unique data directory called C:\data\DB before starting the MongoDB server. We need to create the "data" directory inside the C folder, and we need to create the DB folder inside the data directory. Now, this folder path exists on our Windows operating system. We can run the Mongod command (MongoDB) from any directory.

When we run the Mongod command (Fig. 17.14), we can see the daemon has been started (Fig. 17.15).

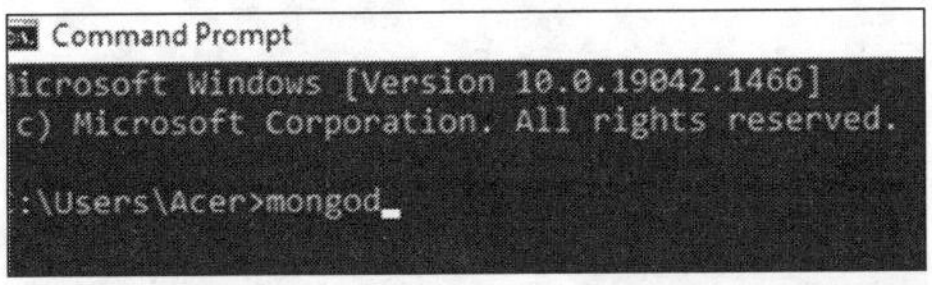

Figure 17.14 Command to start Mongod server

Figure 17.15 Starting the Mongod server

Open one more command prompt to use the Client (Fig. 17.16).

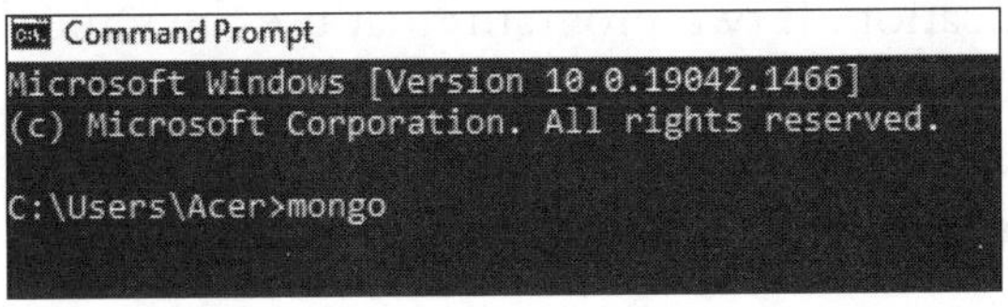

Figure 17.16 Starting the MongoDB Client

Mongo is a shell where we can type all the commands. If it is showing an error (stating that the command is not available), then go to the bin directory of MongoDB and give this command. We can add the bin directory into the System path (which we already did). Ensure that the Mongo services are running (in the earlier command prompt) before running the Mongo shell. We can see the command prompts changed to Mongo shell (Fig. 17.17) after giving the command (Mongo).

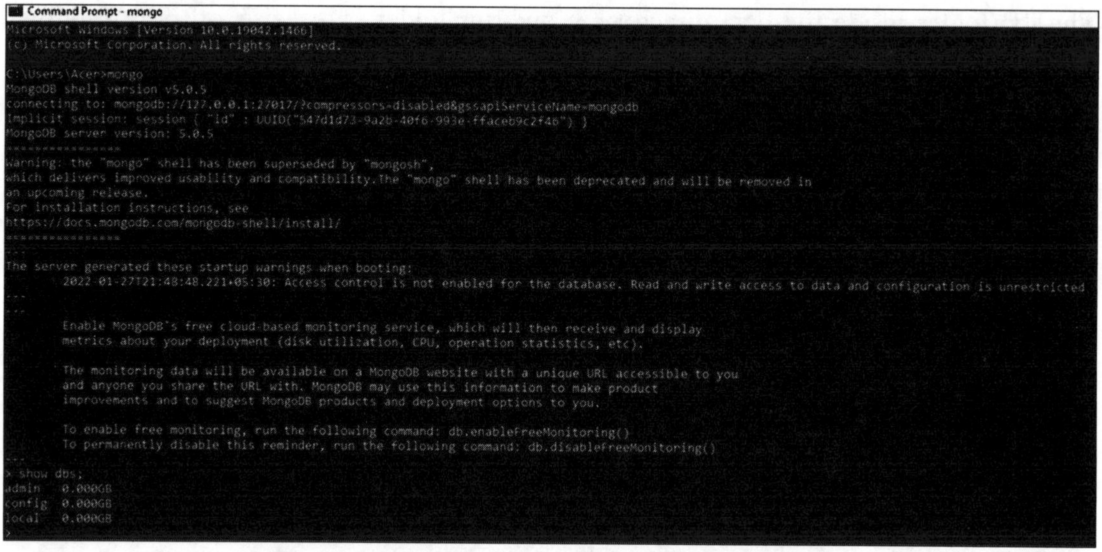

Figure 17.17 MongoDB Client Shell prompt

To show all the databases that are already there, we give the command: show DBS, which will show all the default databases already existing inside MongoDB (Fig. 17.17). It now shows the three default database available in the system (admin, config, and local). While installing MongoDB, we choose Run service (Install MongoDB as a service). Because of this, every time we start the system, the Mongod command automatically runs. So, we need not start the daemon every time. Instead, we can straightaway go to the Mongo shell Command prompt (Mongo Client) and start typing the command.

17.4 MongoDB Schema Design

Unlike relational schema design, MongoDB schema design is quite different. There is no formal method, no algorithms, and no guidelines when it comes to MongoDB schema construction. When it comes to developing a MongoDB schema, it only matters that it works well for the application. If two programs that use the same data are used differently, their schemas may be drastically different. When creating a schema, the following points should be kept in mind: saving the information, good query performance, and a suitable quantity of hardware are required. So, how does a MongoDB document look? Here is an example (Fig. 17.18).

```
{
  userid: 100,
  username: 'joseph',
  useremail: 'joseph31@gmail.com'
}
```

Figure 17.18 Example of a MongoDB document

The above is a primary document that stores a few information fields about a user. Now, let us consider a scenario in which we want to save several emails for each user. For example, we could establish a separate database (tables) of email addresses and the users with whom they are related in the relational world. However, MongoDB provides another easy and efficient option for storing these (Figure 17.19), MongoDB nested document.

```
{
    userid: 20,
    username: 'joseph',
    useremail: [
        'joseph31@gmail.com',
        'joseph7c@xyzuniversity.edu'
    ]
}
```

Figure 17.19 MongoDB nested document

MongoDB is a key-value pair-based NoSQL database. NoSQL means it does not say 'no' to SQL. Instead, it says 'not only SQL', which means it supports not only SQL, but also the other approaches. It is an open-source document database that offers excellent performance and scalability, and data modelling and data management for large datasets in enterprise applications. Auto-scaling is also available in MongoDB. MongoDB is a cross-platform database installed on Windows, Linux, and other operating systems.

A Document is a JSON-style data structure with name-value pairs. As a result, mapping any custom object from any programming language to a MongoDB Document is simple. Documents, as we can see, are JSON representations of custom objects. Therefore, we can avoid excessive JOINS by preserving data as Arrays and Documents (Embedded) within a Document.

Let us look at an example of how we might model the relational user model in MongoDB.

In a document database, a document is a record. A document usually contains information about a single object and its associated metadata. Documents store data in field-value pairs. The values can be of various types and structures, including strings, numbers, dates, arrays, or objects. In addition, documents can be stored in JSON, BSON, and XML formats. For example, a JSON document containing information on a user called Paul is shown in Fig. 17.20.

Working with data in documents is more accessible and straightforward for developers than tables since documents map to data structures in most programming languages. When storing or retrieving data, developers do not have to worry about manually separating it across different tables or manually joining it back together. They do not need to utilize an Object Relational Mapping (ORM) to manipulate the data either. Instead, users can use the data directly in their application to work with it fast.

```
{
    "first_name": "Paul",
    "surname": "Miller",
    "cell": "447557505611",
    "city": "London",
    "profession": ["banking", "finance", "trader"],
    "cars": [
        { "model": "Honda Civic", "year": 1974 },
        { "model": "Mercedes",    "year": 1973 }
    ]
}
```

Figure 17.20 MongoDB relational user model

In the above example, Paul's information is contained in a single document (Fig. 17.20). Let us look at how the same data can be stored in a relational database. We will start by making a table that keeps the user's basic information (Fig. 17.21).

Users Table				
ID	first_name	surname	Cell	City
1001	Paul	Miller	447557505611	London

Figure 17.21 Users Table in RDBMS

Next, we will be constructing another table that keeps the user's Profession (Fig. 17.22), because they can be numerous (there is a one-to-many relationship between a user and Profession). This table also includes User ID for reference (Foreign key). The User ID refers to the ID of the Users Table.

Profession Table		
ID	User ID	Profession
101	1001	banking
102	1001	finance
103	1001	trader

Figure 17.22 Profession Table in RDBMS

A user can maintain (use) multiple cars; we will build another table (Fig. 17.23) that keeps the car owner's information Car Owners Table). In this table, we also include User ID for reference. This User ID refers to the ID of the Users Table.

Car Owners Table			
ID	User ID	Model	Year
201	1001	Honda Civic	1974
202	1001	Mercedes	1973

Figure 17.23 Car Owners Table in RDBMS

This simple example showed how data about a user might be kept in a single document in a document database (MongoDB), which needs three tables in a relational database. A developer can write one query with zero joins to get or update information about a user in the document database. It is simple to interact with the database, and it is also simple to model the data in the database.

17.5 KEY FEATURES OF MONGODB

A database management system is software to store, organize, manage, and retrieve data. Consider it as a collection of massive spreadsheets that systematically collect data. There are different types of databases, and each is usually kept on servers, whether physically in a data center or virtually on cloud infrastructure, as is increasingly the case. Databases exist in various shapes, sizes, and flavors, each built to handle distinct data types. MongoDB, for instance, is a document-based, distributed database designed for day technical coders. Most modern programs use databases, whether on our phone, PC, or the internet. They hold a lot of the data that an app needs to run, and they keep it structured and accessible. NoSQL databases are becoming a more popular option for teams that want to iterate since they can manage ever-changing data types quickly. Furthermore, solutions like MongoDB take advantage of NoSQL's scalability to synchronize different data storage devices.

MongoDB's notion of documents containing sub-documents nested in complex hierarchies is expressive and flexible. Moreover, it has a flexible query model. For example, a user can selectively index some part of a document or a query based on attribute values.

MongoDB may be used as a universal data storage system because data does not fit into a specific relationship. MongoDB data is organized according to a configurable structure. We can quickly rearrange how our data is kept if the needs of our application change. Because MongoDB also provides schema validation, we may lock down our schema as much or as little as we wish. This locking mechanism implies it can handle whatever data structuring requirements we may have now or later in the future.

Associations across data in various tables can be achieved using joins in a relational database, but relationships between nodes are impossible in a hierarchical database. Finally, unlike many other NoSQL databases, MongoDB supports transactions and ensures that reads and writes to multiple documents are atomic. We may feel comfortable that the searches can be consolidated into a single transaction if we need to query data from multiple documents.

MongoDB was created from scratch sources. However, its built-in replication, load balancing, and aggregation capabilities make it a valuable component of modern software design. It can also generate schema recommendations to assist us in making decisions best-suited to MongoDB's document data model.

MongoDB is based on a scale-out architecture, which has grown popular among developers for creating scalable systems with changing data schemas. MongoDB is designed to scale horizontally and vertically, thanks to sharding. As a result, its architecture can distribute the load across multiple instances and accomplish read and write functionality.

MongoDB makes it simple for developers to use a document database to store structured or unstructured data. It stores documents in a JSON-like manner. Most modern programming languages automatically translate this format to native objects, making it logical for developers because they do not have to be concerned about data normalization. MongoDB can also manage massive amounts of data and scale vertically or horizontally to accommodate them. JSON is commonly used for front-end and API communication on the web, and it is even more accessible when the database supports the same standard. MapReduce is an excellent tool for building data pipelines, and MongoDB readily uses MapReduce.

MongoDB was built for people building internet and business applications, who need to evolve quickly and scale elegantly. However, companies and development teams of all sizes use MongoDB for various reasons.

Apart from the majority of the NoSQL default functionality, MongoDB adds a few extra essential and beneficial features: MongoDB is a high-performance database. Support for embedded data models, in particular, minimizes database system I/O traffic. Select queries are also faster because MongoDB indexes provide fast queries. In addition, MongoDB offers a powerful Query Language (Rich Query Language) that supports the most common Create, Read, Update, Delete (CRUD) operations. In addition, keys from embedded documents and arrays can be included in indexes, allowing for faster queries. Text Search and Data Aggregation are other suitable elements of the Query Language.

Users can extract and transform data from MongoDB and load it into a new format or export it to other data sources using native aggregation. Furthermore, MongoDB makes the data highly compatible. It is a database that can be used for anything. MongoDB can handle a wide range of loads within an application and fulfil numerous purposes. It has a flexible schema that can be changed on the fly.

A MongoDB replica set (a group of MongoDB servers) shares the same dataset, ensuring data redundancy and availability. MongoDB's Auto Replication functionality ensures high availability. It also has an automatic failover feature, whereby data is restored from a backup (replica) copy if the server fails. MongoDB's sharding is a powerful feature. Due to sharding, horizontal scalability is possible. Horizontal scalability is built into MongoDB's basic functionality. Data is sharded and replicated across a range of different devices. Starting with 3.4, MongoDB supports creating data zones based on the shard key. MongoDB directs reads and writes covered by a zone, solely to the shards within the zone in a balanced cluster.

MongoDB supports multiple Storage Engines. When we save data in the form of documents (NoSQL) or tables (RDBMS) that hold the data, it is the Storage Engine Data that is preserved in memory and on disc using Storage Engines.

MongoDB comes with an extract, transform, and load (ETL) framework that reduces the need for complicated data pipelines. Data in MongoDB will get replicated across a replica set without a complicated setup. Security features of both authentication and authorization are taken into account.

17.6 RDBMS vs. MongoDB

MongoDB is a considerably better choice for modern-day applications with complicated datasets that change frequently and require a flexible data model that does not need to be created instantly. Figure 17.24 illustrates the differences between RDBMS and MongoDB.

RDBMS	MongoDB
Database	Database
Table	Collection
Row	Document (JSON)
Column	Field
Server (Oracle)	Mongod
Client (MySQL)	Mongo
Index	Index
Joining query	Linking and embedding
Group by	Aggregation pipeline
Triggering	No trigger
Foreign key	No foreign concept
Vertical scaling	Horizontal scaling

Figure 17.24 RDBMS vs. MongoDB

RDBMS is a relational Database Management system, whereas MongoDB is a non-relational document-oriented database. RDBMS is not suitable for hierarchical data storage. MongoDB is highly suitable for hierarchical data storage. RDBMS is vertically scalable (example: increasing RAM), whereas MongoDB is horizontally scalable (adding more servers). RDBMS has predefined schema, whereas MongoDB has dynamic schema. RDBMS is slower in comparison to MongoDB. MongoDB can provide a JavaScript client for querying, which is not possible with RDBMS.

In the screen shown in Fig. 17.25, we executed basic JavaScript commands like division operation, replacing a string, writing and executing a function, which is possible with MongoDB. The above figure also indicates how a syntax error will be thrown while giving the commands.

When modelling products for an e-commerce site, a single product's information can spread across dozens of tables with a completely normalized relational data model. However, if we want a product representation from the database, we will have to construct a complex SQL query with several joins. As a result, developers will need to employ separate software to combine the data into something meaningful.

On the other hand, a document model allows most of a product's information to be represented in a single document. Because MongoDB's query capabilities are tailored to manipulating structured documents, users migrating from relational databases will notice a similar level of query power.

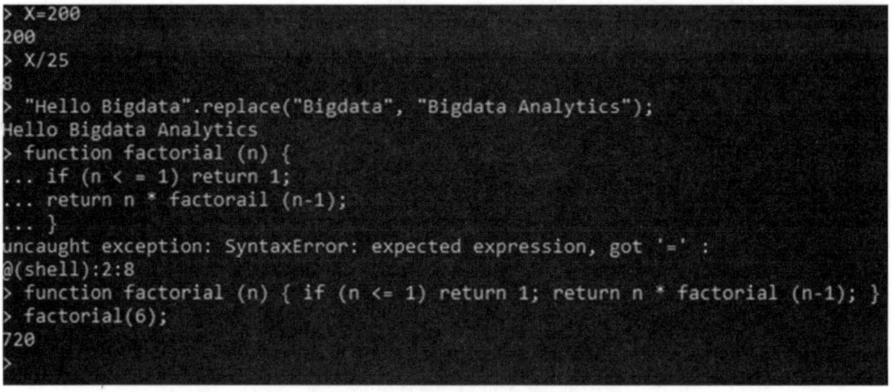

```
> X=200
200
> X/25
8
> "Hello Bigdata".replace("Bigdata", "Bigdata Analytics");
Hello Bigdata Analytics
> function factorial (n) {
... if (n < = 1) return 1;
... return n * factorail (n-1);
... }
uncaught exception: SyntaxError: expected expression, got '=' :
@(shell):2:8
> function factorial (n) { if (n <= 1) return 1; return n * factorial (n-1); }
> factorial(6);
720
>
```

Figure 17.25 JavaScript coding in MongoDB Client prompt

Furthermore, most developers today use object-oriented programming languages and thus want a data store that better translates to objects. The objects defined in the programming language can be saved "as is" in MongoDB, eliminating part of object mappers' complexity. JSON (JavaScript Object Notation) structures are made up of keys and values that can be nested indefinitely deep. They are similar to other programming languages' dictionaries and hash maps.

17.7 MongoDB Query Language (MQL)

MongoDB is a document database that is JSON-oriented (JavaScript Object Notation), though it employs a binary-encoded form of JSON called BSON internally. BSON is a serialized encoding format for JSON, primarily used for document storage and retrieval. Compared to JSON, the BSON format has more data types, such as dates and binary data, supported. MongoDB can be assessed using MongoDB Query Language (MQL). Clients interact with the MongoDB server through this interface. On the MongoDB Shell, developers and database administrators can write MQL commands interactively. In order to execute MQL instructions in client applications, drivers are provided in various programming languages. MQL supports CRUD operations. The results can be sorted, grouped, filtered, and counted via aggregation pipelines. Special functions such as text search and geospatial queries are possible. Multi-document transactions are also supported.

17.8 MongoDB Database, Collection and Documents

Databases, collections, and documents are all necessary components of MongoDB; without them, we will not save data on the server. A database contains a collection (equivalent to the table), and a collection has documents that contain data; they are linked together. Database in MongoDB is called a Database (similar to RDBMS). In the MongoDB context, we can say that database is described as a physical container of collections, which means there will be multiple databases and there will be many collections. A database can have any number of collections. Document in MongoDB is a set of key-value pairs; every document in MongoDB has a unique value key (field) called "-id." MongoDB will add this key automatically for each document. Whenever we insert a document, MongoDB will automatically insert this field, which always has a unique value for all documents. The documents are flexible and they have a dynamic schema, which are user-defined. Since document schemas are user-defined, they are not fixed or static. Documents can hold any data, as long as they are valid data types in MongoDB. Documents within the collection can have different schema or fields. All rows in MongoDB, put together, is called a Document. Indexing is possible in both MongoDB and RDBMS. Join Query is not possible in MongoDB; however, it can be achieved through Linking and Embedding. Group By (Join) in MongoDB is achieved through Aggregation Pipeline. Triggering and Foreign Key concepts are not available in MongoDB.

17.9 MongoDB Server

Mongod.exe is the central server that listens for and receives network requests. When we start the server, we can define the data location. Almost no configuration is required to run the server; nevertheless, there are a few options to "tune" it. Because MongoDB allows the OS to manage memory, this is a purposefully planned feature. With a system call, the data files will be mapped to virtual memory, and the Operating System (OS) will select how to map the data into memory.

17.10 MongoDB Client Through the JavaScript's Shell

The Mongo program (typing mongo in the command prompt) opens a shell and connects to a Mongod process, specified or running locally by default. The shell was created to be similar to the MySQL shell, except it is based on JavaScript and does not require SQL. The syntax of JavaScript is identical to those of C and Java. We should grasp most of the JavaScript examples if we are familiar with either of these.

17.11 CRUD Operation in MongoDB

All actions, including database selection and CRUD, are expressed in JavaScript code in the mongo.exe shell (Fig. 17.26). If we don't want to utilize JavaScript, we can use our favourite dynamic language, PHP or Python, to manage MongoDB.

CRUD Operation	
Create	Add documents to a collection. The unique _id field is automatically added to each document if not specified in the method calls.
Read	Retrieve documents from a collection.
Update	Modify existing documents of a collection.
Delete	Remove documents from a collection.

Figure 17.26 CRUD operation in MongoDB

17.11.1 Creating Database in MongoDB (C of CRUD)

Before we create a database, we need first to learn about database naming restrictions: The database names in MongoDB are case insensitive, but we must remember that they cannot differ solely due to the case of the characters. For windows users, MongoDB database names cannot contain any of the following characters: ^, ", $, *, :, |, and ?. For Unix and Linux users, MongoDB database names cannot contain the following characters: ^, ", and $. MongoDB database names cannot contain null characters (in Windows, Unix, and Linux systems). MongoDB database names cannot be empty and must contain less than 64 characters.

To create a database called "school", give the name of the database ("school") after the command "use". Then, it automatically makes this database and takes us inside. This command will create the database (Fig. 17.27), but when we provide the "show dbs" command, it will show only the old databases and not the new ones ("school"). The newly created database does not display because we need to insert some table to see it using the "show dbs" command. In order to create a collection (table) in the database, the command is `DB.createCollection("Collection_name")`. If we want to create the collection named "students", then the command will be: `db.createCollection("students")`. We can see the collection is created; in typical language, the table is created.

Figure 17.27 Creating database and collection

17.11.2 Creating Collection in MongoDB

Collections hold data in the form of documents, similar to the table in DBMS. Multiple collections can be stored in a single database. MongoDB databases are schema-less. As a result, it is not required for the schema of one document to be like the schema of another document. In other words, a single collection can contain a variety of document kinds.

17.11.3 Listing Down the Databases Available in MongoDB

Now we know the command to create a database. To identify whether our database is there or not, we can check using the command "show dbs". Type the following command (show DBS) in the Mongo shell (Fig. 17.28) to see how many databases your MongoDB server has. There are three default databases: 1. admin, 2. config, and 3. local. Along with this, it also lists the newly created database called "school." According to the MongoDB rule, it cannot show in the list unless we have one record or collection stored inside MongoDB.

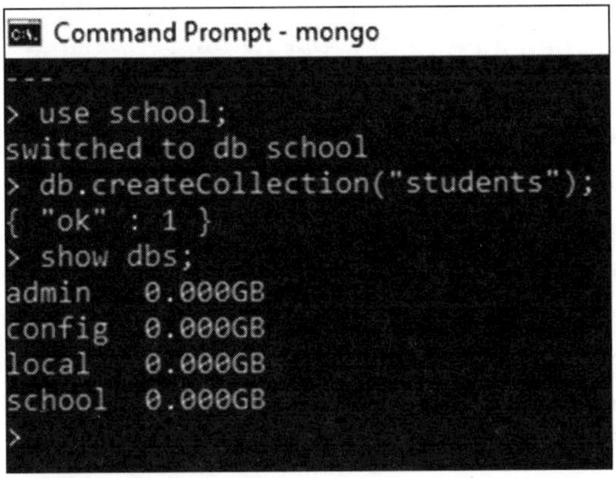

Figure 17.28 Display databases

Collection can also be created on the fly while inserting data (document) into the Collection, using the command `DB.collection_name.insertOne({..})`. The `insertOne()` function stores a single piece of data in the provided Collection. Moreover, we keep our data in the curly braces, or in other words, it is a document. So, this is how the collections can be created using the data.

17.11.4 Inserting Records into Collection (Table)

After creating the database, now we create a collection to store documents. The collection is created using the following syntax: db.createCollection("students").

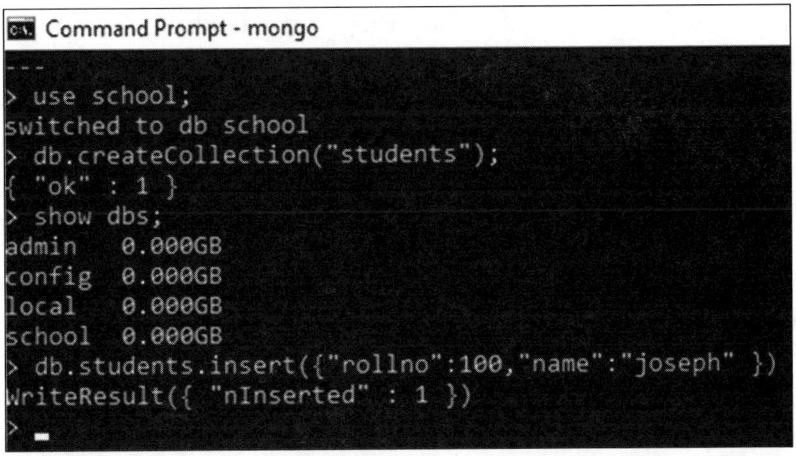

Figure 17.29 Inserting documents into the Collection

In order to insert the data into the collection, DB.collection_name.insert({document}) is used. Let us say the collection name is "students" and then, "insert" and give the parentheses, and inside the parentheses, you give the curly brackets, and you give your values in JSON format. So, inside the curly brackets, we need to provide the key name, so the key name is "rollno" and then a colon (:). Let us give the value 100 here. One more key name is "name" and then a colon (:). Let us give the value here as "joseph". Then, press Enter, which will create this collection (if it already exists) and insert the document into your collection (Fig. 17.29).

In this case, we will make a collection called students, and we insert data in it with the help of the insertOne() function. In other words, {"rollno":100, "name":"joseph"} is a document in the students' Collection, and in this document, the rollno is the key or field, and 100 is the value of this key or field. Similarly, the name is the key or field, and "joseph" is the value of this key or field. After pressing enter, we received a notice (as shown in Fig. 17.28) informing us that the data was successfully entered (i.e., "acknowledge": true) and assigning us an automatically generated id. It is the unique feature of MongoDB, which provides every document with a unique id. Generally, this id is created automatically, but we can also create our id (must be unique).

It would help if we familiarised ourselves with the field naming constraints before proceeding: Strings are used to name the fields. The name of the _id field has been set aside for usage as a primary key. Moreover, this field's value must be unique, immutable, and of any type other than an array. Furthermore, the field name must not contain any null characters. Finally, top-level field names should not begin with the $ sign.

The BSON document can be up to 16MB in size. It ensures that the single document does not consume excessive RAM or bandwidth (during transmission). In addition, MongoDB includes a GridFS API for storing documents with more data than the requested size.

Because MongoDB always retains the order of the fields in the documents, except for the _id field (which always appears first), a single document may include duplicate fields, and field renaming may affect the order of the fields in the documents. Therefore, every document storage in a MongoDB collection must have a unique _id field, similar to a primary key in a relational database. The user or the system can set the value of the _id field (if the user does not establish an _id field, the system will construct an ObjectId for the _id field). Every document's _id field is the initial field. The _id field accepts any BSON type except arrays as a value. The _id field's default type is ObjectId.

We can keep adding as many documents as possible using insert method. In total, we have inserted three documents now with the "rollno" as 100, 110 and 120 respectively (Fig. 17.30).

We can store a set of documents in an Array and then we can insert the array into the collection as shown in Fig. 17.31. We created an array of documents called "Arraystudents" and stored two documents with the "rollno" as 130 and 140 respectively. After that, we used "db.students.insert(Arraystudents)" command to include the two records into the "students" Collection.

```
> db.students.insert({"rollno":100, "name":"Joseph"})
WriteResult({ "nInserted" : 1 })
> db.students.insert({"rollno":110, "name":"Andrea"})
WriteResult({ "nInserted" : 1 })
> db.students.insert({"rollno":120, "name":"Beckey"})
WriteResult({ "nInserted" : 1 })
> db.students.find().pretty()
{
        "_id" : ObjectId("61f6369b4abe6768cd4f0475"),
        "rollno" : 100,
        "name" : "Joseph"
}
{
        "_id" : ObjectId("61f636ca4abe6768cd4f0476"),
        "rollno" : 110,
        "name" : "Andrea"
}
{
        "_id" : ObjectId("61f636ea4abe6768cd4f0477"),
        "rollno" : 120,
        "name" : "Beckey"
}
>
```

Figure 17.30 Inserting multiple documents into the Collection

```
> var Arraystudents =
... [   {"rollno": 130, "name": "Bruce"},
...     {"rollno": 140, "name": "Christina"}
... ];
> db.students.insert(Arraystudents);
BulkWriteResult({
        "writeErrors" : [ ],
        "writeConcernErrors" : [ ],
        "nInserted" : 2,
        "nUpserted" : 0,
        "nMatched" : 0,
        "nModified" : 0,
        "nRemoved" : 0,
        "upserted" : [ ]
})
>
```

Figure 17.31 Inserting multiple documents through Array

Documents inclusions is confirmed by using the find method as shown in Fig. 17.32.

```
> db.students.find().pretty()
{
        "_id" : ObjectId("61f6369b4abe6768cd4f0475"),
        "rollno" : 100,
        "name" : "Joseph"
}
{
        "_id" : ObjectId("61f636ca4abe6768cd4f0476"),
        "rollno" : 110,
        "name" : "Andrea"
}
{
        "_id" : ObjectId("61f636ea4abe6768cd4f0477"),
        "rollno" : 120,
        "name" : "Beckey"
}
{
        "_id" : ObjectId("61f638914abe6768cd4f0478"),
        "rollno" : 130,
        "name" : "Bruce"
}
{
        "_id" : ObjectId("61f638914abe6768cd4f0479"),
        "rollno" : 140,
        "name" : "Christina"
}
>
```

Figure 17.32 Documents insertion confirmation

17.11.5 Showcasing the Current Database Used

If we are unsure which database we are currently using, we can type dbs or db in the command prompt, showing the current database. For us, it shows "school", which is the current database used (Fig. 17.33).

```
Command Prompt - mongo
---
> use school;
switched to db school
> db.createCollection("students");
{ "ok" : 1 }
> show dbs;
admin   0.000GB
config  0.000GB
local   0.000GB
school  0.000GB
> db.students.insert({"rollno":100,"name":"joseph" })
WriteResult({ "nInserted" : 1 })
> db
school
>
```

Figure 17.33 Showcasing the current database in use

17.11.6 Showcasing the Tables (Collections) in the Current Database

To list all the collections inside the database, we need to give the command "show collections" and then the semicolon, and then press the ENTER key, which will show all the collections present inside the database. We have only created one collection, which is "students" inside our "school" database; that is why we see only one collection ("students") here (Fig. 17.34).

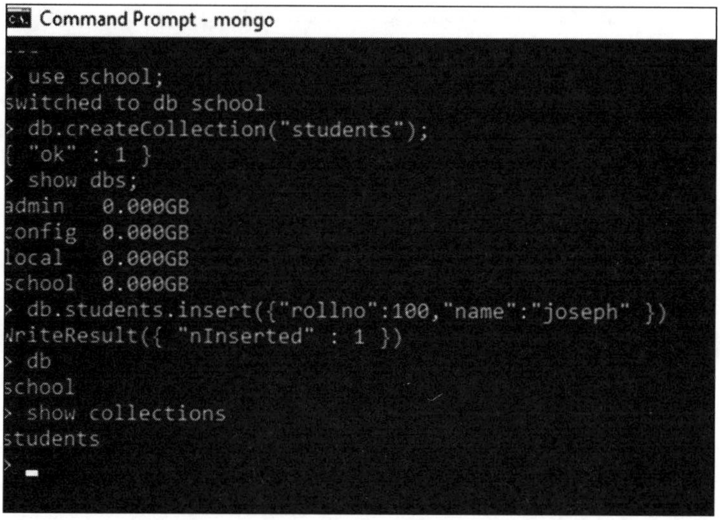

Figure 17.34 Showcasing the collections within the database

17.11.7 Reading Collections in MongoDB (R of CRUD)

To see all the values (documents) present inside the collection, we need to give the command `db.collection_name.find()`. We will see all the documents present inside the collection ("students"). This method will display all the documents in a non-structured way (Fig. 17.35).

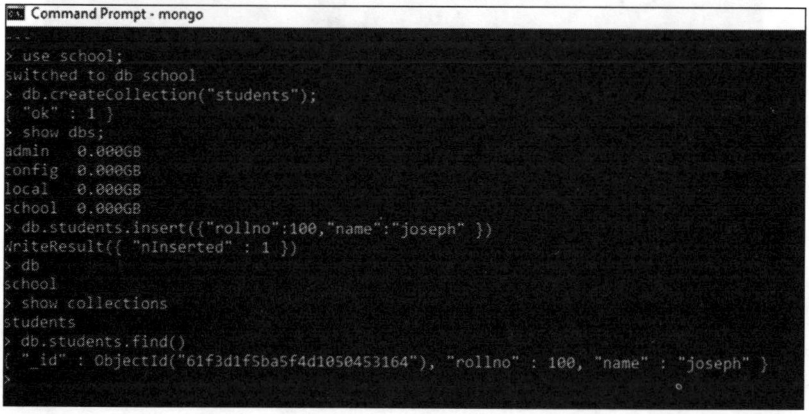

Figure 17.35 Showcasing the documents within the Collection

findOne() method

Apart from the find() method, the findOne() method returns only one document.

    >db.collection_name.findOne()

The example in Fig. 17.36 retrieves the document with the name Beckey from the students collection.

```
> db.students.findOne({name: "Beckey"})
{
        "_id" : ObjectId("61f636ea4abe6768cd4f0477"),
        "rollno": 120
        "name": "Beckey"
}
```

Figure 17.36 The findOne() method

17.11.8 Updating documents in MongoDB (U of CRUD)

The following example will set the new name 'Mercy' of the documents whose name is 'Mercy Jack' (Fig. 17.37).

    >db.students.update({'name':'Mercy'},{$set:{'name':'Mercy Jack'}})

```
(shell):1:46
> db.students.update( {'name': 'Mercy'}, { $set:{'name':'Mercy Jack'} } );
WriteResult({ "nMatched" : 1, "nUpserted" : 0, "nModified" : 1 })
> db.students.find().pretty()

        "_id" : ObjectId("61f6369b4abe6768cd4f0475"),
        "rollno" : 100,
        "name" : "Joseph"

        "_id" : ObjectId("61f636ca4abe6768cd4f0476"),
        "rollno" : 110,
        "name" : "Andrea"

        "_id" : ObjectId("61f636ea4abe6768cd4f0477"),
        "rollno" : 120,
        "name" : "Beckey"

        "_id" : ObjectId("61f638914abe6768cd4f0478"),
        "rollno" : 130,
        "name" : "Bruce"

        "_id" : ObjectId("61f638914abe6768cd4f0479"),
        "rollno" : 140,
        "name" : "Christina"

        "_id" : ObjectId("61f63ab74abe6768cd4f047a"),
        "rollno" : 150,
        "name" : "Mercy Jack"
```

Figure 17.37 Updating document within the collection

MongoDB will only update one document by default. You must set the parameter 'multi' to true to update several documents.

>db.students.update({'name':'Mercy'},{$set:{'title':'Mercy Jack'}}, {multi:true})

17.11.9 Delete Operation in MongoDB (D of CRUD)

We can use the syntax db.collection_name.drop() to drop a particular Collection in MongoDB (Fig. 17.38). This query is an example of a Mongosh method (the name of the MongoDB shell is called Mongosh). This query is not the documentation for driver methods in Node.js or other programming languages. Mongosh methods are similar to traditional mongo shell methods in most circumstances. Some historical techniques, however, are not available in mongosh. Refer to the respective MongoDB Server release documentation for the legacy mongo shell documentation.

Figure 17.38 Dropping a particular collection

We will get an error if we try to dump a collection from a mongosh into the admin or config databases. To remove these collections, connect to the config server and perform the command there.

17.11.10 Dropping (Deleting) a Particular Database

The screenshot below shows how to drop a newly formed database named "students" using the "db.dropDatabase()" function (Fig. 17.39). The database named "Students" is not available while we use "Show dbs" command, indicating that it got dropped already.

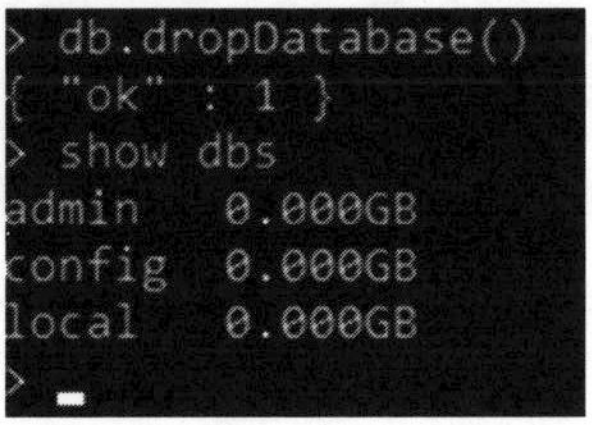

Figure 17.39 Dropping a particular database

Because this operation deletes the presently selected (current use) database, we do not supply a database name in this command. Therefore, if we do not choose a database, the default "test" database will be deleted.

To remove a database that is not in use, check the currently selected database first, using the command "db". Then we may examine the database list with the "display dbs" command. Then use the command "use database name" to pick the database we want to remove. Then, to remove an existing database, use the db.dropDatabase() command.

17.12 Pretty () Method

The `pretty()` method is mostly used to display the result in a more easily readable/formatted way. The command is >db.collection_name.find().pretty().

The following example (Fig. 17.40) retrieves all the documents from the collection named "students" and arranges them in an easy-to-read format.

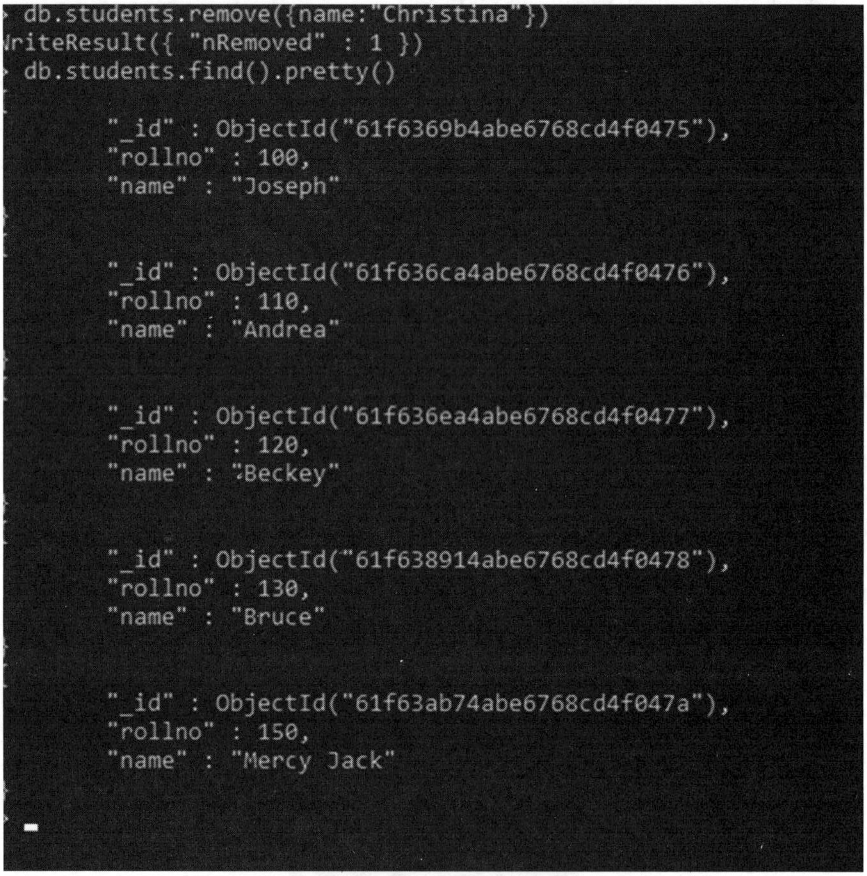

```
> db.students.remove({name:"Christina"})
WriteResult({ "nRemoved" : 1 })
> db.students.find().pretty()
        "_id" : ObjectId("61f6369b4abe6768cd4f0475"),
        "rollno" : 100,
        "name" : "Joseph"


        "_id" : ObjectId("61f636ca4abe6768cd4f0476"),
        "rollno" : 110,
        "name" : "Andrea"


        "_id" : ObjectId("61f636ea4abe6768cd4f0477"),
        "rollno" : 120,
        "name" : "Beckey"


        "_id" : ObjectId("61f638914abe6768cd4f0478"),
        "rollno" : 130,
        "name" : "Bruce"


        "_id" : ObjectId("61f63ab74abe6768cd4f047a"),
        "rollno" : 150,
        "name" : "Mercy Jack"
```

Figure 17.40 Pretty method

17.13 AND in MongoDB

This operator is used to execute a logical AND operation on an array of one or more expressions. It selects or retrieves only those documents in the array that match all of the specified expressions. MongoDB performs an implicit AND operation with a comma-separated set of expressions.

>db.mycol.find({ $and: [{<key1>:<value1>}, { <key2>:<value2>}] })

The following example (Fig. 17.41) will show all the students' detail with rollno as 120 with the name Beckey.

```
> db.students.find({$and:[{"rollno":120},{"name": "Beckey"}]}).pretty()
```

{
  "_id" : ObjectId("61f636ea4abe6768cd4f0477"),
  "rollno": 120,
  "name": "Beckey"
}

Figure 17.41 Result of AND method in MongoDB

Depending on our needs, we can use this operator in methods such as `locate()`, `update()`, and so on. This operator performs the short-circuit evaluation. The $and handles failures in the following way to help the query engine improve queries: Any expression passed to $ that would create an error if evaluated alone, may cause an error in the $and containing the overall expression. MongoDB will not evaluate the remaining expressions in the array if the initial expression of the $and operator evaluates to False. With the help of a comma, you can also use the AND operation implicitly (,).

17.14 OR IN MONGODB

We need to use the "**$or**" keyword to query documents based on the OR condition. The $or operator chooses documents that fulfil at least one of two or more conditions by performing a logical OR operation on an array of two or more expressions. When evaluating the clauses in the $or expression, MongoDB conducts either a collection scan or an index scan. For MongoDB, to assess a $or expression using indexes, all clauses in the $or expression must be supported by indexes. MongoDB will execute a collection scan if this is not the case. Following is the basic syntax of **OR**.

```
>db.collection_name.find(
  {
    $or: [
       {key1: value1}, {key2:value2}
    ]
  }
).pretty()
```

The following example will show all the details with rollno as 100 or the student's name as Andrea (Fig. 17.42).

```
>db.students.find({$or:[{"rollno": 100},{"name: "Andrea"}]}).pretty()
```

```
{
    "_id" : ObjectId("61f636ea4abe6768cd4f0475"),
    "rollno": 100,
    "name": "Joseph"
}
{
    "_id" : ObjectId("61f636ea4abe6768cd4f0476"),
    "rollno": 110,
    "name": "Andrea"
}
```

Figure 17.42 Result of OR method in MongoDB

17.15 USING AND AND OR TOGETHER

The documents with a rollno greater than 110 and whose name is either 'Bruce' or 'Mercy Jack' will be displayed in the following example (Fig. 17.43). The equivalent clause in SQL is **'where rollno >110 AND (name = 'Bruce' OR name= 'Mercy Jack')'**.

```
>db.students.find({"rollno": {$gt:110}, $or: [{"name": "Bruce"},
   {"name": "Mercy Jack"}]}).pretty()
{
 "_id" : ObjectId("61f636ea4abe6768cd4f0478"),
 "rollno": 130,
 "name": "Bruce"
}
{
 "_id" : ObjectId("61f636ea4abe6768cd4f047a"),
 "rollno": 140,
 "name": "Mercy Jack"
}
```

Figure 17.43 Result of AND and OR together in MongoDB

17.16 NOR IN MONGODB

The $nor operator is one of the several logical query operators available in MongoDB. This operator is used to conduct a logical NOR operation on an array of one or more expressions, selecting or retrieving only those documents in the array that do not match all of the specified expressions (Fig. 17.44). $nor is the opposite of $or operation. If $or operation returns True then $nor operation returns False. If $or operation returns False then $nor operation returns True. Depending on our needs, we can use this operator in methods such as `locate()`, `update()`, and so on. The syntax for $nor is as follows:

```
>db.collection_name.find(
    {
        $nor: [ {key1: value1}, {key2:value2} ]
    }
)
```

Figure 17.44 Syntax of NOR method in MongoDB

The following example will retrieve the document(s) whose rollno is not 100 and name is not "Andrea" (Fig. 17.45).

```
db.students.find(
    {
        $nor:[ {"rollno": 100}, {"name": "Andrea"} ]
    }
).pretty()
```

Figure 17.45 NOR method usage in MongoDB

As we can see, the document with rollno 100 is not there in the result below, and the document with the name "Andrea" is also not there (Fig. 17.46).

```
{
    "_id" : ObjectId("61f636ea4abe6768cd4f0477"),
    "rollno": 120,
    "name": "Beckey"
}
{
    "_id" : ObjectId("61f636ea4abe6768cd4f0478"),
    "rollno": 130,
    "name": "Bruce"
}
{
    "_id" : ObjectId("61f636ea4abe6768cd4f047a"),
    "rollno": 140,
    "name": "Mercy Jack"
}
```

Figure 17.46 Result of NOR method

17.17 NOT IN MONGODB

The $not operator is one of the several logical query operators available in MongoDB. This operator performs a logical NOT operation on the specified operator expressions. Only the documents that do not match the supplied term are selected or retrieved. It also covers documents that do not have the field in them. Depending on our needs, we can use this operator in methods such as `locate()`, `update()`, and so on. Always use the $not operator in conjunction with other operators because it cannot independently verify fields or documents, and only impacts other operators. The basic syntax of NOT is as follows (Fig. 17.47).

```
>db.collection_name.find(
{
          $NOT: [ {key1: value1}, {key2:value2} ]
}
).pretty()
```

Figure 17.47 Syntax of NOT method

The document(s) whose rollno is less than 110 will be returned in the example below (Fig. 17.48).

```
> db.students.find( { "rollno": { $not: { $gt: "110" } } } )

{
        "_id" : ObjectId("61f636ea4abe6768cd4f0475"),
        "rollno": 100,
        "name": "Joseph"
}
{
        "_id" : ObjectId("61f636ea4abe6768cd4f0476"),
        "rollno": 110,
        "name": "Andrea"
}
```

Figure 17.48 Result of NOT method

17.18 CREATING AND QUERYING THROUGH INDEXES

Indexes are significant in any database, and it is no different in MongoDB. Performing queries in MongoDB becomes more efficient with the use of Indexes. For example, suppose we have a collection with thousands of documents and no indexes and queries to find specific documents. In that case, MongoDB will have to scan the entire collection to locate the documents. On the other hand, MongoDB would employ indexes to limit the number of documents that could be searched in the collection if we had them. Indexes are one-of-a-kind datasets that store a portion of the data in a collection. Because the data is only partially complete, it is easier to read. This partial set has the value of a single field or a group of fields sorted by field value.

17.18.1 The `createIndex()` method

The `createIndex()` method of MongoDB is used to create an index, `>db.collection_name.createIndex({KEY:1})`. Here, the key is the field's name on which you want to create an index, and one (1) is for ascending order. You must use minus one (−1) to construct an index in descending order.

Create a single-key Index if all queries use the same single key. If you only query on a single key in a given collection, then you need to create just one single-key index for that collection. For example (Fig. 17.49), you might create an index on the rollno in the students collection: `db.students.createIndex( { "rollno": 1 } )`

```
>db.students.createIndex({"rollno":1})
{
            "createdCollectionAutomatically" : false,
            "numIndexesBefore" : 1,
            "numIndexesAfter" : 2,
            "ok" : 1
}

In the createIndex() method, you can pass multiple
fields to create index on various fields.

>db.students.createIndex({"rollno":1, "name": -1 })
```

Figure 17.49 Create Index method

MongoDB creates Compound Indexes to support several different queries. If we sometimes query on only one key and at other times query on that key combined with a second key, creating a compound index is more efficient than creating a single-key index; MongoDB will use the compound index for both queries. So, for example, we might create an index on both rollno and name, `db.students.createIndex( { "rollno": 1, "name": -1 } )`. Then, we can query on just a rollno and query on a rollno combined with the name. In addition, a single compound index on multiple fields can support all the queries that search a "prefix" subset of those fields. The following index on a collection: { x: 1, y: 1, z: 1} can support queries that the following indexes support: { x: 1 } and/or { x: 1, y: 1 }. There are some situations where the prefix indexes may offer better query performance: for example, if z is a large array, the {x: 1, y: 1, z: 1} index can also support many of the same queries as the following index: { x: 1, z: 1 }. The {x: 1, z: 1} index supports both the query and the sort operation, while the {x: 1, y: 1, z: 1} index only supports the query.

17.18.2 MongoDB's `dropIndex()` Method

It allows you to remove a specific index from the specified database.

```
>db.collection_name.dropIndex({KEY:1})
```
Example: > db.students.dropIndex({"rollno":1})

17.18.3 The `dropIndexes()` Method

The `dropIndexes()` is only available as a method on a collection object. This command obtains a write lock on the relevant database, preventing further activities until it completes. The message "non-id indexes dropped for collection" means that it will not drop the default index _id, and we can only drop indexes built by the users. This method deletes multiple (specified) indexes on a collection:

```
>db.collection_name.dropIndexes()
```

Assume we have created two indexes in the named students collection as shown below:

```
> db.students.createIndex({"rollno":1,"name":-1})
```

The following example removes the above-created indexes of students.

```
>db.students.dropIndexes({"rollno":1,"name":-1})
```

17.18.4 The `getIndexes()` Method

This method returns the description of all the indexes in the collection.

The `getIndexes()` method in MongoDB provides an array containing a list of documents that identify and describe the collection's existing indexes. It also includes indexes that are hidden. There are no parameters for this method. Instead, the keys and settings used to generate an index are included in the index information returned by this method. Starting with MongoDB 4.4, the hidden index is available in this function.

17.19 MONGO COMPASS

A compass is an interactive tool, a Graphical User Interface tool (GUI tool) for managing MongoDB for querying, optimizing, and analyzing MongoDB data to get critical insights, to drag and drop for building pipelines, and more. Compass provides everything from schema analysis to index optimization to aggregation pipelines in a single, centralized interface. Compass is open-source and free-to-use, and it runs on macOS, Windows, and Linux. Some of the activities Compass can assist us with are data import and management via a simple interface. We assume the compass app is already installed into the system, as we choose that option while installing MongoDB.

17.19.1 MongoDB Connection

To utilize MongoDB Compass with the MongoDB instance on our remote server, we must first connect to it as if we were using the shell to access the database. We should have already set up the MongoDB server to accept remote connections from our local PC. We can connect to Compass using, Option 1: either a connection string (a single line of text including all necessary database connection information) or Option 2: by manually filling in all connection details. The screen below shows the Option 1 to connect to MongoDB. You need to click "Connect Button" (Fig. 17.50).

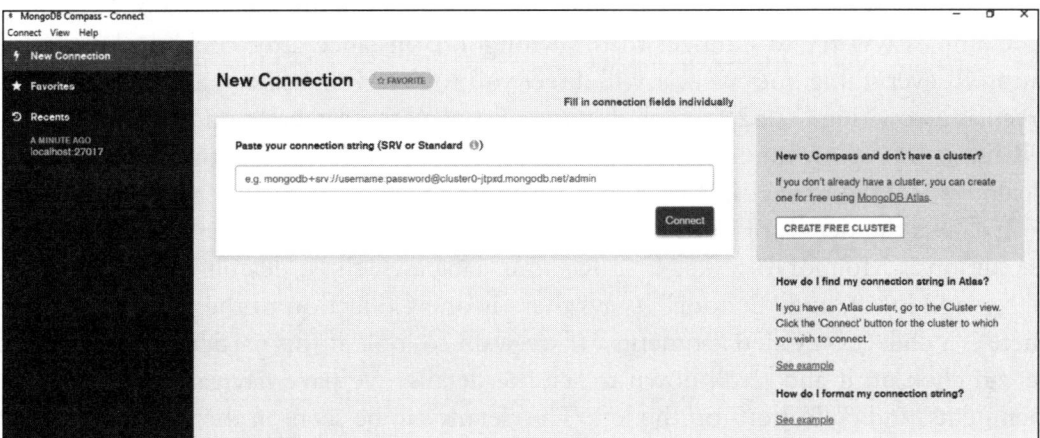

Figure 17.50 Compass Connect screen

The second option is to click "Fill in Connection Fields individually" on the above screen. It will ask for the essential details. In the Hostname column, type the IP address of the remote server where our MongoDB instance is operating (Fig. 17.51). The default name is always localhost; this is the default credential. Unless we have altered the port on which our MongoDB instance listens for connections, leave the default port setting. The default

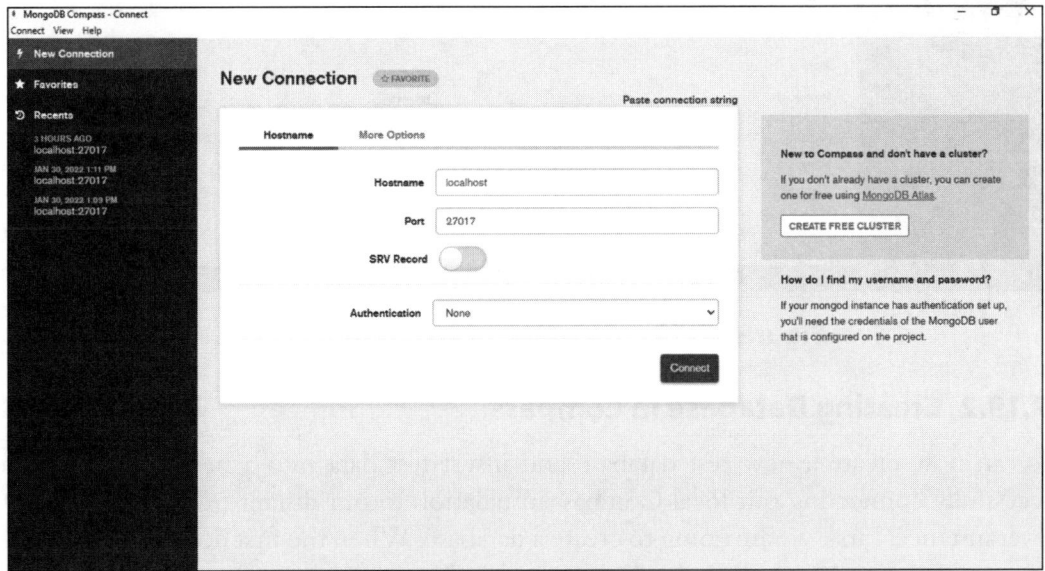

Figure 17.51 Compass Connect screen: Paste connection string

port is always 27017. We may also change the Authentication option to Username/ Password because the secured server with be authentication enabled. After selecting this option, fill in the three new fields with the username of our administrative MongoDB user, the password associated with this account, and the authentication database for this user. Just click on the "Connect" button, and you will see that the Compass application is loaded. MongoDB will always have these three databases defined by default.

Compass will try to connect to the MongoDB instance after clicking the Connect button. If everything goes well, it will direct you to the Home screen and we will get the screen as below (Fig. 17.52), which displays a list of all the databases on the instance. They will also show up on the left panel, alongside high-level details like the database server's IP address and the MongoDB version it is running.

It shows the details of hosting; it says localhost 27017. It is a standalone cluster, and the edition is MongoDB 5.0.5. It shows four databases, three default databases (Admin, config, and local), and "School." It says there is one Collection in the "school" database. There is a collection called "students." If we want to look at this particular user interface, we can click on it and scroll down to see the details. We have navigation for databases, documents, and collections on the left. The details can be seen on the right side.

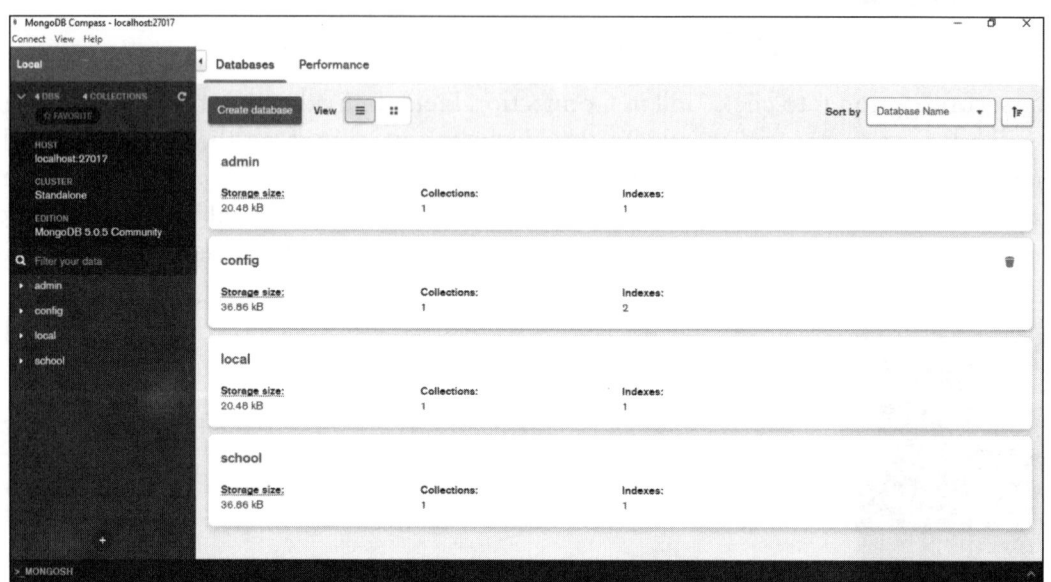

Figure 17.52 Compass database display screen

17.19.2 Creating Database in Compass

We can now create a new test database and insert test data into a new collection after successfully connecting our local Compass installation to our distant (remote) MongoDB server instance. First, we are going to create a database. When the first document is entered into a collection in MongoDB, the database and collection are typically established without an explicit creation process. However, we may also explicitly create a new database. At the top of the Home screen, click the "create Database" button. Alternatively, click the plus sign (+) near the bottom of the left panel. The below screen appears and asks for the essential details about the database to create it.

It asks to submit/enter the name of the database and a name for the Collection. The database name is given as DemoDB (Fig. 17.53).

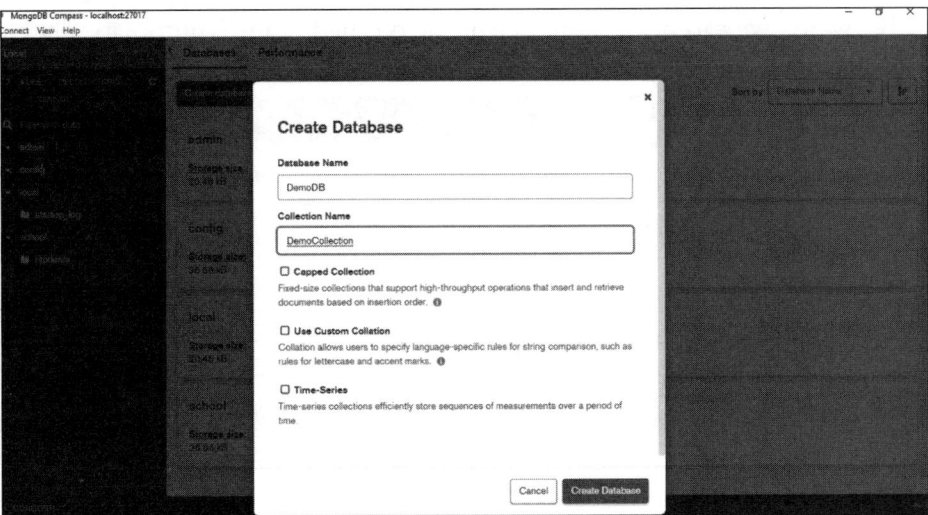

Figure 17.53 Compass database and collection creation

Let us create a new collection: "DemoCollection." Click the button "Create Database" which will create the database and the collection given. Click the "DemoDB" database to reach the database view. Then, click "DemoCollection" to reach the empty collection view (Fig. 17.54).

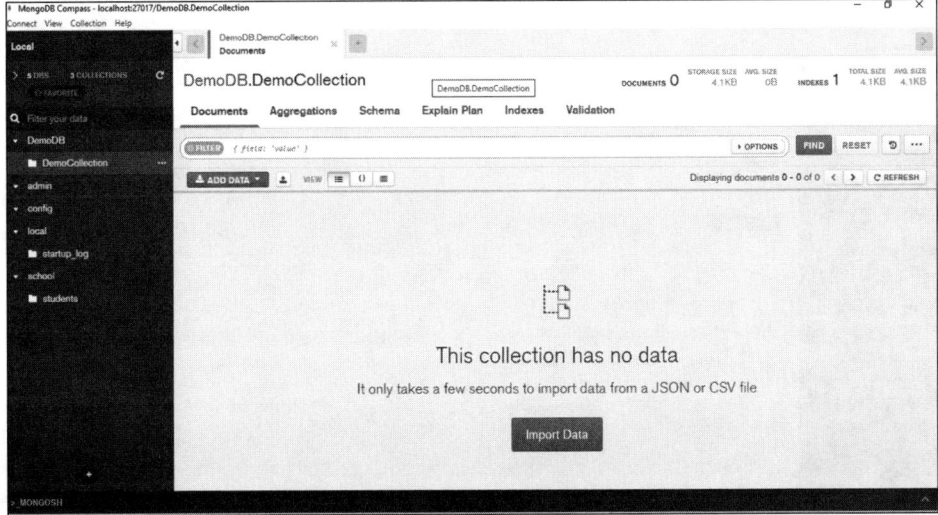

Figure 17.54 Compass Add Data screen

17.19.3 Adding Documents in Compass

"ADD Data" can be clicked to add the document (Fig. 17.54). Thus, we need not give the same fields for all the documents anymore; that is the beauty of MongoDB. When the "ADD Data" button is clicked, the below screen appears (Fig. 17.55), prompting the user to add one or more data (document) into the database. First, we enter one document (data) as below. As we can notice, the default field called "_id" is automatically created.

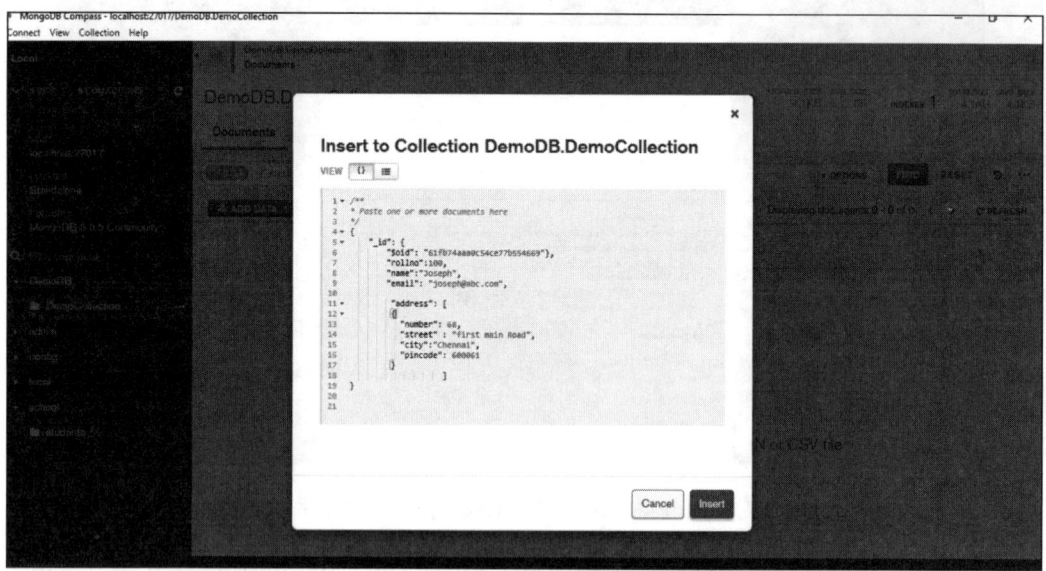

Figure 17.55 Compass Add Data screen: Data entry

When "Insert" button is clicked, we can see that the data (document) gets inserted into the collection as below (Fig. 17.56):

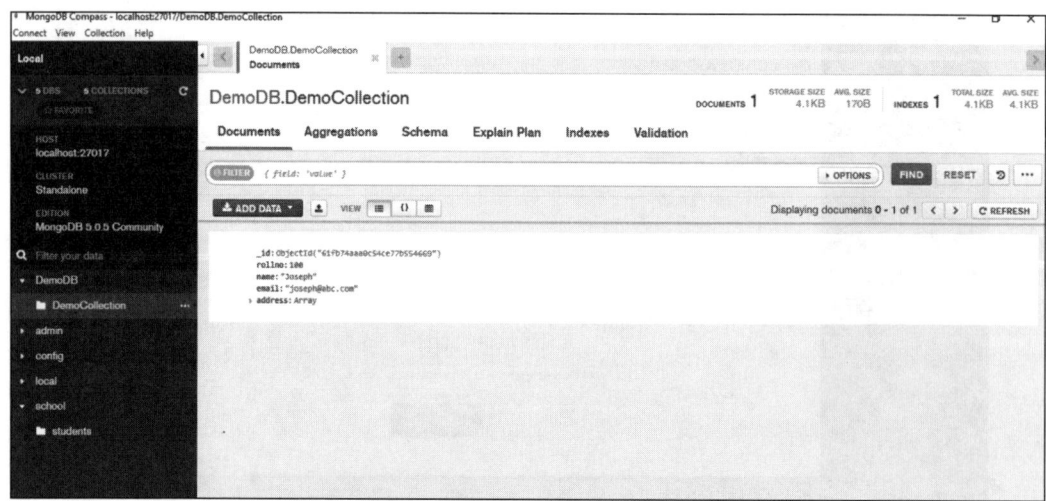

Figure 17.56 Compass Insert Data screen: Data entry

We have added three documents one by one as below, into the collection titled "DemoCollection". You can see "Documents 3" in the screen below indicating that the collection now has three documents (Fig. 17.57).

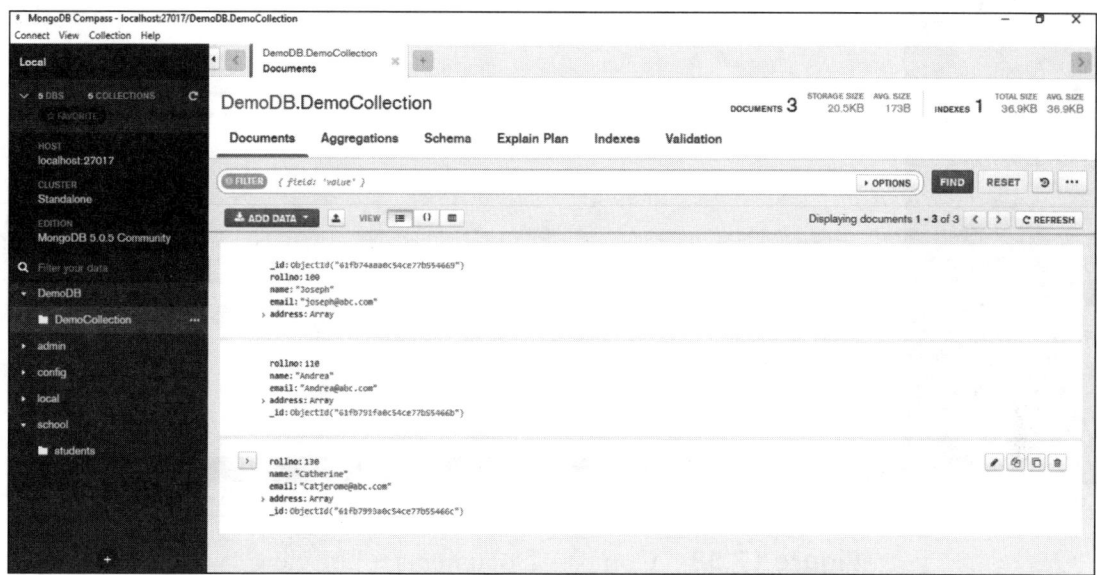

Figure 17.57 Compass Collection with three documents

17.19.4 MongoDB View

MongoDB Compass allows us to browse the data stored in a MongoDB database. It eliminates the need to memorize the names of databases or collections, and it will enable us to quickly go to any database or collection on the MongoDB server. The left panel, which functions as a tree, displays the database's contents, Compass's primary navigation tool. The databases are the top-level nodes, which we can click to show a list of available collections. For example, to go to the "DemoCollection" created in the previous stage, click the "DemoDB" database name, which will display a list of all the collections within it. The data browser panel will load when clicking on the collection name (DemoCollection). Compass will display the first 20 unfiltered results from an empty query on the selected collection by default. A View section to the right of the "Add Data" button contains three different display options. Views are the screens through which we can see the data (documents). We can choose which view we want to use by using the View buttons.

List View

In MongoDB Compass, the Document tab offers three ways to access documents. The default view of the Database in MongoDB Compass is List view (Fig. 17.58).

Individual members of the list will be displayed as documents. In addition, the embedded objects and arrays can be expanded in the list view.

912 • Big Data Analytics

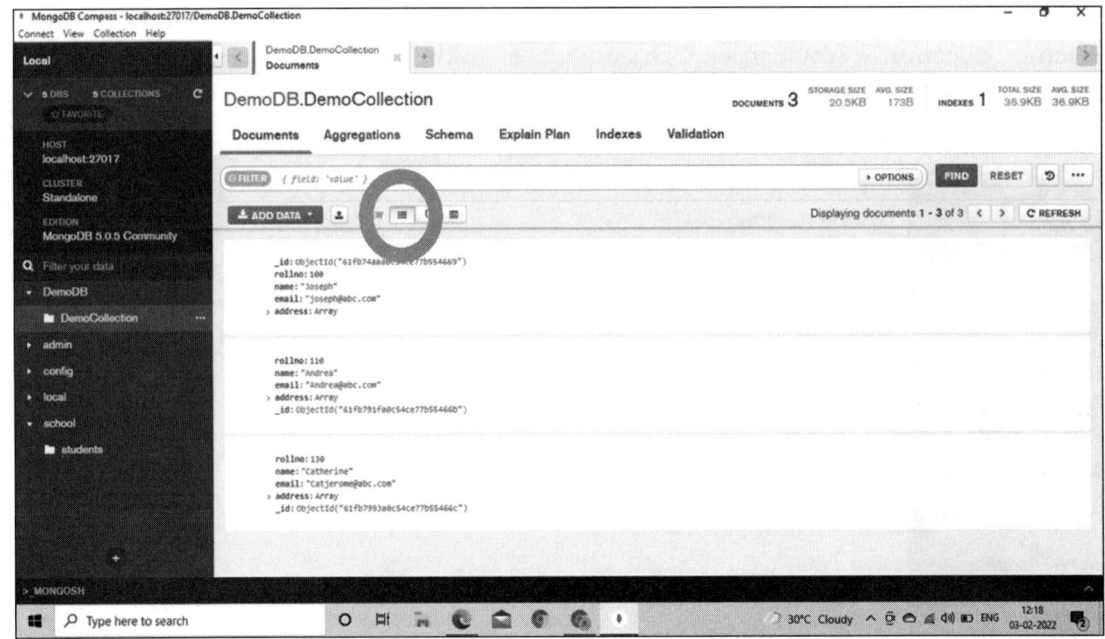

Figure 17.58 Compass Documents – List view

JSON View

Documents will be displayed as fully formed JSON objects in this view (Fig. 17.59).

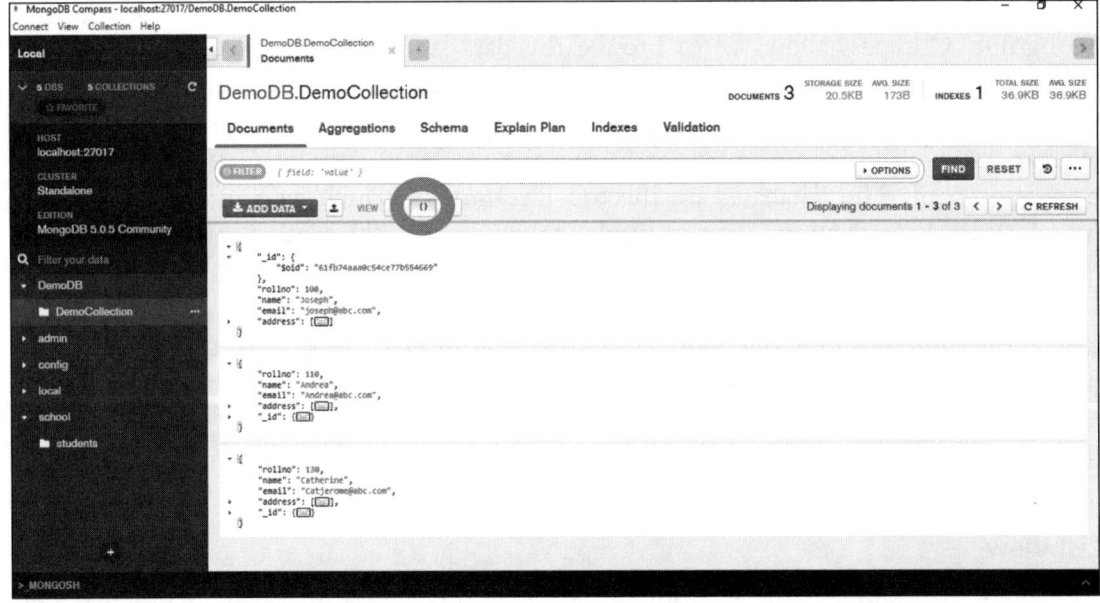

Figure 17.59 Compass Documents – JSON view

MongoDB Compass displays the data types of fields where the correct data types are used with the help of extended JSON in this view.

Table View

The Table view displays documents in a row on a table. In the table, the document fields are shown as a column (Fig. 17.60).

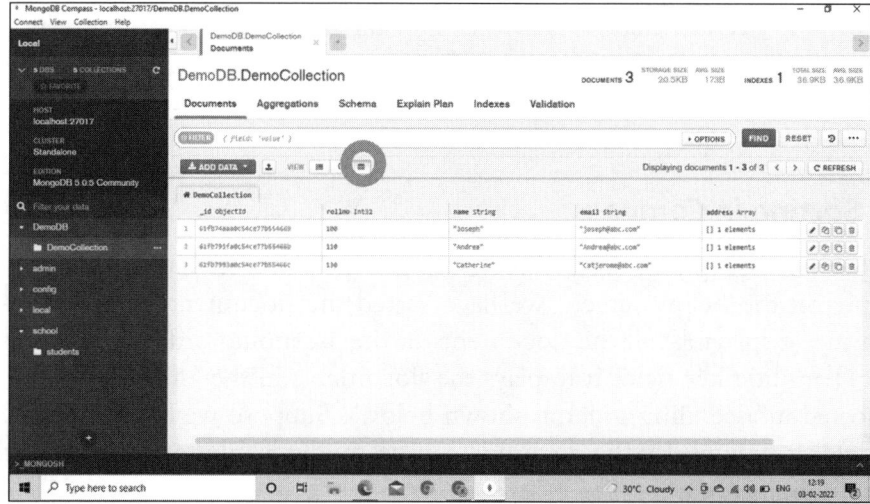

Figure 17.60 Compass Documents – Table view

We may quickly locate documents containing specified field values when using the Table view.

17.19.5 Filters in Compass

Compass also has filtering options (Fig. 17.61), using which data (documents) can be filtered easily. To filter data in the FILTER field, we can use any acceptable query

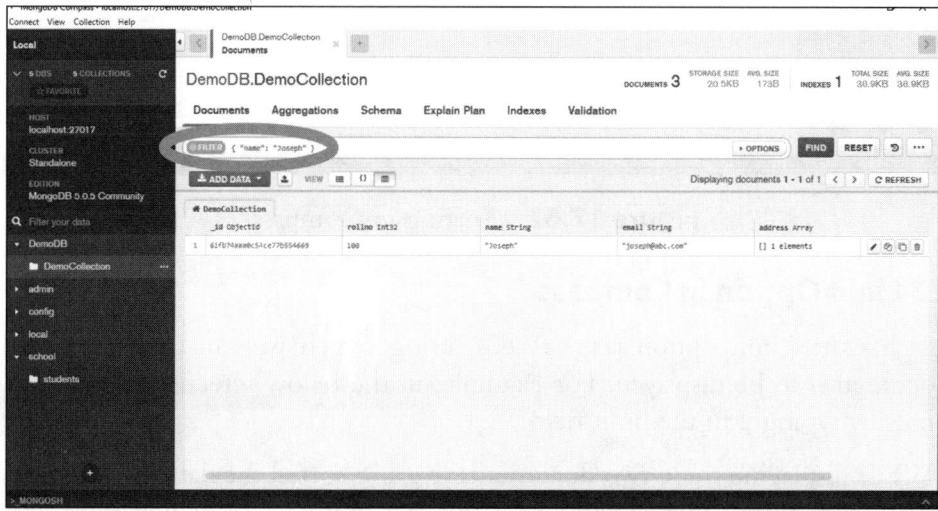

Figure 17.61 Filters in Compass

document that we would use in a search() operation. Compass will change the FILTER badge to red if we make a syntactic error, indicating that the query has an issue. For example, in Fig. 17.60, we have filtered the document which has the name "Joseph" by typing, {"name": "Joseph"} in the filter field.

Click the OPTIONS button near the filtering query bar to see more possibilities. Below the "FILTER" field, the "PROJECT" and "SORT" fields will show. The documents we supply to the find(), and sort() functions in the shell are accepted in both the PROJECT and SORT fields.

17.19.6 Sorting in Compass

Compass has sorting options (Fig. 17.62), using which data (documents) can be sorted. For example, in the below screen, we have sorted the document using the email field by showcasing (displaying) all the documents in the ascending order of email by typing, {"email": 1} in the filter field. It displays the documents in the ascending order of email (email is sorted in ascending order as shown below). Suppose we type {"email": −1} in the filter field. It will display the documents in descending order of the email field.

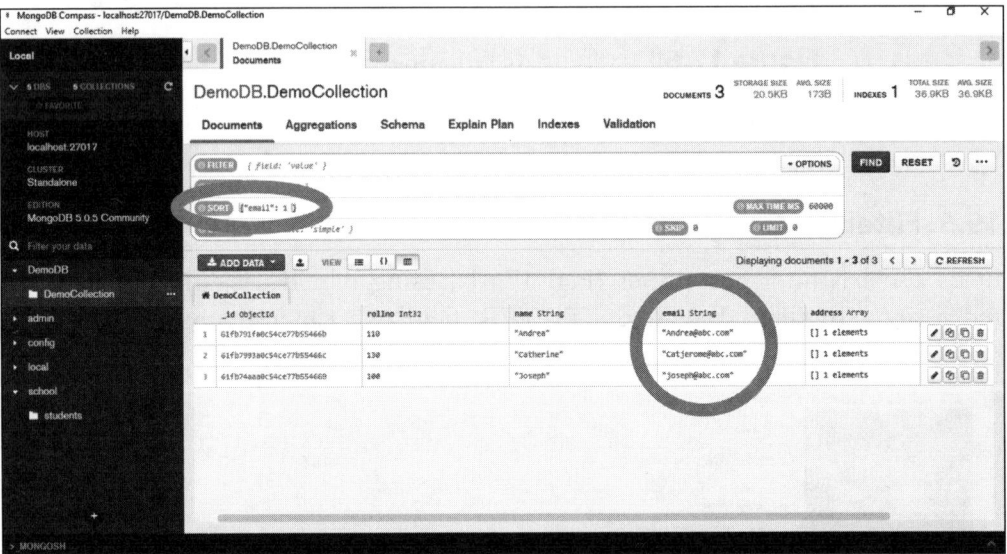

Figure 17.62 Sorting in Compass

17.19.7 Limit Option in Compass

Compass has the Limit option (Fig. 17.63), using which we can limit the number of data (documents) to be displayed. For example, in the below screen, we only show two documents by typing 2 in the limit field.

Note: While displaying these two documents, we also sorted the data (documents) based on email in ascending order. Therefore, if we type Limit as 1, it will show only one document.

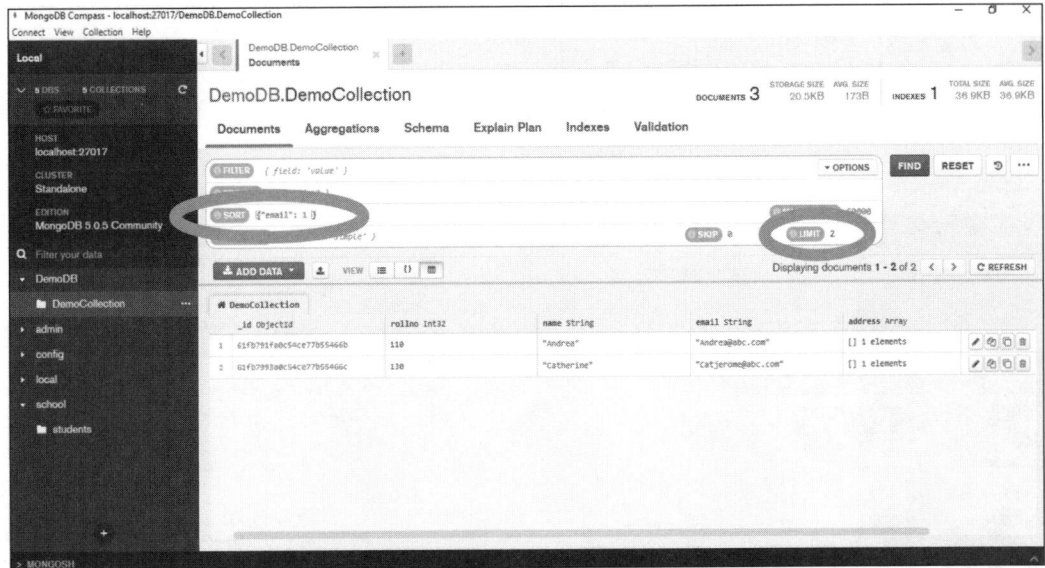

Figure 17.63 Limit options in Compass

17.19.8 Skip Option in Compass

Compass has a Skip option (Fig. 17.64), using which a certain number of data (documents) can be skipped while showing the remaining data (documents). For example, we can skip 1 document (first document) by typing 1 in the skip field as shown in the below screen.

Note: While displaying these two documents, we also sorted the data (documents) based on email in ascending order.

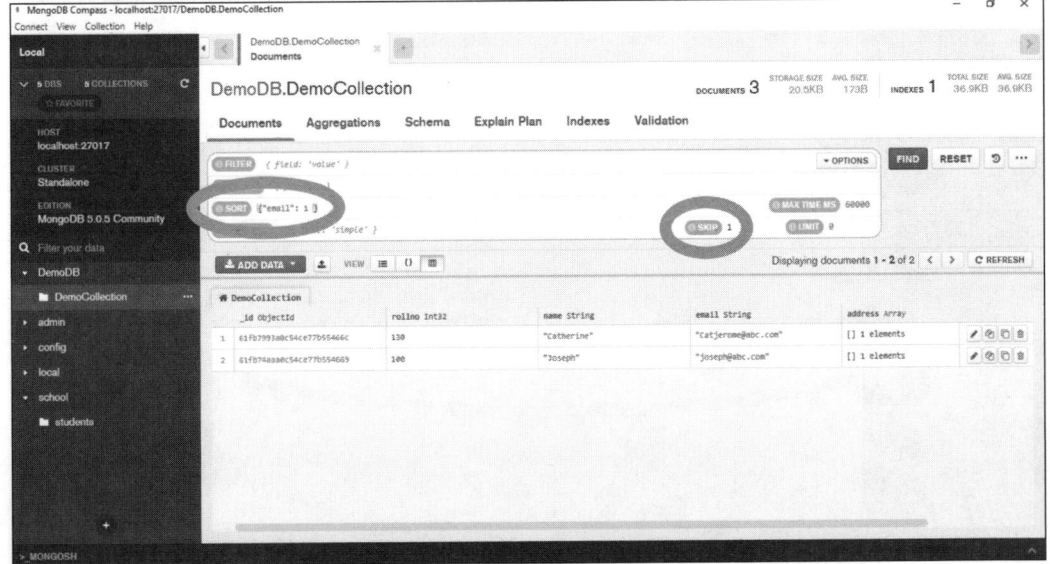

Figure 17.64 Skip options in Compass

17.19.9 Project Option in Compass

Compass has a Project option (Fig. 17.65), using which a specific number field alone can be shown. For example, in the below screen, we are projecting only the name field by giving {"name": 1} in the Project field.

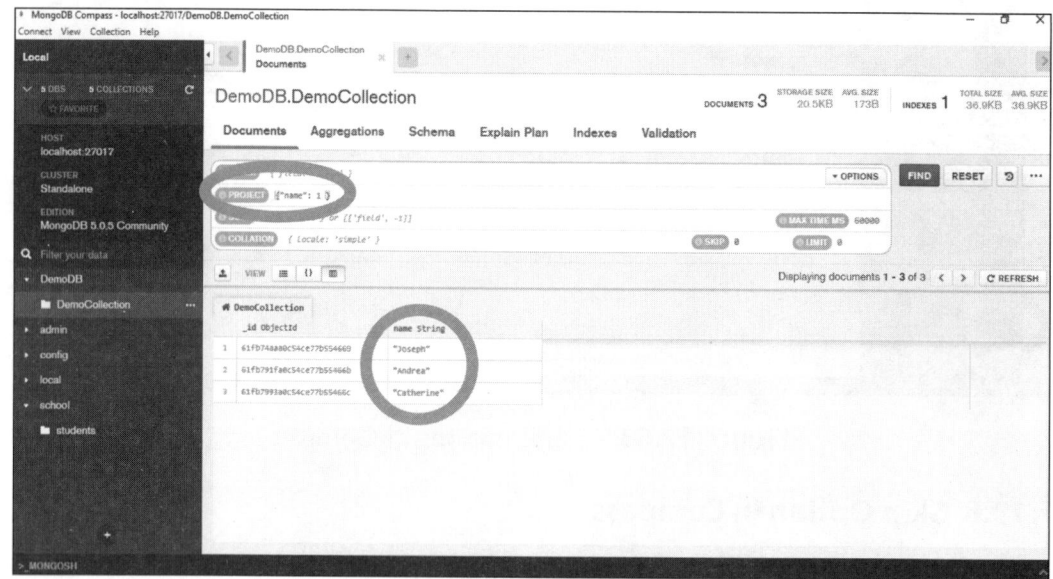

Figure 17.65 Project option in Compass

In the screen shown in Fig. 17.66, we project all the fields, except the name field, by giving {"name": 0} in the Project field.

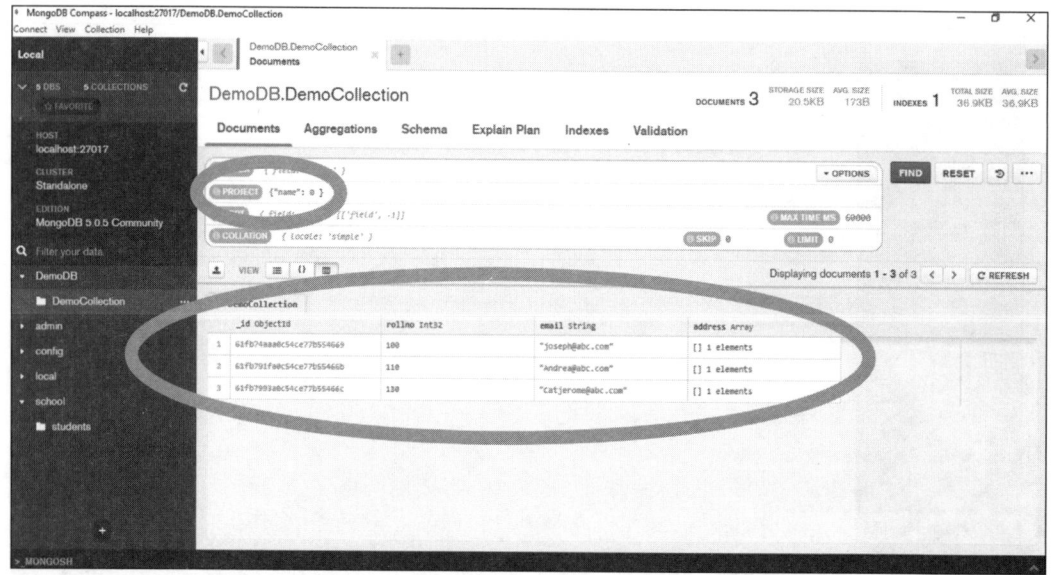

Figure 17.66 Project option results in Compass

17.19.10 Dropping a Database in Compass

To delete a database, click the trash icon that appears when you hover over the name of the database (Fig. 17.67).

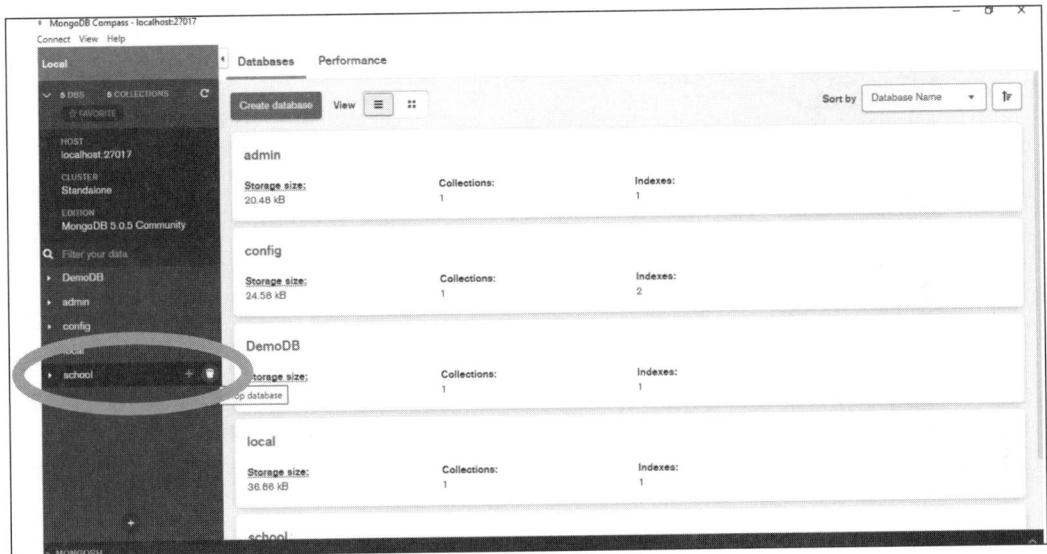

Figure 17.67 Dropping a database option in Compass

A confirmation prompt will be displayed. In the pop-up window, enter the database name that you want to delete (Fig. 17.68). Finally, click the "Drop Database" button to delete the selected database.

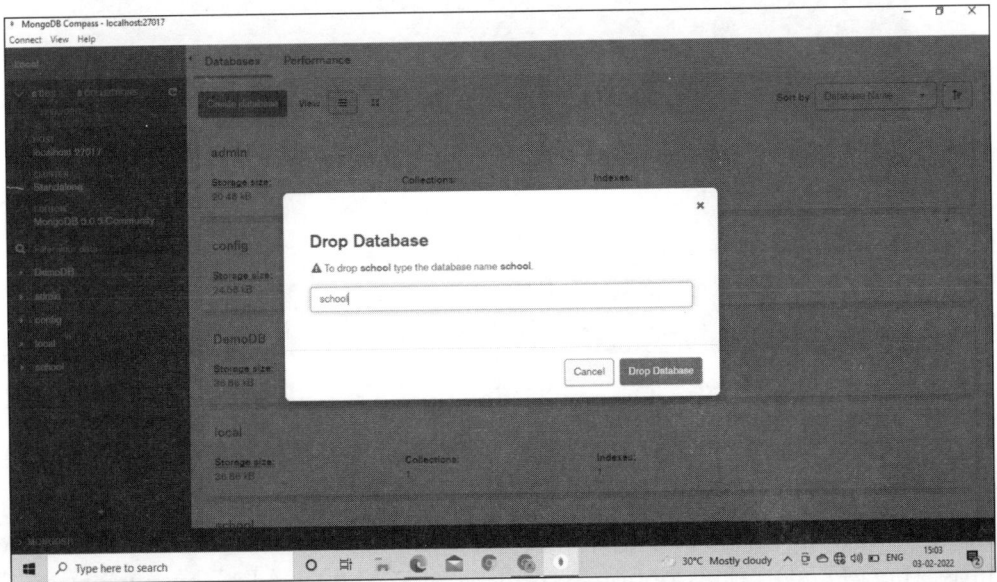

Figure 17.68 Dropping a database pop window in Compass

17.19.11 Dropping a Collection in Compass

To delete a collection, click the bin symbol in the collection pane (Fig. 17.69).

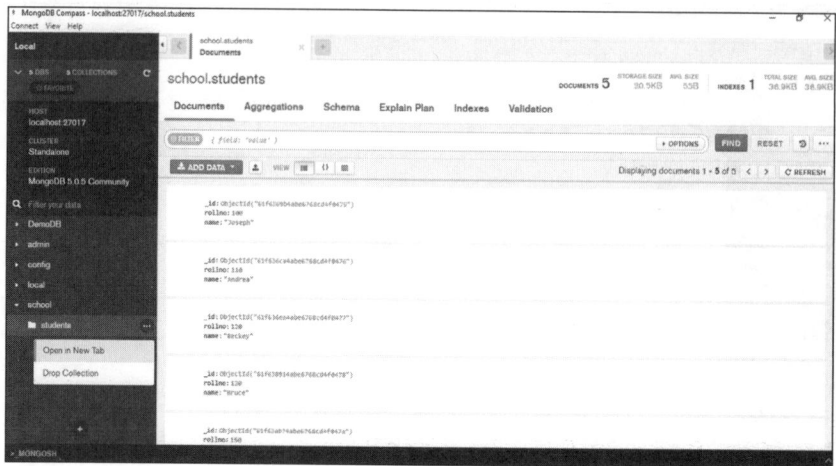

Figure 17.69   Drop collection option in Compass

A dialogue shows when you click the trash symbol, asking for confirmation. In the pop-up dialogue box that appears (Fig. 17.70), type the collection's name that you want to remove from the database. To delete the collection, click the Drop Collection option.

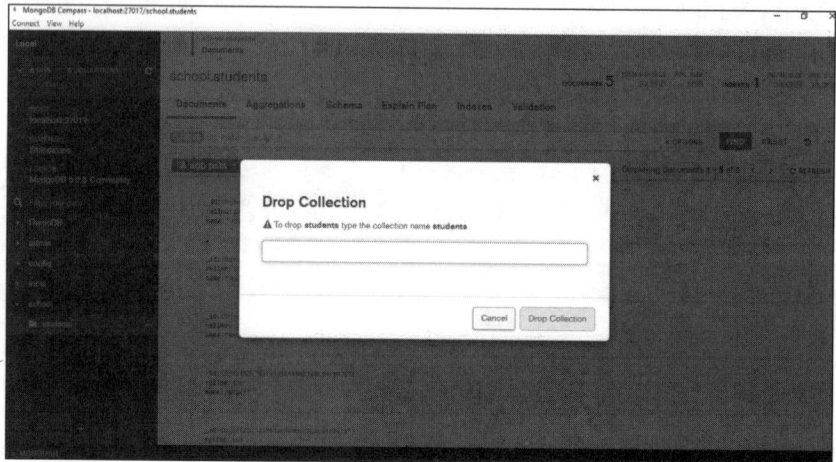

Figure 17.70   Drop collection popup screen in Compass

17.19.12 Importing Documents in Compass

Importing data from JSON and CSV files into a collection has always been simple with Compass (Fig. 17.71). This option is available in "ADD DATA" button option. The below screen appears. Click on "import file", and it will show the next screen with multiple options.

MongoDB • 919

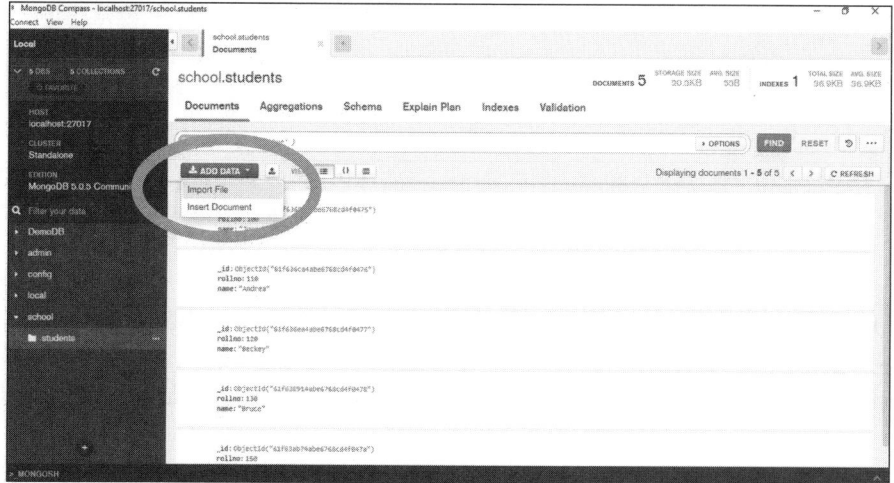

Figure 17.71 Importing options menu in Compass

Options are available to import data in JSON format and CSV format (Fig. 17.72).

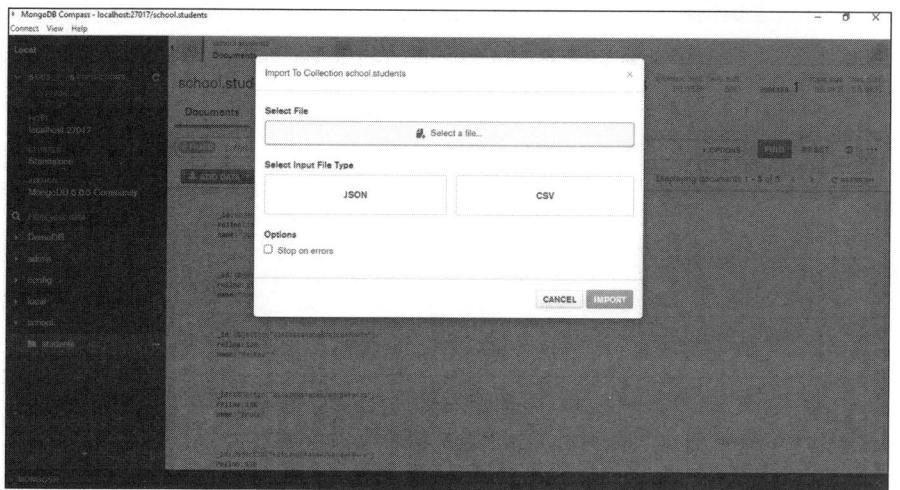

Figure 17.72 Importing CSV, JSON documents in Compass

When it comes to CSV file import, it gives more control over what gets imported. We can now customize the separator used in the CSV file we are trying to import and select which fields should be imported. We can also indicate a data type for each field; if we choose something other than "String," the values will be converted automatically during the import process, eliminating the need for additional batch actions after the import is complete.

17.19.13 Aggregations Option in Compass

Compass has an aggregations option (Fig. 17.73) for creating multi-step aggregation pipelines. This section illustrates how to add sequential aggregating stages to a pipeline.

For example, in the below screen in the first pipeline, we are using the "$match" option to display all the documents with rollno greater than 100 {rollno: ($get:100)}. It shows two records as the output of the first filter with rollno 110 and 130, which displays the document of "Andrea" first and then "Catherine." Note that if the documents do not display right away, we may need to hit the refresh button () to make them appear. Compass will display the filtered documents on the right as a preview of the outcomes of applying the first stage, allowing us to check that each step performs as expected.

The second step/stage is to sort the documents in descending order by name. Using the ADD STAGE button, we can add a new stage. There will be another empty stage row. Select the $sort stage and fill in the stage settings as follows. In the second pipeline, we use the "$sort" option to display all the documents in descending order of the name {name: -1}. It takes the outputs of the first pipeline as input and then performs the sort option to display the two records in descending order of the name field, which shows the document of "Catherine" first and then the document of "Andrea."

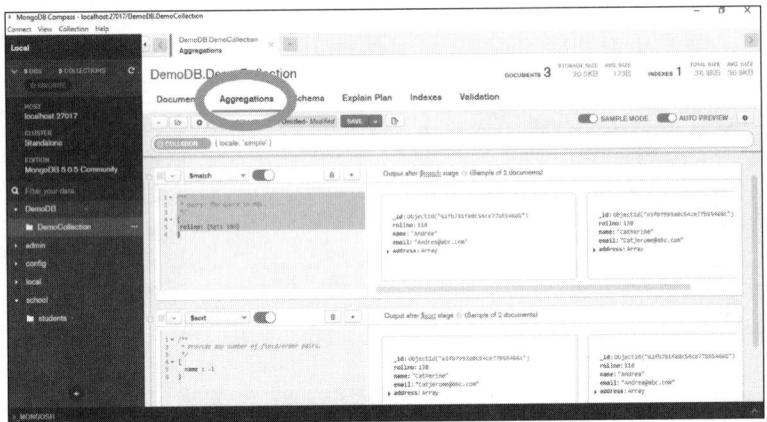

Figure 17.73 Aggregations menu in Compass

We may quickly build aggregations stage by stage with the aggregation pipeline builder without having to worry about the complex syntax of a single aggregation command. In addition, when the SAMPLE MODE switch is enabled, MongoDB Compass will only use a fraction of the input documents, making pipeline development faster when the source dataset is vast. We may check that each stage produces the intended results using the preview pane for each stage. We may also use the flip-switches to disable and enable specific steps to see how the aggregate pipeline works without some of the stages active.

17.19.14 Schema Option in Compass

In this stage, we will learn about Compass's schema visualizer interface (Fig. 17.74), which is a functionality that is available only in Compass. This tool assists us in comprehending the data structure of our collections. Go to the "DemoCollection" view and click the Schema tab to use it. The view will appear empty at first, but when we press the "Analyze" button, Compass will churn the data to expose its shape, size, and content.

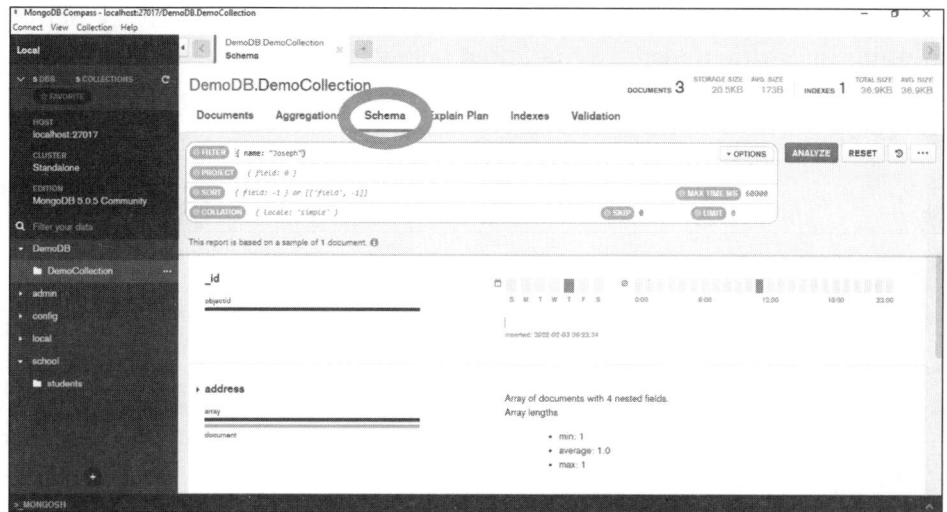

Figure 17.74 Schema menu in Compass

The schema visualizer will show information about the data field in the database for each of the document fields. Now, look at the _id field in the schema visualizer. Every document must have an _id field as a primary key in MongoDB. The schema visualizer in Compass displays when documents were inserted into the database. All of the documents were inserted simultaneously on Thursday afternoon in this example. The entries in a living database, on the other hand, will be spread out over the life of the database's use. This information could help determine how much the database is used during a typical week. Combining schema visualizer and filtering tools allows us to quickly scan the data and the visualizations that emerge, allowing us to study the data without performing complex queries. Schema visualizer helps visualize the database's contents, understand the data, and judge indexes and sharded clusters.

To summarize, MongoDB Compass is a graphical user interface that manages our MongoDB data. We use the tool to establish a new collection, input new documents, filter, and navigate the data, build a multi-stage aggregation pipeline, and use the schema visualization tool to visualize the collection's schema. We have covered only a tiny portion of MongoDB Compass's capabilities. To further understand how Compass can help, you may read the official MongoDB Compass documentation.

17.19.15 Update MongoDB Compass with the Latest Version

The updated version of MongoDB Compass can be used in two ways.

1. At any time, we can download and install the most recent version of MongoDB GUI from MongoDB's official website. To guarantee that Compass GUI is compatible with our system, we must check the S/W and H/W requirements for our OS and the required version of MongoDB Compass.

2. We may update Compass latest version by going to Help → Privacy Settings and activating automatic updates, as indicated below (Fig. 17.75).

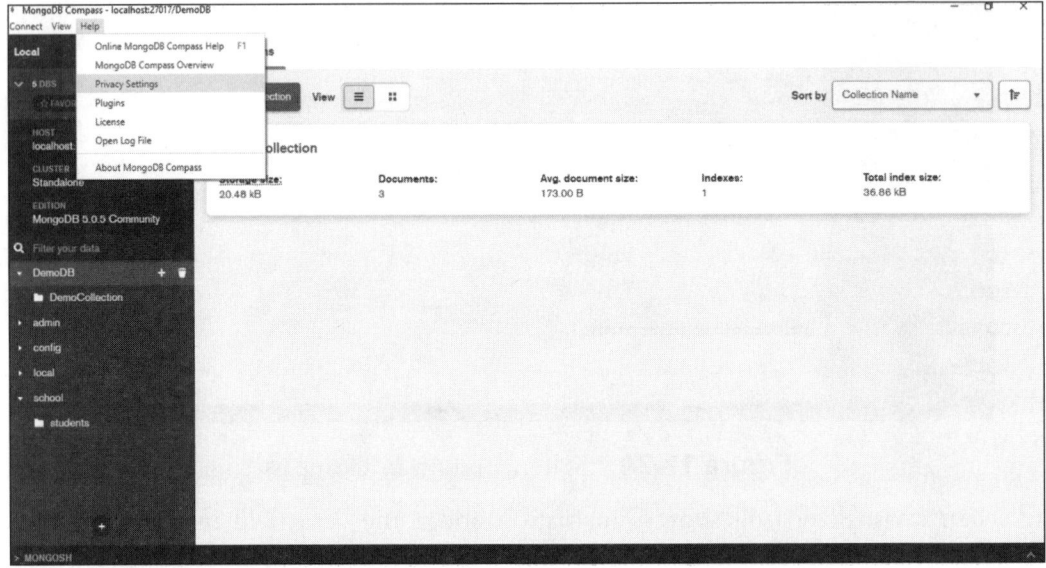

Figure 17.75 Privacy settings menu in Compass

When we click on Help → Privacy Settings, the below screen appears (Fig. 17.76).

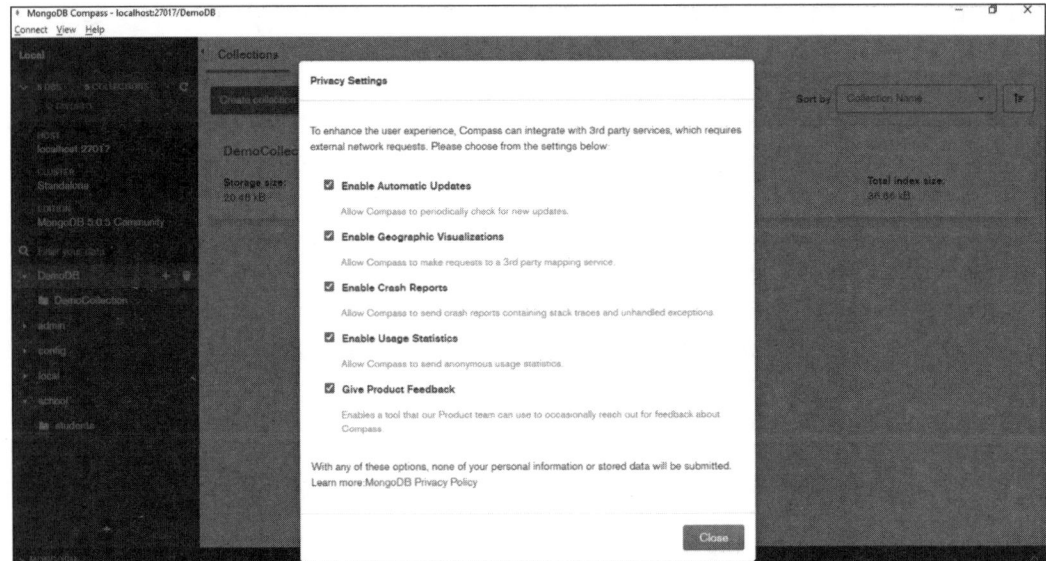

Figure 17.76 Privacy settings options in Compass

We need to select on all the options available and then click "Close" Button. This will ensure the new version is always updated automatically.

SUMMARY

MongoDB is a web application and internet database management system. The data model and persistence mechanisms are designed for high read and write throughput and rapid scaling and failover.

MongoDB was created in early 2007. It was created as part of an attempt to create a platform-as-a-service application software that would be similar to Microsoft Azure. This project was done by a New York-based company named 10gen, which changed its name to MongoDB Inc. Version 5.0 of MongoDB, which was released on July 13, 2021, is the most recent and stable version of MongoDB.

MongoDB replaces the concept of rows in relational data structures with the concept of documents. As a result, it allows developers to change data models with ease.

MongoDB's website has all the installation instructions, and the database is compatible with Windows, Linux, and Mac OS. However, it is worth noting that MongoDB will not run on Windows XP.

Three applications are available inside the bin directory: mongo, mongod, and mongos.

Starting of MongoDB Server

We need to build a unique data directory called C:\data\DB before starting the MongoDB server. Then, when we run the mongod command (MongoDB), we can see the daemon started.

Mongo is a shell where we can type all the commands. If it is showing an error (stating the command is not available), then go to the bin directory of MongoDB and give this command. We can add the bin directory into the System path. Ensure that the Mongo services are running (in the earlier command prompt) before running the Mongo shell.

We can see the command prompts changed to Mongo shell after giving the command (mongo).

To show all the databases already available, we give the command: show dbs, which will show all the default databases already existing inside MongoDB.

Unlike relational schema design, MongoDB schema design is quite different. There is no formal method, no algorithms, and no guidelines when it comes to MongoDB schema construction. For developing a MongoDB schema, it only matters that it works well for our application.

MongoDB is a key-value pair-based NoSQL database. NoSQL means it does not say no to SQL. Instead, it says not only SQL, which means that it supports not only SQL but also the other approaches. It is an open-source document database that offers excellent performance and scalability, and data modeling and data management for large datasets in enterprise applications. Auto-scaling is also available in MongoDB. MongoDB is a cross-platform database installed on Windows, Linux, and other operating systems.

NoSQL databases are becoming a more popular option for teams that want to iterate since they can manage ever-changing data types. Furthermore, solutions like MongoDB take advantage of NoSQL's scalability to synchronize different data storage devices.

MongoDB's notion of documents containing sub-documents nested in complex hierarchies is expressive and flexible. Moreover, it has a flexible query model. For example, a user can selectively index some part of a document or a query based on attribute values.

MongoDB may be used as a universal data storage system because data does not fit into a specific relationship. This feature has various advantages over other database types.

MongoDB data is organized according to a configurable structure. Therefore, we can quickly rearrange how our data is kept if the needs of our application change. This feature helps us to iterate on new ideas much more quickly.

Because MongoDB also provides schema validation, we may lock down our schema as much or as little as we wish. This feature implies it can handle whatever data structuring requirements we may have now or later in the future.

Finally, unlike many other NoSQL databases, MongoDB supports transactions and ensures that reads and writes to multiple documents are atomic. As a result, we may feel comfortable that the searches can be consolidated into a single transaction if we query data from multiple documents.

MongoDB makes it simple for developers to use a document database to store structured or unstructured data. It stores documents in a JSON-like manner. Most modern programming languages automatically translate this format to native objects, making it logical for developers because they do not have to be concerned about data normalization.

In addition, MongoDB offers a powerful Query Language (Rich Query Language) that supports the most common CRUD operations. In addition, keys from embedded documents and arrays can be included in indexes, allowing for faster queries. Text search and data aggregation are other exemplary elements of the Query Language.

A MongoDB replica set (a group of MongoDB servers) shares the same dataset, ensuring data redundancy and availability. MongoDB's Auto Replication functionality ensures high availability. It also has an automatic failover feature, whereby data is restored from a backup (replica) copy if the server fails. MongoDB's sharding is a powerful feature. Due to sharding, horizontal scalability is possible.

MongoDB supports multiple Storage Engines. When we save data in the form of documents (NoSQL) or tables (RDBMS) that hold the data, it is the Storage Engine Data that is preserved in memory and on disc using Storage Engines.

MongoDB comes with an extract, transform, and load (ETL) framework that reduces the need for complicated data pipelines. Data in MongoDB will get replicated across a replica set without a complicated setup. Security features of both authentication and authorization are taken into account.

RDBMS is a relational database management system, whereas MongoDB is a non-relational document-oriented database. RDBMS is not suitable for hierarchical data storage. MongoDB is highly suitable for hierarchical data storage. RDBMS is vertically scalable (example: increasing RAM), whereas MongoDB is horizontally scalable (adding more servers). RDBMS has predefined schema, whereas MongoDB has dynamic schema. RDBMS is slower in comparison to MongoDB. MongoDB can provide a JavaScript client for querying, which is not possible with RDBMS.

MongoDB is a document database that is JSON-oriented (JavaScript Object Notation), though it employs a binary-encoded form of JSON called BSON internally. BSON is a serialized encoding format for JSON, primarily used for document storage and retrieval. Compared to JSON, the BSON format has more data types, such as dates and binary data, supported.

MongoDB can be assessed using MongoDB Query Language (MQL). Clients interact with the MongoDB server through this interface. On the MongoDB shell, developers and database administrators can write MQL commands interactively. In order to execute MQL instructions in client applications, drivers are provided in various programming languages.

MQL supports CRUD operations. Results can be sorted, grouped, filtered, and counted via aggregation pipelines. Special functions such as text search and geospatial queries are possible. Multi-document transactions are also supported.

In the MongoDB context, we can say that the database is described as a physical container of collections, which means there will be multiple databases and many collections. For example, a document in MongoDB is a set of key-value pairs; every document in MongoDB has a unique value key (field) called "-id".

Indexing is possible in both MongoDB and RDBMS. Join Query is not possible in MongoDB; however, it can be achieved through linking and embedding. Group By (Join) in MongoDB is achieved through Aggregation Pipeline. Triggering and Foreign Key concepts are not available in MongoDB.

MongoDB Server: Mongod.exe is the central server that listens for and receives network requests. When we start the server, we can define the data location. Then, the Mongo program (typing Mongo in the command prompt) opens a shell and connects to a Mongod process, specified or running locally by default.

CRUD Operation in MongoDB

All actions, including database selection and CRUD, are expressed in JavaScript code in the mongo.exe shell.

Creating Database in MongoDB (C of CRUD): The database names in MongoDB are case insensitive, but you must remember that they cannot differ solely due to the case of the characters. For Windows users, MongoDB database names cannot contain any of the following characters: ^. ", $, *, :, |, and ?. For Unix and Linux users, MongoDB database names cannot contain the following characters: ^, ", and $. MongoDB database names cannot contain null characters (in Windows, Unix, and Linux systems). MongoDB database names cannot be empty and must contain less than 64 characters.

In order to create a collection (table) in the database, the command used is `db.createCollection("Collection_name")`.

Collection can also be created on the fly while inserting data (document) into the Collection, using the command `db.collection_name.insertOne({..})`. The `insertOne()` function stores a single piece of data in the provided Collection. Moreover, we keep our data in the curly braces, or in other words, it is a document. In order to insert the data into the collection, `db.collection_name.insert({document})` is used.

The BSON document can be up to 16MB in size. It ensures that the single document does not consume excessive RAM or bandwidth (during transmission). MongoDB includes a GridFS API for storing documents with more data than the requested size. For example, we can store a set of documents in an Array and then insert the collection array.

To list all the collections inside the database, we need to give the command "show collections" and then the semicolon, and then press the ENTER key, which will show all the collections present inside the database.

To see all the values (documents) present inside the Collection, we must give the command `db.collection_name.find()`. We will see all the documents present inside the Collection when we give this command.

MongoDB will only update one document by default. Therefore, we must set the parameter 'multi' to true to update several documents.

```
>db.students.update({'name':'Mercy'}, {$set:{'title':'Mercy Jack'}}, {multi:true})
```

We can use the synax `db.collection_name.drop()` to drop a particular collection in MongoDB.

We will get an error if we dump a collection from a Mongos into the admin or config databases.

The command "db" can check the currently selected database. Then we may examine the database list with the "display dbs" command. Then use the command "use database name" to pick the database we want to remove. Then, to remove an existing database, use the `db.dropDatabase()` command.

- **Pretty() Method:** The `pretty()` method is mostly used to display the result in a more easily readable/formatted way: `>db.collection_name.find().pretty()`.
- **AND in MongoDB:** This operator is used to execute a logical AND operation on an array of one or more expressions. It selects or retrieves only those documents in the array that match all of the specified expressions. MongoDB performs an implicit AND operation with a comma-separated set of expressions:
  `>db.mycol.find({ $and: [ {<key1>:<value1>}, { <key2>:<value2>} ] })`
- **OR in MongoDB**: The $or operator chooses documents that fulfil at least one of two or more of the specified expressions. Following is the basic syntax of OR:
  ```
  >db.collection_name.find(
     {
       $or: [
          {key1: value1}, {key2:value2}
       ]
  ```

        }
).pretty()
- **NOR in MongoDB:** This operator is used to conduct a logical NOR operation on an array of one or more expressions, selecting or retrieving only those documents in the array that do not match all specified expressions. $nor is the opposite of $or operation.
- **NOT in MongoDB**: This operator performs a logical NOT operation on the specified operator expressions. Only the documents that do not match the supplied term are selected or retrieved. It also covers documents that do not have the field in them.

Creating and Querying through Indexes

Performing queries in MongoDB becomes more efficient using Indexes. For example, suppose we have a collection with thousands of documents and no indexes and queries to find specific documents. In that case, MongoDB will have to scan the entire Collection to locate the documents. On the other hand, MongoDB would employ indexes to limit the number of documents that could be searched in the Collection if we had them.

- **The `createIndex()` Method**: The `createIndex()` method of MongoDB is used to create an index.
  >db.collection_name.createIndex({KEY:1}). Here, the key is the field's name on which we want to create an index, and one (1) is for ascending order. We must use minus one (−1) to construct an index in descending order.
  MongoDB creates compound indexes to support several different queries. If we sometimes query on only one key and at other times query on that key combined with a second key, creating a compound index is more efficient than creating a single-key index;
- **MongoDB's `dropIndex()` method**: It allows you to remove a specific index from the specified database: >db.collection_name.dropIndex({KEY:1})
- **The `getIndexes()` method:** This method returns the description of all the indexes in the Collection.
- **Mongo Compass:** A compass is an interactive tool, a graphical user interface tool (GUI tool) for managing MongoDB for querying, optimizing, and analyzing MongoDB data to get the critical insights, drag and drop to build pipelines, and more. Compass provides everything from schema analysis to index optimization to aggregation pipelines in a single, centralized interface.
- **MongoDB Connection:** To utilize MongoDB Compass with the MongoDB instance on our remote server, we must first connect to it as if we were using the shell to access the database. We should have already set up the MongoDB server to accept remote connections from our local PC. We can connect to Compass using Option 1: either a connection string (a single line of text including all necessary database connection information) or Option 2: by manually filling in all connection details.

- **MongoDB View:** Views are the screens through which we can see the data (documents). We can choose which view we want to use by using the View buttons. List View: In MongoDB Compass, the Document tab offers three ways to access documents. The default view of the database in MongoDB Compass is List View. Individual members of the list will be displayed as documents.
JSON View: Documents will be displayed as fully formed JSON objects in this view.
Table View: The table view displays documents in a row on a table. In the table, the document fields are shown as a column.
- **Importing documents in Compass:** Importing data from JSON and CSV files into a collection has always been straightforward with Compass. This option is available in the "ADD DATA" button option.

We may quickly build aggregations stage by stage with the aggregation pipeline builder without worrying about the complex syntax of a single aggregation command. In addition, when the SAMPLE MODE switch is enabled, MongoDB Compass will only use a fraction of the input documents, making pipeline development faster when the source dataset is vast.

EXERCISES

Multiple Choice Questions

1. **MongoDB was created as a part of an attempt to create:**
   A. Product-as-a-Service
   B. Technology-as-a-Service
   C. Platform-as-a-Service
   D. Software-as-a-Service
   Answer: C
   Explanation: MongoDB was created in early 2007. It was created as part of an attempt to create a platform-as-a-service application software that would be similar to Microsoft Azure. This project was done by a New York-based company named 10gen, which changed its name to MongoDB Inc. Version 5.0, which was released on July 13, 2021, is the most recent and stable version of MongoDB.

2. **MongoDB replaces the concept of rows in relational data structures with the concept of _____.**
   A. Documents
   B. Collections
   C. Databases
   D. Indexes
   Answer: A
   Explanation: MongoDB replaces the concept of rows in relational data structures with the concept of documents. As a result, it allows developers to change data models with ease.

3. **MongoDB will not run in _____.**
   A. Linux
   B. Mac OS
   C. Windows 10
   D. Windows XP
   Answer: D

Explanation: MongoDB's website has all the installation instructions, and the database is compatible with Windows, Linux, and Mac OS. However, it is worth noting that MongoDB will not run on Windows XP.

4. **MongoDB is a key-value pair-based NoSQL database.**
   A. True   B. False
   Answer: A
   Explanation: MongoDB is a key-value pair-based NoSQL database. NoSQL means it does not say no to SQL. Instead, it says not only SQL, which means it supports only SQL, but also the other approaches. It is an open-source document database that offers excellent performance and scalability, and data modeling and data management for large datasets in enterprise applications.

5. **NoSQL databases are becoming a more popular option for teams that want to iterate since they can manage ever-changing data types.**
   A. True   B. False
   Answer: A
   Explanation: NoSQL databases are becoming a more popular option for teams that want to iterate since they can manage ever-changing data types. Furthermore, solutions like MongoDB take advantage of NoSQL's scalability to synchronize different data storage devices.

5. **In MongoDB, a user needs to index the full document to make use of the indexing.**
   A. True   B. False
   Answer: B
   Explanation: MongoDB's notion of documents containing sub-documents nested in complex hierarchies is expressive and flexible. Moreover, it has a flexible query model. For example, a user can selectively index some part of a document or a query based on attribute values.

6. **MongoDB makes it simple for developers to use a document database to store structured or unstructured data.**
   A. True   B. False
   Answer: A
   Explanation: MongoDB makes it simple for developers to use a document database to store structured or unstructured data. It stores documents in a JSON-like manner. Most modern programming languages automatically translate this format to native objects, making it logical for developers because they do not have to be concerned about data normalization.

7. **Due to this principle, horizontal scalability is possible in MongoDB:**
   A. Racking   B. Sharding
   C. Crunching   D. Merging
   Answer: B

Explanation: A MongoDB replica set (a group of MongoDB servers) shares the same dataset, ensuring data redundancy and availability. MongoDB's Auto Replication functionality ensures high availability. It also has an automatic failover feature, whereby data is restored from a backup (replica) copy if the server fails. MongoDB's sharding is a powerful feature. Due to sharding, horizontal scalability is possible.

8. In MongoDB, data is preserved in memory and on disc using _____.
   A. Racking
   B. Sharding
   C. Crunching
   D. Storage Engine
   Answer: D
   Explanation: MongoDB supports multiple storage engines. When we save data in the form of documents (NoSQL) or tables (RDBMS) that hold the data, it is the Storage Engine Data that is preserved in memory and on disc using Storage Engines.

9. **MongoDB has dynamic Schema.**
   A. True
   B. False
   Answer: A
   Explanation: RDBMS is a relational database management system, whereas MongoDB is a non-relational document-oriented database. RDBMS is not suitable for hierarchical data storage. MongoDB is highly suitable for hierarchical data storage. RDBMS is vertically scalable (example: increasing RAM), whereas MongoDB is horizontally scalable (adding more servers). RDBMS has predefined schema, whereas MongoDB has dynamic schema. RDBMS is slower in comparison to MongoDB. MongoDB can provide a JavaScript client for querying, which is not possible with RDBMS.

10. **Which of the following statement is wrong?**
    A. DBMS is a relational database management system, whereas MongoDB is a non-relational document-oriented database.
    B. RDBMS is not suitable for hierarchical data storage. MongoDB is highly suitable for hierarchical data storage.
    C. RDBMS is horizontally scalable, whereas MongoDB is vertically scalable.
    D. RDBMS has predefined schema, whereas MongoDB has dynamic schema.
    Answer: C
    Explanation: Same as that for Question 9.

11. **MongoDB is a document database that is JSON-oriented. JSON means?**
    A. JavaScript Office Notation
    B. JavaScript Object Notation
    C. JavaScript Object Notification
    D. JavaString Object Notification
    Answer: B
    Explanation: MongoDB is a document database that is JSON-oriented (JavaScript Object Notation), though it employs a binary-encoded form of JSON called BSON internally. BSON is a serialized encoding format for JSON, primarily used for document storage and retrieval. Compared to JSON, the BSON format has more data types, such as dates and binary data, supported.

12. **MQL supports CRUD Operation. In the CRUD Operation, C stands for:**
    A. Create B. Customize
    C. Code   D. Comment
    Answer: A
    Explanation: MQL supports CRUD operations (Create, Read, Update, Delete). Results can be sorted, grouped, filtered, and counted via aggregation pipelines. Special functions such as text search and geospatial queries are possible. Multi-document transactions are also supported.

13. **Join Query is not possible in MongoDB.**
    A. True   B. False
    Answer: A
    Explanation: Indexing is possible in both MongoDB and RDBMS. Join Query is not possible in MongoDB; however, it can be achieved through Linking and Embedding. Group By (Join) in MongoDB is achieved through Aggregation Pipeline. Triggering and Foreign Key concepts are not available in MongoDB.

14. **Triggering is not possible in MongoDB.**
    A. True   B. False
    Answer: A
    Explanation: Same as that for Question 13.

15. **What is the maximum character limit for MongoDB database name?**
    A. 10 Characters   B. 32 Characters
    C. 64 Characters   D. 16 Characters
    Answer: C
    Explanation: The database names in MongoDB are case insensitive, but you must remember that they cannot differ solely due to the case of the characters. For Windows users, MongoDB database names cannot contain any of the following characters: ^, ", $, *, :, |, and ?. For Unix and Linux users, MongoDB database names cannot contain the following characters: ^, ", and $. MongoDB database names cannot contain null characters (in Windows, Unix, and Linux systems). MongoDB database names cannot be empty and must contain less than 64 characters.

16. **In the MongoDB, the BSON document can be up to _____ MB in size.**
    A. 10 MB   B. 32 MB
    C. 64 MB   D. 16 MB
    Answer: D
    Explanation: The BSON document can be up to 16 MB in size. It ensures that the single document does not consume excessive RAM or bandwidth (during transmission). MongoDB includes a GridFS API for storing documents with more data than the requested size. For example, we can store a set of documents in an array and then insert the collection array.

17. **In MongoDB, what is the command to see all the values (documents) present inside the Collection?**
    A. db.showcollections
    B. db.collection_name.find()
    C. use database name
    D. db.mycol.find({ $and: [{<key1>:<value1>}, { <key2>:<value2>}] })

    Answer: B

    Explanation: To list all the collections inside the database, we need to give the command "show collections" and then the semicolon, and then press the ENTER key, which will show all the collections present inside the database. To see all the values (documents) present inside the Collection, we must give the command db.collection_name.find(). We will see all the documents present inside the Collection when we give this command.

18. **This operator selects or retrieves only those documents in the array that match all of the specified expressions:**
    A. NAND   B. NOR
    C. AND   D. OR

    Answer: C

    Explanation: AND in MongoDB – this operator is used to execute a logical AND operation on an array of one or more expressions. It selects or retrieves only those documents in the array that match all of the specified expressions. MongoDB performs an implicit AND operation with a comma-separated set of expressions:
    >db.mycol.find({ $and: [{<key1>:<value1>}, { <key2>:<value2>}] })

19. **This operator chooses documents that fulfil at least one of two or more conditions:**
    A. NAND   B. NOR
    C. AND   D. OR

    Answer: D

    Explanation: OR in MongoDB – the $or operator chooses documents that fulfil at least one of two or more of the specified expressions. Following is the basic syntax of OR.
    >db.collection_name.find(
        {
            $or: [
                {key1: value1}, {key2:value2}
            ]
        }
).pretty()

20. **This operator is used for selecting or retrieving only those documents in the array that do not match all specified expressions:**
    A. NAND
    B. NOR
    C. AND
    D. OR
    Answer: B
    Explanation: NOR in MongoDB - this operator is used to conduct a logical NOR operation on an array of one or more expressions, selecting or retrieving only those documents in the array that do not match all specified expressions. $nor is the opposite of $or operation.

21. **Only the documents that do not match the supplied term are selected or retrieved in:**
    A. NAND
    B. NOT
    C. AND
    D. OR
    Answer: B
    Explanation: NOT in MongoDB – this operator performs a logical NOT operation on the specified operator expressions. Only the documents that do not match the supplied term are selected or retrieved. It also covers documents that do not have the field in them.

22. **This method of MongoDB is used to create an index:**
    A. `createIndex()`
    B. `produceIndex()`
    C. `openIndex()`
    D. `getIndexes()`
    Answer: A
    Explanation: The `createIndex()` method of MongoDB is used to create an index:
    `>db.collection_name.createIndex({KEY:1})`. Here, the key is the field's name on which we want to create an index, and one (1) is for ascending order. We must use minus one (−1) to construct an index in descending order.

23. **This method returns the description of all the indexes in the Collection.**
    A. `createIndex()`
    B. `produceIndex()`
    C. `openIndex()`
    D. `getIndexes()`
    Answer: D
    Explanation: The `getIndexes()` method returns the description of all the indexes in the Collection.

24. **This is an interactive tool, a graphical user interface tool (GUI tool) for managing MongoDB for querying, optimizing, and analyzing MongoDB data:**
    A. MongoDB Connection
    B. MongoDB View
    C. Mongo Compass
    D. Ambari Mongo
    Answer: C

Explanation: Mongo Compass is an interactive tool, a graphical user interface tool (GUI tool) for managing MongoDB for querying, optimizing, and analyzing MongoDB data to get the critical insights, drag and drop to build pipelines, and more. Compass provides everything from schema analysis to index optimization to aggregation pipelines in a single, centralized interface.

25. **These are the screens through which we can see the data (documents):**
    A. MongoDB Connection
    B. MongoDB View
    C. Mongo Compass
    D. Ambari Mongo
    Answer: B
    Explanation: MongoDB Views are the screens through which we can see the data (documents). We can choose which view we want to use by using the View buttons. List View: In MongoDB Compass, the Document tab offers three ways to access documents. The default view of the Database in MongoDB Compass is List View. Individual members of the list will be displayed as documents.
    JSON View: Documents will be displayed as fully formed JSON objects in this view.
    Table View: The table view displays documents in a row on a table. In the table, the document fields are shown as a column.

Short-answer Questions

1. **Write short notes on MongoDB.**
   MongoDB is a key-value pair-based NoSQL database. NoSQL means it does not say no to SQL. Instead, it says not only SQL, which means it supports not only SQL, but also the other approaches. It is an open-source document database that offers excellent performance and scalability, and data modeling and data management for large datasets in enterprise applications. Auto-scaling is also available in MongoDB. MongoDB is a cross-platform database installed on Windows, Linux, and other operating systems.

2. **Write short notes on MongoDB Schema Design.**
   There is no formal method, no algorithms, and no guidelines when it comes to MongoDB schema construction. For developing a MongoDB schema, it only matters that it works well for the application. If two programs that use the same data are used differently, their schemas may be drastically different. When creating a schema, the following points should be kept in mind: saving the information, good query performance, and a suitable quantity of hardware are required.

3. **Write notes on MongoDB document.**
   A document is a JSON-style data structure with name-value pairs. As a result, mapping any custom object from any programming language to a MongoDB document is simple. Documents are JSON representations of custom objects. Documents store data in field-value pairs. The values can be of various types and structures, including strings, numbers, dates, arrays, or objects. In addition, documents can be stored in JSON, BSON, and XML formats.

4. **Write short notes on MongoDB client and explain how to access it.**
   Mongo is a shell where we can type all the commands. If it is showing an error (stating the command is not available), then go to the bin directory of MongoDB and give this command. We can add the bin directory into the System path. Ensure that the Mongo services are running (in the earlier command prompt) before running the mongo shell. We can see the command prompts changed to Mongo shell after giving the command (Mongo).

5. **What is the MongoDB shell command to see all the databases inside MongoDB? What are the default databases of MongoDB?**
   To show all the databases already present, we give the command: show DBS, which will show all the default databases already existing inside MongoDB. There are three default database available in the system – admin, config, and local.

6. **What is a Database in MongoDB?**
   Databases, collections, and documents are all necessary components of MongoDB. Without them, we will not be able to save data on the server. A database contains a collection (equivalent to the table), and a collection has documents that contain data; they are linked together. Database in MongoDB is called a Database (similar to RDBMS). In the MongoDB context, we can say that database is described as a physical container of collections, which means there will be multiple databases and there will be many collections.

7. **What is a Collection in MongoDB?**
   A database can have any number of collections (tables). Document in MongoDB is a set of key-value pairs; every document in MongoDB has a unique value key (field) called "-id". MongoDB will add this key automatically for each document. Whenever we insert a document, MongoDB will automatically insert this field, which always has a unique value for all documents.

8. **What is a Document in MongoDB?**
   All Rows in MongoDB, put together, is called a Document. Documents are flexible and have a dynamic schema, and are user-defined. Since document schemas are user-defined, they are not fixed or static. Documents can hold any data, as long as they are valid data types in MongoDB.

9. **Do a quick comparison of MongoDB and RDBMS.**
   Indexing is possible in both MongoDB and RDBMS. Join Query is not possible in MongoDB; however, it can be achieved through Linking and Embedding. Group By (Join) in MongoDB is achieved through Aggregation Pipeline. Triggering and Foreign Key concepts are not available in MongoDB.

10. **Write notes on MongoDB server.**
    In MongoDB Server, Mongod.exe is the central server that listens for and receives network requests. When we start the server, we can define the data location. Almost

no configuration is required to run the server; nevertheless, there are a few options to "tune" it. Because MongoDB allows the OS to manage memory, this is a purposefully planned feature. With a system call, the data files will be mapped to virtual memory, and the Operating System (OS) will select how to map the data into memory.

11. **How will you create Collection in MongoDB?**
    Collections hold data in the form of documents, similar to the table in DBMS. The collection is created using the following syntax: `db.createCollection("students")`. Collection can also be created on the fly while inserting data (document) into the Collection, using the command `DB.collection_name.insertOne({..})`. The `insertOne()` function stores a single piece of data in the provided Collection.

12. **How data is inserted into the Collection in MongoDB? Give an example.**
    In order to insert data into the collection, `DB.collection_name.insert({document})` is used. Let us say the collection name is "students" and then "insert", and give the parentheses, and inside the parentheses, you give the curly brackets, and you give your values in JSON format. So, inside the curly brackets, we need to provide the key name. Let us say the key name is "rollno" and then a colon(:). Let us give the value 100 here. One more key name is "name" and then a colon(:), Let the value we give here be "joseph". Then, press Enter, and it will create this collection (if it already exists) and insert the document into your collection.

13. **How do we know the current database in use in MongoDB?**
    If we are unsure which database we are currently using, we can type dbs or db in the command prompt, to show the current database.

14. **How to showcase the tables (Collections) in the current database in MongoDB?**
    To list all the collections inside the database, we need to give the command "show collections" and then the semicolon, and then press the ENTER key, which will show all the collections present inside the database.

15. **How to read Collections in MongoDB?**
    To see all the values (documents) present inside the collection, we need to give the command db.collection_name.find(). We will see all the documents present inside the collection ("students"). This method will display all the documents in a non-structured way.

16. **What is the command to set the new name 'Mercy', to a document whose name is 'Mercy Jack'?**
    The following command will set the new name 'Mercy', to a document whose name is 'Mercy Jack'.
    ```
    >db.students.update({'name':'Mercy'},{$set:{'name':'Mercy Jack'}})
    ```

17. **What is the command to set the new name 'Mercy', to of ALL the documents whose name is 'Mercy Jack'?**
    MongoDB will only update one document by default. You must set the parameter 'multi' to true to update several documents.
    `>db.students.update({'name':'Mercy'}, {$set:{'title':'Mercy Jack'}}, {multi:true})`

18. **How can we drop a newly formed database named 'students'?**
    To drop a newly formed database named ' students', use the command 'db.dropDatabase()' function. The database named 'Students' will not be available while we use 'Show dbs' command, indicating that it got dropped already. Because this operation deletes the presently selected (current use) database, we do not supply a database name in this command. Therefore, if we do not choose a database, the default database will be deleted.

19. **What is the purpose of `pretty()` method in MongoDB?**
    The `pretty()` method is mostly used to display the result in a more easily readable/formatted way: `>db.collection_name.find().pretty()`.

20. **How is AND Operator used in MongoDB?**
    This operator is used to execute a logical AND operation on an array of one or more expressions. It selects or retrieves only those documents in the array that match all of the specified expressions. MongoDB performs an implicit AND operation with a comma-separated set of expressions:
    `>db.mycol.find({ $and: [ {<key1>:<value1>}, { <key2>:<value2>} ] })`
    The following example will show all the students' detail with rollno as 120 with the name Beckey:
    `>db.students.find({$and:[{"rollno":120},{"name":"Beckey"}]}).pretty()`

21. **How is OR Operator used in MongoDB?**
    We need to use the "$or" keyword to query documents based on the OR condition. The $or operator chooses documents that fulfil at least one of two or more conditions by performing a logical OR operation on an array of two or more expressions. When evaluating the clauses in the $or expression, MongoDB conducts either a collection scan or index scan. For MongoDB, to assess a $or expression using indexes, all clauses in the $or expression must be supported by indexes. MongoDB will execute a collection scan if this is not the case. Following is the basic syntax of OR:
    ```
    >db.collection_name.find(
        {
            $or: [
                {key1: value1}, {key2:value2}
            ]
    ```

        }
).pretty()

22. **Write a MongoDB query, if the equivalent SQL where clause is 'where rollno >110 AND (name = 'Bruce' OR name= 'Mercy Jack')'.**
    This SQL clause displays the documents with a rollno greater than 110 and whose name is either 'Bruce' or 'Mercy Jack'. The MongoDB query is

    ```
    >db.students.find({"rollno": {$gt:110}, $or: [{"name": "Bruce"},
      {"name": "Mercy Jack"}]}).pretty()
    {
     "_id" : ObjectId("61f636ea4abe6768cd4f0478"),
     "rollno": 130,
     "name": "Bruce"
    }
    {
     "_id" : ObjectId("61f636ea4abe6768cd4f047a"),
     "rollno": 140,
     "name": "Mercy Jack"
    }
    ```

23. **How is NOR operator used in MongoDB?**
    The $nor operator is one of the several logical query operators available in MongoDB. This operator is used to conduct a logical NOR operation on an array of one or more expressions, selecting or retrieving only those documents in the array that do not match all of the specified expressions. $nor is the opposite of $or operation. If $or operation returns True, then $nor operation returns False. If $or operation returns False, then $nor operation returns True.

24. **How is NOT Operator used in MongoDB?**
    The $not operator is one of the several logical query operators available in MongoDB. This operator performs a logical NOT operation on the specified operator expressions. Only the documents that do not match the supplied term are selected or retrieved. It also covers documents that do not have the field in them. Depending on our needs, we can use this operator in methods such as `locate()`, `update()`, and so on. Always use the $not operator in conjunction with other operators because it cannot independently verify fields or documents and only impacts other operators.

25. **Write short notes on indexes in MongoDB.**
    Indexes are significant in any database, and it is no different in MongoDB. Performing queries in MongoDB becomes more efficient with the use of Indexes. For example, suppose we have a collection with thousands of documents and no indexes and queries to find specific documents. In that case, MongoDB will have to scan the entire collection to locate the documents. On the other hand, MongoDB would employ indexes to limit the number of documents that could be searched in the collection if we had them. Indexes are one-of-a-kind datasets that store a portion of

the data in a collection. Because the data is only partially complete, it is easier to read. This partial set has the value of a single field or a group of fields sorted by field value.

26. **How is the `createIndex()` Method used in MongoDB?**
    The `createIndex()` method of MongoDB is used to create an index: `>db.collection_name.createIndex({KEY:1})`. Here, the key is the field's name on which you want to create an index, and one (1) is for ascending order. You must use minus one (−1) to construct an index in descending order. Create a single-key index if all queries use the same single key. If you only query on a single key in a given collection, then you need to create just one single-key index for that collection. For example, you might create an index on the rollno in the students collection: `db.students.createIndex( { "rollno": 1 } )`.

27. **How is MongoDB's `dropIndex()` method used?**
    It allows you to remove a specific index from the specified database:
    `>db.collection_name.dropIndex({KEY:1})`
    Example: `> db.students.dropIndex({"rollno":1})`.

28. **How is the `getIndexes()` method of MongoDB used?**
    This method returns the description of all the indexes in the collection. The `getIndexes()` method in MongoDB provides an array containing a list of documents that identify and describe the collection's existing indexes. It also includes indexes that are hidden. There are no parameters for this method. Instead, the keys and settings used to generate an index are included in the index information returned by this method. Starting with MongoDB 4.4, the hidden index is available in this function.

29. **Write short notes on Mongo Compass.**
    A compass is an interactive tool, a graphical user interface tool (GUI tool) for managing MongoDB for querying, optimizing, and analyzing MongoDB data to get the critical insights, drag and drop to build pipelines, and more. Compass provides everything from schema analysis to index optimization to aggregation pipelines in a single, centralized interface. Compass is open-source and free to use, and it runs on MacOS, Windows, and Linux. Some of the activities Compass can assist us with are data import and management via a simple interface.

Essay-type Questions

1. Write an essay on the key features of MongoDB.
2. Compare RDBMS with MongoDB.
3. Write an essay on MongoDB Database, Collection and Documents.
4. Write an essay on creating Database in MongoDB.
5. How are records inserted into MongoDB Collection (Table)?

CHAPTER **18**

Big Data Visualizations

> **LEARNING OBJECTIVES**
>
> Data visualization includes presenting information visually, such as a map or graph, to facilitate understanding and inference by the human brain. In this chapter, we learn how data visualization realizes its primary objective, which is to make it simpler to spot patterns, trends, and outliers in Big Data sets.

18.1 Introduction

Colours and patterns quickly draw our attention. Red and green, for example, are distinguished easily, as are squares and triangles. Everything in our culture is visual, from television to movies to commercials and art. The phrase "a picture is worth a thousand words" comes to the mind while contemplating on visualization. This is because a picture may describe "what is going on" more quickly, effectively, and frequently than words. Data visualization is another form of visual art that captures and holds our attention.

The graphic display of information and data is known as data visualization. Information graphics, visualization, and statistical graphics are frequently used interchangeably. Data visualization approaches turn data into images with the help of graphical or pictorial representations. The ability to visualize data is crucial for practically every career. Teachers may use it to display exam results of pupils, computer scientists to improve artificial intelligence (AI), and executives to interact with stakeholders. It is also critical in large data initiatives. Businesses want a mechanism to quickly and easily obtain an overview of their data since they collect massive amounts of data every day.

We can rapidly recognize patterns and outliers when we look at a chart. A trend depicts the upward and downward movement of data over time. An outlier is a value or data point that deviates significantly from other data points or values. We can swiftly integrate anything if the information is portrayed pictorially. Taking in enormous volumes of data at a glance allows decision-makers to swiftly see what is going on and what the data has to say.

In the Big Data environment, data visualization tools and technologies are critical for evaluating massive amounts of data and making data-driven choices. Data visualization tools make it simple to see and analyze trends, outliers, and patterns in data by leveraging visual components such as charts, graphs, and maps.

18.2 History of Data Visualization

Before the 17th century, maps mainly used data visualization to depict resources, cities, highways, and other geographic characteristics. However, as the need for more exact mapping and physical measurement grew, better representations were necessary.

In 1644, a Flemish astronomer called Michael Florent Van Langren was credited with creating the first graphic representation of statistical data. The one-dimensional line graph displayed the twelve known estimates of the longitude difference between Toledo and Rome, along with the names of the astronomers who provided the estimates. Of course, Van Langren could have provided this information in a table, but the use of the graph highlights the substantial differences in predictions, which is notable.

Thematic mapping became popular in the 18th century. By the end of the century, attempts had been made to map the geology, economic, and medical data thematically. In addition, abstract function graphs, measurement error, and empirical data collection were also introduced.

Another notable figure from this era is William Playfair, who created many of the most well-known graphs such as line, bar, circle, and pie charts that we use today. In addition, various statistical chart forms, such as scatterplots, time series plots, contour plots, and histograms, were also developed during this period. For example, the Playfair (1821) graph represented wheat prices, weekly pay, and the monarch's reign from 1565 to 1820 for 250 years.

The second part of the nineteenth century was the "Golden Age" for statistical graphics. Two well-known examples of data visualization from that period are John Snow's map of cholera outbreaks during the London epidemic of 1854 and Charles Minard's chart of the number of soldiers in Napoleon's infamous Russian campaign army from 1812, with army location indicated by the X-axis and freezing temperatures indicated at points where frostbite took a fatal toll.

Early in the twentieth century, the growing trend for statistical visualizations hit a little snag. This is the "dark ages of modern data visualization." Statisticians were increasingly preoccupied with exact numbers, believing pictures were too imprecise. Yet even though industrial innovation has shifted away from data visualizations, this period saw a growth in data visualization's appeal among the general public. Using charts and graphs in textbooks, business applications, research, and government swiftly proliferated.

The "rebirth of data visualization" was inspired by the rise of computer processing in the latter part of the twentieth century. Computers enabled statisticians to swiftly and efficiently display data and collect and store increasing volumes of data. During the 1960s and 1970s, researchers like John W Tukey in the United States and Jacques Bertin in France pioneered the science of information visualization in the domains of statistics and mapping, respectively. Then, in the early 1980s, Edward Tufte rose to fame. His seminal book, *The Visual Display of Quantitative Information*, is still frequently utilized in university statistics and data visualization courses today. Tufte introduced us to the sparkline, which condenses the general structure of a trend.

Over the last three decades, the field of data visualization has expanded dramatically, with dozens, if not hundreds, of unique focus areas. As a result, corporations, universities, and individuals may investigate their data in fresh and increasingly creative ways. Dashboards, data discovery tools, scorecard programs, analytics suites, and other software tools have made this possible. Other well-known authors and professors who have contributed to advancing the science and art of data visualization include Alberto Cairo, Stephen Few, and Colin Ware.

This is an exciting and challenging time for data visualization. As we learn new ways to capture, combine, analyze, and visualize data, societal worries about invasions of privacy and the danger of data abuse, both purposeful and inadvertent, emerge. As we approach the digital era, it is exciting and disturbing to think about what the future holds for communities and people.

18.3 BIG DATA VISUALIZATION

As the "age of Big Data" accelerates, visualization will become increasingly vital in making sense of the billions of rows of data created every day. Data visualization assists in the telling of tales by arranging data into a comprehensible style and displaying patterns and outliers. A good visualization emphasizes important information while reducing data noise. Form and function must be appropriately matched for effective data display. The most spectacular visualization may eventually fail to convey the intended information, or it may say volumes. Big Data Visualization extends beyond traditional corporate graphs, histograms, and pie charts to more sophisticated representations such as heat maps and fever charts, allowing decision-makers to explore datasets to discover correlations or unexpected patterns.

Scale is an essential aspect of Big Data visualization. Enterprises now collect and store massive amounts of data that would take an individual, years to read, let alone interpret. In addition, scientists have discovered that the human retina transmits data to the brain at a rate of about ten megabits per second. As a result, Big Data visualization depends on robust computer systems to ingest and analyze raw business data to produce graphical representations that allow humans to absorb and grasp massive volumes of data swiftly.

Data visualization is one of the phases in the data science process that argues that after data has been acquired, analyzed, and modeled, it must be visualized for conclusions to be made. Data visualization is a subset of Data Presentation Architecture (DPA), which aims to search, identify, modify, prepare, and transfer data as efficiently as possible.

Visualization is critical to advanced analytics for the same reasons. For example, when a data scientist builds complex predictive analytics or Machine Learning (ML) algorithms, it is critical to examine the outputs to track outcomes and ensure that models perform as expected. This is because advanced algorithm images are often easier to grasp than numerical outputs.

18.4 Importance of Big Data Visualization

Businesses today gather and retain massive amounts of data that would take humans years to analyze and interpret. Furthermore, the expansion of the Internet of Things is now producing massive volumes of Big Data. As a result, organizations confront a difficulty since this data will only be helpful if it can be used to generate relevant insights.

Big Data visualization promises to enable decision-makers to access, evaluate, analyze, and act on data in near real-time. Decision-makers evaluate data in different ways, of course, but Big Data visualization techniques give a fast and effective way to:

- **Review massive amounts of data:** Rather than spending hours poring over spreadsheets or scrutinizing numerical tables, decision-makers may quickly glance at massive amounts of data when presented graphically and understand what it means.
- **Recognize patterns:** Time-sequence data typically captures trends, but it is not easy to find hidden trends within data, especially when the sources are various and the amount of data is significant. Using the correct Big Data visualization tools, on the other hand, may assist the user in finding these trends rapidly. It goes beyond traditional graphs, bubble plots, histograms, pie charts, and donut charts to more complicated representations like heat maps and box-and-whisker plots, allowing decision-makers to explore datasets for connections or unexpected patterns. A circular chart with a hole in the middle is known as a donut chart. Each graph segment represents a distinct category, and the data are shown as percentages of the total. As you may know, donut charts are frequently used as a fun and exciting way to compare data. When it comes to business, detecting patterns as early as possible is a valuable chance for planning.
- **Disseminate the knowledge to others:** The potential of Big Data visualization to communicate the insights revealed to others is an often-ignored aspect. Valuable insights can be gained due to the ability of data visualization to transfer meaning quickly and clearly, which is necessary for internal and external business presentations.

Big Data approaches may show data of any type, including numbers, trigonometric functions, linear algebra, geometric, essential, and statistical algorithms, in coding, report analytics, and graphical interaction.

18.5 How Does Data Visualization Work?

The core of data visualization science is understanding how humans acquire and interpret information. Amos Tversky and Daniel Kahn collaborated to develop two independent data collection and processing methods.

System 1 is concerned with mental processes that are quick, intuitive, and unconscious. This method is commonly used in everyday life and can assist with activities such as reading the words on a sign, doing elementary math tasks such as adding 2 + 2, identifying the location of a sound's origin, differentiating between colors and so on.

System 2 is connected with cognitive processing that is infrequent, slow, rational, and calculated. This approach will be required in one of the following situations:

- Recalling a person's phone number
- Solving complicated mathematical problems such as 3450 × 24
- Recognizing the meaning of different signs put next to one other
- Recognizing complicated social challenges that need cognitive abilities.

The human brain has adapted to take in and comprehend visual information and is exceptionally good at recognizing visual patterns. This capacity allows people to detect danger and identify other people, including familiar faces like family members and general human faces.

Big Data visualization approaches make use of this ability of the human brain by displaying data in a way that makes it easy for people to interpret it visually, rather than using mathematical analysis, which requires learning and is time-consuming.

Selecting the best visualization strategy for Big Data is crucial for bringing any hidden insights to light.

18.6 Types of Data Visualization

A straightforward bar graph or pie chart is probably the first thing that comes to mind when you think of data visualization. However, simple business tools like pie charts and histograms may not always tell the whole story. Larger, more complex, and more varied datasets may require more exotic visualization techniques.

Although proper visualization may be considered a crucial component of data visualization and a standard starting point for many data graphics, it must be combined with a suitable dataset for optimal results. Simple graphs are just the beginning. Many different visualization techniques present data in attractive and practical ways.

In general, the following are the typical kinds of data visualization. Let us consider the following example. Table 18.1 shows the marks of various students in the subjects: English, Tamil, Maths, Science and Social. With the help of this table, let us understand how various data visualization looks like.

Table 18.1 Marks scored by each student

Name of the Student	English	Tamil	Maths	Science	Social
Mouli	93	90	95	91	85
Christina	85	83	74	80	72
Jasmine	45	42	50	60	60
Melwin	95	90	90	92	85
Jayden	95	93	95	96	97

Line Chart: The line chart is one of the most fundamental and widely used methods. Line charts depict the way how variables can change over time. It is distinguished by its tendency to reflect changes over time or by ordered categories. There should be a minimum of two data records to use a line graph, which can be used to compare trends in a vast volume of data. In addition, it is advised that it should not exceed five polylines in a graph.

Using the data from the Table 18.1, the marks of Christina and Jasmine are visualized. Figure 18.1 shows the line chart.

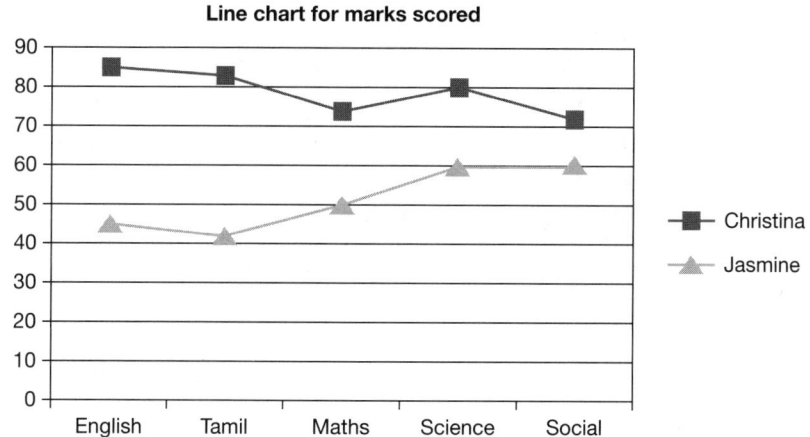

Figure 18.1 Line Chart showing the marks of Christina and Jasmine

Column Chart: Since the human eye is sensitive to height disparities, the column chart uses the column's height to reflect the difference in the data. Column charts are used to show a comparison between values and different categories. It should be emphasized that there should not be too many columns. The drawback of the column chart is that it is suitable only for small and medium-sized data. Figure 18.2 shows how a column chart is used to compare the variables.

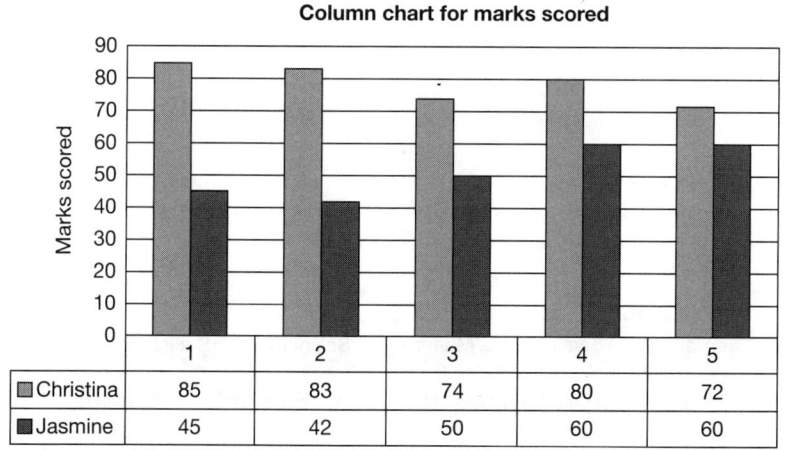

Figure 18.2 Column Chart to compare the marks of Christina and Jasmine

Bar Chart: It is similar to column charts, except that bar charts can have a relatively more significant number of bars. The two axes' location is different compared to the column chart. These bar charts are also used for the comparison of data. With reference to the Table 18.1, a bar chart can be used to compare the marks scored by the students. Figure 18.3 shows how the bar chart looks like.

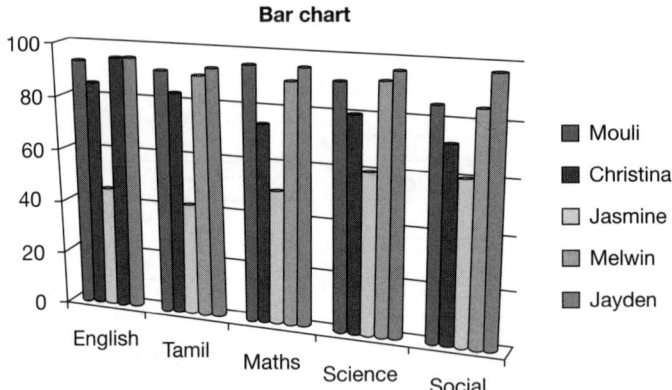

Figure 18.3 Bar Chart showing the comparison of marks

Area Chart: The line chart serves as the foundation for the area chart. It adds color to the line chart's space between the polyline and the axis. Polylines are also called multi-lines. The trend information is better highlighted in the area chart because of the color filling. In this type of chart, the fill color should be somewhat transparent. This transparency will help the user identify overlapping relationships between various series. If there is no transparency, different data series will cover each other. Figure 18.4 shows the area chart for the data in Table 18.1.

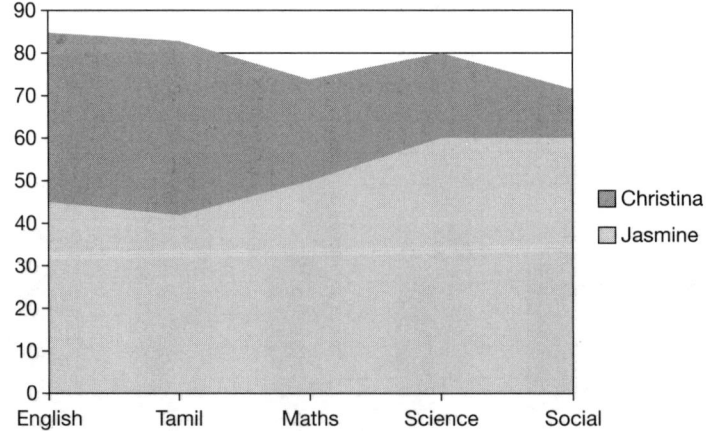

Figure 18.4 Area Chart to show the marks scored by Christina and Jasmine

Pie Chart: A pie chart represents data as a circular graph. The slices in the pie indicate the relative size of the data that is represented pictorially. Numerical and categorical variables are needed for pie chart representation. The word pie indicates the entire part, and the slice indicates a part. Pie charts are frequently used to show the percentages of various classes and compare classifications by arc in various fields.

As the number of series increases, the size of the slices will decrease, and the size differential eventually becomes vague. Hence the pie chart is not suitable if there are numerous series of data. A pie chart can also be turned into a multi-layer one, which reflects the hierarchical relationship and displays the percentage of various categories of data. Figure 18.5 shows the appearance of a pie chart.

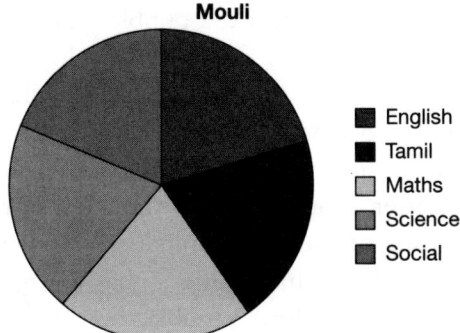

Figure 18.5 Pie Chart showing the marks scored by Mouli

Scatter Plot: In the scatter plot, two variables are represented by two points on a rectangular coordinate system. To distinguish between the values of two separate variables, it employs dots. The variable's value determines where the point is located. We may determine the correlation between the variables by looking at the distribution of the data points. Correlation indicates the dependency of two variables. A massive volume of data is needed to create a scatter plot because the association cannot be identified without huge datasets. Figure 18.6 depicts the way a scatter plot will look like.

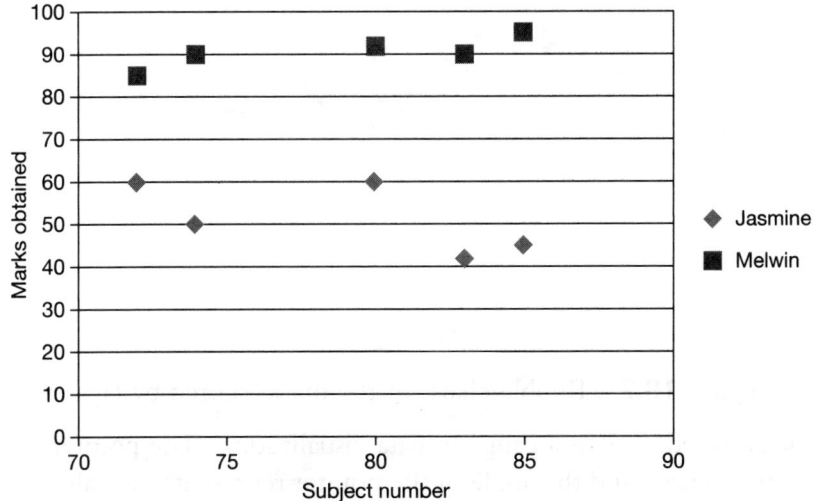

Figure 18.6 Scatter Plot showing the marks scored by Jasmine and Melwin

In the above graph, X axis may represent the subject numbers and Y Axis may represent the marks.

Bubble Chart: A bubble chart is a type of data visualization that displays multiple variables on a two-dimensional plane. Unlike a simple scatter plot, which only shows the relationship between two variables along the horizontal and vertical axes, a bubble chart adds a third variable that is represented by the size of the circles or bubbles. For example, a bubble chart can show the relationship between different subjects, marks, and hours studied (Refer Fig. 18.7). The x-axis and y-axis can represent the subject number and actual marks, respectively, while the size of the bubbles can represent hours spent by the student to study the respective subjects to score the actual marks. A smaller size indicates that the student studied the given subject for fewer hours while a bigger size indicates that the student studied more hours to score the actual marks.

A bubble chart can reveal patterns, trends, and outliers in complex datasets more effectively than a simple scatter plot. It allows the viewer to compare not only the position but also the magnitude of the data points. However, there are some limitations and challenges when using a bubble chart. One is that the area of the bubbles may not be proportional to the value of the third variable, especially if the scale is not linear. Another is that the bubbles may overlap or obscure each other if there are fewer data points or if they are clustered together. Therefore, it is essential to choose an appropriate range and scale for the bubble size and to avoid overcrowding the chart with unnecessary or redundant data. A bubble chart can help show the correlation and distribution of three variables in various fields and contexts. For example, a bubble chart can be used to compare countries' GDP, population, and life expectancy; or to show different products' revenue, profit margin, and market share.

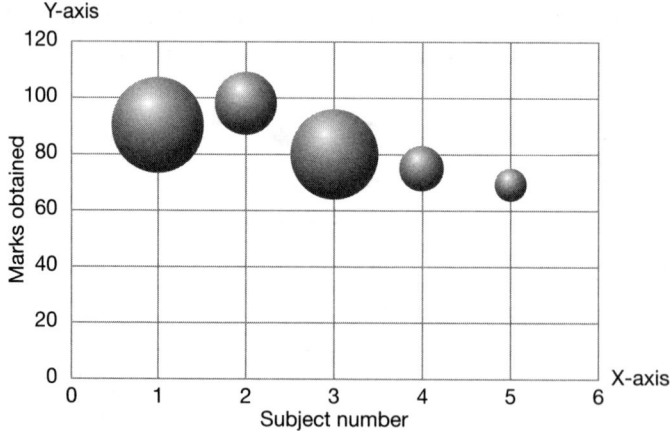

Figure 18.7 Bubble chart for the marks scored by Jayden

Gauge: A materialized chart is a gauge in data visualization. The pointer symbolizes the size, the scale, the metric, and the angle of the pointer represents the value. It can visually display an indicator's progress or current state. The gauge is used for comparing intervals. Figure 18.8 shows how a gauge chart looks like.

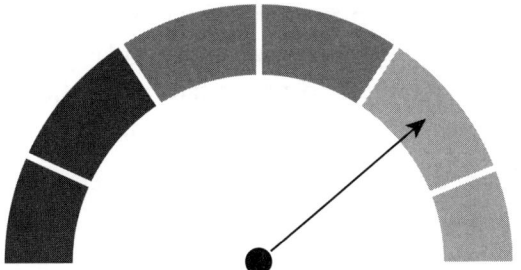

Figure 18.8 Gauge chart

Radar Chart

It compares various quantized variables, such as determining if values are extreme or comparable. They aid in identifying which dataset variables have larger or lower values. Radar diagrams are ideal for displaying work performance. The stacked column design of the radar chart allows for a two-way comparison of the categorization and series and the proportion. Figure 18.9 shows how a radar chart looks like.

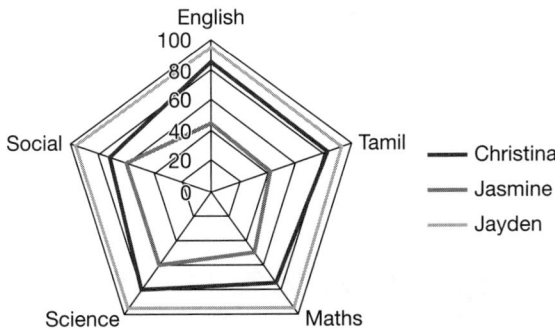

Figure 18.9 Radar chart

Box-and-whisker Plots: An illustration of the distribution of values within measured groups using boxes and whiskers is called a box plot. The locations of the whisker and box ends indicate where most of the data is. Box plots are most frequently used when there are several groups to compare to one another. When there is just one group to the plot, other charts with more detail are favored.

Word Cloud: A visual depiction of text data is a word cloud. It is a colorful image made up of words that resembles a cloud. It may quickly assist readers in perceiving actual content and is used to present a lot of text data.

The word cloud chart needs a lot of data, and there needs to be a lot of discrimination in the data to have an impact. It should be noted that accurate analysis cannot be done with a word cloud.

Cartogram: The limits of a geographic area are distorted by cartograms to communicate alternative variables. Depending on the numeric value of the alternative variable, the boundaries are inflated or deflated.

Dot Distribution Map: A point map is a visual representation of the geographic distribution of data made up of identically sized points placed on a background map. The distribution of points makes it simple to understand how the data is distributed overall. But this is not suitable when we need to focus on a single piece of information.

Gantt Chart: The timing of a task, actual progress, and a comparison to the requirements are displayed clearly in the Gantt chart. The Gantt chart helps the management to identify the progress in a task or project.

Heat Map: The weight of each point within the geographic area is shown on the heatmap. You can use other photos in place of the map as the background layer. Additionally, a heatmap's color typically denotes density.

Highlight Table: Text tables are improved by highlight tables while maintaining their format. They encode ranges of measure value using the pre-attentive visual attribute of color, from lowest to highest. These tables can exhibit sequential or diverging palettes with continuous colors. They can also make use of a graduated color scheme.

Histogram: Using vertical bars on a horizontal line, histograms show how data are distributed over a continuous range or specific period, indicating where values are concentrated. A typical histogram is shown in Fig. 18.10.

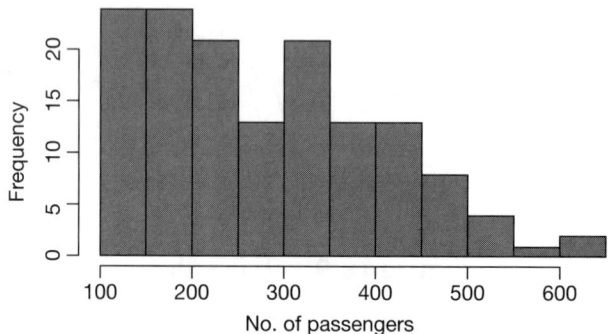

Figure 18.10 Histogram of air passengers

Matrix: The visualization of a matrix resembles a table. Since the data is flat and a table supports two dimensions, duplicate values are shown without being aggregated. Because it offers a stepped pattern, a matrix makes it simpler to present data meaningfully over multiple dimensions. In addition, you can dive deeper into the data because the matrix automatically aggregates the data.

Treemap: This approach uses a nested format to display hierarchical data. Each category's rectangle size is based on how much of the overall group it makes up. When comparing various elements of a whole and there are several categories, treemaps work best.

Wedge Stack Graph: Wedge stack graphs are a type of visual display that uses a radial structure to show hierarchical data. It may be used to illustrate frequency data with multiple levels.

18.7 Challenges of Big Data Visualization

Big Data visualization has the potential to be an incredibly potent business tool, but before a company can use it, there are a few critical challenges that must be resolved.

Availability of visualization experts: Many Big Data visualization tools are made simple enough to be used by everyone in an organization, and they frequently include examples of Big Data visualization suitable for the datasets being analyzed. However, to make the most of some tools, it might be essential to hire a prominent data visualization expert who can choose the finest datasets and visualization types to guarantee that the data is utilized to its fullest potential.

Hardware Resources for Visualization: Big Data visualization is fundamentally a computing activity. To do it rapidly and allow businesses to use real-time data to make choices, it may be necessary to use highly configured computer hardware and quick storage systems or even relocate to the cloud.

Quality of the Data: The accuracy of the insights of the Big Data dramatically depends on the data being visualized. If the data is incomplete or outdated, the results obtained by using any insights from the data will be questionable. To handle this data, metadata, data sources, and any transformations or data cleaning are to be done before storing the data. With the aid of people and procedures, this is possible.

18.8 Introduction to Tableau

Tableau is a fantastic business intelligence and data visualization tool for reporting and analyzing huge volume of data. It was founded in America in 2003. In June 2019, Salesforce bought Tableau. Tableau assists users in producing a variety of graphs, maps, dashboards and stories for the purpose of visualizing and analyzing data to aid in business decision-making. Tableau is one of the most sought-after tools for Business Intelligence as it has many interesting and distinctive features for Business Intelligence.

18.8.1 Features of Tableau

Let us examine some of the key characteristics of Tableau:

- Tableau's powerful data search and exploration helps its users to find answers for important queries.
- To use Tableau, a person need not have any prior programming knowledge. Without previous knowledge about Tableau, a new user can use it to construct visualizations.
- It can link to a number of data sources that are not supported by other BI tools. Users of Tableau can combine and produce reports from many datasets.
- A centralized location to manage all published data sources inside an organization is supported by Tableau Server.

18.8.2 Tableau Product Suite

There are six versions of Tableau out of which three are paid services and three are free. Table 18.2 shows the different versions of Tableau and their prominent features.

Table 18.2 Different versions of Tableau and their features

Product	Version	Features
Tableau Desktop	Paid	Using various charts and graphs, Tableau Desktop assists in the creation of reports, dashboards, and stories. With Tableau Desktop, workbooks and dashboards may be shared privately or publicly.
Tableau Server	Paid	Tableau Server is mostly used in organizations to allow various teams to access workbooks and reports that were prepared using Tableau Desktop applications. Questions can be asked in natural language and the answers that are received will be based on AI which explains the data.
Tableau Online	Paid	The cloud-hosted Tableau Online analytics tool allows users to publish dashboards and share discoveries with anyone. We may connect to cloud databases like Google BigQuery and Amazon Redshift. It automatically updates data from web applications like Salesforce and Google Analytics.
Tableau Public	Free	Although workbooks created using Tableau Public cannot be saved locally, the service is free to use. They can be stored in Tableau's public cloud, which is available to everyone. Any user can download and access the files saved to the cloud because of the lack of privacy options
Tableau Reader	Free	Using this free desktop application Tableau Reader, users can open and interact with reports created on Tableau Desktop.
Tableau Mobile	Free	Users of Tableau Mobile can check data and reports at any time, from any location, using interactive previews. Using the smartphone app, data can be picked, filtered and fine-tuned with the help of a finger.

18.8.3 Installation of Tableau

In this section we shall see how to install Tableau Desktop. This is a paid version but it is given for free as a trial for 13 days.

Step 1: In Google, type Tableau download. The first screen that appears is shown in Fig. 18.11.

Step 2: Once you click the above download option, the screen shown in Fig. 18.12 pops up. Based on the operating system of your computer or laptop or other devices, you can choose the file that has to be downloaded.

Figure 18.11 Screen showing the download option for Tableau Desktop

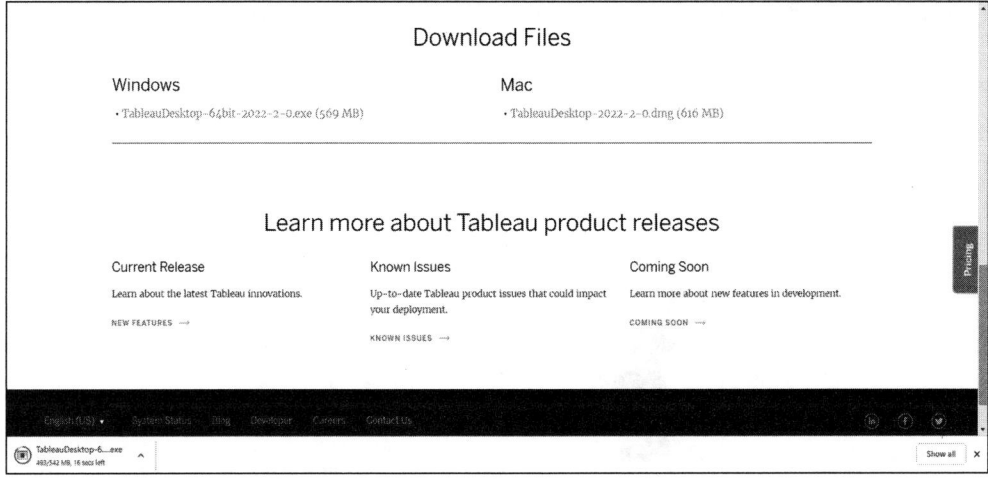

Figure 18.12 Screen showing the option to download Tableau for a particular operating system

Step 3: Once you choose the operating system, the executable file will be downloaded. Then open the downloaded file and start installing the software. Figure 18.13 shows the welcome screen once the executable file is executed. By clicking the agreement, this tool starts getting installed. This is shown in Figure 18.14.

To log in to Tableau, you need to sign-in with the help of your Email ID. This is shown in Figure 18.15. To log in, you need to create an account. If you have already created and trying to create a new log in, a screen showing that you already have an account will be displayed. This is depicted in Figure 18.16.

Figure 18.13 Screen showing the agreement acceptance and installation

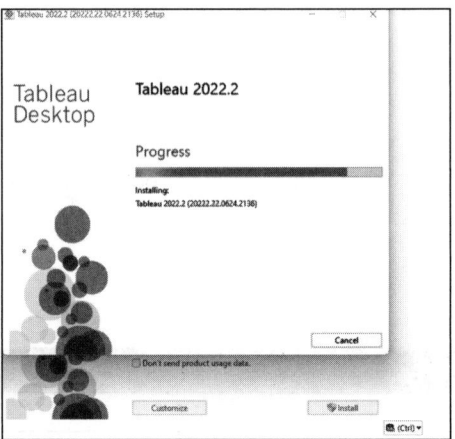

Figure 18.14 Screen showing installation in progress

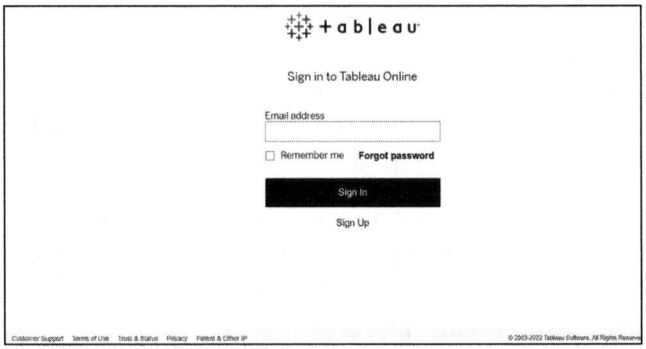

Figure 18.15 Screen showing the log in screen of Tableau

Big Data Visualizations • 955

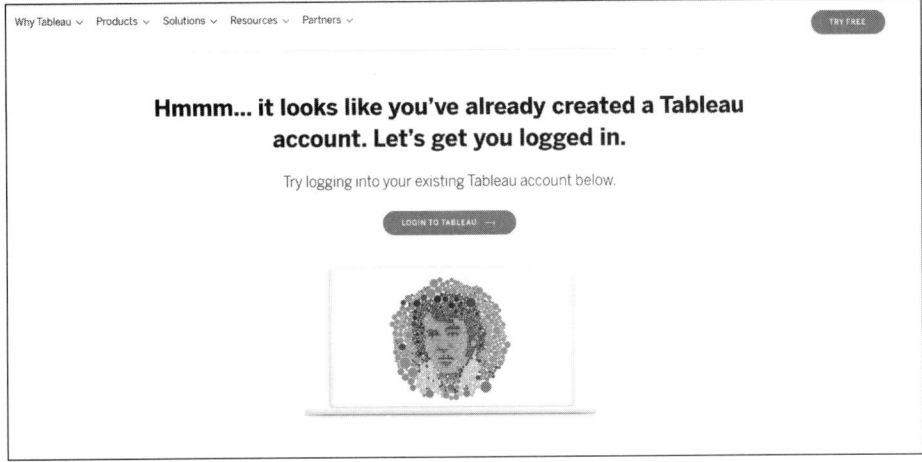

Figure 18.16 Screen showing that the user has already created an account

18.8.4 Tableau for Big Data Visualization

To illustrate visualization of Big Data, in this section we are using the IPL dataset which is available for free download at https://www.kaggle.com/datasets/patrickb1912/ipl-complete-dataset-20082020. You can create your own account in kaggle and download the IPL dataset for free.

To start visualizing the data, first you need to create a worksheet. Once you log in to Tableau, in the home screen you will find an option, New. If you click on that, you will be given a few options as shown in Figure 18.17. From the options, choose Workbook.

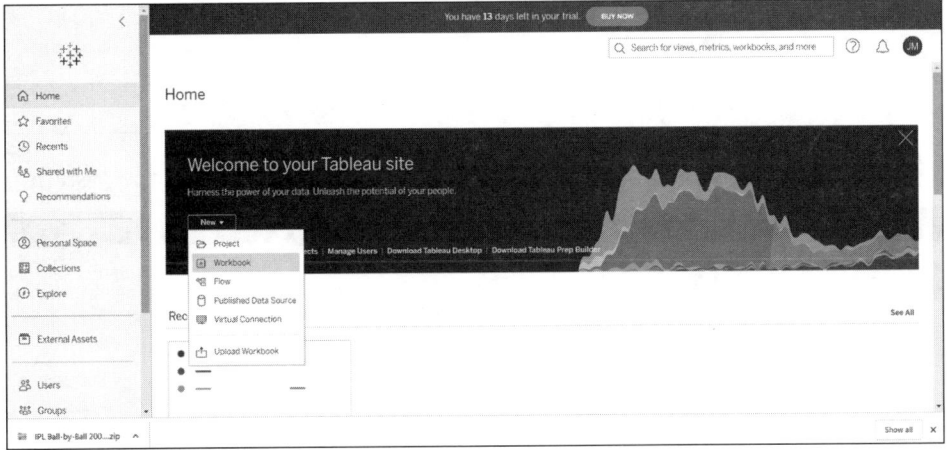

Figure 18.17 Screen depicting the creation of a new worksheet

After creating the worksheet, just connect to the data. Here you can choose your data file from different data sources. Figure 18.18 shows the various ways to choose the dataset. If the data file is in your system, then you can drag and drop the file or browse and upload it. This is shown in Fig. 18.19.

Once the dataset is uploaded, the parameters are seen in the left-most side of the screen. This is shown in Fig. 18.20.

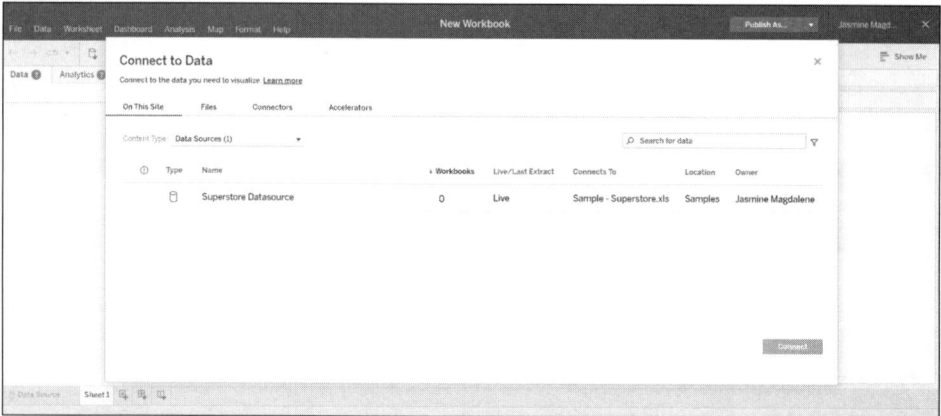

Figure 18.18 Screen showing the options to upload a dataset

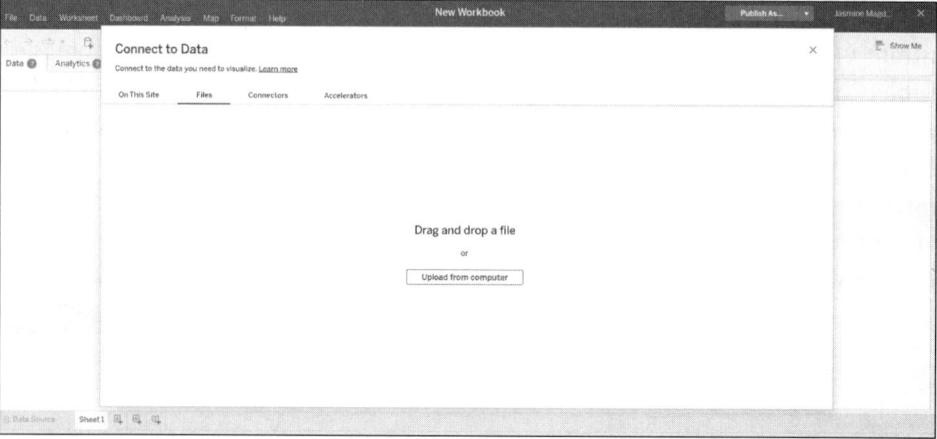

Figure 18.19 Screen showing the way to upload data from the system

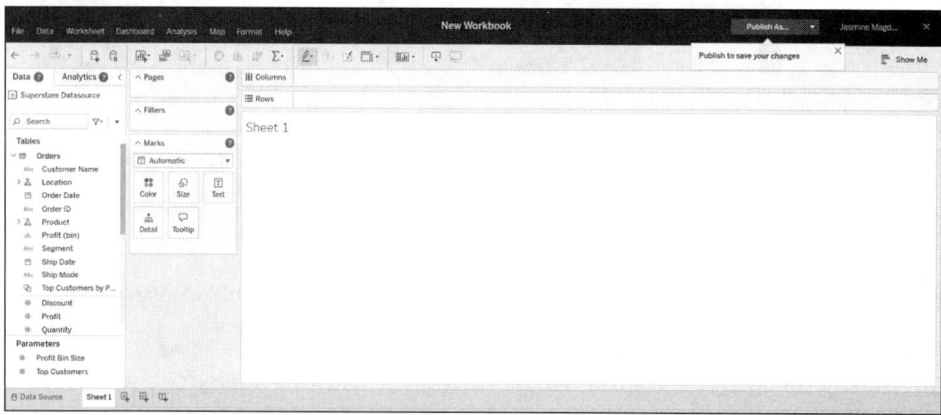

Figure 18.20 Screen showing the parameters in the dataset

Once the data is loaded, the column and the row can be chosen based on the requirement. Here in this example, city is chosen as the column. It should be noted that the column and row should be chosen from different categories. This is shown in Fig. 18.21. The parameter can be dragged and dropped in the column space. The row has to be chosen from the measure values. Figure 18.22 clearly indicates the choosing of parameter to be taken as the row values.

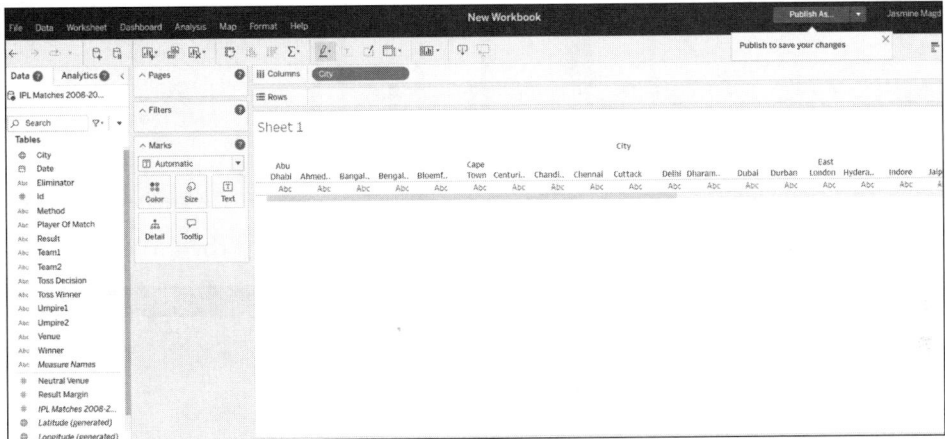

Figure 18.21 Screen showing the column that is chosen

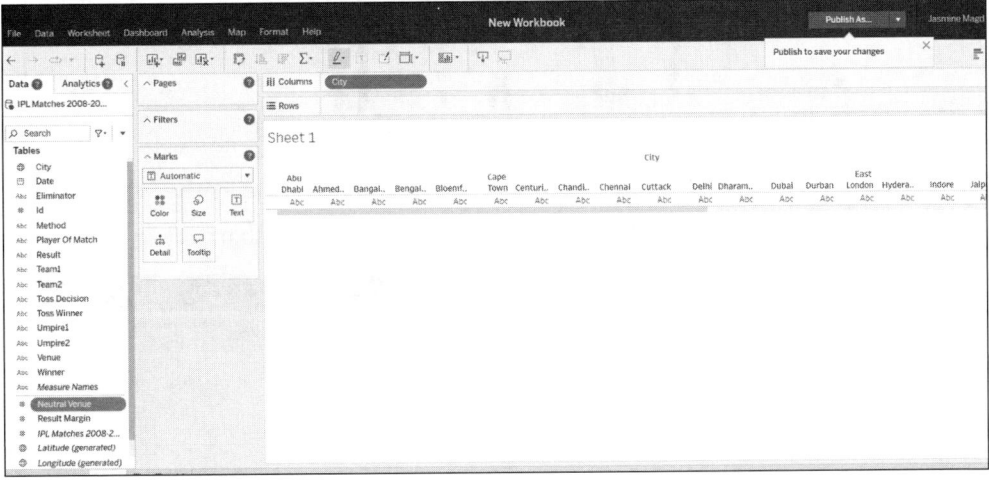

Figure 18.22 Screen showing the selection of the parameter for row

After choosing the column and row, the type of visualization that is needed can be chosen by clicking on the automatic menu. Figure 18.23 shows the column chart with the city and the number of matches played in that city. Other visualization types can be chosen from the automatic menu and the color menu is used to choose the required color of the plot. The various kinds of visualization like bar chart, line chart, area plot and square chart are shown in Figs 18.24 18.25 ,18.26 and 18.27 respectively.

958 ● Big Data Analytics

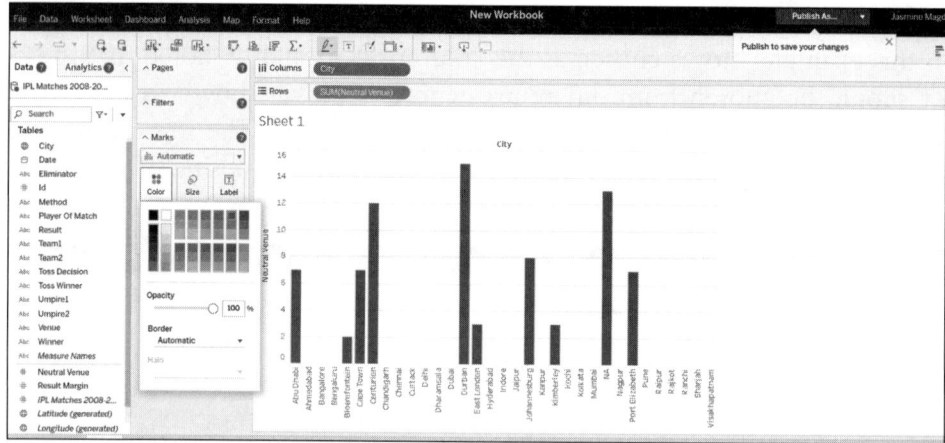

Figure 18.23 Screen showing the Column Chart and the Color Menu

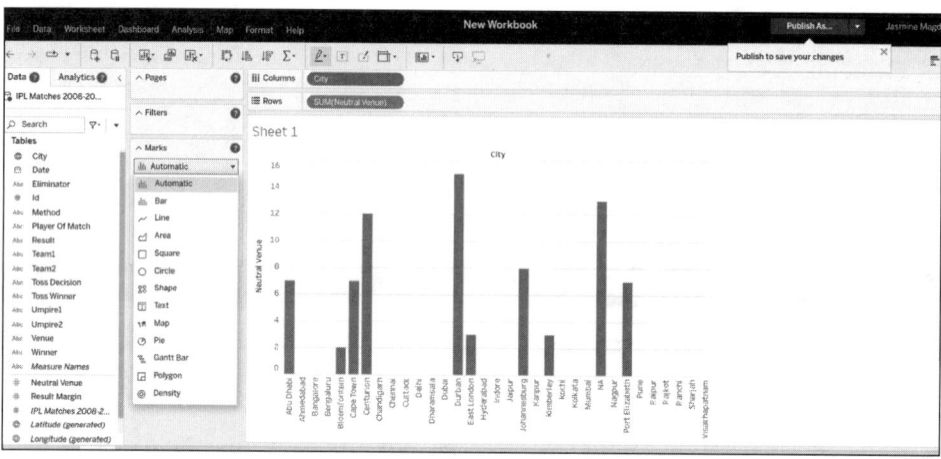

Figure 18.24 Screen showing the Bar Chart

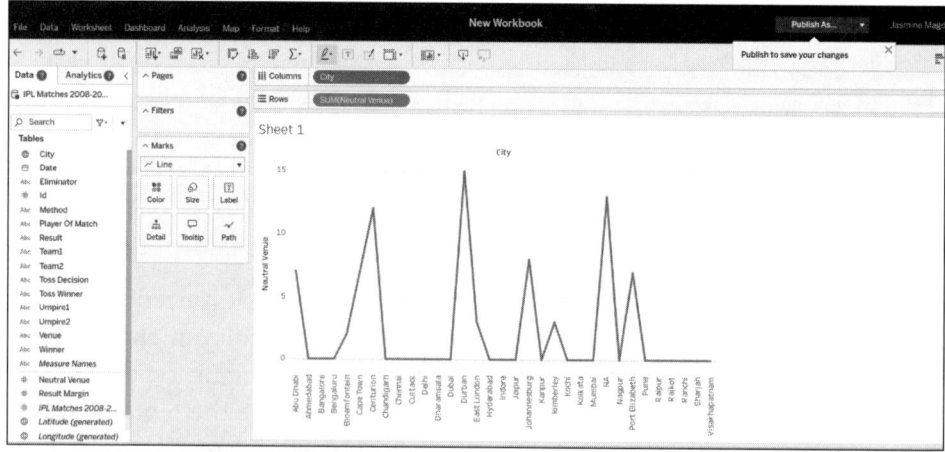

Figure 18.25 Screen showing the Line Chart

Big Data Visualizations • 959

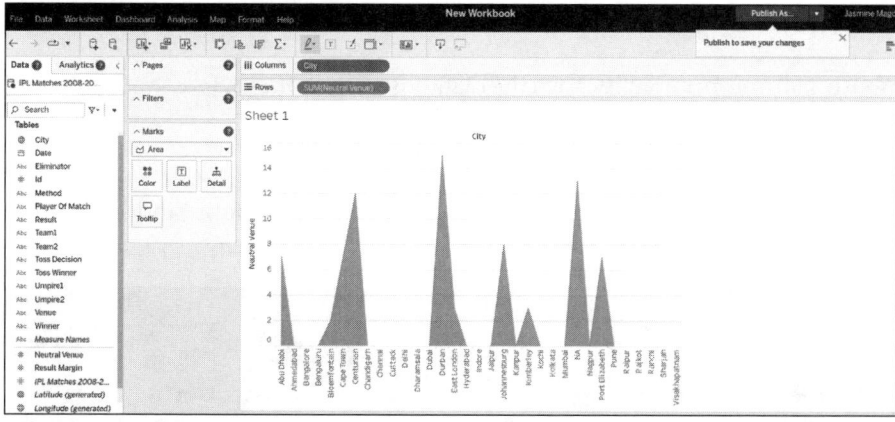

Figure 18.26 Screen showing the Area Chart

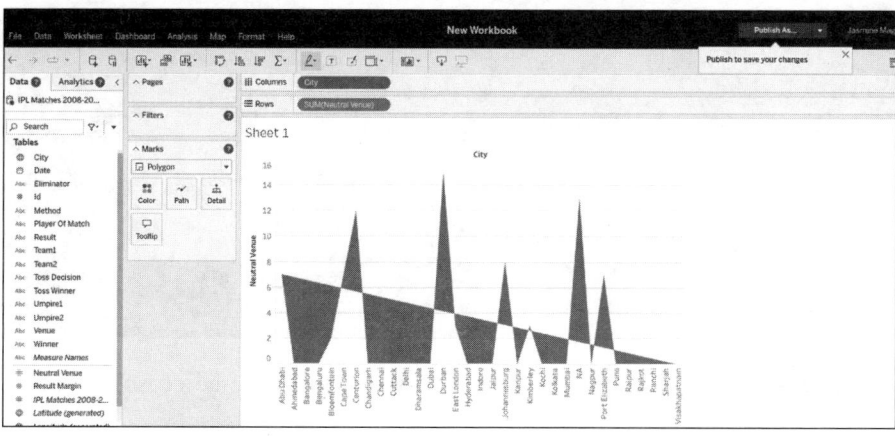

Figure 18.27 Screen showing Square Plot

Tool tip can be added by clicking the Edit Tooltip menu. This is illustrated in Fig. 18.28.

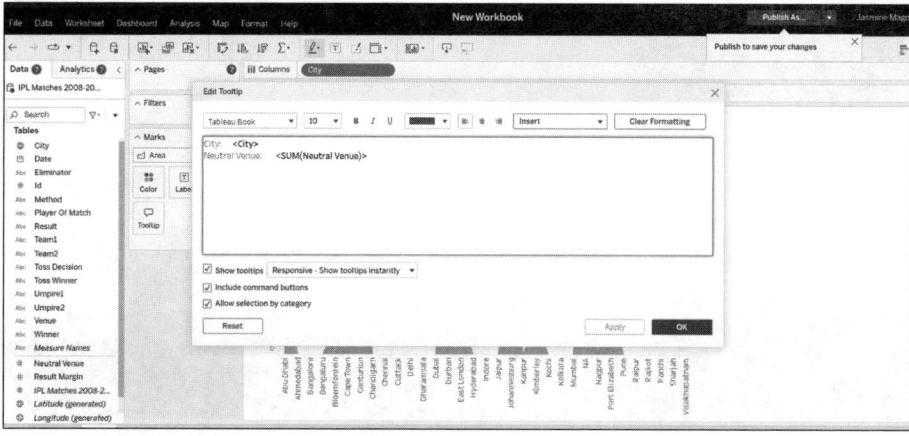

Figure 18.28 Screen showing the way to edit the tool tip

18.9 PYTHON FOR DATA VISUALIZATION

Python is also gaining popularity for Big Data visualization.

18.9.1 Installation of Python

Step 1: To start with, open Microsoft store from the Start menu and download Python 3.7 version from Microsoft app store. This is illustrated as shown in Figs 18.29 and 18.30.

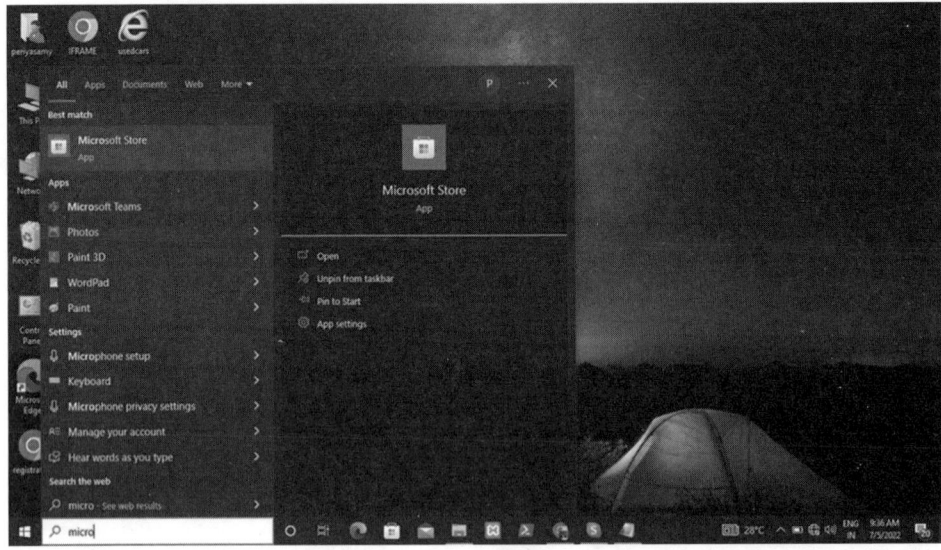

Figure 18.29 Screen showing the way to choose Microsoft store

Figure 18.30 Screen showing the search bar to search for Python installation

Once the file is chosen, it is installed as shown in Fig. 18.31.

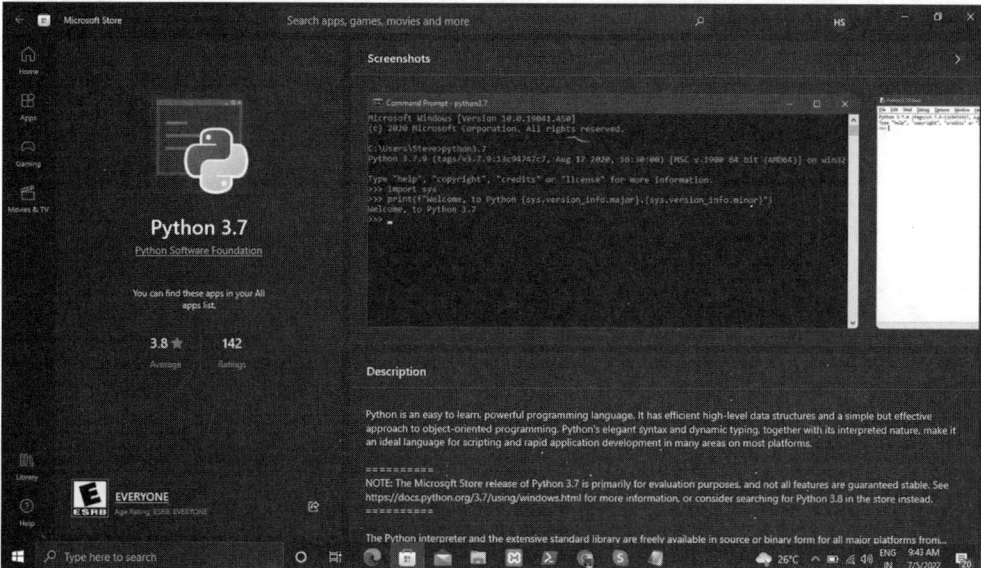

Figure 18.31 Screen depicting the installation of Python

Step 2: Open Windows PowerShell from Start menu. Figure 18.32 shows the way to choose the PowerShell.

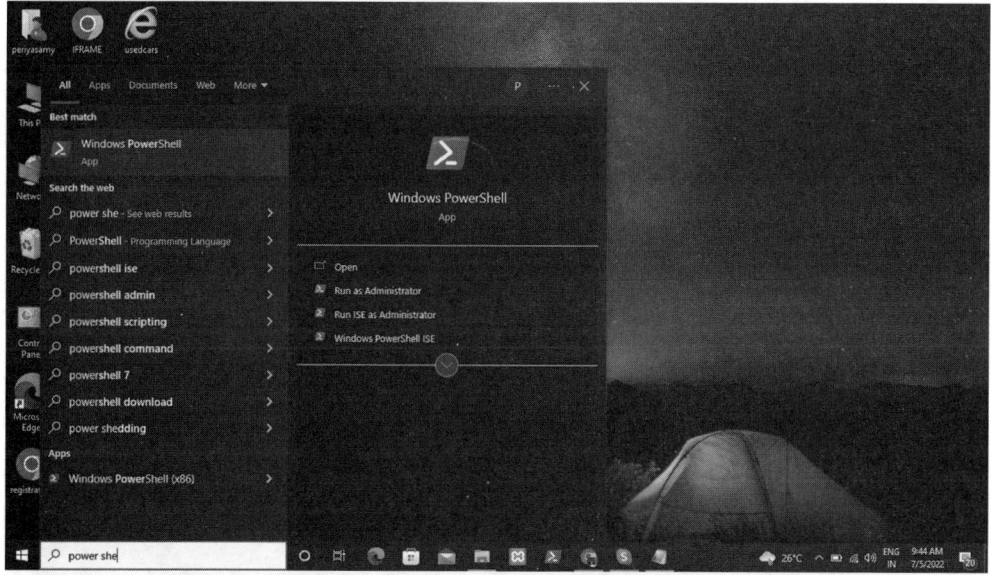

Figure 18.32 Screen showing the option to choose Windows PowerShell

Check whether the Python version is installed in the proper manner by typing Python version. Figure 18.33 shows the checking of the installation for the correct version.

Figure 18.33 Screen to check whether the installation is proper

Step 3: Once the installation of the Python version is checked, the next step is to check the pip installer version. The command `Pip version` is used to perform the same. Figure 18.34 shows the pip version command being used to check the pip version installation.

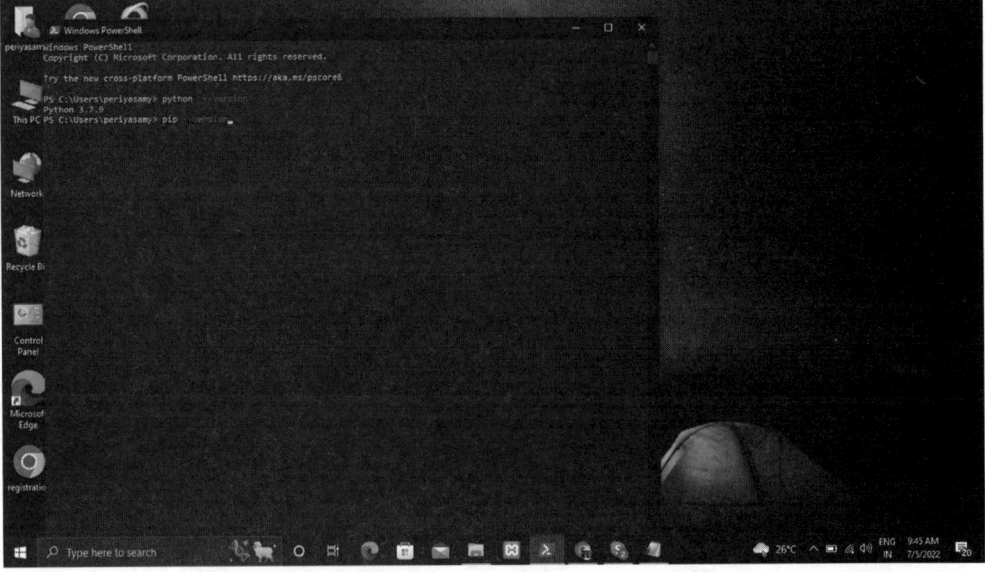

Figure 18.34 Screen showing the command to check the installation of pip version

Step 4: Install packages using pip installer.
Pip installs Pandas.

This is shown in Fig. 18.35. Pandas is a library, which is needed for reading the data.

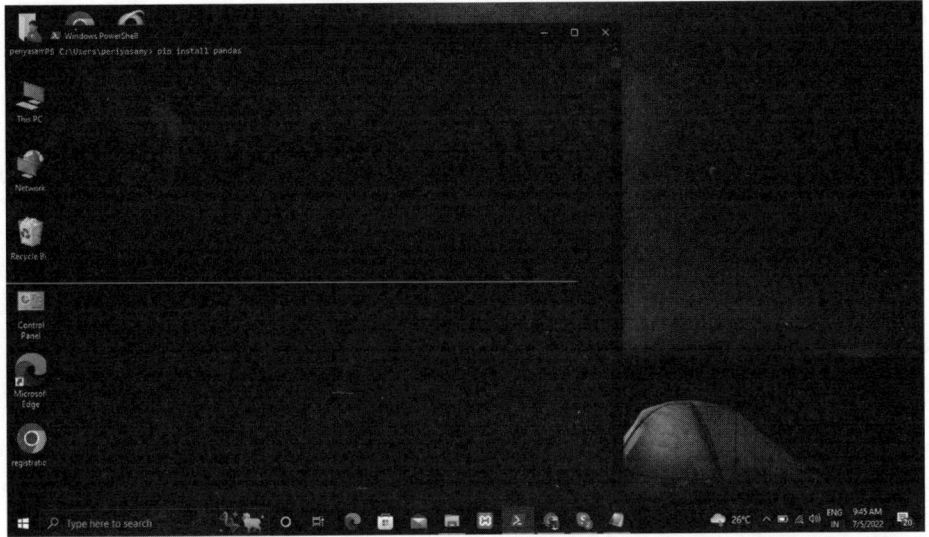

Figure 18.35 Screen showing the installation of Pandas

Step 5: After installing Pandas, install Matplotlib which is needed for different data visualization. This is done by typing the command pip install Matplotlib. Figure 18.36 shows the command that is typed to install Matplotlib.

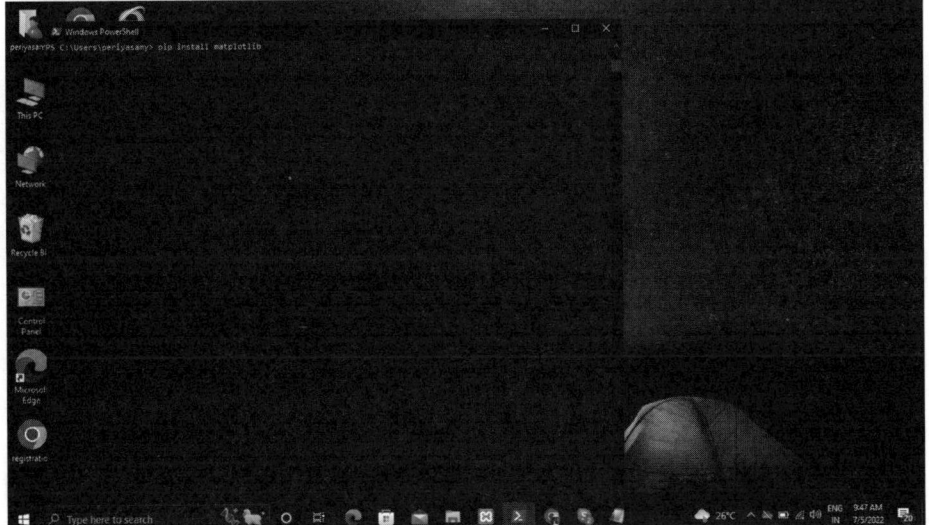

Figure 18.36 Screen showing the installation of Matplotlib

Once these packages are installed, we can start writing programs for visualization. The program for Python data visualization is typed in the notepad or in any text editor. It should be noted that the file must be saved with the extension of .py. It is important the CSV and the program file are stored in the folder which has the same path.

18.9.2 Visualization of Data Using Python

Python provides a wide selection of libraries offering various data display capabilities. Each of these libraries boasts distinctive features and can create various kinds of graphs. Some popular Python libraries for displaying data include Matplotlib, Seaborn, Bokeh, and Plotly. All four have something unique to offer about the presentation and visualization of data. For example, Matplotlib is known for its wide range of plotting options. At the same time, Seaborn focuses on univariate or bivariate exploration using statistical graphics. Bokeh is well-suited to interactive web applications as it generates interactive plots in HTML documents, while Plotly allows users to create publication-quality figures with ease.

18.9.3 Matplotlib

NumPy arrays are the foundation of the user-friendly, low-level data visualization package known as Matplotlib. It includes a number of visualizations, including scatter plots, line plots, and histograms. A lot of flexibility is offered by Matplotlib. Figure 18.37 shows the downloading of Matplotlib.

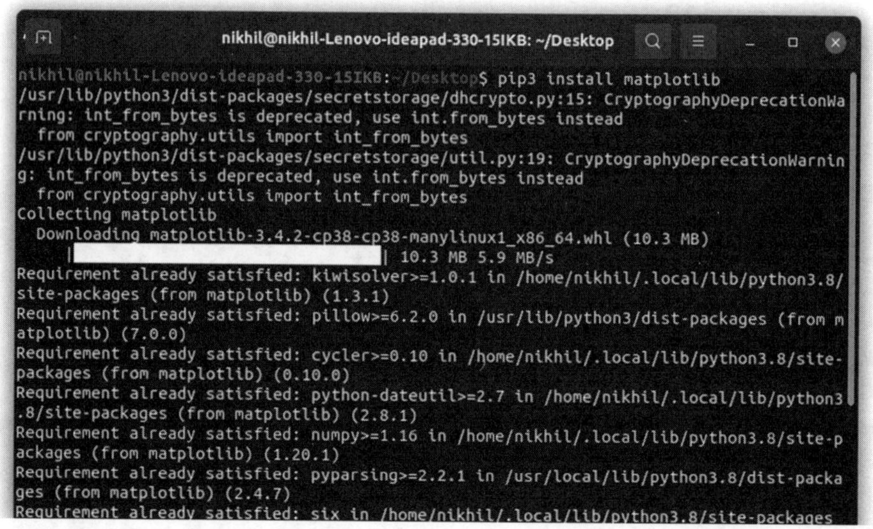

Figure 18.37 Screen showing the download of Matplotlib

Scatter Plot

Dots are used in scatter plots to depict the relationship between variables. Scatter plots are used to observe relationships between variables. To create a scatter plot, use the matplotlib library's `scatter()` method. The following is the program for drawing a scatter plot. The dataset that is taken for illustrating scatter plot is tips.csv.

```
import pandas as pd
import matplotlib.pyplot as plt
# reading the database
```

```
data = pd.read_csv("tips.csv")
# Scatter plot with day against tip
plt.scatter(data['day'], data['tip'])
# Adding Title to the Plot
plt.title("Scatter Plot")
# Setting the X and Y labels
plt.xlabel('Day')
plt.ylabel('Tip')
plt.show()
```

Save the program with an extension of .py., for example scatter.py. To run this program, open it in Windows PowerShell by using the command `python scatter.py`. The output of the above program is shown in Fig. 18.38

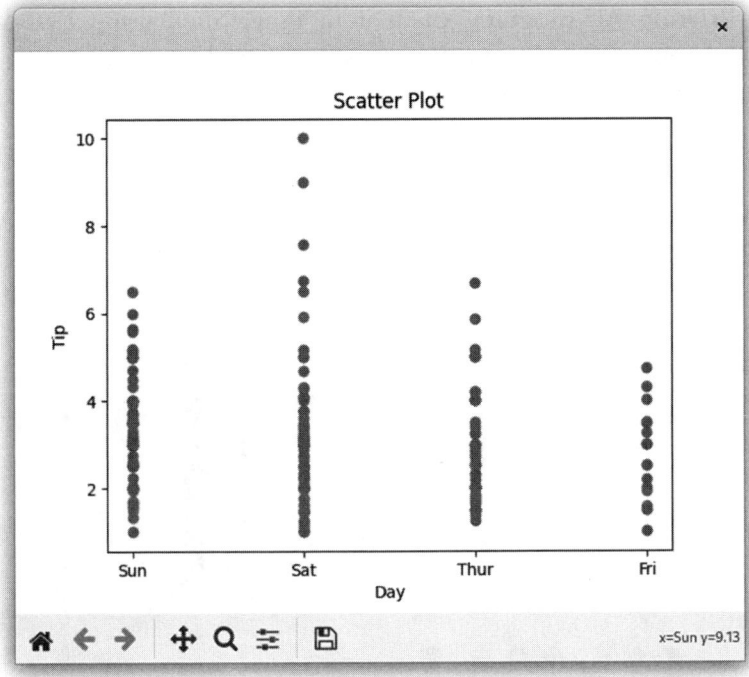

Figure 18.38 Output of the scatter plot program

Color Bar

If we add colors and alter the size of the points, a graph will have more meaning. The scatter function's c and s parameters can be used to do this. The `colorbar()` method can also be used to display the color bar. The following program shows the way a color bar can be created for a given dataset.

```
import pandas as pd
import matplotlib.pyplot as plt
```

```
# reading the database
data = pd.read_csv("tips.csv")
# Scatter plot with day against tip
plt.scatter(data['day'], data['tip'],
c=data['size'],s=data['total_bill'])
# Adding Title to the Plot
plt.title("Scatter Plot")
# Setting the X and Y labels
plt.xlabel('Day')
plt.ylabel('Tip')
plt.colorbar()
plt.show()
```

Once the program is typed, save it with the extension of .py. Here, the file name is given as colorbar.py. To run this program, open it in PowerShell using Python colorbar.py command. The output of the above program is shown in Fig. 18.39.

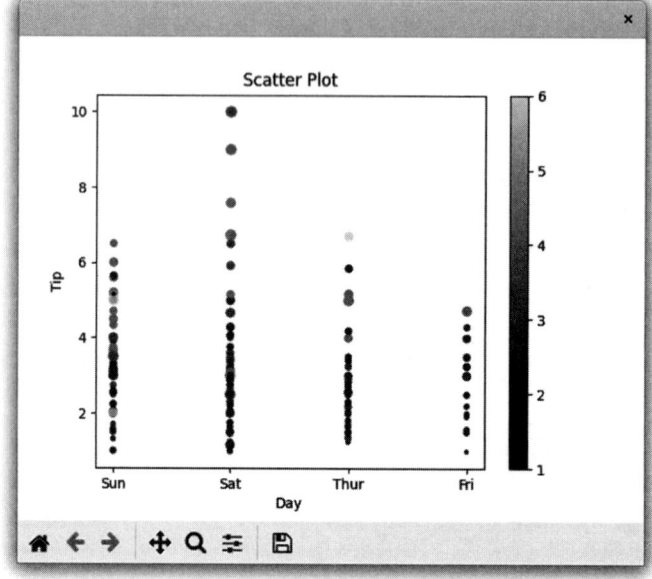

Figure 18.39 Output showing the colorbar plot

Line Chart

A relationship between two pieces of data, X and Y, is shown on different axes using a line chart. The plot() method is used to plot a line chart. Let us look at the example below.

```
import pandas as pd
import matplotlib.pyplot as plt
# reading the database
```

```
data = pd.read_csv("tips.csv")

# Scatter plot with day against tip
plt.plot(data['tip'])
plt.plot(data['size'])

# Adding Title to the Plot
plt.title("Line Chart")

# Setting the X and Y labels
plt.xlabel('Day')
plt.ylabel('Tip')
plt.show()
```

Save this program as linechart.py and open Windows PowerShell using Python linechart.py to run this program. Figure 18.40 shows the output of the above program.

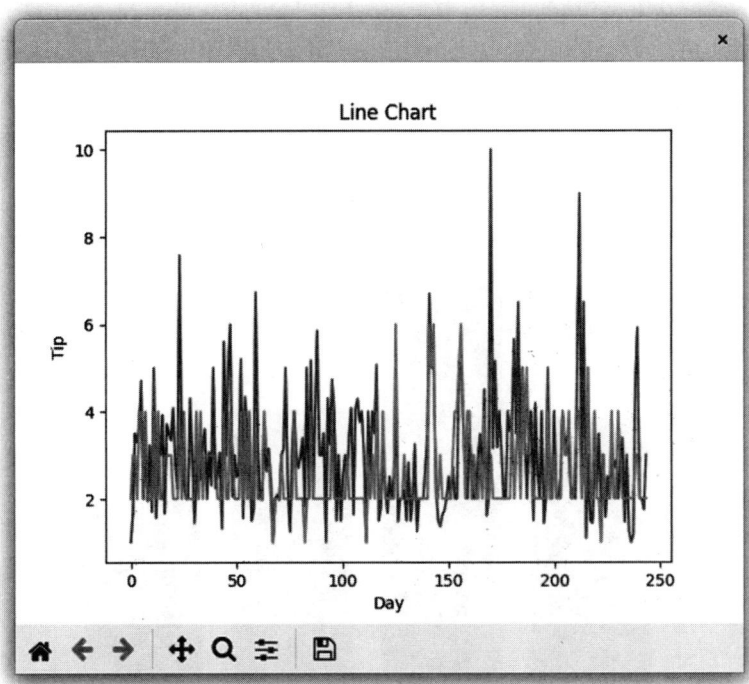

Figure 18.40 Output showing line chart

Bar Plot

A bar plot, often known as a bar chart, is a graph that uses rectangular bars with lengths and heights proportionate to the values they represent to depict a category of data. It can be produced by using the bar() method. The following program is used to create a bar plot.

```
import pandas as pd
import matplotlib.pyplot as plt
# reading the database
data = pd.read_csv("tips.csv")
# Bar chart with day against tip
plt.bar(data['day'], data['tip'])
plt.title("Bar Chart")
# Setting the X and Y labels
plt.xlabel('Day')
plt.ylabel('Tip')
# Adding the legends
plt.show()
```

barchart.py is the file name along with extension that is given to save this progam. To run this program, open PowerShell using Python barchart.py. The output of the program is shown in Fig. 18.41

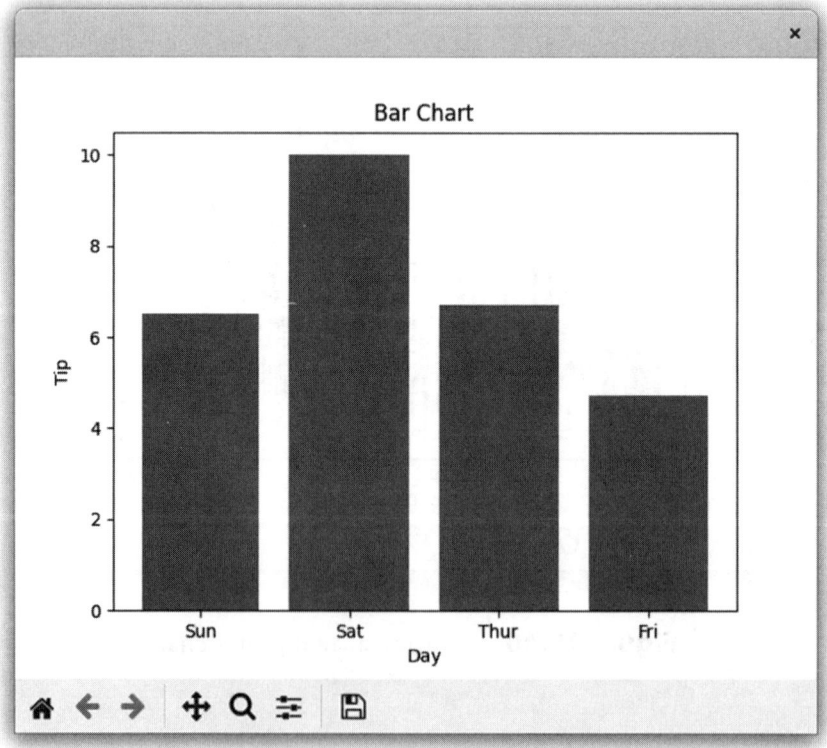

Figure 18.41 Output of the bar chart program

Histogram

A histogram is used to display data in the form of several groupings. It is a particular kind of bar plot where the X-axis shows the bin ranges and the Y-axis provides frequency data. An histogram can be calculated and created using the `hist()` function. When categorical data are passed to a histogram, the frequency of that data is automatically determined. The following program generates a histogram for the tips dataset.

```
import pandas as pd
import matplotlib.pyplot as plt
# reading the database
data = pd.read_csv("tips.csv")
# histogram of total_bills
plt.hist(data['total_bill'])
plt.title("Histogram")
# Adding the legends
plt.show()
```

This program is saved as histogram.py and run by opening the PowerShell using Python histogram.py. Figure 18.42 shows the output of the above program.

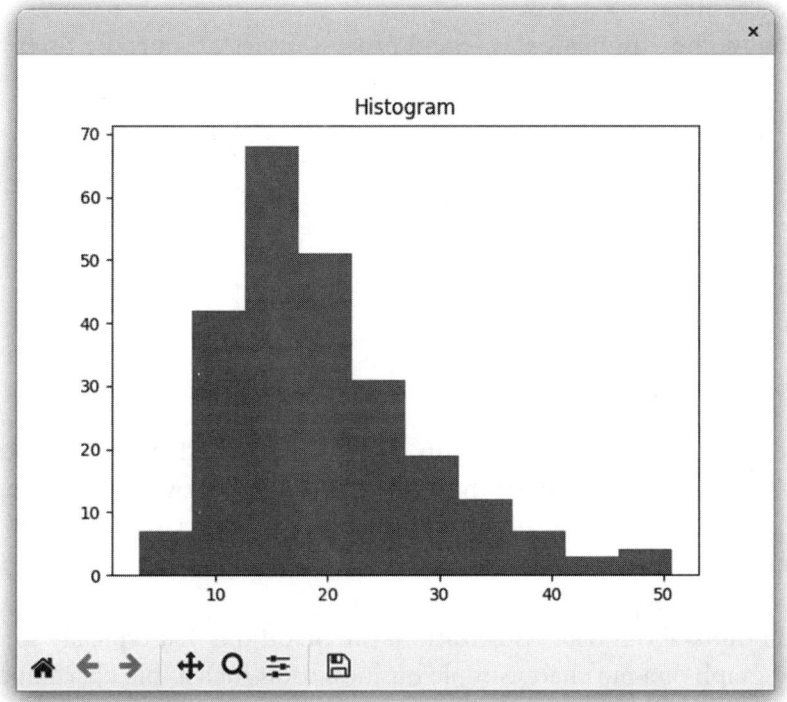

Figure 18.42   Output showing the histogram

SUMMARY

Discussing visualization is important because an image may frequently explain the significance of a given set of data more quickly, effectively, and frequently than words.

Data visualization was primarily used in maps before the 17th century to show resources, cities, roads, and other geographic features. However, better visualizations were required as the need for more precise mapping and physical measurement increased.

For data visualization, this is an exciting and challenging time. The societal concerns related to the invasion of privacy and the possibility of data misuse, both intentionally and unintentionally, are emerging as we learn new ways to gather, aggregate, analyze, and visualize data. As we enter the digital era, it is both exhilarating and unsettling to consider the future implications for individuals and the larger community as a whole.

Big Data visualization goes far beyond the conventional business graphs, histograms, and pie charts to more intricate representations like heat maps and fever charts, allowing decision-makers to study datasets to uncover correlations or unexpected patterns.

Visualization is essential for advanced analytics. For example, it becomes crucial to see the outputs when a data scientist writes advanced predictive analytics or Machine Learning (ML) algorithms to track outcomes and ensure that models operate as planned. This is because sophisticated algorithm visuals are typically more straightforward to understand than numerical results.

Understanding how humans gather and process information is the foundation of data visualization science. Amos Tversky and Daniel Kahn worked together to create two distinct approaches to information collecting and processing.

System 1 concentrates on quick, intuitive, and unconscious mental processes.

This technique is commonly used in daily life and aids with:

- Reading the language on a sign
- Doing simple mathematical problems like adding 2 +2
- Detecting the source from where a sound comes from
- Driving a bicycle
- Distinguishing between colors.

System 2 is concerned with rare, sluggish, logical, calculated thought processing. One of the following situations will need this technique to be followed: Recalling the mobile number of a person, finding the solution for complex mathematical problems like 3450 × 24, identifying the meaning of different signs placed side by side, realizing complex social issues that need cognitive skills.

When you think about data visualization, the first thing that typically springs to mind is a simple bar graph or a pie chart. Simple business tools such as pie charts and histograms, on the other hand, may not necessarily reveal the complete picture. Also, larger, more complicated, and diverse datasets may necessitate more novel display approaches.

Tableau is an excellent business intelligence and data visualization application for reporting on and analyzing massive amounts of data. It was established in 2003 in the

United States. Salesforce acquired Tableau in June 2018. Tableau helps users create a range of graphs, maps, dashboards, and stories to aid in corporate decision-making by visualizing and analyzing data.

EXERCISES

Multiple Choice Questions

1. **This depicts the way how variables can change over some time:**
   A. Line graph
   B. Column chart
   C. Bar chart
   D. Area chart
   Answer: A
   Explanation: A line chart depicts the way how variables can change over time. It is distinguished by a tendency to reflect changes over time or by ordered categories. It should be noted that there should be a minimum of two data records to use a line graph, which can be used to compare trends in a vast volume of data. In addition, it is advised that it should not exceed five polylines in a graph.

2. **The drawback of this chart is that it is suitable only for small and medium-sized data:**
   A. Line graph
   B. Column chart
   C. Bar chart
   D. Area chart
   Answer: B
   Explanation: Since the human eye is sensitive to height disparities, the column chart uses the column's height to reflect the difference in the data. Column charts are used to show a comparison between values and different categories. It should be emphasized that there should not be too many columns. The drawback of the column chart is that it is suitable only for small and medium-sized data.

Short-answer Questions

1. **What is Data Visualization?**
   Data visualization is a form of visual art that captures and holds our attention. The graphic display of information and data is known as data visualization. Information graphics, visualization, and statistical graphics are frequently used interchangeably. Data visualization approaches turn data into images with the help of graphical or pictorial representations.

2. **How is data visualization being used in various fields?**
   The ability to visualize data is crucial for practically every career. Teachers may use it to display the exam results of pupils, computer scientists to improve artificial intelligence (AI), and executives to interact with stakeholders. It is also critical in large data initiatives. Businesses want a mechanism to quickly and easily obtain an overview of their data since they collect massive amounts of data every day.

3. **Describe the features of Tableau.**
   - Tableau's powerful data search and exploration helps its users to find answers for important queries.
   - To use Tableau, a person need not have any prior programming knowledge. Without previous knowledge about Tableau, a new user can use it to construct visualizations.
   - It can link to a number of data sources that are not supported by other BI tools. Users of Tableau can combine and produce reports from many datasets.
4. **Write short notes on Matplotlib.**
   NumPy arrays are the foundation of the user-friendly, low-level data visualization package known as Matplotlib. It includes a number of visualizations, including scatter plots, line plots, and histograms. A lot of flexibility is offered by Matplotlib.

Essay-type Questions

1. Write a short essay on importance of data visualization.
2. How does data visualization work?
3. What are the challenges of Big Data visualization?
4. Write a Python program to draw a bar chart.
5. Write a Python program to draw a scatter chart.

CHAPTER **19**

Business Implementation of Big Data

> **LEARNING OBJECTIVES**
>
> The main objective of this chapter is to discuss the business implementation of Big Data. Big Data Analytics assists businesses in harnessing their data and identifying new possibilities, resulting in wiser company decisions, more effective operations, more profits, and happier consumers. Businesses that combine Big Data with sophisticated analytics benefit in various ways, including cost reduction.

19.1 INTRODUCTION

The rapid growth of linked mobile networks, the Internet of Things, and social networks has resulted in an exponential rise in heterogeneous data collection. As a result, the complexity of semi-structured and unstructured data source channels has increased, ushering in the current digital information era. As the demand grows, and as the rate of data innovation rises, so does the income of Big Data Analytics software. (**Source**: https://www.statista.com/statistics/472934/business-analytics-software-revenue-worldwide).

In addition, the global Big Data and business analytics market size, which was valued at $198.08 billion in 2020, is projected to reach $684.12 billion by 2030, growing at a CAGR of 13.5% from 2021 to 2030. Big Data Analytics is the major part of enterprises as it helps organizations to manage, process, and streamline large datasets in real time while also improving the organization's decision-making capability.(**Source**: Big Data and Business Analytics Market Size, Share | 2030 (alliedmarketresearch.com)).

In 2010, the total amount of information on the globe was nearly two zettabytes, but by 2020, it had risen to 59 zettabytes, and it will continue in the coming decades. The usage of Big Data is on the rise internationally, and enterprises have begun to recognize the relevance of data operations and orchestration to their business performance. The banking industry is the most significant single entity from which data or innovation revenue comes, accounting for nearly 14% of total revenue. Discrete manufacturing comes in second, accounting for over 11.3 percent of total revenue.

Professional services stay at the same level as process manufacturing at 8.2% of total revenue. As the banking industry is the biggest one, identifying the advantages and challenges of data innovation is very essential for every phase. (**Source**: https://assets.researchsquare.com/files/rs-573323/v1/00894662-d20d-4f7c-bcb5-86d9b256f987.pdf?c=1631884261).

19.2 BIG DATA IN BUSINESS

Identifying the type of data you are dealing with is the first step in applying Big Data to a business issue. Structured, unstructured, and semi-structured are the three categories. Customer records and financial transactions are examples of structured data. Social media posts and video recordings are examples of unstructured data. Emails and text messages are examples of semi-structured data.

The second step is to figure out what you want to do with the vast data you have gathered. For example, what business problem do you want to solve with the collected data? For example, it may be used for predictive analytics, which involves predicting the future using previous data.

The third step is to use Big Data to solve the business problem. The data scientist will utilize the information to develop predictions about what may occur in the future. Machine learning algorithms and other statistical approaches can be used to do this. This step aims to look for patterns in the data that may be utilized to forecast future events.

19.2.1 Big Data in Marketing

In recent years, the usage of Big Data in marketing has increased. Companies can now collect and analyze more data than ever before, making more informed decisions regarding their marketing strategy. Customer segmentation, lead creation, and predictive marketing are some of the applications of Big Data.

Customer Segmentation

A seasoned marketer is familiar with customer segmentation. B2B marketers are familiar with segments based on firm size or buying criteria, while marketing for traditional B2C segments based on demographic, psychographic, and behavioral data is taught in introductory college classes. Although these segments have been valuable for decades, the advent of Big Data has given rise to segmentation 2.0. Thanks to a slew of new data sources and enhanced customer segmentation analyses, we are gaining precise facts about audiences worldwide. Marketers may further restrict these client groupings using data obtained from social media, mobile, and other online interactions. Marketers may generate more personalized and targeted information, offers, goods, and services using these smaller groupings or micro-segments. The more significant the potential for actual and meaningful gains, the more direct and tailored a strategy is. While the advantages are apparent, understanding how to leverage Big Data to promote your organization's aims and objectives can be challenging. Fortunately, creativity spreads quickly, and we may learn a lot from others' efforts.

Lead Generation

Big Data is instrumental in generating more and higher quality sales leads. Lead generation has typically been a haphazard and costly affair, but that changes when Big Data is brought in. Big Data analysis turns lead generation into a more structured and predictable process requiring less guesswork and generating more revenue per sales rep. In addition, the ability to quickly collect Big Data sets provides more potential leads. In contrast, AI and Big Data Analytics help identify those leads that are the most likely prospects.

Let us look at how Big Data is affecting lead generation.

Focus on Buyer Personas: You already know who your leads are, but how can you attract more of them? Personas are the only way to target your messaging and lead-generating activities. First, you may use the signup procedure to allow your website to collect information about your customers. It entails gathering consumer information to enrich your database with demographic, social, professional, and interest data. Once you have determined the customer persona, whether it is that of an IT expert, a teen, or a brand manager, you can research what blogs or magazines they read and how you can better support them from a marketing standpoint. This can help you figure out where you should advertise your products and what kind of content/marketing materials you will need to develop.

Personalization in Real-time: Behavioral targeting and product suggestion are two automated ways to give customized information to distinct groups of users on your site. It merely analyzes client search and purchase activity, but it is critical for sending the correct message at the right moment. Such marketing automation platforms like Hubspot and Marketo allow you to personalize your website for visitors in real-time. Then, using the call to action and landing pages, you will be able to identify the needs of each buyer profile and make personalized offers right at the point of contact. Analyze the behavior of leads and consumers to impact the purchase process. This is particularly true in the multi-touch B2B sales process. Along with lead generating, Big Data aids in increasing the efficiency and efficacy of lead creation.

Analyzing client purchasing patterns allows marketers to provide more relevant product suggestions to their customers. An excellent example of a product recommendation is Amazon. Based on your searches, interests, and prior purchase history, it makes better recommendations. Amazon employs market basket analysis (MBA) for cross-selling when it suggests a product. MBA is the most prevalent marketing strategy for determining which items customers buy together. It aids in recommending a product based on one's purchasing history and the purchasing histories of others who have purchased the same item.

Brand Awareness and Positioning: Consumers increasingly demand to view the things they previously bought, both in the real and online worlds. They want merchants and other organizations to deliver the goods they want at the right price, via the right channel, and with a personalized and consistent experience. Another way Big Data may influence marketing is through brand awareness. By giving different categorizations and groupings, Big Data makes it easier to position a brand or product. Data about a brand's growth and client base may assist firms in establishing their brand in the market among the appropriate people. This is the most well-known marketing technique, similar to distinction. Knowing why your brand is famous with which client base may assist in establishing the niche as well as developing a plan that reflects the brand while also attracting the attention of additional customers.

Customer Management: Emphasize centralization, considering cross-channel customer data's fast-paced, fragmented nature. This not only makes your customers' activities and preferences more visible, but also helps you identify your most valuable consumers and populate your backend data with accurate information. This method enables a deeper comprehension to deliver the appropriate message. Once you have figured out how to synthesize it, you can quickly assess the customer's needs – what they are likely to purchase in the future.

Customer engagement, or how customers perceive and interact with your brand, is critical for your marketing activities. Big Data Analytics gives you the insights to make reasonable changes, such as upgrading existing products or boosting revenue per client. Brand awareness is another way Big Data may affect marketing. According to Aberdeen Group's Data-Driven Retail research, "data-driven merchants have a larger yearly rise in brand awareness by 2.7 times (19.1 percent vs. 7.4 percent) when compared to all others." The 360-degree picture provided by Big Data allows marketers to provide customer-specific information when and where it is most successful, improving brand recognition and recall, whether it is online or in-store. Improved customer acquisition is another key benefit of Big Data in marketing. According to a McKinsey study, "intensive users of consumer analytics are 23 times more likely to decisively beat their rivals in terms of new customer acquisition".

Predictive Marketing

Until recently, data analysis was limited to a review of historical performance. While looking back is beneficial, a foresight to what may occur in the future is much better. Using AI and other technologies to collect and evaluate massive data allows for proper predictive analysis. This aids in identifying market possibilities, consumer demands, and new customers and creating timely content and goods for your customers. Big Data and predictive analytics allow you to predict real-world outcomes and take preventive steps.

Uplift modeling: You may better anticipate a lead's behavior based on your gathered data. As a result, you can utilize Uplift Modeling to attract leads with similar demands, anticipate buying obstacles and create solutions to boost the possibility of a sale. For example, use the market basket strategy to mix products/services your target clients prefer to buy together. This will attract and convert leads into clients quickly.

Price fixation: Big Data may give firms information about rivals' prices and inflation rates over time and assist them in understanding the buying power of brand customers so that they can adhere to it without losing money. Although the marketing department does not have direct power over price regulation, they can give suggestions to explain the company's product prices. Furthermore, data on altered pricing can assist the organization in developing the future to clear old product stockpiles during sales or make appropriate price decisions for new items that are expected to be released in the market.

How the Cloud Is Driving Big Data for Marketing

The cloud enables data collection and analysis from various sources, including the web, mobile apps, email, live chat, and even in-store encounters. In cloud computing environments, Big Data may assist marketers in using real-time data. Big Data's ability to receive and analyze real-time data precisely enough to take immediate and effective action is unrivaled by any other technology. This is critical when analyzing GPS, IoT sensors, website visitors, or other real-time data.

It is not easy to foresee successful Big Data solutions in any business without cloud computing. Without the on-demand, self-service, pooled resource, and elastic qualities of cloud computing, it will be impossible to satisfy Big Data's need for computing power and data storage. Beyond these fundamental traits, cloud computing developments continue to assist Big Data marketing endeavors.

Cloud computing, like Big Data, makes virtual machines and containers easier to employ. This allows for workload mobility that would not have been achievable without the cloud. It will enable marketing teams to change workloads, avoid vendor lock-in, cut expenses, and develop innovative solutions that are not possible with physical infrastructure.

In addition to the inherent benefits of cloud technology, cloud service providers such as AWS, Azure, and Google Cloud offer vast markets that make buying, installing, and using Big Data marketing solutions simple. While the "one-click" ease sometimes advertised may be exaggerated, many of these technologies may be up and operating in minutes.

Challenges in Implementing Big Data in Marketing

There is data everywhere. You deal with massive amounts of consumer, operational, and financial data. However, more data is not always better; it must be the appropriate data. Therefore, we should know how to employ analytical instruments. As Big Data expands, so does the amount of time available to make judgments and act on them. Which analytical tools can help you gather and evaluate data and distribute important insights and choices throughout the organization? We need to understand how to get from data to insight to action. How do you transform data into knowledge, once you have it? And how can you put that knowledge to good use in your marketing campaigns?

19.2.2 Big Data in Banking Sector

Big Data enables consumer self-service, one of the essential benefits of banking digitalization. Personal and on-site client-bank communications are no longer necessary. Instead, most banks can obtain all required information on a potential or present client using the tools of Big Data, including that on spending habits, risk profiles, personalization efforts, and motivations for online comments. Big Data analysis allows all of this and more to be extracted from a trove of financial data for each consumer, resulting in a thorough picture of the sector.

Big Data in the banking sector can mainly be used for fraud detection and improving customer contentment.

Fraud Detection

Banks can identify fraud even before it occurs by analyzing data and using statistical computing. Our data is now more exposed to cyber threats than ever before, and it is the most significant problem that a bank confronts. With unique fraud detection algorithms that track and calculate spending and other behavioral patterns, it is possible to recognize and evaluate if a person is on the verge of financial collapse and is lured to defraud banking institutions. Big Data fraud detection is a cutting-edge method of detecting and preventing suspicious conduct by analyzing consumer trends. Even little variations in a consumer's transactions or credit behavior might be evaluated and highlighted as possible fraud. Detecting fraud using data analytics needs specialist expertise and computer resources, but it is now easier than ever, thanks to advances in programming languages and server technology. Organizations may now identify scams before they can be carried out using Big Data Analytics and Machine Learning Algorithms. This is accomplished by recognizing the user's unusual spending habits and forecasting the user's unusual behaviors. Retail banks, investment banks, NBFCs, private equity firms, and other financial institutions have a specialized risk management department that depends on Big Data and Business Intelligence technologies.

Big Data has enabled banks to employ real-time analytics on a broad scale to combat the expanding dangers. For example, banks leverage data mining fraud detection approaches that identify known and novel fraud incidents in real-time, with better accuracy, using distributed Hadoop-based systems that make it feasible to store and analyze enormous datasets cost-effectively and efficiently. (**Source**: https://www.ijera.com/papers/vol11no4/Series-2/A1104020105.pdf).

Fraud costs are increasing more than risk management spending. Financial institutions face a significant threat from fraud, a multi-structured and multi-layered issue. Financial fraud is becoming more complicated and faster, necessitating more robust and more effective protection systems with vital machine learning, data analytics, and predictive capabilities. Financial fraud may be effectively mitigated to assist banks in securing their clients, workers, and reputation while also improving the financial system's resilience. (**Source**: https://assets.kpmg/content/dam/kpmg/xx/pdf/2019/05/global-banking-fraud-survey.pdf).

When correctly implemented as part of a corporation's strategy and operations, the compliance department's technology and data analytics enablement are critical investments in the compliance journey to reduce money and increase performance. (**Source**: https://assets.kpmg/content/dam/kpmg/pa/pdf/compliance-journey-survey-2017.pdf).

Danske Bank, a Nordic financial services leader, collaborated with Think Big Analytics, a Teradata company, to develop and launch a cutting-edge, AI-driven fraud detection platform. The system analyzes tens of thousands of latent variables in real-time, rating millions of online banking transactions to offer actionable information on actual and false fraudulent behavior. As a result, Danske Bank enhanced its overall efficiency and is now prepared for huge savings by drastically decreasing the cost of reviewing false positives. (**Source**: https://www.teradata.com/Press-Releases/2017/Danske-Bank-and-Teradata-Implement-AI).

Customer Contentment

Customer contentment is one of the most important aspects of any organization. Client contentment levels distinguish one bank from another in the commercial banking industry; hence assessing customer contentment is critical. One of the most critical challenges is assuring client satisfaction. Customer retention is crucial for financial organizations, from maintaining the security of their transactions to offering them the most relevant and valuable offers. The information they gather from their clients is now more valuable than ever. Analyzing their clients' data based on several characteristics allows businesses to target their consumers better. Big Data offers the key to unleashing marketing possibilities in the present, highly competitive financial sector. Banks are using advanced analytics to control the total cost of compliance and the risk of non-compliance. However, financial services organizations are still falling behind in using Big Data analysis technologies, indicating that the banking industry has to untap their value creation potential.

Financial businesses acquire data as it is necessary and lucrative to them as anything else. The amount of data created and consumed will only increase as more people generate and consume it. As more industries use Big Data analysis tools, the amount of data generated will grow, and so will its profitability. Financial institutions have realized the worth of their data and are using it. For them, data is like second money. The backbone of the industry's online financial revolution has been Big Data Analytics. Every day, banks discover new methods to use the potential of Big Data Analytics in banking, a journey fueled by technological innovation. Big Data Analytics has now enabled them to save millions, which was unthinkable before.

19.2.3 Big Data in Healthcare Sector

Big Data enables healthcare practitioners and managers to delve deeper into their patients' histories and the treatment they deliver. According to market research, by 2030, the big worldwide data in the healthcare market will be worth $105.73 billion, growing at a compound annual growth rate (CAGR) of 13.85 percent from 2022 to 2030. According to McKinsey, implementing Big Data Analytics successfully in the US healthcare business may generate over $300 billion in annual value. Reduced healthcare spending will account for two-thirds of this benefit.

Public and private entities use three major types of data to market healthcare products and services: health survey data, information about general consumption patterns, and administrative data generated by the healthcare delivery system.

The three critical types of Big Data Analytics capabilities in healthcare, like in many other businesses, are descriptive, predictive, and prescriptive. By monitoring the rate of positive tests in a specific group over time, descriptive analytics may be used to assess how infectious a virus is. Clinicians, healthcare organizations, and health insurance companies utilize predictive analytics to estimate their patients' chances of particular medical illnesses, including heart disease, diabetes, stroke, or COPD. Prescriptive analytics helps healthcare decision-makers improve business outcomes by advising patients or providers on the optimal course of action. They also allow for comparing several "what if" situations to determine the impact of taking one action over another.

Precision diagnosis: Big Data's ability to aggregate information about human health from a range of sources will enable healthcare specialists to be more exact when diagnosing and treating patients, and thus provide a significant impetus to quality healthcare. It aids in the prevention of avoidable illnesses by diagnosing them early on and providing treatment that is more accessible and effective. Patients can receive evidence-based treatment recommended based on previous medical outcomes. In the healthcare business, wearable gadgets and sensors have been launched, which may transmit real-time data to a patient's electronic health record. Apple is one such technology. Apple has created Apple HealthKit, Apple CareKit, and Apple ResearchKit. The primary purpose is to provide iPhone users with the ability to save and retrieve real-time health information on their devices. IoT and Big Data Analytics support tracking of the user's health record. For example, it is used in gadgets monitoring a patient's sleep, exercise, distance walked, or heart rate and blood pressure. Big Data Analytics is also used in pulse oximeters, glucose monitors, and other similar devices.

Cost savings: Big Data lowers treatment costs because it lowers the odds of being subjected to unneeded diagnosis. It aids in predicting epidemic outbreaks and determining what preventive steps may be done to mitigate their consequences. Big Data Analytics in healthcare may also be integrated into predictive analytics software to forecast medical occurrences and enhance patient care quality. Telemedicine lowers the cost of care by reducing hospital admissions, which benefits both the patient and the medical practice. According to a McKinsey report on Big Data in Healthcare, an integrated system has saved an estimated $1.0 billion in fewer office visits and lab testing. A centralized database of electronic patient records would save hospitals and healthcare facilities, much money.

Reduced time to develop a product: Big Data may help product development by lowering the time it takes to design a product or process and bring it to the market. It may also reduce operating expenses, enhance patient outcomes, and encourage innovation.

Reduced patient wait times: Clinical data analytics aims to reduce patient wait times through improved scheduling and staffing, giving patients more options when scheduling appointments and receiving treatment, and lowering re-admission rates by using population health data to predict which patients are most at risk.

Challenges: Capturing data for healthcare companies is a big challenge for Big Data due to a lack of appropriate data governance policies. The data must be clean, precise, and structured adequately to be utilized across several healthcare systems to be more effective.

19.2.4 Big Data in Education Sector

By 2030, the worldwide Big Data Analytics market will reach $57.14 billion, with a CAGR of 15.3 percent. Big Data Analytics is a way businesses study vast amounts of data to extract relevant information such as market trends, client preferences, hidden patterns, and other undiscovered truths that might help them make better decisions. In addition, academic achievement, teacher effectiveness, organizational outreach, and technological efficiency are areas where Big Data changes how schools analyze data and make choices.

Students' performance data, demographic data such as age, ethnicity, and gender, program data such as whether students are full-time or part-time; whether they take classes online, on-campus, or a combination of the two, and perception data are all examples of data that can be used as the data source for the analysis. We can target the correct students, understand their needs, improve the grading system, improve educational quality, monitor students' progress and career paths, and discover the reasons for which they abandon school, by recognizing patterns.

Target the appropriate students: Higher education professionals may use Big Data and analytics to evaluate variables like academic background and geographic location to forecast which prospective students are more likely to enroll once they've been admitted into a program of study. With the introduction of data analytics in the educational sector, institutions may more accurately forecast the type of candidates and study the elements that might influence the application process. Such in-depth understanding may enable educational institutions to adjust their candidate recruiting and funding strategies to accommodate overseas students.

Understanding students' requirements: Data analytics may help EdTech organizations better understand their students' needs by offering insights into how students learn and act. This can assist businesses in developing goods and services that are more likely to suit the wants of their customers. For example, some students learn by just reading, while others may learn better by writing it down, or by watching videos, or through various other means. However, a student must conform to a predetermined structure, which may be incompatible with his preferred learning style, obstructing his development.

Enhanced grading system: Because Big Data is crucial in education, schools may use it to track their students' performance across several disciplines, both individually and collectively, and design suitable solutions to aid their advancement.

Educational quality: Using real-time data, Big Data Analytics helps educational institutions enhance the efficiency of their business operations and facilitate student involvement. Furthermore, numerous decision-makers employ Big Data Analytics to improve marketing methods and boost educational institutes' decision-making capabilities. As a result, the growing need for data-driven choices to enhance the quality of education enables the use of Big Data in the education market.

Students' progress: Predictive analytics may assist instructors in identifying at-risk students and tracking their development over time, and provide them appropriate support. The instructors can use analytics to pinpoint what factors affect students' performance and design practical solutions. Data analytics can help educators better understand the elements that influence their students' success. With a high degree of confidence, learning analysis technologies can forecast their chances of academic achievement and course completion. Data analytics-driven education programs help organizations and mentors understand a student's academic progress and appraise the student's strengths and weaknesses.

Career path: Statistical analysis of students' grades in various disciplines might aid in better directing them and the implementation of study programs. Based on their performance in many subjects and their areas of interest, teachers will be able to advise pupils on which career path to follow. Choosing a professional path may be difficult for even the most outstanding and most reliable performers. Multiple datasets and surveys may be used to follow students and identify which career pathways and courses they should take based on their preferences. If a child wishes to pursue a career in STEM, for example, a model may be developed to help him or her choose high-school courses. Such models will help children to be better prepared for college. Students who are a little hesitant can also be steered to techniques that will help them find their way.

Why do students quit learning: Data analytics opens up a window into the institutional impediments that cause students to leave or end their higher education journeys and also into the institutional supports that are most helpful in advancing student success practices.

The key impediments to Data Analytics in Education include a lack of understanding of the benefits of analytics, the lack of a culture of data-driven choices, and the necessity for a promoter or leader to spearhead the analytics project in educational institutions. Aside from these issues, experts believe that a lack of clarity on privacy laws and inadequate financing also represent substantial obstacles to using data analytics in the education sector.

For extensive data analytics, maintaining data flow is critical. However, accessing data and ensuring data flow is challenging due to inadequate internet connectivity and poorly linked data systems. As a result, using low-quality, poorly structured data for educational analytics will be unproductive.

Another critical and time-consuming obstacle to using Big Data in education is educating and training educators. However, even securing the cooperation and enthusiasm of all instructors and mentors is a significant achievement.

19.3 SECURITY IN BIG DATA

Data is increasingly gaining traction as one of a company's most valuable assets. However, data's increasing relevance and volume have generated a new problem: standard analytic approaches cannot manage it. As a result, the challenge was overcome by developing a new paradigm: Big Data. Organizations have expedited the flow of data for real-time insights and improved decision-making using a variety of sophisticated infrastructure. However, Big Data poses several security threats that might harm businesses. Data breaches might occur if security precautions are not implemented while storing and processing Big Data. While companies must make data more accessible, controlling Big Data is also essential for maintaining customer confidence.

Big Data security refers to the tools and policies to protect data and analytical operations. Big Data security helps secure valuable data against assaults, thefts, and other destructive acts. Companies that use the cloud confront a variety of Big Data security problems. This includes online data theft, ransomware, and distributed denial-of-service (DDoS) assaults that can bring down a system. These risks can have substantial financial consequences for a company, including losses, legal expenses, and penalties or punishments. The aim of Big Data security is simple: keep unauthorized users and intrusions out through firewalls, robust user authentication, end-user training, and intrusion protection and detection technologies. If someone requires access to your data, encrypt it in transit and at rest. Big Data protection technologies must work during three data phases in large data settings, adding another security layer. These data phases are: data ingress (what comes in), stored data (what is saved), and data output (what goes out to apps and reports).

Big Data – Key Security Issues

1. Access controls
2. Endpoint vulnerabilities
3. Data mining solutions
4. Data storage
5. Fake data
6. Lack of security spending
7. Lack of security audits
8. Data cleansing problems
9. Employee theft

19.3.1 User Access Control

The following are four significant challenges to access control: Confidentiality, Integrity, Availability, and Non-Repudiation (CIAR).

Confidentiality: It guarantees that information is only shared with those who need to know. According to confidentiality, any sensitive information should only be shared with a small number of authorized persons. For instance, your credit rating and reputation might soon be ruined if your credit card information and transaction data are shared with unauthorized people (say, hackers). Likewise, a user's transactions with a bank are deemed secure if only the concerned users have access to it; supervisors inside the bank would have some access, subject to acceptable constraints established by local laws.

Integrity: Data integrity refers to the confidence that information is correct and complete. Integrity refers to the prevention of data manipulation. In a nutshell, data integrity relates to its dependability and trustworthiness. It entails maintaining and ensuring the accuracy and consistency of data over its entire life cycle.

Availability: The assurance that the system will be operational when needed. It entails ensuring that individuals who rely on accurate and honest data, have access to it. Ethics and accessibility are related. It may also include a cyberattack, blocking individuals from accessing specific servers or even the entire network.

Non-Repudiation: The assurance that parties will not be able to dispute their involvement in a transaction. We must be able to show that this individual and the nonce created the information, once it is entered into the system.

Companies can assure data integrity while simultaneously protecting data privacy by limiting which data individuals may access or alter. However, controlling access is difficult, especially in more prominent organizations with thousands of employees. User Access Control allows businesses to provide employees, contractors, and third parties access to company data while protecting security, privacy, and compliance. Organizations must have automated robust user access control. Complex user control levels are managed by automation control, which covers the Big Data platform from an inside assault. Access to sensitive data, such as medical records, including personal information, is sometimes restricted by companies. Granular access is a standard option in many businesses. This implies that people can only see and access the information they need. Granular access is not possible with Big Data technology. Copying essential data to a separate large data warehouse is one approach. For example, while accessing data for medical research, just the medical information is copied, not the patient names and addresses.

The transition from on-premise systems to cloud-based services has made dealing with Identity Access Management easier (IAM). IAM is in charge of data flow control through identity, authentication, and authorization. Following relevant ISO standards is an excellent place to ensure that enterprises follow optimal IAM practices.

Vulnerabilities on endpoint devices: Cybercriminals can alter data on endpoint devices and transfer it to data lakes as fictitious data. Endpoint log analysis security solutions must check the endpoints' validity. Hackers can access industrial systems that use sensors to detect process faults. Fraud detection tools are typically used to address such issues. Integrity and reactive security cover all methods, procedures, and documentation relevant to End Point validation and filtering. It also offers real-time security monitoring, including incident response and data forensics.

Data mining solutions: The core of many Big Data settings is data mining. In unstructured data, data mining techniques look for patterns. The issue is that data frequently incorporates personal and financial data. As a result, businesses must add additional security layers to defend themselves from both external and internal dangers.

Data storage: Businesses use Cloud Data Storage to migrate their data and speed up their operations effortlessly. With security difficulties, however, the hazards are multiplied. Even the tiniest oversight in data access management may allow anyone to gain access to a wealth of critical information. As a result, major IT firms choose both on-premise and cloud data storage for security and flexibility. While mission-critical data can be hosted on-premise, less-sensitive data is saved on the cloud for ease of access. However, companies require cybersecurity experts to implement security policies in on-premise databases. Although it increases the cost of managing data in on-premise databases, companies must not take security risks for granted by storing their entire data on the cloud.

Fake data: The production of bogus data is one of the most severe security challenges confronting Big Data today. You can pick the best sort of data processing and apply a range of security measures. However, if you cannot recognize fake data stored within your central repository, you will be exposed to substantial risks that compromise your capacity to secure client data. False flags for false data may also be used to drive inefficient activities that may result in decreased output or restrict other essential business operations. One approach to avoid this is for businesses to be skeptical of the data they are using to improve their business operations. Validating data sources with periodic evaluations and evaluating Machine Learning models with varied test datasets to discover anomalies is an appropriate strategy.

Lack of security spending: Even though significant data security risks have become more visible and dangerous over time, investment in data protection has not seen a proportionate increase. For example, although it was predicted that IT executives would raise spending in this area, average spending remains below what cybersecurity experts suggest for good protection. Data and cybersecurity should account for about 10% of a company's IT expenditure. Unfortunately, there are more breaches every year, and as we uncover new ways to combat these issues, criminals continue to enhance their infiltration tactics. If you do not devote the necessary resources to tackling the problems, preserving your data may become difficult.

Lack of security audits: One of the most severe problems with Big Data security is the failure to conduct proper audits. These audits should be performed regularly to discover security flaws that might endanger a business. Unfortunately, due to a lack of time, money, clarity on security requirements, and skilled employees, this critical work is sometimes postponed or overlooked entirely. Security audits must be conducted on a monthly or quarterly basis. However, they can also be carried out on a department-by-department basis if a company-wide audit would cause significant disruption. According to Forbes, data gathered during an audit may also be in danger; thus, this procedure must be carried out correctly.

Data cleansing problems: When automatic cleaners are used, it becomes clear that Big Data security problems aren't necessarily linked to breaches. Your company may pick from various data cleansing solutions, both manual and automated. However, if an automated data cleansing procedure is based on a defective model, related data properties might be inconsistent. Another significant disadvantage of automated cleaners is that data management people may get complacent. This can lower the quality of your database and also raise the risk of security breaches. Security complacency is one of the significant causes of data breaches worldwide.

Employee theft: Every employee now has access to a certain amount of vital company data thanks to the advancement of data culture. While it promotes data democratization, it also raises the possibility of an employee mistakenly exposing critical information. Employee theft is common in both large and small software organizations. Companies must create legal procedures and secure the network with a virtual private network to prevent employee theft. Furthermore, businesses may utilize Desktop-as-a-Service (DaaS) to eliminate the functionality of data saved on local storage. Data loss by employees is not always unintentional. More than 70% of leaving employees admit to stealing data from the organization. Even more upsetting is that most intellectual property theft by former workers occurs within three months of their notice of departure. This might put your trade secrets, such as customer and staff list, at risk.

Best practices for Big Data security: Create a culture of security and responsibility. Ensure that policies and procedures are appropriately communicated to employees. Implement a disciplinary procedure and make sure employees are aware that they are being watched. Examine your most important information and who has access to it. When an employee leaves, immediately disable their physical access to your network. Implement multiple-layer authentication.

Given the risks mentioned above, it is easy to see why businesses are concerned about Big Data Security. However, many of these issues may be quickly resolved with the correct information, resources, educated workers, a clear coping plan, and a commitment to data integrity and privacy. Businesses will be able to achieve their ultimate objective of utilizing data for better customer experience and retention if there are no risks to Big Data.

19.4 BIG DATA ON CLOUD

The Cloud architecture successfully enables storage, real-time processing, and Big Data analysis at scale and swiftly; therefore, Big Data and Cloud Data are mutually beneficial. Cloud computing stores and analyzes data in the cloud and allows access to distant IT services without installing any IT infrastructure. The fundamental characteristics of cloud computing include on-demand availability of IT resources, extensive network access, resource pooling, flexibility, and measurable service. The internet is utilized to obtain cloud-based services from various cloud providers. Cloud computing's issues include availability, transformation, security concerns, and billing models. Cloud computing is a technique for storing data and information on remote servers and processing it utilizing remote infrastructure. Amazon Web Service (AWS), Microsoft Azure, Google Cloud

Platform, IBM Cloud Services, and other cloud computing manufacturers provide cloud computing services.

Some of the advantages of using cloud computing for Big Data are Elastic scalability, Lower upfront cost, Easy implementation, Easy data experimentation, and Built-in data management tools.

Elastic scalability: The most significant advantage of adopting Cloud storage for Big Data is scalability. Cloud storage may be purchased on a pay-per-use basis. Big Data is also a driving force behind cloud application development. There would be fewer cloud-based apps without Big Data since there would be no genuine need. The existence of Cloud Computing services is mainly due to Big Data. Cloud collects Big Data only because we have services that can take it in and interpret it in seconds. As a result, they are perfect partners because none of them would exist without the other!

Lower upfront cost: We require extensive equipment to handle large data, and the cost grows proportionately with the size of the data. On the other hand, Big Data is built on parallelized architectures that develop linearly and elastically while leveraging pay-per-use and on-demand access mechanisms on the cloud. Data kept in a cloud-based database may aid decision-making processes for enterprises. Thanks to cloud-based Big Data, analysts have more data to work with and the processing ability to handle massive quantities of records with many properties. This has the potential to boost predictability. Big Data has found the public cloud to be an attractive platform. A cloud provides on-demand resources and services, and the firm does not have to construct, own, or operate the infrastructure. As a result, the cloud makes Big Data technology available and inexpensive to businesses.

IaaS as a public cloud: Using a cloud provider's infrastructure for Big Data services provides you access to nearly infinite storage and computation capacity. Enterprise clients may use IaaS to construct cost-effective and scalable IT solutions by letting cloud providers handle the complexities and costs of operating the underlying infrastructure. For example, suppose a client wants to increase his/her company size. He/she can then use the cloud resource as needed rather than purchasing, installing, and integrating hardware.

PaaS as a private cloud: PaaS suppliers are starting to include Big Data technologies like Hadoop and MapReduce into their PaaS services, removing the difficulties of managing independent software and hardware components. Individual PaaS environments, for example, may be used by web developers at every step of development, testing, and hosting. Businesses that build their internal software, on the other hand, can use Platform-as-a-Service to create separate development and testing environments.

SaaS in a hybrid cloud: Many businesses believe they must monitor client feedback, particularly on social media. SaaS suppliers provide the framework for the research and the social media data. The finest example of a firm that uses SaaS is Office software. Accounting, sales, invoicing, and planning tasks may all be completed with SaaS. Businesses may choose to employ one piece of software to handle all of these duties or numerous pieces of software to handle different jobs.

Easy implementation: The cloud is the "easy button" that takes care of all the problematic aspects of Big Data. A Big Data cluster is difficult to put up, maintain, and protect. Cloud natives can work it out, but it shouldn't be a company's fundamental skill. The cloud provider is in charge of most of this infrastructure. Because of the cloud's potential to democratize IT, the company no longer has to consider Big Data as a risky research project.

Easy data experimentation: Cloud technologies make data experimentation straightforward. We may attain the most remarkable results when working with straightforward data. Fortunately, cloud-based model management and data pipeline solutions enable data scientists and engineers to create, test, and publish models and connect and track them in a pipeline. To put it another way, the cloud handles the data "plumbing", so you can focus on the insights that will benefit your business.

Built-in data management tools: Data management is aided by the cloud. It would be helpful if you had a single view of your data, including who owns it, who has access to it, what privacy measures are in place, how good it is, and how it interacts with other data. Emerging cloud technologies include: 1. pre-defined industry data models and metadata systems, 2. apps and devices that allow you to see everything from many systems, 3. cloud vendors and even partners in a single logical perspective.

19.5 BEST PRACTICES IN BIG DATA IMPLEMENTATION

1. **What you want to obtain (achieve) from the data (understand the business needs):** Consider your objectives and how they will help you make decisions. What do you think constitutes a successful analytical result? These examples of primary data analysis questions are crucial for guiding you through the process and supporting you in focusing on the most important findings. Begin by thinking broadly and developing guidelines for particular data-related issues. This method can help you acquire more specific information. While it is easy to defend the need for extensive data analysis, it might be daunting to decide on what to undertake initially. When working with data that your business has never utilized before, there are numerous unknowns, such as unstructured data streams from the web. Which data pieces are valuable? What are the most critical measures that data can produce? What are the quality issues? Because of these unknowns, estimating the expenses and time necessary for achieving success can be difficult.

2. **Treat Big Data problem as a scientific experiment:** An experiment is a technique used to test a hypothesis or establish the efficacy or probability of succeeding in something that has never been done before. Experiments reveal cause-and-effect relationships by illustrating what happens when a particular component changes. A scientific problem

is something you don't understand but can learn more about by experimenting. Observation of scientific occurrences is frequently used to solve scientific challenges. The problem statement summarizes the issue that the study will solve.

4. **Decide what data can be included and what can be missed:** All data is not included in every experiment. The selection of data is critical for data analysis. Concentrate on the data that will be used in the experiment. Once you have gathered the data you will need for a project, figure out what further information you will need and where you can get it. For example, suppose you want to use Big Data Analytics in your business to understand your employees' well-being better. In that case, you will need some more information about their stress levels and information like login–logout time, medical reports, and email reports.

5. **Always start small with Big Data:** Starting small is the key to success. It is a low-risk method to evaluate what Big Data can accomplish for your company and determine how ready you are to use it. First, specify a few basic metrics that won't require much time or data to perform. For example, an online merchant may start by tracking the things each consumer looked at so that if they don't buy, the firm can send them a follow-up offer. A few simple instances like these show the company what data can accomplish. More significantly, this method produces simple data to evaluate the level of lift provided by the analytics. It enables a company to demonstrate the value of a significant investment before making one and better understand how to make a Big Data program pay off in the long run. Successful prototypes can make the necessary backing for significant projects more manageable. Best of all, because the data is better understood and the value is partially established, the entire project will be less hazardous. It is also worth noting that the role of preliminary analytics is to advise you to redirect your efforts, if needed, before considerable time and money is wasted.

6. **Involve all parts of the company in a Big Data initiative:** A Big Data project is not a one-person show; it needs the involvement of all business departments to yield substantial value and insight. Big Data, for example, may help organizations make sense of massive volumes of data to get insight into customer behavior, events, trends, and projections, among other things. This cannot be done by using a data snapshot, which only captures a small percentage of the overall volume of data processed in Big Data. As a result, companies increasingly focus on all types of data from all possible avenues/business units to establish the correct pattern.

7. **First, safeguard the data before analyzing the same:** Data security is crucial in Big Data planning. You will have a subset of data that may be used to gain insight. Data security becomes critical at this stage. When processed and fine-tuned, data becomes more valuable to a business. This highly calibrated output data is private and must be safeguarded. As a result, data security must be considered throughout the Big Data life cycle.

8. **Align with Big Data in the cloud:** Because cloud usage is metered, and Big Data entails many data to be processed, you must be cautious when using it. The cloud, on the other hand, offers various advantages. Provisioning and scaling up on the public cloud may be done instantaneously or quickly. Rapid prototyping is possible with services like Amazon EMR and Google BigQuery. You may build up a development and test environment in hours and utilize it for the testing platform by using a data subset and the numerous tools given by cloud providers like Amazon and Microsoft. Then, once you have figured out an excellent operating model, bring it back on site to do the task. Another benefit of the cloud is that much of your information may be stored there. In that case, you have no reason to move the data on-premises. Many databases and Big Data applications support a variety of data sources from both the cloud and on-premises; so if you are collecting data in the cloud, it is better to leave it there.

9. **Learn and improve data quality over time:** You must constantly be aware of your company's data and its use. Check the health of your data regularly to avoid missing any vital but hidden signals. It is critical to have a strategy before introducing any new technology to your business. Companies must use the above-mentioned Big Data methods in conjunction with enough and correct data to extract value.

10. **Focus on the Business Value:** Your IT crew stands to benefit with Big Data initiatives. Almost all technologists want to work with the latest technological platform. On the other hand, Big Data initiatives are time-consuming and sometimes costly. Do not let your Big Data project become an IT vanity project. Focusing on the business value is the first stage in every endeavor. Align the project with a clear commercial objective. Calculate your return on investment (ROI). Treat your data as an asset once the project is completed. Remember that Big Data is a business initiative, not an IT initiative.

11. **Understand the evolution of technologies around Big Data:** You know your company's goals at this stage, and you know what data you have and what data you don't have. But, how can you put your approach into action? First, you must understand what technologies are available and how they might help your firm achieve better results. Next, start to see the significance of technologies like Hadoop, streaming data services, and complicated event-processing software. Different types of databases, such as in-memory and spatial databases should be considered. Finally, learn about the new tools and approaches that are part of the Big Data ecosystem.

12. **Build an Analytics Culture:** A solid Big Data Analytics program should include change management and training. Employees must think about data and analytics while formulating strategy and addressing business challenges to have the most effect. This will necessitate significant changes in how people and firms function. Employee training is also essential, so they understand how to utilize the tools that help them make sense of the data. Remember that the finest Big Data technology is useless if employees cannot efficiently use it.

13. Avoid bad practices
1. Understand the business need and don't apply obsolete or redundant technology.
2. Don't assume Big Data is the solution for all problems.
3. Don't use the solution of one problem to tackle another problem.

14. Other best practices of Big Data Analytics: You don't need to be perfect before starting the process. Think big for future scalability (focus on the future). Understand that there is no one-size-fits-all. Enable people to learn about the latest technologies around Big Data. Have a regular maintenance plan and use In-Memory Processing.

19.6 LATEST TRENDS IN BIG DATA

19.6.1 Big Data Analytics Will Incorporate Artificial Intelligence

AI refers to a machine's capacity to learn to act like a human by analyzing large amounts of data. The term refers to complementary technologies that can collaborate in significant ways. AI thrives on information. The current trend is to enable AI/ML automation, both for consumer-related issues and internal operations, using Big Data. Without the depth and breadth of Big Data, these automated technologies would not have the training data needed to replace human operations in a company. AI systems learn from patterns and characteristics in their study data by combining vast data with sophisticated, repetitive processing methods. Each time an AI system performs a data processing cycle, it evaluates and measures its performance, gaining new knowledge and uncovering patterns and insights. The acquired information assists enterprises in automating and improving decision-making processes, improving data analysis accuracy, and increasing their efficiency and profitability while simultaneously reducing the costs.

19.6.2 The Use of Blockchain for Data Security Will Increase

Blockchain is gaining popularity to assure secure transactions with little effort. The peer network approves transactions directly, eliminating the need for a third party. In addition, it enables users to store encrypted data on a decentralized, safe network. This greatly simplifies data exchange and auditing while also prohibiting illegal access. E-commerce enterprises have used blockchain for online transactions, though blockchain has also found uses in other fields such as healthcare and security. Data volume has grown exponentially because of the Internet of Things (IoT), posing a security risk. Because blockchain is deemed tamper-proof and hacker-proof, it will be an excellent solution to this problem. In addition, blockchain can give IoT devices anonymous digital identities and enable data exchange between them.

19.6.3 The Internet of Things (IoT) Will Drive Streaming Analytics Adoption

The number of gadgets (things) that can connect to the internet is rapidly increasing. IoT is an internet-connected network of physical objects or "things". Wearable technology, household appliances, autos, and industrial equipment are all examples of these items. The number of interconnected devices is predicted to increase rapidly. As a result, the volume of data created will rise as more gadgets become linked to the internet. To evaluate and interpret the data, streaming analytics will be necessary. Rather than just monitoring data storage and transportation, streaming analytics allows IoT data to be examined and decoded as it is collected in real-time, rather than later. This will enable consumers to take necessary action before a situation worsens. Organizations will benefit significantly from IoT and streaming analytics, such as increased responsiveness and agility. Data from various IoT devices, including sensors, mobile devices, and internal transactional systems, streams in real-time and gives historical and real-time information that may be used to diagnose equipment faults and avoid future problems. This Big Data from Edge and IoT devices necessitates streaming data analytics for data storage and movement tracking. An edge device is a device that provides an entry point into the core network of a service provider. In general, edge devices are normally routers that provide authenticated access (most commonly PPPoA and PPPoE) to faster, more efficient backbone networks. Routers, routing switches, and multiplexers are good examples of edge devices.

19.6.4 The Rise of DataOps

DataOps is a technique and practice based on the DevOps framework, commonly used in software development. DataOps is concerned with the end-to-end data flow through a business, whereas DevOps focuses on continuous technical processes surrounding service delivery. This includes eliminating roadblocks that limit data's usefulness or accessibility and deploying third-party "as-a-service" data solutions. Working with DataOps requires no formal training. Because of the role's development, it is a fantastic chance for anybody with IT knowledge or interest who wants to work on the most exciting and creative projects, which are frequently data projects. There is also a rise in the popularity of "DataOps-as-a-Service" suppliers, who provide on-demand, pay-as-you-go administration of data processes and pipelines. This will decrease the entry hurdles for small and startup businesses with brilliant ideas for new data-driven services but lack the infrastructure to make them a reality. (**Source**: https://www.forbes.com/sites/bernardmarr/2021/02/22/the-4-biggest-trends-in-big-data-and-analytics-right-for-2021/?sh=45abce77df8e).

19.6.5 Data-as-a-Service (DaaS)

DaaS isn't new, it is one of Big Data's lesser-known applications. DaaS is a cloud-based data management solution that provides different integration, storage, processing, and analytics services. All of these services are supplied over the internet. It is handy for employees in large companies who wish to transfer enormous amounts of data between departments but are unable to do it because of technological constraints. For example, downloading music and videos via the internet is akin to Data-as-a-Service. In enterprises, this Data-as-a-Service architecture will serve as a central hub that encourages self-service and boosts productivity. Furthermore, because the data is maintained in one location, it is simple to manage.

Data-as-a-Service is gaining traction thanks to Big Data Analytics. If your company has large data that is helpful to the broader public and you are having trouble keeping and managing it, DaaS can be a lifesaver! Some of the attractive advantages of DaaS include: Data access is made straightforward from any device, anywhere; Data source and utilization at a low cost; and Updates and monitoring are made simple. (**Source**: https://www.datatobiz.com/blog/big-data-trends).

19.6.6 Data Mesh

An enterprise data fabric is supported by a data mesh, an architectural approach. It is a comprehensive way to link all data within an organization, regardless of location, and make it available on demand. A data mesh extends a distributed architecture approach by integrating domain-specific data creation and storage information applicable to users across all domains. By treating data as a product, structured and managed by specialists, Data Mesh provides a framework for enterprises to democratize data access and management. A data mesh technique is worth significant attention for the scalability of the data warehouse concept.

19.6.7 Synthetic Data

Synthetic data are used to train machine learning algorithms. Synthetic datasets are computer-generated simulations that provide a diverse and anonymous source of training data. The data is entirely unknown, and it may be generated using various techniques, such as general conflicting networks or simulators, to provide a near likeness to the real thing. AI engineers gain from higher-performing and more robust models using synthetic datasets. Data scientists have discovered efficient techniques for generating high-quality synthetic data, which could aid firms searching for vast volumes of data to train and create AI and machine learning (ML) models in the future.

19.6.8 Empowerment of Self-service Analytics

Businesses are looking for self-service data analytics solutions as the demand for more fact-based everyday decision-making continues to increase. Many of these choices are data-driven, but not every businessperson is a data specialist. Self-service data analytics solutions allow end-users without a technical background or extensive knowledge of data analytics to access data and create or edit reports and analyses. As a result, more companies are projected to use proper self-service solutions, allowing non-technical business users to gain valuable insights from data in a secure manner. In addition, this means that business users will find it easier to upgrade their skills by learning to use and profit from effective analytics and BI systems, which will lead to improved business outcomes. However, this does not mean that data scientists will become obsolete; instead, they will continue to play an essential role in the coming years.

19.6.9 Data Democratization

Data democratization makes data available to all company sections, not only the managerial and IT departments. The essence of digital transformation is data democratization. This concept of comprehending and accessing data regardless of technical ability might lead to new self-service data analytics solutions. This trend has already become visible with low-code solutions. There are several benefits to data democratization. First, customer intent will become more diversified due to data democratization, allowing many departments to study and exploit datasets. Second, data democratization will lead to the widespread use of efficient technologies like AI analytics and cybersecurity software. Third, employees will better understand the data they have access to, which will reduce misunderstanding that may arise in cross-departmental collaboration. Finally, data democratization shows a broader breadth of intent and increased efficiency, improving many firms' customer-experience. For example, having access to preferred contact information and past shopping data would help your support desk employees to customize your client service.

SUMMARY

The exponential expansion of diverse datasets has emerged from the fast development of linked mobile networks, the Internet of Things, and social networks. As a result, the complexity of semi-structured and unstructured data source channels has increased, ushering in the current digital information era.

Identifying the type of data you are dealing with is the first step in applying Big Data to a business issue. The second step is to figure out what you want to do with the vast data you have gathered. The third step is to use Big Data to solve a business problem.

Big Data is instrumental in generating more and higher-quality sales leads. Lead generation has typically been a haphazard and costly affair, but that changes when Big Data is brought in.

Analyzing client purchasing patterns allows marketers to provide more relevant product suggestions to their customers. Another way Big Data may influence marketing is through brand awareness. By allowing for many categorizations and groupings, Big Data makes positioning a brand or product more manageable.

Customer Management

Emphasize centralization, considering cross-channel customer data's fast-paced, fragmented nature.

Customer engagement, or how customers think about and interact with your business, is crucial to your marketing efforts. Big Data Analytics gives you the insights to make reasonable changes, such as upgrading existing products or boosting revenue per client.

Using AI and other technologies to collect and evaluate massive data allows for accurate predictive analysis.

Big Data may give firms information about rivals' prices and inflation rates over time and assist them in understanding the buying power of brand.

Big Data in the banking sector can mainly be used for fraud detection and improving customer contentment. Banks can identify fraud even before it occurs by analyzing data and using statistical computing. By using advanced analytics, banks can also control the total cost of compliance and the risk of non-compliance.

Big Data enables healthcare practitioners and managers to delve deeper into their patients' histories and the treatment they procide.

Public and private entities use three major types of data to market healthcare products and services: health survey data, information about general consumption patterns, and administrative data generated by the healthcare delivery system.

The three critical types of Big Data Analytics capabilities in healthcare, like in many other businesses, are descriptive, predictive, and prescriptive.

Big Data may help product development by lowering the time to design a product or process and bring it to market. It may also reduce operating expenses, enhance patient outcomes, and encourage innovation.

Clinical data analytics aims to reduce patient wait times by improving scheduling and staffing, giving patients more options when scheduling appointments and receiving treatment, and lowering readmission rates by using population health data to predict which patients are most at risk.

Big Data in Education Sector

Higher education professionals may use Big Data and analytics to evaluate variables like academic background and geographic location to forecast which prospective students are more likely to enroll once they've been admitted into a program of study.

Data analytics may help EdTech organizations better understand their students' needs by offering insights into how students learn and act.

Because Big Data is crucial in education, schools may use it to track their students' performance across several disciplines, both individually and collectively, and design suitable solutions to aid their advancement.

Using real-time data, Big Data Analytics helps educational institutions enhance the efficiency of their business operations and facilitate student involvement.

Predictive analytics may assist instructors in identifying at-risk students and tracking their development over time, allowing them to provide the appropriate support and intervention.

Statistical analysis of students' grades in various disciplines might aid in better directing them and implementing study programs. Furthermore, depending on students' performance and their areas of interest, teachers would be able to advise them on their career paths.

Big Data security refers to the tools and policies to protect data and analytical operations. Big Data security helps secure valuable data against assaults, thefts, and other destructive acts.

Big Data – Key Security Issues

1. Access controls
2. Endpoint vulnerabilities
3. Data mining solutions
4. Data storage
5. Fake data
6. Lack of security spending
7. Lack of security audits
8. Data cleansing problems
9. Employee theft

Big Data on Cloud

The Cloud architecture successfully enables storage, real-time processing, and Big Data analysis at scale and swiftly; therefore, Big Data and Cloud Data are mutually beneficial. Cloud computing stores and analyzes data in the cloud and accesses distant IT services without installing any IT infrastructure. The fundamental characteristics of cloud computing include on-demand availability of IT resources, extensive network access, resource pooling, flexibility, and measurable service.

Some of the advantages of using cloud computing for Big Data are elastic scalability, lower upfront cost, easy implementation, easy data experimentation, and built-in data management tools.

Best Practices in Big Data Implementation

- Make sure you know what you want from the data (understand the business needs)
- Treat Big Data problem as a scientific experiment
- Decide what data can be included and what is missing
- Always start small with Big Data
- Do involve all business sections in a Big Data initiative
- First, safeguard the data before analyzing it
- Align with Big Data in the cloud
- Learn and improve the quality of data over the set period
- Focus on the business value
- Understand the evolution of technologies around Big Data
- Build an analytics culture
- Avoid bad practices
  - Understand the business need and don't apply obsolete or redundant technology.
  - Don't assume Big Data is the solution for all problems.
  - Don't use the solution of one problem to tackle another problem.

Latest Trend in Big Data

- Blockchain will be used more for data security.
- Artificial Intelligence will be an integral part of Big Data Analytics.
- The Internet of Things (IoT) will drive streaming analytics.

- Adoption of DataOps, Data-as-a-Service (DaaS). Self-Service Analytics, Data Democratization, Data Mesh, and Synthetic Data Empowerment.

EXERCISES

Multiple Choice Questions

1. **It guarantees that information is only shared with those who need to know:**
   A. Confidentiality
   B. Integrity
   C. Availability
   D. Non-Repudiation

   Answer: A

   Explanation:
   Confidentiality: It guarantees that information is only shared with those who need to know. According to confidentiality, any sensitive information should only be shared with a small number of authorized persons. For instance, your credit rating and reputation might soon be ruined if your credit card information and transaction data were shared with a few other people (say, hackers). Likewise, a user's transactions with a bank are deemed secure only if connected users have access to it; supervisors inside the bank would have some access, subject to acceptable constraints established by local laws.

2. **This refers to the confidence that information is correct and complete:**
   A. Confidentiality
   B. Integrity
   C. Availability
   D. Non-Repudiation

   Answer: B

   Explanation:
   Integrity: Data integrity refers to the confidence that the information is correct and complete. Integrity refers to the prevention of data manipulation. In a nutshell, data integrity relates to the data's dependability and trustworthiness. It entails maintaining and ensuring the accuracy and consistency of data over its entire life cycle.

3. **The assurance that the system will be operational when needed is called as _____.**
   A. Confidentiality
   B. Integrity
   C. Availability
   D. Non-Repudiation

   Answer: C

   Explanation:
   Availability: The assurance that the system will be operational when needed. It entails ensuring that individuals who rely on accurate and honest data have access to it. Ethics and accessibility are related. It may also include a cyberattack, blocking individuals from accessing specific servers or entering the entire network.

Short-answer Questions

1. **How does Big Data help customer segmentation in marketing?**
   Marketers may restrict client groupings using data obtained from social media, mobile, and other online interactions. They may generate more personalized and targeted information, offers, goods, and services using these smaller groupings or micro-segments. The more significant the potential for actual and meaningful gains, the more direct and tailored a strategy is.

2. **How does Big Data help lead generation in marketing?**
   Big Data is instrumental in generating more and higher-quality sales leads. Lead generation has typically been a haphazard and costly affair, but that changes when Big Data is brought in. Big Data analysis turns lead generation into a more structured and predictable process requiring less guesswork and generating more revenue per sales rep. In addition, the ability to quickly collect Big Data sets provides more potential leads. In contrast, AI and Big Data Analytics help identify those leads that are the most likely prospects.

3. **How does Big Data help to build Brand Awareness in marketing?**
   By giving different categorizations and groupings, Big Data makes it easier to position a brand or product. Data about a brand's growth and client base may assist firms in establishing their brand in the market among the appropriate people. This is the most well-known marketing technique, similar to distinction. Knowing why your brand is famous with which client base may assist in establishing the niche as well as developing a plan that reflects the brand while also attracting the attention of additional customers.

4. **What is Customer Management? How does Big Data help to improve it?**
   Customer engagement, or how customers perceive and interact with your brand, is critical for your marketing activities. Big Data Analytics gives you the insights to make reasonable changes, such as upgrading existing products or boosting revenue per client. Brand awareness is another way Big Data may affect marketing. According to Aberdeen Group's Data-Driven Retail research, "data-driven merchants have a larger yearly rise in brand awareness by 2.7 times (20.1 % vs. 7.4 %) when compared to all others". The 360-degree picture provided by Big Data allows marketers to provide customer-specific information when and where it is most successful, improving brand recognition and recall, whether online or in-store.

5. **What is uplift modeling?**
   Uplift modeling: You may better anticipate a lead's behavior based on your gathered data. As a result, you can utilize Uplift Modeling to attract leads with similar demands, anticipate buying obstacles and create solutions to boost the possibility of a sale. For example, use the market basket strategy to mix products/services your target clients may prefer to buy together. This will attract and convert leads into clients quickly.

6. **What are the challenges in implementing Big Data in marketing?**
   There is data everywhere. You deal with massive amounts of consumer, operational, and financial data. However, more data is not always better; it must be the appropriate data. Therefore, we should know how to employ analytical instruments. As Big Data expands, so does the time available to make judgments and act on them. Hence, we need to identify the right analytical tools that can help us gather and evaluate data and distribute important insights and choices throughout the organization. We need to understand how to gather insights from data and put that knowledge to good use in our marketing campaigns.

7. **How does Big Data help in fraud detection in banking sector?**
   Banks can identify fraud even before it can occur by analyzing data and using statistical computing. Our data is now more exposed to cyber threats than ever before, and it is the most significant problem that a bank confronts. With unique fraud detection algorithms that track and calculate spending and other behavioral patterns, it is possible to recognize and evaluate if a person is on the verge of financial collapse and is lured to defraud banking institutions. Big Data fraud detection is a cutting-edge method of detecting and preventing suspicious conduct by analyzing consumer trends. Even little variations in a consumer's transactions or credit behavior might be evaluated and highlighted as possible fraud.

8. **What are the types of data used by public and private entities to market healthcare products and services?**
   Public and private entities use three major types of data to market healthcare products and services: health survey data, information about general consumption patterns, and administrative data generated by the healthcare delivery system.

9. **How does Big Data help in precision diagnosis in the healthcare sector?**
   Precision diagnosis: Big Data's ability to aggregate information about human health from a range of sources will enable healthcare specialists to be more exact when diagnosing and treating patients. It aids in the prevention of avoidable illnesses by discovering them early on, and keeps the existing medical conditions from worsening, by making therapy more accessible and more effective. Patients can receive evidence-based treatment discovered and recommended based on previous medical outcomes. In the healthcare business, wearable gadgets and sensors have been launched that may transmit real-time data to a patient's electronic health record.

10. **Write short notes on Big Data security.**
    Big Data security refers to the tools and policies to protect data and analytical operations. Big Data security helps secure valuable data against assaults, thefts, and other destructive acts. Companies that use the cloud face a variety of Big Data security problems. This includes online data theft, ransomware, and DDoS assaults that can bring down a system. These risks can have substantial financial consequences for a company, including losses, legal expenses, and penalties or punishments. The aim

of Big Data security is simple: keep unauthorized users and intrusions out through firewalls, robust user authentication, end-user training, and intrusion protection and detection technologies. If someone requires access to your data, encrypt it in transit and at rest. Big Data protection technologies must work during three data phases in large data settings, adding another security layer: data ingress (what comes in), stored data (what is saved), and data output (what goes out to apps and reports).

11. **List down a few key Big Data security issues.**
    1. Access controls
    2. Endpoint vulnerabilities
    3. Data mining solutions
    4. Data storage
    5. Fake data
    6. Lack of security spending
    7. Lack of security audits
    8. Data cleansing problems
    9. Employee theft

12. **What is employee theft?**
    Employee Theft: Every employee now has access to a certain amount of vital company data thanks to the advancement of data culture. While it promotes data democratization, it also raises the possibility of an employee mistakenly exposing critical information. Employee theft is common in both large and small software organizations. Companies must create legal procedures and secure the network with a virtual private network to prevent employee theft. Furthermore, businesses may utilize Desktop-as-a-Service (DaaS) to eliminate the functionality of data saved on local storage. Data loss by employees is not always unintentional. More than 70% of leaving employees admit to stealing data from the organization. Even more upsetting is that most intellectual property theft by former workers occurs within three months of their notice of departure. This might put your trade secrets, such as customer and staff lists at risk.

13. **What are the advantages of using cloud computing for Big Data?**
    Some of the advantages of using cloud computing for Big Data are elastic scalability, lower upfront cost, easy implementation, easy data experimentation, and built-in data management tools.

14. **List down any two best practices in Big Data implementation.**
    1. What you want to obtain (achieve) from the data (understand the business needs): Consider your objectives and how they will help you make decisions. What do you think constitutes a successful analytical result? These examples of primary data analysis questions are crucial for guiding you through the process and supporting you in focusing on the most important findings. Begin by thinking broadly and developing guidelines for particular data-related issues. This method can help you acquire more specific information. While it is easy to defend the need for extensive data analysis, it might be daunting to decide on what to undertake initially. When working with data that your business has never utilized before, there are numerous unknowns, such as unstructured data streams from the web. Which data pieces are

valuable? What are the most critical measures that data can produce? What are the quality issues? Because of these unknowns, estimating the expenses and time necessary for achieving success can be difficult.

2. Treat Big Data problem as a scientific experiment: An experiment is a technique used to test a hypothesis or establish the efficacy or probability of succeeding in something that has never been done before. Experiments reveal cause-and-effect relationships by illustrating what happens when a particular component changes. A scientific problem is something you don't understand but can learn more about by experimenting. Observation of scientific occurrences is frequently used to solve scientific challenges. The problem statement summarizes the issue that the study will solve.

Essay-type Questions

1. Write an essay on usages of Big Data in the field of marketing.
2. How is the cloud driving Big Data for marketing?
3. Write an essay on usages of Big Data in the banking sector.
4. Write an essay on usages of Big Data in healthcare sector.
5. Write an essay on usages of Big Data in education sector.
6. Write an essay on security in Big Data and discuss any five Big Data security issues.
7. Write an essay on Big Data on Cloud.
8. Discuss any five best practices in Big Data implementation.
9. Discuss any five latest trends in Big Data.

CHAPTER **20**

Limitations of Hadoop and Solutions to Overcome Them

LEARNING OBJECTIVES

Although Hadoop is the most powerful Big Data tool, it has several drawbacks, including the inability to handle tiny files, the inability to handle live data reliably, the poor processing speed, the inefficiency of repetitive processing, and the inefficiency of caching. In this chapter, we shall look at the disadvantages of Hadoop that led to the creation of Apache Spark and Apache Flink and discuss several approaches used to overcome Hadoop's shortcomings.

20.1 Introduction

Hadoop is a powerful Big Data tool, but it also has several limitations. It is not suitable to handle small files. Also, it cannot reliably handle live data and has poor processing speed. MapReduce cannot cache results; instead, it retrieves data from HDFS and writes outputs back to the HDFS at both Map and Reduce stages of processing.

20.2 Problem with Small Files

Hadoop's fundamental flaw is that it is not designed for small datasets. Because of its large capacity architecture, the Hadoop distributed file system (HDFS) cannot efficiently support the random reading of small files. The size of a small file is much smaller than the size of an HDFS block (default 128MB). HDFS cannot manage many little files since it is designed to deal with a small number of large files for storing massive datasets rather than a large number of small files. Because it holds the HDFS namespace, the NameNode will get overloaded if there are too many small files. Each file, directory, and block in NameNode's memory takes up a memory element. As a rule of thumb, this memory element is around 150 bytes per file. So, if you have a hundred million files, each of which uses a block, you will need 13.9 GB of RAM. With existing hardware, scaling beyond this point is impossible. Also, in Hadoop, retrieving tiny files is inefficient. It causes numerous disks to search and hop from one data node to another at the backend and this takes a long time.

Solution

1. The solution to Hadoop's drawback of dealing with small files is straightforward. Combine the small files to make larger files, then copy the larger files to HDFS.
2. The inclusion of HAR files (Hadoop Archives) was intended to alleviate the problem of many files putting a strain on the memory of the NameNode. HAR files function by creating a layered filesystem on top of HDFS. HAR files are made using the Hadoop archive command, which performs a MapReduce process to compress the files archived into a limited number of HDFS files. It is not more efficient to read through files in a HAR than reading through files in HDFS. However, it is slower because each HAR file access necessitates reading two index files and the data file.
3. **Sequence Files**: In actuality, sequence files, which employ the filename as the key and the file contents as the value, work exceptionally well to solve the small file problem. We can place files (100 KB) into a single sequence file and then process them in a streaming way using the sequence file by building software for them. Because the sequence file is splitable, MapReduce may break it into parts and work on each part separately.
4. Using HBase to store files is a frequent design strategy for overcoming the HDFS tiny file problem. However, we are not keeping millions of small files in HBase; instead, we are putting the file's binary information into a cell.

20.3 Vulnerability

Hadoop is entirely built in Java, a widely known programming language that has been frequently abused by cyber thieves and implicated in multiple security breaches.

Solution

1. Use tools like Snyk to examine your application's build artifacts and flag any dependencies that are known to be vulnerable. Then, it generates a list of Java security vulnerabilities in the packages you are using as a dashboard in your application.
2. Sensitive information should be handled with caution. Exposing sensitive data such as your client's personal information or credit card details, might be dangerous. However, even a milder example can turn out to be just as dangerous. Exposure of unique identifiers in your system, for example, is a Java security flaw if the identification may be utilized in another request to access more data.

20.4 Long Processing Time

MapReduce reads and writes data to and from the disk in Hadoop. Data is read from and written to the disk at each processing stage. Because disk seeks to require time, the entire operation is exceedingly slow. Hadoop is quite sluggish for processing small amounts of data. It is perfect for Big Data collections. Hadoop's real-time processing speed is limited since it has a batch processing engine at its foundation.

In comparison to newer technologies like Spark and Flink, Hadoop is sluggish. The MapReduce algorithm in Hadoop processes massive datasets using a concurrent and distributed approach. We must do the jobs: Map and Reduce, and MapReduce takes a long time to complete these tasks, resulting in increased latency. In MapReduce, data is disseminated and processed over a cluster, increasing the processing time and slowing it down.

Solution

1. The first step in ensuring optimal Hadoop task performance is to adjust the best memory configuration parameters by monitoring the server's memory utilization. Apache Hadoop includes several memory, storage, CPU, and network settings that can enhance the Hadoop cluster's performance.
2. Make sure the MapReduce job's mapper uses 70% of the heap RAM. When the Map Output is vast, several compression techniques such as LZO, BZIP, Snappy, and others can be used to minimize the intermediate data size. By default, Map Output is not compressed, and to enable compression, use MapReduce.
3. Hadoop Spark has also addressed this issue by processing data in memory. In-memory processing is faster because no time is spent transporting data/processes in and out of the disk. Furthermore, Spark processes everything in memory 100 times quicker than MapReduce. We can also employ Flink because its streaming design allows it to process data quicker than Spark. In addition, Flink is given instructions to process only the data sections that have changed, resulting in a considerable gain in task performance.

20.5 Not Easy to Use

We have to hand-code every action in Hadoop. The first disadvantage is that it is tough to utilize. Second, it expands the number of lines that must be coded. Third, MapReduce does not have an interactive mode; adding one, such as Hive or Pig, makes dealing with it more straightforward for newcomers.

Because Hadoop operates in batch mode, it is tough to debug it. We must give the jar file, the input, and the output file's location in this mode. It is tough to track down the offending code if the application crashes in the middle. Hadoop has 1,20,000 lines of code, the large number of lines produce several bugs, and it takes a long time to execute the program.

Solution

1. When compared to Hadoop, Spark is more user-friendly. This is because of the several APIs available for Java, Scala, Python, and Spark SQL. Spark offers an interactive mode that allows developers and users to get intermediate feedback on queries and other tasks. Spark is simple to program because it has many high-level operators.

In addition, Spark does batch processing, stream processing, and machine learning on the same cluster. Users find it more accessible as a result of this and they can run many workloads on the same infrastructure.

2. A large number of high-level operators are available in Flink. The number of lines of code required to achieve the same effect is reduced due to this.
3. Although Spark and Flink are written in Scala and Java, the implementation is in Scala, resulting in fewer lines of code than Hadoop. As a result, it will take less time to run the application and overcome Hadoop's long-line-of-code constraints.

20.6 Supports Only Batch Processing

Hadoop primarily aids batch processing and does not handle streaming data, resulting in decreased overall performance. Hadoop's MapReduce framework has no significant impact on the Hadoop cluster's memory.

Solution

1. Because Apache Spark provides stream processing, it overcomes this problem. However, Spark stream processing is not as efficient as Flink since it requires micro-batch processing.
2. Flink enhances overall performance by combining streaming and batch processing into a single run-time. In addition, Flink makes machine learning and graph processing quicker by using native closed-loop iteration operators.

20.7 No Delta Iteration

Apache Hadoop is not very efficient in iterative processing because the cyclic data flow is not supported by Hadoop (i.e., a chain of stages in which each output of the previous stage is the input to the next stage).

Solution

1. Apache Spark reads data from RAM rather than disk, improving the efficiency of iterative algorithms that retrieve the same dataset repeatedly. Spark supports iterative processing. Each iteration in Spark must be scheduled and executed individually. It uses a Directed Acyclic Graph (DAG) to do iterative processing. RDDs, or Resilient Distributed Datasets, are a feature of Spark. These are a set of elements distributed over a cluster of nodes. RDDs are created by Spark from HDFS files. We can also cache them, making RDDs reusable. Iterative algorithms perform operations on data repeatedly. As a result, they benefit from the caching of RDDs over iterations.
2. Flink also supports iterative processing. Flink uses a streaming architecture to repeat data. We can tell Flink to handle just the data that changes, which will improve

performance. Flink uses a step function to create iterative algorithms. The step functions are embedded in a particular iteration operator. Iterate and delta iterate are the two variations of this operator. These operators repeat the step function until they reach a terminating condition.

20.8 Security Issues

Managing complicated applications using Hadoop is difficult. Hadoop's setup can be complicated, and users might need help configuring it correctly, leading to security vulnerabilities. The Hadoop ecosystem has many different components that need to be secured, making it hard for a security team to monitor all of them. Overall, Hadoop's security limitations can prevent organizations from using it for sensitive data and lead to data breaches if not properly secured. Because data is crucial to businesses, Hadoop's security function is disabled by default. As a result, the Data Driver must exercise caution while dealing with this security issue and take necessary action. Furthermore, Hadoop uses Kerberos authentication for security, which is challenging to manage. In addition, Kerberos lacks storage and network encryption. Access control lists (ACLs) and typical file permissions paradigms are both supported by HDFS. Third-party suppliers, on the other hand, have made it possible for an organization to use Active Directory Kerberos and LDAP for authentication.

Solution

1. Spark adds a layer of security to Hadoop, allowing it to circumvent these restrictions. For example, we can use HDFS ACLs and file-level permissions if we execute the Spark in HDFS. Additionally, Spark may operate on YARN, allowing it to use Kerberos authentication.
2. Spark encrypts temporary data written to the local drive. It doesn't enable encryption of output data created by apps that use saveashadoopfile or saveastable APIs. For RPC connections, Spark uses AES-based encryption. To enable encryption, we should enable RPC authentication. It should be set up correctly.

SUMMARY

The necessity for Spark and Flink increases due to Hadoop's limitations. As a result, these systems become more user-friendly while dealing with large amounts of data. Furthermore, Spark allows for in-memory data processing, which speeds up the process. Flink enhances overall performance by combining streaming and batch processing into a single run-time. Spark gives you a security benefit. As a result, alternative Big Data technologies such as Apache Spark and Flink may be used to overcome all of Hadoop's constraints. However, these solutions employ Hadoop's HDFS as a backend since it is still a reliable data storage system.

EXERCISES

Multiple Choice Question

1. **Which of the following is not a disadvantage of Hadoop System?**
   A. Ability to handle tiny files   B. Processing speed
   C. Caching issue   D. Replication issue
   Answer: D
   Explanation: Although Hadoop is the most powerful Big Data tool, it has several drawbacks, including the inability to handle tiny files, inability to handle live data reliably, poor processing speed, inefficiency of repetitive processing, and inefficiency of caching.

Short-answer Questions

1. **What are all the problems related to vulnerability in Hadoop? How can it be overcome?**
   Hadoop is entirely built in Java, a widely known programming language that has been frequently abused by cyber thieves and implicated in multiple security breaches.
   Solution
   1. Use some tools like Snyk to examine your application's build artifacts and flag any dependencies that are known to be vulnerable. Then, it generates a list of Java security vulnerabilities in the packages you are using as a dashboard in your application.
   2. Sensitive information should be handled with caution. Exposing sensitive data such as your client's personal information or credit card details, might be dangerous. However, even milder examples might be just as dangerous. Exposure of unique identifiers in your system, for example, is a Java security flaw if the identification may be utilized in another request to access more data.

2. **Hadoop supports only batch processing. How can this difficulty be overcome?**
   Hadoop primarily aids batch processing and does not handle streaming data, resulting in decreased overall performance. Hadoop's MapReduce framework has no significant impact on the Hadoop cluster's memory.
   Solution
   Because Apache Spark provides stream processing, it overcomes this problem. However, Spark stream processing is not as efficient as Flink since it requires micro-batch processing. Flink enhances overall performance by combining streaming and batch processing into a single run-time. In addition, Flink makes machine learning and graph processing quicker by using native closed-loop iteration operators.

3. **What are all the problems related to security in Hadoop? How can they be overcome?**

Managing complicated applications using Hadoop is difficult. Hadoop's setup can be complicated, and users might need help configuring it correctly, leading to security vulnerabilities. The Hadoop ecosystem has many different components that need to be secured, making it hard for a security team to monitor all of them. Overall, Hadoop's security limitations can prevent organizations from using it for sensitive data and lead to data breaches if not properly secured. Because data is crucial to businesses, Hadoop's security function is disabled by default. As a result, the Data Driver must exercise caution while dealing with this security issue and take necessary action. Furthermore, Hadoop uses Kerberos authentication for security, which is challenging to manage. In addition, Kerberos lacks storage and network encryption. Access control lists (ACLs) and typical file permissions paradigms are both supported by HDFS. Third-party suppliers, on the other hand, have made it possible for an organization to use Active Directory Kerberos and LDAP for authentication.

Solution

Spark adds a layer of security to Hadoop, allowing it to circumvent these restrictions. For example, we can use HDFS ACLs and file-level permissions if we execute the Spark in HDFS. Additionally, Spark may operate on YARN, allowing it to use Kerberos authentication.

Spark encrypts temporary data written to the local drive. It does not enable encryption of output data created by apps that use saveashadoopfile or saveastable APIs. For RPC connections, Spark uses AES-based encryption. To enable encryption, we should enable RPC authentication. It should be set up correctly.

Essay-type Questions

1. What are the problems with small files in Hadoop? How can these problems be overcome?

2. What are the problems related to Processing Time in Hadoop? How can the problems be overcome?

3. Hadoop is difficult to use. How can this problem be overcome?

CHAPTER **21**

Big Data Case Studies

> **LEARNING OBJECTIVES**
>
> In this chapter, case studies of Big Data implementations for retail, logistics, manufacturing, travel industry have been discussed.

21.1 Applications of Big Data in the Retail Industry

21.1.1 Customer Segmentation

Customer segmentation is a popular retail approach that divides customers into smaller groups based on criteria such as demographics, purchasing behavior, and preferences. Big Data Analytics is vital in helping retailers to process massive volumes of data to uncover patterns and insights that can be used to produce personalized marketing messages and offers for each segment.

According to a report by McKinsey & Company, personalized and relevant communication can increase customer satisfaction and sales by up to 15%. Additionally, a study by Segment (a leading customer data platform) found that companies that use customer data analytics for segmentation and personalization can increase their marketing efficiency by up to 30 %.

Amazon is a prominent example of a company that uses Big Data Analytics to segment its customers and provide personalized product recommendations. Its recommendation system is powered by machine learning algorithms that analyze customer browsing and purchase history to predict their interests and preferences. As a result, Amazon's recommendation engine drives up to 35 % of its sales. Furthermore, Big Data Analytics allows merchants to track client behavior patterns such as frequency of visits, time of day they shop, and devices used. This information can be used to personalize marketing messages and offers for each customer segment, optimizing the timing and delivery of their marketing messages to maximize engagement. Customer segmentation is crucial for retailers looking to improve customer engagement, loyalty, and retention. Big Data

Analytics enables retailers to process massive volumes of Big Data to uncover patterns and insights that can be used to develop personalized marketing messages and offers for each segment, thereby improving the customer experience and generating sales.

References

1. https://www.mckinsey.com/industries/retail/our-insights/personalizing-the-customer-experience-driving-differentiation-in-retail. Accessed April 24, 2023.
2. Segment. (2022). *The 2022 State of Personalization Report*. Retrieved from https://segment.com/state-of-personalization-report/. Accessed April 27, 2023.
3. Amazon. (2022). *Personalized Recommendations*. Retrieved from https://aws.amazon.com/personalize/. Accessed April 27, 2023.

21.1.2 Inventory Management

Inventory management is critical in retail operations, and Big Data Analytics plays a growing role in optimizing inventory levels based on demand estimates and sales histories. Retailers may effectively estimate demand for their items and alter inventory levels accordingly by analyzing massive volumes of data in real time, eliminating overstocking and understocking problems.

Walmart is well-known for using Big Data to optimize inventory levels and reduce out-of-stock situations. For example, Walmart can watch sales patterns across thousands of stores using a sophisticated data analytics system and alter inventory levels accordingly. This allows Walmart to reduce the chance of popular products going out of supply, which can result in lost sales and customer unhappiness. Walmart uses Big Data to optimize its inventory management by analyzing historical sales data to predict future demand. Using machine learning algorithms and predictive analytics, Walmart can identify trends and patterns in sales data and use this information to adjust its inventory levels in real time. This ensures that Walmart has sufficient inventory to meet customer demand without excess inventory, which can bind up valuable resources and increase costs.

Additionally, Walmart uses Big Data to optimize its supply chain, ensuring that products are delivered to stores quickly and effectively. By using data analytics to track shipping times and delivery schedules, Walmart can adjust its inventory levels to ensure that products arrive at the store when needed. This helps Walmart minimize the time spent in product transit and reduce the risk of out-of-stock situations.

Big Data Analytics plays an increasingly important role in inventory management for retailers. Walmart is leveraging this technology to optimize its operations. By accurately predicting demand and adjusting inventory levels accordingly, Walmart has been able to reduce costs, improve customer satisfaction, and maintain its top position as one of the world's leading retailers.

References

1. *Five ways Walmart uses bigdata*: Retrieved from https://chainstoreage.com/operations/five-ways-walmart-uses-big-data. Accessed April 24, 2023.

2. https://www.rtinsights.com/walmart-cloud-inventory-management-real-time-data/. Accessed April 24, 2023.
3. *Walmart's inventory management*: Retrieved from https://panmore.com/walmart-inventory-management. Accessed April 24, 2023.
4. *How Walmart enhances its inventory, supply chain through AI*: Retrieved from https://www.ciodive.com/news/walmart-AI-ML-retail/638582/. Accessed April 24, 2023.

21.1.3 Price Optimization

Price optimization is a critical aspect of retail operations, and Big Data Analytics is increasingly vital in helping retailers determine the optimal prices for their products. Retailers can stay competitive by analyzing massive volumes of data in real time and identifying characteristics such as competitive prices, customer demand, and sales history.

Macy's is a leading department store chain that uses Big Data to optimize its prices and increase sales. By leveraging sophisticated data analytics tools, Macy's tracks prices of similar products offered by competitors and adjust its prices to remain competitive. This enables Macy's to attract price-sensitive customers and maintain its position in the market.

Macy's also uses Big Data to analyze customer demand and buying behavior to determine the optimal price points for its products. By tracking customer interactions with different product categories and monitoring sales data, Macy's can identify price sensitivity levels and adjust its prices accordingly. This helps Macy's maximize profits and achieve sales goals while meeting customer demand.

Furthermore, Macy's uses Big Data to establish dynamic pricing, allowing it to modify prices in real time in response to changing market conditions. Macy's stays competitive and maximizes earnings by analyzing market trends and adjusting prices in real time using machine learning algorithms and predictive analytics.

In conclusion, Big Data Analytics is increasingly vital in price optimization for retailers. Macy's is a prime example of a company leveraging this technology to optimize its operations. By tracking competitor prices, analyzing customer demand, and implementing dynamic pricing, Macy's can stay competitive, maximize profits, and maintain its position as a leading department store chain.

References

1. *5 Ways Macy's is Harnessing Data and Analytics*: Retrieved from: https://risnews.com/5-ways-macys-harnessing-data-and-analytics. Accessed April 24, 2023.
2. *Macy's Is Changing The Shopping Experience With Big Data Analytics*: Retrieved from https://datafloq.com/read/macys-changing-shopping-experience-big-data-analyt/. Accessed April 24, 2023.

21.1.4 Fraud Detection

Fraud detection is a critical aspect of retail operations, and Big Data Analytics is increasingly vital in helping retailers detect and prevent fraudulent activities. Retailers may spot patterns and abnormalities that suggest fraudulent transactions, take action to avert losses and maintain customer trust by analyzing Big Data in real time.

Target is a leading retailer that uses Big Data to detect fraudulent transactions and prevent losses. By leveraging sophisticated data analytics tools, Target can track customer behavior across its stores and online channels and identify patterns that indicate fraudulent activities. This includes monitoring suspicious purchases, unusual account activity, and abnormal behavior patterns.

Furthermore, Target also uses Big Data to implement fraud prevention measures, such as machine learning algorithms and predictive analytics, which can identify potential fraud before it occurs. By analyzing vast amounts of transaction data in real time, Target can identify suspicious activities and take action to prevent losses, such as blocking transactions and alerting security teams.

In addition to credit card fraud, Target also uses Big Data to prevent return fraud, which occurs when customers return products that were stolen or purchased fraudulently. By tracking customer return patterns and analyzing historical data, Target can identify patterns of fraudulent returns and take action to prevent losses, such as implementing stricter return policies and requiring proof of purchase for all returns.

In conclusion, Big Data Analytics is increasingly vital in fraud detection for retailers. Target is a prime example of leveraging this technology to protect its bottom line and maintain customer trust. By tracking customer behavior and analyzing transaction data in real time, Target can detect and prevent fraudulent activities and take action to prevent losses and maintain customer loyalty.

Reference

1. *On Target: Rethinking The Retail Website*: Retrieved from: https://www.forbes.com/sites/hbsworkingknowledge/2018/12/04/on-target-rethinking-the-retail-website/?sh=a08a4a916fb1. Accessed April 24, 2023.

21.1.5 Supply Chain Optimization

Supply chain optimization is a crucial aspect of retail operations, and Big Data Analytics is increasingly vital in helping retailers optimize their supply chain operations. By analyzing real-time data, retailers can identify inefficiencies and constraints in their supply chain and take steps to reduce costs and increase efficiency.

Zara uses Big Data to optimize its supply chain and reduce lead times. By leveraging sophisticated data analytics tools, Zara can track every aspect of its supply chain, including transportation, warehousing, and logistics, and identify areas for improvement. This includes analyzing production capacity, shipping times, and inventory levels.

One of the critical ways Zara uses Big Data to optimize its supply chain is through its fast fashion strategy, which involves producing and delivering new clothing designs in small batches rapidly. By analyzing sales data and customer feedback in real time, Zara can quickly identify popular designs and adjust production levels accordingly. This allows Zara to minimize overstocking and reduce lead times, which improves efficiency and reduces costs.

Furthermore, Zara also uses Big Data to optimize its logistics operations, such as routing and scheduling. For example, Zara can optimize logistics operations by analyzing data on transportation routes, delivery times, and traffic patterns to reduce transportation costs and reduce delivery times. This includes utilizing predictive analytics and real-time data to predict demand and modify production schedules accordingly.

In conclusion, Big Data Analytics is increasingly vital in supply chain optimization for retailers. Zara is leveraging this technology to improve efficiency and reduce costs. By analyzing every aspect of its supply chain operations, from production to transportation to logistics, Zara can identify inefficiencies and take action to optimize its operations, reduce lead times, and maintain its position as a leading fashion retailer.

References

1. Kumar, P. (2021). "Big Data Analytics in Supply Chain Management: An Overview", in *Digital Twin Technologies and Applications in Industry* 4.0 (pp. 263–281). Springer, Singapore.
2. Lee, K., Lee, H., Kim, H., and Lee, H. (2019). "Supply Chain Management with Big Data Analytics", *Big Data Research*, 16, 100–110.
3. McAfee, A., and Brynjolfsson, E. (2012). "Big Data: The Management Revolution", *Harvard Business Review*, 90(10), 60–68.
4. Öztürk, S. (2020). "Using Big Data Analytics in Supply Chain Management: A Literature Review", *Journal of Engineering and Technology Management*, 58, 101583.
5. Sheffi, Y. (2018). *The power of Zara's fast fashion supply chain*. Retrieved from https://hbr.org/2018/03/the-power-of-zaras-fast-fashion-supply-chain. Accessed April 24, 2023.

21.1.6 Predictive Analytics

Predictive analytics is an influential tool retailers use to anticipate customer behavior, such as purchasing patterns and product preferences. By analyzing actual time data, retailers can identify patterns and trends that indicate customer demand and adjust their product offerings accordingly.

Tesco is a leading retailer that uses Big Data to predict customer demand and optimize its product offerings. By leveraging sophisticated data analytics tools, Tesco can track customer behavior across its stores and online channels and identify patterns that indicate customer demand. This includes monitoring product searches, purchase history, and customer feedback.

One of the critical ways Tesco uses Big Data to predict customer demand is through its Clubcard loyalty program. By analyzing customer purchases and preferences data, Tesco can stock popular products, offer personalized discounts and promotions, and introduce new products that align with customer preferences.

Furthermore, Tesco uses Big Data to optimize its product offerings and improve customer satisfaction. By analyzing customer feedback and reviews, Tesco can identify improvement areas and address customer concerns. This includes improving product quality, offering better customer service, and introducing new products that meet customer needs.

In addition to improving customer satisfaction, predictive analytics helps Tesco reduce costs and improve efficiency. By anticipating customer demand, Tesco can optimize its inventory levels and reduce waste, which improves efficiency and reduces costs.

Thus, Big Data Analytics is increasingly vital in predictive analytics for retailers. Tesco is a prime example of a company leveraging this technology to improve customer satisfaction, reduce costs, and maintain its position as a leading retailer. By analyzing customer behavior and adjusting its product offerings accordingly, Tesco can anticipate demand, reduce waste, and provide a better shopping experience for its customers.

References

1. Marr, B. (2016). "How Tesco is using Big Data to keep customers coming back for more", *Forbes*.
2. Patterson, D. (2018). "Tesco: How one retail giant has revolutionised grocery shopping with Big Data".
3. Rosencrance, L. (2016). "Predictive analytics: How Tesco uses it to steer its business", *Computerworld*, UK.
4. Carter, J. (2016). "Tesco boosts profits with predictive analytics", *TechRadar*.

21.1.7 Customer Experience

Customer experience is a critical aspect of retail, and Big Data is vital in personalizing the customer experience. By analyzing vast data, retailers can gain insight into consumer behavior and preferences and use this knowledge to provide personalized recommendations, offers, and promotions.

Sephora (beauty industry) uses Big Data to personalize its online shopping experience and provide product recommendations. Sephora's online platform collects data on customer behavior, such as browsing history, search queries, and purchase history, and uses this information to provide personalized product recommendations.

One of the critical ways Sephora uses Big Data to personalize the customer experience is through its Beauty Insider loyalty program. Sephora can identify patterns and trends that indicate customer preferences by tracking customer purchases and preferences and adjusting its product offerings accordingly. This includes stocking popular products, offering personalized discounts and promotions, and introducing new products that align with customer preferences.

Sephora also uses Big Data to personalize its online shopping experience. By analyzing customer behavior and preferences, Sephora can provide personalized product recommendations and offer a seamless shopping experience across multiple channels, such as its website, mobile app, and social media platforms.

Furthermore, Sephora uses Big Data to improve its customer service and support. Sephora can identify improvement areas and address customer concerns by analyzing customer feedback and reviews. This includes improving product quality, offering better customer service, and introducing new products that meet customer needs.

In conclusion, Big Data Analytics plays an increasingly important role in personalizing the customer experience for retailers. Sephora is a prime example of a company leveraging this technology to improve customer satisfaction and loyalty. By analyzing customer behavior and preferences and providing personalized recommendations and support, Sephora can provide a better customer shopping experience and maintain its position as the industry's foremost retailer.

References

1. *Big Data and the Future of Retail*: Retrieved from: https://www.mytotalretail.com/article/big-data-and-the-future-of-retail/. Accessed April 28, 2023.
2. *Data: The Secret Weapon for Customer Satisfaction*: Retrieved from: https://contentsquare.com/blog/data-secret-weapon-customer-satisfaction/. Accessed April 28, 2023.
3. *Sephora Asia details its journey to data-driven decision making*: Retrieved from: https://www.cmo.com.au/article/645205/sephora-asia-details-its-journey-data-driven-decision-making/. Accessed April 28, 2023.
4. *Sephora Marketing Analytics Success Story*: Retrieved from: https://www.takethiscourse.net/sephora-marketing-analytics-success-story/. Accessed April 28, 2023.

21.1.8 Social Media Analysis

Social media helps retailers to understand customer opinions, trends, and preferences. By analyzing social media data, retailers can gain valuable insights into customer behavior and adjust their marketing strategies and product offerings accordingly. Nike is a company that uses Big Data to analyze social media data and gain insights into customer preferences and behavior.

One of the ways Nike uses Big Data for social media analysis is through sentiment analysis. By analyzing customer feedback and reviews on social media platforms, Nike can identify patterns and trends in customer sentiment towards its brand and products. This helps Nike understand which products are popular and which are not, and adjust its product offerings accordingly.

Another way Nike uses Big Data for social media analysis is through social listening. For example, Nike can gain insights into customer opinions and preferences by monitoring social media platforms for mentions of its brand and products. This includes identifying which products are popular and which ones are not and understanding what customers say about the quality, design, and functionality of its products.

Nike also uses social media analysis to inform its marketing strategies. By analyzing social media data, Nike can identify the most effective marketing campaigns and adjust its strategies as required. This includes identifying which channels are most effective for reaching its target audience and what types of content are most engaging.

Furthermore, Nike uses social media analysis to engage with customers and build brand loyalty. By responding to customer feedback and reviews on social media platforms,

Nike shows customers that it values their opinions and is committed to providing a positive customer experience. This helps to build customer loyalty and trust in the Nike brand.

Big Data Analytics is increasingly vital in retailers' social media analysis. Nike is leveraging this technology to gain insights into customer preferences and behavior. By analyzing social media data and adjusting its marketing strategies and product offerings accordingly, Nike can maintain its top position as a leading retailer in the sportswear industry and continue providing a positive customer experience.

References

1. Retalon. (2022). *5 Vital Considerations for Big Data Analytics in Retail*: Retrieved from: https://retalon.com/blog/big-data-analytics-in-retail. Accessed April 24, 2023.
2. *5 ways Tesco uses Big Data Analytics*: Retrieved from: https://www.analyticssteps.com/blogs/5-ways-tesco-uses-big-data-analytics. Accessed April 24, 2023.
3. *How Nike Is Using Data to Sell Directly to Customers*: Retrieved from: https://bernardmarr.com/how-nike-is-using-data-to-sell-directly-to-customers/#:~:text=Nike%27s%20data%20analytics%20systems%20are,services%2C%20and%20improve%20business%20processes. Accessed April 24, 2023.

21.1.9 Store Layout Optimization

The layout and design of a store can have a significant impact on customer behavior and sales. By optimizing the store layout based on customer behavior and preferences, retailers can improve the customer experience and increase sales. Walmart is one such company that uses Big Data to optimize its store layout and improve customer flow.

Walmart collects and analyzes data on customer behavior, such as traffic patterns, product placements, and checkout times. This data is then used to optimize the layout and design of Walmart stores, aiming to improve the customer experience and increase sales. For example, Walmart may adjust the placement of products based on customer demand or rearrange the store layout to improve customer flow and reduce wait times.

One of the ways Walmart uses Big Data to optimize its store layout is through the use of heat maps. Heat maps show the store areas customers most frequently visit, allowing Walmart to identify which products are most popular and which areas are underutilized. This information can then be used to adjust the store's layout to improve customer flow and increase sales.

Walmart also uses Big Data to optimize the checkout process. By analyzing checkout times and wait times, Walmart can identify areas where customers may be experiencing long wait times and adjust the store layout or the number of cash registers accordingly. This helps to reduce wait times and improve the overall customer experience.

In addition to optimizing the layout of its physical stores, Walmart also uses Big Data to optimize its online store layout. By analyzing customer behavior and preferences on its website, Walmart can adjust the layout of its online store to improve the customer experience and increase sales. This includes adjusting the placement of products, optimizing the search function, and providing personalized recommendations based on customer browsing and purchase history.

In conclusion, Big Data Analytics is increasingly vital in store layout optimization for retailers. Walmart is leveraging this technology to improve the customer experience and increase sales. By analyzing customer behavior and preferences and adjusting the layout of its stores and website accordingly, Walmart strives maintain its position as a leading retailer and continue to provide a positive customer experience.

References

1. *How Big Data Analysis helped increase Walmart Sales turnover*: Retrieved from: https://www.projectpro.io/article/how-big-data-analysis-helped-increase-walmarts-sales-turnover/109. Accessed April 28, 2023.
2. *Wal-Mart works to use Big Data to improve checkout process, manage supply chain*: Retrieved from: https://talkbusiness.net/2017/08/wal-mart-works-to-use-big-data-to-improve-checkout-process-manage-supply-chain/. Accessed April 28, 2023.
3. *Walmart: Big Data Analytics at the world's biggest retailer*: Retrieved from: https://bernardmarr.com/walmart-big-data-analytics-at-the-worlds-biggest-retailer/. Accessed April 28, 2023.

21.2 Applications of Big Data in the Logistics Industry

21.2.1 Route Optimization

Route optimization is an essential application of Big Data Analytics for retailers and transportation companies. Companies can optimize their delivery routes, reduce transportation costs, and improve overall efficiency by analyzing various factors such as traffic patterns, weather forecasts, and delivery schedules.

UPS, one of the largest delivery corporations in the world, optimizes its delivery routes using ORION (On-Road Integrated Optimization and Navigation). ORION optimizes UPS delivery routes using data analysis, machine learning, and algorithmic decision-making.

ORION considers various factors such as package size and weight, customer delivery time windows, traffic patterns, and even the number of left-turns on a delivery route (since left turns are considered unsafe and wasteful on right-hand driving roads such as those in the U.S.). By optimizing these factors, ORION can reduce the total number of miles traveled by UPS drivers, saving millions of gallons of fuel and lowering carbon emissions.

The system constantly learns from driver feedback and adapts to traffic patterns and delivery schedule changes. ORION also provides drivers with turn-by-turn navigation instructions and real-time traffic updates, enabling them to make faster and more efficient deliveries.

In addition to UPS, other retailers and transportation companies use similar systems to optimize delivery routes and reduce transportation costs. By leveraging Big Data Analytics, these companies can improve operational efficiency, reduce environmental impact, and provide better customer service.

References

1. UPS ORION: https://about.ups.com/us/en/newsroom/press-releases/innovation-driven/ups-to-enhance-orion-with-continuous-delivery-route-optimization.html. Accessed April 24, 2023.
2. *AI And Advanced Analytics In Shipping And Logistics*: AI and Advanced Analytics in Shipping and Logistics: An interview with Gregory Brown and Laura Patel, UPS (forbes.com). Accessed April 24, 2023.

21.2.2 Supply Chain Visibility

Supply chain visibility refers to tracking shipments in real time, monitoring their progress, and identifying any potential bottlenecks or delays in the supply chain. By leveraging Big Data Analytics, companies can gain valuable insights into their supply chain operations and make informed decisions to improve efficiency and reduce costs.

One example of a company using Big Data to improve supply chain visibility is Maersk Line, the world's largest container shipping company. Maersk Line utilizes TradeLens, a digital platform with blockchain technology and Big Data Analytics, to provide real-time visibility to its shipping containers. The platform allows Maersk Line and its customers to track their shipments in real time, monitor their progress, and identify potential issues or delays. Consequently, Maersk Line can optimize its operations, reduce costs, and increase customer satisfaction by enhancing supply chain visibility.

According to a case study published by IBM, Maersk Line has seen significant benefits from using TradeLens. The platform has helped the company reduce manual processes and paperwork, improve efficiency and collaboration with partners, and increase supply chain visibility. For example, by using TradeLens, Maersk Line reduced the time taken for transporting flowers from Kenya to the Netherlands from two weeks to four days.

References

1. *Maersk and IBM Introduce TradeLens Blockchain Shipping Solution*: Retrieved from: https://newsroom.ibm.com/2018-08-09-Maersk-and-IBM-Introduce-TradeLens-Blockchain-Shipping-Solution. Accessed April 28, 2023.
2. *Maersk and digital revolution in shipping industry*: Retrieved from: https://d3.harvard.edu/platform-digit/submission/maersk-and-digital-revolution-in-shipping-industry/. Accessed April 28, 2023.

21.2.3 Risk Management

Big Data Analytics is helping to improve risk management in the transportation business. Companies can detect possible dangers and proactively mitigate them with the help of predictive analytics and machine learning algorithms.

Delta Airlines, for example, uses Big Data to forecast weather trends and reduce the impact of weather-related flight interruptions. The organization has created a system that integrates data from many sources, such as satellites, radar, and other weather sensors, to predict weather patterns reliably.

Using this system, Delta Airlines can make real-time decisions about flight schedules, rerouting flights, and adjusting operations to minimize disruptions caused by weather events. This helps the company to improve the overall customer experience by reducing the impact of weather-related delays and cancellations.

In addition to weather-related risks, Big Data Analytics can assist transportation businesses in managing cyber threats, supply chain disruptions, and operational risks. Companies can identify potential hazards and proactively mitigate them by analyzing large volumes of data.

References

1. *How a team of meteorologists protects passengers and their schedules*: Retrieved from: https://cluballiance.aaa.com/the-extra-mile/articles/prepare/travel/meteorologists-protects-passengers-and-their-schedules. Accessed April 29, 2023.
2. Saravanan, A. M. (2020). "Role of Big Data Analytics in risk management in the transportation industry", *International Journal of Data Science*, 5(1), 1–9.

21.2.4 Fleet Management

Fleet management involves monitoring and controlling a company's fleet of vehicles to improve efficiency and reduce costs. Big Data Analytics can collect and analyze data from various sources, such as sensors, GPS tracking, and maintenance logs, to optimize fleet performance and reduce downtime. For example, Caterpillar uses predictive analytics to monitor the performance of its heavy machinery and predict maintenance needs, allowing the company to schedule maintenance proactively and reduce downtime.

Caterpillar's system collects data from sensors on its machinery and sends it to a cloud-based analytics platform. The platform employs machine learning algorithms to analyze data and identify patterns that may indicate maintenance issues. The system can also identify anomalies that may indicate a problem, and alert technicians to take corrective action. By proactively scheduling maintenance, Caterpillar has reduced downtime and improved efficiency, saving the company millions of dollars.

In addition, fleet management systems can also optimize routing and scheduling to reduce fuel costs and improve delivery times. For instance, UPS uses Big Data Analytics to optimize its delivery routes and reduce fuel consumption. The company's proprietary routing software considers traffic patterns, delivery windows, and driver availability to create the most efficient route for each driver.

Overall, fleet management is an essential aspect of many industries, and Big Data Analytics can provide valuable insights and improvements to optimize efficiency, reduce costs, and improve performance.

Reference

1. *How Caterpillar uses Machine Learning to Produce Real ROI*: Retrieved from: https://d3.harvard.edu/platform-rctom/submission/how-caterpillar-uses-machine-learning-to-produce-real-roi/. Accessed April 29, 2023.

21.2.5 Warehouse Optimization

Warehouse optimization involves using Big Data Analytics to improve warehouse operations, such as inventory accuracy and order processing times. By leveraging data, retailers can gain insights into warehouse operations, which help to identify inefficiencies and improvement areas.

One of the best examples of warehouse optimization using Big Data is Amazon. Amazon uses algorithms, sensors, and data analysis to optimize its warehouse operations. For instance, the company uses Kiva robots to automate moving products around its warehouses. These robots are equipped with sensors that can detect products and guide the robots to the correct location. Additionally, Amazon uses predictive analytics to forecast demand and optimize inventory levels. This ensures that the products are available in the warehouse when needed, which helps reduce delivery times.

Another way Amazon optimizes its warehouse operations is by analyzing customer data to predict which products are likely to be ordered together. This allows the company to place related products in the exact location, improving the efficiency of the order-picking process.

In summary, warehouse optimization using Big Data Analytics can help retailers improve inventory accuracy, reduce order processing times, and ultimately improve customer satisfaction. Amazon is an excellent example of a company that has successfully leveraged Big Data to optimize its warehouse operations and improve efficiency.

References

1. *Amazon's Super-Efficient Warehouses*: Retrieved from: https://www.palletmarketinc.com/blog/how-amazon-makes-their-warehouses-hyper-efficient. Accessed April 29, 2023.
2. *How algorithms run Amazon's warehouses*: Retrieved from: https://www.bbc.com/future/article/20150818-how-algorithms-run-amazons-warehouses. Accessed April 29, 2023.

21.2.6 Pricing Optimization

Pricing optimization is a critical area where Big Data Analytics can offer valuable insights to businesses. By analyzing customer behavior, market trends, and competitor pricing, companies can set the optimal price for their products or services to maximize profits while remaining competitive.

One notable example of a company using Big Data Analytics for pricing optimization is Uber Freight. The company uses a dynamic pricing model that employs data analytics to determine the optimal price for each shipment based on supply and demand, distance, and route efficacy. This helps Uber Freight offer competitive pricing to its customers while ensuring profitability.

The pricing optimization process involves collecting and analyzing large volumes of data, including historical pricing data, market trends, and customer behavior. Companies can identify patterns and trends by analyzing this data to devise their pricing strategies. This can result in increased sales, improved customer satisfaction, and higher profits.

In conclusion, Big Data Analytics can play a significant role in pricing optimization for businesses, and companies that effectively leverage this technology can gain a competitive advantage in their industries.

References

1. *How does Uber's pricing work?*: Retrieved from: https://www.uber.com/en-gb/blog/uber-dynamic-pricing/#:~:text=That%27s%20because%20of%20our%20dynamic,price%20during%20particularly%20busy%20periods. Accessed April 29, 2023.
2. *Uber and its Use of Dynamic Pricing*: Retrieved from: https://www.insitetrack.com/uber-and-its-use-of-dynamic-pricing-unfair-or-smart-business/. Accessed April 29, 2023.
3. *3 Pricing Lessons from Uber*: Retrieved from: https://www.pricingsolutions.com/pricing-blog/lessons-in-pricing-from-uber/. Accessed April 29, 2023.

21.2.7 Quality Control

Quality control is a critical aspect of the manufacturing process, which ensures that products meet the required quality standards before they reach customers. Big Data Analytics can monitor quality control processes in real time, identify defects, and improve product quality. One company that has successfully implemented Big Data Analytics in its quality control processes is Nestlé.

Nestlé monitors its production processes using Big Data Analytics and identifies potential issues that could impact product quality and safety.

The company collects data from various sources, including sensors on production equipment, quality control checks, and customer feedback. This data is then analyzed using machine learning algorithms to identify patterns and trends and detect any anomalies indicating a quality issue.

By using Big Data Analytics, Nestlé has improved its quality control processes and reduced the risk of product recalls. The company has also been able to identify areas for improvement and make changes to its production processes to improve product quality further.

In conclusion, Big Data Analytics can play a crucial role in quality control processes by providing real-time monitoring, early detection of defects, and insights for process improvement. Companies like Nestlé have successfully implemented Big Data Analytics in their quality control processes to improve product quality and safety.

References

1. *Nestlé Quality Assurance Center*: Retrieved from https://www.nqaclabs.com/. Accessed April 29, 2023.
2. Sivarajah, U., Kamal, M. M., Irani, Z., and Weerakkody, V. (2017). "Critical analysis of Big Data challenges and analytical methods", *Journal of Business Research*, 70, 263–286.

21.2.8 Environmental Sustainability

Various logistics and transportation companies are utilizing Big Data Analytics to reduce the environmental impact of their operations. For example, Maersk Line, a global container shipping company, has developed a data analytics tool called "Carbon Calculator" to monitor and reduce carbon emissions. This tool analyzes data from various sources, such as vessel performance data, fuel consumption data, and cargo data, to estimate the carbon footprint of each shipment. Maersk Line uses this information to optimize its shipping routes, reduce fuel consumption, and lower carbon emissions.

Various organizations have recognized Maersk Line's Carbon Calculator. Maersk Line has won several awards, including the 2017 Green Supply Chain Award and the 2018 Lloyd's List Intelligence Innovation Award. Maersk Line's carbon emissions have decreased by 46% since 2007, and the company has set a goal to achieve net-zero emissions by 2050.

In addition to Maersk Line, other companies such as UPS and FedEx are also using Big Data Analytics to reduce their carbon footprint and promote environmental sustainability. These businesses are utilizing data analytics to optimize their delivery routes, decrease their petroleum consumption, and enhance the efficacy of their operations.

References

1. *Emissions Dashboard: Enhanced carbon footprint analysis*: Retrieved from: https://www.maersk.com/digital-solutions/emissions-dashboard. Accessed April 29, 2023.
2. *Maersk launches digital dashboard to track carbon emissions*: Retrieved from: https://www.joc.com/article/maersk-launches-digital-dashboard-track-carbon-emissions_20210603.html. Accessed April 29, 2023.
3. *Maersk rolls out new digital tool to track CO2 emissions*: Retrieved from: https://www.offshore-energy.biz/maersk-rolls-out-new-digital-tool-to-track-co2-emissions/. Accessed April 29, 2023.

21.3 Applications of Big Data in the Manufacturing Industry

21.3.1 Predictive Maintenance

Predictive maintenance is an essential application of Big Data Analytics in manufacturing. By monitoring machine data such as sensor readings and historical performance, manufacturers can identify potential issues before they occur and schedule preventative maintenance, reducing downtime and increasing productivity.

One example of a company using Big Data Analytics for predictive maintenance is General Electric (GE). GE uses a software platform called Predix to collect and analyze data from its aircraft engines. The system uses machine learning algorithms to predict potential issues and alert maintenance crews, allowing them to address the problem before it causes a critical failure.

In addition to improving maintenance efficiency, predictive maintenance can also reduce costs associated with unplanned downtime and prolong the lifespan of machinery. As such, it is becoming an increasingly important tool for manufacturers seeking to optimize their operations.

References

1. *Project Predictive Maintenance*: Retrieved from: https://www.ge.com/research/project/predictive-maintenance. Accessed April 29, 2023.
2. *5 Steps to Reaching Smart Predictive Maintenance*: Retrieved from: https://www.ge.com/digital/blog/5-steps-reaching-smart-predictive-maintenance. Accessed April 29, 2023.
3. *Predictive Maintenance at General Electric*: Retrieved from: https://sparrow.dev/predictive-maintenance-at-general-electric/. Accessed April 29, 2023.

21.3.2 Quality Control

Procter & Gamble (P&G), one of the largest consumer goods companies in the world, uses Big Data Analytics to improve their product quality and production processes. By collecting and analyzing data from sensors and other sources, P&G can monitor the quality of their products in real time and detect any issues early on. This allows the company to quickly identify and correct the problem, minimizing waste and improving efficiency.

P&G also uses Big Data to optimize its production processes, reducing the likelihood of quality issues in the first place. For example, the company can identify patterns and optimize their processes by analyzing temperature, humidity, and machine performance data. This leads to more consistent product quality and reduced costs.

Furthermore, P&G also leverages Big Data Analytics to improve their supply chain operations. They analyze data from suppliers, transportation, and warehousing to identify potential bottlenecks and improve efficiency.

By utilizing Big Data Analytics, P&G has improved product quality, reduced costs, and increased the efficiency of production and supply chain operations.

References

1. *Big Data Strategy of Procter & Gamble: Turning Big Data into Big Value*: Retrieved from: https://www.icmrindia.org/casestudies/catalogue/IT%20and%20Systems/ITSY091.htm. Accessed April 29, 2023.
2. *Big Data Strategy of Procter & Gamble: Turning Big Data into Big Value*: Retrieved from: https://www.sutori.com/en/story/big-data-strategy-of-procter-gamble-turning-big-data-into-big-value--TeymYfnFawThYdvr8zM84DWY. Accessed April 29, 2023.

3. *Analytics: The real-world use of Big Data in manufacturing*: Retrieved from: https://www.ibm.com/downloads/cas/ONBGKB82. Accessed April 29, 2023.

21.3.3 Supply Chain Optimization

Nestlé, one of the world's largest food and beverage companies, leverages Big Data to optimize their supply chain operations. The company uses advanced analytics to analyze its supply chain data, including demand forecasting, inventory levels, and logistics performance. With these insights, Nestlé can optimize their production and distribution processes, reduce waste, and improve efficiency.

For instance, Nestlé uses Big Data to optimize their inventory management, ensuring the right amount of products at suitable locations to meet customer demand while minimizing inventory costs. They also use Big Data to optimize their logistics operations, such as transportation planning and route optimization, to reduce costs and improve delivery times.

By leveraging Big Data, Nestlé has optimized their global supply chain, reducing logistics costs by 10–15% while improving customer service. In addition, Nestlé has improved their sustainability efforts, reducing greenhouse gas emissions by 6% in their logistics operations.

Reference

1. *Nestlé accelerates sustainable*: Retrieved from: https://supplychaindigital.com/digital-supply-chain/nestle-accelerates-sustainable-packaging-initiatives. Accessed April 29, 2023.

21.3.4 Production Optimization

Production optimization involves identifying and eliminating inefficiencies in the manufacturing process to improve productivity, reduce waste, and increase profits. Big Data Analytics can monitor production processes, identify bottlenecks, and improve efficiency.

For instance, Ford uses Big Data to optimize its manufacturing processes. The company collects data from over 100 sensors on its assembly lines and uses machine-learning algorithms to identify bottlenecks and predict equipment failures before they occur. This allows Ford to optimize its production processes, reduce downtime, and improve product quality.

Moreover, Big Data Analytics can help manufacturers identify waste-reduction opportunities in energy consumption, raw material utilization, and transportation. By optimizing these areas, manufacturers can reduce costs and increase profitability.

In conclusion, Big Data Analytics can significantly improve the manufacturing industry's productivity and efficiency by providing insights into production processes, identifying inefficiencies, and enabling optimization.

References

1. *How Ford Motor Company Handles Big Data*: Retrieved from: https://www.industryweek.com/technology-and-iiot/article/21246494/how-ford-motor-company-handles-big-data. Accessed April 29, 2023.
2. *The Amazing Ways The Ford Motor Company Uses Artificial Intelligence And Machine Learning*: Retrieved from: https://www.forbes.com/sites/bernardmarr/2019/05/17/the-amazing-ways-the-ford-motor-company-uses-artificial-intelligence-and-machine-learning/?sh=3bcf5eb5e49a. Accessed April 29, 2023.

21.3.5 Energy Efficiency

Big Data Analytics can help manufacturing companies monitor and optimize energy usage, leading to cost savings and improved sustainability.

Dow Chemical: Dow Chemical uses Big Data Analytics to identify energy-saving opportunities in its facilities. They use sensors and analytics to monitor energy usage and identify areas where they can reduce energy consumption. This has helped Dow Chemical to save millions of dollars in energy costs.

Intel: Intel uses Big Data Analytics to optimize energy usage in its data centers. They employ analytics to monitor real-time energy consumption and identify opportunities to reduce it. This has helped Intel to reduce its energy usage by 38% and save $633 million in energy costs.

Toyota: Toyota uses Big Data Analytics to optimize energy usage in its manufacturing facilities. They use analytics to monitor real-time energy consumption and identify opportunities to reduce it. This has helped Toyota to reduce its energy usage by 35% and save millions of dollars in energy costs.

General Electric: General Electric uses Big Data Analytics to optimize energy usage in their manufacturing facilities. They use analytics to monitor real-time energy consumption and identify opportunities to reduce it. This has helped General Electric to reduce its energy usage by 30% and save millions of dollars in energy costs.

Johnson Controls: Johnson Controls uses Big Data Analytics to optimize building energy usage. They use sensors and analytics to monitor energy usage and identify areas where they can reduce energy consumption. This has helped Johnson Controls to reduce energy usage by up to 25% in some buildings.

In conclusion, Big Data Analytics can help manufacturing companies monitor and optimize their energy usage, leading to cost savings and improved sustainability. By using sensors and analytics to monitor energy usage in real time, companies can identify opportunities to reduce energy consumption and make more informed decisions about energy usage.

References

1. *Dow Chemical continues success in energy efficiency*: Retrieved from: https://www.reliableplant.com/Read/16097/dow-chemical-continues-success-in-energy-efficiency. Accessed April 29, 2023.
2. *Data Center Energy Efficiency with Intel® Power Management Technologies*: Retrieved from: https://www.intel.in/content/www/in/en/software/intel-it-power-management-technologies-case-study.html. Accessed April 29, 2023.
3. *Growing revenues by 5% while reducing CO_2 emissions by 33%*: Retrieved from: https://toyota-forklifts.eu/about-toyota/news-and-editorials/growing-revenues-by-5-while-reducing-co2-emissions-by-33/. Accessed April 29, 2023.
4. *Part 1: Energy Efficiency is Our Future*: Retrieved from: https://www.ge.com/news/reports/part-1-energy-efficiency-is-our-future. Accessed April 29, 2023.
5. *Our leading energy-saving solutions benefit the planet and your business*: Retrieved from: https://www.johnsoncontrols.com/services-and-support/energy-and-efficiency-solutions. Accessed April 29, 2023.

21.3.6 Product Development

In order to gain insight into consumer preferences and behaviors, Nike employs Big Data Analytics to acquire and analyze customer data from various sources, including social media, customer reviews, and online behavior. The company uses this data to develop new products that better meet the needs of its customers and improve their overall experience.

For instance, Nike's data-driven approach to product development helped them launch their Flyknit technology, which uses a single piece of woven material to create a lightweight, comfortable, and supportive shoe. The idea for Flyknit came from Nike's customer feedback analysis and the desire for a more personalized and customizable shoe. By leveraging Big Data, Nike created a product that met the needs of its customers and became a significant success.

Nike also uses Big Data to inform its marketing strategies, creating more personalized and targeted campaigns that resonate with its audience. This has helped the company to better connect with its customers and increase brand loyalty.

References

1. *Here's How Nike Is Turning Data into Unrivaled Customer Experiences*: Retrieved from: https://nextgencx.wbresearch.com/blog/nike-data-unrivaled-customer-experiences-strategy. Accessed April 29, 2023.
2. *How Nike Is Using Data to Sell Directly to Customers*: Retrieved from: https://bernardmarr.com/how-nike-is-using-data-to-sell-directly-to-customers/. Accessed April 29, 2023.
3. *Nike: It's Data Analytics, Just Do It*: Retrieved from: https://d3.harvard.edu/platform-digit/submission/nike-its-data-analytics-just-do-it/. Accessed April 29, 2023.

21.3.7 Risk Management

Big Data Analytics can help manufacturers identify and mitigate potential business risks, leading to significant cost savings and improved safety. For example, in the case of BP, they use Big Data to monitor their offshore oil rigs and prevent potential environmental disasters. BP collects and analyzes vast amounts of data from sensors, weather forecasts, and other sources to identify potential risks such as equipment failures, human errors, and natural disasters, allowing them to take proactive actions/measures to prevent/avoid accidents before they occur.

Furthermore, BP uses predictive analytics to identify patterns and trends in its data, allowing it to make informed decisions about risk management and improve its overall safety culture. For instance, the company uses machine learning algorithms to analyze data from its drilling operations, helping to identify the factors that lead to successful drilling and reduce the likelihood of adverse incidents.

Big Data Analytics can also help manufacturers to comply with regulatory requirements and minimize the potential impact of accidents. By analyzing past data (historical data) and simulating different scenarios, companies like BP can identify potential (possible) risks and develop risk contingency plans to minimize the impact of accidents or environmental disasters.

References

1. *Energy with purpose*: Retrieved from: https://www.bp.com/content/dam/bp/business-sites/en/global/corporate/pdfs/sustainability/group-reports/bp-sustainability-report-2019.pdf. Accessed April 29, 2023.
2. *Big Data Analytics in oil and gas industry*: An emerging trend: Retrieved from: https://www.sciencedirect.com/science/article/pii/S2405656118301421. Accessed April 29, 2023.
3. *What do you need to know about data analytics in the oil and gas industry?*: Retrieved from: https://addepto.com/blog/data-analytics-in-the-oil-and-gas-industry/. Accessed April 29, 2023.

21.3.8 Warranty Analytics

Warranty analytics is an essential application of Big Data in the manufacturing industry. By analyzing warranty data, manufacturers can gain insights into the performance and quality of their products, as well as identify common issues and areas for improvement. This can help them to reduce warranty claims, improve customer satisfaction, and ultimately increase profits.

Caterpillar, a leading manufacturer of heavy equipment, is one company that has leveraged warranty analytics to improve its products. The company uses Big Data to analyze warranty data and identify failure patterns in its equipment. This information is used to improve the design and production processes and plan preventive maintenance schedules to reduce customer downtime.

In addition to improving product quality, warranty analytics can help manufacturers identify opportunities for cost savings. By analyzing warranty data, companies can identify components that fail more frequently than expected, allowing them to negotiate better pricing with suppliers or adjust production processes to reduce costs.

Overall, warranty analytics is a valuable tool for manufacturers looking to improve their product quality, reduce warranty claims, and increase profitability.

Reference

1. *Building Value with Big Data*: Retrieved from: https://www.caterpillar.com/en/news/caterpillarNews/2022/ar-big-data.html. Accessed April 29, 2023.

21.3.9 Customer Analytics

Utilizing Big Data Analytics, manufacturers can gain insights into customer preferences, behavior, and purchasing patterns, which can be used to tailor marketing and sales efforts to specific consumers or customer segments. As a result, manufacturers can create more personalized and effective marketing campaigns by understanding what customers want and need, increasing sales and customer satisfaction.

John Deere, a leading agricultural equipment manufacturer, uses Big Data Analytics to analyze customer data and develop targeted marketing campaigns. By leveraging customer data, John Deere can gain insights into what features and capabilities their customers value most in their products, which allows them to tailor/customize their marketing messages and product offerings accordingly. This has led to improved customer engagement and increased sales for the company.

In addition to marketing and sales, customer analytics can also be used to improve customer service and support. By analyzing customer data, manufacturers can gain insights into common customer issues and complaints, allowing them to address these issues and improve customer satisfaction proactively.

References

1. *How Data-Driven John Deere Wins the Market*: Retrieved from: https://www.esri.com/about/newsroom/publications/wherenext/john-deere-market-development-with-location-intelligence/. Accessed 29 April 2023.
2. *Big Data in Agriculture and how we do it at John Deere*: Retrieved from: https://h2020-demeter.eu/big-data-in-agriculture-and-how-we-do-it-at-john-deere/. Accessed 29 April 2023.

21.4 APPLICATIONS OF BIG DATA IN THE TRAVEL INDUSTRY

21.4.1 Customer Service

Using Big Data Analytics, Delta Airlines enhances customer service by providing personalized assistance via its mobile app. The airline's mobile app uses Data Analysis to provide passengers with real-time information and personalized recommendations based on travel history and preferences. For example, the app can use flight information and past preferences to suggest in-flight meal options and seat upgrades.

Moreover, Delta Airlines uses Big Data to analyze customer feedback and complaints to identify patterns and areas for improvement in its customer service. The airline also uses predictive analytics to anticipate customer needs and address potential issues before they arise.

By leveraging Big Data Analytics, Delta Airlines can provide a more personalized and efficient customer service experience, increasing customer satisfaction and loyalty.

References

1. *Big Data Takes Flight at Delta Air Lines*: Retrieved form: https://d3.harvard.edu/platform-digit/submission/big-data-takes-flight-at-delta-air-lines/. Accessed 29 April 2023.
2. *Delta crew leveraging Big Data to personalise in-flight experience*: Retrieved from: https://www.futuretravelexperience.com/2017/05/delta-crew-leveraging-big-data-to-personalise-in-flight-experience/. Accessed 29 April 2023.
3. *How Airlines are Using Big Data*: Retrieved from: https://medium.com/@exastax/how-airlines-are-using-big-data-6bf47bb27d90. Accessed 29 April 2023.

21.4.2 Predictive Maintenance

In the travel industry, predictive maintenance using Big Data Analytics can help prevent equipment failures and minimize downtime. GE Aviation is one company that uses Big Data to predict maintenance issues in its aircraft engines. The company uses data from engine sensors to monitor engine performance and identify potential problems. Then, the data is analyzed using machine learning algorithms, which can detect patterns and anomalies that may indicate a potential issue. This allows the airlines to schedule maintenance proactively, reducing the risk of unexpected downtime and flight cancellations.

In addition to reducing downtime, predictive maintenance helps in cost saving by enabling the airlines to schedule maintenance more efficiently and avoid unnecessary repairs. It also improves safety by identifying potential issues before they become critical.

Other companies in the travel industry are also exploring the use of predictive maintenance. For example, United Airlines uses Big Data to predict aircraft maintenance issues, while Amtrak uses predictive analytics to monitor trains and identify potential issues before they occur.

Overall, predictive maintenance using Big Data Analytics has the potential to revolutionize maintenance in the travel industry, improving safety, reducing downtime, and cutting costs.

References

1. *Predictive maintenance and condition monitoring*: Retrieved from: https://www.infineon.com/cms/en/applications/industrial/condition-monitoring-and-predictive-analytics/?gclid=Cj0KCQjwgLOiBhC7ARIsAIeetVDRsKwE-9KloDKyr598fzLU31rBr

pAphWPSuA65jQv0iS4VDfujEtQaAl_WEALw_wcB&gclsrc=aw.ds. Accessed 29 April 2023.
2. *The value of Big Data to MROS*: Retrieved from: https://www.aerospacetechreview.com/the-value-of-big-data-to-mros/. Accessed 29 April 2023.

21.4.3 Weather Forecasting

Weather is one of the significant factors affecting airline operations. Using Big Data Analytics, airlines can access real-time weather data to enhance their operations. Airlines can use weather data to optimize their flight routes, reduce delays, and ensure safe operations. For instance, United Airlines uses Big Data Analytics to optimize its operations by analyzing weather data in real time. They use various data sources, including satellite images, radar data and weather models, to predict weather patterns and fine-tune their flight schedules and routes. This approach helps United Airlines to improve customer satisfaction, reduce costs, and improve safety by avoiding potentially dangerous weather conditions.

In addition to optimizing flight schedules and routes, airlines can use weather data to regulate fuel consumption, reduce emissions, and minimize environmental impact. For example, airlines can use weather data to determine the optimal flight altitude and speed to minimize fuel consumption and emissions. This approach can help airlines reduce operating costs and contribute to a more sustainable aviation industry.

References

1. *United Airlines to Employ FlightAware's Predictive Data*: Retrieved from: https://airlinegeeks.com/2020/09/25/united-airlines-to-employ-flightaware-s-predictive-data/. Accessed 29 April 2023.
2. *Aviation weather forecast solutions*: Retrieved from: https://www.ibm.com/weather/industries/aviation. Accessed 29 April 2023.
3. *Weather Forecasting: How Does Big Data Analytics Magnify it*: Retrieved from: https://www.analyticssteps.com/blogs/weather-forecasting-how-do-big-data-analytics-magnify-it. Accessed 29 April 2023.

21.4.4 Customer Sentiment Analysis

Hilton Hotels & Resorts uses Big Data Analytics to obtain insights from customer feedback and enhance the guest experience. The hotel chain uses a social listening tool to monitor online conversations about its brand and analyze customer sentiment data such as social media posts and reviews. This data helps Hilton understand customer needs and preferences, identify areas for improvement, and create targeted marketing campaigns.

Moreover, Hilton also collects and analyzes customer data from its loyalty program, Hilton Honors, to personalize the guest experience. As a result, Hilton can provide personalized customer recommendations and offers to improve customer loyalty and satisfaction.

Big Data Analytics has helped Hilton improve its guest experience and drive revenue growth. For example, Hilton's revenue per available room (RevPAR) increased by 2.7% in the first quarter of 2021, partly due to its focus on personalized guest experiences through customer data analytics.

References

1. *Social media analytics: Extracting and visualizing Hilton hotel ratings and reviews from TripAdvisor*: Retrieved from: https://www.researchgate.net/publication/321077978_Social_media_analytics_Extracting_and_visualizing_Hilton_hotel_ratings_and_reviews_from_TripAdvisor. Accessed 29 April 2023.
2. *Case Study: How Hilton uses social listening to win customers*: Retrieved from: https://awario.com/blog/hilton-social-media-case-study/. Accessed 29 April 2023.

21.4.5 Destination Management

Big Data Analytics has been used in the travel industry to help manage destinations and improve tourism experiences. Destination management organizations (DMOs) can use Big Data Analytics to collect, analyze and interpret a vast amount of data related to tourism activities, visitor behaviors, and patterns to help them make informed decisions that can enhance their tourist experience.

For example, the Singapore Tourism Board (STB) has been using Big Data Analytics to provide real-time insights into tourism activities. STB uses Big Data Analytics to analyze tourist data such as hotel occupancy rates, visitor arrivals, spending patterns, foot traffic, and reviews to optimize tourism offerings and improve the overall tourist experience. These insights enable STB to adjust its tourism strategies in real time, providing visitors with relevant information and improving the overall tourism experience.

Moreover, DMOs can use Big Data Analytics to target specific tourist segments effectively. For example, by analyzing data on tourists' preferences and behavior, DMOs can create customized packages and services that appeal to their specific needs. This improves the overall tourist experience and leads to increased tourism revenue.

Big Data Analytics can help DMOs to enhance the overall tourist experience by analyzing and interpreting vast amounts of tourist data. It helps DMOs to provide customized services, optimize tourism offerings, and make informed decisions to attract more tourists.

References

1. *Singapore Tourism Board – Strategy Towards 2020*: Retrieved from: https://www.thinkdigital.travel/opinion/singapore-tourism-board-strategy-towards-2020. Accessed 29 April 2023.
2. *How the Singapore Tourism Board uses data to personalize tourism*: Retrieved from: https://govinsider.asia/intl-en/article/how-the-singapore-tourism-board-uses-data-to-personalise-tourism. Accessed 29 April 2023.

21.4.6 Operational Efficiency

Hertz (a car rental company) employs Big Data Analytics to optimize its rental car fleet and increase operational efficiency. By analyzing historical rental data, weather patterns, and other factors, Hertz can predict demand and adjust its fleet accordingly, ensuring that the correct number and type of vehicles are available at suitable locations.

Moreover, the company uses GPS tracking and telematics devices to monitor the performance and condition of its vehicles in real time, allowing it to proactively identify maintenance issues and schedule repairs, reducing downtime and improving the overall customer experience.

Hertz's use of Big Data Analytics has improved operational efficiency, reduced costs, and increased revenue. The company has reduced its inventory by optimizing its fleet, saving on storage and maintenance costs while increasing revenue by providing better customer service and improving the overall rental experience.

References

1. *How Big Data is giving Hertz a big advantage*: Retrieved from: https://www.ciosummits.com/media/pdf/solution_spotlight/IBM_big-data-giving-hertz-advantage.pdf. Accessed 29 April 2023.
2. *What is the role of Big Data in transforming on-demand vehicle rental sector*. Retrieved from: https://customerthink.com/what-is-the-role-of-big-data-in-transforming-on-demand-vehicle-rental-sector/. Accessed 29 April 2023.

21.4.7 Revenue Management

Revenue management is vital to the travel industry, and Big Data Analytics can significantly optimize revenue. By analyzing data such as demand, pricing, and customer behavior, companies can develop strategies to maximize revenue and profits.

Marriott International is one example of a company that uses Big Data to optimize revenue management. By analyzing data such as room demand, pricing, and inventory, Marriott can adjust its pricing and availability in real time to maximize revenue. The company also uses predictive analytics to forecast demand and adjusts pricing accordingly.

In addition to Marriott, other companies in the travel industry, such as airlines, online travel agencies, and car rental companies, also use Big Data Analytics to optimize revenue management. For example, American Airlines uses Big Data to optimize its pricing and inventory management, while Expedia uses Big Data to analyze customer behavior and improve its pricing and promotions.

Overall, Big Data Analytics can play a crucial role in revenue management in the travel industry by helping companies optimize pricing, availability, and inventory to maximize revenue and profits.

References

1. *Marriott International Increases Revenue by Implementing a Group Pricing Optimizer*. Retrieved from: https://www.jstor.org/stable/40599237. Accessed 29 April 2023.

2. *Hotel revenue management: Strategies to boost topline revenue*: Retrieved from: https://www.siteminder.com/r/hotel-revenue-management-strategies/. Accessed 29 April 2023.

SUMMARY

Big Data is gaining popularity, and many industries have started implementing Big Data solutions in a phased manner rather than as a big-bang implementation. Although these implementations can be done within 4 to 10 weeks, it is essential that the various stakeholders in the system collaborate properly for the implementation to be successful and gain mass adoption. That is why industries are implementing Big Data in the pilot mode. The pilot mode helps the stakeholders check the new technology's functionality and helps them to keep up and gain more business, customer confidence, and scalability.

Appendix A

Model Questions

SET I

Duration: 3 Hrs   Max Marks: 75

Part-A (10 × 1 = 10)

Answer ALL the Questions

1. In _____ stage, referential integrity, performance tuning, indexing, and triggers are defined.
   A. Conceptual Data model   B. Logical Data model
   C. Physical Data model   D. Hierarchical Data model

2. Frequency distribution, variability, and measures of central tendency are some types of _____.
   A. Confirmatory Analysis   B. Descriptive Analysis
   C. Exploratory Analysis   D. Predictive Analysis

3. A data present in Word document is an example of _____.
   A. Structured Data   B. Unstructured Data
   C. Semi-structured Data   D. Mixed Data

4. _____ was the first search engine to systematically sort, store, and retrieve large amounts of data.
   A. Google   B. Microsoft Edge
   C. Yahoo   D. Apache Lucene

5. _____ is a part of Apache open-source project that helps customers to create scalable "Machine Learning" Algorithms.
   A. Tableau   B. Apache Spark
   C. Apache Hive   D. Apache Mahout

6. _____ is the common name of a software that runs above the physical server (hardware) or host.
   A. Hypervisor   B. Cloud
   C. Virtual Software   D. Supervisor

7. To check the list of Hadoop services that are up and running, we can use _____ command.
   A. Rmdir   B. Chmod
   C. JPS   D. LS

8. _____ performs the transformation operations like column pruning, reordering on the execution plan, and improving efficiency and scalability.
   A. Hive Driver
   B. Hive Optimizer
   C. HiveServer2
   D. Hive Compiler

9. The three phases of Spark Streaming in the correct order are_____.
   A. Processing, Data Storage and Gathering
   B. Processing, Gathering and Data Storage
   C. Gathering, Data Storage and Processing
   D. Gathering, Processing, and Data Storage

10. _____ helps for bootstrapping Cassandra
    A. Data Node
    B. Data Center
    C. Cluster
    D. Seeds Node

Part-B (5 × 2 = 10)

Answer ALL the Questions

1. What is Qualitative Data?
2. What do you mean by Inferential Analysis?
3. What are Type 1 and Type 2 Hypervisors?
4. List down the three main components of HBase architecture
5. What is the meaning of NoSQL?

Part-C (5 × 5 = 25)

Answer Any FIVE Questions

1. What is Clustering? Explain connectivity-based clustering in brief.
2. Give a brief account on tokenization with examples.
3. Write short notes on the five *V*'s of Big Data.
4. How is security in Hadoop taken care of?
5. Write short notes on Hive table and its types.
6. Give a brief account on Spark streaming.
7. Write a Python program to draw a bar chart.

Part-D (3 × 10 = 30)

Answer Any THREE Questions

1. Explain Forecasting in detail.
2. Write an essay on the different types of Big Data.
3. Elaborate on Hadoop key-value pair.
4. Give a detailed account on the architecture of HBase.
5. Illustrate cluster management in Spark.

SET II

Duration: 3 Hrs **Max Marks: 75**

Part-A (10 × 1 = 10)

Answer ALL the Questions

1. _____ organizes data elements and standardizes how they relate to one another. It emulates a possible real-world scenario.
   A. Data Discovery B. Data Preparation
   C. Data Presentation D. Data Model

2. "feels" and "feeling" is converted to "feel" in _____.
   A. Tokenization B. Lower Casing
   C. Stemming D. Lemmatization

3. Data should add _____ to the end customer in order to have business impactful insights.
   A. Volume B. Velocity
   C. Variety D. Value

4. Hadoop daemon runs in a separate Java process in _____ mode.
   A. Standalone B. Pseudo-distributed
   C. Fully distributed D. Redistributed

5. The default block size of HDFS is _____.
   A. 128 KB B. 646 MB
   C. 646 KB D. 128 MB

6. _____ runs on 8080 port and is mainly used for administration purpose.
   A. Virtual Box B. Ambari
   C. Cloud Era D. VMWare work station

7. Which of the following commands is used for creating a new file on HDFS with size 0 bytes?
   A. tail B. touch
   C. touchz D. appendToFile

8. HBase uses _____ as a database.
   A. HMaster B. Data Node
   C. Region D. ZooKeeper

9. In BASE properties of NoSQL, S stands for _____.
   A. Schema-less B. Sharding
   C. Scalability D. Soft State

10. _____ depicts the way how variables can change over some time.
    A. Line Graph B. Column Chart
    C. Bar Chart D. Area Chart

Part-B (5 × 2 = 10)

Answer ALL the Questions

1. Define Data Analytics.
2. What is Stop-word removal?
3. What is the role of Pig Optimizer?
4. List down a few Use Cases of Cassandra.
5. What is Data Visualization?

Part-C (5 × 5 = 25)

Answer Any FIVE Questions

1. Write any three applications of Text Analytics.
2. Write short notes on Flume.
3. What are the advantages of using Hadoop?
4. Explain Hadoop ecosystem and its five major components.
5. Give a brief account on Region split in HBase.
6. Write short notes on Gossip in Cassandra.
7. What are all the problems related to Vulnerability in Hadoop? How are they overcome?

Part-D (3x10=30)

Answer Any THREE Questions

1. Explain typical Analytical Architecture in detail.
2. Explain HDFS Architecture in detail with its various components.
3. How can an internal/managed table be created in Hive? How is data loaded into a HIVE Table?
4. Write an essay on interpreting Pig Scripts.
5. Elucidate on the usages of Big Data in the field of marketing.

SET III

Duration: 3 Hrs **Max Marks: 75**

Part-A (10 × 1 = 10)

Answer ALL the Questions

1. _____ refers to computing infrastructure and resources, including software and data, stored on remote servers that users can access via the Internet.
   A. Algorithm
   B. Batch Processing
   C. Behavioral Analytics
   D. Cloud Computing

2. _____ is used by organizations to determine which independent or predictor variables (input) hold the most influence on over-dependent (output) variable.
   A. Regression Modelling
   B. Classification Modelling
   C. Clustering Model
   D. Outliers Model

3. Hadoop runs on a cluster of computers inside a _____.
   A. Cluster
   B. Rack
   C. Computer
   D. Laptop

4. Pig belongs to which layer of Hadoop ecosystem?
   A. Data Ingestion Layer
   B. Data Storage Layer
   C. Processing engine Layer
   D. Analysis Layer

5. Apache Hadoop uses _____ for managing security.
   A. Hive
   B. Kerberos
   C. ZooKeeper
   D. MapReduce

6. _____ is another security feature provided by Hartonworks in a data platform.
   A. Ambari Console
   B. Oracle Virtualbox
   C. VMWare Workstation
   D. Kerberos

7. We won't be able to compute the outcome if any of the machines fails to produce output. This is called as_____.
   A. Critical Path Problem
   B. Problem of Reliability
   C. Equal Split issue
   D. Single Split Failure

8. _____ helps to convert Pig Latin into MapReduce.
   A. Pig Optimizer
   B. Pig Compiler
   C. Pig Engine
   D. Pig Interpreter

9. _____ is equivalent to a schema or database in a relational paradigm.
   A. Cluster
   B. Keyspace
   C. Column Family
   D. Rows

10. Which of the following is not a disadvantage of Hadoop system?
    A. Ability to handle tiny files
    B. Processing speed
    C. Caching issue
    D. Replication issue

Part-B (5 × 2 = 10)

Answer ALL the Questions

1. What is data aggregation?
2. What is veracity?
3. Write short notes on the key-value pair of MapReduce.

4. What is Micro Batching in Spark SQL?
5. Define Node, and Data Center in Cassandra.

Part-C (5 × 5 = 25)
Answer Any FIVE Questions
1. Briefly explain Data Lake.
2. Write short notes on Rack Awareness Algorithm.
3. Explain the different flavors of Hadoop.
4. How does tuning the number of MapReduce help in Hadoop optimization?
5. Explain any five Pig built-in eval functions.
6. Explain the Architecture components of Cassandra.
7. List down a few key Big Data security issues.

Part-D (3 × 10 = 30)
Answer Any THREE Questions
1. Give a detailed account on the various predictive analytics algorithms.
2. Explain HDFS blocks formation, data replication and rack awareness in detail.
3. Explain about the architecture of HIVE in detail.
4. Illustrate the workflow in HIVE.
5. Elaborate on Cassandra and its features.

Appendix B

Capstone Projects

Project 1 (HDFS)
Design and build a data visualization tool in Excel for HDFS that can provide an interactive and intuitive view of the data stored in HDFS. First write a Java program to export data from HDFS to the local directory excel file. Another Java program should access and query the data from Excel sheet, use various visualization techniques (e.g., charts, graphs, maps, dashboards) to display the data in a meaningful way. You can use Fusion Chart for the same.

Submission Guidelines
The submitted program file should have the following program headers:
Roll No.
Name
Assignment number
Specific compilation/execution flags (if required)
Copying from friends/web will lead to strict penalties.

Project 2 (HDFS)
Create a tool that allows users to connect to HDFS data sources from Excel and perform various tasks such as querying, importing, exporting, updating, and analyzing HDFS data. The tool can leverage the CData Excel Add-in for HDFS, which provides a simple way to access HDFS data from Excel. The tool can also use the QUERY formula to automate spreadsheet operations based on HDFS data. The project can demonstrate how to use Excel as a powerful interface for working with Big Data stored in HDFS.

Submission Guidelines
The submitted program file should have the following program headers:
Roll No.
Name
Assignment number
Specific compilation/execution flags (if required)
Copying from friends/web will lead to strict penalties.

Project 3 (MapReduce)

Group similar documents based on their content using MapReduce. A possible solution is to use a term frequency-inverse document frequency (TF-IDF) approach to compute the similarity between documents and apply a clustering algorithm such as k-means or hierarchical clustering on the MapReduce framework.

Submission Guidelines

The submitted program file should have the following program headers:
Roll No.
Name
Assignment number
Specific compilation/execution flags (if required)
Copying from friends/web will lead to strict penalties.

Project 4 (MapReduce)

Sort a large amount of data using MapReduce. A possible solution is to use a partitioning-based sorting algorithm such as quicksort or mergesort on the MapReduce framework, where each mapper sorts a subset of data and each reducer merges the sorted subsets.

Submission Guidelines

The submitted program file should have the following program headers:
Roll No.
Name
Assignment number
Specific compilation/execution flags (if required)
Copying from friends/web will lead to strict penalties.

Project 5 (Data ingestion using Sqoop)

Create a data pipeline that imports data from a relational database into HDFS and performs some analysis on it. Sqoop is a tool that allows transferring data between Hadoop and relational databases. HDFS is a distributed file system that stores data in Hadoop clusters.

The project could involve the following steps:

- Identify a relational database source that contains some interesting data, such as customer transactions, product reviews, social media posts, etc.
- Use Sqoop to import the data from the relational database into HDFS. Specify the appropriate parameters for Sqoop, such as the connection string, the table name, the number of mappers, the target directory, etc.
- Verify that the data is successfully imported into HDFS by using commands such as 'hdfs dfs -ls' or 'hdfs dfs -cat'.
- Perform some analysis on the data using tools such as Hive, Pig, Spark, etc. For example, you could calculate some statistics, perform some aggregations, join some tables, filter some records, etc.

- Write a report that describes the data source, the Sqoop import process, the analysis results, and any challenges or insights you encountered during the project.

Submission Guidelines
The submitted program file should have the following program headers:
Roll No.
Name
Assignment number
Specific compilation/execution flags (if required)
Copying from friends/web will lead to strict penalties.

Project 6 (Data ingestion using Flume)
Design and implement a data pipeline that collects and analyzes your Facebook data in real time using FLUME. HDFS can be used to store and manage the Facebook data in a distributed and fault-tolerant manner. Read the data from HDFS and perform sentiment analysis and display the result.

Submission Guidelines
The submitted program file should have the following program headers:
Roll No.
Name
Assignment number
Specific compilation/execution flags (if required)
Copying from friends/web will lead to strict penalties.

Project 7 (HIVE)
Design and build a data visualization tool in Excel for HIVE that can provide an interactive and intuitive view of the data stored in HIVE. First, write a Java program to export data from HIVE to the local directory excel file. Another Java program should access and query the data from an Excel sheet. Use various visualization techniques (e.g., charts, graphs, maps, dashboards) to display the data in a meaningful way. You can use Fusion Chart for the same.

Submission Guidelines
The submitted program file should have the following program headers:
Roll No.
Name
Assignment number
Specific compilation/execution flags (if required)
Copying from friends/web will lead to strict penalties.

Project 8 (HIVE and HDFS)
Create a data warehouse and perform analytical queries on a large-scale dataset. HIVE is a data warehouse software that facilitates reading, writing, and managing large datasets

residing in distributed storage using SQL. HDFS is a distributed file system that provides high-throughput access to application data.

The project could consist of the following steps:

- Choose a suitable dataset that is available in a structured or semi-structured format, such as JSON, CSV, XML, etc. The dataset should be large enough to demonstrate the scalability and performance of HIVE and HDFS. For example, one could use the Yelp dataset (https://www.yelp.com/dataset) that contains information about businesses, reviews, users, etc.
- Upload the dataset to HDFS using the Hadoop command-line interface or a graphical user interface such as Hue (https://gethue.com/). The dataset should be split into multiple files and stored across different nodes in the cluster.
- Create a database and tables in HIVE using the HIVE query language (HQL). The tables should correspond to the schema of the dataset and specify the location of the data files in HDFS. For example, one could create a table for businesses with columns such as business_id, name, address, categories, etc.
- Load the data from HDFS into HIVE tables using the LOAD DATA command or by specifying the external table property. The data should be stored in a compressed and optimized format such as ORC (https://orc.apache.org/) or Parquet (https://parquet.apache.org/) to improve query performance and reduce storage space.
- Perform analytical queries on the HIVE tables using HQL or a graphical user interface such as Hue. The queries should answer some interesting questions or provide some insights about the dataset. For example, one could query the average rating of businesses by category, the most popular keywords in reviews, the distribution of users by location, etc.
- Evaluate the performance of HIVE and HDFS by measuring metrics such as query execution time, resource utilization, scalability, fault tolerance, etc.

Project 9 (HBase and Excel)

Create a dashboard that analyzes the performance of a large-scale distributed database system using HBase. HBase is a NoSQL database that runs on top of Hadoop and provides fast and scalable access to Big Data. Excel is a spreadsheet application that can be used for data preparation, transformation, visualization and reporting.

The steps for this project are:

- Install and configure HBase on a cluster of machines or use a cloud service that offers HBase as a service.
- Load some sample data into HBase tables using the HBase shell or a client API such as Java or Python.
- Use the HBase metrics system to collect and export various metrics about the database system, such as read/write latency, throughput, compaction, garbage collection, etc.
- Import the metrics data into Excel using the Power Query feature or a custom connector.

- Use Excel formulas, functions, charts, slicers and pivot tables to analyze and visualize the metrics data and identify any performance issues or bottlenecks in the database system.
- Create a dashboard in Excel that summarizes the key findings and recommendations for improving the database performance.
- Write a report that explains the purpose, methodology, results and conclusion of the project.

Project 10 (Cassandra)

Create a data analysis tool that can import and export data from Cassandra to Excel, and vice-versa. The tool can use the CData Excel Add-in for Cassandra and the CData ODBC Driver for Cassandra to connect with live Cassandra data and perform various operations such as reading, writing, updating, filtering, and querying data. The tool can also leverage Excel's features such as charts, pivot tables, and formulas to analyze and visualize the Cassandra data. The project can demonstrate how to use Microsoft Query and parameters to create dynamic queries that can be refreshed based on user input. The project can also compare the performance and scalability of Cassandra and Excel for different types of data and queries.

Appendix C

Model Syllabi

MODEL SYLLABUS 1

Credits: 5

Contacts per week: 3 lectures

Module I

Data Models and Analysis: Object-based data models; Record-based data models; Types of data (nominal, ordinal, discrete and continuous); Nature of data (transaction, social, and machine data); Data analysis methods (correlation, regression); Clustering and classification; Evolution of analytic scalability; Business drivers for analytics; Typical analytical architecture; Analytic processes and tools; Data analytic life-cycle; Key roles for successful analytic projects; Modern-day Intelligence.

Fundamentals of Big Data: Big Data concepts and terminology; Big Data types; Big Data Analytics; Distributed file system in Big Data; Big Data characteristics; Challenges of processing Big Data; Drivers for Big Data; Big Data Analysis framework; Approaches for Big Data Analysis; Understanding text analytics and Big Data; Predictive analysis of Big Data; Procedural vs. Functional programming models for Big Data; Big Data integration process; Big Data technology landscape; Big Data key roles.

Module II

Fundamentals of Hadoop: Problems with traditional large-scale systems; History of Hadoop; Why Hadoop?; Different flavors of Hadoop; Different modes of Hadoop; Core components of Hadoop; Hadoop ecosystem (data ingestion layer, data storage layer, processing engine, analysis layer, and management and coordination layer); HDFS architecture; Data integrity in Hadoop; Data locality in Hadoop; Limitations of Hadoop; Apache Hadoop and RDBMS; Problems with small files in Hadoop; Security in Hadoop; Hadoop 1.0 vs. 2.0; Zeppelin architecture; NoSQL concepts.

HDFS: Virtualization; HDFS command line interface (basic commands); VMware vs. VirtualBox; HDFS features; HDFS architecture; HDFS read request; HDFS write request; HDFS blocks; Data racks; Block replication; Rack awareness algorithm; Data integrity in

HDFS; Data locality in HDFS; Distributed cache in HDFS; HDFS serialization; Directory creation in HDFS; Connecting HDFS from Python.

Module III

MapReduce: Features; Advantages of MapReduce; A real-world problem; Real-time use cases of MapReduce; MapReduce phases (splitting, mapping, shuffling, reducing); Word count example; MapReduce job; Hadoop mapper; Hadoop reducer; Hadoop key-value pair; Input format in MapReduce; Input split in MapReduce; Hadoop record reader; MapReduce partitioner; Shuffling and sorting in MapReduce; Hadoop output formats; Input split vs. HDFS block in MapReduce; Map-only jobs; Hadoop speculative execution; Hadoop counters; Hadoop optimization; MapReduce performance tuning; Introduction to YARN.

Module IV

HIVE: Need for Hive; Features of Hive; Limitations of Hive; Hive architecture; Workflow in Hive; Hive vs. Traditional database; Categorization of data in Hive; Creating and using database; Creating table; Adding data into table; Interacting with HDFS using Hive; Hive commands: Loading, Filtering and Grouping; Data types and operators in Hive; Relational operators in Hive; Arithmetic and logical operators in Hive; Hive complex operators; Four types of joins; Map join and bucket join.

NoSQL: NoSQL definition; Types of NoSQL databases (column family databases, key-value pair database, document store, graph database); Examples of NoSQL databases; Advantages of NoSQL databases; NoSQL usage; SQL vs. NoSQL; New SQL; ACID and BASE properties; Two-phase commit; Schema, sharding and share-nothing architecture; Four basic strategies for shard structure; Brewer's CAP Theorem; Cassandra – Definition and features; Key structures in Cassandra; Architecture of MongoDB.

Module V

Big Data Visualization: History of data visualization; Big Data visualization; Importance of Big Data visualization; How does data visualization work?; Types of data visualization; Challenges of Big Data visualization; Introduction to Tableau.

Business implementation of Big Data: Big Data in business; Big Data in marketing (customer segmentation, lead generation, predictive marketing); How the cloud is driving Big Data for marketing; Challenges in implementing Big Data in marketing; Big Data in the banking sector (fraud detection, customer contentment); Big Data in healthcare sector; Big Data in education sector; Security in Big Data; Big Data on cloud; Best practices in Big Data implementation; Latest trend in Big Data.

Model Syllabus 2

Credits: 5

Contacts per week: 3 lectures

Module I

Data Models and Analysis: Object-based data models; Record-based data models; Types of data (nominal, ordinal, discrete and continuous); Nature of data (transaction, social, and machine data); Data analysis methods (correlation, regression); Clustering and classification; Evolution of analytic scalability; Business drivers for analytics; Typical analytical architecture; Analytic processes and tools; Data analytic life-cycle; Key roles for successful analytic projects; Modern-day Intelligence.

Fundamentals of Big Data: Big Data concepts and terminology; Big Data types; Big Data Analytics; Distributed file system in Big Data; Big Data characteristics; Challenges of processing Big Data; Drivers for Big Data; Big Data Analysis framework; Approaches for Big Data Analysis; Understanding text analytics and Big Data; Predictive analysis of Big Data; Procedural vs. Functional programming models for Big Data; Big Data integration process; Big Data technology landscape; Big Data key roles.

Module II

Fundamentals of Hadoop: Problems with traditional large-scale systems; History of Hadoop; Why Hadoop?; Different flavors of Hadoop; Different modes of Hadoop; Core components of Hadoop; Hadoop ecosystem (data ingestion layer, data storage layer, processing engine, analysis layer, and management and coordination layer); HDFS architecture; Data integrity in Hadoop; Data locality in Hadoop; Limitations of Hadoop; Apache Hadoop and RDBMS; Problems with small files in Hadoop; Security in Hadoop; Hadoop 1.0 vs. 2.0; Zeppelin architecture; NoSQL concepts.

HDFS: Virtualization; HDFS command line interface (basic commands); VMware vs. VirtualBox; HDFS features; HDFS architecture; HDFS read request; HDFS write request; HDFS blocks; Data racks; Block replication; Rack awareness algorithm; Data integrity in HDFS; Data locality in HDFS; Distributed cache in HDFS; HDFS serialization; Directory creation in HDFS; Connecting HDFS from Python.

Module III

MapReduce: Features; Advantages of MapReduce; A real-world problem; Real-time use cases of MapReduce; MapReduce phases (splitting, mapping, shuffling, reducing); Word count example; MapReduce job; Hadoop mapper; Hadoop reducer; Hadoop key-value pair; Input format in MapReduce; Input split in MapReduce; Hadoop record reader; MapReduce partitioner; Shuffling and sorting in MapReduce; Hadoop output formats; Input split vs. HDFS block in MapReduce; Map-only jobs; Hadoop speculative execution; Hadoop counters; Hadoop optimization; MapReduce performance tuning; Introduction to YARN.

Module IV

HIVE: Need for Hive; Features of Hive; Limitations of Hive; Hive architecture; Workflow in Hive; Hive vs. Traditional database; Categorization of data in Hive; Creating and using database; Creating table; Adding data into table; Interacting with HDFS using Hive; Hive commands: Loading, Filtering and Grouping; Data types and operators in Hive; Relational operators in Hive; Arithmetic and logical operators in Hive; Hive complex operators; Four types of joins; Map join and bucket join.

HBase: Features of HBase; Architecture of HBase; Managing large datasets with HBase; HBase compaction; Schema design; Load balancing; Data recovery; HBase crash recovery; Creating HBase tables; Adding data to tables; Scanning tables; Altering table; Deleting table; Disabling and enabling table; Truncating and dropping table; Defining external table; Hive and HBase integration; Advanced indexing in HBase; Filters; Comparison operators; Counters; Co-processor.

Module V

Big Data Visualization: History of data visualization; Big Data visualization; Importance of Big Data visualization; How does data visualization work?; Types of data visualization; Challenges of Big Data visualization; Introduction to Tableau.

Business implementation of Big Data: Big Data in business; Big Data in marketing (customer segmentation, lead generation, predictive marketing); How the cloud is driving Big Data for marketing; Challenges in implementing Big Data in marketing; Big Data in the banking sector (fraud detection, customer contentment); Big Data in healthcare sector; Big Data in education sector; Security in Big Data; Big Data on cloud; Best practices in Big Data implementation; Latest trend in Big Data.

Model Syllabus 3

Credits: 5

Contacts per week: 3 lectures

Module I

Data Models and Analysis: Object-based data models; Record-based data models; Types of data (nominal, ordinal, discrete and continuous); Nature of data (transaction, social, and machine data); Data analysis methods (correlation, regression); Clustering and classification; Evolution of analytic scalability; Business drivers for analytics; Typical analytical architecture; Analytic processes and tools; Data analytic life-cycle; Key roles for successful analytic projects; Modern-day Intelligence.

Fundamentals of Big Data: Big Data concepts and terminology; Big Data types; Big Data Analytics; Distributed file system in Big Data; Big Data characteristics; Challenges of processing Big Data; Drivers for Big Data; Big Data Analysis framework; Approaches for Big Data Analysis; Understanding text analytics and Big Data; Predictive analysis of Big Data; Procedural vs. Functional programming models for Big Data; Big Data integration process; Big Data technology landscape; Big Data key roles.

Module II

Fundamentals of Hadoop: Problems with traditional large-scale systems; History of Hadoop; Why Hadoop?; Different flavors of Hadoop; Different modes of Hadoop; Core components of Hadoop; Hadoop ecosystem (data ingestion layer, data storage layer, processing engine, analysis layer, and management and coordination layer); HDFS architecture; Data integrity in Hadoop; Data locality in Hadoop; Limitations of Hadoop; Apache Hadoop and RDBMS; Problems with small files in Hadoop; Security in Hadoop; Hadoop 1.0 vs. 2.0; Zeppelin architecture; NoSQL concepts.

HDFS: Virtualization; HDFS command line interface (basic commands); VMware vs. VirtualBox; HDFS features; HDFS architecture; HDFS read request; HDFS write request; HDFS blocks; Data racks; Block replication; Rack awareness algorithm; Data integrity in HDFS; Data locality in HDFS; Distributed cache in HDFS; HDFS serialization; Directory creation in HDFS; Connecting HDFS from Python.

Module III

MapReduce: Features; Advantages of MapReduce; A real-world problem; Real-time use cases of MapReduce; MapReduce phases (splitting, mapping, shuffling, reducing); Word count example; MapReduce job; Hadoop mapper; Hadoop reducer; Hadoop key-value pair; Input format in MapReduce; Input split in MapReduce; Hadoop record reader; MapReduce partitioner; Shuffling and sorting in MapReduce; Hadoop output formats; Input split vs. HDFS block in MapReduce; Map-only jobs; Hadoop speculative execution; Hadoop counters; Hadoop optimization; MapReduce performance tuning; Introduction to YARN.

Spark: History of Spark; Spark ecosystem; Supporting languages; Spark core; Spark SQL; Spark streaming; Spark MLlib; Spark Graph X; SparkR; Cluster management; Design principles for Apache Spark; Advantages of Spark; Disadvantages of Apache Spark; Apache Spark physical architecture; Apache Spark layered architecture (RDD, DAG); Ways to create RDD in Spark; Paired RDD; Dazzling features of Spark RDD; Persistence and caching mechanisms in Apache Spark; Operations of Apache Spark RDD; Apache Spark RDD limitations; Need for DAG in Apache Spark; Working Principle of DAG in Spark; Applications of Apache Spark; Spark in real-world; Use cases of Spark; Spark vs. Hadoop.

Module IV

NoSQL: NoSQL definition; Types of NoSQL databases (column family databases, key-value pair database, document store, graph database); Examples of NoSQL databases; Advantages of NoSQL databases; NoSQL usage; SQL vs. NoSQL; New SQL; ACID and BASE properties; Two-phase commit; Schema, sharding and share-nothing architecture; Four basic strategies for shard structure; Brewer's CAP Theorem; Cassandra – Definition and features; Key structures in Cassandra; Architecture of MongoDB.

MongoDB: MongoDB history; MongoDB schema design; MongoDB key features; RDBMS vs. MongoDB; MongoDB Query Language (MQL); MongoDB Database; Collection and Documents; MongoDB Server; CRUD Operation in MongoDB; Showcasing the current database used; Showcasing the tables (collections) in the current database; Reading collections in MongoDB (R of CRUD); Updating documents in MongoDB (U of CRUD); Delete operation in MongoDB (D of CRUD); Dropping (deleting) a particular database; `Pretty()` method; AND in MongoDB; OR in MongoDB; Using AND and OR together; NOR in MongoDB; NOT in MongoDB; Creating and querying through indexes.

Module V

Big Data Visualization: History of data visualization; Big Data visualization; Importance of Big Data visualization; How does data visualization work?; Types of data visualization; Challenges of Big Data visualization; Introduction to Tableau.

Business implementation of Big Data: Big Data in business; Big Data in marketing (customer segmentation, lead generation, predictive marketing); How the cloud is driving

Big Data for marketing; Challenges in implementing Big Data in marketing; Big Data in the banking sector (fraud detection, customer contentment); Big Data in healthcare sector; Big Data in education sector; Security in Big Data; Big Data on cloud; Best practices in Big Data implementation; Latest trend in Big Data.

Limitations of Hadoop: Problem with small files – vulnerable, processing time is slow, not easy to use, supports only batch processing, no delta interaction, security problem.

Case Studies: Insurance sector; Retail sector; Healthcare sector.

Index

A

A/B testing, 127
ACID and BASE Models, 229
ACID method, 751
ACK (DigestAckMessage), 830
ACK2 (DigestAck2Message), 831
Adaptive Query Execution (AQE), 652
Algorithm, 98
Amazon DynamoDB, 737
Ambari administration, 289
Analytic processes and tools, 67
Analytic scalability, 26
Analytical architecture, 64
ANSI SQL compliance, 653
Anti-entropy, 844
Apache Ambari, 204
Apache Drill, 203
Apache Flume, 442
    Architecture, 443
Apache Impala, 194, 466
Apache Kafka, 455
    Features of, 456
Apache Mahout, 202
Apache Mesos, 660
Apache NiFi, 195, 467
Apache Pig User-Defined Functions, 626
Apache Pig, 607
    Architecture, 608
    Features of, 608
Apache Samza, 590
Apache Spark, 589
    Architecture of, 681
    Design principles, 662
    Latency issues, 589
    Need for DAG in, 695
    Physical architecture, 677f
    Physical execution plan, 678f
    Persistence and caching mechanism in, 687
    Streaming, 589
Apache Storm, 195
Artificial intelligence, 98
Atomicity, 749
Attribute, 5
Audio analytics, 105

B

Backup node, 313
Bar chart, 15
BASE model, 752
Batch processing, 99
Batch-based data ingestion (BBDI), 427
Behavioral analytics, 99
Big Data analysis framework, 125
Big Data applications, 1009
    in the logistics industry, 1017
    in the manufacturing industry, 1022
    in the retail industry, 1009
    in the travel industry, 1028
Big Data architecture, 150
    Analysis layer, 151
    Storage layer, 151
Big Data implementation, 973
    Best practices in, 988
Big Data in Banking Sector, 977
    Fraud detection, 978
Big Data in Business, 974
Big Data in Education Sector, 981
Big Data in Healthcare Sector, 979
    Precision diagnosis, 980
Big Data in Marketing, 974
    Challenges in implementing, 977
    Customer segmentation, 974
    Focus on buyer personas, 975
    Lead generation, 975
    Predictive marketing, 976
Big Data integration process, 147
Big Data on Cloud, 986
Big Data processing activities, 98
    Data computing and analysis, 98
    Data consumption and visualization, 98

Suffixes *f* and *t* have been inserted after the page numbers, where applicable, to indicate figure and table entries respectively.

Data mining, 98
Data storing, 98
Big Data storage, 151
Big Data Visualizations, 940
    Importance of, 943
    Types of, 944
Binary data, 12
Bivariate analysis, 129
Bivariate data, 14
Block cache, 527
Bloom filter, 847
Box plot, 17
Brokers, 458
BucketCache, 529
Business drivers for analytics, 62
Business intelligence (BI), 76
ByteOrderPartitioner, 834

C

Cache migration pattern, 857
CAP Theorem, 229, 764
Cassandra Batch, 812
Cassandra Commit Log, 834
Cassandra data model, 791
Cassandra Query Language (CQL), 798
Cassandra read process, 852
Cassandra server, 797f
Cassandra, 196, 766, 791
    Architecture of, 824
    Features of, 827
    Peer-to-peer approach, 828
Catalyst optimization, 656
Categorical data, 11
Categorization of data in Hive, 497
Causal consistency, 771
Challenges of conventional systems, 66
Change Data Capture (CDC), 195
Chukwa, 193
Classification model, 140
Classification, 25
Cloud computing, 28, 99
Cloudera Manager, 204
Cluster management, 659
Clustered computing, 99
Clustering model, 140
Clustering, 22, 105, 137
    Centroid-based, 23
    Connectivity-based, 22

    Density-based, 24
    Distribution-based, 24
Column family databases, 737
Column family, 805
Column tombstone, 841
Commit phase, 754
Commit-request phase, 754
Compaction, 840
    Strategies, 840
    Types, 841
Confirmatory data analysis, 129
Consistency, 749
Consumer group, 459
Consumers, 459
Content enrichment, 138
Continuous data, 11
Correlation, 19
Cost-based optimizer, 656

D

Data aggregation, 99
Data analysis, 99, 199
Data analyst, 155
Data analytics, 64, 99
Data cleansing, 99
Data democratization, 994
Data discovery, 72
Data engineer, 157
Data ingestion layer, 191
Data ingestion types, 426
Data integrity in Hadoop, 210
Data interpretation, 137
Data lake, 99
Data locality in MapReduce, 361
Data management, 64, 104
Data mart, 99
Data Mesh, 993
Data mining, 99
Data models, 3
    Conceptual, 3
    Logical, 3
Data nodes, 206, 313
Data processing, 100
Data racks, 208
Data relationships, 3
Data science, 77, 100
Data scientist, 100, 156
Data size, 100

Data storage layer, 195
Data types in Cassandra, 808
Data warehouse, 100, 152
DataOps, 992
Dataset, 100
Denormalization, 814
Descriptive analysis, 128
Digitization, 114
Dimensional model, 10
Dimensionality of data, 14
Directed Acyclic Graph (DAG), 683, 695
Discrete data, 11
Distributed cache in Apache Hadoop, 215
Document store, 740
Durability, 751
Dynamic partition pruning, 653

E

Elastic scalability, 769, 987
Empowerment of self-service analytics, 993
Entity, 5
Entity-relationship data model, 5
ELT, 148, 149*t*, 153
ETL, 100, 148, 149*t*
Exploratory data analysis, 128

F

Fact table, 10
Fan-in flow, 448
Fan-out structure, 447*f*
Filter hierarchy, 563
Flume, 194
Forecasting, 22
Frequency distribution, 128
Functional programming model, 146

G

Gossip and failure detection, 829
Graph database, 741
Grid computing, 28
Grunt, 613

H

Hadoop class path, 210
Hadoop counters, 397
Hadoop ingestion, 426
Hadoop input format, 383
Hadoop key-value pair, 381
Hadoop metrics, 210
Hadoop optimization, 399
Hadoop reducer, 379
Hadoop speculative execution, 396
Hadoop streaming, 588, 599
Hadoop Yarn, 660
Hadoop, 179
    Data locality in, 211
    Flavors of, 188
    Fully distributed mode, 189
    Hadoop ecosystem, 191
    Hadoop framework, 191
    Ingestion tools in, 193
    Inter-rack, 211
    Intra-rack, 211
    Limitations of, 1002
    Modes of, 188
    Pseudo-distributed mode, 189
    Safe mode, 220
    Standalone mode, 188
    Why Hadoop, 187*t*
Hashing, 540
HBase compaction, 534
HBase coprocessor, 546
HBase crash recovery, 544
HBase filters, 563
HBase row-key design, 538
    Conciseness, 538
    Hot-spotting, 539
HBase, 196, 523, 737
    Architecture of, 525
    Features of, 524
HDFS block replication, 207, 317
HDFS blocks, 207, 316
HDFS Command Line Interface, 300
HDFS Features, 306
HDFS read request, 313
HDFS write request, 314
HDFS, 190, 196
    Architecture, 204
    Data integrity, 319
    Data locality, 320
    Serialization, 322
    Web UI, 323
Heat map, 18
HFile, 529
HIndex features, 560

Hinted handoff, 842
Histogram, 16
Hive clients, 480
Hive commands – Loading, Filtering, Grouping, 502
Hive Compiler, 481
Hive data types, 496
Hive Driver, 481
Hive logical operators, 506
Hive services, 480
Hive vs. Traditional database, 485
Hive, 477
    Architecture, 480
    Features of, 478
    Limitations of, 479
    Workflow in, 483
HiveServer2, 481
HMaster, 525
Hortonworks, 204
Hyper table, 737
Hypervisor, 265
    Type 1 and Type 2, 265f

I

Impala, 466
Improvements in Deep Learning using Hydrogen, 653
Inferential analysis, 129
Information extraction (IE), 136
Information retrieval (IR), 136
InputSplit, 385
Intelligent data analysis (IDA), 78
Interactive Pig shell, 609
Internet of Things, 100
Interpreting Pig scripts, 611
Isolation, 750

K

Kafka producers, 461
Kafka replication, 460
Kafka, 194
Key-value pairs, 739
Key-value store, 739

L

Lambda architecture data ingestion, 428
Latest trends in Big Data, 991

Lazy evaluation, 666
Lemmatization, 133
Leveled compaction strategy (LCS), 840t
Line chart, 15
Load balancing policy (LBP), 847
Load balancing, 543
Lookup table, 763
LruBlockCache, 528

M

Machine learning, 101
Machine-generated data, 100
Major compaction, 536
Making Pigs fly, 628
MAP R Control System, 204
MapOnly job in MapReduce, 394
Mapper job, 378
Mapping phase, 367
    Combiner, 368
    Mapper, 367
    Partitioner, 368
MapReduce combiner, 389
MapReduce job, 377
MapReduce Partitioner, 388
MapReduce vs. Spark, 650t
MapReduce, 29, 190, 197, 357
Massively parallel processing (MPP), 27
Master observer, 547
Mem table, 776
MemStore, 529
Memtable flush, 837
Merkle tree, 776
Metadata, 101, 482
Minor compaction, 535
Model building, 74
Mongo Compass, 906
MongoDB, 776, 874
    AND operator in, 900
    Key features of, 887
    Updating documents in, 898
MongoDB connection, 906
MongoDB Query Language (MQL), 890
MongoDB server, 882, 891
MongoDB View, 911
Multivariate analysis, 129
Multivariate data, 14
Murmur3Partitioner, 834

N

Name Node, 205
Natural language processing (NLP), 127
Nature of data, 12
    Machine data, 13
    Social data, 13
Negative correlation, 20
Network diagrams, 18
Network topology strategy, 803
NewSQL, 747
NoSQL databases, 735
    Types of, 737
NoSQL definition, 737
NoSQL, 101

O

Object-based data models, 5
Object-oriented data model, 5
ODBC, 201
Oozie, 204
Operationalize phase, 74
Optimizing Pig scripts, 628
Outliers model, 141

P

Pandas UDF API improvements, 653
Parallel processing, 360
Parsing, 135
    Chunking, 135
    Deep parsing, 136
    Shallow parsing, 135
Partition index, 857
Partition summary, 856
Partitioning horizontal and vertical data, 757
Part-of-speech tagging, 134
Phases of data analytic life-cycle, 71
Pie chart, 16
Pig executive engine, 611
Pig Latin statements, 618
Pig Latin, 607
    Data model of, 615
Pig, 200
    Built-in functions, 624
    Pig arithmetic operators, 619
    Pig comparison operators, 621

Pig compiler, 611
Pig data types, 616
Pig optimizer, 610
Pig parser, 609
Pig relational operators, 621
Pigs eat anything, 616
Poor partitioning, 389
Positive correlation, 19
Post-decision phase, 754
Predictive analysis, 138
Predictive analytics algorithms, 142
    Clustering algorithms, 143
    Decision trees, 142
    Deep learning, 143
    Density-based clustering, 143
    Ensemble method, 143
    Fuzzy logic algorithm, 144
    Hierarchical-based clustering, 143
    K-Nearest Neighbour (KNN), 144
    Linear regression algorithms, 142
    Logistic regression algorithms, 142
    Neural network, 144
    Random forest, 142
    Support vector machine (SVM), 145
Predictive analytics models, 139
Predictive analytics, 107
    Gradient boosted model (GBM), 108
    K-means, 108
    Random forest model, 107
`Pretty()` method, 900
Problem with small files, 1002
Processing layer, 197

Q

Qlik, 70
Qualitative data, 11
    Nominal data, 12
    Ordinal data, 12
Quantitative data, 11
Quasi-structured data, 103

R

Rack awareness algorithm, 208, 318
Random partitioner, 833
Read repair, 845
Real-time analytics, 589

Real-time data ingestion (RTDI), 427
Record Reader, 367
Record-based data models, 6
    Hierarchical model, 6
    Network model, 7
    Relational model, 9
Reducing phase, 369
Region observer, 547
Region server, 525
Region split, 541
Regression modelling, 140
Regression, 21
Relational DBMS, 735
Relational operators in Hive QL, 503
Relationship, 5
Replication strategy, 802
Reporting vs. Analysis, 30
Resilient distributed dataset, 681
Reverse row-key, 539
Row cache, 838
Row tombstone, 841

S

Salting, 539
Schema design, 537
Schema of column families, 541
Schema option in Compass, 920
Schema, 756
Secondary Name Node, 205
Security in Big Data, 983
    Best practices for, 986
Semi-structured data, 102
Sentiment analysis, 105
Session store, 745
Sharding, 757
    Directory-based sharding, 763
    Feature-based shard, 760
    Key-based sharding, 761
    Range-based sharding, 762
Share nothing architecture, 757
Shuffling and sorting in MapReduce, 391
Shuffling, 368
Size tiered compaction strategy (STCS), 840t
Slab allocator, 837
SlabCache, 529
Snitch, 831
Snowflake schema, 10
Social media analytics, 106

Sorted strings tables, 832
Spark 3.0, 652
Spark core engine, 224
Spark ecosystem, 653
    Spark core, 655
    Spark SQL, 202, 224, 649, 655
Spark GraphX, 202, 649, 658
Spark is potential, 667
Spark MLlib, 658
Spark RDD, 682f
    Features of, 685
    Ways to create RDD in Spark, 684
Spark streaming, 202, 224, 657
Spark, 198, 648
    Advantages of, 663
    Disadvantages of, 667
    Ways to create RDD, 684
SparkR, 659
    Advantages of, 659
Splitting, 366
Spurious correlation, 21
SQL vs. NoSQL, 747
Sqoop, 193, 430
    Export, 439
    Functionalities, 431
    Importing, 436
    Incremental import, 439
Staged event-driven architecture (SEDA), 854
Stemming, 133
Stochastic (or statistical) POS tagger, 135
Stream computing, 594
Strict consistency, 771
Structured data, 101
Summarization, 137
Synthetic data, 993

T

Table schema, 537
Tableau, 203, 951
    Features of, 951
Tall vs. Wide tables, 541
Temporal patterns, 817
Text analytics, 104
Text categorization, 137
Text extraction, 105
Text index, 136
Text mining process, 130
Text mining, 136

Text preprocessing, 131
The issue with small files, 215
Thread pooling, 593
Time window compaction strategy (TWCS), 840t
Timestamps, 540
Tokenization, 131
Traditional large-scale systems, 179
Tunable consistency, 770
Tuples, 10
Two-phase commit, 753
Types of analytics, 67
    Descriptive analytics, 67
    Diagnostic analytics, 67
    Predictive analytics, 68
    Prescriptive analytics, 68
Types of data, 11

U

Univariate analysis, 129
Univariate data, 14
Unstructured data, 101, 103
Unsupervised learning, 141
User profile store, 746

V

V's of Big Data, 101, 181
    Value, 111, 182

Variety, 111, 182
Velocity, 111, 182
Veracity, 111, 182
Volume, 111, 181
Video content analytics (VCA), 106
VirtualBox, 275
Virtualization, 264
    Enabling, 281
Visualization, 101
VMware, 266
    Workstation, 266

W

WAL observer, 547
Word cloud, 17
Write-Ahead log (WAL), 527

Y

Yarn, 198
Yet Another Resource Navigator (YARN), 222, 402

Z

Zeppelin, 226
Zero correlation, 20
ZooKeeper, 203, 458, 525, 531